KV-031-053

a

So-Sz Volume 18

The World Book Encyclopedia

WORLD
BOOK
a Scott Fetzer company
Chicago
www.worldbookonline.com

The World Book Encyclopedia

World Book, Inc.
233 North Michigan Avenue
Chicago, IL 60601
U.S.A.

www.worldbookonline.com

About the cover design

The encyclopedia is available in both traditional and SPINESCAPE bindings. The SPINESCAPE design for the 2008 edition—*The Global City*—combines images of two of the world's largest cities, New York City and Tokyo. Both are world centers of business and culture that glow with light and energy at night. For the first time in history, the majority of people on the planet live in cities. *The Global City* highlights a major goal of World Book, to bring knowledge of the world's people and how they live to its readers.

© Jim Lopes, Shutterstock; © Chad Ehlers, Stone/Getty Images; © Comstock/SuperStock; © Photonica/Getty Images

Library of Congress Cataloging-in-Publication Data

The World Book encyclopedia.
    p. cm.
    Summary: "A 22-volume, highly illustrated, A-Z general encyclopedia for all ages, featuring sections on how to use World Book, other research aids, pronunciation key, a student guide to better writing, speaking, and research skills, and comprehensive index"--Provided by publisher.
    Includes bibliographical references and index.
    ISBN 978-0-7166-0108-1
    1. Encyclopedias and dictionaries. I. World Book, Inc.
AE5.W55 2008
031--dc22
              2007022003

FSC

Mixed Sources
Product group from well-managed forests, controlled sources and recycled wood or fiber

Cert no. SCS-COC-00648
www.fsc.org
© 1996 Forest Stewardship Council

Printed in the United States of America

08 5 4 3 2 1

Soap. See Detergent and soap.

Soap Box Derby is a coasting race for small motorless racing cars. The derby received its name because at one time many of the cars were built from wooden soap boxes. Beginners from ages 9 to 16 race in the Stock division. More advanced racers, ages 9 to 16, compete in the Kit Car division. The most advanced racers, from ages 11 to 16, compete in the Masters division. The contestants must build their own cars. Rules govern the size, weight, and cost of the racer. Contestants first compete in local races. Winners qualify for the All-American Soap Box Derby held every August in Akron, Ohio. Racers from the United States, Canada, and other countries enter the derby each year. The first race was held in 1934 in Dayton, Ohio. It was moved to Akron in 1935.

Critically reviewed by the All-American Soap Box Derby

Soap opera is daily serial melodrama that originated in the United States on radio and then became popular on daytime television in many countries. Soap operas received the name because soap manufacturers first sponsored them on radio. For many years, a number of critics considered soap operas, though popular, to be a low type of mass-market entertainment. However, many critics have re-evaluated soap operas, assessing them as one of the few original American art forms.

The first soap opera, "Painted Dreams," premiered on radio in 1930. It failed because it included too much advertising to emotionally involve its audience. Other, better-crafted serials quickly followed, such as "The Guiding Light," "Backstage Wife," and "The Romance of Helen Trent" in the United States, and "The Archers" in the United Kingdom. The first major soap opera on television, "Search for Tomorrow," appeared in 1951 in the United States. The United Kingdom's first important TV soap opera, "Coronation Street," began in 1960.

The early American soap operas emphasized situations in which women's desires were central to the story, often focusing on themes of romance and family life. During the late 1960's and early 1970's, such soap operas as "One Life to Live" and "All My Children" expanded their content to include social issues. Episodes dealt with abortion, war, domestic violence, and child abuse, usually from the viewpoint of female psychology.

By the mid-1980's, a number of soap operas had gained a worldwide audience. Sometimes, as in Russia, soap operas captured more viewers than any other television show. Newer shows, including the British series "EastEnders" and the Australian series "Neighbours," concentrated less on the psychology of female characters and more on sociology in their vivid portrayals of a community's ethnic and class issues.

In the 1980's, such American soap operas as "General Hospital" and "Days of Our Lives" began to challenge gender cliches. These shows portrayed troubled women seeking ways to combine strength, sexuality, and ability. In the 1990's, however, TV soap operas began to turn back to earlier gender stereotypes. Some shows demoted the importance of female characters and focused on gangsters, thus glamorizing male domination and violence. Mature men and women virtually disappeared from some series, which featured teenaged characters.

By the early 2000's, soap operas had fallen into a state of uncertainty. Talk shows and other programs replaced many soap operas, and the form struggled to recapture the innovation of the late 1900's.   Martha Nochimson

See also **Radio** (The Golden Age of Broadcasting).

Soap plant is a tall herb of California that reaches a height of about 8 feet (2.4 meters). It grows from a bulb and has tufted leaves and white flowers streaked with purple. The leaves may be up to 28 inches (71 centimeters) long. The flowers spread open in the afternoon. Indians used the bulb as a kind of soap. They also roasted and ate the bulbs.   Anton A. Reznicek

Scientific classification. The soap plant belongs to the agave family, Agavaceae. It is *Chlorogalum pomeridianum.*

Soapberry is the name of 13 species of trees or shrubs found in tropical and subtropical areas of Asia and North and South America, and on islands in the Pacific Ocean. These plants bear fruits that are most commonly yellowish-brown with a leathery covering. Each fruit is made up of two or three round lobes. The fruits and leaves contain a soapy substance called *saponin.* They produce a lather when rubbed in water and can be used as a substitute for soap. Soapberry plants are cultivated from seeds or from cuttings planted in the early spring. They grow well in dry, sandy soil.

The most common Asian species is the *Chinese soapberry.* It is found from India to China and Japan. A species that is called *soapberry* or *false dogwood* is found in the Americas. It ranges from the southern United States to Argentina. One variety of this species is evergreen. Another variety is *deciduous*—that is, it loses its leaves every fall. It is found from Mexico to Kansas, Missouri, Louisiana, and northern Florida.   Thomas B. Croat

Scientific classification. Soapberries belong to the soapberry family, Sapindaceae. They make up the genus *Sapindus.* The scientific name for the Chinese soapberry is *S. mukorossi.* The American soapberry is *S. saponaria.*

See also **Tree** (Broadleaf and needleleaf trees [picture]).

Soapstone, also known as *steatite,* is a soft rock composed mostly of the mineral talc. It feels soapy or oily and varies from white to gray and grayish-green.

Soapstone has many industrial uses. It is a good electric insulator and can easily be cut into various shapes. Because soapstone is not affected by high temperatures, or acids, it is used for laboratory table tops, sinks, and some chemical equipment. Powdered soapstone is added to cosmetics, paper, and paint as a filler to improve these products. For example, soapstone gives paper a smooth surface. Tailors use pieces of soapstone called *French chalk* to mark cloth.

Soapstone is formed in the earth by changes in the structure and composition of an *igneous* rock such as peridotite (see **Igneous rock**). These changes occur at low temperature and moderate pressure in the presence of water. Other kinds of rock that usually occur along with soapstone include dolomite and serpentinite. Soapstone, a *metamorphic* rock, forms in layers that vary greatly in thickness.

The United States ranks among the leading soapstone producers. Deposits occur in several states, including California, New York, North Carolina, and Virginia. Other countries that produce soapstone include Canada, France, and Italy.   John C. Butler

See also **Metamorphic rock; Talc.**

Sobieski, John. See John III Sobieski.

© David Lean, Allsport

Allsport

Soccer is the world's most popular team sport. The goalkeeper, shown here diving toward the ball, tries to prevent the ball from going into his goal. The opposing players, shown here kicking and leaping, try to control the ball for their team.

Soccer

Soccer is the world's most popular sport. It is the national sport of most European and Latin American countries, and of many other nations. Millions of people in more than 200 countries play soccer. Soccer's most famous international competition, the World Cup, is held every four years for both men and women.

In a soccer game, two teams of 11 players try to kick or head a ball into each other's goal without using their hands. The team that scores the most goals wins. Players must kick the ball or hit it with their head or body. Only the goalkeepers can touch the ball with their hands.

Soccer as it is played today developed in the United Kingdom during the 1800's and quickly spread to many other countries. Until the mid-1900's, the game was not greatly popular in the United States. But today, it is one of the nation's fastest-growing sports.

In the United Kingdom and many other countries, soccer is called *football* or *association football*. The word *soccer* comes from *assoc.,* an abbreviation for *association*.

The field and equipment

The field is rectangular and may vary in size. In international competition, it measures from 100 to 130 yards (91 to 119 meters) long and from 65 to 100 yards (59 to 91 meters) wide. The boundary lines on the sides of the field are called *touch lines*. Those on each end are called *goal lines*. The goals stand in the center of the goal line. Each goal measures 24 feet (7.3 meters) wide and 8 feet (2.4 meters) high. The *penalty area* is a rectangle in front

Jim Moorhouse, the contributor of this article, is Director of Communications for U.S. Soccer.

of each goal. It is 132 feet (40.2 meters) wide and extends 54 feet (16.5 meters) in front of the goal. Defending players are penalized if they break certain rules while in their own penalty area.

The *goal area* is a smaller rectangle that measures 60 feet (18 meters) wide and extends 18 feet (5.5 meters) in front of the goal. Attacking players cannot come into contact with the goalkeeper in this area unless the goalkeeper is holding the ball and has both feet on the ground. For the names and sizes of other sections of a soccer field, and the names of other lines, see the field diagram with this article.

The ball is made of leather or other approved material and is inflated with air. A soccer ball used for adult games measures from 27 to 28 inches (69 to 71 centimeters) in circumference and weighs from 14 to 16 ounces (396 to 453 grams). Children generally use a ball with a circumference of about 25 inches (64 centimeters).

The uniform consists of a shirt, shorts, calf-length socks, and shoes with cleats. Some soccer players wear shin guards. The goalkeeper's shirt differs in color from those worn by the other players of both sides and by the referee.

Players and officials

The players of a soccer team—except for the goalkeeper, who normally remains within the penalty area— use certain formations for offensive or defensive strategy. The score of the game often determines a team's strategy. For example, a team that is ahead may use a formation based on defense. A team that is behind may choose one that emphasizes offense. Some formations are designed to take advantage of the weaknesses of the opposing team. Other formations center around the special abilities of a star player.

One popular formation is the 4-4-2. The first line of this formation has four defenders, the second line consists of four midfielders, and the third line has two forwards. A number of other formations are also used in soccer. For example, the 3-5-2 is popular with many teams throughout the world. This formation uses three defenders, five midfielders, and two forwards.

International soccer rules allow a team to substitute up to three players during a game, regardless of how many players are injured. Under international rules, a player who has been substituted for may not return to the game. College and high school teams in the United States and Canada allow an unlimited number of substitutions, with players allowed to return to the game after they have been substituted for.

The forwards have the primary responsibility for scoring goals. They are sometimes called *strikers*. They must be exceptionally skillful with the ball, pass accurately, *dribble* (nudge the ball ahead with the feet while running down the field), and shoot accurately. A good forward can fake an opponent out of position and then score a goal with the head or foot. Forwards may also put pressure on the opposing team's players when possession of the ball is lost.

The midfielders, also called *halfbacks,* unite the offense and the defense. These players have a role in every play and require exceptional physical endurance. Midfielders sometimes score goals, but they must always be in position to help the defense.

The defenders, sometimes called *fullbacks,* form the last line of defense in front of the goalkeeper. A defender tries to take the ball away from the other team and pass it to a midfielder to start an attack. A defender called a *sweeper* tries to intercept passes by roaming from side to side behind or in front of other defenders.

The goalkeeper has perhaps the most difficult job. A goalkeeper must move quickly to all parts of the penalty area to stop shots or take the ball from an opponent. After stopping a shot, a good goalkeeper controls the ball and starts an attack by kicking or throwing the ball to a teammate. The goalkeeper is the only player who may touch the ball with the hands or arms.

The officials. A referee and two referee's assistants officiate most games throughout the world. In high school and college games in the United States, two referees or a referee and two assistants may be used. The referee serves as the timekeeper and enforces the rules. This official decides all disputes and may put a player out of the game for repeated fouling. The assistants help decide which team gets possession of the ball after it goes out of bounds. The assistants also signal the referee when they see a player commit a foul. They cannot, however, make decisions. The assistants only assist the referee, who has the sole responsibility for calling fouls and breaches of conduct.

How soccer is played

Soccer games played according to international rules are divided into two 45-minute halves, with a brief rest period between halves. College games in the United States also consist of two 45-minute periods. Leagues of younger teams adjust the length of games according to the physical abilities of the players.

In some leagues, the teams play an overtime period if the score is tied at the end of regulation time. If the teams are still tied after the overtime, each may shoot a series of five *penalty kicks* at the goal. The team that scores the most goals out of five, or gains an unbeatable

A soccer field This diagram shows the players of a soccer team in a 4-3-3 formation on the rectangular field. Most teams use this line-up at the start of a game and then shift to other formations.

WORLD BOOK diagram

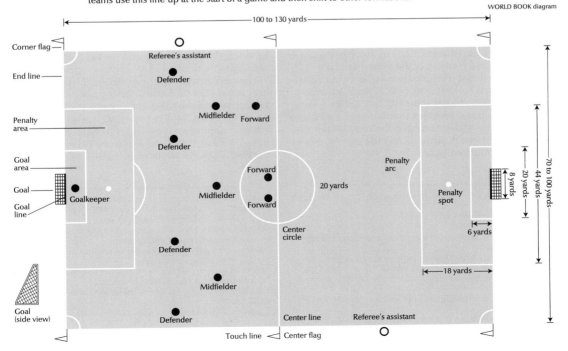

advantage after each team has taken the same number of kicks, is declared the winner.

Starting the game. A soccer game begins with a *kickoff* in the center of the field. The opposing captains flip a coin to decide which team will kick off. The other team kicks off to start the second half, when the teams change goals. After a goal, play resumes with a kickoff by the team scored upon.

The kickoff takes place in the center of the field on the halfway line. The players line up in their half of the field. No player on the defensive team can enter the center circle until play has started. To start play, the kicking team must move the ball forward at least the distance of its circumference. The player who kicks off may not touch the ball again until another player has touched it. No player on the defensive team may enter the center circle until the ball has rolled at least the distance of its circumference.

The ball in play. After the kickoff, the ball remains in play unless it completely crosses a goal line or a touch line. There are no time outs in soccer unless the referee calls one after a player has been injured or for some other reason that the referee feels requires stopping the clock.

The attacking team tries to advance the ball into the opposing team's territory. The attackers then try to pass the ball to a player who is in a good position to score a goal. A player may kick or hit the ball into the goal with any part of the body except the hands and arms.

The defending players constantly shift their positions to break up attacks. They try to cover their opponents, intercept passes, and take the ball away. Hard body contact is permitted only when it results from an attempt to kick the ball or hit it with the head.

Restarts. If the ball goes out of bounds, play is restarted with a *corner kick,* a *goal kick,* or a *throw-in.* The referee, assisted by the referee's assistants, decides which type of restart is used.

If the ball crosses the goal line without going into the goal, play resumes with either a corner kick or a goal kick. A corner kick, which is made by an offensive player, takes place if a member of the defensive team touched the ball last. The offensive player kicks the ball from the nearest corner of the field. A goal kick occurs if an offensive player touched the ball last. A defensive player restarts play with a kick from inside the goal area in the half of the goal area nearest the point where the ball went out. A goal kick must clear the penalty area before it can be touched again.

A throw-in takes place if a player knocks the ball over a touch line. An opposing player throws the ball back into play. The thrower must have both feet on the ground, either on or behind the touch line. The throw must be made with both hands from above and behind the head.

Fouls. A player who repeatedly commits fouls may be sent off the field for the rest of the game. No substitute is allowed for such a player, and a team must then play one person short for the remainder of the game. After most fouls, the referee awards a free kick to the other team. This kick may be a *penalty kick,* a *direct free kick,* or an *indirect free kick.*

A penalty kick is awarded if the defending team commits one of nine fouls within its penalty area. These fouls are (1) deliberately kicking or trying to kick an opponent, (2) tripping an opponent, (3) jumping at an opponent, (4) violently charging into an opponent, (5) charging into an opponent from behind, (6) striking an opponent, (7) holding an opponent, (8) pushing an opponent, or (9) deliberately touching the ball with the hands or arms. The opposing team takes the kick from the *penalty spot,* which is 12 yards (11 meters) directly in front of the goal. All the players, except the kicker and the opposing goalkeeper, must be outside the penalty area and 10 yards (9 meters) from the ball when the kick is taken.

A direct free kick may be awarded for one of the nine fouls committed anywhere on the field except the penalty area. This kick is taken toward the offending team's goal from the point where the foul occurred. Opponents must be at least 10 yards (9 meters) from the ball when it is kicked, but they can try to block it.

An indirect free kick is awarded for dangerous play, such as (1) kicking the ball when the goalkeeper is holding it, (2) *obstructing* (blocking) an opponent, (3) charging an opponent in an otherwise legal manner when the ball is not within playing distance, or (4) unsportsmanlike conduct. The kicker kicks the ball toward the offending team's goal, but the ball must touch at least one other player before entering the goal. All opponents must be at least 10 yards (9 meters) from the ball, but they can attempt to block it.

The referee also awards an indirect free kick if a player is *offside.* Generally, an attacking player is offside when between the ball and the goal line in the opponent's half of the field. However, the player is not offside if (1) two opponents were closer to their goal line than the player was, (2) the player is in the player's own half of the field, or (3) the player received the ball from a cor-

Soccer terms

Center means to pass the ball into the penalty area from near a touchline.
Charge is the legal use of the shoulder to push an opponent off balance.
Dribbling means to move the ball while running by nudging it along with the feet.
Drop ball is a way of restarting play after the game has been stopped for a reason other than a foul, such as an injury. The referee drops the ball to the ground between two opposing players.
Half-volley is a kick made just as the ball bounces off the ground.
Hands is a rule violation that occurs when a player deliberately touches the ball with the hands or arms.

Marking means guarding an opponent.
Obstruction is a violation that occurs when a player deliberately runs or stands in an opponent's path.
Overlap occurs when a defender moves far down the field past an offensive forward to help the attack.
Save occurs when the goalkeeper or another player prevents the ball from going into the goal.
Screen means to maintain control of the ball by keeping the body between the ball and an opponent.
Tackle means using the feet or shoulder to take the ball from an opponent.
Trap occurs when a player uses the feet, thighs, or chest to stop the ball and gain control of it.
Volley is a kick made while the ball is in the air.

Some soccer skills Soccer players must control the ball without using their hands. Players use their feet, head, legs, and chest to advance the ball or to pass it to a teammate. Defensive players use their feet to kick or hook the ball from an opponent, a maneuver called *tackling*.

WORLD BOOK illustration by David Cunningham

ner kick, a goal kick, a throw-in, or a *drop ball*. The *Soccer terms* table with this article defines a drop ball.

Soccer skills

Soccer requires a variety of skills. They include (1) kicking, (2) passing, (3) heading, (4) dribbling and faking, and (5) tackling.

Kicking is the most important skill in soccer. It involves shooting at the goal, putting the ball in play, or putting the ball into a particular area of the field. A good player can kick the ball accurately in many ways with either foot.

In most cases, kicking the ball with the instep is the most effective method. A player can control the accuracy, distance, and power of a kick better with the instep than in any other way. In certain situations, however, a player might use the outer or inner side of the foot or even the heel.

Soccer players generally try to kick the ball so that it travels just above the field. Players put their nonkicking foot next to the ball. They keep their head down and

their eyes on the ball. Then they swing their kicking leg with the toes pointed downward and kick the ball squarely with the instep. After the foot strikes the ball, the leg should straighten and follow through. This action makes the ball travel in the right direction.

A player usually stops the ball before kicking it. Kicking a moving ball lessens the player's control over the direction of the kick.

Passing the ball among teammates enables a team to move into scoring position and keep possession. A player tries to pass the ball so that it travels just above or on the ground. Occasionally, the ball may have to be kicked over the head of a defending player. Short passes generally are more effective than long ones, which involve a larger margin for error.

Heading means hitting the ball with the head. It sometimes is the only legal way a player can reach the ball in the air. A player may use the head to pass the ball, intercept an opponent's pass, or shoot at the goal. Good players can head the ball long distances with great power and accuracy.

 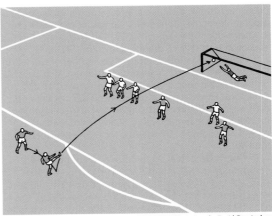

WORLD BOOK illustrations by David Cunningham

Offensive plays in soccer are designed to move the ball into scoring position. The diagrams above show how teamwork and ball control can lead to a goal. By moving the ball quickly, the offensive team pulls the defense out of position, setting up a good shot at the goal. In the diagram on the left, Player 1 kicks the ball to Player 2 and then breaks toward the goal. Player 2 kicks a return pass to Player 1. The defender has moved to protect against a shot by Player 2, giving Player 1 a good opportunity to score. The diagram on the right illustrates an *indirect free kick*, which is awarded after certain violations by the opposing team. A player puts the ball in play by passing to a teammate, who kicks it over the defenders and out of reach of the goalkeeper.

Some referee signals   The referee enforces the rules during a soccer game. This official stops play after a violation or an injury and uses a hand signal to indicate how the action will resume. The referee holds up a colored card to warn or expel a player for repeated fouling or for unsportsmanlike conduct.

WORLD BOOK illustration by David Cunningham

Penalty kick   Direct free kick   Indirect free kick   Goal kick   Corner kick   Warning or expulsion

When heading, a player jumps up, snaps the head forward, and hits the ball with the forehead. A ball that hits the top or back of the head may stun the player.

Dribbling enables players to keep possession of the ball while running. While dribbling, a player can pass or shoot the ball if an opponent threatens to take it away. Faking makes dribbling more effective. A player may fool an opponent by faking a pass or a shot and then dribbling. The player may also fake a dribble in one direction and then dribble in another.

Tackling involves using the feet to kick or hook the ball away from an opponent. An ideal tackle involves little or no body contact and leaves the defending player or a teammate in control of the ball. In a *sliding tackle,* a player slides along the ground with one leg extended and takes the ball from an opponent.

Soccer competition

Soccer is played on several levels throughout the world. Professional teams provide the most popular competition in many countries. Semiprofessional teams compete for pay, but play only on a part-time basis. Amateur athletes play in interclub soccer competition and are not paid. Many colleges and high schools include soccer as part of their athletic program.

The Fédération Internationale de Football Association (FIFA) governs soccer in all parts of the world. It consists of the national soccer associations of more than 200 countries. These associations include U.S. Soccer and the Canadian Soccer Association. Most soccer games, including those in the United States and Canada, are played according to international rules established by the FIFA.

In North America. As in other parts of the world, competition in the United States is divided into divisions, based on the skill level of the teams. The highest level is the Division I Major League Soccer (MLS). The MLS features a number of well-known American and international players. The United Soccer Leagues (USL) has more than 100 affiliated clubs. It includes the Division II A-League, the Division III D3 Pro League semiprofessional league, and the Premier Development League (PDL), an amateur Division IV league. As in Europe, teams that meet certain standards can advance into a higher division from season to season. The USL also has youth and women's semiprofessional leagues.

The national governing body for soccer in the United States is U.S. Soccer. It has its headquarters in Chicago. Besides staging national and international tournaments, the federation organizes and manages 11 national teams that represent the United States in competitions throughout the world, including the Summer Olympic Games and the World Cup.

The United States Youth Soccer Association, a branch of U.S. Soccer, conducts national, state, and regional championships for boys and girls up to the age of 19. The American Youth Soccer Organization, an independent group, holds regional championships and sponsors teams that compete with teams from other countries.

The Canadian Soccer Association holds national and international tournaments. It also conducts national, provincial, and regional championships and sponsors teams that represent Canada in world competition.

In Europe and Latin America. Most countries in Europe and Latin America have professional or semiprofessional soccer leagues. These leagues consist of a number of divisions for teams of varying ability. At the end of the season, two or three teams from each division may move into a stronger or weaker division, depending on their record. The winner of the top division is the country's national champion.

International competition includes the World Cup, held every four years. The national all-star teams of 32 nations compete in the men's tournament and those of 16 nations compete in the women's tournament. All member nations of FIFA may compete in qualifying rounds held two years before the championship. These rounds determine which teams will join the host nation and the previous champion in the final tournament.

European club teams compete annually in the Union of European Football Associations (UEFA) Champions League. This tournament begins with almost 100 teams and determines the European club champion. The UEFA Cup is a tournament for clubs that did not qualify for, or were eliminated from, the Champions League.

South American teams compete in a tournament called the Copa Liberadores. North and Central American domestic champions compete for the Confederation of North, Central American and Caribbean Association Football (CONCACAF) Champions Cup. The winners of the two tournaments meet for the Interamerican Cup.

National teams from throughout the world compete

FIFA World Cup championship games

Men

Year		Location
1930	Uruguay 4, Argentina 2	Montevideo, Uruguay
1934	Italy 2, Czechoslovakia 1	Rome
1938	Italy 4, Hungary 2	Paris
1950	Uruguay 2, Brazil 1	Rio de Janeiro, Brazil
1954	West Germany 3, Hungary 2	Bern, Switzerland
1958	Brazil 5, Sweden 2	Stockholm, Sweden
1962	Brazil 3, Czechoslovakia 1	Santiago, Chile
1966	England 4, West Germany 2	London
1970	Brazil 4, Italy 1	Mexico City
1974	West Germany 2, Netherlands 1	Munich, West Germany
1978	Argentina 3, Netherlands 1	Buenos Aires, Argentina
1982	Italy 3, West Germany 1	Madrid, Spain
1986	Argentina 3, West Germany 2	Mexico City
1990	West Germany 1, Argentina 0	Rome
1994	Brazil 0, Italy 0*	Pasadena, United States
1998	France 3, Brazil 0	St-Denis, France
2002	Brazil 2, Germany 0	Yokohama, Japan
2006	Italy 1, France 1‡	Berlin, Germany

Women

Year		Location
1991	United States 2, Finland 0	Guangzhou, China
1995	Norway 2, Germany 0	Stockholm, Sweden
1999	United States 0, China 0†	Pasadena, United States
2003	Germany 2, Sweden 1	Carson, United States
2007	Germany 2, Brazil 0	Shanghai, China

*Brazil won 3-2 on penalty kicks.   ‡ Italy won 5-3 on penalty kicks.
†United States won 5-4 on penalty kicks.

in events similar to the FIFA World Cup. The European Championships are held every four years. Every two years, competition is held for the Copa America in South America, the Gold Cup in North and Central America, and the African Nations Cup in Africa.

History

A game similar to soccer was probably played in China as early as 400 B.C. In the A.D. 200's, the Romans played a game in which two teams tried to score by ad-vancing the ball across a line on the field. The players passed the ball to one another but did not kick it. London children of the 1100's played a form of soccer.

In the early 1800's, many English schools played a game that resembled soccer. Players added many rules that changed the game, but each school interpreted the rules differently. In 1848, a group of school representatives met at Trinity College in Cambridge and drew up the first set of soccer rules. In 1863, representatives of English soccer clubs founded the Football Association.

Soccer began to spread throughout the world in the late 1800's. By 1900, associations had been established in Belgium, Chile, Denmark, Italy, the Netherlands, and Switzerland. In 1904, the national associations founded the Fédération Internationale de Football Association. The Canadian Soccer Association was established in 1912, and the United States Soccer Federation in 1913. In 1930, the first World Cup was played in Montevideo, Uruguay. Since then, the World Cup has been held every four years except during World War II (1939-1945), when the games were suspended. In 1991, the first women's World Cup was played in Guangzhou, China.

Both professional and amateur soccer grew in popularity during the late 1900's. By the early 2000's, amateur soccer had become one of the fastest growing team sports in high schools in the United States and many other countries. Soccer competition at the college level had also gained in popularity.   Jim Moorhouse

Related articles in *World Book* include:

Africa (picture)	Latin America (Recreation;
Beckham, David	picture)
Brazil (Recreation; picture)	Pelé
England (Recreation)	World Cup
Hamm, Mia	

Outline

I. The field equipment
  A. The field   C. The uniform
  B. The ball
II. Players and officials
  A. The forwards
  B. The midfielders
  C. The defenders
  D. The goalkeeper
  E. The officials
III. How soccer is played
  A. Starting the game   C. Restarts
  B. The ball in play   D. Fouls
IV. Soccer skills
  A. Kicking
  B. Passing
  C. Heading
  D. Dribbling
  E. Tackling
V. Soccer competition
  A. In North America
  B. In Europe and Latin America
  C. International competition
VI. History

Additional resources

Allaway, Roger, and others. *The Encyclopedia of American Soccer History.* Scarecrow, 2001.
Crouch, Terry. *The World Cup: The Complete History.* Aurum Pr., 2002.
Fortanasce, Vincent. *Life Lessons from Soccer: What Your Child Can Learn On and Off the Field.* Fireside Paperbacks, 2001.
Gifford, Clive. *Soccer.* Kingfisher Bks., 2002. Younger readers.
Mackin, Bob. *Soccer the Winning Way.* Greystone Bks., 2001. Younger readers.

. The Newberry Library, Chicago
Soccer became popular in England during the late 1800's. Before the construction of large stadiums in the 1900's, crowds of spectators stood along the sidelines.

Social change refers to any significant change in the structure of society. Short-lived changes, such as changes in the employment rate, do not produce social change. Nor do fads, fashions, or temporary changes in ideas and behavior. The election of a new president is not social change. But replacement of the presidency with a dictatorship changes the structure of government and is thus a social change. Most sociologists recognize four main types of social change.

One type of social change involves changes in the number and variety of positions and social roles. When we say that an industrial society is more complex than a peasant society, we mean that it has many new and specialized jobs, such as computer programming, conducting cancer research, and piloting a spacecraft.

A second kind of change occurs in the obligations or duties attached to positions. For example, parents are no longer responsible for educating their children. They give this job to teachers and schools.

These two types of change lead to a third type—new ways of organizing social activities. The establishment of kindergartens occurred partly because the children of working mothers needed care. Other educational changes took place in response to rising educational aspirations and occupational needs. For example, community, or junior, colleges were established for advanced—but not university-level—education.

A fourth kind of social change involves the redistribution of facilities and rewards, such as power, education, income, and respect. In 1950, for example, about half the people in the United States with substandard incomes were nonwhites. Today, about a third of the nation's poor are nonwhites.

Sometimes societies evolve gradually. At other times, they change abruptly, as in times of revolution. Change can result from planning, or it can be unintentional. Every society changes, but not all change at the same rate or in the same direction. Revolutionary change is often accompanied by violence. Most changes benefit some people more than they benefit others, and they may penalize some people. For this reason, some resistance to change is inevitable. Many social changes have had both beneficial and undesirable consequences.

When change improves conditions, people's expectations grow. They become dissatisfied with current achievements and demand more. Sometimes they demand changes in the law. But when people believe that their grievances cannot be corrected within the system, they call for more radical change—for revolution.

People have long sought simple explanations for change, often emphasizing single factors. The German social philosopher Karl Marx claimed the economy is the prime source of social change. Today, scholars believe such explanations do not account for the complicated events of social change. Many scholars think societies are systems. Change in one part, they believe, leads to change in other parts, with no one part having priority. For example, the car—a product of technological change—created changes in where people live and work, and in their leisure activities.   Harriet Zuckerman

See also **Culture** (How cultures change); **Social role;** **Sociology** (Social change).

Social class is a group of people who share a common status or position in society. Social classes represent differences in wealth, power, employment, family background, and other qualities. These qualities indicate a person's *socioeconomic status*—that is, his or her position in society as measured by social and economic factors. The process by which populations are divided into classes is called *social stratification.* All societies have some form of social stratification.

Because of their common experience, members of a social class often share similar values, behaviors, and political beliefs. In some cases, members of a social class work together to pursue collective goals. For instance, workers in an industry may form a labor union to seek improvements in wages, working conditions, and standard of living. The collective actions of a class can bring about significant social change or even revolution. See **Labor movement; Revolution; Social change.**

Class structure. The system of social classes in a society is called the *class structure.* At the top of the class structure are the wealthiest people and people who have significant power and influence in society. The middle of the class structure includes people who have secure jobs and a comfortable standard of living. Most people in the United States and other developed countries identify with this category, which is often called the *middle class.* Below this category are people who work low-paying jobs or who are temporarily unemployed. This group is sometimes called the *lower class* or *working class.*

The boundaries between social classes vary from one country to another. In most Western democracies—including the United States, the United Kingdom, and Canada—the class structure is largely informal. Such countries allow for some degree of *social mobility.* In other words, it is possible for a person to move from one class to another through his or her actions and achievements.

In some countries, however, each person is born into a certain social class and has an *ascribed* (assigned) social status. In such cases, moving to another class may be difficult or impossible. A class with extremely rigid boundaries is sometimes called a *caste.* In India, for instance, people have traditionally been organized into castes that determine their social status and influence what occupations they might hold. Under this system, children almost always occupy the same class position as their parents. See **Caste; India** (Social structure).

Communism has long promoted the ideal of a "classless" society, in which there are no distinctions based on social class. But in China and other Communist nations—just as in non-Communist nations—certain groups of people, such as government officials, have had much more power, wealth, and prestige than others. See **Communism** (Communism in theory).

How people are categorized. Social scientists have used a variety of methods to compare and rank individuals and groups.

The German philosopher Karl Marx, in the 1800's, identified two classes in a capitalist system. One class, called the *capitalist class* or the *bourgeoisie,* controlled the resources needed to hire workers and to produce goods. The other, the working class or *proletariat,* consisted of people whose chief resource was their own labor. In this system, classes are distinct groups that are

© Gerry Penny, AFP/Getty Images

Members of a social class often share similar values, behaviors, and customs. The formally dressed people shown here are gathered at a British social event, the Royal Ascot horse races.

defined primarily by their relationships to one another. Marx believed that the relationship between the bourgeoisie and the proletariat was marked by a *class struggle*. He believed that the struggle would end—and classes would disappear—when workers seized control of industry and the government. See **Communism** (The ideas of Marx); **Marx, Karl.**

Many social scientists categorize people based on the amount of money they have. Traditionally, people with more money have ranked higher in the class structure than people with less money. However, wealth is usually just one of several factors that determines a person's status. Other factors include education, occupation, and community involvement. Firefighters and members of government, for instance, are highly regarded in most societies, even though their incomes may not be especially high. People whose jobs require leadership, responsibility, or special expertise usually have high status.

Some scholars use *life chances* as an indicator of social class. Life chances, as described by the German sociologist Max Weber, reflect the sets of resources, opportunities, and choices available to a person. A person's life chances depend largely on money, education, and support from family and the community.

Every society consists of members of numerous cultural groups, sometimes called *identity groups*. Such groups may be distinguished by race, ethnicity, sex, religion, or cultural practices. Although these groups are distinct from social classes, they may still contribute to the process of social stratification. For instance, widespread discrimination against women or minority

groups can limit job opportunities and drive people into lower classes.

Debate over classes. Some sociologists believe that social classes benefit society. A society, they argue, must have a system of rewards that encourages people to undertake certain essential jobs. Many important occupations involve high levels of stress and require advanced education and training. People may be unlikely to pursue such jobs unless they are rewarded with a high income. As a result, these sociologists claim that varying levels of income—and therefore different social classes—help ensure that workers are available for all of society's necessary jobs.

Other sociologists claim that social classes are not a necessary part of society. They argue that large differences in income or prestige only benefit people at the top of the class structure. Most social scientists have opinions somewhere between these two positions. They believe that some social stratification may be necessary for society. However, they also believe that large differences between upper and lower classes do not benefit society. 　　　　Philip N. Cohen

See also **Aristocracy; Middle class; Minority group; Poverty.**

Additional resources

Brooks, David. *Bobos in Paradise: The New Upper Class and How They Got There.* Simon & Schuster, 2001.
Payne, Geoff, ed. *Social Divisions.* St. Martin's, 2000.
Perelman, Michael. *Class Warfare in the Information Age.* 1998. Reprint. St. Martin's, 1999.
Zweig, Michael. *The Working Class Majority.* ILR Pr., 2000.
Zweig, Michael, ed. *What's Class Got to Do with It? American Society in the Twenty-First Century.* ILR Pr., 2004.

Social Darwinism is the belief that people in society compete for survival and that superior individuals, social groups, and races are those which become powerful and wealthy. Social Darwinism applies Charles R. Darwin's theories on evolution to the development of society. Darwin, a British naturalist, published his theories in 1859 in the book *The Origin of Species* (see **Evolution** [Darwin's theory]). He believed all plants and animals had *evolved* (developed naturally) from a few common ancestors. He proposed that evolution occurred through a process called *natural selection.* In this process, the organisms best suited to their environment are the ones most likely to survive and produce organisms like themselves.

Social Darwinism applies the idea of natural selection to society, trying to explain differences in achievement and wealth among people. According to the theory, individuals or groups must compete with one another to survive. The principles of natural selection favor the survival of the fittest members of society. Such individuals or groups adapt successfully to the social environment, while those that are unfit fail to adapt successfully.

Social Darwinists assert that those individuals best able to survive show their fitness by accumulating property, wealth, and social status. Poverty, according to the theory, proves an individual's or group's unfitness.

Social Darwinism has been criticized by a large number of social scientists because the theory fails to consider that some people inherit power and influence merely by being born into wealthy families. Critics claim these people or groups owe their good fortune more to their higher social rank than to any natural superiority.

Social Darwinism developed as an important social theory in the late 1800's. Herbert Spencer, a British philosopher, first proposed the theory. William Graham Sumner, an American sociologist, helped make social Darwinism popular in the United States. The theory had lost much of its influence by the early 1900's. But some social scientists still study it.   Irving M. Zeitlin

See also **Spencer, Herbert; Sumner, William Graham.**

Social insect. See Animal (Group living); Ant (Life in an ant colony); Bee (The honey bee colony; Kinds of bees); Termite; Wasp.

Social legislation. See Child labor; Housing; Labor movement; Medicaid; Medicare; Social security; Women's movement (Contemporary women's movements).

Social psychology is the study of how the thoughts, feelings, and behavior of individuals are influenced by the actual, imagined, or implied presence of other people. Social psychologists examine how situations and people combine to affect what people think, feel, and do. Studies and experiments by social psychologists have produced many important findings about human behavior. Social psychologists investigate a wide variety of social interactions and behaviors. These include how people form impressions of themselves and others, stereotyping and prejudice, leadership and group behavior, *altruism* (concern or help for others), the formation of close personal relationships, and aggression.

For example, psychologists may be interested in why people help each other. Many psychologists focus on how the personality characteristics of individuals lead them to help others. However, social psychologists also examine how aspects of a situation, such as the presence of other people or the possibility of rewards, may influence a person's decision to help another.

Social psychologists have found that other people and groups can have great influence on how people think and act. For example, individuals will tend to go along with a decision made by a group even when they privately disagree. People also have a strong tendency to obey the commands of authority figures, such as military officers or police. Experiments by social psychologists show that people will often obey commands from authorities even when those commands cause others to suffer. Social psychologists also observe that people are highly motivated to protect cherished freedoms for themselves, but people tend to help strangers only when they have time to spare. Social psychologists studying group behavior have found that conflict within a group is often reduced when the members must cooperate to achieve a particular goal.

The German-born American psychologist Kurt Lewin is recognized as the founder of social psychology. The findings of social psychologists have influenced important legal decisions, particularly those concerning discrimination. The research of social psychologists Kenneth Clark and Mamie Phipps Clark in the 1950's documented the harm of racial segregation to the self-image of black children. Their research was cited in *Brown v. Board of Education of Topeka,* the 1954 decision by the Supreme Court of the United States that ended racial segregation in U.S. public schools.

Sarah J. Gervais and Theresa K. Vescio

Related articles in *World Book* include:

Social role is a position that an individual or group occupies in a community. Such positions guide the behavior of people in the community and influence the relationships they have with one another.

Social roles are shaped by the beliefs and practices of the community. They are not instinctive. Social roles vary from one culture to another. For example, the primary social roles for women in some societies are wife and mother. But other societies offer women a wider variety of roles from which to choose.

A person typically occupies numerous social roles during his or her lifetime. For instance, a woman may be a daughter to her parents, a wife to her husband, a mother to her children, and a worker to her employer.

Some roles—such as those of student or hospital patient—are occupied by almost all members of society at some time. Other roles—such as those of teacher or doctor—are occupied only by certain individuals who have specialized training.

A person may experience problems if the demands of one social role interfere with those of another. This situation is called *role conflict.* For example, being out of town on a business trip (role as worker) may keep a person from attending his or her child's school play (role as parent).   Ron Mallon

See also **Behavior; Personality; Sexuality** (Gender roles); **Social psychology.**

Social science. Scholars generally identify three categories of knowledge: (1) the natural sciences and mathematics, (2) the humanities, and (3) the social sciences. The natural sciences concern nature and the physical world. The humanities try to interpret the meaning of life rather than to describe the physical world or society. The social sciences focus on our life with other people in groups.

The social sciences include anthropology, economics, history, political science, sociology, social psychology, criminology, and law. Some scholars also regard education, ethics, and philosophy as social sciences. Certain studies in other fields, such as biology, geography, medicine, art, and linguistics, may be said to fall within the broad category of the social sciences.

Relationship to natural sciences. Scholars in the social sciences have developed certain ways of studying people and their institutions. Generally these scholars have borrowed from the natural sciences the methods they use to describe and explain the observed behavior of human society. Their observations of the regularity of human behavior lead scholars in the social sciences to form *hypotheses* (propositions) and then to test the validity of these hypotheses.

The social sciences are still a comparatively new field of learning. History and geography have existed as separate disciplines for a long time. But attempts to systematically study human behavior are new, and most scholars doubt that the scientific method can be used with complete success to understand any aspect of society. They see a wide gulf between the exact nature of the natural sciences and the inexact nature of the social sciences. One of the most powerful tools of the natural sciences is the controlled experiment. Such a method is difficult to use in experiments involving human beings.

Relationship to humanities. The interdependence of the social sciences and the humanities is important. In a social science, the scholar must consider the underlying values of a society, which are stated by the scholars of the humanities. For instance, suppose a political scientist wishes to determine scientifically whether an authoritarian or a representative form of political organization and control would best serve a particular community. The scholar must first learn the importance the community attaches to such values as the right of the individual to differ with authority, or to have a voice in policy and laws. Then the principles that guide its political action can be assessed.   Charles M. Bonjean

Related articles in *World Book* include:

Anthropology	Education	History	Psychology
Archaeology	Ethics	Law	Social psy-
Civics	Geography	Linguistics	chology
Criminology	Geopolitics	Philosophy	Social studies
Economics	Government	Political sci-	Sociology
		ence	

Social security is a government program that helps workers and retired workers and their families achieve a degree of economic security. Social security programs provide payments to help replace income lost as a result of retirement, unemployment, disability, or death. All industrialized nations, as well as many less developed countries, offer some form of social security. In many countries, social security programs are funded by *payroll taxes*—sometimes called *social security contributions*—paid by workers and employers.

Social security differs from *welfare,* or *public assistance.* Social security pays benefits to individuals and their families largely on the basis of their work histories. Welfare, on the other hand, aids the poor largely on the basis of financial need. See **Welfare.**

Social Security in the United States

The United States government provides its main social security benefits through the *old-age, survivors, disability, and hospital insurance* (OASDHI) program—commonly known as Social Security, with two capital letters.

Social Security Administration

A United States Social Security card carries an individual's name and Social Security number. The number enables the Social Security Administration to record the person's earnings.

The program consists of two parts: (1) old-age, survivors, and disability insurance (OASDI) and (2) Medicare. The U.S. government administers OASDI through an independent agency called the Social Security Administration (SSA). The Centers for Medicare and Medicaid Services, an agency of the U.S. Department of Health and Human Services, manages Medicare.

Social Security covers most U.S. workers, including nearly all workers in private industry and most public employees. Workers in jobs covered by the program are required to have a Social Security number. This number enables the SSA to keep a record of the worker's earnings. Any U.S. resident may apply for a Social Security number, and a printed Social Security card, at a local Social Security office. Applicants must present proof of age and citizenship or alien status.

Social Security does not cover some state and municipal employees and certain self-employed people. It also does not cover some foreign workers admitted temporarily to the United States. Most workers who are not covered by Social Security contribute to other retirement and disability funds.

Old-age, survivors, and disability insurance forms the foundation of the U.S. Social Security program. It provides payments to workers or their families after the workers reach a certain age, die, or become disabled.

Eligibility. Workers or their families become eligible for OASDI benefits after the workers earn a specified number of *work credits*—also called *quarters of coverage*—in jobs covered by Social Security. The number of work credits people receive depends on the amount of money they make per year. But workers may receive no more than four work credits per year, no matter how much money they earn.

A worker earns full and permanent OASDI coverage if he or she has a total of 40 work credits. A worker or a worker's family may also receive benefits based on the number of credits earned between the age of 21 and the year of the worker's disability or death. Other eligibility rules apply if a worker becomes disabled before the age of 31 and in certain other cases.

Benefits. To collect OASDI benefits, individuals and families must file a claim with the Social Security Administration. Benefits are paid monthly, except for lump-sum death payments.

Insured workers may collect full retirement benefits when they reach the *full retirement age,* as defined by the government. Beginning in 2003, the retirement age began to increase gradually from 65 to 67. It will rise by two months per year until it reaches age 66 by 2009, and then it will remain fixed through 2020. After 2020, it will increase gradually to age 67 by 2027. Workers age 62 and older may choose to collect retirement benefits before they reach the full retirement age. However, such workers receive a permanently reduced benefit.

To collect disability benefits, workers must have a severe physical or mental condition that affects their ability to perform the activities of everyday life. The condition must have lasted at least 12 months, or it must be expected to last that long or to result in death.

Social Security also provides benefits to the families of retired workers or workers with disabilities. Spouses may collect full benefits when they reach the full retirement age. A spouse's full benefit equals 50 percent of

U.S. social security programs

This chart shows major social security programs, how they are financed, and the agencies that administer them. The programs pay benefits to individuals—and their families—largely on the basis of work histories. Benefits are paid monthly, except for lump-sum death benefits.

WORLD BOOK illustrations by David Cunningham

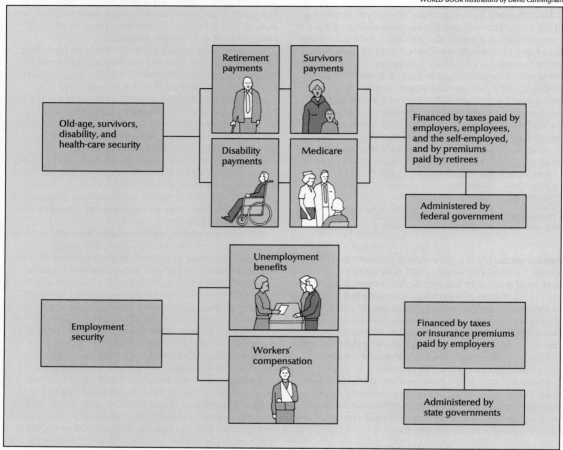

the worker's benefit. Spouses may collect reduced benefits as early as age 62. If a spouse has his or her own working record, he or she may choose between collecting worker's benefits or collecting spouse's benefits. Under certain conditions, additional benefits may be paid to a worker's child, to a spouse or other adult who provides care for a worker's child, or to a former spouse.

When an insured worker dies—either before or after retirement—the worker's dependents may be eligible for a monthly survivors benefit. Payments are based on the benefits the worker was receiving at the time of death or would have received at retirement. The spouse also receives a small single lump-sum payment after the worker's death to help cover funeral expenses.

How benefits are figured. The amount workers receive in OASDI benefits depends on their average lifetime earnings, over a maximum of 35 years, in jobs covered by Social Security. A worker who has paid a large amount in Social Security taxes receives a greater benefit than a worker who has paid less. However, workers with lower lifetime earnings collect benefits that are greater in proportion to their earnings. When calculat-

ing OASDI benefits, the government *wage-indexes* the worker's covered earnings—that is, it adjusts the earnings record to reflect the average increase in wages over time. The government also raises benefits to reflect increases in the cost of living.

Workers who choose to collect retirement benefits before the full retirement age receive reduced benefits. The amount of reduction depends on their age at retirement. Workers who retire at age 62, for instance, collect 75 percent of the full monthly amount. Workers who retire after the age of 62 receive a higher monthly benefit. People who work beyond the normal retirement age without claiming benefits collect a bonus called the *deferred retirement credit.* This bonus provides an eventual increase in benefits to make up for the years that fully eligible workers did not claim benefits.

Total benefits payable on a worker's earnings record each month may not exceed an amount called the *maximum family benefit.* This amount varies from 150 to 180 percent of the worker's basic monthly benefit. When the total benefits exceed the maximum, each individual benefit is proportionately reduced. Some higher-income individuals and couples must pay federal income tax on their benefits. This tax revenue helps finance the Social Security program.

Medicare is a government health insurance program that covers nearly all people age 65 or older. It also covers certain people with kidney disease and people who have received Social Security disability benefits or Railroad Retirement Board disability benefits for at least two years. The program includes hospital insurance, medical insurance, and prescription drug coverage.

Hospital insurance helps pay for hospital care, certain skilled nursing facility care, and home health services. Medicare also has an optional *hospice* benefit for terminally ill patients. Hospice care is a type of home-centered health care for people dying of an incurable illness. People entitled to Social Security or Railroad Retirement Board benefits automatically qualify for hospital insurance at age 65, even if they continue to work.

Medical insurance helps pay the cost of physicians' services and certain other costs that hospital insurance does not cover. Almost all Medicare beneficiaries participate in medical insurance.

Prescription drug coverage helps people pay for generic and brand-name prescription drugs. Members have a choice of plans, operated by private companies, that provide different types of drug coverage. Each state government determines the selection of available plans.

People age 65 or older who are ineligible for retirement benefits may obtain Medicare coverage by paying a monthly premium. For certain low-income individuals who are disabled or age 65 or older, a welfare program called Medicaid pays some or all of the medical expenses and premiums that Medicare beneficiaries usually must pay. Individual states administer their own state Medicaid programs and provide most of the funding.

Financing Social Security. A payroll tax shared equally by employers and workers finances the OASDHI program. This payroll tax is called the Federal Insurance Contributions Act (FICA) tax. Each worker's annual income, up to a certain fixed amount, is subject to the tax. This amount, called the *wage base,* is the same for each employee and changes from year to year, depending on the cost of living. Self-employed workers also pay a FICA tax, but they are allowed tax deductions that result in their getting back half the amount paid. All earnings of all workers are subject to the Medicare portion of the FICA tax.

Employers deduct the FICA tax from workers' income each pay period, add an equal contribution, and then send the amount periodically to the Department of the Treasury. The department distributes most of the money to the Old-Age and Survivors Insurance Trust Fund and the Disability Insurance Trust Fund, and these funds pay the appropriate benefits. The rest of the FICA revenue goes to the Hospital Insurance Trust Fund, which finances Medicare's hospital insurance. The U.S. government's general revenues pay most of the cost of Medicare's medical insurance. Participants in the program pay the rest through monthly premiums.

Funding issues. The FICA required to keep the Social Security system solvent continually changes and Congress has always periodically adjusted the program. In 1983, Congress passed legislation that sought to protect the financial health of the Social Security system over the next 75 years. For the first time, Congress reduced future benefits while it raised taxes to boost future revenue. The law accelerated parts of a previously scheduled tax increase and expanded the categories of workers covered under Social Security. It required all federal employees hired after 1983 to join the system. The law also required some higher-income retirees to pay federal income taxes on up to 50 percent of their benefits. The resulting revenues were added to the Social Security trust funds. In addition, the law required a gradual rise in the full retirement age.

From the mid-1960's through the mid-1980's, the tax-paying labor force was enlarged by the entry of the *baby boom generation*—that is, the group of people born during a period of high birth rates from 1946 to 1964. As a result, during the late 1900's, the number of workers paying taxes into the Social Security system grew more rapidly than the number of retirees collecting from the system.

Social Security's covered labor force is expected to remain about three times as large as the population of beneficiaries until about 2010. Soon after that, however, large numbers of baby boom retirees will begin to collect retirement benefits, which will draw heavily from the Social Security trust funds. The Social Security Administration estimates that these funds may be exhausted by about 2040.

Proposed changes. To address funding problems, Congress has considered a number of changes to Social Security. Suggested changes have included increases in tax rates, changes in the ways benefits are calculated, and reductions in benefits for higher-income workers. Many people favor further expansion of the categories of workers who must participate in Social Security, more increases in the retirement age, or further rises in the percentage of benefits that are subject to income taxes. Some proposals involved the movement of Social Security funds into individual investment accounts.

Other U.S. programs

Workers in the United States may receive other social security benefits through *unemployment insurance* and *workers' compensation* programs.

Unemployment insurance provides weekly payments to workers who have lost their jobs through no fault of their own and are seeking work. It covers civilian federal employees, former military personnel, and most workers in commerce and industry who are not self-employed. It also covers state and local government workers and workers in nonprofit organizations.

The state governments administer the unemployment insurance system and determine the benefits. But federal law requires that state programs meet certain standards. Unemployment insurance is financed chiefly by a payroll tax on employers. The states determine the rate employers must pay. In a few states, employees also contribute.

To qualify for benefits, an unemployed person must have worked for a certain period in a job covered by unemployment insurance, or must have earned a certain amount of income, or both. Unemployed workers must apply for benefits at a state unemployment office. They also must register for employment and be willing to take a suitable job.

Unemployment benefits vary. Most states base them on the person's average earnings during a specified number of months prior to unemployment. Benefits generally equal about half the worker's full-time weekly pay, within minimum and maximum limits. A few states pay extra benefits to workers with dependents. The period during which workers may collect benefits also varies. All states extend the maximum benefit period during times of high statewide unemployment.

The Tax Reform Act of 1986 made all unemployment benefits subject to federal income tax. In addition, some states require recipients to pay state income tax on their benefits.

Workers' compensation provides medical benefits and payments for lost wages to workers who suffer a work-related injury or illness. It also pays death benefits to the dependents of workers who die from a job-related injury or disease. Most states require employers to provide workers' compensation coverage. But some states limit coverage for farm and domestic workers, as well as for workers in small businesses.

Most workers' compensation programs are administered by state agencies known as *workers' compensation boards* or *industrial commissions.* Many employers obtain coverage for their employees through insurance companies or by establishing their own insurance funds. Some states provide a fund through which employers may obtain coverage. Most limit the size of benefit payments and may limit the benefit period or the total paid to any individual. Injured workers normally receive about two-thirds of their salary while disabled.

Social security in Canada

Canada's social security system has three main parts: (1) the Old Age Security program, (2) the Canada Pension Plan, and (3) unemployment insurance. A government department called Human Resources and Social Development Canada administers the country's social security programs.

The Old Age Security program provides a modest retirement income to people age 65 or older who have lived in Canada for at least 10 years. To receive this pension outside Canada, the person must have lived in Canada for at least 20 years. Beneficiaries are paid benefits regardless of their work records. Benefits, which are paid monthly, rise automatically with the country's cost of living. Low-income beneficiaries receive an additional benefit called the Guaranteed Income Supplement.

The Canada Pension Plan provides additional monthly benefits to retired workers, workers with disabilities and their children, and the spouse and children of deceased workers. The plan also provides a death benefit in a single payment to the estate of a covered deceased worker. Workers must be 60 or older to collect a retirement pension under the plan. Retirement benefits are based on workers' earnings and their contributions to the plan. The plan is financed by a payroll deduction. Employers and workers pay separate taxes on the worker's earnings. Self-employed workers pay both the employer's and worker's shares.

Participation in the plan is required for all workers from the ages of 18 to 60 who earn more than an annual minimum. Workers from 60 to 70 continue to participate if they are not yet receiving a retirement pension

under the plan. Workers in the province of Quebec do not participate in the plan. Instead, they are covered by a similar program, called the Quebec Pension Plan.

To qualify for disability and survivors benefits, workers must have contributed to the pension plan for a specified period. Such benefits equal a fixed amount plus a percentage of the retirement pension to which the worker would be entitled. Benefits are adjusted yearly to reflect increases in the cost of living.

Unemployment insurance covers almost all Canadian workers. To receive benefits, an unemployed worker must have worked in an insured job for a minimum number of weeks. The number of weeks depends on how long the person has worked and on the unemployment rate in the region where the worker lives. Generally, the weeks worked must fall within the year before the person filed for benefits. The worker also must have worked a minimum number of hours per week or earned a minimum amount of money per week. Some unemployed workers are eligible for maternity, illness, and parental benefits. Unemployment insurance is financed by premiums paid by employers and employees. Premiums are paid into the Unemployment Insurance Account, which is administered by Human Resources and Social Development Canada.

Social security in other countries

Social security systems vary from one country to another. In the United Kingdom, the government provides a *basic state pension* for people above a certain age who have paid taxes into the National Insurance system. People who have contributed large amounts to the National Insurance system may also be eligible for a *state second pension.* In addition, the British government provides unemployment insurance and a *minimum pension* for people in need.

In Australia, the government provides unemployment insurance and two main programs for retirement income. The first is a *federal means-tested pension,* which covers nearly all workers and is supported by general government funds. The second is a system of individual accounts that employers are required by law to support. In Japan, there is a social security council that oversees programs to ensure that all Japanese people can maintain an adequate standard of living. In India, the government does not have a universal social security system. Instead, a number of laws provide benefits for different segments of the nation's workforce.

In many less developed countries, there is no social security system. Retired workers and workers with disabilities in such countries may have to rely on their children or other relatives for financial security.

History

The Industrial Revolution of the 1700's and early 1800's led to the development of social insurance in Europe. During this period, many people moved from rural areas to cities and found work in factories. Most of the workers received low wages, and many labored under dangerous working conditions. In many cases, workers were unable to save for old age because their wages were so low. If they became disabled in job-related accidents or lost their jobs during business slumps, workers and their families suffered hardships.

During the late 1800's, Germany began to adopt laws to improve conditions for workers. The German government established the first sickness insurance law in 1833 and the first workers' compensation act in 1884. By 1889, Germany had passed the first compulsory old-age and disability insurance program.

By the early 1900's, most European countries had enacted basic social security programs similar to Germany's. The United Kingdom adopted its social security system in 1908. Australia introduced its program the same year.

The United States was one of the last major industrialized nations to establish a social security system. In 1911, Wisconsin passed the first state workers' compensation law to be held constitutional. At that time, most Americans believed the government should not have to care for the aged, the needy, or people with disabilities. But such attitudes changed during the Great Depression of the 1930's. Many Americans realized that economic misfortune could result from events over which workers had no control.

In 1935, the U.S. Congress passed the Social Security Act, which formed the basis of the U.S. Social Security system. It provided cash benefits only to retired workers in commerce and industry. In 1939, Congress amended the act to include benefits for wives and dependent children of deceased workers. In 1950, the act began to cover many farm and domestic workers, nonprofessional self-employed workers, and many state and municipal employees. Coverage became nearly universal in 1956, when lawyers and other professional workers came under the system. Congress added disability insurance to the system in 1956 and set up Medicare in 1965.

Canada's system began in 1940, when the Canadian Parliament passed the Unemployment Insurance Act. Parliament amended the act in 1971 to cover nearly all employees. The Canada Pension Plan went into effect in 1966, and the payment of retirement benefits began in 1967. The Quebec Pension Plan was established in 1965.

Teresa Ghilarducci

Related articles in *World Book* include:

Medicare	Social Security Administration
Old age	Unemployment insurance
Pension	Workers' compensation
Retirement	

Additional resources

Altman, Nancy J. *The Battle for Social Security: From FDR's Vision to Bush's Gamble.* Wiley, 2005.
Béland, Daniel. *Social Security: History and Politics from the New Deal to the Privatization Debate.* Univ. Pr. of Kans., 2005.
Jasper, Margaret C. *Social Security Law.* 2nd ed. Oceana, 2004.
Tomkiel, Stanley A., III. *The Social Security Benefits Handbook.* 4th ed. Sphinx, 2004.

Social Security Administration (SSA), an independent agency of the United States government, administers the nation's Social Security program. This program provides retirement, disability, and death benefits for working Americans and their families. Under the plan, retired or disabled workers or their dependents or survivors receive monthly cash payments. The SSA administers the Supplemental Security Income (SSI) program, which guarantees an annual income to needy people who are 65 or over, blind, or disabled. The Social Security program was created in 1935.

The Social Security Administration became an independent federal agency in 1995. Before then, it had been part of the U.S. Department of Health and Human Services. See also **Social security.**

Critically reviewed by the Social Security Administration

Social settlement. See Settlement house.

Social studies is a program of study in elementary and high school. Social studies deals with the individuals, groups, and institutions that make up human society.

Social studies includes many of the *social sciences,* the fields of study concerned with people in society. For example, students in social studies classes study anthropology to learn about world cultures. They study sociology to investigate social relationships and groups. The students learn economics to discover how people make and distribute goods. They also study geography to find out where and how people live, history to gain knowledge of the past, and political science to understand different forms of government. In some programs, students study philosophy, psychology, religion, and art.

The term *social studies* first gained widespread use about 1916. That year, the Committee on Social Studies of the National Education Association issued a report on such studies. The committee defined social studies as studies that enable students to understand others and become good citizens.

Goals. A major goal of social studies programs is to provide knowledge of the world and its peoples. Social studies students investigate their own and other cultures to determine the similarities and differences. Early programs concentrated on the cultures of the United States and western Europe. Today, social studies courses also cover many other cultures.

Educators design social studies programs to teach four chief types of skills: (1) study skills, (2) intellectual skills, (3) group work skills, and (4) social skills. Study skills help students gather information from books, maps, and other materials. Intellectual skills enable them to define and analyze problems. Group work skills help students operate effectively in committees and other groups. Social skills help them get along with others.

Social studies programs are also designed to help students develop certain attitudes and beliefs, such as respect for others and a sense of fairness. However, educators, parents, and community leaders often differ on what values these programs should stress.

Methods. Educators sometimes organize social studies content around key concepts. For example, a teacher may base a unit on the concept of justice, an important idea in political science. Another unit might deal with the concept of region, as used by geographers.

Social studies teachers encourage students to ask questions and to seek answers for themselves. This method, sometimes called the *discovery method* or *inquiry method,* teaches young people how to think, rather than what to think.   Francis P. Hunkins

Related articles in *World Book* include:

Anthropology	Geography	Political science
Civics	Government	Social science
Economics	History	Sociology

Social welfare. See Welfare; Philanthropy.

Social work is a profession that administers a wide range of social services and programs. Specially trained people called *social workers* provide counseling, support, guidance, and other services to people in need.

The goal of such assistance by social workers is to help people resolve their psychological and social problems and attain their full potential. Social workers also try to improve living conditions by participating in programs to prevent such problems as drug addiction, mental illness, poor housing, and neglect or abuse of children or the elderly.

Most social work programs are financed by government agencies or private organizations. Most social workers are employed in family service agencies, hospitals, clinics, drug abuse centers, nursing homes, settlement houses, schools, prisons, and various business offices and industrial workplaces. Some social workers have a private practice and provide counseling for a fee.

Methods of social work

Traditionally, social work has consisted of three basic approaches—*casework, group work,* and *community organization work.* Casework involves direct contact between a social worker and the individuals and families being helped. Group work involves programs in which the social worker deals with several persons at the same time. Community organization work focuses on neighborhoods and their large groups of people. Since the mid-1900's, social workers have increasingly combined the three basic approaches.

Fields of social work

There are five major fields of social work: (1) family and child welfare, (2) health, (3) mental health, (4) corrections, and (5) schools.

Family and child welfare includes services to families during times when physical or mental illness, unemployment, or other situations seriously disrupt family life. Social workers in this field give divorce counseling, provide therapy for married couples and families, and lead programs that teach people how to improve their family life. The Alliance for Children and Families coordinates family service agencies in communities throughout North America.

Child welfare programs provide such services as adoption, day care, foster child care, and care for children with disabilities. Child welfare workers also aid physically or emotionally abused children and their families. The Child Welfare League of America organizes agencies that offer support services for abused or neglected children and their families.

Health. Medical social workers help patients and their families in clinics, hospitals, and other health care facilities. They help physicians by providing information about the social and economic background of patients. Such problems as inadequate housing and lack of money for medicine may cause or aggravate illness. Medical social workers help patients and their families deal with the impact of illness and death. They also counsel patients who have been discharged, to help them return to everyday life. Many medical social workers specialize in a particular area. These areas include maternal and child care, the care of dying patients, and counseling victims of a certain disease, such as cancer.

Mental health. Social work in mental health includes aid to people suffering from mental and emotional stress. Social workers in this field also provide many of the same kinds of services offered by medical social workers. Many receive training in *psychotherapy,* the treatment of mental or emotional disorders by psychological methods.

Corrections includes programs concerned with the prevention of crime and the rehabilitation of criminals. Social workers in the field of corrections also counsel people who are on probation or parole.

Schools. Social work is part of the program in schools on all levels, from nursery school through college. It includes services to students in special schools for emotionally disturbed and disabled individuals. Social workers in schools provide vocational counseling

WORLD BOOK photo by Dan Miller

Casework involves direct contact between the social worker and the individuals and families being helped. Casework is one of the basic methods of social work. Other basic methods include group work and community organization work.

and help with personal problems. They also assist students who have learning difficulties and help them work to their potential.

Other fields of social work offer assistance in a wide variety of situations. Many social workers help elderly people obtain financial assistance, medical care, and services that enable them to live as independently as possible. Social workers in clinics and community treatment centers counsel alcoholics and drug abusers.

Some social workers aid people in public housing projects and help find dwellings for families made homeless by urban crises. Social workers employed by corporations and labor unions provide a variety of work-related services, including health counseling and retirement planning.

Other social workers practice *social planning*. This field involves organizing and developing programs that deliver social services. Still others specialize in researching social service issues.

History

Social work became a profession with the founding of the first social service agencies in the late 1800's. Before that time, the needy relied upon charitable individuals and certain religious groups and fraternal societies for assistance.

Social service agencies began in response to changes that took place in society during the Industrial Revolution, a period of great industrial development that had begun in the 1700's. During this period, the growth of populations and industries, together with a movement of people from rural areas to cities, brought such problems as overcrowding, unemployment, and poverty.

One of the first social service agencies was the Charity Organization Society, founded in London in 1869. Its counselors, called "friendly visitors," went as volunteers to the homes of needy people and performed services, some of which were similar to those of present-day social workers. Such services later became known as casework. Charity Organization Societies also were founded in the United States and Canada.

Another type of social service agency that began in the late 1800's was the *settlement house*. These centers worked to improve living conditions in city neighborhoods and helped immigrants deal with the problems that come with living in a new country. Group work and community organization work developed out of the settlement house movement.

The New York School of Philanthropy was the first school to train people for jobs with social agencies. This school, now the Columbia University School of Social Work, was founded by the United States' Charity Organization Society in 1898 in New York City. By the early 1900's, a large number of state and local governments in the United States had started to provide social services financed by tax funds. The United States government created the Social Security program in 1935, during the Great Depression. Under this program, the government became a major source of public aid. See Social security.

Americans who have made important contributions to social work's development include Jane Addams, Mary E. Richmond, Grace L. Coyle, Gordon Hamilton, and Bertha Reynolds. Addams was a leader of the settlement

house movement. Richmond wrote the first scientific study of casework techniques in social work, *Social Diagnosis* (1917). Coyle helped develop group practice in social work. Hamilton built on Richmond's work and formulated one of the major approaches to casework. This approach stressed the importance of establishing specific goals for individuals receiving help. Reynolds, through her teaching and leadership, showed how social work could be used to influence public policy.

Careers

Social work offers a variety of job opportunities. Most professional social workers deal directly with the people they serve. Others work as administrators, supervisors, planners, researchers, or teachers. *Paraprofessional* social workers do not require full professional training. They work as assistants to professional personnel, and some of them volunteer their services.

Professional social workers have at least a bachelor's degree in social work. Many jobs require a person to have a master's or doctor's degree in social work. More than 100 schools in the United States and Canada offer a master's degree in social work, and more than 400 colleges offer a bachelor's degree in the subject. Many junior and community colleges have two-year training programs for paraprofessional jobs. In addition, a number of agencies and organizations provide on-the-job training.   Ann Hartman

Related articles in *World Book* include:

Organizations

Big Brothers/Big Sisters of America
Jewish community centers
Junior Leagues
Red Cross
Salvation Army
Social Workers, National Association of
Travelers Aid International
United Way of America

Other related articles

Addams, Jane	Lathrop, Julia C.
Alinsky, Saul D.	Riis, Jacob A.
Breckinridge, Sophonisba	Settlement house
Child welfare	Wald, Lillian D.
Day, Dorothy	Welfare
Hull House	

Additional resources

Gibelman, Margaret. *What Social Workers Do.* 2nd ed. National Assn. of Social Workers, 2004.
Grobman, Linda M., ed. *Days in the Lives of Social Workers.* 3rd ed. White Hat Communications, 2005.
Morales, Armando T., and Sheafor, B. W. *The Many Faces of Social Workers.* Allyn & Bacon, 2002.
Sowers, Karen M., and Thyer, B. A. *Getting Your MSW: How to Survive and Thrive in a Social Work Program.* Lyceum Bks., Inc., 2006.
Van Wormer, Katherine. *Introduction to Social Welfare and Social Work: The U.S. in Global Perspective.* Brooks/Cole, 2006.
Woodside, Marianne R., and McClam, Tricia. *An Introduction to Human Services.* 5th ed. Brooks/Cole, 2006.

Social Workers, National Association of, is a professional organization devoted to the improvement of social work practices and standards. The organization works to promote the social work profession, advance the practice of social work, and shape public policy. The association was formed in 1955 by the merger of seven organizations. The association's publications include *The*

Encyclopedia of Social Work, four professional journals, a monthly newspaper, and many books dealing with the professional needs of its members. The National Association of Social Workers has headquarters in Washington, D.C.

Critically reviewed by the National Association of Social Workers

Socialism refers to economic and political arrangements that emphasize public or community ownership of *productive property.* Productive property includes land, factories, and other property used to produce goods and services. All societies have practiced some form of public ownership. But the term *socialism,* as it is used today, first appeared in Europe in the 1800's. At that time, socialist thinkers contrasted the idea of socialism with the newly developed idea of capitalism. Many socialists were also concerned by the disruptions in people's lives caused by the Industrial Revolution, a period of rapid industrialization that had begun in the 1700's.

Eventually, many countries adopted socialist policies. These policies included government control of the economy and the establishment of vast social welfare programs to aid the needy. By the 1990's, many people had begun to associate socialist policies with a lack of economic flexibility. As a result, numerous political parties that once called themselves socialist stopped doing so. Nevertheless, many institutions inspired by socialist ideas remained and kept the support of most citizens.

Early socialist ideas. In the 1800's, thinkers who favored socialism claimed it was a traditional economic system and perhaps a more natural one than capitalism. They pointed out, for example, that much property served public purposes in ancient Greece and Rome, in Europe during the Middle Ages, and in Christian monasteries. Public or communal ownership applied especially to natural resources and to large enterprises that required community cooperation.

The early socialists saw community ownership as an answer to poverty, great inequalities of wealth, and social unrest. The French journalist and politician Pierre J. Proudhon considered the establishment of any kind of private property as a theft from the community. The Welsh-born socialist leader Robert Owen believed that the sharing of property created social harmony and progress, in contrast to the competition and conflict generated by private property and capitalism.

Such ideas influenced political movements for protecting the working class. In the mid-1800's, for example, the French socialist leader Louis Blanc began a French workers' movement that was based on socialist ideas. The movement gave rise not only to labor unions but also to socialist political parties. Similar developments later occurred in all industrialized countries.

Karl Marx, a German philosopher and economist, became the most influential socialist. His thinking was critical of French socialists, who focused on the moral questions of property and advocated reforms to achieve social justice. Marx proposed a type of socialism that his supporters called "scientific" and "revolutionary."

Marx's writings include the *Communist Manifesto* (1848), which he wrote with the German journalist Friedrich Engels. The work held that civilization had reached its condition at that time by an inevitable process that began with the invention of private property. The existence of private property divided society into owners and workers. According to Marx, conflict between those classes drove civilization to adopt capitalism. But Marx thought capitalism soon would fall apart because of its defects, including a tendency to produce economic depressions. The working class would then use socialism to dismantle capitalism's foundation of private property.

The *Communist Manifesto* served as the political platform for an organization called the First International (originally known as the International Workingmen's Association). This organization united several labor and socialist groups.

The First International brought together socialists from many countries at its first congress, which was held in London in 1865. Marx and Engels inspired the meeting. Socialists at the congress hammered out a common doctrine that included insistence on revolution instead of gradual reform, the elimination of private ownership of productive property, and the establishment of *state socialism* (authoritarian rule by the working class). The First International did not include all socialists, however.

UPI/Corbis-Bettmann

American socialist Eugene V. Debs, *shown speaking here,* gave many antiwar speeches during World War I (1914-1918). Debs ran five times as the socialist candidate for president of the United States but received few votes. Socialism has never been as strong in the United States as in many other countries.

Moderate socialism developed in a variety of ways from the mid-1800's through the early 1900's. For example, the Fabian Society was founded in the United Kingdom in 1884. Its members taught that socialist goals could be achieved gradually through a series of reforms. Similar movements appeared in other countries. In both Europe and the United States, some reformers advocated Christian socialism, which stressed biblical ideas of shared property and a common good.

In the United States, Christian socialists and labor activists united to form the Socialist Party in 1901. Socialists in labor were led by Eugene V. Debs and Victor L. Berger. Debs ran for president of the United States as the Socialist Party candidate in 1904, 1908, 1912, and 1920. Each time, he received less than 6 percent of the popular vote. Berger and several other socialists served in Congress.

Events of the late 1800's and early 1900's led many socialists to break with the Communists. The working-class revolution that Marx had expected failed to occur. In Europe, such everyday concerns as job safety, employment benefits, better wages, and social welfare occupied workers' attention. Even many Marxists began to argue that achieving socialism should be *evolutionary* (gradual) rather than revolutionary. These socialists were led by such thinkers as the German writer and politician Eduard Bernstein. Bernstein claimed socialism must be achieved within a democratic system. Socialists should make members of the middle class their allies and strive for practical reforms instead of revolutionary change.

The Second International, organized at a meeting in Paris in 1889, highlighted this new moderation. Bernstein and other evolutionary socialists dominated the Paris meeting.

World Wars I and II. In World War I (1914-1918), the Allies, who included France, Russia, the United Kingdom, and the United States, defeated the Central Powers, including Germany and Austria-Hungary. During the war, the international spirit of the Second International virtually disappeared. This change occurred partly because most socialist parties of the warring nations of Europe supported their own governments. But even more important may have been the war's role in bringing Communists to power in Russia in 1917.

The war brought economic hardship and political unrest to Russia. Russian Communists led by V. I. Lenin took advantage of these conditions to gain control of Russia's government. Lenin became the nation's dictator. With his followers, he transformed Russia into the first self-described socialist state, the Union of Soviet Socialist Republics. Its political and economic principles became known as Marxism-Leninism. However, not all socialists throughout the world approved of the Soviet Union. Some socialists criticized the Soviets for their authoritarian methods and radical policies.

During the early 1900's, socialist parties also came to power in Australia, Denmark, France, Italy, Sweden, and the United Kingdom. In the United States, Norman M. Thomas ran as the Socialist Party's candidate for president several times. In 1932, he received about 2 percent of the popular vote. Some scholars argue that his campaigns influenced the policies of President Franklin D. Roosevelt's New Deal, especially those designed to help the nation recover from the Great Depression.

In World War II (1939-1945), the Allies, who included the Soviet Union, the United Kingdom, and the United States, defeated the Axis Powers, who included Germany, Italy, and Japan. The major socialist groups and parties of the Allied countries supported their nations' war efforts. Nazi Germany occupied much of Europe during the war, and socialists played a key role in the European resistance to the Nazi occupation. Socialists became the targets of German dictator Adolf Hitler and of Benito Mussolini's Fascist government in Italy.

After the war, socialist parties made gains around the world. In 1945, for example, the Labour Party in the United Kingdom won control of the government on a platform of largely socialist policies. These policies led to the nationalization of much of the nation's economy, including the coal mining, iron and steel, railroad, and trucking industries. Similar socialist successes occurred in nearly every nation of Europe and in many of the independent countries of Latin America and Asia. Socialists also played a central role in establishing and developing the nation of Israel.

The Cold War. The Soviet Union took advantage of political disorder following World War II to establish authoritarian Communist governments in Eastern Europe. Other governments that followed the Soviet pattern appeared around the world, including in China in 1945 and Cuba in 1959. The new governments, like that of the Soviet Union, described their countries as "socialist" states.

Non-Communist socialists in democratic nations found themselves caught between the two sides of the Cold War, a period of international hostility that developed after World War II. The Cold War pitted the Communist nations, led by the Soviet Union, against the non-Communist nations, led by the United States. The Cold War sharpened the division between moderate socialist groups and Communism. It also weakened the appeal of moderate socialism in nations where many people identified it with Communism. This weakening occurred especially in the United States, where support for socialist policies and ideas fell sharply in the 1940's and 1950's. Many socialists criticized Communists for accepting the brutal dictatorship of Soviet leader Joseph Stalin.

The New Left. The 1960's and 1970's saw the rise of a new type of socialism called the New Left in many countries. In the United States, this new socialism was represented by such thinkers as philosopher Herbert Marcuse, who criticized the effects of advertising on consumers in capitalist societies; linguist and educator Noam Chomsky, who saw large capitalist corporations as a threat to personal freedom; and political scientist Michael Harrington, who advocated the gradual establishment of extensive welfare programs.

In Czechoslovakia, Yugoslavia, and other Communist countries, the New Left favored liberal reforms and a rethinking of Marxism-Leninism. In Czechoslovakia in 1968, Communist Party leader Alexander Dubček introduced what became known as "socialism with a human face." This type of socialism restored freedom of the press and other civil liberties. Dubček's reforms, known as the "Prague spring," ended later that year when troops from the Soviet Union and other Communist countries invaded Czechoslovakia.

In both Eastern and Western countries during the

1960's and 1970's, socialism influenced the civil rights movement, the youth culture, and the peace movement. The thinking of those years rejected large-scale state socialism in favor of a focus on socialist policies for local communities.

During the 1960's and 1970's, socialism also had wide appeal in less developed countries. Many newly independent nations viewed socialist policies as a means to speed their economic and political development. Nations that experimented with socialist policies included Kenya and Tanzania in Africa, Egypt and Iraq in the Middle East, Mexico and Chile in the Americas, and India and Burma (now Myanmar) in Asia. In the late 1900's, the economies of many rapidly industrializing nations, including Indonesia, Thailand, and China, blended aspects of socialism and capitalism. For example, they maintained state ownership of rail transport and the petroleum industry. But they also encouraged private ownership of many types of productive property.

The fall of the Soviet Union. In 1991, the Soviet Union broke apart into a number of separate countries, most of which rejected Communism. About the same time, many of the countries of Eastern Europe also set up non-Communist governments.

Some people saw the fall of Communism in Eastern Europe as proof of socialism's inferiority. However, socialists could still point to new successes. In the late 1900's, for example, socialist or formerly socialist parties came to power in the United Kingdom, France, Germany, and many other nations. In addition, aspects of traditional socialist policies had become permanent features throughout the world. Numerous countries, for example, had adopted extensive social welfare programs.

Despite socialism's numerous successes, the movement became difficult to define and identify after the fall of the Soviet Union. A large number of the "socialist" parties that came to power in the 1990's rejected the socialist label.

Today, socialists throughout the world disagree on many doctrines they once held in common. For example, many still advocate that the government plan and administer a nation's economy. Others support small-scale cooperatives instead of state-owned industries and believe that, in general, government involvement in citizens' private lives should be kept to a minimum.

The focus of socialism has also changed. In the 1800's, socialists saw socialism as a rival to capitalism. Today, many socialists see value in some aspects of capitalism. Traditionally, socialists focused on issues important to workers. Today, many also focus on issues important to the middle class, including women's rights, consumer safety, and the environment. Some socialists and former socialists see these changes as evidence of socialism's failure. Others see it as evidence that the movement has achieved many of its goals.   Stephen Schneck

Related articles in *World Book* include:

Additional resources

Bronner, Stephen E. *Socialism Unbound.* 2nd ed. Westview, 2000.
Buckingham, Peter H., ed. *Expectations for the Millennium: American Socialist Visions of the Future.* Greenwood, 2002.
Lipset, Seymour M., and Marks, Gary. *It Didn't Happen Here: Why Socialism Failed in the United States.* Norton, 2000.
Muravchik, Joshua. *Heaven on Earth: The Rise and Fall of Socialism.* Encounter Bks., 2002.

Socialization, in the behavioral sciences, refers to the complex process by which individuals come to learn and perform behavior expected of them by society. Socialization teaches habits, ideas, attitudes, and values. Behavioral scientists—anthropologists, psychologists, and sociologists—regard socialization as one of the principal ways by which societies perpetuate themselves. Through socialization, culture is transmitted from one generation to the next.

Learning plays an important part in socialization. A person must acquire a wide range of information and skills to participate in the activities of a family, a play group, a school group, a business, or a political system. From the family, children learn such basic functions as speaking, toilet management, and eating properly. They also learn the basic values, beliefs, and goals of the family. For example, they learn what it is to be male or female, what to believe as truth and falsehood, and what to value in human relations.

Socialization is a deliberate process when individuals are told what to do or how to act. But much socialization that occurs is unconscious. For example, children learn many basic attitudes and values by observing other people, especially their parents or older brothers or sisters.

Behavioral scientists study socialization because of three basic characteristics common to all human beings. First, infants cannot live unaided and must depend heavily on others. Second, people must learn most of the behavior that is necessary for survival. Third, people must learn to control their relations with one another by living according to shared values and roles.

In most societies, socialization begins in infancy and continues throughout a person's life. Other agencies, especially the school, have taken over some of the socialization functions of the family. As individuals advance through successive stages of school, they continually discard some attitudes and roles and take on new ones. Other important elements that influence an individual's social behavior include friends and co-workers, religious institutions, television, motion pictures, and various kinds of reading matter.

While the family and other institutions have a strong impact on the child, the individual also influences these institutions in important ways. For example, the infant influences its parents through its ingenuity, moods, and wants. Thus, socialization should not be viewed as a one-way process. At the same time, individuals continuously socialize one another to their separate expectations.   Kenneth J. Gergen

See also **Culture; Social psychology; Social role.**

Additional resources

Berk, Laura E. *Awakening Children's Minds: How Parents and Teachers Can Make a Difference.* 2001. Reprint. Oxford, 2004.
Perret-Clermont, Anne-Nelly, and others, eds. *Joining Society.* Cambridge, 2004.

Société Radio-Canada. See Canadian Broadcasting Corporation.

Society. See Culture (Culture and society); Sociology.

Society for the Advancement of Education was organized in 1939 to publish information on problems and trends in education. It publishes *USA Today,* a monthly magazine that deals with aspects of American life. The society has several thousand members. Its headquarters are in Valley Stream, New York.

Critically reviewed by the Society for the Advancement of Education

Society for the Preservation and Encouragement of Barber Shop Quartet Singing in America. See Barbershop quartet singing.

Society for the Prevention of Cruelty to Animals (SPCA) is the name of many organizations throughout the world that work to foster and promote animal welfare. These anticruelty, or humane, societies help enforce animal protection laws by investigating reports of the mistreatment of animals. Anticruelty societies also maintain shelters and adoption services for lost or unwanted animals. Originally, most anticruelty societies were founded chiefly to protect work animals. Today, these organizations work primarily to protect pets.

The first anticruelty society was founded in 1824 in England. In 1866, Henry Bergh, a New York philanthropist, founded the first such society in the United States, the American Society for the Prevention of Cruelty to Animals (ASPCA). The New York legislature chartered the ASPCA the same year. It became a model for other anticruelty societies that were later founded in the United States.

Today, the United States has about 1,000 local anticruelty societies. Many of these anticruelty societies maintain animal hospitals and humane education programs. In addition, many of the societies perform low-cost birth

WORLD BOOK photo by Steven Spicer

A pet ambulance is used to carry injured, unwanted, or mistreated animals to hospitals and shelters operated by the Society for the Prevention of Cruelty to Animals.

control operations to prevent pet overpopulation.

Critically reviewed by the American Society for the Prevention of Cruelty to Animals

Society Islands is a group of islands located in the Pacific Ocean. The island group is part of French Polynesia, an overseas possession of France. It lies slightly northeast of the Cook Islands, about 4,200 miles (6,760 kilometers) southwest of San Francisco. Samuel Wallis claimed the islands for Britain in 1767. But Louis-Antoine de Bougainville claimed them for France in 1768. The group became a French protectorate in 1842, and a colony in 1880.

The Society Islands group consists of 14 islands. Tahiti and Raiatea are the largest islands. The Society Islands cover an area of 613 square miles (1,587 square kilometers) and have a population of about 215,000. For location, see **Pacific Islands** (map).

Ancient volcanoes form many high peaks, making the land rough and mountainous. Some of the islands are low coral atolls. Papeete, on Tahiti, is the capital of French Polynesia. It has an appearance somewhat similar to France's cities.   Robert C. Kiste

See also **French Polynesia; Tahiti.**

Society of Friends. See Quakers.

Society of Jesus. See Jesuits.

Society of the Cincinnati. See Cincinnati, Society of the.

Sociobiology is the study of the biological basis for the social behavior of human beings and other animals. Sociobiologists try to determine the function of various types of behavior in the life of an animal. They also seek to discover how aggression, communication, and other types of social behavior originated and have changed through countless generations.

Social behavior has traditionally been studied by experts in such fields as *ethology* (the study of animal behavior), anthropology, psychology, and sociology. Sociobiologists use information and ideas from these fields, but they examine social behavior primarily in terms of modern theories of genetics and evolution. Many sociobiologists believe that the results of their studies will someday revolutionize sociology and the other social sciences.

Sociobiology is based on the theory that the central process of life is the struggle of genes to reproduce themselves. According to this theory, an organism inherits tendencies to develop certain types of behavior. These behavior patterns increase the animal's chances of transmitting its genes to the next generation.

Sociobiologists believe an animal can pass on its genes not only by reproducing but also by helping related animals, such as brothers and sisters, survive and reproduce. For example, a worker bee may sting an intruder to protect the hive. The act of stinging kills the worker bee but it protects the queen bee, which has many of the same genes. The queen bee will pass on these genes to her offspring. Sociobiologists have discovered that the more closely two animals are related genetically, the more likely one is to sacrifice itself to protect the other. These scientists speculate that self-sacrificing behavior in human beings may also have a genetic basis.

Some biologists argue that sociobiological explanations of social behavior in animals cannot be applied to human social behavior. These critics point out that human behavior, unlike animal behavior, is highly changeable and is affected by many cultural and environmental influences. Sociobiologists recognize the importance of such influences. However, they insist that human behavior cannot be understood properly without consideration of genetic factors as well.

Arthur Caplan

See also **Evolutionary psychology; Wilson, Edward Osborne.**

Additional resources

Alcock, John. *The Triumph of Sociobiology.* Oxford, 2001.
Durham, William H. *Coevolution: Genes, Culture, and Human Diversity.* Stanford, 1991.
Segerstråle, Ullica. *Defenders of the Truth: The Battle for Science in the Sociobiology Debate and Beyond.* 2000. Reprint. Oxford, 2001.
Turner, Jonathan H. *Human Institutions: A Theory of Societal Evolution.* Rowman & Littlefield, 2003.

Sociology is the study of the individuals, groups, and institutions that make up human society. The field of sociology covers an extremely broad range that includes every aspect of human social life. Sociologists observe and record how people relate to one another and to their environments. They also study the formation of groups; the causes of various forms of social behavior; and the role of churches, schools, and other institutions within a society. Sociology is a social science and is closely related to anthropology, psychology, and other social sciences.

Most sociological studies deal with the predominant attitudes, behavior, and types of relationships within a society. A society is a group of people who have a similar cultural background and live in a specific geographical area. Each society has a *social structure*—that is, a network of interrelationships among individuals and groups. Sociologists study these relationships to determine their effect on the overall function of the society.

Sociological data can also help explain the causes of crime, poverty, and other social problems. The field of *applied sociology* deals with the use of this knowledge to develop solutions for such problems.

Sociologists formulate theories based on observations of various aspects of society. They use scientific methods to test these theories, but few sociological studies can be conducted in a laboratory under controlled conditions. Nevertheless, in many studies, sociologists can achieve results that are nearly as precise as those results achieved through the use of laboratory methods.

What sociologists study

Many elements determine the general social conditions of a society. These elements can be classified into five major areas: (1) population characteristics, (2) social behavior, (3) social institutions, (4) cultural influences, and (5) social change.

Population characteristics determine the general social patterns of a group of individuals who live within a certain geographical area. There are two principal kinds of population studies, *demography* and *human ecology.*

Demography is the systematic study of the size, composition, and distribution of human populations. Demographers compile and analyze various statistics, including people's ages, birth and death rates, marriage rates, ethnic backgrounds, and migration patterns. Many demographic studies explain the effects of social conditions on the size and composition of a population. For example, several studies of the 1900's found a direct correspondence between the growth of science, medicine, and industry and a decline in the death rate.

Human ecology deals mainly with the structure of urban environments and their patterns of settlement and growth. Studies in human ecology explain why and how cities and other communities grow and change.

Social behavior is studied extensively in the field of sociology. Social psychologists usually work with small groups and observe attitude change, conformity, leadership, morale, and other forms of behavior. They also study *social interaction,* which is the way the members of a group respond to one another and to other groups. In addition, sociologists examine the results of conflicts between groups, such as crime, social movements, and war.

In most societies, standards of behavior are passed on from one generation to the next. Sociologists and psychologists observe how people adjust their behavior to conform to these standards, a process called *socialization.*

Sociologists also study *social roles* and *status.* A social role is the function or expected behavior of an individual within a group. Status is a person's importance or rank.

Social institutions consist of organized relationships among people and tend to perform a specific function within a society. These institutions include business organizations, churches, governments, hospitals, and schools. Each institution has a direct effect on the society in which it exists. For example, the attitudes and

Some major subdivisions of sociological study

Criminology is the study of criminal behavior and the causes of crime. Criminologists also develop various methods of crime prevention.
Demography is the study of the size, composition, and distribution of human populations.
Deviance is the study of behavior that departs from or challenges social norms, and of the people and institutions that attempt to control such behavior.
Human ecology deals with the structure of urban environments and their patterns of settlement and growth.
Political sociology is concerned with how people gain and use power within a political system, and the rise of various political movements.
Social psychology deals with the individual's social behavior and relationships with others in a society.
Sociolinguistics studies the way people use language in a variety of social situations.
Sociology of education is concerned with understanding how educational institutions transmit a society's cultural attitudes and traditions.
Sociology of knowledge is the study of a society's myths, philosophies, and sciences and their effect on attitudes and behavior.
Sociology of law studies the relationships between a society's legal code and various social patterns, such as economic concerns, cultural traditions, and family relationships.
Urban sociology deals with the social conditions and problems of cities. This field includes the study of race relations and city planning.

University of Chicago (WORLD BOOK photo by Dan Miller)

Sociology students work on various research projects under the guidance of their professors. During class, the students discuss the information they have gained from these studies.

WORLD BOOK photo by Dan Miller

Market researchers often use sociological data and techniques. This woman is using a computer to gather data on consumer buying habits for a marketing study.

the goals of an entire society are influenced by the transmission of learning and knowledge in educational institutions. Some branches of sociology study the influence of one particular type of institution. These branches include the sociology of the family and the sociology of law.

Sociologists also study relationships among institutions. For example, sociologists try to discover whether distinct types of social classes and governments are associated with particular systems of economic production.

Cultural influences help unify a society and regulate its social life. These influences also give people a common base of communication and understanding. The culture of a society includes its arts, customs, language, knowledge, and religious beliefs. Sociologists study the effect of each of these elements on social conditions and behavior. For example, religious beliefs may determine the moral code of a society. Sociological studies focus on the way this code regulates social behavior and the role the code plays in the establishment of a society's laws.

Social change is any significant alteration in the social conditions and patterns of behavior in a society. Such a change may be caused by fashions, inventions, revolutions, wars, and other events and activities. Technological developments have led to many social changes. A number of sociological studies have concentrated on the changes in education, social values, and settlement patterns that occur in newly industrialized nations.

Methods of sociological research

Sociological theories must be tested and verified before they can be considered reliable. Sociologists use three chief methods to test theories. These methods are (1) surveys, (2) controlled experiments, and (3) field observation.

Surveys, sometimes called *public opinion polls,* are the most widely used method of sociological research. They measure people's attitudes about various subjects. Sociologists often use surveys to determine the relationship between a certain viewpoint and such factors as age, education, and sex.

Most surveys are conducted by the use of questionnaires prepared by sociologists. These questionnaires consist of clearly worded questions about the participant's background and his or her opinions on the subject being studied.

The sociologist selects the group of individuals to be questioned. This group, called a *sample,* may be chosen at random or may be selected to represent a particular segment of the population. The sociologist questions the participants personally or by telephone, or mails the questionnaires to the participants. In most cases, sociologists use computers to analyze the survey results.

Surveys provide information on voting behavior, consumer buying habits, racial prejudice, and many other human attitudes and activities. Surveys are also used by sociologists to pinpoint particular social problems and to evaluate social conditions within a specific community.

Controlled experiments are used primarily in the study of small groups. Some of these experiments are conducted in a laboratory. In most cases, two or more highly similar groups of people are studied. The groups differ in one principal feature, which is called a *variable.* The variable may be age, sex, economic background, or any other identifiable characteristic. The sociologist observes each group to learn if the variable produces a significant difference in the attitudes and behavior of its members.

For example, a sociologist may theorize that groups of people of the same sex solve problems more effectively than coeducational groups. To test this theory, three groups might be studied. The first group would consist only of women, the second of men, and the third of an equal number of both. The groups must be similar in such factors as age, education, and social background. All the groups receive identical problems and instructions. If the groups composed of members of one sex perform better consistently, the theory has been verified. In most cases, however, sociologists test theories more extensively before forming any general conclusions.

Field observation usually involves a sociologist's living in the community that he or she is studying. Information is gathered primarily through observation and conversations with members of the community. The sociologist also may participate in a variety of social functions and political activities during the period of study.

The community's institutions and culture are studied, along with the attitudes, behavior, and interactions of its members. The sociologist then draws general conclusions about the community's social conditions and records these findings in a report called a *case study*. Case studies provide reference material for sociologists who are studying similar communities. Such information is also used in *comparative sociology*, a field concerned with examining the similarities and differences among societies.

History

Early sociological thought. The study of human society dates back to ancient times, but it was not considered a science until the early 1800's. At that time, the French philosopher Auguste Comte created the term *sociology*. Comte developed the theory of *positivism*, which held that social behavior and events could be observed and measured scientifically and expressed in the form of scientific laws.

Many sociological theories were suggested during the 1800's. Several of them were *single-factor theories*, which emphasized one factor as the controlling element of the social order. One of the most historically important single-factor theories was *economic determinism*, which was developed by two German social thinkers, Friedrich Engels and Karl Marx. This theory states that economic factors control all social patterns and institutions. Economic determinism forms much of the basis of Communism.

During the mid-1800's, sociological thought was greatly influenced by the theory of evolution. The British philosopher Herbert Spencer concluded that the development of human society was a gradual process of evolution from lower to higher forms, much like biological evolution.

Development of social research. During the late 1800's, many sociologists rejected social evolution and shifted to a more scientific study of society. The French sociologist Émile Durkheim was one of the first social thinkers to use scientific research methods. Durkheim conducted an extensive study of suicide. He collected demographic information from various nations and studied the relationship between their suicide rates and such factors as religion and marital status.

In the early 1900's, the German sociologist Max Weber concluded that sociological theories must be generalizations. Weber devised a method of study in which he compiled all the typical characteristics of a specific group of people. These characteristics formed what Weber called an *ideal type*. Weber based general conclusions about the group as a whole on this ideal type.

Several new schools of sociological thought gained prominence during the 1920's. They included *diffusionism, functionalism,* and *structuralism.*

Diffusionism stressed the influence that individual societies have on each other. Diffusionists believed that social change occurred because a society adopted various cultural traits of other societies.

Functionalism viewed society as a network of institutions, such as marriage and religion, that are related to and dependent on one another. According to the theory of functionalism, a measurable change in one institution would then cause a change in the others.

Structuralism emphasized the social structure as the major influence on society. Structuralist thinkers developed the idea that social roles and status determined much human behavior.

A sociological theory that was called *structural-functionalism* also developed during the 1920's. This philosophy, which included elements of both structuralism and functionalism, was advanced in the 1930's by the American sociologist Talcott Parsons. The theory of structural-functionalism dominated sociology until the mid-1900's.

Modern sociology. During the mid-1900's, sociology became an increasingly specialized field. In general, sociologists shifted from making conclusions about overall social conditions to studying specific groups or types of people within a society. Such groups as business executives, women who work outside the home, and street gangs have been the subject of sociological studies.

Sociologists also began to rely more heavily on scientific research methods. The survey method has been greatly improved, and the use of computers has increased the efficiency of evaluating survey results. Sociologists also have developed better methods of selecting samples.

Changes in life styles and social conditions during the 1960's and 1970's have been the subject of many sociological studies. Various theories have been formed by sociologists on such developments as the drug culture, the youth movement, and the feminist movement.

Since the 1950's, a growing number of sociologists in the United States have called for greater efforts in the field of applied sociology. These men and women believe that sociologists have an obligation to work toward the solution of social problems and the establishment of social justice.

Today, the fields of study in which sociologists are most active include social mobility and the rise and survival of social organizations. Many sociologists are also studying international systems of interdependence and dominance and social influences on the development of science. In addition, a number of earlier theoretical approaches to sociology, including the Marxist approach, have regained significant influence in the field of sociology.

Careers

Most careers in sociology require a master's or doctor's degree. However, people who have a bachelor's degree in sociology may find positions as interviewers or research assistants. A majority of sociologists work for educational institutions. However, some are employed by government agencies and business organizations.

Colleges and universities employ about 70 percent of the sociologists with Ph.D.'s. Some of these individuals devote most of their time to research programs and to teaching sociology to undergraduate and graduate students. Students often gain experience by assisting their professors with research projects. Community colleges and high schools also employ sociology teachers, most of whom have a master's degree.

Government agencies are employing an increasing number of sociologists to study the general conditions and needs of communities. The findings of these sociologists are used in determining government policies on housing, education, safety, and other matters of civic concern.

Some city governments employ sociologists as *city planners.* These experts study such problems as slum housing, transportation, and traffic congestion. They then propose solutions for the problems and plan future development of the city.

Business companies employ many sociologists in the field of *market research.* Market researchers conduct surveys on consumer buying habits to help firms predict sales of products. Professional sociologists prepare these surveys, but people with little or no sociological background may conduct the interviews. Some businesses also hire sociologists to study problems concerning employee relations and motivation.

Career opportunities in sociology are also available in various other areas. Further information about careers in sociology can be obtained from the American Sociological Association, based in Washington, DC.

Neil J. Smelser

Related articles in *World Book* include:

Sociologists

Balch, Emily G.
Comte, Auguste
Du Bois, W. E. B.
Durkheim, Émile
Engels, Friedrich
Frazier, E. Franklin
Johnson, Charles S.
Marx, Karl

Merton, Robert K.
Myrdal, Gunnar
Pareto, Vilfredo
Parsons, Talcott
Spencer, Herbert
Sumner, William G.
Weber, Max

Related studies

Anthropology
Criminology
Demography
Ecology
Psychology

Social psychology
Social science
Social work
Sociobiology

Other related articles

Alienation
Assimilation
Baby boom generation
Behavior

Caste
City
City planning
Civil disobedience

Collective behavior
Community
Crime
Criminology
Culture
Custom
Ethnic group
Family
Group dynamics
Homelessness
Human relations
Juvenile court
Juvenile delinquency
Market research
Middle class
Minority group
Mores
Population

Poverty
Power (social)
Prejudice
Public opinion
Public opinion poll
Racism
Riot
Segregation
Social change
Social class
Social role
Socialization
Statistics
Tribe
Unemployment
Urban renewal
Vital statistics

Additional resources

Borgatta, Edgar F., and Montgomery, R. J. V., eds. *Encyclopedia of Sociology.* 5 vols. 2nd ed. Macmillan Reference, 2000.
Glover, David M. *The Young Oxford Book of the Human Being: The Body, the Mind, and the Way We Live.* Oxford, 1997. Includes a section on sociology.
Howard, Eve L. *Classic Readings in Sociology.* 2nd ed. Wadsworth Pub., 2002.
Johnson, Allan G. *The Blackwell Dictionary of Sociology.* 2nd ed. Blackwell, 2000.
Kornblum, William, and Smith, C. D. *Sociology in a Changing World.* 5th ed. Harcourt Coll., 2000.
Smelser, Neil J. *Sociology.* 5th ed. Prentice Hall, 1995.

Socrates, SAHK ruh TEEZ (about 470-399 B.C.) was a Greek philosopher and teacher. Socrates was one of the most original, influential, and controversial figures in ancient Greek philosophy and in the history of Western thought.

Before Socrates, Greek philosophy focused on the nature and origin of the universe. He redirected philosophy toward a consideration of moral problems and how people should best live their lives. Socrates urged his fellow Greeks to consider as the most important things in life the moral character of their souls and the search for knowledge of moral ideas like justice. He was credited with saying "the unexamined life is not worth living." Socrates's teachings, combined with his noble life and calm acceptance of death, have made him the model of what it is to be a philosopher.

The Socratic problem. Because Socrates wrote nothing, our only knowledge of his ideas comes from other Greek writers. The most important sources are the dialogues written by one of his followers, Plato. Also important are the writings of the historian Xenophon; the comedy *Clouds,* by the playwright Aristophanes; and writings of Plato's pupil Aristotle. The difficulty of determining the character and beliefs of Socrates based on these sources is referred to as "the Socratic problem." The most common understanding of Socrates comes from Plato's dialogues, which communicate the force of Socrates's intellect and character. Plato's *Apology of Socrates* is regarded as a reliable representation of Socrates's defense of his life at his trial. His *Euthyphro* and *Laches* are probably true to the spirit of Socrates's philosophical method. See **Plato** (Plato's writings).

Socrates's life. Socrates was born near Athens, and spent most of his life in Athens. His wife, Xanthippe, was supposedly ill-tempered. They had three sons. Socrates spent most of his time in conversations with a wide range of Athenians, but mostly with young men. Plato distinguished Socrates from the professional teachers of the day, who were called Sophists. Plato emphasized that Socrates did not accept money from his listeners. As a result, Socrates was very poor. Socrates was famous for his self-control and also for his indifference to physical comfort. Supposedly, he once stood in one spot for a day and night puzzling over a philosophical problem.

Many Athenians were annoyed by Socrates's constant examination of their moral assumptions. Plato showed Socrates engaging leading Athenian citizens in conversation. These people entered the conversations believing that they knew the nature of such virtues as piety or courage. But Socrates soon showed them that their beliefs were contradictory or confused. He also criticized some assumptions of the Athenian democratic system.

Hostility arose in Athens toward Socrates. At the age of 70, Socrates was brought to trial and charged with "not believing in the gods the state believes in, and introducing different new divine powers; and also for corrupting the young." Socrates was convicted and sentenced to death. He could have escaped from prison, but he felt morally obligated to follow the court's decision, even if it was unjust. His arguments for his action are recorded in Plato's *Crito.* Plato's *Phaedo* describes Socrates's calm in the face of death and his drinking of the poison, hemlock, which the Athenians used for the death penalty.

Although Socrates's conviction was unjust, there was some truth to the charges against him. Socrates apparently observed the religious rites of Athens and believed in divine power. But Plato's *Euthyphro* indicates that Socrates would not accept stories that showed the gods behaving in an immoral manner. Socrates also claimed to have received a "divine sign" that kept him from committing immoral actions. In addition, his repeated demonstration of the weak reasoning behind most people's moral beliefs could be seen as teaching the young to reject the morals accepted by Athenian society. In fact, Socrates's ultimate goal was to encourage people to devote their lives to considering how to live morally.

The Socratic method. As a philosopher, Socrates is more important for his philosophical methods than for any specific doctrine. The dialogue form was probably invented by Plato to portray the *Socratic method* or *dialectic.* The method consisted of asking questions like "What is courage?" of people who were confident of the answer. Socrates, claiming ignorance of the answers to the questions, would gradually show the people's beliefs to be contradictory. Socrates did not answer his questions, though much could be learned from the course of the discussion.

Socrates was the first philosopher to make a clear distinction between body and soul and to place higher value on the soul. His examination of such moral ideas as piety and courage represent an important first attempt to arrive at universal definitions of terms. He believed that a person must have a knowledge of moral ideas to act morally.   Carl A. Huffman

See also **Philosophy** (Ancient philosophy); **Law** (The influence of ancient Greece); **Plato.**

Additional resources

Brann, Eva T. H. *The Music of the Republic: Essays on Socrates' Conversations and Plato's Writings.* Paul Dry Bks., 2004.
Brickhouse, Thomas C., and Smith, N. D. *The Philosophy of Socrates.* Westview, 2000. *The Trial and Execution of Socrates.* Oxford, 2002.
Phillips, Christopher. *Six Questions of Socrates.* Norton, 2004.
Rudebusch, George. *Socrates, Pleasure, and Value.* 1999. Reprint. Oxford, 2002.

Sod house is a house with walls built of blocks of sod or turf in horizontal layers. Sod houses were constructed by early settlers on open plains where there were no trees to supply lumber. For a description of sod houses and how they were built, see **Western frontier life in America** (Shelter); **Nebraska** (Territorial days; picture).

Soda is the common name for a group of compounds that contain sodium. These sodium compounds are manufactured from common salt (NaCl), which is made up of sodium and chlorine. See **Sodium.**

A common sodium compound is *sodium carbonate*

Detail of *The Death of Socrates* (1787), an oil painting on canvas; The Metropolitan Museum of Art, New York City, Wolfe Fund, 1931. Catherine Lorillard Wolfe Collection

Socrates prepares to carry out his death sentence by drinking a cup of hemlock in this painting by Jacques Louis David. The artist showed Socrates's followers in great despair. Socrates made a toast to the gods and drank the bitter poison. He met death with the same calm and self-control with which he had lived.

(Na$_2$CO$_3$), known as *sal soda, washing soda,* and *soda ash.* It comes in crystals or white powder and has a strong alkaline reaction. This means that it neutralizes acids. Sodium carbonate is used in the manufacture of glass, soap, and paper. It is also used as a disinfectant, a cleaning agent, and a water softener.

Sodium bicarbonate (NaHCO$_3$) is a popular soda used in cooking and in medicines. It is also known as *baking soda* or *saleratus.* Baking powder contains sodium bicarbonate, which acts as a leavening agent because it causes bread, biscuits, or pastries to rise in baking. Seidlitz powders, used to relieve excess stomach acid, also contain sodium bicarbonate. See **Baking powder.**

Sodium hydroxide (NaOH) is a sodium compound also known as c*austic soda* or *lye.* It is widely used in the manufacture of industrial chemicals, rayon, paper, and soap. The compound is also used in the production of aluminum and in petroleum refining.   Clark L. Fields

See also **Glass** (Composition of glass).

Soddy, Frederick (1877-1956), a British chemist, received the 1921 Nobel Prize in chemistry for his atomic structure research. He and New Zealand-born physicist Ernest Rutherford showed that radioactive elements disintegrate into other chemical elements as they emit radioactivity. Soddy gave the name *isotopes* to atoms of the same element with different weights (see **Isotope**).

Soddy was born on Sept. 2, 1877, in Eastbourne, Sussex, and studied at Oxford University. He taught at Oxford, Aberdeen University, and the University of Glasgow. He died on Sept. 22, 1956.   Bruce R. Wheaton

Sodium is a silvery-white metallic element that has many important uses. It is a soft metal, and can easily be molded or cut with a knife. Sodium belongs to a group of chemical elements that are called the *alkali metals.*

Where sodium is found. Sodium is the sixth most common chemical element in the earth's crust. It makes up about 2.8 percent of the crust. Sodium never occurs *pure*—that is, as a separate element—in nature. It combines with many other elements, forming *compounds.* To obtain pure sodium, the metal must be *extracted* (removed) from its compounds.

One of the most familiar sodium compounds is *sodium chloride,* which is common table salt. It can be found in dry lake beds, underground, and in seawater. Countries with large deposits of sodium chloride include Belarus, China, France, Germany, India, Russia, Ukraine, the United Kingdom, and the United States.

Such minerals as borax and cryolite contain sodium. Many plants and the bodies of animals contain small amounts of sodium. The human body needs a certain amount of sodium to maintain a normal flow of water between the body fluids and the cells. Sodium also plays a part in tissue formation and muscle contraction.

A number of studies have shown that the foods in a balanced diet contain enough sodium for the body's normal needs, without the addition of table salt. In fact, some studies have indicated that too much sodium in a person's diet can lead to high blood pressure.

Uses. Sodium compounds have many uses in industry, medicine, agriculture, and photography. Manufacturers use *sodium borate* (borax) in making ceramics, soaps, water softeners, and many other products (see **Borax**). *Sodium hydroxide* (caustic soda, or lye) is an important industrial alkali used in refining petroleum and

in making paper, soaps, and textiles. *Sodium carbonate* (soda ash or washing soda) is used in the manufacture of *sodium bicarbonate* (baking soda). Many people take sodium bicarbonate to relieve an overly acid stomach. *Sodium nitrate* (Chile saltpeter) is a valuable fertilizer. Photographers use *sodium thiosulfate* (hypo) to fix photographic images on paper.

Pure sodium also has industrial uses. Finely divided sodium is used as a *catalyst* (substance that causes a chemical reaction) in the making of some types of synthetic rubber. Some nuclear power plants use sodium in liquid form to cool nuclear reactors. Sodium is also used to produce such metals as titanium and zirconium.

Extracting sodium. In 1807, the English chemist Sir Humphry Davy became the first person to obtain pure sodium. He used electric current to extract the metal from sodium hydroxide.

Manufacturers still use electric current to obtain sodium. The process is called *electrolysis.* In this process, a current is passed through a molten sodium compound, such as sodium chloride. The current separates the compound into chlorine gas and sodium metal. See **Electrolysis.**

Chemical properties. Pure sodium is extremely active chemically. Sodium immediately combines with oxygen when it is exposed to the air. As a result, the element loses its shiny appearance and becomes dull. Sodium's bright surface can be seen only after it has been newly cut or extracted. Sodium weighs less than water. It *decomposes* (breaks up) water, producing hydrogen gas and sodium hydroxide. This chemical reaction is extremely violent. It produces much heat that often causes the hydrogen to ignite.

Sodium also reacts quickly with such other nonmetals as chlorine and fluorine, and it forms alloys with many metals. Liquid ammonia dissolves sodium, forming a dark-blue solution. A test to determine whether a material contains sodium is to hold the substance in a flame. If sodium is present, the flame will burn a bright yellow.

Sodium must be handled and stored with extreme care. In laboratories, small amounts are stored under kerosene in airtight bottles. The kerosene prevents air or moisture from reaching the metal. Large quantities of sodium in brick form are stored and shipped in airtight, moisture-free barrels. Sodium is also shipped in sealed tank cars. The metal is melted and poured into the tanks. The sodium hardens during shipping, and must be melted again before it can be removed.

Sodium has the chemical symbol Na. Its *atomic number* (number of protons in its nucleus) is 11. Its *relative atomic mass* is 22.989770. An element's relative atomic mass equals its *mass* (amount of matter) divided by $\frac{1}{12}$ of the mass of an atom of carbon 12, the most abundant form of carbon. The melting point of sodium is 97.8 °C, and its boiling point is 881 °C.   Duward F. Shriver

Related articles in *World Book* include:

Alkali	Carbonate	Salt, Chemical	Sodium hydroxide
Bicarbonate of soda	Chloride	Saltpeter	
	Nitrite	Soda	Thiopental
Borax	Salt		

Sodium hydroxide, also called lye or caustic soda, is an important industrial chemical. It is the main ingredient in many commercial drain cleaners and oven cleaners. It is also used to make soap and paper. Sodium hydroxide is a solid, white material that readily absorbs moisture. It produces extremely corrosive solutions. Sodium hydroxide, both as a solid and in solution, can severely damage skin if it comes into contact with it. If splashed into eyes, sodium hydroxide solution can cause blindness in a few seconds. Sodium hydroxide is produced from brine by electrolysis (see **Electrolysis**). Its chemical formula is NaOH. See also **Alkali**.

Robert J. Ouellette

Sodium pentothal. See Thiopental.

Sodom and Gomorrah, *SAHD uhm, guh MAWR uh,* were two Biblical cities located near the Dead Sea. Genesis 18-19 tells the story of how God destroyed Sodom and Gomorrah with fire and brimstone because the people were wicked.

The Hebrew leader Abraham pleaded with God not to destroy Sodom. Abraham said that if only some righteous people were found in the city, God should be merciful and spare it. But when not even 10 righteous people were found in Sodom, God decided to destroy both Sodom and Gomorrah. God first sent two angels to rescue Abraham's nephew, Lot, who was living in Sodom. The angels warned Lot and his wife and two daughters to flee the city and not look back. But Lot's wife turned to see the fiery destruction of Sodom and Gomorrah. According to Genesis 19:26, she was immediately changed into a pillar of salt as punishment for her disobedience.

Eric M. Meyers

See also **Lot**.

Sofia, *SOH fee uh* or *soh FEE uh* (pop. 1,173,988), is the capital and largest city of Bulgaria, and the country's chief economic and cultural center. The city lies in western Bulgaria and is surrounded by the Balkan Mountains and other ranges. For location, see **Bulgaria** (map).

The Alexander Nevsky Cathedral, built in the late 1800's to celebrate Bulgaria's liberation from Turkish rule, stands in the center of Sofia. The National Museum and the ancient churches of St. George and St. Sofia are in the city's old section. This section has winding, narrow streets, and its small houses are jammed closely together. In contrast, modern sections of Sofia have wide avenues and high-rise apartment buildings. Most of the people of Sofia live in apartments.

Sofia is the site of the National Assembly Building, the National Theater, the National Library, and the former Royal Palace. The University of Sofia and the Bulgarian Academy of Sciences are also in the city.

About a fifth of Bulgaria's industry is in Sofia. Industry and transportation employ over half the city's workers. Sofia's industries include food processing; the manufacture of textiles and clothing; and the production of machinery, electric equipment, and metals. Nearby farms provide fruit, vegetables, and dairy products for the city. Streetcars and buses furnish public transportation.

The Roman Emperor Trajan founded the city in the early A.D. 100's. The Huns, led by Attila, destroyed it in 447. A short time later, Sofia became part of the Byzantine Empire. The Bulgarians conquered the city in 809, but the Byzantines regained control of it in 1018. In 1382, the Ottomans made Sofia part of their empire. The city again came under Bulgarian rule in 1878, when Russia helped Bulgarian rebels defeat the Ottomans. Bulgaria became an independent nation that same year, and Sofia was named the capital.

Joseph F. Viesti, FPG

Sofia is the capital and largest city of Bulgaria. Modern high-rise buildings line the Maria-Luisa Boulevard. Streetcars provide transportation for many of Sofia's residents.

Since the mid-1900's, thousands of people from rural areas have moved to Sofia in search of jobs. As a result, the city's population has grown rapidly. To prevent overcrowding in Sofia, city planners have built apartment buildings and shopping facilities in the city's suburban areas.

Vojtech Mastny

See also **Bulgaria** (picture).

Soft-coated wheaten terrier is a breed of dog that originated in Ireland. Farmers used it to drive cattle, to guard houses and barns, and to kill rats and other pests. This terrier is related to the Irish and Kerry blue terriers.

Soft-coated wheaten terrier puppies are dark brown

© Callea Photo

The soft-coated wheaten terrier comes from Ireland.

or brownish-red. The adults have a rich wheat-colored coat of soft, wavy hair. In many of these terriers, the tails are *docked* (cut short). The dogs stand about 19 inches (48 centimeters) high and weigh from 35 to 45 pounds (16 to 20 kilograms).

Critically reviewed by the American Kennel Club

Soft drink is a flavored, nonalcoholic beverage prepared with carbonated water. Soft drinks are called *soft* to distinguish them from *hard* (alcoholic) drinks. Soft drinks are also called soda pop, soda, or pop. Cola is by far the most widely consumed soft drink. Other flavors include lemon-lime, orange, ginger ale, and root beer.

Soft drinks are popular in many countries throughout the world. In the United States, people consume more soft drinks than any other type of beverage. On the average, people in the United States drink about 56 gallons (201 liters) of soft drinks per person annually.

How soft drinks are made. Soft drinks consist of carbonated water and syrup. Carbonated water is produced by adding carbon dioxide gas to water under pressure. The gas makes the water bubble and fizz. In most cases, syrup is made of a *concentrate* and sweeteners. A concentrate includes a blend of flavor and acid. Concentrates for most soft drinks also include coloring. Syrup can also be prepared directly from individual ingredients.

Many of the flavorings found in soft drinks come from such natural sources as fruit juices and oils obtained from roots, citrus fruit peels, and leaves of various plants. Some flavorings are artificial, though many are similar to natural flavorings in taste. Citric acid and phosphoric acid give soft drinks a tart taste. Caramel provides the brown color of most cola drinks. Other types of soft drinks use a variety of natural and artificial colors. The sweetener may come from corn, sugar beets, or sugar cane. Low-calorie sweeteners, such as saccharin, aspartame, acesulfame-K, and sucralose, are used in diet soft drinks (see **Artificial sweetener**).

Soft drinks are generally distributed by the *franchise system.* Under this system, a soft drink company produces the soft drink concentrate or syrup and sells it to a bottler. The bottler adds carbonated water to the syrup, or carbonated water and sweetener to the concentrate, to make the soft drink. Then the bottler cans or bottles the drink and sells it. Under the terms of the franchise, each bottling firm agrees to follow certain formulas established by the soft drink company. In return, the bottler receives exclusive rights from the soft drink company to sell a particular soft drink in a specific area. See **Franchise.**

History. Many soft drinks, especially colas, had their start in the late 1800s in the southern United States. Drugstore soda fountains originally sold many of the beverages as tonics. Individual druggists mixed their own special tonics as syrups. It later became popular to add soda water—that is, carbonated water—to these syrups before drinking them. Many restaurants still dispense soft drinks in much the same way, using equipment that mixes the soft drink syrup with carbonated water at the time the beverage is sold. Soon, the druggists discovered that there was a market for soft drinks in bottles, and they began to sell the beverages door-to-door and in grocery stores.

In time, syrup makers founded larger soft drink com-

panies and started to sell their syrup to bottlers. Today, the main soft drink companies in the world include Cadbury Schweppes plc; the Coca-Cola Company; PepsiCo, Inc.; and Royal Crown Cola Company, Inc.

Soft drink consumption has increased significantly since the mid-1960's. Since then, soft drink companies have made their products available in more convenient packages, such as metal cans and many types of glass and plastic containers. In addition, beverage makers have developed a wider variety of soft drinks, including diet and low-sodium drinks.   Theresa S. Chamblee

See also **Coca-Cola Company; PepsiCo, Inc.**

Soft-shelled crab. See **Blue crab.**

Softball is a popular game throughout the world. Softball resembles baseball, but the rules of the sports differ in several ways. Softball pitching must be underhand. Softball requires less space and equipment, and regulation games last seven innings instead of nine. A softball is also larger than a baseball.

Types of softball. There are two types of softball games, *slow pitch* and *fast pitch.* Slow-pitch games account for about 90 percent of the softball competition in the United States. In slow-pitch games, pitchers must throw the ball slowly enough to make it arch on its way to the batter. Teams have 10 players—a pitcher, a catcher, and eight fielders. Nine positions are the same as those in baseball. On most teams, the 10th person plays as a fourth outfielder. Many slow-pitch teams play with balls about 12 inches (30 centimeters) in circumference. Others use 11- or 16-inch (28- or 41-centimeter) balls. Slow-pitch rules prohibit bunting and base stealing.

Fast-pitch teams use a 12-inch ball, and some players can pitch it more than 85 miles (137 kilometers) per hour. Teams have nine players who play the same positions as those in baseball. Batters may bunt, and runners may steal bases after the ball leaves the pitcher's hand.

Field and equipment. The infield in softball is smaller than that in baseball. The bases lie 65 feet (19.8 meters) apart in adult slow-pitch games, and 60 feet (18.3 meters) apart in adult fast-pitch games. The pitcher stands 46 feet (14 meters) from home plate in men's fast-pitch games and 43 feet (13.1 meters) away in women's

© Ingram Publishing/SuperStock

Softball is a team game that resembles baseball. In softball, the pitcher must throw the ball to the batter underhanded.

Pitching a softball

All softball pitches are thrown underhand. The series of pictures at the right shows a typical right-handed fast pitch. Start with both feet on the pitcher's plate. Then raise the right hand over the head and swing the arm back and down. At the same time, step forward with the left foot, keeping the right foot on the plate. As the right arm swings forward, release the ball and follow through.

WORLD BOOK illustrations by David Cunningham

games. The distance is 50 feet (15 meters) for men's and women's slow pitch.

Softballs are filled with a soft material called *kapok,* a mixture of cork and rubber, a plastic material called *polyurethane,* or other materials. They can have a cover of cowhide, horsehide, or synthetic material. Softball bats may be made of such materials as wood, metal, plastic, or fiberglass. Softball bats cannot be thicker than 2 ¼ inches (5.7 centimeters) or longer than 34 inches (86.4 centimeters). All players may wear gloves, but only catchers and first basemen may wear padded mitts.

History. Softball was developed as an indoor game in 1887 by George W. Hancock in Chicago. He used a 17-inch (43-centimeter) ball whose seams looked like ridges because they were turned to the outside. In 1895, Lewis

Rober of the Minneapolis Fire Department adapted the game for outdoor play. Rober used a 12-inch ball that had a cover like that of a baseball.

In 1933, the Amateur Softball Association (ASA) was founded to govern and promote softball in the United States. The ASA set up a committee that established one set of rules now used by teams in all parts of the world. The International Softball Federation, founded in 1952, governs international competition. It has more than 125 countries, whose teams compete in annual regional, national, and international tournaments.

Critically reviewed by the Amateur Softball Association

See also **Baseball.**

Softwood. See Lumber (Softwood lumber); **Tree** (Needleleaf trees; Needleleaf forests); **Wood.**

A softball field

The diagram at the right shows the approximate positions of the players in men's and women's slow-pitch softball. The outfield and the foul territories extend beyond the area shown to the boundaries of the playing area. A diagram of the home-plate area appears below.

WORLD BOOK diagrams by Arthur Grebetz

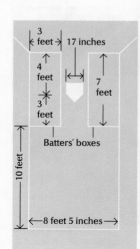

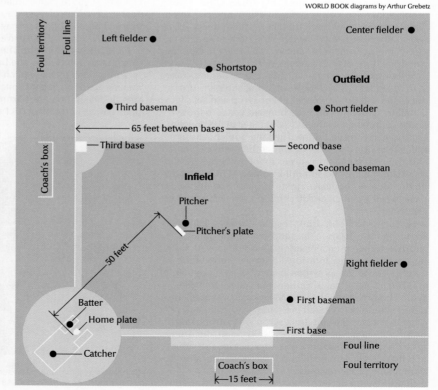

Soil is an important natural resource that covers much of the earth's land surface. Most life on the earth depends upon the soil as a direct or indirect source of food. Plants are rooted in the soil and obtain *nutrients* (nourishing substances) from it. Animals get nutrients from plants or from animals that eat plants. Certain microbes in the soil cause dead organisms to decay, which helps return nutrients to the soil. In addition, many kinds of animals find shelter in the soil.

Soil contains mineral and organic particles, other plant and animal matter, and air and water. The contents of soil change constantly. There are many kinds of soils, and each has certain characteristics, including color and composition. The kind of soil in an area helps determine how well crops grow there. Soil forms slowly and is destroyed easily, and so it must be conserved so it can continue to support life.

Soil scientists, called *pedologists,* use the term *polypedons* for the bodies of individual kinds of soil in a geographic area. Polypedons can be indefinitely large, but some have a surface area of only about 10.8 square feet (1 square meter). Some polypedons measure less than 5 inches (13 centimeters) deep. Others are more than 4 feet (1.2 meters) deep.

Composition of soils

The mineral and organic particles in soil are called *soil particles.* Water and air occupy the spaces between the particles. Plants and animals live in these *pore spaces.* Plant roots also grow through the pore spaces.

Minerals supply nutrients to green plants. Particles called *sands, silts,* and *clays* make up most of the mineral content of soils.

Sands and silts are particles of such minerals as quartz and feldspars. Clays consist of illite, kaolin, micas, vermiculite, and other minerals. Trace amounts of many minerals add nutrients, including calcium, phosphorus, and potassium, to the soil. Most soils are called *mineral soils* because more than 80 percent of their soil particles are minerals.

Plant and animal matter consists of organic material in various stages of decay. Many organisms also live in the soil. These soil organisms include plant roots, microbes, and such animals as worms, insects, and small mammals. Bacteria, fungi, and other microbes *decompose* (break down) dead plants and animals. Many soil organisms help mineral and organic particles *aggregate* (come together) and form clumps of soil. Roots, burrowing animals, and natural weathering break apart large clumps of soil.

Decaying organic material releases nutrients into the soil. In addition, some organic material combines with mineral particles. Other decaying material forms organic soil particles called *humus.* Most humus is black or dark brown, and it holds large amounts of water. Only 6 to 12 percent of the volume of particles in most mineral soils is organic. However, these small quantities greatly increase a soil's ability to support plant life. In some soils,

called *organic soils,* more than 20 percent of the soil particles are organic.

Water that enters the soil dissolves minerals and nutrients and forms a *soil solution.* Much of the solution drains away, but some remains in the pore spaces. Green plants obtain water and some nutrients by absorbing soil solution through their roots.

Air replaces the water that drains from the larger pore spaces. Soil organisms live best in soils that contain almost equal amounts of air and water.

How soil is formed

Soil begins to form when environmental forces break down rocks and similar materials that lie on or near the earth's surface. Pedologists call the resulting matter *parent material.* As soil develops through the centuries, organic material collects, and the soil resembles the parent material less and less. Glaciers, rivers, wind, and other environmental forces may move parent material and soil from one area to another.

Soils are constantly being formed and destroyed. Some processes, such as wind and water erosion, may quickly destroy soils that took thousands of years to form.

Soil formation differs according to the effects of various environmental factors. These factors include (1) kinds of parent material, (2) climate, (3) land surface features, (4) plants and animals, and (5) time.

Kinds of parent material. The type of parent material helps determine the kinds of mineral particles in a soil. A process called *weathering* breaks down parent material into mineral particles. There are two kinds of weathering, *physical disintegration* and *chemical decomposition.* Physical disintegration is caused by ice, rain, and other forces. They wear down rocks into smaller particles that have the same composition as the parent material. Sand and silt result from physical disintegration.

Chemical decomposition mainly affects rocks that are easily weathered. In this kind of weathering, the rock's chemical structure breaks down, as when water dissolves certain minerals in a rock. Chemical decomposition results in elements and in chemical compounds and elements that differ from the parent material. Some of these substances dissolve in the soil solution and become available as plant nutrients. Others recombine and form clay particles or other new minerals.

The mineral content of parent material also affects the kinds of plants that grow in a soil. For example, some plants, including azaleas and rhododendrons, grow best in acid soils that contain large amounts of iron.

Effects of climate. Climate affects the amount of biological and chemical activity in a soil, including the kinds and rates of weathering. For example, physical disintegration is the main form of weathering in cool, dry climates. Higher temperatures and humidity encourage chemical decomposition as well as disintegration. In addition, decaying and most other soil activities require warm, moist conditions. These activities slow down or even stop in cold weather. Therefore, soils in cool, dry climates tend to be shallower and less developed than those in warm, humid regions.

Effects of land surface features also influence the amount of soil development in an area. For example,

Taylor J. Johnston, the contributor of this article, is Associate Dean of the College of Agriculture and Natural Resources and Professor of Crop and Soil Sciences at Michigan State University.

water running off the land erodes the soil and exposes new rock to weathering. Also, soils on slopes erode more rapidly than those on flat areas. They generally have less time to form and therefore develop less than do soils on flat terrains.

Effects of plants and animals. Soil organisms and organic material help soil develop, and they also protect it from erosion. The death and decay of plants and animals add organic material to the soil. This organic material helps the soil support new organisms. Soils that have a cover of vegetation and contain large amounts of organic material are not easily eroded.

Effects of time. Soils that are exposed to intense soil formation processes for long periods of time become deep and well developed. Soils that erode quickly or have been protected from such processes for a long time are much less developed.

Characteristics of soils

The method and rate of soil formation differs throughout a body of soil. As a result, the soil develops layers. These layers are called *soil horizons.* Soil horizons may be thick or thin, and they may resemble or differ from the surrounding horizons. The boundaries between the layers can be distinct or barely noticeable.

Most soils include three major horizons. The upper two, called the *A* and *B* horizons, are the most highly developed layers. The A horizon is also known as *topsoil.* The lowest horizon, called the *C* horizon or the *subsoil,* is exposed to little weathering. Its composition resembles that of the parent material. Pedologists describe soils by the characteristics of the soil horizons, including (1) color, (2) texture, (3) structure, and (4) chemical conditions.

Color. Soils range in color from yellow and red to dark brown and black. The color of a soil helps pedologists estimate the amounts of air, water, organic matter, and certain elements in the soil. For example, a red color may indicate that iron compounds are present in the soil.

Texture of a soil depends on the size of its mineral particles. Sands are the largest particles. The individual grains can be seen and felt. Silts are just large enough to be seen, and clays are microscopic. Pedologists divide soils into textural classes according to the amounts of sand, silt, and clay in a soil. For example, the mineral portions of soils classified as *loam* contain from 7 to 27 percent clay and less than 52 percent sand. In *silty clay,* more than 40 percent of the mineral particles are clay, and more than 40 percent are silt. Texture helps determine how thoroughly water drains from a soil. Sands promote drainage better than clays.

How soil is formed Soil formation depends on several factors that act together. They include (1) the rock from which the soil forms, (2) the climate, (3) plants and animals, and (4) time. Soils form slowly and continuously. The illustrations below show how a typical soil forms and develops through the centuries.

WORLD BOOK diagrams by Cynthia Fujii

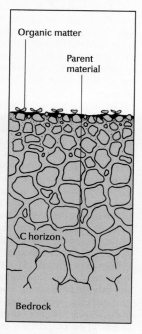
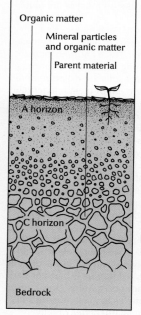
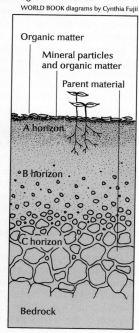

Soil begins to form when rain, ice, freezing and thawing, and other environmental forces break down rocks and similar materials. The resulting matter, called *parent material,* breaks down further into mineral particles.

Simple organisms live on rocks that are *decomposing* (decaying). Plantlike *lichens* produce acids that help decompose the rocks. When the organisms die, organic matter collects among the mineral particles.

Layers called *horizons* appear as soil develops. The top layer, or *A horizon,* has more organic matter than the others and becomes deep enough to support plant roots. The lowest layer, or *C horizon,* resembles the parent material.

A well-developed soil can support a healthy cover of vegetation. It also may include a middle layer, called the *B horizon.* This horizon contains minerals that have been washed down in drainage waters from the soil's surface.

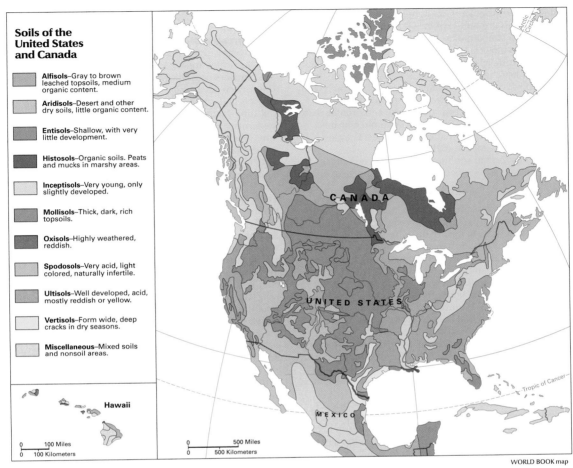

Soils of the United States and Canada

Alfisols—Gray to brown leached topsoils, medium organic content.

Aridisols—Desert and other dry soils, little organic content.

Entisols—Shallow, with very little development.

Histosols—Organic soils. Peats and mucks in marshy areas.

Inceptisols—Very young, only slightly developed.

Mollisols—Thick, dark, rich topsoils.

Oxisols—Highly weathered, reddish.

Spodosols—Very acid, light colored, naturally infertile.

Ultisols—Well developed, acid, mostly reddish or yellow.

Vertisols—Form wide, deep cracks in dry seasons.

Miscellaneous—Mixed soils and nonsoil areas.

Hawaii

0   100 Miles
0   100 Kilometers

0   500 Miles
0   500 Kilometers

WORLD BOOK map

Structure. When soil particles aggregate, they form clumps of soil that are called *peds*. Most peds range from less than $\frac{1}{2}$ to 6 inches (1.3 to 15 centimeters) in diameter. Their shape and arrangement determine a soil's structure. The ability of peds and soil particles to stick together and hold their shape is called *consistence*.

Most soils contain two or more kinds of structures. Some soils have no definite structure. In some such soils, the peds lack a definite shape or arrangement. In others, the particles do not aggregate.

There are three main kinds of soil structures: (1) platelike, (2) prismlike, and (3) blocklike. Platelike peds are thin, horizontal plates that occur in any horizon. Prismlike peds are column-shaped subsoil structures. Blocklike peds look like blocks with flat or curved sides. Large, flat-sided, blocklike peds commonly occur in subsoils. Small, rounded, blocklike peds make up most topsoils. They contain more organic matter and hold water and nutrients better than do larger peds.

Chemical conditions. Soils can be acid, alkaline, or neutral. The amounts of acid and alkali in a soil influence the biological and chemical processes that take place there. Highly acid or alkaline soils can harm many plants. Neutral soils support most of the biological and chemical processes, including the process by which green plants obtain many nutrients. This process is called *cati-*

on exchange. Many nutrients and other elements dissolve in the soil solution, forming positively charged particles called *cations*. The negatively charged clay and humus attract some cations and prevent them from being *leached* (washed away) from the topsoil by drainage waters. The solution that remains in the soil contains other cations. Nutrient cations on the clay and humus and those in the soil solution change places with nonnutrient cations that are on roots. The roots can then absorb the nutrients.

How soils are classified

Pedologists classify soils according to the characteristics of a polypedon. The Soil Survey Staff of the United States Department of Agriculture uses a system that consists of 10 *orders* (groups) of soils. They are (1) alfisols, (2) aridisols, (3) entisols, (4) histosols, (5) inceptisols, (6) mollisols, (7) oxisols, (8) spodosols, (9) ultisols, and (10) vertisols.

Alfisols develop under forests and grasslands in humid climates. Some agricultural soils are alfisols.

Aridisols occur in dry regions and contain small amounts of organic matter. Desert soils are aridisols.

Entisols show little development. They resemble the parent material and occur in many climates.

Histosols are organic soils. They form in water-saturated environments, including swamps and bogs.

Inceptisols are only slightly developed. They are more common in subhumid and humid climates, but also occur in most other kinds of climates.

Mollisols develop in prairie regions. They have thick, organically rich topsoils.

Oxisols are the most chemically weathered soils. They have a reddish color and occur in tropical regions.

Spodosols contain iron, aluminum, and organic matter in their B horizons. They form in humid climates.

Ultisols occur in warm, humid climates. They are moist, well-developed, acid soils.

Vertisols form in subhumid and arid warm climates. They develop wide, deep cracks during dry seasons.

Soil conservation

The soils of farmlands, grazing lands, and forestlands provide many products and recreational areas. Soil conservationists work to ensure the wise use of these soils.

Wise use of farmlands involves maintaining a high level of nutrients and organic matter in cultivated soils. Farmers add organic matter to the soil by plowing under certain green plants. They also add fertilizers and rotate crops to replace nutrients that leaching and growing plants remove. In addition, farmers plow and plant their fields in ways that control erosion. See **Conservation** (picture: Soil conservation).

Grazing lands that have been overgrazed also suffer from erosion. Overgrazing decreases the amounts of plant life and organic matter in the soil, and the soil erodes easily. Ranchers conserve grazing lands by limiting the time that their herds graze in one area.

Forestlands also must be protected from erosion. In some cases, foresters leave unusable branches and other parts of trees on the forest floor to add organic matter to the soil. In addition, foresters develop large groups of trees whose roots protect the soil by holding it in place against wind and water erosion.

Taylor J. Johnston

Related articles. See the *Natural resources* or *Economy* section of the country, state, and province articles. See also:

Agronomy	Fertilizer
Alkali	Gardening
Clay	Humus
Conservation (Soil conserva-	Irrigation
tion)	Loam
Drainage	Loess
Dust Bowl	Permafrost
Earthworm	Sand
Environmental pollution (Soil	Silt
pollution)	Soil bank
Erosion	Topsoil
Farm and farming	

Additional resources

Bial, Raymond. *A Handful of Dirt.* Walker, 2000. Younger readers.
Lal, Rattan, ed. *Encyclopedia of Soil Science.* Marcel Dekker, 2002.
Singer, Michael J., and Munns, D. N. *Soils.* 6th ed. Prentice Hall, 2006.
Wolfe, David W. *Tales from the Underground.* Perseus Pub., 2001.

Soil bank was a United States federal government program designed to reduce crop surpluses by taking croplands out of production from 1 to 10 years. The program provided government payments to farmers who agreed to take designated cropland out of production. The bank

was adopted in 1956, but was replaced by other programs in the early 1960's.

Soil Conservation Service was an agency of the United States Department of Agriculture from 1935 to 1994. Its professional conservationists helped farmers and ranchers prevent soil erosion from water and wind. The service gave assistance through soil-conservation districts and other state and federal agencies. It made soil surveys, developed conservation plans for individual farms, and helped land users install antierosion systems. The agency also managed a national program of flood prevention, irrigation, and watershed protection. In 1994, the agency was replaced by the Natural Resources Conservation Service.

Critically reviewed by the Department of Agriculture

Soil pollution. See Environmental pollution (Soil pollution).

Soilless agriculture. See Hydroponics.

Sokol, *SOH kawl,* is an international organization that stresses physical fitness and moral strength. The organization has no political or religious connections, and people of any age may join. Sokol was founded in Prague, in what is now the Czech Republic, in 1862. It has chapters in Australia, Canada, the United States, South America, and Europe. The American Sokol Organization was founded in 1865. National headquarters are in East Orange, New Jersey.

Critically reviewed by the American Sokol Organization

Solanum, *soh LAY nuhm,* is an important group of plants in the nightshade family. Over 1,000 species of herbs and shrubs are included in the group. They grow throughout the world but are especially abundant in warm and tropical regions of North and South America, Africa, and Australia. Some plants are cultivated for their showy flowers and others for their edible parts. Some species contain medicinal compounds.

Two of the most common species of solanum are the *potato plant* and the *eggplant.* The *horse nettle* and *buffalo bur* are spiny, troublesome weeds native to the United States. The *kangaroo apple* was once used as food by the Aborigines in Australia. Several species, including the *bittersweet* and the *common nightshade,* have been used in ointments and other medicines.

William G. D'Arcy

Scientific classification. Solanums belong to the nightshade family, Solanaceae.

Related articles in *World Book* include:

Bittersweet	Flowering tobacco	Painted-tongue
Eggplant	Nightshade	Potato

Solar cell. See Electric eye; Semiconductor; Solar energy (Photovoltaic conversion).

Solar day. See Day.

Solar eclipse. See Eclipse.

Solar energy is a term that usually means the direct use of sunlight to produce heat or electric power. The sun's energy is plentiful, but it is thinly distributed over a large area and must be collected and concentrated to produce usable power. As a result, solar energy is a more expensive power source than fossil fuels for most applications. Solar technology is improving rapidly, though. Someday, it may provide a clean and abundant source of power.

There are two chief ways that sunlight may be converted into electric power: (1) directly, in a process called *photovoltaic conversion,* or (2) by *solar thermal conversion,* which converts light to heat and then to electric power. Most solar thermal devices heat water to produce steam, which drives a steam turbine.

Nearly all the energy that we use is actually solar energy—energy from the sun. For example, solar energy stored in plants millions of years ago makes up such *fossil fuels* as coal, petroleum, and natural gas. Hydroelectric power plants harness the energy of moving water, and there would be no moving water without the sun. The sun's heat evaporates moisture so that it falls back to earth as rain and other forms of precipitation. The sun also powers the air currents that cause the wind to blow. This article, however, discusses only solar electric and solar heating technologies. For information on other forms of solar energy, see the articles on the fossil fuels, such as **Coal** and **Petroleum,** and the articles on other forms of power, such as **Water power** and **Wind power.**

Photovoltaic conversion

Devices called *photovoltaic cells* or *solar cells* produce electric current directly from sunlight. This ability results from the *photovoltaic effect,* a phenomenon in which the energy in sunlight causes electric charges to flow through layers of a conductive material to produce a useful electric current.

The development of photovoltaic cells. The French physicist Alexandre Edmond Becquerel discovered the photovoltaic effect in 1839. He immersed two metal plates in a solution and observed a small voltage when one plate was exposed to sunlight. The first photovoltaic cells were made of a semimetallic element called selenium. Selenium cells could convert only 1 percent of sunlight to electric power, so they remained just a curiosity for many years.

In 1954, scientists at Bell Telephone Laboratories (now part of Lucent Technologies) invented the first photovoltaic cell that could produce a useful amount of electric power. The Bell scientists, chemist Calvin S. Fuller and physicists Daryl M. Chapin and Gerald L. Pearson, developed a solar cell with an efficiency of 6 percent, six times better than the best selenium cells. A solar cell's efficiency measures the percentage of sunlight striking the cell that it turns into electric power. The Bell scientists made their cell from purified silicon, the material used to make computer chips. Silicon is a *semiconductor*—that is, a material that conducts electric current better than an insulator but not as well as a conductor.

How a photovoltaic cell is made. The most common type of photovoltaic cells are *crystalline silicon cells,* so named because every atom in the cell is part of a single crystal structure. To make a crystalline silicon cell, a manufacturer begins with a thin wafer of silicon that has been *doped* (treated) with an impurity. The impurity, usually the element boron, is called a *p-type dopant,* the *p* standing for *positive.* The addition of the dopant causes local *deficits* (shortages) of electrons, called *holes,* to appear in the material. The doped material is called a *p-type material.* A hole can pass from one atom to another and migrate around the crystal.

An *n-type dopant (n* for *negative),* such as phosphorous, is then *diffused* (spread out) part way into the p-type material. The addition of this dopant produces local

How a photovoltaic cell produces energy

Artwork adapted courtesy of Solar Energy Research Institute

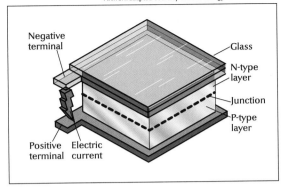

A photovoltaic cell produces electric current when exposed to sunlight. The most common such cell consists of a thin wafer of silicon treated with impurities to create a *p-type* layer with local deficits of electrons and an *n-type* layer with local excesses of electrons. An electrode is joined to each of the layers. Current will flow through a wire connecting the two electrodes.

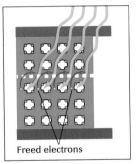

The absorption of light energy in the p-type layer near the *junction,* where the p- and n-type layers join, frees electrons in the p-type layer. The electrons jump across the junction to collect at the negative electrode.

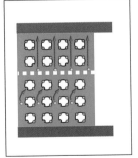

The loss of electrons from the p-type layer produces local deficits, called *holes,* in the layer. Other electrons fill the holes, creating holes in the atoms from which they have come. In this way, the holes migrate from atom to atom.

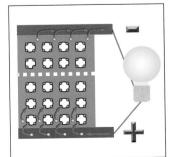

When a wire connects the two terminals, electrons flow from the negative terminal to the positive one, creating electric current. The electrons will then fill some holes in the p-type layer. Electrons will migrate through the cell as long as the cell absorbs light.

excesses of electrons. This layer is then called the *n-type material*. A *potential* (difference in electrical charge) is thus set up between the two layers. When sunlight strikes the photovoltaic cell, the light's energy forces the negative and positive charges in the semiconductor to separate and to accumulate at electrodes joined to each of the two layers. An electric current will then flow through a wire connecting the two electrodes.

Using photovoltaic cells. For most applications, engineers wire together many cells in a grouping called a *module* to produce a desired voltage. Multiple modules may be connected in an arrangement called an *array* to produce the required current for the application. Silicon cell efficiencies have reached 25 percent without special equipment to concentrate sunlight. Compound photovoltaic cells combined with solar concentrating systems have achieved 35 percent efficiency. Researchers have also made solar cells from a number of other semiconductor materials.

Today, solar cells provide power for spacecraft and artificial satellites, handheld calculators, and wristwatches. Solar cells are also used for electric power generation in remote areas, where extending power lines would be difficult or costly. Most photovoltaic systems require a storage facility, which normally consists of batteries. Excess energy is stored in the batteries during the day and extracted as needed during the night.

Other solar cells. Researchers are also studying solar cells called *photoelectrochemical cells*. The simplest such cell is similar to the device made by Becquerel in 1839. However, today's cells are much more stable and efficient. In addition to producing electric current, photoelectrochemical cells can be used to chemically split water directly into oxygen and hydrogen gas. The hydrogen can then be burned as fuel.

Solar thermal conversion

Solar thermal conversion systems, also called *solar concentrators*, use one or more reflectors to concentrate solar energy to extremely high levels. There are three major kinds of systems: (1) parabolic trough systems, (2) parabolic dish systems, and (3) central receivers.

Parabolic trough systems are the simplest of the solar thermal systems. A *parabola* is a type of curve. In such a system, a *parabolic* (curved) trough covered with rows of reflectors moves to track the sun. The reflectors focus sunlight to a line that strikes a fluid-filled pipe at

How solar energy heats a house

WORLD BOOK illustrations by Oxford Illustrators Limited

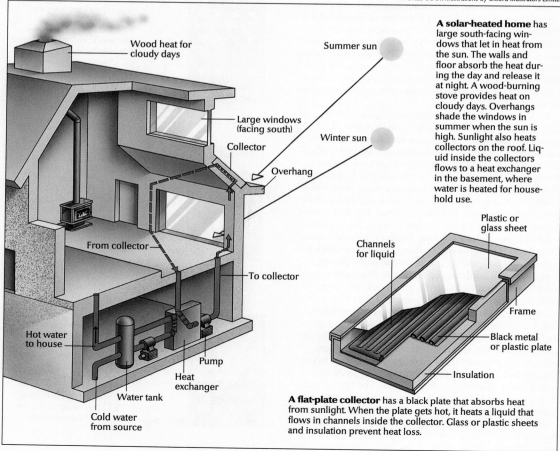

A solar-heated home has large south-facing windows that let in heat from the sun. The walls and floor absorb the heat during the day and release it at night. A wood-burning stove provides heat on cloudy days. Overhangs shade the windows in summer when the sun is high. Sunlight also heats collectors on the roof. Liquid inside the collectors flows to a heat exchanger in the basement, where water is heated for household use.

A flat-plate collector has a black plate that absorbs heat from sunlight. When the plate gets hot, it heats a liquid that flows in channels inside the collector. Glass or plastic sheets and insulation prevent heat loss.

Advanced Photovoltaic Systems

A solar power plant in Davis, California, uses photovoltaic cells to capture energy from the sun. When the sun shines on a cell, an electric current flows from one side of the cell to the other.

the center of the trough. The fluid in the pipe is a heat-absorbing substance that may reach temperatures above 750 °F (400 °C). The heat can be used to make steam to generate electric power or to merely heat water. Trough systems can concentrate solar radiation to 100 times the intensity of normal sunlight. Power plants using this technology in southern California provide about 350 megawatts of electric power per year—enough for a community of about 350,000 people.

Parabolic dish systems resemble parabolic trough systems except that they focus light to a point instead of a line. Parabolic dish systems have reflectors arrayed along the contour of a bowl-shaped structure called a *dish*. Such systems can achieve concentrations up to 10,000 times the intensity of normal sunlight.

Central receiver systems use an array of sun-tracking mirrors, called *heliostats*, that reflect light onto a single central tower called a *receiver*. A central receiver system called Solar Two operates in the Mojave Desert near Barstow, California. It has 1,926 heliostats that focus sunlight on a single receiver. The receiver is filled with a mixture of molten sodium and potassium salts, which holds heat longer than other fluids. After the molten salt is heated, the system pumps it into insulated tanks. When power is needed, the molten salt is pumped into a device called a *heat exchanger*, where it produces steam that turns a turbine. Solar Two's storage capability enables it to operate even after dark or when the sun is covered by clouds. The plant supplies 10 megawatts of electrical power. Other central receiver test facilities operate in Almería, Spain, and Rehovot, Israel.

Solar heating

Solar heating requires an efficient absorber to collect sunlight and convert it to heat. The absorber may be as simple as a coating of black paint, or it may be a textured, heat-absorbing ceramic. A good absorber collects 95 percent or more of the solar radiation while emitting 20 percent or less of the heat energy an ordinary hot surface would.

There are several methods of solar heating. One common method uses windows as solar collectors, as in a greenhouse. The windows trap the sun's heat, and the heat passes back through the windows, roof, and walls slowly.

The simplest solar collectors are *flat-plate collectors*. The plates are fixed, and the sun shines on them at various angles as it moves. The sun heats fluid inside the plates to a temperature of up to 212 °F (100 °C). The hot fluid flows to a heat exchanger, a device like an automobile radiator through which water circulates, and transfers its heat to the water. The hot water is used to warm buildings in a conventional hot-water heating system or to heat their hot-water supplies.

Another kind of collector, designed specifically for heating air, is the *transpired solar collector*. Such collectors consist of flat or ridged plates pierced by an array of small holes. Air is drawn through the holes and is heated by the sun-warmed plates. As much as 80 percent of the solar energy collected by the plates is transferred to the air stream.

A *solar furnace* is a type of solar collector that concentrates sunlight to produce temperatures high enough for use in industrial processes. Scientists use solar furnaces to process steel, ceramics, and other materials; to *pump* (provide energy for) solid-state lasers; and to destroy hazardous wastes. One such furnace operates at the National Renewable Energy Laboratory in Golden, Colorado. In the Colorado installation, a single mirror tracks the sun and directs solar radiation into a series of concentrating mirrors. The mirrors reflect the beam of light through a system of *attenuators* and *shutters,* devices that control the intensity of the beam and turn it on and off. This solar furnace has achieved concentrations of light 50,000 times greater than that of normal sunlight. Such highly focused energy can heat materials to temperatures as high as 6300 °F (3500 °C). Other solar furnaces operate in France, Germany, Israel, Spain, Switzerland, and Uzbekistan.   J. Roland Pitts

See also **Electric eye; Energy supply; Greenhouse; Photochemistry; Sun** (Energy output).

Additional resources

Boyle, Godfrey, ed. *Renewable Energy.* 2nd ed. Oxford, 2004.
Graham, Ian. *Solar Power.* Raintree Steck-Vaughn, 1999. Younger readers.
Green, Martin. *Power to the People.* New South Wales Univ. Pr., 2000.
Kryza, Frank T. *The Power of Light.* McGraw, 2003.
Markvart, Tomas, ed. *Solar Electricity.* 2nd ed. Wiley, 2000.
Perlin, John. *From Space to Earth: The Story of Solar Electricity.* aatec, 1999.

Solar furnace. See **Solar energy** (Solar heating).
Solar heating. See **Solar energy** (Solar heating).
Solar plexus is a common name for the *celiac plexus,* a network of nerves in back of the stomach. The solar plexus is part of the autonomic nervous system. This system controls the abdominal *viscera* (internal organs). Nerve threads of the autonomic nervous system connect by branches with organs of the abdominal cavity. A blow on a spot between the navel and breastbone, a little to the right, is called the solar plexus punch. A fighter can be knocked out by this punch if it is hard enough. The exact manner in which this occurs has not been determined. The solar plexus first became well known in 1897 as a result of the championship boxing match between James Corbett and Robert Fitzsimmons. Fitzsimmons knocked out Corbett with a blow to the solar plexus.   Delmas J. Allen

See also **Nervous system.**

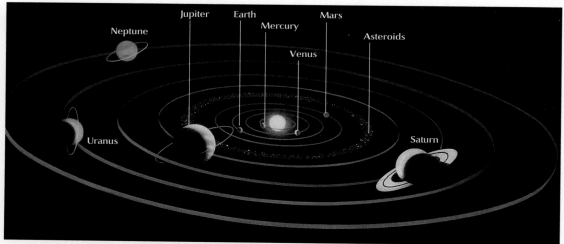

Neptune   Jupiter   Earth   Mars   Mercury   Asteroids   Venus   Uranus   Saturn

The solar system includes many different objects that travel around the sun. These objects vary from planets much larger than Earth to tiny meteoroids and dust particles.

Solar system is a group of heavenly bodies consisting of a star and the planets and other objects orbiting around it. We are most familiar with our own solar system, which includes Earth and the other objects that orbit the sun. Besides the sun, Earth, and Earth's moon, many objects in our solar system are visible to the unaided eye. These objects include the planets Mercury, Venus, Mars, Jupiter, and Saturn; the brightest asteroids; and occasional comets and meteors. Many more objects in the solar system can be seen with telescopes.

Since the 1990's, astronomers have discovered many planets orbiting distant stars, though the planets cannot be seen directly. By studying the masses and orbits of these planets, astronomers hope to learn more about solar systems in general. For example, our own solar system contains four small, rocky planets near the sun—Mercury, Venus, Earth, and Mars—and four giant, gaseous planets farther out—Jupiter, Saturn, Uranus, and Neptune. Astronomers were surprised to find that other stars have giant, gaseous planets in close orbits.

Our solar system

Our solar system includes the sun and all the objects that revolve around it. Astronomers have different ideas about how to classify these objects. The International Astronomical Union, the recognized authority in naming heavenly bodies, divides them into three major classes: (1) planets, (2) dwarf planets, and (3) small solar system bodies. Small solar system bodies include comets, asteroids, and meteoroids. The solar system also includes all the satellites or moons of these objects and a thin cloud of gas and dust known as the *interplanetary medium.*

The sun is the largest and most important object in our solar system. It contains 99.8 percent of the solar system's *mass* (quantity of matter). It provides most of the heat, light, and other energy that makes life possible. The sun's outer layers are hot and stormy. The hot gases and electrically charged particles in those layers continually stream into space and often burst out in solar eruptions. This flow of gases and particles forms the

solar wind, which bathes everything in the solar system.

Planets orbit the sun in oval-shaped paths called *ellipses,* according to a law of planetary motion discovered by the German astronomer Johannes Kepler in the early 1600's. The sun is slightly off to the side of the center of each ellipse at a point called a *focus.* The focus is actually a point inside the sun—but off its center—called the *barycenter* of the solar system.

The inner four planets consist chiefly of iron and rock. They are known as the *terrestrial* (Earthlike) planets because they are somewhat similar in size and composition. The four outer planets are giant worlds with thick, gaseous outer layers. Almost all their mass consists of hydrogen and helium, giving them compositions more like that of the sun than that of Earth. Beneath their outer layers, the giant planets have no solid surfaces. The pressure of their thick atmospheres turns their insides liquid, though they may have rocky cores.

Dwarf planets are round objects smaller than planets that also orbit the sun. Unlike a planet, a dwarf planet lacks the gravitational pull to sweep other objects from the area of its orbit. As a result, dwarf planets are found among populations of smaller bodies. The dwarf planet Ceres, for example, orbits in a region of space called the *Main Belt* between the orbits of Mars and Jupiter. Ceres shares the Main Belt with millions of smaller asteroids.

Other dwarf planets orbit mainly beyond Neptune in a region known as the Kuiper belt. They share this region with many smaller icy bodies. Together, these objects are known as the *Kuiper belt objects* (KBO's). Compared to the planets, KBO's tend to follow irregular, elongated orbits. Dwarf planets of the Kuiper belt include Pluto and Eris, originally known by the designation 2003 UB_{313}.

Moons orbit all the planets except Mercury and Venus. The inner planets have few moons. Earth has one, and Mars has two tiny satellites. The giant outer planets, however, resemble small solar systems, with many moons orbiting each planet. Jupiter has at least 63 moons. Jupiter's four largest moons are known as the Galilean satellites because the Italian astronomer Galileo discovered them in 1610 with one of the first telescopes. The largest Galilean satellite—and the largest satellite in the solar system—is Ganymede, which is even bigger than Mercury. Saturn has at least 60 moons. The largest of Saturn's moons, Titan, has an atmosphere thicker than Earth's and a diameter larger than that of Mercury. Uranus has at least 27 moons, and Neptune has at least 13. The giant planets probably have more small moons not yet discovered.

Many dwarf planets, asteroids, and other bodies also have smaller moons. Pluto's moon Charon measures half Pluto's diameter. Eris's moon Dysnomia measures around ⅛ Eris's diameter.

Rings of dust, rock, and ice chunks encircle all the giant planets. Saturn's rings are the most familiar, but thin rings also surround Jupiter, Uranus, and Neptune.

Comets are snowballs composed mainly of ice and rock. When a comet approaches the sun, some of the ice in its *nucleus* (center) turns into gas. The gas shoots out of the sunlit side of the comet. The solar wind then carries the gas outward, forming it into a long tail.

Astronomers divide comets into two main types, *long-period comets*, which take 200 years or more to orbit the sun, and *short-period comets*, which complete their orbits in fewer than 200 years. The two types come from two regions at the edges of the solar system. Long-period comets originate in the *Oort* (pronounced *oort* or *ohrt*) *cloud,* a cluster of comets far beyond the orbit of Pluto. The Oort cloud was named for the Dutch astronomer Jan H. Oort, who first suggested its existence. Short-period comets come from the Kuiper belt. Many of the objects in the Oort cloud and the Kuiper belt may be chunks of rock and ice known as *planetesimals* left over from the formation of the solar system.

Asteroids are rocky or metallic objects smaller than planets. Some have elliptical orbits that pass inside the orbit of Earth or even that of Mercury. Others travel on a circular path among the outer planets. Most asteroids circle the sun in the Main Belt. The belt contains over 200 asteroids larger than 60 miles (100 kilometers) in diameter. Scientists estimate that there are over 750,000 asteroids in the belt with diameters larger than ⅗ mile (1 kilometer). There are millions of smaller asteroids.

Meteoroids are chunks of metal or rock smaller than asteroids. When meteoroids plunge into Earth's atmosphere, they form bright streaks of light called *meteors* as they disintegrate. Some meteoroids reach the ground, and then they become known as *meteorites.* Most meteoroids are broken chunks of asteroids that resulted from collisions in the Main Belt. During the 1990's, astronomers discovered a number of meteoroids that came from Mars and from the moon. Many tiny meteoroids are dust from the tails of comets.

Heliosphere is a vast, teardrop-shaped region of space containing electrically charged particles given off by the sun. Scientists do not know the exact distance to the *heliopause,* the limit of the heliosphere. Many astronomers think that the heliopause is about 9 billion miles (15 billion kilometers) from the sun at the blunt end of the "teardrop."

Formation of our solar system

Many scientists believe that our solar system formed from a giant, rotating cloud of gas and dust known as the *solar nebula.* According to this theory, the solar nebula began to collapse because of its own gravity. Some astronomers speculate that a nearby *supernova* (exploding star) triggered the collapse. As the nebula contracted, it spun faster and flattened into a disk.

The nebular theory indicates that particles within the flattened disk then collided and stuck together to form asteroid-sized objects called planetesimals. Some of these planetesimals combined to become the eight large planets. Other planetesimals formed moons, asteroids, and comets. The planets and asteroids all revolve around the sun in the same direction, and in more or less the same plane, because they originally formed from this flattened disk.

Most of the material in the solar nebula, however, was pulled toward the center and formed the sun. According to the theory, the pressure at the center became great enough to trigger the nuclear reactions that power the sun. Eventually, solar eruptions occurred, producing a solar wind. In the inner solar system, the wind was so powerful that it swept away most of the lighter elements—hydrogen and helium. In the outer regions of the solar system, however, the solar wind was much weaker. As a result, much more hydrogen and helium remained on the outer planets. This process explains why the inner planets are small, rocky worlds and the outer planets are giant balls composed almost entirely of hydrogen and helium.

Other solar systems

Several other stars have disk-shaped clouds around them that seem to be developing solar systems. In 1983, an infrared telescope in space photographed such a disk around Vega, the brightest star in the constellation Lyra. This discovery represented the first direct evidence of such material around any star except the sun. In the 2000's, astronomers detected water vapor in some disks, within the region where Earthlike planets could form.

Astronomers have discovered more than 200 planets orbiting other stars. In most cases, they found only one planet per star. Most of the planets are likely giant and gaseous with no solid surface. In 2007, astronomers reported the discovery of a planet only about five times as massive as Earth.   Jay M. Pasachoff

Related articles in *World Book* include:

Asteroid	Jupiter	Neptune
Astronomy	Kepler, Johannes	Oort cloud
Bode's law	Kuiper belt	Planet
Ceres	Mars	Pluto
Comet	Mercury	Satellite
Earth	Meteor	Saturn
Galaxy	Milky Way	Star
Gravitation	Moon	Sun
Interstellar	Nebular	Uranus
medium	hypothesis	Venus

Additional resources

Level I
Ride, Sally, and O'Shaughnessy, T. E. *Exploring Our Solar System.* Crown, 2003.
World Book's Solar System & Space Exploration Library. 10 vols. World Book, 2006.

Level II
Lang, Kenneth R. *The Cambridge Guide to the Solar System.* Cambridge, 2003.

Solar wind is a continuous flow of particles from the sun. Its chief cause is the expansion of gases in the *co-*

rona, the outermost atmosphere of the sun. The corona's high temperature, which averages about 4,000,000 °F (2,200,000 °C), heats the gases and causes them to expand. Many of the gas atoms collide as they are heated. As a result, they lose their electrons, which have a negative electric charge. The atoms thereby become *ions* (electrically charged atoms) with a positive charge. The electrons and ions--mostly hydrogen ions--make up the solar wind.

The velocity of the solar wind ranges from 155 to 625 miles (250 to 1,000 kilometers) per second. The solar wind has a density of about 82 ions per cubic inch (5 ions per cubic centimeter). It is responsible for a variety of occurrences in the solar system. For example, the *magnetosphere,* a region of strong magnetic forces surrounding the earth, is pushed into a teardrop shape by the solar wind as it streams past the earth. The magnetosphere prevents particles of the solar wind from reaching the surface of the earth. The blowing of the solar wind against a comet produces an *ion tail,* which is one of the various types of tails that comets have. Ion tails are long and straight and consist of ionized material that the solar wind has blown off the comet.

In 1959, the Soviet Luna 2 spacecraft confirmed the existence of the solar wind and made the first measurements of its properties. Several American spacecraft have also had equipment that studied this wind. The Apollo 11 and Apollo 12 astronauts placed large metal screens called *foils* on the moon to collect solar wind particles. The moon has no magnetosphere, and so the particles reach its surface. The astronauts brought the foils back to the earth for analysis. In 1984, the Active Magnetospheric Particle Tracer Explorer (AMPTE) space mission produced an artificial comet as part of a series of experiments designed to study the solar wind and magnetosphere. The mission was conducted by the United Kingdom, the United States, and West Germany.

Studies of stars other than the sun show that gases also stream away from them. As a result, astronomers believe many stars produce winds, called *stellar winds,* that resemble the solar wind. Ken G. Libbrecht

See also **Heliosphere; Magnetic storm.**

Solder, *SAHD uhr,* is a metal alloy used to join metal surfaces together (see **Alloy**). It is also used to mend metal objects. To be effective, the solder must melt more easily than the metals to which it is applied and must adhere to the materials being joined.

There are two types of solder, hard and soft. Hard solders will melt only at high temperatures. The advantage of hard solders is their strength and the fact that they can be pressed or hammered into various shapes without breaking. Some hard solders are drawn out into long threads, and others are pressed into sheets. The most common hard solder is silver solder, which consists of silver, copper, and zinc. Many copper alloys also are used as hard solders.

Soft solders will melt at low temperatures. But they are weak and cannot be hammered without breaking. The most common soft solders include various alloys of tin and lead. These alloys also contain other metals, such as antimony, cadmium, bismuth, and silver.

Researchers have developed many special solders for joining unusual material combinations, such as glass and ceramics. These solders combine the chemical ele-

ment indium with either tin or silver. Gold-based solders are used in the assembly and sealing of semiconductor devices. Melvin Bernstein

Soldier. See **Army; Army, U.S.; Rank, Military.**

Sole is the name of a family of flatfishes that have twisted skulls so that both eyes are on the same side of the body. Soles live in warm seas near shores. Their eyes are small and are set close together. Their mouth is crooked. The sole's body is flat and oval shaped.

The *European sole* grows from 10 to 26 inches (25 to 66 centimeters) long, and usually weighs about 1 pound (0.5 kilogram). The *common American sole,* also called

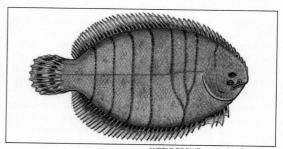

WORLD BOOK illustration by John F. Eggert

The sole has a flat, oval-shaped body with both eyes on one side of the head. The American sole, *shown here,* is used as food.

hogchoker, lives along the eastern coast of North America. It may travel far up rivers. The American sole is often used as food. Some kinds of flounder that live along coasts are also called soles. Robert R. Rofen

Scientific classification. Soles form the sole family, Soleidae. The scientific name for the American sole is *Trinectes maculatus.* The European sole is *Solea solea.*

See also **Flounder.**

Solenodon, *suh LEE nuh dahn,* is a rare animal that looks like a long-nosed rat. The *yellow-headed solenodon* lives in Cuba, and the *brown solenodon* is found in Haiti. The solenodon lives in dens and hollow logs, and it comes out for food only at night. It scratches for insects with its long claws. The solenodon weighs about $2\frac{1}{2}$ pounds (1 kilogram) and grows about 2 feet (61 centimeters) long, including its stiff, scaly tail, which is 10 inches (25 centimeters) long. It has a long, pointed

Varin-Visage from Jacana

The rare solenodon looks like a long-nosed rat. It is a shy animal and rarely comes above ground in daylight hours.

snout and short, coarse hair. The solenodon is bad tempered, and its saliva is poisonous.   Hugh H. Genoways

Scientific classification. The solenodon is in the family Solenodontidae. The Haitian solenodon is *Solenodon paradoxus.* The Cuban solenodon is *S. cubanus.*

Soleri, *soh LEH ree,* **Paolo,** *PAH oh loh* (1919-   ), is an Italian-born architect and urban planner. He became famous for his theories of preserving the environment. Soleri believes that, to protect nature's resources, cities should be built on as little land as possible.

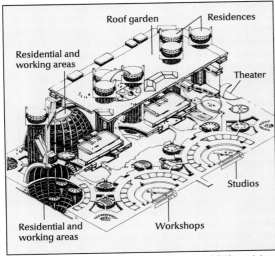

Roof garden   Residences
Residential and working areas
Theater
Studios
Residential and working areas   Workshops

Reprinted from *Arcology* by Paolo Soleri by permission of The M.I.T. Press, Cambridge, Mass.

Soleri's experimental cities are designed on many vertical levels to save land. Soleri planned the community of Arcosanti, *above,* to occupy only a few acres. He believes that society must develop such communities to preserve the environment.

According to Soleri, an urban center should be a single structure surrounded by open land used for agriculture and recreation. He calls such a city an *arcology,* a term formed by combining parts of the words *architecture* and *ecology.* In 1970, Soleri began to build his first experimental city, called Arcosanti, near Prescott, Arizona. He designed Arcosanti for a population of 5,000.

Soleri has also proposed designs for other urban environments. As in Arcosanti, all housing, business, and industrial facilities would be located within a single gigantic structure. Such cities would use shuttle systems and moving walkways instead of automobiles. Nuclear and solar power would provide energy. Soleri's designs for these cities indicate his concern for pure geometric forms, and his faith in technology and machines.

Soleri was born in Turin, Italy. He came to the United States in 1947 to study with architect Frank Lloyd Wright. In 1956, Soleri settled in Arizona, where he built structures half hidden in the earth. He built some structures by forming the earth into a desired shape, pouring concrete over it, and then removing the earth to expose the interior space.   Nicholas Adams

Solicitor. See Lawyer.

Solicitor general. See Justice, Department of; Supreme Court of the United States (The court in action); Canada, Government of (The Cabinet).

Solid, in mathematics, is a geometric figure with the three dimensions of length, breadth, and thickness. Some solids are named from the shapes of their surfaces, such as cubes, cylinders, cones, and spheres. In physics, solid refers to one of the three basic *states* (forms) in which matter may exist. The other states are *liquid* and *gaseous.* The state of each body of matter is classified according to the power of its molecules to resist forces that may change its shape. A solid has a fixed shape and volume because its molecules cannot move freely.   John K. Beem

Related articles in *World Book* include:

Archimedean solid	Cylinder	Molecule
Cohesion	Gas	Prism
Cone	Liquid	Pyramid
Cube	Matter (Solids)	Sphere

Solid geometry. See Geometry.

Solid-state physics, also called *condensed-matter physics,* deals with the physical properties of solid materials. These properties include magnetism, *luminescence* (giving off light), mechanical strength, and the conduction of electric current and heat. Solid-state physicists try to understand the properties of solids by studying the arrangement and motion of the atoms and electrons that make them up.

Most solids are composed of atoms arranged in an orderly pattern called a *crystal* (see **Crystal**). The basic building block of a crystal is the *unit cell,* which is repeated over and over. Physicists beam electrons, X rays, or neutrons at crystals to learn how the atoms or molecules are arranged.

Much of the progress in solid-state physics has been made by preparing extremely pure single crystals of various substances and studying their properties. The detailed structure of the electron distribution of a solid can be determined in this way. The information learned from such relatively ideal materials provides a better understanding of common materials and helps people create new materials with superior properties.

The field of solid-state physics has grown rapidly since about 1946 because of its importance to industry and its scientific interest. More people are involved in it than in any other area of physics. Achievements of solid-state physics include the development of transistors and other devices that are made of semiconductors and are used in electronic circuits. Solid-state physicists have also made semiconductor lasers, solar batteries, solid *luminescent sources* (devices that change electric power directly into light), and sensitive detectors for many types of radiation. The electrical, computer, communications, and space industries make use of solid-state technology.

A knowledge of the *quantum theory* is essential in studying solid-state physics. The theory forms the basis of understanding the structure of atoms and molecules and the forces that bind them together to form crystals.

Quantum theory has given an understanding of one of the most remarkable properties to be studied in solid-state physics, *superconductivity.* In normal metals, voltage must be applied and power used up to keep an electric current flowing. But in a superconductor, a current will flow indefinitely with no voltage applied and no power used up. Superconductivity is exhibited by many metals and alloys, and by certain ceramic materials, at extremely low temperatures.

Solid-state physics presents scientists with many other challenging problems. Some of the problems being studied involve the interaction of light from intense laser beams with matter. Other areas of research include the conversion of electric energy into light, and improving materials for semiconductor lasers and other light sources. Methods of solid-state physics are also being applied to the transfer of energy and electric charge in organic systems important in biology.   B. Jensen

Related articles in *World Book* include:

Computer chip	Quantum	Superconductivity
Cryogenics	mechanics	Transistor
	Semiconductor	Zone melting

Solidarity. See Poland (History); Wałęsa, Lech.

Solitaire is the name of many card games that are played by one person. Solitaire is usually played with a standard deck of 52 playing cards. In the most popular

WORLD BOOK photo by Dan Miller

In Klondike solitaire, the player stacks the cards into piles by suit and in order, *top,* and by alternate color and rank, *bottom.*

kind of solitaire, known as *Klondike solitaire,* the player deals seven cards in a horizontal row, the first one faceup, and the rest facedown. Then the player deals a card faceup on the second card, and a card facedown on each of the remaining five cards. The deal continues until all seven piles have a card facing up. The row of seven piles is called the *tableau.*

One faceup card may be moved on top of a second faceup card if it is one lower in rank and the opposite color of the second card. Any cards that have been placed on the first card move with it to the second card.

When an ace is exposed, it is put in a row above the main piles. The aces are known as *foundations.* The object is to stack all the cards by suits and in order in the top piles, from ace to king. The top card in any pile in the tableau may be moved to the top row if it can be placed on the card ranking just below it in the same suit. A facedown card that becomes the top card in a tableau pile may be turned faceup. If a tableau pile becomes empty, a king may be moved to the space. Undealt cards are turned over one at a time. Each is either played on a pile or placed faceup on a discard pile. The player may only go through the deck once.   R. Wayne Schmittberger

Solomon, *SAHL uh muhn* (? -928? B.C.), was the third king of ancient Israel. He ruled from about 965 B.C. until his death. Solomon was the son of King David and Bathsheba. David had unified Israel and conquered many of

its neighboring states. Solomon ruled this extensive kingdom, apparently without using military force.

Solomon was responsible for many public works, including the Temple and palace in his capital of Jerusalem. These magnificent structures served to establish the authority of the laws and government of Israel.

Information about Solomon comes chiefly from Biblical accounts in I Kings 1-11. The Bible describes Solomon's unique role in the history of Israel. He was an international leader who reorganized and developed the large kingdom his father had conquered. Solomon apparently ruled with great diplomacy and personal wisdom. His reputation as a wise man probably comes from his skill in dealing with a variety of people in various difficult situations. According to a tradition that developed after his reign, he composed many songs and proverbs as well as three books of the Hebrew Bible—Ecclesiastes, Proverbs, and the Song of Solomon.

Solomon's success in maintaining his empire was based on his administrative skills. He reorganized the various government departments his father had established. He also organized Israel into 12 districts and appointed his own *prefect* (governor) for each one.

Solomon helped establish peace on Israel's borders. According to the Bible, he carried out this policy by marrying or taking as mistresses many women from nearby states, including the daughter of the powerful pharaoh of Egypt. Solomon also formed a close alliance with Hiram, the king of Tyre, a Phoenician city on the Mediterranean Sea. Hiram sent Solomon building materials from Lebanon in return for agricultural products from Israel. The two kings also collaborated in building a navy and in organizing large trading fleets.

After Solomon's death, his son Rehoboam became king. However, most of the tribes of Israel rebelled against Rehoboam's rule and formed a new kingdom. Jeroboam, the leader of the revolt, became their king. Rehoboam remained king only of the southernmost tribes. Some historians believe that the other tribes rejected Rehoboam because Solomon had imposed forced labor and heavy taxes on them. Solomon had used this money and labor to carry out his numerous building projects.   Carol L. Meyers

See also **David; Phoenicia** (The spread of Phoenician influence).

Solomon Islands is an island country in the South Pacific Ocean. Its largest islands are Choiseul, Guadalcanal, Malaita, New Georgia, San Cristobal, and Santa Isabel. Its many other islands include Bellona, Rennell, and the Santa Cruz Islands.

The country's largest islands are part of an island chain that is also called the Solomon Islands. But not all the islands in the chain belong to the country. Bougainville, Buka, and a few smaller islands in the northern part of the chain are part of Papua New Guinea.

The Solomon Islands lies about 1,000 miles (1,610 kilometers) northeast of Australia. It has a land area of 11,157 square miles (28,896 square kilometers). The country spreads over about 230,000 square miles (600,000 square kilometers) of ocean. About 510,000 people live in the Solomon Islands.

The United Kingdom ruled the Solomons from 1893 to 1978. Honiara, on Guadalcanal, is the Solomons' capital and largest community. It has a population of about

A small village in the Solomon Islands has houses on stilts to keep the dwellings cool. Most Solomon Islanders live in rural villages. The one shown here is near Honiara, the nation's capital, on Guadalcanal Island.

Cameramann International, Ltd. from Marilyn Gartman

30,000. The Solomon Islands dollar is the country's basic unit of currency. "God Save Our Solomon Islands" is the national anthem. For a picture of the country's flag, see **Flag** (Flags of Asia and the Pacific).

Government. The Solomon Islands is a parliamentary democracy and a member of the Commonwealth of Nations (see **Commonwealth of Nations**). A governor general represents the British monarch in the Solomon Islands. A 50-member Parliament makes the country's laws. The people elect the members of Parliament to four-year terms. A prime minister heads the government. Parliament elects the prime minister from among its own members. A Cabinet helps the prime minister run the government. The governor general appoints Cabinet members based on the recommendation of the prime minister. The Solomon Islands is divided into nine provinces, each of which is governed by an elected assembly.

People. Most Solomon Islanders are Melanesians, and about 85 percent of them live in rural villages. Many of the people build houses on stilts to keep the dwellings cool. The main foods of the people include chicken, fish, pork, coconuts, sweet potatoes, and *taro,* a tropical plant with one or more edible rootlike stems.

Although English is the official language of the Solomon Islands, about 90 languages are spoken among the Melanesians. The islanders also speak Solomons Pidgin, a form of Pidgin English, which helps them cross language barriers (see **Pidgin English**). About 80 percent of the people are Protestants. The other islanders are Roman Catholics or follow local traditional beliefs. The nation has about 350 elementary schools and about 20 high schools. Students may attend college locally, at the College of Higher Education. Some islanders go to universities in Papua New Guinea and Fiji.

Land and climate. The country's main islands were formed by volcanoes. They are rugged, mountainous, and covered with tropical plants. The islands range from 90 to 120 miles (140 to 190 kilometers) long and from 20 to 30 miles (32 to 48 kilometers) wide. Each island has a central spine of mountains. Some of the mountains are more than 4,000 feet (1,200 meters) high. The land drops sharply to the sea on one side of the island and gently to a narrow coastal strip on the other. Some of the outlying islands are *atolls* (ring-shaped coral reefs).

Rainfall in the Solomon Islands varies from 60 to 200 inches (150 to 500 centimeters) annually. Temperatures range from 70 to 90 °F (21 to 32 °C).

Economy. Fish, timber, palm oil, cocoa, and *copra* (dried coconut meat) are the main products of the Solomon Islands. Japan buys much of the fish and timber exported by the country. The Solomon Islands imports food, machinery, manufactured goods, and gasoline from Australia, Japan, Malaysia, Singapore, and the United Kingdom. The country has good shipping services, but it has few roads. Air routes connect the Solomon Islands with Australia and other neighboring islands. The government publishes a weekly newspaper and broadcasts radio programs in both English and Pidgin English.

WORLD BOOK maps

Solomon Islands

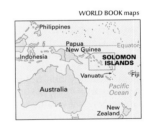

- ⊛ National capital
- • Town or village
- + Elevation above sea level
- — International boundary
- — Road

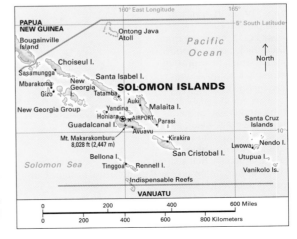

History. Scholars believe the Solomon Islands were first settled about 6,000 years ago by people from New Guinea. In 1568, the Spanish explorer Álvaro de Mendaña became the first European to reach the islands. Few other Europeans went there for the next 200 years. From 1870 to 1911, Europeans recruited nearly 30,000 islanders to work on plantations in Fiji and in Queensland, Australia. Some were recruited by force and treated harshly. In 1893, the United Kingdom took control of most of the Solomons. By 1899, the United Kingdom had made all the Solomons part of a protectorate.

In 1942 and 1943, during World War II, fierce fighting took place between Allied and Japanese forces on Guadalcanal and other islands. The Solomon Islands became independent on July 7, 1978.

Many Malaitans moved to Guadalcanal during and after World War II. Over time, resentment grew between the Malaitans and native Guadalcanal islanders. Fighting erupted between militias of the two groups in early 2000. In June, members of the Malaita Eagle Force (MEF), one of the militias, seized Prime Minister Bartholomew Ulufa'alu and forced him to resign. The MEF felt he was too sympathetic to the Guadalcanal islanders. Parliament elected Manasseh Sogavare, the opposition leader, as prime minister. The militias signed a peace agreement in October 2000. In 2001, the people elected a new Parliament. Sir Allan Kemakeza became prime minister.

In 2003, violence increased between Guadalcanal islanders and Malaitans. In July, Australia led a multinational peacekeeping force to the islands. A year later, the force had restored order. In 2006, Solomon Islanders elected a new Parliament, which then elected Snyder Rini prime minister. Rini resigned following public protests, and Parliament chose Sogavare to replace him.

Geoffrey M. White

See also **Guadalcanal Island; Honiara; World War II** (The South Pacific).

Solomon Islands are a chain of islands in the South Pacific Ocean northeast of Australia. The southern islands are part of a country called the Solomon Islands. The northern islands are part of Papua New Guinea. See **Papua New Guinea; Solomon Islands.**   David A. M. Lea

Solomon's-seal, *SAHL uh muhnz,* is the name of a large group of hardy plants that grow in the temperate zones of North America, Europe, and Asia. The plants get their name from their thick, creeping rootstalks, which bear growth scars that resemble the mystic seal of Solomon.

A Solomon's-seal has a long, arching stem that gives it a graceful appearance. It bears round berries that may be blue or

© E. A. James, N.H.P.A.
Solomon's-seal

black. Greenish, bell-shaped flowers grow at the bases of the leaves. Solomon's-seal plants grow best in shady places and in rich, moist soil.   Kenneth A. Nicely

Scientific classification. Solomon's-seal plants belong to the butcher's broom family, Ruscaceae. They make up the genus *Polygonatum.*

Solon, *SOH luhn* or *SOH lahn* (639?-559? B.C.), was a famous lawmaker. He was known as one of the *seven wise men of Greece.* Solon was born in Athens of a noble family. He first became known as a poet. His poems played a great part in urging the Athenians to regain the island of Salamis, which had long been in foreign hands. He was given command of the forces sent to take back the island, and he quickly conquered it. Afterward, Solon was elected an *archon* (chief government official) of Athens and was given authority to change the laws.

Athens badly needed political and economic reforms. A few citizens had most of the wealth. Farmers had been forced to mortgage their lands and to borrow money, offering themselves and their families as security. Solon passed a law that canceled the debts and mortgages. He also changed the money system to make foreign trade easier and made a law banning the export of grain.

Solon's constitutional reforms redivided the citizens into four classes according to income. Citizens of all classes were allowed to participate in the assembly and the public law courts. Solon established a council of 400 to take over the political powers of the Areopagus and set up popular courts in which citizens could appeal the officials' decisions (see **Areopagus**). He kept the old provisions that allowed only the three higher classes to hold public office, and only the highest class to hold the archonship. These provisions continued the oligarchy, but his reforms were a step toward democracy.

Solon asked the Athenians to keep his laws for 10 years. He then left Athens. When he returned 10 years later, he found the city fighting a civil war. Soon afterward, Pisistratus seized control. After opposing Pisistratus, Solon retired from public life.   Ronald P. Legon

Solow, Robert Merton (1924-   ), is an American economist known for his contributions to the theory of economic growth. In his book *Growth Theory: An Exposition* (1970), he explained the relationship between the different resources necessary for economic production. The resources include labor, technology, and such productive goods as buildings and machinery. Solow concluded that advances in technology stimulate growth more than increases in other resources do. He won the 1987 Nobel Prize in economics for this research.

Solow was born Aug. 23, 1924, in New York City. He graduated from Harvard University and earned a Ph.D. degree there. In 1949, he joined the faculty of Massachusetts Institute of Technology. Solow has written on many economic topics, including the distribution of income and the theory of capital. His books include *Capital Theory and the Rate of Return* (1963) and *The Sources of Unemployment in the United States* (1964).   Barry W. Poulson

Solstice, *SAHL stihs,* is one of the two moments each year when the sun is at either its northernmost or southernmost position. The sun appears directly overhead at different latitudes during the year because of the tilt of Earth's axis of rotation. The axis is tilted at an angle of 23°27' in relation to the plane of Earth's orbit.

One solstice occurs on June 20, 21, or 22, when the sun reaches its most northerly point, directly overhead at the Tropic of Cancer (23°27' north latitude). At the other solstice, on December 21 or 22, the sun appears at its most southerly position, directly overhead at the Tropic of Capricorn (23°27' south latitude).

In the Northern Hemisphere, the June solstice is

known as the *summer solstice,* and the December solstice is called the *winter solstice.* The day of the summer solstice in the Northern Hemisphere marks the start of summer. The summer solstice occurs on or near the longest day of the year. Similarly, the winter solstice occurs on or near the shortest day of the year and marks the start of winter. In the Southern Hemisphere, summer and winter are reversed.   Jay M. Pasachoff

See also **Equinox; Season; Tropic of Cancer; Tropic of Capricorn.**

Solti, *SHOHL tee,* **Sir Georg** (1912-1997), was a leading symphony orchestra and opera conductor. He won fame for his interpretations of romantic works, especially the symphonies of Anton Bruckner and Gustav Mahler and the operas of Richard Wagner.

Solti was born on Oct. 21, 1912, in Budapest, Hungary. He worked at the Budapest Opera House from 1930 until World War II began in 1939. From that year until the war ended in 1945, he lived in Switzerland. Solti then worked in Germany, serving as music director of the Bavarian State Opera from 1946 to 1952 and as conductor of the Frankfurt Opera from 1952 to 1961. In that year, Solti became music director of Covent Garden in London, retaining this post until 1971. Solti was music director of the Chicago Symphony Orchestra from 1969 until 1991. Solti was knighted by Queen Elizabeth II of Britain in 1971 and became a British subject in 1972. He was artistic director of the London Philharmonic from 1979 to 1983. Solti wrote an autobiography, *Memoirs* (1997).

Charles H. Webb

Solution is a mixture of two or more individual substances that cannot be separated by a mechanical means, such as filtration. There are three basic kinds of solutions: (1) liquid, (2) solid, and (3) gaseous.

Liquid solutions result when a liquid, a solid, or a gas is dissolved in a liquid. Examples are water mixed with alcohol, and sugar dissolved in coffee. Two liquids that can form a solution are said to be *miscible.* This ability depends on the liquids' chemical properties and on such physical conditions as temperature and atmospheric pressure. Some liquid blends are more miscible than others. Water and alcohol are completely miscible because any amount of the two substances produces a solution. Oil and water are partly miscible because only a small amount of each will dissolve in the other.

Gases and solids that dissolve in a liquid are said to be *soluble.* The substance that is dissolved is the *solute,* and the substance that causes dissolution is the *solvent* (see **Solvent**). A given volume of a solvent at a particular temperature can dissolve only a certain amount of solute. For example, a given amount of water can dissolve only a certain amount of salt. Any additional salt remains undissolved in the water. The ability of a substance to dissolve in another is called its *solubility.* The solubility of most solids depends on the chemical properties of the substances and on the temperature of the liquid solution. For gases, solubility also depends on pressure.

Solid solutions, in most cases, form when liquid solutions freeze. For example, a mixture of melted copper and zinc cools to form brass, a solid solution. Sterling silver, another solid solution, results when melted silver and copper are mixed and cooled.

Gaseous solutions result from the mixture of gases. Air, a gaseous solution, is a mixture of nitrogen and oxygen, plus smaller amounts of argon and carbon dioxide. Physical conditions do not affect the ability of gases to form a solution.   John B. Butt

Solvent, *SAHL vuhnt,* is a substance that dissolves another substance to form a solution. The term *solvent* is also used to refer to the substance in a solution that is present in the greater amount. The substance present in the lesser amount is called the *solute.*

Most solvents and the solutions they form are liquids, but there are some solutions of gases or solids. Water is the most common solvent and it forms various solutions. Other common solvents include acetone and alcohol. In most cases, the molecules of a solvent and the substance it dissolves are similar. For example, water will dissolve acetone or ethanol but not oil, which is dissolved instead by gasoline.

Solvents have many industrial and scientific applications. They are used in the production of cleaning fluids and such coatings as inks and paints. Solvents also are important in the manufacture of nylon, polyethylene, and many other synthetic fibers. In addition, they are useful for *extraction.* This technique involves the transfer of a solute from one solution into a second solvent for further separation. The solute may be a useful by-product or an impurity. Extraction is used in analytical chemistry, chemical purification, and petroleum refining.

Marye Anne Fox

Related articles in *World Book* include:

Acetone	Furfural	Solution
Alcohol	Paint	Turpentine
Chloroform		

Solzhenitsyn, *SAWL zhuh NEET sihn,* **Alexander** (1918-   ), is a Russian novelist. He was awarded the 1970 Nobel Prize for literature.

Alexander Isaevich Solzhenitsyn was born on Dec. 11, 1918, in Kislovodsk. He served four years in the Soviet Army during World War II (1939-1945). Russia was part of the Soviet Union from 1922 to 1991. In 1945, while Solzhenitsyn was still in the army, he was falsely accused of a political crime. He spent eight years in labor camps and three years in exile.

Solzhenitsyn's novels reflect his prison and war experiences. *One Day in the Life of Ivan Denisovich* (1962) and *The First Circle* (1964) have prison settings. *Cancer Ward* (1966) takes place in a hospital. Using the prison and the hospital as symbols of society, the author dramatizes the contrast between revolutionary ideals and harsh political reality. His heroes express the triumph of dignity over tyranny and suffering. Solzhenitsyn also wrote a historical novel, *August 1914* (1971), about the first days of World War I in 1914. A revised version published in 1989 included emphasis on the historical meaning of the February Revolution of 1917.

Throughout the 1960's and early 1970's, the Soviet government accused Solzhenitsyn of slandering his country in his writings. The government intensified its attacks on the author following the publication in Paris of volume one of Solzhenitsyn's three-volume *The Gulag Archipelago, 1918-1956* in 1973. The book is a study of the Soviet prison camp system. Volume two of *The Gulag Archipelago* was published in 1975, and volume three in 1976. In 1974, the government revoked Solzhenitsyn's citizenship and deported him. He lived in Switzerland for about two years and then settled in the

United States in 1976. Solzhenitsyn described his final years in the Soviet Union in the autobiographies *Invisible Allies* (1971) and *The Oak and the Calf* (1975). In 1990, the Soviet government restored his citizenship. In 1994, Solzhenitsyn returned to Russia to live.   Anna Lisa Crone

Additional resources

Pearce, Joseph. *Solzhenitsyn.* Baker Bks., 2001.
Thomas, D. M. *Alexander Solzhenitsyn.* St. Martin's, 1998.

Somalia, *soh MAH lee uh* or *soh MAHL yuh,* is the easternmost country on the mainland of Africa. Its coastline, which runs along the Gulf of Aden and the Indian Ocean, forms the outer edge of the "horn" of Africa.

Almost all of Somalia's people are Sunni Muslims and speak the Somali language. Somalia's capital and largest city is Mogadishu. The country's official name is the Somali Democratic Republic. Somalia became an independent nation in 1960. Before then, the United Kingdom ruled the northern part, and Italy ruled the south.

Government. Somalia has not had an effective government since 1991, when rebels overthrew the country's military leaders. In 2000, a conference of traditional, religious, and business leaders elected a transitional national assembly for Somalia. But many faction leaders opposed this government, and it never gained control over the country. In 2004, Somali politicians and faction leaders agreed to establish a new transitional government. A new national assembly, with 275 members, was created. The northern part of Somalia, which declared independence in 1991 as Somaliland, is not represented in this assembly. The assembly elects a president, and the president appoints a prime minister.

People. About 95 percent of Somalia's people share the same language, culture, and religion. But they are sharply divided according to traditional clan groupings. Most Somalis belong to one of four clans that together are known as the Samaal. The Samaal are primarily nomadic herders. Members of two other clans, called the Sab (or Saab), live along the rivers in southern Somalia. Most Sab are farmers. Many Somalis are loyal only to their clan. Fighting between clans has been common.

Many Somalis live in the neighboring countries of Ethiopia, Djibouti, and Kenya. Minority groups living in Somalia include Arabs, Indians, Italians, and Pakistanis.

Except for the coastlands, small trade centers, and cultivated areas, much of Somalia is unsettled. Nomads

Facts in brief

Capital: Mogadishu.
Official language: Somali.
Area: 246,201 mi² (637,657 km²). *Greatest distances*—north-south, 950 mi (1,529 km); east-west, 730 mi (1,175 km). *Coastline*—1,800 mi (2,408 km).
Elevation: *Highest*—Mount Surud Ad, 7,900 ft (2,408 m) above sea level. *Lowest*—sea level along the coast.
Population: *Estimated 2008 population*—9,007,000; density, 37 per mi² (14 per km²); distribution, 65 percent rural, 35 percent urban.
Chief products: *Agriculture*—bananas, grains, livestock products, sugar cane. *Manufacturing*—processed foods, sugar.
Flag: The light blue flag has a large white star in the center. The colors come from the United Nations flag. See **Flag** (picture: Flags of Africa).
Money: *Basic unit*—Somali shilling. One hundred cents equal one shilling. Somaliland's basic unit is the Somaliland shilling.

make up about half the population. They live in small, collapsible shelters that have arched wooden braces covered with skins and grass mats. Their chief foods are milk and camel and goat meat. They also eat rice and other grains. Many people in Somalia enjoy drinking tea.

In much of Somalia, the people wear traditional clothing that consists of a piece of brightly colored cloth draped over the body like a toga. Many men wear a kilt-like garment called a *lungi* or a *ma'owey.* In the cities and towns, some people wear clothing similar to that worn in Europe and North America.

The official language of Somalia is called Somali. Some Somalis also use Arabic, English, or Italian.

Less than 20 percent of all Somali children attend school. Most of Somalia's adults cannot read or write. The Somali National University is in Mogadishu. Somalia also has several technical institutes.

Somali craftworkers make fine leather goods, such as handbags and dagger sheaths. The people enjoy soccer and other sports and games. Reciting poetry and chanting are favorite forms of entertainment. Many of the poems and chants tell of love, death, or war, or of a prized possession such as a horse or camel.

Land and climate. Dry, grassy plains cover almost all of Somalia. A mountain ridge rises behind a narrow

Somalia

——	International boundary
——	Road
——	Railroad
⊛	National capital
•	Other city or town
+	Elevation above sea level

WORLD BOOK maps

coastal plain in the north. Altitudes in some parts of northern Somalia reach more than 7,000 feet (2,100 meters) above sea level. The flat central and southern areas of Somalia have an average altitude of less than 600 feet (180 meters) above sea level.

The average temperature ranges from 85 to 105 °F (29 to 41 °C) in northern Somalia, and from 65 to 105 °F (18 to 41 °C) in the south. Average annual rainfall is about 11 inches (28 centimeters). Rainfall is seldom more than 20 inches (51 centimeters) a year, even in the south, the wettest region. Parts of the north receive only 2 to 3 inches (5 to 8 centimeters) of rain a year. In general, rain falls during two seasons—from March to May, and from October to December. But droughts occur frequently.

Most of the land in Somalia is generally suitable only for grazing livestock. However, in the south, two major rivers—the Jubba and the Shabeelle—provide water for irrigation. Farmers in this region grow crops.

Somalia has a wide variety of plant and animal life. Acacia thorntrees, aloes, baobabs, candelabras, and incense trees grow in the drier parts of the country. Such plants as kapok, mangrove, and papaya grow along the rivers. Wild animals include the crocodile, elephant, gazelle, giraffe, hippopotamus, hyena, and lion.

Economy. Somalia has limited economic resources. Its economy has long been based on the herding of camels, cattle, goats, and sheep. During Somalia's colonial period, Italian settlers established banana plantations along the Shabeelle and Jubba rivers. Somalis continue to grow such crops as bananas and sugar cane. Other crops include corn and sorghum.

Fishing employs a few people, mainly in the north. Somalia has a few light industries, such as sugar refining and cotton milling. The country has gypsum, iron ore, and uranium deposits, but they have not been mined.

The chief exports include animal hides and skins; bananas; and camels, goats, and sheep. Imports include construction materials, food, and petroleum products.

Somalia has no railways. Most travel is by truck or bus. The country's 13,700 miles (22,048 kilometers) of roads include about 1,600 miles (2,575 kilometers) of all-weather roads. A number of cities have airports. Small air charter firms provide most air transportation.

History. The land that is now northern Somalia was well known in the ancient world because of its location on a major trade route between the Mediterranean Sea and lands to the east. During the 800's or 900's, Somalis began to move south from the Gulf of Aden coast, and Arabs and Persians began to establish settlements along the Indian Ocean coast. The Somalis were probably converted to Islam by about 1100.

Most of the Somali-inhabited area came under colonial rule in the 1800's. In the mid-1880's, the British took over much of northern Somalia, which became British Somaliland. The Italians gained control of most of the Indian Ocean coast in the 1880's and 1890's. They gradually advanced inland toward Ethiopia and established the colony of Italian Somaliland. In the early 1900's, Somali nationalists led by Sayyid Muhammad Abdille Hassan fought against British, Italian, and Ethiopian forces.

Italy conquered Ethiopia in 1936. Italian Somaliland then became part of the Italian East African Empire, based in Ethiopia. In 1940, Italy entered World War II and seized British Somaliland. But the British drove the

Shostal

Mogadishu, the capital of Somalia, lies on the country's southern coast. The city has Arab- and Western-style buildings.

Italians out of eastern Africa in 1941. A British military administration was temporarily set up in British Somaliland and Italian Somaliland. In 1948, Ethiopia regained its Ogaden region, where many Somali people live.

In 1950, the United Nations ruled that Italian Somaliland should be placed in the care of Italy for 10 years, after which it was to become independent. At the same time, Somalis in British Somaliland were demanding self-government. In the summer of 1960, the United Kingdom and Italy granted their Somali territories independence. The two territories united to form the independent state of Somalia on July 1, 1960. The new government encouraged national expansion, particularly into the Somali-inhabited areas of Ethiopia, Kenya, and French Somaliland (now Djibouti). This action led to tension between Somalia and all three of its neighbors.

Somalia experienced economic difficulties, and many people felt that only a few individuals and clans were benefiting from independence. These concerns prompted military officers, led by Major General Mohamed Siad Barre, to seize control of the government in 1969. All Somali land, transport systems, electrical plants, banks, schools, and medical services came under government control. Many of these changes took place in the midst of a serious drought in the mid-1970's.

More problems followed when Somalia encouraged antigovernment Somali rebels in Ethiopia in 1974. Fighting broke out between Somalia and Ethiopia. In 1977 and 1978, Somali forces took over the Ogaden region of Ethiopia. But Ethiopian forces pushed back the Somalis, leaving Somalia militarily weak. In 1988, Ethiopia and Somalia signed a peace agreement, ending the fighting.

In 1991, a rebel group called the United Somali Congress (USC) overthrew Somalia's military regime and took control of the capital. Fighting broke out in and around Mogadishu between USC factions. Other rebel groups gained power in other parts of Somalia. One group, the Somali National Movement, declared the independence of northern Somalia, calling it the Somaliland Republic. But other countries did not recognize it.

Drought and a disruption of food production and distribution caused by the fighting led to widespread starvation. Other countries and international relief groups sent food to Somalia. But Somalia had no government to protect the food, and armed criminals stole much of it.

By December 1992, about 270,000 Somalis had starved to death. That month, the United Nations (UN) Security Council sent a coalition of military forces from several countries to Somalia. Led by the United States, the coalition provided security for relief organizations and helped get large amounts of food to needy people.

In 1993, UN troops replaced most coalition forces. Mohammed Farah Aidid, a clan leader, accused UN officials of favoring his rivals. His forces killed several UN peacekeepers. The UN then shelled Aidid's headquarters in Mogadishu. Fighting between Aidid's forces and UN troops, including U.S. forces, heightened tension.

United States forces were withdrawn from Somalia in 1994 to help promote a negotiated settlement. Rival clan leaders signed a peace accord at a UN-sponsored conference that year. The agreement called for a cease-fire and formation of a transitional government. But fighting continued. In 1995, the UN's remaining forces left Somalia. Talks held in 1997 also failed to stop the fighting. In 1998, the region of Puntland in northeastern Somalia declared itself an *autonomous* (self-governing) state.

A conference of about 2,000 Somali leaders elected a transitional national assembly for Somalia in 2000. The assembly elected a president, who appointed a prime minister. This government had little control of the country outside Mogadishu. Several faction leaders refused to support the government and remained in control of various parts of Somalia. Somaliland continued to claim independence, and both Somaliland and Puntland continued to maintain separate governments. In 2002, the Somali government and more than 20 faction leaders agreed to a cease-fire. But some fighting continued.

In 2004, Somali politicians and the major faction leaders signed an agreement in Kenya to establish a new transitional government. Somaliland did not participate, but Puntland did. A national assembly was created later that year. The assembly elected a president, who appointed a prime minister. The new government stayed in Kenya until 2005. The Somali parliament met in Baydhabo in 2006, though it had little control over Somalia.

Also in 2004, an undersea Indian Ocean earthquake generated a series of large ocean waves called a *tsunami*. It killed about 300 people in Somalia.

An Islamic militia gained control of Mogadishu in June 2006 and began to rule the city under the Shari`ah (Islamic law). In late 2006, the militia gradually gained control of most of southern Somalia. The Somali government still held Baydhabo. In December, Somali government and Ethiopian forces regained control of southern Somalia, though some fighting continued.

Stephen K. Commins

See also **Mogadishu; Puntland; Somaliland.**

Somaliland, *soh MAH lee land,* is a self-governing state in the "horn" of Africa, between Ethiopia and the Gulf of Aden. Somaliland's full name is the Somaliland Republic. It declared independence from the country of Somalia in 1991. However, no countries recognize Somaliland as an independent state. Internationally, Somaliland is recognized as part of Somalia. For the location of Somaliland, see **Somalia** (map).

During the late 1800's and much of the 1900's, the name *Somaliland* was used for three European colonies in eastern Africa. These colonies were British Somaliland, Italian Somaliland, and French Somaliland (now the country of Djibouti). In 1960, British Somaliland and Italian Somaliland gained independence and united to form the Somali Republic, also called Somalia. When Somalia's central government collapsed in 1991 during a civil war, northern clan leaders declared independence, calling their new state the Somaliland Republic. Somaliland has its own constitution and its own currency, and it has held democratic elections for president and parliament. Since 1997, Somaliland has been peaceful.

Most Somalilanders are Muslims, and the countryside is dotted with small Islamic religious schools. About half the people of Somaliland raise camels, cattle, sheep, and goats for local needs and for export to the Middle East. In the west, where there is more rainfall, farmers grow cereals, fruits, and vegetables.

Somaliland has a busy port and a modern airfield at Berbera, two universities, and a booming cellular telephone industry. The capital city of Hargeysa, which was bombed in 1988, is being rebuilt with financial help from Somalis living overseas.   Lee V. Cassanelli

Somnus. See Hypnos.

Somoza García, Anastasio, *soh MOH sah gahr SEE uh, AH nah STAH syoh* (1896-1956), was a Nicaraguan dictator who ruled his country for 20 years before he was assassinated on Sept. 29, 1956. Somoza controlled Nicaragua's government, armed forces, and economy and used his power to become rich. He crushed all opposition and did not allow freedom of expression.

Somoza was born on Feb. 1, 1896, in San Marcos, Nicaragua, the son of a small rancher. He studied at Peirce Union Business College (now Peirce Junior College) in Philadelphia, then returned to Nicaragua and became a tax collector. He joined a revolutionary movement led by his wife's uncle, Juan Batista Sacasa. He became minister of war in 1932, after Sacasa was elected president.

In 1934, Somoza gained a reputation as a ruthless man when he had Augusto Sandino, a popular guerrilla fighter, killed by the National Guard. In 1936, Somoza drove Sacasa from power. Somoza was elected president later that year in an election controlled by his troops. He resigned as president in 1947 but forced his successors to rule as he wished. He became president again in 1950.

Somoza improved Nicaragua's agriculture, cattle raising, and mining. He also expanded port facilities and built new highways, houses, hospitals, power plants, railroads, and schools. Somoza's sons, Luis Somoza Debayle and Anastasio Somoza Debayle, served as presidents of Nicaragua from the 1950's through the 1970's.

Thomas G. Mathews

See also **Nicaragua** (The Somoza period).

Sonar, *SOH nahr,* is a system that uses sound energy to locate objects; measure their distance, direction, and speed; and even produce pictures of them. The word *sonar* comes from the phrase *so*und *n*avigation *a*nd *r*anging.

Sound travels through water better than radio waves or light do, and so it is useful for exploring and monitoring oceans. The word *sonar* is most often associated with devices for finding submarines. But sonar systems are also used for many other purposes, including *imag-*

ing (creating pictures of) the seafloor, spotting schools of fish, and tracking whales. Sonar systems are also found in nature. For example, dolphins, porpoises, some bats, and some whales use a form of sonar, known as *echolocation,* to find food and to avoid obstacles.

How sonar works. There are two types of sonar: (1) active, and (2) passive. *Active sonar systems* purposely radiate sound into the water. Such a system includes an underwater device called a *projector* that converts electrical signals into sound waves. The system sends out short sounds, called *pings,* that allow for more accurate location of objects than sounds of longer duration. Each ping travels from the projector through the water until it strikes an object. Objects reflect and scatter the sound in various directions. The sound reflected by an object back to the sonar is called an *echo.* An underwater device known as a *hydrophone* converts the echo from sound to electrical signals. In modern sonar systems, a computer analyzes the echoes and processes them to obtain information about the object. Such information includes distance, speed, size, and direction.

The distance to an object of interest, called a *target,* is known as its *range.* Because sound travels at roughly 1 mile (1.6 kilometers) per second through water, a ping that returns after 2 seconds has traveled 2 miles—1 mile to the target and 1 mile back. Thus, the target's range is 1 mile. The speed of the target can be determined by measuring the *frequency* of the echo and comparing it to that of the signal that was sent. The frequency of a sound is the number of sound waves that pass a given point each second. An object moving away from the projector will return a sound of lower frequency, and an approaching object will cause a shift to a higher frequency. This phenomenon is called the *Doppler effect,* and the frequency change is known as a *Doppler shift.* The faster the target is moving, the greater this shift.

Passive sonar systems do not employ a projector but instead receive sounds radiated by other sources. These systems usually combine the sound information from several hydrophones to determine the direction of a sound. Active sonar is better for determining target range. But submarine crews prefer using passive sonar, because by not putting any sound in the water, they do not reveal their own position.

Other uses. Sonar has many other applications besides its use in the ocean. For example, physicians can use a form of sonar called *ultrasound,* which operates at frequencies above the range of human hearing, to diagnose heart disease or to produce images of a *fetus* (unborn baby).

History. Many scientists consider the first known reference to the idea of sonar to be an observation on the properties of sound made by the great Italian artist and scientist Leonardo da Vinci. In 1490, he wrote, "If you cause your ship to stop, and place the head of a long tube in the water and place the outer extremity to your ear, you will hear ships at a great distance from you." Naval scientists in France, the United Kingdom, and the United States experimented with underwater sonar during World War I (1914-1918). In the 1920's and 1930's, scientists and engineers developed practical sonar systems that were used in World War II (1939-1945). Since then, engineers have continued to improve the sensitivity and accuracy of sonar systems. The use of sonar for scientific and commercial purposes has grown.   Jeffrey L. Krolik

See also **Bat** (How bats navigate); **Dolphin** (The bodies of dolphins); **Ultrasound.**

Sonata, *suh NAH tuh,* is an instrumental composition that consists of several movements. A sonata has contrasts in tempo and key, but its movements are related to one another in thematic material. Sonatas composed after the mid-1700's are made up of either three or four movements. The typical classical sonata begins with a brilliant *allegro* (lively movement). The second movement is slow, rhythmic, and lyrical. The optional third movement is usually light and graceful, and it may be in dance form or in the form of a *scherzo* (playful piece). The last movement, or *finale,* is in a quick, bright tempo. Symphonies, string quartets, and long works for solo instruments use the classical sonata pattern.

Thomas W. Tunks

See also **Classical music** (Sonata); **Minuet.**

Sondheim, *SAHND hym,* **Stephen** (1930-   ), is one of the most creative and praised composers and lyricists in the American musical theater. Sondheim's sophisticated scores feature brilliant, often witty lyrics and complex, unsentimental music. Sondheim has won many awards, including the 1985 Pulitzer Prize for drama for *Sunday in the Park with George* (1984). He also won the 1990 Academy Award for his song "Sooner or Later" from the motion picture *Dick Tracy* (1990).

Stephen Joshua Sondheim was born on March 22, 1930, in New York City. He gained early recognition as a lyricist with *West Side Story* (1957), with music by the American composer Leonard Bernstein. Sondheim next wrote the lyrics for *Gypsy* (1959), with music by the American composer Jule Styne. Sondheim wrote his first complete score to be performed on Broadway, *A Funny Thing Happened on the Way to the Forum,* in 1962. He pieced this broad comedy together from various ancient Roman comedies. Sondheim's other significant musicals include *Anyone Can Whistle* (1964), *Do I*

WORLD BOOK illustration by Kim Downing

A fishing boat uses sonar to detect schools of fish. The sonar sends out a pulse of sound and receives echoes from the fish and the ocean bottom.

Hear a Waltz? (1965), *Company* (1970), *Follies* (1971), *A Little Night Music* (1973), *Pacific Overtures* (1976), *Sweeney Todd: The Demon Barber of Fleet Street* (1979), *Into the Woods* (1987), and *Assassins* (1991). Don B. Wilmeth

Song is a musical composition for one or more voices. It is performed with or without accompaniment. Most songs are written in a fairly simple style.

Songs are the oldest musical form and have been found in all cultures. The earliest surviving songs, which date from the late A.D. 800's, are hymns known as *Gregorian chants*. These songs had Latin texts and were used in religious services. The earliest known *secular* (nonreligious) songs date from the 1100's. Between the 1100's and the 1600's, poets and singers called *troubadours* and *trouvères* in France and *minnesingers* and *meistersingers* in Germany composed works that glorified romantic love and heroic deeds.

Early songs were composed in the *monophonic* style —that is, they were written with one vocal part and no accompaniment. Composers took the first steps toward *polyphonic* songs—those with two or more parts—when they added a second vocal line to Gregorian chants.

The *chanson* became one of the main song styles of the 1400's. Chansons were written for several vocal parts. Most of these songs had a French text, and many were about chivalry and love. In the mid-1500's, the *madrigal* became the most important type of art song. Most madrigals had many vocal parts and were settings of serious literary texts. A new song style in Italy in the early 1600's, called *monody,* greatly influenced the development of the art song. Pieces in this new style had one part that was sung to a simple accompaniment.

In Germany during the late 1700's, the monodic style led to the development of songs called *lieder.* Lieder used German poetry as lyrics. Most were written for a solo singer and piano accompaniment. Lieder flourished in Germany in the 1800's. An important body of sentimental, popular songs also developed in the late 1700's and the 1800's. Many of these works came from the musical stage. Others were published as sheet music.

In the 1890's and early 1900's, a popular-music publishing industry, called Tin Pan Alley, emerged in the United States. This industry became responsible for the composition and sale of vast numbers of popular songs. Tin Pan Alley composers also wrote for the stage and later for motion pictures and recordings. Other styles of popular music in the 1900's also relied heavily on song. For example, a vast majority of rock compositions are songs, and many instrumental jazz improvisations are based on songs. Katherine K. Preston

Related articles in *World Book* include:

Folk music	Lieder	Popular music	Spiritual
Hymn	Madrigal	Singing	

Song dynasty, *soong,* also spelled *Sung,* ruled China from 960 to 1279. Great urban and commercial expansion took place in China during this period. Better farming practices and varieties of rice were introduced. Under the Song, a type of handheld gun and movable type for printing—inventions that would change the course of history—were developed. Shipbuilding, tea processing, porcelain manufacture, and metalworking advanced. Scholarship and education flourished. Artists began to paint the dramatic landscapes that characterize much classic Chinese art. Many Chinese endured poverty and hardships under the Song. However, scholars believe China was probably the wealthiest and most advanced nation in the world at that time.

The practice of awarding government positions based on scholarly merit gained in importance during the Song period. The government recruited administrators through civil service exams that tested literary skills and knowledge of classical Confucian philosophy. These scholar-officials had great power and took part in policy debates in the emperor's court. *Neo-Confucianism,* which combined the moral standards of traditional Confucianism with elements of Buddhism and Taoism, emerged during the Song period. The philosopher Zhu Xi was largely responsible for the development of this new Confucianism. The Song dynasty established Neo-Confucianism as the official state philosophy, and all later Chinese dynasties continued to support it.

Commerce flourished during the Song period. The Song became the world's first government to use paper money as a standard form of currency. Wealthy Chinese people flocked to cities, where they enjoyed fine restaurants and tea houses, and where musicians, storytellers, puppeteers, jugglers, and acrobats entertained them.

The Song dynasty rose to power in 960, following a series of short-lived military dynasties. Zhao Kuangyin, a general and the first Song emperor, unified China under a strong central government. The Song faced frequent attacks by peoples from the north, such as the Khitans. In 1126, the Jurchens seized the Song capital in northern China. After that, the Song held only the southern half of China. The dynasty that ruled from 960 to 1127 is often called the Northern Song, and the dynasty that ruled after 1127 is often called the Southern Song. In 1279, the Song dynasty ended when the Mongols conquered all of China and established the Yuan dynasty. Grant Hardy

See also **China** (The Song dynasty); **Painting** (Chinese painting).

Song of Hiawatha. See Longfellow, Henry Wadsworth (Narrative poems).

Song of Roland. See Roland.

Song of Solomon is a poetic book of the Hebrew Bible, or Old Testament. Another name for the book is *Canticles.* The book's Hebrew name is translated as *Song of Songs,* which means best or greatest song. This name refers to the exceptional beauty of the love poems that make up the book. The book's association with King Solomon derives from his being mentioned in the book, and from his many marriages and romantic alliances.

The Song of Solomon refers explicitly to human love and sexuality, which is unusual in religious literature. For this reason, Jewish and Christian traditions have tended to view the book as allegory. It has been considered a representation of God's love for the Hebrew people, or Christ's love for the church. But most scholars recognize the book's origins in the language of human love. The poems are similar to the love songs written in ancient Egypt. The book's exotic and vivid imagery presents an expression of mutual love between a man and woman in a garden setting. Carol L. Meyers

Songbird. See **Bird** (Calls and songs). See also *Related articles* at the end of the **Bird** article.

Songhai Empire, *sawng GY* or *SAWNG hy,* was a trading state in West Africa that reached its peak in the 1400's and 1500's. The Songhai Empire extended from

The Songhai Empire about 1500

This map shows in yellow the Songhai Empire at the height of its power. During the reign of Emperor Askia Muhammad, the empire stretched from the Atlantic coast to what is now central Nigeria. The Songhai controlled important trade routes that made the empire the richest in West Africa. The gray lines are the boundaries of present-day countries.

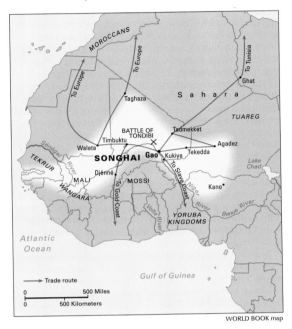

WORLD BOOK map

what is now central Nigeria to the Atlantic coast and included parts of what are now Burkina Faso, Gambia, Guinea, Mali, Mauritania, Niger, and Senegal. Gao, the capital, stood on the Niger River.

Songhai's roots date back to at least the 700's. The empire developed from large towns around Kukiya, near the present-day Mali-Niger border. By the 1000's, Gao had become the center of a kingdom known as Kaw-Kaw. During the 1400's, Kaw-Kaw expanded to become the vast and rich Songhai Empire. Songhai became powerful chiefly by controlling trade across the Sahara. Most of Songhai's people farmed, fished, or traded. The traders exchanged gold and other West African products for goods from Europe and southwest Asia.

Two kings, Sunni Ali and Askia Muhammad, strengthened the empire more than any others. Sunni Ali, a great military leader, ruled from 1464 to 1492. His army conquered Timbuktu and Djénné, two large West African trading centers (see **Djénné; Timbuktu**). Askia Muhammad, also known as Askia I or Askia the Great, became king in 1493. Songhai reached its greatest size under his reign. He encouraged the spread of Islam and governed Songhai according to strict Muslim law. He also expanded trade. Askia's son deposed him in 1528. The empire's power declined after a Moroccan army defeated Songhai at the Battle of Tondibi in 1591. Kevin C. MacDonald

See also **Askia Muhammad; Sunni Ali.**

Sonic boom is a loud noise caused by an object—usually an airplane—flying at a supersonic speed. To a person on the ground, it may sound like a clap of thunder. The noise results from a shock wave produced by the plane. A shock wave is a pressure disturbance that builds up around a plane flying at a supersonic speed. It results from a change in the air-flow pattern around the plane's leading edges. Sonic booms cannot hurt people, but they may damage plaster walls and break windows. A plane reaching the speed of sound is said to be crossing the *sound,* or *sonic, barrier.* Captain Charles E. Yeager of the U.S. Air Force became the first person to break the barrier. He did so in a Bell X-1 rocket plane on Oct. 14, 1947. See also **Aerodynamics** (Shock waves); **Shock wave; Yeager, Charles Elwood.**   Thomas A. Griffy

Sonnet is a 14-line poem with a fixed pattern of meter and rhyme. Its name is an Italian word meaning *a little song.* In the Italian sonnet, the *octave* (first eight lines) states a theme or experience and the *sestet* (final six lines) responds to or comments on the theme. The octave rhyme scheme is *abbaabba* (lines one, four, five, and eight rhyme; and lines two, three, six, and seven rhyme). The sestet rhyme scheme is often *cdecde.*

During the Italian Renaissance (the A.D. 1200's and 1300's), poets wrote groups of love poems called *sonnet sequences.* Dante addressed sonnets to Beatrice, and Petrarch wrote them to Laura. The French court poet Pierre de Ronsard wrote *Sonnets for Hélène* (1578).

English poets brought back this form from their travels abroad. Sonnets by Sir Thomas Wyatt and Henry Howard, Earl of Surrey, were published in *Tottel's Miscellany* (1557). For his *Amoretti* (1595), Edmund Spenser invented his own rhyme scheme. But the form used by William Shakespeare is identified as the English sonnet. It consists of three *quatrains* (four-line stanzas) followed by a *couplet* (two-line stanza), rhyming *abab cdcd efef gg.* By the time his *Sonnets* was published in 1609, the writing of sonnet sequences was out of fashion.

Few sonnets were written in English during the next 200 years. But in the mid-1600's, John Milton wrote a few great sonnets. The Romantic poets revived the form in the early 1800's. Later in the 1800's, Elizabeth Barrett Browning wrote love poems to her husband in the sequence *Sonnets from the Portuguese.* Gerard Manley Hopkins explored the limits of the form in "The Windhover" (1877). Many American poets of the 1900's wrote sonnets, including Edna St. Vincent Millay, E. E. Cummings, John Berryman, and Robert Lowell.   Paul B. Diehl

Each poet discussed in this article has a separate article in *World Book.* See also **Poetry** (Forms).

Sonoran Desert, *suh NOHR uhn,* is the largest desert in North America. It covers approximately 120,000 square miles (310,000 square kilometers) in northwestern Mexico and the southwestern United States. Parts of the desert lie in the states of Baja California and Sonora in Mexico and Arizona and California in the United States. The desert contains many landforms, including *basin and range* formations (parallel mountain ranges with valleys between them); *playas* (flat, dry lake beds); *arroyos* (dry stream beds); deep river valleys; inactive volcanoes; and sandy beaches. It also has the largest system of sand dunes in North America.

Temperatures in the Sonoran Desert vary widely depending upon the time of day, season, and location. Although the average temperature is above 65 °F (18 °C), temperatures can drop below freezing in northern regions and exceed 120 °F (49 °C) in southern regions. The average annual rainfall is about 5 to 12 inches (13 to 30 centimeters). Because the desert has both summer and winter rainy seasons, it has a greater variety of plants and animals than any other desert in the world.

Several million people make their home in the Sonoran Desert. The largest cities in the desert include Mexicali, Baja California; Hermosillo, Sonora; and Phoenix and Tucson, Arizona.   Christina B. Kennedy

Sons of Liberty was a group of patriotic societies that sprang up in the American Colonies before the Revolutionary War (1775-1783). They began as secret societies but later came into the open. They fought against the Stamp Tax of 1765, opposed the importation of British goods after the passage of the Townshend Acts in 1767, and led resistance to the Tea Act of 1773. They were active from South Carolina to New Hampshire and supported the calling of the Continental Congress.

During the American Civil War (1861-1865), some members of a group known as *Copperheads* began to call themselves the *Sons of Liberty.* They were Northern sympathizers with the South and were charged with planning to overthrow the government of President Abraham Lincoln. See **Copperheads.**   Richard D. Brown

Sons of the American Revolution is a patriotic organization. Its members are male descendants of people who served in the Revolutionary War in America, or who contributed to establishing the independence of the United States. Constitution Day, Flag Day, and Bill of Rights Day were established through the group's efforts. The society was founded on April 30, 1889. Its official name is the National Society of the Sons of the American Revolution. Its headquarters are in Louisville, Kentucky.   Critically reviewed by the Sons of the American Revolution

Sontag, *SAHN tahg,* **Susan** (1933-2004), was an American essayist and novelist. Her works strongly influenced experimental art during the 1960's and 1970's.

Sontag is perhaps best known for a collection of essays called *Against Interpretation* (1966). In these essays, she argued that people should experience art with their emotions and senses, rather than analyze it intellectually. Her essay collection *Styles of Radical Will* (1969) deals with the effects of drugs and pornography on art. In *Illness as Metaphor* (1978), Sontag examines how different illnesses generate cultural metaphors. Her essays on alienation and photography appear in *On Photography* (1978). Essays on literature and film were published in *Under the Sign of Saturn* (1980). She provided cultural analysis in *AIDS and Its Metaphors* (1989). In *Regarding the Pain of Others* (2003), Sontag discusses the impact of images of violence on modern society.

Sontag's novels *The Benefactor* (1963) and *Death Kit* (1967) deal with characters who are separated from reality because they cannot distinguish between it and their dream worlds. *The Volcano Lover* (1992) is a historical work about the British admiral Horatio Nelson and his lover, Emma Hamilton. *In America* (2000) describes the adventures of a Polish actress in California in the late 1800's. Sontag's short stories were collected in *I, etcetera* (1978). She was born on Jan. 16, 1933, in New York City and died there on Dec. 28, 2004.   Victor A. Kramer

Sony Corporation, a Japanese manufacturer, is one of the world's leading producers of communications and information technology products for consumers and businesses. Sony's products include batteries, cellular telephones, compact disc players, computers, computer chips, DVD-video players, radios, televisions, and video game consoles. The company also has divisions that produce musical recordings and motion pictures. Sony Corporation has headquarters in Tokyo.

Sony traces its origins to 1945, when Masaru Ibuka, a Japanese engineer and inventor, opened a manufacturing facility called Tokyo Telecommunications Research Institute in Tokyo. In 1946, Ibuka, together with his friend Akio Morita, incorporated the factory as Tokyo Telecommunications Engineering Corporation. The company was renamed Sony Corporation in 1958.

The company produced Japan's first tape recorder in 1950, and its first transistor radio in 1955. In 1975, Sony produced the first videocassette recorder for home use. In 1982, Sony introduced the world's first compact disc player.   Critically reviewed by Sony Corporation of America

Soo Canals permit ships to pass between Lakes Superior and Huron. They are on the border between the United States and Canada. About 85 to 90 percent of the tonnage on the canals is eastbound. Iron ore, grain, and coal make up most of the eastbound cargo. Coal, stone, and oil are the chief products carried on westbound ships. About 85 million tons (77 million metric tons) of cargo pass through these canals annually. Ice closes the Soo Canals from about mid-December to early April.

The St. Marys River forms a natural connection between Lakes Superior and Huron. Early trappers sometimes "ran the rapids" to cross from one lake to the other. However, they usually carried their canoes and furs around the rough water. In 1798, the Hudson's Bay Company completed a canal with a single lock that permitted canoes and flat-bottomed boats to pass up the river. American troops destroyed the lock during the War of 1812. After 1839, ships were moved around the rapids on rollers. A railroad was built in 1850.

The American canals. Increasing shipments of iron and copper during the late 1800's created a need for better transportation between Lakes Superior and Huron. A federal grant enabled Michigan to complete a canal with a lock in 1855. The U.S. government took over the canal's administration in 1881 and abolished tolls.

The American canals, also called the St. Marys Falls Canal and Locks, are about 1 ¾ miles (2.8 kilometers) long. Davis lock, opened in 1914, and Sabin lock, opened in 1919, are in the North Canal. The South Canal includes MacArthur lock, opened in 1943, and the Poe lock, opened in 1968. The Poe lock, 110 feet (34 meters) wide, is the widest of the American canals. It handles vessels up to 105 feet (30 meters) wide and 1,000 feet (300 meters) long. The 1968 lock replaced a smaller Poe lock, which was torn down in 1962.

The Canadian canal, completed in 1895, is 1 ¾₀ miles (2 kilometers) long and 150 feet (46 meters) wide. Until the Davis lock was built, the larger lake ships used the Canadian canal, also called the Sault Sainte Marie Canal.

The 2-mile (3-kilometer) International Bridge carries traffic across the St. Marys River at Sault Ste. Marie. The bridge opened in 1962.   John Edwin Coffman

See also **Lake Huron.**

Soochow. See Suzhou.

Soot is a black or dark brown substance found in smoke. Soot consists chiefly of particles of carbon.

Soo Canals

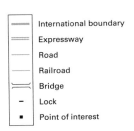

- ▬▬ International boundary
- ══ Expressway
- — Road
- — Railroad
- ⋈ Bridge
- – Lock
- ■ Point of interest

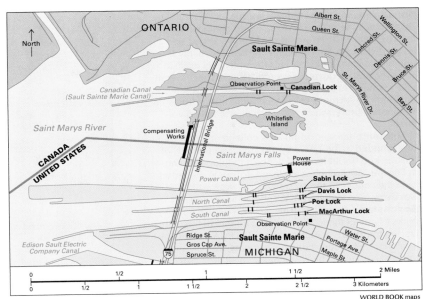

WORLD BOOK maps

These particles have a diameter less than ¹⁄₆₀ the width of a human hair. They form when carbon-containing fuels, such as coal, wood, or oil, do not burn completely.

Airborne soot is a form of air pollution. It sticks to any surface it touches. Soot can harm the respiratory system, particularly the lungs. It can also cause widespread damage to property. Smoke blowing through a city leaves soot on buildings. This soot can eventually damage the buildings' surfaces by reacting chemically with them.

However, soot is valuable as a *pigment* (coloring matter). Two kinds of soot used as pigments are bister and lampblack. Bister, a shiny brown powder containing dried tar, is the kind of soot found nearest to wood fires. Lampblack, a black soot, is found farther from such fires. Lampblack also is produced in the incomplete burning of such fuels as oil and natural gas.   David J. Kolaz

See also **Fire** (What fire produces).

Sophists, *SAFH ihsts,* were educators who traveled from city to city teaching for pay in the city-states of Greece during the second half of the 400's B.C. They taught many subjects, but their main subject was persuasive public speaking, which was crucial in such democracies as Athens. They claimed to teach virtue, which they defined as being successful in the world.

Sophists did not cling to a specific set of beliefs. For example, some Sophists believed that laws should be rejected in favor of the natural right of the strong. But others recognized that human law, though unnatural, was essential for a secure society.

Much of our knowledge of the Sophists comes from dialogues written by the great Greek philosopher Plato. Plato presents the Sophists as largely uninterested in the truth and only concerned with making money. His influence has led to the modern meaning of *sophist* as someone who uses clever but misleading reasoning.

Sophists included Protagoras, Gorgias, and Critias. Protagoras believed that arguments of equal force could be built for the opposing sides of any issue. Gorgias was the premier teacher of rhetoric of his time. Critias argued that the gods were inventions whose purpose was to inspire fear of wrongdoing.   Carl A. Huffman

Sophocles, *SAHF uh KLEEZ* (about 496-406 B.C.), was one of the three great Greek writers of tragedy. The others were Aeschylus and Euripides.

Sophocles's plays deal with a struggle of a strong individual against fate. In most of them, this person chooses a course of action that the chorus and the lesser characters do not support. This course costs the individual suffering or death, but it makes the person nobler and somehow benefits humanity. Sophocles did not create ordinary characters who could be used to criticize conventional morality as Euripides did. The Greek philosopher Aristotle said Sophocles portrayed people as they should be and Euripides portrayed people as they are.

Artistically and in their dramatic construction, the plays of Sophocles are more finished than those of Aeschylus or Euripides, and Aristotle regarded Sophocles's works as models. Sophocles added a third actor, fixed the size of the chorus at 15, and used scene painting. His plays show intrigue and suspense. Of the more than 120 plays Sophocles wrote, 7 complete ones have survived. These are *Ajax, Antigone, Trachinian Woman, Oedipus Rex, Electra, Philoctetes,* and *Oedipus at Colonus.* Part of a play called *The Trackers* was found in 1907.

Sophocles was born at Colonus, near Athens. His tragedies earned many prizes in drama competitions. He served as a general and as a member of delegations to other states. He was also active in the religious life of Athens. Sophocles wrote one of his greatest plays, *Oedipus at Colonus,* when he was nearly 90.   Luci Berkowitz

See also **Antigone; Drama** (Greek drama); **Greek literature; Oedipus.**

Additional resources

Beer, Josh. *Sophocles and the Tragedy of Athenian Democracy.* Praeger, 2004.
Nardo, Don, ed. *Readings on Sophocles.* Greenhaven, 1997.

Sor Juana. See Juana Inés de la Cruz.

Sorbonne, *sawr BAHN,* was a world-famous college in Paris. Until 1970, it formed the liberal arts and sciences division of the University of Paris. The name Sorbonne was frequently used for the university itself. In 1970, the French government reorganized the university into 13 units. Three of these units use the Sorbonne buildings for lectures. One of the buildings includes the Sorbonne library, which has more than 3 million volumes.

The Sorbonne was originally a college of theology. It was founded in the 1200's by the theologian Robert of Sorbon and became one of the best theological schools in Europe. The French statesman Cardinal Richelieu rebuilt the college in the 1600's.   P. A. McGinley

Sorcery. See Witchcraft (Witchcraft as sorcery).

Sorenstam, Annika (1970-   ), a Swedish golfer, ranks as one of the leading woman golfers in the world. During the 1990's, Sorenstam won 18 LPGA (Ladies Professional Golf Association) tournaments, more than any other player on the tour. She has won all four major tournaments on the LPGA tour—the United States Women's Open in 1995, 1996, and 2006; the Kraft Nabisco Championship in 2001, 2002, and 2005; the LPGA Championship in 2003, 2004, and 2005; and the British Women's Open in 2003.

In 2001, Sorenstam tied an LPGA record by winning four consecutively scheduled tournaments. In 2002, Sorenstam won 11 tournaments, the most in a single year by a professional woman golfer since 1964.

Sorenstam was born on Oct. 9, 1970, in Stockholm, Sweden. She was a member of the Swedish national team from 1987 to 1992. While attending the University of Arizona, she won the National Collegiate Athletic Association (NCAA) championship in 1991. Sorenstam turned professional in 1992 and competed on the Women Professional Golfers' European Tour. She joined the LPGA tour in 1994.

In 2003, Sorenstam became the first woman golfer since Babe Didrikson Zaharias in 1945 to play in a tournament on the men's professional tour in the United States. She played the first two rounds of the Bank of American Colonial tournament but did not qualify to play in the final two rounds.   Marino A. Parascenzo

See also **Golf** (picture: Golf stars of today).

Sorghum, *SAWR guhm,* is the name of a group of tropical grasses from Africa and Asia. In regions that have a warm summer climate, farmers grow some of them for syrup, grain, broom fiber, and animal feed. The common varieties of sorghum have thick, solid stalks and look like corn plants. But their flowers grow in branched clusters at the tips of the stems.

Farmers plant and grow sorghums in much the same manner as they do corn. About 9 million acres (3.6 million hectares) of sorghum are planted in the United States each year, especially in the Great Plains region. All sorghums fall into four main groups. These groups are (1) grain sorghums, (2) sweet sorghums, (3) grassy sorghums, and (4) broomcorn.

Grain sorghums are grown especially for their round, starchy seeds. The grain is used for feeding animals. Some grain sorghums grow to 15 feet (5 meters) high. Plant breeders have developed shorter varieties that can be harvested with a combine. In India, Africa,

Jeff Simon, Bruce Coleman Ltd.

Grain sorghums are grown for their round, starchy seeds. Many farmers use the grain as feed for animals.

and China, the grain is ground and made into pancakes or mush for food. Common grain sorghums include durra, milo, and kafir (see **Grain sorghum; Kafir**).

Sweet sorghums, also called *sorgos,* have sweet, juicy stems. They are grown especially for the production of sorghum syrup. This syrup is made by pressing the juice out of the stems with rollers and boiling it down to the proper thickness. Animal feed and silage can also be made from sweet sorghums.

Grassy sorghums are used for green feed and hay. *Sudan grass* is tall and has thin stalks. It grows quickly and may reach 10 feet (3 meters) in height. It serves as excellent summer pasturage (see **Sudan grass**). *Johnson grass* grows as a weed in the southern United States. It resembles Sudan grass but spreads by creeping rootstocks. Johnson grass is a pest on land needed for cotton or other row crops. But it is excellent cattle feed.

Broomcorn is a sorghum grown for the *brush* (branches) of the seed cluster used in making brooms.

Donald J. Reid

Scientific classification. The sorghums belong to the grass family, Poaceae or Gramineae. Grain sorghums, sweet sorghums, and broomcorn are *Sorghum bicolor.* Sudan grass is *S. x drummondii.* Johnson grass is *S. halepense.*

Soroptimist International, *suh RAHP tuh mihst,* is the world's largest service organization for business, executive, and professional women. It has about 95,000 members in clubs in approximately 120 countries. Membership is by invitation. The clubs support programs that advance the status and human rights of women and girls. The programs include cash awards to improve education and training, measures to prevent domestic violence, and recognition of young women for volunteer actions to improve their communities.

The organization consists of four federations—Soroptimist International of the Americas, Soroptimist International of Europe, Soroptimist International of Great Britain and Ireland, and Soroptimist International of the

South West Pacific. The first club was chartered in 1921 in Oakland, California. The American federation has its headquarters in Philadelphia. The headquarters of Soroptimist International are in Cambridge, England.

Critically reviewed by Soroptimist International of the Americas

Sorority is a society of women or girls. In most sororities, the members are college or university students and graduates. Sororities, like fraternities, are often called *Greek-letter societies.* Most form their names by combining two or three Greek letters. The word *sorority* comes from the Latin word *soror,* which means *sister.*

There are four kinds of sororities: (1) *general,* also called *social;* (2) *professional;* (3) *honor societies;* and (4) *recognition societies.* General sororities are the most common. One of their main purposes is to help members meet new friends. They also encourage high academic standards, carry on charitable and educational programs, and sponsor social activities. Many sororities have their own houses in which the members live.

Professional societies consist of people with the same academic interest, such as journalism. Honor societies enroll people with exceptional academic records. Members of recognition societies have done outstanding work in a specific area. Some of them also admit men.

The branch of a sorority at a particular school is called a *chapter.* Most general sororities have a national headquarters that advises local chapters and promotes the broad interests of the organization. Many individual sororities belong to the National Panhellenic Conference, which has headquarters in Indianapolis. This conference promotes cooperation among national sororities. Most universities and colleges have an intersorority council to regulate general sororities on campus.

Many school clubs, the forerunners of sororities, were formed during the 1800's. Adelphean began as a literary society at Wesleyan College, in Macon, Georgia, in 1851. It adopted the name Alpha Delta Pi in 1905. Pi Beta Phi was organized as I. C. Sorosis at Monmouth College in Monmouth, Illinois, in 1867. Pi Beta Phi was the first organization of college women established on a national basis. Kappa Alpha Theta was the first group founded as a women's Greek-letter society. It began in 1870 at DePauw University in Greencastle, Indiana. Gamma Phi Beta, founded in 1874 at Syracuse University in Syracuse, New York, was the first to use the name *sorority.*

Critically reviewed by National Panhellenic Conference

Soros, George (1930-　　　), is a Hungarian-born American businessman who became famous for his wealth and *philanthropy* (charity). Soros made his fortune as an investor in currencies.

Soros was born in Budapest, Hungary, on Aug. 12, 1930. In 1947, he left Hungary to study at the London School of Economics in England. He graduated in 1952 with a bachelor's degree.

In 1956, Soros moved to the United States and eventually made his fortune there. Soros became an American citizen in 1961. In the late 1970's and the 1980's, he established foundations with his own money to help people in the Soviet Union, Hungary, and other Eastern European countries. After the Soviet Union broke up into a number of independent countries in 1991, Soros gave money to help the new nations establish democratic institutions. Soros has written several books. They include *Underwriting Democracy* (1991), *The Crisis of Global Capitalism* (1998), and *The Bubble of American Supremacy* (2003).　　John C. Schmeltzer

Sorrel, *SAWR uhl,* is the name of several species of herbs. These plants have juicy leaves and stems that contain oxalic acid. This gives them a sour taste.

WORLD BOOK illustration by Carol A. Brozman
Red sorrel

The *red sorrel,* also called *common sorrel* and *sheep sorrel,* is native to North America, Europe, and Asia. It grows about 1 foot (30 centimeters) high. The plant has arrow-shaped leaves and clusters of small reddish or greenish flowers. The name *red sorrel* comes from the plant's masses of triangular red seeds. Red sorrel is a troublesome weed. Its presence means that the land needs lime.

The *garden sorrel* measures about 3 feet (90 centimeters) in height. Native to Europe and Asia, the garden sorrel is sometimes grown in North America for its edible leaves.　　Harold D. Coble

Scientific classification. Sorrels belong to the buckwheat family, Polygonaceae. The red sorrel is *Rumex acetosella.* The garden sorrel is *Rumex acetosa.*

Sorrel-tree. See Sourwood.

SOS is the Morse code call for help. It was once widely used by ships and aircraft in distress. SOS does not stand for anything. It was chosen as a distress signal because it was convenient to send by telegraph. The international code for SOS consists of three dots, three dashes, and three dots. See also **Morse code.**

Sosa, Sammy (1968-　　　), became one of the most exciting home-run hitters in baseball history. Sosa is the first major league player to hit at least 60 home runs in three different seasons. He hit 66 in 1998, 63 in 1999, and 64 in 2001. Sosa hit 50 home runs in 2000, the most in the major leagues. He led the National League with 49 home runs in 2002. In 2007, Sosa became the fifth player in major league history to hit 600 career home runs.

Sosa was selected as the National League's Most Valuable Player for the 1998 season. He led the major leagues in runs batted in (RBI's) in 1998 with 158 and in 2001 with 160, the third most in a season in modern National League history. Sosa plays right field. He bats and throws right-handed.

Samuel Sosa was born in San Pedro de Macorís in the Dominican Republic on Nov. 12, 1968. He started his major league career with the Texas Rangers in 1989. Later in 1989, he was traded to the Chicago White Sox. The White Sox traded him to the Chicago Cubs in 1992. Sosa was suspended for seven games in 2003 for illegally using cork in a bat during a game. The Cubs traded Sosa to the Baltimore Orioles in 2005. Sosa did not play major league baseball in 2006. He joined the Texas Rangers for the 2007 season.　　Dave Nightingale

Soto, Hernando de. See De Soto, Hernando.

Soul. See **Mythology** (Tylor's theory); **Plato** (Plato's philosophy); **Reincarnation; Religion** (A doctrine of salvation).

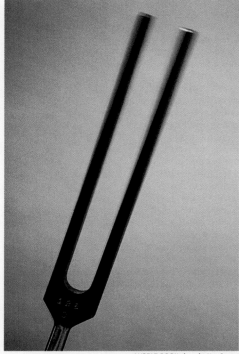

WORLD BOOK photo by Ken Sexton

A tone-producing tuning fork

Jerry Herman, FPG

A male frog sounding a mating call

Dennis Hallinan, FPG

Trombonists in a marching band

All sounds are produced by vibrations. When a tuning fork is struck, the vibration of its prongs generates a tone. A frog croaks by forcing air over its vocal cords, making them vibrate. A trombone produces sound when the player causes the air inside the instrument to vibrate.

Sound

Sound is a sensation that we hear. A sound originates in the vibration of an object. This vibration, in turn, makes the air or some other substance surrounding the object vibrate. The vibrations in the substance travel as waves, moving outward from the object in all directions. When the waves enter our ears, our organs of hearing translate them into nerve impulses. The impulses travel to the brain, which interprets them as a sound. The term *sound* also refers to the traveling waves.

Waves of sound can travel in any kind of substance. Most of the sounds that we hear travel in air, which scientists classify as a gas. But sound can also travel in liquids and solids. Sound travels most rapidly in solids, and more rapidly in liquids than in gases.

A substance in which sound waves travel is called a *sound medium.* Where no sound medium is present, there can be no sound. There is no sound in outer space because outer space contains no sound medium.

How some familiar sounds are produced

The human voice is produced in the *larynx,* a part of the throat. Two small folds of tissue stretch across the lar-

Ilene J. Busch-Vishniac, the contributor of this article, is Dean of the Whiting School of Engineering at Johns Hopkins University.

ynx. These folds, the *vocal cords,* have a slitlike opening between them. When we speak, muscles in the larynx tighten the vocal cords, narrowing the opening. Air from the lungs rushes past the tightened cords, causing them to vibrate. The vibrations produce the vocal sounds. The tighter the vocal cords are, the more rapidly they vibrate and the higher are the sounds produced.

Animal sounds. Birds, frogs, and almost all mammals have vocal cords or similar structures. These animals therefore make sounds as people do. But many animals produce sounds in different ways. A dolphin produces clicks and whistles in air-filled pouches connected to its *blowhole,* a nostril in the top of its head. Bees buzz as they fly because their wings move rapidly. The wings make the air vibrate, producing the buzzing sound. Other insects produce sounds by rubbing one body part against another. A cricket "sings" by scraping parts of its front wings together.

Some kinds of fishes vibrate a *swim bladder* or *air bladder,* a baglike organ below the backbone. The vibrations produce clucks, croaks, grunts, and other sounds. Certain kinds of shellfish produce clicks by striking their claws together.

Musical sounds are produced in various ways. Certain instruments make sounds when struck. For example, when a drummer hits the membrane of a drum, the membrane vibrates, producing sound. Xylophones have a series of bars, each of which sounds a particular note when struck.

A stringed instrument, such as a cello, violin, or harp, produces sound when a player makes one or more of its strings vibrate. This vibration causes parts of the instrument's body to vibrate, creating sound waves in the air.

A wind instrument, such as a clarinet, flute, or trumpet, generates sound when a player makes a column of air inside the instrument vibrate. A clarinet has a flat, thin part called a *reed* attached to its mouthpiece. The reed vibrates when a player blows across it. The vibration of the reed, in turn, makes the air column vibrate. The column of air in a flute vibrates when a musician blows across a hole in the flute's mouthpiece. In a trumpet, the vibrating lips of the player make the air column vibrate.

Noises are unpleasant, annoying, and distracting sounds. Many manufactured products are noisy. An automobile makes noise when its engine vibrates and makes other parts of the vehicle vibrate. Natural events also create noise. Thunder occurs when lightning heats the air, causing the air to vibrate. Some noises consist of *impulsive sounds*—that is, sounds that start suddenly and end quickly. Impulsive sounds include the crack of a gunshot and the bang of a firecracker.

The nature of sound

Sound waves resemble the waves that travel across the surface of a body of water. You can create such surface waves by dropping a small pebble into a tub of water. When the pebble strikes the surface, the water will react by producing a series of waves. You will see the waves as expanding circles with the pebble's point of entry in the center.

But there is a major difference between the shape of water waves and the shape of sound waves. Water waves travel in two dimensions, moving along the plane of the water's surface. Sound waves, by contrast, travel in three dimensions. Although you cannot see sound waves, you can imagine them as expanding spheres with the vibrating object in the center.

An individual sound wave consists of a region in which the sound medium is denser than normal and a region in which the medium is less dense than normal. As a vibrating object moves outward from its position of rest, it compresses the medium, making it denser. The resulting region of compression is called a *condensation.* As the vibrating object then moves inward, the medium fills in the space formerly occupied by the object. The resulting region, called a *rarefaction,* is less dense than normal. As the object continues to move outward and inward, a succession of condensations and rarefactions travels away from the object.

Scientists describe sound in terms of (1) frequency and pitch, (2) wavelength, (3) intensity and loudness, and (4) quality.

Frequency and pitch. The *frequency* of a sound is the number of waves that pass a given point each second. The more rapidly an object vibrates, the greater is the frequency of the sound that it makes. Scientists use a unit called the *hertz* to measure frequency. One hertz equals one *cycle* (vibration, or sound wave) per second.

The frequency of a sound determines its *pitch*—the degree of highness or lowness of the sound as we hear it. A high-pitched sound has a higher frequency than a low-pitched sound.

Most people can hear sounds that have frequencies from about 20 to 20,000 hertz. Bats, dogs, and many other kinds of animals can hear sounds with frequencies much higher than 20,000 hertz.

Terms used in the study of sound

Acoustics is the science of sound and its effects on people.
Condensation is a region in a sound wave in which the sound medium is denser than normal.
Decibel (dB) is the unit used to measure the intensity of a sound. A 3,000-hertz tone of 0 dB is the softest sound that a normal human ear can hear.
Frequency of a sound is the number of sound waves that pass a given point each second.
Hertz is the unit used to measure the frequency of sound waves. One hertz equals one *cycle* (vibration, or sound wave) per second.
Intensity of a sound is a measure of the power of its waves.
Loudness refers to how strong a sound seems when we hear it.
Noise is sound that is unpleasant, annoying, and distracting.
Pitch is the degree of highness or lowness of a sound as we hear it.
Rarefaction is a region in a sound wave in which the density of the sound medium is less than normal.
Resonance frequency is the frequency at which an object would vibrate naturally if disturbed.
Sound medium is a substance in which sound waves travel. Air, for example, is a sound medium.
Sound quality, also called *timbre,* is a characteristic of musical sounds. Sound quality distinguishes between notes of the same frequency and intensity that are produced by different musical instruments.
Ultrasound is sound with frequencies above the range of human hearing—that is, above about 20,000 hertz.
Wavelength is the distance between any point on a wave and the corresponding point on the next wave.

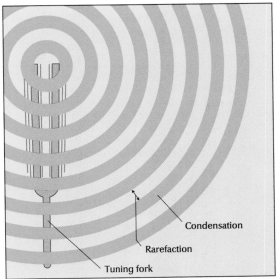

Condensation

Rarefaction

Tuning fork

WORLD BOOK diagram by Mark Swindle

Sound waves form when a vibrating object causes the surrounding *medium* (substance) to vibrate. As the object moves outward, it produces a region of compression called a *condensation.* As the object then moves inward, a region of expansion known as a *rarefaction* forms. Sound waves consist of the series of condensations and rarefactions generated by the object.

Sounds from different sources have different frequencies. For example, the sound of jingling keys ranges from 700 to 15,000 hertz. Human voices produce frequencies from about 85 to 1,100 hertz. The tones of a piano have frequencies from about 30 to 15,000 hertz.

Musicians use various techniques to change the pitch of the tones produced by their instruments. For example, a trumpet player presses and releases valves that shorten or lengthen the vibrating column of air inside the instrument. A short column produces a high-frequency, high-pitched sound. A long column results in a note of low frequency and low pitch.

Wavelength is the distance between any point on one wave and the corresponding point on the next wave. Wavelength is related to frequency: The greater the frequency of a wave, the shorter the wavelength.

Intensity and loudness. The *intensity* of a sound is a measure of the power of its sound waves. Sound intensity can be defined as the amount of sound power striking a unit of surface area—such as a square millimeter of the surface of an eardrum. Sound intensity can also be defined in terms of energy. Because power is a rate of energy flow, sound intensity is also a measure of the sound energy striking a unit of surface area each second. Scientists commonly refer to a sound's intensity as its *sound pressure level.*

Sound intensity depends partly on the *amplitude* of the vibrations creating the waves. Amplitude is the longest distance that an object moves from its position of rest as it vibrates. For an object vibrating at a given frequency, intensity increases as amplitude increases.

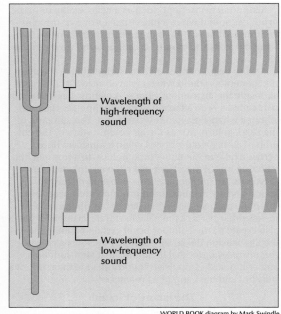

WORLD BOOK diagram by Mark Swindle

Frequency of sound waves is the number of condensations or rarefactions produced by a vibrating object each second. The more rapidly an object vibrates, the higher will be the frequency. As the frequency increases, the *wavelength* decreases. The frequency of a sound determines its pitch. High-pitched sounds have higher frequencies than low-pitched sounds.

Some common frequency ranges

Scientists use a unit called the *hertz* to measure frequency. One hertz equals one *cycle* (vibration) per second. This graph shows the range of frequencies, in hertz, that people and some animals can *emit* (give off) and receive. Many animals hear frequencies far above those heard by people.

WORLD BOOK graph

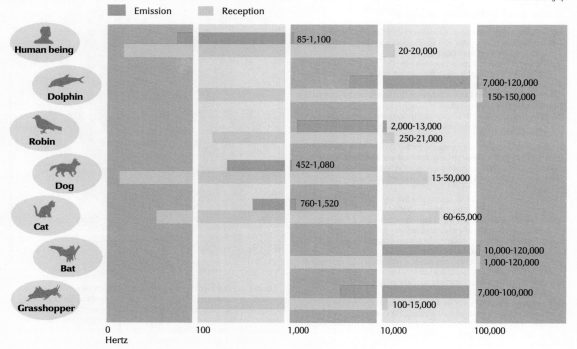

Scientists use a unit called the *decibel* (dB) to measure sound intensity. An increase of 10 dB represents a tenfold increase in power. Thus, a 50-dB sound delivers 10 times as much power per unit of area as a 40-dB sound.

A 3,000-hertz tone of 0 dB marks the *threshold of audibility*—the softest sound that the normal human ear can hear. A whisper amounts to about 20 dB. Ordinary conversation occurs at about 60 dB. Loud rock music can produce up to 120 dB. A level of 140 dB is the *threshold of pain.* Sounds of 140 dB or more can make a person's ears hurt.

Loudness refers to how strong a sound seems to be when we hear it. For sounds of a given frequency, the more intense a sound is, the louder it seems. But equally intense sounds that have different frequencies are not equally loud. The ear has a low sensitivity to sounds near the upper and lower ends of the range of frequencies we can hear. Thus, a high-frequency or low-frequency sound does not seem as loud as a sound of the same intensity in the middle of the frequency range.

Scientists often use a unit called the *phon* (pronounced *FAHN)* to measure loudness. Measured in phons, the loudness of a tone is equal to the intensity level in decibels of a 1,000-hertz tone that seems equally loud. For example, a tone with an intensity of 80 dB and a frequency of 20 hertz seems as loud as a 20-dB tone with a frequency of 1,000 hertz. Thus, the 80-dB tone has a loudness level of 20 phons.

Sound quality, or *timbre,* distinguishes between sounds of the same pitch and intensity produced by different musical instruments. Almost every musical sound is a combination of the actual tone sounded and a number of higher tones related to it. The tone played is the *fundamental.* The higher tones are *overtones.*

In many musical instruments, the overtones are *harmonics.* The frequency of a harmonic is an *integer multiple* of the frequency of the fundamental. That is, the frequency of the harmonic equals the fundamental frequency multiplied by an *integer* (whole number).

Suppose, for example, a violinist plays the note A above middle C. The A string of the violin will produce the fundamental by vibrating at 440 hertz over its entire length. The string will also produce a harmonic by vibrating in two segments, each equal to half the length of the string. Each segment will vibrate at a rate equal to twice the fundamental frequency—that is, at 880 hertz. The string will produce another harmonic by vibrating in three segments, each equal to one-third of the string's length. The frequency of this harmonic will be three times that of the fundamental, or 1,320 hertz. Other harmonics will have frequencies of four and more times that of the fundamental.

The number, intensity, and frequency of the overtones help determine the characteristic sound quality of an instrument. A note on the flute sounds soft and sweet because it has only a few weak harmonics. The same note played on the trumpet sounds powerful and bright because it has many strong overtones.

How sound behaves

The speed of sound depends on the medium's density and its *compressibility,* a measure of how easily it can be squeezed into a smaller volume. If two mediums are equally dense, but one is more compressible than

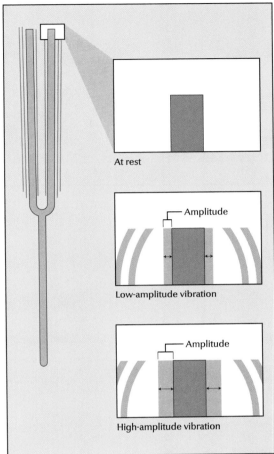

At rest

Amplitude

Low-amplitude vibration

Amplitude

High-amplitude vibration

Amplitude is the maximum distance that a vibrating object moves from its position of rest as it vibrates. For a given sound source, the intensity increases as the amplitude becomes larger.

the other, sound will travel more slowly through the more compressible medium. If two mediums are equally compressible, but one is denser than the other, sound will travel more slowly through the denser medium.

In general, liquids and solids are denser than air. But they are also much less compressible. Therefore, sound

The speed of sound in various mediums

Medium	Speed	
	In feet per second	In meters per second
Air at 59 °F (15 °C)	1,116	340
Aluminum	16,000	5,000
Brick	11,980	3,650
Distilled water at 77 °F (25 °C)	4,908	1,496
Glass	14,900	4,540
Seawater at 77 °F (25 °C)	5,023	1,531
Steel	17,100	5,200
Wood (maple)	13,480	4,110

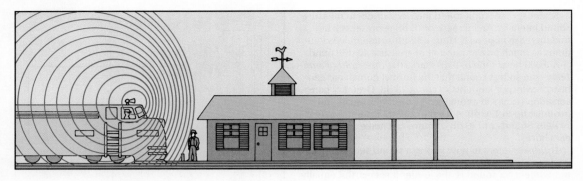

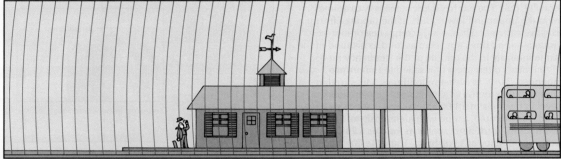

WORLD BOOK diagrams by Bill and Judie Anderson

The Doppler effect is an apparent change in pitch produced by moving objects. For example, the pitch of a train whistle appears higher as the train approaches and lower as the train moves away. As the train approaches, *top,* sound waves from the whistle are crowded together, producing a higher apparent pitch to the listener on the platform. As the train moves away, *bottom,* the waves are spread out, producing a lower apparent pitch. The people on the train hear a uniform pitch.

travels faster through liquids and solids than it does through air.

At sea level and a temperature of 59 °F (15 °C), sound travels in air at a speed of 1,116 feet (340 meters) per second. As the air temperature increases, the speed of sound also increases. For example, sound travels 1,268 feet (386 meters) per second in air at 212 °F (100 °C).

The speed of sound is related to frequency and wavelength by the equation: $v = f \times \lambda$, where v is the speed of sound, f is frequency, and λ (the Greek letter lambda) is wavelength. Thus, for example, where the speed of sound is 1,116 feet (340 meters) per second, the musical note A—whose frequency is 440 hertz—has a wavelength of about $2\frac{1}{2}$ feet (0.8 meter).

The Doppler effect. You may have noticed that the pitch of a train whistle is relatively high as the train approaches and relatively low as the train passes and moves away. The sound waves produced by the whistle travel through the air at a constant speed, regardless of the speed of the train. But as the train approaches, each successive wave produced by the whistle travels a shorter distance to your ears. The decrease in distance causes the waves to arrive more frequently than they would if the train were not moving. Thus, the frequency, and therefore the pitch, of the whistle is higher than it would be if the train were standing still.

As the train moves away, each successive sound wave created by the whistle travels a longer distance to your ears. The increase in distance causes the waves to arrive

less frequently, producing a lower pitch.

This apparent change in pitch produced by moving objects is called the *Doppler effect.* A listener on the train does not experience this effect because the train is not moving relative to him or her.

Supersonic speed. Jet airplanes sometimes fly at *supersonic* speeds—that is, faster than the speed of sound. A supersonic plane creates *shock waves,* strong pressure disturbances that build up around the aircraft and travel slightly faster than less intense sound. When the shock waves from the plane sweep over people on the ground, the people hear a loud noise that is known as a *sonic boom.*

Reflection. If you shout toward a large brick wall that is at least 30 feet (9 meters) away, you will hear an echo. The echo will occur because the wall will reflect most of the sound waves that you create when you shout.

Generally, when sound waves in one medium strike a large object of another medium, some of the sound is reflected. The remainder enters the new medium. The speed of sound in the two mediums and the densities of the mediums help determine the amount of reflection. If the speed differs greatly in the two mediums and their densities are much different, most of the sound will be reflected. Sound waves travel much more slowly through air than through brick, and brick is much denser than air. Thus, when you shout at the brick wall, most of the sound is reflected.

Refraction. When sound waves leave one medium

and enter another, the waves can be *refracted* (bent). For refraction to occur, the waves must enter the second medium at an angle other than 90°, and the speed of sound must be different in the two mediums. If sound travels more slowly in the second medium, the waves will bend toward the *normal.* The normal is an imaginary line perpendicular to the boundary between the mediums. If sound travels faster in the second medium, the waves will bend away from the normal.

Refraction can also occur in a single medium if the speed of sound is not the same throughout the medium. In this kind of medium, sound waves will bend toward a region in which the speed of sound is lower. Such refraction accounts for the fact that sounds carry farther at night than during a sunny day. During the day, air near the ground is warmer than the air above. Because the speed of sound is lower in the cooler air, the waves bend upward. As a result, the sound near the ground is relatively weak. But at night, air near the ground becomes cooler than the air above. Sound waves bend toward the ground, and so sound near the ground can be heard over longer distances.

Diffraction. When sound waves pass through a doorway, they spread out around its edges. The spreading of waves as they pass by the edge of an obstacle or through an opening is called *diffraction.* Diffraction enables you to hear a sound from around a corner.

Resonance. Any object will vibrate if it is disturbed. This natural vibration is called *resonance,* and its fre-

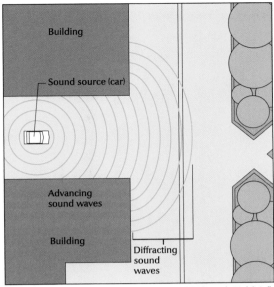

WORLD BOOK diagram by Mark Swindle

Diffraction is the spreading out of waves as they pass by the edge of an obstacle or through an opening. Diffraction enables the sound produced by the approaching car shown here to be heard around the corners of the buildings at the intersection.

Refraction of sound waves When sound waves leave one medium and enter another in which the speed of sound differs, the waves are *refracted*—that is, their direction is altered. Sound waves can be refracted away from or toward the *normal,* an imaginary line perpendicular to the boundary between the mediums.

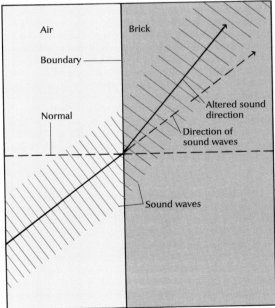

WORLD BOOK diagram by Bill and Judie Anderson

Refraction away from the normal. If sound waves in one medium enter another medium in which sound travels faster, the waves will be refracted away from the normal. For example, sound waves passing from air into brick are refracted away from the normal because sound travels faster in brick than in air.

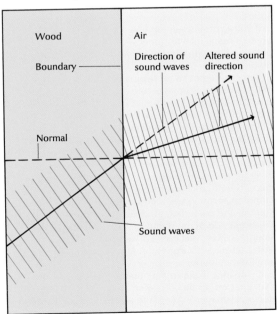

WORLD BOOK diagram by Bill and Judie Anderson

Refraction toward the normal. If sound waves in one medium enter another medium in which sound travels slower, the waves will be refracted toward the normal. For example, sound waves passing from wood into air are refracted toward the normal because sound travels slower in air than in wood.

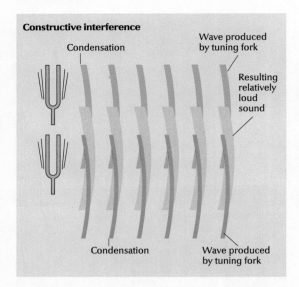

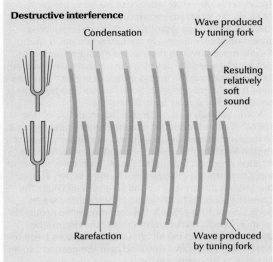

WORLD BOOK diagrams by Linda Kinnaman

Interference is a result of an overlapping of sound waves whose frequencies are the same, or nearly the same. In a *constructive interference* of two waves, *above left,* the condensations of the waves overlap. The sound of the resulting wave is louder than the sound that would be produced by either of the original waves alone. In *destructive interference,* condensations overlap with rarefactions. The result is either silence or, *above right,* a sound that is softer than what would be produced by the louder of the original waves.

quency is the object's *resonance frequency.* The quality of the sound produced by the vibration depends on the shape of the object and the material of which it is made. For example, a thin goblet will ring if struck with a fingernail, but a block of wood will make only a brief, dull sound.

If you apply a small force to a vibrating object at the object's resonance frequency, you will increase the amplitude of the vibration. The amplitude can become quite large.

You can demonstrate resonance with a tuning fork and a tube that is open at one end. The length of the tube must be one-fourth as long as the wavelength of the sound produced by the fork.

First, hold the tuning fork away from the tube and strike the fork. The fork will make a soft sound. Then strike the fork again and hold it above the open end of the tube. The sound waves will travel down the column of air inside the tube, and the closed end will reflect them. The original waves and the reflected waves will combine, forming *standing waves* in the tube. The air column and the tuning fork will be *in resonance,* and so the amplitude of the standing waves will grow. The standing waves will cause the surrounding air to vibrate with a larger and larger amplitude, resulting in a louder and louder sound.

Resonance makes most musical instruments louder than they would be otherwise. A wind instrument produces resonance in the same way as a tuning fork and tube. A violin produces a resonance between its strings, its body, and the space inside its body.

Beats. If two tones that have slightly different frequencies are sounded at the same time, you will hear a single tone. This tone will become louder and softer at regular intervals. The variations in loudness are called

beats. The number of beats per second, called the *beat frequency,* equals the difference between the frequencies of the two tones. For example, if a 256-hertz tone and a 257-hertz tone are sounded together, you will hear one beat each second.

Beats occur because the sound waves of the two tones overlap and interfere with each other in a certain way. An interference of waves is called *constructive* if the condensations of the waves of one tone coincide with the condensations of the waves of the other tone. When constructive interference occurs, the waves reinforce each other, producing a louder sound. But if the condensations of one tone coincide with the rarefactions of the other tone, the interference is *destructive,* resulting in a weaker sound or silence. And if periods of constructive and destructive interference alternate, the loudness of the sound increases and decreases periodically, producing beats.

Working with sound

Controlling sound. The science of *acoustics* deals with sound and its effects on people. We are continually exposed to noise from a variety of sources, such as airplanes, construction projects, factories, motor vehicles, and household appliances. People exposed to loud noise for long periods may suffer temporary or permanent loss of hearing. Loud sounds of short duration, such as the noise of a gunshot or a firecracker, can also damage the ear. Constant noise—even if it is not extremely loud—can cause fatigue, headaches, hearing loss, irritability, nausea, and tension.

Acoustical engineers have developed many ways to quiet noise. For example, mufflers help quiet automobile engines. In buildings, thick, heavy walls and well-sealed doors and windows can block out noise. In addition, industrial workers and other people exposed to intense noise can wear earplugs to help prevent hearing loss.

Acoustical engineers also provide good conditions for producing and listening to speech and music. For example, they work to control *reverberation*—the bouncing back and forth of sound against the ceiling, walls, floor, and other surfaces of an auditorium. Some reverberation is necessary to produce pleasing sounds. But too much reverberation can blur the voice of a speaker or the sound of an instrument. Engineers use such sound-absorbing items as carpets, draperies, acoustical tiles, and upholstered furniture to control reverberation.

Using sound. Sound has many uses in science and industry. Geophysicists use sound in exploring for minerals and petroleum. In one technique, they set off a small explosion on or just below the earth's surface. The resulting sound waves bounce off underground layers of rock. The nature of each echo and the time the echo takes to reach the surface indicate the type and thickness of each rock layer present. Geophysicists can thus locate possible mineral- or oil-bearing rock formations. A device called *sonar* uses sound waves to detect underwater objects. Fishing boats use sonar to detect schools of fish. Warships can locate enemy submarines with sonar.

There are many uses for *ultrasound,* sound with frequencies above the range of human hearing. Techni-

Intensity of some common sounds

The unit used to measure the intensity level of a sound is called the *decibel.* A 3,000-hertz tone of zero decibels is the weakest sound the human ear can hear. Sounds of 140 decibels or more produce pain in the ear and may damage the delicate tissues.

WORLD BOOK chart

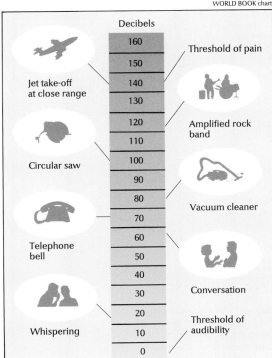

Decibels

160	Threshold of pain
150	
Jet take-off 140	
at close range 130	
120	Amplified rock
110	band
Circular saw 100	
90	
80	Vacuum cleaner
70	
60	
Telephone 50	
bell 40	
30	Conversation
20	
Whispering 10	Threshold of audibility
0	

cians use ultrasound to clean watches and other delicate instruments. Manufacturers use ultrasonic waves to detect flaws in metals, plastics, and other materials. Physicians can diagnose brain tumors, gallstones, liver diseases, and other disorders with ultrasound. Ultrasound also provides a relatively safe means to check the development of unborn children. In addition, doctors use ultrasound to break up kidney stones nonsurgically.

Scientists and engineers have developed several devices for recording and reproducing sound. These devices include the microphone, the speaker, and the amplifier. A *microphone* changes sound waves into electric signals that correspond to the pattern of the waves. A *speaker* changes electric signals, such as those produced by a microphone, back into sound. An *amplifier* strengthens the electric signals, making them powerful enough to operate the speaker.

In recording music, engineers make two or more separate recordings from microphones placed at various points around the sound source or sources. When these recordings are played back together, they produce *stereophonic sound.* This kind of sound has qualities of depth and direction that are similar to those of the original sound. To reproduce stereophonic sound, a sound system must have two or more amplifiers and speakers.

History

Early ideas about sound. The study of sound began in ancient times. As early as the 500's B.C., Pythagoras, a Greek philosopher and mathematician, experimented on the sounds of vibrating strings. About 400 B.C., a Greek scholar named Archytas may have observed that faster motions result in higher pitched sounds. About 50 years later, the Greek philosopher Aristotle suggested that the movement of air carries sound to our ears. From then until about A.D. 1300, most investigation of sound dealt with its relationship to music.

The study of waves. European scientists did not begin extensive experiments on the nature of sound until the early 1600's. About that time, Italian astronomer and physicist Galileo demonstrated that the frequency of sound waves determines their pitch. Galileo scraped a chisel across a brass plate and noticed this action often produced a screech. During the screech, filings would gather as lines on the plate. Galileo reasoned that waves within the plate concentrated the filings into the lines. He then worked out the mathematical relationship between the spacing of the lines and the frequency and pitch of the screeches.

About 1640, Marin Mersenne, a French mathematician, attempted to measure the speed of sound in air. About 20 years later, the Irish chemist and physicist Robert Boyle demonstrated that sound waves must travel in a medium. Boyle showed that a ringing bell could not be heard as easily if placed in a jar from which almost all the air had been removed. During the late 1600's, the English scientist Isaac Newton formulated a relationship between the speed of sound in a medium and the density and compressibility of the medium.

In the mid-1700's, Daniel Bernoulli, a Swiss mathematician, explained that a string could vibrate at more than one frequency at the same time. In the early 1800's, French mathematician Jean Baptiste Fourier developed a mathematical technique for analyzing waves. Fourier's technique can break down complex sound waves into the pure, single-frequency tones that make them up. During the 1860's, Hermann von Helmholtz, a German physicist and physiologist, investigated the perception of sound.

The recording of sound. In 1877, American inventor Thomas A. Edison invented the first practical phonograph. This device recorded sound on tinfoil wrapped around a small metal cylinder, and it could replay the sound. In 1887, Emile Berliner, a German immigrant to the United States, invented a phonograph that used discs instead of cylinders. Stereophonic phonographs and discs appeared in 1958. Audio compact discs were introduced in Japan and Europe in 1982, and in the United States in 1983.

Tape recorders were in wide use in the radio and recording industries by 1950. In the mid-1950's, manufacturers began to produce stereophonic tape recorders for use in the home. By the mid-1960's, tape cassettes were competing with phonograph records.

Synchronized sound came to motion pictures in the mid-1920's, when engineers in Germany and the United States demonstrated a few systems. In these systems, the sound from a disc was mechanically matched with the film. This method was soon replaced by one in which the sound was recorded on the film. The sound-on-film system is still in use.

Modern acoustics. In 1878, the British physicist Lord Rayleigh described many of the important principles of acoustics in the book *The Theory of Sound.* Although many properties of sound have thus been long established, the science of acoustics has continued to expand into new areas. In the 1940's, Georg von Békésy, an American physicist and physiologist, showed how the ear distinguishes between sounds. In the 1960's, the field of *environmental acoustics* expanded rapidly in response to concern over the physical and psychological effects of noise.

Acoustical research of the 1970's included the study of new uses of ultrasound and the development of better ultrasonic equipment. During the 1980's, research included the development of computers that can understand and reproduce speech.

By the early 2000's, two important areas of acoustics were active noise cancellation (ANC) and active structural-acoustic control (ASAC). In the simplest form of ANC, a speaker produces sound waves that interfere destructively with the waves of an unwanted sound. As a result, the sound from the speaker cancels out the unwanted sound. In ASAC, a device called an *actuator* applies force to an object whose vibration is producing an unwanted sound. The force changes the nature of the vibration, making the resulting sound less objectionable.

Ilene J. Busch-Vishniac

Related articles in *World Book* include:

Principles of sound

Acoustics	Larynx
Decibel	Noise
Doppler effect	Pitch
Ear	Tone
Echo	Ultrasound
Harmonics	Vibration
Hertz	Voice
Interference	Waves

Sound instruments and devices

Camcorder	Motion picture	Tape recorder
Cellular telephone	Oscilloscope	Telephone
Compact disc	Phonograph	Television
Dictating machine	Radio	Transducer
DVD	Sonar	Tuning fork
Electronics	Speaker	Videotape
Fathometer	Stereophonic	recorder
Hearing aid	sound system	Voiceprint
Microphone	Stethoscope	

Other related articles

Aerodynamics (Shock waves)	Insulation (Insulation against
Bell, Alexander G.	sound)
Berliner, Emile	Mach, Ernst
Deafness	Muffler
Edison, Thomas A.	Music
Frequency modulation	Phonetics
Helmholtz, Hermann	Recording industry
	Singing

Outline

I. How some familiar sounds are produced
  A. The human voice   C. Musical sounds
  B. Animal sounds   D. Noises
II. The nature of sound
  A. Frequency and pitch
  B. Wavelength
  C. Intensity and loudness
  D. Sound quality
III. How sound behaves
  A. The speed of sound   D. Diffraction
  B. Reflection   E. Resonance
  C. Refraction   F. Beats
IV. Working with sound
  A. Controlling sound
  B. Using sound
V. History

Questions

How does a vibrating object produce sound waves?
Why does sound travel faster through liquids and solids than through air?
How do wind instruments generate tones?
Why do acoustical engineers try to control the amount of reverberation in auditoriums?
What is the frequency of a sound? The wavelength?
What characteristic of sound do scientists measure in decibels?
Why do sounds carry farther at night than during a sunny day?
What causes echoes?
Why does a note on the flute sound different from the same note played on a trumpet?
Why are sound waves absent in outer space?

Additional resources

Level I
Farndon, John. *Sound and Hearing.* Benchmark Bks., 2001.
Parker, Steve. *Light and Sound.* Raintree, 2001.
Riley, Peter D. *Sound.* Gareth Stevens, 2002.
Wright, Lynne. *The Science of Noise.* Raintree, 2000.

Level II
Crocker, Malcolm J., ed. *Encyclopedia of Acoustics.* 4 vols. Wiley, 1997.
Everest, F. Alton. *Master Handbook of Acoustics.* 4th ed. TAB, 2000.
Kruth, Patricia, and Stobart, Henry, eds. *Sound.* Cambridge, 2000.
Mullin, William J., and others. *Fundamentals of Sound with Applications to Speech and Hearing.* Allyn & Bacon, 2003.

Sound spectrograph. See Voiceprint.
Soundproofing. See Acoustics; Insulation.
Sourgum. See Tupelo.
Sourwood is a tree native to the woods of the southern part of the United States. It grows as far north as

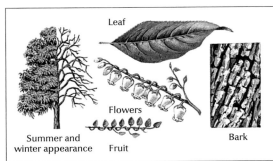

WORLD BOOK illustration by Chris Skilton

The sourwood is a beautiful American tree that bears clusters of small, bell-shaped flowers during the summertime.

Pennsylvania, Indiana, and Ohio. The name *sourwood* comes from the taste of its leaves and twigs, which hunters, hikers, and campers sometimes chew when they are thirsty. The sourwood is also called the *sorrel-tree,* from an Old French word that means *sour.*

The sourwood may reach a height of 50 to 60 feet (15 to 18 meters). It has reddish-gray bark and smooth, oblong leaves. In summer, it bears graceful clusters of small, bell-shaped, white flowers, which are soon followed by little downy capsules. In spring, the foliage is bronze-green, but in autumn it turns a brilliant scarlet. The wood is sometimes used to make handles for tools. Sourwood leaves furnish a black dye.   James L. Luteyn

Scientific classification. The sourwood belongs to the heath family, Ericaceae. Its scientific name is *Oxydendrum arboreum.*

Sousa, John Philip (1854-1932), was a famous American composer and bandmaster. Sousa wrote many kinds of music, including operettas, orchestral suites, songs, waltzes, and a symphonic poem. But his fame rests on his marches, and he became known throughout the world as the "March King."

Sousa took the rather simple form of the military march and gave it a personal style and new rhythmic and melodic vitality. The best known of his 136 marches include "Semper Fidelis," "The Washington Post," "El Capitan," "Thunderer," "The High School Cadets," "Liberty Bell," "Manhattan Beach," "Hands Across the Sea," and "The Stars and Stripes Forever."

Sousa also wrote five novels. His autobiography is titled *Marching Along* (1928).

Sousa was born on Nov. 6, 1854, in Washington, D.C. His parents could not afford to send him to Europe to study music. But Sousa later said, "I feel I am better off as it is ... for I may therefore consider myself a truly American composer."

After studying violin and harmony, Sousa began his professional career at the age of 17, playing in theater and dance orchestras and touring with a variety show. In 1876, he played in Jacques Offenbach's orchestra when the famous French composer toured the United States. Soon afterward, Sousa wrote an operetta, *The Smugglers,* the first of many that he wrote in the next 35 years. Sousa was one of the first Americans to compose operettas. He wrote both the words and the music. His most successful operetta was *El Capitan* (1896).

Sousa was appointed leader of the United States Marine Band in 1880 and made the band into one of the

finest in the world. Some of the marches that made him famous were written for it. In 1892, he obtained his discharge from the Marine Corps and formed his own band.

"Sousa's Band" quickly became famous throughout America and Europe. He was honored wherever he traveled. In England, King Edward VII decorated him with the Victorian Order. In 1900, the Ameri-

Bettmann Archive

John Philip Sousa

can writer Rupert Hughes wrote, "There is probably no other composer in the world with a popularity equal to that of Sousa." In 1910 and 1911, the band made a triumphal world tour. From 1917 to 1919, Sousa served as bandmaster for the United States Navy. He died on March 6, 1932.   Stewart L. Ross

Sousaphone. See Tuba.

Souster, Raymond (1921-   ), is a Canadian poet. He uses direct, simple language to make uncomplicated statements. Most of Souster's poems concern Toronto, where he was born and grew up. He writes about that city with both irony and sympathy.

Souster won the Governor General's Award for the collection *The Colour of the Times* (1964). In 1952, Souster helped found Contact Press, which published the work of modern Canadian poets. He also edited several anthologies of Canadian verse, including *New Wave Canada: The New Explosion in Canadian Poetry* (1966). Eight volumes of Souster's *Collected Poems* cover his verse from 1955 to 1995. His later collections include *Take Me Out to the Ballgame* (2002). Souster has written two novels, *The Winter of Time* (1949), under the pen name Raymond Holmes, and *On Target* (1973), under the pen name John Holmes. Souster was born on Jan. 15, 1921.   Laurie R. Ricou

Souter, *SOO tuhr,* **David Hackett** (1939-   ), became an associate justice of the Supreme Court of the United States in 1990. President George H. W. Bush appointed him to fill the vacancy created by the retirement of Justice William J. Brennan, Jr.

As a Supreme Court justice, Souter has become known as a moderate. But he has often sided with the liberal justices on issues facing the court.

Souter was born on Sept. 17, 1939, in Melrose, Massachusetts. He graduated from Harvard College in 1961 and spent two years at Oxford University as a Rhodes scholar. Rhodes scholarships enable top students from the United States and other nations to study at Oxford. In 1966, Souter graduated from Harvard Law School.

Souter was appointed attorney general of New Hampshire in 1976. In 1978, he was named associate justice of the state's Superior Court. In 1983, Souter was appointed to the Supreme Court of New Hampshire. Bush named him to serve as a judge of the United States Court of Appeals for the First Circuit in April 1990. Souter joined the Supreme Court of the United States in October 1990.   Dennis J. Hutchinson

See also **Supreme Court of the United States.**

South, The. See United States (Regions).

© Gerald Cubitt

Cape Town, South Africa's legislative capital and oldest city, lies at the foot of the Cape Mountains in a setting of striking natural beauty. The city's location on the country's southwest coast and its excellent harbor make Cape Town an important shipping and trading center.

South Africa

South Africa is a country at the southern tip of the continent of Africa. The country has a wealth of natural resources, especially minerals, and it is the most highly industrialized nation in Africa. South Africa also has great geographical variety and natural beauty.

South Africa was the last nation in Africa ruled by a white minority. From the late 1940's to the early 1990's, the white government enforced a policy of rigid racial segregation called *apartheid* (pronounced *ah PAHRT hayt).* Under apartheid, the government denied voting rights and other rights to the black majority. Many South Africans and people throughout the world opposed apartheid. Protests against it often led to violence.

In 1990 and 1991, South Africa repealed most of the main laws on which apartheid was based. In 1993, the country extended voting rights to all races, and democratic elections were held the next year. After those elections, South Africa's white leaders handed over power to the country's first multiracial government. Nelson Mandela, a civil rights leader who had spent 27 years in prison, became South Africa's first black president.

Government

South Africa has three capitals. Parliament meets in Cape Town, the legislative capital. All executive departments of the government have their headquarters in Pretoria, the administrative capital. The Supreme Court of Appeal meets in Bloemfontein, the judicial capital.

South Africa adopted a temporary constitution in 1993. It provided for a new government that took office in May 1994, following the country's first all-race elec-

tions. In 1996, South Africa adopted a new Constitution. Most of this Constitution, which includes a wide-ranging bill of rights, took effect in 1997.

National government. South Africa's Parliament makes the country's laws, which must be signed by the president to take effect. Parliament consists of two houses: the National Assembly and the National Council of Provinces. The National Assembly has at least 350 members and no more than 400 members, elected for five-year terms. Under certain conditions, the Assembly may be dissolved before the members serve their full terms. The National Council of Provinces represents the interests of South Africa's provinces at the national level. Each of the nine provincial legislatures chooses 10 delegates to send to the National Council. The proportion of seats a political party holds in the provincial legislature determines how many of the 10 delegates to the National Council come from that party.

A president, elected by the National Assembly from among its members, heads South Africa's government. A Cabinet assists the president in running the government. The Cabinet includes the deputy president and the ministers in charge of government departments. The president chooses the members of the Cabinet and assigns them their duties. Cabinet members are chosen mainly from the members of the National Assembly.

South Africa's court system includes the Constitutional Court, the Supreme Court of Appeal, several High Courts, and local courts run by magistrates. In addition, *traditional leaders,* the heads of South Africa's black African ethnic groups, may hear and decide matters of customary law in their own courts.

South Africa's highest court in all constitutional matters is the Constitutional Court, which meets in Johannesburg. The Constitutional Court settles disputes between national, provincial, and local governments that involve the Constitution. It also decides if constitutional amendments passed by Parliament and laws approved by Parliament and provincial legislatures are legal. In addition, it can determine whether the conduct of the president is constitutional. Members of the Constitutional Court are appointed by the president of South Africa to 12-year terms.

South Africa's Supreme Court of Appeal, in Bloemfontein, hears appeals from the High Courts. The Supreme Court of Appeal is South Africa's highest court except in constitutional matters.

The government has set up several independent national institutions to strengthen the country's democracy. They include the Human Rights Commission; the Commission for the Promotion and Protection of the Rights of Cultural, Religious and Linguistic Communities; the Commission for Gender Equality; and the Independent Electoral Commission. In addition, a Council of Traditional Leaders advises the government on the role of traditional leaders and on customary law.

Provincial government. Before 1994, South Africa was divided into 4 provinces and 10 areas called *homelands.* The provinces were (1) Cape Province, (2) Natal, (3) Orange Free State, and (4) Transvaal. The homelands were reserved for black Africans. The South African government granted independence to four homelands and allowed the other six a degree of self-government. But none of the homelands had much real power, and black Africans strongly opposed the homeland system.

The 1993 Constitution dissolved the 4 provinces and 10 homelands. In their place, 9 new provinces were created. These provinces are (1) Eastern Cape, (2) Free State, (3) Gauteng, (4) KwaZulu-Natal, (5) Limpopo, (6) Mpumalanga, (7) Northern Cape, (8) North West, and (9) Western Cape. Each province is governed by a provincial legislature of from 30 to 80 members. The legislature elects the premier of the province.

Local government under apartheid was racially segregated, with separate areas for whites and blacks. After apartheid ended, South Africa redrew its local government boundaries to merge previously segregated areas. Today, the country is divided into 6 metropolitan municipalities and 47 district municipalities. The district municipalities are further divided into 231 local municipalities. An elected council governs each municipality. The municipalities include both urban and rural areas.

Political parties. The largest political parties in South Africa are the African National Congress (ANC), the Democratic Alliance (DA), and the Inkatha Freedom Party (IFP). The ANC was founded in 1912 to promote the rights of black Africans. Although illegal from 1960 until 1990, it served as the main political voice for blacks, who were not allowed to vote. Its supporters now include people from all ethnic groups. The DA is supported mainly by white voters. Most members of the IFP belong to the black Zulu ethnic group.

Armed forces. The South African National Defence Force combines the forces of the army, navy, and air force. Men and women of all racial and ethnic groups serve in the National Defence Force. All service is voluntary. Before 1994, most officers in the armed forces were white. The number of black African soldiers and officers increased when armies of the black homelands became part of the National Defence Force. The force also absorbed the military wings of the ANC and another black political group, the Pan-Africanist Congress (PAC).

People

Racial and ethnic groups. From the late 1940's to the early 1990's, the government enforced a policy of racial segregation called *apartheid. Apartheid* means *separateness* in Afrikaans, a language spoken in South Africa. Under apartheid, the government officially categorized the people into four main racial groups: (1) African (black), (2) white, (3) Coloured (mixed-race), and (4) Asian. The government segregated the groups in housing, education, and employment, and in the use of transportation and other public facilities. Even after apartheid ended, the four groups remained generally separated. This separation is slowly diminishing.

Black Africans, often called simply Africans or blacks, make up 79 percent of South Africa's total population. The ancestors of black Africans moved into what is now eastern South Africa from the north between about A.D. 200 and 1000.

Although black Africans live throughout the country, the largest group, the Zulu, make their homes mainly in KwaZulu-Natal. The second largest group, the Xhosa, live mostly in Eastern Cape. The Sotho are the third largest black group. The southern Sotho live in eastern Free State. The northern Sotho reside in Limpopo. The western Sotho or Tswana, related to the people of Botswana, live near the border of that country.

Whites make up 10 percent of South Africa's people. About 60 percent of the white population call themselves Afrikaners. Their ancestors came chiefly from the Netherlands in the late 1600's, though some came from Germany and France. Until the 1900's, most Afrikaners lived on farms and were known as Boers. *Boer* is a Dutch word that means *farmer.*

Today, most Afrikaners live in cities, but they still make up most of the white population in rural areas. English-speaking whites account for about 40 percent of the white population. Their ancestors came chiefly from England, Ireland, and Scotland beginning in the early 1800's.

Coloureds make up 9 percent of South Africa's population. Their ancestors include the Khoikhoi and San peoples of western South Africa; African and Asian slaves brought to the country by whites; white settlers; and passing sailors, soldiers, and travelers. Most Coloured people live in Western Cape and Northern Cape provinces.

Asians—almost all of whom are people of Indian ancestry—make up 2 percent of the country's population. The ancestors of most of them came from India between 1860 and 1911 to work on sugar plantations in Natal (now KwaZulu-Natal). Plantation owners imported them as *indentured laborers,* workers contracted to work for a set time for a particular employer. South Africa also has a few people with Chinese ancestry.

Languages. South Africa has 11 official languages. They are (1) Afrikaans, (2) English, (3) Ndebele (which

South Africa in brief

Capitals: Cape Town (legislative), Pretoria (administrative), Bloemfontein (judicial).
Official languages: South Africa's 11 official languages are (1) Afrikaans, (2) English, (3) Ndebele (isiNdebele), (4) Sepedi, (5) Sesotho, (6) Swazi (siSwati), (7) Tsonga (Xitsonga), (8) Tswana (Setswana), (9) Venda (Tshivenda), (10) Xhosa (isiXhosa), and (11) Zulu (isiZulu).
Official name: Republic of South Africa.
National anthem: Combined version of "Nkosi Sikelel' iAfrika" and "Die Stem van Suid-Afrika/The Call of South Africa."
Largest municipalities: (2001 census)

Johannesburg	3,225,810
eThekwini (Durban)	3,090,117
Cape Town	2,893,251
Ekurhuleni (East Rand)	2,480,282

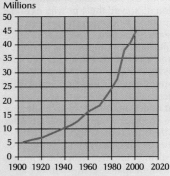

South Africa's flag, adopted in 1994, represents the country's peoples coming together in unity.

Coat of arms was adopted in 2000. The motto, in an ancient South African language, means *diverse people unite.*

Land and climate

Land: South Africa lies at the southern tip of Africa, with a coastline on the Indian and Atlantic oceans. The country borders Namibia, Botswana, Zimbabwe, Mozambique, and Swaziland, and it completely surrounds the country of Lesotho. South Africa's interior is mostly plateau. Coastal lowlands lie in the east. The Cape Mountains are in the far south. The Namib Desert stretches along the west coast. The Kalahari Desert covers much of the northwest interior. South Africa's main rivers include the Orange and its branch, the Vaal.

Area: 471,445 mi² (1,221,037 km²). *Greatest distances*—east-west, 1,010 mi (1,625 km); north-south, 875 mi (1,408 km). *Coastline*—about 1,836 mi (2,954 km).
Elevation: *Highest*—Champagne Castle, 11,072 ft (3,375 m) above sea level. *Lowest*—sea level.

Climate: South Africa's climate is generally mild and sunny. The Cape Mountains Region has warm, dry summers and cool, wet winters. Much of the Coastal Strip has hot, humid summers and dry, sunny winters. In the Plateau, summer days are hot, but the nights are cool. The winter is cold. The deserts are hot and dry. Only about a fourth of South Africa receives more than 25 inches (64 centimeters) of rain yearly. More rain falls in the east than in the west.

Government

Form of government: Parliamentary republic.
Head of government: President.
Legislature: Parliament of two houses: National Assembly (350 to 400 members); National Council of Provinces (90 members).
Executive: President (elected by the National Assembly) and Cabinet.
Judiciary: Constitutional Court is highest court in constitutional matters; Supreme Court of Appeal is highest court in other matters.
Political subdivisions: Nine provinces.

People

Population: *2008 estimate*—47,114,000. *2001 census*—44,819,778.
Population density: 100 per mi² (39 per km²).
Distribution: 58 percent urban, 42 percent rural.
Major ethnic/national groups: 79 percent black African (mainly Zulu, Xhosa, and Sotho); 10 percent white; 9 percent Coloured (mixed race); 2 percent Asian (mostly Indian).
Major religions: 40 percent Protestant; 40 percent African Independent churches; 8 percent Roman Catholic; less than 2 percent each of Hindu, Muslim, Jewish, and traditional African religions.

Population trend
Millions

Year	Population
1950	13,683,000
1955	15,385,000
1960	17,396,000
1965	19,832,000
1970	22,458,000
1975	25,669,000
1980	29,170,000
1985	33,043,000
1990	37,066,000
1996	40,583,573
2001	44,819,778

Sources: United Nations estimates; Statistics South Africa.

Economy

Chief products: *Agriculture*—apples, beef cattle, chickens and eggs, corn, sheep, sugar cane, wheat, wool. *Manufacturing*—chemicals, fabricated metal products, iron and steel, petroleum products, processed foods and beverages, textiles, transportation equipment. *Mining*—chromite, coal, copper, diamonds, gold, iron ore, limestone, manganese, phosphate, platinum, uranium, vanadium.
Money: *Basic unit*—rand. One hundred cents equal one rand.
International trade: *Major exports*—corn, diamonds, gold, metals and minerals, sugar, wool. *Major imports*—chemicals, machinery, petroleum and petroleum products, transportation equipment. *Major trading partners*—Germany, Japan, United Kingdom, United States.

Africans call isiNdebele), (4) Sepedi, (5) Sesotho, (6) Swazi (siSwati), (7) Tsonga (Xitsonga), (8) Tswana (Setswana), (9) Venda (Tshivenda), (10) Xhosa (isiXhosa), and (11) Zulu (isiZulu). All these languages except Afrikaans and English are black African languages belonging to the Bantu group. Afrikaans developed from Dutch, but it also has words from other European languages and from Asian and African languages. South African English resembles British English with the addition of some words from Afrikaans and Bantu languages.

About 60 percent of South Africa's white people use Afrikaans as their first language, as do about 80 percent of the Coloured population. The other whites and Coloureds speak English as their first language. Many black Africans speak Bantu languages, and many also speak English or Afrikaans. Most Indians and Chinese speak English, as well as one or more Asian languages.

For many years, English and Afrikaans were South Africa's only two official languages, and the only two used in government. English remains the chief language used in business, industry, and government. However, by law, all government documents must be printed in at least 2 of the country's 11 official languages. Also, the law calls for spoken government transactions to occur in any official language a speaker chooses.

© Gisela Damm, eStock Photo

Cattle graze near the Drakensberg mountains in eastern South Africa. About 45 percent of the country's people reside in rural areas. Many earn their living through agriculture.

Ways of life

The differing cultural backgrounds of South Africa's people have created contrasting ways of life. In addition, the inequalities created by apartheid and white domination have profoundly affected how people live.

South Africa's racial groups are no longer segregated by law. But black Africans, Coloureds, and Asians still face much unofficial discrimination. Some schools and housing remain segregated by custom. Whites generally enjoy a higher standard of living than other groups do. A growing number of black Africans, Indians, and Coloureds hold executive and professional positions. But most in these groups struggle to earn a living.

Black Africans. The average *per capita* (per person) income of black Africans is about one-fifth that of whites. Large numbers of black Africans are unemployed, and many lack adequate housing. Many still live in areas that were formerly black homelands.

During the apartheid years, strict controls prevented black Africans from leaving the homelands. Agricultural production in the homelands was difficult because of overcrowding, poor soils, and overgrazed pastureland. Many adults, especially men, sought jobs in the cities to support their families. Only black Africans who found jobs with urban employers were permitted to live temporarily in cities. Even then, apartheid laws restricted them to segregated neighborhoods, many of which were far from the center of town.

In the mid-1980's, the government repealed the laws that kept black Africans out of the cities. In 1994, the government ended the homelands system. Today, about 50 percent of black Africans live in urban areas. Many still live in previously segregated black neighborhoods. Others have moved into formerly all-white neighborhoods. Still others have built makeshift shelters on empty land inside the city limits and on land along major roads leading into the cities.

Whites. About 90 percent of white South Africans live in urban areas. Many whites enjoy a relatively high standard of living. Most white families live in single-family homes in suburban areas, and many employ household help who are not white.

Afrikaners and English-speaking whites have traditionally led separate lives. Many still live in different towns and suburbs, go to different schools, and belong to different churches and other organizations. But these distinctions are gradually breaking down. Before 1994, Afrikaners held most government jobs in South Africa. They still control most of the nation's agriculture. English-speaking whites dominate business and industry.

Coloureds. About 85 percent of South Africa's Coloureds live in cities. The Coloured community began in what is now Western Cape, and many Coloureds still live there. In cities, many Coloureds have jobs as servants, factory laborers, or craftworkers. In rural areas, many work in agriculture.

Asians. More than 95 percent of South Africa's Asians live in cities. Indians make up almost all the Asian population. Most Indians live in KwaZulu-Natal. Many are poor and work in factories or grow vegetables for city markets. But some are prosperous doctors, industrialists, lawyers, merchants, and government officials.

Food and drink vary among the people of South Africa. Whites eat foods similar to those eaten by Americans and Europeans. They also enjoy traditional specialties, such as *boerewors,* an Afrikaner sausage. *Braaivleis* (barbecues) are particularly popular. Coloureds have a diet similar to that of whites, but less costly. Indians often cook *curries,* dishes of eggs, fish, meat, or vegetables in a spicy sauce. The basic food of most black Africans is *mealies* (corn), eaten as a porridge. Wealthier black Africans eat the same foods as whites and Coloureds. Many poor people suffer from a shortage of protein and vitamins. Popular beverages include coffee, tea, beer, wine, and soft drinks.

Recreation. Many South Africans love sports, and the country's mild climate enables people to spend

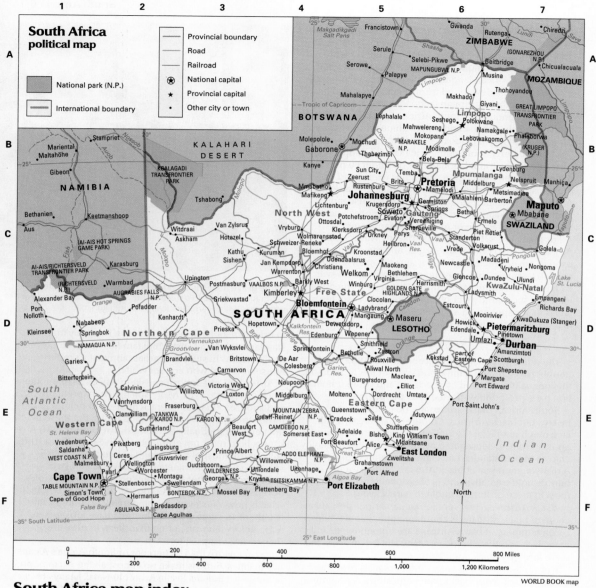

South Africa map index

Provinces

Eastern Cape	.6,436,756	.E	4
Free State	.2,706,754	.D	4
Gauteng	.8,837,157	.C	5
KwaZulu-Natal	.9,426,018	.D	6
Limpopo	.5,273,647	.A	6
Mpuma-langa	.3,122,977	.B	6
Northern Cape	.822,720	.D	2
North West	.3,669,339	.C	4
Western Cape	.4,524,316	.F	2

Municipalities*

Abaqulusi	.191,001	.C	7
Albert Luthuli	.187,929	.C	7
Aganang	.147,676	.B	6
Blouberg	.161,316	.A	6
Buffalo City	.701,884	.E	5
Bushbuck-ridge	.499,701	.B	7
Cape Town	.2,893,251	.F	1
Dr. JS Moroka	.243,304	.B	6

See footnotes at end of index.

Drakenstein ...194,421 ..F 2

Ekurhuleni (East Rand)	.2,480,282	.C	6
eMalahleni	.276,406	.C	6
Emfuleni	.658,425	.C	5
Emnambithi/Ladysmith	.225,449	.D	6
Engcobo	.148,396	.E	5
eThekwini (Durban)	.3,090,117	.D	7
Greater Giyani	.237,425	.B	7
Greater Grob-lersdal	.220,733	.B	6
Greater Letaba	.220,121	.B	6
Greater Taung	.182,167	.C	4
Greater Tubatse	.270,125	.B	6
Greater Tzaneen	.375,581	.B	6
Hibiscus Coast	.218,175	.E	6
Highveld East	.221,750	.C	6
Hlabisa	.176,879	.D	7
Intsika Yethu	.194,219	.E	5
Johannes-burg	.3,225,810	.C	5
Jozini	.184,092	.C	7

King Sabata Dalind-yebo ...415,237 ..E 6

Klerksdorp	.359,206	.C	5
KwaDukuza	.158,586	.D	7
Lepelle-Nkumpi	.227,961	.B	6
Lukanji	.184,541	.E	5
Madibeng	.338,266	.B	5
Mafikeng	.259,478	.C	4
Makhado	.497,083	.A	6
Makhudu-thamaga	.262,885	.B	6
Maluti a Phofung	.360,775	.D	6
Mangaung	.645,438	.D	5
Matjhabeng	.408,170	.C	5
Mbhashe	.253,381	.E	6
Mbizana	.245,415	.E	6
Mbombela	.474,803	.B	7
Merafong City	.210,478	.C	5
Mhlontlo	.196,677	.E	6
Mnquma	.287,765	.E	5
Mogala-kwena	.298,453	.B	6
Mogale City	.289,720	.C	5
Moqhaka	.167,895	.C	5
Moretele	.177,907	.B	5
Moses Kotane	.236,842	.B	5

| | | | |
|---|---|---|---|
| Msinga | .168,031 | .D | 6 |
| Msunduzi | .553,223 | .D | 6 |
| Ndwedwe | .152,479 | .D | 6 |
| Nelson Man-dela (Port Elizabeth) | .1,005,776 | .F | 4 |
| Newcastle | .332,980 | .C | 6 |
| Nkomazi | .334,418 | .B | 7 |
| Nongoma | .198,441 | .C | 7 |
| Nyandeni | .281,244 | .E | 6 |
| Polokwane | .508,271 | .B | 6 |
| Qaukeni | .255,370 | .E | 6 |
| Rustenburg | .395,539 | .B | 5 |
| Sol Plaatje | .201,462 | .D | 4 |
| Thembisile | .258,862 | .B | 6 |
| Thulamela | .584,560 | .A | 6 |
| Tshwane (Pretoria) | .1,985,984 | .B | 5 |
| Ulundi | .212,965 | .C | 7 |
| uMhlathuze | .289,186 | .D | 7 |
| uMlalazi | .221,070 | .D | 7 |
| Umzimvubu | .376,053 | .D | 9 |
| Umzumbe | .193,762 | .D | 9 |
| Umzimkhulu | .174,338 | .D | 9 |

Cities and towns†

Akasia‡	.B	6	
Alberton‡	.C	5	
Alexandra‡	.C	5	
Aliwal North	.D	5	

| | | | |
|---|---|---|---|
| Barberton | .C | 7 | |
| Beaufort West | .E | 3 | |
| Bela-Bela | .B | 6 | |
| Benoni‡ | .C | 5 | |
| Bethlehem | .D | 5 | |
| Bisho | .E | 5 | |
| Bloemfontein | .D | 5 | |
| Bloemhof | .C | 4 | |
| Boksburg‡ | .C | 5 | |
| Botshabelo‡ | .D | 5 | |
| Brakpan‡ | .C | 5 | |
| Brits | .B | 5 | |
| Cape Town | .F | 1 | |
| Carletonville | .C | 5 | |
| Carnarvon | .E | 3 | |
| Christiana | .C | 4 | |
| Colesberg | .D | 4 | |
| Cradock | .E | 4 | |
| Cullinan‡ | .B | 6 | |
| Dayeyton‡ | .C | 5 | |
| De Aar | .D | 4 | |
| Durban | .D | 7 | |
| East London | .E | 5 | |
| Edendale | .D | 6 | |
| eMalahleni | .C | 6 | |
| eMbalenhle‡ | .C | 6 | |
| Ermelo | .C | 6 | |
| Estcourt | .D | 6 | |
| Evaton | .C | 5 | |
| Galeshewe‡ | .D | 4 | |

(Index continued on page 613.)

WORLD BOOK map

© David & Peter Turnley, Corbis

Association football (soccer) is South Africa's most popular sport. The country's mild climate enables people to spend much of their leisure time participating in outdoor sports.

© Robin Laurance, Impact Photos

A high school in Germiston, a town near Johannesburg, enrolls students of all races. Many schools in South Africa were once segregated but became racially integrated starting in the 1990's.

much of their leisure time outdoors. Association football (soccer) is the country's most popular sport. Cricket and rugby football are traditional sports among white South Africans, although people of other races also participate. Tennis, bowls (lawn bowling), golf, field hockey, boxing, athletics (track and field), and water sports are popular among all racial groups. Many black Africans excel in boxing and in athletic events, such as long-distance running. On weekends and holidays, city dwellers flock to the beaches or tour their country's national parks and game reserves.

For many years, black and white South Africans had to compete in separate sports events and could not attend the same restaurants and theaters. From the 1970's to 1990, the government slowly lifted these restrictions. Some segregation still exists, especially in private sports clubs, even though it is illegal.

Education. Until 1991, most South African students attended racially separate public schools where far more money per child was spent to educate white children than black children. Since then, many black children have begun to attend previously all-white public schools. In large cities, schools that were formerly all white have become integrated. South Africa's private schools are integrated.

Many areas—especially rural ones—have a shortage of schools. All children from ages 7 through 16 are required to attend school. Until 1981, the law did not re-

quire black children to go to school, and many received little education. Today, about 100 percent of whites, 95 percent of Asians, 90 percent of Coloureds, and 75 percent of black Africans can read and write.

South Africa has about 20 universities. Most of the country's institutions of higher education were originally segregated. Since the mid-1980's, qualified students of any race have been permitted to attend any university that will accept them. An increasing number of black Africans, Indians, and Coloureds attend formerly all-white schools.

Religion. About 80 percent of South Africa's people are Christians. Many of the country's churches belong to the South African Council of Churches, which played an important role in the struggle against apartheid.

About 15 million people belong to *African independent churches*. Nearly all of the 15 million are black Africans. African independent churches combine Christian and traditional African beliefs. The largest African independent church is the Zion Christian Church, with more than 4 million members.

Most Afrikaners, as well as many Coloureds and black Africans, belong to a family of churches called the Dutch Reformed churches. These churches have about 3 million members. Other large Christian churches are the Anglican, Roman Catholic, Methodist, Presbyterian, Congregational, and Lutheran churches. These churches have members from all ethnic groups.

The Great Limpopo Transfrontier Park, which lies partly in eastern South Africa, is a famous game reserve. Many wild animals, such as impalas, *shown here,* elephants, lions, and zebras, roam in this park.

A small number of black Africans follow traditional African religions, which often involve prayer to the spirits of ancestors. About half of all Asians are Hindu, about one-fourth Muslim, and one-fourth Christian. A small number of Coloureds known as Cape Malays are Muslims. Fewer than 100,000 South Africans are Jews.

The arts. South Africa's National Arts Council distributes public funds to artists, cultural institutions, and private nonprofit groups. There are state-sponsored theaters in Bloemfontein, Cape Town, Durban, and Pretoria. Private companies also perform in many areas.

South Africa has produced outstanding artists in ballet, music, painting, sculpture, and other fields. One of the best-known performing groups is the black vocal group Ladysmith Black Mambazo. The singers perform in a humming style called *mbube,* which is influenced by European and African American harmonies and vocal traditions but retains black African rhythms.

Much South African literature reflects political and social tensions. After the Anglo-Boer War of 1899-1902, Afrikaner poets expressed sorrow over the British conquest of land occupied by Afrikaners. They included Jan F. E. Celliers, Jacob Daniel du Toit (also called Totius), Christiaan Louis Leipoldt, and Eugène Nielsen Marais, who also won critical praise for his writings on nature.

Since the mid-1900's, many South African writers have dealt with racial themes. They include poet and essayist Breyten Breytenbach and novelist André Brink. Both wrote in Afrikaans. Major English-language authors include the novelists Peter Abrahams, J. M. Coetzee, Nadine Gordimer, Es'kia Mphahlele (also known as Ezekiel Mphahlele), Njabulo S. Ndebele, and Alan Paton; playwright Athol Fugard; the poets Oswald Mbuyiseni Mtshali, Sipho Sepamla, and Mongane Wally Serote; and the nonfiction author Mark Mathabane. Gordimer won the 1991 Nobel Prize in literature. Coetzee won it in 2003.

Land and climate

South Africa has five main geographic regions: (1) the Plateau, (2) the Coastal Strip, (3) the Cape Mountains Region, (4) the Namib Desert, and (5) the Kalahari Desert. There are slight climatic variations among these regions, but most of the country has a mild, sunny climate.

The Plateau covers most of the interior of South Africa. In much of the Plateau, summer days are hot, but nights are cool. In winter, the days are crisp and clear, and the nights are cold. Winter temperatures throughout most of the Plateau can drop below freezing.

The Great Escarpment, a semicircular series of cliffs and mountains, rims the Plateau and separates it from the coastal regions. The escarpment reaches its greatest heights—more than 11,000 feet (3,350 meters) above sea level—in the Drakensberg mountain range in the east. The highest point, Champagne Castle, is in the Drakensberg. It stands 11,072 feet (3,375 meters) high.

The Plateau slopes gradually downward from the Great Escarpment. The Plateau has three chief subregions: (1) the Highveld, (2) the Middleveld, and (3) the Transvaal Basin. The Highveld occupies all the Plateau except for the northwestern and northeastern corners. It lies mostly between 4,000 and 6,000 feet (1,200 and 1,800 meters) above sea level and consists largely of flat, grass-covered land. In places, flat-topped mountains rise above the plain. The area of the Highveld around Johannesburg is called the Witwatersrand. It covers more than 1,000 square miles (2,600 square kilometers) and has rich gold deposits. This area is the nation's chief industrial and business center. Farmers in the Highveld raise cattle, corn, fruits, potatoes, and wheat.

The Middleveld, in the northwestern Plateau, averages less than 4,000 feet (1,200 meters) above sea level. It is a dry, flat area and serves largely as ranch country.

The Transvaal Basin forms the Plateau's northeastern part. It averages less than 4,000 feet above sea level but has mountain ranges more than 6,000 feet (1,800 meters) high. The area is largely a rolling grassland with scattered thorn trees. Farmers raise citrus and other fruits, corn, and tobacco. Elephants, leopards, lions, rhinoceroses, zebras, and other wild animals roam in the Great Limpopo Transfrontier Park, a famous game reserve. This park was established in 2002 by merging Kruger National Park in South Africa with nearby national parks in Mozambique and Zimbabwe. The park is one of the region's most popular tourist attractions.

The Coastal Strip extends along the southeast coast from Mozambique to the Cape Mountains Region. Except in the northeast, the region has little low-lying land. In the Durban area, for example, the land rises to 2,000 feet (610 meters) within 20 miles (32 kilometers) of the sea. Much of the Coastal Strip has hot, humid summers and dry, sunny winters. Chief crops include bananas, citrus fruits, sugar cane, and vegetables. Durban is a major industrial center, port, and resort area.

The Cape Mountains Region stretches from the Coastal Strip to the Namib Desert. Mountain ranges in the west and south meet northeast of the great port city of Cape Town. Between the mountains and the Great Escarpment lie two dry plateaus—the Little Karoo and the Great Karoo. There, farmers grow wine grapes and other fruits on irrigated land. They also grow wheat and raise sheep and ostriches. The Cape Mountains Region has warm, dry summers and cool, wet winters.

The Namib and Kalahari deserts. The Namib lies along the Atlantic Ocean north of the Cape Mountains Region and extends into Namibia. The Kalahari lies north of the Middleveld and extends into Botswana. Small bands of hunters and gatherers used to roam the deserts, living on the plants and animals they found.

Rivers. South Africa's longest river is the Orange River. It begins in Lesotho and flows westward about 1,300 miles (2,100 kilometers) into the Atlantic. The Vaal River, the Orange's largest branch, rises in Mpumalanga. It flows about 750 miles (1,210 kilometers) before joining the Orange in Northern Cape. The Limpopo River begins in Gauteng and winds about 1,000 miles (1,600 kilometers) across northern and northeastern South Africa and Mozambique before emptying into the Indian Ocean. South Africa also has many shorter rivers. Waterfalls, sand bars, and shallow water make even the longest rivers useless for shipping.

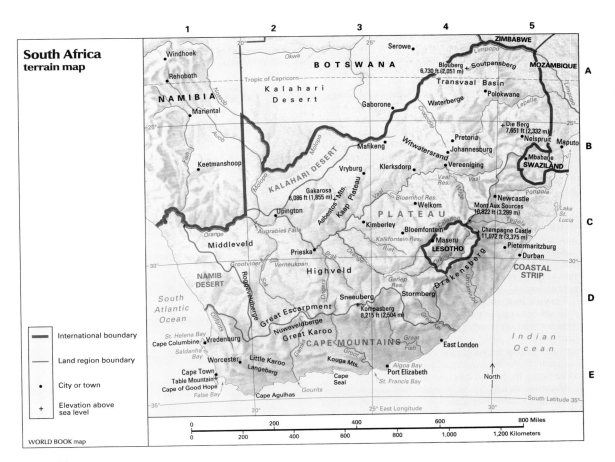

South Africa terrain map

WORLD BOOK map

International boundary	
Land region boundary	
•	City or town
+	Elevation above sea level

Physical features

Algoa Bay ....E 3	Crocodile River ....A 4	Grootvloer (salt flat) ....D 2	Molopo River ....B 2	St. Francis Bay ....E 3
Asbestos Mountains ...C 3	Die Berg (mountain) ....B 5	Highveld (plateau) ....D 3	Mont Aux Sources	St. Helena Bay ....D 1
Augrabies Falls ....C 2	Drakensberg	Kaap Plateau ....C 3	(mountain) ....C 4	Sneeuberg (range) ......D 3
Bloemhof Reservoir ....C 3	(mountains) ....D 4	Kalahari Desert ....B 2	Namib Desert ....D 1	Table Mountain ....E 1
Blouberg (mountain) ....A 4	False Bay ....E 1	Kompasberg	Nuweveldberge	Transvaal Basin ....A 4
Caledon River ....C 4	Gakarosa (mountain) ...C 3	(mountain) ....D 3	(range) ....D 2	Tugela River ....C 5
Cape Agulhas ....E 2	Gariep Reservoir ....D 3	Kouga Mountains ....E 3	Olifants River ....D 1	Vaal River ....B 4
Cape Columbine ....E 1	Great Escarpment ......D 2	Lake St. Lucia ....C 5	Orange River ....C 1	Vaal Reservoir ....B 4
Cape Mountains ....E 3	Great Fish River ....E 4	Lepelle River ....A 5	Pongola River ....C 5	Verneukpan (salt flat) ..C 2
Cape of Good Hope .....E 1	Great Karoo (plateau) ...D 2	Limpopo River ....A 4	Rand, see	Wilge River ....C 4
Champagne Castle	Great Kei River ....D 4	Little Karoo (plateau) ...E 2	Witwatersrand	Witwatersrand
(mountain) ....C 4	Groot River ....E 3	Middleveld (plateau) ....C 1	Saldanha Bay ....E 1	(ridge) ....B 4

Economy

South Africa is the richest, most economically developed country in Africa. It occupies only about 4 percent of the continent's area and has about 5 percent of its people. Yet the value of goods and services that South Africa produces is about 25 percent of the value of goods and services from all African nations combined.

From the 1950's through the 1970's, South Africa experienced spectacular economic growth. Many people from other countries invested in South African businesses. In the 1980's, an economic slowdown and international opposition to apartheid led to the withdrawal of some foreign investments. Some countries reduced or ended trade with South Africa. After the repeal of apartheid in the early 1990's, foreign trade and investment increased. Beginning in the 1990's, however, the AIDS disease spread rapidly and began to hinder growth.

For many years, South Africa's apartheid government owned many businesses and appointed white South Africans to run them. It also passed laws that reserved the best positions in both industry and government for white employees. Today, whites still hold nearly all the executive, professional, and technical jobs. But an increasing number of black Africans, Coloureds, and Indians have moved into these jobs.

Black African workers are generally less educated than whites and receive far lower wages. In 1979, the government for the first time recognized labor unions formed by black African workers. In 1985, many of these unions formed the Congress of South African Trade Unions, which successfully fought for higher wages.

Natural resources. South Africa has long been famous for its vast deposits of gold and diamonds. It also has large supplies of chromite, coal, copper, iron ore, manganese, platinum, silver, and uranium. Although no oil has been discovered in the country, some oil is produced from coal. There are also natural gas deposits near the country's shore.

South Africa is less fortunate in some other natural resources. Only a third of the farmland receives enough rain to grow crops easily. South Africa also has poor forest resources.

Service industries are economic activities that provide services rather than produce goods. Such industries account for nearly two-thirds of South Africa's *gross domestic product* (GDP), the value of all goods and services produced within the country. They include community, government, and personal services, as well as banking, trade, and transportation.

Manufacturing. South Africa's chief manufactured products include chemicals, clothing and textiles, iron and steel and other metals, metal products, motor vehicles, petroleum products, and processed foods. Most factories are in the Cape Town, Durban, Johannesburg, Port Elizabeth, and Pretoria areas.

Mining. Large gold deposits were discovered in South Africa in the 1880's, and gold has been the main force behind the country's growth ever since. Gold mining has attracted huge foreign investments and has led to the development of the transportation and manufacturing facilities in South Africa. Many of the mineworkers come from neighboring countries.

South Africa produces more gold than any other country, supplying about a sixth of the gold mined in the world each year. South Africa is also a major producer of chromite, coal, copper, diamonds, iron ore, limestone, manganese, phosphate, platinum, uranium, and vanadium.

Agriculture. South Africa's farmers produce almost all the food needed by its people. The leading crops include apples, bananas, corn, grapefruit, grapes, lemons, oranges, potatoes, sugar cane, and wheat. South Africa has an extensive sheep industry, and wool is an important agricultural export. Other leading farm products include beef and dairy cattle, chickens, eggs, milk, and wine.

South Africa has two main types of farming—that practiced mainly by whites and that practiced mainly by black Africans. White farmers use modern methods and raise products chiefly for the market. Black farm families produce food mainly for their own needs. Black farms are generally much smaller than white farms. Production on black farms has been extremely low because, for

South Africa's gross domestic product

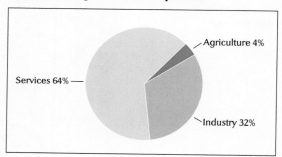

Services 64% — Agriculture 4% — Industry 32%

The gross domestic product (GDP) of South Africa was $159,886,000,000 in 2003. The GDP is the total value of goods and services produced within a country in a year. *Services* include community, government, and personal services; finance, insurance, real estate, and business services; trade, restaurants, and hotels; and transportation and communication. *Industry* includes construction, manufacturing, mining, and utilities. *Agriculture* includes agriculture, forestry, and fishing.

Production and workers by economic activities

Economic activities	Percent of GDP produced	Employed workers	
		Number of people	Percent of total
Community, government, & personal services	21	3,450,000	30
Manufacturing	20	1,634,000	14
Finance, insurance, real estate, & business services	20	1,079,000	9
Trade, restaurants, & hotels	14	2,451,000	21
Transportation & communication	10	563,000	5
Mining	7	503,000	4
Agriculture, forestry, & fishing	4	1,197,000	10
Construction	2	626,000	5
Utilities	2	86,000	1
Total*	100	11,589,000	100

*Figures may not add up to 100 percent due to rounding.
Figures are for 2003.
Sources: South African Reserve Bank; Statistics South Africa; International Monetary Fund.

© Piers Cavendish, Impact Photos

Gold mining has been a major force behind South Africa's economic growth since the 1880's. The country supplies about a sixth of the gold mined in the world each year.

many years, blacks were confined to areas where the land was poor. In addition, most black farmers could not afford modern equipment. Since 1994, the government has redistributed some of the country's farmland.

Fishing industry. South Africa's coastal waters yield about 827,000 tons (750,000 metric tons) of fish and shellfish a year. Important catches include anchovies, hake, and herring. Overfishing has reduced the once-plentiful supplies of fish in offshore waters, and so the government has set limits on catching certain types of fish.

Energy sources. Most of South Africa's electric power comes from plants that burn coal. A nuclear power plant in Cape Town produces a small amount of electric power. Eskom, South Africa's state-owned power utility, is one of the largest utilities in the world. South Africa exports electric power to other countries in southern Africa.

The country does not produce enough petroleum to support its needs, so it must import oil. South African refineries produce gasoline and other fuels from coal.

International trade. South Africa's chief trade partners—besides other African countries—include Germany, Japan, the United Kingdom, and the United States. Chief exports include corn, diamonds, fruits, gold, metals and minerals, sugar, and wool. Machinery and transportation equipment make up more than one-third of the value of the country's imports. Other imports include chemicals, manufactured goods, and petroleum.

Transportation. South Africa has the best transportation system in Africa. Paved roads crisscross much of the country. Most of the roads in the former black homelands remain unpaved. Most white families own at least one automobile. Most blacks rely on buses and trains. The country's freight and long-distance passenger railroads are operated by a government-owned company called Spoornet. South African Airways, British Airways, Comair, and other airlines provide domestic and international service. Cape Town, Durban, and Johannesburg have major airports. South Africa has six large, well-equipped seaports—Cape Town, Durban, East London, Port Elizabeth, Richards Bay, and Saldanha.

Communication. The *Sowetan,* published in Johannesburg, is an English-language newspaper for black Africans. It has the largest circulation of any daily paper in the country. Other large English-language dailies are *The Citizen* and *The Star,* also published in Johannesburg, and *Cape Argus,* published in Cape Town. The largest Afrikaans-language dailies are *Beeld* of Johannesburg and *Die Burger* of Cape Town.

A government agency called the Independent Broadcasting Authority (IBA) directs the licensing and regulating of all radio and television stations. The South African Broadcasting Corporation (SABC) provides most of the country's public broadcasting. The country also has privately owned stations. Radio and TV shows are broadcast in English, Afrikaans, and a number of black African languages. The government runs the postal and telegraph systems. In 1997, it partially privatized the national telephone company.

History

Early days. For thousands of years, the San, who were descendants of prehistoric Africans, were the only inhabitants of the region. They moved about in small bands hunting animals and gathering wild plants for food. Around the A.D. 100's, a related group called the Khoikhoi began to move into the area from the north. By about 500, they occupied what is now western South Africa. The Khoikhoi raised cattle and sheep and settled in communities. When Europeans arrived in the 1600's, they called the San *Bushmen* and the Khoikhoi *Hottentots.* Both of these European terms are now considered offensive. The two groups have come to be known collectively as the Khoisan.

In the A.D. 200's, peoples who spoke various Bantu languages began to move into the area that is now eastern South Africa. These groups migrated from the north. They raised cattle, grew grain, made tools and weapons out of iron, and traded among themselves.

By the 500's, some of the Bantu-speaking people had begun to group together and form chiefdoms. Each chiefdom was headed by a wealthy chief who regulated trade, controlled cattle ownership, and settled disputes. Within the chiefdoms, senior men exercised authority over individual homesteads. After the 1200's, some of the chiefdoms grew to become powerful. Such chiefdoms included those of the Sotho-Tswana and those of the Nguni.

Arrival of Europeans. Portuguese sailors were the first Europeans to see what is now South Africa. They sighted it in 1488, when they rounded the Cape of Good Hope in their search for a sea route east to India.

The first European settlers arrived in 1652. They worked for the Dutch East India Company, a powerful Dutch trading company. The company sent the settlers, headed by Jan van Riebeeck, to set up a base at the present site of Cape Town. The base was to serve as a station where company ships could pick up supplies on the way to and from the East Indies. The company imported slaves—mostly from Southeast Asia—to do manual labor at the base and to work on its nearby farms.

Starting in 1657, the Dutch East India Company allowed some employees to start their own farms. These people became known as *Boers* (farmers). In 1679, the company also began to offer free passage and land to new settlers from Europe. More Dutch farmers, as well as French and German settlers, arrived. By 1700, whites occupied most of the good farmland around Cape Town. Then, they moved into drier areas and became sheep and cattle ranchers. As the white territory expanded, the Khoikhoi and San population declined. White settlers killed some in conflicts and forced many others out of the area. Many Khoikhoi and San also died of diseases, such as smallpox. Most survivors became servants of the whites and intermarried with them.

During this period, the Dutch language spoken in the area began to change. It incorporated words and sounds from the languages of other European settlers, and from Southeast Asian slaves and San and Khoikhoi servants. A new language, called Afrikaans, developed.

About 1770, white settlers spread into the area occupied by the Xhosa, a Bantu-speaking people, in what is now Eastern Cape. The whites called the Xhosa *Kaffirs,* which is now considered an offensive term. Between 1779 and 1879, the settlers and the Xhosa fought several wars in which the settlers took land from the Xhosa.

By the end of the 1700's, the whites had spread about 300 miles (480 kilometers) north and more than 500 miles (800 kilometers) east of Cape Town. The area became a colony known as the Cape Colony. It had a total population of about 60,000. Nearly 20,000 were whites. The rest consisted mostly of Khoikhoi, San, and slaves.

The Zulu and the Mfecane. Between 1818 and 1828, the Zulu kingdom grew to be the most powerful black African kingdom in southern Africa. This kingdom, established by the Zulu leader Shaka, covered most of what is now KwaZulu-Natal. It incorporated a number of Nguni chiefdoms. As the Zulu kingdom grew in size and power, many Nguni peoples fled to other parts of southeastern Africa. The refugees often came into conflict with other peoples during their migrations. This period of forced migrations and battles, known as the *Mfecane* (or *Difaqane),* led to the emergence of new kingdoms, including the Sotho, Swazi, and Ndebele. Other groups, however, were wiped out. The destruction and chaos caused by the Mfecane made it easier for white settlers to eventually expand eastward from the Cape.

British rule. In 1795, after France conquered the Netherlands, British troops occupied the Cape Colony to keep it out of French hands. The British returned the colony to the Dutch in 1803 but reoccupied it in 1806. A treaty between the British and the Dutch in 1814 formally recognized the Cape as a British colony. Thousands of British settlers arrived in 1820. They occupied land that the previous white settlers had taken from the Xhosa.

The Boers soon came to resent British colonial rule. The government made English the colony's only official language in 1828. That same year, the Khoikhoi and Coloured people received the same legal rights as whites. In 1834, the United Kingdom freed all slaves throughout its empire, ruining a number of Boer farmers who depended on slave labor to work their fields.

Many Boers decided to leave the Cape Colony to get away from British rule. Beginning in 1836, several thousand made a historic journey called the Great Trek. They loaded their belongings into ox-drawn covered wagons and headed inland. They traveled into lands occupied by Bantu-speaking peoples, including the Zulu kingdom. The Boers defeated the Zulu and other groups and set-

tled in what became Natal, the Orange Free State, and the Transvaal. The British annexed Natal in 1843 but recognized Boer independence in the Transvaal in 1852 and in the Orange Free State in 1854. In 1858, the Boers in the Transvaal named their government the South African Republic, or SAR.

In Natal and the Boer republics, whites claimed the best land and steadily extended their control over black Africans and Coloureds. In Natal, the British imported Indians to work as indentured laborers on sugar plantations.

Discovery of diamonds and gold. In the late 1860's, diamonds were discovered in South Africa. The richest deposits were found at the site of present-day Kimberley. Miners and fortune seekers from the United Kingdom and elsewhere flocked to the area. Both the British and the Boers claimed the area. In 1871, the United Kingdom annexed it, and it became part of the Cape Colony.

Diamonds began an economic revolution in South Africa and made the region more strategically and commercially important to the United Kingdom. To strengthen its authority over the region, the United Kingdom annexed the Transvaal in 1877.

The British also extended their authority over black African chiefdoms that were still independent. By 1879, the British had conquered the Xhosa, and the Zulu kingdom remained the region's only major African state. The British saw the Zulu as a threat to the eventual confederation of South Africa's colonies, and so they invaded Zulu territory in January 1879. Although the Zulu defeated the British at Isandhlwana later that month, the British army crushed the Zulu in July. By 1898, British rule extended over all independent black African groups.

In 1880, the Transvaal Boers rose in revolt against the British in the Anglo-Boer War of 1880-1881. This struggle is also called the Anglo-Transvaal War. After several victories, the Boers finally defeated the British in a battle on Majuba Hill in 1881. The British agreed to withdraw from the Transvaal. The Boers thus regained independence in the Transvaal and again named it the South African Republic (SAR).

In 1886, the Witwatersrand gold field was discovered north of the Vaal River, where Johannesburg now stands. Fortune seekers rushed to the area. By 1895, these *Uitlanders* (foreigners) made up about half of the SAR's white male population. To maintain control, the Boers restricted the political rights of the Uitlanders, most of whom were British. As a result, tension grew between the United Kingdom and the SAR.

In 1895, Cecil Rhodes, the prime minister of the Cape Colony, plotted to overthrow the government of the SAR. He sent a force led by Leander Jameson, a Scottish-born government administrator, to invade the republic. But the Boers captured the invaders, and the so-called Jameson Raid failed. Relations between the British and the SAR grew more strained. In 1899, the SAR and the Orange Free State declared war on the United Kingdom. During the Anglo-Boer War of 1899-1902 (often called the Boer War or the South African War), the Boers fought bravely against huge odds. They finally surrendered in 1902. The two Boer republics then became British colonies.

The Union of South Africa. The United Kingdom gave colonial self-government to the Transvaal in 1906 and to the Orange Free State in 1907. The Cape Colony and Natal already had self-rule. In 1910, the four colonies formed the Union of South Africa, a self-governing country within the British Empire. The Union's Constitution gave whites almost complete power.

Several black African, Coloured, and Indian groups tried to defend themselves against repression by the white government. A lawyer from India, Mohandas K. Gandhi, worked for greater rights for Indians in South Africa. Gandhi urged the Indians to defy unjust laws, such as a law requiring them to register and be fingerprinted. Gandhi's methods of nonviolent resistance resulted in the Indians' gaining some additional rights. Using the same methods, Gandhi later helped India gain independence from British rule.

Gandhi's example helped inspire black Africans to found the South African Native National Congress (SANNC) in 1912. The SANNC's purpose was to work for black African rights. In 1923, the SANNC shortened its name to the African National Congress (ANC).

In World War I (1914-1918), the British Empire and its allies fought the Central Powers, led by Austria-Hungary and Germany. Two Boer generals, Louis Botha and Jan Christiaan Smuts, led South African forces against Germany. Botha seized German South West Africa (now Namibia) from Germany in 1915, and Smuts drove the Germans from German East Africa (now Tanzania) in 1917. In 1920, the League of Nations, a forerunner of the United Nations, gave South Africa control of South West Africa. Botha and Smuts were the first prime ministers of the Union of South Africa. Botha served from 1910 to 1919. Smuts served from 1919 to 1924, and from 1939 to 1948.

The rise of Afrikaner nationalism. Botha and Smuts had fought the British in the Anglo-Boer War of 1899-1902. But as prime ministers, they tried to unite Afrikaners (as the Boers came to be called) and English-speaking whites. Many Afrikaner authors and religious leaders, however, urged their people to consider themselves a nation. They said Afrikaners had a heroic history, a rich culture, and a God-given mission to rule South Africa. In 1914, James Barry Munnik Hertzog, another Boer general who had fought the British, founded the National Party to promote these ideas.

In 1924, the National Party and the Labour Party joined forces and won control of the government. Hertzog became prime minister. During the next 15 years, he achieved many Afrikaner goals. Afrikaans became an official language along with English. Industries were developed to reduce dependence on British imports. In 1931, South Africa gained full independence as a member of the Commonwealth of Nations, an association of the United Kingdom and some of its former colonies.

In 1934, Hertzog joined with Smuts to form a United Party government. Whites benefited under this coalition government, but black Africans did not. For example, black Africans in Cape Province, who had retained the right to vote after the Union was formed, lost most of their voting rights. The government also passed laws that made it difficult for black Africans to live in cities. In contrast, it made city jobs available for poor Afrikaners, who were leaving their farms in search of work.

Cooperation between Smuts and Hertzog ended at the start of World War II (1939-1945). Hertzog wanted South Africa to be neutral. But Smuts wanted the country to join the United Kingdom and the other Allies against Germany. Smuts won the bitter debate in Parliament and became prime minister again in 1939. During the war, South Africans fought in Ethiopia, northern Africa, and Europe. After the war, South Africa became a founding member of the United Nations (UN).

Apartheid. During World War II, Daniel François Malan, a strong supporter of Afrikaner nationalism, reorganized the National Party. The party came to power, under Malan, in 1948. It began the apartheid program, under which racial groups were legally segregated and given different rights and privileges. Hendrik F. Verwoerd, who served as minister of native affairs from 1950 to 1958 and prime minister from 1958 to 1966, was the main architect of the apartheid state. His government began a program that gave the police and the military extensive powers to enforce apartheid.

Opposition to the Nationalists' racial policies grew. The ANC played the main role in this opposition. In the 1950's, the ANC, along with Coloured and Indian groups and white liberals, demanded reforms through boycotts, rallies, and strikes. The government crushed each campaign. In 1959, some black Africans left the ANC and formed the Pan-Africanist Congress (PAC) because they opposed the ANC's alliances with white groups. They wanted an all-black government instead. PAC first targeted the laws that required black Africans to carry *passes* (identity papers). These laws restricted black Africans from moving freely around the country. PAC leaders told blacks to appear on March 21, 1960, at police stations without their passes—and so invite arrest. In most places, the police broke up the crowd without incident. But at Sharpeville, near Johannesburg, the police

Important dates in South Africa

A.D. 200's Bantu-speaking farmers began to enter eastern South Africa from the north. They were the ancestors of present-day South Africa's black African population.

1652 The first Dutch settlers arrived at the site of Cape Town.

1814 The Cape Colony officially became a British colony.

1818-1828 The Zulu leader Shaka built a powerful kingdom in present-day KwaZulu-Natal.

1836 Boers left Cape Colony on the Great Trek.

1843 Natal became a British colony.

1852 The Transvaal became a Boer republic.

1854 The Orange Free State became a Boer republic.

1867 Diamonds were discovered near what is now Kimberley.

1877 The United Kingdom annexed the Transvaal.

1879 The United Kingdom defeated the Zulu kingdom.

1880-1881 The Transvaal Boers defeated the British in the first Anglo-Boer War (also called the Anglo-Transvaal War).

1886 Gold was discovered near Johannesburg.

1899-1902 The United Kingdom defeated the Boers in the second Anglo-Boer War (also called the Boer War or South African War).

1910 The Union of South Africa was formed.

1912 Black Africans founded the African National Congress.

1948-1994 The National Party governed South Africa.

1961 South Africa became a republic.

1976 Black Africans began widespread protests against the South African government.

1990-1991 The South African government repealed many laws that had formed the legal basis of apartheid.

1994 South Africa held its first all-race elections. Nelson Mandela was elected as the nation's first black president.

1999 Thabo Mbeki succeeded Mandela as the second democratically elected president.

opened fire and killed 69 black Africans. The government then banned both the ANC and PAC.

Opposition to apartheid also came from outside South Africa. Many leaders of the Commonwealth of Nations strongly criticized South Africa's apartheid policies. On May 31, 1961, South Africa became a republic and left the Commonwealth. In 1966, the UN voted to end the country's control over South West Africa. South Africa called the UN action illegal and ignored it.

In the 1960's, South Africa's government introduced its homeland policy. In an attempt to make South Africa a "white" nation, the government set aside separate areas for each racial group. The government granted limited self-rule—and in some cases, full independence—to the black African homelands (also called *bantustans*).

Verwoerd was killed in 1966 by a mentally ill government messenger. Apartheid policies continued under Verwoerd's successor, Balthazar Johannes Vorster. By the 1970's, opposition to white rule was increasing both inside and outside the country. In June 1976, thousands of black African schoolchildren in Soweto (now part of Johannesburg) marched to protest a policy that required some of their classes to be taught in Afrikaans. Police opened fire on the children, killing two and wounding several of them. Disturbances followed in many parts of the country, and several clashes erupted between black Africans and the police. At least 575 people, almost all of them blacks, were killed.

The dismantling of apartheid. Vorster's successor, P. W. Botha, realized that apartheid was causing South Africa's economy to suffer. In the late 1970's, the Botha government repealed some apartheid laws. It lifted restrictions against multiracial sports. It also abolished most of the *job reservation system,* which had reserved certain jobs for certain races.

In an attempt to gain Coloured and Indian support, Botha proposed a new constitution. White South Africans approved it in 1983, and it went into effect in 1984. The new Constitution restructured Parliament to include representation for whites, Coloureds, and Indians. The Constitution also combined the offices of the prime minister and state president under the office of state president. Botha became state president.

The new Constitution, like the one it replaced, made no provision for black African representation in Parliament or in other parts of the national government. Also, like the old Constitution, it excluded black Africans from voting in national elections. To protest their exclusion from the government, blacks staged many labor strikes, demonstrations, and riots. The protesters targeted whites, black police officers, and other blacks regarded as government collaborators. Many people, mostly blacks, were killed in these clashes. At the same time, military branches of the ANC and PAC carried out guerrilla attacks on government targets. To keep control and stop the violence, the South African government declared a national state of emergency in 1986. Under the state of emergency, the government was allowed to arrest and hold people without charging them.

Many countries expressed opposition to apartheid by reducing economic ties with South Africa. In 1986, the European Community, the Commonwealth of Nations, and the United States enacted *sanctions* (bans) on certain kinds of trade with South Africa. Some companies

© Mike Persson, Getty Images

Nelson Mandela, *left,* takes the oath of office for the presidency of South Africa in May 1994. Mandela was elected president in the country's first elections open to all races.

ended or limited their business in South Africa.

In 1986, the South African government repealed more apartheid laws. It permitted black Africans, Coloureds, and Asians to attend white universities. The government also permitted interracial marriages, which apartheid laws had forbidden. It repealed the laws requiring black Africans to carry passes and allowed them to live in cities without special permission. As a result, more than 1 million black Africans moved to the cities. But many apartheid regulations continued. Black Africans were still excluded from participation in government.

In 1988, after several years of talks with major Western powers, South Africa agreed to withdraw from Namibia. In 1990, Namibia gained full independence.

In 1989, F. W. de Klerk became state president. De Klerk realized that white minority rule could not continue in South Africa without great risk of civil war.

In February 1990, de Klerk ended South Africa's state of emergency and lifted the bans on political organizations, including the ANC and PAC. Later that month, de Klerk released Nelson Mandela, the most famous member of the ANC, from prison. Mandela had been arrested in 1962 and sentenced to life imprisonment in 1964 for sabotage and conspiracy against the South African government. While in prison, Mandela had become a symbol of the black struggle for racial justice. In May 1990, the government held its first formal talks with the ANC. Mandela met with de Klerk several times after that to discuss political change in South Africa.

Despite these events, violence continued in South Africa. Some violence resulted from white reactions to de Klerk's reforms, and other fighting broke out between rival black African groups. Much of the violence occurred between supporters of the Xhosa-dominated ANC and the Zulu-dominated Inkatha Freedom Party. Thousands of people were killed in the conflicts.

In 1990 and 1991, the South African government repealed most of the remaining laws that had formed the legal basis of apartheid. In 1991, the government, the ANC, and other groups began holding talks on a new constitution. In 1993, the government adopted an interim constitution that gave South Africa's blacks full voting rights. The country held its first elections open to all races in 1994. The ANC won nearly two-thirds of the

National Assembly seats, and the Assembly elected Nelson Mandela president. Politically motivated violence then decreased. In 1994, South Africa resumed full participation in the UN and rejoined the Commonwealth.

Recent developments. In 1995, the government appointed a panel called the Truth and Reconciliation Commission to gather information about human rights violations during the apartheid years. Desmond Tutu, a former Anglican archbishop and winner of the 1984 Nobel Peace Prize, headed the commission. In a report issued in 1998, the commission said the apartheid-era government had committed "gross violations of human rights," including kidnapping and murders. The report also criticized opposition groups, including the ANC, holding them responsible for killings and torture. The commission issued its final report in 2003.

In 1996, South Africa adopted a new Constitution. It provides for a strong presidency and includes a wide-ranging bill of rights. Among the rights it guarantees are freedom of religion, belief, and opinion; freedom of expression, including freedom of the press; and freedom of political activity. It also establishes the right to adequate housing, food, water, education, and health care.

In 1997, Mandela resigned as ANC head. He was replaced by South Africa's deputy president, Thabo Mbeki. In 1999, Mandela retired as president of South Africa. In elections that year, the ANC won a majority in the National Assembly. The Assembly elected Mbeki president. In 2004, the ANC again won a majority of Assembly seats, and the Assembly reelected Mbeki as president.

During the 1990's, AIDS became a major problem in South Africa. More people in South Africa are infected with HIV, the virus that causes AIDS, than in any other country. By 2000, more than 10 percent of the population was infected with HIV. Christopher Saunders

Related articles in *World Book* include:

Biographies

Barnard, Christiaan
  Neethling
Biko, Steve
Botha, Louis
Botha, P. W.
Coetzee, J. M.
De Klerk, Frederik Willem
Fugard, Athol
Gandhi, Mohandas
  Karamchand
Gordimer, Nadine
Hertzog, James Barry Munnik
Kruger, Paul
Luthuli, Albert John
Malan, Daniel François
Mandela, Nelson
Masekela, Hugh
Mbeki, Thabo
Paton, Alan
Rhodes, Cecil John
Shaka
Smuts, Jan Christiaan
Sullivan, Leon Howard
Tutu, Desmond
Verwoerd, Hendrik
Vorster, Balthazar

Cities

Bloemfontein
Cape Town
Durban
Johannesburg
Kimberley
Pietermaritzburg
Port Elizabeth
Pretoria
Soweto

People

Afrikaners
Bantu
Khoikhoi
San
Xhosa
Zulu

Physical features

Cape of Good
  Hope
Drakensberg
Great Limpopo
  Transfrontier
  Park
Kalahari Desert
Limpopo River
Orange River

Other related articles

Africa
African National
  Congress
Anglo-Boer Wars
Apartheid
Cape Colony
Drakensberg
Inkatha Freedom
  Party
Lesotho
Namibia
Natal
Orange Free State
Southern African
  Large Telescope
Transvaal
Truth commission
United Nations
  (Working for
  self-government)

Outline

I. Government
  A. National government
  B. Provincial government
  C. Local government
  D. Political parties
  E. Armed forces

II. People
  A. Racial & ethnic groups
  B. Languages

III. Ways of life
  A. Food and drink
  B. Recreation
  C. Education
  D. Religion
  E. The arts

IV. Land and climate
  A. The Plateau
  B. The Coastal Strip
  C. The Cape Mountains
    Region
  D. The Namib and Kalahari
    deserts
  E. Rivers

V. Economy
  A. Natural resources
  B. Service industries
  C. Manufacturing
  D. Mining
  E. Agriculture
  F. Fishing industry
  G. Energy sources
  H. International trade
  I. Transportation
  J. Communication

VI. History

Questions

How did South Africa achieve spectacular industrial growth?
What land region covers most of South Africa's interior?
What was apartheid? How did it affect black Africans, Coloureds, and Indians in South Africa?
Who were the Boers?
How does life differ among South Africa's racial groups?
What was the Great Trek?
What are some black African ethnic groups in South Africa?

Additional resources

Afolayan, Funso S. *Culture and Customs of South Africa.* Greenwood, 2004.
Blauer, Ettagale, and Lauré, Jason. *South Africa.* Rev ed. Children's Pr., 2006. Younger readers.
Davenport, T. R. H., and Saunders, Christopher. *South Africa: A Modern History.* 5th ed. St. Martin's, 2000.
Feinstein, Charles H. *An Economic History of South Africa.* Cambridge, 2005.

© Giacomo Pirozzi, Panos Pictures

AIDS prevention is a major goal in South Africa, where over 10 percent of the population is infected with the virus that causes the disease. These boys are reading a pamphlet about AIDS.

Rio de Janeiro, Brazil, on Guanabara Bay, is one of South America's most scenic cities. A famous statue of Jesus overlooks Rio from Corcovado Mountain. Most South Americans live in cities.

South America

South America is the fourth largest continent in area. Only Asia, Africa, and North America are larger. It ranks fifth among the continents in population. Asia, Europe, Africa, and North America all have more people. South America covers about 12 percent of the world's land area and has about 6 percent of the total world population. The continent is divided into 12 independent countries and 2 other political units.

South America has nearly every type of landscape and climate. The world's largest tropical rain forest grows in the Amazon River Basin, which occupies about two-fifths of the continent and contains an estimated 50 percent of Earth's plant and animal species. The Atacama Desert in northern Chile is one of the driest places on Earth. Snowy peaks and active volcanoes rise along the crest of the lofty Andes Mountains of western South America. In Argentina, Uruguay, and Venezuela, rolling grasslands stretch as far as the eye can see. South America's varied landscape also includes spectacular water-falls, huge lakes, and rocky, windswept islands.

The continent has abundant natural resources, including rich farmlands, vast timberlands, and some of the largest deposits of valuable minerals in the world. Many South American countries, however, have not taken full advantage of their natural riches.

The countries of South America vary in their level of economic development. Most of them rely on exports of minerals and agricultural products to provide income. They must import many manufactured goods, including machinery, chemicals, and fuels. Brazil is the continent's industrial giant. It produces and exports airplanes, mo-tor vehicles, motor-vehicle parts, and other goods.

About four-fifths of South America's people live in ur-ban areas. South America's urban population has soared since the mid-1900's. This tremendous growth has oc-curred as millions of poor rural people have come to the cities in search of better economic opportunities.

The standard of living in South America varies greatly. It is much higher in predominantly middle-class coun-tries, such as Argentina and Uruguay, than in Bolivia, where most of the people struggle to earn a living. All South American countries have a small class of wealthy landowners, factory owners, and political and military leaders. But the vast majority of the people are poor. Since the mid-1900's, the gap between rich and poor has widened. But there is a growing middle class in the large cities. It consists of professional people, business people, government employees, and skilled workers.

South America is part of Latin America, a large cultur-al region that also includes Central America, Mexico, and the West Indies. This article discusses South Ameri-ca's land, climate, animal and plant life, and economy.

Facts in brief

James Wiley, the contributor of this article, is Associate Profes-sor of Geography at Hofstra University. This article was critically reviewed by Brian P. Owensby, Associate Professor of History at the University of Virginia.

Area: 6,886,000 mi^2 (17,835,000 km^2). *Greatest distances*—north-south, 4,750 mi (7,645 km); east-west, 3,200 mi (5,150 km). *Coastline*—20,000 mi (32,000 km).
Population: *Estimated 2008 population*—385,200,000; density, 56 per mi^2 (22 per km^2).
Elevation: *Highest*—Aconcagua in Argentina, 22,835 ft (6,960 m) above sea level. *Lowest*—Valdés Peninsula in Argentina, 131 ft (40 m) below sea level.
Physical features: *Chief mountain ranges*—Andes, Brazilian Highlands, Guiana Highlands. *Chief rivers*—Amazon, Madeira, Magdalena, Orinoco, Paraguay, Paraná, Pilcomayo, Purus, São Francisco, Uruguay. *Chief gulfs*—Darién, Guayaquil, San Jorge, San Matías, Venezuela. *Chief islands*—Falkland Islands, Gala-pagos Islands, Marajó, Tierra del Fuego. *Chief lakes*—Maracai-bo, Mirim, Poopó, Titicaca. *Largest deserts*—Atacama, Patago-nia. *Highest waterfalls*—Angel, Cuquenán.
Number of countries: 12.

The Altiplano is a high, windswept plateau between two mountain ranges in western South America. Most of this region lies in Bolivia. These llamas are grazing on the Altiplano in southern Bolivia.

© Borchi Massimo, 4Corners Images

Dense rain forests cover most of the Amazon River Basin, an area that includes northwestern Brazil and parts of Colombia, Ecuador, Peru, and Bolivia. This photograph shows Manu National Park, part of the Manu Biosphere Reserve, in southeastern Peru.

© Gregory G. Dimijian, Photo Researchers

For discussions of the people, way of life, arts, and history of South America and the rest of Latin America, see **Latin America** and the articles on each of the independent countries and dependencies in South America.

The land

South America covers about 6,886,000 square miles (17,835,000 square kilometers)—about one-eighth of the world's land area. The northern three-fourths of the continent lies in the tropics. The equator crosses South America about 400 miles (640 kilometers) north of the continent's widest point. Cape Horn, the southernmost tip of South America, lies about 600 miles (970 kilometers) from Antarctica.

South America is almost totally surrounded by water. The Caribbean Sea lies to the north. The Atlantic Ocean

Independent countries of South America*

Map key	Name	Area In mi²	Area In km²	Population	Capital	Date of independence
L 5	**Argentina**	1,073,519	2,780,400	39,746,000	Buenos Aires	1816
I 5	**Bolivia**	424,165	1,098,581	9,764,000	La Paz; Sucre	1825
H 7	**Brazil**	3,287,613	8,514,877	193,540,000	Brasília	1822
K 4	**Chile**	291,930	756,096	16,763,000	Santiago	1818
F 4	**Colombia**	439,737	1,138,914	43,127,000	Bogotá	1819
G 3	**Ecuador**	109,484	283,561	13,832,000	Quito	1830
E 6	**Guyana**	83,000	214,969	753,000	Georgetown	1966
J 6	**Paraguay**	157,048	406,752	6,352,000	Asunción	1811
H 4	**Peru**	496,225	1,285,216	29,180,000	Lima	1821
E 7	**Suriname**	63,251	163,820	458,000	Paramaribo	1975
L 7	**Uruguay**	68,037	176,215	3,370,000	Montevideo	1828
E 5	**Venezuela**	352,145	912,050	28,112,000	Caracas	1830

Dependencies in South America*

Map key	Name	Area In mi²	Area In km²	Population	Status
O 6	**Falkland Islands**	4,700	12,173	3,000	British overseas territory
F 7	**French Guiana**	35,135	91,000	200,000	Overseas department of France

*Each country and dependency has a separate article in *World Book*.
Populations are 2008 estimates based on the latest figures from official government and United Nations sources.

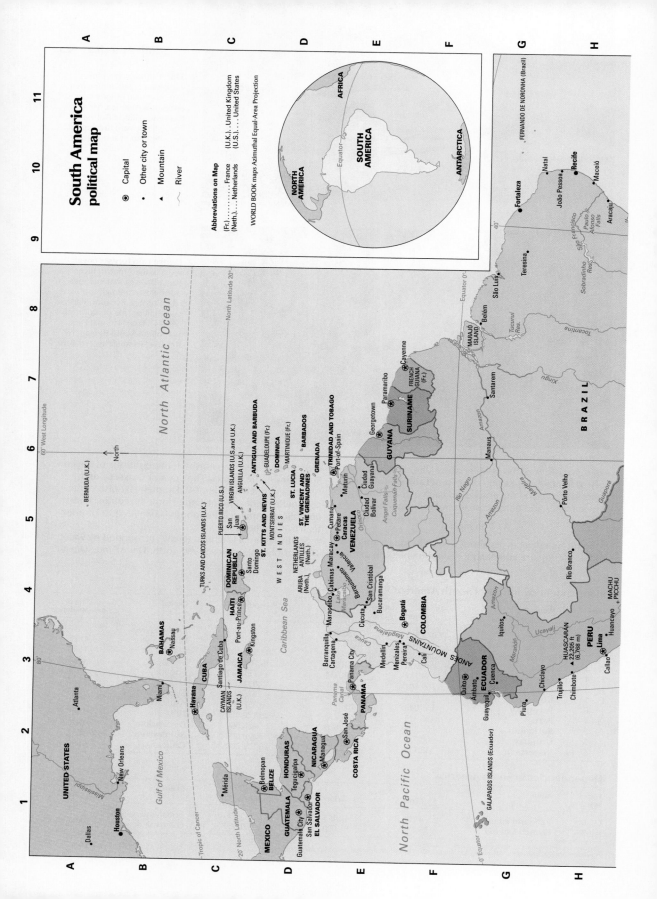

South America
political map

⊕ Capital
• Other city or town
▲ Mountain
〰 River

Abbreviations on Map

(Fr.)..........France   (U.K.)....United Kingdom
(Neth.)....Netherlands   (U.S.)....United States

WORLD BOOK maps Azimuthal Equal-Area Projection

NORTH AMERICA

SOUTH AMERICA

AFRICA

Equator

ANTARCTICA

North Atlantic Ocean

North Pacific Ocean

Caribbean Sea

Gulf of Mexico

UNITED STATES

Dallas
Atlanta
New Orleans
Houston
Mississippi
Miami

BERMUDA (U.K.)

North Latitude 20°
Tropic of Cancer
20° North Latitude

MEXICO
Mérida
BELIZE
Belmopan
GUATEMALA
Guatemala City
EL SALVADOR
San Salvador
HONDURAS
Tegucigalpa
NICARAGUA
Managua
COSTA RICA
San José
PANAMA
Panama City
Panama Canal

BAHAMAS
Nassau
CUBA
Havana
Santiago de Cuba
CAYMAN ISLANDS (U.K.)
JAMAICA
Kingston
HAITI
Port-au-Prince
DOMINICAN REPUBLIC
Santo Domingo

TURKS AND CAICOS ISLANDS (U.K.)
PUERTO RICO (U.S.)
San Juan
VIRGIN ISLANDS (U.S. and U.K.)
ANGUILLA (U.K.)
ST. KITTS AND NEVIS
MONTSERRAT (U.K.)
ANTIGUA AND BARBUDA
GUADELOUPE (Fr.)
DOMINICA
MARTINIQUE (Fr.)
ST. LUCIA
ST. VINCENT AND THE GRENADINES
BARBADOS
GRENADA
TRINIDAD AND TOBAGO
Port-of-Spain

WEST INDIES

NETHERLANDS ANTILLES (Neth.)
ARUBA (Neth.)

60° West Longitude
North

COLOMBIA
Bogotá
Barranquilla
Cartagena
Medellín
Manizales
Pereira
Cali
Bucaramanga
San Cristóbal
Cúcuta
Magdalena
Cauca

VENEZUELA
Caracas
Maracaibo
Lake Maracaibo
Maracay
Valencia
Cabimas
Barquisimeto
Petare
Cumaná
Maturín
Ciudad Bolívar
Ciudad Guayana
Orinoco
Angel Falls
Cuquenah Falls

GUYANA
Georgetown
SURINAME
Paramaribo
FRENCH GUIANA (Fr.)
Cayenne

Equator 0°

BRAZIL
Manaus
Santarém
Belém
MARAJÓ ISLAND
Tucuruí Res.
Xingu
Tocantins
São Luís
Teresina
Fortaleza
Natal
João Pessoa
Recife
Maceió
Aracaju
FERNANDO DE NORONHA (Brazil)
São Francisco
Paulo Afonso Falls
Sobradinho Res.
Amazon
Rio Negro
Madeira
Guaporé
Pôrto Velho
Rio Branco

ECUADOR
Quito
Guayaquil
Cuenca
Ambato
GALAPAGOS ISLANDS (Ecuador)

PERU
Lima
Callao
Iquitos
Chiclayo
Trujillo
Chimbote
Piura
Huancayo
HUASCARÁN
▲ 22,205 ft
(6,768 m)
MACHU PICCHU
Marañón
Ucayali
Amazon

ANDES MOUNTAINS

80°

40°

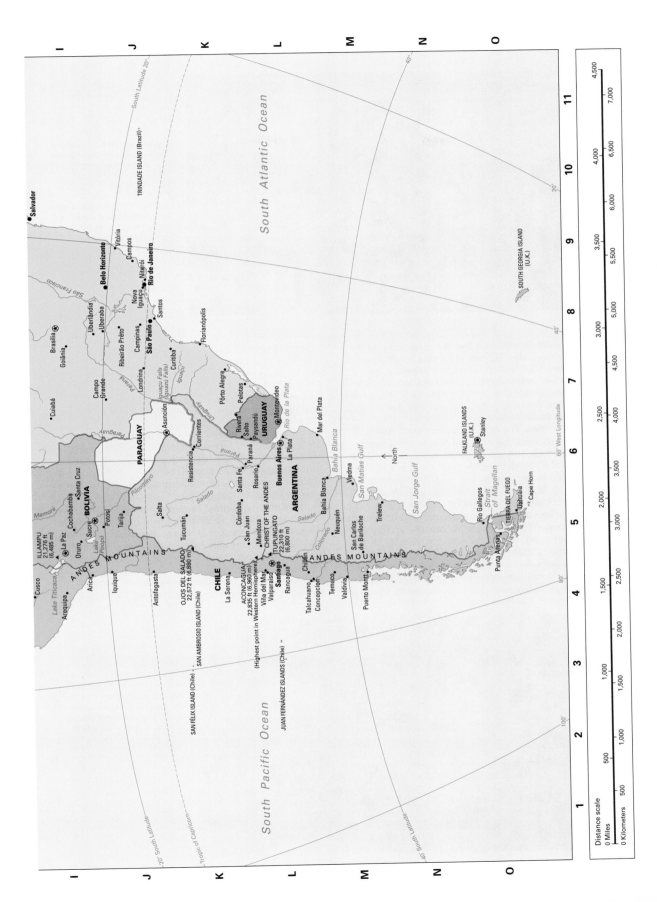

Snow-capped Aconcagua, the highest peak in the Western Hemisphere, rises 22,835 feet (6,960 meters) in the Andes Mountains in Argentina. The rugged Andes, which extend along the length of western South America, are the world's longest mountain range above sea level.

borders South America on the northeast and east. To the south, the Drake Passage separates South America from Antarctica. The Pacific Ocean washes up against the continent's west coast. South America borders land only at the Isthmus of Panama. This narrow strip of land links Central America with Colombia, in the northwestern part of South America.

Land regions. The land surface of South America broadly resembles that of North America. Both continents have high, rugged mountain ranges in the west, vast central plains drained by mighty rivers, and older, less rugged mountains in the east. South America has three major land regions: (1) the Andes Mountains, (2) the Central Plains, and (3) the Eastern Highlands.

The Andes Mountains form a region of jagged, snow-covered peaks; broad, grassy plateaus; steep slopes; and glacier-filled valleys. The Andes stretch for about 4,500 miles (7,200 kilometers), from Venezuela in the north to Tierra del Fuego in the south. The Andes are the longest mountain range above sea level and the second highest mountain range in the world. The Mid-

Atlantic Ridge, which rises from the bottom of the Atlantic Ocean, is longer, and the Himalaya in Asia are higher, than the Andes are. Many Andean peaks rise over 20,000 feet (6,100 meters) above sea level. Aconcagua, in Argentina, is the tallest mountain in the Western Hemisphere. It stands 22,835 feet (6,960 meters) above sea level.

The activity of *tectonic plates* along the western coast of South America formed the Andes over the past 10 million to 15 million years. Tectonic plates are huge, rigid pieces of Earth's crust. Their movements and interactions continue to cause volcanic eruptions and earthquakes in the Andean region.

The Andes have great economic importance for several South American countries. The mountains contain large deposits of valuable minerals, including copper, gold, lead, tin, and zinc. Farmers cultivate coffee in the rich volcanic soils on the slopes of the Andes. In the high mountain valleys and plateaus, the farmers grow thousands of distinct varieties of potatoes and such grains as barley, quinoa, rye, and wheat. Farmers also

The Gran Chaco, a region of hardwood scrub forest, covers portions of Argentina, Bolivia, and Paraguay. This photograph of the Gran Chaco in Bolivia shows a tree known locally as the *toborochi.* During the dry season, the toborochi retains water in its trunk.

South America terrain map

Land region boundary
International boundary
• City
+ Elevation above sea level
▽ Depression

WORLD BOOK map

Physical features

Aconcagua (mountain) ....F 3
Amazon River ....B 4
Andes Mountains ....F 3
Angel Falls ....A 4
Atacama Desert ....E 3
Brazilian Highlands ....D 5
Cape Horn ....H 4
Caribbean Sea ....A 3
Cauca River ....A 2
Central Plains ....C 3
Chimborazo (mountain) ....B 2

Cuquenán Falls ....B 4
Eastern Highlands ......C 5
El Misti (mountain) ....D 3
Falkland Islands ....H 4
Galapagos Islands ......B 1
Gran Chaco (region) ....E 4
Guiana Highlands ......B 4
Gulf of Darién ....A 2
Gulf of Guayaquil ......C 1
Gulf of Venezuela ......A 3
Huascarán (mountain) ..C 2
Iguaçu (Iguazú) Falls ..E 5
Iguaçu River ....E 5
Juan Fernández Islands ....F 2

La Guajira Peninsula ....A 3
Lake Maracaibo ....A 3
Lake Poopó ....D 3
Lake Titicaca ....D 3
Llanos (plains) ....A 3
Magdalena River ....A 3
Marajó Island ....B 6
Mirim Lake ....F 5
Nevado del Ruiz (volcano) ....B 2
Ojos del Salado (mountain) ....E 3
Orinoco River ....A 4
Pampas (plain) ....F 4

Paraguay River ....E 4
Paraná River ....E 4
Patagonia (plateau) ....G 3
Pico da Bandeira (mountain) ....E 6
Pilcomayo River ....E 4
Point Aguja ....C 2
Purus River ....C 4
Río de la Plata (estuary) ....F 5
San Jorge Gulf ....G 4
San Matías Gulf ....G 4
São Francisco River ....C 6

Selva (region) ....C 3
Serra do Espinhaço (mountains) ....D 6
Sertão (region) ....C 7
South Georgia Island ....H 6
Strait of Magellan ......H 3
Tierra del Fuego (islands) ....H 4
Tupungato (mountain) ....F 3
Ucayali River ....C 3
Uruguay River ....E 5
Valdés Peninsula ....G 4

© Jacques Jangoux from Peter Arnold, Inc.

The Guiana Highlands lie north of the Amazon River Basin. They consist of open grasslands with scattered trees, *shown here,* and tropical forests. Few people live in the region.

raise cattle and sheep for meat and wool.

At their widest point, the Andes divide into two mountain chains. Between these chains lies the Altiplano, a high plateau region that is cold, windswept, and nearly treeless. The Altiplano covers southeastern Peru, western Bolivia, northeastern Chile, and northwestern Argentina. It is a difficult region to farm because few crops grow well at such high elevations.

The Central Plains extend eastward from the Andes, covering about three-fifths of South America. They are drained by huge river systems that empty into the Atlantic. Four large areas make up the Central Plains. One of these areas consists of rolling grasslands called the Llanos (pronounced *YAH nohs),* in the Orinoco River Basin of Colombia and Venezuela. These grassy plains with scattered trees provide grazing land for many large cattle ranches. Another area of the Central Plains is a lowland region called Selva, covered by tropical rain forest, in the Amazon River Basin of Bolivia, Brazil, and Peru. The third area, the Gran Chaco, consists of a hardwood scrub forest in north-central Argentina, western Paraguay, and southeastern Bolivia. The fourth area is the vast grassland of Argentina and Uruguay called the Pampas. Its fertile soil supports many farms and ranches.

The Eastern Highlands actually consist of two separate areas—the Guiana Highlands and the Brazilian Highlands. The broad Amazon River Basin separates the two areas. Mountains in the Eastern Highlands are much lower and older than the Andes.

The Guiana Highlands rise north of the Amazon basin. They lie about 3,000 to 5,000 feet (900 to 1,500 meters) above sea level. Tropical forests and open grasslands cover the region. The Guiana Highlands are thinly populated and largely undeveloped.

The Brazilian Highlands stretch south of the Amazon region to southeastern Brazil, covering nearly a fourth of the continent. The highest mountain in this region, Pico da Bandeira, rises 9,482 feet (2,890 meters) northeast of Rio de Janeiro. Most of the Brazilian Highlands, however, consist of rounded hills and flat tablelands between

1,000 and 3,000 feet (300 and 900 meters) above sea level. The southern Brazilian Highlands have fertile farms, fine cattle ranches, and rich mineral deposits.

Rivers. Five large river systems drain most of South America. These river systems are (1) the Amazon, (2) the Río de la Plata, (3) the Magdalena-Cauca, (4) the Orinoco, and (5) the São Francisco.

The Amazon River system drains about 2,700,000 square miles (7,000,000 square kilometers) of land—the world's largest drainage basin. The Amazon carries about one-fifth of the world's fresh river water. It flows some 4,000 miles (6,437 kilometers) from the Peruvian Andes to the Atlantic. Only Africa's Nile River is longer. Oceangoing ships can navigate the Amazon as far upstream as Iquitos, Peru.

The Río de la Plata system is made up of the Paraná, Paraguay, and Uruguay rivers. It provides inland water routes for Argentina, Bolivia, Brazil, Paraguay, and Uruguay. The system empties into the Río de la Plata, a bay on the southeastern coast of South America. The Itaipú Dam power plant lies on the Paraná between Paraguay and Brazil. With a generating capacity of about 12 ½ million kilowatts of electric power, the power plant is the world's largest hydroelectric plant.

The Magdalena and Cauca rivers flow northward through two fertile farming valleys in Colombia. The Cauca River flows into the Magdalena, which empties into the Caribbean Sea.

The Orinoco River runs in a broad arc through Venezuela to the Atlantic. For part of its length, the Orinoco forms the border between Colombia and Venezuela. The lower Orinoco crosses the Llanos, a productive ranching area in central Venezuela. Oceangoing ships travel up the Orinoco to load iron ore at the Venezuelan river port of Ciudad Guayana.

The São Francisco River stretches for nearly 2,000 miles (3,200 kilometers) through northeastern Brazil. It flows northeastward through a large, drought-prone region and then turns toward the southeast and empties into the Atlantic. It is a broad, navigable waterway along about 900 miles (1,400 kilometers) of its middle course. Several large hydroelectric power plants generate electric power on the São Francisco.

Lakes. South America has few large lakes. Lake Maracaibo in Venezuela is the continent's largest. It covers 5,217 square miles (13,512 square kilometers). A short, narrow channel links Lake Maracaibo with the Gulf of Venezuela. Oil wells operate in the lake and along its shores.

Lake Titicaca, in the Andes, is the highest navigable lake in the world. It lies on the border between Bolivia and Peru at an elevation of 12,507 feet (3,812 meters). Crops that normally could not survive at such a high altitude grow in the area because the waters of Lake Titicaca warm the air.

Waterfalls. South America has many spectacular waterfalls. Angel Falls, in eastern Venezuela, has a longer drop than any other waterfall in the world. The water plunges 3,212 feet (979 meters) down a cliff, lands as a heavy mist, and drains into the Churún River. The world's second highest waterfall, Cuquenán Falls, also lies in southeastern Venezuela. There, the Cuquenán River drops 2,000 feet (610 meters).

Iguaçu Falls (spelled Iguazú in Argentina) are on the

Lake Titicaca, on the border between Bolivia and Peru, is the world's highest navigable lake at 12,507 feet (3,812 meters) above sea level. Local people use reeds growing on the lakeshore to make canoes like the one shown here.

border between Argentina and Brazil. Many people consider these falls the most magnificent natural sight in South America. The Iguaçu River forms Iguaçu Falls when it plunges 237 feet (72 meters) along an arc about 2 miles (3.2 kilometers) wide. See **Brazil** (picture).

Tropical rain forests cover more than a third of South America. Dense rain forests blanket most of the warm, wet Amazon River Basin and the northeast and northwest coasts of the continent. Many valuable forest products come from the lush Amazon region.

Large areas of coastal rain forest in Brazil have been cleared for farming and ranching. In such forests, most of the soil's fertility comes from decaying leaves. As a result, the soil of the rain forest is thin and poor.

Deserts. A coastal desert extends from southern Ecuador, along the coast of Peru, to meet the Atacama Desert of northern Chile. A much smaller desert covers the northern part of Colombia's border with Venezuela. Patagonia, in southern Argentina, is a semidesert region. The Sertão of northeastern Brazil is a dry area covered with thorny bushes and low trees. Increasingly frequent droughts threaten to create a new desert there.

Coastline and islands. South America's long coastline has few natural harbors or bays. The best natural harbor is at Rio de Janeiro. Other bays include Todos os Santos Bay at Salvador, Brazil; the Gulf of Darién off Colombia's Caribbean coast; the mouths of the Amazon and the Río de la Plata on the Atlantic; and Ecuador's Gulf of Guayaquil on the Pacific.

South America includes several major island groups. The largest is the Tierra del Fuego group. These islands lie across the Strait of Magellan from the southernmost tip of the mainland. Argentina and Chile own them. Chile also owns the Juan Fernández Islands in the Pacific, about 400 miles (640 kilometers) off Chile's coast. The Falkland Islands, an overseas territory of the United Kingdom, lie in the South Atlantic about 320 miles (515 kilometers) east of the southern coast of Argentina. Argentina also claims these islands and calls them the *Islas Malvinas*. The Falklands and Tierra del Fuego have valuable sheep-grazing lands. The Galapagos Islands belong to Ecuador and lie in the Pacific about 600 miles (970 kilometers) off the coast of that country. They are the

home of huge tortoises, sea turtles, and many other unusual animals. Marajó, an island at the mouth of the Amazon River, belongs to Brazil. Herders raise water buffaloes on this flat, grassy island.

Climate

South America has a wide variety of climates. They range from the dry desert conditions of northern Chile to the heavy rains along the windswept southwestern coast. Steamy heat characterizes the tropical rain forest of the Amazon basin, while icy cold air surrounds the lofty, snow-capped peaks of the Andes. In general, how-

Spectacular Angel Falls, in eastern Venezuela, has a longer drop than any other waterfall in the world. It plunges 3,212 feet (979 meters) down a cliff into the Churún River.

Perito Moreno Glacier, *shown here,* is in southern Patagonia, a rugged, wind-swept region of southern South America. Perito Moreno and other glaciers are major attractions at Los Glaciares National Park in Argentina.

© Damm Fridmar, 4Corners Images

WORLD BOOK map

The climate of South America

South America has a wide range of climates. Most of the continent receives ample rain. However, the Atacama Desert in northern Chile is one of the driest places on Earth. This map and legend show what the climate is like throughout the continent.

Tropical wet–Always hot and wet. Heavy precipitation well distributed throughout year.

Tropical wet and dry– Always hot, with alternate wet and dry seasons. Heavy precipitation in wet season.

Semiarid–Hot to cold. Great changes in temperature from day to night except in coastal areas. Light precipitation.

Desert–Hot to cool. Great changes in temperature from day to night except in coastal areas. Very little precipitation.

Subtropical dry summer– Hot, dry summers and mild, rainy winters. Moderate precipitation in winter.

Humid subtropical–Warm to hot summers and cool winters. Moderate precipitation in all seasons.

Humid oceanic–Moderately warm summers and generally cool winters. Moderate precipitation in all seasons.

Highland–Climate depends on altitude. Climates at various altitudes are like those found in flat terrain.

Average January temperatures

Most of South America has hot or warm weather in January. January is a summer month south of the equator.

Average July temperatures

July is a winter month south of the equator. South America's coldest weather occurs in the Andes and the far south.

Average yearly precipitation

Much of South America receives heavy or moderate rainfall. Drier areas are found in Argentina, Chile, and Peru.

WORLD BOOK maps

ever, most of the continent has warm weather the year around. Only in the high Andes is it always cold.

The hottest weather in South America occurs in Argentina's Gran Chaco, where the temperature reaches 110 °F (43 °C). Temperatures in the Amazon region generally range from 70 to 90 °F (21 to 32 °C) and rarely reach 100 °F (38 °C). South of the equator, summer lasts from late December to late March, and winter runs from late June to late September. In the far south of Argentina, the temperature generally ranges from 40 °F (4 °C) in July to 60 °F (16 °C) in January, but it has dropped to as low as –27 °F (–33 °C).

Most of South America receives ample rain. Rainfall averages more than 80 inches (200 centimeters) a year in four areas: (1) coastal French Guiana, Guyana, and Suriname; (2) the Amazon River Basin; (3) southwestern Chile; and (4) the coasts of Colombia and northern Ecuador. Quibdo, Colombia, the rainiest place in South America, receives more than 350 inches (890 centimeters) of rain a year. Even the wettest regions of the continent generally have a dry season, however, when there is plenty of sunshine between downpours.

In southwestern Chile, humid westerly winds blow in from the Pacific and drop most of their moisture as rain before crossing the Andes. As a result, the area east of the Andes is dry. For example, the plateaus of Patagonia, in southeastern Argentina, receive only about 10 inches (25 centimeters) of rain a year.

Coastal Peru and northern Chile are among the driest places on Earth. Arica, the northern port city of Chile, receives an average of only ³⁄₁₀₀ inch (0.76 millimeter) of rain a year. The dry conditions in this part of the continent result from the cold Peru Current, which flows northward from Antarctica and travels along the coast. This current cools the air. Because such cool air cannot hold much moisture, little rain falls in the region.

At irregular periods, usually every two to seven years, the northward Peru Current weakens and stronger warm waters flow southward along the coast. This event is called *El Niño* (Spanish for *the child*). It usually occurs around Christmas, and its name refers to the Christ child. El Niño creates changes in the atmosphere that lead to torrential downpours in the usually dry region. The changes also disrupt marine life, hurting the local fishing industry. See El Niño.

Animal and plant life

Animals. South America has a great variety of animals, including about a fourth of all known kinds of mammals. However, it does not have such huge animals or such large herds of wild animals as are found in Africa. South America's largest wild land animal is the hoglike tapir, which lives in the Amazon region and grows about as large as a pony.

The Amazon River Basin has the greatest variety of animals on the continent. These include the capybara, the world's largest rodent, which grows up to about 4 feet (1.2 meters) long. Trees in the rain forest provide homes for many kinds of monkeys. Other unusual forest dwellers include the armadillo, the giant anteater, and the sloth. The Amazon is also the home of the green anaconda, one of the world's largest snakes. It may grow up to 30 feet (9 meters) long.

The manatee, a large water mammal, lives in the Amazon River. Amazon manatees weigh from 700 to 1,000 pounds (350 to 500 kilograms). Another large inhabitant of the river is the arapaima fish, which grows more than 7 feet (2.1 meters) long and commonly weighs more than 200 pounds (90 kilograms). Piranha also swim in the river. A school of these small fish may attack a much larger

animal and devour its flesh, leaving only the bones.

Many kinds of birds live in South America. They include egrets, flamingos, hummingbirds, parrots, and toucans. The large, ostrichlike rhea lives in the Argentine Pampas. Ecuador's Galapagos Islands support giant tortoises, sea turtles, crabs, iguanas, and a great variety of birds. Many of these animals are *endemic* species, meaning that they live nowhere else on Earth.

The vicuña and the guanaco, two wild members of the camel family, live high in the Andes. Scientists believe the alpaca and the llama, which were *domesticated* (tamed) in South America, may be descended from the

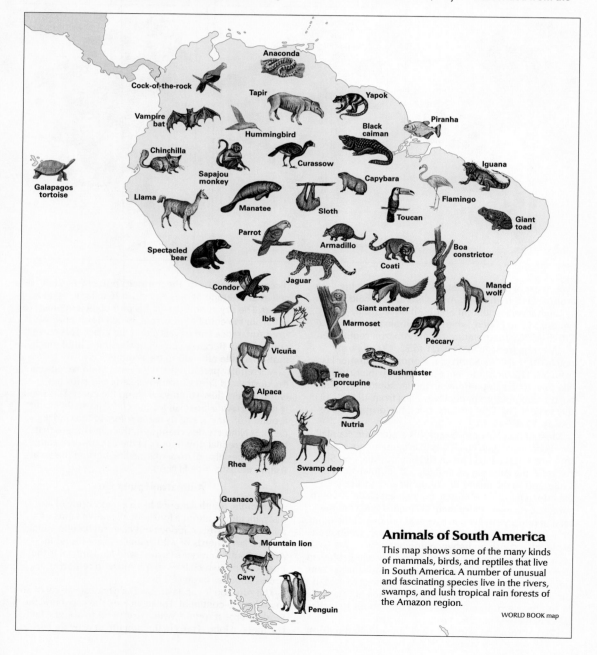

Animals of South America

This map shows some of the many kinds of mammals, birds, and reptiles that live in South America. A number of unusual and fascinating species live in the rivers, swamps, and lush tropical rain forests of the Amazon region.

WORLD BOOK map

guanaco. Alpacas produce fine wool. Llamas can carry loads of as much as 130 pounds (60 kilograms). The guinea pig also was domesticated in South America.

Plants. South America has a great variety of plants, many of which grow on no other continent. The Amazon River Basin, sometimes referred to as "the green ocean," contains tens of thousands of plant species. Countless kinds of orchids and more than 2,500 types of trees grow in the Amazon rain forest. Many of the trees are hardwoods, including mahogany and rosewood, which are used in making fine furniture. The wood of some South American trees is so dense that it does not float.

Other useful trees that grow in the Amazon River Basin include the rubber tree, the towering Brazil-nut tree, and the cacao tree, which produces beans used to make cocoa and chocolate.

Many valuable plants live in other parts of South America as well. The sisal plant grows in dry northeastern Brazil. It produces fibers used in making twine. The pineapple plant also grows in this region, as does the carnauba palm, which produces lubricating and polishing waxes. Coca shrubs grow in the subtropical forests. Their leaves are the source both of illegal cocaine and of other, legal drugs used in medicine. *Quinine,* a drug

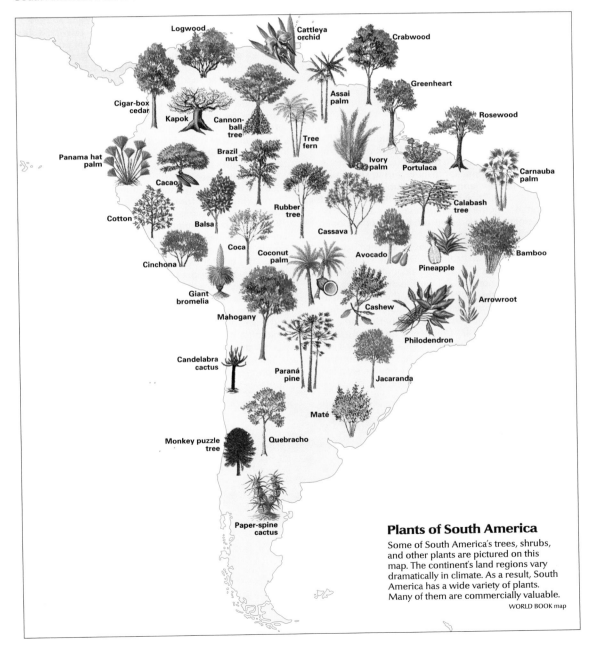

Plants of South America

Some of South America's trees, shrubs, and other plants are pictured on this map. The continent's land regions vary dramatically in climate. As a result, South America has a wide variety of plants. Many of them are commercially valuable.

WORLD BOOK map

used to treat malaria, comes from the cinchona tree found in Ecuador and Peru. Ecuador is the world's largest producer of balsa, a lightweight wood. Tannin, a chemical used in tanning hides and making inks and dyes, comes from the quebracho tree of Argentina and Paraguay. The softwood of the Paraná pine of southern Brazil is used in the construction industry.

Several commercially valuable plants were brought to South America from other continents. These useful plants include bananas and coffee—two of South America's most important export crops. In the mid-1800's, people brought the eucalyptus tree from Australia to South America. It has become common over much of the continent and is a valuable source of firewood.

Economy

South America has abundant natural resources. These include vast stretches of fertile land; raw materials, such as hardwoods and minerals, used in manufacturing; and plentiful energy resources, such as natural gas and petroleum. However, many of these resources remain undeveloped.

All the countries of South America have developing economies. Argentina, Brazil, Chile, Uruguay, and Venezuela have the most developed economies, which include successful modern manufacturing industries. Other nations have smaller manufacturing sectors and rely upon a narrow range of agricultural and mineral exports for income. They purchase manufactured goods from overseas. Some also import food and energy resources. Bolivia and Paraguay are the least developed nations on the continent.

In general, the countries of South America have a lower *gross domestic product* (GDP)—the value of all goods and services produced in a country in a year—than do North American and European countries. The *per capita GDP*—the GDP divided by the total population—is an indication of a country's standard of living. In 2004, 5 of the 12 countries in South America had a per capita GDP above $3,000. Chile's was the highest, at $5,839. That same year, the per capita GDP of the United States was $40,245. In all of South America's countries, wealth is unevenly distributed. A few people earn far more than the per capita average, but a great majority earn far less.

Agriculture. About four-fifths of South America's land could be used for agriculture. However, only about one-third is actually used for agriculture, and most of that serves as pasture for grazing animals. Most land in South America is divided into large properties called *latifundios,* which are owned by a small percentage of the population. Latifundios include *haciendas* (large farms or country estates); plantations, often owned by foreign companies; and technologically sophisticated farms controlled by *agribusinesses* (companies that produce, transport, distribute, and sell farm products).

Small properties called *minifundios* greatly outnumber the latifundios. Minifundios generally provide a single family with food. They often employ traditional farming methods that rely upon human and animal labor. Minifundios cover much less of South America's good farmland than latifundios do.

Millions of rural South Americans do not own any land. They work for wages on the latifundios or as *share-croppers,* receiving a percentage of the crops they raise as payment. Since the mid-1900's, many rural South Americans have moved to cities in search of better job opportunities. By the early 2000's, only about one-fifth of the continent's population lived in rural areas.

During the colonial period, which lasted from the 1500's to the 1800's in South America, farmers grew crops primarily for foreign markets. Each country produced just a few crops, such as cacao, coffee, cotton, and sugar. The invention of refrigerated shipping in the late 1800's made it possible to transport such perishable goods as fruits and meats over long distances.

Today, Ecuador exports more bananas than any other country in the world. Colombia is a leading banana exporter as well. Argentina, Brazil, and Colombia produce beef for European markets. Brazil and Colombia are among the world's leading exporters of coffee. Wheat and corn are the chief grains produced for consumption in South America. Farmers also cultivate potatoes and rice for domestic markets.

Since the late 1900's, many farmers have begun growing nontraditional crops. Several countries, including

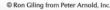
© Ron Giling from Peter Arnold, Inc.

Modern farming methods have become common on large farms in South America. These men in Suriname are using a combine to harvest rice. Altogether, large farms cover much more of South America's good farmland than small farms do.

Colombia, cultivate flowers for sale in North America and Europe. Chile produces kiwi fruit, citrus fruits, and grapes for export during the winter months in the Northern Hemisphere. Argentina and Chile produce wine grapes, and soybeans for animal feed are a chief export of Argentina and Brazil.

Many farmers earn high profits cultivating such illegal crops as coca, used to produce cocaine; poppies, used to make heroin; and marijuana. Efforts to encourage growers to substitute legal crops for illegal ones often fail because the illegal crops earn high profits.

Manufacturing. Until the 1800's, Spain and Portugal hindered the development of manufacturing in South America, preferring instead to export the continent's raw materials. During the 1800's and early 1900's, newly independent countries continued this practice. At the same time, such nations as the United Kingdom and the United States discouraged the development of South American industry. In doing so, they hoped to limit local competition with their own manufactured goods. It was not until the 1930's and 1940's that South American countries began manufacturing goods for domestic use and for export to North America and Europe. Argentina, Brazil, and Chile emerged as the most industrialized nations.

In the early and mid-1900's, South American governments closely controlled their national economies. They often owned manufacturing firms, as well as airlines, banks, and utility companies. Governments tried to protect their industries from foreign competition by imposing *tariffs* (taxes) on imports and giving *subsidies* (aid payments) to domestic firms. They had to take out loans to pay these subsidies. In the 1980's, many countries could not repay their loans, which led to a debt crisis. Following the crisis, nations began to *privatize* their industries. Privatization involves the sale of government-owned industries or portions of them to private, often foreign, companies.

Today, governments encourage the manufacture of goods for export, and South America makes a greater variety of products than ever before. Brazil, one of the world's leading industrial countries, produces airplanes, automobiles, military weapons, and televisions. São Paolo, Brazil, is South America's chief manufacturing center. In most other South American nations, manufacturing includes such consumer goods as beverages, furniture, processed foods, shoes, and textiles.

Several countries have created *export processing zones* where foreign-owned factories operate. These

Agriculture and fishing in South America

This map and legend show the major uses of land in South America. The map locates the chief agricultural products. The most important crops and livestock appear in large type. The map also shows the major fishing areas and kinds of fish caught.

Commercial agriculture

Subsistence agriculture

Cereals and livestock

Grazing land

Chiefly forestland

Generally unproductive land

Fishing

factories employ many South Americans. The multinational firms that own them benefit from favorable taxation policies and lower labor costs.

Mining. The mountains of South America have long been a source of mineral wealth. Deposits of gold and silver attracted the Spanish and Portuguese to the area in colonial times. Today, the Amazon River Basin is another significant source of mineral wealth.

South America's mineral resources are distributed unevenly. Paraguay possesses few useful minerals. Brazil and Venezuela are leading producers of iron ore, and Brazil mines large amounts of manganese. Brazil, Guyana, Suriname, and Venezuela are among world leaders in mining bauxite, used to make aluminum. Chile is a major source of copper, mined in the Atacama Desert. Peru has copper deposits and exports zinc as well. Colombia is a leading source of emeralds, and Amazonian gold is emerging as a significant export.

Global demand for the continent's energy resources, particularly oil and natural gas, has increased since the late 1900's. Venezuela is one of the world's top exporters of oil. Argentina, Colombia, and Ecuador also export oil, while Argentina and Bolivia export large quantities of natural gas.

Mining generates great wealth for a small portion of the population and for large corporations. Because mining is highly mechanized, it creates only a few jobs. It does, however, cause substantial environmental damage. For example, mercury and other toxins used to process mineral ores pollute South America's water.

Forestry and fishing. Brazil is South America's chief producer of forestry products. All the countries in the Amazon River Basin have forestry industries that produce such hardwoods as greenheart, mahogany, and rosewood. Builders use the extremely dense greenheart, found in the Guiana Highlands, to construct ships and piers. Softwood pine trees grow in southern South America.

South American forests yield many products besides wood. These include coconuts, dates, edible nuts, oils, and ingredients used to make medicines and other pharmaceutical products. The sap of rubber trees, which grow naturally in the Amazon rain forest, is used to make rubber tires. This sap is called *latex*.

During the debt crisis of the late 1900's, many countries leased land to foreign logging firms that cut down vast areas of trees. Large-scale logging caused such environmental problems as soil erosion, water pollution,

Mining and manufacturing in South America

This map locates South America's chief mineral resources and manufacturing centers. Major mineral-producing areas are indicated in large type, and lesser ones in small type. Manufacturing centers are printed in red.

WORLD BOOK map

Petroleum is a valuable export of several South American countries. Lake Maracaibo, in northwestern Venezuela, has many oil wells, *shown here.* Argentina, Colombia, and Ecuador also export oil.

© Georg Gerster, Photo Researchers

and the extinction of some species of animals, plants, and microbes. Since then, many South American countries have begun to plant trees in *afforestation* and *reforestation* programs.

Chile and Peru have South America's most valuable fishing industries. The cool Peru Current (also called the Humboldt Current), which flows along South America's west coast, is rich in *plankton* and other small organisms that many fish eat. The anchovetta, a fish used to make oil and animal feed, is one important commercial variety. Both freshwater and ocean fish provide protein in the diets of many South Americans. But decades of overfishing have reduced fish stocks worldwide and caused a decline in South America's fishing industry since the late 1900's.

Service industries employ more than half of South America's work force. They include banking, commercial sales, government services, health care, and tourism. Many service jobs, such as cleaning and food preparation, require few skills and pay low wages. Such industries as data processing, legal services, and telecommunications, which require high levels of education, are becoming increasingly important.

South American cities are home to many underemployed people who lack full-time jobs. They often work in the *informal economy* that exists outside of government control and taxation structures. The informal economy provides low-cost services to many South American professional people, who earn less than their counterparts in North America and Europe. The informal economy also includes such illegal activities as *prostitution* (the performance of sexual acts for payment) and the sale of illegal drugs.

International trade. The countries of North America and Europe have long ranked as South America's leading trading partners. International trade between South American countries is also important. In addition, Middle Eastern countries buy many South American products. Trade with such Pacific nations as Australia, China, Japan, and South Korea has increased since the late 1900's, as the economies of those countries have grown stronger. Major exports of South America include agricultural, forest, and mineral products. Some major imports are chemicals, foodstuffs, fuels, machinery, and transportation equipment.

All the countries of South America are members of the World Trade Organization (WTO), which sets rules for international trade and works to reduce trade barriers between countries. In 1991, Argentina, Brazil, Paraguay, and Uruguay formed a trade association called Mercosur. Mercosur strives to increase trade among members and promotes closer commercial ties with the European Union. The Andean Community, another trade association, was founded by Bolivia, Colombia, Ecuador, Peru, and Venezuela. The Andean Community has had less success increasing trade among members because several of its members produce similar goods. Venezuela withdrew from the group in 2006.

Transportation. The geography of South America presents many obstacles to transportation. Rugged mountains, dense rain forests, and harsh deserts make it difficult to construct efficient transportation systems. The continent lacks extensive rail lines. Those railroads that do exist are aging lines in need of modernization. For this reason, ships carry most of South America's imports and exports. Cargo and passenger boats travel up and down the Amazon River. Chile uses ferries to link its central region to the far south, where the irregular coastline has no paved roads.

Airlines provide passenger service within and between countries and transport some cargo. Most South Americans cannot afford to fly, nor do they own automobiles. For them, buses offer a cheap alternative. Bus-

© Graham French, Masterfile

Boats are an important means of transportation for people and goods in South America. The cargo ships and fishing boats shown here are docked at Valparaíso, Chile's leading seaport.

es travel extensively throughout the continent, on mountain roads as well as on highways. They are also the primary means of transportation in urban areas. Long-distance buses in Argentina, Brazil, Chile, and Peru provide comfortable transportation. The number of automobiles in South America is increasing, and traffic congestion and air pollution are problems in large cities. Subway systems operate in a few major cities.

Increased trade between South American nations has made it necessary to improve transportation within the continent. Countries have begun to cooperate to integrate their transportation systems and build roads to carry goods across borders and to the coast. Chile is building a huge port facility called a *megaport* on its northern coast at Mejillones. The megaport will serve as a point of access to the Pacific Ocean for Argentina, Bolivia, Brazil, and Chile.

Communication. Books, magazines, and newspapers are important means of communication in South America. In most countries, at least 90 percent of adults can read and write. Radio and television are other major means of communication.

Television has grown in significance, especially in urban areas, where it is common even in poor neighborhoods. In 2005, Venezuela launched Telesur, a TV network that broadcasts news from a Latin American point of view. Argentina, Cuba, and Uruguay also own shares of Telesur. Soccer matches and soap operas called *telenovelas* are the most popular television programs in South America.

Telephone service extends to all but the most remote communities in South America. A growing number of people use cellular phones to do their daily business. Since the mid-1990's, use of the Internet has grown.

James Wiley

Critically reviewed by Brian P. Owensby

Related articles in *World Book* include:

Characteristic animal life

Alpaca	Manatee	Tapir
Anaconda	Parrot	Toucan
Arapaima	Piranha	Turtle (Kinds of
Capybara	Rhea (bird)	turtles)
Guanaco	Sloth	Vicuña
Llama		

Characteristic plant life

Balsa	Coca	Quebracho
Cacao	Orchid	Sisal
Cinchona		

Countries and other political units

See the separate articles on South American countries and other political units listed in the table with this article.

Islands

Galapagos Islands	Marajó
Juan Fernández	Tierra del Fuego

Mountains

Aconcagua	El Misti
Andes Mountains	Ojos del Salado
Chimborazo	Pinchincha
Cotopaxi	

Plains and deserts

Atacama Desert	Pampas
Gran Chaco	Patagonia

Rivers, lakes, and waterfalls

Amazon River	Lake Titicaca	Río de la Plata
Angel Falls	Madeira River	São Francisco
Cuquenán Falls	Orinoco River	River
Iguaçu Falls	Paraguay River	Uruguay River
Lake Maracaibo	Paraná River	

Other related articles

Amazon rain forest	Magellan, Strait of
Andean Community	Mercosur
Cape Horn	Pan American Highway
El Niño	Rain forest
Latin America	

Outline

I. **The land**
   A. Land regions
   B. Rivers
   C. Lakes
   D. Waterfalls
   E. Tropical rain forests
   F. Deserts
   G. Coastline and islands
II. **Climate**
III. **Animal and plant life**
   A. Animals
   B. Plants
IV. **Economy**
   A. Agriculture
   B. Manufacturing
   C. Mining
   D. Forestry and fishing
   E. Service industries
   F. International trade
   G. Transportation
   H. Communication

Questions

What percentage of the world's plant species grow in the Amazon River Basin?

What are three animals domesticated in South America?

Why are ships an important means of transportation in South America?

What is Mercosur? The Andean Community?

Which countries of South America have the most developed economies?

What are South America's three major land regions, and how does the continent's land surface resemble that of North America?

What portion of the world's fresh river water does the Amazon River carry?

How does *El Niño* affect the weather in coastal Peru and northern Chile?

What are *latifundios* and *minifundios?*

How much of the land in South America is used for pasture and other agricultural purposes?

Additional resources

Level I

Petersen, David. *South America.* Children's Pr., 1998.
Sammis, Fran. *South America.* Benchmark Bks., 2000.
Sayre, April P. *South America.* 21st Century Bks., 1999. *South America, Surprise!* Millbrook, 2003.

Level II

Archer, Christon I., ed. *The Wars of Independence in Spanish America.* Scholarly Resources, 2000.
Heenan, Patrick, and Lamontagne, Monique, eds. *The South America Handbook.* Fitzroy Dearborn, 2002.
Lavallée, Danièle. *The First South Americans.* Univ. of Ut. Pr., 2000.
Parodi, Carlos A. *The Politics of South American Boundaries.* Praeger, 2002.
Santana, Gui, ed. *Tourism in South America.* Haworth Hospitality Pr., 2001.
South America, Central America, and the Caribbean. Europa. Published annually.
Wilbert, Johannes, ed. *Encyclopedia of World Cultures, Vol. 7: South America.* Macmillan, 1994.

WORLD BOOK map

Adelaide is South Australia's largest city. The Adelaide Festival Centre, *shown here,* hosts performing arts events.

© Taxi from Getty Images

South American ostrich. See Rhea (bird).

South Arabia, Federation of. See Yemen (History).

South Australia is a state in south-central Australia. It faces a bay called the Great Australian Bight and the Indian Ocean, which is called the Southern Ocean in Australia. The state covers an area of about 380,000 square miles (984,000 square kilometers), which is about one-eighth the total area of Australia. Adelaide is South Australia's capital and largest city.

Land and climate. The Adelaide and southeastern coastal regions of South Australia are flat, fertile lands. The Flinders, Gawler, and Mount Lofty mountain ranges are in the south-central section of the state. In the central and north regions, the Everard and Musgrave ranges surround a desert plain and several large salt lakes. The Nullarbor Plain covers much of the western part. Mount Woodroffe, the state's highest point, rises 4,724 feet (1,440 meters) above sea level.

The Murray River is Australia's longest permanently flowing river. It rises near the eastern border of Victoria and flows for 1,609 miles (2,589 kilometers). It crosses eastern South Australia before it empties into the Indian Ocean at Goolwa, south of Adelaide. South Australia's yearly temperature averages 71 °F (22 °C). Less than 10 inches (25 centimeters) of rain falls annually in all but the state's southern region.

People. The 2001 Australian census reported that South Australia had 1,467,261 people. About three-fourths of the state's people live in the Adelaide area. Today, most residents are of British descent. Since World War II (1939-1945), many southern Europeans have moved to South Australia.

All children ages 6 to 15 must attend school. Adelaide has three universities with numerous campuses.

Economy. South Australia has excellent farming and grazing land. Wheat, barley, canola, alfalfa, and oats are grown on the Eyre and Yorke peninsulas and the Port Pirie and Adelaide plains in the south. Irrigated orchards and vineyards grow along the Murray River. The Clare Valley, north of Adelaide, also has vineyards. Many cattle and sheep graze in the northern, western, and eastern areas, and wool is an important industry.

Such valuable minerals as iron ore and copper are mined in the central area. Many of the world's opals come from the north-central region of Coober Pedy and Andamooka. Petroleum is mined in the Cooper Basin, and natural gas is found in the Otway Basin. Plantations in the southeast produce commercial timber. Most manufacturing is on the plains near Adelaide. Leading products include automobiles, chemicals, household and electronic appliances, machinery, and paper products. The state's tuna industry centers around Port Lincoln.

Government. The governor of South Australia represents the British monarch. The premier, who is the leader of the majority party of the Legislature, leads the state government. The Legislature consists of a 22-member Legislative Council and a 47-member House of Assembly. Voters elect members of the upper house to eight-year terms and lower house members to four-year terms. A Cabinet of 13 ministers directs the policy and administration of the government. Voters elect 11 members to the national House of Representatives and 12 senators to the national Senate in Canberra. All Australian citizens who are 18 years of age or older must vote.

History. The British navigator Matthew Flinders made the first lengthy exploration along the South Australia coast in 1802. In 1829 and 1830, the British explorer Charles Sturt explored the Murray River and inland areas. Mineral discoveries and the growth of wheat farming and the wool industry helped South Australia grow in the 1800's. In 1856, the people were given self-government. In 1901, South Australia joined five other colonies to form the Commonwealth of Australia. After about 1950, immigration rapidly increased the state's population and its ethnic diversity. Kym Tilbrook

See also **Adelaide; Lake Eyre; Murray River.**

South Bend (pop. 107,789; met. area pop. 316,663) is one of the largest cities in Indiana. It lies in the north-central part of the state, south of the Michigan state line. It is named for its location at the southernmost point of the Indiana bend in the St. Joseph River (see **Indiana** [political map]). Its factories make transportation equipment, rubber and plastic products, tools, and metalworking machinery. The city is a regional commercial, retail, and medical center. It is the county seat of St. Joseph County.

The University of Notre Dame, St. Mary's College, and Bethel College are near South Bend. A regional campus of Indiana University is in the city.

In 1823, Alexis Coquillard, a fur trader, founded South Bend. He called it Big St. Joseph Station. The name was later changed to South Bend. The village was incorporated in 1835 and became a city in 1865. South Bend has a mayor-council government. Nancy J. Sulok

See also **Notre Dame, University of.**

© Jack Alterman

Charleston is the second largest city in South Carolina and the state's chief port. This historic Southern city is known for its stately homes, some dating back to colonial and pre-Civil War days.

South Carolina   *The Palmetto State*

South Carolina is the smallest state in the Deep South region of the United States. In spite of its size, South Carolina is an important manufacturing and farming state. It is one of the leading states in the nation in the manufacture of textiles. South Carolina also raises one of the largest tobacco crops in the United States. Most South Carolina workers are employed in service industries, which include trade, health care, and government. Tourism is also important to the economy of South Carolina.

More than half the people of South Carolina live in urban areas. Columbia is the capital and largest city in the state. South Carolina still has many features of the South of pre-Civil War days. Graceful buildings erected before the war still stand in Beaufort, Charleston, and other cities. Large plantations, which were once the backbone of the South's economy, remain in parts of South Carolina. The state's many beautiful flower gardens recall the leisurely life of the South that existed before the Civil War.

The eastern part of South Carolina is a lowland that borders the Atlantic Ocean. In the west, the land rises to

The contributors of this article are Charles F. Kovacik, Professor of Geography at the University of South Carolina; and George C. Rogers, Jr., former Chairman of the Department of History at the University of South Carolina.

sand hills, and then to mountains. The people of South Carolina call the eastern part of the state the *Low Country.* They call the western part of the state the *Up Country.*

South Carolina was named for King Charles I of England, in 1629. *Carolina* is a Latin form of *Charles.* The word *South* was added in 1730, when North and South Carolina became separate colonies.

Many important battles of the Revolutionary War in America (1775-1783) were fought in South Carolina. Colonial victories in the Battle of Kings Mountain and the Battle of Cowpens were turning points of the war in the South. South Carolina may have earned its nickname, the *Palmetto State,* as the result of certain events that occurred during the Revolutionary War. In 1776, colonists in a small fort built of palmetto logs defeated a British fleet that tried to capture Charleston Harbor. The next day, William Moultrie, the colonial commander, saw a column of smoke rising from a burning British ship. The shape of the smoke reminded Moultrie of the palmetto tree, which grows widely in South Carolina. These wartime events supposedly gave South Carolina its nickname.

South Carolina was the first state to *secede* (withdraw) from the Union before the Civil War (1861-1865). It did so on Dec. 20, 1860. Confederate troops fired the first shot of the Civil War when they attacked Fort Sumter in Charleston Harbor on April 12, 1861.

Wendell Metzen, Bruce Coleman Inc.

Sunbathers relax on one of the sandy beaches of Hilton Head Island, a leading South Carolina resort. The state's warm climate and long ocean shoreline make it a popular vacationland.

Interesting facts about South Carolina

WORLD BOOK illustrations by Kevin Chadwick

The first musical society in America, the St. Cecilia Society, was established in Charleston in 1762.

The Fireproof Building, completed in Charleston in 1826, was the first building in the United States constructed to withstand fire. It was designed by Robert Mills, the architect of the Washington Monument. The building currently houses the Historical Society of South Carolina.

The Fireproof Building

"Heart of pine" houses, built in South Carolina in colonial times, still stand today. Timber was so plentiful during the state's early days that "sapwood" was thrown away, and only the hearts of pine trees were used. This wood is said to keep indefinitely.

The first museum in the American Colonies was opened by the Charleston Library Society in 1773. The museum featured objects related to the natural history of South Carolina.

The reformed branch of Judaism in America originated in Charleston in 1824 with the Reformed Society of Israelites.

The first commercial tea farm in the United States was established at Summerville in 1890 by Charles Shepard.

The first steam locomotive to be placed in regular passenger and freight service was the *Best Friend of Charleston.* This locomotive, built for the South Carolina Canal and Rail Road Company, made its first run on Christmas Day in 1830.

The *Best Friend of Charleston*

David R. Frazier

Marine recruits march at the Parris Island Marine Corps Recruit Depot. The base trains most Marine Corps recruits from the eastern half of the United States.

South Carolina Department of Parks, Recreation, and Tourism

Forest-covered mountains rise in South Carolina's *Up Country.* This area includes the Piedmont and Blue Ridge regions in the northwestern third of the state. Elevations in the Up Country range from about 400 feet (120 meters) to about 3,600 feet (1,100 meters) above sea level.

South Carolina in brief

Symbols of South Carolina

The state flag, adopted in 1861, bears a palmetto tree and a crescent. The state seal, authorized in 1776, displays two scenes. In the scene on the left, a palmetto over a dead oak symbolizes the defense in 1776 of the palmetto-log fort on Sullivan's Island against the United Kingdom's oaken ships. On the right, a woman walking on a sword-covered beach represents hope overcoming danger.

State flag

State seal

South Carolina (brown) ranks 40th in size among all the states and 11th in size among the Southern States (yellow).

General information

Statehood: May 23, 1788, the 8th state.
State abbreviations: S.C. (traditional); SC (postal).
State mottoes: *Animis Opibusque Parati* (Prepared In Mind and Resources); *Dum Spiro Spero* (While I Breathe, I Hope).
State song: "Carolina." Words by Henry Timrod; music by Anne Custis Burgess (one of two state songs).

The State House is in Columbia, the capital of South Carolina since 1790. Charleston served as capital from 1670 to 1790.

Land and climate

Area: 31,117 mi² (80,593 km²), including 1,006 mi² (2,605 km²) of inland water but excluding 72 mi² (186 km²) of coastal water.
Elevation: *Highest*—Sassafras Mountain, 3,560 ft (1,085 m) above sea level. *Lowest*—sea level along the coast.
Coastline: 187 mi (301 km).
Record high temperature: 111 °F (44 °C) in Blackville on Sept. 4, 1925, in Calhoun Falls on Sept. 8, 1925, and in Camden on June 28, 1954.
Record low temperature: −19 °F (−28 °C) was recorded at Caesars Head on Jan. 21, 1985.
Average July temperature: 80 °F (27 °C).
Average January temperature: 45 °F (7 °C).
Average yearly precipitation: 48 in (122 cm).

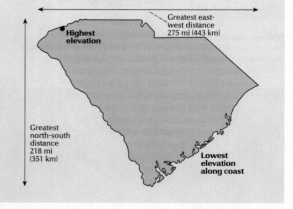

Greatest east-west distance 275 mi (443 km)

Highest elevation

Greatest north-south distance 218 mi (351 km)

Lowest elevation along coast

Important dates

The English established the first permanent European settlement in South Carolina at Albemarle Point.

| 1521 | 1670 | 1788 | 1861 |

Francisco Gordillo of Spain explored the Carolina coast.

South Carolina became the 8th state on May 23.

The Civil War began on April 12 when Confederate forces fired on Fort Sumter.

State bird
Carolina wren

State flower
Yellow jessamine

State tree
Sabal palmetto

People

Population: 4,012,012
Rank among the states: 26th
Density: 129 per mi² (50 per km²), U.S. average 78 per mi² (30 per km²)
Distribution: 60 percent urban, 40 percent rural
Largest cities in South Carolina

Columbia	116,278
Charleston	96,650
North Charleston	79,641
Greenville	56,002
Rock Hill	49,765
Mount Pleasant†	47,609

†Unincorporated place.
Source: 2000 census.

Population trend

Millions

Source: U.S. Census Bureau.

Year	Population
2000	4,012,012
1990	3,486,703
1980	3,122,814
1970	2,590,713
1960	2,382,594
1950	2,117,027
1940	1,899,804
1930	1,738,765
1920	1,683,724
1910	1,515,400
1900	1,340,316
1890	1,151,149
1880	995,577
1870	705,606
1860	703,708
1850	668,507
1840	594,398
1830	581,185
1820	502,741
1810	415,115
1800	345,591
1790	249,073

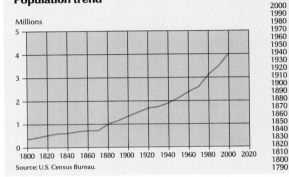

Economy

Chief products

Agriculture: beef cattle, broilers, cotton, eggs, greenhouse and nursery products, soybeans, tobacco, turkeys.
Manufacturing: chemicals, machinery, plastics and rubber products, textiles, transportation equipment.
Mining: crushed stone, portland cement.

Gross domestic product

Value of goods and services produced in 2004: $131,492,000,000. *Services* include community, business, and personal services; finance; government; trade; and transportation and communication. *Industry* includes construction, manufacturing, mining, and utilities. *Agriculture* includes agriculture, fishing, and forestry.

Source: U.S. Bureau of Economic Analysis.

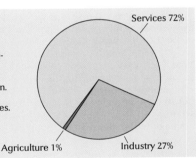

Services 72%
Agriculture 1%
Industry 27%

Government

State government

Governor: 4-year term
State senators: 46; 4-year terms
State representatives: 124; 2-year terms
Counties: 46

Federal government

United States senators: 2
United States representatives: 6
Electoral votes: 8

Sources of information

For information about tourism, write to: South Carolina Department of Parks, Recreation & Tourism, 1205 Pendleton Street, Columbia, SC 29201. The Web site at http://www.discoversouthcarolina.com also provides information.
For information on the economy, write to: South Carolina Department of Commerce, P.O. Box 927, Columbia, SC 29202.
The state's official Web site at http://www.sc.gov also provides a gateway to much information on South Carolina's economy, government, and history.

The Santee-Cooper navigational project and hydroelectric dam was completed.

Hurricane Hugo killed 18 people and caused $5 billion in property damage in the state.

| 1895 | 1941 | 1953 | 1989 | 2003 |

South Carolina adopted its present constitution.

Operations began at the Savannah River Atomic Energy Plant near Aiken.

Congaree National Park, the first national park in the state, was established.

Population. The 2000 United States census reported that South Carolina had 4,012,012 people. The state's population had increased 15 percent over the 1990 census figure, 3,486,703. According to the 2000 census, South Carolina ranks 26th in population among the 50 states.

The state has 10 metropolitan areas (see **Metropolitan area**). About 75 percent of the population lives in these areas. Eight metropolitan areas are entirely within the state. Parts of the Augusta (Georgia)-Richmond County (Georgia) and the Charlotte (North Carolina)-Gastonia (North Carolina)-Concord (North Carolina) metropolitan areas extend into South Carolina. For the names and populations of the metropolitan areas, see the *Index* to the political map of South Carolina.

The largest cities in South Carolina, in order of size, are Columbia, Charleston, North Charleston, and Greenville. They are the only cities with a population of more than 50,000.

Many of South Carolina's people are descendants of early settlers to the state. About 30 percent of the state's people are African Americans. Other large population groups in the state include people of German, Irish, English, Scotch-Irish, and American Indian descent.

Schools. In colonial times, most of the children in South Carolina were educated at home or in private schools. In 1710, the colonial government established semipublic schools that were called *free schools*. These schools were free to poor children, but other youngsters paid tuition.

In 1811, the state legislature approved a plan to set up free schools in all parts of South Carolina. But not enough money was put aside to run the schools. There were few free schools except in the largest towns in the state. The 1868 Constitution called for free public schools for all children. But the legislature failed to provide enough money for the schools. Finally, the 1895 Constitution provided tax support for statewide public schools.

Like other Southern States, South Carolina had sepa-

Population density

South Carolina's most densely populated areas lie in and around the state's largest cities. Parts of the state, including the southwest, are thinly populated.

Persons per sq. mi.	Persons per km²
More than 250	More than 100
125 to 250	50 to 100
50 to 125	20 to 50
Less than 50	Less than 20

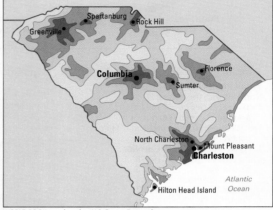

WORLD BOOK map; based on U.S. Census Bureau data.

rate schools for blacks and whites for many years. In 1954, the Supreme Court of the United States ruled that public school segregation on the basis of race is unconstitutional. The first racial integration in South Carolina public schools took place in Charleston in 1963. By 1970, South Carolina's public school districts had been integrated. Children from age 5 to 17 must attend school. For the number of students and teachers in the state, see **Education** (table).

A superintendent of education and a State Board of Education head the South Carolina public school system. The board has 17 members. The governor appoints one member from the state *at large* (as a whole). The

© David R. Frazier

Citadel Military College in Charleston is a state-controlled institution. Students at the college learn the fundamentals of military training, strategy, and tactics.

other members are appointed by the state legislators from each of South Carolina's 16 *judicial* (court) circuits. Board members serve four-year terms. The voters elect the superintendent to a four-year term.

Libraries. South Carolina had the first government-supported lending library in the 13 original colonies. The library opened in Charleston in 1698 but closed a few years later. In 1840, the University of South Carolina built the nation's first separate college library building. Today, South Carolina has public library service in each of its 46 counties.

Museums. The Charleston Museum, founded in 1773, is one of the oldest museums in the United States. It has natural history, anthropology, and colonial history exhibits. The South Carolina State Museum in Columbia has exhibits dealing with art, cultural history, natural history, science, and technology. The Museum of York County in Rock Hill has a large collection of African mammals and a planetarium. Bob Jones University Museum & Gallery in Greenville has a collection of paintings on religion. Other art museums in the state include the Columbia Museum of Art, the Gibbes Museum of Art in Charleston, and the Greenville County Museum of Art in Greenville.

South Carolina Botanical Garden at Clemson University

The historic Hunt Family Cabin is part of the Pioneer Complex at the South Carolina Botanical Garden at Clemson University. The cabin, built about 1825, was moved to this site in 1955.

Universities and colleges

This table lists the universities and colleges in South Carolina that grant bachelor's or advanced degrees and are accredited by the Southern Association of Colleges and Schools.

Name	Mailing address	Name	Mailing address
Allen University	Columbia	Lander University	Greenwood
Anderson University	Anderson	Limestone College	Gaffney
Benedict College	Columbia	Lutheran Theological Southern Seminary	Columbia
Charleston, College of	Charleston	Morris College	Sumter
Charleston Southern University	Charleston	Newberry College	Newberry
Citadel, The Military College of South Carolina	Charleston	North Greenville University	Tigerville
Claflin University	Orangeburg	Presbyterian College	Clinton
Clemson University	Clemson	Sherman College of Straight Chiropractic	Spartanburg
Coastal Carolina University	Conway	South Carolina, Medical University of	Charleston
Coker College	Hartsville	South Carolina, University of	*
Columbia College	Columbia	South Carolina State University	Orangeburg
Columbia International University	Columbia	South University	Columbia
Converse College	Spartanburg	Southern Wesleyan University	Central
Erskine College	Due West	Voorhes College	Denmark
Francis Marion University	Florence	Winthrop University	Rock Hill
Furman University	Greenville	Wofford College	Spartanburg

*For campuses, see **South Carolina, University of.**

University of South Carolina, Columbia

The University of South Carolina was chartered in 1801 as South Carolina College. Shown here is the East Campus, part of the university's main campus in Columbia. The East Campus has a large central mall with high-rise academic buildings on either side.

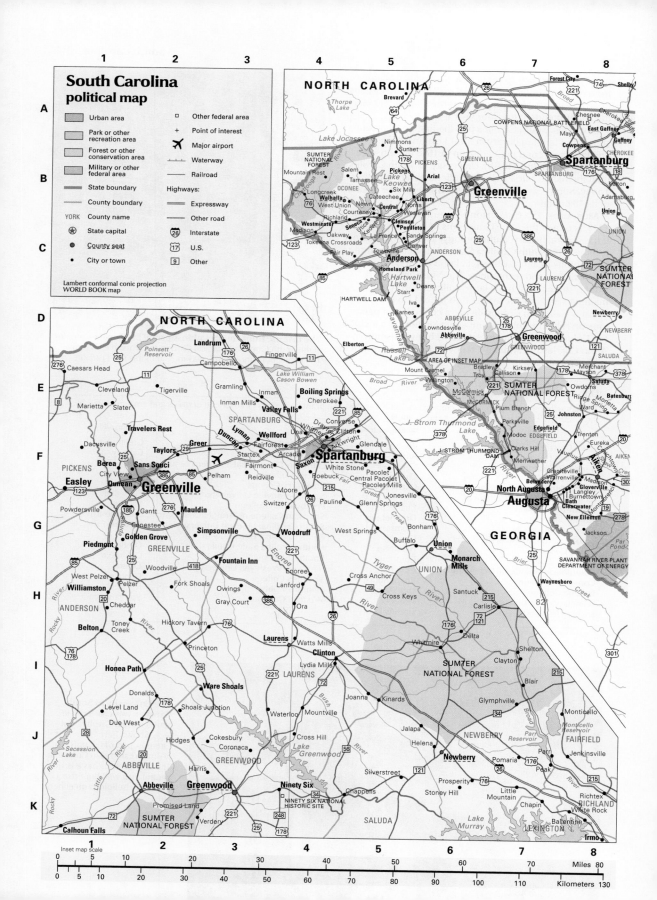

South Carolina
political map

Urban area

Park or other recreation area

Forest or other conservation area

Military or other federal area

State boundary

County boundary

YORK County name

State capital

County seat

City or town

Other federal area

Point of interest

Major airport

Waterway

Railroad

Highways:

Expressway

Other road

26 Interstate

17 U.S.

9 Other

Lambert conformal conic projection
WORLD BOOK map

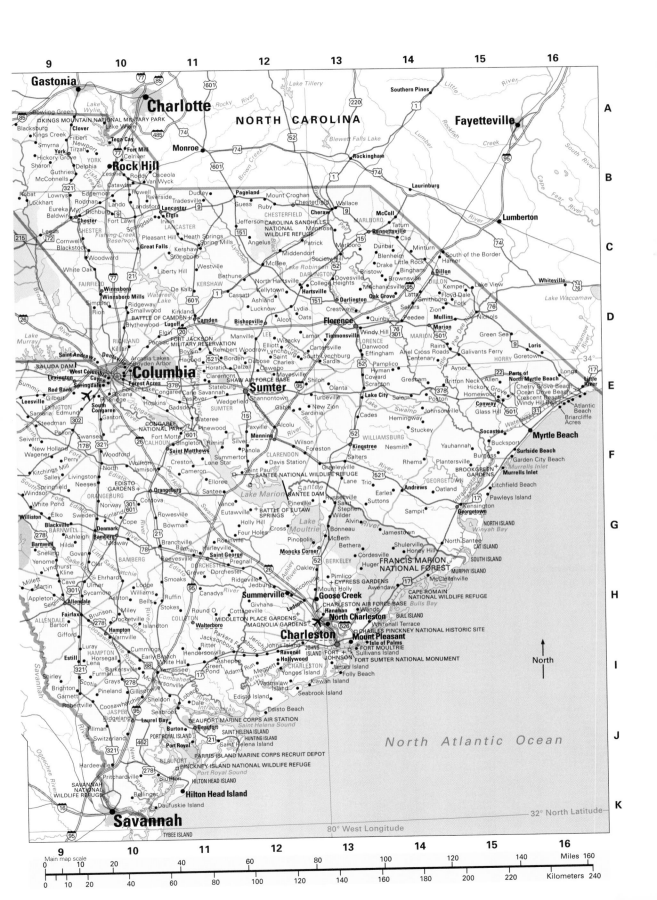

South Carolina map index

Metropolitan areas

Counties

Cities towns, and other populated places

*Does not appear on map; key shows general location.
†Census designated place—unincorporated, but recognized as a significant settled community by the U.S. Census Bureau.

°County seat.
Source: 2000 census. Metropolitan area figures are based on 2003 Office of Management and Budget reorganization of 2000 census data. Places without population figures are unincorporated areas.

Columbia Metropolitan Convention & Visitors Bureau

Columbia is South Carolina's capital, largest city, and commercial center. The city stands in the center of the state. Downtown Columbia includes Finlay Park with its unusual artificial waterfall, *shown in the foreground*. The popular park is the site of concerts, festivals, and other events.

Visitor's guide

South Carolina's attractions include wide, sparkling beaches, excellent golf courses, beautiful gardens, numerous historic sites, and charming cities. Abundant wildlife in South Carolina's fields and streams provides exciting action for hunters and fishing enthusiasts.

Among the favorite annual events in South Carolina are the Carolina Cup, a *steeplechase* (horse race) that takes place in Camden in late March, and the Carolina Dodge Dealers 500, a stock car race that is run in Darlington in May.

South Carolina Dept. of Parks, Recreation & Tourism

The Grand Strand at Myrtle Beach

South Carolina Dept. of Parks, Recreation & Tourism

Golfing on Hilton Head Island

Places to visit

Following are brief descriptions of some of South Carolina's many interesting places to visit:

Battlegrounds recall South Carolina's part in the Revolutionary War. *Kings Mountain National Military Park,* near Blacksburg, and *Cowpens National Battlefield,* near Gaffney, mark the sites of major Revolutionary War battles.

Beaches along South Carolina's Atlantic Coast offer swimming and sunbathing. The coastal area is also popular with vacationers for its golf courses and entertainment facilities. Myrtle Beach is the state's most famous beach. Other beaches, from north to south, include Cherry Grove, Ocean Drive, Crescent, Atlantic, Windy Hill, Isle of Palms, Folly, Kiawah Island, Seabrook Island, Edisto Island, Hunting Island, and Hilton Head Island.

Charles Towne Landing, near Charleston, marks the area where South Carolina's first permanent English settlement was established. It includes a replica of a colonial trading ship and the Animal Forest, which features animals native to the state in 1670.

Fort Moultrie, on Sullivan's Island, was the site of a brave defense by colonists against a British invasion during the Revolutionary War.

Fort Sumter, in Charleston Harbor, is the place where the Civil War began in 1861.

Gardens offer a glimpse of the beauty of South Carolina. Brookgreen Gardens, north of Georgetown, are a showplace of art and nature on the site of four former rice plantations. These gardens display hundreds of sculptures among plants typical of South Carolina. Middleton Place Gardens, near Charleston, are the oldest formal landscaped gardens in America. These gardens were begun in 1741 and feature azaleas, camellias, ancient oaks, and a pair of butterfly lakes. Magnolia Gardens, near Charleston, are part of Magnolia Plantation, which dates from the late 1600's. Magnolia Gardens include an herb garden, the Barbados Tropical Garden, and the Audubon Swamp Garden, which features cypress and tupelo trees in a swamp crossed by bridges, boardwalks, and dikes. Other beautiful gardens in the state include Cypress Gardens near Charleston, Edisto Gardens in Orangeburg, Swan Lake Iris Gardens in Sumter, and the Botanical Gardens at Clemson University.

National forests. South Carolina has two national forests—Francis Marion, near Charleston, and Sumter, which covers two areas in the Piedmont and one area in the Blue Ridge Mountains. Visitors to Sumter have the opportunity to raft down the Chattooga River.

State parks and forests. South Carolina has 46 state parks and historic sites, and 4 state forests. For information, write to South Carolina State Park Service, 1205 Pendleton Street, Columbia, SC 29201.

Annual events

January-June

Lowcountry Oyster Festival in Charleston (February); Garden Tours, statewide (February-May); Aiken Triple Crown in Aiken (March); Canadian-American Days in Myrtle Beach (March); Plantation Tours, statewide (March-May); Carolina Cup in Camden (March); Verizon Heritage in Hilton Head (April); Governor's Frog Jump Festival in Springfield (Saturday before Easter); Family Circle Cup in Charleston (April); Carolina Dodge Dealers 500 in Darlington (May); Bravo Arts Festival in Hilton Head (May); Gullah Festival in Beaufort (May); Pontiac GMC Freedom Weekend Aloft in Anderson (May); Spoleto Festival U.S.A. in Charleston (May-June); Sun-Fun Festival in Myrtle Beach (June).

July-December

Pageland Watermelon Festival in Pageland (July); Jubilee: Festival of Heritage in Columbia (August); Aiken's Makin' in Aiken (September); Scottish Games and Highland Gathering in Mount Pleasant (September); Come Horse Around Festival in Camden (September); Beaufort Shrimp Festival in Beaufort (October); State Fair in Columbia (October); Colonial Cup in Camden (November); Chitlin Strut in Salley (November); Colonial Christmas in Camden (December).

SouthCarolina Dept. of Parks, Recreation, & Tourism

Revolutionary War reenactment near Blacksburg

South Carolina Dept. of Parks, Recreation, & Tourism

Fort Sumter in Charleston Harbor

South Carolina Dept. of Parks, Recreation, & Tourism

Sculpture garden at Brookgreen Gardens in Murrells Inlet

© Robert Clark, Transparencies

State Fair in Columbia

Land regions. South Carolina has three main land regions: (1) the Atlantic Coastal Plain, (2) the Piedmont, and (3) the Blue Ridge. South Carolinians call the easternmost portion of the coastal plain the *Low Country*, and they call the Piedmont and Blue Ridge the *Up Country*.

The Atlantic Coastal Plain is a lowland that covers the southeastern two-thirds of South Carolina. It is part of the plain of the same name that stretches from New York to Florida. In South Carolina, the land rises gradually from southeast to northwest. One section of this plain, the Outer Coastal Plain, extends 50 to 70 miles (80 to 113 kilometers) inland from the coast, and is flat and broken by rivers. Swamps cover much of the land near the coast and extend far inland along the rivers. Another area, the Inner Coastal Plain, is hilly and rolling. A belt of forest called the Pine Barrens covers part of the central Atlantic Coastal Plain. A series of sand hills runs from southwest to northeast through Aiken, Columbia, Camden, and Cheraw, marking the western edge of the plain. These sand hills form part of an ancient beach, and indicate that the Atlantic Coastal Plain once lay under the ocean.

The Piedmont covers most of northwestern South Carolina. It is part of a land region that extends from New York to Alabama. The boundary between the Piedmont and the coastal plain is called the Fall Line. It forms the eastern edge of the Piedmont in South Carolina. The Fall Line is a zone where rivers tumble from higher land to the low-lying Atlantic Coastal Plain (see **Fall line**). In the southeast, the South Carolina Piedmont is a rolling upland with elevations from 400 to 1,200 feet (120 to 370 meters) above sea level. It rises to a hilly area 1,400 feet (430 meters) above sea level at its western edge.

The Piedmont slopes from northwest to southeast, which causes rivers in the region to flow rapidly. The swift-running rivers have been a major source of hydro-electric power. This power has helped make the Piedmont an important manufacturing area.

The Blue Ridge covers the northwestern corner of South Carolina. It is part of a larger region of the same name that runs from southern Pennsylvania to northern Georgia. The Blue Ridge Mountains, part of the Appalachian Mountain system, give the region its name. The Blue Ridge Mountains of South Carolina are less rugged and more easily crossed than those of North Carolina. Few peaks in South Carolina rise more than 3,000 feet (910 meters), and all are topped with forests. Sassafras Mountain, the highest point in the state, rises 3,560 feet (1,085 meters) above sea level in the Blue Ridge.

Coastline of South Carolina has many wide bays and inlets. Measured in a straight line, the state's general coastline totals 187 miles (301 kilometers). If all the coastal area washed by water were measured, the coastline would total 2,876 miles (4,628 kilometers). Important bays and harbors along the coast include, from north to south, Little River Inlet, Winyah Bay, Bulls Bay, Charleston Harbor, St. Helena Sound, and Port Royal Sound. The northern part of the coastline, from North Carolina to Winyah Bay, is called the Grand Strand. It has an almost unbroken beach. South of Winyah Bay, saltwater marshes cover much of the coastal area, and tidal rivers cut far inland. Here, the Santee River forms the largest delta on the east coast. Many islands lie along the coast. They include, from north to south, Pawleys Island, Bull Island, Isle of Palms, Sullivans Island, Kiawah Island, Edisto Island, Hunting Island, Fripp Island, Hilton Head Island, and Daufuskie Island. Parris Island, near Beaufort, is a major United States Marine training center.

Rivers, waterfalls, and lakes. Many large rivers cross South Carolina from northwest to southeast. The largest, the Santee, drains about 40 percent of the

© David R. Frazier

The Blue Ridge Mountains, part of South Carolina's Up Country, cut across the northwestern corner of the state.

Land regions of South Carolina

WORLD BOOK map

Map index

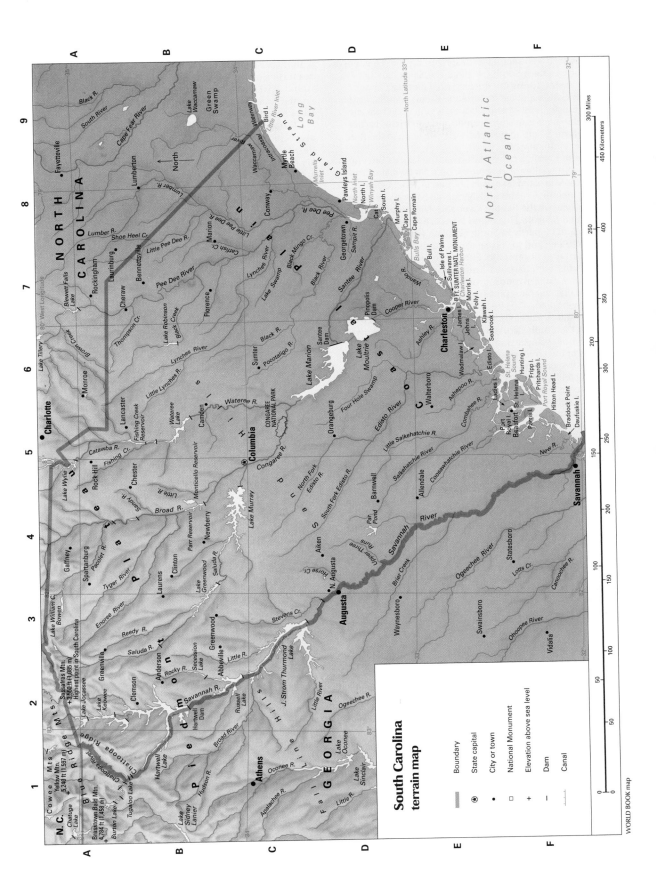

South Carolina
terrain map

Boundary

⊛ State capital

• City or town

□ National Monument

+ Elevation above sea level

| Dam

Canal

WORLD BOOK map

state's area. The second largest river, the Pee Dee, flows through eastern South Carolina. The Savannah River, third in size, forms the border with Georgia. Other South Carolina rivers include the Broad, Saluda, Combahee, Edisto, Ashley, and Cooper. Rivers that cross the Fall Line have a series of rapids and waterfalls. Larger and more beautiful waterfalls may be seen in the Blue Ridge Mountains.

South Carolina has no large natural lakes. Dams form many large lakes or reservoirs. Lake Marion, the largest artificially created lake, was created in 1942. Other reservoirs include Greenwood, Moultrie, Murray, Wateree, and Wylie on the Santee River and its tributaries. Hartwell and J. Strom Thurmond lakes are on the Savannah River and lie partly in South Carolina and partly in Georgia. Keowee and Jocassee are on Savannah tributaries.

Plant and animal life. Forests cover almost two-thirds of South Carolina. Trees found in the state include beeches, cottonwoods, cypresses, hemlocks, hickories, magnolias, maples, pines, oaks, sweet gums, and yellow-poplars.

Palmettos, yuccas, and other subtropical plants grow along the South Carolina coast. Thick growths of dwarf white honeysuckle and sweet bay spread over large areas in the Low Country. Spanish moss hangs from many live oak and cypress trees. Other South Carolina plants include yellow jessamine, the state flower, and the Venus's-flytrap, a rare insect-trapping plant that grows wild only in North and South Carolina. Patches of azaleas, mountain laurels, and rhododendrons blanket the South Carolina mountainsides in spring.

Large numbers of white-tailed deer live in the Piedmont and Coastal Plain forests. A few black bears and alligators inhabit swamps near the coast. Fox squirrels, foxes, and some wildcats live in the state's inland forests. Opossums, raccoons, and cottontail rabbits may be found throughout the state. More than 450 kinds of birds, including wild turkeys, mourning doves, quail, and ducks, live in South Carolina. Few other states have so many kinds of birds.

Bottlenose dolphins, sharks, sperm whales, and giant sea turtles often swim in South Carolina's coastal waters. About 350 kinds of saltwater fishes live in the state's coastal waters and salt marshes. Freshwater streams and lakes have bass, bream, rockfish, and trout.

Climate. South Carolina has a warm climate. The state's July temperatures average about 81 °F (27 °C) in the south and about 72 °F (22 °C) in the northwest. January temperatures average about 51 °F (11 °C) in the south and about 41 °F (5 °C) in the northwest. South Carolina's record high temperature, 111 °F (44 °C), was recorded in Blackville on Sept. 4, 1925; in Calhoun Falls on Sept. 8, 1925; and in Camden on June 28, 1954. The state's record low, –19 °F (–28 °C), was recorded at Caesars Head on Jan. 21, 1985.

Yearly *precipitation* (rain, melted snow, and other forms of moisture) in most parts of South Carolina averages about 45 inches (114 centimeters). The mountains receive more than 70 inches (178 centimeters) of precipitation annually. South Carolina gets little snow. Annual snowfall ranges from about 7 inches (18 centimeters) in the mountains to light traces of snow in the south.

Average monthly weather

	Charleston					Spartanburg				
	Temperatures				Days of rain or snow	Temperatures				Days of rain or snow
	°F		°C			°F		°C		
	High	Low	High	Low		High	Low	High	Low	
Jan.	59	37	15	3	11	50	31	10	–1	11
Feb.	62	39	17	4	9	55	34	13	1	9
Mar.	69	46	21	8	10	63	41	17	5	11
Apr.	76	52	24	11	7	71	47	22	8	9
May	83	61	28	16	9	78	56	26	13	10
June	88	69	31	21	11	85	64	29	18	10
July	91	73	33	23	14	89	69	32	21	12
Aug.	89	72	32	22	13	87	68	31	20	10
Sept.	85	67	29	19	10	81	62	27	17	9
Oct.	77	55	25	13	6	71	50	22	10	7
Nov.	70	46	21	8	7	61	41	16	5	9
Dec.	62	39	17	4	9	53	34	12	1	10

Average January temperatures

South Carolina has mild winters. The southern portion is the warmest. Temperatures decline to the northwest.

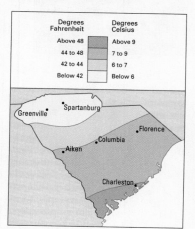

Degrees Fahrenheit	Degrees Celsius
Above 48	Above 9
44 to 48	7 to 9
42 to 44	6 to 7
Below 42	Below 6

Average July temperatures

Summers are warm in South Carolina, with generally even temperatures. The northwest is slightly cooler.

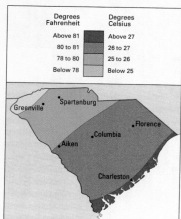

Degrees Fahrenheit	Degrees Celsius
Above 81	Above 27
80 to 81	26 to 27
78 to 80	25 to 26
Below 78	Below 25

Average yearly precipitation

Rainfall is usually abundant throughout the state. The southeast and the northwest receive the most precipitation.

WORLD BOOK maps

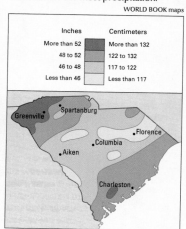

Inches	Centimeters
More than 52	More than 132
48 to 52	122 to 132
46 to 48	117 to 122
Less than 46	Less than 117

A variety of elements contribute to the strength of South Carolina's economy. Service industries, from trade to tourism, provide jobs for the vast majority of the state's workers. But manufacturing remains one of South Carolina's most important economic activities. Chemicals and transportation equipment are the state's most valuable manufactured items.

Natural resources of South Carolina include rich soils, minerals, vast forests, and a plentiful water supply.

Soils. The best soils in the state are in the Inner Coastal Plain section of the Atlantic Coastal Plain. Deposits of silt from rivers have left a black loam along the river valleys. The red to brown Piedmont soils are generally less fertile.

Minerals. Large deposits of *kaolin* (a kind of clay) occur in Aiken County. The Atlantic Coastal Plain region also has deposits of limestone, peat, and sand and gravel. The Piedmont and Blue Ridge areas have clays, granite, mica, sand, talc, topaz, and vermiculite.

Forests cover almost two-thirds of South Carolina's land area. Loblollies and other pines, oaks, hickories, dogwoods, and red maples grow in the Piedmont. Slash and longleaf pines, oaks, hickories, magnolias, and bay trees are common in the Coastal Plain. Baldcypresses, black tupelos, sweet gums, and yellow-poplars grow in the swamps. Hemlocks are common in the Blue Ridge Mountains, and palmettos grow along the coast.

Service industries account for the largest part of South Carolina's *gross domestic product*—the total value of all goods and services produced in the state in a year. Most of these industries are concentrated in the metropolitan areas. Retail trade and personal services benefit greatly from tourism. The beaches, golf courses, and fashionable resort hotels of Myrtle Beach and Hilton Head attract visitors the year around. Tourism in Charleston focuses on the city's colonial and antebellum heritage and architecture. Spending by tourists adds more than $10 billion to the state's economy each year.

Community, business, and personal services ranks first among South Carolina's service industry groups in terms of the gross domestic product. This group forms the leading source of employment in the state. These services consist of a variety of establishments, including engineering firms, private health care, and repair shops.

Trade, restaurants, and hotels ranks second among the service industry groups. The wholesale trade of automobiles, groceries, and machinery is important in the state. Major retail establishments in South Carolina include automobile dealerships, discount stores, and grocery stores. Many restaurants and hotels are in Charleston, Columbia, Greenville, and Myrtle Beach.

Ranking third among South Carolina's service industry groups are (1) finance, insurance, and real estate and (2) government. These groups each account for a roughly equal share of the gross domestic product.

Real estate plays an important part in South Carolina's economy because of the large amounts of money involved in the buying and selling of homes. Many banks are in Columbia, Charleston, and Greenville.

Government includes public schools and hospitals, and military bases. South Carolina is the home of several military bases. These bases include Marine Corps Recruit Depot Parris Island, and Fort Jackson, which has a U.S. Army Training Center, near Columbia. State government offices are based in Columbia. The public school system is a major employer.

Transportation and communication ranks fifth among South Carolina's service industry groups. Charleston, a major East Coast port, is the home of many large shipping companies. Telephone companies are an important part of the communications industry. More information about transportation and communication appears later in this section.

Manufacturing. Goods that are manufactured in South Carolina have a *value added by manufacture* of about $35 billion annually. Value added by manufacture represents the increase in value of raw materials after they become finished products.

Production and workers by economic activities

Economic activities	Percent of GDP* produced	Employed workers Number of people	Employed workers Percent of total
Community, business, & personal services	18	631,400	27
Manufacturing	18	277,700	12
Trade, restaurants, & hotels	17	533,800	23
Government	16	379,100	16
Finance, insurance, & real estate	16	178,700	8
Construction	6	163,400	7
Transportation & communication	5	94,100	4
Utilities	3	12,200	1
Agriculture	1	46,100	2
Mining	†	2,300	†
Total	100	2,318,800	100

*GDP = gross domestic product, the total value of goods and services produced in a year.
†Less than one-half of 1 percent.
Figures are for 2004; employment figures include full- and part-time workers.
Source: *World Book* estimates based on data from U.S. Bureau of Economic Analysis.

Art B'Arazien, Shostal

Textiles are a leading manufactured product of South Carolina. Most textile factories are in the northwest part of the state. This worker operates a weaving machine at a textile mill in Prosperity.

Chemicals are South Carolina's leading manufacturing product in terms of value added by manufacture. The leading sectors of the state's chemical industry include dyes, *pharmaceuticals* (medicinal drugs), plastic resins, and synthetic fibers. Leading centers of chemical manufacturing include Charleston, Columbia, Greenville, and Spartanburg.

Transportation equipment is the state's second-leading manufacture. Motor vehicles and parts are the leading products of the transportation sector. BMW, one of Europe's top automakers, has a plant in Greer.

Plastics and rubber products rank third among South Carolina's manufactured products. The state's factories produce plastic sheets and rubber tires. The North American headquarters of Michelin, a major manufacturer of tires and other products, is in South Greenville.

Machinery is the fourth leading manufactured product in South Carolina. Engines, transmission equipment, and turbines are the leading products in this category.

Textiles are an important manufactured product in the state. South Carolina ranks among the leading textile-producing states. The state's textile manufacturers produce a wide variety of fabrics from blends of natural fibers, as well as from synthetic fibers. Most of South Carolina's textile factories are found in the northwestern part of the state.

South Carolina's other manufactured goods include electrical equipment, fabricated metal products, paper products, and processed foods.

Agriculture. South Carolina has approximately 24,000 farms. Farmland covers about a fourth of the state's total area. Much of the rest is covered by forests. Forestry is an important economic activity for many of the state's people.

Livestock products provide more than half of South Carolina's farm income. *Broilers* (young, tender chickens) are the state's most valuable farm product. Cattle, eggs, hogs, and turkeys are also an important source of livestock income. The northern half of South Carolina has the most poultry and egg farms. Beef and dairy cattle are found throughout the state. Hogs are raised primarily in the eastern part of the state.

Crops provide nearly half of South Carolina's agricultural income. Greenhouse and nursery plants are the most valuable crop in South Carolina. Shrubs, flowers, and young plants grown in greenhouses and nurseries, and turf grass are major sources of agricultural income in the state. Tobacco is the state's second leading crop. South Carolina ranks among the leading tobacco-growing states. The eastern part of the state produces most of the tobacco. Farmers also raise significant amounts of corn, cotton, and soybeans. Other important crops in South Carolina include nuts, peaches, tomatoes, watermelons, and wheat.

Mining. Crushed stone and portland cement are South Carolina's most valuable mined products. Crushed stone is mined throughout the state. South Carolina is a leading producer of portland cement. South Carolina is also a leading producer of fire clays, kaolin, masonry cement, mica, and vermiculite.

Fishing industry. South Carolina has an annual fish catch valued at about $20 million. Shrimp is South Carolina's most valuable catch. Other catches include clams, crabs, oysters, and snapper. The Charleston and Mount Pleasant areas form the state's leading fishing port.

South Carolina Department of Parks, Recreation, and Tourism

Tobacco is one of South Carolina's most important farm products. The state is a leading United States tobacco grower.

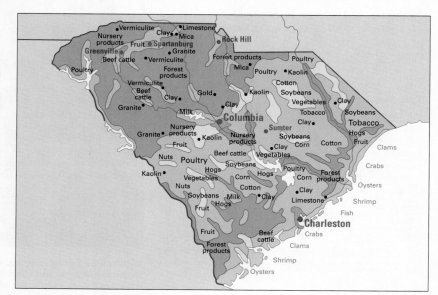

Economy of South Carolina

This map shows the economic uses of land in South Carolina and where the state's leading farm, mineral, and forest products are produced. Major manufacturing centers are shown in red.

Mostly cropland

Woodland mixed with cropland and grazing

Mostly forest land

Marsh and swamp land

Urban area

• Manufacturing center

• Mineral deposit

© Bill Barley, Shostal

The V. C. Sumner Nuclear Power Plant near Columbia is one of several nuclear facilities in South Carolina. Nuclear power plants provide about 50 percent of the state's electric power.

Electric power and utilities. South Carolina's utilities provide electric, gas, and water service. About 50 percent of South Carolina's electric power is generated by plants that use nuclear energy. About 40 percent of the state's electric power comes from plants that burn coal. Most of the remaining power comes from hydroelectric plants and plants that burn natural gas.

Transportation. South Carolina has about 66,000 miles (106,000 kilometers) of roads and highways. Thirteen rail lines provide freight service on about 2,400 miles (3,860 kilometers) of railroads in the state. South Carolina's chief airports are at Charleston, Columbia, Greenville-Spartanburg, and Myrtle Beach. The state's leading seaports are Charleston and Georgetown. The Atlantic Intracoastal Waterway is the chief inland shipping route (see **Atlantic Intracoastal Waterway**).

Communication. About 90 newspapers, including about 15 dailies, are published in South Carolina. The *South Carolina Weekly Journal,* the state's first newspaper, was published for only six months, sometime between 1730 and 1732. Today, the largest daily papers include *The Greenville News, The Post and Courier* of Charleston, and *The State* of Columbia.

The state's first radio station, WSPA, began operating in Spartanburg in 1930. WCOS-TV, the first television station, opened in Columbia in 1953. The state now has about 245 radio stations and 20 TV stations. Many communities have access to cable TV and the Internet.

Government

Constitution of South Carolina was adopted in 1895. The state's six earlier constitutions were adopted in 1776, 1778, 1790, 1861, 1865, and 1868.

The Constitution has been *amended* (changed) about 350 times. The state legislature or a constitutional convention may propose an amendment. An amendment proposed by the legislature requires approval by two-thirds of the members of both the Senate and House of Representatives. Next, the amendment must have the approval of a majority of the people voting on it in a statewide election. To become law, the amendment must then be approved by a majority of members of the state legislature.

A two-thirds vote in each house of the legislature is required to call a constitutional convention. The convention also must be approved by a majority of the people voting on the issue in a statewide election.

Executive. The governor of South Carolina is elected to a four-year term. The governor may not serve more than two terms in a row.

South Carolina voters also elect the lieutenant governor, adjutant general, attorney general, commissioner of agriculture, comptroller general, secretary of state, state treasurer, and superintendent of education. All these officials serve four-year terms.

Legislature, called the General Assembly, consists of a 46-member Senate and a 124-member House of Representatives. Members of both houses are elected from single-member districts. Senators serve four-year terms, and representatives two-year terms.

Until the mid-1960's, one senator was elected from each of the state's 46 counties. In 1965, a special federal court ordered the legislature to *reapportion* (redivide) the Senate to provide equal representation based on population. The court approved a temporary plan for the 1966 elections, and all senators were elected to two-year terms. In 1968, the court approved the legislature's plan of electing 46 senators from 20 districts. In 1972, the legislature reduced the number of senatorial districts from 20 to 16. In 1983, the number of districts was increased to 46.

The legislature meets each year, starting on the second Tuesday in January. The legislature must adjourn by the first Thursday in June. Any extension of the session requires two-thirds approval by both houses. The governor may call special sessions.

Courts. The Supreme Court is South Carolina's highest court. It has a chief justice and four associate justices. The justices are elected by the legislature to 10-year terms. The South Carolina Court of Appeals shares appellate jurisdiction with the Supreme Court. The Court of Appeals has nine judges elected by the legislature to six-year terms. Circuit courts of common pleas and general sessions are the chief trial courts. The legislature elects 46 circuit court judges to six-year terms. Supreme Court justices are usually chosen from among the circuit court judges. Circuit court judges are often chosen from the legislature.

Magistrates' courts hear minor civil and criminal cases. The magistrates who head these courts are appointed by the governor, with the approval of the state Senate.

Local government. County governments in South Carolina are headed by boards of county commissioners, county councils, or similar local boards. County commissioners or council members and their assistants carry out such functions as enforcing laws and regulating taxes. Many of the county councils appoint professional administrators to direct the county government agencies. Chief county officials include the auditor, clerk of court, county attorney, sheriff, and treasurer.

South Carolina's cities and towns operate under charters. Most of the state's larger cities have the council-manager form of government. Most of the smaller cities have the mayor-council form.

Revenue. Taxes account for about two-fifths of the state government's *general revenue* (income). Most of the rest comes from federal grants and other U.S. government programs. A general sales tax and a personal income tax each provide about a third of the state's tax revenue. Other important sources of tax revenue include taxes on alcoholic beverages, business licenses, corporation licenses, inheritances, insurance premiums, mo-

tor fuels, motor vehicle licenses, public utilities, and tobacco products. South Carolina uses funds from the motor-fuels tax to build and maintain highways.

Politics. The Democratic Party has controlled South Carolina politics throughout most of the state's history. But the Republican Party gained strength during the 1950's and 1960's. In 1964, Senator Strom Thurmond of South Carolina resigned from the Democratic Party and became a Republican. In 1974, James B. Edwards became the first Republican to be elected governor of the state in 100 years.

From 1880 through 1964, Democratic candidates won South Carolina's electoral votes in every presidential election except 1948. Senator Thurmond, the candidate of the States' Rights Democratic (Dixiecrat) Party, won the votes in 1948. Since 1964, the Republican candidate has won the state's electoral votes in almost all the presidential elections. For South Carolina's voting record in presidential elections, see **Electoral College** (table).

The state governors of South Carolina

Governor	Party	Term	Governor	Party	Term
John Rutledge*	None	1776-1778	Benjamin F. Perry	Democratic	1865
Rawlins Lowndes*	None	1778-1779	James L. Orr	Democratic	1865-1868
John Rutledge	None	1779-1782	Robert K. Scott	Republican	1868-1872
John Mathews	None	1782-1783	Franklin J. Moses, Jr.	Republican	1872-1874
Benjamin Guerard	None	1783-1785	Daniel H. Chamberlain	Republican	1874-1876
William Moultrie	None	1785-1787	Wade Hampton	Democratic	1876-1879
Thomas Pinckney	None	1787-1789	William D. Simpson	Democratic	1879-1880
Charles Pinckney	None	1789-1792	Thomas B. Jeter	Democratic	1880
William Moultrie	Federalist	1792-1794	Johnson Hagood	Democratic	1880-1882
Arnoldus Vander Horst	Federalist	1794-1796	Hugh S. Thompson	Democratic	1882-1886
Charles Pinckney	Dem.-Rep.**	1796-1798	John C. Sheppard	Democratic	1886
Edward Rutledge	Dem.-Rep.	1798-1800	John P. Richardson	Democratic	1886-1890
John Drayton	Dem.-Rep.	1800-1802	Benjamin R. Tillman	Democratic	1890-1894
James B. Richardson	Dem.-Rep.	1802-1804	John G. Evans	Democratic	1894-1897
Paul Hamilton	Dem.-Rep.	1804-1806	William H. Ellerbe	Democratic	1897-1899
Charles Pinckney	Dem.-Rep.	1806-1808	Miles B. McSweeney	Democratic	1899-1903
John Drayton	Dem.-Rep.	1808-1810	Duncan C. Heyward	Democratic	1903-1907
Henry Middleton	Dem.-Rep.	1810-1812	Martin F. Ansel	Democratic	1907-1911
Joseph Alston	Dem.-Rep.	1812-1814	Coleman L. Blease	Democratic	1911-1915
David R. Williams	Dem.-Rep.	1814-1816	Charles A. Smith	Democratic	1915
Andrew Pickens	Dem.-Rep.	1816-1818	Richard I. Manning	Democratic	1915-1919
John Geddes	Dem.-Rep.	1818-1820	Robert A. Cooper	Democratic	1919-1922
Thomas Bennett	Dem.-Rep.	1820-1822	Wilson G. Harvey	Democratic	1922-1923
John L. Wilson	Dem.-Rep.	1822-1824	Thomas G. McLeod	Democratic	1923-1927
Richard I. Manning	Dem.-Rep.	1824-1826	John G. Richards	Democratic	1927-1931
John Taylor	Dem.-Rep.	1826-1828	Ibra C. Blackwood	Democratic	1931-1935
Stephen D. Miller	Democratic	1828-1830	Olin D. Johnston	Democratic	1935-1939
James Hamilton, Jr.	Democratic	1830-1832	Burnet R. Maybank	Democratic	1939-1941
Robert Y. Hayne	Democratic	1832-1834	J. Emile Harley	Democratic	1941-1942
George McDuffie	Democratic	1834-1836	Richard M. Jefferies	Democratic	1942-1943
Pierce M. Butler	Democratic	1836-1838	Olin D. Johnston	Democratic	1943-1945
Patrick Noble	Democratic	1838-1840	Ransome J. Williams	Democratic	1945-1947
B. K. Henagan	Democratic	1840	Strom Thurmond	Democratic	1947-1951
John P. Richardson	Democratic	1840-1842	James F. Byrnes	Democratic	1951-1955
James H. Hammond	Democratic	1842-1844	George B. Timmerman, Jr.	Democratic	1955-1959
William Aiken	Democratic	1844-1846	Ernest F. Hollings	Democratic	1959-1963
David Johnson	Democratic	1846-1848	Donald S. Russell	Democratic	1963-1965
Whitemarsh B. Seabrook	Democratic	1848-1850	Robert E. McNair	Democratic	1965-1971
John H. Means	Democratic	1850-1852	John C. West	Democratic	1971-1975
John L. Manning	Democratic	1852-1854	James B. Edwards	Republican	1975-1979
James H. Adams	Democratic	1854-1856	Richard W. Riley	Democratic	1979-1987
Robert F. W. Allston	Democratic	1856-1858	Carroll A. Campbell, Jr.	Republican	1987-1995
William H. Gist	Democratic	1858-1860	David Beasley	Republican	1995-1999
Francis W. Pickens	Democratic	1860-1862	Jim Hodges	Democratic	1999-2003
Milledge L. Bonham	Democratic	1862-1864	Mark Sanford	Republican	2003-
Andrew G. Magrath	Democratic	1864-1865			

*From 1776 to 1779, the chief executive of South Carolina was called the president.   **Democratic-Republican

Indian days. More than 30 Indian tribes lived in what is now South Carolina before white settlers came. The chief tribes were the Catawba, Cherokee, and Yamasee (or Yemasee). The Catawba belonged to the Siouan Indian language family, the Cherokee to the Iroquoian language family, and the Yamasee to the Muskhogean language family. The Indians lived in semipermanent log shelters. Most of them raised crops.

Exploration and settlement. In 1521, Francisco Gordillo led a Spanish expedition that explored the Carolina coast. Gordillo came from Spanish-held Santo Domingo in the Dominican Republic. In 1526, Lucas Vásquez de Ayllón, a judge from Santo Domingo on the island of Hispaniola, founded the first European settlement in what is now the United States. He named it San Miguel de Gualdape. Ayllón led about 600 people from Hispaniola to what historians believe may have been the coast of present-day Georgia or South Carolina. The colony lasted only about half a year. Disease and bad weather forced the settlers to return to Hispaniola. Between 1562 and 1565, French explorers tried to settle at Port Royal and at another place farther south. They failed, partly because they lacked food.

England claimed the entire North American mainland in the early 1600's. The English based their claim on John Cabot's voyage to America in 1497 (see **Cabot, John**). In 1629, King Charles I of England granted North American land to Sir Robert Heath. Part of the grant was a strip of land that included what are now the states of South Carolina and North Carolina. The strip extended to the Pacific Ocean. The land was named *Province of Carolana* (land of Charles). The spelling was changed to *Carolina* in 1663. Heath made no attempts to establish settlements in the area of Carolina.

In 1663, King Charles II granted Carolina to eight English noblemen called *lords proprietors.* In 1669, the proprietors sent settlers to America. The settlers arrived in 1670 and set up South Carolina's first permanent white settlement at Albemarle Point, near what is now Charleston. The colonists moved to Oyster Point in 1680, and named the settlement Charles Town. The spelling was changed to *Charleston* in 1783.

Colonial days. The proprietors wanted to limit self-government in Carolina. They also failed to protect the settlers when enemies threatened the colony. During Queen Anne's War (1702-1713), the colonists turned back French and Spanish forces at Charleston. They successfully defended themselves against attacks by the Yamasee Indians and against several pirate raids between 1715 and 1718. During these battles, the colonists received little help from the powerful proprietors. In 1719, the proprietors rejected laws requested by the colonists. As a result, the colonists rebelled that year.

The South Carolina area was Britain's southern line of defense against French and Spanish attacks. Partly as a result, King George I was willing to accept the overthrow of proprietary rule in 1719 and to make South Carolina a royal colony. Britain ruled the colony, but allowed the people self-government. North and South Carolina had separate governors since 1710. In 1729, the British government bought the property rights of the proprietors. In 1732, the southern part of South Carolina became the colony of Georgia.

During the mid-1700's, many South Carolinians moved

Bettmann Archive

Blackbeard, a fierce British pirate, terrorized the Carolina and Virginia coasts in 1717 and 1718. He received his name from his habit of braiding his long, black beard.

from coastal settlements to the Up Country. The Up Country population was also increased by waves of settlers from Pennsylvania and Virginia. By 1775, about 70,000 whites and about 100,000 blacks lived in South Carolina. Most of the blacks were slaves.

The Revolutionary War. During the 1760's, Britain passed a series of laws that caused unrest in South Carolina and the other American colonies. Most of these laws set up new taxes or restricted colonial trade. Some South Carolinians, called *Tories,* urged loyalty to Britain in spite of the laws. But the majority of the people, called *Whigs,* favored independence.

The Revolutionary War began in Massachusetts in 1775. South Carolina became the scene of many important battles. In June 1776, British land and sea forces attacked Charleston. But the colonists defeated the British in the Battle of Sullivan's Island. A second British attack on Charleston was turned back in 1779. The British captured the city in 1780. In August of that year, the British defeated colonial troops under General Horatio Gates at Camden. The British and their Tory allies then controlled most of South Carolina. Colonial victories in the Battle of Kings Mountain (Oct. 7, 1780) and at Cowpens (Jan. 17, 1781) turned the tide of war in the South. In 1781, colonial troops under General Nathanael Greene drove the main British army from South Carolina to Virginia. The South Carolina militia forced smaller British units from

The Battle of Kings Mountain was fought on Oct. 7, 1780. The battle marked a turning point in the Revolutionary War in the southern part of the U.S. An army of 900 American frontiersmen defeated and captured or killed 1,100 British troops.

Anne S. K. Brown Military Collection, Brown University Library

the area. Famous leaders of the militia included Francis Marion, called the *Swamp Fox;* Thomas Sumter, called the *Gamecock;* and Andrew Pickens. The British evacuated Charleston in 1782. During the war, more than 200 battles or smaller fights took place in the state. Most were fought between bands of Whigs and Tories.

On July 9, 1778, South Carolina *ratified* (approved) the Articles of Confederation, the forerunner of the United States Constitution. South Carolina became the eighth state of the Union on May 23, 1788, when it ratified the U.S. Constitution.

Nullification. South Carolina strongly supported states' rights and free trade. The state's people opposed federal tariffs because South Carolina's economy depended heavily on trade with European nations. Tariffs, of course, discouraged this trade. A depression hit the United States in 1819, and South Carolinians blamed federal tariffs for their economic problems. In 1828, Congress passed a law that raised tariffs even higher than before. This law was called the "tariff of abominations." Reaction against the federal government spread throughout the state. In 1828, Vice President John C. Calhoun, a South Carolinian, wrote the South Carolina Exposition. This document declared that no state was bound by a federal law which the state regarded as unconstitutional. After another high tariff law was passed in 1832, South Carolina adopted an *Ordinance of Nullification.* This ordinance declared the tariff acts of 1828 and 1832 "null and void." President Andrew Jackson threatened to send troops to South Carolina to enforce the law. But Congress passed a compromise tariff bill in 1833, and the state repealed the Ordinance of Nullification. See **Nullification.**

The Civil War. Shortly after the nullification crisis, an antislavery movement gained strength in the North. In 1850, a dispute between the North and South arose over whether slavery should be allowed in parts of the West. South Carolina threatened to *secede* (withdraw) from the Union. But little support came from other Southern states, and South Carolina took no further action. On

Nov. 6, 1860, Abraham Lincoln, a Northern Republican, was elected president. South Carolina feared Lincoln would use federal power to abolish slavery. On Dec. 20, 1860, South Carolina became the first state to secede from the Union. By the spring of 1861, 10 other Southern states had joined the secession movement and had formed the Confederate States of America (see **Confederate States of America**).

The Civil War began on April 12, 1861, when Confederate troops fired on Fort Sumter in Charleston Harbor. Fighting raged along the South Carolina coast throughout the war. A blockade of Charleston Harbor by the Union fleet ruined South Carolina's economy. In 1865, Union troops led by William T. Sherman destroyed many plantations in the state. Much of Columbia, the capital, burned while Union troops occupied it. About a fourth of the 63,000 troops from South Carolina died during the war.

Reconstruction. During the Reconstruction period after the Civil War, Union troops occupied South Carolina and the other Southern states. The Republican Party in the state was made up chiefly of blacks, Union sympathizers from the South called *scalawags,* and former Northerners called *carpetbaggers.* The Republicans controlled the government during part of the Reconstruction period, and had the support of the Union troops. In 1868, South Carolina adopted a new state constitution. It gave blacks the right to vote. Congress readmitted South Carolina to the Union on June 25, 1868.

In 1876, Wade Hampton, a Democrat and a Confederate cavalry hero, defeated the Republican candidate for governor. The Republicans challenged the election results, and South Carolina had rival state governments for several months. President Rutherford B. Hayes withdrew the federal troops from South Carolina in March 1877. Republican power then collapsed, and the Democrats gained control of the state.

Industrial growth began in South Carolina during the late 1800's. Farm profits had declined greatly after the Civil War. The decline was caused chiefly by compe-

Historic South Carolina

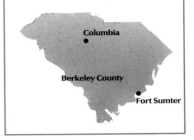

General Francis Marion, known as the *Swamp Fox,* led daring raids against the British in South Carolina during the Revolutionary War. He was born in Berkeley County.

Santee Dam, completed in 1941, harnessed the Santee River to provide hydroelectric power. The dam also opened an abandoned canal to navigation.

Slave markets flourished in South Carolina and other Southern states in the years before the Civil War. By 1860, South Carolina had about 402,000 slaves, more than half the state's population.

The first permanent settlement in South Carolina was established at Albemarle Point in 1670. It moved to Oyster Point, now Charleston, in 1680.

The Civil War began on April 12, 1861, when Confederate batteries shelled Fort Sumter in Charleston Harbor. Federal troops surrendered on April 13 and withdrew from the fort the next day.

Important dates in South Carolina

WORLD BOOK illustrations by Kevin Chadwick

1521 Francisco Gordillo of Spain explored the Carolina coast.

1670 English settlers established the first permanent white settlement in South Carolina, at Albemarle Point.

1719 South Carolina became a separate royal province.

1780 American forces won the Battle of Kings Mountain, a turning point in the Revolutionary War.

1788 South Carolina became the 8th state on May 23.

1832 South Carolina passed the Ordinance of Nullification.

1860 South Carolina seceded from the Union on Dec. 20.

1861 The Civil War began on April 12 when Confederate forces fired on Fort Sumter.

1868 South Carolina was readmitted to the Union.

1877 Reconstruction ended in South Carolina.

1895 South Carolina adopted its present constitution.

1953 Operations began at the Savannah River Plant, which produces nuclear materials.

1970 Three blacks won election to the state House of Representatives. They became the first blacks to serve in South Carolina's House since 1902.

1974 James B. Edwards became the first Republican to be elected governor since 1874.

1983 The Reverend I. DeQuincey Newman became the first black elected to the state Senate since 1888.

1989 Hurricane Hugo struck South Carolina, killing 18 people and causing $5 billion in property damage.

2003 Congaree National Park, the first national park in the state, was established.

© Weiner, Gamma/Liaison

Hurricane Hugo struck South Carolina in September 1989. The hurricane caused $5 billion in property damage in the state. This house was damaged by the hurricane. It stood in Charleston, one of the hardest hit areas.

tition from many new farms in the Western United States. About 1880, South Carolina business owners began expanding the textile industry. Hydroelectric power, rather than direct water power, became the source of energy for many textile mills. Thousands of poor farmers welcomed the chance to work in the mills, even at low wages. A number of textile companies moved from the North to South Carolina, partly to take advantage of this inexpensive labor.

During the late 1800's, a group of Democrats called *Tillmanites* gained control of South Carolina politics. The group was led by Benjamin R. Tillman. Before 1890, a group called the Bourbon Democrats ran South Carolina politics. The Bourbon Democrats were lawyers, planters, and business executives whose strength was in the Low Country. Owners of small farms, especially those in the Up Country, protested the Bourbon rule after farm prices dropped. Tillman campaigned for widespread reforms in state government, and was elected governor in 1890. The Tillmanites rewrote the state Constitution, and all but eliminated black voting rights. Tillman became a U.S. senator in 1895, and remained a powerful force in South Carolina politics until his death in 1918.

After the United States entered World War I in 1917, the state's textile mills produced large amounts of cloth for the armed forces. By 1920, the textile industry employed about 54,600 workers and was still growing.

The boll weevil damaged much cotton in South Carolina during the 1920's. Many farmers began raising other crops, including fruits, tobacco, and wheat. But cotton remained the main farm product. The Great Depression of the 1930's caused widespread unemployment in South Carolina. Economic conditions improved as the Depression eased in the late 1930's.

The mid-1900's brought great economic growth to South Carolina as the state shifted from a chiefly agricultural to a more industrial economy. In 1941, the South Carolina Public Service Authority completed the Santee-Cooper navigational canal and power dam between the Santee and Cooper rivers. This $57-million project supplied electric power and helped industry. During World War II (1939-1945), many military bases were established in the state. Some remained open after the war.

In 1953, operations began at the Savannah River Plant

of the Atomic Energy Commission near Aiken. This plant, now operated by Westinghouse Savannah River Company for the Department of Energy, helped the state become a leader in producing nuclear materials.

During the 1960's, South Carolina industry continued to expand, largely through programs sponsored by the State Development Board. Various companies built manufacturing facilities worth nearly $4 billion.

In the mid-1900's, the Democratic Party lost much of its traditional control of South Carolina politics. In 1948, Governor Strom Thurmond of South Carolina was nominated for president by the States' Rights Democratic (Dixiecrat) Party. Thurmond received the electoral votes of four states—Alabama, Louisiana, Mississippi, and South Carolina. In the 1952, 1956, and 1960 presidential elections, the Democrats barely won South Carolina. Then, in 1964, the state's electoral votes went to the Republican candidate, Barry M. Goldwater, by a large majority. The state also supported Republican Richard M. Nixon for president in 1968. Thurmond, who had first been elected to the U.S. Senate in 1954, left the Democratic Party in 1964 and became a Republican. In the mid-1900's, several Republicans were elected to the state legislature and some were elected mayors and city council members.

Since the late 1940's, South Carolina blacks have been voting in growing numbers. During the 1960's, blacks were elected to several local offices, including city council member and school trustee. In 1970, three blacks won election to the state House of Representatives, becoming the first blacks to serve as representatives since 1902.

South Carolina schools changed greatly following the 1954 decision of the Supreme Court of the United States prohibiting compulsory school segregation. Traditionally, the state had operated separate schools for blacks and whites. In the 1960's, most of South Carolina's school districts became integrated.

The late 1900's. During the early 1970's, Republicans increasingly began to offer candidates at almost all levels of government. Many of these candidates sought offices traditionally held by Democrats without opposition. In 1972, Nixon carried South Carolina again. In 1974, James B. Edwards became the first Republican to be elected governor of the state in 100 years. Thurmond continued to win reelection to the U.S. Senate. In 1996, he won his eighth term. He was then 93 and the oldest person ever to serve in Congress. In 1983, I. DeQuincey Newman, a Methodist minister, became the first black to serve in the state Senate since 1888.

Black and white Republicans continued to take a larger role in state politics. More and more African American voters supported the Democratic Party. As a result, a growing number of black candidates were elected and were having an influence on party policies.

South Carolina worked to encourage further industrial growth. At the same time, the state became increasingly concerned about air and water pollution.

In the 1980's, South Carolina began working to provide better education for its students. In 1984, the state passed the Education Improvement Act. This act raised the state's education standards and provided more money for elementary and secondary education.

In September 1989, Hurricane Hugo struck the state. Charleston and other parts of the central coast were especially hard hit. The hurricane killed 18 people in South Carolina and caused $5 billion in property damage.

The early 2000's. After almost 50 years in the Senate, Strom Thurmond retired in January 2003, at age 100. He died the following June.

In late 2003, President George W. Bush signed legislation designating Congaree Swamp National Monument a national park. Congaree National Park, which lies southeast of Columbia in central South Carolina, became the first national park in the state.

Charles F. Kovacik and George C. Rogers, Jr.

Study aids

Related articles in *World Book* include:

Biographies

Allston, Washington	Middleton, Arthur
Butler, Pierce	Moultrie, William
Byrnes, James F.	Pinckney, Charles
Calhoun, John C.	Pinckney, Charles C.
Gadsden (family)	Pinckney, Eliza Lucas
Grimké (family)	Pinckney, Thomas
Hampton, Wade	Rutledge, Edward
Hayne, Robert Y.	Rutledge, John
Heyward, DuBose	Smalls, Robert
Heyward, Thomas, Jr.	Thurmond, Strom
Jackson, Andrew	Vesey, Denmark
Longstreet, James	Watson, John B.
Lynch, Thomas, Jr.	Westmoreland, William
Marion, Francis	Childs

Cities

Charleston	Columbia

History

Civil War, American	Fort Sumter
Confederate States of	Nullification
America	Reconstruction
Fort Moultrie	Revolutionary War in America

Physical features

Atlantic Intracoastal	Piedmont Region
Waterway	Savannah River
Blue Ridge Mountains	

Other related articles

Fort Sumter National Monument
Parris Island Marine Corps Recruit Depot

Outline

I. People
 A. Population
 B. Schools
 C. Libraries
 D. Museums
II. Visitor's guide
 A. Places to visit
 B. Annual events
III. Land and climate
 A. Land regions
 B. Coastline
 C. Rivers, waterfalls, and lakes
 D. Plant and animal life
 E. Climate
IV. Economy
 A. Natural resources
 B. Service industries
 C. Manufacturing
 D. Agriculture
 E. Mining
 F. Fishing industry
 G. Electric power and utilities
 H. Transportation
 I. Communication
V. Government
 A. Constitution
 B. Executive
 C. Legislature
 D. Courts
 E. Local government
 F. Revenue
 G. Politics
VI. History

Questions

Where did the Civil War begin?
What are South Carolina's four largest cities?
What were *free schools?*
What are some of the plants native to South Carolina?
Why is South Carolina called the *Palmetto State?*
When was the Santee-Cooper Project completed?
Who were the *lords proprietors?*
What is South Carolina's chief economic activity?
Where was the state's first permanent white settlement?
What are the three main land regions in the state?

Additional resources

Level I
Blashfield, Jean. *The South Carolina Colony.* Child's World, 2004.
Fredeen, Charles. *South Carolina.* 2nd ed. Lerner, 2002.
Hoffman, Nancy. *South Carolina.* Benchmark Bks., 2001.
Weatherly, Myra S. *South Carolina.* Children's Pr., 2002.

Level II
Anzilotti, Cara. *In the Affairs of the World: Women, Patriarchy, and Power in Colonial South Carolina.* Greenwood, 2002.
Edgar, Walter B. *South Carolina.* Univ. of S.C. Pr., 1998.
Kovacik, Charles F., and Winberry, J. J. *South Carolina.* Univ. of S.C. Pr., 1989. A geographical study.
Morgan, Philip D. *Slave Counterpoint: Black Culture in the Eighteenth-Century Chesapeake and Lowcountry.* Univ. of N.C. Pr., 1998.
Waldrep, George C. *Southern Workers and the Search for Community: Spartanburg County, South Carolina.* Univ. of Ill. Pr., 2000.

South Carolina, University of, is a state-supported coeducational system of higher education. Its campus in Columbia, South Carolina, has colleges of applied professional sciences, business administration, criminal justice, education, engineering, health, humanities and social sciences, journalism and mass communications, library and information science, nursing, pharmacy, science and mathematics, and social work; schools of law and medicine; and a graduate school. The university also has four-year campuses in Aiken, Beaufort, and Spartanburg, and four campuses that focus mainly on the first two years of undergraduate study. The university grants bachelor's, master's, and doctor's degrees. It was chartered in 1801 as South Carolina College.

Critically reviewed by the University of South Carolina

See also **South Carolina** (Libraries; picture).

South China Sea. See China Sea.

Lee Foster, FPG

Mount Rushmore National Memorial, near Rapid City, South Dakota, honors the United States Presidents George Washington, Thomas Jefferson, Theodore Roosevelt, and Abraham Lincoln.

South Dakota   *The Mount Rushmore State*

South Dakota is a Midwestern state of the United States. It is an area of many startling and beautiful physical contrasts. The Missouri River flows south through the middle of South Dakota. Low hills, lakes formed by ancient glaciers, and vast stretches of fertile cropland lie east of the Missouri River. West of the river are deep canyons and rolling plains. The Black Hills rise abruptly in the southwestern part of the state. Southeast of the Black Hills are the ravines, ridges, and many-colored cliffs of the Badlands. South Dakota is sometimes called the *Land of Infinite Variety* because of the many great differences in the state's landscape.

Pierre, in central South Dakota, is the state capital. Sioux Falls ranks as the largest city. It lies in the southeastern part of the state.

Farming plays a leading role in the economy of South

Dakota. Farms and ranches occupy about 90 percent of the state. Sprawling livestock ranches lie in the western part of South Dakota. Smaller livestock farms and most of the state's crop farms lie in eastern South Dakota.

Service industries also play an important role in South Dakota's economy. An increasingly large number of people are employed in such activities as education, health care, banking, and trade.

Millions of tourists visit South Dakota every year. The Black Hills rank among one of the most popular vacationlands in the United States. The chief attraction in the Black Hills is Mount Rushmore National Memorial, which is also called the *Shrine of Democracy.* Heads of U.S. Presidents George Washington, Thomas Jefferson, Theodore Roosevelt, and Abraham Lincoln, 60 feet (18 meters) high, have been carved out of a granite mountain. The Mount Rushmore memorial is one of the largest sculptures in the world. Nearby, an even larger statue of the Sioux leader Crazy Horse is being blasted out of a mountain.

Gold was discovered in the Black Hills in 1874. In 1876, the rich Homestake *lode* (deposit) was discovered

The contributors of this article are Orville E. Gab, Assistant Professor of Geography at South Dakota State University, and David A. Wolff, Associate Professor of History at Black Hills State University.

Interesting facts about South Dakota

WORLD BOOK illustrations by Kevin Chadwick

South Dakota was either the 39th or 40th state, but no one will ever know for certain where it fits in the order of admission. In 1889, when both North and South Dakota were ready to be admitted into the Union, President Benjamin Harrison shuffled the admission papers so that one state could not claim precedence over the other. Today, the two states are ranked alphabetically, making North Dakota the 39th state and South Dakota the 40th.

South Dakota statehood

The geographic center of the United States, including Alaska and Hawaii, is in western South Dakota, 17 miles (27 kilometers) west of Castle Rock.

The world's largest natural indoor warm-water pool, called Evans Plunge, is in Hot Springs.

Experiments with buffaloes and Brahman cattle conducted in Belle Fourche have resulted in the breeding of an unusual new animal, the *brahmalo.*

South Dakota has more buffaloes than any other state in the United States. Privately owned and publicly owned herds in the state include thousands of buffaloes.

Buffaloes

David R. Frazier

A mesa rises in western South Dakota. *Mesas* are isolated hills or mountains with flat tops and steep sides. They are among the many interesting land formations found in South Dakota.

in the state. Until its closure in 2001, the Homestake mine was one of the world's greatest gold producers. Today, the leading mined products in South Dakota include crushed stone, granite, and sand and gravel.

A French trader established the first permanent settlement in South Dakota in 1817. Until the 1850's, all white settlement was along the Missouri River and was related to the fur trade. Agricultural settlement began in the 1850's. The population soared during the late 1870's and 1880's in the stampede for gold as well as a rush for farmland and rangeland. The state's history includes such famous Wild West figures as Calamity Jane, Wild Bill Hickok, Crazy Horse, and Sitting Bull. It also includes many farm families and townspeople who endured droughts, depressions, and blizzards to make South Dakota an important agricultural state.

South Dakota was named for the Sioux Indians who once roamed the region. The Sioux called themselves *Dakota* or *Lakota,* meaning *allies* or *friends.* South Dakota's official nickname is the *Mount Rushmore State.* The coyote is the state animal of South Dakota, and the state is also known as the *Coyote State.*

South Dakota Tourism

Sioux Falls is the largest city in South Dakota. The city, which lies in the southeastern part of the state, is the leading commercial and livestock center in South Dakota.

South Dakota in brief

Symbols of South Dakota

The state flag, adopted in 1992, bears the state seal. The design for the seal was adopted in 1885, four years before South Dakota became a state. On the seal, a farmer plowing symbolizes agriculture. Cattle feeding on the plain stand for ranching and dairying, and a smelting furnace represents the mining industry. A riverboat, symbolizing transportation and commerce, steams along the Missouri River.

State flag

State seal

South Dakota (brown) ranks 16th in size among all the states and 4th among the Midwestern States (yellow).

General information

Statehood: Nov. 2, 1889, the 40th state.
State abbreviations: S. Dak. or S.D. (traditional); SD (postal).
State motto: *Under God the People Rule.*
State song: "Hail, South Dakota." Words and music by Deecort Hammit.

The State Capitol is in Pierre, South Dakota's capital since 1889. Capitals of the Dakota Territory included Yankton (1861-1883) and Bismarck, now in North Dakota (1883-1889).

Land and climate

Area: 77,122 mi² (199,744 km²), including 1,225 mi² (3,174 km²) of inland water.
Elevation: *Highest*—Harney Peak, 7,242 ft (2,207 m) above sea level. *Lowest*—Big Stone Lake, 962 ft (293 m) above sea level.
Record high temperature: 120 °F (49 °C) at Gann Valley (also spelled Gannvalley) on July 5, 1936.
Record low temperature: −58 °F (−50 °C) at McIntosh on Feb. 17, 1936.
Average July temperature: 74 °F (23 °C).
Average January temperature: 16 °F (−9 °C).
Average yearly precipitation: 18 in (46 cm).

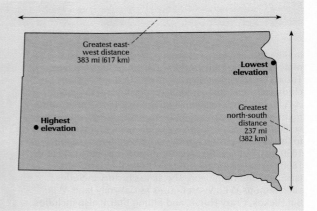

Greatest east-west distance 383 mi (617 km)

Lowest elevation

Greatest north-south distance 237 mi (382 km)

Highest elevation

Important dates

The United States acquired South Dakota through the Louisiana Purchase.

Congress created the Dakota Territory.

Gold was discovered in the Black Hills.

| 1743 | 1803 | 1817 | 1861 | 1874 |

François and Louis-Joseph La Vérendrye became the first known white people to explore the South Dakota region.

Joseph La Framboise established the first permanent white settlement at what is now Fort Pierre.

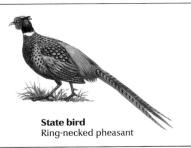

State bird
Ring-necked pheasant

State flower
Pasqueflower

State tree
Black Hills
spruce

People

Population: 754,844
Rank among the states: 46th
Population density: 10 per mi² (4 per
km²), U.S. average, 78 per mi² (30 per
km²)
Distribution: 52 percent urban, 48 per-
cent rural
Largest cities in South Dakota

Sioux Falls	123,975
Rapid City	59,607
Aberdeen	24,658
Watertown	20,237
Brookings	18,504
Mitchell	14,558

Source: 2000 census.

Population trend

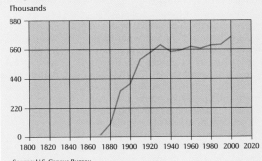

Thousands

Source: U.S. Census Bureau.

Year	Population
2000	754,844
1990	696,004
1980	690,768
1970	666,257
1960	680,514
1950	652,740
1940	642,961
1930	692,849
1920	636,547
1910	583,888
1900	401,570
1890	348,600
1880	98,268
1870	11,776

Economy

Chief products

Agriculture: beef cattle, corn, hay,
hogs, milk, sheep, soybeans,
wheat, wool.
Manufacturing: computer and electronic products, fabricated metal
products, food products, machinery, transportation equipment.
Mining: cement, crushed stone,
granite, natural gas, petroleum,
sand and gravel.

Gross domestic product

Value of goods and services produced in 2004: $29,699,000,000.
Services include community, business, and personal services; finance; government; trade; and
transportation and communication. *Industry* includes construction, manufacturing, mining, and
utilities. *Agriculture* includes agriculture, fishing, and forestry.

Source: U.S. Bureau of Economic Analysis.

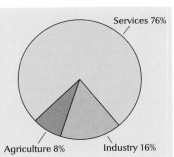

Services 76%

Agriculture 8%   Industry 16%

Government

State government

Governor: 4-year term
State senators: 35; 2-year terms
State representatives: 70; 2-year terms
Counties: 66

Federal government

United States senators: 2
United States representatives: 1
Electoral votes: 3

Sources of information

For information about tourism, write to: Office of Tourism, Capitol
Lake Plaza, 711 E. Wells Avenue, Pierre, SD 57501-3369. The Web
site at http://www.TravelSD.com also provides information.
For information on the economy, write to: Governor's Office of
Economic Development, 711 E. Wells Avenue, Pierre, SD 57501-
3369.
The state's official Web site at http://www.state.sd.us also provides
a gateway to much information on South Dakota's economy, government, and history.

South Dakota became the
40th state on November 2.

The U.S. Supreme Court ordered the federal government to pay
$105 million to eight Sioux tribes for land seized in 1877.

1889   **1944**   **1980**   **2001**

Congress authorized the construction of Fort Randall,
Oahe, Gavins Point, and Big Bend dams.

The Homestake
gold mine closed.

Population. The 2000 United States census reported that South Dakota had 754,844 people. The state's population had increased 8 ½ percent over the 1990 figure, which was 696,004. According to the 2000 census, South Dakota ranks 46th in population among the 50 states.

About 40 percent of South Dakota's people live in metropolitan areas. The state has three metropolitan areas—Rapid City; Sioux City, Iowa; and Sioux Falls. For the population of these three metropolitan areas, see the *Index* to the political map of South Dakota.

South Dakota has no great manufacturing industries to prompt the growth of large cities. Only Aberdeen, Rapid City, Sioux Falls, and Watertown have more than 20,000 people. Most towns were established to serve surrounding agricultural regions and are east of the Missouri River, in the state's chief farming area. Many towns also have grown up in the Black Hills, where mining once prospered and the tourist industry flourishes.

More than 8 percent of South Dakota's people are of American Indian descent, a higher percentage than in any state except Alaska and New Mexico. South Dakota's other large population groups include people of German, Norwegian, Irish, and English descent. African Americans, Asians, and Hispanic Americans together account for less than 3 percent of the state's population.

Schools. The first schoolhouse in the South Dakota region opened in 1860 in Bon Homme. The building was torn down after three months, and its logs were used in a stockade built for protection against Indian attacks. The first territorial legislature authorized a public school system in 1862. In 1864, a superintendent of public instruction was appointed.

Today, a state Board of Education sets policies for the public schools and post-secondary vocational schools. The governor appoints the nine board members, with state Senate approval, to four-year terms. The secretary of the Department of Education serves as the board's executive officer. Children must attend school from age 6 through 15. For the number of students and teachers, see **Education** (table).

Libraries. South Dakota's first libraries were established in the 1880's. Today, the state's largest libraries are at the University of South Dakota in Vermillion and South Dakota State University in Brookings. Siouxland Libraries is South Dakota's largest public library system. The South Dakota State Library has collections on art and on the history of South Dakota, as well as a large braille and talking-book collection. The South Dakota Library Network, an automated library system, can be used by libraries throughout the state.

Museums. The Cultural Heritage Center in Pierre houses the museum of the South Dakota State Historical Society. The National Music Museum in Vermillion displays rare musical instruments. Other state museums include the Museum of Geology at the School of Mines and Technology in Rapid City, the South Dakota National Guard Museum in Pierre, and the South Dakota Art Museum and the State Agricultural Heritage Museum at South Dakota State University in Brookings. City museums include the Adams Museum and House in Deadwood, displaying pioneer items, and the Journey Museum in Rapid City, which explores Black Hills history.

Universities and colleges

This table lists the universities and colleges in South Dakota that grant bachelor's or advanced degrees and are accredited by the North Central Association of Colleges and Schools.

Name	Mailing address
Augustana College	Sioux Falls
Black Hills State University	Spearfish
Colorado Technical University	Sioux Falls
Dakota State University	Madison
Dakota Wesleyan University	Mitchell
Mount Marty College	Yankton
National American University	Rapid City
North American Baptist Seminary	Sioux Falls
Northern State University	Aberdeen
Oglala Lakota College	Kyle
Presentation College	Aberdeen
Si Tanka University	Eagle Butte
Sinte Gleska University	Mission
Sioux Falls, University of	Sioux Falls
South Dakota, University of	Vermillion
South Dakota School of Mines and Technology	Rapid City
South Dakota State University	Brookings

Population density

South Dakota is one of the most thinly populated states. Nearly half of the people live in rural areas. Most of the urban population is in the eastern part of the state.

Persons per sq. mi.	Persons per km²
More than 25	More than 10
10 to 25	4 to 10
5 to 10	2 to 4
Less than 5	Less than 2

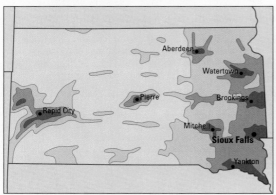

WORLD BOOK map; based on U.S. Census Bureau data.

Ken Olson, University of South Dakota

The University of South Dakota, in Vermillion, is the oldest public university in the state. It was founded in 1862.

South Dakota map index

Metropolitan areas

Counties

Cities and towns

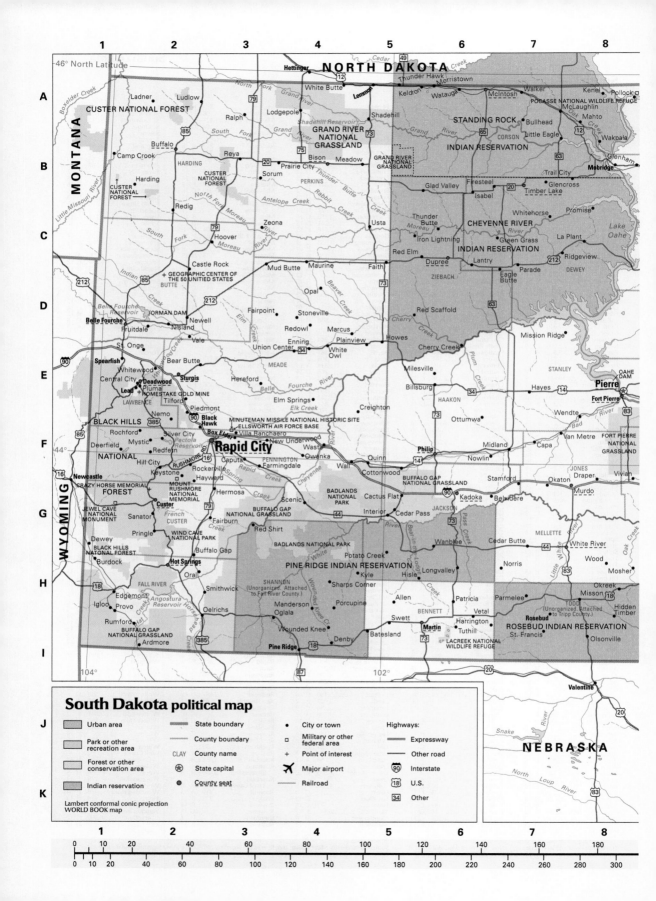

South Dakota political map

Legend:

- Urban area
- Park or other recreation area
- Forest or other conservation area
- Indian reservation

- State boundary
- County boundary
- CLAY County name
- ● City or town
- □ Military or other federal area
- + Point of interest
- ✈ Major airport
- ⊛ State capital
- ● County seat
- Railroad

Highways:
- Expressway
- Other road
- 90 Interstate
- 18 U.S.
- 34 Other

Lambert conformal conic projection
WORLD BOOK map

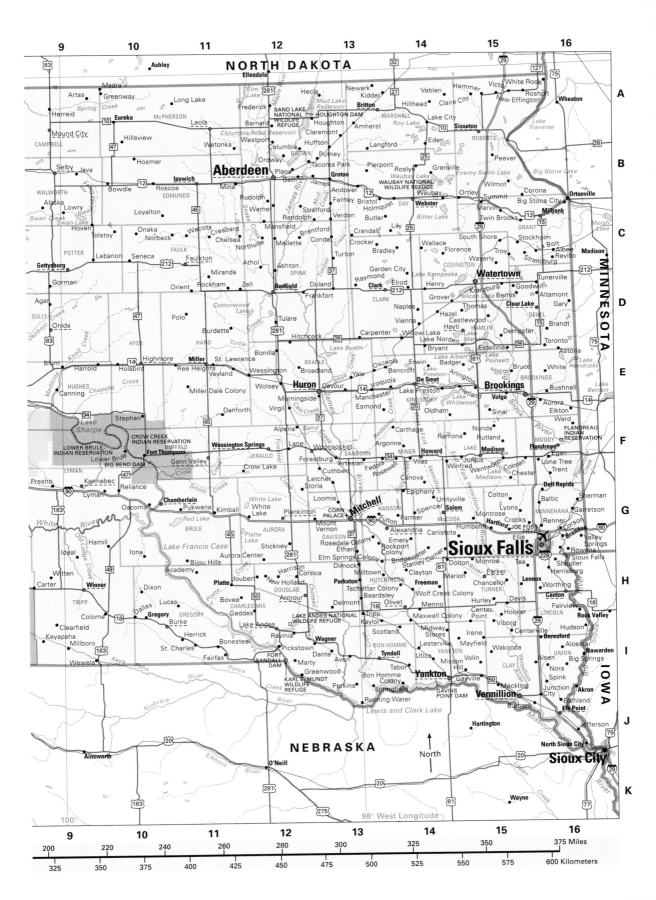

Each year, millions of visitors choose the national parks and memorials in South Dakota as a vacation destination. All of these destinations are in the Black Hills and Badlands areas, where visitors can also visit Custer State Park, home to one of the world's largest publicly owned buffalo herds. Other state parks and recreation areas offer breathtaking scenery, wildlife viewing, hiking, biking, bird-watching, water recreation, and camping. South Dakota communities stage such cultural events as powwows, rodeos, and pioneer celebrations.

Buffalo herd in Custer State Park

© Robert E. Pelham, Bruce Coleman Inc.

Corn Palace in Mitchell

South Dakota Department of Highways

Places to visit

Following are brief descriptions of some of South Dakota's many interesting places to visit.

Corn Palace, in Mitchell, is redecorated every fall with murals made of different colors of corn, grains, and grasses. Concerts, dances, and many other events are held in the building.

Crazy Horse Memorial, near Mount Rushmore National Monument, is a mountain carving in progress. When complete, it will be the world's largest sculpture. Korczak Ziolkowski began the carving in 1948. Members of Ziolkowski's family have continued the work since his death in 1982. The memorial also includes the Indian Museum of North America.

Deadwood, in the Black Hills, was a brawling mining town in the Old West. Reminders of its early days include legalized gambling, renovated buildings and streets, and Mount Moriah Cemetery, where such famous Wild West figures as Wild Bill Hickok and Calamity Jane are buried.

"Great Lakes of South Dakota" are formed by four massive dams on the Missouri River. The lakes—Francis Case, Lewis and Clark, Oahe, and Sharpe—offer water recreation.

National forests, parks, memorials, monuments, and grasslands. South Dakota shares Black Hills National Forest with Wyoming, and Custer National Forest with Montana. The federal government also administers Badlands National Park, Wind Cave National Park, Mount Rushmore National Memorial, and Jewel Cave National Monument. Each of these places has a separate article in *World Book.* Three areas have been designated as national grasslands. These areas—Buffalo Gap, Fort Pierre, and Grand River—offer bird-watching, hiking, and camping.

State parks. For information about South Dakota's many state parks and recreation areas., write to Department of Game, Fish and Parks, 523 E. Capitol Avenue, Pierre, SD 57501-3182.

Bob McNerling, Taurus

Badlands National Park

South Dakota Tourism

Rodeo at Days of '76 in Deadwood

Annual events

January-July

Black Hills Stock Show and Rodeo in Rapid City (January-February); Black Hills Horse Expo in Rapid City (April); Schmeckfest in Freeman (April); New Frontier Bull Ride in Presho (May); Sioux Empire Ribfest in Sioux Falls (June); Fort Sisseton Historical Festival at Fort Sisseton State Park (July); Mount Rushmore Independence Day Celebration in Keystone (July); Days of '76 in Deadwood (July).

August-December

Sturgis Motorcycle Rally in Sturgis (August); Riverboat Days in Yankton (August); Oak Lake Bluegrass Jamboree in Astoria (August); Great Dakota Wine Fest in Vermillion (September); Spirit of the West Festival in Sioux Falls (September); Black Hills Pow Wow in Rapid City (October); Capitol Christmas in Pierre (November-December).

South Dakota Office of Tourism

Capitol Christmas in Pierre

© Vance Henry, Taurus

The Black Hills region of South Dakota is an area of dramatic beauty. The trees covering the mountain slopes look black when seen from the plains.

Land regions. South Dakota has three major land regions. They are: (1) the Central Lowlands, (2) the Great Plains, and (3) the Black Hills.

The Central Lowlands, in eastern South Dakota, cover about a third of the state. A series of glaciers crossed this region during the most recent ice age, which ended about 11,500 years ago. The glaciers leveled off high places, filled in valleys, and created lakes. Most of the lakes of the Central Lowlands are in the eastern part of the region, which early French fur traders named the *Coteau des Prairies* (Prairie Hills).

The Coteau des Prairies is a plateau that rises abruptly from its surrounding landscape. Its northeastern corner ends at an *escarpment* (steep slope) along the Minnesota River Valley. The state's lowest point is in this valley, near Big Stone Lake. The western part of the Coteau des Prairies ends in another escarpment, along the edge of the James River Lowland.

The James River Lowland is a flat to slightly rolling lowland that occupies the western section of the Central Lowlands region. The James River Lowland extends in a wide belt down the width of the state, and the James River winds through it. The lowland's surface is covered with materials deposited by glaciers called *drift* and with windblown soil particles called *loess.*

In southeastern South Dakota, just south of the James River Lowland, are three ridges of drift-covered limestone bedrock. These ridges—James, Turkey, and Yankton ridges—form an *end moraine* or *terminal moraine.* They mark the end point to which glaciers advanced in the region.

The Great Plains cover most of the western two-thirds of South Dakota. The region is also called the Missouri Plateau. It is part of the immense highland that extends from northern Canada to southern Texas (see **Great Plains**).

The Coteau du Missouri, an area of hills and valleys, forms the eastern edge of the Great Plains. The Coteau du Missouri extends west to the Missouri River Valley. The Missouri River flows through the middle of South Dakota from north to south. The valley through which the Missouri flows is often called the Missouri River Trench because of its steep slopes and narrow width. Among the chief features of the land west of the Missouri are smooth, rounded hills; plateaus; and *buttes* (steep, flat-topped hills that stand alone).

In the southern part of the Great Plains region lie the nation's most famous badlands. Badlands are regions of small, steep hills and deep gullies formed primarily by water erosion. See **Badlands**.

Just south of the badlands is the Sand Hills area. This area is an extension of the Sand Hills section of Nebraska. In this area, sand piled up by the wind formed into sand dunes, and the dunes have become *fixed* (stationary).

The Black Hills are a low, isolated mountain group in southwestern South Dakota. The region has great

Land regions of South Dakota

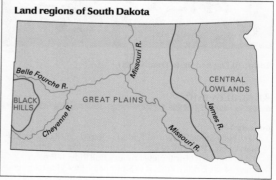

WORLD BOOK map

Map index

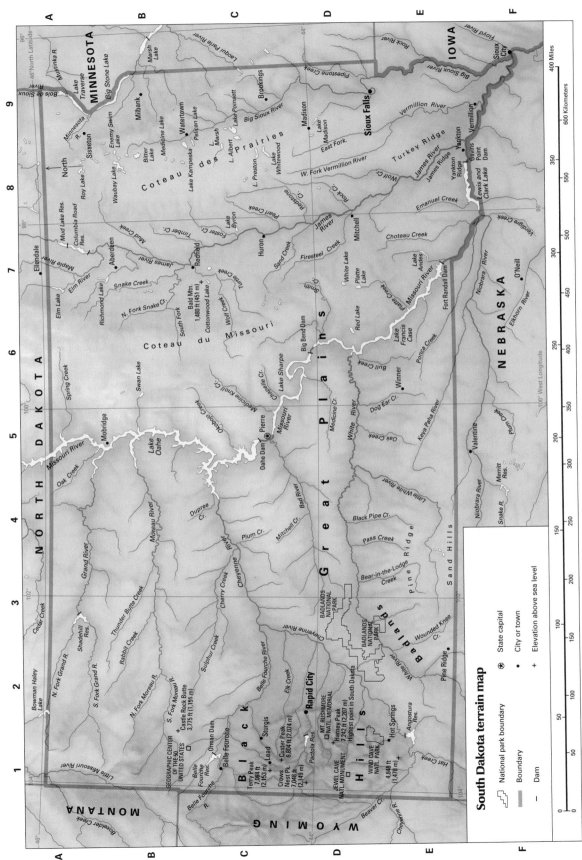

South Dakota terrain map

National park boundary
Boundary
Dam

⊛ State capital
• City or town
+ Elevation above sea level

WORLD BOOK map

Falls of the Big Sioux River flow near the city of Sioux Falls. The Big Sioux River winds through the Central Lowlands region in eastern South Dakota and joins the Missouri River.

beauty, with deep canyons and towering rock formations. The Black Hills also have rich mineral deposits, and thick forests of tall pines, spruces, and other trees. The state's highest point—7,242-foot (2,207-meter) Harney Peak—rises in the Black Hills. See **Black Hills.**

Rivers and lakes. The Missouri River is the state's most important river. The Missouri and its branches drain all of the state except the northeastern corner. The Missouri's western branches include the Cheyenne, Grand, Moreau, and White rivers. The Big Sioux, James, and Vermillion rivers join the Missouri in the eastern part of South Dakota.

Most of the state's lakes were formed by glaciers at the end of the most recent ice age, which ended about 11,500 years ago. A series of glacial lakes stretches across eastern South Dakota. The state's biggest lakes are created by four dams on the Missouri River. The largest lake is Lake Oahe, 250 miles (402 kilometers) long, created by Oahe Dam. Fort Randall Dam created Lake Francis Case, 140 miles (225 kilometers) long. Lake Sharpe, a reservoir formed by Big Bend Dam, is 80 miles (130 kilometers) long. Gavins Point Dam forms Lewis and Clark Lake, which is 25 miles (40 kilometers) long.

Medicine Lake, near Florence in Codington County, has a salt content of more than 4 percent, compared with about 3 ½ percent for seawater. Its water was once believed to have medicinal qualities.

Plant and animal life. Forests cover about 3 percent of South Dakota. Trees in the Black Hills include junipers, pines, and spruces. Such hardwood trees as ashes and oaks are scattered across the rest of the state.

The American pasqueflower, South Dakota's state flower, blooms on hillsides in early spring. Black-eyed

Susans, goldenrod, mariposa lilies, poppies, sunflowers, and wild orange geraniums grow on the eastern prairies. Cactus plants are common in western South Dakota. Bluebells, forget-me-nots, lady's-slippers, and larkspurs blossom in the Black Hills.

White-tailed deer live in all parts of South Dakota. They are most numerous in the Black Hills and in the woodlands of the Missouri River Valley. Pronghorns roam the land west of the Missouri. Mule deer graze in the rocky butte and canyon areas of the west. Bighorn sheep, elks, and Rocky Mountain goats live in the Black Hills. Thousands of buffaloes roam in various areas. South Dakota has more buffaloes than any other state.

The ring-necked pheasant, the state bird, is found throughout South Dakota. Hungarian partridges nest in northern parts of the state, and sage grouse in the extreme northwest. Sharp-tailed grouse and prairie chickens are found chiefly west of the Missouri River. Wild turkeys feed in the Black Hills.

Bass, bluegills, crappies, perch, walleyed pike, and other fishes are abundant in the glacial lakes of northeastern South Dakota. Among the fishes in the Missouri River and its branches are bass, catfish, northern pike, paddlefish, sauger, sturgeon, and walleyed pike. Brook, brown, and rainbow trout are found in the rivers and lakes of the Black Hills.

Climate. South Dakota has great ranges in temperatures. Temperatures in excess of 100 °F (38 °C) occur every summer. But even the hottest days are seldom uncomfortable, because the humidity is low. Below-zero temperatures are common on midwinter mornings.

Average July temperatures in South Dakota range from 78 °F (26 °C) in the south-central part of the state to 68 °F (20 °C) in the Black Hills. The record high, 120 °F (49 °C), was set at Gann Valley (also spelled Gannvalley) on July 5, 1936. Average January temperatures range from 10 °F (–12 °C) in the northeast to 22 °F (–6 °C) in the southwest. The record low, –58 °F (–50 °C), was set at McIntosh on Feb. 17, 1936.

The state's annual *precipitation* (rain, melted snow, and other forms of moisture) ranges from about 13 inches (33 centimeters) in the northwest to about 25 inches (64 centimeters) in the southeast. Most of the rain falls in the growing season, from April through September. The heaviest snowfalls occur in February and early March.

Average monthly weather

	Rapid City						Sioux Falls					
	Temperatures				Days of rain or snow		Temperatures				Days of rain or snow
	°F		°C				°F		°C			
	High	Low	High	Low			High	Low	High	Low	
Jan.	34	11	1	–12	6	Jan.	25	3	–4	–16	6
Feb.	39	16	4	–9	7	Feb.	32	10	0	–12	7
Mar.	47	23	8	–5	8	Mar.	44	21	7	–6	8
Apr.	57	32	14	0	10	Apr.	59	33	15	1	9
May	67	43	19	6	12	May	71	45	22	7	11
June	77	52	25	11	12	June	81	55	27	13	11
July	86	58	30	14	9	July	86	60	30	16	10
Aug.	86	57	30	14	8	Aug.	83	58	28	14	9
Sept.	75	46	24	8	6	Sept.	74	48	23	9	8
Oct.	62	35	17	2	6	Oct.	61	35	16	2	6
Nov.	49	22	9	–6	6	Nov.	42	21	6	–6	6
Dec.	36	13	2	–11	5	Dec.	29	8	–2	–13	6

Average January temperatures

South Dakota has a broad range of temperatures during the winter. The northeast has the coldest weather.

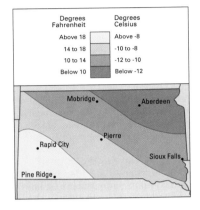

Average July temperatures

South Dakota has warm summers with low humidity. Temperatures are the highest in the southeastern section.

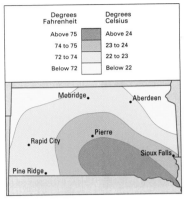

Average yearly precipitation

Western South Dakota generally has the least amount of precipitation. The east is the wettest portion of the state.

WORLD BOOK maps

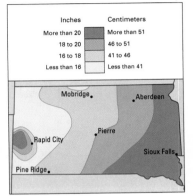

Economy

Agriculture contributes a larger portion of the *gross domestic product* of South Dakota than it does for most other states. Gross domestic product is the total value of all goods and services produced in the state in a year. South Dakota's leading farm products are beef cattle, corn, soybeans, and wheat. Many of the state's other industries rely on farm products. For example, food processing is an important manufacturing activity, and the distribution of food products is the most important type of wholesale trade.

Sioux Falls is an important financial center. The federal government employs many people on Indian reservations, military establishments, and national parklands in the state. Each year, the millions of tourists who come to South Dakota contribute more than $1 billion to the state's economy.

Natural resources. South Dakota's most precious natural resource is its fertile soil. The state also has rich mineral resources. Most of the forest reserves are in the Black Hills.

Soil. Rich soils that developed from glacial materials cover most of eastern South Dakota. These soils are loamy and range in color from dark brown to black. A belt of *loess*—yellow-brown soil composed of tiny mineral particles—stretches along the east bank of the Missouri River. A deep deposit of loess also covers the lower Big Sioux River Basin in the eastern part of the state. The soils of eastern South Dakota are good for growing corn, wheat, and other crops. Most of the soils west of the Missouri River were formed from the weathering of shales. These soils make good grazing lands.

Minerals. South Dakota's northwestern counties have deposits of *lignite,* a low-grade coal. Much of western South Dakota lies in the great Williston Basin. This basin is a rich petroleum reservoir that extends across North Dakota and eastern Montana and into Canada. From the 1870's to the early 2000's, the Homestake lode, a rich vein of gold ore in the Black Hills, yielded millions of tons of the ore. But yields decreased in the late 1990's,

Production and workers by economic activities

Economic activities	Percent of GDP* produced	Employed workers Number of people	Employed workers Percent of total
Finance, insurance, & real estate	26	45,800	9
Community, business, & personal services	17	145,000	27
Trade, restaurants, & hotels	15	119,700	23
Government	13	80,700	15
Manufacturing	10	40,700	8
Agriculture	8	40,400	8
Transportation & communication	5	22,100	4
Construction	4	31,400	6
Utilities	2	2,100	†
Mining	†	1,200	†
Total	**100**	**529,100**	**100**

*GDP = gross domestic product, the total value of goods and services produced in a year.
†Less than one-half of 1 percent.
Figures are for 2004; employment figures include full- and part-time workers.
Source: *World Book* estimates based on data from U.S. Bureau of Economic Analysis.

and major gold operations there came to an end. Gold mining continues in the state, but on a small scale. Other mined products in South Dakota include cement, clays, crushed stone, feldspar, granite, gypsum, iron ore, mica, quartz, sand and gravel, and silver.

Forests cover about 4 percent of South Dakota. Most of the forests lie in the Black Hills and contain chiefly cone-bearing trees, including junipers, ponderosa pines, and spruces. Ashes, cottonwoods, oaks, and other hardwoods are scattered throughout the state.

Service industries contribute the largest portion of South Dakota's gross domestic product. Service industries are concentrated in the state's largest cities.

Finance, insurance, and real estate ranks as South

A worker processes cheese at a plant in Milbank. Food processing, which includes cheese making, is a leading manufacturing activity in South Dakota.

Dakota's leading service industry group in terms of the gross domestic product. Sioux Falls is the state's leading financial center. Citigroup Inc., the largest financial services company in the United States, has some of its operations based in Sioux Falls. Several other financial companies are also based in the city. The buying and selling of homes is the main activity in the state's real estate industry.

Ranking second among service industry groups is community, business, and personal services. This group consists of a variety of businesses, including private health care, law firms, and repair shops.

Trade, restaurants, and hotels ranks third in terms of the gross domestic product. The wholesale trade of groceries and farm products is especially important in the state. Retail businesses include automobile dealerships, discount stores, and food stores. Many of the state's motels and restaurants are concentrated near Sioux Falls and leading tourist sites, such as Mount Rushmore.

Government ranks fourth among the state's service industry groups. Government services include the operation of public schools and hospitals, military bases, and Indian reservations. The public school system is one of South Dakota's leading employers. Two of the nation's largest Indian reservations are in South Dakota.

Transportation and communication ranks fifth among the state's service industry groups. Trucking companies and railroads play a major role in the economy because the state lies a great distance from most major markets. More information about transportation and communication appears later in this section.

Manufacturing. Goods manufactured in South Dakota have a *value added by manufacture* of approximately $4 ½ billion yearly. This figure represents the increase in value of raw materials after they become finished products.

Food products are South Dakota's leading type of manufactured product in terms of value added by manufacture. Meat processing and packing is the most important food-processing industry in South Dakota. The largest plant is in Sioux Falls. Other meat processing and packing plants are in Mitchell and Yankton. Poultry is dressed and packed in Huron and Watertown. Dairy-processing plants operate in Lake Norden, Milbank, Rapid City, Sioux Falls, and many other towns.

Machinery production ranks second in terms of value added by manufacture. Farming and construction equipment are the leading types of machinery produced.

Other products made in South Dakota include computers and electronics, fabricated metal products, and transportation equipment. Computers are manufactured in North Sioux City. Architectural and structural metals are the state's most valuable fabricated metal products. Major types of transportation equipment made in the state include truck trailers and motor vehicle parts. The state's factories also produce furniture, plastics and rubber products, printed materials, and wood products.

Agriculture. Farmland covers about 90 percent of South Dakota's land area. The state has about 31,000 farms and ranches. Larger farms lie in the western and central parts of South Dakota, while smaller farms lie in the eastern part of the state. Irrigation is used on many farms in both the eastern and western parts of the state.

Economy of South Dakota

This map shows the economic uses of land in South Dakota and where the leading farm and mineral products are produced. Major manufacturing centers are shown in red.

- Mostly cropland
- Cropland mixed with woodland
- Mostly grazing land with some cropland
- Shrubland with some grazing
- Forest land
- • Manufacturing center
- • Mineral deposit

WORLD BOOK map

Livestock and livestock products account for about 60 percent of South Dakota's farm income. South Dakota is a major producer of beef cattle, hogs, lambs, and sheep. Pastures cover approximately 24 million acres (10 million hectares), or about half the state. Beef cattle graze on the enormous ranches of the western section. The ranchers often ship their calves and yearlings to cattle ranchers called *feeders* in eastern South Dakota or in neighboring states. The feeders fatten the young cattle on grains before sending them to market. Sheep are raised throughout South Dakota, especially in the eastern and northwest parts of the state. The state is a leader in wool production. Most of the state's chickens, eggs, geese, and turkeys are produced in the east. Farmers raise dairy cattle throughout the east, and milk is an important source of farm income.

Crops account for about 40 percent of the state's agricultural income. Corn, soybeans, and wheat are South Dakota's leading crops. The eastern part of the state is the chief region for growing corn and soybeans. However, these two crops are grown in other parts of the state as well. Spring wheat is produced mainly in the northern part of South Dakota, and winter wheat is grown mainly in the central part of the state. South Dakota ranks among the leading states in the production of spring wheat. South Dakota is also among the chief producers of flaxseed, hay, oats, rye, and sunflower seeds.

Mining. South Dakota's most important mined products include granite, cement, crushed stone, sand and gravel, petroleum, and natural gas. Quarries in Grant County provide granite. Cement, formed from a mixture of clays and limestone, is produced in Pennington County. Crushed stone is produced in the southeastern and southwestern parts of the state. Most of the sand and gravel comes from pits in the eastern part of the state. Much of the crushed stone and sand and gravel is used in construction. Custer, Dewey, Fall River, and Harding counties are the centers of South Dakota's oil and natural gas production.

Until the early 2000's, South Dakota had ranked as one of the leading gold-producing states. The Homestake mine at Lead was one of the largest gold mines in the Western Hemisphere. It produced huge amounts of gold ore since the first ore was mined in 1876. However, due to declining yield and decreasing gold prices, the mine's owners closed it at the end of 2001. Minor gold-mining operations continue in the state.

Electric power and utilities. South Dakota's utilities provide electric, gas, and water service. Hydroelectric projects and plants that burn coal each produce nearly half of the state's electric power. A small amount also comes from plants that burn natural gas or petroleum. Four huge Missouri River dams—Big Bend, Fort Randall, Gavins Point, and Oahe—supply most of the state's hydroelectric power (see **Fort Randall Dam**).

Transportation. The wide Missouri River provided the first great highway into South Dakota. Early explorers, fur traders, and missionaries sailed up the river in canoes or flat-bottomed boats. In 1874, gold was discovered in the Black Hills. Prospectors carved trails into the region as they rushed to the gold fields in stagecoaches and oxcarts. In 1872, the first railroad to enter South Dakota reached Vermillion. By 1880, two rail lines crossed eastern South Dakota to the Missouri River. A railroad reached the Black Hills in 1885.

Today, 11 railroads provide freight service on about 1,900 miles (3,100 kilometers) of operational rail lines in South Dakota. No passenger railroads cross the state. The state has about 84,000 miles (135,000 kilometers) of roads and highways. Sioux Falls has the state's largest airport.

Communication. South Dakota's first newspaper, the *Dakota Democrat,* began in Sioux Falls in 1859. The oldest newspaper still published in the state is the *Yankton Press and Dakotan.* It was founded as the *Weekly Dakotian* in 1861 and became a daily in 1875. South Dakota has about 140 newspapers, of which about 10 are dailies. Daily papers with the largest circulations include the *Argus Leader* of Sioux Falls and the *Rapid City Journal.*

The South Dakota School of Mines and Technology established the state's first radio station, WCAT. The station was licensed in Rapid City in 1922. The first television station, KELO, began operating in Sioux Falls in 1953. Today, more than 80 radio stations and 20 television stations serve the state. Cable and satellite television systems and Internet providers serve many communities.

Artstreet

Fort Randall Dam crosses the Missouri River near the South Dakota-Nebraska border. It is one of four dams that make up South Dakota's Missouri Basin Program. The dams provide electric power, flood control, and irrigation throughout the basin.

Constitution. South Dakota is still governed under its original Constitution, adopted in 1889. But the document has been *amended* (changed) many times.

A proposed amendment to the Constitution must be placed on the ballot in a regular statewide election. It may be proposed and placed on the ballot in any of three ways: (1) The Legislature may propose it by a majority vote in each house. (2) A group of citizens may propose an amendment by *initiative.* In this method, the citizens submit a *petition* (formal request) signed by at least 10 percent of the number of people who voted in the last election for governor. (3) A constitutional convention, approved by a three-fourths majority vote in both the House of Representatives and the Senate of the South Dakota Legislature, may propose an amendment. In order to become part of the Constitution, an amendment must be approved by a majority of the citizens voting on the issue.

Executive. The governor of South Dakota is elected to a four-year term and may not serve more than two terms in a row. Other elected officials include the lieutenant governor, secretary of state, attorney general, commissioner of school and public lands, treasurer, and auditor. They are also elected to four-year terms and may serve no more than two terms in succession.

Legislature consists of a 35-member Senate and a 70-member House of Representatives. Voters in each of the state's 35 legislative districts elect 1 senator and 2 representatives. Members of both houses serve two-year terms and may serve no more than four terms in the same house in succession.

Legislative sessions begin on the second Tuesday in January. Sessions last 35 days in even-numbered years and 40 days in odd-numbered years. The Legislature or the governor may call special legislative sessions.

In 1898, South Dakota became the first state to adopt the *initiative* and the *referendum,* actions that give voters a certain amount of direct control over lawmaking. The state's voters can pass laws directly through their power of initiative. If 5 percent of the number of people who voted in the last election for governor sign a petition for the adoption of a law, the measure is then put on a statewide ballot.

The referendum allows voters to accept or reject measures approved by the Legislature. Any law passed by the Legislature must be submitted to the people if 5 percent of the number voting in the last election for governor sign a petition asking that a vote on the law be taken. The petition asking for the vote must be completed within 90 days after the adjournment of the Legislature that passed the law. See **Initiative and referendum.**

Courts. The state Supreme Court is the highest court in South Dakota. This court has five justices appointed by the governor. After a justice has served three years, the people vote to retain or dismiss the justice. Such a vote is then repeated after every eight years of service. Every four years, the justices select one of their number to be the chief justice of the Supreme Court.

South Dakota is divided into seven judicial districts. Voters in each of these judicial districts elect at least four circuit court judges. Circuit court judges serve eight-year terms.

Local government. South Dakota has 66 counties. All of the counties are governed by county commissions.

Each county commission consists of a board of three to five members elected to four-year terms. Other elected county officials include the state's attorney, auditor, coroner, register of deeds, sheriff, and treasurer.

South Dakota has hundreds of cities and towns. The state Constitution allows them the power of *home rule.* That is, cities and towns may operate under their own charters and adopt their own form of government. Counties in South Dakota may also adopt home rule. Most cities in South Dakota have the mayor-council form of government.

Revenue. Taxes bring in about one-third of the state government's *general revenue* (income). Most of the rest of the general revenue comes from federal grants and programs. A general sales tax accounts for about one-half of the tax revenue in South Dakota. Other major sources of tax revenue include taxes on legalized gambling, motor fuels, and motor vehicle licenses. The state does not tax property or personal incomes. Only banks and other financial institutions in South Dakota pay corporation taxes.

Politics. South Dakota voters have strongly favored the Republican Party throughout most of the state's history. Republicans have won most of the elections for governor, and Republicans also have won the state's electoral votes in most presidential elections. For the state's voting record in presidential elections, see **Electoral College** (table). In the 1960's, South Dakota began to show signs of being a two-party state. Since then, the Democratic Party has continued to draw voter support. But the Republicans remain the largest party.

The governors of South Dakota

	Party	Term
Arthur C. Mellette	Republican	1869-1893
Charles H. Sheldon	Republican	1893-1897
Andrew E. Lee	Populist	1897-1901
Charles N. Herreid	Republican	1901-1905
Samuel H. Elrod	Republican	1905-1907
Coe I. Crawford	Republican	1907-1909
Robert S. Vessey	Republican	1909-1913
Frank M. Byrne	Republican	1913-1917
Peter Norbeck	Republican	1917-1921
W. H. McMaster	Republican	1921-1925
Carl Gunderson	Republican	1925-1927
W. J. Bulow	Democratic	1927-1931
Warren Green	Republican	1931-1933
Thomas "Tom" Berry	Democratic	1933-1937
Leslie Jensen	Republican	1937-1939
Harlan J. Bushfield	Republican	1939-1943
M. Q. Sharpe	Republican	1943-1947
George T. Mickelson	Republican	1947-1951
Sigurd Anderson	Republican	1951-1955
Joseph J. Foss	Republican	1955-1959
Ralph Herseth	Democratic	1959-1961
Archie Gubbrud	Republican	1961-1965
Nils Boe	Republican	1965-1969
Frank L. Farrar	Republican	1969-1971
Richard F. Kneip	Democratic	1971-1978
Harvey L. Wollman	Democratic	1978-1979
William J. Janklow	Republican	1979-1987
George S. Mickelson	Republican	1987-1993
Walter Dale Miller	Republican	1993-1995
William J. Janklow	Republican	1995-2003
Mike Rounds	Republican	2003-

Early days. Four major Indian tribes lived in the South Dakota region before white explorers first arrived. The Kiowa occupied the Black Hills region, and the Arikara lived along the Missouri River, near the mouth of the Cheyenne River. The Cheyenne Indians came to the region from the northeast and moved to the White River and Black Hills area, displacing the Kiowa. The Sioux, or Lakota and Dakota, came to South Dakota from what is now Minnesota, beginning in the 1700's. They were hunters and warriors who followed the buffalo herds. They eventually pushed most other Indian groups out of South Dakota.

Exploration and fur trade. In 1682, René-Robert Cavelier, Sieur de La Salle, claimed for France all the land drained by the Mississippi River system. This vast territory included what is now South Dakota, because the waters of the Missouri River flow into the Mississippi.

The French-Canadian explorers François and Louis-Joseph La Vérendrye were the first white people known to have visited the South Dakota area. In 1743, the two brothers buried a small lead plate near the site of present-day Fort Pierre to prove they had been there. Schoolchildren found the plate in 1913, and the South Dakota State Historical Museum now owns it.

In 1762, France gave its land west of the Mississippi River to Spain. Spain returned it to France in 1800. In 1803, the United States bought this territory, called Louisiana, from France (see **Louisiana Purchase**).

About 1785, Pierre Dorion, a French fur trader, arrived in the lower James River Valley, near what is now Yankton. He became the first white person to settle permanently in the South Dakota region.

In 1804, President Thomas Jefferson sent Meriwether Lewis and William Clark to explore the Louisiana Territory and to blaze a trail to the Pacific Ocean. In August, the explorers camped in the South Dakota region for the first time, near what is now Elk Point. They followed the Missouri River through the region. Lewis and Clark passed through again in 1806 on their return from the Pacific. Their reports of the abundant fur-bearing animals in the region attracted an increased number of fur traders. The explorers had also established friendly relations with many Indian tribes.

The most important trading post was built in 1817 at the mouth of the Bad River, on the site of present-day Fort Pierre. This lonely post became the first permanent settlement in the South Dakota region. It was established by Joseph La Framboise, a French trader.

The first large-scale military action against South Dakota Indians took place in 1823. The Arikara tribe attacked a fur-trading party led by General William Ashley, lieutenant governor of Missouri. The federal government sent troops under Colonel Henry Leavenworth to punish the tribe. The Sioux, traditional enemies of the Arikara, joined in fighting them.

In 1831, the steamboat *Yellowstone* sailed up the Missouri River from St. Louis to Fort Tecumseh (now Fort Pierre). It proved steamboats could travel the upper Missouri. This development further spurred the fur trade in South Dakota. Large cargoes could be shipped in far less time than it took for flat-bottomed boats that were moved by the river currents. The fur trade thrived for several years but began to decline by 1850. The number of fur-bearing animals had started to decrease, and the demand for furs fell as silk became more fashionable.

Agricultural settlement. The land that became North Dakota and South Dakota was part of the Missouri Territory between 1812 and 1834. The eastern section later belonged, in turn, to the Michigan, Wisconsin, Iowa, and Minnesota territories. The western section remained part of the Missouri Territory until 1854, when it became part of the Nebraska Territory.

Before the 1850's, all white settlement in the South Dakota region had been along the Missouri River and had been related to the fur trade. Agricultural settlement began in the eastern section during the late 1850's.

In 1857, the U.S. Congress passed the Minnesota statehood bill. This bill set the new state's western border east of the Big Sioux River. But nothing was done about the rich farmland westward to the Missouri River. Some business people and politicians saw a chance to make money. They quickly formed land companies, gained control of choice locations, and laid out townsites. Settlements were established at Sioux Falls, Medary, Flandreau, and other points.

In 1858, a group of Sioux called the Yankton Sioux signed a treaty with the government giving up their land in the southeastern corner between the Big Sioux and Missouri rivers. The opening of this land attracted more settlers to the South Dakota region. Yankton, Vermillion, and Bon Homme were founded in 1859.

Territorial days. Congress created the Dakota Territory in 1861. It consisted of present-day North and South Dakota and much of Montana and Wyoming. William Jayne was the first governor of the Dakota Territory, and Yankton was the capital.

Indian wars prevented rapid settlement of the territory during the 1860's. One of the most important wars was Red Cloud's War, named for the Sioux leader Red Cloud. The government planned to build a road across the Powder River country to newly discovered gold fields in Montana. Red Cloud believed the road would ruin the Indians' hunting grounds. In 1866, the Sioux attacked troops sent to make a survey for the road. The Indians continued their raids until 1868, when the government met their demands. In the Treaty of Fort Laramie signed that year, the government agreed to give up its military posts in the Powder River country. The government also promised not to build any roads through the area without making payment to the Indians. The treaty created the Great Sioux Reservation, which covered all the land in present-day South Dakota west of the Missouri River.

In 1874, a military expedition led by Lieutenant Colonel George A. Custer entered the Black Hills in what the Sioux believed was a violation of the Treaty of Fort Laramie. The government had ordered the expedition to find a suitable site for a fort. The soldiers discovered gold near the present town of Custer. The news brought a rush of prospectors to the area. In 1876, prospectors discovered far richer deposits of gold between the present towns of Lead and Deadwood. Another stampede of gold seekers followed. The town of Deadwood sprang up as the center of mining operations. It became a brawling, wide-open town, with a reputation as the most lawless settlement on the frontier. Wild Bill Hickok, Calamity Jane, and other citizens of Deadwood became famous Wild West figures.

Historic South Dakota

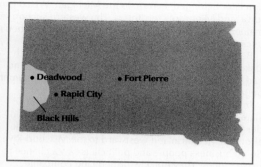

The *Yellowstone* sailed up the Missouri River to Fort Tecumseh (now Fort Pierre) in 1831, proving that steamboats could travel on the upper Missouri.

Gold was discovered in the Black Hills in 1874, when Lieutenant Colonel George A. Custer led an expedition in the area. South Dakota remained a leading gold-producing state until the early 2000's.

The La Vérendrye brothers were the first explorers of South Dakota. In 1743, they buried a small lead plate near the site of present-day Fort Pierre as proof of their visit. The plate was found in 1913.

Mount Rushmore National Monument, a huge carving on a granite cliff, was begun in 1927 and completed in 1941.

The Battle of Wounded Knee, in which more than 200 Sioux Indians were killed by federal troops, took place in 1890.

Important dates in South Dakota

WORLD BOOK illustrations by Kevin Chadwick

1682 René-Robert Cavelier, Sieur de La Salle, claimed for France all the land drained by the Mississippi River. This land included the South Dakota region.

1743 François La Vérendrye and Louis-Joseph La Vérendrye were the first white people known to visit the South Dakota region.

1803 The United States acquired South Dakota through the Louisiana Purchase.

1804, 1806 Meriwether Lewis and William Clark passed through South Dakota on their expedition to and from the Pacific Ocean.

1817 Joseph La Framboise established the first permanent settlement in South Dakota at what is now Fort Pierre.

1861 The U.S. Congress created the Dakota Territory.

1868 The Treaty of Fort Laramie ended Red Cloud's War.

1874 Gold was discovered in the Black Hills.

1889 South Dakota became the 40th state of the United States on November 2.

1927 Gutzon Borglum began work on Mount Rushmore National Memorial. The monument was completed in 1941.

1930's South Dakota suffered its worst drought.

1944 Congress authorized construction of Fort Randall, Oahe, Gavins Point, and Big Bend dams.

1973 A group of armed Indians seized the village of Wounded Knee and occupied it for 71 days.

1980 The U.S. Supreme Court ordered the federal government to pay South Dakota Indian tribes $105 million for land seized by the government in 1877.

1989 Legalized gambling began in Deadwood.

2001 The Homestake gold mine closed.

Deadwood sprang up in 1876 after rich gold deposits were discovered in the Black Hills. A wave of prospectors rushed to the area, and Deadwood gained a reputation as the most brawling, lawless settlement on the frontier.

Bettmann Archive

The invasion of the Black Hills by white settlers caused a series of Indian uprisings led by Crazy Horse and Sitting Bull. In 1877, the U.S. government took possession of the Black Hills from the Sioux Indians. Most of the Sioux surrendered and settled on reservations west of the Missouri River. On the reservations, the Sioux had to give up their old lifestyle of following the buffalo. In 1889, a Paiute Indian named Wovoka started a religious movement called the Ghost Dance. Many Sioux became involved in this movement, which promised to restore the Indians' old way of life.

Government officials misinterpreted the Ghost Dance. They considered it a threat to white settlers and called in military forces. In 1890, Indian police sent to arrest Sitting Bull wound up killing him after his followers resisted the arrest. Some of his followers then joined Chief Big Foot's band of Sioux on the Cheyenne River. Federal troops caught up with the Indians and took them to a cavalry camp on Wounded Knee Creek. There, they tried to disarm the Sioux. A gun went off, and the soldiers began firing. They killed more than 200 people, including Big Foot. Wounded Knee marked the end of large-scale resistance by Indians on the northern plains. See **Indian wars** (Wounded Knee).

Statehood. A great land boom followed the discovery of gold in the Black Hills. Thousands came to seek gold. But many more came to farm in other sections of South Dakota. An enormous land rush began in 1878. Between 1878 and 1887, farmers and speculators poured into South Dakota in what became known as the Great Dakota Boom. They acquired more than 24 million acres (9.7 million hectares) of public lands offered by the government.

In 1870, the region had a population of less than 12,000. By 1890, the population had soared to 348,600. Most of the settlers came from neighboring states, but many came from Germany, Norway, Russia, the United Kingdom, and other European countries.

Railroad building also boomed during this period. By 1880, two railroads had crossed eastern South Dakota to the Missouri River. In 1886, a railroad reached the Black Hills. Many towns sprang up along the rail lines. During the late 1870's and the 1880's, cattle ranchers entered the open rangeland west of the Missouri. The rush of miners and merchants to the Black Hills and the needs of the Indian agencies and military posts had created a heavy demand for meat.

During the 1870's, a movement began to divide the Dakota Territory into two parts. The major population centers had grown up far apart—in the northeastern and southeastern corners of the territory. The two groups of settlers wanted to develop separate governments. In February 1889, Congress set the present boundary between South Dakota and North Dakota. It also passed an *enabling act,* which allowed the two regions to set up the machinery to become states (see **Enabling act**). On Nov. 2, 1889, North Dakota and South Dakota entered the Union as the 39th and 40th states. South Dakotans elected Arthur C. Mellette, a Republican, as their first governor. Pierre became the state capital in 1889, shortly after South Dakota gained statehood.

The early 1900's. The population of South Dakota had climbed to almost 350,000 by the time it became a state. But little growth occurred during the first 10 years of statehood. A severe drought began in 1889 and lasted until 1897. In 1890, part of the state's Great Sioux Reservation was opened to settlement, but few settlers came.

Prosperity returned to South Dakota in the early

1900's. The drought had ended, and prices for farm crops were good. The government opened more Indian lands in the west, and thousands of settlers poured into the state. Some of this land was offered through great land lotteries. People registered for land and received claims if they were lucky in the lottery drawings. Special trains brought people from all parts of the United States to take part in the lotteries.

By 1910, the population had soared to almost 584,000. Between 1900 and 1910, the railroads added more than 1,100 miles (1,770 kilometers) of track in the state. Most of the track was laid west of the Missouri River to serve the state's growing sheep and cattle ranches.

Boom-and-bust economy. Throughout South Dakota's history, the state's *boom-and-bust economy* has affected its development. In a boom-and-bust economy, periods of great prosperity alternate with periods of economic decline and many business failures. The boom of the first 10 years of the 1900's ended in 1911, when another drought began.

The state government soon began a program designed to protect the people from the hardships of economic slumps. In 1915, state lawmakers passed a law guaranteeing the safety of bank deposits. Later, the state lent millions of dollars to farmers. It also bought a coal mine, built a cement-making plant, and operated an insurance program against damage by hail. South Dakota abandoned most of these businesses by the 1930's.

Another economic boom began during the late 1910's. The prices of South Dakota's farm products increased after the United States entered World War I (1914-1918). Crops grew well during the 1920's.

After 1925, the state's economy suffered because of lower farm prices and bank failures. Then, in 1930, the worst drought and grasshopper plague in South Dakota's history began. Except for some relief in 1932 and 1935, the drought lasted for 10 years. It was accompanied by great dust storms called *black blizzards*. In addition, the entire nation was hit by the Great Depression. Prices for South Dakota's farm products sank lower and lower. The population of the state also began to decline. In 1930, South Dakota's population had reached a record 692,849. By 1940, it had fallen to 642,961.

The federal government provided money and jobs to help the distressed farmers. The Civilian Conservation Corps (CCC) gave thousands of young men jobs in the forests of the Black Hills. The Works Progress Administration (WPA), later called Work Projects Administration, provided money to build bridges, buildings, and other projects. The government also helped South Dakota farmers plant wheatlands with grasses whose roots reach deep for moisture and hold the soil in place.

In stark contrast to the hard times elsewhere in the state, Lead and Deadwood experienced prosperity in the 1930's. An increase by the federal government in the price of gold set off a small boom at the Homestake mine. Many unemployed men found work there.

The mid-1900's. During World War II (1939-1945), South Dakota farmers broke production records in supplying food. The increased use of machinery enabled farmers to do more work but, at the same time, made many farmworkers jobless. Thousands of farmworkers moved to towns and cities in search of jobs, but many could not find employment. As a result, large numbers

Don Polovich, *Rapid City Journal*

Floodwaters swept across Rapid City and the surrounding area in 1972 after rains caused Canyon Lake Dam to burst. The flood killed 238 people and caused about $165 million in damage.

of people—mostly young people—left the state. To decrease its dependence on farming, South Dakota started a drive to broaden its economy. This effort included developing the Missouri River Basin, increasing tourism, and attracting new industry.

In 1944, Congress authorized the Missouri River Basin Project (now the Pick-Sloan Missouri Basin Program). This huge program was designed to provide electric power, flood control, and irrigation throughout the basin. Part of the project called for construction of four hydroelectric dams on the Missouri River in South Dakota. By 1966, all four dams—Big Bend, Fort Randall, Gavins Point, and Oahe—were producing hydroelectric power. The dams created Francis Case, Lewis and Clark, Oahe, and Sharpe lakes, which became known as the "Great Lakes of South Dakota." These lakes, along with many new highways, attracted additional tourists to the state. Tourism became South Dakota's second largest industry, after agriculture.

During the Cold War, the government built a number of defense projects in South Dakota. These projects included Ellsworth Air Force Base near Rapid City, which had bombers and missiles. However, the government removed all the missiles in the first half of the 1990's.

In 1972, floodwaters swept across Rapid City and the surrounding area after heavy rains caused Rapid City's Canyon Lake Dam to burst. The flood killed 238 people and caused an estimated $165 million in damage.

In 1973, the village of Wounded Knee was seized by about 200 armed Indians, including members of the American Indian Movement (AIM). The action was designed to protest federal policies concerning Indians, and was also the result of a tribal dispute among the Oglala Sioux band of the Teton Sioux. During the occupation, several gunfights broke out between the occupiers and federal authorities. The occupation lasted 71 days and resulted in 2 deaths and more than 300 arrests. Government officials promised to study the protesters' complaints.

The late 1900's. The departure of young people slowed in the 1970's, but it continued to remain a concern. The state broadened its economy, and new jobs were created in commerce and industry. In the mid-1980's, agriculture suffered from low farm prices and high interest rates. Some farmers lost their land. By the early 1990's, farmers' incomes had begun to rise again.

In 1980, the Supreme Court of the United States ordered the U.S. government to pay about $105 million to eight Sioux Indian tribes. The payment was for Indian land in the Black Hills seized by the government in 1877. But the Sioux refused the money and are seeking return of the land.

In 1987, South Dakota began its state lottery. In 1989, the town of Deadwood legalized casino gambling. In the 1990's, taxes on legalized gambling became an important source of the state's revenue.

The early 2000's. In 2003, former governor William J. Janklow, the state's only member of the U.S. House of Representatives, killed a motorcyclist in a traffic accident. He was convicted of manslaughter, reckless driving, running a stop sign, and speeding. In 2004, he was fined and sentenced to 100 days in prison. He resigned from the House, and the state held a special election to replace him. Orville E. Gab and David A. Wolff

Related articles in *World Book* include:

Biographies

Calamity Jane	La Vérendrye, Sieur de
Crazy Horse	Lawrence, Ernest O.
Custer, George A.	McGovern, George S.
Daschle, Tom	Sitting Bull
Gall	Spotted Tail
Hickok, Wild Bill	Ward, Joseph

Cities

Pierre
Rapid City
Sioux Falls

History

Indian wars	Western frontier life
Lewis and Clark expedition	in America
Louisiana Purchase	Wounded Knee
Sioux Indians	

Physical features

Badlands	Great Plains
Black Hills	Minnesota River
Fort Randall Dam	Missouri River

Other related articles

Badlands National Park
Jewel Cave National Monument
Midwestern States
Mount Rushmore National Memorial
Wind Cave National Park

Outline

I. People
  A. Population
  B. Schools
  C. Libraries
  D. Museums
II. Visitor's guide
  A. Places to visit
  B. Annual events
III. Land and climate
  A. Land regions
  B. Rivers and lakes
  C. Plant and animal life
  D. Climate
IV. Economy
  A. Natural resources
  B. Service industries
  C. Manufacturing
  D. Agriculture
  E. Mining
  F. Electric power and utilities
  G. Transportation
  H. Communication
V. Government
  A. Constitution
  B. Executive
  C. Legislature
  D. Courts
  E. Local government
  F. Revenue
  G. Politics
VI. History

Additional resources

Level I
Santella, Andrew. *Mount Rushmore.* Children's Pr., 1999.
Shepherd, Donna W. *South Dakota.* Children's Pr., 2001.
Sirvaitis, Karen. *South Dakota.* 2nd ed. Lerner, 2002.

Level II
Bettelyoun, Susan B., and Waggoner, Josephine. *With My Own Eyes: A Lakota Woman Tells Her People's History.* Univ. of Neb. Pr., 1998.
Gries, John, P. *Roadside Geology of South Dakota.* Mountain Pr. Pub. Co., 1996.
Miller, John E. *Looking for History on Highway 14.* 1993. Reprint. S. Dak. State Hist. Soc., 2001.
Nelson, Paula M. *After the West Was Won: Homesteaders and Town Builders in Western South Dakota, 1900-1917.* Univ. of Ia. Pr., 1986. *The Prairie Winnows Out Its Own: The West River Country of South Dakota in the Years of Depression and Dust.* 1996.
Raventon, Edward. *Island in the Plains: A Black Hills Natural History.* 1994. Reprint. Johnson Bks., 2003.

South Dakota, University of, is a state-supported coeducational school in Vermillion, South Dakota. It has a college of arts and sciences and a college of fine arts. The university also has schools of business, education, law, and medicine; a graduate school; and a division of continuing education. Courses lead to bachelor's, master's, and doctor's degrees. The university was founded in 1862. Critically reviewed by the University of South Dakota

South Dakota State University is a state-controlled coeducational university in Brookings, South Dakota. It has colleges of agriculture and biological sciences, arts and science, education and counseling, engineering, family and consumer sciences, general studies, nursing, and pharmacy. It also has a graduate school. South Dakota State University grants associate, bachelor's, master's, and doctor's degrees. It was founded in 1881 as a land-grant school.

Critically reviewed by South Dakota State University

South Korea. See Korea, South.

South Pole is a term used for several invisible surface points in the Antarctic region. The best known is the *south geographic pole.* But other important south poles include the *instantaneous south pole,* the *south pole of balance,* the *south magnetic pole,* and the *geomagnetic south pole.*

The south geographic pole lies near the center of Antarctica at the point where all of Earth's lines of longitude meet. It is on 9,200 feet (2,800 meters) of glacial ice. Explorer Roald Amundsen of Norway beat Robert Scott of the United Kingdom to the south geographic pole in 1911 by five weeks. In 1956, the United States established a permanent scientific base called the Amundsen-Scott South Pole Station at the pole.

The instantaneous south pole lies at the point where Earth's *axis* (an imaginary line through Earth) meets the surface. Earth wobbles slowly as it turns on its axis, causing the instantaneous south pole to move. This pole takes about 14 months to move counterclockwise around an irregular path called the *Chandler Circle.* The diameter of the path varies from less than 1 foot (30 centimeters) to about 70 feet (21 meters).

The south pole of balance lies at the center of the Chandler Circle. Its position locates the south geographic pole. It has moved about 6 inches (15 centimeters) toward Australia each year since 1900.

The south magnetic pole is the farthest point on Earth in the direction of magnetic south. This pole may move as much as 5 to 10 miles (8 to 16 kilometers) in a year. Today, the pole lies off the coast of Wilkes Land. For location, see **Antarctica** (terrain map).

The geomagnetic south pole lies about 900 miles (1,400 kilometers) from the south geographic pole, toward Vincennes Bay. In the upper atmosphere, the magnetic field of Earth is directed upward and away from this point.   Sankar Chatterjee

Related articles in *World Book* include:

Amundsen, Roald	Earth (How Earth moves)
Antarctic Circle	Exploration (The exploration
Antarctica (Human activities)	of Antarctica)
Balchen, Bernt	Midnight sun
Byrd, Richard E.	Scott, Robert F.

South Sea Islands. See Pacific Islands.

South West Africa. See Namibia.

Southampton, *sowth AMP tuhn,* is a major seaport in the southern part of England, one of the United Kingdom's political divisions. The city lies on the River Test, near where the river flows into the English Channel (see **England** [political map]). Southampton, a unitary authority with all local government powers within its boundaries, had a population of 217,478 at the 2001 census.

Docks stand along Southampton's waterfront. The city is a center of cargo shipping and also of passenger traffic by sea between the United Kingdom and continental Europe. It is also a center for manufacturing, marine engineering, business services, health care, and tourism. The city is the home of the University of Southampton. Landmarks of Southampton include a number of medieval buildings and Bar Gate—part of a wall that encircled the city during the Middle Ages (the period from about the 400's through the 1400's).

The Romans founded a settlement at what is now Southampton shortly after they invaded the island of Great Britain in the A.D. 40's. It became a major seaport in the Middle Ages.   Peter R. Mounfield

Southampton Island, *sowth AMP tuhn,* is an island in Canada's territory of Nunavut. It lies between Hudson Bay and Foxe Basin (see **Canada** [political map]). It is 210 miles (338 kilometers) long and 150 miles (241 kilometers) wide, and it covers 15,913 square miles (41,214 square kilometers). Cliffs rise about 1,300 feet (400 meters) on the island's rugged northern shore. The southern area is *tundra* (cold, dry, treeless marshland). About 750 people live in Coral Harbour, the island's only community. The island has two bird sanctuaries.

G. Peter Kershaw

Southeast Asia includes the peninsula and islands east of India and Bangladesh and south of China. The region consists of Brunei, Cambodia, East Timor, Laos, Malaysia, Myanmar, the Philippines, Singapore, Thailand, Vietnam, and most of Indonesia.

Most of Southeast Asia's approximately 575 million people have Chinese or Malay ancestors. About three-fifths of the people live in rural areas. The region's largest urban centers surround the cities of Bangkok, Thailand; Jakarta, Indonesia; and Manila, Philippines. Buddhism and Islam are the area's major religions. Most Filipinos are Christians.

Southeast Asia has rich, fertile soil. Its main agricultural products are rubber, rice, tea, and spices. The region's forests produce most of the world's teak. The coastal waters yield large quantities of fish. Parts of the area have rich petroleum deposits and tin and gem mines. Since the mid-1980's, the manufacture of export goods has greatly contributed to rapid economic growth in Indonesia, Malaysia, Singapore, and Thailand.

Europeans, attracted by the area's natural riches, began to take over Southeast Asia in the 1500's. The United Kingdom, France, the Netherlands, Portugal, Spain, and the United States all have ruled parts of Southeast Asia. Only Thailand escaped foreign control. After World War II (1939-1945), the Philippines and the major British colonies gained independence peacefully. Elsewhere in Southeast Asia, several different groups fought for their independence.

In the 1950's, what had been the colony of French Indochina was divided into Cambodia, Laos, North Vietnam, and South Vietnam. In 1975, Communist North Vietnam conquered South Vietnam after the long and bitter Vietnam War. The Communists unified North and South Vietnam into the single country of Vietnam.

Frederick T. Temple

For more details on Southeast Asia, see **Asia** (Way of life in Southeast Asia). See also the separate articles for each country in Southeast Asia, and **Association of Southeast Asian Nations; Indochina; Vietnam War.**

K. Hisham, Bruce Coleman Inc.

Southampton is one of the United Kingdom's major ports and also is a center of shipbuilding. In this picture, the luxury ocean liner *Queen Elizabeth 2* is docked at Southampton for repairs.

Southeast Asia

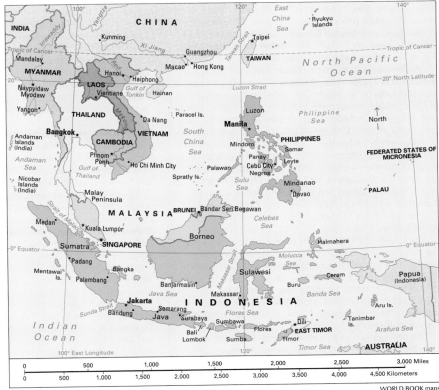

WORLD BOOK maps

★ Capital

• Other city or town

——— International boundary

Southeast Asia Treaty Organization (SEATO) was an alliance of eight nations that signed the Southeast Asia Collective Defense Treaty in Manila, the Philippines, on Sept. 8, 1954. The members were Australia, the United Kingdom, France, New Zealand, Pakistan, the Philippines, Thailand, and the United States. Pakistan withdrew in 1972. SEATO was dissolved in 1977.

The treaty was initiated by the United States after Communist forces defeated France in Indochina (present-day Vietnam, Laos, and Cambodia). The United States claimed that the alliance was needed to prevent the expansion of Communist influence in Southeast Asia. Under the terms of the treaty, member states agreed to help defend one another—as well as other designated nations—against military aggression. This aggression included threats both from other nations and from forces within member nations.

SEATO did not become an effective alliance. It failed partly because many Asian states, including India, Indonesia, and Japan, did not join. Also, SEATO's members disagreed on the extent of the Communist threat and on how to meet it. Only Australia, New Zealand, and Thailand sent combat troops to support the intervention of the United States in the Vietnam War (1957-1975).

Joseph Camilleri

See also **Cold War** (The death of Stalin).

Southern African Large Telescope (SALT) ranks as the largest visible-light telescope in the Southern Hemisphere. SALT's *primary* (main) mirror measures an average of 34 feet (10 meters) across. The telescope lies near Sutherland, South Africa, about 175 miles (280 kilo-

meters) northeast of Cape Town. SALT can detect objects a billion times fainter than those that are visible to the unaided eye. Astronomers can use it to study some of the most distant known objects in the universe.

SALT's primary mirror consists of 91 smaller *hexagonal* (six-sided) mirrors arranged to form part of a large, spherical bowl. Unlike many other large telescopes, SALT does not tilt its mirror to track a star, galaxy, or other object as it moves across the sky. Instead, instruments at the telescope's *focus* move to follow the object. The focus is the place where rays of light meet after being reflected by the mirror. SALT can track an object for a few hours. This design enables SALT to observe about 70 percent of Earth's southern sky without the complex and expensive machinery needed to tilt the mirror.

SALT is supported by a partnership that includes institutions in South Africa, the United States, Poland, Germany, the United Kingdom, and New Zealand. The telescope opened in 2005. Richard E. Griffiths

Southern Baptist Convention is a large Baptist denomination. The Convention has about 16 million members who worship in more than 41,000 churches in the United States. Southern Baptists sponsor about 5,000 home missionaries who serve the United States, Canada, Guam, and the Caribbean. The organization also sponsors more than 5,000 foreign missionaries in more than 150 other countries.

The Southern Baptist Convention has 41 state conventions and fellowships that help support 6 seminaries, 49 colleges and universities, 3 Bible schools, and 3 academies. The state conventions also help support hospitals, children's homes, and homes for the aging. Many of the denomination's offices are in Nashville, Tennessee.

The Southern Baptist Convention was organized in Augusta, Georgia, in 1845. For more information about Baptist doctrine and history, see **Baptists.**

Critically reviewed by the Southern Baptist Convention

Southern California, University of, is a coeducational private university in Los Angeles. It is one of the largest private universities in the western United States. The university includes 17 professional schools in addition to the central College of Letters, Arts, and Sciences. The University of Southern California grants bachelor's, master's, and doctor's degrees. It has a full graduate program, a summer session, and evening and extension programs. It also offers Air Force and Naval Reserve Officers Training Corps programs. The university supports a marine science center on Catalina Island and has teaching facilities in Sacramento, California, and in Washington, D.C.

The University of Southern California is well known for its programs in business administration, cinema-television, engineering, gerontology, journalism, linguistics, music, public administration, and social work. It is also famous for its major research programs. Researchers and physicians study and treat cancer patients at the university's Kenneth Norris Jr. Cancer Hospital and Research Institute.

The university was founded in 1880. It is the oldest major private university in the western United States.

Critically reviewed by the University of Southern California

Southern Christian Leadership Conference (SCLC) is a civil rights organization in the United States. The SCLC works to achieve equal rights for African Americans and other minority groups through nonviolent civil protest and community development programs. The SCLC also focuses on internal problems of the African American community, including crime and drug abuse. Most SCLC affiliates are church and civil rights groups.

Membership in the SCLC is open to all, but most of the organization's leaders are African American Protestant ministers. The SCLC is financed by contributions from individuals and groups. It also receives grants from foundations.

Martin Luther King, Jr., and other civil rights leaders founded the SCLC in 1957 to coordinate civil rights work in the South. King headed the SCLC from 1957 until his assassination in 1968. Headquarters are in Atlanta, Georgia.   Alton Hornsby, Jr.

See also **Abernathy, Ralph D.; Jackson, Jesse L.; King, Martin Luther, Jr.**

Southern Cross is a famous *constellation* (group of stars) in the Southern Hemisphere. It is also called the *Crux,* which is Latin for *cross.* The constellation gets its name from the outline of a cross formed by its four brightest stars. The star farthest to the south, the brightest star in the constellation, is of the first *magnitude* (measure of a star's brightness). The eastern and northern stars are of the second magnitude, and the western star is of the third magnitude. See **Magnitude.**

The four stars of the Southern Cross are not arranged in the exact form of a cross, and the constellation is sometimes difficult to pick out if one has not seen it before. The upper and lower stars of the constellation,

which form the "upright" of the cross, point to the South Pole of the sky. The Southern Cross appears too far south to be seen in the United States, with the exception of a few places.

The Southern Cross was visible in ancient Babylonia and Greece, where people considered it a part of the constellation Centaurus. The cross has gradually shifted toward the south in the sky as a result of Earth's *precession*—that is, the circular motion of Earth's axis.

Sumner Starrfield

Southern Methodist University is a private coeducational school in Dallas. It has schools of the arts, business, continuing education, engineering, humanities and sciences, law, and theology. The university grants bachelor's, master's, and doctor's degrees.

The university was founded in 1911 by the United Methodist Church. It opened in 1915.

Critically reviewed by Southern Methodist University

Southern Ocean is the body of water that surrounds Antarctica. The Southern Ocean covers about 8.5 million square miles (22 million square kilometers). It is the world's fourth largest ocean, ranking behind the Pacific, Atlantic, and Indian oceans. The Southern Ocean has also been referred to as the *Antarctic Ocean.*

Scientists long disagreed about whether the waters surrounding Antarctica should be considered an ocean. Oceanographers referred to those waters as the Southern Ocean, but geographers regarded the waters as extensions of the Pacific, Atlantic, and Indian oceans. In 2000, the International Hydrographic Organization (IHO), a group of major maritime nations, proposed that the waters around Antarctica be recognized as the Southern Ocean.

Boundaries. The southern boundary of the Southern Ocean is the coastline of Antarctica. The IHO set the northern boundary at 60° south latitude. That is also the northern boundary specified in the Antarctic Treaty, the most important international agreement on the use and the protection of Antarctica. That treaty took effect in 1961.

There is a natural border between the surface waters of the Southern Ocean and those of the Pacific, Atlantic, and Indian oceans. However, that border is too indefinite to be useful as an official boundary. The border is an imaginary line where the cold waters of the Southern Ocean meet the warmer waters of the other three oceans. It is known as the *Antarctic Convergence* (AAC) or the *polar front.* The AAC would not be useful as an official boundary because it shifts back and forth with the seasons and from year to year. Its general location ranges from 48° to 60° south latitude.

Two large seas, the Weddell Sea and the Ross Sea, extend far into Antarctica. Permanent ice in those two seas reaches as far south as 80° to 85° south latitude.

A land mass known as the Antarctic Peninsula extends

Facts in brief

Area: About 8.5 million mi² (22 million km²)
Average depth: 14,800 ft (4,500 m).
Greatest depth: 23,737 ft (7,235 m), at the southern end of the South Sandwich Trench.
Surface temperatures: *Highest*—30 to 43 °F (−1 to 6 °C).
Lowest—28 to 30 °F (−2 to −1 °C).

Southern Ocean

The Southern Ocean joins the South Atlantic, Indian, and South Pacific oceans at 60° south latitude, and it surrounds the continent of Antarctica.

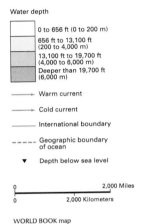

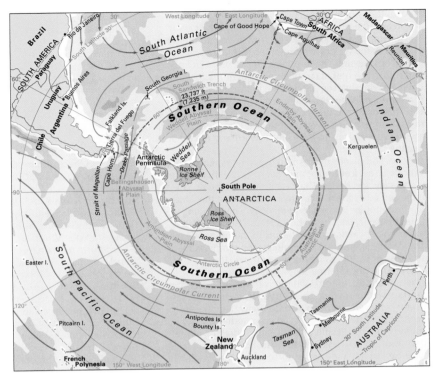

WORLD BOOK map

from Antarctica toward South America. Many islands are clustered around the peninsula.

People in Australia commonly use the term *Southern Ocean* to refer to all waters south of Australia. Those waters include part of the Indian Ocean.

The ocean floor. The continental shelf surrounding Antarctica is narrow and deep at its outer edge. The depth there ranges from about 1,300 to 2,600 feet (400 to 790 meters). By contrast, the depth of the shelf around other continents is less than 600 feet (200 meters). Antarctica's shelf edge is so deep because massive amounts of ice press the continent down.

The floor of the Southern Ocean includes five major *basins* (broad, deep regions): the Amundsen Abyssal Plain, the Australian-Antarctic Basin, the Bellingshausen Abyssal Plain, the Enderby Abyssal Plain, and the Weddell Abyssal Plain. Some areas of those basins reach depths of more than 16,400 feet (5,000 meters). The greatest depth in the Southern Ocean lies 23,737 feet (7,235 meters) below sea level at the southern end of the South Sandwich Trench.

Temperature. The Southern Ocean is often cold. At a latitude of 70° south, the sun never rises during midwinter, which occurs in June and July. In midsummer, which occurs in December and January, the sun never sets.

The surface waters reach their lowest temperatures of 28 to 30 °F (−2 or −1 °C) in August and their highest temperatures of 30 to 43 °F (−1 to 6 °C) in February. The lowest temperatures generally occur near Antarctica, and the highest temperatures near 60° south latitude.

Surface seawater freezes during the winter. As the water freezes, salts come out of the ice. The surrounding waters become more salty and thus more dense. During the winter, the surface waters freeze as far north as 55° south latitude on the Atlantic side and 65° south latitude on the Pacific side. During the summer, the sea ice retreats to about 67° to 70° south latitude.

Winds. The average wind speed between 40° and 67° south latitude is roughly 35 miles per hour (mph), or 55 kilometers per hour (kph)—higher than at any other place in the world. The winds there are *prevailing westerlies*—that is, they come from the west. They blow eastward in a circle around Antarctica.

Winds that blow away from Antarctica can reach tremendous speeds. Those winds, known as *katabatic winds,* originate high on the mass of ice that covers Antarctica. At that location, the air becomes extremely cold and dense. Due to the force of gravity, the heavy air then moves down the slopes at ever increasing speeds. The katabatic winds reach their maximum speeds in excess of 100 mph (160 kph) as they move down valleys and out over the Southern Ocean. The winds blow across the ocean more than 100 miles (160 kilometers) from some parts of Antarctica. The term *katabatic* comes from a Greek word meaning *to go down.*

Currents. The prevailing westerlies drive waters of the Southern Ocean eastward around Antarctica as the Antarctic Circumpolar Current. That current extends from north of the AAC to about 67° south latitude. The current transports about 4.6 billion cubic feet (130 million cubic meters) of water per second. That is approximately 100 times the flow of water from all the world's rivers. The current reaches depths of 9,800 feet (3,000 meters).

At latitudes higher than 67° south latitude and near Antarctica, the prevailing winds blow from the east. Those winds cause a narrow current to flow to the west on the surface waters around much of Antarctica.

Water masses. The Southern Ocean plays an important role in the global circulation of *water masses,* layers of water with different circulation patterns. The Antarctic Circumpolar Water is a major mass in the Southern Ocean. It occurs at depths of about 980 to 9,800 feet (300 to 3,000 meters). This water circulates from west to east around Antarctica and mixes northward into the other oceans.

At several places near Antarctica, and especially in the Weddell Sea, freezing at the ocean surface makes the water salty and dense. That water flows to the ocean floor and away from Antarctica, mixing with the Antarctic Circumpolar Water along the way. The resulting mass of water, known as the Antarctic Bottom Water, mixes and spreads into the basins of the other oceans. The Antarctic Bottom Water affects the temperature and saltiness of waters as far north as the equator.

The Antarctic Intermediate Water forms at the AAC when Antarctic Bottom Water mixes with cold, fresh water released by melting ice. The Antarctic Intermediate Water is therefore cooler and less salty than the Antarctic Bottom Water. The Antarctic Intermediate Water spreads into the Pacific, Atlantic, and Indian oceans at depths of 1,300 to 3,900 feet (400 to 1,200 meters). Its effects can be detected as far north as the North Atlantic Ocean.

Commercial resources of the Southern Ocean include fish and small shrimplike animals known as *krill.* Much of the krill caught is used as fish meal or animal feed. Many people eat krill that has been cut up into small pieces or made into a paste.

Whaling crews once hunted whales in the Southern Ocean. But in 1963, the International Whaling Commission (IWC) banned the killing of humpback whales in the Southern Hemisphere. The IWC banned the killing of blue whales in those waters in 1967. In 1994, the IWC declared that no commercial whaling would be allowed in Antarctic waters.

The floor of the Southern Ocean may contain much oil and gas. However, prospectors have not yet explored extensively for those resources. The severe conditions in the ocean would make the oil and gas expensive to bring to the surface.

Scientific research. In the early 2000's, many international scientific groups were studying the Southern Ocean. Major research topics included the ability of the ocean to dissolve carbon dioxide (CO_2). That topic is related to the issue of *global warming,* an increase in the average temperature of Earth's surface. Human activities are responsible for most of the warming that has occurred. The chief activity contributing to global warming has been the burning of *fossil fuels*—coal, oil, and natural gas. The burning of those fuels has increased the amount of CO_2 in the atmosphere. CO_2 is a *greenhouse gas,* one that contributes to global warming through a complex process involving sunlight, gases, and particles in the atmosphere. The Southern Ocean and the other oceans can dissolve some of the CO_2 that enters the atmosphere, thereby reducing the amount of global warming that will occur.

Global warming may affect the Southern Ocean and other areas of high latitude more than regions of low latitude. Satellites have already detected huge chunks of ice breaking free from Antarctica. Increases in the amount of ice in the Southern Ocean could lead to a rise in the sea level throughout the world.

Other researchers are studying how an increase in ultraviolet radiation might harm living things in the Southern Ocean. A layer of a gas called *ozone* in the upper atmosphere shields Earth from 95 to 99 percent of the sun's ultraviolet rays. But since the late 1970's, scientists have observed a thinning of the ozone layer over Antarctica and the Southern Ocean.   Dana R. Kester

See also **Antarctica; Global warming; Krill; Ocean; Ozone hole.**

Southern States are Alabama, Arkansas, Delaware, Florida, Georgia, Kentucky, Louisiana, Maryland, Mississippi, North Carolina, South Carolina, Tennessee, Virginia, and West Virginia.

For information on this region, see **United States** (Regions). See also the articles on the states that make up the region.

Southey, *SOW thee* or *SUHTH ee,* **Robert** (1774-1843), was poet laureate of England from 1813 until his death. He is chiefly remembered for a few ballads, including "The Battle of Blenheim" (1798), and for his association with poets William Wordsworth and Samuel Taylor Coleridge.

Critics consider Southey a better prose writer than poet. He wrote much history and biography, including the *Life of Nelson* (1813). His prose collection *The Doctor* (1834-1847) popularized the fairy tale "The Three Bears." Southey also wrote long verse romances, including *Thalaba, the Destroyer* (1801) and *The Curse of Kehama* (1810). The exotic, especially Asian, settings of these poems provided much of their appeal for Southey's readers. These works use Muslim and Hindu myths, and influenced Percy Shelley and other poets.

Southey was born on Aug. 12, 1774, in Bristol. He and Coleridge supported ideals that had inspired the American and French revolutions. They planned with another friend, Robert Lovell, to establish a utopian community in the United States. The project failed because of a lack of financial support. Southey later became conservative and supported the English monarchy, for which he was attacked in satires by poet Lord Byron, especially "The Vision of Judgment" (1822).   Frederick W. Shilstone

Southwestern States are Arizona, New Mexico, Oklahoma, and Texas. Arizona and New Mexico are also sometimes considered Rocky Mountain States, as well as Southwestern States.

For information on the Southwestern States region, see **United States** (Regions). See also the articles on the states that make up the region.

Sovereign. See Pound.

Sovereignty. The name *sovereign* was first applied to kings. Everyone in a kingdom was a subject of the king. The king himself was usually *sovereign,* which means *subject to no one.* Few kings are left in the world, but the idea of sovereignty remains. Today, national states are considered subject to no one, and therefore sovereign. A sovereign country can conduct its own affairs, enter into treaties, declare war, or adopt any other course of action without another nation's consent. Small countries are sometimes sovereign in name only. They shape their policies and conduct their affairs to suit the desires or needs of a stronger nation. The United States is a sovereign nation, but the 50 states which compose it do not have full sovereignty.   Robert J. Pranger

Soviet, *SOH vee eht,* is a Russian word that means *council.* Russian revolutionary groups were known as soviets. The first soviets were formed during the Russian workers' revolution in 1905. Soviets were formed throughout Russia after the downfall of the czar in March 1917. These soviets were councils made up of workers, peasants, and soldiers. These councils rallied groups of people to support the Socialist plan for setting up a Russian government. In 1917, Communists led by V. I. Lenin gained control of the soviets and of Russia. In 1922, the Soviet Union, officially known as the Union of Soviet Socialist Republics, was formed under Russia's leadership. The Soviet Union broke up into a number of independent countries in 1991.   Zvi Gitelman

Soviet Union. See Union of Soviet Socialist Republics.

Sow. See Hog.

Sow bug. See Wood louse.

Soweto, *suh WAY toh,* is South Africa's largest urban black African community. It is part of Johannesburg, the largest city in South Africa. Soweto has approximately 900,000 people—about one-fourth of the total population of Johannesburg.

Soweto consists mainly of residences—apartment buildings, *hostels* (inexpensive lodgings), houses, and shacks. People from a number of ethnic groups live in Soweto. The community has a university campus, a major soccer stadium, and the largest hospital in Africa.

Soweto is made up of areas called *townships* or *suburbs.* These areas were set up in stages starting in the early 1900's. South Africa's government relocated many thousands of black Africans to the townships as they were created. These people had come to the Johannesburg area mainly from rural regions in search of work. Many townships were set up under a racial segregation policy called *apartheid,* which lasted from the late 1940's to the early 1990's (see **Apartheid**). The name *Soweto,* adopted in 1963, comes from the first letters of each of the words *South Western Townships.* Soweto became part of Johannesburg in 1995.   Phillip L. Bonner

Sowthistle is the name of a group of weeds that grow wild in Europe. Several species of sowthistles have been introduced into the United States, where they have become a nuisance in gardens and fields. The *annual sowthistle* grows 2 to 3 feet (61 to 91 centimeters) high and has a branching stem. It contains a milky juice, and its flower heads resemble those of dandelions. Another type of sowthistle is the *perennial sowthistle.* Sowthistles are among the most troublesome weeds.

          Harold D. Coble

Peter Ward, Bruce Coleman Ltd.
Perennial sowthistle

Scientific classification. Sowthistles belong to the composite family, Asteraceae or Compositae. The scientific name for the annual sowthistle is *Sonchus oleraceus.* The perennial sowthistle is *S. arvensis.*

Soybean is a plant that serves as a vital source of food and provides raw materials for industry. Much of the world's vegetable oil and livestock feed come from soybeans. Manufacturers use the plant to make such products as paint and cosmetics.

The soybean yields one of the cheapest and most useful sources of protein. However, the kinds of proteins in soybeans differ from those in other protein-rich foods, such as beef, chicken, and fish (see **Protein** [Proteins in the diet]).

People in many countries eat soybeans instead of such other protein sources as meat, eggs, and cheese. *Tofu,* a food made from soybean curd, is popular in eastern Asia and other regions (see **Tofu**). In addition, soybean oil contains no cholesterol, and it has one of the lowest levels of saturated fat among vegetable oils.

People sometimes refer to the soybean as the *soya,* or *soja, bean.* Because soybeans live for only one year, they belong to a group of plants known as *annuals.* Soybeans also belong to the same scientific family as peas. Plants in this family are called *legumes* (see **Legume**).

The United States grows more soybeans than any other country. In fact, soybeans rank as the second largest U.S. crop, next to corn. Other important soybean producers around the world include Argentina, Brazil, and China.

The soybean plant

Growers typically plant soybeans in the spring. After six to eight weeks, small flowers appear on the plants. The flowers may be purple or white, depending on the variety of soybean plant. Soybean flowers develop for about two weeks, and some of them produce pods. Each pod contains two or three seeds, also called *beans.* As the seeds develop and mature, the plant's leaves turn yellow and drop to the ground. At maturity, most soybean plants stand from 2 to 4 feet (61 to 122 centimeters) tall.

Farmers cultivate many types of soybeans. Scientists have developed the types now used by crossing different soybean varieties or by altering the plants' *genes* (units of heredity). These methods produce soybean plants with special characteristics, such as light-colored seeds, resistance to disease, and increased yield.

The soybean plant is covered with short, fine, brown or gray hairs. The pods range in color from light yellow to shades of gray, brown, and black. Soybean seeds have a round or oval shape with yellow, green, brown, black, or speckled coloring, depending on the variety.

Farmers cultivate two main groups of soybeans: *commercial soybeans* and *vegetable-type soybeans.* Processors use commercial soybean varieties to make meal and oil. Most of these varieties have yellow or buff-colored seeds. The seeds measure about ¼ inch (5 to 7 millimeters) in diameter. Commercial soybeans make up most of the world's soybean crop. Vegetable-type soybeans are eaten as a vegetable or are used to produce bean sprouts. Most vegetable-type soybeans have green seeds. These seeds grow somewhat larger than the seeds of commercial soybeans.

International Harvester

Harvesting soybeans with a combine, *shown here,* cuts the plants and threshes and cleans the seeds in one operation. Soybeans are harvested in late summer or early fall.

WORLD BOOK illustration by James Teason

The soybean plant stands from 2 to 4 feet (61 to 122 centimeters) high. Each of its pods contains two or three seeds, or *beans,* which grow for 30 to 40 days.

Soybean products

Soybean meal and oil rank as the most important soy products. Many countries use a process called *solvent extraction* to make meal and oil. In this process, specialized machines first clean and dehull the seeds. Then rollers crush the seeds into flakes. Crude oil is *extracted* (removed) from the flakes by a *solvent,* a substance that can dissolve other substances. After the oil has been removed, the flakes are called *soybean meal* or, more commonly, *soy meal.*

Soy meal. Most of the world's soybean meal serves as food for animals. Manufacturers heat the flakes and make them into high-protein feed for cattle, hogs, and poultry. Food for house pets also contains soybeans.

Soybean meal comes in many foods that people eat. Processors can grind the meal into fine *soy flour* or coarser *soy grits.* Baby food, cereals, and various low-calorie products contain soy flour. Soy grits are used in candy and such processed meats as patties and sausages. Both soy flour and grits go into baked goods and pet foods.

Processors make a number of other products through further processing of soy flour. For example, they produce *soy protein concentrate* by extracting about a sixth of the nonprotein content from soy flour. This creamy concentrate can be made into a powder or a grainy substance. Processors use the concentrate in baby food, cereals, and processed meats. A product called *isolated soy protein* is made by removing about a fourth of the nonprotein content from soy flour. Isolated soy protein helps provide firmness and protein in various processed foods, especially meats.

A number of soy products make up a group of foods called *textured vegetable protein* (TVP). Processors chemically treat these foods to look and taste like meat so they will appeal to consumers. TVP foods can be mixed with meat or eaten alone. They cost less than meat and contain more protein. TVP products consist of either *extruded soy protein* or *spun soy protein.*

To make extruded soy protein, processors *extrude* (push) soy flour from machines in the same way that people squeeze toothpaste from tubes. The machine shapes the soy flour into small meatlike pieces. The product may be dried before being packaged for sale. Extruded soy protein becomes moist and chewy when the consumer adds water. People generally mix this food with ground meat.

To make spun soy protein, processors spin isolated soy protein into fibers. Spun soy products resemble such meats as beef, chicken, and ham. People buy them in canned, dried, and frozen form.

Many food items contain soy meal but do not consist entirely of treated soybeans. These products, called *soy derivatives,* include food flavorings, soy milk, and soy sauce. Manufacturers also use soy meal to make such products as fertilizer, fire extinguisher fluid, insect sprays, and paint.

Soy oil. Manufacturers make crude soybean oil into three basic products: (1) technical refined oil, (2) edible refined oil, and (3) lecithin.

Technical refined oil is produced by putting crude soy oil through several processes. First, manufacturers

Composition of soybeans

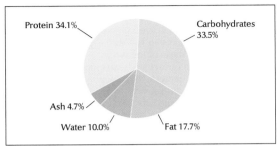

Protein 34.1%
Carbohydrates 33.5%
Ash 4.7%
Water 10.0%
Fat 17.7%

Source: U.S. Agricultural Research Service.

purify the crude oil by adding a mixture of water and a chemical called an *alkali*. Next, they wash and dry the oil. They then bleach the oil using absorbent clay and pass the bleached oil through a filter, producing technical refined oil. Such products as candles, disinfectants, linoleum, soaps, and varnishes contain technical refined oil.

Manufacturers make edible refined oil by deodorizing technical refined oil. They heat and steam the technical refined oil to remove its unpleasant odor and flavor. Oil derived from soybeans ranks as the most widely used edible oil in the world.

Processors often use edible oil to make products for commercial baking and frying. They also use the oil to manufacture cooking oils for home use and in making margarine, mayonnaise, salad dressings, and other food products. In addition, edible refined oil provides an ingredient for such products as adhesive tape, carbon paper, various drugs and explosives, and leather softeners.

Lecithin, a sticky substance, is extracted after mixing crude soy oil with water. Manufacturers use soybean lecithin in making candy, ice cream, and baking products. They also use it to produce chemicals, cosmetics, and textiles.

Growing soybeans

Soybean farming most often takes place in areas with fertile, well-drained soil. A good soybean crop requires at least 20 inches (51 centimeters) of rain during the growing season.

Farmers generally plant soybeans in spring. Most plant them in rows 20 to 30 inches (51 to 76 centimeters) apart. They space the seeds in each row 1 to 1 ½ inches (25 to 38 millimeters) apart and 1 to 2 inches (25 to 51 millimeters) deep. Farmers control weeds by means of cultivating machines and *herbicides* (chemical weed-killers) and by rotating soybeans with other crops. Like other legumes, soybeans obtain nitrogen from the air by means of bacteria growing on their roots. Thus they do not require nitrogen fertilizers.

Most farmers harvest soybeans in late summer or early fall. They use a machine called a *combine,* which cuts, threshes, and cleans the seeds in one operation. Farmers sell the harvested seeds to owners of storage elevators, to food manufacturers, and to other buyers. The buyers then ship the crop to processing plants or directly export it to other countries.

Leading soybean-growing states

Bushels of soybeans produced in a year

Iowa — 446,475,000 bushels
Illinois — 444,407,000 bushels
Minnesota — 261,142,000 bushels
Indiana — 243,518,000 bushels
Nebraska — 193,152,000 bushels
Missouri — 179,742,000 bushels
Ohio — 174,520,000 bushels
South Dakota — 127,457,000 bushels
Arkansas — 110,723,000 bushels
North Dakota — 85,783,000 bushels

One bushel equals 60 pounds (27 kilograms).
Figures are for a three-year average, 2002-2004.
Sources: U.S. Department of Agriculture.

Soybeans are grown in few areas of the world. The United States is the leading soybean-growing country. Other major producers include Argentina, Brazil, and China. Soybeans are also produced in Canada, India, Indonesia, Italy, and Paraguay.

Major soybean-producing area

Other soybean-producing area

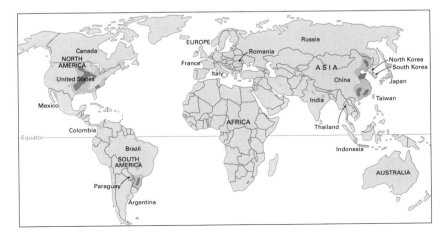

WORLD BOOK map

How soybeans are processed

Soybeans are processed into flakes and oil in an operation called *solvent extraction*. The flakes and oil are made into such products as meal for livestock and oil for cooking.

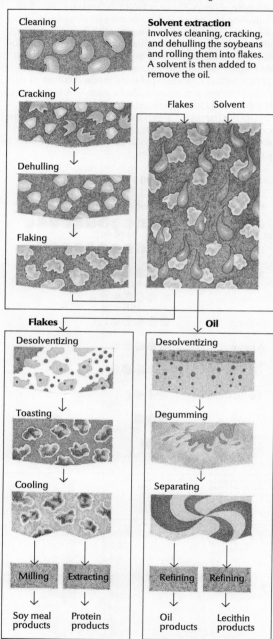

Cleaning

Cracking

Dehulling

Flaking

Solvent extraction involves cleaning, cracking, and dehulling the soybeans and rolling them into flakes. A solvent is then added to remove the oil.

Flakes   Solvent

Flakes

Desolventizing

Toasting

Cooling

Milling   Extracting

Soy meal products   Protein products

Oil

Desolventizing

Degumming

Separating

Refining   Refining

Oil products   Lecithin products

WORLD BOOK diagram

Flake processing removes the solvent by forcing steam through the flakes. The flakes are then toasted and cooled. The flakes may be milled to make soy meal products, or the protein may be extracted and used in food products.

Oil processing removes the solvent by heating the oil until the solvent vaporizes. Water is then added in a process called *degumming,* which helps separate lecithin from the oil. The oil and lecithin are then refined.

Diseases and pests. Dozens of diseases and pests attack soybeans. They include fungal diseases, bacterial diseases, and insects. Fungal diseases may attack the plants' roots, stems, or leaves. One of the most dangerous fungal diseases, *Asian soybean rust,* has spread from Asia to other parts of the world.

Bacterial diseases affect soybeans most severely during wet years. The bacteria that cause *bacterial blight* live in the soil and in diseased soybean plants. They enter healthy plants through the leaves. Wet spots form on the leaves and turn brown. Patches of leaf tissue die and fall out, and the entire leaf may die. *Bacterial pustule* involves *pustules* (small bumps filled with fluid) that form on the leaves.

Many animal pests attack soybeans, but few present serious threats. Common pests include the *bean leaf beetle, soybean aphid, stink bug,* and *velvetbean caterpillar.* Other threats to soybeans include viruses and tiny worms called *nematodes.*

Farmers use several methods to control diseases and pests. They may employ pesticide chemicals. For example, a special *fungicide* chemical can kill the fungus that causes Asian soybean rust. Farmers may spray this fungicide on the soybeans from the ground or from an airplane flying about 12 feet (3.7 meters) above the plants' leaves. The spraying of *insecticides* on soybean plants can kill many of the insect pests.

Overuse of pesticides, has proved harmful to the environment. As a result, many farmers now prefer to combat soybean diseases and pests by cultivating varieties resistant to those attackers. Scientists have created many resistant varieties by altering the plants' genes.

Growers also can prevent pests by using simple field management practices. For example, workers control the spread of insects by merely removing dead leaves and other debris where insects lay their eggs.

History

Soybeans rank among the oldest crops raised by human beings. Historians believe the plant first grew in eastern Asia. Soybeans were mentioned in Chinese literature about 3,000 years ago. The ancient Chinese considered soybeans their most important crop and one of the five sacred grains necessary for life.

Soybeans spread slowly to other parts of the world. People introduced the plants into Europe and North America during the 1600's and 1700's. Farmers in these areas first used soybeans as a food crop for livestock. During the 1930's, manufacturers widely introduced soybean products into human foods. Farmers soon grew soybean plants chiefly for their seeds.

Soybeans provide a vital tool for easing the world's food shortage. Soybeans grown on 1 acre (0.4 hectare) of land can provide about 10 times as much protein as can beef cattle raised on the same land. Soybeans yield more protein than most other vegetables or grains, making soybean cultivation one of the most efficient uses of land. More and more people have become aware of the protein value of the soybean and rely on it to supply their protein needs.   Daniel F. Austin

Scientific classification. The soybean belongs to the pea family, Fabaceae or Leguminosae. The scientific name for the cultivated soybean is *Glycine max.*

See also **Julian, Percy L.; Protein; Tofu.**

Soyer brothers were important American painters known for realistic scenes of city life in the 1930's. Raphael Soyer (1899-1987) and Moses Soyer (1899-1974) remained close in style and subject matter throughout their careers. They both specialized in depicting the working lives of anonymous, middle-class residents of the Lower East Side of New York City. Their most famous paintings movingly show the difficulty of surviving economically in an urban environment during the Great Depression of the 1930's.

Many of the Soyers' paintings portray unglamorous working women. Raphael's painting *Office Girls* (1936) is typical of their work. It shows women crowded on a city street but isolated in their individual struggles, reflected in their grim expressions. Other paintings of this period include Raphael's *Mission* (1933) and Moses's *Out of Work* (1937). Their later work includes Raphael's *Avenue of the Americas* (1970) and Moses's *Ballet Studio* (1955).

The Soyers were twin brothers who were born in Borisoglebsk, Russia. They immigrated with their family to the United States in 1912, settling in New York City. Both came to prominence during the late 1920's. Their

Office Girls (1936), an oil painting on canvas; Whitney Museum of American Art, New York City

A painting by Raphael Soyer shows a realistic city street scene. Soyer painted many pictures of unglamorous women in urban settings. His brother Moses painted similar pictures.

early art showed their admiration for the realistic style of the American painters George Bellows, Thomas Eakins, and Robert Henri. The Soyers also produced prints and drawings as well as paintings of friends and family members. Another brother, Isaac Soyer (1902-1981), also painted realistic scenes of urban life. Deborah Leveton

Soyinka, *shaw YIHN kuh* or *shaw ihn KAH,* **Wole,** *WOH lay* (1934-), won the 1986 Nobel Prize in literature. Soyinka, a Nigerian, was the first African writer to win the prize. Soyinka writes in English but draws from

the philosophy, religion, and language of the Yoruba people of southwestern Nigeria. He has written novels, poems, and nonfiction, but he is best known for his plays.

One of Soyinka's major plays, *The Road* (1965), explores colonialism and human responsibility. It also deals with the relationships between the lower and the middle classes, and between Yoruba religion and Christianity. Soyinka attacks European colonialism in his plays *Kongi's Harvest* (1965) and *A Play of Giants* (1984). However, his focus in these plays is on the forces within African society that permit dictatorship.

Soyinka believes that artists must sometimes take political action. In 1967, the Nigerian government arrested Soyinka because he tried to stop the civil war in Nigeria. He was jailed for about two years. *The Man Died: Prison Notes of Wole Soyinka* (1972) is his account of how he survived in prison. In *The Open Sore of a Continent* (1996), Soyinka analyzes Nigeria's political and social problems. He also wrote a memoir, *You Must Set Forth at Dawn* (2006).

Akinwande Oluwole Soyinka was born on July 13, 1934, in Abeokuta, Nigeria. "Wole" is an abbreviated form of his middle name. Peter Nazareth

Spaak, *spahk,* **Paul-Henri** (1899-1972), was a European statesman and the first Socialist prime minister of Belgium. He helped guide the redevelopment of Europe after World War II (1939-1945).

Spaak was born on Jan. 25, 1899, near Brussels. His political career as a Socialist leader began in the Belgian Chamber of Deputies in 1932. Starting in 1935, Spaak served in several Cabinet posts, most often as foreign minister. He served as Belgium's prime minister from 1938 to 1939, briefly in 1946, and from 1947 to 1949. Spaak also worked to establish Benelux. This economic union of Belgium, the Netherlands, and Luxembourg was organized in 1944. Spaak presided over the first session of the United Nations General Assembly in 1946.

In 1952, Spaak was elected president of the Assembly of the European Coal and Steel Community. From 1957 to 1961, he served as secretary-general of the North Atlantic Treaty Organization (NATO). Spaak died on July 31, 1972. Janet L. Polasky

Spaatz, *spahts,* **Carl** (1891-1974), was a distinguished combat leader of the United States Army Air Forces (AAF) in World War II (1939-1945). He pioneered the AAF's strategic bombing doctrine, which emphasized the bombing of enemy industrial sites.

In 1942, Spaatz became commander of the Eighth Air Force in England. In 1943, he was promoted to lieutenant general and took command of the Northwest African Air Forces. This combined U.S.-British force supported the conquest of Tunisia and the invasions of Sicily and Italy. Spaatz then led the U.S. Strategic Air Forces in Europe for the final assault on Germany in 1944 and 1945. See **World War II** (The air war).

After the victory in Europe, Spaatz went to the Pacific, where his air forces bombed Japan. He commanded the Army Air Forces in 1946, and he became the first chief of staff of the newly independent U.S. Air Force in 1947.

Spaatz was born on June 28, 1891, in Boyertown, Pennsylvania. He graduated from the U.S. Military Academy in 1914. Spaatz died on July 4, 1974. Adrian R. Lewis

Space. See **Space exploration** (What is space?).

NASA

United States astronauts landed on the moon six times between 1969 and 1972. In this photograph, Apollo 16 astronaut
John W. Young salutes a U.S. flag on the moon's surface.

U.S. Geological Survey

Space probes travel far into space to gather information about
moons, planets, comets, and stars. A Voyager probe took this
photograph of Io, a moon of Jupiter.

Space exploration

Space exploration is our human response to curiosity about Earth, the moon, the planets, the sun and other
stars, and the galaxies. Piloted and unpiloted space vehicles venture far beyond the boundaries of Earth to collect valuable information about the universe. Human beings have visited the moon and have lived in space
stations for long periods. Space exploration helps us see
Earth in its true relation with the rest of the universe.
Such exploration could reveal how the sun, the planets,
and the stars were formed and whether life exists beyond our own world.

The space age began on Oct. 4, 1957. On that day, the

*James Oberg, the contributor of this article, is a space flight
engineer, author, and lecturer.*

Soviet Union launched Sputnik (later referred to as Sputnik 1), the first artificial satellite to orbit Earth. The first
human space flight was made on April 12, 1961, when
Yuri A. Gagarin, a Soviet cosmonaut, orbited Earth in the
spaceship Vostok (later called Vostok 1).

Remotely controlled vehicles called *space probes*
have vastly expanded our knowledge of outer space, the
planets, and the stars. In 1959, one Soviet probe passed
close to the moon and another hit the moon. A United
States probe flew past Venus in 1962. In 1974 and 1976,
the United States launched two German probes that
passed inside the orbit of Mercury, close to the sun.
Two other U.S. probes landed on Mars in 1976. In addition to studying planets and their moons, space probes
have investigated comets and asteroids.

The first human voyage to the moon began on Dec.
21, 1968, when the United States launched the Apollo 8
spacecraft. It orbited the moon 10 times and returned
safely to Earth. On July 20, 1969, U.S. astronauts Neil

NASA

Shuttle astronauts have performed many challenging missions in space. In 1992, three astronauts worked outside the shuttle Endeavour to capture a communications satellite.

A. Armstrong and Buzz Aldrin landed their Apollo 11 lunar module on the moon. Armstrong became the first person to set foot on the moon. United States astronauts made five more landings on the moon before the Apollo lunar program ended in 1972.

During the 1970's, astronauts and cosmonauts developed skills for living in space aboard the Skylab and Salyut space stations. In 1987 and 1988, two Soviet cosmonauts spent 366 consecutive days in orbit.

On April 12, 1981, the U.S. space shuttle Columbia blasted off. It was the first reusable spaceship and the first spacecraft able to land at an ordinary airfield. On Jan. 28, 1986, a tragic accident occurred. The U.S. space shuttle Challenger tore apart in midair, killing all seven astronauts aboard. The shuttle was redesigned, and flights resumed in 1988. Another tragedy struck on Feb. 1, 2003, when the Columbia broke apart as it reentered Earth's atmosphere. All seven crew members died. The United States did not launch a shuttle again until 2005.

In the early years of the space age, the United States and the Soviet Union were engaged in an intense rivalry called the Cold War. As a result, the two nations competed with each other in developing space programs. In

Important dates in the history of space exploration

1926 American scientist Robert H. Goddard launched the world's first liquid-propellant rocket.

1957 (Oct. 4) The Soviet Union launched Sputnik (later referred to as Sputnik 1), the first artificial satellite.

1958 The National Aeronautics and Space Administration (NASA) was formed.

1959 (Sept. 12) The Soviet Union launched Luna 2, the first space probe to hit the moon.

1961 (April 12) Soviet cosmonaut Yuri A. Gagarin became the first person to orbit the earth.

1961 (May 5) Alan B. Shepard, Jr., became the first U.S. astronaut in space.

1962 (Feb. 20) John H. Glenn, Jr., became the first U.S. astronaut to orbit the earth.

1963 (June 16) Soviet cosmonaut Valentina Tereshkova became the first woman in space.

1964 (Oct. 12) The Soviet Union launched Voskhod (later called Voskhod 1), the first multiperson space capsule.

1968 (Dec. 21) The United States launched Apollo 8, the first manned space mission to orbit the moon.

1969 (July 20) U.S. astronauts Neil A. Armstrong and Buzz Aldrin made the first manned lunar landing.

1970 (Aug. 17) The Soviet Union launched Venera 7, which became the first space probe to transmit data from Venus's surface after it landed on Dec. 15, 1970.

1971 (June 7) Soviet cosmonauts boarded Salyut 1, making it the first manned orbiting space station.

1975 (June 8) The Soviet Union launched the probe Venera 9, the first spacecraft to photograph the surface of Venus.

1975 (July 15) The United States and the Soviet Union launched the first international manned space mission.

1975 (Aug. 20) The United States launched the probe Viking 1. This probe, along with a second probe called Viking 2, landed on Mars in 1976 and sent back photos and data.

1977 (Aug. 20) The United States launched the probe Voyager 2, which flew past and photographed Jupiter in 1979, Saturn in 1981, Uranus in 1986, and Neptune in 1989.

1981 (April 12) The United States launched the space shuttle Columbia, the first reusable manned spacecraft.

1985 (July 2) The European Space Agency launched the probe Giotto, which passed Halley's Comet on March 14, 1986, photographed the comet's nucleus, and sent back data.

1986 (Jan. 28) The U.S. space shuttle Challenger was destroyed in an accident in midair, killing all seven crew members.

1989 (Oct. 18) The United States launched the probe Galileo, which reached Jupiter in 1995. Galileo transmitted information about Jupiter and its satellites.

1990 (Aug. 10) The U.S. space probe Magellan began to orbit Venus and return radar images of the planet's surface.

1995 (March 22) Cosmonaut Valery Polyakov spent a record 438 days in space on the Russian space station Mir.

1996 The United States launched the probe Pathfinder, which landed on Mars on July 4, 1997. The probe and a remote-controlled vehicle sent back photos and data.

1996 (Nov. 7) The United States launched the Mars Global Surveyor probe to map the planet. The probe began to orbit Mars in September 1997.

1997 (Oct. 15) The United States launched the space probe Cassini, which reached Saturn in 2004.

2003 (Feb. 1) The U.S. space shuttle Columbia was destroyed in an accident in midair, killing all seven crew members.

2003 (Oct. 15) Yang Liwei became the first person launched into space by China.

2004 (June 21) Scaled Composites of Mojave, California, became the first private company to launch a person into space.

the 1960's and 1970's, this "space race" drove both nations to tremendous exploratory efforts.

A major dispute in the development of space programs has been the proper balance of manned and unmanned exploration. Some experts favor unmanned

Space exploration terms

Artificial satellite is a manufactured object that orbits the earth or any other body in space.

Astronaut is a general term for any space traveler, particularly one from the United States.

Booster is the rocket that provides most or all of the energy for the launch of a spacecraft.

Cosmonaut is an astronaut from the former Soviet Union or the present Commonwealth of Independent States.

Entry is the phase of a space flight during which the vehicle is moving through a planet's atmosphere before landing.

Escape velocity is the minimum speed a spacecraft must reach to overcome the pull of gravity.

Extravehicular activity, or **EVA,** refers to activities performed outside a vehicle in outer space.

Heat shield is that part of a spacecraft designed to protect the vehicle from heat during atmospheric entry. The shield may consist of tiles or other types of insulation.

Launch vehicle is a rocket used to launch a spacecraft or satellite into space.

Launch window is the period when a spacecraft's target—such as a planet or a satellite—is properly lined up with the launch point, creating an efficient flight path.

Lox, or **liquid oxygen,** consists of oxygen cooled to a temperature of −297 °F (−183 °C), at which it becomes a liquid. It is a common source of oxygen to use in burning rocket fuel.

Microgravity refers to those conditions that occur during orbital flight when a spacecraft's contents and crew float freely, without the feeling of weight that gravity normally produces.

Mission control is a facility on the ground that supervises a space flight.

Module is a section of a spacecraft that can be disconnected and separated from other sections.

Orbit is the path of a spacecraft or a heavenly body as it revolves around a planet or other body.

Orbital velocity is the minimum velocity needed to maintain an orbit around the earth or some other body.

Oxidizer is the substance in a rocket propellant that provides the oxygen needed to make the fuel burn in the airlessness of space.

Payload is the cargo carried into space aboard a spacecraft, including passengers and instruments.

Propellant is the material burned by a rocket to generate thrust. It generally consists of both fuel and an oxidizer.

Sounding rocket is a rocket that carries scientific instruments into the upper atmosphere or into space near the earth.

Space probe is an unmanned spacecraft sent to explore other planets, celestial bodies, or interplanetary space.

Space shuttle is a reusable space vehicle that takes off like a rocket and lands like an airplane.

Space station is an orbiting spacecraft designed to be occupied by teams of astronauts or cosmonauts over a long period.

Stage is a section of a rocket having its own engine.

Telemetry is the use of radio signals to receive information from spacecraft in flight.

Thrust is the push given to a rocket by the expulsion of the gases created by burning fuel.

---

probes because they may be cheaper, safer, and faster than manned vehicles. They note that probes can make trips that would be too risky for human beings to attempt. On the other hand, probes generally cannot react to unexpected occurrences. Today, most space planners favor a combined, balanced strategy of unmanned probes and manned expeditions. Probes can visit uncharted regions of space or patrol familiar regions where the data to be gathered fall within expected limits. But in some cases, people must follow the probes and use human ingenuity, flexibility, and courage to explore the mysteries of the universe.

What is space?

Space is the near-emptiness in which all objects in the universe move. The planets and the stars are tiny dots compared with the vast expanse of space.

The beginning of space. The earth is surrounded by air, which makes up its atmosphere. As the distance from the earth increases, the air becomes thinner. There is no clear boundary between the atmosphere and outer space. But most experts say that space begins somewhere beyond 60 miles (95 kilometers) above the earth.

Outer space just above the atmosphere is not entirely empty. It contains some particles of air, as well as space dust and occasional chunks of metallic or stony matter called *meteoroids.* Various kinds of radiation flow freely. Thousands of spacecraft known as *artificial satellites* have been launched into this region of space.

The earth's *magnetic field,* the space around the planet in which its magnetism can be observed, extends far out beyond the atmosphere. The magnetic field traps electrically charged particles from outer space, forming zones of radiation called the *Van Allen belts.*

The region of space in which the earth's magnetic field controls the motion of charged particles is called the *magnetosphere.* It is shaped like a teardrop, with the point extending away from the sun. Beyond this region, the earth's magnetic field is overpowered by that of the sun. But even such vast distances are not beyond the reach of the earth's gravity. As far as 1 million miles (1.6

million kilometers) from the earth, this gravity can keep a satellite orbiting the planet instead of flying off into space.

Space between the planets is called *interplanetary space.* The sun's gravity controls the motion of the planets in this region. That is why the planets orbit the sun.

Huge distances usually separate objects moving through interplanetary space. For example, the earth revolves around the sun at a distance of about 93 million miles (150 million kilometers). Venus moves in an orbit 68 million miles (110 million kilometers) from the sun. Venus is the planet that comes closest to the earth—25 million miles (40 million kilometers) away—whenever it passes directly between the earth and the sun. But this is still 100 times as far away as the moon.

Space between the stars is called *interstellar space.* Distances in this region are so great that astronomers do not describe them in miles or kilometers. Instead, scientists measure the distance between stars in units called *light-years.* For example, the nearest star to the sun is Proxima Centauri, 4.2 light-years away. A light-year equals 5.88 trillion miles (9.46 trillion kilometers). This is the distance light travels in one year at its speed of 186,282 miles (299,792 kilometers) per second.

Various gases, thin clouds of extremely cold dust, and a few escaped comets float between the stars. Interstellar space also contains many objects not yet discovered.

Kinds of earth orbits

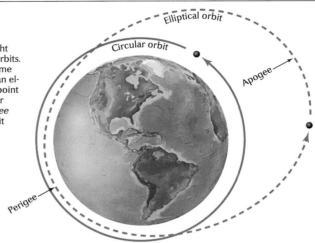

Circular and elliptical orbits. The diagram at the right shows the difference between circular and elliptical orbits. In a circular orbit, a spacecraft always travels at the same speed and stays the same distance from the earth. In an elliptical orbit, a spacecraft goes fastest at *perigee* (the point closest to the earth) and then slows as it swings farther from the earth. The spacecraft travels slowest at *apogee* (the point farthest from the earth), but it speeds up as it curves back closer to the earth.

An inclined orbit forms an angle with the equator. In the diagrams below, the red lines show the orbit, and the blue lines represent the spacecraft's path as mapped on the earth. Because the earth rotates, the spacecraft does not pass over the same points on the earth during each orbit. As a result, the path of the spacecraft appears as crisscrossed lines on the earth.

First orbit

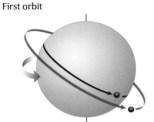

Fourth orbit

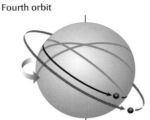

Eighth orbit

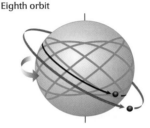

A polar orbit carries a spacecraft over the North and South poles. As the earth rotates, the spacecraft passes over different points on the earth during each orbit, as shown in the diagrams below. A polar orbit is useful for scientific satellites such as Nimbus. By orbiting almost directly over the poles, Nimbus can photograph the entire earth once a day.

First orbit

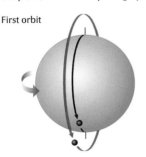

Fourth orbit

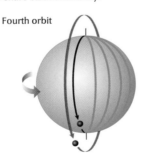

Eighth orbit

A geosynchronous orbit carries a spacecraft around the earth once every day. The diagram below shows the path of a Syncom communications satellite. As mapped on the earth, the path is a figure eight, because the orbit is slightly inclined. If the craft were launched directly in line with the equator, it would stay above one spot on the earth without moving north or south.

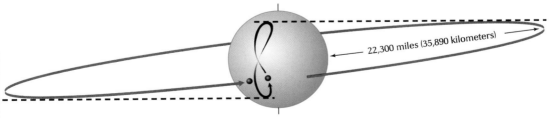

22,300 miles (35,890 kilometers)

Getting into space and back

Overcoming gravity is the biggest problem for a space mission. A spacecraft must be launched at a particular *velocity* (speed and direction).

Gravity gives everything on the earth its weight and accelerates free-falling objects downward. At the surface of the earth, acceleration due to gravity, called *g,* is about 32 feet (10 meters) per second each second.

A powerful rocket called a *launch vehicle* or *booster* helps a spacecraft overcome gravity. All launch vehicles have two or more rocket sections known as *stages.* The first stage must provide enough *thrust* (pushing force) to leave the earth's surface. To do so, this stage's thrust must exceed the weight of the entire launch vehicle and the spacecraft. The booster generates thrust by burning fuel and then expelling gases. Rocket engines run on a special mixture called *propellant.* Propellant consists of solid or liquid fuel and an *oxidizer,* a substance that supplies the oxygen needed to make the fuel burn in the airlessness of outer space. *Lox,* or *liquid oxygen,* is a frequently used oxidizer.

The minimum velocity required to overcome gravity and stay in orbit is called *orbital velocity.* At a rate of acceleration of 3 g's, or three times the acceleration due to gravity, a vehicle reaches orbital velocity in about nine minutes. At an altitude of 120 miles (190 kilometers),

Launch vehicles that made history

The vehicles shown on this page helped the United States and the Soviet Union achieve milestones in the exploration of space. The United States no longer builds these rockets, but Russia continues to use the Soviet A Class design in the Soyuz rocket on the facing page.

WORLD BOOK illustrations by Oxford Illustrators Limited

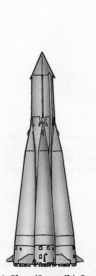
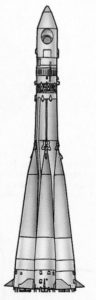

Jupiter C, U.S. Lifted Explorer I, the first U.S. satellite, in 1958. 68 feet (21 meters)

Mercury-Redstone, U.S. Launched Alan Shepard in 1961. 83 feet (25 meters)

A Class (Sputnik), Soviet Boosted Sputnik 1, the first artificial satellite, in 1957. 98 feet (29 meters)

A Class (Vostok), Soviet Carried Yuri Gagarin, the first person to orbit the earth, in 1961. 126 feet (38 meters)

Saturn 5, U.S. Launched Neil Armstrong, the first person to set foot on the moon, in 1969. 363 feet (111 meters)

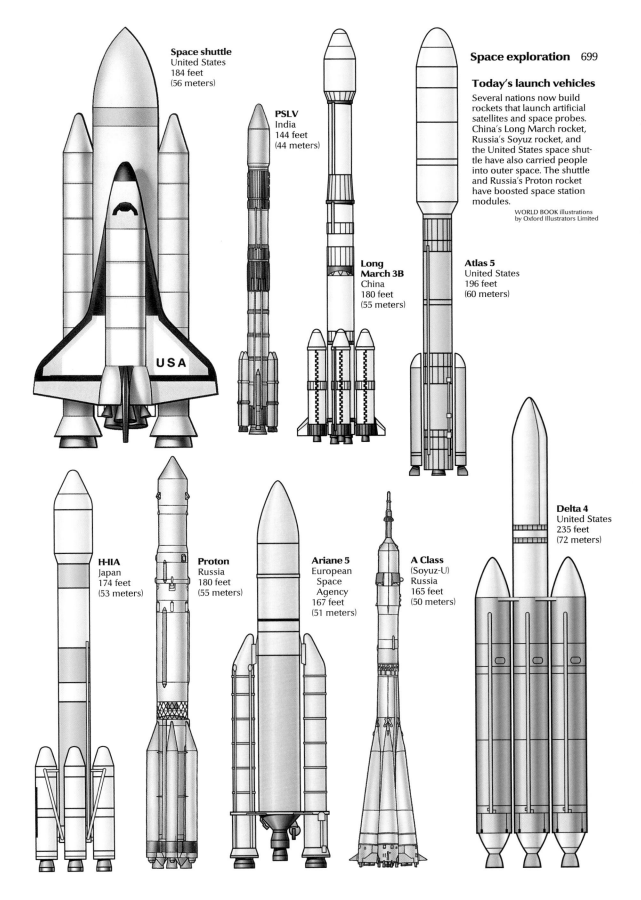

Space shuttle
United States
184 feet
(56 meters)

PSLV
India
144 feet
(44 meters)

Long March 3B
China
180 feet
(55 meters)

Today's launch vehicles

Several nations now build rockets that launch artificial satellites and space probes. China's Long March rocket, Russia's Soyuz rocket, and the United States space shuttle have also carried people into outer space. The shuttle and Russia's Proton rocket have boosted space station modules.

WORLD BOOK illustrations
by Oxford Illustrators Limited

Atlas 5
United States
196 feet
(60 meters)

USA

H-IIA
Japan
174 feet
(53 meters)

Proton
Russia
180 feet
(55 meters)

Ariane 5
European
Space
Agency
167 feet
(51 meters)

A Class
(Soyuz-U)
Russia
165 feet
(50 meters)

Delta 4
United States
235 feet
(72 meters)

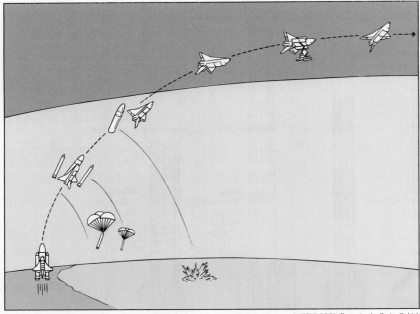

WORLD BOOK illustration by Zorica Dabich

The space shuttle takes off by using the fuel in its solid rocket boosters and external tank. After the fuel has been used, the boosters return to the earth by parachute and the tank falls into the ocean. In orbit, the spacecraft's payload bay doors are opened for such purposes as releasing or retrieving a satellite.

the speed needed for a spacecraft to maintain orbital velocity and thus stay in orbit is about 5 miles (8 kilometers) per second.

In many rocket launches, a truck or tractor moves the rocket and its *payload* (cargo) to the launch pad. At the launch pad, the rocket is moved into position over a flame pit, and workers load propellants into the rocket through special pipes.

At launch time, the rocket's first-stage engines ignite until their combined thrust exceeds the rocket's weight.

The thrust causes the vehicle to lift off the launch pad. If the rocket is a multistage model, the first stage falls away a few minutes later, after its propellant has been used up. The second stage then begins to fire. A few minutes later, it, too, runs out of propellant and falls away. If needed, a small *upper stage* rocket then fires until orbital velocity is achieved.

The launch of a space shuttle is slightly different. The shuttle has solid-propellant boosters in addition to its main rocket engines, which burn liquid propellant. The

WORLD BOOK illustration by Zorica Dabich

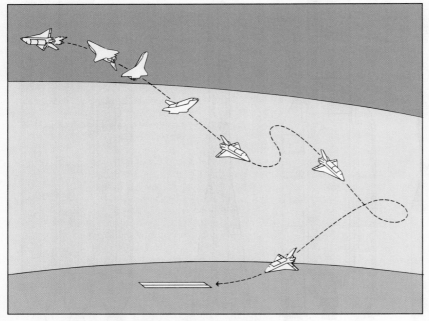

The orbiter returns to the earth by firing two engines that reduce its speed. The spacecraft enters the earth's atmosphere at a speed of more than 16,000 miles (25,800 kilometers) per hour and maneuvers into landing position. It lands on a runway at a speed of about 200 miles (320 kilometers) per hour.

boosters combined with the main engines provide the thrust to lift the vehicle off the launch pad. After slightly more than two minutes of flight, the boosters separate from the shuttle and return to the earth by parachute. The main engines continue to fire until the shuttle has almost reached orbital velocity. Small engines on the shuttle push it the remainder of the way to orbital velocity.

To reach a higher altitude, a spacecraft must make another rocket firing to increase its speed. When the spacecraft reaches a speed about 40 percent faster than orbital velocity, it achieves *escape velocity,* the speed necessary to break free of the earth's gravity.

Returning to the earth involves the problem of decreasing the spacecraft's great speed. To do this, an orbiting spacecraft uses small rockets to redirect its flight path into the upper atmosphere. This action is called *deorbit.* A spacecraft returning to the earth from the moon or from another planet also aims its path to skim the upper atmosphere. Air resistance then provides the rest of the necessary *deceleration* (speed reduction).

At the high speeds associated with reentering the atmosphere from space, air cannot flow out of the way of the onrushing spacecraft fast enough. Instead, molecules of air pile up in front of it and become tightly compressed. This squeezing heats the air to a temperature of more than 10,000 °F (5,500 °C), hotter than the surface of the sun. The resulting heat that bathes the spacecraft would burn up an unprotected vehicle in seconds. Insulating plates of quartz fiber glued to the skin of some spacecraft create a *heat shield* that protects against the fierce heat. Refrigeration may also be used. Early spacecraft had *ablative shields* that absorbed heat by burning off, layer by layer, and vaporizing.

Many people mistakenly believe that the spacecraft skin is heated through friction with the air. Technically, this belief is not accurate. The air is too thin and its speed across the spacecraft's surface is too low to cause much friction.

For unmanned space probes, deceleration forces can be as great as 60 to 90 g's, or 60 to 90 times the acceleration due to gravity, lasting about 10 to 20 seconds. Space shuttles use their wings to skim the atmosphere and stretch the slowdown period to more than 15 minutes, thereby reducing the deceleration force to about $1\frac{1}{2}$ g's.

When the spacecraft has lost much of its speed, it falls freely through the air. Parachutes slow it further, and a small rocket may be fired in the final seconds of descent to soften the impact of landing. Some spacecraft, including the space shuttle, use their wings to glide to a runway and land like an airplane. The early U.S. space capsules used the cushioning of water and "splashed down" into the ocean.

Living in space

When people orbit the earth or travel to the moon, they must live temporarily in space. Conditions there differ greatly from those on the earth. Space has no air, and temperatures reach extremes of heat and cold. The sun gives off dangerous radiation. Various types of matter also create hazards in space. For example, particles of dust called *micrometeoroids* threaten vehicles with destructive high-speed impacts. *Debris* (trash) from previous space missions can also damage spacecraft.

On the earth, the atmosphere serves as a natural shield against many of these threats. But in space, astronauts and equipment need other forms of protection. They must also endure the physical effects of space travel and protect themselves from high acceleration forces during launch and landing.

The basic needs of astronauts in space must also be met. These needs include breathing, eating and drinking, elimination of body wastes, and sleeping.

Protection against the dangers of space

Engineers working with specialists in space medicine have eliminated or greatly reduced most of the known hazards of living in space. Space vehicles usually have double hulls for protection against impacts. A particle striking the outer hull disintegrates and thus does not damage the inner hull.

Astronauts are protected from radiation in a number of ways. Missions in earth orbit remain in naturally protected regions, such as the earth's magnetic field. Filters installed on spacecraft windows protect the astronauts from blinding ultraviolet rays.

The crew must also be protected from the intense heat and other physical effects of launch and landing.

Space vehicles require a heat shield to resist high temperatures and sturdy construction to endure crushing acceleration forces. In addition, the astronauts must be seated in such a way that the blood supply will not be pulled from their head to their lower body, causing dizziness or unconsciousness.

Aboard a spacecraft, temperatures climb because of the heat given off by electrical devices and by the crew's bodies. A set of equipment called a *thermal control system* regulates the temperature. The system pumps fluids warmed by the cabin environment into radiator panels, which discharge the excess heat into space. The cooled fluids are pumped back into coils in the cabin.

Microgravity

Once in orbit, the space vehicle and everything inside it experience a condition called *microgravity.* The vehicle and its contents fall freely, resulting in an apparently weightless floating aboard the spacecraft. For this reason, microgravity is also referred to as *zero gravity.* However, both terms are technically incorrect. The gravitation in orbit is only slightly less than the gravitation on the earth. The spacecraft and its contents continuously fall toward the earth. But because of the vehicle's tremendous forward speed, the earth's surface curves away as the vehicle falls toward it. The continuous falling seems to eliminate the weight of everything inside the spacecraft. For this reason, the condition is sometimes referred to as *weightlessness.*

Microgravity has major effects on both equipment and people. For example, fuel does not drain from tanks in microgravity, so it must be squeezed out by high-pressure gas. Hot air does not rise in microgravity, so

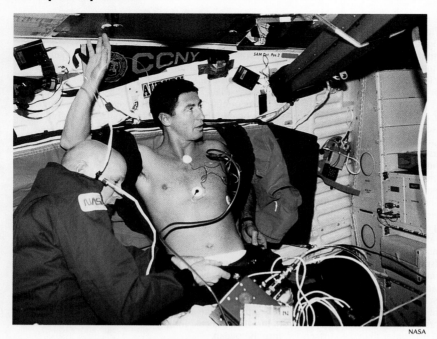

NASA

Recording medical information on a spacecraft enables physicians to identify any abnormal changes in the body that could indicate physical disorders or stress.

air circulation must be driven by fans. Particles of dust and droplets of water float throughout the cabin and only settle in filters on the fans.

The human body reacts to microgravity in a number of ways. In the first several days of a mission, about half of all space travelers suffer from persistent nausea, sometimes accompanied by vomiting. Most experts believe that this "space sickness," called *space adaptation syndrome,* is the body's natural reaction to microgravity. Drugs to prevent motion sickness can provide some relief for the symptoms of space adaptation syndrome,

and the condition generally passes in a few days.

Microgravity also confuses an astronaut's *vestibular system*—that is, the organs of balance in the inner ear—by preventing it from sensing differences in direction. After a few days in space, the vestibular system disregards all directional signals. Soon after an astronaut returns to the earth, the organs of balance resume normal operation.

Over a period of days or weeks, an astronaut's body experiences *deconditioning.* In this process, muscles grow weak from lack of use, and the heart and blood

NASA

Microgravity, the apparent weightlessness in space, has a variety of effects. This special chair and helmet are used to study how microgravity affects a person's sense of direction.

NASA

An apparently weightless floating makes some tasks challenging inside an orbiting spacecraft. In this photograph, a shuttle astronaut struggles with a floating computer printout.

vessels "get lazy." Strenuous exercise helps prevent deconditioning. Space travelers ride exercise bikes, use treadmills, and perform other types of physical activity.

After many months in space, a process called *demineralization* weakens the bones. Most physicians believe that demineralization results from the absence of stress on the bones in a weightless environment. The experiences of Soviet cosmonauts who spent long periods in orbit showed that vigorous exercise and a special diet can minimize demineralization.

Meeting basic needs in space

Manned space vehicles have life-support systems designed to meet all the physical needs of the crew members. In addition, astronauts can carry portable life-support systems in backpacks when they work outside the main spacecraft.

Breathing. A manned spacecraft must have a source of oxygen for the crew to breathe and a means of removing carbon dioxide, which the crew exhales. Manned space vehicles use a mixture of oxygen and nitrogen similar to the earth's atmosphere at sea level. Fans circulate air through the cabin and over containers filled with pellets of a chemical called lithium hydroxide. These pellets absorb carbon dioxide from the air. Carbon dioxide can also be combined with other chemicals for disposal. Charcoal filters help control odors.

Eating and drinking. The food on a spacecraft must be nutritious, easy to prepare, and convenient to store. On early missions, astronauts ate *freeze-dried foods*—that is, frozen foods with the water removed. To eat, the astronauts simply mixed water into the food. Packaging consisted of plastic tubes. The astronauts used straws to add the water.

Over the years, the food available to space travelers became more appetizing. Today, astronauts enjoy ready-to-eat meals much like convenience foods on the earth. Many space vehicles have facilities for heating frozen and chilled food.

Water for drinking is an important requirement for a space mission. On space shuttles, devices called *fuel cells* produce pure water as they generate electricity for the spacecraft. On long missions, water must be recycled and reused as much as possible. Dehumidifiers remove moisture from exhaled air. On space stations, this water is usually reused for washing.

Eliminating body wastes. The collection and disposal of body wastes in microgravity poses a major challenge. Astronauts use a device that resembles a toilet seat. Air flow produces suction that moves the wastes into collection equipment under the seat. On small spacecraft, crew members use funnels for urine and plastic bags for solid wastes. While working outside the spacecraft, astronauts wear special equipment to contain body wastes.

Bathing. The simplest bathing method aboard a spacecraft is a sponge bath with wet towels. Astronauts on early space stations used a fully enclosed, collapsible plastic shower stall. This allowed the astronauts to spray their bodies with water, then vacuum the stall and towel themselves dry. Newer space stations have permanent shower stalls.

Sleeping. Space travelers can sleep in special sleeping bags with straps that press them to the soft surface and to a pillow. However, most astronauts prefer to sleep floating in the air, with only a few straps to keep them from bouncing around the cabin. Astronauts may wear blindfolds to block the sunlight that streams in the windows periodically during orbit. Typically, sleep duration in space is about the same as that on the earth.

Recreation on long space flights is important to the mental health of the astronauts. Sightseeing out the spacecraft window is a favorite pastime. Space stations have small collections of books, tapes, and computer games. Exercise also provides relaxation.

Controlling inventory and trash. Keeping track of the thousands of items used during a mission poses a major challenge in space. Drawers and lockers hold

NASA

To sleep aboard a spacecraft, astronauts can zip themselves into sleeping bags strapped to the wall. Blindfolds block the sunlight that streams in the windows periodically during orbit.

Recreational activities are important to the mental health of people traveling or living in space for long periods. These Soviet cosmonauts enjoyed guitar music aboard the space station Mir.

ITAR-Tass from Sovfoto

some materials. Other equipment is strapped to the walls, ceilings, and floors. Computer-generated lists keep track of what is stored where, and computerized systems check the storage and replacement of materials. The crew aboard the spacecraft may stow trash in unused sections of the vehicle, throw it overboard to burn up harmlessly in the atmosphere, or bring it back to the earth for disposal.

Communicating with the earth

Communication between astronauts in space and *mission control,* the facility on the earth that supervises their space flight, occurs in many ways. The astronauts and mission controllers can talk to each other by radio. Television pictures can travel between space vehicles and the earth. Computers, sensors, and other equipment continuously send signals to the earth for monitoring. Facsimile machines on spacecraft also can receive information from the earth.

Working in space

Once a space vehicle reaches its orbit, the crew members begin to carry out the goals of their mission. They perform a variety of tasks both inside and outside the spacecraft.

Navigation, guidance, and control. Astronauts use computerized navigation systems and make sightings on stars to determine their position and direction. On the earth, sophisticated tracking systems measure the spacecraft's location in relation to the earth. Astronauts typically use small firings of the spacecraft's rockets to tilt the vehicle or to push it in the desired direction. Computers monitor these changes to ensure they are done accurately.

Activating equipment. Much of the equipment on a space vehicle is turned off or tied down during launch.

Once in space, the astronauts must set up and turn on the equipment. At the end of the mission, they must secure it for landing.

Conducting scientific observations and research. Astronauts use special instruments to observe the earth, the stars, and the sun. They also experiment with the effects of microgravity on various materials, plants, animals, and themselves.

Docking. As a spacecraft approaches a target, such as a space station or an artificial satellite, radar helps the crew members control the craft's course and speed. Once the spacecraft reaches the correct position beside the target, it *docks* (joins) with the target by connecting special equipment. Such a meeting in space is called a *rendezvous.* A space shuttle can also use its robot arm to make contact with targets.

Maintaining and repairing equipment. The thousands of pieces of equipment on a modern space vehicle are extremely reliable, but some of them still break down. Accidents damage some equipment. Other units must be replaced when they get old. Astronauts must find out what has gone wrong, locate the failed unit, and repair or replace it.

Assembling space stations. Astronauts may serve as construction workers in space, assembling a space station from components carried up in the shuttle. On existing space stations, crews often must add new sections or set up new antennas and solar panels. Power and air connectors must be hooked up inside and outside the station.

Leaving the spacecraft. At times, astronauts must go outside the spacecraft to perform certain tasks. Working outside a vehicle in space is called *extravehicular activity* (*EVA*). To prepare for EVA, astronauts put on their space suits and move to a special two-doored chamber called an *air lock.* They then release the air from the air lock,

NASA

A mission control facility on the earth supervises the activities of astronauts in space. From this center, flight directors communicate with astronauts through the use of television pictures, radio transmissions, computers, and other monitoring equipment.

open the outer hatch, and leave the spacecraft. When the astronauts return, they close the outer door and let air into the air lock. Then they open the inner door into the rest of the spacecraft, where they remove their space suits.

A space suit can keep an astronaut alive for six to eight hours. The suit is made from many layers of flexible, airtight materials, such as nylon and Teflon. It provides protection against heat, cold, and space particles.

Tight mechanical seals connect the pieces of the space suit. Equipment in a backpack provides oxygen and removes carbon dioxide and moisture. A radio enables the astronaut to communicate with other crew members and with the earth. The helmet must allow good visibility while at the same time blocking harmful solar radiation. Gloves are a crucial part of the space suit. They must be thin and flexible enough for the astronaut to feel small objects and to handle tools.

NASA

Flying free in space, an astronaut becomes a human satellite. A jet-powered backpack first used in 1984 allows astronauts to maneuver outside the spacecraft without a safety line.

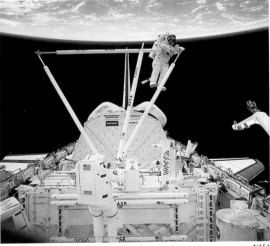

NASA

Astronauts work outside their spacecraft on certain tasks. In this photograph, shuttle astronauts practice assembly techniques that might be used to build a space station in orbit.

As people began to dream of flying above the earth's surface, they realized that objects in the sky could become destinations for human travelers. In the early 1600's, the German astronomer and mathematician Johannes Kepler became the first scientist to describe travel to other worlds. He also developed the laws of planetary motion that explain the orbits of bodies in space. See **Kepler, Johannes.**

The English scientist Sir Isaac Newton described the *laws of motion* in a work published in 1687. These laws enabled scientists to predict the kinds of flight paths needed to orbit the earth and to reach other worlds. Newton also described how an artificial satellite could remain in orbit. His third law, which states that for every action there is an equal and opposite reaction, explains why a rocket works. See **Motion** (Newton's laws of motion); **Newton, Sir Isaac.**

Early dreams of space flight. During the 1700's, scientists realized that air got thinner at higher altitudes. This meant that air probably was entirely absent between the earth and other worlds, so wings would be useless. Many imaginative writers proposed fanciful techniques for travel to these worlds.

In 1903, Konstantin E. Tsiolkovsky, a Russian high-school teacher, completed the first scientific paper on the use of rockets for space travel. Several years later, Robert H. Goddard of the United States and Hermann Oberth of Germany awakened wider scientific interest in space travel. Working independently, these three men addressed many of the technical problems of rocketry and space travel. Together, they are known as the fathers of space flight.

In 1919, Goddard explained how rockets could be used to explore the upper atmosphere in his paper "A Method of Reaching Extreme Altitudes." The paper also described a way of firing a rocket to the moon. In a book called *The Rocket into Interplanetary Space* (1923), Oberth discussed many technical problems of space flight. He even described what a spaceship would be like. Tsiolkovsky wrote a series of new studies in the 1920's. These works included detailed descriptions of multistage rockets.

The first space rockets. During the 1930's, rocket research went forward in the United States, Germany, and the Soviet Union. Goddard's team had built the world's first liquid-propellant rocket in 1926, despite a lack of support from the U.S. government. German and Soviet rocket scientists received funding from their governments to develop military missiles.

In 1942, during World War II, German rocket experts under the direction of Wernher von Braun developed the V-2 guided missile. Thousands of V-2's were fired against European cities, especially London, causing widespread destruction and loss of life.

After World War II ended in 1945, many German rocket engineers went to work for the U.S. government

New York Public Library

The dream of space travel led people to design strange spaceships. About 1780, a French inventor thought this spaceship might use a balloon, a parachute, and movable wings.

Bettmann Archive

A "moon train," *shown here,* was described by French novelist Jules Verne in 1865. He imagined the spacecraft as a series of cars that would carry travelers between the earth and the moon.

to help develop military missiles. The U.S. Navy worked on larger rockets, such as the Aerobee and the Viking. In 1949, the rocket team built and tested the world's first two-stage rocket, with a V-2 missile as a first stage and a small WAC Corporal rocket as a second stage. This rocket reached an altitude of 250 miles (400 kilometers).

By 1947, the Soviet Union had secretly begun a massive program to develop long-range military missiles. In the 1940's, the small but influential British Interplanetary Society published accurate plans for manned lunar landing vehicles, space suits, and orbital rendezvous. A U.S. group, the American Rocket Society, concentrated on missile engineering. In 1950, a new International Astronautical Federation began to hold annual conferences.

The first artificial satellites. In 1955, both the United States and the Soviet Union announced plans to launch artificial satellites with scientific instruments on board. The satellites were to be sent into orbit as part of the International Geophysical Year, a period of international cooperation in scientific research beginning in July 1957. The Soviets provided detailed descriptions of the radio equipment to be included on their satellite. But the Soviet rocket program had been kept secret until that time. As a result, many people in other countries did not believe that the Soviets had the advanced technology required for space exploration.

Then, on Oct. 4, 1957, the Soviets stunned the world by succeeding in their promise—and by doing so ahead of the United States. Only six weeks earlier, the Soviet two-stage R-7 missile had made its first 5,000-mile (8,000-kilometer) flight. This time, it carried Sputnik (later referred to as Sputnik 1), the first artificial satellite. *Sputnik* means *traveling companion* in Russian. The R-7 booster hurled the 184-pound (83-kilogram) satellite and its main rocket stage into orbit around the earth. Radio listeners worldwide picked up Sputnik's characteristic "beep-beep" signal.

The space race begins. The Western world reacted to the launch of Sputnik with surprise, fear, and respect.

United Press Int.

The first successful liquid-propellant rocket was launched in 1926 by Robert H. Goddard, an American scientist, *shown here.* The rocket burned gasoline and liquid oxygen.

Soviet Premier Nikita S. Khrushchev ordered massive funding of follow-up projects that would continue to amaze and dazzle the world. In the United States, leaders vowed to do whatever was needed to catch up. Thus the "space race" began.

More Soviet successes followed. A month after Sputnik, another satellite, Sputnik 2, carried a dog named Laika into space. The flight proved that animals could

Marshall Space Flight Center, NASA

A captured German V-2 guided missile from World War II, like those shown in this photograph, was used to launch a U.S. WAC Corporal rocket in 1949. The rocket soared to what was then a record height of 250 miles (400 kilometers).

survive the unknown effects of microgravity. In 1959, Luna 2 became the first probe to hit the moon. Later that year, Luna 3 photographed the far side of the moon, which cannot be seen from Earth.

The first United States satellite was Explorer 1, launched on Jan. 31, 1958. This satellite was followed by Vanguard 1, which was launched on March 17, 1958. These and later U.S. satellites were much smaller than their Soviet counterparts because the rockets the United States used to carry satellites were smaller and less powerful than those used by the Soviet Union. The Soviet Union's rockets gave it an early lead in the space race. Because bigger rockets would be needed for manned lunar flight, both the United States and the Soviet Union began major programs of rocket design, construction, and testing.

Organizing and managing space activities. A key to the ultimate success of U.S. space programs was centralized planning. In 1958, a civilian space agency called the National Aeronautics and Space Administration (NASA) was established. NASA absorbed various aviation researchers and military space laboratories. The formation of NASA helped forge agreement among competing interests, including military branches, universities, the aerospace industry, and politicians.

Soviet space activities, on the other hand, were coordinated by special executive commissions. These commissions tried to tie together various space units from military and industrial groups, as well as competing experts and scientists. But the commissions did not coordinate Soviet activities effectively enough to meet the complex challenges of the space race.

Space probes

A *space probe* is an unmanned device sent to explore space. A probe may operate far out in space, or it may orbit or land on a planet or a moon. It may make a one-way journey, or it may bring samples and data back to Earth. Most probes transmit data from space by radio in a process called *telemetry.*

Lunar and planetary probes that land on their targets may be classified according to their landing method. *Impact vehicles* make no attempt to slow down as they approach the target. *Hard-landers* have cushioned instrument packages that can survive the impact of a hard landing. *Soft-landers* touch down gently. *Penetrators* ram deeply into the surface of a target.

How a space probe carries out its mission. Probes explore space in a number of ways. A probe makes observations of temperature, radiation, and objects in space. A probe also observes nearby objects. In addition, a space probe exposes material from Earth to the conditions of space so that scientists can observe the effects. A probe may also perform experiments on its surroundings, such as releasing chemicals or digging into surface dirt. Finally, a probe's motion enables controllers

on Earth to determine conditions in space. Changes in course and speed can provide information about atmospheric density and gravity fields.

Early unmanned explorations. Beginning in the 1940's, devices called *sounding rockets* carried scientific instruments into the upper atmosphere and into nearby space. They discovered many new phenomena and took the first photographs of Earth from space.

The 1957 launch of Sputnik 1 marked the beginning of the space age. Sputnik 1 carried only a few instruments and transmitters, but it paved the way for the sophisticated probes that would later explore space.

Many early satellites probed uncharted regions of space. During the late 1950's and the 1960's, the Explorer satellites of the United States and the Kosmos satellites of the Soviet Union analyzed the space environment between Earth and the moon. United States Pegasus satellites recorded the impacts of micrometeorites. During the early 1970's, Soviet Prognoz satellites studied the sun. See **Satellite, Artificial.**

Lunar probes. In 1958, both the United States and the Soviet Union began to launch probes toward the

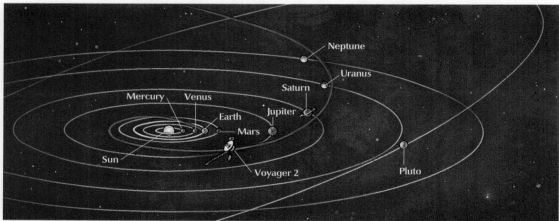

WORLD BOOK illustration by Ken Tiessen, Koralik Associates

The space probe Voyager 2 was launched on Aug. 20, 1977. Its path through the solar system is shown in red in this diagram. Voyager 2 flew past and photographed Jupiter in 1979, Saturn in 1981, Uranus in 1986, and Neptune in 1989.

moon. The first probe to come close to the moon was Luna 1, launched by the Soviet Union on Jan. 2, 1959. It passed within about 3,700 miles (6,000 kilometers) of the moon and went into orbit around the sun. The United States conducted its own lunar fly-by two months later with the probe Pioneer 4. The Soviet Luna 2 probe, launched on Sept. 12, 1959, was the first probe to hit the moon. One month later, Luna 3 circled behind the moon and photographed its hidden far side.

The Soviet Union began to test lunar hard-landers in 1963. After many failures, they succeeded with Luna 9, launched in January 1966. The U.S. Surveyor program made a series of successful soft landings beginning in 1966. Between 1970 and 1972, three Soviet probes returned lunar soil samples to Earth in small capsules.

Two of them sent remote-controlled jeeps called *Lunokhods,* which traveled across the lunar surface.

Beginning in 1966, the United States sent five probes called Lunar Orbiters into orbit to photograph the moon's surface. The Lunar Orbiters revealed the existence of irregular "bumps" of gravity in the moon's gravitational field caused by dense material buried beneath the lunar seas. These areas of tightly packed matter were called *mascons,* which stood for *mass concentrations.* If the mascons had not been discovered, they might have interfered with the Apollo missions that sent astronauts to the moon.

The United States space probe Clementine orbited the moon from February to May 1994. The probe photographed the moon extensively. In addition, Clemen-

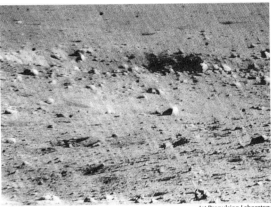

Jet Propulsion Laboratory

Surveyor 1, *left,* made a soft landing on the moon on June 2, 1966. It took about 11,000 pictures of the lunar surface, including the one above.

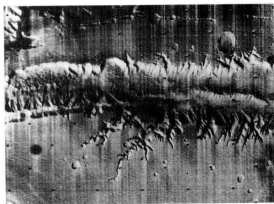

NASA

Mariner 9, *left,* was the first probe to orbit Mars. It photographed a canyon, *above,* from an altitude of 1,225 miles (1,971 kilometers) in 1973.

Jet Propulsion Laboratory

Voyager 2, *left,* flew past Jupiter in July 1979. The space probe took many photographs of the planet, including the one shown above.

Jet Propulsion Laboratory

Magellan, *left,* reached Venus in August 1990. The space probe used radar to create this image of a volcano on the planet's surface, *above.*

tine measured the height and depth of mountains, craters, and other features, and gathered data on mascons. From January 1998 to July 1999, another U.S. probe, Lunar Prospector, orbited over the moon's poles. The probe found strong evidence of large amounts of frozen water mixed with the soil at both poles.

The SMART-1 probe went into orbit around the moon in November 2004. SMART-1 was built and launched by the European Space Agency (ESA), an association of European nations. The craft's instruments were designed to investigate the moon's origin and conduct a detailed survey of the chemical elements on the lunar surface.

Solar probes. Beginning in 1965, the United States launched a series of small Pioneer probes into orbit around the sun to study solar radiation. In 1974 and 1976, the United States launched two German-built Helios probes. These probes passed inside the orbit of Mercury to measure solar radiation. The Ulysses probe was launched in 1990 by the United States and the ESA. In 1994, Ulysses became the first probe to observe the sun from an orbit over the sun's poles.

Probes to Mars. The Soviet Union launched the first probes aimed at another planet, two Mars probes, in 1960. However, neither probe reached orbit. After more Soviet failures, the United States launched two Mariner probes toward Mars in 1964. Mariner 4 flew past the planet on July 14, 1965, and sent back remarkable photographs and measurements. The probe showed that the atmosphere of Mars was much thinner than expected, and the surface resembled that of the moon.

In 1971, the Soviet probe Mars 3 dropped a capsule that made the first soft landing on Mars. But the capsule failed to return usable data. That same year, the U.S. probe Mariner 9 reached Mars and photographed most of the planet's surface. It also passed near and photographed Mars's two small moons, Phobos and Deimos.

Two U.S. probes, Viking 1 and Viking 2, landed in 1976 and operated for years, measuring surface weather and conducting complex experiments to detect life forms. The probes found no evidence of life.

In 1992, the United States launched the probe Mars Observer. In 1993, NASA lost contact with the probe three days before it would have orbited Mars. Contact was never restored, and the probe was presumed lost.

The United States launched the Pathfinder probe in December 1996. The probe landed on Mars on July 4, 1997. Two days later, a six-wheeled vehicle called Sojourner rolled down a ramp from the probe to the surface. The vehicle was only 24.5 inches long, 18.7 inches wide, and 10.9 inches high (63 by 48 by 28 centimeters). Its mass was 11.5 kilograms, equivalent to a weight of 25.4 pounds on Earth. The vehicle used a device called an alpha proton X-ray spectrometer to gather data on the chemical makeup of rocks and soil. Sojourner transmitted this information to Pathfinder, and the probe relayed the information to the earth. Scientists on Earth controlled Sojourner. However, because radio signals take about 10 minutes to travel from Earth to Mars, the scientists could not control Sojourner in *real time*—that is, as the vehicle moved. To avoid obstacles, Sojourner used a number of automatic devices.

In 1996, the United States launched a probe called the Mars Global Surveyor to map the planet's surface. The probe used a laser device to determine the elevation of

the Martian surface. That instrument produced maps of the entire surface that are accurate to within 3 feet (1 meter) of elevation. Another instrument determined the composition of some of the minerals on the surface. A camera revealed layered sediments that may have been deposited in liquid water, and small gullies that appear to have been carved by water.

In 2001, the United States launched the Mars Odyssey probe to Mars. The spacecraft carried instruments to help identify minerals on the surface, to search for evidence of water and ice beneath the surface, and to measure radiation that might harm any future explorers. In 2002, Mars Odyssey found vast amounts of ice within 3 feet (1 meter) of the surface, most of it near the south pole.

In 2003, three probes were launched to Mars, one by the ESA and two by the United States. The ESA's Mars Express probe went into orbit around the planet in December 2003. It transmitted stunning pictures of the planet's surface, confirmed the presence of water ice in the planet's southern region, and detected methane in the Martian atmosphere, a possible indicator of life. Mars Express carried a lander called Beagle 2 that failed to land safely and was lost.

The United States launched rovers nicknamed Spirit and Opportunity. In January 2004, Spirit landed in Gusev Crater, and Opportunity landed in an area called Meridiani Planum. The rovers used cameras and other instruments to analyze soil and rocks. In March 2004, U.S. scientists concluded that Meridiani Planum once held large amounts of liquid water. Opportunity's analysis had shown that the rock there contained minerals and structures normally found in Earth rocks that formed in water.

In August 2005, the United States launched the Mars Reconnaissance Orbiter, which arrived in orbit around Mars in March 2006. The craft was designed to study the planet's structure and atmosphere and to identify potential landing sites for future lander and rover missions.

Probes to Venus and Mercury. The Soviet Union launched the first probes toward Venus in 1961, but these attempts failed. The first successful probe to fly past Venus and return data was the U.S. Mariner 2, on Dec. 14, 1962. Mariner 5 flew past Venus in 1967 and returned important data. Mariner 10 passed Venus and then made three passes near Mercury in 1974 and 1975.

Soviet attempts to obtain data from Venus finally succeeded in 1967. Venera 4 dropped a probe by parachute, and it transmitted data from the planet's extremely dense atmosphere. In 1970, Venera 7 reached the surface of the planet, still functioning. Between 1975 and 1985, several other probes landed and conducted observations for up to 110 minutes before the temperature and pressure destroyed them. In 1978, the United States sent two probes to Venus, Pioneer Venus 1 and 2. Pioneer Venus 1 was an orbiter. Pioneer Venus 2 dropped four probes into the planet's atmosphere.

Probes that orbited Venus generated rough maps of its surface by bouncing radio waves off the ground. Pioneer Venus 1 mapped most of the surface to a *resolution* of about 50 miles (80 kilometers). This means that objects at least 50 miles apart showed distinctly on the map. In 1983, two Soviet probes carried radar systems that mapped most of the planet's northern hemisphere to a resolution of 0.9 mile (1.5 kilometers). In 1990, the U.S. probe Magellan mapped almost the entire surface to a resolution of about 330 feet (100 meters).

In 2004, the United States launched the Messenger probe to Mercury. Beginning in 2011, the probe was to orbit the planet for one Earth year, studying its geography, composition, interior structure, and magnetic field.

The ESA Venus Express probe, launched in 2005, went into orbit around Venus in 2006. The probe carried instruments used to study Venus's atmosphere in detail.

Probes to Jupiter and beyond must meet special challenges. Radiation belts near Jupiter are so intense that camera lenses and computer circuits must be shielded to prevent damage. The dim sunlight at the outer planets requires lengthy camera exposures, and the vast distances mean that radio commands take hours to reach the probes.

Probes have visited Jupiter, Saturn, Uranus, and Neptune. The United States sent the probes Pioneer 10 and 11 to Jupiter in 1972 and 1973. After observing Jupiter, Pioneer 11 was sent to Saturn, arriving in 1979. This probe was renamed Pioneer-Saturn.

From 1979 to 1981, sophisticated Voyager probes provided much more detailed data on Jupiter and Saturn. They still explore space. Voyager 2 flew past Uranus in January 1986 and Neptune in August 1989. The probes sent back spectacular photos of the outer planets and their rings and moons, and recorded a great deal of scientific data. Active volcanoes were found on Io, a moon of Jupiter, and geysers were discovered on Triton, a moon of Neptune. Other moons exhibited bizarre ice and rock formations.

The Galileo space probe, launched on a mission to Jupiter by the United States in 1989, was far more sophisticated than earlier planetary probes. It consisted of two parts—an atmosphere probe and a larger orbiting spacecraft. On the way to Jupiter, Galileo flew past the asteroids Gaspra and Ida. In July 1995, the atmosphere probe separated from the spacecraft. Both parts reached Jupiter five months later. As planned, the probe plunged into Jupiter's atmosphere. The spacecraft orbited Jupiter until 2003, studying the planet, its satellites, and its rings.

In 1997, the United States launched the Cassini probe to investigate Saturn, its rings, and satellites. Cassini began orbiting Saturn in 2004. It then released an ESA probe called Huygens that landed on Saturn's moon Titan in 2005.

In 2006, U.S. scientists launched the New Horizons probe to make the first close observations of Pluto. The probe was expected to fly by Pluto in 2015.

Probes to comets. Two Soviet probes flew past Venus and dropped instruments into its atmosphere, then intercepted Halley's Comet as it passed by the sun in 1986. In 1985, ESA launched its first interplanetary probe, called Giotto. It passed closer to the comet's nucleus than any other probe and returned dramatic close-up images. Japan also sent two small probes. After several years of inactivity, Giotto was reactivated to fly past the comet Grigg-Skjellerup in July 1992.

The United States did not send a probe to Halley's Comet due to budget limitations. But NASA scientists used a small probe already in space, the International Sun-Earth Explorer 3 satellite, to explore another comet. In 1983, the satellite's course was shifted into interplane-tary space, and it was renamed the International Cometary Explorer. On Sept. 11, 1985, it passed a comet named Giacobini-Zinner, becoming the first probe to reach a comet.

In 1999, NASA launched a probe called Stardust to visit Comet Wild 2. In 2004, Stardust passed near the comet and gathered samples from the cloud of dust and gas surrounding the comet's nucleus. Stardust returned the samples to Earth in 2006. Also in 2004, the European Space Agency launched the Rosetta spacecraft, which was to go into orbit around Comet Churyumov-Gerasimenko in 2014. Rosetta carried a small probe designed to land on the comet's nucleus.

In 2005, the United States launched the Deep Impact spacecraft to Comet Tempel 1. The craft consisted of two smaller probes: an *impactor* and a *flyby craft*. The impactor intentionally slammed into the comet's nucleus, while the flyby craft recorded the crash. Analyzing the debris ejected by the collision enabled scientists to study the comet's composition.

Probes to asteroids. NASA launched the Near Earth Asteroid Rendezvous (NEAR) probe in 1996. In 1997, the probe flew within 753 miles (1,216 kilometers) of the asteroid Mathilde. NEAR flew past the asteroid Eros at a distance of 2,378 miles (3,829 kilometers) in 1998. It went into orbit around Eros in 2000. The probe, renamed NEAR-Shoemaker in honor of the American astronomer Eugene Shoemaker, landed on Eros in 2001.

In October 1998, NASA launched a probe called Deep Space 1 (DS1). The probe flew within only about 16 miles (26 kilometers) of the asteroid Braille in July 1999.

The flight of DS1 successfully tested several new types of equipment for space probes. This equipment included a navigation system that operates automatically, rather than under the direction of people and computers on Earth. Also included was an ion rocket, which operates by shooting electrically charged particles called ions out its nozzle.

In 2005, Japan's Hayabusa probe visited the asteroid Itokawa. Despite the failure of several of its systems, the craft managed to transmit detailed pictures of the asteroid and to land briefly on its surface.

Human beings enter space

In 1958, scientists in the United States and the Soviet Union began serious efforts to design a spacecraft that could carry human beings. Both nations chose to develop a wingless capsule atop a launch vehicle that would consist of a modified long-range missile.

The prospect of human beings traveling in space greatly worried scientists. Tests with animals had shown that space travel probably involved no physical danger, but there were serious concerns about possible psychological hazards. Some experts feared that the stresses of launch, flight, and landing might drive a space traveler to terror or unconsciousness.

Vostok and Mercury: The first human beings in space

The Soviet Union's Vostok (East) program and the Mercury program of the United States represented the first efforts to send a human being into space. The Vos-

ITAR-Tass from Sovfoto

Soviet cosmonaut Yuri A. Gagarin, *right,* became the first person in space on April 12, 1961. Gagarin's Vostok spacecraft completed one orbit of the earth. The flight lasted 108 minutes.

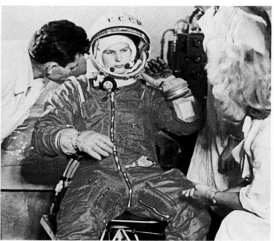

RIA-Novosti from Sovfoto

Soviet cosmonaut Valentina Tereshkova became the first woman in space on June 16, 1963. Tereshkova orbited the earth for almost three days aboard the Vostok 6 space capsule.

tok capsule weighed about 10,000 pounds (4,500 kilograms). It was to be carried into orbit atop a modified R-7 missile. The capsule consisted of a spherical pilot's cabin and a cylindrical *service module,* the section containing the propulsion system. An ejection seat was designed to provide an escape for the astronaut in case of a mishap during launch. The life-support system used a mixture of oxygen and nitrogen similar to the atmosphere at sea level.

The U.S. Mercury capsule weighed about 3,000 pounds (1,360 kilograms) and was to be carried into space atop a Redstone or Atlas rocket. The cone-shaped capsule would use parachutes to land in the ocean, where the water would provide extra cushioning. The Mercury's life-support system used pure oxygen at low pressure. If a booster malfunction occurred during launch, the capsule and pilot would be pulled free by a solid-fuel rocket attached to the nose of the capsule.

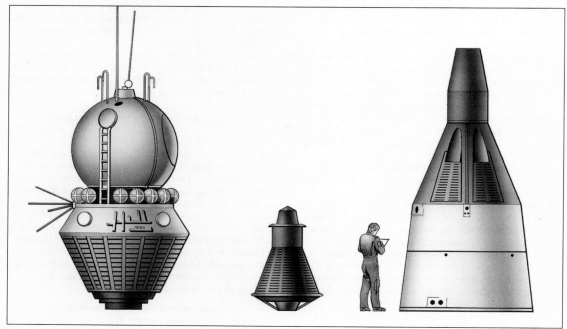

WORLD BOOK illustrations by Oxford Illustrators Limited

Early manned spacecraft. The Soviet Vostok capsule, *left,* stood about 16 feet (4.9 meters) high. The U.S. Mercury capsule, *center,* was 9 ½ feet (2.9 meters) high. Each vehicle carried one space pilot. The U.S. Gemini spacecraft, *right,* stood 19 feet (5.8 meters) high and held two astronauts.

While U.S. plans proceeded in the glare of publicity, Soviet developments took place in great secrecy. Both nations made unmanned orbital tests in 1960 and 1961, some of which suffered booster failures. Both nations also sent animals into space during this period. One animal was a chimpanzee named Ham, who made an 18-minute flight in a Mercury capsule on Jan. 31, 1961.

The first fatality in a manned space program occurred on March 23, 1961. A Soviet cosmonaut trainee named Valentin V. Bondarenko burned to death in a pressure chamber fire. Soviet officials covered up the accident.

The first human being in space was a Soviet air force pilot named Yuri A. Gagarin. He was launched aboard Vostok (later referred to as Vostok 1) on April 12, 1961. In 108 minutes, Gagarin orbited the earth once and returned safely. An automatic flight control system managed the spacecraft's operations during the entire flight. A 25-hour, 17-orbit flight by cosmonaut Gherman Titov aboard Vostok 2 followed in August of that year.

The Mercury program made its first manned flight on May 5, 1961, when a Redstone rocket launched astronaut Alan B. Shepard, Jr., in a capsule he named Freedom 7. Shepard flew a 15-minute suborbital mission— that is, a mission that did not reach the speed and altitude required to orbit the earth.

A suborbital flight on July 21, 1961, by astronaut Virgil I. Grissom almost ended tragically. The Mercury capsule's side hatch opened too soon after splashdown in the Atlantic Ocean, and the spacecraft rapidly filled with water. Grissom managed to swim to safety.

On Feb. 20, 1962, John H. Glenn, Jr., became the first American to orbit the earth. Glenn completed three orbits in less than five hours. He pointed his capsule in different directions, tested its various systems, and observed the earth.

NASA

Mercury astronaut Walter M. Schirra, Jr., orbited the earth six times on Oct. 2, 1962. This photograph shows workers inserting Schirra into his snug Mercury capsule.

Three months later, astronaut M. Scott Carpenter repeated Glenn's three-orbit mission. A six-orbit mission by Walter M. Schirra, Jr., in October 1962 further extended the testing of the Mercury spacecraft. The final Mercury mission took place in May 1963, with Gordon Cooper aboard. The mission lasted 1 ½ days.

Meanwhile, the Soviet Union continued to launch Vostok missions. In August 1962, Vostok 3 and Vostok 4 lifted off just a day apart and passed near each other in space. Another two capsules—Vostok 5 and Vostok 6— were launched in June 1963. One of the pilots spent al-

NASA

The first seven U.S. astronauts, selected for the Mercury program, were, *left to right,* M. Scott Carpenter, Gordon Cooper, John H. Glenn, Jr., Virgil I. Grissom, Walter M. Schirra, Jr., Alan B. Shepard, Jr., and Donald K. Slayton.

Voskhod 2 carried Soviet cosmonauts Pavel I. Belyayev, *far left,* and Alexei A. Leonov into space on March 18, 1965. Leonov became the first human being to walk in space.

most five days in orbit, a new record. The other pilot, Valentina Tereshkova, became the first woman in space.

Voskhod and Gemini: The first multiperson space flights

In 1961, the United States announced the Gemini program, which would send two astronauts into space in an enlarged version of the Mercury capsule. This announcement spurred Soviet planners to modify their Vostok capsule to carry up to three cosmonauts. Political pressure to upstage U.S. efforts was so intense that Soviet engineers sacrificed certain safety features, such as ejection seats, to enlarge the capsule.

The world's first multiperson space capsule, Voskhod (Sunrise)—later referred to as Voskhod 1—was launched on Oct. 12, 1964. Cosmonauts Vladimir M. Komarov, Konstantin P. Feoktistov, and Boris B. Yegorov spent 24 hours in orbit. They became the first space travelers to land inside their capsule on the ground, rather than in the ocean.

In March 1965, cosmonaut Alexei A. Leonov stepped through an inflatable air lock attached to Voskhod 2 to become the first person to walk in space. After the capsule's autopilot failed, Leonov and Pavel I. Belyayev had to land it manually. They missed their planned landing zone and came down in an isolated forest. The cosmonauts had to fend off hungry wolves until rescuers reached them the following day.

The first manned Gemini mission, Gemini 3, was launched on March 23, 1965. Astronauts Grissom and John W. Young used the capsule's maneuvering rockets to alter its path through space. With Gemini 4, launched on June 3, 1965, copilot Edward H. White II became the first American to walk in space. The astronauts aboard

Gemini 5, launched on Aug. 21, 1965, spent almost eight days in space, a record achieved by using fuel cells to generate electricity.

Gemini 6 was originally intended to link up with an Agena rocket sent into space a few hours earlier. After the unmanned Agena was lost in a booster failure, NASA combined Gemini 6 with an already scheduled 14-day Gemini 7 mission. Gemini 7 was launched as planned, on Dec. 4, 1965, and Gemini 6 took off 11 days later. Within hours, Schirra and Thomas P. Stafford moved their spacecraft to within 1 foot (30 centimeters) of Gemini 7 and its crew, Frank Borman and James A. Lovell, Jr. The two spacecraft orbited the earth together for several hours before separating.

On March 16, 1966, Gemini 8 completed the world's first docking of two space vehicles when it linked up with an Agena rocket in space. However, the spacecraft went into a violent tumble. Astronauts Neil A. Armstrong and David R. Scott managed to regain control of the spacecraft and make an emergency splashdown in the western Pacific Ocean.

Additional tests of docking and extravehicular activity took place on the remaining four Gemini missions. On these missions, astronauts and flight controllers also gained vital experience in preparation for the tremendous challenges of manned lunar flight.

Apollo: Mission to the moon

The race to the moon dominated the space race of the 1960's. In a 1961 address to Congress, President John F. Kennedy called for the United States to commit itself to "landing a man on the moon and returning him safely to the earth" before the 1960's ended. This goal was intended to show the superiority of U.S. science, engi-

NASA

neering, management, and political leadership.

NASA considered several proposals for a manned lunar mission. The agency selected a plan known as *lunar-orbit rendezvous*. A spacecraft would carry three astronauts to an orbit around the moon. Two of the astronauts would then descend to the lunar surface.

The spacecraft would consist of three parts, or modules—*a command module (CM), a service module (SM),* and a *lunar module (LM)*, which was originally called the *lunar excursion module (LEM)*. The cone-shaped CM would be the spacecraft's main control center. The SM would contain fuel, oxygen, water, and the spacecraft's electric power system and propulsion system. The CM and SM would be joined for almost the entire mission as the *command/service module (CSM)*.

Only the LM would land on the moon. This module would consist of two sections—a *descent stage* and an *ascent stage*. The two stages would descend to the lunar surface as a single unit, but only the ascent stage would leave the moon. A Saturn 5 booster would launch the spacecraft toward the moon. As the craft approached the moon, rockets on the SM would adjust its course so that it would go into a lunar orbit. With the craft in orbit, the LM would separate from the CSM and carry the two astronauts to the surface. After the astronauts completed their activities on the moon, the LM's ascent stage would blast off from the descent stage and rendezvous with the CSM.

After the returning astronauts entered the command module, the CSM would cast off the LM's ascent stage. The CSM would then return to the earth. As the craft approached the earth, the CM would separate from the SM and would splash down in the ocean.

Lunar-orbit rendezvous would be complex but relatively economical. The mission would save a tremendous amount of fuel by landing only the small LM on the moon and then launching only its ascent stage.

Making ready. Tragedy struck during preparations for the first manned Apollo flight, a trial run in low earth orbit. During a ground test on Jan. 27, 1967, a flash fire inside the sealed CM killed astronauts Grissom, White, and Roger B. Chaffee. An electrical short circuit probably started the fire, and the pure oxygen atmosphere caused it to burn fiercely.

A few months later, the Soviet space program also suffered a disaster. The Soyuz (Union) 1 capsule was launched with Vladimir Komarov aboard as pilot. It was supposed to link up with a second manned spaceship, but Soyuz 1 developed problems and the second ship was never launched. Controllers ordered Soyuz 1 to return to the earth. But a parachute failure caused the capsule to crash, killing Komarov.

While the Apollo CSM and the Soyuz capsule were being redesigned, unmanned tests took place as planned. The United States launched the first Saturn 5 booster on Nov. 9, 1967, with complete success. Early in 1968, an LM was sent into orbit, where it test-fired its engines. Soyuz vehicles linked up automatically in orbit in 1967 and 1968.

Orbiting the moon. By late 1968, the United States had redesigned the Apollo CSM. However, the lunar module remained far behind schedule.

NASA officials knew about Soviet preparations for a manned lunar fly-by. To beat the Soviets, NASA decided to fly a manned mission to orbit the moon, without an LM. The orbital mission would also test navigation and communication around the moon.

Apollo 8, the first manned expedition to the moon, blasted off from the Kennedy Space Center near Cape Canaveral, Florida, on Dec. 21, 1968. Hundreds of thousands of people crowded nearby beaches to watch the launch. The spacecraft carried astronauts Borman, Lovell, and William A. Anders. After three days, the crew fired the SM engine to change course into a lunar orbit. They made observations and took photographs, then headed back to the earth. Apollo 8 landed safely in the

NASA

Apollo 11 blasted off on July 16, 1969, *above*. The illustration on this page shows the operations used to send the Apollo spacecraft to the moon. After the lunar module (LM) landed (16), the astronauts performed a number of scientific tasks on the moon. To leave the moon, part of the LM lifted off and docked with the orbiting command/service module. Then the LM crew moved into the command/service module, the LM was disconnected, and the command/service module returned to the earth.

11 Command/service module reduces speed to enter lunar orbit

Parking orbit

14 Lunar module separates

Moon North Pole

17 Command/service module remains in orbit

12 Crew makes navigation measurements

16 Landing on the moon

15 Lunar module descends

13 Two astronauts transfer to lunar module

10 Course corrected

9 Third stage separates from spacecraft

8 Docking with lunar module

7 Command/service module turns around

6 Spacecraft separates

Parking orbit

Earth North Pole

Liftoff

1

2

3

4 Third stage and spacecraft enter parking orbit

5 Third stage reignites to send spacecraft to the moon

Second stage separates and third stage ignites

First stage separates and second stage ignites

Wide World

The first step on the moon. As U.S. astronaut Neil A. Armstrong, *above,* took the historic step on July 20, 1969, he said: "That's one small step for a man, one giant leap for mankind." The event was televised to the earth. A plaque, *below,* was attached to the lunar module's descent stage, which was left on the moon.

NASA

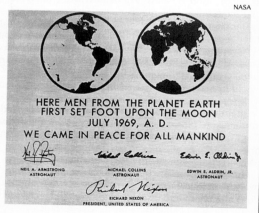

HERE MEN FROM THE PLANET EARTH
FIRST SET FOOT UPON THE MOON
JULY 1969, A. D.
WE CAME IN PEACE FOR ALL MANKIND

NEIL A. ARMSTRONG
ASTRONAUT

MICHAEL COLLINS
ASTRONAUT

EDWIN E. ALDRIN, JR.
ASTRONAUT

RICHARD NIXON
PRESIDENT, UNITED STATES OF AMERICA

Pacific Ocean near Hawaii on December 27.

Two additional test flights were made to ensure the safety and effectiveness of the lunar module. The LM was tested in low orbit around the earth by the Apollo 9 astronauts and in lunar orbit by the Apollo 10 crew.

Landing on the moon. Apollo 11 was the first mission to land astronauts on the moon. It blasted off on July 16, 1969, carrying three astronauts—Neil A. Armstrong, Edwin E. (Buzz) Aldrin, Jr., and Michael Collins.

The first two stages of a Saturn 5 rocket carried the spacecraft to an altitude of 115 miles (185 kilometers) and a speed of 15,400 miles (24,800 kilometers) per hour, just short of orbital velocity. The third stage fired briefly to accelerate the vehicle to the required speed. It then shut down while the vehicle coasted in orbit. The astronauts checked the spacecraft and lined up the flight path for the trip to the moon. The third stage was then restarted, increasing the speed to an escape velocity of 24,300 miles (39,100 kilometers) per hour. On the way to the moon, the crew pulled the CSM away from the Saturn rocket. They turned the CSM around and docked it to the LM, which was still attached to the Saturn. The linked vehicles then pulled free of the Saturn.

For three days, Apollo 11 coasted toward the moon. As the spaceship traveled farther from the earth, the pull of the earth's gravity became weaker. But the earth's gravity constantly tugged at the spacecraft, slowing it down. By the time the ship was 215,000 miles (346,000 kilometers) from the earth, its speed had dropped to 2,000 miles (3,200 kilometers) per hour. But then the moon's gravity became stronger than the earth's, and the craft picked up speed again.

Apollo 11 was aimed to pass directly behind the moon. However, it was moving much too fast for the moon's weak gravity to capture it. A braking rocket burn changed its course into a low lunar orbit.

Once in lunar orbit, Armstrong and Aldrin separated the LM from the CSM. They fired the LM's descent stage and began the landing maneuver. They used the LM's rockets to slow its descent. Collins remained in the CSM.

To help NASA mission controllers recognize voice signals from the CSM and the LM, the astronauts used different call signs for the two vehicles. They called the CSM *Columbia* and the LM *Eagle*.

The LM's computer controlled all landing maneuvers, but the pilot could override the computer if something unexpected occurred. For the final touchdown, Armstrong looked out the window and selected a level landing site. Probes extended down from the LM's landing legs and signaled when the LM was about 5 feet (1.5 meters) above the surface. The engine shut off, and the LM touched down at a lowland called the Sea of Tranquility on July 20, 1969. Aldrin radioed a brief report on the vehicle's status. Moments later, Armstrong radioed back his famous announcement: "Houston, Tranquility Base here. The *Eagle* has landed."

Exploring the moon. Immediately after the LM touched down, the astronauts performed a complete check to make sure that the landing had not damaged

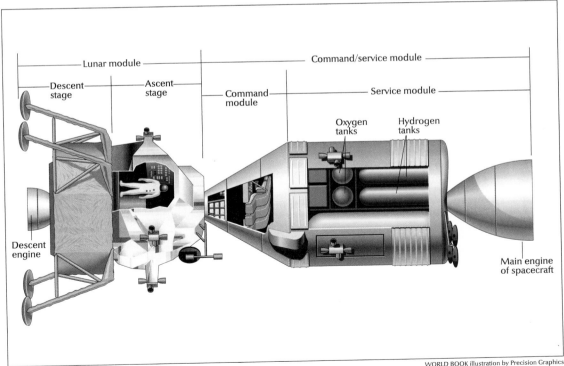

WORLD BOOK illustration by Precision Graphics

The Apollo spacecraft, *shown here,* carried three astronauts in its command module (viewed from beneath the flight couches) into orbit around the moon. Two of them then boarded the lunar module, which separated from the command/service module and descended to the surface.

any equipment. Then they prepared to go outside.

Armstrong and Aldrin had worn space suits during the landing. They transferred their air hoses from a cabin supply to their backpack units, then released the air from the cabin and opened a small hatch below their front windows. First Armstrong and then Aldrin crawled backward through the hatch. They descended a ladder mounted on one of the LM's legs to a wide pad at the base of the leg.

A television camera mounted on the side of the LM sent blurred images of the astronauts back to the earth. Armstrong stepped off the pad onto the moon and said, "That's one small step for a man, one giant leap for mankind." Most of the huge TV audience did not hear Armstrong say the word *a* before *man* because of a gap in the transmission.

The astronauts had no trouble adjusting to the weak lunar gravity. They found rocks and soil samples and photographed their positions before picking them up. The astronauts also set up automatic science equipment on the moon. Meanwhile, from the orbiting CSM, Collins conducted various scientific observations and took photographs.

Returning to the earth. The LM's descent stage served as a launch pad for the ascent stage liftoff. To lighten the spacecraft, the crew left all extra equipment behind, including backpacks and cameras. The ascent stage rocketed into orbit, where it linked up with the waiting CSM. The astronauts transferred samples and film into the CSM, then cast off the LM ascent stage. The crew fired the on-board rocket again to push the CSM out of lunar orbit and set their course for the earth.

The CM splashed down in the Pacific Ocean on July 24. NASA immediately put the lunar material, the astronauts, and all equipment that had been exposed to the lunar environment into isolation. The purpose of the isolation, which lasted about 17 days for the astronauts, was to determine whether any germs or other harmful material had been brought from the moon. Nothing harmful was found.

The second flight to the moon was as successful as the first. The Apollo 12 LM made a precision landing on the lunar surface on Nov. 19, 1969. Astronauts Charles (Pete) Conrad, Jr., and Alan L. Bean walked to a landed space probe, Surveyor 3, and retrieved samples for study.

The flight of Apollo 13, which was supposed to result in the third lunar landing, almost ended in disaster. The flight, from April 11 to 17, 1970, became a mission to save the lives of three astronauts—James A. Lovell, Jr., Fred W. Haise, Jr., and John L. Swigert, Jr.

During the spacecraft's approach to the moon, one of the two oxygen tanks in the SM exploded. The blast also disabled the remaining tank. The tanks provided both breathing oxygen and fuel for the electrical power systems of the CM and the SM. Moments later, Swigert reported "OK, Houston, we've had a problem."

After the explosion, flight controllers at Mission Control in Houston quickly realized that the astronauts probably did not have enough oxygen and battery power to get them back to the earth. The flight controllers ordered the crew to power up the LM, which was still docked with the CSM. The crew then shut down the CSM, saving its power supply until power would be needed for descent to the earth. The LM had its own power and oxygen supplies, but it was not designed to

NASA

The first people on the moon were U.S. astronauts Neil A. Armstrong, who took this picture, and Buzz Aldrin, *shown here,* next to a seismograph. A television camera and a United States flag are in the background. Their lunar module, *Eagle,* stands at the right.

support three astronauts. The astronauts used only minimal electric power during the 3-day return trip to the earth, and all three of them survived.

A NASA investigation later determined the cause of the tank explosion. Months before the launch, wires leading to a fan thermostat inside the tank had been tested at too high a voltage. As a result, the wire's insulation had burned off. When the fan was turned on during the flight, the wires short-circuited. The short caused a fire in the pure oxygen environment of the tank, resulting in the explosion. The blast blew off one side of the SM and broke the feed line to the other tank.

Other moon landings. Apollo astronauts landed on the moon six times between 1969 and 1972. Each mission brought various instruments to the moon, which usually included a *seismograph*—a device that detects and records moonquakes and other small movements of the moon's crust. On later missions, mission controllers sent the empty Saturn third stage and the discarded LM ascent stage hurtling to the moon's surface to create seismic waves. These waves provided information about the moon's internal structure.

An important task of the Apollo astronauts was the recovery of samples from the lunar surface for study. On some flights, they used drills to collect soil samples to a depth of 10 feet (3 meters). Astronauts gathered about 840 pounds (384 kilograms) of samples. Some missions launched small scientific satellites near the moon.

After investigating the Apollo 13 accident, NASA redesigned the CM and SM. The inquiry and modifications set back the Apollo 14 mission from October 1970 to January 1971. The Apollo 14 LM, carrying astronauts Alan B. Shepard, Jr., and Edgar D. Mitchell, landed near Fra Mauro Crater on February 5. Fra Mauro had originally been the target for Apollo 13.

Apollo 15 landed near the Apennine Mountains of the moon on July 30, 1971. Astronauts David R. Scott and James B. Irwin became the first astronauts to drive across the moon's surface. They drove a battery-powered *lunar roving vehicle,* often called the *lunar rover,* more than 17 miles (27 kilometers). Apollo 16, carrying John W. Young and Charles M. Duke, Jr., landed in the

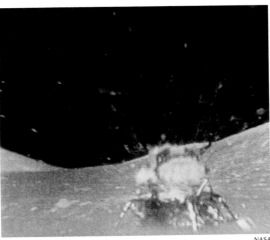

NASA

An Apollo lunar module blasts off from the moon in this photo taken from a TV transmission. After liftoff, the lunar module (LM) went into an orbit around the moon that was lower than that of the command/service module (CSM). When the two spacecraft were in the proper positions, the LM went into the same orbit as the CSM. The CSM then docked with the LM.

Descartes region on April 20, 1972. The last lunar mission, Apollo 17, landed in the Taurus Mountains on Dec. 11, 1972. Eugene A. Cernan and Harrison H. Schmitt rode the LM to the surface on this mission.

The Apollo expeditions achieved the goal of demonstrating U.S. technological superiority, and the race to the moon ended with a clear-cut U.S. triumph. Apollo provided unique scientific data, much of which would have been impossible to gather through the use of probes alone. The data enabled scientists to study the origin of the moon and the inner planets of the solar system with much greater certainty than ever before. In addition, the Apollo program forced hundreds of industrial and research teams to develop new tools and technologies that were later applied to more ordinary tasks. For example, microelectronics and new medical

NASA

After splashdown, three balloons righted the Apollo 11 spacecraft in the water, and an orange collar helped keep it afloat.

NASA

A lunar roving vehicle, also called a *lunar rover,* carried Apollo 15 astronauts David R. Scott and James B. Irwin more than 17 miles (27 kilometers). The photo above shows Irwin working with the vehicle near the landing site. Mount Hadley, in the Apennine Mountains, rises in the background.

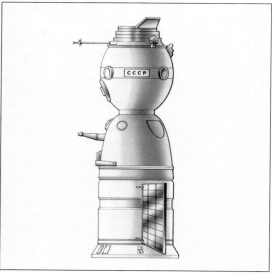

WORLD BOOK illustration by Oxford Illustrators Limited

The Soviet Soyuz spacecraft could carry three cosmonauts. The capsule stood 23 3/8 feet (7.1 meters) high.

monitoring equipment were developed as a result of the Apollo program. These advancements enriched the U.S. economy. Most importantly, the Apollo missions stirred people's imagination and raised their awareness of the earth's place in the universe.

Soviet attempts to reach the moon

Officials in the Soviet Union publicly denied there had ever been a Soviet equivalent to the Apollo program. This official story became widely accepted around the world. But in the late 1980's, the Soviet Union began to release new information indicating that the Soviet government actually had an ambitious lunar program that failed.

Soviet plans for manned lunar flight may have been hampered by a lack of central authority. Rivalry among different spacecraft design teams and other space organizations prevented cooperation. The Soviet equivalent of the Apollo CSM was a two-person lunar modification of the Soyuz capsule, called the L-1. The Soviet lunar module, the L-3, resembled the LM developed in the United States. However, it would carry only one cosmonaut. The Soviet booster, the N-1, was bigger than the Saturn 5 but less powerful, because it used less efficient fuels.

Manned Soviet L-1 capsules were scheduled to fly past the moon as part of a test program. This program was planned for 1966 and 1967, well before the United

NASA

The Apollo-Soyuz Test Project featured the docking of a U.S. Apollo capsule with a Soviet Soyuz capsule in earth orbit. The U.S. astronauts and Soviet cosmonauts visited each other and conducted scientific experiments. The photograph at the left shows astronaut Donald K. Slayton, *left,* cosmonaut Alexei A. Leonov, *center,* and astronaut Thomas P. Stafford, *right,* aboard the Soyuz spacecraft.

States could attempt a lunar landing. The Soviet Union conducted unmanned test flights under the cover name *Zond.* Three pairs of Soviet cosmonauts trained for a lunar mission.

The Soviet moon ships had serious problems. Many of the boosters for the L-1 lunar fly-by blew up. In addition, the unmanned L-1 spacecraft developed serious flaws. It was still too dangerous to allow cosmonauts aboard. Soviet efforts to reach the moon were also frustrated by the continued failure of the giant N-1 booster. Four secret test flights were made between 1969 and 1972. However, all of the vehicles exploded.

The Apollo-Soyuz Test Project

In 1972, the United States and the Soviet Union agreed to participate in the first international manned space mission. They planned to perform an orbital rendezvous between a Soviet Soyuz capsule and a U.S. Apollo capsule. The Apollo-Soyuz Test Project began on July 15, 1975. The Apollo capsule, commanded by Thomas P. Stafford, successfully linked up with the Soyuz capsule, commanded by Alexei A. Leonov.

Space stations

A *space station* is a place where people can live and work in space for long periods. It orbits the earth, usually about 200 to 300 miles (300 to 480 kilometers) high. A space station may serve as an observatory, laboratory, factory, workshop, warehouse, and fuel depot. Space stations are much larger than manned spacecraft, so they provide more comforts. Manned spacecraft may transport people between the earth and the space station. Unmanned spacecraft may supply the station with food, water, equipment, and mail.

Small space stations can be built on the earth and launched into orbit by large rockets. Larger stations are assembled in space. Rockets or space shuttles carry *modules* (sections) of the station into space, where astronauts assemble them. Old modules can be replaced, and new modules can be added to expand the station.

A space station has at least one *docking port* to which a visiting spacecraft can attach itself. Most docking ports consist of a rimmed doorway called a *hatch* that can connect with a hatch on the visiting spacecraft to form an airtight seal. When the two hatches open, they form a pressurized tunnel between the station and the visiting spacecraft.

The main tasks of a space station crew involve scientific research. For example, they might analyze the effects of microgravity on various materials, investigate the earth's surface, or study the stars and planets.

Astronauts at a space station also devote much of their time to the assembly of equipment and the expansion of the station's facilities. This includes erecting beams, connecting electrical and gas lines, and welding permanent joints between sections of the station. The crew must also fix or replace broken equipment.

Salyut and Skylab

In the 1960's, missions to the moon dominated the U.S. and Soviet space programs. But both countries also developed simple space stations during this period. These early stations had a cylindrical shape, with a docking port at one end and solar power panels sticking out from the sides. The stations were designed to hold enough air, food, and water to last for about 6 to 12 months. The manned spacecraft originally built for lunar flight—the U.S. Apollo and the Soviet Soyuz—were modified to transport people to the space stations.

Salyut. The Soviet Union launched the first space station, Salyut (Salute) 1, on April 19, 1971. It consisted of a single module with one docking port. On June 7, 1971, three cosmonauts—Georgi T. Dobrovolsky, Victor I. Pat- sayev, and Vladislav N. Volkov—linked their Soyuz 11 spacecraft with Salyut 1. They spent 23 days aboard the space station, making medical observations and performing experiments. In a tragic accident, the air leaked out of the Soyuz 11 spacecraft during the return journey, killing all three cosmonauts.

In 1974, Salyut 3 hosted a 15-day mission to photograph the earth. Salyut 4 received two missions in 1975. The second lasted 63 days. In 1976, Salyut 5 repeated the Salyut 3 photography mission.

In 1977, the Soviet Union launched Salyut 6. It had two docking ports, one at either end of the main module. This new design enabled a space station crew to receive a visit from a second crew or a resupply vehicle. A modified, unmanned Soyuz spacecraft called Progress began delivering new supplies and equipment to Salyut 6 in January 1978. Thus it became the first space station to be resupplied and refueled. These capabilities greatly extended the useful life of space stations and enabled crews to repair and modernize them. Spare parts and more advanced instruments could be sent to the stations as needed. Salyut 6 operated for almost five years. It received visits by 16 crews, who spent up to six months in orbit. Between 1982 and 1986, Salyut 7 housed expeditions lasting up to eight months.

Skylab. The first U.S. space station was Skylab, launched into orbit by a Saturn 5 booster on May 14, 1973. Skylab was built from the empty third stage of a Saturn 5 rocket, with an attached air lock module, docking port, and solar telescope.

Astronauts Pete Conrad, Joseph P. Kerwin, and Paul J. Weitz arrived at Skylab on May 25. The station had suffered damage during launch, losing most of its thermal insulation and one of its two solar power panels. In addition, debris had jammed the other solar panel so it could not open. The crew worked outside the station several times to free the stuck panel. The success of this 28-day expedition proved the usefulness of people in space for the repair and maintenance of space stations.

Two more crews carried out Skylab missions. These astronauts continued to operate the station while conducting medical experiments, photographing the earth, and observing the sun. The second mission lasted 59 days, and the third ran for 84 days.

United States space officials hoped to keep Skylab in orbit long enough to host a space shuttle mission. However, the station fell from its orbit in July 1979 and broke apart. Fragments of the station landed in western Australia and in the Indian Ocean.

Skylab Skylab, the first U.S. manned space laboratory, orbited the earth from 1973 to 1979. Astronauts traveled to Skylab in Apollo spacecraft, as shown here. Solar panels provided electric energy. Skylab lost one set of panels during launch (see photo).

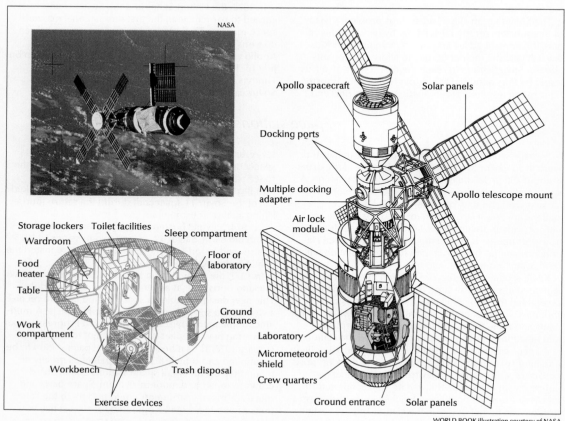

NASA

Apollo spacecraft

Solar panels

Docking ports

Multiple docking adapter

Apollo telescope mount

Air lock module

Laboratory

Micrometeoroid shield

Crew quarters

Ground entrance

Solar panels

Storage lockers Toilet facilities Sleep compartment

Wardroom

Floor of laboratory

Food heater

Table

Ground entrance

Work compartment

Workbench Trash disposal

Exercise devices

WORLD BOOK illustration courtesy of NASA

Mir

The Soviet space station Mir (Peace) was launched on Feb. 20, 1986. Mir featured two docking ports—one at each end—and four other hatches. They were designed for the attachment of laboratory modules, with the original Mir serving as the hub and the modules looking like the spokes of a wheel. Mir also had modernized equipment and improved solar power panels. Following the launch of Mir, the Soviet Union sent three laboratory modules into orbit, where they docked with the core module. Many cosmonauts spent several months aboard Mir.

Russia took over the operation of Mir after the Soviet Union broke apart in 1991. In 1995, U.S. space shuttles began to dock with Mir. Russia connected an additional science module to Mir in 1995 and another in 1996, completing the station.

A dangerous accident occurred in June 1997. A cosmonaut was practicing maneuvers that would dock a supply craft with the station. The craft collided with a module of Mir called Spektr. As a result of the accident, Mir had to operate on reduced power. In July 1997, Russia sent emergency supplies and equipment to Mir.

In March 2001, Russia destroyed Mir by guiding it into Earth's atmosphere. Much of the station burned during this journey, and the remainder fell into the Pacific Ocean.

The International Space Station

In 1984, President Ronald Reagan authorized the building of a large, permanent space station "within a decade." Designs for the station changed often, and the estimated cost increased. The promised completion date slipped later and later.

In 1993, President Bill Clinton directed NASA to redesign the proposed station to reduce the cost and the time it would take to build. The United States, Brazil, Canada, Japan, Russia, and the ESA would become partners in a program to build what would be known as the International Space Station.

Construction of the space station began in 1998. Russia launched the first module, called Zarya, in November that year. A month later, the space shuttle Endeavour carried the module Unity into orbit and docked it with Zarya. A crew of one American astronaut and two Russian cosmonauts moved into the International Space Station in 2000.

A historic docking occurred in 1995, when the United States space shuttle Atlantis, *left,* became the first U.S. spacecraft to link up with Russia's space station Mir, *right.* The station had been in orbit around the earth since 1986. A camera mounted in a Russian Soyuz spacecraft took this photograph.

NASA

Space shuttles

During the 1950's and the 1960's, aviation researchers worked to develop winged rocket planes. Advocates of winged spaceplanes pointed out that such vehicles could land on ordinary airfields. Adding wings to a spacecraft increases the vehicle's weight, but wings make landing the vehicle much easier and cheaper than splashdowns at sea. Ocean landings require many ships and aircraft, and the salt water usually damages the spacecraft beyond repair.

NASA began to develop a reusable space shuttle while the Apollo program was still underway. In 1972, U.S. President Richard M. Nixon signed an executive order that officially started the space shuttle project. The shuttles were designed to blast off like a rocket and land like an airplane, making up to 100 missions.

The space shuttle system consists of three parts: (1) an orbiter, (2) an external tank, and (3) two solid rocket boosters. The nose of the winged orbiter houses the pressurized crew cabin. From the flight deck at the front of the orbiter, pilots can look through the front and side windows. The middeck, located under the flight deck, contains additional seats, equipment lockers, food systems, sleeping facilities, and a small toilet compartment. An air lock links the middeck with the *payload bay,* the area that holds the cargo. The tail of the orbiter houses the main engines and a smaller set of engines used for maneuvering in space.

The external tank is attached to the orbiter's belly. It contains the liquid propellants used by the main engines. Two rocket boosters are strapped to the sides of the external tank. They contain solid propellants.

The designers of the space shuttle had to overcome a number of major technological challenges. The shuttle's main engines had to be reusable for many missions. The shuttle needed a flexible but reliable system of computer control. And it required a new type of heat shield that could withstand many reentries into the earth's atmosphere.

The shuttle era begins

In 1977, NASA conducted flight tests of the first space shuttle, Enterprise, with a modified 747 jumbo jet. The jet carried the orbiter into the air and back on several flights and released it in midair on several more.

The shuttle's first orbital mission began on April 12, 1981. That day, the shuttle Columbia was launched, with astronauts John W. Young and Robert L. Crippen at the controls. The 54-hour mission went perfectly. Seven

The first space shuttle mission blasted off from Cape Canaveral, Florida, on April 12, 1981. The shuttle, called Columbia, carried U.S. astronauts John W. Young and Robert L. Crippen on a 54-hour orbital flight. Columbia landed safely two days later at Edwards Air Force Base in California.

months later, the vehicle made a second orbital flight, proving that a spacecraft could be reused.

Although the first four shuttle flights each carried only two pilots, the crew size was soon expanded to four, and later to seven or eight. Besides the two pilots, shuttle crews included *mission specialists* (experts in the operation of the shuttle) and *payload specialists* (experts in the scientific research to be performed).

The large capacity of the space shuttle's orbiter opened the possibility of including other passengers besides NASA astronauts and scientists. Citizens who participated in shuttle missions included representatives of the companies launching payloads and members of the U.S. Congress.

In 1984, NASA created a special "Space Flight Participant" program to offer the opportunity of space travel to more Americans. President Reagan announced that the first participant would be a schoolteacher. Later flights were expected to carry journalists, artists, and other interested civilians.

Types of shuttle missions

Space shuttles carry artificial satellites, space probes, and other heavy loads into orbit around the earth. In addition to launch operations, the shuttles can retrieve artificial satellites that need servicing. Astronauts aboard the shuttle can repair the satellites and then return them to orbit. Shuttle crews can also conduct many kinds of scientific experiments and observations.

Commercial satellite launches. The first launch of a payload for a customer took place in November 1982.

The shuttle Columbia launched two communications satellites. Solid-rocket boosters helped the satellites climb to their designated orbits. Many later satellite launches followed. NASA discovered that using the space shuttle to launch satellites was more flexible than it had expected. However, the length of time required to ready each space shuttle for its next launch was also greater than NASA planners had expected and sometimes caused expensive delays.

Military missions. About one-fourth of the shuttle missions during the 1980's were conducted for military purposes. Astronauts on these missions sent special observation satellites into orbit and tested various military instruments. To prevent the discovery of information about the capabilities of these satellites, unusual secrecy surrounded the missions. NASA did not reveal launch times of the missions in advance or release any conversations between mission control and the astronauts in space. In the early 1990's, the United States phased out the use of shuttles for such missions and resumed the use of cheaper, single-use rockets.

Repair missions. The space shuttle enables astronauts to retrieve, repair, and relaunch broken satellites. This important capability was first demonstrated in April 1984, when two astronauts from the shuttle Challenger repaired the Solar Maximum Mission satellite—the only solar observatory in orbit. This success underscored the flexibility and capability of human beings in space. Astronauts have repaired several other satellites in space.

In 1993, a crew from the shuttle Endeavour repaired the orbiting Hubble Space Telescope. After the telescope had been launched in 1990, NASA engineers discovered an error in its primary mirror. The Endeavour astronauts installed optical equipment that canceled out the effect of the error. The crew also replaced certain scientific instruments, the solar panels, and the *gyroscopes,* devices used in pointing the telescope.

Spacelab missions. Spacelab was a facility that enabled shuttle crews to perform a wide variety of scientific experiments in space. Spacelab was built as a part of the space shuttle program by the European Space Agency. The first Spacelab mission was launched in 1983 in the space shuttle Columbia. In 1998, the same shuttle carried Spacelab on its last mission. Each mission focused on research in a certain area of science or technology, such as astronomy, the life sciences, and microgravity.

Spacelab consisted of a manned space laboratory and several separate platforms called *pallets.* The pressurized laboratory was connected to the crew compartment by a tunnel. It had facilities for scientists to conduct experiments in manufacturing, medicine, the production of biological materials, and other areas. The pallets carried large scientific instruments that were used to conduct experiments in astronomy and other fields. Scientists operated the instruments from the laboratory, from the shuttle's orbiter, or from the ground. Spacelab facilities were shared by the European Space Agency and the United States.

The Challenger disaster

The 10th launch of the space shuttle Challenger was scheduled as the 25th space shuttle mission. Francis R. (Dick) Scobee was the mission commander. The crew in-

NASA

Sally K. Ride became the first U.S. woman in space on June 18, 1983. In this photograph, Ride eats a meal on the shuttle Challenger during her second shuttle flight in October 1984.

cluded Christa McAuliffe, a high-school teacher from New Hampshire. The five other crew members were Gregory B. Jarvis, Ronald E. McNair, Ellison S. Onizuka, Judith A. Resnik, and Michael J. Smith.

After several launch delays, NASA officials overruled the concerns of engineers and ordered a liftoff on a cold morning, Jan. 28, 1986. The mission ended in tragedy. Challenger disintegrated into a ball of fire 73 seconds into flight, at an altitude of 46,000 feet (14,020 meters) and at about twice the speed of sound.

Strictly speaking, Challenger did not explode. Instead, various structural failures caused the spacecraft to break apart. Although Challenger disintegrated almost without warning, the crew may have briefly been aware that

something was wrong. The crew cabin tore loose from the rest of the shuttle and soared through the air. It took almost three minutes for the cabin to fall to the Atlantic Ocean, where it smashed on impact, killing the seven crew members.

All shuttle missions were halted while a special commission appointed by President Reagan determined the cause of the accident and what could be done to prevent such disasters from happening again. In June 1986, the commission reported that the accident was caused by a failure of *O rings* in the shuttle's right solid rocket booster. These rubber rings sealed the joint between the two lower segments of the booster. Design flaws in the joint and unusually cold weather during launch caused the O rings to allow hot gases to leak out of the booster through the joint. Flames from within the booster streamed past the failed seal and quickly expanded the small hole. The flaming gases then burned a hole in the shuttle's external fuel tank. The flames also cut away one of the supporting beams that held the booster to the side of the external tank. The booster tore loose and ruptured the tank. Propellants from the tank formed a giant fireball as structural failures ripped the vehicle apart.

The commission said NASA's decision to launch the shuttle was flawed. Top-level decision-makers had not been informed of problems with the joints and O rings or of the possible damaging effects of cold weather.

Shuttle designers made several technical modifications, including an improved O-ring design and the addition of a crew bail-out system. Although such a system would not work in all cases, it could save the lives of shuttle crew members in some situations. Procedural changes included stricter safety reviews and more restrictive launching conditions.

Back into space

Space shuttle flights resumed with the launch of the redesigned shuttle Discovery on Sept. 29, 1988. Over the next few years, several long-delayed missions were carried out. Astronauts launched many unmanned probes, such as Galileo, Magellan, and Ulysses. A number of sci-

NASA

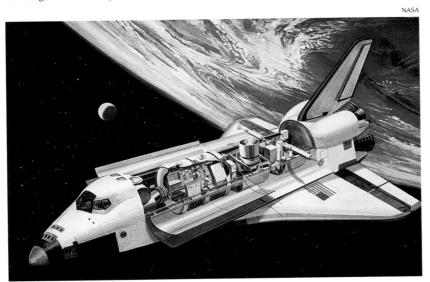

Spacelab, a space laboratory built by the European Space Agency, is carried by the space shuttle in this illustration. The laboratory was designed for four scientists to conduct experiments in an apparently weightless environment.

entific research satellites were placed into orbit, including the Hubble Space Telescope, the Compton Gamma Ray Observatory, and the Upper Atmosphere Research Satellite.

Shuttles also launched military and communications satellites. Spacelab research missions studied astronomy and space medicine. Officials worked out a less ambitious launch schedule, and major delays became less frequent. NASA also improved the shuttle fleet. New computers and life-support hardware were installed. A drag parachute and new brakes made landings easier to control. The automatic flight control system and computerized life-support systems were also improved.

Docking with Mir

Spacecraft from the United States and Russia resumed joint operations in 1995, 20 years after the Apollo-Soyuz mission. On June 29, after three years of negotiations, planning, and practice missions, the space shuttle Atlantis docked with Russia's Mir space station.

Atlantis carried a replacement crew of Russian cosmonauts to Mir and brought the station's former crew home to Earth. Among the returning crew members was astronaut Norman Thagard, who had ridden a Russian rocket to Mir on March 14, 1995. Thagard had spent 115 days in space, breaking the previous U.S. record of 84 days in space.

On March 22, 1995, three cosmonauts who were on Mir when Thagard arrived had made their return voyage to Earth. They included Valery Polyakov, who set an international record of 438 days in space.

Unlike the largely symbolic Apollo-Soyuz mission, the Atlantis-Mir docking was the first in a series of missions. Astronauts began regular visits to Mir, carried up and back by shuttles. The shuttles delivered replacement parts and scientific equipment, as well as water, food, and air. In addition, the astronauts and cosmonauts began to test techniques to be used to build and maintain the International Space Station.

On July 15, 1996, astronaut Shannon Lucid, aboard Mir, broke Thagard's record by spending her 116th consecutive day in space. Lucid had been launched aboard Atlantis on March 22, 1996, and had been on Mir since March 23. On Sept. 7, 1996, Lucid broke the women's record of 168 consecutive days in space. That record had been set by cosmonaut Yelena Kondakova in 1995. On September 26, Lucid returned to Earth aboard Atlantis, having spent 188 consecutive days in space.

The Soviet space shuttle

The Soviet Union carried out its own shuttle program in great secrecy during the 1980's. The Soviet shuttle, Buran (Snowstorm), resembled the U.S. shuttle, but Soviet engineers made many modifications. For example, Buran had no main engines on board. Instead, an expendable booster provided all its launching power.

On Nov. 15, 1988, a heavy booster called Energia carried Buran into orbit without a crew. An automatic flight control system managed the two-orbit flight. Buran landed on a runway at the Baykonur Cosmodrome in Kazakhstan, then part of the Soviet Union.

Beginning in 1989, shortages of funds caused long delays in further development of the Buran program. In 1993, work on the program ended.

The Columbia disaster

Disaster struck the U.S. shuttle fleet again on Feb. 1, 2003, when Columbia, the fleet's oldest shuttle, broke apart over the southwestern United States as it reentered Earth's atmosphere. The flight was Columbia's 28th launch and the shuttle fleet's 113th mission. The accident occurred about 16 minutes before the shuttle was due to land. All seven crew members died. The crew consisted of Rick Husband, the mission commander; Ilan Ramon, the first Israeli astronaut; and Michael Anderson, David M. Brown, Kalpana Chawla, Laurel Clark, and William McCool. NASA halted shuttle flights and appointed an independent commission to investigate the accident.

In 2003, the commission reported that the accident had been caused by a chunk of foam insulation that broke away from the shuttle's external fuel tank and struck Columbia's left wing at high speed shortly after liftoff. The impact created a hole in the heat-resistant panels that protected the wing from high temperatures during reentry. As the shuttle reentered Earth's atmosphere, the hole allowed superheated air to enter the wing and damage its internal structure. Eventually, the wing was destroyed, and the shuttle went out of control and broke apart.

The report called for NASA to develop systems for inspecting and repairing protective tiles and panels while the shuttle is in orbit. It recommended reinforcing the panels and working to limit or prevent the shedding of foam from the external fuel tank. The report also criticized NASA management, concluding that pressure to meet budgets and deadlines had contributed to a decline in the safety of the shuttle program.

In 2004, President George W. Bush announced plans to retire the United States shuttle fleet by 2010, after the completion of the International Space Station. He proposed replacing the shuttle with a new craft that could carry astronauts to the moon and, eventually, to Mars.

Return to flight

After working for over two years to improve the safety of the space shuttle program, NASA launched the shuttle Discovery on July 26, 2005. During the launch, the external fuel tank shed a chunk of foam nearly as large as the one that had fatally damaged Columbia. The foam did not appear to strike Discovery, but the incident led NASA officials to suspend further shuttle launches.

The Discovery astronauts continued on their mission to deliver supplies and perform repairs to the International Space Station. The crew also tested methods of inspecting and repairing the shuttle's heat shield in orbit. They used laser imaging equipment mounted on a robotic arm to scan the heat-resistant tiles for damage.

The inspections revealed that two strips of material used to fill the gaps between the tiles had come loose. Engineers worried that the dangling strips could cause the craft to overheat. Mission managers sent U.S. astronaut Stephen K. Robinson out on a robotic arm to remove the fabric, the first heat shield repair in orbit in shuttle history. The shuttle landed safely on August 9.

Discovery visited the station again during the next shuttle flight in July 2006. No major safety problems arose. In September, the shuttle Atlantis completed the first of a series of regular missions to continue assembly of the station.

A number of nations have developed rocket and space programs smaller than the U.S. and Russian programs. Most of them concentrate on single applications such as the launching of scientific satellites.

European nations. Several European nations built boosters to launch small scientific research satellites. In 1965, France became the first nation in western Europe to launch a satellite. The United Kingdom sent another satellite into orbit in 1971.

In 1975, the European Space Agency (ESA) was organized. Its western European member nations combine their financial and scientific resources in the development of spacecraft, instruments, and experiments. ESA supervised the construction of Spacelab, launched the space probe Giotto toward Halley's Comet, and built the Ulysses solar probe. ESA also developed a series of Ariane booster rockets to launch communications satellites for paying customers. By the late 1980's, Ariane rockets were launching more commercial satellites than U.S. rockets were. ESA spacecraft lift off from Kourou in French Guiana, on the northern coast of South America. See **European Space Agency.**

Besides its activities as an ESA member, Germany independently built two solar probes called Helios. These probes were launched in 1974 and 1976. The probes flew within 28 million miles (45 million kilometers) of the sun—closer than any other probe had reached.

Japan became the fourth nation in space when it launched a satellite in February 1970. The nation's space program blossomed in the 1980's. In 1985, Japan fired two probes toward Halley's Comet. Two separate programs developed a family of small, efficient space boosters. The H-1 rocket, a medium-sized booster with liquid hydrogen fuel, also became operational. In 1990, Japan launched a lunar probe.

In 1994, Japan launched its first heavy-lifting booster, the H-2. In 1996, an H-2 lofted the Advanced Earth Observing Satellite. The satellite began to gather data on Earth's lands, seas, and atmosphere.

Japan sends small scientific research satellites into orbit from Kagoshima Space Center on the island of Kyushu. Rockets carrying larger satellites take off from Tanegashima Space Center on Tanega Island, about 60 miles (95 kilometers) to the south. Japan is developing a laboratory module for the International Space Station.

China. In April 1970, China sent its first satellite into space aboard a CZ-1 launcher. In the 1980's, China developed impressive space technology that included liquid-hydrogen engines, powerful Long March rockets, and recoverable satellites. China launches spacecraft from three sites—Jiuquan, Taiyuan, and Xichang.

In the 1990's, China began developing the Shenzhou, a spacecraft designed to carry astronauts. The Shenzhou resembles Russia's Soyuz capsule. In October 2003, China became the third nation to launch a person into

European Space Agency

The Ariane 5 rocket is used chiefly to launch commercial satellites. The rocket was developed by the European Space Agency and a group of European companies known as Arianespace.

space. Chinese astronaut Yang Liwei orbited Earth aboard a Shenzhou craft for 21 hours. Another Shenzhou craft carried two astronauts into orbit on a five-day mission in October 2005. Astronauts in the Chinese space program are sometimes called *taikonauts.*

India first launched a satellite into orbit in July 1980. The Indian Space Research Organisation builds boosters. India launches rockets from the island of Sriharikota, off its eastern coast.

Canada has an active space research program and a communications satellite program. Canada took part in the U.S. space shuttle program by designing and building the shuttle's robot arm. It also built a larger robot arm that was installed on the International Space Station.

Other nations. Israel sent its first satellite into orbit in 1988. Australia has launched modified U.S. rockets from Woomera, in central Australia. Italy has launched United States rockets from the San Marco platform in the Indian Ocean, located off the coast of Kenya. Several countries, including Brazil, Sweden, and South Africa, have sent scientific sounding rockets into space.

Plans for the future

In the early 2000's, scientists and engineers were developing new kinds of spacecraft and more efficient rockets. Industrial researchers were working on manufacturing techniques that would use the space environment to advantage. Encouraged by the commercial potential of space activities, private companies had begun to provide launch services.

Developing new spacecraft. Several organizations were developing technologies for a craft that would replace the space shuttles after 2010. These organizations included NASA, ESA, Japan's National Space Development Agency, and several private companies. Their chief objective was to cut flight costs. One way to achieve this goal would be to develop a *reusable launch vehicle* (RLV). All the main parts of an RLV would be reused, giving the craft an advantage over a shuttle.

A shuttle's main fuel tank drops away after use and so must be replaced for each flight. In one RLV design, a special airplane would carry a spacecraft to a high altitude and release it. The spacecraft would then fire its own rockets to go into orbit. After completing its mission, the craft would land as an airplane does. Another type of RLV would be a *single-stage-to-orbit* (SSTO) craft—a vehicle that would take off by itself and not discard any components.

In the early 2000's, NASA officials decided that an RLV replacement for the shuttle would prove too difficult to develop by 2010. In the meantime, the agency concentrated on developing the Crew Exploration Vehicle (CEV), a capsule-shaped spacecraft that would carry crew and light cargo to and from the International Space Station. A partially recoverable booster would carry the CEV into space. The agency planned to eventually use the CEV to transport crew to the moon and to Mars.

In 2006, NASA invested in two private companies to help them build spacecraft that could deliver crew and cargo to the International Space Station. The companies were Space Exploration Technologies, also known as SpaceX, of El Segundo, California, and Rocketplane-Kistler of Oklahoma City, Oklahoma.

Developing more efficient rockets. Scientists and engineers are working on alternatives to fuel-burning rockets. Two main alternatives are (1) the *ion rocket* and (2) the *nuclear rocket.* For a given amount of fuel, both alternatives can create at least twice as much acceleration as a fuel-burning rocket. In addition, both can operate for a long time before running out of fuel. Neither ion rockets nor nuclear rockets would launch spacecraft; they would create thrust after fuel-burning boosters had performed that task.

An ion rocket is an electrical device. Electric energy heats a fuel, converts its atoms to *ions* (electrically charged atoms), and expels the ions to create thrust. Designers have already used small ion rockets to keep communications satellites in position above Earth and to propel experimental space probes.

A nuclear rocket uses heat from a nuclear reactor to change a liquid fuel into a gas and expel the gas. This kind of rocket would not be practical as a launcher as some radioactive materials might escape into the atmosphere. But, a small nuclear rocket that continuously created thrust could reduce mission times to other planets.

Expanding space activities. Two major areas of space utilization have been the gathering and communication of information. Satellites monitor weather systems on Earth, and space probes gather information on the other planets and the sun. Since the 1960's, communications satellites have regularly relayed television signals between points on Earth's surface.

The next major area of space utilization may be the manufacture of medicinal and industrial products. Manufacturers may use the low gravity, high-vacuum environment of space to create substances that are purer or

Scaled Composites, LLC

SpaceShipOne, a rocket launched from an airplane, soared to an altitude of over 62 miles (100 kilometers) on June 21, 2004, becoming the first privately funded, piloted craft to reach space.

stronger than those produced on Earth. These substances might include drugs; *semiconductors,* the materials of which computer chips are made; and special *alloys* (mixtures of metals).

Private launch services. Many private companies have begun to develop launch services to compete with the national and international organizations. One firm, Sea Launch Company, boosted a communications satellite from a floating platform in the Pacific Ocean in October 1999. The company used a Ukrainian-built Zenit rocket to launch the satellite. Corporations in the United States, Russia, Norway, and Ukraine own Sea Launch.

On June 21, 2004, Scaled Composites of Mojave, California, became the first private company to launch a person into space. The company's rocket, called SpaceShipOne, carried American test pilot Michael Melvill more than 62 miles (100 kilometers) above Earth on a brief suborbital test flight. The rocket was launched from a specially designed airplane called the White Knight. SpaceShipOne went on to win the Ansari X Prize with successful launches on Sept. 29 and Oct. 4, 2004. The $10 million prize was designed to stimulate interest in private space travel.   James Oberg

Related articles in *World Book.* For information on the astronauts and cosmonauts and on how they are selected and trained, see **Astronaut.** For details on how rockets work and how they are used in space exploration, see **Rocket.** For information on artificial satellites, see **Satellite, Artificial.** See also the following articles:

Biographies

For biographies of astronauts and cosmonauts, see the *Related articles* listed in the **Astronaut** article. See also **Goddard, Robert H.,** and **Von Braun, Wernher.**

Organizations

American Institute of Aeronautics and Astronautics
European Space Agency
National Aeronautics and Space Administration

Other related articles

Aerospace medicine	Eros
Astronomy (Space probes)	Exobiology
Cape Canaveral	Galileo
Cassini	Gravitation
Cosmic rays	Guided missile

Hubble Space Telescope
International Space Station
Jet propulsion
Jet Propulsion Laboratory
Jodrell Bank Observatory
Johnson Space Center
Jupiter (History of Jupiter
study)
Kennedy Space Center
Life (The search for life on
other planets)
Map (Mapmaking and
modern technology)
Mars (Observation by
spacecraft)
Mercury (Flights to Mercury)

Meteor
Mir
Moon
Orbit
Planet
Radar (In space travel)
Radiation
Relativity
Satellite (Spacecraft missions)
Saturn (Flights to Saturn)
SETI Institute
Solar system
Sun (Studying the sun)
Telemetry
Venus (Flights to Venus)
Voyager

Outline

I. **What is space?**
A. The beginning of space
B. Space between the planets
C. Space between the stars
II. **Getting into space and back**
A. Preparing the spacecraft
B. Overcoming gravity
C. Returning to the earth
III. **Living in space**
A. Protection against the dangers of space
B. Microgravity
C. Meeting basic needs in space
D. Communicating with the earth
E. Working in space
IV. **The dawn of the space age**
A. Early dreams of space flight
B. The first space rockets
C. The first artificial satellites
D. The space race begins
E. Organizing and managing
space activities
V. **Space probes**
A. How a space probe car-   E. Probes to Mars
ries out its mission   F. Probes to Venus
B. Early unmanned   G. Probes to Jupiter and
explorations   beyond
C. Lunar probes   H. Probes to comets
D. Solar probes
VI. **Human beings enter space**
A. Vostok and Mercury: The first human
beings in space
B. Voskhod and Gemini: The first multiperson
space flights
C. Apollo: Mission to the moon
D. Soviet attempts to reach the moon
E. The Apollo-Soyuz Test Project
VII. **Space stations**
A. Salyut and Skylab
B. Mir
C. The International Space Station
VIII. **Space shuttles**
A. The shuttle era begins
B. Types of shuttle missions
C. The Challenger disaster
D. Back into space
E. Docking with Mir
F. The Soviet space shuttle
G. The Columbia disaster
IX. **Other nations in space**
A. European nations   D. India
B. Japan   E. Canada
C. China   F. Other nations
X. **Plans for the future**
A. Developing new spacecraft
B. Developing more efficient rockets
C. Expanding space activities
D. Private launch services

Questions

What is microgravity? How does microgravity affect space
travelers?
How does a rocket generate thrust?
What was the first international manned space mission? When
did it begin?
Who was the first person to set foot on the moon? When did
this achievement occur?
What device allows astronauts to maneuver outside a spacecraft
without a safety line?
What was the first space station to be resupplied and refueled
in orbit?
Why would a nuclear rocket be impractical as a booster?
Who was the first woman in space?
How did the "space race" begin?
How far above Earth does Earth's atmosphere end and space
begin?

Additional resources

Level I

Ackroyd, Peter. *Escape from Earth*. DK Pub., 2003.
Bredeson, Carmen. *Our Space Program*. Millbrook, 1999.
Carlisle, Rodney P. *Exploring Space*. Facts on File, 2005.
Johnstone, Michael. *In Space*. Candlewick Pr., 1999.
Nicolson, Cynthia P. *Exploring Space*. Kids Can Pr., 2000.

Level II

Angelo, Joseph A., Jr. *Encyclopedia of Space Exploration*. Facts
on File, 2000.
Chaikin, Andrew. *Space*. Firefly Bks., 2004.
Crouch, Tom D. *Aiming for the Stars: The Dreamers and Doers
of the Space Age*. Smithsonian Institution, 1999.
Freeman, Marsha. *Challenges of Human Space Exploration*.
Springer-Verlag, 2000.
Mudgway, Douglas J. *Big Dish: Building America's Deep Space
Connection to the Planets*. Univ. Pr. of Fla., 2005.

Space travel. See Space exploration.

Spaghetti. See Pasta.

Spahn, Warren (1921-2003), became one of the greatest pitchers in baseball history. During his major league
career, he won 363 games, more than any other left-
handed pitcher. Spahn won 20 or more games in one
season 13 times, and he led the National League in
games won eight different times. Spahn set the major
league record for the most shut outs by a left-handed
pitcher, 63.

Warren Edward Spahn was born on April 23, 1921, in
Buffalo, New York. He played for the Boston Braves—lat-
er the Milwaukee Braves—from 1942 to 1964. In 1965,
Spahn pitched for the New York Mets and San Francisco
Giants. He retired from baseball after the 1965 season.
Spahn was elected to the National Baseball Hall of Fame
in 1973. He died on Nov. 24, 2003.   Dave Nightingale

Spaight, *spayt,* **Richard Dobbs** (1758-1802), was a
North Carolina signer of the Constitution of the United
States. At the Constitutional Convention of 1787, Spaight
was one of the few delegates to attend every session. He
also helped win *ratification* (approval) of the Constitution
by North Carolina.

Spaight was born on March 25, 1758, in New Bern,
North Carolina, and educated in Ireland. He served in
the North Carolina legislature for much of the 1780's,
and he served in the Congress of the Confederation
from 1783 to 1785. Spaight was governor of North Carolina from 1792 to 1795 and a member of the United
States House of Representatives from 1798 to 1801. He
died on Sept. 6, 1802, from a wound he received in a
duel with John Stanly, a political rival.   Joan R. Gundersen

ZEFA

Spain is famous for its beautiful castles, many of which were built during the Middle Ages. The castle shown here, in central Spain near Toledo, dates from the mid-1400's.

Spain

Spain is a country in western Europe famous for its colorful bullfights, sunny climate, historic cities, and beautiful castles. Spain was once a great empire with colonies throughout the world. Spanish language and culture took root and became a part of the culture of many nations. Today, Spain is a prosperous nation with a well-developed economy based on service industries and manufacturing.

Spain is one of the largest countries in Europe in area. Spain occupies about five-sixths of the Iberian Peninsula, which lies in southwestern Europe between the Atlantic Ocean and the Mediterranean Sea. Portugal occu-

The contributors of this article are Carla Rahn Phillips, Professor of History at the University of Minnesota, and William D. Phillips, Jr., Professor of History at the University of Minnesota.

pies the rest of the peninsula. Spain also includes the Balearic Islands in the Mediterranean Sea and the Canary Islands in the Atlantic Ocean. Madrid, Spain's capital and largest city, stands in the center of the country.

Spain ranks among the major manufacturing nations of Europe. Most Spaniards live in cities, and modern urban ways of life have become commonplace. Many of the country's old customs, such as taking a *siesta* (nap or rest) after lunch, are disappearing.

Spain is one of the world's leading tourist countries. Each year, millions of people visit Spain's sunny Mediterranean beaches and islands, the rocky Atlantic coast, and the castles and churches that stand in historic Spanish cities.

On Spain's northeastern border, the mighty Pyrenees Mountains separate Spain from France. These mountains once formed a great barrier to overland travel be-

ZEFA

Madrid, Spain's capital and largest city, is one of the chief commercial, cultural, and industrial centers of the country. The Plaza de Cibeles, *shown here,* is one of the city's major crossroads.

Nik Wheeler

The "running of the bulls" is a well-known tradition in the festival of San Fermín in Pamplona. Bulls and people race through the streets to the bull ring, where bullfights later take place.

tween the Iberian Peninsula and the rest of Europe. Africa lies only about 8 miles (13 kilometers) south of Spain across the Strait of Gibraltar.

Most of Spain lies on a high, dry plateau called the Meseta. Hills and mountains rise throughout the Meseta, and north of it mountains extend across the peninsula. In spite of Spain's rugged landscape and limited resources, the Spaniards established one of the largest empires in world history.

In the A.D. 700's, Arabs and other Muslim people from northern Africa conquered most of Spain. They held control for hundreds of years. In the 1000's, Spanish Christians began to drive the Muslims from the country. The Christians finally defeated the Muslims in 1492. That same year, Christopher Columbus, an Italian navigator in the service of Spain, reached America—sailing in Spanish ships.

Columbus's voyage touched off a great age of Spanish exploration and conquest. The Spaniards built an empire that included much of western South America and southern North America, as well as lands in Africa, Asia, and Europe.

Beginning in the late 1500's, economic difficulties, wars with other countries, and civil wars weakened Spain. The country held most of its empire until the early 1800's, however. Without its empire, Spain became poor. The country lagged behind most of its European neighbors until the mid-1900's.

In the late 1930's, a bloody civil war tore Spain apart. The war brought General Francisco Franco to power as dictator. Franco controlled the country until his death in 1975. Spain became a democracy after Franco died.

For population and other key statistics, see the *Spain in brief* feature in this article.

Spain in brief

Capital: Madrid.
Official language: Castilian Spanish; Catalan, Galician, and Basque are official languages in provinces where they are widely spoken. About 17 percent of population speaks Catalan, 8 percent Galician, and 2 percent Basque; most people also speak Spanish.
National anthem: "Marcha Real" ("The Royal March").
Largest cities: (2001 census)

   Madrid (2,938,723)   Seville (684,633)
   Barcelona (1,503,884)   Saragossa (614,905)
   Valencia (738,441)   Málaga (524,414)

Spain's state flag, used by the government, was adopted in 1981. The civil flag, used by the people, has no coat of arms.

Coat of arms was adopted in 1981. The symbols on the shield represent Aragon, Castile, and other historic kingdoms of Spain.

Land and climate

Land: Spain occupies five-sixths of the Iberian Peninsula in far southwestern Europe. The other one-sixth is occupied by Portugal. Spain also includes the Balearic Islands in the Mediterranean Sea and the Canary Islands in the Atlantic Ocean. The country borders France, Portugal, the Atlantic Ocean, and the Mediterranean Sea. A plateau called the Meseta is the largest land region of Spain. Hills and mountains rise throughout the plateau. North of the plateau, mountains extend across the country. The Pyrenees Mountains in the northeast form Spain's border with France. Spain's chief rivers include the Ebro, Guadalquivir, and Tagus.

Area: 195,365 mi² (505,992 km²), including Balearic and Canary Islands. *Greatest distances*—east-west, 646 mi (1,040 km); north-south, 547 mi (880 km). *Coastline*—2,345 mi (3,774 km).

Elevation: *Highest*—Pico de Teide, 12,198 ft (3,718 m) above sea level, in Canary Islands. *Lowest*—sea level along the coast.
Climate: Most of Spain has hot, sunny summers and cold winters. In the interior, average temperatures rise above 80 °F (27 °C) in July and fall below 30 °F (–1 °C) in January. The northern mountains have somewhat cooler summers and warmer winters. The Mediterranean coast, Balearic Islands, and Canary Islands have warmer weather than the rest of the country.

Government

Form of government: Parliamentary monarchy.
Head of state: King.
Head of government: Prime minister.
Legislature: Parliament of two houses—the Chamber of Deputies (350 members) and the Senate (about 260 members). The Chamber of Deputies is more powerful than the Senate.
Executive: Prime minister; Cabinet selected by the prime minister.
Political subdivisions: 50 provinces in 17 regions.

People

Population: *2008 estimate*—44,687,000. *2001 census*—40,847,371.
Population density: 229 per mi² (88 per km²).
Distribution: 77 percent urban, 23 percent rural.
Major ethnic/national groups: About 95 percent Spanish (including Catalans, Basques, and others who have long lived in Spain). Some citizens of other European countries, Moroccans, and Latin Americans.
Major religion: About 95 percent Roman Catholic.

Population trend

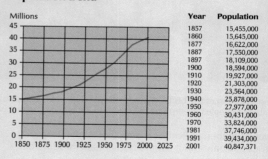

Year	Population
1857	15,455,000
1860	15,645,000
1877	16,622,000
1887	17,550,000
1897	18,109,000
1900	18,594,000
1910	19,927,000
1920	21,303,000
1930	23,564,000
1940	25,878,000
1950	27,977,000
1960	30,431,000
1970	33,824,000
1981	37,746,000
1991	39,434,000
2001	40,847,371

Economy

Chief products: *Agriculture*—barley, hogs, milk, olives, oranges, potatoes, sheep, sugar beets, tomatoes, wheat, wine. *Fishing*—mussels, sardines, squid. *Manufacturing*—automobiles, chemicals, iron and steel, machinery, ships, shoes, textiles.
Money: *Basic unit*—euro. One hundred cents equal one euro. The peseta was taken out of circulation in 2002.
International trade: *Major exports*—automobiles, fruit, iron and steel, petroleum products, textiles. *Major imports*—automobiles, chemicals, corn, electrical equipment, machinery, petroleum, primary metals, soybeans. *Major trading partners*—China, France, Germany, Italy, Japan, Mexico, Netherlands, Portugal, United Kingdom, United States.

Government

Spain has a democratic form of government called a parliamentary monarchy. The main public officials are a king, a prime minister, and members of a Cabinet and a parliament.

The king is head of state. He does not have a direct role in the operations of the government, but he has an advisory role in matters of government policies. The king represents the country at important diplomatic and ceremonial affairs. Juan Carlos I, who became king of Spain in 1975, played an important part in the process that changed Spain from a dictatorship to a democracy.

The prime minister leads the national government. The prime minister heads a Cabinet, a group of officials that carries out the day-to-day operations of the government. The leader of the political party that holds the most seats in parliament becomes prime minister.

The parliament of Spain, called the Cortes, makes the country's laws. The Cortes is a two-house legislature. It consists of a 350-member lower house called the Chamber of Deputies and an upper house called the Senate with about 260 members. The people elect all of the deputies and most of the senators. The regional governments appoint about a fifth of the senators. The members of both houses serve four-year terms. Spaniards who are 18 years old or older may vote.

Local government. Spain is divided into 50 provinces. Mainland Spain consists of 47 provinces; the Canary Islands consist of 2; and the Balearic Islands, 1. A governor appointed by the national government leads each province.

The Constitution of 1978 grouped the provinces into 17 regions called *autonomous* (self-ruling) communities. Each autonomous community has its own popularly elected government and wide powers in areas such as education and culture. Spain's national government controls national defense and foreign policy, but many other responsibilities are shared by the national and regional governments. Cities and towns have mayors and town councils, elected by popular vote.

Political parties. The Popular Party and the Socialist Workers' Party are the largest political parties in Spain. Other important parties include the United Left and the Convergence and Union. The United Left is a coalition of several left-wing parties, including the Communist Party of Spain. Convergence and Union is a coalition of two parties that promote a separate identity for the region of Catalonia. The Basque region has its own local parties.

Courts. Spain's highest court is the Supreme Court. There are also 17 territorial courts, 52 provincial courts, local courts, military courts, and a constitutional court.

Armed forces of Spain consist of an army, a navy, and an air force. About 150,000 people serve in the country's armed forces.

People

The people of Spain live in an increasingly modern and urban society. Their standard of living is high. Most Spaniards today eat better, dress better, live in better homes, and receive more education and better health care than their parents and grandparents.

Spain is a modern, industrial nation, but it maintains strong ties to traditional ways. Most Spaniards lived in rural areas before the country's rapid economic development in the 1950's and 1960's. Many of the people owned small farms. Others worked on large estates. The people in each region of the country, such as Andalusia in the south or Galicia in northwestern Spain, felt great loyalty to their region. The nation's greatest unifying force was the Roman Catholic Church. Almost all Spaniards were Roman Catholics, and a Catholic church stood in the center of most villages.

Regionalism and Roman Catholicism remain important forces in Spanish life. But rapid economic and social change has reduced the influence of these forces on many of the people.

Ancestry and population. People have lived in what is now Spain for more than 100,000 years. About 5,000 years ago, a people known as Iberians occupied much of Spain. During the next 4,000 years, other groups came to Spain as conquerors, settlers, or traders. Phoenicians, the first of these groups, were followed by Celts, Greeks, Carthaginians, Romans, Jews, Germanic peoples, and Muslims. Each group mixed with other peoples in Spain and thus helped shape the ancestry of the present-day Spanish people.

Most of Spain's people live in cities. The country has two cities with more than a million people. These cities are Madrid, the nation's capital and largest city, and Barcelona. At the time of the 2001 census, Spain had 19 other cities with populations of more than 200,000 people. See the separate articles on Spanish cities that are listed in the *Related articles* at the end of this article.

Language. Castilian Spanish is the official language of Spain, and it is the language that is spoken by most of the people. Pronunciation varies slightly from one region of the country to another. See **Spanish language**.

In three northern regions of Spain—Catalonia, the Basque provinces, and Galicia—a second official language is used in addition to Castilian Spanish. Many people in Catalonia speak Catalan, a language similar to the Provençal tongue of southern France. Some Basques speak Euskara, also called Basque, which is not known to be related to any other language. In Galicia, most people speak Galician, a language related to Portuguese.

City life. The majority of Spain's people live in cities and follow modern, urban ways of life. Almost all city people live in apartments, and many of them own rather than rent their dwellings. Almost all city homes have electric power. Many families own automobiles, television sets, and computers. But the people also suffer from such problems as pollution and traffic jams.

A number of age-old customs survive alongside the latest trends. Until the late 1900's, most Spanish factories, stores, and offices closed for three-hour lunch breaks and then stayed open until 7 p.m. or later. Some businesses still keep these hours. Some Spaniards still take a siesta after lunch, though most people no longer follow this custom. Spaniards enjoy a *paseo* (walk) before their evening meal, which they often do not eat until 10 or 11 p.m. Spanish people also go to sidewalk cafes, bars, and clubs, where they visit with friends and drink coffee, soft drinks, or wine.

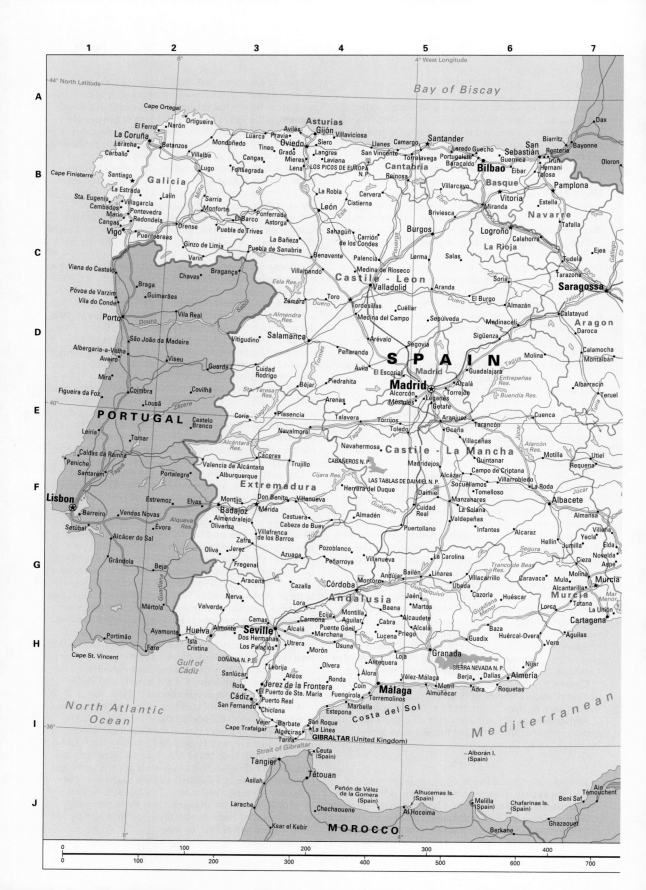

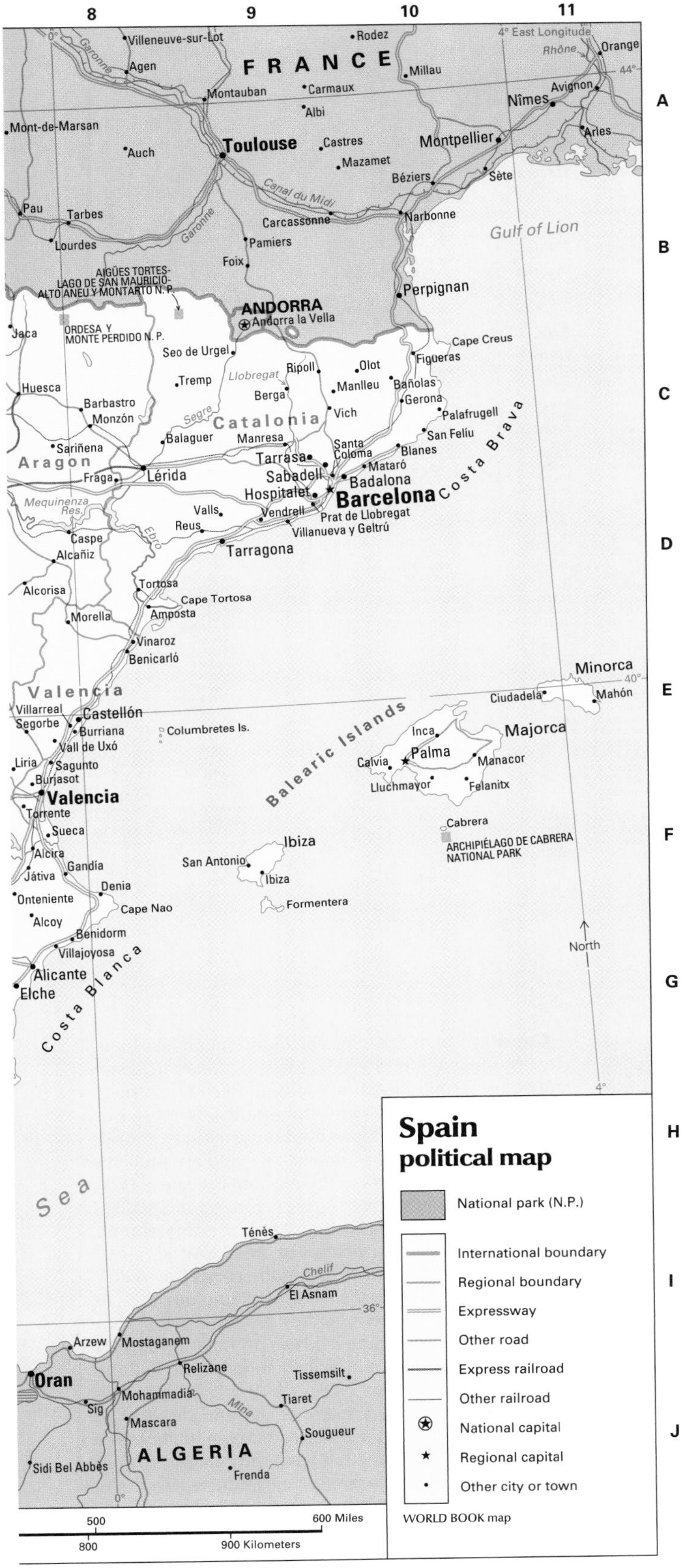

Spain map index

Regions

Map key	Name	Population	Area In mi²	Area In km²
G 4	**Andalusia**	7,357,558	33,694	87,268
C 8	**Aragon**	1,204,215	18,405	47,669
B 4	**Asturias**	1,062,998	4,079	10,565
E 10	**Balearic Islands**	841,669	1,936	5,014
B 6	**Basque (País Vasco)**	2,082,587	2,803	7,261
†	**Canary Islands**	1,694,477	2,808	7,273
B 5	**Cantabria**	535,131	2,042	5,289
E 5	**Castile-La Mancha**	1,760,516	30,589	79,226
C 5	**Castile-Leon**	2,456,474	36,350	94,147
C 9	**Catalonia**	6,343110	12,328	31,930
F 5	**Extremadura**	1,058,503	16,063	41,602
B 2	**Galicia**	2,695,880	11,365	29,434
C 6	**La Rioja**	276,702	1,944	5,034
E 5	**Madrid**	5,423,384	3,087	7,995
H 7	**Murcia**	1,197,646	4,369	11,317
C 7	**Navarre**	555,829	4,024	10,421
E 8	**Valencia**	4,162,776	8,998	23,305

Cities and towns‡

Adra	21,983	I 6
Aguilar	13,421	H 4
Águilas	27,771	H 7
Alaquás*	27,733	F 8
Albacete	148,934	F 7
Alcalá [de Guadaira]	57,426	H 3
Alcalá [de Henares]	176,434	E 5
Alcalá [la Real]	21,296	H 5
Alcantarilla	34,303	G 7
Alcaudete	11,154	H 5
Alcazar [de San Juan]	26,403	F 5
Alzira	39,668	F 8
Alcobendas*	92,090	E 5
Alcorcón	153,100	E 5
Alcorisa	3,339	D 8
Alcoy	58,358	F 8
Aldaia*	24,800	E 8
Alfafar*	18,622	E 8
Algeciras	101,468	I 4
Algemesí*	24,563	E 8
Alicante	284,580	G 8
Almansa	23,531	F 7
Almazora*	17,331	E 8
Almen-dralejo	27,521	F 3
Almería	166,328	H 6
Almonte	17,827	H 3
Almuñécar	21,420	I 5
Álora	12,363	I 4
Amorebieta-Etxano*	16,182	B 6
Amposta	16,865	D 8
Andoain*	13,814	B 6
Andújar	36,455	G 5
Antequera	40,289	H 4
Aranda [de Duero]	29,942	C 5
Aranjuez	40,797	E 5
Arcos [de la Frontera]	27,849	H 3
Arganda*	33,432	E 5
Arrecife	44,980	†
Arteixo*	23,306	B 1
Arucas	32,466	†
Aspe	16,631	G 7
Astorga	12,242	C 3
Ávila	49,712	D 4
Avilés	83,185	A 4
Ayamonte	16,604	H 2
Badajoz	133,519	F 3
Badalona	205,836	D 10
Baena	19,155	H 5
Baeza*	15,091	G 4
Bailén	17,593	G 5
Balaguer	13,359	C 8
Bañolas	14,232	C 10
Baracaldo (Barakaldo)	94,478	B 6
Barbastro	15,053	C 8
Barbate	21,815	I 3
Barcelona	1,503,884	D 10
Basauri*	45,085	B 6
Baza	21,808	H 6
Béjar	15,123	E 4
Benavente	16,590	C 4
Benicarló	20,542,	E 8
Benidorm	51,873	G 8
Berga	14,678	C 9
Berja	13,312	H 6
Bermeo*	16,938	B 6
Betanzos	12,510	B 2
Bilbao	349,972	B 6
Blanes	30,693	C 10
Boadilla del Monte*	27,443	D 5
Boiro*	17,748	B 2
Burgos	166,187	C 5
Burjasot	35,330	F 8
Burlada*	17,164	B 6
Burriana	26,757	E 8
Cabra	20,598	H 5
Cáceres	82,716	F 3
Cádiz	133,363	I 3
Calahorra	20,528	C 6
Calatayud	18,019	D 7
Callosa de Segura*	15,805	G 7
Calviá	35,977	E 10
Camargo	24,498	B 5
Camas	24,966	H 3
Cambados	13,385	B 1
Campo de Criptana	13,184	F 6
Cangas	23,981	C 1
Cangas [del Narcea]	16,511	B 3
Caravaca	22,963	G 6
Carballo	28,142	B 1
Carcagente*	19,508	F 8
Carmona	25,794	H 4
Cartagena	184,686	H 7
Castelldefels*	46,428	D 9
Castellón [de la Plana]	147,667	E 8
Castrillon*	22,501	B 4
Catarroja*	20,990	F 8
Cerdanyola*	53,343	D 9
Ceuta	71,505	I 4
Chiclana [de la Frontera]	61,028	I 3
Cieza	33,017	G 7
Ciudadela	23.103	E 11
Ciudad Real	63,251	F 5
Ciudad Rodrigo	13,991	D 3
Coín	17,388	I 4
Collado Villalba*	47,001	D 5
Córdoba	308,072	G 4
Coria	12,086	E 3
Coria del Río*	24,040	H 3
Cornella de Llobregat*	79,979	D 9
Corvera de Asturias*	15,885	B 3
Coslada*	77,884	E 5
Crevillent*	24,786	G 7
Cuenca	46,341	E 6
Cullera*	20,379	F 8
Daimiel	17,095	F 5
Dalías	3,625	H 6
Denia	33,342	F 8
Don Benito	31,538	F 3
Dos Hermanas	101,988	H 3
Durango*	25,003	B 6
Écija	36,896	H 4
Éibar	28,219	B 6
Ejea [de los Caballeros]	16,048	C 7
El Arahal*	18,365	H 3
Elche	194,767	G 7
Elda	51,593	G 7
El Ejido*	57,877	H 6
El Ferroll	77,950	B 2
Elgóibar*	10,440	B 6
El Puerto de Santa Maria	76,236	I 3
El Viso del Alcor*	16,333	H 4
Ermúa*	16,795	B 6
Esplugas de Llobregat*	45,127	D 9
Estella	13,024	B 6
Estepona	43,109	I 4
Felanitx	14,882	F 10
Fene*	14,496	B 2
Figueras	33,064	C 10
Fraga	12,100	D 8
Fuengirola	49,675	I 4
Fuenla-brada*	182,705	E 5
Galdakao*	29,544	B 6
Gandia	59,850	F 8
Gava*	39,815	D 9
Gerona (Girona)	74,879	C 10
Galapagar*	25,559	D 5

See footnotes at end of index.

Getafe ....151,479 ..E 5
Gijón ....266,419 ..B 4
Grado ....11,454 ..B 3
Granada ....240,661 ..H 5
Granollers* ......53,105 ..D 9
Guadalajara ......68,248 ..E 6
Guadix ....18,188 ..H 6
Guecho ....82,285 ..B 6
Guernica ....B 6
Hellín ....27,553 ..G 7
Hernani ....18,287 ..B 6
Hospitalet ....239,019 ..D 9
Huelva ....142,284 ..H 3
Huércal-Overa ....14,850 ..H 6
Huesca ....46,243 ..C 8
Ibi* ....21,798 ..G 8
Ibiza (Eivissa) ..34,826 ..F 9
Igualada* ....33,049 ..D 9
Inca ....23,029 ..E 10
Irún ....56,601 ..B 6
Isla Cristina ....18,189 ..H 2
Jaca ....11,398 ..C 7
Jaén ....112,590 ..G 5
Játiva (Xàtiva) ..25,736 ..F 8
Jerez ....183,273 ..I 3
Jerez [de los
  Caballeros] ...9,492 ..G 3
Jumilla ....22,113 ..G 7
La Carolina ......14,780 ..G 5
La Coruña ....236,379 ..B 2
La Estrada ....22,308 ..B 2
La Laguna ....128,822 ...†
Lalín ....19,869 ..B 2
La Línea ....59,437 ..I 4
Langreo
  (Sama)* ....45,731 ..B 4
La Orotava ....37,738 ...†
La Puebla
  del Río* ......10,499 ..H 3
Laracha ....10,596 ..B 2
Laredo ....12,559 ..B 5
La Rinconada* ....29,282 ..H 3
La Roda ....13,959 ..F 6
La Solana ....15,047 ..F 5
Las Palmas ....354,863 ...†
La Unión ....14,541 ..H 7
Laviana ....14,531 ..B 4
Lebrija ....24,121 ..H 3
Leganés ....173,584 ..E 5
Lejona* ....28,381 ..B 6
Lena ....13,573 ..B 4
León ....130,916 ..B 4
Lérida ....112,199 ..C 8
Linares ....57,578 ..G 5
Liria ....17,211 ..F 7
Llanes ....13,276 ..B 4
Lluchmayor ....24,277 ..E 10
Logroño ....133,058 ..C 6
Loja ....20,060 ..H 5
Lora [del Río] ...18,281 ..H 4
Lorca ....77,477 ..H 7
Los Palacios
  [y Villa-
  franca] ....33,045 ..H 3
Los Realejos .....33,438 ...†
Lucena ....37,028 ..H 5
Lugo ....88,414 ..B 2
Madrid ....2,938,723 ..E 5

Mahón ....23,315 ..E 11
Mairena del
  Aljarafe* .....35,833 ..H 3
Málaga ....524,414 ..I 5
Manacor ....31,255 ..E 10
Manises* ....25,685 ..E 8
Manlleu ....17,532 ..C 10
Manresa ....63,981 ..C 9
Manzanares ....17,917 ..F 5
Marbella ....100,036 ..I 4
Marchena ....17,850 ..H 4
Marín ....24,997 ..C 1
Marratxí* ....23,410 ..F 10
Martorell* ....23,023 ..D 9
Martos ....22,356 ..H 5
Mataró ....106,358 ..C 10
Medina
  del Campo .....19,907 ..D 4
Medina
  Sidonia* ......10,728 ..I 4
Melilla ....66,411 ..J 6
Mérida ....50,271 ..F 3
Mieres ....47,719 ..B 4
Mijas* ....46,232 ..I 4
Miranda
  [de Ebro] .....35,925 ..B 6
Mislata* ....40,548 ..F 8
Moaña* ....17,887 ..C 1
Molina de
  Segural ....46,905 ..G 7
Mollet* ....47,270 ..D 9
Moncada* ....18,631 ..F 8
Moncada i
  Reixae* ....28,295 ..D 9
Mondragón* ....23,118 ..B 6
Monforte ....19,091 ..C 2
Montijo ....15,253 ..F 3
Montilla ....22,925 ..H 4
Montoro ....9,407 ..G 5
Monzón ....14,920 ..C 8
Morón ....27,710 ..H 4
Móstoles ....196,524 ..E 5
Motril ....51,298 ..H 5
Mula ....14,611 ..G 7
Murcia ....370,745 ..G 7
Narón ....32,204 ..B 2
Navalmoral
  [de la Mata] ..15,237 ..E 4
Níjar ....17,824 ..H 6
Novelda ....24,800 ..G 7
Noia* ....14,217 ..C 1
Olesa de
  Montserrat* ...17,987 ..D 9
Oliva* ....21,003 ..G 7
Onda* ....20,019 ..F 8
Olot ....28,060 ..C 10
Ontinyent ....32,664 ..F 8
Orense ....107,510 ..C 2
Orihuela* ....54,390 ..G 7
Oritgueira* ......8,172 ..A 2
Osuna ....16,848 ..H 4
Oviedo ....201,154 ..B 4
Paiporta* ....18,860 ..F 8
Palafrugell ......18,322 ..C 10
Palencia ....79,797 ..C 4
Palma ....333,801 ..E 10
Palma del
  Río* ....19,072 ..H 3

Pamplona ....183,964 ..B 7
Parla* ....79,213 ..E 5
Paterna* ....46,974 ..E 8
Peñarroya
  [-Pueblo-
  nuevo] ....12,440 ..G 4
Petrer* ....30,138 ..G 7
Pinos
  Puente* ....13,422 ..H 5
Pinto* ....31,340 ..E 5
Plascencia ....36,690 ..E 3
Ponferrada ....62,175 ..C 3
Pontevedra ....74,942 ..C 2
Portugalete ......51,066 ..B 6
Pozoblanco ....16,369 ..G 4
Pozuelo de
  Alarcón* ......68,214 ..E 5
Prat del
  Llobregat .....61,818 ..C 9
Pravia ....9,226 ..B 3
Premiá de
  Mar* ....26,334 ..D 9
Priego [de
  Córdoba] ......22,378 ..H 5
Ponteareas ....19,011 ..C 2
Puente Genil .....28,004 ..H 4
Puerto de la
  Cruz ....26,441 ...†
Puerto Real ......35,783 ..I 3
Puertollano ......48,086 ..F 5
Quart de
  Poblet* ....25,305 ..F 8
Redondela ....29,003 ..C 2
Reinosa ....10,694 ..B 5
Rentería ....38,224 ..B 7
Requena ....19,135 ..F 7
Reus ....89,006 ..C 9
Rincón de la
  Victoria* .....25,302 ..H 5
Ripoll ....10,597 ..C 9
Ripollet* ....30,235 ..D 9
Rivas-Vacia-
  madrid* ....35,742 ..D 5
Ronda ....34,468 ..H 4
Roquetas ....50,096 ..H 6
Rota ....25,053 ..I 3
Rubí* ....61,159 ..D 9
Sabadell ....183,788 ..C 9
Sagunto ....56,471 ..E 8
Salamanca ....156,368 ..D 4
Salt* ....21,238 ..C 10
San Andrés del
  Rabanedo* .....26,054 ..C 4
San Fernando .....88,073 ..I 3
San Fernando
  de Henares* ...36,244 ..E 5
San Juan
  de Aznal-
  farache* ......19,340 ..H 3
San Martín
  del Rey
  Aurelio* ......20,247 ..B 3
San Roque ....23,436 ..I 4
San Sebas-
  tián ....178,377 ..B 6
San Sebas-
  tián de
  los Reyes* ....61,884 ..E 5

San Vicente
  [de la
  Barquera] .....4,391 ..B 5
San Vicente
  del
  Raspeig* ......39,666 ..G 7
Sanlúcar
  [de Barra-
  meda] ....60,254 ..H 3
Santa Coloma
  [de Gra-
  manet] ....112,992 ..C 10
Santa Cruz ....188,477 ...†
Sant Adriá
  de Besós* .....31,939 ..D 9
Santa Eugenia
  [de Ribeira] ..26,086 ..B 1
Santa Eulalia
  del Río* ......19,808 ..F 9
Santander ....180,717 ..B 5
Santa Per-
  petua de
  Mogoda* ....20,479 ..D 9
Santa Pola* ......19,782 ..G 8
Sant Boi de
  Llobregat* ....78,738 ..D 9
Sant Cugat* ......60,265 ..D 9
Sant Feliú [de
  Guixols] ......17,994 ..C 10
Sant Feliú de
  Llobregat* ....40,042 ..C 9
Santiago ....90,188 ..B 2
Sant Joan
  Despí* ....40,042 ..D 9
Santurtzi* ....47,173 ..B 6
Sant Vicenç
  dels Horts* ...24,694 ..D 9
Sanxenxo* ....16,098 ..C 1
Saragossa ....614,905 ..C 7
Sarriá ....12,887 ..B 2
Segovia ....54,368 ..D 5
Sestao* ....31,773 ..B 6
Seville ....684,633 ..H 3
Siero* ....47,890 ..B 4
Silla* ....16,208 ..F 8
Socuéllamos ......11,667 ..F 6
Soria ....35,151 ..C 6
Sueca ....25,371 ..F 8
Tabernes
  de la
  Valldigna* ....16,523 ..G 8
Talavera
  [de la
  Reina] ....75,369 ..E 4
Tarazona ....10,580 ..C 7
Tarifa ....15,670 ..I 3
Tarragona ....113,129 ..D 9
Terrassa ....173,775 ..C 9
Telde ....87,949 ...†
Teruel ....31,158 ..E 7
Tineo ....12,598 ..B 3
Toledo ....68,382 ..E 5
Tolosa ....17,642 ..B 6
Tomelloso ....30,654 ..F 6
Torre-
  Pacheco* ......24,332 ..H 7
Torredon-
  jimeno* ....13,649 ..H 5

Torrejon
  [de Ardoz] ...97,887 ..E 5
Torrelavega ......55,477 ..B 5
Torremolinos .....44,772 ..I 4
Torrente ....65,417 ..F 8
Torrevieja* ......50,953 ..G 8
Tortosa ....28,933 ..D 8
Totana ....24,657 ..G 7
Tres Cantos* .....36,927 ..D 5
Tudela ....29,918 ..C 7
Túy (Tui)* ....16,042 ..C 1
Úbeda ....32,926 ..G 5
Ubrique* ....17,396 ..I 4
Urnieta* ....5,518 ..B 6
Utiel ....11,500 ..F 7
Utrera ....45,175 ..H 3
Valdemoro* ....33,169 ..D 5
Valdepeñas ....26,269 ..F 5
Valencia ....738,441 ..F 8
Valladolid ....316,580 ..C 4
Vall de Uxó ......28,964 ..E 8
Valls ....20,232 ..D 9
Valverde
  [del
  Camino] ....12,431 ..H 3
Vejer [de la
  Frontera] .....12,540 ..I 3
Vélez-
  Málaga ....57,142 ..H 5
Vendrell ....23,744 ..D 9
Vich (Vic) ....32,703 ..C 10
Vigo ....280,186 ..C 1
Viladecáns* ......56,841 ..D 9
Vilaseca* ....13,353 ..E 7
Villablino* ......12,459 ..B 3
Villacarrillo ....11,021 ..G 6
Villafranca
  de los
  Barros ....12,487 ..G 3
Villafranca
  del
  Panadés* ......31,248 ..D 9
Villagarcía ......33,496 ..B 1
Villajoyosa ......23,657 ..G 8
Villamartín* .....11,953 ..I 3
Villanueva
  [de
  Córdoba] ......9,781 ..G 4
Villanueva
  [de la
  Serena] ....24,092 ..F 4
Villanueva y
  Geltrú ....54,230 ..D 9
Villareal ....42,442 ..E 8
Villarro-
  bledo ....22,725 ..F 6
Villaviciosa .....13,951 ..B 4
Villena ....32,654 ..G 7
Vinaroz ....22,113 ..E 8
Vitoria ....216,852 ..B 6
Vívero* ....15,240 ..A 2
Xirivella
  (Chirivella)* ..30,824 ..F 7
Yecla ....30,824 ..G 7
Zafra ....15,253 ..G 3
Zamora ....64,845 ..D 4
Zarauz* ....21,078 ..B 6
Zumárraga* ....10,175 ..B 6

*Does not appear on map; key shows general location.
†Does not appear on map; in Canary Islands in Atlantic Ocean off northwest Africa.
‡Populations are for municipalities, which may include some rural areas as well as the city or town.
Source: 2001 census.

Sabine Weiss, Rapho Guillumette

The Basques of northern Spain are one of the nation's many regional population groups. Each group has folk dances, *shown here,* and other customs that differ from those of all the others.

Country life in Spain has changed much less than city life. Since the mid-1900's, expanded electrical service, better farming methods, and modern equipment have helped make life easier for Spanish farmers. But agriculture has fallen far behind industry in economic importance, and rural standards of living are much lower than those in the cities. Throughout the late 1900's, hundreds of thousands of farmers moved to Spanish cities or to other countries to try to find employment.

Most farmers live in villages or small towns. Every morning and evening they travel the roads between their homes and the fields, either walking or riding in vehicles. Unlike city people, they take only a short lunch break. But the evening paseo is as popular in rural areas as in the cities. Rural people also enjoy sitting in their town or village square.

Most rural homes are made of clay and stone. In some regions, the walls are covered with whitewashed plaster for added protection from the sun. Most houses have gently sloping tile roofs. Many homes rise directly

Population density

This map shows the population distribution in Spain. About two-thirds of the people live in cities. Madrid and Barcelona are the most heavily populated urban centers.

Major urban centers

● More than 1 million inhabitants

● 500,000 to 1 million inhabitants

● Less than 500,000 inhabitants

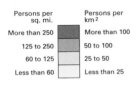

Persons per sq. mi.	Persons per km²
More than 250	More than 100
125 to 250	50 to 100
60 to 125	25 to 50
Less than 60	Less than 25

WORLD BOOK map

from the street or from a narrow sidewalk, and many have iron grillwork over the windows.

Food and drink. Spaniards enjoy seafood, which is plentiful in the coastal waters and inexpensive. A popular dish is *paella.* It consists of such foods as shrimp, lobster, chicken, ham, and vegetables, all combined with rice that has been cooked with a flavoring called *saffron.* Other favorite Spanish dishes include squids, crabs, sardines, and fried baby eels. A popular dish during warm weather is *gazpacho,* a cold soup made of strained tomatoes, onions, garlic, olive oil, and spices. Spaniards serve gazpacho sprinkled with bread cubes and chopped cucumbers, onions, and tomatoes.

Popular meats among Spaniards include beef, chicken, goat, lamb, pork, and rabbit. Bread baked in round or oval loaves is eaten plain or with cheese or butter.

Almost every region of Spain produces wine, and most Spaniards drink wine with all meals except breakfast. They also enjoy a drink called *sangría,* which consists of wine, soda water, fruit juice, and fruit. Other popular beverages include soft drinks, strong black coffee, and thick hot chocolate. The hot chocolate is usually served with deep-fried strips of dough called *churros.*

Recreation. Spaniards spend much of their leisure time outdoors. They like to sit for hours visiting at sidewalk cafes or in town or village squares. Summer vacations at the country's beautiful beaches have become popular. On weekends, city people often drive into the Spanish countryside for picnics or overnight trips.

Soccer is Spain's most popular sport, and many cities have a soccer stadium that seats 100,000 or more fans. Bullfighting is Spain's best-known and most unusual spectacle. Most cities have at least one bull ring, and leading matadors are national heroes.

Religion. About 95 percent of the people in Spain are Roman Catholics. Some Muslims, Protestants, and Jews

Guido Cozzi, Bruce Coleman, Inc.

A street in downtown Madrid bustles with activity. The main streets of Spain's capital are usually filled with crowds. Most of the people of Spain live in cities.

also live in Spain. During most of the period from 1851 to 1978, Roman Catholicism was the state religion of Spain. During that time, the government of Spain restricted the rights of non-Catholics in some ways. For example, non-Catholics were not allowed to try to win new followers for their religions, and only marriage ceremonies performed by the Roman Catholic Church were legal.

Spain adopted a new Constitution in 1978. Under provisions of the Constitution, Spain has no state religion, and people of all faiths are allowed complete religious freedom.

Religious holidays. The most important Spanish holiday period is Holy Week, celebrated the week before Easter with parades and other special events. Spaniards also hold celebrations to honor their local *patrón* (guardian) saint. Many of these celebrations last several days. People decorate the streets, build bonfires, dance and sing, set off fireworks, and hold parades, bullfights, and beauty contests.

One of the best-known celebrations is the *fiesta* (festival) of San Fermín, celebrated each July in Pamplona. As part of the festivities, each morning for eight days bulls are turned loose in streets leading to the bull ring. People run in front of the animals and into the ring, where bullfights are held later in the day.

Education. The Spanish government operates a system of primary and secondary schools that provide free public education. But there are also Roman Catholic schools and nonreligious private schools at the primary and secondary levels.

Spanish children from the ages of 6 to 16 must go to school. Children ages 6 through 12 attend primary schools. Secondary schools, for ages 12 through 16, are divided into two two-year courses of study. Students ages 16 through 18 may continue their education in either a vocational training school or a college preparatory school.

Spain has about 60 public and private universities. Its leading universities include the Complutensian University of Madrid and the University of Barcelona.

Museums and libraries. The Prado in Madrid, Spain's best-known museum, contains one of the world's finest art collections. It features works by such great Spanish painters as Francisco Goya and Diego Velázquez, as well as works by many foreign artists. Madrid's other art museums include the Reina Sofía art museum and the Thyssen-Bornemisza Museum, which has an outstanding collection of European paintings from the 1200's to the 1900's. Madrid also has the Museum of the Americas; the National Archaeological Museum; the Royal Palace; and the Army, Navy, and Municipal museums.

Most of Spain's major cities have museums that exhibit art from the surrounding region. The best known of these museums are the Provincial Archaeological Museum in Seville and the Museum of Catalan Art in Barcelona. In Toledo, the house of the great painter El Greco has been made into a museum that exhibits many of his works. Other notable Spanish museums include the Picasso Museum in Barcelona, devoted to the work of painter Pablo Picasso, and the Guggenheim Museum in

Michael Kuh, Rapho Guillumette

Spanish children take part in a Roman Catholic festival in Toledo. Most Spaniards belong to the Catholic Church.

Bilbao, a museum of modern art.

Spain's largest library is the National Library in Madrid. The Municipal Periodical Library of Madrid owns one of the most complete collections of periodicals in the world. Millions of records and important documents of Spanish history are preserved in the Archives of the Indies in Seville; the General Archives of the Kingdom in Simancas, near Valladolid; and the National Historical Archives in Madrid.

The arts

Spain has a rich artistic tradition and has produced some of the world's finest painters and writers. Spanish arts flourished during a Golden Age in the 1500's and 1600's, when the country ranked among the world's leading powers. Spain's arts then declined somewhat, but a rebirth occurred during the 1900's.

Literature. The oldest Spanish writings still in existence are *The Poem of the Cid* and *The Play of the Wise Men.* Scholars believe both works date from the 1100's, but they do not know who wrote them. *The Poem of the Cid* describes the deeds of one of Spain's national heroes, El Cid (see **Cid, The**). Only part of *The Play of the Wise Men* has been preserved. It tells of the visit of the Three Wise Men to the Christ child.

Spanish writers produced some of their best-known literature during the Golden Age. For example, Miguel de Cervantes wrote the novel *Don Quixote,* one of the world's greatest literary works. Playwright Pedro Calde-

The Alhambra, a famous fortified palace in Granada, is known for its beautiful inner courtyards, such as the Court of the Lions, *shown here.* The Alhambra was built between 1248 and 1354.

rón de la Barca vividly dramatized life's dreams and realities in his famous play *Life Is a Dream.* Spain's leading writers of the early and middle 1900's included essayists José Ortega y Gasset and Miguel de Unamuno, playwrights Antonio Buero Vallejo and Federico García Lorca, novelist Camilo José Cela, and poet Juan Ramón Jiménez. See **Spanish literature.**

Painting. Spain's leading painters during the Golden Age included El Greco, Bartolomé Esteban Murillo, and Diego Velázquez. Francisco Goya, one of the first masters of modern art, painted during the late 1700's and early 1800's.

Spain's most famous artist of the 1900's was Pablo Picasso. He created fine sculptures, drawings, graphics, and ceramics in addition to his paintings. Other leading Spanish painters of the early and middle 1900's included Salvador Dali, Juan Gris, and Joan Miró. In the late 1900's, the country's best-known artist was probably Antonio Tàpies, who created abstract multimedia paintings.

Architecture in Spain reflects the influence of various peoples who once controlled the country. Some aqueducts, bridges, and other structures built by the ancient Romans are still in use in Spain, and the ruins of other Roman structures can be seen throughout the country. *Mosques* (houses of worship) built by the Muslims stand in some southern cities, though most of these buildings are now Roman Catholic churches. The huge cathedral in Córdoba was built as a mosque in the 700's. More than 1,000 pillars of granite, jasper, marble, and onyx support its arches. The Muslims also built fortified palaces, the most famous of which is the magnificent Alhambra in Granada (see **Alhambra**).

Spain has about 1,400 castles and palaces. The Escorial, a combination burial place, church, college, monastery, and palace, stands about 30 miles (48 kilometers) northwest of Madrid. It was built in the 1500's and is one of the world's largest buildings. The gray granite structure covers almost 400,000 square feet (37,000 square meters) and has 300 rooms, 88 fountains, and 86 staircases. The tombs of many Spanish monarchs are in the Escorial. See **Escorial.**

About 10 miles (16 kilometers) from the Escorial is the Valley of the Fallen, another burial place and monastery. The burial chamber lies inside a mountain. About 46,000 men who died in the Spanish Civil War are buried there. The body of dictator Francisco Franco is also buried there. A cross 500 feet (150 meters) high, cut from a single piece of stone, stands on top of the mountain.

The Gothic cathedral in Seville is the third largest church in Europe. Only St. Peter's Basilica in Rome and the basilica in Lourdes, France, are larger. The Seville cathedral measures 380 feet (116 meters) long and 250 feet (76 meters) wide, and the cathedral's tower is 400 feet (120 meters) high.

Music. During the 1700's, Spanish composers created a form of light opera known as *zarzuela.* It combines singing with spoken words. Spain's best-known musicians of the early and middle 1900's included cellist Pablo Casals, composer Manuel de Falla, and classical guitarist Andrés Segovia. In the late 1900's and early 2000's, Spanish tenors José Carreras and Placido Domingo ranked among the world's leading opera singers.

Folk singing and dancing have long been popular in Spain, and the people of each region have their own special songs and dances. Musicians provide accompaniment on castanets, guitars, and tambourines. Such Spanish dances as the bolero, fandango, and flamenco have become world famous.

Motion pictures. Spain's first well-known director in the mid-1900's was Luis Buñuel. He made two famous Surrealistic films with the painter Salvador Dali in 1929 and 1930. During most of the Franco dictatorship, Buñuel worked in self-exile in France and Mexico. He gained international attention in the 1950's for his realistic and often cynical films about modern society.

Carlos Saura's films won several international prizes from the 1960's through the 1980's and established him as the leading Spanish filmmaker of his time. Pedro Almodóvar directed several internationally acclaimed comedies in the late 1900's. Almodóvar's success made international stars of such actors as Carmen Maura and Antonio Banderas.

The flamenco is one of the many lively Spanish folk dances. Flamenco dancers are usually accompanied by guitarists.

Robert Frerck, Woodfin Camp & Associates

The snow-capped Pyrenees Mountains form the border between Spain and France. They lie at the eastern end of Spain's Northern Mountains region.

The land

Spain has seven land regions: (1) the Meseta, (2) the Northern Mountains, (3) the Ebro Basin, (4) the Coastal Plains, (5) the Guadalquivir Basin, (6) the Balearic Islands, and (7) the Canary Islands. Mainland Spain covers about five-sixths of the Iberian Peninsula. Portugal occupies the rest.

The Meseta is a huge, dry plateau that ranks as the largest region of Spain. It consists mainly of plains broken by hills and low mountains. Higher mountains rise on the north, east, and south. To the west, the Meseta extends into Portugal. Mainland Spain's highest peak, 11,411-foot (3,478-meter) Mulhacén, stands in the Sierra Nevada range on the southern edge of the region. Irrigation has improved farm yields in the driest areas of the Meseta.

Forests grow on the mountains and hills, but only small, scattered shrubs and flowering plants grow on most of the plains. Goats and sheep graze in the highlands.

Most of Spain's major rivers rise in the Meseta. The longest river, the Tagus, flows 626 miles (1,007 kilometers) from the eastern Meseta through Portugal to the Atlantic Ocean. The Guadalquivir flows 400 miles (640 kilometers) from the southern Meseta to the Atlantic Ocean.

The Northern Mountains cross northernmost Spain from the Atlantic Ocean to the Coastal Plains. The region consists of mountain ranges in Galicia, in the west; the Cantabrian Mountains, in the central area; and the Pyrenees Mountains, which separate Spain from France, in the east. The Galician and Cantabrian mountains rise sharply from the sea along most of the Atlantic coast.

Forests cover many of the slopes in the region, and many short, swift-flowing rivers plunge through the mountains. Much of the region is pastureland, but some crops are grown on terraced fields.

The Ebro Basin consists of broad plains that extend along the Ebro River in northeastern Spain. The Ebro, which is one of Spain's longest rivers, flows 565 miles (909 kilometers) from the Northern Mountains to the Mediterranean Sea. The basin has dry soil, but irrigation has turned it into an important agricultural region.

The Coastal Plains stretch along Spain's entire Mediterranean coast. The region consists of fertile plains broken by hills that extend to the sea. It is a rich agricultural area. Farmers along the coast have used rivers that cut through the plains to build irrigation systems.

The Guadalquivir Basin lies in southwestern Spain. It spreads out along the Guadalquivir River to the Atlantic Ocean. The basin is a dry but extremely fertile region in the hottest part of the country. Farmers depend on irrigation to water their crops.

The Balearic Islands lie from about 50 to 150 miles (80 to 240 kilometers) east of mainland Spain in the Mediterranean Sea. Five major islands and many smaller ones make up the group. The three largest islands, in order of size, are Majorca, Minorca, and Ibiza. Majorca is a fertile island with a low mountain range along its

Dave Bartruff

The Meseta is a high plateau that covers most of Spain. Many hills and low mountains rise from the dry plains that stretch across most of the region.

northwest coast. Plains stretch from the mountains to hills on the southeast coast. Minorca is mostly flat, with wooded hills in the center. Ibiza is hilly. Both smaller islands are much less fertile than Majorca.

The Canary Islands lie in the Atlantic Ocean about 60 to 270 miles (96 to 432 kilometers) off the northwest coast of Africa. They include seven major islands. The largest are, in order of size, Tenerife, Fuerteventura, and Gran Canaria. Pico de Teide, Spain's highest mountain, rises 12,198 feet (3,718 meters) in the center of Tenerife. Gran Canaria has central mountains and rich valleys. Las Palmas, the largest city of the Canary Islands, lies on Gran Canaria. Fuerteventura is flatter, drier, and less populated than Tenerife and Gran Canaria.

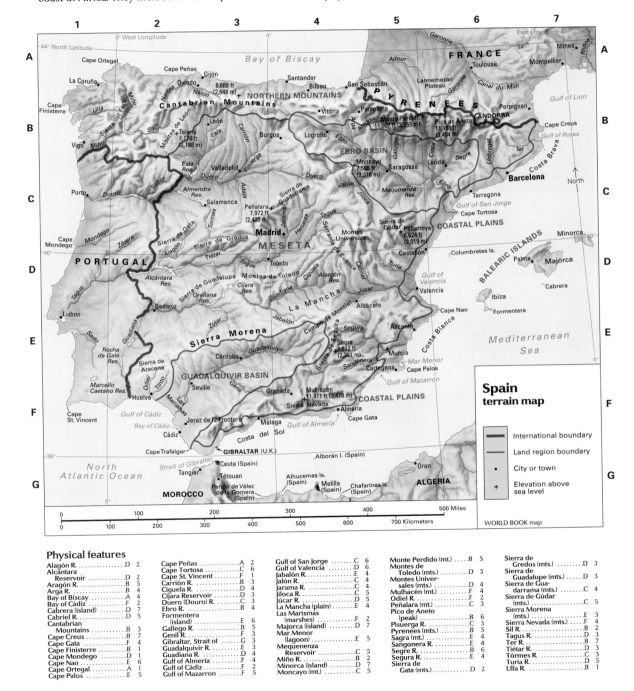

Physical features

Climate

The Meseta and other inland regions of Spain have dry, sunny weather throughout the year. These regions, which make up most of Spain, have hot summers and cold winters. The average temperature for some areas rises above 80 °F (27 °C) in July, the hottest month. It may fall below 30 °F (–1 °C) in January, the coldest month.

Summer and winter droughts—broken only by occasional rainstorms—are common. In addition, steady winds often whip up the dry soil. Snow covers upper mountain slopes in the Meseta region during most of the winter.

Mild, rainy winters alternate with hot, dry, sunny summers in the Coastal Plains and the Balearic Islands. The average January temperature rarely falls below 40 °F (4 °C), and the average July temperature usually rises to almost 80 °F (27 °C).

Short, heavy rainstorms are common in winter. But summer droughts last up to three months in some areas. The dry, sunny summers attract millions of vacationers to the Balearic Islands and to Costa Brava, Costa del Sol, and other famous resort areas along Spain's Mediterranean coast. The Canary Islands, also a popular vacation area, have mild to warm temperatures all year.

Winds from the Atlantic Ocean bring mild, wet weather to the Northern Mountains in all seasons. The region has Spain's heaviest *precipitation* (rain, snow, and other forms of moisture). Rain falls much of the time throughout the year, usually in a steady drizzle. There are many cloudy, humid days, and fog and mist often roll in from the sea. This region's heaviest precipitation comes in winter, when the upper mountain ranges usually build up deep snow. In January, the average temperature in the region rarely falls below 40 °F (4 °C), and the average July temperature seldom rises above 70 °F (21 °C).

J. Alex Langley, DPI

Spain's sunny Mediterranean coast has many resort areas, such as the Costa Brava, *shown here,* that attract millions of vacationers each summer. Almost all Spain has hot, dry summers.

Average monthly weather

	Madrid					Seville			
	Temperatures °F		°C		Days of rain or snow	Temperatures °F		°C		Days of rain or snow
	High	Low	High	Low		High	Low	High	Low	
Jan.	57	24	14	−4	9	67	35	19	2	8
Feb.	61	27	16	−3	9	71	35	22	2	9
Mar.	68	30	20	−1	11	77	39	25	4	9
Apr.	76	34	24	1	9	84	43	29	6	8
May	84	40	29	4	9	94	48	34	9	5
June	91	47	33	8	6	101	55	38	13	2
July	96	53	36	12	3	107	60	42	16	0
Aug.	96	54	36	12	2	107	61	42	16	0
Sept.	89	45	32	7	6	101	56	38	13	3
Oct.	77	37	25	3	8	91	48	33	9	5
Nov.	63	30	17	−1	10	76	39	24	4	9
Dec.	57	25	14	−4	9	68	34	20	1	8

Average January temperatures

January is Spain's coldest month. Temperatures are lowest in the northern inland regions.

Degrees Fahrenheit	Degrees Celsius
Above 43	Above 6
40 to 43	4 to 6
36 to 40	2 to 4
Below 36	Below 2

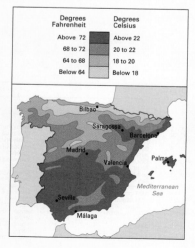

Average July temperatures

July is Spain's hottest month. Summer temperatures are highest in the southern two-thirds of the country.

Degrees Fahrenheit	Degrees Celsius
Above 72	Above 22
68 to 72	20 to 22
64 to 68	18 to 20
Below 64	Below 18

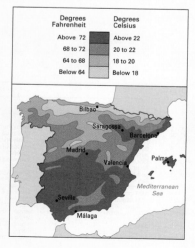

Average yearly precipitation

Precipitation levels vary throughout Spain. Mountainous areas in the north receive the most rain and snow.

WORLD BOOK maps

Inches	Centimeters
More than 40	More than 100
32 to 40	80 to 100
24 to 32	60 to 80
Less than 24	Less than 60

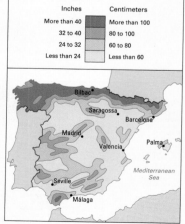

Economy

Spain plays an important role in the economy of Europe. Agriculture sustained the country for many years, and Spain still ranks among the world's leading producers of citrus fruits, olives, and wine. Tourism thrives on Spain's rich history and contributes much to the economy. However, a variety of modern enterprises have become the backbone of the country's economy.

During the 1950's and 1960's, Spain transformed itself into a modern industrial nation. During this period, the country's annual production of goods and services more than tripled. In 1950, about half of Spain's workers were engaged in agriculture, forestry, or fishing. Today, about two-thirds of the workers are employed in services, about a third in industry, and only a small fraction in agriculture.

Natural resources. Spain is poor in natural resources. Most of Spain has poor soil and limited rainfall, which make it difficult to raise crops. The country lacks many important industrial raw materials.

One of Spain's chief mined resources is the high-grade iron ore found in the Cantabrian Mountains. The mountains also contain coal, but the deposits are mostly of low quality. Other products mined in Spain include copper, lead, mercury, potash, pyrite, uranium, and zinc.

Thick forests once covered much of Spain, but most of the trees were cut down through the years. Since the 1960's, government planting programs have increased the amount of forested lands.

Service industries are economic activities that provide services rather than produce goods. About two-thirds of the workers in Spain are employed in service industries. Service industries are especially important to the economies of the largest cities.

Community, government, and personal services form the leading group of service industries in Spain. This industry group includes such economic activities as edu-

A. Gutierreze from Carl Östman

Spanish steel mills, such as this one in northern Spain, supply the nation's automobile, shipbuilding, and other important industries. Spain's steel production has increased greatly since the 1950's as part of the rapid industrial growth in the country.

cation and health care, public administration and the military, and data processing. It also includes smaller services, such as dry cleaning and automobile repairing. Madrid is the most important center for community, government, and personal services.

Trade, restaurants, and hotels form another important group of service industries in Spain. Barcelona is a major center of trade. Large amounts of textiles, wine, and citrus fruit are exported from the city. Seville also has a large wine and citrus fruit trade. Bilbao is the main distribution area for iron and steel. Saragossa is a leading city in the wholesale trade of machinery, and Cartagena is a center of trade for agricultural products. Madrid is the most important city for trade, restaurants, and hotels because of its large population and large number of tourists.

Other groups of service industries include finance, insurance, real estate, and business services, and transportation and communication. Transportation and communication are discussed later in this section.

Tourism contributes greatly to Spain's economy. Tourist activities benefit the country's service industries, especially trade, restaurants, and hotels. Tens of millions of tourists visit Spain each year. Visitors are drawn to Spain by its resorts on the warm, sunny Mediterranean coast and by its bullfights, castles, and colorful festivals.

The Spanish government encourages the growth of tourism, and it operates schools that train hotel managers, tour guides, chefs, and other people involved in tourism activities. The government also closely supervises the quality of services offered tourists.

Manufacturing. Spain ranks among the world's leading producers of automobiles. Other important manufactured products include cement, chemical products, iron and steel, machinery, plastics, rubber goods, ships, shoes and other clothing, and textiles. Barcelona, Bilbao,

PHOTRI

Olive orchards are cultivated in the southern Meseta, *shown here,* and many other regions of Spain. Olives are a major Spanish product, and Spain ranks as a leading olive-growing country.

and Madrid are the country's chief industrial centers. Most of Spain's steel mills and shipyards are in the northern provinces. The Barcelona area manufactures cotton and woolen textiles and shoes. Madrid has electronics and other high-technology industries. Major motor vehicle plants are in Barcelona, Madrid, Saragossa, Valencia, and Valladolid.

The government controls much of the production in the steel industry and in certain other major industries. But most factories in Spain are privately owned and operated. Companies and individuals from other countries invest heavily in Spanish industries. They are attracted by the low labor costs, low tax rates, and other favorable conditions for investment in Spain.

Agriculture. About 50 percent of the land in Spain is used for farming, either as cropland or as pastureland. Raising crops in most regions has always been a challenge because of the poor soil and dry climate.

Spain's chief farm products include barley, milk, sugar beets, wheat, and wine grapes. Other important products include corn, onions, potatoes, sunflower seeds, tomatoes, and wool. The country ranks among the world's leading producers of lemons and limes, olives, oranges, and wine. Grain crops grow mainly in Spain's northern regions. Farmers in the south and east produce most of the country's grapes, olives, and oranges and other citrus fruits. Bananas grow in the Canary Islands. Sheep are the chief livestock in Spain. The country's other important farm animals include beef and dairy cattle, chickens, goats, and pigs.

About two-thirds of all Spanish farmers own farms. The rest work as hired hands or tenants on large farms. Less than 1 percent of all landowners hold about 50 percent of Spain's farmland. The poorest 50 percent of landowners own about 5 percent of the country's farmland. Small farmers own most of the farmland in the north of Spain. In the south, wealthy landlords hold most of the land.

During the late 1900's, the government introduced modern methods and equipment to Spanish agriculture. The total area of irrigated farmland and the number of tractors have increased greatly. Such advances have increased farm production.

Fishing. Spain ranks as one of Europe's leading fishing countries. The chief fish and shellfish caught include anchovies, hake, mackerel, octopuses, sardines, squids, and tuna. Much of the catch comes from waters off Spain's northern coast. Fishing crews collect large amounts of mussels along the northern coast.

Spain's gross domestic product

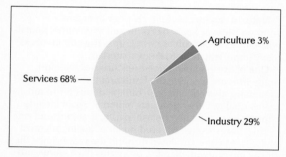

Agriculture 3%

Services 68% —

Industry 29%

Spain's gross domestic product (GDP) was $653,115,000,000 in 2002. The GDP is the total value of goods and services produced within a country in a year. *Services* include community, government, and personal services; finance, insurance, real estate, and business services; trade, restaurants, and hotels; and transportation and communication. *Industry* includes construction, manufacturing, mining, and utilities. *Agriculture* includes agriculture, forestry, and fishing.

Oranges, an important Spanish product, are packed in crates for shipment to markets in Spain and many other countries. The orange crop comes mostly from southern and eastern Spain.

Production and workers by economic activities

Economic activities	Percent of GDP produced	Employed workers	
		Number of people	Percent of total
Community, government, & personal services	20	3,968,800	24
Finance, insurance, real estate, & business services	20	1,693,800	10
Trade, restaurants, & hotels	19	3,571,200	22
Manufacturing	16	2,999,100	18
Construction	9	1,913,200	12
Transportation & communication	9	993,700	6
Agriculture, forestry, & fishing	3	961,300	6
Utilities	3	91,500	1
Mining	*	63,200	*
Total†	100	16,255,800	100

*Less than one-half of 1 percent.
†Figures do not add up to 100 percent due to rounding.
Figures are for 2002.
Sources: Spain's National Institute of Statistics; International Monetary Fund.

Mining. Spain has a wide variety of mineral resources but only small deposits of most minerals. The country is, however, one of the world's leading producers of mercury. Spain's other important mined products include coal, copper, gold, iron ore, lead, potash, pyrite, quartz, tin, uranium, and zinc.

Energy sources. Spain has small reserves of natural gas and oil. Spain imports nearly all of its petroleum, mainly from Libya, Mexico, Russia, and Saudi Arabia.

Plants that burn coal, petroleum, or natural gas produce about 60 percent of Spain's electric power. Nuclear plants provide about 25 percent of the country's power. Hydroelectric plants supply about 10 percent, and wind power generates about 5 percent.

International trade. Spain has always imported more goods than it has exported because of its limited natural resources. But the income from Spain's tourist business makes up for most of this imbalance.

Automobiles rank as Spain's chief export. Other leading exports include citrus fruits, iron and steel, petroleum products, textiles, and wine. Petroleum is Spain's chief import. Other major imports include corn and soybeans. Like most industrial countries, Spain imports some kinds of machinery and chemicals and exports others. Spain's main trading partners include Belgium, China, France, Germany, Italy, Japan, Mexico, the Netherlands, Portugal, the United Kingdom, and the United States.

Spain belongs to the European Union (EU), an association of European nations that work for economic and political cooperation among themselves. The union's members have made a great deal of progress toward uniting their resources into a single economy. There are almost no trade barriers among the members. Spain and most other members of the EU adopted a common currency called the *euro* in 1999. The euro replaced the national currencies, including Spain's peseta, in 2002.

Transportation and communication. Spain has a good network of paved highways. Most Spanish families own an automobile. Trucks carry most of the freight transported within the country. The government-owned Spanish National Railways operates an extensive railway system, including some high-speed trains.

Iberia Air Lines, also owned by the government, flies throughout Spain, to North and South America, and to many Western European cities. Many privately owned airlines also serve the country. The chief international airports include Madrid; Palma de Majorca; Barcelona; Málaga; and Las Palmas and Santa Cruz de Tenerife in the Canary Islands.

Spanish ships carry about a third of the freight transported between Spain and other nations. These ships also sail between Spanish ports, carrying about a third of the freight transported within the country. Algeciras, Barcelona, and Bilbao are the nation's largest ports.

Both the government and private companies operate postal services, radio stations, and television stations in Spain. The country has about 90 daily newspapers with a wide variety of political opinions. The largest include *ABC, El Mundo, El País, La Vanguardia,* and *Marca.* Thousands of magazines and weekly newspapers are published in Spain.

Economy of Spain

This map shows the economic uses of land in Spain. It also shows the country's main farm, mineral, and fishing products. The map also includes Spain's most important manufacturing centers.

Irrigated cropland

Other cropland

Mostly grazing land

Forest land

Generally unproductive land

Fishing

● Manufacturing center

• Mineral deposit

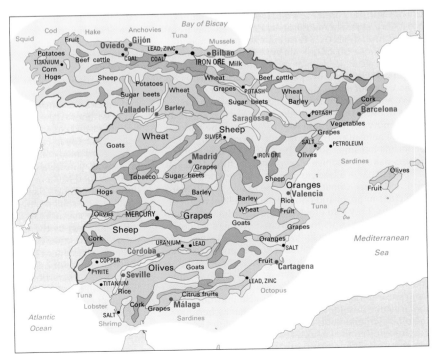

WORLD BOOK map

Ancient Roman structures can still be seen in Spain. The Romans controlled Spain for more than 400 years. They erected many bridges, buildings, and other structures, including the aqueduct in Segovia that is shown in this photo.

History

Early days. More than 100,000 years ago, people lived in what is now Spain. At the beginning of recorded history—about 5,000 years ago—a people known as Iberians occupied much of Spain. They farmed and built villages and towns.

Phoenicians, who lived on the eastern shore of the Mediterranean, began to establish colonies along Spain's east and south coasts in the 1000's B.C. The Phoenicians carried on a flourishing trade with their colonies. Some of the cities they built, such as Cádiz and Málaga, have lasted to the present day.

Celtic peoples moved into Spain from the north about 900 B.C. and again about 600 B.C. They settled in northern Spain. Greeks landed in Spain about 600 B.C. and later established trading posts along the east coast.

During the 400's B.C., the powerful northern African city of Carthage conquered much of Spain. Hannibal, the great Carthaginian general, attacked Roman Italy from Spain during the 200's B.C. But the Romans defeated Hannibal in the Second Punic War (218-201 B.C.) and drove all Carthaginian forces from Spain.

Roman conquest of Spain began during the Second Punic War. But it took the mighty Roman army almost 200 years to conquer the stubborn, freedom-loving tribes of every region of Spain. Rome also conquered what is now Portugal, and for the first time the entire Iberian Peninsula came under one government. The peninsula became a Roman province called *Hispania*. Spain's name in Spanish, *España*, comes from *Hispania*.

Spain became a leading province of the Roman Empire, and many Romans went there to live. The Romans built cities in Spain and constructed excellent roads to all regions. They also erected huge aqueducts that carried water from rivers to dry areas. Several of Rome's greatest emperors—including Hadrian and Trajan—were born in Spain. Such outstanding Roman authors as Martial and Seneca also came from Spain.

The Romans introduced Latin into the province, and the Spanish language gradually developed from the Latin spoken there. Christianity was also introduced into the province during Roman rule. Christianity became the official religion of the province—and of the Roman Empire—during the late A.D. 300's. About the same time, the empire split into two parts—the East Roman Empire and the West Roman Empire. Spain became part of the West Roman Empire.

Germanic rule. During the 400's, invading Germanic tribes swept across the West Roman Empire and helped bring about its collapse in 476. One tribe, the Visigoths, invaded Spain and conquered the entire peninsula by 573. The Visigoths set up a monarchy in Spain that was the first separate and independent government to rule the entire peninsula. The Visigoths, who were Christians, tried to establish a civilization like that of the Romans. But continued fighting among the Visigoth nobles and repeated revolts of the nobles against the kings weakened the nation.

Muslim control. The Visigoths ruled Spain until the early 700's, when the Arabs, Berbers, and other Muslim peoples from northern Africa invaded the country. The invasion began in 711, and the Muslims conquered almost all the Visigoth kingdom by 718. Only the narrow mountainous region across far northern Spain remained free of Muslim rule.

The Muslims practiced the religion of Islam. Following the Muslim conquest, many Spanish people converted to Islam. The Muslims had a more advanced culture than did most of medieval Europe. The Muslims had made great discoveries in mathematics, medicine, and other fields of study. They had also preserved many of the writings of the ancient Greek, Roman, and Middle Eastern civilizations. In Spain, the Muslims made these works available to European scholars. The Muslims also constructed many buildings in Spain, including beautiful *mosques* (houses of worship) and fortified palaces.

The unified Muslim government of Spain collapsed during the early 1000's because of internal conflicts. The country then split into many small Muslim states and independent cities.

Reconquest by the Christian kingdoms. Groups of Visigoths and other Christians in far northern Spain remained independent following the Muslim conquest. These groups formed a series of kingdoms that extended from Spain's northwest coast to the Mediterranean Sea. During the 1000's, these kingdoms began to expand and push the Muslims southward.

Castile, in north-central Spain, became the strongest of the growing Christian kingdoms, and its soldiers led the fight against the Muslims. A Castilian known as El Cid emerged as the champion of the Christian cause. He became one of Spain's national heroes (see **Cid, The**).

During the 1100's, several Spanish kings set up a Cortes (parliament) to strengthen their support among the people. Each Cortes brought representatives of the middle class, the nobility, and the Roman Catholic Church into the government. But the Spanish kings gave little or no power to the Cortes.

Also during the 1100's, the region that is now northern Portugal gained its independence from Castile. By the mid-1200's, Portugal controlled all its present-day territory. Meanwhile, Spanish Christians continued to fight the Muslims. By the late 1200's, the Muslim territory in Spain had been reduced to the Kingdom of Granada in the south. The Christian kingdoms of Aragon, Navarre, and Castile controlled the rest of what is now Spain. Aragon ruled most of eastern Spain and the Balearic Islands. Navarre ruled a small area northwest of Aragon. Castile controlled the rest of Spain. It remained Spain's largest and most powerful kingdom throughout the 1300's and most of the 1400's.

Union of the Spanish kingdoms. In 1469, Prince Ferdinand of Aragon married Princess Isabella of Castile. Isabella became queen of Castile in 1474, and Ferdinand became king of Aragon in 1479. Almost all of what is now Spain thus came under their rule.

Ferdinand and Isabella wanted to create a strong, united Spain. They considered Jews and Muslims to be a threat to this goal. In 1480, they established the Spanish Inquisition, a court that imprisoned or killed Christians suspected of not following the church's teachings. The Inquisition continued for over 300 years. Also in the 1480's, Ferdinand and Isabella began to drive the Muslims from Granada. Their troops defeated the Muslims in 1492. That same year, the last of the Spanish Jews who would not convert to Christianity were driven from the country. But some Jews who had converted practiced Judaism in secret, risking the wrath of the Inquisition. Ferdinand seized the small Kingdom of Navarre in 1512 to complete the union of Spain.

The Spanish Empire. In 1492, while working to unify Spain, Ferdinand and Isabella sent the Italian navigator Christopher Columbus on the voyage that took him to America. During the next 50 years, Spanish explorers, soldiers, and adventurers flocked to the New World. The Spanish explorer Vasco Núñez de Balboa crossed Central America in 1513 and became the first European to see the eastern shore of the Pacific Ocean. Hernando Cortés conquered the mighty Aztec nation of Mexico in 1521. By 1533, the huge Inca empire of western South America had fallen to Francisco Pizarro. These men and other Spaniards explored much of South America and southern North America.

By 1550, Spain controlled Mexico, Central America, nearly all the West Indies, part of what is now the southwestern United States, and much of western South America. In the Treaty of Tordesillas, signed in 1494, Spain and Portugal agreed to a line that divided the New World between them. But the two powers could not secure the land because England, France, and the Netherlands claimed much of it. See **Line of Demarcation**.

While its empire grew in America, Spain seized territories in Europe and Africa. Spanish troops conquered the French province of Rousillon, much of Italy, the Canary Islands, and land in northern Africa.

In 1516, a grandson of Ferdinand and Isabella became King Charles I of Spain. Charles had ruled the Low Countries (what are now Belgium, Luxembourg, and the Netherlands), and he brought these lands into the Spanish empire. His father belonged to the Habsburg royal family, rulers of the Holy Roman Empire in central Europe. Charles became Holy Roman emperor in 1519. He ruled the empire as Charles V and Spain as Charles I.

The Spanish Empire reached its height during the reign of Charles's son, Philip II, who became king in 1556. In 1580, Philip II of Spain enforced his claim to the Portuguese throne by invading and conquering the country. Spain gained control of the Philippine Islands during the late 1500's. Spain also fought to defend western Europe from the expanding Ottoman Empire. Philip's rule brought the beginning of the Golden Age of Spanish art, a time when writers and painters created some of Spain's greatest artistic works.

The Spanish decline. Although Philip ruled a worldwide empire and Spain was the strongest nation in Europe, signs of strain began to appear. Wars, inflation, and poor economic management weakened the country's economy. Philip's attempts to slow or stop the advance of Protestantism in Europe met serious opposition

Important dates in Spain

1000's B.C. The Phoenicians began to colonize Spain.
400's B.C. The Carthaginians conquered much of Spain.
200's B.C. The Romans drove the Carthaginians from Spain.
A.D. 400's The Visigoths took Spain from the Romans.
711-718 The Muslims conquered almost all Spain.
1000's Christian kingdoms began to drive the Muslims from Spain.
1479 The kingdoms of Aragon and Castile united, bringing almost all of what is now Spain under one rule.
1492 Spanish forces conquered Granada, the last center of Muslim control in Spain. Christopher Columbus sailed to America and claimed it for Spain.
1512 King Ferdinand V seized the Kingdom of Navarre, completing the unification of what is now Spain.
1556-1598 The Spanish Empire reached its height during the reign of Philip II.
1588 The English navy defeated the Spanish Armada.
1808 Napoleon's armies seized Madrid.
1808-1814 Spanish, Portuguese, and English forces drove the French from Spain during the Peninsular War.
1810-1825 All Spain's American colonies except Cuba and Puerto Rico revolted and declared their independence. By this time, Spain had lost almost all its empire.
1898 Spain lost Cuba, Puerto Rico, and the Philippines in the Spanish-American War.
1931 King Alfonso XIII fled the country and Spain became a democratic republic.
1936-1939 The Spanish Civil War was fought. It brought General Francisco Franco to power as dictator of Spain.
1950's and 1960's Spain achieved one of the highest rates of economic growth in the world.
1975 Franco died. Spaniards began setting up a new, democratic government to replace his dictatorship.
1978 Spaniards approved a new Constitution based on democratic principles.
1982 Spain joined the North Atlantic Treaty Organization.
1986 Spain joined the European Community, an economic organization that became the basis of the European Union.

from the Netherlands and England. In the 1560's, the Netherlands rebelled against Spain. In 1588, Philip II launched a great Spanish Armada of about 130 ships in an unsuccessful attempt to conquer England. English ships repelled the armada, and storms destroyed many of the Spanish ships during the retreat. Only about two-thirds of the armada made it back to Spain.

In the 1600's, Spain was weakened by wars, rebellions, economic crises, and weak rulers. Fighting in the Netherlands continued into the early 1600's. Spain heavily financed the Roman Catholic cause in the Thirty Years' War (1618-1648). It also fought wars with France and faced rebellions in Portugal and the region of Catalonia in northern Spain.

The last Spanish Habsburg, Charles II, had no children of his own. In 1700, he named a French duke, Philip of Anjou, as heir to the Spanish throne. Philip was a grandson of France's King Louis XIV, who reigned in France from 1643 to 1715. Philip was also descended from the Spanish Habsburgs through intermarriage between the Spanish and French royal families. When Charles II died later in 1700, Philip became King Philip V of Spain, the first Spanish ruler from the French Bourbon family.

The succession of Philip V touched off the War of the Spanish Succession (1701-1714). France fought England, the Netherlands, and other European nations that opposed French control of the Spanish crown. France lost the war. Under the peace treaty, Philip remained king of Spain, but Spain lost all its possessions in Europe. In addition, the United Kingdom received Gibraltar and the Balearic island of Minorca. See **Succession wars.**

Bourbon reforms. During the 1700's, the Bourbon rulers of Spain carried out many government reforms. They lowered taxes and collected them more fairly. The Bourbon rulers also built roads and other public works, and the economy began to grow. Meanwhile, strong ties developed between Spain and France because the rulers of both countries were Bourbons.

Conflict with the United Kingdom. In the 1700's, Spain and the United Kingdom challenged each other for colonial power in the Americas. In addition, Spain wanted to regain Gibraltar and Minorca from the United Kingdom. As a result, Spain joined several other European nations in wars with the United Kingdom.

Spain also declared war against the United Kingdom in the Revolutionary War in America (1775-1783). In 1779, Spanish troops invaded Florida, which Spain had lost to the United Kingdom in 1763. The Treaty of Paris, which ended the Revolutionary War in 1783, returned Florida to Spanish control. It also recognized Spain's control of Minorca, which Spanish troops had taken in 1782. British forces recaptured Minorca in 1798, but the United Kingdom returned the island to Spain in 1802. The warfare against the United Kingdom weakened Spain.

French conquest. Napoleon Bonaparte seized control of France in 1799. At first, he allied France with Spain. But in 1808, French forces invaded Spain and quickly gained control of the government. Napoleon forced Ferdinand VII to give up the Spanish throne and named Joseph Bonaparte, his brother, king of Spain.

The Spanish people bitterly resisted the French occupation. They struck back with a hit-and-run method of fighting called a *guerrilla* (little war), a word used ever since to describe such fighting. This opposition triggered the Peninsular War later in 1808, when the United Kingdom joined Spain and Portugal against France. The French were driven from the peninsula in 1814.

During the Peninsular War, the Spanish Cortes—

Spanish Empire in 1588   The Spanish Empire in 1588, at the height of Spain's power, included large areas of the Americas, European and African possessions, and the Philippines. Portugal was united with Spain in 1580, but the Portuguese colonies remained under Portuguese control.

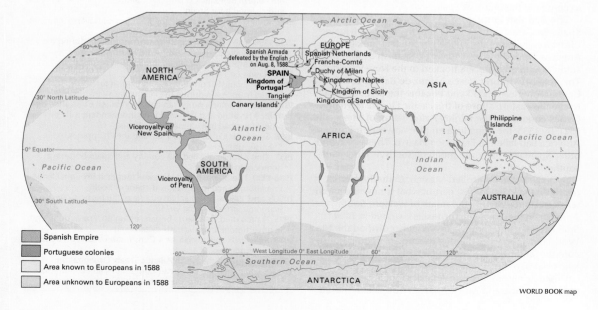

WORLD BOOK map

Launch of Fireships Against Spanish Armada (about 1588), an oil painting
by an unknown artist; National Maritime Museum, Greenwich, England

The defeat of the Spanish Armada in 1588 damaged the prestige of Spain, then the world's most
powerful nation. English ships, *right,* launched flaming boats against the armada, *left,* to divide it
and make it easier to attack. Later, storms destroyed many Spanish ships as they retreated.

which had fled from Madrid to southern Spain—drew
up a new constitution for the country. The new constitution reduced the power of the Roman Catholic Church
and increased individual rights and freedoms. But it continued the Spanish monarchy. Supporters of the constitution were known as *liberals.*

Loss of the empire. King Ferdinand VII returned to
the Spanish throne in 1814. He repealed the new constitution and persecuted the liberals. He also tried to regain control of Spain's overseas empire. During the Peninsular War, most of Spain's American colonies had
revolted and declared their independence.

In 1820, Spanish troops at Cádiz refused to leave on
an expedition to reconquer the American colonies. The
mutiny spread quickly into a countrywide military revolt.
Ferdinand put down the uprising—with the help of
French troops—in 1823. But Spain remained torn politically between Ferdinand's supporters and the liberals.
By 1825, Spain had lost all its overseas possessions except Cuba, Puerto Rico, several outposts in Africa, the
Philippines, and the island of Guam.

The reign of Isabella II. In 1833, Ferdinand's daughter succeeded him to the throne as Isabella II. Her reign
was opposed by the Carlists, a group that wanted Ferdinand's oldest brother, Don Carlos, to be king. The liberals supported Isabella. Quarreling among Carlists, liberals, and other political groups created disorder
throughout Isabella's reign. In 1868, a group of army officers led a revolt that quickly gained support and forced
the queen and her family to leave the country.

Six years of political unrest followed the overthrow of
Isabella. A republican government was established in
1873, but civil war broke out between the Carlists and
the liberals. The army overthrew the new government in
1874 and, in 1875, brought Isabella's son back to Spain
to become King Alfonso XII. He ruled until 1885.

The reign of Alfonso XIII. Alfonso XII died six
months before his son, Alfonso XIII, was born in 1886.
Young Alfonso's mother, María Cristina of Austria, ruled
in his place until he became old enough to take the
throne in 1902.

Spain's most important remaining colonies, Cuba and
the Philippines, rebelled in the 1890's. The United States
supported Cuba and declared war on Spain in April
1898. In August, the Spanish-American War ended with
Spain's defeat. Spain gave Cuba its independence and
surrendered Guam, the Philippines, and Puerto Rico to
the United States. All that remained of the once mighty
Spanish Empire were a few tiny outposts in northern
Africa. See **Spanish-American War.**

During the late 1800's and early 1900's, the power of
the Cortes and the prime minister increased. At the
same time, Spanish political parties and labor unions
gained more and more power. Control of the government alternated between liberals and conservatives,
who favored authoritarian government. Radicals, who
wanted extreme reforms, and labor union leaders organized frequent protests against the government.

Spain remained neutral in World War I (1914-1918)
and profited greatly by selling industrial goods to the
warring nations. But the end of the war caused widespread unemployment in Spain, and Spaniards who had

jobs earned low wages. These conditions added to an already growing discontent with Alfonso's rule.

In 1912, Spain gained control over parts of Morocco (see **Morocco** [French and Spanish control]). But the Moroccans would not submit to Spanish authority. In 1921, they revolted and killed more than 10,000 Spanish troops. This disastrous incident caused bitter disputes in Spain, and these disputes became more intense as the fighting continued in Morocco. Coupled with Spain's political unrest and poor economy, the Moroccan situation led to strikes and violence throughout Spain.

In 1923, General Miguel Primo de Rivera headed a military revolt to take over the government and restore order in Spain. King Alfonso supported the rebels, and Primo became prime minister with the power of a dictator. Primo restored order in Morocco and Spain. He also promised to reestablish constitutional government in Spain but repeatedly delayed. The army finally turned against Primo in 1930, and he was forced to resign.

After the Primo dictatorship fell, a movement for a republican form of government gained strength in Spain. Supporters of the movement included liberals, socialists, and others who did not want a monarchy. The strength of support for the movement forced King Alfonso to allow free elections. Municipal elections were held in April 1931, and the people voted overwhelmingly for republican candidates. Alfonso then left the country, but he refused to give up his claim to the throne.

The Spanish republic. Republican leaders took control of the government after Alfonso left Spain. They called for a parliamentary election to be held in June 1931. Liberals, socialists, and other republican groups won a huge majority in the Cortes. The new Cortes immediately began work on a democratic constitution, which was approved in December 1931. That same month, the Cortes elected Niceto Alcalá Zamora, a leading liberal, as the first president of the republic.

The republicans had won control of the government, but political unrest continued in the country. Some Spaniards still favored a monarchy. In addition, the vari-

ous republican groups were only loosely united. Radical leaders agitated for the overthrow of the government and created uprisings in various sections of the country. The worldwide Great Depression of the 1930's added to these difficulties as Spain's exports fell and poverty spread among the people.

The new government reduced the power of the Roman Catholic Church and gave greater power to the labor unions. It took over estates held by aristocrats and greatly increased the wages of farmworkers. In 1932, the Cortes yielded to demands from nationalists in Catalonia and granted the region limited self-government. Other regions then demanded similar freedom.

The actions of the republican government created opposition among increasing numbers of Spaniards, especially conservatives. The conservatives supported the Roman Catholic Church and wanted Spain to become a monarchy again. The government called for a parliamentary election in 1933. In the election, a newly formed conservative party emerged as the most powerful political force in Spain. This party was the Confederación Española de Derechas Autónomas (Spanish Confederation of Autonomous Rightist Parties), called the CEDA.

Late in 1934, socialists and Catalan nationalists led an uprising against the government. The uprising quickly spread throughout Spain. Government forces put down the revolt, but they killed more than 1,000 people in the process. The political division in Spain then widened. Army leaders, monarchists, and Catholic groups made up the Right. Communists, socialists, labor unions, and liberal groups formed the Left.

President Alcalá dissolved the Cortes in February 1936 and called an election to try to unite the republic. Forces of the Left joined in an alliance called the Popular Front and won the election by a slight margin. Their victory touched off increased violence in Spain. Rightists and Leftists fought in the streets. Armed bands dragged opponents from their homes and murdered them. Political assassinations became common.

Civil war. In July 1936, Spanish army units stationed in Morocco proclaimed a revolution against Spain's government. About half of the army units in Spain then rose in revolt, and they soon won control of about a third of the country. The rebels hoped to overthrow the government quickly and restore order in Spain. But Popular Front forces took up arms against the military.

In late September, rebel leaders chose General Francisco Franco as their commander in chief. By this time, the revolt had developed into a full-scale civil war. Franco's forces became known as Nationalists or Rebels. They were supported by Spain's fascist political party, the Falange Española (Spanish Phalanx). The forces that fought to save the republic were called Republicans. Both sides killed civilians and prisoners in a violent, bloody conflict that raged across Spain for three years.

The Spanish Civil War drew international attention. Nazi Germany and Fascist Italy supported Franco's forces, and the Communist Soviet Union aided the Republicans. Republican sympathizers from the United States and many other countries joined the International Brigades that Communists formed to fight in Spain.

By the end of 1937, the Nationalists clearly held the

The monarchs of Spain

In 1469, Prince Ferdinand of Aragon married Princess Isabella of Castile. The princess became Queen Isabella I* of Castile in 1474. Ferdinand became King Ferdinand II of Aragon in 1479. Most of what is now Spain thus came under the rule of the two monarchs. Isabella died in 1504. By the time Ferdinand died in 1516, he had brought all of what is now Spain under his control as Ferdinand V.*

Name	Reign	Name	Reign
Charles I		Charles III	1759-1788
(Holy		Charles IV	1788-1808
Roman		Ferdinand VII	1808
Emperor		Joseph	
Charles V*)	1516-1556	Bonaparte	1808-1813
* Philip II	1556-1598	Ferdinand VII	1814-1833
Philip III	1598-1621	Isabella II	1833-1868
Philip IV	1621-1665	Amadeo	1870-1873
Charles II	1665-1700	Alfonso XII	1875-1885
* Philip V	1700-1724	*Alfonso XIII	1886-1931
Louis I	1724	*Juan Carlos I	1975-
* Philip V	1724-1746		
Ferdinand VI	1746-1759		

*Has a separate biography in *World Book.*

upper hand in Spain. They had taken most of western Spain in the summer of 1936 and were gradually pushing the Republican forces to the east and north. The Soviet Union ended large-scale aid to the Republicans in 1938, and Franco launched a mighty offensive against Republican armies that same year.

Franco entered Madrid, one of the last Loyalist strongholds, on March 28, 1939. The remaining Loyalist forces throughout Spain surrendered by the end of the month, and Franco announced on April 1 that the war had ended. Several hundred thousand Spaniards had died in the war, and much of Spain lay in ruins. A dictatorship under Franco replaced the short-lived republic.

World War II (1939-1945) broke out five months after the Spanish Civil War ended. Officially, Spain remained neutral in the war. But Franco drew closer to Germany after the fall of France in 1940, when it seemed that Germany would win the war. Late in 1942, however, the tide of war began to turn against Germany. Franco then became friendlier toward the United Kingdom, the United States, and other Allied countries.

Involvement in the Cold War. In 1945, the Soviet Union launched a campaign calling for international opposition to Franco and for the overthrow of his government. Western nations supported this campaign because of Franco's dictatorial policies and because of his support of Germany and Italy in World War II. Nearly all major countries broke off diplomatic relations with Spain in 1945 and 1946.

In 1947, Franco announced that a king would succeed him upon his death or retirement. Franco hoped this announcement would reduce international criticism of his rule. But it was the growing Cold War—the struggle between Communist and non-Communist nations—that finally led the Western powers to ease their stand against Spain during the late 1940's.

Franco strongly opposed the Communist nations, and the United States sought his help to strengthen the defense of Western Europe. In 1953, Spain and the United States signed a 10-year military and economic agreement. Franco allowed the United States to build Air Force and Navy bases in Spain, and the United States gave Spain more than $1 billion in grants and loans. The agreement has been renewed for shorter periods ever since, though U.S. aid to Spain has been greatly reduced. In 1992, U.S. air bases in Spain were closed. A naval base and a few small military facilities still operate.

Growth and discontent. During the 1950's and 1960's, Spain achieved one of the highest rates of economic growth in the world. The nation's automobile, construction, and steel industries boomed, and the Spanish tourist trade flourished. As a result, the standard of living of most Spaniards rose rapidly.

During the mid-1960's, the government began to ease some restrictions on personal freedom. In 1966, for example, it relaxed its strict censorship of the press. But protests against the government erupted. Student demonstrations began in 1968 at the universities of Barcelona and Madrid. During the 1960's and 1970's, people in some Spanish regions protested against Spain's national government. Some in the Basque provinces demanded independence for their region.

United Press Int.

Francisco Franco was dictator of Spain from 1939 until his death in 1975. This photograph shows him reviewing troops during a parade held in 1970. Prince Juan Carlos, *left,* became king of Spain after Franco died.

Other Basques did not favor independence but called for greater control over their government affairs. Some people in the regions of Catalonia, Valencia, Andalusia, and Galicia also called for more control over their government affairs. In the late 1960's, a Basque organization named Euskadi ta Askatasuna (ETA), which favored independence, began a terrorist campaign against the Spanish government. Under Franco, many Basques and other Spaniards were arrested for revolutionary activities.

Political changes. Franco died in November 1975. Spain then entered a period of major political change. It quickly began a process of establishing a democratic government to replace Franco's dictatorship.

In 1969, Franco had declared that Prince Juan Carlos would become king of Spain after Franco's death or retirement. Juan Carlos is a grandson of King Alfonso XIII, who left Spain in 1931. Juan Carlos became king two days after Franco died. In 1976, he made Adolfo Suárez González prime minister. Juan Carlos, Suárez, and most other Spaniards favored changing Spain's government from a dictatorship to a democracy.

In 1976, Spain's new government ended Franco's ban on political parties other than his own. In 1977, the government held elections in which several political parties competed for seats in the parliament. This marked the first time since 1936 that the people of Spain were given a choice of candidates in parliamentary elections. In the elections, the Union of the Democratic Center, headed by Prime Minister Suárez, won the most seats.

In 1978, the voters of Spain approved a new constitution based on democratic principles. In elections held after the adoption of the Constitution, the Union of the Democratic Center again won the most seats in parliament. In 1981, Suárez resigned as prime minister. Juan Carlos appointed Leopoldo Calvo Sotelo of the Union of the Democratic Center to succeed Suárez.

Spain's democratic government began a process of increasing local government power in the country's regions. In 1980, people in the Basque provinces and Catalonia elected regional parliaments. Since then, the people of all other regions have also elected parliaments. Basque separatists, however, continued their terrorist campaign for complete independence.

In elections in 1982, the Socialist Workers' Party won the most seats in parliament. Felipe González, the party's leader, became prime minister. The elections gave Spain its first leftist government since 1939. The Socialist Workers' Party won again in 1986, 1989, and 1993, and González remained prime minister.

In 1986, Spain joined the European Community (EC), an economic organization of European nations. In 1993, Spain and the other EC countries formed the European Union, which works for both economic and political cooperation among its members (see **European Union**).

Recent developments. In 1996 elections, the center-right Popular Party won the most seats in parliament. Its leader, José María Aznar, became prime minister. The Basque separatist group ETA declared a cease-fire in 1998 but resumed terrorist attacks in 2000. Elections that year again gave the Popular Party most of the seats in parliament, and Aznar remained prime minister.

In March 2004, bombs exploded on commuter trains in Madrid, killing nearly 200 people. The government charged Islamic terrorists with the attacks. In elections held shortly after the attacks, the Socialist Workers' Party won control of parliament. The leader of the Socialists, José Luiz Rodríguez Zapatero, became prime minister.

In early 2006, ETA declared a permanent cease-fire and pledged to use nonviolent means to achieve its goals. But ETA claimed responsibility for a bomb attack at a Madrid airport in December 2006. In response to the bombing, Zapatero suspended peace talks with ETA.

Carla Rahn Phillips and William D. Phillips, Jr.

Related articles. See **Spanish literature** with its list of *Related articles.* See also:

Monarchs

See the biographies of the monarchs whose names are marked with an asterisk in the table *The monarchs of Spain,* in this article.

Political and military leaders

Alba, Duke of
Franco, Francisco

Torquemada, Tomás de

Explorers and conquerors

Alvarado, Pedro de
Ayllón, Lucas Vásquez de
Balboa, Vasco N. de
Cabeza de Vaca, Álvar N.
Columbus, Christopher
Coronado, Francisco V. de
Cortés, Hernán
De Soto, Hernando

Jiménez de Quesada, Gonzalo
Menéndez de Avilés, Pedro
Narváez, Pánfilo de
Oñate, Juan de
Orellana, Francisco de
Pizarro, Francisco
Ponce de León, Juan

Cities

Barcelona
Cádiz
Cartagena

Córdoba
Granada
Madrid

Saragossa
Seville

Toledo
Valencia

History

Aztec (The Spanish conquest)
Boabdil
Bourbon
Castile and Aragon
Cid, The
Colonialism
Equatorial Guinea

European Union
Exploration
Falange Española
Granada
Iberia
Inquisition
Latin America (History)

Line of Demarcation
Monroe Doctrine (Origins)
Spanish-American War
Spanish Armada

Spanish Civil War
Spanish Main
Succession wars
Trafalgar, Battle of

Physical features

Balearic Islands
Bay of Biscay
Canary Islands

Majorca
Mediterranean
  Sea

Pyrenees
Tagus River

Other related articles

Alcazar
Alhambra
Andorra
Basques
Bolero
Bullfighting
Castanets
Castle (picture)

Christmas (In
  Spain)
Cork
Don Juan
Escorial
Europe (picture)
Flag (picture: His-
  torical flags of
  the world)

Flamenco
Furniture (Spain)
Gaudi, Antonio
Loyola, Saint
  Ignatius
Montserrat
Peseta
Spanish language

Outline

I. Government
  A. The king
  B. The prime minister
  C. The parliament
  D. Local government

  E. Political parties
  F. Courts
  G. Armed forces

II. People
  A. Ancestry and
    population
  B. Language
  C. City life
  D. Country life
  E. Food and drink

  F. Recreation
  G. Religion
  H. Religious holidays
  I. Education
  J. Museums and libraries

III. The arts
  A. Literature
  B. Painting
  C. Architecture

  D. Music
  E. Motion pictures

IV. The land
  A. The Meseta
  B. The Northern
    Mountains
  C. The Ebro Basin

  D. The Coastal Plains
  E. The Guadalquivir Basin
  F. The Balearic Islands
  G. The Canary Islands

V. Climate

VI. Economy
  A. Natural resources
  B. Service industries
  C. Tourism
  D. Manufacturing
  E. Agriculture
  F. Fishing

  G. Mining
  H. Energy sources
  I. International trade
  J. Transportation and
    communication

VII. History

Questions

Who were the early peoples who lived in what is now Spain?
How does Spain's government promote tourism?
What is the Meseta?
What is Spain's official form of government?
When was the Golden Age of Spanish art?
When did Francisco Franco rule as dictator of Spain?
When did Spain change from being chiefly an agricultural country into an industrial nation?
When did the Spanish Empire reach its height?
What were the two sides in the Spanish Civil War?

Additional resources

Barton, Simon. *A History of Spain.* Palgrave, 2003.
Carr, Raymond, ed. *Spain: A History.* Oxford, 2000.
Gunther, Richard, and others. *Democracy in Modern Spain.* Yale, 2004.
Jordan, Barry. *Spanish Culture and Society.* Oxford, 2002.
Settle, Mary L. *Spanish Recognitions: The Roads to the Present.* Norton, 2004.
Thomas, Hugh. *Rivers of Gold: The Rise of the Spanish Empire, from Columbus to Magellan.* Random Hse., 2003.

Spalato. See Split.

Spallanzani, SPAH *luhn ZAH nee,* **Lazzaro,** *LAHD dzah roh* (1729-1799), an Italian experimental biologist, showed that the air carries microscopic life. He also showed that microscopic life in food can be killed by boiling. Spallanzani was the first to watch isolated bacterial cells divide. He found that bats can dodge strings even when blind, and that salamanders can replace damaged limbs. He was born in Scandiano, and took orders in the Roman Catholic Church. He taught at the University of Padua.   Eric Howard Christianson

Span. See Bridge.

Spandex is a highly elastic manufactured fiber. It is made of a chainlike arrangement of soft, stretchable segments of the plastics material *polyurethane* with stiffer segments in-between. When the fibers are relaxed, they stretch easily and can extend up to five times their original length. But as they are stretched, the stiff segments align and maintain strength. Manufacturers vary the lengths of the soft and stiff segments to produce fibers of differing strength and elasticity.

No fabric is made entirely of spandex. Instead, spandex is always used in combination with other fibers. Fabrics that contain spandex are lightweight and resistant to deterioration from perspiration and detergents. They are used to make such clothing as athletic wear, foundation garments, and support hose.   Richard V. Gregory

Spaniel is a large family of dogs. The American Kennel Club recognizes 10 spaniel breeds: the *American water, clumber, cocker, English cocker, English springer, field, Irish water, Sussex,* and *Welsh springer* spaniels, and the *Brittany.* Two dogs, the *English toy spaniel* and the *cavalier King Charles spaniel,* may be related to the others. But another toy dog, the *Japanese chin,* is probably not related to these spaniels.

The spaniel family probably descended from a Spanish dog, and its name comes from the word *Spain.* All spaniels except the toys are sporting dogs. The spaniel has a gentle and friendly disposition, and likes to hunt in the fields. Spaniels are fine companions as well as good hunters. They make excellent pets. Most spaniels have long, silky coats. In general, spaniels have long ears; rather large, round eyes; broad, domed skulls; and sturdy bodies and legs.

All the spaniel breeds except the Brittany hunt game in much the same way. They search the ground within gun range of the hunter. When a spaniel smells game, it rushes in to *flush* it, or make it fly or run. When the game is flushed and the hunter shoots, the spaniel waits for the command, finds the game, and then brings it back to the hunter.

Critically reviewed by the American Spaniel Club

For a list of separate articles in *World Book* on each spaniel breed, see **Dog** (table; pictures: Sporting dogs).

Spanish, language. See **Spanish language.**

Spanish America is the name sometimes given to the Spanish-speaking parts of Latin America. It includes Central America, except Belize; South America, except Brazil and the Guianas; Mexico; Cuba; Puerto Rico; the Dominican Republic; and certain islands of the West Indies. See also **Latin America.**

Spanish-American War marked the emergence of the United States as a world power. This brief conflict between the United States and Spain took place between April and August 1898, over the issue of the liberation of Cuba. In the course of the war, the United States won Guam, Puerto Rico, and the Philippine Islands.

Background of the war

Spanish misrule. Until about 1860, American expansionists had hoped to acquire Cuba. After the Civil War, interest in annexation dwindled, but Americans continued to be displeased by Spanish misrule. A long and exhausting uprising took place in the 1870's. In 1895, during a depression that made conditions worse, a revolution broke out again and threatened to go on endlessly. The Spanish forces were not powerful enough to put down the insurrection, and the rebels were not strong enough to win.

American intervention. American newspapers, especially the "yellow press" of William Randolph Hearst and Joseph Pulitzer, printed sensational accounts of Spanish oppression, and carried seriously exaggerated reports that a quarter of the population had died. They continually agitated for intervention. Many Americans regarded conditions in Cuba as intolerable and began to demand that the United States intervene. A few felt that the United States should also acquire naval and military bases and become an imperial power.

In November 1897, President McKinley pressured Spain into granting Cuba limited self-government within the Spanish empire. The rebels wanted nothing less than independence, and continued to fight. Meanwhile, pro-Spanish mobs in Havana rioted in protest against self-government. To protect Americans from the rioters, the battleship *Maine* arrived in Havana harbor January 25, 1898. On February 15, an explosion blew up the ship and killed about 260 persons on board. The outraged American public immediately blamed Spain for the explosion, but today many historians believe it was accidental and occurred inside the ship.

"Remember the *Maine"* became a popular slogan, but forces already in operation did more to bring about actual war. In March, President McKinley sent three notes to Spain, demanding full independence for Cuba. Spain granted an armistice. On April 19, Congress passed overwhelmingly a joint resolution asserting that Cuba was independent. In addition, the resolution disavowed any American intention to acquire the island, and authorized the use of the army and navy to force Spanish withdrawal. On April 25, the United States formally declared that a state of war existed with Spain as of April 21.

Chief events

Manila Bay. The first important battle of the war took place in the Philippines. The Asiatic Squadron of six ships under Commodore George Dewey sailed from Hong Kong to Manila Bay. On May 1, 1898, it destroyed the entire Spanish fleet of 10 vessels without the loss of an American life or serious damage to any American ship. Then Dewey blockaded Manila harbor while he waited for U.S. troops to arrive.

Cuban blockade. Meanwhile, the North Atlantic Squadron under Rear Admiral William T. Sampson had begun a partial blockade of Cuba while scouting in the Caribbean Sea for a fleet that had left Spain under Admiral Pascual Cervera y Topete. Finally, on May 28, American ships located Cervera's fleet, which had anchored in the landlocked harbor of Santiago de Cuba, on the southeastern part of the island. While the navy placed a blockading force outside the harbor, the army hastily prepared to send an expeditionary force to assault Santiago by land.

Land battles. On June 22, Major General William R. Shafter began landing 15,000 troops at Daiquirí and Siboney, near Santiago. The Spaniards offered little resistance during the landing and deploying of troops. Joyful newspaper reports of this helped make celebrities of the Rough Rider Regiment and its commanders, Colonel Leonard Wood and Lieutenant Colonel Theodore Roosevelt.

General Shafter launched a full-scale two-pronged assault against Santiago on July 1. He sent nearly half of his men against a small Spanish force strongly defending a stone fort at El Caney. The remainder made a frontal assault on the main Spanish defenses at Kettle Hill and San Juan Hill. By nightfall, the Americans had taken the ridges commanding Santiago, but they had suffered 1,600 casualties. Both black and white Americans fought in the campaign. First Lieutenant John J. Pershing wrote: "White regiments, black regiments … fought shoulder to shoulder, unmindful of race or color … and mindful only of their common duty as Americans."

As soon as Santiago came under siege, the governor of Cuba ordered Admiral Cervera to run the naval blockade to try to save his ships. Cervera led the ships out on July 3, heading in single file westward along the Cuban coast. The pursuing American naval vessels, commanded by Commodore Winfield S. Schley, sank or forced the beaching of every one of them. Again no serious damage occurred to any American vessel.

After days of negotiations, Santiago surrendered on July 17. On July 25, Major General Nelson A. Miles began an invasion of Puerto Rico which met almost no opposition. Several contingents of U.S. troops arrived in the Philippines. On August 13, they entered and occupied Manila, thus keeping the Filipino patriots out. The cables had been cut, and Dewey did not realize that an armistice had been signed the previous day.

Results of the war

The peace treaty. Sentiment grew within the United States to keep the spoils of war, except for Cuba. In the Treaty of Paris, signed Dec. 10, 1898, Spain granted Cuba its freedom. Spain ceded Guam, Puerto Rico, and the Philippines to the United States. The United States, in turn, paid Spain $20 million for the Philippine Islands. See **Philippines** (History).

Anti-imperialism. Many people in the United States did not like their nation's new position as a colonial power. These *anti-imperialists* opposed the annexations. They did not wish to hold subject peoples by force, run the risk of becoming involved in further wars, or face competition from colonial products or workers. Their forces were so strong in the Senate that it ratified the peace treaty by only one vote on Feb. 6, 1899.

Other results. The United States had to put down a long and bloody insurrection in the Philippines, strengthen its defenses, build more powerful battleships, and reorganize the army to remedy serious weaknesses revealed by the war. The war also showed the need for a canal through the Isthmus of Panama, which

The Charge of the Rough Riders at San Juan Hill (1898), an oil painting on canvas by Frederic Remington; Remington Art Museum, Ogdensburg, New York. All rights reserved.

The Rough Rider regiment won fame for its charge up Kettle Hill in Cuba in 1898. Lieutenant Colonel Theodore Roosevelt, *on horseback,* led the assault. The Kettle Hill charge helped the Americans win the Battle of San Juan Hill and so became identified with a similar attack there.

The chief battles of the Spanish-American War took place around Santiago de Cuba. The U.S. Army and Navy played key roles in the war.

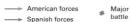
→ American forces
→ Spanish forces
✳ Major battle

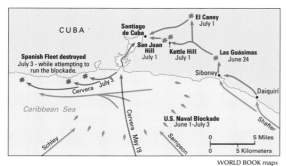

WORLD BOOK maps

separated the Caribbean Sea from the Pacific Ocean. The Spanish-American War thus led to the building of the Panama Canal. Frank Freidel

Related articles in *World Book* include:

Cuba
Dewey, George
Maine (ship)
McKinley, William (The Spanish-American War [1898])
Miles, Nelson A.
Puerto Rico
Roosevelt, Theodore
Sampson, William T.
Wood, Leonard

Additional resources

Berner, Brad K. *The Spanish-American War.* Scarecrow, 1998.
Golay, Michael. *Spanish-American War.* 2nd ed. Facts on File, 2003. Younger readers.
Musicant, Ivan. *Empire by Default: The Spanish-American War and the Dawn of the American Century.* Henry Holt, 1998.

Spanish Armada was a fleet of armed ships that tried to invade England in 1588. The Spanish fleet has often

been called the *Invincible Armada,* supposedly because the Spaniards thought it could not be defeated. But the English fleet defeated the Armada. The failure of the Armada was a great blow to the prestige of Spain, then the world's most powerful country. Spain remained a major power after the battle, but English merchants and sailors challenged the Spaniards with greater confidence throughout the world.

Background to battle. Bad feeling between Spain and England had existed since the 1560's. Spain was taking gold and silver from lands it had claimed in the Americas, and England wanted some of this wealth. Queen Elizabeth I encouraged Francis Drake and other English seamen to raid Spanish ships and towns, even though the countries were officially at peace.

Religious differences also caused conflict between the two nations. Spain was a Roman Catholic country, and most of England was Protestant. In the 1560's, the English began to aid the Dutch Protestants who were rebelling against Spanish rule (see **Netherlands** [Freedom from Spain]). In the early 1580's, King Philip II of Spain started planning to send a fleet and army to invade England. He hoped to end the English raids and to make England a Catholic country.

The two fleets. Philip began to assemble the Armada in January 1586. Spain built many new warships and armed its existing ones more heavily. It also rented many foreign ships. In 1587, Francis Drake raided Cádiz harbor in Spain and destroyed about 30 ships. The Armada was brought together in May 1588, at the Portuguese port of Lisbon, which at that time was ruled by Spain. The fleet had about 130 ships and more than 29,000 men, most of them soldiers. Some of the ships lacked guns and experienced gunners, and others lacked ammunition because they were only transport ships. Philip named the Duke of Medina Sidonia to command the Armada. The duke was an experienced military planner but an inexperienced seaman.

Oil painting on canvas by an unknown artist; National Maritime Museum, Greenwich, England

The Spanish Armada was a fleet of heavily armed ships that was defeated by the English fleet in 1588. This painting of the 1500's shows the Armada in battle against England. The ship in the center foreground is a Spanish *galleass*—a heavy, low-built warship powered by both sails and oars.

Meanwhile, England armed many of its merchant vessels and added them to its warships. England's fleet had about 200 ships and nearly 16,000 men, most of them sailors rather than soldiers. Admiral Lord Howard of Effingham commanded the fleet. His squadron leaders included Drake, John Hawkins, and Martin Frobisher.

The battle. The Armada left Lisbon on May 30, 1588. It entered the English Channel on July 30 and fought long-range gun duels with English warships during the next few days. On August 6, it anchored at Calais, France. Medina Sidonia had planned to meet barges carrying Spanish troops from nearby Dunkerque, a port then in the Netherlands. But Dutch gunboats prevented the barges from meeting the Armada. This act doomed the Armada to failure.

In the early hours of August 8, the English sent eight *fire ships* (vessels filled with gunpowder and set on fire) toward the Armada. The Spanish ships sailed out to sea to escape the flames. Later that morning, about 60 English ships attacked an equal number of Spanish ships off the French port of Gravelines. The English sank two Spanish ships and damaged others.

The Armada fled to the North Sea. It returned to Spain by sailing north around the islands of Great Britain and Ireland. Heavy winds wrecked many of its ships off Ireland's coast.   Carla Rahn Phillips and William D. Phillips, Jr.

See also **Drake, Sir Francis; Elizabeth I; Philip II** (of Spain).

Spanish bayonet is a general name for shrubby and treelike yuccas that grow in many dry regions of North America. The name is often used in particular for a low, slender yucca tree that grows in the southern part of the United States and in Mexico and the West Indies. It may grow to about 25 feet (8 meters) but usually is much smaller. It has long, flat, bayonetlike leaves, $2\frac{1}{2}$ feet (76 centimeters) long and 2 to 3 inches (5 to 8 centimeters) wide. The Spanish bayonet bears cream-white flowers that are sometimes tinted green or purple. The flowers are about $2\frac{1}{2}$ inches (6 centimeters) wide and are shaped like deep bowls. The leaves are a source of fiber for rope. See also **Yucca.**   Philip W. Rundel

Scientific classification. The Spanish bayonet is in the agave family, Agavaceae. Its scientific name is *Yucca aloifolia.*

Spanish Civil War (1936 to 1939) was fought between the forces of Spain's democratically elected, liberal government and conservative rebels. The war cost the lives of hundreds of thousands of Spaniards and set the stage for a dictatorship that lasted more than 35 years.

The conservative or *right-wing* forces that rebelled against the government were known as Nationalists. They included military leaders, parts of the Roman Catholic Church, groups that wanted Spain to become a monarchy again, and *fascists.* The fascists were members of a political party called the *Falange Española* (Spanish Phalanx). Like similar groups in Germany and Italy, the fascists wanted to set up a dictatorship.

The forces that fought on the side of the government were known as Republicans. They included a variety of liberal or *left-wing* groups, such as socialists, Communists, and *anarchists* (those who believe people should live without government).

Much of the world viewed the Spanish Civil War as a contest between democracy and fascism. It became a major source of concern for many nations, which be-

lieved that the outcome could determine the balance of power in Europe. Many people who felt strongly about the war held fund-raising rallies and publicized the international issues at stake in Spain's domestic conflict.

Background to the war. From 1923 to 1930, General Miguel Primo ruled Spain with the power of a dictator. King Alfonso XIII supported his government. By the end of Primo's time in power, the movement for a republican form of government had gained strength in Spain. Supporters of the movement included liberals, socialists, and other people who did not want a monarchy. The strength of popular support forced Alfonso to allow free elections. In April 1931, the people voted overwhelmingly for republican candidates in city elections. Following the elections, Alfonso left the country, though he refused to give up his claim to the throne. Republican leaders then took control of the government and established what became known as the Second Republic.

The left-wing alliance of republicans and socialists that ruled Spain between 1931 and 1933 attempted to transform Spain's social, economic, and political institutions. Some policies, including certain land reforms and the establishment of an eight-hour work day, threatened the upper classes who owned Spain's land and industries. The government tried to reduce the long-standing influence of the Roman Catholic Church in Spanish society and politics. The government also adopted controversial measures aimed at reforming the armed forces.

These reforms created opposition to the government among many Spaniards, especially conservatives. In parliamentary elections held in 1933, an alliance of moderate and right-wing parties gained control of the government. The new government tried to reverse the progressive reforms of the earlier administration.

Elections held in February 1936 returned the liberals

© Hulton Getty from Liaison

The Spanish Civil War pitted conservative rebels, called Nationalists, against Spain's elected Republican government. In this photo, Nationalist troops guard captured Republican soldiers.

The Spanish Civil War

The Nationalists quickly captured about a third of Spain. Republicans held most of the country's industrial areas and large cities, including Spain's capital, Madrid. The superior military strength of the Nationalists eventually triumphed.

✳ Major battle

⟶ Major Republican campaign

⟶ Major Nationalist campaign

▨ Areas held by Nationalists Oct. 1936

▨ Areas gained by Nationalists Oct. 1937

▨ Areas gained by Nationalists July 1938

☐ Areas gained by Nationalists March 1939

WORLD BOOK map

to power in an alliance of left-wing parties known as the Popular Front. In the late spring, a series of strikes, violent public demonstrations, and political assassinations caused most Spaniards to lose faith in the Popular Front.

Rebellion leads to civil war. On July 17, 1936, Spanish army units in Morocco launched a rebellion against the Spanish government. The revolt soon spread to Spain itself. The rebels hoped to overthrow the government quickly and to restore order in Spain. But Republican forces took up arms against the military. Within four days after the start of the uprising, the rebels controlled about a third of Spain. The Republicans controlled Spain's industrial centers and most of its densely populated towns and cities, including the capital, Madrid.

On both sides, a wave of terror and repression followed the military uprising. The Nationalists shot thousands of workers and Republican supporters living in areas under their control. In the Republican zone, thousands of civilians were executed by working-class groups fearful of a reaction from rebel supporters.

In some areas held by Republicans, workers belonging to anarchist and other left-wing organizations dismantled existing government institutions. They replaced them with agricultural and industrial *collectives*—that is, groups jointly owned by their workers—and with bodies known as *people's committees* that intended to rule on behalf of the working classes.

In late July 1936, the Nationalists set up a government in Burgos called the Junta de Defensa Nacional (Council of National Defense). In September, this group chose Francisco Franco to serve as head of both the armed forces and the Nationalist government. Franco and his advisers based the new government on fascist and conservative principles and created a prominent role in the government for the Roman Catholic Church. By the end of 1937, all the forces on the Nationalist side had joined together under Franco's leadership.

Foreign assistance. In August 1936, France, Germany, Italy, the United Kingdom, and other European

countries agreed not to intervene in the war. The French and British in particular feared that interference by other countries in the Spanish conflict could cause the war to spread to the rest of Europe. As a result of the agreement, the United Kingdom and France—both supporters of the Republican government—did not provide it with aid. However, Germany's Nazi government and Italy's Fascist government both violated the agreement. Germany provided military aid to the Nationalists in exchange for certain mining rights. Italy supplied military equipment and troops to help Franco's army.

The Soviet Union sent the Republicans food, clothing, and military equipment in exchange for most of Spain's gold reserves. No Soviet troops were sent, but the Soviet-led organization known as the Comintern recruited volunteers from around the world to fight for the Republicans in groups called the International Brigades.

Progress of the war. Early in the war, the Nationalists demonstrated superior military strength. By the first week of November 1936, rebel troops were closing in on Madrid, hoping to occupy the capital quickly. The determined resistance of the city's population, supported by newly organized units of the International Brigades and Republican troops, stopped the Nationalist advance. The Republicans also defeated the Nationalists at the Jarama River near Madrid in February 1937 and at Guadalajara in March. But they lost the coastal city of Málaga to the Nationalists on February 8.

With the Madrid front stalled, Franco decided to launch a major offensive in the north. As part of this operation, on April 26, 1937, bombers of the German Condor Legion attacked the small market town of Guernica. They destroyed much of the town center and killed over 1,500 civilians, according to most estimates. News of the bombing generated a storm of international protests and demonstrations, and the incident became known as a symbol of fascist brutality. The Spanish painter Pablo Picasso captured the terror of the bombing in his masterpiece *Guernica.* See **Picasso, Pablo** (illustration).

The Nationalists continued their northern assault. The city of Bilbao fell in June. A few months later, the Nationalists conquered the northern coastal areas and industrial regions that had been under Republican control. A major Nationalist offensive launched in the region of Aragon in March 1938 led farther into Republican territory. Franco's army pushed east through the region and reached the Mediterranean Sea by mid-April, cutting the Republican-controlled zone in two.

Franco's advance on Valencia was interrupted by the Republican army's last major offensive, the Battle of the Ebro. This battle, fought from July to November 1938, was the longest of the war. Despite early Republican gains, the Nationalists eventually halted the attack. The Republican defeat paved the way for the Nationalists' march on Catalonia in the northeast. By the end of January 1939, most of the region, including Barcelona, was in Nationalist hands. Republican troops and civilian supporters retreated toward the Spanish-French frontier.

Republican forces were plagued by disagreements among themselves throughout the war. By 1939, internal disputes had split the Republicans into two camps. The government of Juan Negrín, who had come to power in 1937, wanted to continue fighting. But an alliance of left-wing parties considered further resistance useless. In March, this group set up its own government in Madrid. Shortly afterward, Negrín's government collapsed.

As street fighting broke out between pro- and anti-Communist forces in Madrid and elsewhere, representatives of the new government sought in vain to negotiate a surrender with the Nationalists. On March 28, Franco's troops began entering the capital. The remaining Republican forces throughout Spain surrendered, and Franco announced on April 1 that the war was over.

Results of the war. The Spanish Civil War resulted in widespread destruction. Estimates of the numbers of people killed during the conflict vary. Many experts estimate that from 600,000 to 800,000 people died as a result of the war, including deaths caused by combat, bombing, execution, and starvation.

Following the war, Franco established a harsh right-wing dictatorship. Franco had thousands of Republican supporters executed and outlawed all political parties but his own. Spain did not return to democracy until after Franco's death in 1975.   George R. Esenwein

See also Franco, Francisco; Spain (History [Civil war]).

Spanish fly. See Spanishfly.

Spanish Inquisition. See Inquisition; Torquemada, Tomás de.

Spanish language is the official language of Spain. It is also the official language of most Latin American countries and one of the two official languages of Puerto Rico. About 14 ½ million Spanish-speaking people live in the United States. Most of them reside in Florida and the Southwest. About 297 million people worldwide speak Spanish, the most popular Romance language (see **Romance languages**).

The Spanish spoken in Spain is often called *Castilian Spanish*. The Spanish used in Latin America is known as *American Spanish*. Castilian Spanish and American Spanish are basically the same but have a few differences in pronunciation and vocabulary.

Many English words come from Spanish. They include *alfalfa, alligator, armada, cargo, cork, lariat, lasso,* *mosquito, potato, ranch, rodeo, tobacco, tomato, tornado,* and *vanilla.* Some states and many U.S. cities have Spanish names. Among them are *California, Florida, Nevada, Los Angeles, San Antonio,* and *San Francisco.*

Spanish pronunciation

Spanish is one of the most phonetic of all languages. That is, its pronunciation follows its spelling closely. See **Phonetics** (Phonetics and spelling).

Vowels. Spanish has only five basic vowel sounds. These sounds are represented by the letters *a, e, i* or *y, o,* and *u.* The following table gives the approximate English sound for each Spanish vowel:

Spanish vowel	Approximate sound in English
a	*a* in *father*
e	*e* in *they*
i or *y*	*i* in *machine*
o	*o* in *owe*
u	*oo* in *moon*

Consonants. Spanish has four consonant sounds not found in English. They are *ch, ll, ñ,* and *rr.* Their pronunciation corresponds roughly to the English pronunciation of *ch* in *church; lli* in *million; ny* in *canyon;* and a *trilled* (rolled) *r,* a sound that does not exist in American English. People who speak American Spanish pronounce the consonants *c* (when it is followed by *e* or *i*) and *z* as English-speaking people pronounce the *s* in *sink.* People who speak Castilian Spanish pronounce them like the *th* in *think.* The letter *h* is not pronounced in Spanish. The consonants *b* and *v* are generally pronounced like a *b.*

Spanish grammar

Nouns and adjectives. All Spanish nouns are either masculine or feminine. Most nouns that name male human beings or male animals, or that end in *-o, -l,* or *-r,* are masculine. Most nouns that name female human beings or female animals, or that end in *-a, -d,* or *-ión,* are feminine. For example, *padre* (father), *libro* (book), *papel* (paper), and *calor* (heat) are masculine. *Madre* (mother), *pluma* (pen), *felicidad* (happiness), and *revolución* (revolution) are feminine. Plurals of nouns and adjectives are formed by adding *-s* to those that end in vowels and *-es* to those ending in consonants.

Adjectives must agree in *gender* (masculine or feminine) and in *number* (singular or plural) with the nouns they modify. Thus, many adjectives have four forms. *Sombrero pequeño* means *small hat, casa pequeña* means *small house, sombreros pequeños* means *small hats,* and *casas pequeñas* means *small houses.*

Verbs. Spanish has 15 commonly used tenses, 8 simple and 7 *perfect,* or compound (see **Tense**). The simple tenses are formed by adding endings to the stem of the verb or to the infinitive. The perfect tenses are formed by using the appropriate simple tense of *haber* (to have) followed by a past participle of the verb.

Spanish verbs are classified according to the endings of their infinitives. They fall into three groups: *-ar* verbs, such as *andar* (to walk); *-er* verbs, such as *correr* (to run); and *-ir* verbs, such as *vivir* (to live).

Word order in Spanish is similar to that of English. Two exceptions are the positions of object pronouns and descriptive adjectives in Spanish sentences. Object pronouns usually come before the verb in Spanish. In

Spanish words and phrases

¿adónde va usted? *ah DOHN day vAH oo STAYD,* where are you going?
ayer, *ah YEHR,* yesterday
bien, *BYEHN,* well
bueno, *BWAY noh,* good
buenos días, *BWAY nohs DEE ahs,* good morning
¿cómo está usted? *KOH moheh STAH oo STAYD,* how are you?
¿cómo se llama usted? *KOH moh sayl YAH mah oo STAYD,* what is your name?
gracias, *GRAH syahs,* thanks, thank you
hasta luego, *AH stahl WAY goh,* good-by (until later)
hombre, *OHM bray,* man
hoy, *oy,* today
mañana, *mahn YAH nah,* morning, tomorrow
me llamo Juan, *mayl YAH moh HWAHN,* my name is John
mucho, *MOO choh,* much, a lot
mujer, *moo HEHR,* woman
muy bien, *MWEE BYEHN,* very well
pequeño, *pay KAYN yoh,* small
por favor, *POHR fah BOHR,* please
¿qué hora es? *kay OHR ah EHS,* what time is it?
señor, *sayn YOHR,* sir, Mr.
señora, *sayn YOH rah,* lady, Mrs.
señorita, *sayn yoh REE tah,* young lady, Miss
sí, *SEE,* yes
son las dos, *SOHN lahs DOHS,* it is two o'clock
tengo hambre, *TEHNG goh AHM bray,* I am hungry

the English sentence *She greeted us,* the verb (*greeted*) comes before the object pronoun (*us*). In Spanish, this sentence becomes *Ella nos saludó* (*She us greeted*). Descriptive adjectives in Spanish usually follow the nouns they modify. In the English sentence *We live in a white house,* the descriptive adjective (*white*) comes before the noun (*house*). In Spanish, this sentence becomes *Vivimos en una casa blanca* (*We live in a house white*).

A Spanish sentence is made negative by placing *no* before the verb. An *interrogative sentence,* which asks a question, is formed by placing the subject after the verb. A Spanish interrogative sentence has an inverted question mark before the first word, and a regular question mark after the last. This construction enables readers to recognize a question as soon as they begin reading it. The following are the affirmative, negative, and interrogative forms of the English sentence *Charles lives here:* Affirmative—*Carlos vive aquí;* Negative—*Carlos no vive aquí;* Interrogative—*¿Vive Carlos aquí?*

Development

Beginnings. The Spanish language developed from Latin, the language of the Roman Empire. During the 200's and 100's B.C., Roman armies conquered the *Iberian Peninsula* (present-day Spain and Portugal). The Iberians gradually adopted their conquerors' language, *vulgar* (common) Latin.

In the early 400's, Germanic tribes, called Goths, invaded the Iberian Peninsula. The Goths controlled the peninsula until 711, but they had little influence on the language. In 711, the Arabic-speaking Moors conquered all but a small part of the peninsula. They ruled most of the region until the mid-1200's. The Moors added about 700 Arabic words to vulgar Latin. But the language changed little in sound and structure.

Castilian Spanish. Spanish began to emerge as an independent language from Latin in the period from 950 to 1000. Like other languages, Spanish developed sever-

al dialects. During the 1200's, the Spanish province of Castile became an important literary, military, and political center. The influence of Castile spread, and the Castilian dialect was soon the accepted form of Spanish in most parts of the Iberian Peninsula.

Two other dialects became separate languages during this period. The *Galician-Portuguese* dialect developed in the western part of the Iberian Peninsula. This dialect was the basis of Portuguese, which began in the late 1100's (see **Portuguese language**). The *Catalan* dialect survived in northeastern Spain and grew into the Catalan language.

American Spanish developed in what is now Latin America as Spanish colonists, conquerors, and missionaries began settling there in the 1500's. Spanish to a large extent replaced many of the Indian languages that were spoken in Latin America, including those of the Aztec, Inca, and Maya.   Richard P. Kinkade

See also **Spain** (Language).

Additional resources

Berlitz, Charles. *Spanish Step-by-Step.* 1979. Reprint. Wynwood, 1990.
Kattán-Ibarra, Juan. *Spanish Grammar.* Rev. ed. Teach Yourself, 2003.
Penny, Ralph J. *A History of the Spanish Language.* 2nd ed. Cambridge, 2002.
Zagona, Karen. *The Syntax of Spanish.* Cambridge, 2002.

Spanish literature is one of the richest and most varied of all European literatures. Spanish writers have combined a strong individuality with an openness to the Western traditions of Europe and the Eastern traditions of North Africa. As a result, they have produced a literature characterized by its originality, vibrant wit, realism, color, humor, and lyricism.

Two historical periods have been especially important in their influence on Spanish literature. The Romans occupied the Spanish peninsula for about 600 years, beginning in the 200's B.C. The main heritage they left to Spain was the Latin language, particularly *vernacular Latin,* the form used by the common people. Vernacular Latin gave birth to the Romance languages, three of which became the most common Spanish dialects— Castilian, Galician-Portuguese, and Catalan (see **Spanish language** [Development]). From the A.D. 700's through the 1400's, Christians fought Muslim Moors for control of Spain. This long struggle created a strongly religious patriotism that inspired some of the world's finest religious poetry and prose.

The greatest period of Spanish literature began about the mid-1500's and lasted until the late 1600's. This period, called the Golden Age, brought a flowering of fiction, poetry, and drama. Spain's most outstanding and best-known writer, Miguel de Cervantes, the author of the novel *Don Quixote,* lived during this period.

This article discusses literature written in the Spanish language by authors in Spain. For information about literature written in the Spanish language by authors in the Americas, see **Latin American literature**.

The Middle Ages

Early medieval literature. Lyric poetry existed in Spain as early as the A.D. 900's. The first lyric poems, called *jarchas,* are short refrains added to Arabic or Hebrew poems called *muwashshahas.* Jarchas were written in characters from the Hebrew and Arabic alphabets, but the language was a Mozarabic dialect of Spanish. The Mozarabs were Christian Spaniards living under Moorish rule. Jarchas may be the oldest form of lyric poetry in a Romance language. The poems express the sadness of a young woman who misses her absent lover, or of a young woman who longs for love.

Almost all the early Spanish epic poems have been lost. The only one that has survived in nearly complete form is the *Poem of the Cid.* It tells of the adventures of a Castilian hero, Rodrigo Díaz de Vivar. *The Cid* is more realistic than epics written in other countries during the Middle Ages. It was written about 1140, or perhaps in the early 1200's. See **Cid, The.**

Minstrels called *juglares* recited epic poems in town squares and also performed satirical plays called *juegos de escarnio.* Early medieval Spanish drama is not well known. Only a fragment of a religious drama from the middle to late 1100's, *The Play of the Three Wise Men,* has survived. During the 1100's, Spanish lyric poetry came under the influence of the poems of the Provençal troubadours of southern France. The early poetry of two related dialects, Galician and Portuguese, was modeled on Provençal poetry. The Galician-Portuguese works, consisting of short *cantigas* (songs) and longer poems, were collected and preserved in three famous medieval *cancioneiros* (anthologies). From this period came Gonzalo de Berceo, the first Spanish poet known by name. He wrote *Miracles of Our Lady,* a series of poems about the miracles of the Virgin Mary.

The Castilian king Alfonso X, called *the Wise,* helped promote early Spanish prose. In the late 1200's, two long historical works were begun under Alfonso's direction—*General Chronicle of Spain,* a history of Spain; and *General History,* a world history. The king also supported the scientific and philosophical interests of the school of translators at Toledo, which introduced Ptolemy, Aristotle, and other ancient writers to western Europe. In addition, Alfonso is remembered for his Galician cantigas that were dedicated to the Virgin Mary.

The earliest known prose fiction in Spain included a collection of *apologues* (moral tales) in Latin. They were published in about 1100 by Pedro Alfonso under the title *Scholar's Guide.* During the 1200's, several collections of tales were translated into Spanish from Arabic and other languages. These works included *Calila and Dimna* (1251) and *Sendebar* (1253). In the early 1300's, Spanish prose began to take on a more distinctive character with the writings of Don Juan Manuel, nephew of Alfonso the Wise. Don Juan Manuel wrote many works on a wide variety of subjects. His greatest achievement was *Count Lucanor* (1335), a collection of moral tales.

The poetry of the scholars began to decline during the 1300's. Juan Ruiz, the *archpriest* (chief priest) of the town of Hita in Castile, preserved the verse form of the clerics to some extent in his unique work, *The Book of Good Love* (1330, enlarged 1343). The book offers a vivid picture of many details of Spanish life in the 1300's, telling about food, musical instruments, songs, love affairs, and monastic and tavern customs. Ruiz invented a famous character named Trotaconventos, an old hag who serves as a go-between for the lovers.

The 1400's. A wide view of the lyric poetry of the late 1300's and the 1400's appeared in the *Cancionero de Baena* and the *Cancionero de Stúñiga.* The Italian poets Dante, Petrarch, and Giovanni Boccaccio influenced the poetry. But the spirit of the Middle Ages survived in many anonymous *romances* (ballads). Some scholars believe these romances were fragments of epic songs that were meant to be sung or recited. They have been preserved through oral tradition in Spain, Spanish America, and Morocco, and among Sephardic Jews.

Three great poets wrote in the 1400's: (1) Íñigo López de Mendoza, better known as the Marquis of Santillana; (2) Juan de Mena; and (3) Jorge Manrique. Santillana wrote sonnets in the Italian style and elaborate, courtly *serranillas* (pastoral poems). He also wrote an important letter concerning the poetry of the times. Mena wrote *The Labyrinth of Fate* (1444), an allegorical work of 297 stanzas inspired by Dante and several ancient writers. Manrique wrote the *Coplas* (1476), a moving and sophisticated elegy on the death of his father.

Several events of literary importance took place during the late 1400's. Printing was introduced in Spain, probably in Saragossa in 1473. In 1492, Antonio de Nebrija published his *Castilian Grammar,* the first book written on the rules of a modern European language. The theater took its first steps toward *secular* (nonreligious) dramas before 1500. Juan del Encina and Lucas Fernández wrote Christmas and Easter plays, as well as pastoral and folk dramas.

Other new trends in Spanish literature appeared in such prose works as Diego de San Pedro's *The Prison of Love* (1492) and the Catalan book of chivalry, *Tirant lo Blanch* (begun about 1460 and published in 1490), by Joanot Martorell and Martí Joan de Galba. The long novel of chivalry called *Amadís of Gaul,* known since the 1300's, was printed, probably for the first time, in 1508. Part of it was written by Garci Ordóñez (or Rodríguez) de Montalvo. See **Amadís of Gaul.**

The masterpiece generally known as *La Celestina* appeared in the late 1400's. The first known edition was published as an anonymous novel in dialogue form. Its 16 acts appeared under the title *Comedia de Calisto y Melibea* in 1499. Three years later it was expanded to 21 acts and titled *Tragicomedia de Calisto y Melibea.* The author of at least part—and possibly all—of the work was Fernando de Rojas. *La Celestina* combines medieval theology with a Renaissance conception of life and love. The central character is Celestina, a witchlike go-between who brings together two lovers, Calisto and Melibea. The main characters lose their lives one by one. Melibea's father closes the work with a tragic lament in which he questions the emptiness of his world.

The Golden Age

The 1500's. The spirit of the Italian Renaissance spread through Spanish literature in the 1500's. During this time, literary expression was in constant conflict with the Inquisition, an institution established by the Roman Catholic Church to seek out and punish people who opposed church teachings. Many Spaniards were influenced by Desiderius Erasmus, a Dutch scholar and priest who worked for reform of the church. His ideas were present in the philosophical writings of Juan Luis Vives and the brothers Alfonso and Juan de Valdés.

Poetry. During the early 1500's, Juan Boscán and Garcilaso de la Vega introduced the meters, verse forms, and themes of Italian Renaissance poetry, which soon dominated Spanish poetry. But Cristóbal de Castillejo and Gregorio Silvestre, among others, preserved the Castilian tradition of writing shorter verse lines. Spanish poetry is indebted not only to such other Spaniards as Hernando de Acuña and Gutierre de Cetina, but also to the Portuguese poets Francisco Sá de Miranda and Luis de Camões. Camões' great epic poem *Os Lusíadas* (1572) is a masterpiece in the style of Italian epics.

There were two main poetic schools after the mid-1500's—the Castilian school of Salamanca and the Andalusian school of Seville. Poets of both schools wrote in the style of the Italian poet Petrarch. However, a certain serenity and a more cautious use of metaphor characterized the school of Salamanca and its representatives—Fray (Brother) Luis de León, Pedro Malón de Chaide, and Francisco de la Torre. Poets of the school of Seville included Fernando de Herrera, Baltasar de Alcázar, Francisco de Rioja, Juan de Jáuregui, and Juan de Arguijo. Through the use of colorful images, they developed a concern for the formal possibilities of language that led to the baroque style of the 1600's.

Another important aspect of Spanish poetry of the 1500's was the lyrical expression of *mystics*—people who seek a union of the soul with God. Saint John of the Cross was the major mystic poet. Saint Teresa of Avila contributed several prose works, including her autobiography, to mystical literature. Two similar writers were Fray Luis de Granada, author of *Introduction to the Symbol of Faith* (1582), and Fray Luis de León, a professor at the University of Salamanca who was persecuted by the Inquisition. León wrote religious poetry and the prose masterpiece *The Names of Christ* (1583).

Medieval epics survived in the 1500's, not only in the romances but also in books of chivalry. The epic glorification of people and events continued in long poems by Luis de Zapata, Luis Barahona de Soto, and Bernardo de Balbuena, and in Alonso de Ercilla y Zúñiga's important *La Araucana* (1569-1589). This epic poem told of the conflicts between the Indians of Chile and the Spaniards. All these poets wrote in the Italian narrative style.

Prose. The *pastoral novel* became popular during the Renaissance. Pastoral novels idealized rural life and the lives of shepherds and simple country people. *Diana* (1559?) by Jorge de Montemayor and *Diana in Love* (1564) by Gaspar Gil Polo are still well-known Spanish pastoral novels. Cervantes' first long work, *La Galatea* (1585), and Lope de Vega's *La Arcadia* (1598) later followed the fashion of pastoral fiction.

The *picaresque novel* was by far the most important contribution of Spanish Golden Age fiction to world literature. This type of novel presented society through the eyes of a *pícaro* (rogue) and usually included biting satire or moral commentary. The first picaresque novel, according to some critics, was *Lazarillo de Tormes* (1554). This anonymous work was written in the form of a short autobiography. It details the struggles of Lazarillo, a boy of humble birth who makes his way by cunning and treachery as he serves a blind beggar, a greedy priest, a starving nobleman, and other representative social types. The work moralizes on the episodes of his life, and it is especially aggressive in its satire of the church. Lazarillo became a famous character and in-

spired sequels in Spain and elsewhere in Europe.

Drama. The Spanish theater developed slowly during most of the 1500's. In 1517, Bartolomé de Torres Naharro published a collection of plays with a prologue on dramatic theory, *Propalladia.* Gil Vicente of Portugal wrote plays in Spanish, such as *La Comedia del Viudo* (1514) and *Amadís de Gaula* (1533). The actor-playwright Lope de Rueda created the *paso,* a short farce that ridiculed the daily life of his time. Juan de la Cueva was the first author to take his plots from Spanish history or from popular narrative songs called ballads.

The 1600's. Following *Lazarillo,* the most outstanding Spanish picaresque novel is *Guzmán de Alfarache* (first part, 1599; second part, 1604) by Mateo Alemán. *Guzmán* is more detailed than *Lazarillo* and presents a more bitter, pessimistic view of life by showing that neither human nature nor conditions of life can be changed. The picaresque novel quickly became a tradition. Francisco López de Úbeda created a female rogue in *La pícara Justina* (1605). Vicente Espinel wrote *Marcos de Obregón* (1618). The poet and satirist Francisco de Quevedo wrote the aggressive and skeptical novel *Life of the Swindler* (1626). Quevedo also became famous for his satirical *Visions* (1627) and his theological and philosophical essays.

A contrast to the realism of the picaresque novel was the idealism of Cervantes' masterpiece, *Don Quixote* (first part, 1605; second part, 1615). This story of a country landowner who considers himself a knight is filled with humor and pathos. The novel contrasts idealistic and practical approaches to life, and it examines the differences between appearances and reality. But Cervantes went beyond his times and gave his characters and themes universal qualities that extend to all humanity. Cervantes is not well known as a dramatist, but his *entremeses* (one-act comedies) are among his best works.

Lope de Vega was the leading Golden Age dramatist. He emerged in the late 1500's as a uniquely prolific and gifted literary figure. He wrote popular works that mix tragic and comic elements. The topics of Lope's dramas had various origins. As the creator of a national drama, he drew on historical events and glorified national heroes. He also created rulers who had divine characteristics and were concerned with justice. Some of Lope's plays were "cloak-and-sword" dramas of intrigue, with love and honor as the sources of dramatic conflict. Others were light plays with complicated plots in which his qualities of poet and dramatist stand out. The *bobo* (fool) of earlier comedies became a constant character in Lope's plays in the form of the *gracioso,* the witty counterpart of the hero. Two of his greatest dramas were *Fuenteovejuna* (1619) and *Justice Without Revenge* (1634).

Another dramatist who wrote in the style and spirit of Lope was Tirso de Molina, whose *The Trickster of Seville* (1630) was the first dramatized version of the Don Juan legend. Guillén de Castro wrote a famous play, *The Cid's Youth* (1618?), about Spain's national hero. Other notable playwrights were the Mexican-born Juan Ruiz de Alarcón, Juan Pérez de Montalbán, Francisco de Rojas Zorrilla, and Agustín Moreto.

At the beginning of the 1600's, the world of art sought new forms of expression. Artists tended toward greater ornamentation and density in their works. The resulting style was called *baroque* (see **Baroque**). In Spain, there were two literary examples of this trend—*conceptismo* and *culteranismo*.

Conceptismo featured a subtle and ambiguous use of figures of speech. Authors elaborated upon complex metaphors called *conceptos* (conceits) to create complicated and original views of life. Quevedo and Baltasar Gracián represented this trend.

Culteranismo was a movement led by Luis de Góngora. The movement was also known as *gongorismo*. Góngora created lyric poetry full of color, imagery, and musical linguistic effects. His long and complex poems, *Polifemo and Galatea* (1613?) and the unfinished *Solitudes,* as well as his sonnets, ballads, and short compositions, became models for new developments in literature. Other poets who cultivated culteranismo were Pedro Soto de Rojas; Juan de Tassis y Peralta, the Count of Villamediana; and Luis Carrillo y Sotomayor.

Drama was also influenced by the Baroque style. Pedro Calderón de la Barca succeeded Lope de Vega as the leading Spanish dramatist. He is sometimes considered a more skillful playwright than Lope for the construction of his intricate plots. Calderón dramatized the dreams and realities of life in a brilliant work, *Life Is a Dream* (1635). The theme of honor and the conflict between love and jealousy were topics often explored by Calderón. His historical and religious dramas showed his versatility. Calderón's *autos sacramentales* (religious plays on the theme of the Eucharist) reflected culteranismo combined with the spirit of the Counter Reformation, a reform movement within the Roman Catholic Church following the Reformation. Calderón used symbolism to express in solemn verse philosophical explorations of life and death, original sin, and free will. His best-known autos include *The Feast of King Belshazzar* (1634) and *The Great Theater of the World* (1649?).

Neoclassicism, Romanticism, and Realism

The 1700's. By the end of the 1600's, Spain had declined politically, economically, and artistically. Philip V, a Frenchman, became king of Spain in 1700 and began the Bourbon dynasty of rulers. With French rulers in Spain and the beginning of the Enlightenment in the rest of Europe, it was inevitable that Spanish literature would assume new directions.

Neoclassicism, a style strongly influenced by Greek and Roman literature, was the most important literary trend of the 1700's. Many writers tried to refine Spanish literature along the lines of French Classicism, eliminating the ornamental excesses of much Baroque literature. See **Classicism.**

Benito Jerónimo Feijoo, a Benedictine friar, wrote on almost every branch of learning in his nine-volume *Universal Theater of Criticism* (1726-1740) and five-volume *Erudite and Interesting Letters* (1742-1760). Ignacio de Luzán supported the Neoclassical ideas of reason, proper behavior, and moral sense in *Poetics* (1737), a work that attempts to systematize literary principles.

The major novel of the time was *History of the Famous Preacher, Friar Gerund de Campazas* (first part, 1758; second part, 1768) by the Jesuit José Francisco de Isla. Two of Spain's important writers of the 1700's were José Cadalso and Gaspar Melchor de Jovellanos. Cadalso satirized the defects he saw in Spaniards in a collection of letters between fictional people, *Moroccan*

Spanish literature from the 1100's

Masters of Spanish literature from the 1100's to the present rank among the greatest literary figures in the world. Spain's Golden Age, a period during the 1500's and 1600's, produced some of the finest drama, poetry, and fiction ever written.

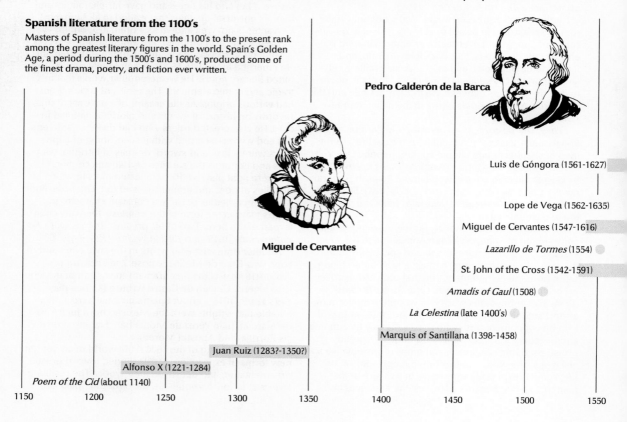

Pedro Calderón de la Barca

Miguel de Cervantes

Luis de Góngora (1561-1627)

Lope de Vega (1562-1635)

Miguel de Cervantes (1547-1616)

Lazarillo de Tormes (1554)

St. John of the Cross (1542-1591)

Amadís of Gaul (1508)

La Celestina (late 1400's)

Marquis of Santillana (1398-1458)

Juan Ruiz (1283?-1350?)

Alfonso X (1221-1284)

Poem of the Cid (about 1140)

1150   1200   1250   1300   1350   1400   1450   1500   1550

Letters (written about 1774, published in 1789). Jovellanos was a poet, essayist, and economist who wrote on ways to reform the country.

Neoclassicism began to heavily influence Spanish drama in the mid-1700's. Playwrights who wrote in this style included Nicolás Fernández de Moratín and his son, Leandro Fernández de Moratín; Vicente García de la Huerta; and José Cadalso. Two of the best poets, Juan Meléndez Valdés and Nicasio Álvarez de Cienfuegos, wrote lyrical works that displayed refined tastes.

The 1800's. Spanish authors continued the Neoclassical style in the early 1800's. Leandro Fernández de Moratín was the most accomplished writer of Neoclassical comedy. His most famous play was *The Maiden's Consent* (1806). The poet Manuel José Quintana belonged to the Neoclassical school. His odes and long poems had a strong patriotic sentiment. The works of Juan Nicasio Gallego resembled those of Quintana. Manuel Bretón de los Herreros wrote dozens of satirical, realistic comedies in the manner of the younger Moratín.

Romantic impulses had existed in Spanish literature since the 1700's. These impulses intensified after the death of the conservative King Ferdinand VII in 1833. A new liberal atmosphere prevailed in Spain, and exiled Romantic authors returned to Spain from elsewhere in Europe carrying new influences.

Ángel de Saavedra, the Duke of Rivas, assured the success of Romantic theater with his Romantic tragedy *Don Álvaro or the Force of Destiny* in 1835. Antonio García Gutiérrez scored a triumph with his historical tragedy *The Troubadour* (1836). Francisco Martínez de la Rosa and Juan Eugenio Hartzenbusch wrote plays that

reflected the rebellion, melancholy, and passion of Spanish Romanticism. José Zorrilla's *Don Juan Tenorio* (1844) became one of the greatest successes of the Spanish stage. There were echoes of the Romantic fervor in Manuel Tamayo y Baus's *A New Play* (1867) and in José Echegaray y Eizaguirre's *The Great Go-Between* (1881). A concern for social justice, evident in *Juan José* (1895) by Joaquín Dicenta, highlighted the Spanish stage of the late 1800's.

Romantic prose had its greatest stylist in Mariano José de Larra, who published penetrating articles in the daily press that criticized Spain's many problems. His acute observations were directed at political, social, and literary events. He turned progressively more bitter and frustrated with life, and killed himself in 1837.

Among Spain's most distinguished poets of the 1800's were José de Espronceda and Gustavo Adolfo Bécquer. Two of Espronceda's poems, *The Student from Salamanca* (1836-1839) and the unfinished *Devil World,* are the richest expressions of Spanish Romantic anguish and social protest.

Bécquer's simple, airy lyric poetry contains elements of Romanticism. He is often considered the most sensitive Spanish poet of the 1800's, and he represents the country's transition to modern poetry.

Two poets, Ramón de Campoamor and Gaspar Núñez de Arce, represented a reaction to Romantic passion. Campoamor wrote short philosophical and skeptical poems that he called *doloras* and *humoradas.* Núñez de Arce expressed an aggressive patriotism in *War Cries* (1875). Rosalía de Castro wrote delicate lyrics, mostly in Galician. Her collection of poems in Castilian, *On the*

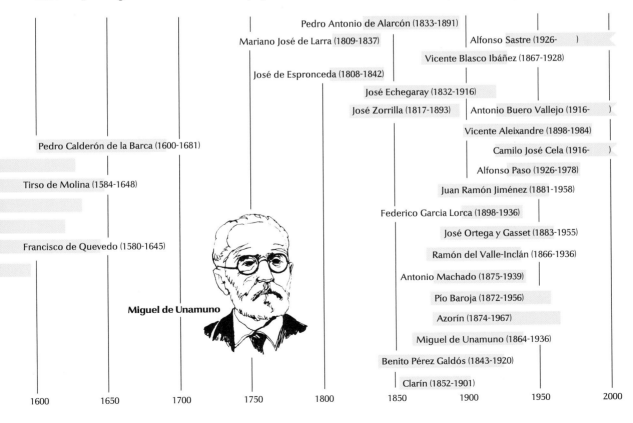

Pedro Antonio de Alarcón (1833-1891)

Mariano José de Larra (1809-1837)

Alfonso Sastre (1926-   )

Vicente Blasco Ibáñez (1867-1928)

José de Espronceda (1808-1842)

José Echegaray (1832-1916)

José Zorrilla (1817-1893)

Antonio Buero Vallejo (1916-   )

Vicente Aleixandre (1898-1984)

Pedro Calderón de la Barca (1600-1681)

Camilo José Cela (1916-   )

Alfonso Paso (1926-1978)

Tirso de Molina (1584-1648)

Juan Ramón Jiménez (1881-1958)

Federico Garcia Lorca (1898-1936)

José Ortega y Gasset (1883-1955)

Francisco de Quevedo (1580-1645)

Ramón del Valle-Inclán (1866-1936)

Antonio Machado (1875-1939)

Pío Baroja (1872-1956)

Azorín (1874-1967)

Miguel de Unamuno

Miguel de Unamuno (1864-1936)

Benito Pérez Galdós (1843-1920)

Clarín (1852-1901)

1600   1650   1700   1750   1800   1850   1900   1950   2000

Shores of the River Sar (1884), helped make her one of the most respected poets of the 1800's.

Romanticism in Catalonia led to a revival of literature in the Catalan language during the last half of the 1800's. It produced such excellent poets as Jacint Verdaguer and Joan Maragall, and such dramatists as Ángel Guimerá.

Short prose sketches of regional customs and manners reached a peak of popularity in the mid-1800's. This type of literature was called *costumbrismo,* and the writers of costumbrismo were called *costumbristas.* Costumbrista writers included Larra, Ramón de Mesonero Romanos, and Serafín Estébanez Calderón (known as El Solitario). Mesonero, who called himself El Curioso Parlante, wrote articles about Madrid and published them in several collections. Estébanez described typical scenes and people from Andalusia in articles published as *Andalusian Scenes* (1847).

Elements of the costumbrista article can be found in some realistic novels, which developed in the mid-1800's. Cecilia Böhl de Faber, who wrote under the name of Fernán Caballero, brought costumbrismo to the novel in *The Seagull* (1849). Pedro Antonio de Alarcón wrote about Andalusian characters in his charming story *The Three-Cornered Hat* (1874). Juan Valera, one of the most cultured writers of the 1800's, wrote the psychologically complex *Pepita Jiménez* (1874).

Realistic regional novels dominated the second half of the 1800's. José María de Pereda's *The Upper Cliffs* (1895) was a costumbrista novel about life on Spain's northern coast. *Marta and Maria* (1883) by Armando Palacio Valdés dealt with the conflict of mystic and worldly virtues set against the detailed description of a small town in the region of Asturias. Emilia Pardo Bazán wrote *The Ulloa Estate* (1886), a sparkling narrative of local traditions and politics in the interior of Galicia. Vicente Blasco Ibáñez earned his literary reputation in the late 1800's with *The Cabin* (1898) and other novels about life in his native Valencia. However, he gained international popularity in the early 1900's for his novel inspired by the terror of World War I, *The Four Horsemen of the Apocalypse* (1916).

The literary critic Leopoldo Alas, who wrote under the name of Clarín, created one of the best novels of the 1800's in Spain—the sensitive and powerful *La Regenta* (1884-1885). But Spain's greatest novelist of the 1800's, and the best author of fiction since Cervantes, was Benito Pérez Galdós. Galdós wrote about 80 novels and about 25 plays. In the five series of novels that make up the *Episodios nacionales,* he novelized Spanish history from the Battle of Trafalgar (1805) until the late 1800's. Many of his works were novels of ideas that dealt with religion and the structure of society. Galdós created profound characterizations—particularly his main female characters, as can be seen in his masterpiece, *Fortunata and Jacinta* (1886-1887). He showed unusual awareness of the depth of human psychology. Galdós wrote about all levels of society, and his novels provided clear insight into the life of Madrid.

The 1900's

The Generation of 1898 was a group of writers who appeared on the literary scene about the time of the Spanish-American War. These writers played an important part in the history of Spanish literature.

In the Spanish-American War, which was fought in 1898, Spain lost the last parts of its once mighty empire. The corruption of Spain's ruling class and the loss of its overseas colonies led many Spaniards to examine the nation's culture and civilization. The problem was whether Spain's cultural heritage could be adapted to the progress of modern Europe, and if it was original and creative enough to survive. From this examination of the Spanish character and past came a philosophical, historical, and artistic awakening that produced rich artistic expression.

Many types of writers contributed to the national renaissance of creative genius that dominated Spanish letters during the early 1900's. Miguel de Unamuno expressed romantic and philosophical grief in his essay *The Tragic Sense of Life* (1913), in his poetry, and in such novels as *Mist* (1914). Unamuno is often considered a forerunner of the philosophical movement called Existentialism. The unique prose of José Martínez Ruiz, who called himself Azorín, included delicate and melancholic descriptions of Spanish landscape and history. Pío Baroja became a leading Spanish novelist of the early 1900's. He showed sensitive heroes shifting between failure and triumph in *Zalacaín the Adventurer* (1909) and *The Tree of Knowledge* (1911).

The poetry of Antonio Machado portrayed the severe spirit and landscape of Castile. Ramiro de Maeztu expressed himself in biting journalism. The beautiful and original prose of Ramón María del Valle-Inclán appeared in *Autumn Sonata* (1902). He invented a drama of distortion and exaggeration called the *esperpento.* In the esperpento *Bohemian Lights* (1924), he saw Spain as a grotesque distortion of normalcy.

Spain's literary past was rediscovered, interpreted, edited, and published by a group of scholars at the Center of Historical Studies in Madrid. These scholars included Ramón Menéndez Pidal, Américo Castro, Tomás Navarro Tomás, and José Fernández Montesinos. They continued the work of Marcelino Menéndez y Pelayo, the great scholar and critic of the late 1800's.

Two fine novelists succeeded the Generation of 1898. Gabriel Miró wrote extremely lyrical prose, and Ramón Pérez de Ayala was one of the most intellectual novelists of his day. Noted essayists included the Catalan philosopher and art critic Eugenio d'Ors, and the internationally recognized philosopher, historian, and critic José Ortega y Gasset.

Modernism. While the generation of 1898 was trying to discover the spirit of Spain, lyric poetry was undergoing a renewal through a literary school called *Modernism.* This school was inspired by the work of the Nicaraguan poet Rubén Darío and the French Symbolists (see **Latin American literature** [Modernism]). The Modernists joined the richness of form, musicality, and expression of the Spanish language with new poetic concepts and created a wealth of lyric poetry.

The school of Modernism was represented by Manuel Machado and Gregorio Martínez Sierra. Although short-lived, it inspired poetry of a quality and intensity that has been unequaled in Spanish literature during the 1900's. Modernist writers included Juan Ramón Jiménez. Jiménez also wrote poetic prose, best exemplified in his beautiful *Platero and I* (1914).

Drama during the early 1900's was dominated by Jacinto Benavente. His best-known plays are the comedy *The Bonds of Interest* (1907) and the domestic tragedy *The Passion Flower* (1913). The brothers Serafín and Joaquín Álvarez Quintero wrote amusing plays about Andalusian life. The plays of José María Péman and the verse dramas of Eduardo Marquina dealt patriotically with Spanish national themes. The costumbrista plays of Carlos Arniches and the farces of Pedro Muñoz Seca pleased audiences of the time.

An outstanding figure of the period was the dramatist and poet Federico García Lorca. He wrote three intensely lyrical tragedies of rural life—*Blood Wedding* (1933), *Yerma* (1934), and *The House of Bernarda Alba* (1936).

The Generation of 1927. During the 1920's and 1930's, several poets turned to the traditional ballad or to complex, colorful gongorism for inspiration. These poets, who celebrated the 300th anniversary of Luis de Góngora's death in 1627, became known as the Generation of 1927. They included Pedro Salinas, Jorge Guillén, León Felipe, Gerardo Diego, Federico García Lorca, Dámaso Alonso, Luis Cernuda, Rafael Alberti, and Vicente Aleixandre.

In the 1930's, Miguel Hernández, Leopoldo Panero, Luis Rosales, Luis Felipe Vivanco, and Germán Bleiberg represented a return to the formal poetry of the Renaissance. But their works reveal the anguish often present in love poetry. Prose writers of note included Ramón Gómez de la Serna and Benjamín Jarnés.

Spanish literature today. The Spanish Civil War (1936-1939) caused a break in Spanish literature. Some writers, notably García Lorca, were killed and others were exiled. The world of Spanish letters took some time to recover. Many writers, including the novelists Francisco Ayala and Ramón Sender and the playwright Alejandro Casona, developed their work in exile. After the war, the dark novel *The Family of Pascual Duarte* (1942) by Camilo José Cela was published, followed by Carmen Laforet's existential novel *Nothing* (1944) and Cela's *The Hive* (1951).

Many young authors emerged in the 1950's. Their work was initially characterized by social realism but later moved into more daring and experimental areas. Some of the major novels since the mid-1950's have included *The Jarama River* (1956) by Rafael Sánchez Ferlioso, *Time of Silence* (1962) by Luis Martín Santos, Ana María Matute's *Soldiers Cry at Night* (1964), *Five Hours with Mario* (1966) by Miguel Delibes, Juan Goytisolo's *The Revenge of Count Julian* (1970), *The Saga/Flight of J. B.* (1972) by Gonzalo Torrente Ballester, *If They Tell You I Fell Down* (1973) by Juan Marsé, the four-volume *Antagonia* (1973-1981) by Luis Goytisolo, *The Truth About the Savolta Case* (1975), by Eduardo Mendoza, and Carmen Martín Gaite's *The Back Room* (1978).

Following the death of Spanish dictator Francisco Franco in 1975, Spain returned to democracy during a period from 1975 to 1982 called "the Transition." A number of novels expressed the richness of modern Spanish life following the Transition. They include *I'll Treat You Like a Queen* (1983) by Rosa Montero, *Heart So White* (1993) by Javier Marías, *Stories from the Kronen Bar* (1994), by José Angel Mañas, and *The Polish Horseman* (1991) and *Full Moon* (1997) by Antonio Muñoz Molina. Manuel Vázquez Montalbán has written a popular se-

ries of detective stories featuring a private investigator named Pepe Carvalho, who appears in such novels as *Off Side* (2000) and *Murder in the Central Committee* (2002). Arturo Pérez-Reverte has also gained popularity for such mystery and historical novels as *The Fencing Master* (1999). The theater was represented by playwrights who wrote in a wide variety of styles. Miguel Mihura wrote hilarious farces of everyday life. Antonio Buero Vallejo initiated the modern interest in serious theater with his *History of a Staircase* (1949). Alfonso Sastre wrote philosophical and political plays, while Alfonso Paso became popular for his social comedies. Fernando Arrabal gained international attention for his controversial and experimental plays. José Martín Recuerda wrote powerful studies of values in Spanish society.

Poets who began writing after 1939 tended toward simpler forms of expression than those favored by the poets of the Generation of 1927. José Luis Cano and Dionisio Ridruejo wrote thoughtful and beautiful poems. Gabriel Celaya, Blas de Otero, and others reflected social concerns similar to the novelists of the period. Some poets, including Claudio Rodríguez and Carlos Bousoño, were less interested in social realism. In the 1970's and 1980's, the generation of poets known as the *novísimos* rejected social concerns, instead displaying interest in more personal, intimate, and intellectual matters. Guillermo Carnero and Luis Antonio de Villena were poets of this generation. In the late 1900's and early 2000's, Luis García Montero, Ana Rosetti, and Alejandro Duque Amusco have written poems of great beauty and power.   David Thatcher Gies

Related articles in *World Book* include:

Outline

Questions

How did *costumbrismo* affect the novel of the mid-1800's?
When did Neoclassicism develop in Spanish literature?
What are *culteranismo* and *conceptismo*?
What are the characteristics of the picaresque novel?
How did Alfonso the Wise contribute to medieval Spanish literature?
Who were considered the two most important dramatists of the

Golden Age of Spanish literature?
What was the Generation of 1898?
How is *The Cid* different from other medieval epics?
Why did Spanish literature assume new directions in the 1700's?
What are *jarchas?*

Additional resources

Bleiberg, German, and others, eds. *Dictionary of the Literature of the Iberian Peninsula.* 2 vols. Greenwood, 1993.
Chandler, Richard E., and Schwartz, Kessel. *A New History of Spanish Literature.* Rev. ed. La. State Univ. Pr., 1991.
Debicki, Andrew P. *Spanish Poetry of the Twentieth Century.* Univ. Pr. of Ky., 1994.
Gies, David Thatcher, ed. *The Cambridge History of Spanish Literature.* Cambridge, 2004.

Spanish Main was the name English traders and pirates gave to the northern coast of South America and to the Caribbean Sea and its islands. Spain had gained control of the entire Caribbean region by 1550. *Spanish Main* comes from the term *Spanish mainland,* which referred to what are now Colombia and Venezuela. English sailors later shortened the name to *Spanish Main.*

Michael L. Conniff

Spanish moss is a hanging plant that lives from the southeastern United States to Argentina and Chile. It commonly hangs from trees, cliffs, and even telephone lines. Its grayish, hairlike stems can grow over 20 feet (6 meters) in length but usually measure 3 to 4 feet (0.9 to 1.2 meters) long. Spanish moss also has long, narrow, silver-gray leaf blades and small yellow-green flowers.

Spanish moss is not a true moss but an *epiphyte.* Epiphytes are plants that grow on other plants and make their own food. Spanish moss has no roots. Instead, it absorbs water from the air and gets nutrients from airborne dust. The plant normally reproduces through a process called *vegetative propagation.* In this process, wind tears up the plants and spreads the torn parts to other areas, where they start to grow.

People use Spanish moss flowers for decoration. Birds favor the plant's tough, flexible stems as a material for building nests. Other names for Spanish moss include *graybeard* and *Louisiana moss.* Thomas B. Croat

Scientific classification. Spanish moss belongs to the bromeliad family, Bromeliaceae. Its scientific name is *Tillandsia usneoides.*

See also **Bromeliad; Epiphyte.**

Spanish Phalanx. See **Falange Española.**

Spanish Sahara. See **Western Sahara.**

Spanish Succession, War of the. See **Succession wars.**

Spanishfly is a type of blister beetle, not a true fly. Spanishflies are found throughout Europe. They are about ¾ inch (19 millimeters) long and often are metallic green or bronze in color. A dangerous chemical called *cantharidin* can be extracted from their bodies. It is used as a *vesicant* (blistering agent) and as a skin irritant. When taken internally, cantharidin may increase a person's blood circulation. David J. Shetlar

Scientific classification. The Spanishfly is in the blister beetle family, Meloidae. It is *Lytta vesicatoria.*

Spark, Muriel (1918-2006), was a Scottish author best known for her short novels. Spark filled her fiction with witty dialogue, eccentric characters, and unusual events. These elements are often humorous, but Spark used them to explore serious moral questions.

Spark's best-known novel is *The Prime of Miss Jean Brodie* (1961). The central character is a romantic, domineering teacher at a Scottish girls' school. The analysis of this character reflects Spark's interest in unusual personalities. *The Mandelbaum Gate* (1965) is one of Spark's few long novels. Set in modern Jerusalem, its complex plot involves a large and diverse cast of characters. Her other popular short novels include *Memento Mori* (1959), *The Ballad of Peckham Rye* (1960), *The Girls of Slender Means* (1963), and *Aiding and Abetting* (2001). She also wrote the political satire *The Abbess of Crewe* (1974) and the comic novels *The Takeover* (1976), *A Far Cry from Kensington* (1988), and *The Finishing School* (2004). Her short stories were collected in *The Stories of Muriel Spark* (1985) and *Open to the Public* (1997).

Muriel Sarah Camberg was born in Edinburgh, Scotland, on Feb. 1, 1918. She married Sydney Oswald Spark, a teacher, in 1937. Spark converted to the Roman Catholic Church in 1954. She often dealt with religious issues in her fiction. Spark wrote poetry, plays, children's books, literary criticism, and *Child of Light* (1951), a biography of the English author Mary Shelley. Spark also edited the letters of several English writers of the 1800's. *Curriculum Vitae* (1993) is her autobiography. In 1993, Queen Elizabeth II made Spark a Dame Commander in the Order of the British Empire. Dame Muriel Spark died on April 13, 2006. Jane Marcus

Spark plug. See **Ignition; Automobile** (The engine diagram).

Sparkman, John Jackson (1899-1985), an Alabama Democrat, served in the United States House of Representatives from 1937 to 1947 and in the U.S. Senate from 1947 to 1979. He was the Democratic nominee for vice president of the United States in 1952. Sparkman became chairman of the Senate Foreign Relations Committee in 1975. In Congress, Sparkman generally supported the policies of the Democratic presidents except in civil rights policies. He usually backed Republican presidents Dwight D. Eisenhower, Richard M. Nixon, and Gerald R. Ford on foreign policy. Sparkman was born on Dec. 20, 1899, near Hartselle, Alabama. He died on Nov. 16, 1985.

James I. Lengle

Sparrow is the name of many small, common birds. The name comes from the Anglo-Saxon word *spearwa,* which probably was a general term for all small birds. Sparrows are found throughout most of the world. About 50 species live in North and South America.

Most American sparrows are plain, brownish birds about 6 inches (15 centimeters) long. Many are noted for their musical songs, including the *song sparrow, vesper sparrow, lark sparrow, white-crowned sparrow, white-throated sparrow, fox sparrow,* and *Lincoln's sparrow.*

Sparrows have large feet that are well-adapted for scratching for seeds, their chief food. They feed insects to their young. American sparrows build nests on the ground, in clumps of grass, in bushes, or in low trees, but seldom far from the ground. But the *chipping sparrow* nests as high as 25 feet (8 meters) above the ground in evergreens. A sparrow's nest is a compact, well-built, open structure made of grasses, plant fibers, and sometimes small twigs. The female lays four or five white eggs marked with reddish-brown. The eggs hatch in 11 to 14 days, and the young leave the nest 8 to 10 days later. Both the male and the female care for the young.

American sparrows live almost everywhere. For ex-

Song sparrow
Mealospiza melodia
Found throughout most of North America
Body length: 5 to 7 inches
(13 to 18 centimeters)

Lark sparrow
Chondestes grammacus
Found from southern Canada
to El Salvador
Body length 5 $\frac{1}{2}$ to 6 $\frac{3}{4}$ inches
(14 to 17 centimeters)

House sparrow
Passer domesticus
Found throughout the temperate
zones of the world
Body length: 5 $\frac{1}{2}$ to 6 $\frac{1}{4}$ inches
(14 to 16 centimeters)

WORLD BOOK
illustrations by
Guy Tudor

ample, song sparrows live in bushy areas, fox sparrows in forests, swamp sparrows in marshes, vesper sparrows in prairies, and sage sparrows in deserts. Those sparrows that breed in northern North America may migrate south in winter, some as far as Mexico and Central America. However, even among migrant species, older males often spend the winter near their breeding area.

The common *house sparrow* was brought to America from Europe in 1853. It now lives in most of the populated areas of Canada, the United States, Central America, and western South America.   Edward H. Burtt, Jr.

Scientific classification. American sparrows belong to the family Emberizidae. The song sparrow is *Mealospiza melodia;* Lincoln's sparrow, *M. lincolnii;* and the swamp sparrow, *M. georgiana.* The white-throated sparrow is *Zonotrichia albicollis,* and the white-crowned sparrow is *Z. leucophrys.* The chipping sparrow is *Spizella passerina;* the fox sparrow, *Passerella iliaca;* the vesper sparrow, *Pooecetes gramineus;* and the sage sparrow, *Amphispiza belli.* The house sparrow belongs to the family Passeridae. Its scientific name is *Passer domesticus.*

See also **Bird** (pictures: Birds of urban areas; Birds of grasslands); **House sparrow.**

Sparrowhawk is the name of more than 20 species of small birds related to hawks. Sparrowhawks got their name because they eat mostly sparrows and other small birds. They also prey on larger birds and small animals. Sparrowhawks live in Africa, Asia, Europe, and Australia. They have short, broad wings and a long, slim tail. These features help them swerve in the air to catch prey.

The *European sparrowhawk* lives in Africa, central Asia, and Europe. The male European sparrowhawk has a gray back and a whitish spot on the back of the neck. Its white breast is marked with reddish-brown bars. The female has a brown back and a white breast with dark gray or dark brown bars. Males measure about 12 inches (30 centimeters) long, and females measure

about 15 inches (38 centimeters). Most European sparrowhawks build their nests in evergreen trees. The female lays three to six whitish eggs spotted with brown.

The American kestrel is sometimes called the American sparrowhawk. It is actually more closely related to falcons than to hawks (see **Kestrel**).   Richard D. Brown

Scientific classification. Sparrowhawks belong to the family Accipitridae. The scientific name for the European sparrowhawk is *Accipiter nisus.*

See also **Hawk.**

E. V. Breeze Jones, Bruce Coleman Inc.

A sparrowhawk preys on sparrows and other small birds. Sparrowhawks live in Africa, Asia, Australia, and Europe.

Spars. See Coast Guard, United States (Women in the Coast Guard).

Sparta, also called Lacedaemon, LAS *ih DEE muhn* or LAS *ih DY mohn,* the capital of Laconia, was once the most powerful city-state of ancient Greece. It was famous for its military power and its loyal soldiers. The greatest honor that could come to a Spartan was to die in defense of the country. Endurance, a scorn of luxuries, and unyielding firmness are still spoken of as Spartan virtues.

The land. Sparta lay in a lovely, sheltered valley on the bank of the Eurotas River (see map). It was protected on three sides by mountains. The climate was mild, and the soil was fertile and well watered. Sparta had few mineral resources. Spartans obtained marble and a little iron from nearby Mount Taygetus.

The people belonged to three classes. The Spartans themselves were descended from the Dorians, a people who invaded the Greek peninsula in the 1100's B.C. They were the ruling class of Sparta and were the only ones who had full rights of citizenship. They enslaved the earlier Greek peoples of Laconia, the Achaeans and Ionians. These enslaved Greeks, known as *helots* (pronounced *HEHL uhts),* outnumbered the Spartans. Some of the non-Spartan Greeks escaped enslavement. They were not citizens, but they lived in Sparta as free people. This group was known as the *perioeci* (also spelled *perioikoi,* pronounced *PEHR ee OY koy).*

The numbers of the three classes during Sparta's long history are not well known. Some historians estimate that at the height of Spartan power there were about 10,000 citizens, an unknown number of perioeci, and about 200,000 helots.

Way of life. Spartan citizens could engage only in agriculture. A few aristocrats owned their own land. However, a majority of the citizens held state-owned plots. Citizens who could not make enough from their estate to support their family and pay the taxes lost their land to someone who could make it pay. They also lost their citizenship. Because citizens could not carry on manufacturing or trade, the perioeci took over these pursuits. Some of them grew wealthy.

The helots farmed the soil, and they had to give a fixed amount of produce, probably half of what they grew, to their master. The helots bitterly resented their lot, and revolts were not unusual. Once a year, the Spartans officially declared war on the helots, so that they could kill any who seemed rebellious without breaking the law against murder.

Every Spartan male belonged to the state from the time of his birth. A committee of elders inspected each male infant. Those who were not physically sound were taken to the mountains and left to die of exposure to the elements. A boy was left to the care of his mother until he was 7 years of age, when he was enrolled in a company of 15 members, all of whom were kept under strict discipline. From the age of 7, every boy had to take his meals with his company in a public dining hall. The bravest boy in a company was made captain. The others obeyed his commands and bore such punishments as he decided they should have.

When the boys were 12, their undergarments were taken away and only one outer garment a year was allowed them. Their beds consisted of the tops of reeds, which they gathered with their own hands and without knives. Spartans did not consider the arts of reading and writing necessary. Boys learned the *Iliad* and songs of war and religion, but leaping, running, wrestling, and wielding a weapon with grace and accuracy were held much more important. Between the ages of 20 and 30, Spartan men served as cadets who policed the country, kept the helots in order, and exacted disciplined obedience from the enslaved people.

At 30, a Spartan male attained full maturity and enjoyed the rights and duties of citizenship. He might marry, attend meetings of the assembly, and hold public office. He continued to train and eat with the members of his company. At 60, his military career ended, and he worked either in public affairs or in training the young. As a result of this system, the Spartan men became tough, proud, disciplined, and noted for obstinate conservatism and for brevity and directness of speech.

Spartan women, on the other hand, lived the freest life of any women in Greece. As girls, they engaged in athletics, and as women, they ran their own households. They engaged in business, and many became wealthy and influential. Aristotle tells us that women owned two-fifths of the land in Sparta.

History. The Dorians who settled in Sparta extended their control over all Laconia at an early date. In the 700's B.C., they conquered Messenia, the rich farming region to the west of Mount Taygetus. Sparta failed to conquer the cities of Arcadia but forced them to enter the Peloponnesian League. The members of the league were obliged to follow Sparta in war. By 500 B.C., this league included most of the cities in southern and central Greece.

Sparta conquered Athens, the leader of the powerful Athenian Empire, in the hard-fought Peloponnesian War. In 404 B.C., the Athenians were forced to accept a humiliating peace treaty. But the leadership won by Sparta was short-lived. The Spartans ruled over the other Greek states so cruelly that they revolted. At the battle of Leuctra, in 371 B.C., the people of Thebes decisively defeated the Spartans. Thebes then liberated the Messenians and crippled Spartan power forever. In 146 B.C., Sparta came under the control of Rome.

There is a modern town of Sparta near the site of the ancient city. It was laid out about 1835 and made the capital of the modern political division of Laconia. Excavations have been made on the old site, and much valu-

WORLD BOOK maps

Sparta was the most powerful city-state of ancient Greece, and the capital of Laconia. By 500 B.C., Sparta had forced nearby city-states to enter the Peloponnesian League.

able material has been discovered from the early city's history.   Peter Krentz

Related articles in *World Book* include:

Dorians	Lycurgus
Greece, Ancient (Government;	Lysander
History)	Messenia
Leonidas I	Peloponnesian War

Spartacus, *SPAHR tuh kuhs* (? -71 B.C.), led a great slave revolt against the Roman Republic. The rebellion lasted from 73 B.C. to 71 B.C.

Spartacus was born in Thrace, a region northeast of Greece. He was a member of a group of nomadic herders and later served in the Roman army. Spartacus deserted the army but was captured and enslaved. The Romans trained him as a gladiator to fight other gladiators and wild beasts in the arena for the people's entertainment (see **Gladiator**).

In 73 B.C., Spartacus and other gladiators rebelled against Roman authority at the town of Capua, in what is now southern Italy. The rebels took refuge on nearby Mount Vesuvius and soon organized an army of about 70,000 runaway slaves. Commanded by Spartacus, the army defeated the Roman forces and gained control over much of central and southern Italy.

In 72 B.C., the rebels divided into two groups. The Romans defeated one group in Italy. Spartacus led the other rebels to victory against a Roman army in Cisalpine Gaul (now northern Italy). In 71 B.C., Spartacus's army returned to the south. Roman forces commanded by Marcus Licinius Crassus defeated the rebel army (see **Crassus, Marcus Licinius**). Spartacus was killed in the battle.   William G. Sinnigen

Spartina, *spahr TYN uh,* is the name of a group of 16 species of grasses native to North America, South America, western Europe, and northern Africa. Most of these species grow primarily in marshes.

A species of spartina called *smooth cordgrass* is the dominant plant in marshes along the Atlantic and Gulf coasts of the United States. Along the shoreline, it usually grows from about 3 to 7 feet (1 to 2 meters) high. Smooth cordgrass spreads quickly and can gradually turn *tidal flats* (land uncovered at low tide) into marshes. Such marshes provide food and shelter for the young of commercially important species of fish. The marshes also help protect shorelines from the erosive forces of waves generated by storms and hurricanes.

WORLD BOOK illustration by
Bob Bampton, Bernard Thornton Artists

Smooth cordgrass is a common species of spartina.

People have introduced spartina to coastal areas around the world to create or restore marshes.

         Irving A. Mendelssohn

Scientific classification. Spartina grasses make up the genus *Spartina* in the grass family, Poaceae or Gramineae. The scientific name for smooth cordgrass is *S. alterniflora.*

Spastic paralysis is a condition in which there is poor control over the muscles as a result of damage to the *central nervous system* (brain and spinal cord). The damage that causes the condition can occur at or before birth. Spastic paralysis can also develop after birth if an infection such as meningitis damages the brain, or if damage results from strokes, skull fractures, or other injuries.

The part of the central nervous system that is damaged and the amount of damage done determine which muscles are affected and how severely. Sometimes the damage is so slight that the individual may have only a little clumsiness, a slight loss of balance, or a slight speech difficulty. In severe cases, victims cannot walk. Or they may walk on their toes with their feet turned inward, their knees together, and with one leg crossing over in front of the other, in the typical "scissors gait." Spastic paralysis can affect all the muscles. The face, the tongue, and even the muscles that control breathing may be affected. This may result in uncontrollable grimacing, drooling, and difficulty in speaking.

Some people suffering from spastic paralysis are completely normal, except for their difficulties in controlling the affected muscles. However, in other cases, brain injury affects intelligence. Even mental retardation may occur. Nevertheless, some people with spastic paralysis have above-average intelligence.

The damage to the nervous system cannot be cured, but the use of the muscles can be improved through surgery, training, and the use of crutches and braces. Spastic patients can be taught to speak more effectively, to care for themselves, and to earn their own living. In the mid-1970's, surgeons began using brain pacemakers to treat spastic paralysis. The pacemaker electrically stimulates the *cerebellum,* a part of the brain, and helps relieve spastic paralysis in some patients.

The spastic patient should be treated as a normal person, except for the special training that may be required to improve muscle use. For example, spastic children should be encouraged to play with other children. People should understand that spastic paralysis is not a communicable disease, that it is not inherited, and that it is not a form of mental illness.   Marianne Schuelein

See also **Cerebral palsy.**

Spavin, *SPAV uhn,* is a common name for two unrelated diseases that affect the hocks of horses. The hock is the ankle joint of the hind leg. *Bone spavin,* or *true spavin,* is a bony growth usually on the inner, lower part of the joint. It is caused by a lack of certain minerals in the bones. *Bog spavin* is a swelling of a capsule of tissue of the main joint. It is believed to exist at birth and seldom causes trouble. The two diseases are seldom curable. But bone spavin can be treated, often by corrective shoeing of the horse, to end lameness and to keep the growth from enlarging.   Steven D. Price

Spawn is a word that refers to the eggs of fishes, mollusks, amphibians, and other animals. Usually such eggs are produced in great numbers because many are eaten by aquatic animals. The eggs do not have shells and must be kept in water to prevent them from drying out. The eggs of certain fishes, particularly the sturgeon, are used to make caviar. Spawn from fishes is also called *roe,* particularly when used as human food. See also **Caviar; Fish** (How fish reproduce); **Salmon** (The life of a salmon); **Sturgeon.**   John J. Poluhowich

SPCA. See Society for the Prevention of Cruelty to Animals.

Speaker is an electric device that reproduces sound. Speakers form part of stereophonic sound systems, radios, cassette players, and television sets. They also are part of public address systems and equipment used to amplify sound created by musicians.

Most speakers have three main parts: (1) a coil of wire called a *voice coil,* (2) a permanent magnet, and (3) a cone-shaped piece of paper or plastic called a *diaphragm.* Waves of electric current from an amplifier pass through the voice coil, producing varying magnetic forces in the coil. The magnetic forces move the coil back and forth within the permanent magnet in rapid vibrations. The diaphragm, attached to the voice coil, vibrates with it. The vibrations of the diaphragm make vibrations in the air. These air vibrations are sound waves.

Some equipment has several speakers, each of which reproduces either lower-pitched or higher-pitched sounds. A speaker that reproduces lower-pitched sounds is a *woofer.* A speaker that reproduces higher-pitched sounds is a *tweeter.* In general, a system of woofers and tweeters provides sound reproduction of higher quality than a single speaker. Speakers in such systems are mounted in wooden cabinets. The size and shape of these cabinets can influence the tone quality of the sounds.   Ken C. Pohlmann

See also **Radio** (The speaker); **Stereophonic sound system.**

Speaker is the presiding officer in the lower house of several national, state, and provincial legislatures. The duties of the office differ in various legislatures.

In the United States, the speaker of the House of Representatives can wield great power. The speaker is the leader of his or her political party in the House, as well as the presiding officer. The speaker need not be a member of the House, but no nonmember has ever held the post. The speaker is expected to use the office to promote the party. He or she ranks next after the vice president in order of presidential succession.

The early speakers considered themselves simply as presiding officers and tried to be impartial. Henry Clay, who was elected speaker in 1811, started the practice of using the office for party purposes. The office gained much political force under the strong personalities of Thomas B. Reed, who served from 1889 to 1891 and again from 1895 to 1899, and Joseph G. Cannon, who served from 1903 to 1911. At times, the speaker has been considered almost as important as the president.

In 1910, the speaker was removed from the Committee on Rules, and the speaker's official right to appoint committees was taken away. Committee chairmen became more important than before, as they took over much of the power that had been lost by the speaker. In the 1970's, the speaker's powers were increased, making the speaker more important in national legislation. Another man with a forceful personality, Newt Gingrich, served as speaker from 1995 to 1999 and was one of the most powerful speakers since 1910. He demonstrated his power, in part, by persuading his fellow Republicans to allow him to choose the heads of key House committees. For a list of speakers and other information, see **House of Representatives.**

In the United Kingdom, a speaker has presided over the House of Commons since at least 1377. The speaker should be a model of impartiality. He or she must rule according to the will of the majority but never permit the minority to be abused. The House elects each new speaker. It is the custom to reelect the same speaker in all Parliaments until the person dies or retires.

The office of speaker in the House of Commons has great dignity. When the speaker retires, he or she becomes a member of the nobility.   Kenneth Janda

Speaker, Tris (1888-1958), an American baseball player, was known as the "Gray Eagle" because of his gray hair and his speed in playing center field. Speaker revolutionized outfield defense by playing close to the infield and catching balls that normally fell in for base hits. His great speed enabled him to run back and catch balls hit over his head. Speaker holds the American League record for career putouts by an outfielder with 6,794. He had a powerful throwing arm and led American League outfielders in assists for five seasons. In addition, Speaker holds the major league record for two-base hits with 793.

Tristram E. Speaker was born on April 4, 1888, in Hubbard, Texas. He played with the Boston Red Sox from 1907 to 1915 and with the Cleveland Indians from 1916 to 1926. He also managed the Indians from 1919 to 1926. Speaker had a lifetime batting average of .344. Speaker was elected to the National Baseball Hall of Fame in 1937. He died on Dec. 8, 1958.   Jack Lang

Speaking in tongues. See Pentecostal churches.

Spear is one of the oldest weapons known to human beings. People have used spears for hunting and in warfare since prehistoric times. A spear consists of a long pole or shaft with a sharply pointed head. The earliest spears were wooden shafts that had one end sharpened to a point. Later spears had heads made of animal bone, chipped stone, bronze, and iron.

In warfare, spears can be used in two basic ways. They can either be hurled or used for stabbing. Ancient Greek warriors often carried two spears—a light spear for throwing and a heavier one for close combat.

Throughout history, various types of spears have been used by infantry and cavalry. For example, spears as long as 20 feet (6 meters) were carried by Greek foot soldiers and helped make the *phalanx,* introduced by the Greeks in the 600's B.C., an effective military formation (see **Army** [Ancient armies]). A similar weapon, known as a *pike,* became popular with infantry during the Renaissance in Europe. During the Middle Ages, which began about A.D. 400, knights on horseback fought with strong, heavy spears called *lances.* Lances were widely used among European cavalry soldiers until about 1600.

The use of spears for close combat declined during the 1700's, with the increasing popularity of the bayonet. Today, spears are still used for hunting, fishing, and warfare in some parts of the world.   Joseph Goering

See also **Javelin; Spearfishing.**

Speare, Elizabeth George (1908-1994), was an American author of historical fiction for children. Her novels *The Witch of Blackbird Pond* (1958) and *The Bronze Bow* (1961) won the 1959 and 1962 Newbery medals. *The Witch of Blackbird Pond* is a romantic novel set in the late 1680's that portrays the unrest in New England during the era of the witch trials. *The Bronze Bow* is a re-creation of events in the Middle East during the time of Jesus Christ.

Speare's first novel was *Calico Captive* (1957), based on a true story about a New England girl and her family who were kidnapped by Indians and taken to Canada in the mid-1700's. *The Sign of the Beaver* (1983) is set in Maine during the 1700's. It is a sympathetic account of the conflict between Indian values and the values of the early settlers as well as the story of a friendship between two boys of different backgrounds. Speare also wrote the nonfiction *Life in Colonial America* (1963) and the adult novel *Prospering* (1967). In 1989, she received the Laura Ingalls Wilder Award for her contribution to children's literature. Speare was born on Nov. 11, 1908, in Melrose, Massachusetts. She died on Nov. 15, 1994.

Jill P. May

Spearfishing is the sport of hunting fish underwater with a spear or a gun that shoots a spear. Spearfishing enthusiasts hunt in rivers, lakes, and oceans in many parts of the world. They use the fish chiefly as food. Some biologists use spearfishing techniques when marking fish for research purposes, but these scientists do not harm the fish.

Basic spearfishing equipment includes a face mask, a *snorkel* (breathing tube), swim fins, and one of several kinds of hunting devices. Such devices include (1) pole spears, (2) powered spear guns, and (3) Hawaiian slings.

Pole spears, the simplest spearfishing devices, are fiberglass, metal, or wooden rods that measure up to 10 feet (3 meters) long. They have one or more sharp metal points at one end. The hunter jabs the spear into the fish or shoots it forward using an attached elastic loop.

Rubber-powered spear guns are the most widely used devices for spearfishing. A steel spear from 2 to 6 feet (0.6 to 1.8 meters) long rests on top of the barrel of the gun. The spear is held in place by a catch connected to the trigger. The front end of the gun has one or more rubber loops attached to it. The hunter stretches the

loops back and hooks them into notches in the spear. When the hunter pulls the trigger, the spear is released and the loops propel it forward with great force. Other types of spear guns are powered by springs, compressed air or gas, or an explosive charge.

Hawaiian slings consist of a short, open tube with an elastic loop fastened across one end. The hunter shoots a steel spear from this device much as a person shoots a pebble from a slingshot. The spear measures about 6 feet (1.8 meters) long, and its shaft fits through the tube and rests against the loop. The hunter grasps the tube with one hand and holds the loop and the spear with the other. To fire the spear, the hunter stretches the loop and releases it.

Spearheads have sharp hooks called *barbs*. The barbs hold the spear in place after it has penetrated a fish. A line attaches a spear to a spear gun and prevents a speared fish from escaping. A spearhead containing an explosive charge is used only to protect the hunter from a shark or to take very large fish.

Most spearfishing enthusiasts can dive to a depth of about 20 feet (6 meters). However, they must return to the surface for breath after less than a minute. Some of the more skilled divers can go as deep as 100 feet (30 meters) and stay underwater for about two minutes. A snorkel enables hunters to swim at the surface of the water and spot their prey before diving. Some people who do spearfishing use *scuba* (*s*elf-*c*ontained *u*nderwater *b*reathing *a*pparatus) equipment. Scuba divers breathe air from metal tanks strapped on their backs. They can stay underwater for as long as an hour.

In certain areas of the world, the law prohibits spearfishing with scuba gear. In some areas, powered guns are outlawed. Several states of the United States prohibit all spearfishing. Arthur H. Ullrich, Jr.

See also **Skin diving.**

Spearmint is a type of mint plant that grows in most of the temperate regions of the world. It yields an oil

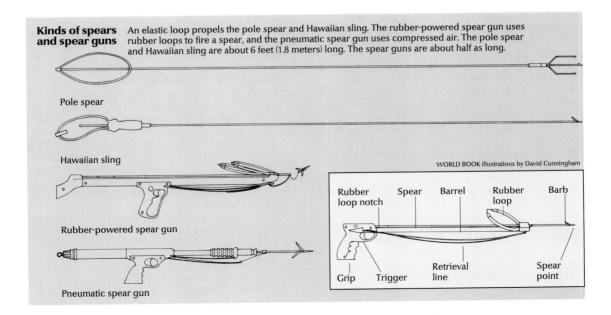

Kinds of spears and spear guns An elastic loop propels the pole spear and Hawaiian sling. The rubber-powered spear gun uses rubber loops to fire a spear, and the pneumatic spear gun uses compressed air. The pole spear and Hawaiian sling are about 6 feet (1.8 meters) long. The spear guns are about half as long.

Pole spear

Hawaiian sling

WORLD BOOK illustrations by David Cunningham

Rubber-powered spear gun

Pneumatic spear gun

Rubber loop notch   Spear   Barrel   Rubber loop   Barb

Grip   Trigger   Retrieval line   Spear point

used in making perfumes, medicine, chewing gum, candies, and mint jelly or sauce. It has smooth, erect stems 1 to 2 feet (30 to 61 centimeters) high, topped with spikes of lavender or white flowers. Most spearmints in the United States grow in Idaho, Indiana, Michigan, Washington, and Wisconsin.

Lyle E. Craker

WORLD BOOK illustration by Lorraine Epstein

Spearmint

Scientific classification. The spearmint belongs to the mint family, Lamiaceae or Labiatae. Its scientific name is *Mentha spicata.*

Special Drawing Rights are reserve assets entered in the books of the International Monetary Fund (IMF) as credits for member nations. A member may use this special account to obtain needed foreign currency from another member. Special Drawing Rights are often called "SDR's" or "paper gold." They are not real money and have no gold backing, but they have a full guarantee of gold value. Member nations may transfer SDR's among themselves to settle debts.

The IMF first created Special Drawing Rights in 1969 to supplement international reserves of gold and national currencies, especially the United States dollar. SDR's represented a more reliable and internationally better controlled medium of exchange. Gold supplies could no longer meet the demand for reserve backing.

In addition, the dollar had two drawbacks. Some Europeans thought its use as an international currency gave the United States too much power in international finance. Some Americans thought a dollar-based exchange placed too much international responsibility on U.S. domestic economic policy.   Robert M. Stern

See also **International Monetary Fund; Money** (International finance).

Special education is instruction designed to help both disabled and gifted children use their full learning ability. The youngsters who need such education to get the most from school are called *exceptional children.*

In the past, many people thought that the best way to help children with disabilities was to wait until they were 6 or 7 years old to educate them and then educate them in classrooms or schools separate from nondisabled children. Today, however, most educators believe children with disabilities need special attention early in life. Most children with disabilities and children at great risk of being disabled receive educational services during the preschool years. Special education services for some children begin soon after birth.

Most educators also believe that children with disabilities and nondisabled children should be taught together whenever possible. Isolating children with disabilities may lower their self-esteem and may reduce their ability to deal with other people. In addition, nondisabled children can learn much about personal courage and perseverance from children with disabilities.

The practice of integrating children with disabilities into regular school programs is called *mainstreaming.* Students with disabilities attend special classrooms or

schools only if their need for very specialized services makes mainstreaming impossible.

Many children with disabilities attend regular classes most of the school day. They work with a specially trained teacher for part of each day to overcome their disability. These sessions may be held in a classroom called a *resource room,* which may be equipped with such materials as braille typewriters and relief maps for blind students. Other students with disabilities attend special classes most of the day but join the rest of the children for certain activities. For example, youngsters with mental retardation may join other children who do not have retardation for art and physical education.

In the United States, the Education for All Handicapped Children Act of 1975 and the 1990 amendments to the act support special education. They require the states to provide free special education for all children with disabilities from birth to 21 years of age. The act also directs that these children be taught in the "least restrictive environment" possible, given their special needs. About 7 percent of the nation's children need special education because they have physical or mental disabilities or are emotionally disturbed. Between 3 and 5 percent of U.S. children could benefit from special education programs because they are gifted. Federal law encourages the states to establish programs for gifted children. In Canada, each province establishes its own guidelines for special education programs.

Children with physical disabilities may be unable to walk; have difficulty hearing or seeing; or have such illnesses as kidney failure, cancer, or heart disease. Many need special education only part of the time because, with certain equipment, they do well in regular classrooms. For example, a child in a wheelchair may need a desk that has been altered and laboratory equipment placed at a level the child can reach. Children with poor vision may require books with large print.

Other physical disabilities may require especially intensive instruction. Deaf children, for example, need training to learn lip reading and sign language. Many blind children learn braille. Children with physical disabilities often can participate with the nondisabled when they are taught to use computers and other computer-based instruments. These devices allow children with physical disabilities to communicate efficiently.

Children with mental disabilities may have mental retardation, or they may have normal intelligence but be hampered by a learning disability.

Children with mental retardation learn more slowly than other children. Educators have designed special programs to teach students with mild mental retardation such subjects as reading, writing, and arithmetic. Children with moderate or severe mental retardation must have special training to prepare them for employment and for caring for themselves and their homes when they become adults.

Children with learning disabilities may have average or even superior intelligence, but they have difficulty mastering certain skills. Most learning disabilities are due to minor *dysfunctions* (abnormalities) of the central nervous system. Such dysfunctions interfere with the brain's ability to use information transmitted by the senses. Many children with learning disabilities have great difficulty learning to read, spell, or write, or to solve arithmetic problems. Others are *hyperactive.* These children cannot sit still in class and have trouble controlling their behavior. Most such children succeed in regular classes if given special help to overcome their disabilities.

Children with emotional disturbances have great problems relating to other people in socially acceptable ways. Some children with emotional disturbances are withdrawn and may not even speak to other people. Other troubled students may argue, fight, or otherwise disrupt classroom activities. Some emotionally disturbed children should be hospitalized for psychiatric care. However, many of these children are able to attend regular schools if they receive special education and psychological counseling.

Gifted children may be unusually intelligent or have exceptional ability in art, mathematics, or another area. Special education helps such children develop their talents while they get a well-rounded education. Many schools provide special activities and materials that encourage gifted children to develop at their own rate in regular classrooms.   Jeannette E. Fleischner

Related articles in *World Book* include:

Attention deficit disorder	Education (Special education)
Blindness (Education and training)	Gifted children
	Learning disabilities
Deafness (Education)	Mental retardation
Disability	(Treatment)
Dyslexia	

Additional resources

Reynolds, Cecil R., and Fletcher-Janzen, Elaine, eds. *Concise Encyclopedia of Special Education.* 2nd ed. Wiley, 2002.
Sanna, Ellyn. *Special Education Teacher.* Mason Crest, 2003. A career guide.

Special Libraries Association is an international organization of professional librarians and information specialists who serve institutions that use or produce specialized information. Such institutions include companies, associations, government agencies, museums, and colleges and universities. The Special Libraries Association, also called the SLA, helps its members develop professionally and assists them with research and public relations.

The Special Libraries Association publishes a monthly newsletter, a quarterly journal, and a variety of books, manuals, and self-study course materials. The organization was founded in 1909. Headquarters are in Washington, D.C.   Critically reviewed by the Special Libraries Association

Special Olympics is a year-round international program of athletic training and competition for children and adults with mental retardation. Special Olympics features sports events modeled on those of the Olympic Games. More than 90 countries take part in Special Olympics programs.

Special Olympics provides opportunities for training and competition in such sports as basketball, bowling, canoeing, cycling, floor hockey, gymnastics, horseback riding, ice skating, powerlifting, roller skating, skiing, soccer, softball, swimming, table tennis, team handball, tennis, track and field, and volleyball. Participants compete in different divisions depending on their age and ability. The athletes train in programs offered through their schools or communities.

In the United States, Special Olympics games at local, area, and state levels are held every year. In other coun-

tries, national Special Olympics Games are held every year or every other year. The International Special Olympics Games consist of summer games and winter games, which occur by turns every two years.

Special Olympics was created in 1968 by Eunice Kennedy Shriver, executive vice president of the Joseph P. Kennedy, Jr., Foundation. Headquarters of Special Olympics International are in Washington, D.C.
Critically reviewed by Special Olympics International

Special prosecutor. See Independent counsel.
Species. See Classification, Scientific (Groups in classification).
Specific gravity. See Density.
Specific heat. See Heat (Changes in temperature; pictures).
Spectator, The. See Addison, Joseph.
Spectrometer, *spehk TRAHM uh tuhr,* is an instrument that spreads out light and other types of electromagnetic waves into a spectrum and displays it for study. The atoms or molecules of all substances give off light when heated to high temperatures. The pattern of light given off is different for every substance. No two substances have the same spectrum. Thus, experts can identify a substance or determine its chemical composition by analyzing its spectrum.

Spectrometers are used to examine a wide range of materials. Industrial chemists use these instruments to detect impurities in steel and other metal alloys. Spectrometers enable astronomers to study the chemical composition of the stars. Spectrometers are also used to identify chemical substances found at the scene of a crime and to detect pollutants in the air and water.

A typical spectrometer is enclosed by a container that

AP/Wide World
The Special Olympics sponsors a World Summer Games competition that includes such team sports as soccer, *shown here.*

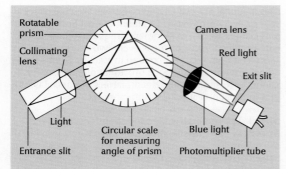

Rotatable prism

Collimating lens

Camera lens

Red light

Exit slit

Light

Circular scale for measuring angle of prism

Blue light

Entrance slit

Photomultiplier tube

WORLD BOOK diagram

How a typical spectrometer works. Light enters through a narrow slit, as shown in the diagram above. A collimating lens causes the light to become a beam of parallel rays. A prism then spreads the rays into a pattern of different colors, such as blue and red. Only one color of light can pass through the exit slit at a time, and it is focused on the slit by a camera lens. The prism must be rotated to bring the other color into the slit. A photomultiplier tube measures the brightness of light leaving the slit.

keeps out light not being studied. Light enters through the narrow entrance slit and passes through a *collimating lens*. This lens causes the light to become a beam of parallel light rays. The parallel light then travels through a prism, where it is broken up into a spectrum. A lens focuses the light on the exit slit. Only one color of light can pass through this slit at a time. Therefore, the prism must be rotated to bring the other colors into the exit slit and to scan the entire spectrum. A circular scale records the angle of the prism, from which the wavelength of the light can be determined.

Some spectrometers have a flat mirror called a *grating* instead of a prism. The surface of a grating is lined with thousands of narrow, parallel grooves. Upon striking a grating, a parallel beam of light spreads out into a spectrum. See **Diffraction** (Uses of diffraction).

There are several kinds of spectrometers. A *spectroscope* has a telescope for visual observation of a spectrum. A *spectrograph* photographs a spectrum by recording its image on a photographic plate. A *spectrophotometer* scans a spectrum and measures the bright-

ness of each of its colors. Many spectrophotometers have a *photomultiplier tube* that produces an electric current proportional in strength to the brightness of the light that is being measured. Sandra M. Faber

See also **Light** (The spectrum of light sources); **Mass spectrometry; Telescope** (What telescopes do).

Spectrophotometer. See **Color** (The CIE system of color specification); **Crime laboratory** (Analyzing the evidence); **Spectrometer.**

Spectrum is a band of visible light or any other kind of electromagnetic radiation arranged in order of wavelength. Electromagnetic radiation can be thought of as consisting of waves of electricity and magnetism. Wavelength is the distance between successive wave crests.

A rainbow is a spectrum: Its colors appear in the order of their wavelength. Red has the longest visible wavelength, violet the shortest. The energy of electromagnetic radiation is directly related to its wavelength: the longer the wavelength, the lower the energy. Thus, particles of red light have less energy than particles of violet light. Particles of light are known as *photons*.

Any object can absorb and *emit* (give off) electromagnetic radiation. The spectrum of this radiation depends on the substance's composition and temperature. Thus, by studying the spectrum of an object, scientists can determine its composition and temperature.

About 1915, the Danish physicist Niels Bohr explained what happens when an atom absorbs or emits electromagnetic radiation. He based his explanation on the most common kind of hydrogen atom, which consists of one proton at the center and one electron in an orbit around the proton. The electron can occupy any of an infinite number of possible orbits. Each orbit is associated with a given level of energy, with lower-energy orbits nearer the proton. When the electron absorbs electromagnetic radiation, it jumps from a lower orbit—one nearer the proton—to a higher orbit. When the electron jumps from a higher orbit to a lower orbit, it emits electromagnetic radiation. Jay M. Pasachoff

See also **Electromagnetic waves; Light** (The spectrum of light sources); **Rainbow; Spectrometer.**

Speech has several definitions. It may mean the act of speaking, the forms of speech, the content of speech or what is spoken, the language of a nation or group of na-

WORLD BOOK diagrams by Precision Graphics

White light

Emission lines on screen

Cloud of gas

Prism

Emission lines

Absorption lines

Prism

Absorption lines on screen

The spectrum of light from a gas cloud reveals the composition of the gas. White light, containing all the colors of the rainbow, enters the cloud. The gas absorbs light energy that represents certain colors. Some of the light that continues forward passes through a slit in a wall and is broken up by a prism. When the light strikes a screen, the absorbed colors are replaced by dark *absorption lines.* The gas also loses energy by sending out light representing the same colors. Light viewed from the side of the cloud appears as *emission lines.* These absorption and emission lines identify the gas as hydrogen.

tions, or the dialect peculiar to a region or locality.

The act of speaking uses an *audible code* and a *visible code* to produce messages. The audible code consists of *phonation,* the creation of sound, and *articulation,* the shaping of sound into understandable language. The visible code consists of eye contact, facial expressions, hand gestures, and other types of body movement.

The forms of speech may be informal or formal. Informal speeches include conversation and storytelling. Formal speeches include lectures, debates, orations, dramas, and broadcasts. Speeches may inform, persuade, or entertain.

The content of speech includes *what* is spoken whether it is from memory, text, or *impromptu* (without preparation). A speech may contain a speaker's ideas or arguments, supporting evidence, emotional pleas, or remarks that attract an audience's attention, such as jokes.

Language is the different sounds made by people to communicate. *Dialects* are variations in pronunciation, word choice, or accent between groups of people who speak a common language.

The average child learns to speak by imitating other people. It is important that a child hear proper speech. Parents should note any speech difficulties, such as lisping or stuttering, in their children. If such difficulties occur, parents should take the child to a competent authority on speech problems. Speech clinics can offer helpful advice.   James M. Copeland

Related articles in *World Book* include:

Communication
Dialect
Language
Lisping

Pronunciation
Public speaking
Speech therapy
Stuttering

Speech, Freedom of. See Freedom of speech.

Speech therapy, also called *speech-language pathology,* is a profession concerned with the evaluation and treatment of speech and language problems. Experts in this field are called *speech-language pathologists.* They work with children and adults whose speech interferes with communication, calls attention to itself, and frustrates both speaker and listener. These specialists also do research on the normal development and production of speech and language, and on the causes of speech disorders. Speech-language pathologists who work with patients are sometimes known as speech therapists or speech clinicians.

Types and causes of speech defects. There are five main types of speech defects: (1) articulation problems, such as the inability to produce certain sounds; (2) stuttering, *cluttering* (rapid, slurred speech), and other fluency problems; (3) voice disorders, including problems of pitch, voice quality, and volume; (4) delayed speech, characterized by a child's slow language development; and (5) *aphasia,* the partial or total loss of the ability to speak or understand language.

About 6 percent of the people in the United States have some kind of speech defect. Of that group, about 60 percent have articulation problems, 12 percent have fluency difficulties, and 8 percent have voice disorders. The remaining 20 percent have delayed speech, aphasia, or multiple speech problems.

Some speech defects result from a physical condition, such as brain damage, cleft palate, a disease of the larynx, or partial or complete deafness. Other speech defects may be related to a person's environment. For example, a child who receives little encouragement to talk at home may not develop normal speech skills. Severe emotional conflicts, such as pressure to succeed or a lack of love, can also lead to speech difficulties.

Diagnosis. In many schools, speech-language pathologists test students regularly for speech disorders. If students have a speech problem, they receive therapy at the school, or they go to a speech clinic for treatment. Many physicians, psychologists, and teachers refer people with speech defects to such clinics.

Speech-language pathologists diagnose their patients' speech problems and try to learn their causes. They take detailed case histories and give their patients special speech, language, and hearing tests. A patient may need medical or psychological treatment in addition to speech therapy.

Treatment. The speech-language pathologist first gains the confidence of the patient. For the best results, the individual should enjoy being with the therapist and want to follow instructions.

The method of treatment varies from case to case. The speech-language pathologist must consider the age of the patient, the case history, the type of speech disorder, and the data gained during therapy. The therapist talks to the patient's family, teachers, and others who have close contact. The success of the treatment depends largely on the cooperation of these people.

Most children develop speech habits until about the age of 8. Thus, when working with a young patient, the therapist uses methods that help stimulate the development of good speech habits. With older patients, the therapist must use corrective measures. First, the patients must be helped to identify their speech problems and to tell the difference between their speech and normal speech. Many therapists use audio and video recording machines. Patients who mispronounce the "r" sound may be able to identify their error by listening to themselves on a tape recorder and by watching the movement of their lips and tongue on a video screen. The therapist pronounces the sound correctly, and the patient hears and sees the difference. During the second stage of treatment, the therapist teaches the patient new speech skills. Tongue exercises and speech drills may be used. After the patients have improved their speech, they learn to use their skills in everyday situations.

Speech therapy may be given individually or in groups. Therapists put patients in groups if they think that contact with people who have similar defects will bring rapid improvement. Many people feel more at home and less self-conscious in a group than when alone with a therapist. They also receive encouragement by listening to others and by hearing the improvement of members of the group. Most patients with complex speech problems, such as aphasia, receive individual therapy. Some patients attend both kinds of sessions.

History. People have studied speech and speech problems for more than 2,000 years. However, little progress in the treatment of speech defects occurred until the 1700's and 1800's. During the 1700's, speech specialists worked mostly with the deaf. Successful teachers of the deaf included Thomas Braidwood, a Scottish mathematician. Braidwood taught his students to talk by starting with simple sounds and then progressing to syllables and, finally, words. The 1800's brought much research into the causes and treatment of stuttering. In 1817, Jean Marie Itard, a French physician, declared that stuttering resulted from a weakness of the tongue and larynx nerves. He recommended exercises to cure stutterers. During the late 1800's, Adolf Kussmaul, a German physician, wrote about the physical and psychological causes of stuttering. Today, speech-language pathologists agree that there is no single cause.

Speech therapy became a profession in the early 1900's. In Europe, it was associated with the medical profession. During the 1920's, schools for training speech therapists opened in several European countries. In the United States, speech therapy became closely allied with education, psychology, and speech. Several colleges opened speech clinics during the 1920's. The organization that later became the American Speech and Hearing Association was founded in 1925.

During World War II (1939-1945), many servicemen developed speech defects as a result of war injuries. The need for speech rehabilitation services attracted large numbers of men and women to the profession of speech therapy. Many speech clinics opened, and research increased into speech problems and their causes. Since the end of World War II, the field of speech therapy has expanded rapidly.

Careers. Many universities offer undergraduate and graduate training in speech-language pathology. Men and women who plan a career in this field should have a master's degree. Those who intend to teach in a college or university or to direct a clinic or research program usually have a Ph.D. degree.

Undergraduate students interested in speech therapy take courses in biology, linguistics, psychology, physics, introductory speech correction, and related fields. Graduate training covers five main areas: (1) development of speech, hearing, and language; (2) evaluation of speech production, language abilities, and auditory skills; (3) the nature of speech disorders; (4) treatment procedures; and (5) research techniques.

Most speech-language pathologists work in schools. Others are employed by private institutions, including hospitals, specialized community speech and hearing centers, and university speech clinics. Some speech-language pathologists conduct their research in private institutes. An increasing number of speech-language pathologists are entering private practice. Further information can be obtained from the American Speech-Language-Hearing Association, which has its headquarters in Rockville, Maryland.   Hugo H. Gregory

See also **Aphasia; Cleft palate; Lisping; Speech; Stuttering.**

Additional resources

Kent, Susan. *Let's Talk About Stuttering.* PowerKids Pr., 2000. Younger readers.

Martin, Katherine L. *Does My Child Have a Speech Problem?* Chicago Review Pr., 1997

Speed. See Methamphetamine.

Speed. See Light (The speed of light); Motion; Sound (The speed of sound); Velocity.

Speed reading is the ability to read rapidly and with good understanding. Many students and other people who need to do a great deal of reading take courses to increase their reading speed and improve their comprehension.

There are many ways of learning speed reading. A machine that flashes words on a screen at increasing rates helps some readers practice their eye movements. Drills and workbooks assist some people in mastering certain activities or skills. However, the most important changes to be made are mental, not physical.

Speed-reading courses teach how to eliminate or control certain habits that tend to slow or distract readers. One such habit is *vocalizing,* in which the reader pronounces each word or syllable silently. Another habit is *regressing,* in which the reader goes back to reread lines. A third bad habit is unnecessarily *fixating* (pausing) at long words that the reader already knows.

There are three good habits that can speed up a person's reading rate and improve comprehension at the same time. The first is setting a definite purpose for reading, such as digging out facts, skimming for ideas, or enjoying a good story. The second is for the reader to push his or her reading speed to a level of slight discomfort, but not to complete confusion. Third and most importantly, the reader should concentrate and give full attention to the text. These habits together help reading efficiency, whether the material is interesting and well written, or not.   J. Michael Bennett

Speed skating. See Ice skating; Roller skating.

Speedboat. See Motorboat racing (pictures).

Speedometer, *spee DAHM uh tuhr,* is an instrument that indicates the speed of an automobile or other vehicle. The speedometer display may show speed in miles per hour, kilometers per hour, or both.

There are two types of speedometers: (1) *electronic speedometers* and (2) *mechanical speedometers.*

An electronic speedometer consists of a *speed-sending unit,* a *signal conditioner,* and an electronic digital or analog *readout.* The speed-sending unit is connected to the transmission and sends an optical, electric, or magnetic signal to the signal conditioner. In most cases, the signal is a series of pulses that vary in proportion to the vehicle's speed. The signal conditioner translates the signal and sends it to the electronic readout, which then displays the vehicle's speed.

A mechanical speedometer indicates speed by means of a dial and a pointer. This type of speedometer is driven by a flexible shaft connected to a set of gears in the vehicle's transmission. When the vehicle moves, the gears in the transmission turn a core inside the shaft. The core is attached directly to a permanent magnet that lies near a metal cylinder called a *speedcup.* The revolving magnet sets up a rotating magnetic field that pulls the speedcup and its attached pointer in the same direction that the magnetic field is turning. A hairspring keeps the speedcup steady. The pointer on the speedcup comes to rest where the hairspring balances the force of the revolving magnet. When the vehicle speeds up, the magnet increases its pull on the speedcup, and the speedometer registers a higher speed. When the vehicle stops, the hairspring pulls the pointer back to zero.

A device called an *odometer* registers the total distance traveled by a vehicle. Many speedometers have a *trip odometer* that can be reset to zero at the beginning of a trip. Manufacturers typically design mechanical speedometers so that 1,000 revolutions of the flexible

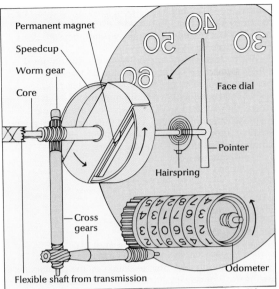

Permanent magnet
Speedcup
Worm gear
Core
Face dial
Pointer
Hairspring
Cross gears
Odometer
Flexible shaft from transmission

WORLD BOOK illustration by Mas Nakagawa

A mechanical speedometer can be used to show the speed of a vehicle. As the vehicle moves, gears in its transmission turn a core inside a flexible shaft. The core turns a permanent magnet, which rotates a speedcup and pointer on the speedometer dial. The pointer stops when a hairspring balances the force of the magnet. An odometer registers the total distance traveled.

shaft will register 1 mile (1.6 kilometers) on the odometer. In electronic speedometers, a specific number of pulses—usually 4,000—equals 1 mile. Thus, electronic odometers convert the number of pulses from the speed-sending unit into the total distance traveled.

William H. Haverdink

See also **Pedometer; Tachometer.**

Speedwriting is the registered trademark for a widely used rapid writing system. It employs letters of the alphabet instead of symbols.

In Speedwriting, all words are written as they sound. Thus, *you* is written *u; are* is *r; eye* is *i.* A whole syllable may be represented by a letter or a punctuation mark. The letter *a* expresses the sound of *ate.* Thus, *late* is *la; bait* is *ba.* The letter *r* expresses the sound *re.* Thus, *rebate* is *rba.* The capital letter *C* expresses the sound *ch.* Thus, *check* is written *Cc.* A hyphen represents the past tense verb ending *ed.* Thus, *checked* is *Cc-.* A dot in the middle of the line stands for the word *a.*

Brief forms or abbreviations represent some frequently used words. All other words are written according to basic Speedwriting principles. A person using Speedwriting writes the sentence, *"Your rebate check will reach you in a few days,"* as:

u rba Cc l rC u n · fu ds

The main advantage of Speedwriting is the use of the alphabet to represent sounds. Therefore, students can take dictation at the rate of about 80 to 100 words per minute after only six to eight weeks of training. They can transcribe their notes easily because the notes are in their regular handwriting.

Emma B. Dearborn, a shorthand teacher in Darien, Connecticut, originated Speedwriting in 1923. Joe M.

Pullis, a business education professor, developed the Regency System of Speedwriting in 1984.

Chris Katsaropoulos

See also **Shorthand.**

Speer, *shpayr,* **Albert** (1905-1981), directed the production of weapons in Nazi Germany during World War II (1939-1945). He served as an adviser to Nazi dictator Adolf Hitler from 1933 to 1945.

Speer was born on March 9, 1905, in Mannheim, Germany. He became an architect and joined the Nazi Party in 1931. From 1933 to 1942, Speer designed monuments and decorations for rallies to promote the Nazi government. In 1942, Hitler put Speer in charge of arms production. Speer greatly increased weapons output. He used slave labor in German factories.

By March 1945, it was obvious that Germany would lose the war. Hitler did not want any enemy troops to use Germany's industries, and so he ordered Speer to have the German Army destroy the industries. However, Speer knew that the German people would need the industries after the war. He refused to obey Hitler's order.

In 1945, after Germany surrendered, Speer was put on trial as a war criminal at Nuremberg, Germany. He admitted responsibility for using slave labor and was sentenced to 20 years in prison. Speer completed his term in 1966. He wrote *Inside the Third Reich* (1969), an important book about Nazi leaders. Speer died on Sept. 1, 1981.

Daniel Clayton

Speleology is the scientific study of caves. Scientists who make such studies are called *speleologists.* People who explore and map caves as a hobby are called *spelunkers.* Many cave explorers belong to the National Speleological Society. See also **Cave.**

Nicholas C. Crawford

Spell. See **Magic** (Magical words).

Spelling is the way we combine letters to write words. Learning to spell correctly is part of learning a language. The English language has over 40 sounds, called *phonemes,* but only 26 letters to represent them. Nevertheless, the several hundred thousand words of the English language can all be spelled with these 26 letters. Correct spelling, like correct speaking, is more than a sign of a person's education. Spelling helps a person communicate thoughts in writing, so others will know quickly and easily what is meant. Any system of spelling and the art and study of spelling are called *orthography.*

To understand how an alphabet-based spelling system works, say the word *bat* aloud. Listen carefully for the three sounds that blend together to make up the spoken word. Now, write the word instead of saying it. First, write the letter that stands for the beginning sound of the word, *b.* Next, write the letter that stands for the middle sound, *a.* Finally, write the letter that stands for the final sound, *t.* The letters *b-a-t* repeat in the same order the three original sounds of the spoken word. Spelling is simply the method of writing letters for spoken sounds. But the historical development of the English language has resulted in many spellings that do not follow the way the words are pronounced.

Learning to spell

Many people make spelling more difficult than is necessary. They try to learn their spelling by speaking, as one would spell in a spelling bee (spelldown), and they

100 spelling demons

absence	familiar	pageant
ache	fasten	perform
again	February	permanent
aggravate	forfeit	pleasant
ally	friend	possessive
already	fulfill	prairie
among	genius	professor
analysis	government	pursue
angle	grammar	quantity
answer	guarantee	raise
arctic	guess	receipt
awkward	height	repeat
believe	history	restaurant
bicycle	hour	rhyme
boundary	innocent	schedule
burglar	interfere	seize
business	laboratory	separate
cafeteria	leisure	siege
ceiling	library	sophomore
cemetery	license	succeed
chocolate	maneuver	sugar
colonel	mathematics	surgeon
column	medal	sympathize
committee	millionaire	temporary
counterfeit	minute	tragedy
courteous	muscle	typical
dealt	mystery	vacuum
desperate	necessary	vegetable
develop	noticeable	wear
discipline	occasion	weird
eighth	often	whether
enough	optimistic	would
existence	original	yacht
expense		

forget that writing is the only place in which spelling can possibly matter. They spend time and effort on words that they are unlikely ever to write and whose meanings are vague to them. They emphasize spelling drill and spelling rules, but they neglect to work out an effective method of learning to spell new words. Experts estimate that over 80 percent of all English words are spelled according to regular patterns. Of the 20 percent of irregularly spelled words, only about 3 percent are used commonly enough to require that their spelling be memorized.

Base words. The first problem in learning to spell is deciding which words are the most important. The average person uses fewer than 25,000 words in speaking, and even fewer in writing.

About 2,000 *base words* will satisfy over 90 percent of the writing needs of the average eighth-grade student. An additional 1,000 base words, or 3,000 in all, will take care of 95 percent of the writing needs of the average adult. An example of a base word is *danger*. Some words that can be formed from this base include *dangerous* and *endanger*.

The student should first learn to spell the 3,000 base words. Then the student can add spellings for other words. There are two main sources for base words. One is the writing of adults, and the other is the writing of children. Many words occur in both groups. Most spelling textbooks include lists of words of both groups.

Thousands of words have been studied to make up the lists of base words. For example, *about* is used by adults and by children as early as the first grade. *Absorb*

is used by adults, but it is seldom used by children before they are in the eighth grade. *Abrupt* is often used by adults but is seldom used by young people before high school.

Methods of study. The difference between good spellers and poor spellers can often be traced to one problem: finding an effective *method* of learning to spell. Good spellers have some method for studying words they want to spell. Poor spellers are frequently helpless with a new word. When they try to learn a new spelling, they usually use poor methods. Here are 10 common steps used by good spellers:

1. Looking at the word.
2. Copying the word.
3. Remembering how the word looks.
4. Listening to the pronunciation of the word.
5. Pronouncing the word.
6. Dividing the word into syllables.
7. Saying the letters of the word in order.
8. Writing the word to get its "feel."
9. Studying the difficult parts of the word.
10. Using the word in a meaningful sentence.

Remembering trick phrases, such as "the princi*pal* is a *pal*," is not a good substitute for an effective learning method. A few spelling tricks, such as remembering "station*ery*" with "pap*er*," may be helpful with particularly hard words. But too many tricks can be confusing.

Few people would use all of the 10 steps listed above, but people who want to improve their spelling can use some combination of these steps. Once the combination has been selected, it should be tested and changed if necessary. Then the combination can become a regular part of people's learning habits. Visualizing the word, or remembering how it looks, should probably be part of everyone's combination. A combination of steps for learning to spell a word suggested by an authority on spelling is given below:

1. Understand the use, meaning, and pronunciation of the word.
2. Visualize the word.
3. Note the spelling of the word.
4. Write the word carefully and neatly.
5. Check the spelling of the word.
6. Use the word as often as possible in writing.

Spelling rules have many exceptions. Nevertheless, knowing the basic spelling rules can often improve a person's spelling.

Many words come from a base word. Words derived from *develop*, for example, include *develops, developed, development, developing,* and *developer*. These new forms are made with a *suffix* added at the end of a word. Some rules for spelling correctly with suffixes are:

1. Drop the final *e* in a word before a suffix beginning with a vowel. For example, *love* + *ing* is *loving*. An exception to this rule is *dyeing*.
2. Keep the final *e* in a word before a suffix beginning with a consonant. For example, *sure* + *ly* is *surely*.
3. When a word ends in *y* preceded by a consonant, change the *y* to *i* before adding a suffix (unless the suffix begins with *i*). For example, *plenty* + *ful* is *plentiful*.
4. When a one-syllable word ends in a consonant preceded by a single vowel, double the consonant before a suffix beginning with a vowel. For example, *run* + *er* becomes *runner*.
5. In American English, when a word has more than one syllable, double the consonant only if the accent of the word is on the last syllable. For example, *admit* + *ed* is *admitted*.

Prefixes are added to the beginning of words. Three

common prefixes are *dis-, mis-,* and *un-.* When they are added to a word beginning with the same letter, there will be two *s*'s or *n*'s. For example, *mis + spell* is *misspell.*

One of the biggest spelling problems comes from the use of *ei* and *ie.* Some words are spelled with *ei,* such as *receive.* Some words are spelled with *ie,* such as *believe.* A spelling rule to remember is: "Use *i* before *e* except after *c* or when it is sounded like *a,* as in *neighbor* and *weigh.*" Exceptions include *either* and *seize.*

Adding new words

One way people can increase the number of words they can spell is to learn the spelling of words derived from a base word. For example, *trust* is a base word. A number of words, such as *mistrust, trusting,* and *trustee,* come from this base word. A similar method is to learn the *root meanings* of words. The root of a word is its basic form. For example, the verbal root *port* comes from the Latin word for *carry.* Knowing this helps to learn the spelling and meaning of such words as *portage, import, export, report, porter,* and *deport.*

A more important way of learning to spell new words is to learn the habit of using a dictionary. On seeing a new word, look it up in the dictionary and study its spelling and pronunciation. The dictionary also gives root meanings of words. See **Dictionary.**

Sometimes a word has two or more different spellings. For example, *enrollment* and *enrolment* are both correct spellings. Usually, a dictionary gives the *preferred spelling* first. But this does not mean that the alternate spelling is wrong. There are also many differences between American and British spellings. For example, the American *labor* is the British *labour.*

Spelling demons

Spelling demons often have an irregular arrangement of letters and need special study. *Fasten* is a spelling demon. Many people who misspell this word write it *fasen,* because they do not sound the *t* in *fasten* when speaking the word. Another demon is *friend.* People often write it *freind,* because the word has the sound of *e.*

There are also many words in English that have *silent letters.* The *k* in *knee* and *knight,* for example, is not pronounced. The reason for this mismatch between pronunciation and spelling is that in earlier stages of English the *k*-sound in these words was pronounced audibly. The pronunciation changed over time, but the spelling was already fixed. Another source for silent letters is the borrowing of words from another language, such as *pneumonia* (from the Greek word for *lung*).

Many spelling demons are *homophones,* or words that sound alike but have different meanings. For example, *pray* and *prey* are often misspelled because they sound alike. Other homophones include *to, too,* and *two.* Failing to pronounce a word accurately and distinctly is a frequent cause of error. The word *government* is an example. People who say *gov-er-ment* may spell the word without the first *n.*

Simplified spelling

Many attempts have been made to simplify the spelling of English words. The aim of most plans is to spell a word exactly as it is pronounced. For example, under these plans the word *though* would be spelled *tho,* and the word *knock* would be spelled *nok.*

There have been two chief arguments against such changes. The first is that simplified spelling would destroy the familiar pattern of words and cause confusion. The second is that the pronunciation of words changes continuously. Changes in pronunciation can occur rapidly or slowly. Words would soon become unrecognizable if the spelling were changed to meet each new change in pronunciation. Anja Wanner

See also **Abbreviation; Alphabet.**

Spellman, Francis Joseph (1889-1967), served as archbishop of New York City from 1939 until his death on Dec. 2, 1967. In that position, he became one of the most powerful and influential religious figures in the United States. Spellman was famous for his energy and his ability to consolidate power, raise money for charities, and administer a huge and complex diocese. His Alfred E. Smith Memorial Foundation Dinner became one of the most significant annual political banquets in the country. While archbishop, Spellman was also vicar of the U.S. armed services.

Spellman was born on May 4, 1889, in Whitman, Massachusetts. He was ordained a priest for the archdiocese of Boston in 1916. Spellman was appointed to the Secretariat of State at the Vatican in 1925. There he became friendly with Cardinal Eugenio Pacelli, later Pope Pius XII. Spellman became a bishop in 1932. Pius XII appointed him archbishop of New York City and named him a cardinal in 1946. David G. Schultenover

Spelunker. See Speleology.

Spencer, Anna Garlin (1851-1931), was an American reformer, minister, and educator. She was actively involved in the woman suffrage movement. She also worked to promote world peace, to ban the sale of liquor, and to strengthen family life. She was a founding member of the Woman's Peace Party and an active member of several other women's organizations. Her books included *Woman's Share in Social Culture* (1913) and *The Family and Its Members* (1923).

Anna Garlin was born in Attleboro, Massachusetts, on May 17, 1851. In 1878, she married William H. Spencer, a Unitarian minister. In 1891, she became minister of the Bell Street Chapel in Providence, Rhode Island. She was the state's first woman minister. As an educator, she held positions at a number of institutions, including the New York School of Philanthropy. Anna Spencer died on Feb. 12, 1931. Melanie S. Gustafson

See also **Woman suffrage.**

Spencer, Lady Diana. See Diana, Princess of Wales.

Spencer, Herbert (1820-1903), was an English philosopher. He attempted to work out a comprehensive philosophy based on the scientific discoveries of his day. Spencer was greatly influenced by the English naturalist Charles Darwin. He applied his own and Darwin's fundamental law—the idea of *evolution* (gradual development)—to biology, psychology, sociology, and other fields. Spencer's major works include *First Principles* (1862) and *Principles of Ethics* (1879-1893).

In his work on biology, Spencer traced the development of life from its lowest recognizable form up to human beings. He believed that the great law of nature is the constant interaction of forces which tend to change all forms from the simple to the complex. He explained that the mind of human beings has developed in this way, advancing from the simple automatic responses of lower animals to the reasoning processes of human beings. Spencer claimed that knowledge was of two kinds: (1) knowledge gained by the individual, and (2) knowledge gained by the race. He said that intuition, or knowledge learned unconsciously, was the inherited knowledge or experience of the race. He also believed that there is a basic and final reality beyond our knowledge, which he called the Unknowable.

Spencer was born in Derby on April 27, 1820. He was a delicate child. His first interest was biology, but he turned to engineering. From 1837 to 1841, he worked as an engineer for the London and Birmingham Railway. Later he served as an editor for the *Economist.* Spencer left the *Economist* in 1853 to pursue his philosophical career, which met with great popular success. He died on Dec. 8, 1903.   Karl Ameriks

Spender, Stephen (1909-1995), was an English poet. His best-known poetry is a blend of traditional Romanticism and thoroughly modern subject matter and attitudes. Thus, he found in an express train the sort of beauty earlier Romantic poets found in waterfalls and sunsets. In "The Express," he wrote:

> Ah, like a comet through flame, she moves entranced,
> Wrapt in her music no bird song, no, nor bough
> Breaking with honey buds, shall ever equal.

Spender was born on Feb. 28, 1909, in London. He attended Oxford University and there gained recognition in the 1930's as one of a group of poets led by his friend W. H. Auden.

Spender's *Journals: 1939-1983* and his *Collected Poems: 1928-1985* were published in 1983 and 1986, respectively. His criticism was collected in *The Destructive Element* (1935), *The Creative Element* (1953), and *The Making of a Poem* (1962). Spender also wrote drama, fiction, and translations, as well as the autobiographical *World Within World* (1951). Queen Elizabeth II knighted him in 1983, and he became known as Sir Stephen Spender. He died on July 16, 1995.   William Harmon

Spengler, *SPEHNG gluhr,* **Oswald** (1880-1936), was a German philosopher of history. In *The Decline of the West* (1918-1922), he held that the key to history is the law of societies and civilizations, which rise and fall in cycles. By studying developments in science and the arts as well as other aspects of history, he concluded that Western civilization was in a period of decay (see **Civilization** [Why civilizations rise and fall]). Spengler was born on May 29, 1880, in Blankenburg, near Braunschweig, Germany. He died on May 8, 1936.

Joseph Martin Hernon, Jr.

Spenser, Edmund (1552?-1599), was a great Elizabethan poet. His epic poem, *The Faerie Queene,* though never finished, is a masterpiece of English literature. Spenser completed only 6 of the 12 *books* (sections) he planned for this work.

Spenser's life. Spenser was born in London. He entered Pembroke Hall at Cambridge University in 1569. At Cambridge, he received a strong background in the classics. He also was influenced there by the anti-Roman Catholic feelings and stern moral beliefs of John Young, master of Pembroke Hall. These views were later reflected in Spenser's poems. In his works, he blended classical literary themes and conventions with Christian moralism, and revealed his strong English patriotic feelings. After leaving Cambridge, Spenser served as secretary to Young, who had left Pembroke Hall to become bishop of Rochester. Soon afterward, Spenser entered the service of Robert Dudley, the powerful Earl of Leicester.

In 1580, Spenser became secretary to Lord Grey of Wilton, the governor of Ireland. From 1580 until a month before his death in 1599, Spenser visited England no more than twice, to supervise publication of *The Faerie Queene.* The first three books of *The Faerie Queene* were published in 1590. Spenser dedicated them to Queen Elizabeth, who awarded him a yearly pension.

In 1594, Spenser married Elizabeth Boyle, the daughter of an Irish landowner. The second three books of *The Faerie Queene* appeared in 1596. Spenser was appointed sheriff of Cork in 1598, and late that year was sent to England with reports on the Irish uprisings. He became ill and died in London on Jan. 13, 1599. Part of the seventh book of *The Faerie Queene* was published in 1609.

The Faerie Queene is an *allegory* (extended metaphor) filled with personifications of abstract ideas, such as pride, hypocrisy, and faith. In writing *The Faerie Queene,* Spenser was influenced by the works of the English poet Geoffrey Chaucer and two Italian epics of the 1500's, Ludovico Ariosto's *Orlando Furioso* and Torquato Tasso's *Jerusalem Delivered. The Faerie Queene* also demonstrates the qualities a gentleman should have, reflecting the tradition of the *courtesy book.* The main character in each of the six books gradually develops a desired virtue—holiness, temperance, chastity, friendship, justice, or courtesy. Spenser included both moral and political allegory in *The Faerie Queene.* He wrote in a distinctive pattern, now called the *Spenserian stanza,* consisting of eight pentameter lines followed by an alexandrine.

Spenser's other poems. Spenser's first major poem, *The Shepheardes Calender* (1579), made his reputation. It consists of 12 pastoral *eclogues* (short poems about country life written as dialogues between shepherds). *Colin Clouts Come Home Againe* (1595) records a visit to London and the royal court that Spenser made with Sir Walter Raleigh. *Amoretti* (1595) is Spenser's famous *cycle* (series) of 89 love sonnets. *Epithalamion* (1595) is a great poem about marriage. It describes the events of an Irish wedding day and is a blend of classical and Christian traditions.   John N. King

Additional resources

Hadfield, Andrew, ed. *The Cambridge Companion to Spenser.* Cambridge, 2001.
Pugh, Syrithe. *Spenser and Ovid.* Ashgate Pub. Ltd., 2004.

Sperm. See Reproduction; Reproduction, Human.

Sperm whale is the largest of the toothed whales, a group that includes belugas and narwhals. Sperm whales live in all oceans. Males grow about 60 feet (18 meters) long, and females to about 40 feet (12 meters). Only certain baleen whales, a group that has thin plates called *baleen* in the mouth rather than teeth, are larger.

Sperm whales range in color from brownish-black to dark gray. They have a low, thick hump on the back and a series of ridges between the hump and the tail. A sperm whale's huge head makes up about a third of the total body length. The head is filled with *spermaceti,* an oily substance once widely used for making candles, and *sperm oil,* once used as a lubricant.

Sperm whales live in temperate and tropical waters. Mature males swim north or south to cooler waters in spring. Females and young whales stay in groups in the lower latitudes. The whales feed mainly on large squid. They often dive deeper than 3,300 feet (1,000 meters) and can remain submerged for more than an hour. They breathe through a single *blowhole* (nostril) on the left front of the head.

Sperm whales were hunted to near-extinction in the 1800's and 1900's, mainly for their meat and spermaceti. A waxy substance called *ambergris* sometimes forms in the whale's intestines. It was once highly valued as a base for perfumes. The International Whaling Commission banned most sperm whale hunting in 1984.

Bernd Würsig

Scientific classification. The sperm whale is in the family Physeteridae, suborder Odontoceti, order Cetacea. Its scientific name is *Physeter macrocephalus.*

See also **Whale** (picture: Some kinds of whales).

Spermaceti, *SPUR muh SEHT ee* or *SPUR muh SEE tee,* is a waxy material obtained from the enormous head of the sperm whale. Some spermaceti also comes from the bottlenose whale. Spermaceti once was used to make candles. It also has been used as a lubricant and as an ingredient of some salves and face creams.

Scientists are not certain exactly how the whale uses spermaceti. The substance probably focuses the sounds that the whale produces to locate prey.   John K. B. Ford

See also **Sperm whale.**

Sperry, Elmer Ambrose (1860-1930), was an American scientist, inventor, and manufacturer. He is best known for developing the gyroscope for use in navigation (see **Gyroscope**). His enterprises included the manufacture of arc lamps in Chicago, of electric railways in Cleveland, and of gyroscopes in New York City.

Sperry was born in Cortland, New York, on Oct. 12, 1860. He studied at the State Normal and Training School and at Cornell University. While in college, he built an arc lamp with a dynamo to run it. The lamp was much more efficient than any other then used to light streets. At the age of 19, Sperry set up his first factory in Chicago to produce his lamps. Forty years after that, he developed a beacon and searchlights later used by many armies and navies. In the meantime, he also developed electrical mining equipment, automobiles, and streetcars.

Sperry used the gyroscope in 1911 to develop a new kind of compass for ships. The increase in the amount of steel used in shipbuilding had made magnetic compasses unreliable. Sperry's gyrocompass successfully solved this problem (see **Gyrocompass**). The gyroscopic stabilizer for aircraft, which Sperry devised with his son Lawrence, was successfully demonstrated in 1914. From his gyrocompass, Sperry developed the gyropilot, which steers a ship automatically. Later he installed giant gyroscopes that could steady the rolling motions of ships. After the United States entered World War I (1914-1918), Sperry developed a number of instruments for gun control. These inventions increased the effectiveness and range of gunfire and torpedoes. Sperry

also produced an aerial torpedo that was controlled by a gyroscope. He died on June 16, 1930.

Today's naval gunnery methods would be impossible without the inventions that grew out of Sperry's original gyroscope. During World War II (1939-1945), the gyroscope was used in many complex military instruments, such as naval gunsights. Sperry's inventions were equally important for aircraft navigation.   Tom D. Crouch

Sphagnum moss. See Peat moss.

Sphalerite, *SFAL uh ryt* or *SFAY luh ryt,* is the most important zinc ore. It consists of zinc and sulfur. Sphalerite occurs in many colors, including black, red, yellow, white, and various shades of brown. The mineral has a peculiar luster, which may cause it to resemble hardened tree sap. Some varieties of sphalerite are *triboluminescent*—that is, they give off flashes of orange light when a sharp metal object is run across them. A rotten egg odor results from scratching the mineral. Major deposits of sphalerite occur in Mexico, eastern Europe, Spain, England, and the United States. Sphalerite is sometimes called *zinc blende.* See also **Zinc.**

David F. Hess

Sphere is a solid figure shaped like a ball or globe. The term *sphere* comes from the Greek word *sphaira,* meaning *ball.* In geometry, mathematicians define a sphere as a set of all points in space a certain distance from a fixed point called the *center.* This means that a sphere is a solid figure bounded by a single surface. The surface has no edges or boundaries, and each of the points on the surface is the same distance from the center.

The *radius* of a sphere is the distance from the center to the surface. The radius also can be defined as any straight line drawn from the center to the surface. The *diameter* of a sphere is twice the radius. It also is any

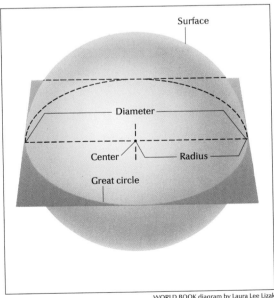

WORLD BOOK diagram by Laura Lee Lizak

A sphere is a solid, globelike figure. Its *surface* consists of all points a certain distance from a fixed point called the *center.* The *radius* is the distance from the center to the surface. The *diameter* equals twice this distance. If a *plane* (flat surface) passes through the center, it produces a *great circle.*

straight line drawn through the center whose ends stop at the surface. A *secant* is any line that cuts through a sphere. A *chord* is any line that joins two points on the sphere.

If a *plane* (flat surface) passes through the center of a sphere, the plane produces a *great circle* of the sphere. The radius and diameter of a great circle are the same as the radius and diameter of the sphere. A great circle cuts a sphere in half. Each half is called a *hemisphere*.

The area of the surface of a sphere can be found by using the following formula:

$$\text{Surface} = 4\pi r^2$$

In the formula, the letter *r* stands for the radius. An approximate value for π is 3.1416. The surface computed with this formula will appear in square units, such as square inches or square centimeters.

The volume of a sphere can be calculated with the formula:

$$\text{Volume} = \tfrac{4}{3}\pi r^3$$

The letter *r* again represents the radius of the sphere. The volume computed with this formula will appear in cubic units, such as cubic inches or cubic centimeters.

John K. Beem

See also **Circle; Geometry** (Euclidean geometry); **Pi.**

Spheroid is a solid figure that resembles a sphere but is not perfectly round. Earth is an *oblate* spheroid because it is wider at the equator than it is long between the poles. A football is a *prolate* spheroid, being longer than it is wide. John K. Beem

Sphinx, *sfihngks,* is an imaginary creature of ancient myths. The Egyptians, Greeks, and peoples of the Near East all had stories about such creatures. According to various tales, the sphinx had the body of a lion and the head of a human, falcon, or ram. Some sphinxes also had wings and a serpent tail.

The term *sphinx* is a Greek word that originally referred to an imaginary evil monster. The ancient Greeks used the term to describe the huge stone statues of lions with human heads that they saw during their visits to Egypt.

Egyptian sphinxes. Most Egyptian sphinxes had the head of a man and the body, feet, and tail of a lion. Others had heads of rams or falcons. Egyptians often made statues of sphinxes to honor a king or queen. The sculptors modeled the face of such a sphinx after the honored person. Egyptian art frequently showed kings as lions conquering their enemies, and sphinxes became symbols of royal protection. Statues of sphinxes often lined avenues leading to temples, such as those near the great temple at Karnak. Other sphinxes represented the god Horus, the sky god and sun god who was thought to be a protector of the king.

The largest, oldest, and most famous sphinx statue, called the *Great Sphinx,* lies in the desert near Giza, Egypt. The monument stretches 240 feet (73 meters) long and stands about 66 feet (20 meters) high. The width of its face measures 13 feet 8 inches (4.17 meters). Egyptians built the Great Sphinx about 4,500 years ago. They carved its head and body directly out of a giant rock in a limestone formation and cut stone blocks to form the paws and legs. This limestone formation had supplied much of the stone used to build several great pyramids.

The Great Sphinx wears a royal headdress and lies near the pyramid of King Khafre. Historians believe that the sphinx's face is a portrait of Khafre, who probably had the monument built.

Sand has often buried the Great Sphinx up to its neck. King Thutmose IV of Egypt (who ruled about 1400 to 1390 B.C.) cleared the sand away, supposedly after dreaming that the god Horus asked him to do so. During modern times, workers removed the sand in 1818, 1886, 1926, and 1938.

© Andrew Bayuk

The Great Sphinx is a huge limestone statue that sits in the desert near Giza, Egypt. This sphinx, which has a human head and a lion's body, stretches 240 feet (73 meters) long and rises about 66 feet (20 meters) high. Egyptians built the monument about 4,500 years ago.

The Metropolitan Museum of Art, New York City, Hewitt Fund, 1911;
Munsey Fund, 1936, 1938; and anonymous gift, 1951

The sphinx in Greek mythology had a woman's head, a lion's body, two wings, and a serpent tail. This stone statue of a Greek sphinx was carved about 540 B.C.

Through the years, desert sand, wind, rain, and sun have worn away part of the stone of the Great Sphinx. A broken section of the head indicates that it may have been used as a target for gun practice at various times. In the 1970's, scientists began efforts to preserve the crumbling stone of the Great Sphinx by treating it with special chemicals.

The Greek sphinx had the head of a woman, the body of a lion, a serpent tail, and wings. In the Greek myths, the most famous sphinx occurs in the story of Oedipus. The Sphinx lived on a high rock outside the city of Thebes. When anyone passed by, she asked a riddle: What has one voice and becomes four-footed, two-footed, and three-footed? The Sphinx destroyed everyone who could not answer correctly.

When Oedipus passed by on his way to Thebes, the Sphinx asked him the riddle. Oedipus replied: Man, who crawls on all fours as a baby, then walks on two legs, and finally needs a cane in old age. The Sphinx became furious because Oedipus had solved the riddle and jumped off the rock to her death.

Other sphinxes. Pictures, sculptures, and statues of sphinxes existed in parts of the ancient world besides Egypt and Greece. For example, sphinxes have been found in the remains of such ancient civilizations as Assyria and Phoenicia in the Near East and those of Asia Minor (now Turkey). Many of these sphinxes were made of pottery or metal.

Like the Egyptians, other ancient peoples decorated tombs and temples with carvings or pictures of sphinxes. These ancient peoples probably intended the sphinxes to serve as guardians of sacred places.

Leonard H. Lesko

See also **Cairo** (picture: The Egyptian Museum).

Sphinx moth. See Hawk moth.

Sphygmomanometer. See Blood pressure.

Spica, *SPY kuh,* is the brightest star in the constellation Virgo. Spica is best seen in the evening sky during spring. It is located about 220 light-years from Earth and gives off as much light as about 2,400 suns (see **Light-year**).   David H. Levy

Spice is the name given to various food seasonings made from plants. Spices have a sharp taste and odor. Some spices are valued for their taste, and others for their smell. People throughout the world flavor their foods and beverages with spices. Common spices include pepper, nutmeg, cloves, ginger, allspice, mace, mustard, and cinnamon.

Spices have little in common except their use. They come from different parts of plants and from different parts of the world. For example, cloves come from the bud, cinnamon from the bark, and pepper and nutmeg from the fruit of each plant. Ginger comes from the root and mustard from the seed.

Spice plants grow in many tropical countries. The Moluccas, or Spice Islands, in Indonesia are a famous source of cloves, nutmeg, or mace. Vanilla grows in South America. Many people prefer to grow spice plants such as sage, marjoram, and thyme in their own gardens. They then dry the plants for later use. Some common spice plants grow indoors if they are placed in pots in sunny windows.

Spices have little food value because they are eaten in limited quantity. But they do increase the appetite and aid in digestion. Excessive consumption of spices can sometimes be harmful to the body. Before foods were refrigerated or canned, spices were used to make tainted foods taste better and last longer.

Spices have played an important part in history. The Italian cities of Genoa and Venice became powerful because they were at the center of the spice trade with the East. When Columbus and the early explorers set sail across unknown seas, they were interested in discovering an all-water route to the spice lands of the East. Even in modern times, spices are important to us.

Chemists have identified many of the chemical compounds responsible for the taste and odor of spices. Some of these flavors can now be made synthetically.

James E. Simon

Related articles in *World Book* include:

Allspice	Coriander	Nutmeg
Anise	Cumin	Paprika
Caper	Curry	Pepper
Caraway	Fennel	Saffron
Cardamom	Ginger	Sage
Cayenne pepper	Mace	Tarragon
Cinnamon	Marjoram	Thyme
Clove	Mustard	Turmeric

Spice Islands. See Indonesia (The Molucca Islands).

Black and yellow garden spider *(Argiope aurantia);* © Mark Gibson, Index Stock

A beautiful spider web consists of silk spun from the spider's own body. The silk threads on this web resemble beaded necklaces. Spiders use webs to catch insects.

Spider

Spider is an eight-legged animal that spins silk. About half of all known *species* (kinds) of spiders make silk webs. These webs range in appearance from simple jumbles of threads to complex, often beautiful designs. Spiders use their webs to catch insects for food.

All spiders have fangs, and all except a few have poison glands. Spiders use their fangs and poison glands to kill prey. A spider's bite can paralyze or kill insects and other small animals. Although spiders feed mostly on insects, larger spiders may occasionally capture and eat tadpoles, small frogs, fish, birds, or even mice. Spiders frequently eat each other. Most female spiders are larger and stronger than male spiders, and they may attack males or young of their own species.

Spiders live anywhere they can find food. They thrive in fields, woods, swamps, caves, and deserts. One species, the *European water spider,* spends most of life underwater. Other species live on beaches between high and low tides so that they lie under salt water for part of each day. Some spiders thrive in houses, barns, or other buildings. Others prefer the outsides of buildings—on walls, on window screens, or in the corners of doors and windows. Spiders often live near lights that attract insects at night.

Many people think spiders are insects. However, spiders differ from insects in a number of ways. Ants, bees, beetles, and other insects have six legs. Spiders have eight. Most insects also have wings and *antennae* (feelers), but spiders do not. Biologists classify spiders as *arachnids.* Other arachnids include scorpions, ticks, and the spiderlike daddy longlegs (also called *harvestmen).* Both arachnids and insects belong to a large group of animals called *arthropods,* which have jointed legs and a stiff outside shell or skin.

Scientists arrange the thousands of spider species into more than 100 classifications called *families.* One family, the *liphistiids,* consists of primitive burrowing spiders. Liphistiids have abdomens that are visibly divided into segments. In all other kinds of spiders, the abdomens do not show segmentation. Scientists divide nonsegmented spiders into *araneomorphs,* or *true spiders,* and *mygalomorphs.* More than 90 percent of all spider species belong to the true spider group. Mygalomorphs include tarantulas.

Jonathan A. Coddington, the contributor of this article, is Senior Scientist in the Department of Entomology at the Smithsonian Institution's National Museum of Natural History.

Another way to group spiders divides them into *web-building spiders,* which make webs to trap insects; and *hunting spiders,* which catch prey without webs. Hunting spiders catch food in a variety of ways. *Jumping spiders,* for example, sneak up and jump on prey. *Crab spiders* ambush their victims.

This article will describe the body of a spider, how a spider makes and uses its silk, and the life of a spider. It will then discuss different spider families and the ways spiders and people have interacted.

The spider's body

Some spiders are smaller than the head of a pin. Others grow as large as a person's hand. One South American tarantula can measure more than 10 inches (25 centimeters) long with its legs extended.

Interesting facts about spiders

Goliath birdeater tarantula *(Theraphosa blondi);* © John Mitchell, Photo Researchers

The goliath birdeater tarantula ranks as one of the world's largest spiders. With its legs extended, it can measure more than 10 inches (25 centimeters) long. The tarantula shown here has captured a baby bird.

An ogre-faced spider traps insects in a small web of sticky silk. The spider stretches the web to several times its normal size and sweeps it over the insect.

Ogre-faced spider *(Deinopis spinosus);*
WORLD BOOK illustration by Jack Kunz

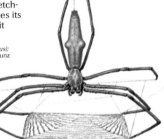

European water spider *(Argyroneta aquatica);* © O.S.F./Animals Animals

The European water spider lives mostly underwater. This animal "breathes" by carrying air bubbles on its abdomen. The water spider also encloses its underwater web in air bubbles.

Jumping spider *(Phidippus clarus);* © Kim Taylor, Nature Picture Library

A jumping spider catches prey by pouncing on it. Jumping spiders can leap more than 40 times the length of their bodies. The spider shown here is attacking a beelike insect called a hoverfly.

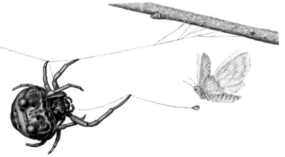

Bolas spider *(Mastophora cornigera);* WORLD BOOK illustration by Jack Kunz

A bolas spider does not trap its insects in a web. Instead, it spins a line of silk with a ball of sticky silk at the end. The spider swings the line at an insect and traps it on the sticky ball.

Spiders may be short and fat, long and thin, round, oblong, or flat. Their legs range from short and stubby to long and thin. Most spiders have brown, gray, or black coloring. But some types are as colorful as the loveliest butterflies. For many tiny spiders, people must use a microscope to clearly see the color patterns.

A spider has no bones. Its tough, mostly rigid skin serves as a protective outer skeleton. Fine hairs sprout from a spider's skin. Many spiders also have bumps and *spines* (outgrowths of skin) on their bodies.

A spider's body has two main sections, the *cephalothorax*, which consists of the fused head and *thorax* (middle section), and the abdomen. A thin waist called the *pedicel* connects the cephalothorax and abdomen.

Eyes. A spider's eyes lie on top and near the front of its head. The size, number, and position of the eyes vary among different species. Most species have eight eyes, arranged in two rows of four each. Other kinds have six, four, or two eyes. Some spiders have better vision than others. For example, hunting spiders have good eye-sight at short distances, which enables them to see prey and mates. Web-building spiders generally have poor eyesight. They use their eyes to detect changes in light. Some species of spiders that live in caves or other dark places have no eyes at all.

Mouth. A spider's mouth opening lies below its eyes. Spiders do not have chewing mouthparts, and they swallow only liquids. Extensions around the mouth form a short "straw" through which the spider sucks the body fluid of its victim.

A spider eats the solid tissue of its prey by predigesting it. First, the spider vomits digestive juices on its prey to dissolve the tissue. Then the spider drinks the liquid and repeats the process.

Chelicerae *(kuh LIHS uh ree)* are a pair of mouthparts that the spider uses to seize, crush, and kill its prey. The chelicerae are above the spider's mouth opening and just below its eyes. Each chelicera ends in a sharp, hard, hollow fang. An opening at the tip of the fang connects to the poison glands. When a spider stabs an insect with

Wolf spider *(Lycosa punctulata)*; WORLD BOOK illustrations by Jack Kunz

The body of a spider

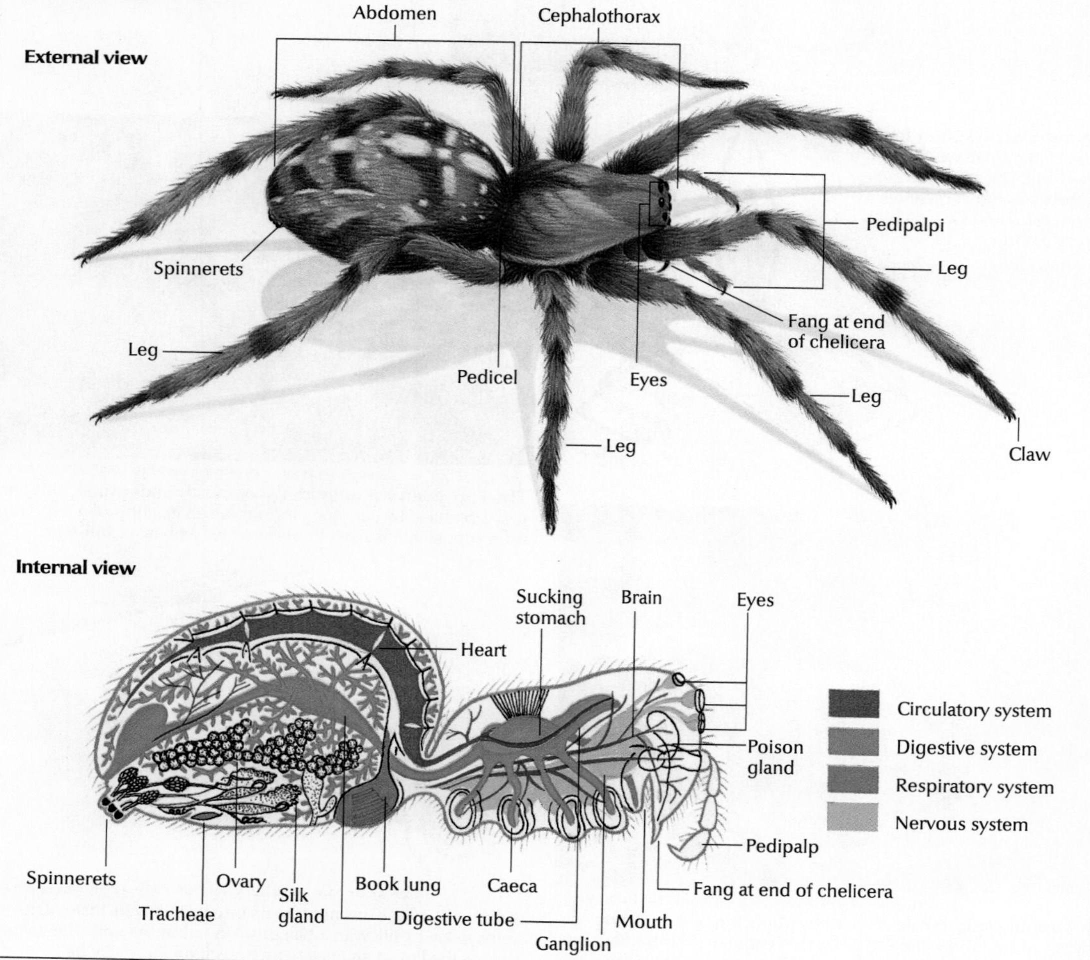

External view

- Abdomen
- Cephalothorax
- Spinnerets
- Pedipalpi
- Leg
- Fang at end of chelicera
- Leg
- Pedicel
- Eyes
- Leg
- Claw
- Leg

Internal view

- Heart
- Sucking stomach
- Brain
- Eyes
- Poison gland
- Pedipalp
- Fang at end of chelicera
- Mouth
- Ganglion
- Caeca
- Digestive tube
- Book lung
- Silk gland
- Ovary
- Tracheae
- Spinnerets

- Circulatory system
- Digestive system
- Respiratory system
- Nervous system

its chelicerae, poison squirts through the fang into the wound to paralyze or kill the victim. Some spiders use their chelicerae to dig burrows in the ground.

The fangs of true spiders point crosswise and move toward each other. True spiders have poison glands in their cephalothorax. The fangs of tarantulas and other mygalomorphs point straight down from the head and move parallel to each other. Mygalomorphs have poison glands in their chelicerae.

Pedipalpi *(PEHD uh PAL py),* also called *palps,* are a pair of projecting parts that look like small legs attached to each side of the spider's mouth. Each pedipalp has six *segments* (parts). The segment on each palp closest to the body forms one side of the mouth. In most spiders, the mouth segment bears a sharp plate with toothed edges. The spider uses this plate to cut and crush food. In adult male spiders, the last segment of each pedipalp bears a reproductive organ.

Legs. A spider has four pairs of legs, which are attached to its cephalothorax. Each leg has seven seg-

ments. The tip of the last segment has two or three claws. A brush of hairs called a *scopula* may surround the claws. The scopula sticks even to smooth surfaces and helps the spider walk on ceilings and walls.

Each leg is also covered with various kinds of sensitive hairs that serve as organs of touch and smell. Some hairs pick up vibrations from the ground or air. Others detect chemicals in the environment.

When a spider walks, the first and third leg on one side of its body move with the second and fourth leg on the other side. Spiders lack muscles in one leg joint and squirt blood into their legs to make them extend while walking. If a spider's body does not contain enough fluids, its blood pressure drops. The legs then curl up under its body, and the animal cannot walk.

Respiratory system. Spiders have two kinds of breathing organs—*tracheae (TRAY kee ee)* and *book lungs*. Tracheae, small tubes found in almost all kinds of true spiders, carry air to the body tissues. Air enters the tubes through one or, rarely, two openings called *spiracles* on the abdomen.

Book lungs are cavities in the spider's abdomen. Air enters the cavities through a tiny slit on each side and near the front of the abdomen. The wall of each cavity consists of 15 or more thin, flat sheets of tissue arranged like the pages of a book. Blood covers the inner sides of the sheets, and air covers the outer sides. Oxygen passes through the sheets into the blood, while carbon dioxide passes out of the sheets. Most true spiders have one pair of book lungs. Mygalomorphs have two pairs.

The *European water spider* lives mostly underwater. This animal "breathes" in water by carrying air bubbles on its abdomen. It fills its underwater web with air bubbles, which gradually push all the water out of the web. The spider can survive on air from these bubbles for up to several months, if necessary. It then has to return to the surface to gather more bubbles.

Circulatory system. Spider blood contains many pale blood cells and has a slightly bluish color. The heart consists of a long, slender tube in the abdomen that pumps blood to the body. The blood drains back to the heart through open passages instead of veins, as in the human body. If a spider's skin is broken, it may quickly bleed to death.

Digestive system. A digestive tube extends the length of the spider's body. In the cephalothorax, the tube is larger and is surrounded by an organ called the *sucking stomach.* Powerful muscles attached to the stomach alternately squeeze and expand it, causing a strong sucking action. The sucking pulls the liquid food through the stomach into the intestine. Digestive juices break the food into molecules small enough to pass through the walls of the intestine into the blood. The blood then distributes the food to all parts of the body. Food is also pulled through the stomach into fingerlike storage cavities called *ceca,* also spelled *caeca (SEE kuh).* The ability to store food in the caeca helps enable spiders to go for months without eating.

Nervous system. The spider's central nervous system lies in the cephalothorax. It includes the brain, which is linked to a large group of nerve cells called the *ganglion.* Nerve fibers from the brain and ganglion run throughout the body. These fibers carry information to the brain from sense organs on the head, legs, and other

WORLD BOOK illustrations by Jack Kunz

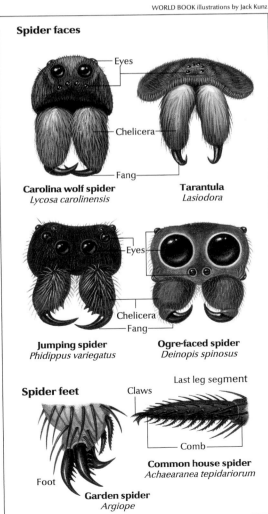

Spider faces

Eyes

Chelicera

Fang

Carolina wolf spider
Lycosa carolinensis

Tarantula
Lasiodora

Eyes

Chelicera
Fang

Jumping spider
Phidippus variegatus

Ogre-faced spider
Deinopis spinosus

Last leg segment

Spider feet

Claws

Comb

Common house spider
Achaearanea tepidariorum

Foot

Garden spider
Argiope

Spider silk

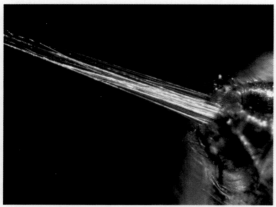

© Hans Pfletschinger from Peter Arnold, Inc.

A spider spins silk with fingerlike spinnerets on the rear of its abdomen. Liquid silk made in the silk glands flows through the spinnerets to the outside, where it hardens into threads.

© M. A. Chappell, Animals Animals

Threads of sticky spider silk look like beaded necklaces. The threads trap insects, which stick to the silk. Oil on the spider's body prevents the silk from sticking to the spider.

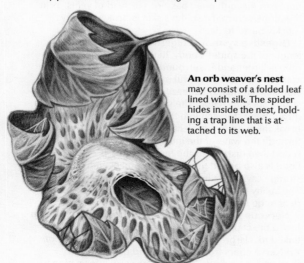

An orb weaver's nest may consist of a folded leaf lined with silk. The spider hides inside the nest, holding a trap line that is attached to its web.

WORLD BOOK illustration by Carol A. Brozman

body parts. The brain can also send signals through the nerve fibers to control the body's activities.

The spider's silk

Spider silk consists of protein. The silk cannot be dissolved in water, and it ranks as the strongest natural fiber known.

How spiders make silk. Silk glands in the spider's abdomen make silk. As a group, spiders have eight kinds of silk glands, each of which produces a different type of silk. However, no species of spider has all eight kinds. Every spider has at least two kinds of silk glands, and most species have five. Some silk glands produce a liquid silk that dries outside the body. Other glands create a silk that stays sticky.

The spider spins silk with short, fingerlike structures called *spinnerets* on the rear of the abdomen. Most kinds of spiders have six spinnerets, but some have four or two. The tip of a spinneret contains the *spinning field*. As many as 100 tubelike *spinning spigots* cover the surface of each spinning field. Each spigot serves one silk gland. Liquid silk flows from the silk glands through these spigots to the outside. As the liquid silk comes out, it hardens. Using different spinnerets and spigots, a spider may combine silk from different silk glands and produce a thin thread or a thick, wide band.

In addition, some spiders can make a sticky thread that looks like a beaded necklace. To do this, the spider spins a dry thread and coats it with sticky silk. The sticky silk then contracts into a series of tiny beads along the thread.

Some kinds of spiders have another spinning organ called the *cribellum*. It lies almost flat against the abdomen, just in front of the spinnerets. Hundreds or thousands of spigots cover the cribellum, producing extremely thin fibers of silk. Spiders with a cribellum also have a special row of curved hairs called a *calamistrum* on their hind legs. Spiders use the calamistrum to comb sticky silk from the cribellum onto dry silk from the spinnerets. This combination of threads forms a flat or tubular mesh of microscopic fibers called a *hackled band*. The mesh entangles the bristles, spines, and claws of insects and other small prey.

How spiders use silk. Spiders, including those that do not build webs, depend on silk in so many ways that they could not live without it. Wherever a spider goes, it spins a silk thread behind itself. This thread is called a *dragline*. The dragline is also called a "lifeline" because it can help the spider to escape from enemies. Spiders use their draglines to lower themselves to the ground from high places. When in danger, a spider can drop on its dragline and hide in the grass. Or the spider can simply hang in the air until the danger has passed, then climb back up the dragline.

Spiders also can use a special kind of fine silk to spin tiny bundles of sticky threads called *attachment disks*. Attachment disks cement the spiders' draglines and webs to various surfaces.

Each kind of web-building spider makes a different type of silk *retreat* (nest) as its home. Some *wandering spiders* rest each day in a leaf that they fold around themselves and line with silk. Other spiders dig burrows in the ground and line them with silk. Still others build retreats in the center or at the sides of their webs.

Many web-building spiders wrap silk lines or sticky bands around their prey as they capture them. Some *orb weavers* wrap their victims with wide sheets like mummy wrappings so the victims cannot escape.

The life of a spider

Most spiders live less than one year. But large species can live longer. Some female tarantulas have survived more than 20 years in captivity. Spiders become adults at different times of the year. Some mature and mate in the fall and then die during the winter. Their eggs do not hatch until spring. Others live through the winter, mate and lay eggs in the spring, and then die.

Except during mating, most spiders are loners. But some species live in social groups. Certain kinds of spiders live together on a communal web. In one tropical species, for example, tens of thousands of spiders may share a web 25 feet (7.6 meters) long and 6 to 8 feet (1.8 to 2.4 meters) wide. Other spiders live close to one another in large groups, but each individual has its own web.

Courtship and mating. As soon as a male spider matures, he seeks a mate. Most male spiders perform courtship activities to identify themselves and to woo females. In web-building spiders, the males usually pluck and vibrate the female's web. Some male hunting spiders wave their legs or vibrate the ground in a courtship dance. Male jumping spiders use the colored hairs on

their legs to attract females. In certain spiders, the male presents the female with a captured fly before mating.

Before he mates, the male spider spins a silk platform called a *sperm web.* He deposits a drop of sperm from his abdomen on the platform. Then he fills the organs at the tips of his pedipalpi with sperm. He uses the pedipalpi to transfer the sperm to a female during mating. After mating, the female stores the sperm in her body. When she lays her eggs, weeks or even months later, the sperm fertilize the eggs. Female spiders do not usually eat the males after mating, as some people believe.

Eggs. The number of eggs that a female spider lays at one time varies with her size. Females of many species lay about 100 eggs. But some of the smallest spiders lay just 1 egg, while some of the largest lay more than 2,000.

In most species, the mother spider encloses the eggs in a silken egg sac. This sac consists of several kinds of silk, including one type used only for egg sacs. Egg sacs can have a complex structure with an outer papery layer, an inner threadlike layer, and a soft core to support the eggs.

In many species, the mother dies soon after making the egg sac. In other species, mothers remain with the eggs until they hatch. Some spiders keep the sac in their web. Others attach the sac to leaves or plants. Still others carry it with them. A female *wolf spider* attaches the sac to her spinnerets and drags it behind her. *Fishing spiders* carry the sac with their fangs.

Spider reproduction

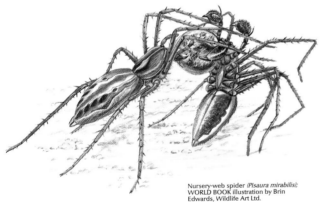

Nursery-web spider *(Pisaura mirabilis);* WORLD BOOK illustration by Brin Edwards, Wildlife Art Ltd.

Spider courtship sometimes includes an elaborate ritual. This illustration shows a male nursery-web spider, *right,* presenting a female, *left,* with a captured fly that he has wrapped in silk. The two spiders will mate after completing the ritual.

Thinlegged wolf spiders *(Pardosa milvina);* WORLD BOOK illustrations by Jack J. Kunz

A mother wolf spider carries her spiderlings on her back for a short time after they hatch. Wolf spiders take more care of their young than do most other kinds of spiders.

WORLD BOOK illustration by John F. Eggert

Spiderlings hatch from eggs inside the egg sac. One by one, they leave the sac through a tiny hole that they tear in its side. Most spiderlings immediately begin spinning draglines. Many then move to other areas, often by *ballooning,* a method of traveling along air currents.

Kite spider *(Gasteracantha sanguinolenta);* © Anthony Bannister, Corbis

A kite spider belongs to a group of orb weavers with distinctive spines on the abdomen. This African spider has a largely yellow abdomen with reddish spines and dark markings.

Bowl-and-doily spider *(Frontinella pyramitela);* © John Anderson, Animals Animals

A bowl-and-doily spider has bright yellow markings on its abdomen. This sheet-web weaver spins an unusual web that consists of a bowl-shaped sheet above a flat sheet.

Spiderlings hatch inside the egg sac. They do not leave the sac immediately because they are not yet able to walk or spin silk. After *molting* (shedding their skin) once inside the egg sac, the spiderlings are developed enough to leave. But they remain in the sac until warm weather arrives. If the eggs are laid in autumn, the spiderlings stay inside their egg sac until spring. After leaving the sac, most spiderlings begin spinning draglines. In a few species, the spiderlings remain for a time in the mother's web and share the food she captures.

Many spiderlings move far away from their birthplace. To do this, a spiderling climbs to the top of a twig or some other high perch and tilts its abdomen up into the air. It then pulls silk threads out of its spinnerets. The wind catches the threads and carries the spiderling into the air. This method of traveling is called *ballooning.* A spiderling may travel a great distance by ballooning. Sailors more than 200 miles (320 kilometers) from land have seen ballooning spiders. But most ballooners travel less than a mile or kilometer.

Spiderlings must molt to grow larger. First they make a new, larger skin just beneath their old skin. The tight old skin splits. The animal then wriggles out of the old skin and plumps up the new skin until it hardens. Most kinds of spiders molt from four to twelve times before becoming adults. When mature, most spiders stop molting. Female tarantulas and a few others continue to molt even after they become adults.

Enemies of spiders consist mainly of birds, insects, and other spiders. *Pirate spiders* eat only other spiders. Wasps rank among the spider's worst enemies. Predators also include lizards, snakes, frogs, toads, fish, or any other animals that eat insects. In addition, spiders suffer from fungal infections and from flies and wasps that live as parasites inside the spiders' bodies.

Mexican redknee tarantula *(Brachypelma smithi);* © William Ervin, Photo Researchers

A Mexican redknee tarantula rests on a leaf. Its legs have black, red, and yellow bands. Tarantulas rank as the largest spiders. The creature shown here lives in a forest in Costa Rica.

Redback spider *(Latrodectus hasselti);* © Carol Buchanan, Alamy Images

A redback spider has a striking red mark on both the top and bottom of its abdomen. This poisonous spider lives in Australia. It belongs to the group of spiders called tangled-web weavers.

Web-building spiders

Web-building spiders catch food by spinning webs to trap insects. A web-building spider does not usually become caught in its own web. When walking across the web, it grasps the silk lines with a special hooked claw on each foot.

Tangled-web weavers spin the simplest type of web. It consists of a jumble of threads attached to supports, such as the corner of a ceiling. *Cobwebs* are old tangled webs that have collected dust and dirt.

Cellar spiders spin tangled webs in dark, empty parts of buildings. One cellar spider that looks like a daddy longlegs has thin legs more than 2 inches (5 centimeters) long.

Cobweb weavers spin a tangled web with a tightly woven sheet of silk in the middle. The sheet serves as an insect trap and as the spider's hideout. Also called *comb-footed spiders,* these spiders have a comb of hairs on their fourth pair of legs. They use the comb to throw liquid silk over an insect and trap it. The *black widow* spiders belong to the cobweb weaver group.

Ogre-faced spiders, also called *net-casting spiders,* make webs that consist of a small, sticky mesh supported by a structure of dry silk. The sticky mesh consists mostly of hackled bands. The spider hangs upside down from the dry silk and holds the sticky mesh with its four front legs. When an insect crawls or flies near, the spider stretches the mesh to several times its normal size and sweeps it over the insect.

Funnel weavers live in large webs that they spin in tall grass, under rocks or logs, or in water. The bottom of the web, in which the spider hides, is shaped like a funnel. The top part of the spider's web forms a large sheet of silk spread out over the grass, soil, or other surface. When an insect lands on the sheet, the spider runs out of the funnel and pounces on the victim.

Carolina wolf spider *(Lycosa carolinensis);* © Paul & Joyce Berquist, Animals Animals

A Carolina wolf spider has a large, hairy body. The creature shown here, in Arizona, is feeding on an insect. Wolf spiders are excellent hunters and can run swiftly in search of food.

Artificial spider silk may provide manufacturers with an extremely strong and durable industrial fiber. The artificial spider silk shown here was produced by scientists in Munich, Germany.

© Matthias Schrader, Landov

Linyphiids, sometimes called *money spiders,* weave flat sheets of silk between blades of grass or branches of shrubs or trees. Many of these spiders also spin a mesh of crisscrossed threads above the sheet web. When a flying insect hits the mesh, it falls onto the sheet. Often, an insect will fly into the sheet web. The spider, which hangs beneath the web, quickly runs to the insect and pulls it through the webbing. Sheet webs last a long time because the spider repairs any damaged parts.

Scientists typically divide linyphiids into two basic groups, *dwarf weavers* and *sheet-web weavers.* The tiny dwarf weavers usually measure less than ⅒ inch (2.5 millimeters) long. Sheet-web weavers generally grow larger and often have patterns on their abdomens.

Orb weavers build the most beautifully patterned webs of all. They weave their round webs in open areas, often between tree branches or flower stems. Threads of dry silk extend from an orb web's center like the spokes of a wheel. Coiling lines of sticky silk connect the spokes and serve as an insect trap.

Some orb weavers lie in wait for their prey in the center of the web. Others attach a signal line to the center. These spiders hide in a retreat near the web and hold on to the signal line. When an insect lands in the web, the line vibrates. The spider then darts out and captures the insect. Most orb weavers spin a new web every night. It takes about 30 minutes. Such spiders often eat their old webs to reuse the silk and to consume any tiny insects stuck in the web. Other orb weavers repair or replace damaged parts of their webs.

The *bolas spiders* spin a single line of silk with a ball of sticky silk at the end. This ball attracts certain kinds of male moths. When the moth flies near, a bolas spider will whirl the line and trap the moth on the sticky ball.

Hunting spiders

Hunting spiders typically creep up on their prey or lie in wait and pounce on it. The strong chelicerae of hunting spiders help them overpower victims. Most seem to locate prey using vibrations transmitted through the ground. A few hunters have large eyes and can see their prey from a distance. Tarantulas have poor vision. They use a system of silk lines radiating from their retreats to both alert them of passing prey and to trip up prey. Some hunting spiders spin simple web nets that stretch out along the ground and stop insects.

Jumping spiders sneak up and pounce on their prey. These spiders have short legs, but they can jump more than 40 times the length of their bodies. Male jumping spiders rank among the most colorful of all spiders. Thick, colored hairs cover their bodies, especially on their first pair of legs. Jumping spiders possess excellent vision, and the males use their colors to attract females.

Tarantulas rank as the world's largest spiders. The biggest ones live in South American jungles. Great numbers of tarantulas also inhabit dry regions of Mexico and the southwestern United States. Many tarantula species dig burrows. A California tarantula builds a *turret* (small tower) of grass and twigs at the entrance to its burrow. This spider then sits just below the rim and waits for insects to pass within striking distance. A few kinds of tarantulas live in trees.

Nursery-web spiders, sometimes called *fishing spiders,* live near water and hunt aquatic insects, small fish, and tadpoles. These spiders have large bodies and long, thin legs. Because of their light weight, many can walk on water without sinking. They also can dive underwater for short periods. Many females in this group build special webs for their young.

Wolf spiders thrive in a variety of environments and are excellent hunters. Many kinds have large, hairy bodies, and run swiftly in search of food. Other kinds live near water and resemble fishing spiders in appearance and habits. Still others live in burrows, while some spin funnel-shaped webs.

Spiders and people

How spiders help people. Spiders have helped people for thousands of years by eating harmful insects, including flies, mosquitoes, and such crop pests as aphids and grasshoppers. Spiders rank among the most important predators of these insects.

Scientists believe spider silk and venom will also prove useful to human beings. Spider silk, though extremely fine, has great strength and durability. Biologists study the microscopic structure of this silk to understand its unusual properties. They also study how spiders make the silk by using only a few kinds of proteins dissolved in water. Such studies may help manufacturers develop new ways of producing extremely strong industrial fibers.

Spider venom can affect the human nervous system in many ways, and scientists have learned much about the nervous system by studying the effects of spider venom. Knowledge gained from these studies may lead to cures for illnesses of the nervous system, including Parkinson disease.

Manufacturers also hope to use spider venoms to make new kinds of insecticides. Collectively, the many different spider venoms may contain thousands of compounds that are highly poisonous to insects but harmless to people or other animals.

Dangerous spiders. Only a few kinds of spiders can inflict bites severe enough to endanger people. The most dangerous spider groups include the *recluses* and the *widows* of North America, the *redbacks* and *funnel-web spiders* of Australia, and the *button spiders* of Africa. The bites of these spiders can cause severe pain, but they rarely prove fatal. Moreover, spiders rarely bite people unless seriously threatened.

Spiders in the home. Many people have a fear of spiders, known as *arachnophobia,* and do not want spiders in their homes. Web-building spiders often live well hidden indoors and rarely touch floors or walls. As a result, pesticides may not prove effective. A good way to control spiders indoors is to eliminate insects from the home. Spiders will not infest houses in which they can find no food.   Jonathan A. Coddington

Scientific classification. Spiders belong to the phylum Arthropoda and the class Arachnida. They make up the spider order, Araneae. Liphistiids make up their own family, Liphistiidae. True spiders include the cobweb weaver family, Theridiidae; the crab spider family, Thomisidae; the dwarf and sheet-web weaver family, Linyphiidae; the funnel weaver family, Agelenidae; the hackled orb weaver family, Uloboridae; the jumping spider family, Salticidae; the nursery-web spider family, Pisauridae; the ogre-faced spider family, Deinopidae; the orb weaver family, Araneidae; and the wolf spider family, Lycosidae. Mygalomorphs include the purse-web spider family, Atypidae, and the tarantula family, Theraphosidae.

Additional resources

Foelix, Rainer F. *Biology of Spiders*. 2nd ed. Oxford, 1996.
Mason, Adrienne. *The World of the Spider*. Sierra Club, 1999.
O'Toole, Christopher, ed. *Firefly Encyclopedia of Insects and Spiders*. Firefly Bks., 2002.
Simon, Seymour. *Spiders*. HarperCollins, 2003. Younger readers.

Spider monkey is any of several large monkeys noted for using the tail as an extra limb. Spider monkeys can hang by the tail and even pick up objects by curling the tail around them. These animals sometimes hang upside down by grasping a branch with all four long, slender limbs and the tail. This position makes the monkeys resemble huge spiders. Spider monkeys often use their arms to swing from branch to branch. Only Asian primates called gibbons can swing through trees faster.

Spider monkeys inhabit tropical forests from central Mexico to central Bolivia. They live in groups of up to 35 individuals and spend most of their time in high branches, where they eat fruits, seeds, and other plant matter. Various species have black, brown, golden, reddish, or tan fur. Adults weigh from 10 to 19 pounds (5 to 8.6 kilograms) and grow almost 2 feet (61 centimeters) long, not including the tail. A spider monkey's hands have four long fingers and an extremely small thumb.

Spider monkeys rank among the most threatened of the New World monkeys. They have been hunted to extinction in certain areas of the Amazon Basin.
          Roderic B. Mast and Russell A. Mittermeier

Scientific classification. Spider monkeys belong to the New World monkey family, Cebidae. They make up the genus *Ateles.*

See also **Animal** (Animals of the tropical forests [picture]); **Monkey** (picture).

Spiderwort, *SPY duhr WURT,* is the common name for a group of mostly tropical plants. Some are ornamental plants. The leaves of the spiderworts are often grasslike and sometimes striped. The flowers may be blue, white, or purple. They are fragile and may dissolve into watery jelly. They have weak stems. Some spiderworts grow erect, and some run along the ground. They are perennials. The *common spiderwort* is the best-known of the erect plants. An example of creeping spiderwort is the *wandering-jew* (see **Wandering-jew**).   Thomas B. Croat

Scientific classification. Spiderworts belong to the spiderwort family, Commelinaceae. The scientific name for the common spiderwort is *Tradescantia virginiana.*

Spielberg, Steven (1946-   ), is an American motion-picture director and producer. Several of his films rank among the highest grossing movies in history. Spielberg is a superb technician, especially expert in propelling his stories forward with breathless style.

Spielberg's films tend to fall into two categories. One is light entertainment movies that appeal primarily to youthful audiences. Most of his commercial hits fall into this category. They include *Jaws* (1975), *Close Encounters of the Third Kind* (1977), *E.T.: The Extra-Terrestrial* (1982), and *Jurassic Park* (1993) and its sequel *The Lost World* (1997), and *War of the Worlds* (2005). His other popular films include the "Indiana Jones" trilogy of *Raiders of the Lost Ark* (1981), *Indiana Jones and the Temple of Doom* (1984), and *Indiana Jones and the Last Crusade* (1989). He also produced the horror films *Poltergeist* (1982) and *Gremlins* (1984), and the fantasy *Back to the Future* (1985). In addition, Spielberg directed the comedies *Catch Me If You Can* (2002) and *The Terminal* (2004).

The second category consists of more serious works. *Schindler's List* (1993) is a drama set during the Holocaust in Europe (see **Holocaust**). Spielberg won the Academy Award as best director for the film, which also won the best picture award. He won the Academy Award as best director for *Saving Private Ryan* (1998), a realistic story of battle during World War II. His serious films include *The Color Purple* (1985), *Empire of the Sun* (1987), *A.I. Artificial Intelligence* (2001), *Minority Report* (2002), and *Munich* (2005).

Spielberg was born on Dec. 18, 1947, in Cincinnati, Ohio. Unlike most of his peers, he is largely self-taught. He began making movies in his teens. He dropped out of college after his low-budget, amateur films led to a TV contract with Universal Studios. In 2002, Spielberg completed his college work and received a B.A. degree in film and electronic arts from California State University, Long Beach. Spielberg first gained attention with the suspense TV movie *Duel* (1971). In 1994, he joined with entertainment executives Jeffrey Katzenberg and David Geffen to form DreamWorks SKG, a new film studio.

In 1994, Spielberg established the Survivors of the Shoah Visual History Foundation. Its mission is to record on videotape firsthand accounts of survivors, rescuers, and other eyewitnesses of the Holocaust. It distributes the material with a goal of promoting tolerance and cultural understanding.   Louis Giannetti

See also **Motion picture** (picture: *Jurassic Park*).

Spikenard, *SPYK nuhrd,* also called *nard,* is a plant that grows in China and the Himalaya. Its long, narrow root yields a vital oil once commonly used in perfume. A cluster of stems about 2 inches (5 centimeters) long grows from the top of the root. The flowers are purplish.

An unrelated shrub, the *American spikenard,* is found from southern Canada to northern Mexico. It grows to about 6 feet (1.8 meters) high and has brown to purple flowers. American Indians once used its roots and *rhizomes* (root stems) medicinally.   James E. Simon

Scientific classification. The spikenard is in the valerian family, Valerianaceae. It is *Nardostachys jatamansi.* The American spikenard is in the ginseng family, Araliaceae. It is *Aralia racemosa.*

Spina bifida, *SPY nuh BIHF uh duh,* is a spinal defect present at birth. The spine encloses and protects the spinal cord. In spina bifida, the spinal cord does not form properly and the vertebrae and skin cannot enclose it.

There are several types of spina bifida, and they vary in severity. The most familiar and serious type is *open spina bifida,* also called *meningomyelocele* (pronounced *muh NIHNG goh MY uh luh seel).* This form of spina bifida

can be life-threatening during infancy and causes mild to severe disabilities in all who survive. In addition to spinal defects, open spina bifida is characterized by abnormalities of the brain and of the muscles and skin that lie over the spine. At birth, the baby has an opening in the skin over the middle or lower part of the back.

Open spina bifida results from an error in the development of the embryo that occurs early in pregnancy. This error may have various causes, including the use of alcohol or certain medications by the pregnant woman.

Infants with open spina bifida require various types of surgery, including surgery immediately after birth to close the open spine. Without treatment, most infants will die within a few years or become severely disabled.

Disabilities common in people born with open spina bifida include paralysis or weakness of the legs and lack of bowel or bladder control. Many infants also have *hydrocephalus* (*HY droh SEHF uh luhs),* an enlargement of the head due to blockage of fluid flow from the brain. These infants require surgery to prevent brain damage.

Ultrasound tests during pregnancy usually can detect open spina bifida in a fetus. *Folic acid,* also called *folate,* may often prevent open spina bifida. Ideally, a woman should take this vitamin in the month or two before she becomes pregnant and in the first three months of the pregnancy. See **Folic acid.**   John F. McLaughlin

Spinach is a popular garden vegetable. It produces a thick cluster of wide, succulent leaves that people eat raw or cooked. Spinach is related to beets, Swiss chard, and the weed lamb's-quarters. Spinach originally came from southwest Asia. The Persians used it as medicine. The English grew it as early as 1500, and Americans cultivated it during colonial times.

Spinach is a low-growing *annual* that must be replanted each year. It grows fast, preferably in a cool season. Spinach can withstand frost but not heat. Gardeners should cultivate spinach in a fertile, sandy loam, sowing the seeds in spring and harvesting the crop in about three months. Spinach is high in vitamins and minerals. It provides an excellent source of vitamins A and C. The vegetable also acts as a mild laxative.   Albert Liptay

Scientific classification. Spinach belongs to the goosefoot family, Chenopodiaceae. Its scientific name is *Spinacea oleracea.*

See also **Vegetable** (picture).

Spine is the part of the skeleton that extends down the center of the back. It is made up of a column of bones called *vertebrae.* The spine plays an important role in posture and movement, and it also protects the spinal cord. The spine is also called the *spinal column, vertebral column,* or *backbone.* Animals with a spine are called *vertebrates.*

The human spine consists of 33 vertebrae, but some of them grow together in adults. There are 7 *cervical* (neck), 12 *thoracic* (chest), 5 *lumbar* (lower back), 5 *sacral* (hip region), and 4 *coccygeal* (tailbone region) vertebrae. The vertebrae are held in place by muscles and strong connective tissue called *ligaments.* Most vertebrae have fibrous *intervertebral disks* (also spelled *discs)* between them to absorb shock and enable the spine to bend.

The spine normally has a slight curve. Abnormal curvatures may be present at birth. They may also result from disease, poor posture, or a strain on the muscles attached to the spine. *Scoliosis* occurs when the spine curves sideways. *Kyphosis,* or hunchback, is a forward bending of the thoracic vertebrae that often affects elderly people. *Lordosis,* or *swayback,* is an exaggerated curvature of the lumbar vertebrae.

Fractured cervical vertebrae may injure the spinal cord, resulting in a loss of sensation, paralysis, or even death. *Whiplash* is an injury to the muscles and ligaments attached to cervical vertebrae. It occurs when a sudden force—such as a rear-end car accident—throws the head backward. As people age, the inner part of an intervertebral disk may stick out through the outer part. This condition is called a *disk herniation.* Arthritis and *degeneration* (breakdown) of intervertebral disks may cause low back pain. Nerve compression from a herniated disk or other conditions may cause *sciatica* (pain racing down the leg). Frank E. Fumich

Related articles in *World Book.* See the Trans-Vision three-

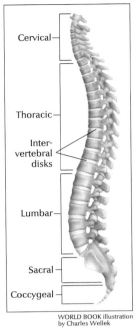

Cervical

Thoracic

Intervertebral disks

Lumbar

Sacral

Coccygeal

WORLD BOOK illustration by Charles Wellek
Divisions of the spine

dimensional picture in **Human body.** See also:

Backache	Nervous system	Scoliosis
Cerebrospinal fluid	Paralysis	Spina bifida
Hunchback	Sciatica	Whiplash

Spinet, *SPIHN iht,* is a keyboard musical instrument that was popular from the 1500's to the 1700's. Many spinets look like miniature grand pianos. A spinet operates like a *harpsichord,* though its sound is not as rich (see **Harpsichord**). A spinet has wire strings plucked by quills or pieces of leather when the keys are pressed down. The word *spinet* may have come from the Italian *spina,* which means *thorn,* and may refer to the quills. *Spinet* is also the name of a small upright piano. See also **Piano** (Upright pianos). F. E. Kirby

Spingarn, *SPIHN gahrn,* **Joel Elias,** *JOH ehl ih LY uhs* (1875-1939), an American literary critic, was one of the first white leaders of the National Association for the Advancement of Colored People (NAACP). In 1914, as chairman of the board of the NAACP, Spingarn established an award to be given annually to an outstanding African American. The award is called the Spingarn Medal.

Spingarn was born in New York City on May 17, 1875. He taught literature at Columbia University from 1899 to 1911. His critical works include *A History of Literary Criticism in the Renaissance* (1899) and *The New Criticism* (1911). He encouraged the works of African American writers during the Harlem Renaissance, a period of intense black literary activity in the early 1900's. Spingarn died on July 26, 1939. Alton Hornsby, Jr.

Spingarn Medal, *SPIHN gahrn,* is an annual award that was instituted by the National Association for the

Winners of the Spingarn Medal

Year	Medal winners	Field of achievement	Year	Medal winners	Field of achievement
1915	*Ernest E. Just	Research in biology	1945	*Paul Robeson	Singing and acting
1916	Charles Young	Organization of the Liberian constabulary	1946	*Thurgood Marshall	Equality before the law
			1947	*Percy L. Julian	Commercial chemistry
1917	*Harry T. Burleigh	Creative music	1948	Channing H. Tobias	Civil liberties
1918	W. S. Braithwaite	Literature	1949	*Ralph J. Bunche	UN mediator, Palestine
1919	Archibald H. Grimké	Politics and literature	1950	Charles H. Houston†	Law; education
1920	*William E. B. Du Bois	Founding of Pan-African Conferences	1951	Mabel K. Staupers	Equal rights for African American nurses
1921	Charles S. Gilpin	Drama	1952	Harry T. Moore†	Civil liberties
1922	Mary B. Talbert	Helped create Frederick Douglass Shrine	1953	Paul R. Williams	Architecture
			1954	*Theodore K. Lawless	Dermatology
1923	*George W. Carver	Agricultural chemistry	1955	Carl Murphy	Publishing
1924	*Roland Hayes	Concert singing	1956	*Jackie Robinson	Major league baseball
1925	*James Weldon Johnson	Literature	1957	*Martin Luther King, Jr.	Civil rights
1926	*Carter G. Woodson	History	1958	Daisy Bates	Arkansas NAACP
1927	Anthony Overton	Life insurance		Minnijean Brown	First African American students
1928	*Charles W. Chesnutt	Literature		Ernest Green	to attend Little Rock (Arkansas) Central High School
1929	Mordecai W. Johnson	Education, Howard U.		Thelma Mothershed	sas) Central High School
1930	Henry A. Hunt	Education in the South		Melba Patillo	
1931	Richard B. Harrison	Drama		Gloria Ray	
1932	*Robert R. Moton	Educational work		Terrence Roberts	
1933	Max Yergen	Interracial work in South Africa		Jefferson Thomas	
1934	William T. B. Williams	Education, Tuskegee Institute		Carlotta Walls	
1935	*Mary McLeod Bethune	Education	1959	*Duke Ellington	Creative music
1936	*John Hope†	Education, Atlanta U.	1960	*Langston Hughes	Literature
1937	*Walter F. White	Civil rights	1961	*Kenneth B. Clark	Psychology
1938	No award given.		1962	*Robert C. Weaver	Government
1939	*Marian Anderson	Concert singing	1963	*Medgar W. Evers†	Equal rights for African Americans in Mississippi
1940	Louis T. Wright	Surgery and civic affairs			
1941	*Richard Wright	Literature	1964	*Roy Wilkins	Civil rights
1942	*A. Philip Randolph	Labor and civic affairs	1965	*Leontyne Price	Opera singing
1943	*William H. Hastie	Civil rights	1966	*John H. Johnson	Publishing
1944	*Charles R. Drew	Medicine	1967	*Edward W. Brooke	Government

*Has a separate biography in *World Book.*   †Awarded posthumously.

(Continued on page 794)

Winners of the Spingarn Medal (continued)

Year	Medal winners	Field of achievement	Year	Medal winners	Field of achievement
1968	Sammy Davis, Jr.	Entertainment	1986	*Benjamin L. Hooks	Civil rights
1969	Clarence M. Mitchell, Jr.	Fair housing legislation	1987	Percy E. Sutton	Law; politics; business
1970	*Jacob Lawrence	Paintings of African American life	1988	Frederick Patterson	Education
			1989	*Jesse Jackson	Civil rights; politics
1971	*Leon H. Sullivan	Equal economic opportunities for blacks	1990	*L. Douglas Wilder	Politics
			1991	*Colin L. Powell	Military
1972	*Gordon Parks	Photography, film, literature, music	1992	*Barbara C. Jordan	Politics
			1993	Dorothy I. Height	Equality and human rights
1973	Wilson C. Riles	Education	1994	*Maya Angelou	Literature
1974	Damon J. Keith	Law	1995	*John Hope Franklin	History
1975	*Henry (Hank) Aaron	Baseball	1996	A. Leon Higginbotham, Jr.	Law
1976	*Alvin Ailey	Modern dance	1997	*Carl T. Rowan	Journalism
1977	*Alex Haley	Literature	1998	*Myrlie Evers-Williams	Civil rights
1978	*Andrew J. Young, Jr.	Domestic and international affairs	1999	Earl G. Graves	Publishing
			2000	*Oprah Winfrey	Television; publishing
1979	*Rosa L. Parks	Civil rights	2001	*Vernon E. Jordan, Jr.	Civil rights
1980	Rayford W. Logan	History; education	2002	John R. Lewis	Civil rights
1981	*Coleman Young	Government	2003	Constance Baker Motley	Law
1982	*Benjamin E. Mays	Education; theology	2004	Robert L. Carter	Law
1983	*Lena Horne	Entertainment	2005	Oliver W. Hill	Civil rights
1984	*Tom Bradley	Law; public and political leadership	2006	Benjamin S. Carson, Sr.	Medicine
			2007	John Conyers, Jr.	Politics; civil rights
1985	*Bill Cosby	Entertainment; education			

*Has a separate biography in *World Book*. †Awarded posthumously.

Advancement of Colored People (NAACP) in 1914. The award was named for Joel Elias Spingarn, who was then chairman of the NAACP's board of directors. Gold medals are given each year to the black American who reached the highest achievement in his or her field in the previous year or over time. See also **National Association for the Advancement of Colored People; Spingarn, Joel E.**   Nancy J. Weiss

Spinning is the process of making threads by twisting together plant or animal fibers. It is one of the most ancient arts. For thousands of years, yarn was spun by means of a *spindle*. This consisted of little more than a smooth stick from 9 to 15 inches (23 to 38 centimeters) long. It had a notch at one end for catching the thread, and a stone or baked clay bowl, called a *whorl*, to help make the spindle spin, like a top. The spinner turned the spindle by rolling it against the thigh. Ancient Egyptians used such spindles to make thread for fine cloth.

Ancient spinners in India and South America used finer spindles, usually in a bowl or on the ground. They spun cotton from combed rolls. Wool or flax fibers were wound around a stick called the *distaff*.

Early spinning wheels included the *great wheel* and the *Saxony wheel*. The great wheel, developed in India around 500 B.C., was the first spinning device to have a mechanized spindle. A drive band connected to a large wheel turned the spindle. The great wheel was used in Europe by the Middle Ages. The Saxony wheel, developed in Germany in the late 1400's and early 1500's, featured a foot pedal that turned the spindle. A distaff carried the material to be spun. The material was drawn off the distaff by hand. The fineness of the thread produced by the great wheel and the Saxony wheel depended on the speed with which the twisting thread was drawn out. Very fine thread required two spinnings. New England housewives used both wheels during colonial times.

The spinning jenny was invented by James Hargreaves in about 1764. This machine could spin more than one thread at a time. But it produced coarse thread

rather than fine thread. No one really knows the origin of the term *jenny*. See **Spinning jenny.**

The water frame was a cotton-spinning machine patented by Richard Arkwright in 1769. This machine made it much easier to spin cotton thread for the *warp,* the lengthwise threads in a piece of cloth. Arkwright's frame drew cotton from the carding machine in a fine, hard-twisted thread suitable for the warp.

The mule, introduced by Samuel Crompton in 1779, combined principles of the spinning wheel and the water frame. It was widely used to produce muslin and so was called the muslin wheel. Some mules had more than 1,000 spindles. Mules produced fine, uniform yarn.

New spinning machines helped bring about that change in history known as the Industrial Revolution, when machines began to take the place of hand workers. The increased output of spinning factories created a demand for more cotton. This need led to the invention of Eli Whitney's cotton gin. With more thread to weave, the weavers developed better and faster power looms. Then came machines to knit, to make lace, or embroider, to cut out patterns, and finally to sew cloth into finished garments in large quantities.

Cotton spinning in a present-day factory is a typical example of most spinning. After the raw cotton has been cleaned and blended, it usually goes through an air duct system to the carding machines. These machines have huge rollers covered with wire teeth. Here the tangled fibers are straightened out and made to lie in straight, even rows. Then the fibers are rolled over and over one another to form *slivers* (pronounced *SLY vuhrs)*, which look like loose ropes of soft cotton yarn. A sliver goes through the processes of *drawing, slubbing,* and *roving,* by which it is made finer, more even, and stronger. Spinning machines perform these operations and give the thread the required firmness and strength.

New machines have been invented to spin the old natural fibers, such as flax and hemp, and new machines are being made for other fibers, such as kapok and ramie. Machines may be developed that will make cloth directly without first spinning thread. Laurence F. Gross

Related articles in *World Book* include:

Arkwright, Sir Richard
Cotton (Spinning; picture)
Crompton, Samuel
Hargreaves, James

Industrial Revolution (Spinning machines)
Thread

Spinning jenny is a machine for spinning yarn. It played an important role in the mechanization of textile production. Like the spinning wheel, it may be operated by a treadle or by hand. But unlike the spinning wheel, it can spin more than one yarn at a time. The idea for multiple-yarn spinning was conceived about 1764 by James Hargreaves, an English weaver. In 1770, he patented a machine that could spin 16 yarns at a time. See also **Hargreaves, James** (with picture). Richard F. Hirsh

Spinone Italiano is a large, rugged breed of dog developed in Italy during ancient times. The dog stands about 22 to 28 inches (56 to 71 centimeters) high at the shoulders and weighs from 61 to 85 pounds (28 to 39 kilograms). It has a muscular body with a deep chest and a thick, wiry coat. Spinoni can be white, brown and white, or orange and white in color, and many possess solid brown or orange patches. The dog has a distinctive long head with hanging ears, a wiry mustache, and a tufted beard. Its eyes have a sweet expression. Spinoni have served as hunting dogs for many centuries, helping hunters retrieve prey. They can hunt in all environments and are good swimmers. Spinoni are also gentle, intelligent, loyal dogs that can make excellent family pets. Critically reviewed by the Spinone Club of America

Spinoza, *spih NOH zuh,* **Baruch,** *buh ROOK* (1632-1677), was a Dutch philosopher. He was also called Benedict, the Latin form of Baruch.

Spinoza was born on Nov. 24, 1632, in Amsterdam of Portuguese-Jewish parents. He early acquired the reputation of a freethinker and was excommunicated by the Amsterdam Jewish community in 1656. He then lived in several towns in the Netherlands, earning a living as a lens grinder. Throughout his career, Spinoza supported religious toleration and political liberalism. He prized his independence, rejecting offers of a pension from King Louis XIV of France and of a university professorship in Germany. Although he was respected by many, Spinoza was controversial because of his radical and unorthodox views on religion, philosophy, and politics.

Spinoza's philosophy was strongly influenced by the French philosopher René Descartes and by such medieval Jewish philosophers as Moses Maimonides. Spinoza accepted Descartes's view that thought and matter are the basic categories of reality. The physical world is nothing but bits of matter moving and interacting according to general *causal laws*—that is, laws of cause and effect. However, in his masterpiece, *The Ethics* (published shortly after his death), Spinoza developed Descartes's ideas in radically unconventional ways. Spinoza stated that God is not some transcendent, supernatural being but is identical with Nature, and that "God or Nature" is the only substance. Thought and matter are two of God's infinite *attributes* (qualities), and all finite things, such as human minds and bodies, are only modes or effects of the attributes of God.

Spinoza argued that there are no exceptions to Nature's causal principles. He denied that human beings—or even God—act with free will. He maintained, however, that human happiness and freedom of mind can be attained by rational understanding of our place in Nature and of our subjection to its laws—particularly the laws of the mind's passion.

Spinoza published the *Theological-Political Treatise* anonymously in 1670. In it, he argued that the Bible is not literally of divine origin but is a work of human literature. It is, moreover, not a source of scientific, historical, or philosophical truths, but only of some basic universal moral precepts approved by reason. The most important of these precepts is to love one's fellow human beings and act with charity and justice. For Spinoza, these are the principles of "true religion." Spinoza argued that religions based on what he considered a fictional humanlike conception of God are just organized superstition. They represent a threat to personal well-being and the peace of the state. Spinoza was harshly condemned by both religious and secular authorities for these views. Spinoza died on Feb. 21, 1677. Steven Nadler

See also **Philosophy** (Modern philosophy).

Spiny anteater. See Echidna.

Spiny puffer. See Porcupinefish.

Spire is an architectural term used to describe the tapering structure at the top of a tower. Spires first became popular in Europe during Romanesque times in the A.D. 1100's. They reached their most developed form in the Gothic period that followed. Spires most often appeared on cathedral and church towers. Some skyscrapers built in the early 1900's had spires. William J. Hennessey

For pictures of spires, see **Coventry; Gothic art; Notre Dame, Cathedral of; Rouen; Sainte-Anne-de-Beaupré.**

Spirea, *spy REE uh,* also spelled *spiraea,* is a group of herbs and shrubs in the rose family that bear white, pink, or rose-colored flowers. Spireas grow in the temperate and cold regions of the Northern Hemisphere. Gardeners raise them as ornamental plants.

Vanhoutte spirea, one of the best known species, is a hardy shrub with thick, deep green foliage. Thunberg spirea has more delicate leaves. The hardhack, or steeplebush, another spirea, can be planted in masses. Its flowers grow in narrow, crowded clusters. The plum-leaved spirea is known as *bridal wreath.* It has white flowers and sometimes grows more than 6 feet (1.8 meters) tall. The troublesome weed meadowsweet, another notable species, grows in New England. Spireas grow well in good soil but need plenty of moisture and full exposure to the sun. Tim D. Davis

Scientific classification. Spireas make up the genus *Spiraea* in the rose family, Rosaceae. Vanhoutte spirea is *Spiraea x vanhouttei.* Thunberg spirea is *S. thunbergii.* Hardhack is *S. tomentosa.* Bridal wreath is *S. prunifolia.* Meadowsweet is *S. latifolia.*

See also **Bridal wreath.**

Spirit of '76 is a famous patriotic scene painted about 1875 by American artist Archibald M. Willard. It shows a fife player and two drummers leading American troops in a battle of the Revolutionary War in America (1775-1783). Willard painted several versions of the scene.

Willard first drew *The Spirit of '76* as a humorous sketch called "Yankee Doodle." Later, Willard painted a serious version of the sketch that was displayed at the Philadelphia Centennial Exhibition of 1876. Willard used

Detail of an oil painting on canvas (about 1875) by Archibald M. Willard; Board of Selectmen, Abbot Hall, Marblehead, Massachusetts

The Spirit of '76 shows two drummers and a fife player leading American troops during a Revolutionary War battle.

friends and relatives as models in the various versions of the painting.   Sarah Burns

Spiritual is a type of religious song made famous by the African Americans of the southern United States. Spirituals are emotional songs and have a strong rhythm. They are especially moving when sung by a group. A leader sometimes sings one or two lines alone, and a chorus comes in with the refrain. Spiritual singers often emphasize the rhythm by clapping their hands.

The melodies used in spirituals are sometimes said to have originated in Africa. However, many spirituals are unrelated to African songs. Such spirituals reflect a direct relationship to evangelistic preaching among poor Southern whites that began at a Kentucky camp meeting in 1800. These "revivals" also encouraged "white spirituals." The blacks' love for song led them to put their feelings into their singing at worship and at work.

The slaves based most of their spirituals upon characters and stories from the Bible. The manner in which these stories are told in black spirituals shows a colorful imagination and a simple faith. Many slaves thought of themselves as modern children of Israel and sought freedom from bondage. Their songs were appealing and sincere. Well-known spirituals include "Go Down, Moses," "Deep River," and "Swing Low, Sweet Chariot."

Spirituals were little known outside the Southern States until after the blacks were freed from slavery. In 1871, spirituals were introduced to other parts of the United States by a group of African Americans called the Jubilee Singers, of Fisk University. They traveled throughout the United States, and to England and Germany, giving concerts to raise money for their school. Other black schools followed their example. The black quartets from Hampton Institute and Tuskegee Institute (now Tuskegee University) became famous.

Spirituals are now one of the best-known forms of American music. Major writers of spirituals include the African American composers Harry Thacker Burleigh, William Dawson, and Hall Johnson. Such African American singers as Marian Anderson, Roland Hayes, and William Warfield helped make spirituals popular.

Leonard W. Van Camp

See also **Burleigh, Harry Thacker.**

Spiritualism is the belief that spirits of the dead can communicate with the living. It exists worldwide in various forms. In the United States, the modern spiritualist movement began in 1848. That year, Katherine and Margaret Fox, two sisters from Hydesville, New York, near Rochester, heard knocking in their home. They could not attribute the knocking to any material source. The sisters devised a code to interpret the noises to communicate with the spirit they believed was sending them messages. The events at Hydesville led to the formation of many independent churches and philosophical organizations to advance the ideas of spiritualism.

Beliefs. Spiritualists believe that human beings are made up of body, soul, and spirit. At death, the body ceases to exist, but the spirit continues to exist because it is encased in the soul. According to spiritualists, communication between the physical and spiritual world does not end with physical death. Spiritualists also claim that after death the spirit moves through several *extraterrestrial* levels of existence—that is, levels outside of the earth. These levels range from *purgation* (punishment) for the wicked to freedom from all suffering for the good. In the extraterrestrial state, the spiritual being can improve and move upward toward the highest plane of existence.

The medium. To communicate with departed spirits, spiritualists sometimes meet in small gatherings called *séances.* During a séance, several persons sit at a table and touch hands. An individual, usually called a *medium* but sometimes called an *instrument* or a *channel,* leads the séance. The medium helps the group concentrate their thoughts on the person they wish to contact, usually a deceased friend or relative. The spirit of the deceased supposedly shows its presence by making rapping sounds, moving objects in the room, or by speaking through the medium. A medium also may meet with one person to channel communication between a particular spirit and that person.

Mediums who communicate the words of the spirit sometimes use such devices as a *Ouija board* or a board called a *planchette* to spell out messages. *Materializing mediums* claim that their powers can make the spirit appear in solid form. *Physical manifestation mediums* supposedly enable the spirit to move objects or to play musical instruments.

Spiritualism and religion. Although many scientists dispute spiritualist claims, spiritualists defend their beliefs. They claim that communication between the living and the dead has been scientifically verified. Spiritualists regard their beliefs as an authentic religion based on moral and philosophical principles. Many attend churches that belong to the National Spiritualist Association of Churches. But most forms of Christianity do not agree with spiritualism's main teaching that the spirits of the dead communicate with people on earth.

Susan M. Setta

See also **Ghost; Trance.**

Additional resources

Schwartz, Gary E., and Simon, W. L. *The Afterlife Experiments.* Simon & Schuster, 2002. A study of mediums and their communication with the dead.
Spirit Summonings. Time-Life Bks., 1989.

Spiritualists. See Abstract art.
Spirometer, *spy RAHM uh tuhr,* is an instrument used to measure the volume of air a person can breathe. Physicians use spirometers to diagnose certain respiratory disorders and to evaluate treatment.

A common type of spirometer consists of an air-filled cylinder, closed at its upper end and open at its lower end. This cylinder floats in the water-filled space between two other cylinders. The air-filled cylinder is connected to the lungs by a tube with a mouthpiece at one end. When a person exhales, the air in this cylinder increases, and the cylinder floats higher in the water. As the patient inhales, air leaves the cylinder, and it falls. The movements of the air cylinder are recorded on a strip of paper called a *spirogram.* Electronic spirometers show results on a display screen or paper printout.

A spirometer can measure changes in the volume of air in the lungs. Inflammation and tumors reduce the capacity of the lungs. The instrument also shows the speed at which air moves in and out of the lungs. Such diseases as asthma and bronchitis narrow the air passages, reducing the rate of air flow.   Michael G. Levitzky
Spitz is the name of a family of dogs of far northern descent. Breeds in the spitz family include the Akita, Alaskan malamute, chow chow, Finnish spitz, Keeshond, Norwegian elkhound, Pomeranian, Samoyed, and schipperke. All have sturdy bodies, pointed ears, and thick, harsh coats. Many have curled tails that fall over their hindquarters. Each of the breeds named has an article in *World Book.*   Critically reviewed by the American Kennel Club
Spitzer, Lyman, Jr. (1914-1997), an American astrophysicist, pioneered the use of telescopes in space. His research focused on *plasmas,* forms of matter made up of electrically charged atomic particles. Spitzer studied plasmas in outer space and also in laboratories on Earth.

In his 1946 paper "Astronomical Advantages of an Extra-Terrestrial Observatory," Spitzer made the first convincing proposal for sending a telescope into space. Earth's atmosphere interferes with the light reaching the planet's surface from outer space. Spitzer argued that a telescope orbiting above the atmosphere, therefore, could perform important observations not possible with ground-based telescopes. Spitzer's ideas eventually led to the launch of the Hubble Space Telescope in 1990.

Much of Spitzer's astrophysical research concerned the *interstellar medium,* the gas and dust in the space between the stars. He also led efforts to create hot plasmas in Earth laboratories, becoming the founding director of the Princeton Plasma Physics Laboratory in 1951.

Spitzer was born June 26, 1914, in Toledo, Ohio. In 1938, he earned a Ph.D. degree from Princeton University. He joined the faculty of Yale University in 1939. In 1947, he returned to Princeton, working there until his death on March 31, 1997. The Spitzer Space Telescope, launched by the National Aeronautics and Space Administration in 2003, was named for him.   James S. Sweitzer
Spleen is a soft, purplish organ behind and to the left of the stomach in human beings. A person's spleen is about the size of his or her fist. Scientists do not fully understand the spleen's functions. However, the organ plays a part in the circulatory and the immune systems.

The spleen helps filter useless substances from the blood. Blood cells form in the bone marrow and circulate in the body for some time before they die. Blood passing through the spleen travels through a maze of spongelike spaces called *sinusoids.* There, large cells called *macrophages* surround and destroy old or damaged blood cells. The spleen also helps the body fight infection. Macrophages in the spleen rid the blood of certain parasites and bacteria. In addition, the spleen contains clumps of white blood cells called *lymphocytes,* which release special proteins into the blood. These proteins, called *antibodies,* weaken or kill bacteria, viruses, and other organisms that cause infection.

Sometimes, surgeons remove a patient's spleen in an operation called a *splenectomy.* The spleen may be removed if it is damaged or overactive, or if the patient has cancer of the lymphatic system. A person's spleen may be damaged by a blow to the abdomen, causing a serious loss of blood. In most cases, surgeons can repair a damaged spleen. But a splenectomy is sometimes necessary to stop the bleeding.

The spleen may also become overactive and filter useful substances from the blood. The loss of these substances may result in anemia, bleeding, or infection. In some cases, a splenectomy improves or corrects the disorder. Cancer of the lymphatic system may also affect the spleen, thus requiring surgical removal of the organ.

A splenectomy causes no noticeable ill effects in most patients. But in a few patients, especially children, removal of the spleen leads to serious infection. For this reason, a patient who has had a splenectomy should receive a special vaccination that reduces the chances of infection.   David D. Oakes

See also **Iron** (How bodies use iron); **Lymphatic system** (picture).
Split (pop. 190,000) is a city in southern Croatia that developed from an ancient Roman town. It lies along the Adriatic Sea (see **Croatia** [map]). The city's name in Italian is Spalato. Split was originally built about A.D. 295 within the walls of the palace of the Roman Emperor Diocletian. The remains of the palace still stand in what is now the center of Split. They provide a fine example of Roman architecture. Today, Split is an important seaport and center of industry—especially shipbuilding. A large hydroelectric power plant is nearby.   Sabrina P. Ramet
Spock, Benjamin McLane (1903-1998), an American pediatrician, became famous for his books on child care. Spock's best-known book, *Common Sense Book of Baby and Child Care* (1946), was translated into over 25 languages. For later editions, the book's title was shortened to *Baby and Child Care.* His other books include *Feeding Your Baby and Child* (1955), *Baby's First Year* (1955), *Dr. Spock Talks with Mothers* (1961), *Problems of Parents* (1962), and *Caring for Your Disabled Child* (1965). These works had a tremendous influence on parents during the 1950's and the 1960's, especially in the United States.

In the 1960's, Spock became an active opponent of United States involvement in the Vietnam War. In 1968, he was convicted on charges of conspiring to counsel young men to avoid the military draft. He appealed the verdict. In 1969, the United States Court of Appeals for the First Circuit reversed his conviction.

Spokane is Washington's second largest city—after Seattle—and a center of commerce and transportation. Spokane lies on the Spokane River in the far eastern part of the state. Buildings along the river include the modern sloping convention center, *center*. The landmark clock tower at the far right of the picture stands in Riverfront Park and dates from 1902.

Allan Bisson

Spock was born in New Haven, Connecticut. He graduated from Yale University and received his medical degree from Columbia University. Dale C. Smith

Spoils system is the practice of giving public offices as political rewards for party services. The system is used in many countries. When a new political party comes to power, its leaders place many of their faithful followers in government offices. Many people consider this justifiable when a party places able persons in high offices where policy is to be made. They feel the victorious party must shape policies to satisfy its supporters. But many people feel the practice is unjustifiable when leaders dismiss able persons from positions that are not of a policymaking type to make room for others whose chief or only merit consists of their having demonstrated their strong support of the party.

It was once widely thought that the spoils system in the United States first came into general use during the presidency of Andrew Jackson. Recent studies show that President Thomas Jefferson, a Democratic-Republican, followed a policy of not appointing Federalists to government offices. However, Jackson's friend, Senator William L. Marcy of New York, popularized the slogan "to the victor belong the spoils of the enemy."

By 1840, the spoils system was widely used in federal, state, and local governments. In 1883, a civil service law made it illegal to fill some federal offices by the spoils system. Since then, federal civil service legislation has greatly expanded. Many cities and states also make education and experience the basis of appointment to public office. In a series of three decisions—in 1976, 1980, and 1990—the Supreme Court of the United States ruled that low-level government workers may not be hired, promoted, transferred, or fired based on their support or nonsupport of a political party. Charles O. Jones

See also **Civil service** (History); **Grant, Ulysses S.** (Political corruption); **Jackson, Andrew** (The spoils system); **Patronage.**

Spokane, *spoh KAN* (pop. 195,629; met. area pop. 417,939), is an important commercial center in eastern Washington. It ranks second to Seattle among the state's largest cities. Spokane is the transportation center of the Inland Northwest. This rich agricultural, lumber, and mining area covers part of eastern Washington, northern Idaho, western Montana, and northeastern Oregon. Spokane, the seat of Spokane County, lies on the Spokane River, about 15 miles (24 kilometers) west of the Idaho border (see **Washington** [political map]).

In 1810, the Canadian North West Company established a fur trading post called Spokane House near what is now Spokane. Permanent settlers came to the area in 1871. They were attracted by the falls of the Spokane River as a possible source of water power. They named their settlement Spokane Falls. The word *Spokane* is the name of an Indian tribe that lived in the area.

Description. Two waterfalls in the center of the city furnish hydroelectric power and add to Spokane's beauty. Riverfront Park, located at the falls, provides open space and recreational facilities. Other attractions include a symphony orchestra, the Grace Campbell Memorial House and the Northwest Museum of Arts and Culture, which houses one of the world's largest collections of materials of the plateau Indian group. Educational institutions in the city include Gonzaga University, Whitworth College, Spokane Falls Community College, and a campus of Washington State University.

Economy. Service industries, such as wholesale and retail trade, employ many Spokane workers. The city has about 500 manufacturing firms. Their products include aircraft parts, computer equipment, fabricated metal machinery, food products, lumber and wood products, and primary metals.

Spokane International Airport lies southwest of the city. Passenger and freight trains also serve Spokane.

Government and history. A mayor and a seven-member city council govern Spokane. Voters elect the mayor and a council president in a citywide election. Voters also elect two council members from each of the city's three districts.

Spokane Indians lived in what is now the Spokane area when white people first arrived there in the early 1800's. Spokane Falls was founded in 1871. A railroad first reached the community in 1881, and Spokane Falls also received a city charter that year. The discovery of silver and other minerals in the area attracted new settlers and businesses. A fire destroyed the city's business district in 1889, but the people rebuilt their community. They renamed it Spokane in 1891.

During the late 1890's, Spokane grew as a railroad center. New silver and lead mines opened nearby in northern Idaho during the early 1900's and increased Spokane's importance as a mining community. Immigrants from Europe helped boost the city's population from 36,848 in 1900 to 104,402 in 1910. During World War II (1939-1945), Spokane served as a base for training pilots and as a center of aluminum production. The city's population reached 181,608 in 1960, but many people moved to the suburban areas in the 1960's and 1970's.

In 1974, Spokane held a world's fair called Expo '74. In preparation for the fair, many redevelopment projects were carried out along the banks of the Spokane River. Riverfront Park was one such project. Several structures built for the fair became permanent features of the city, including an opera house and a convention center.

A major new shopping mall was completed near Riverfront Park in 2001. The mall, River Park Square, brought new growth to the area.   Chris Peck

For the monthly weather in Spokane, see **Washington** (Climate).

Sponge is an animal that lives at the bottom of oceans and other bodies of water. Sponges do not have heads, arms, or internal organs. They live attached to rocks, plants, and other objects beneath the water's surface. Adult sponges do not move about from one place to another, and many sponges look like plants. For these reasons, people once regarded sponges as plants. But today, scientists classify sponges as animals. Like most animals, sponges eat their food. They cannot manufacture their own food, as do plants.

There are about 5,000 species of sponges. Most of them live in oceans, but a few species are found in lakes, rivers, and other bodies of fresh water. Sponges can live in both shallow and deep water. Most *marine* (ocean-dwelling) sponges inhabit warm or tropical seas.

Sponges rank among the oldest kinds of animals. Fossils have been found of marine sponges that lived more than 500 million years ago. For centuries, people have used sponges for cleaning and bathing. The skeletons of certain sponges make good cleaning tools because they are soft and absorb large amounts of water. However, most cleaning sponges are artificially produced.

Recently, scientists have discovered chemical compounds in sponges that may be used in medicines to fight cancer and other diseases. Because sponges harbor large populations of bacteria in their body tissues, the bacteria may produce many of these compounds. Such important discoveries have led to an increased amount of research involving sponges.

The bodies of sponges

Sponges vary widely in shape, color, and size. Some sponges are round while others are shaped like vases. Many simply follow the shape of the object on which they grow, forming a living crust. Marine sponges range in color from bright yellow, orange, or purple, to gray or brown. Sponges of the same species may be of many different colors. Most freshwater sponges are green, purple, or gray. The smallest sponges measure less than 1 inch (2.5 centimeters) in diameter. The largest grow to more than 4 feet (1.2 meters) in diameter.

Body openings. A sponge has two types of openings on its body surface: (1) small pores called *ostia,* and (2) a large *osculum.* The sponge's ostia allow water to enter its body, and the osculum allows water to leave the body. Among more advanced sponges, a network of canals transports water entering through the ostia to all parts of the sponge. The water brings tiny plants and animals into the sponge. These tiny organisms are the sponge's food. Waste products—along with water—leave the sponge through the osculum.

Special cells. The canals that pass into the sponge's body lead into many small chambers. These small chambers in the sponge are lined with cells called *choanocytes,* also known as *collar cells.* Each of these cells has a delicate tissue, or collar, that acts like a net to trap food particles. Each collar cell also bears a long threadlike structure called a *flagellum.* The sponge's flagella whip around, and this action creates the water currents that flow through the body of the sponge.

The body of a sponge also contains other types of cells. Some of these cells form tissue that covers the body and the walls of canals inside the body. Other types of cells travel freely within the sponge. These cells have many different functions. For example, some heal injuries to the body, and others play a major role in reproduction. Still others produce material for the sponge's skeleton.

Skeleton. Sponges have several types of skeletons. Most sponges have a mineral skeleton made up of tiny, needlelike *spicules.* The spicules may be of either *calcium carbonate* (limestone) or *silica,* a glasslike mineral. In bath sponges, the skeleton consists only of fibers of a tan-colored protein called *spongin.* The skeleton of spongin fibers is what remains after a bath sponge dies and its cells are removed. Many sponges have a skeleton of both mineral spicules and spongin fibers. In other sponges, the skeleton consists of silica spicules, spongin fibers, and a massive base of limestone crystals.

The sponge's skeleton forms a framework that supports and protects the body. Spicules may be organized into bundles that form strong, geometric networks. In many sponges, numerous spicules grow around the osculum. These spicules protect the sponge from animals that try to eat it or enter its body.

Some kinds of sponges There are more than 5,000 species of sponges. Most sponges live in the ocean, but a few species are found in fresh water. Size, shape, and color vary widely among the many species of sponges, as shown by these photographs.

David Waselle, Journalism Services
Purple tube sponge

David Waselle, Journalism Services
Sulfur sponge

Al Grotell
Sheepswool sponge

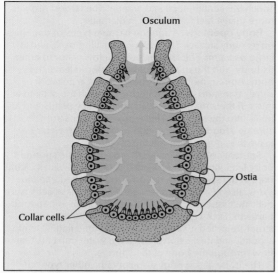

Osculum

Ostia

Collar cells

WORLD BOOK illustration by Arthur Grebetz

A sponge's body has many openings and passages that allow water to flow through the animal, as shown in this cross section. *Collar cells* trap and digest food particles in the water.

How sponges reproduce

Sponges reproduce both *sexually* and *asexually*. In sexual reproduction, a new sponge develops from the joining of two sex cells. In asexual reproduction, a new sponge is formed by methods that do not involve sex cells. Most sponges also have the ability to replace lost or injured body parts by growing new ones. This process is called *regeneration.*

Sexual reproduction in sponges begins when an *egg* (female sex cell) starts to grow inside the parent sponge's body. At first, the egg absorbs food from surrounding body fluids. Later, it engulfs cells called *nurse cells,* which provide food reserves. When fully grown, the egg is fertilized by a *sperm* (male sex cell). Some sponges produce both eggs and sperm. In these species, the egg may be fertilized by a sperm from the same animal. Other species produce either eggs or sperm only. In these species, another sponge releases sperm into the surrounding water. A sperm enters the parent sponge's body by way of the ostia and canal network and fertilizes the egg.

After the egg is fertilized, it gradually develops into a *larva* (immature animal form). The larva is covered with cells that have flagella. The flagella beat rapidly, enabling the larva to swim outward through the parent's canal system, aided by water currents. The larva leaves the sponge through the osculum and swims around from a few hours to a few days. It then attaches itself to some suitable surface at the bottom of the body of water and develops into an adult sponge.

Asexual reproduction in sponges may occur in a variety of ways. In every case, however, it involves cells called *archaeocytes.* These cells have no specialized functions. Instead, they have the capacity to develop into any type of cell in the sponge's body. During asexual reproduction, a group of archaeocytes grow into every

type of cell needed to form a new sponge.

Sponges may reproduce asexually by *budding.* In this process, buds or branches filled with archaeocytes grow on the parent sponge. These growths may break away from or fall off the parent sponge or remain attached to it. The growths develop into new sponges.

Some marine sponges and most freshwater sponges also may reproduce asexually by forming *gemmules.* Gemmules are budlike structures that consist of a group of archaeocytes within a tough shell of spongin. Many gemmules are reinforced by spicules. Gemmules typically form in response to either cold or hot weather. Protected within the gemmule shell, the archaeocytes can survive periods of drought or freezing temperatures, though the parent sponge may die. Gemmules "hatch" when more favorable weather returns. The archaeocytes then spread out on a solid surface and develop into a new sponge.

Regeneration. The developmental abilities of archaeocytes give sponges remarkable powers of regeneration. Even if large parts of a sponge's body are lost or damaged, they may be replaced or repaired. In laboratory experiments, scientists have pressed sponges through extremely fine cloth so that the sponges' bodies break up into separate cells or clumps of cells. When the cells are replaced in water, they first migrate together to form rounded cell clusters. Then the cell clusters reorganize to form complete sponges again.

Kinds of sponges

Sponges make up a *phylum* (major group) of animals called Porifera, which comes from a Latin word meaning *pore-bearer.* Zoologists divide sponges into three classes, based chiefly on common skeletal features.

Sponges with a limestone skeleton belong to the class Calcarea. Most species in this class inhabit shallow parts of oceans, but some have been found at depths of up to 13,000 feet (4,000 meters). The tiny sponge called *Sycon* belongs to this group.

A second class, Hexactinellida, consists of marine sponges with a silica skeleton. These species are commonly called *glass sponges.* Their spicules form beautiful geometric patterns. Glass sponges live up to 23,000 feet (7,000 meters) beneath the ocean's surface. The *Venus's-flower-basket* is a typical kind of glass sponge.

All freshwater sponges and most of the best-known marine sponges are in the class Demospongiae. Most of these animals have a skeleton of silica or spongin or of both substances. One kind of sponge in this class, the *boring sponge,* bores into coral, seashells, and other hard structures. This activity helps shape such marine environments as coral reefs and seacoasts. Other marine species in this group include the red-beard sponge, the sheepswool sponge, and bath sponges.

Some ocean sponges have a skeleton of silica and spongin with a thick base of limestone. Scientists include these sponges, sometimes called *coralline sponges,* in either the class Calcarea or Demospongiae. Many coralline sponges live in underwater caves. They are closely related to marine sponges that lived hundreds of millions of years ago.   Frederick W. Harrison

Scientific classification. Sponges make up the phylum Porifera, which is divided into the classes Calcarea, Demospongiae, and Hexactinellida.

Spontaneous generation refers to the theory that certain forms of life, such as flies, worms, and mice, can develop directly from nonliving things, such as mud and decaying flesh. This theory dates to prehistoric times and was widely accepted for thousands of years. It was challenged by scientific experiments, such as those performed by the Italian biologist Francesco Redi in 1668. Redi demonstrated that *maggots* (the young of flies) did not appear in meat from which adult flies were excluded. Previously, many people had believed that flies developed from decaying meat.

The theory of spontaneous generation was largely abandoned in the mid-1800's. By then, improvements in microscopes and other scientific instruments had enabled scientists to see the eggs and sperm of higher animals, the *ovules* (eggs) and pollen of plants, and bacteria and other microorganisms. For example, in the mid-1800's, the French scientist Louis Pasteur observed reproduction and growth in microorganisms. He demonstrated that the microorganisms would grow in sterilized broth only if the broth was first exposed to air that contained their *spores* (reproductive cells). Pasteur's discoveries led to the development of the *cell theory* of the origin of living matter. The cell theory states that all life originates from preexisting living material.

Today, most scientists believe that spontaneous generation took place at least once—when certain chemicals came together to form the first simple living organism more than 3 billion years ago. This process is not thought to be occurring in nature today because conditions on the earth no longer favor such chemical combinations. In addition, any simple organisms that did form in this way would almost certainly fail to compete successfully against more complex existing organisms. However, laboratory experiments since the mid-1900's have showed that many molecules found in living organisms can be *synthesized* (produced artificially). Most biologists believe that it will eventually be possible to produce simple forms of life in the laboratory.

Jerry A. Coyne

See also Life (The origin of life [The theory of spontaneous generation]); **Biogenesis.**

Spoon-billed catfish. See Paddlefish.

Spoonbill. See Shoveler.

Spoonbill is a long-legged wading bird that has a spoon-shaped bill. The bird swings its bill from side to side in the water to search for food. Spoonbills usually eat fish, water insects, and small crabs. Most spoonbills are white. The color of the bill, face, and legs varies with the species. These birds live in warm *wetlands* (marshy regions), and some migrate to nest. Spoonbills are related to herons, storks, and flamingos.

The *roseate spoonbill* is the most colorful spoonbill. Its neck and upper back are white. The other feathers are rosy-pink, turning to red on the wings. Roseate spoonbills nest in colonies and return year after year to the same place. The nest is a platform of sticks placed in low trees or shrubs. Females lay three or four eggs, which are white spotted with olive-brown. The roseate spoonbill lives in warm areas of the Americas.

Five other species of spoonbills live in Africa, Asia, Australia, and Europe. The *black-faced,* or *lesser, spoonbill* is endangered.　　James J. Dinsmore

Scientific classification. Spoonbills are members of the ibis

© Ralph A. Reinhold, Animals Animals

The spoonbill is a wading bird that swings its spoon-shaped bill from side to side in the water in search of food. The roseate spoonbill, *above,* lives in the warmer regions of the Americas.

family, Threskiornithidae. The scientific name of the roseate spoonbill is *Ajaia ajaja.* The black-faced spoonbill is *Platalea minor.*

Spore is a tiny, specialized structure that is able to grow into an organism. Nearly all kinds of plants, plus certain kinds of algae, bacteria, fungi, and protozoans, form spores. Spores help an organism or its species survive and move from place to place.

Spores vary greatly in size and shape, but most consist of one microscopic cell. Some fungi produce complex, multicelled spores. Spores contain protoplasm and food. Some spores have a thick wall and can remain *dormant* (inactive) for several months. These features help such spores withstand harsh weather, chemicals, and other conditions that might otherwise kill the organism. Spores called *zoospores* have tails and can swim. Others may move from place to place on air currents.

Plant spores. Plants produce spores during one stage of their complex life cycle called *alternation of generations* (see **Alternation of generations**). Plants form spores in a number of ways. Some plants grow a structure called a *sporangium* in which the spores develop. Examples of sporangia include the capsules that grow upright on moss plants and on the undersides of fern leaves. After the spores mature, they are released by the sporangia and scattered. If the spores are in a favorable environment, they *germinate* (start to grow). The protoplasm then breaks through the spore wall and begins to develop. Plants that bear spores in this way usually produce many spores at a time, but only a few of the spores live and germinate.

In some plants, such as ferns and mosses, the spores grow into a new plant called a *gametophyte.* The gametophyte does not resemble the parent plant. It produces *gametes* (sex cells). The gametes unite and produce a plant called a *sporophyte.* The sporophyte resembles the original parent plant. The sporophyte produces spores, and the cycle begins again. See **Fern.**

Seed plants have a reproductive cycle somewhat like that of ferns and mosses. But their spores are produced as a step in seed formation. The female reproductive organ of a seed plant produces spores called *megaspores,* and the male reproductive organ produces

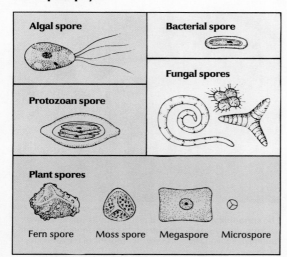

Algal spore

Bacterial spore

Protozoan spore

Fungal spores

Plant spores

Fern spore   Moss spore   Megaspore   Microspore

WORLD BOOK illustrations by Marion Pahl

Some kinds of spores. Plants, algae, fungi, bacteria, and protozoans form spores that vary in size and shape. Most consist of a single cell, although some fungal spores have many cells.

spores called *microspores.* Each megaspore stays inside the female reproductive organ and grows into a tiny gametophyte that produces an egg cell. Each microspore grows into a pollen grain, which becomes a gametophyte that produces two sperm cells. After pollination, a sperm cell unites with an egg cell, and a seed begins to develop. See **Seed** (How seeds develop).

Algal and fungal spores. Certain kinds of algae and fungi produce spores that function like seeds. These organisms bear sporangia that contain spores. The mature spores burst out of the sporangia and are widely scattered. The spores that germinate grow directly into a new alga or fungus. See **Fungi** (How a fungus lives).

Bacterial spores. Certain types of bacteria form spores as a means of protection. A bacterial spore is a bacteria cell that has developed a thickened cell wall and has become dormant. Some bacterial spores can withstand boiling water and thus hamper the sterilization of various foods.

Protozoan spores. Certain protozoans form protective spores by a type of cell division. Most of the protozoans are parasites in animals, and they move from animal to animal as spores. One common spore-forming protozoan causes the disease malaria.   Darrell J. Weber

See also **Plant** (How plants reproduce); **Protozoan** (Reproduction); **Reproduction** (Through asexual reproduction).

Sporophyte. See **Alternation of generations; Liverwort.**

Sport utility vehicle (SUV) is a popular passenger vehicle that is taller and larger than a normal car. An SUV combines the features of a station wagon and a truck. Like a station wagon, an SUV has a combined compartment for passengers and cargo, a rear door, and no separate trunk. But like a truck, an SUV features elevated driver seating and extra ground clearance.

Most SUV's have *four-wheel drive*—that is, a drive system that delivers the engine's power to all four wheels. Four-wheel drive provides good traction on steep hills,

rough or wet roads, and muddy trails. SUV's with four-wheel drive can be used for off-road travel, and so they are popular with skiers, hunters, and other outdoor enthusiasts. But most people use SUV's for everyday travel on paved roads. Manufacturers have begun producing SUV's without four-wheel drive for such mainstream drivers. Some vehicles, called *crossover vehicles,* look like SUV's, but their performance and fuel efficiency are more like those of a regular automobile.

Military jeeps, first used in the 1940's, were the forerunners of today's SUV's (see **Jeep**). The first commercial SUV was the 1962 Jeep Wagoneer.   Barry Winfield

Sporting dogs. See **Dog** (table: Breeds of purebred dogs; pictures: Sporting dogs).

Sports are organized athletic activities played individually or in teams. Most sports can be played by men and women and boys and girls. Many people participate in sports as amateurs for personal enjoyment, the love of competition, or as a healthful form of exercise.

Sports provide entertainment for people throughout the world. Large crowds attend sporting events in person. Millions of sports fans also follow their favorite teams and athletes by listening to play-by-play accounts of games on radio or watching competition on television.   William F. Reed

Related articles in *World Book* include:

Ball games

Baseball	Field hockey	Little League	Soccer
Basketball	Football	Baseball	Softball
Beach volley-	Golf	Platform	Squash
ball	Handball	tennis	Table tennis
Billiards	Jai alai	Polo	Team handball
Bowling	Lacrosse	Racquetball	Tennis
Cricket	Lawn bowling	Rugby football	Volleyball
Croquet			

Ice and snow sports

Biathlon	Ice skating	Skeleton	Snowboarding
Bobsledding	Iceboating	[sports]	Snowmobiling
Curling	Luge	Skiing	Tobogganing
Hockey	Ringette		

Water sports

Birling	Fishing	Sailing	Swimming
Boating	Rafting	Skin diving	Water polo
Canoeing	Rowing	Surfing	Water-skiing
Diving			

Other sports

Archery	Gymnastics	Kickboxing	Shuffleboard
Automobile	Hang gliding	Martial arts	Skateboarding
racing	Hiking	Mountain	Skydiving
Badminton	Horse racing	climbing	Spearfishing
Bicycle racing	Horseshoe	Quoits	Track and field
Boxing	pitching	Racing	Trapshooting
Climbing	Hot rod	Rodeo	Triathlon
Falconry	Hunting	Roller skating	Weightlifting
Fencing	Judo	Running	Wrestling
Glider			

Sports organizations

Amateur Athletic Union
Fellowship of Christian Athletes
International Olympic Committee
National Collegiate Athletic Association
Sokol

Other related articles

America's Cup	Baton twirling	Commonwealth
Balloon	Cheerleading	Games

Sports car is an automobile designed more for performance than for carrying passengers or luggage. Sports cars are known for their speed, handling, and appearance. They feature special equipment, and manufacturers make only limited numbers of them. As a result, they cost more than most other cars. Famous sports cars include the Chevrolet Corvette of the United States, the Lamborghini Diablo of Italy, the MGB and Triumph TR-7 of the United Kingdom, and the Nissan 300ZX of Japan.

Characteristics. Most sports cars are two-seaters with low, streamlined bodies that enable them to cut through the air easily. Consequently, these cars can accelerate more quickly than other automobiles do. Sports cars have wide tires and firm springs. These features enable the cars to get a firm grip on the road and therefore turn through corners faster. Also, sports cars typically weigh less than other automobiles. Their low weight gives them improved engine performance and makes it easier for them to change direction or slow down.

Sports cars often serve as a means of testing new automotive technology. For example, automakers have used sports cars to test four-wheel steering.

History. Automobiles began to be driven as sporting vehicles in the late 1800's. At that time, rich enthusiasts started racing one another from town to town. The first formally organized race took place in France in 1895. This race and others like it helped encourage the development of the automobile, and soon special cars were built for racing. Today, automobiles do not have to compete in any motor sport to be considered sports cars.

Many of the names of the early sports cars have disappeared, among them De Dion-Bouton, Deutz, Hispano-Suiza, Horch, and Itala. But others still appear on cars today, including Benz, Peugeot, and Vauxhall.

Automobiles in the United States in the early 1900's were light, rugged, and powerful. Well-known models of the time included the Chadwick Great Six, the Lozier Briarcliff, the Mercer Type 35 Raceabout, and the Stutz Bearcat. As time went by, however, the size of cars increased. By the 1930's, the only sports cars made in the United States were the Auburn, Cord, and Duesenberg, and the same company made all three.

By the 1940's, stock car racing had become the most popular motor sport in the United States. But in the late 1940's and early 1950's, there was a revival of interest in light, quick cars. A number of small, short-lived businesses sprang up to produce sports cars—among them the Kaiser Darrin and the Woodill Wildfire.

In 1953, the General Motors Corporation launched the Corvette. The Ford Motor Company responded with the Thunderbird in 1954, but Ford eventually turned the "T-bird" into a four-seater sedan. Thus, the Corvette remained the only true sports car made in the United States until the Chrysler Corporation introduced the Dodge Viper in 1992.

Meanwhile, sports car production was fairly strong in Europe before and after World War II (1939-1945). Among the most important sports cars made in the United Kingdom were the MG, Austin-Healey, and Triumph.

© General Motors and Wieck Photo Database

Chevrolet Corvette—United States

© Automobili Lamborghini U.S.A., Inc.

Lamborghini Gallardo—Italy

© Porsche Cars North America, Inc.

Porsche Carrera GT—Germany

Beginning in the late 1940's, such names as Jaguar of the United Kingdom, Ferrari of Italy, and Porsche of Germany became well known for racing and sports cars.

In the 1960's, the Japanese auto industry introduced its first sports cars, including the Honda S800 and Toyota 2000GT. Since then, Japanese automakers have built generations of fast, reliable sports cars. Among these are the Nissan 300ZX, Toyota Supra, and Mazda RX-7.

Since 2000, several automakers have made cars with vastly increased engine power. This increase makes sports cars potentially more dangerous and difficult to control. Fortunately, advanced stability control systems have also become more common. The Audi R8 is typical of the modern sports car, with all-wheel drive and all-aluminum construction.   Barry Winfield

See also **Automobile racing** (Sports car racing).

Sports medicine is a field that provides health care for physically active people. Its main purpose is to minimize the risk of injury and to treat effectively injuries that do occur. Sports medicine draws on the knowledge of many specialists, including physicians, athletic trainers, physiologists, and physical educators. These experts aid in determining the kind of training needed to help athletes perform to their highest capabilities without injury. Experts in sports medicine also evaluate coaching methods, the enforcement of regulations, and the design and use of athletic equipment and facilities.

Many organized athletic teams have an arrangement

with a doctor who functions as the team physician. This physician arranges for preseason physical examinations, and medical attention for team members during the season. On many teams, an athletic trainer provides first aid and emergency care to injured players. After an injury, the team physician and trainer provide a rehabilitation program so the injured athlete may return to play as quickly as possible. Surgery is usually performed by an orthopedic surgeon. Sports medicine has led to improved diagnosis and treatment of common problems, including knee injuries and muscle strains, which affect the general public as well as athletes.   Bruce Reider

Spot is a popular sport fish found in shallow coastal waters, estuaries, and sounds along the Atlantic and Gulf of Mexico coasts. Most spots measure from 6 to 10 inches (15 to 25 centimeters) long and weigh about ½ pound (0.2 kilogram). The fish is bluish above and silvery below, and it has a small dark spot on the shoulder. The

WORLD BOOK illustration by Colin Newman, Linden Artists, Ltd.
The spot is named for the spot on its shoulder.

upper side of the fish has from 12 to 15 yellowish stripes. The spot has value as a food fish, as a bait fish, and as pet food.   Tomio Iwamoto

Scientific classification. The spot belongs to the family Sciaenidae. It is *Leiostomus xanthurus.*

Spotswood, Alexander (1676-1740), was a lieutenant governor of colonial Virginia. He took office in 1710. He tried to regulate the fur trade with the Indians, and he favored the inspection of tobacco to prevent the export of inferior goods. He tried to protect the colony from Indian raids. Spotswood encouraged settlement along the colony's western frontier and led many expeditions over the Blue Ridge Mountains. He quarreled with the council of the Virginia colony over many of his policies. He retired to his estate in Spotsylvania County in 1722 after being removed as lieutenant governor. Spotswood was born in Tangier, Morocco. He died on June 7, 1740.

Fred W. Anderson

Spotted fever, Rocky Mountain. See Rocky Mountain spotted fever.

Spotted knapweed is a flowering plant that has become a harmful weed. The plant, native to Europe and western Asia, now grows widely in North America. It often invades grasslands, driving out native vegetation by spreading rapidly and by releasing into the soil a poisonous substance called *cnicin* (pronounced *NY sihn).* Spotted knapweed does not prevent soil erosion as well as native plants, and its spread may lead to erosion damage. Pasturelands overrun by the weed cannot easily support livestock, which prefer to eat the native plants.

Spotted knapweed has one or more slender, upright stems that stand about 1 to 3 feet (30 to 90 centimeters)

tall. Its flowers usually range from pink to purple in color, though some are white. Black-tipped *bracts* (modified leaves) lie below the flowers' petals, giving the blossoms a "spotted" appearance. Spotted knapweed can multiply rapidly because it produces more than 1,000 seeds per plant. Seeds may sprout from spring through fall. Those that begin to grow in the fall produce a group of leaves called a *rosette* before winter. The weed then remains inactive until spring, when it resumes growth. Spotted knapweed can live for two or more years.

People first brought the plant to North America in the late 1800's. Since then, the weed has infested millions of acres or hectares of land there.   James S. Miller

Scientific classification. Spotted knapweed belongs to the composite family, Asteraceae or Compositae. Its scientific name is *Centaurea biebersteinii.*

Spotted owl is an owl that lives in forested mountains of western North America. It also inhabits the southwestern United States and Mexico. This owl has become the center of a dispute between conservationists and the timber industry over the use of Pacific Coast forests.

Spotted owls are dark brown with white spots across the back of the head and white blotches on the breast and abdomen. They stand about 18 inches (46 centimeters) tall and weigh about 20 ounces (565 grams). Spotted owls nest in large cavities or deserted nests in trees, or on ledges in caves or cliffs. Unlike most types of owls, spotted owls have little fear of human beings.

The spotted owl that has been the major source of controversy is a subspecies called the *northern spotted owl.* The centuries-old forests that it inhabits are a major source of timber. The U.S. Fish and Wildlife Service classified this owl as a threatened subspecies in 1990, mostly because logging was destroying the owl's natural habitat. In 1994, to protect the owl and other wildlife, the U.S. government began limiting logging in large areas of federal forests in Washington, Oregon, and northern California. Conservationists have criticized the government for not preserving enough forestland and for failing to take additional measures to prevent the owl from eventually dying out. Prologging groups argue that the government's actions have cost many jobs in the forest products industry, and further conservation efforts could eliminate more.   Eric Forsman

Scientific classification. Spotted owls belong to the family Strigidae. The northern spotted owl is *Strix occidentalis caurina.*

Spotted Tail (1823?-1881) was a leader of the Brulé band of the Lakota Sioux Indians. In the early 1860's, he led his band against white settlers but later supported peaceful relations between the Lakota and the United States government.

In 1868, Spotted Tail and other Lakota leaders signed the Treaty of Fort Laramie, which forbade whites to occupy or build roads through Lakota territory. This region included parts of present-day North and South Dakota, Montana, and Wyoming. Miners violated the treaty

Detail of oil painting on canvas (1887) by Henry Ulke; National Collection of Fine Arts, Smithsonian Institution, Washington, D.C.

Spotted Tail

when they poured into the Black Hills during the gold rush of 1874, and several Indian uprisings resulted. Spotted Tail did not take part in the fighting and worked for a peaceful solution. In 1877, the U.S. government took possession of the Black Hills from the Lakota. In 1878, Spotted Tail and his people settled on the Rosebud reservation in what is now South Dakota. On Aug. 5, 1881, he was killed by Crow Dog, a rival Brulé leader.

Spotted Tail was born near Fort Laramie in Wyoming. The Rosebud Sioux tribal university in Mission, South Dakota, has his Indian name, *Sinte Gleska.*   Jeffrey Ostler

See also **Indian wars** (Wars on the Plains).

Sprain is an injury to a ligament or to the tissue that covers a joint. Ligaments are bands of fibers that hold the joint's bones in position (see **Ligament**). The tissue that covers the joint is the *capsule.* Most sprains result from a sudden wrench that stretches or tears the tissues of the ligaments or capsule. Ankle and wrist sprains are most common, but a person may sprain any joint.

A sprain is usually extremely painful. The injured part often swells and turns black and blue. Doctors may prescribe rest, elevation of the injured part, or the application of cold compresses or elastic bandages to reduce swelling. Special types of exercise also may help reduce swelling and speed recovery.   Bruce Reider

Sprat is one of the smaller sea fish in the herring family. Sprat grow to 8 inches (20 centimeters) long. They live in European coastal waters from the Baltic and North seas to the Mediterranean and Black seas. They have a flattened body with a saw-toothed edge along the belly. Sprat are important food fish. They are eaten fresh or smoked. Some are canned in oil as *brisling sardines.* Others are processed for oil and fish meal.

Robert R. Rofen

Scientific classification. The European sprat is *Sprattus sprattus.*

See also **Herring; Sardine.**

Spreadsheet is a computer program used to organize numerical and other data in rows and columns, and then to perform calculations involving the rows and columns of numbers. Its many uses include mathematical, financial, scientific, and non-numerical work. *Spreadsheet* also refers to a body of data created by means of a spreadsheet program, and to a display of such data. The first spreadsheet program, VisiCalc, was introduced in 1978 for use on the Apple II personal computer. Spreadsheet programs used today include Microsoft Excel, Lotus 1-2-3, and Corel Quattro Pro.

The term *spreadsheet* comes from the accountant's spreadsheet—a large piece of lined paper used to list and analyze financial information. Spreadsheet programs have almost completely replaced such paper documents. These programs can perform simple and complex mathematical operations. They make it easy to insert, delete, change, reorganize, analyze, and search for information. Repetitive tasks can be automated through *macros,* small programs written by the user and stored with the spreadsheet data.

The accompanying illustration shows two versions of a spreadsheet displayed on a computer. The intersection of a column and a row is called a *cell.* The currently selected cell is C8. Formulas link cells so that a change in one cell automatically changes all related cells. For example, the number in cell C8 is based on a formula that tells the computer to multiply the number in B8 by 10. When the user changes the number in B8, the numbers in C8 and other related cells change automatically.

Spreadsheets can link cells in one *worksheet* (set of rows and columns) with cells in other worksheets. These worksheets may be stored in a single file as a *workbook.* A corporation might create a workbook to evaluate ways it might invest in its divisions. Changing certain cells in the corporate worksheet would automatically change cells in divisional worksheets.   William T. Verts

Microsoft Corporation (WORLD BOOK photo)

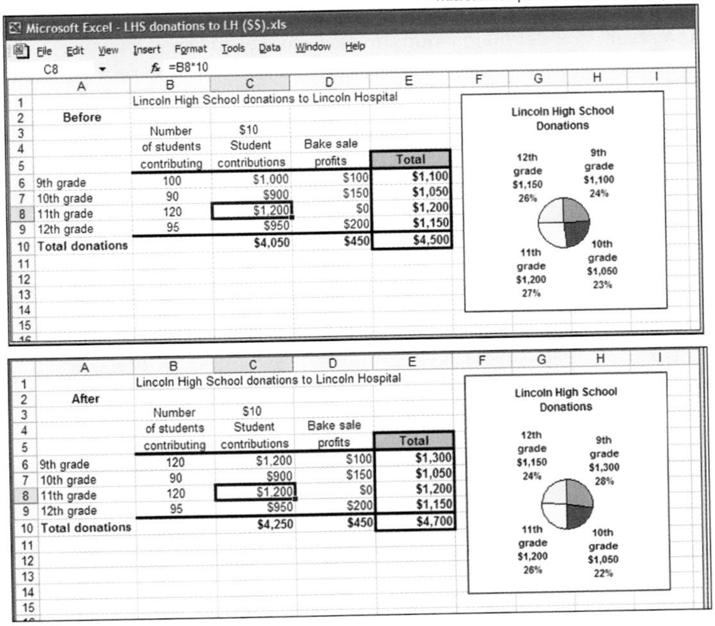

A spreadsheet program can add up columns of numbers and perform other calculations based on formulas entered by the computer user. When the user changes one number involved in a formula, the computer automatically recalculates. These spreadsheet displays show how the program reports results. The bottom display is a later version of the top display. Columns in both displays are linked by the formulas:

Column C = Column B × 10, and
Column E =
Column C + Column D.

The bottom display shows how the computer recalculated when the user changed the number of ninth-graders contributing from 100 to 120. This program can display data in graphs. These graphs help a user see, at a glance, how changing the number of ninth-graders altered the proportion of the total donations provided by each of the four classes.

Spring is a natural source of water that flows from the ground. Water from rain and melting snow seeps into the ground. It filters through pores and cracks in the soil into rock layers and eventually reaches a layer through which it cannot pass. This water held underground is called *ground water*. Gravity may force the water to rise until it finds a way out to the surface to form a spring.

Springs are found in mountains, hills, and valleys. They are often found at the foot of a cliff or slope or where a crack or fault reaches the surface. Hundreds of springs pour from walls of Idaho's Snake River Canyon.

The largest springs are found in limestone regions where the water flows underground in cavelike chan-

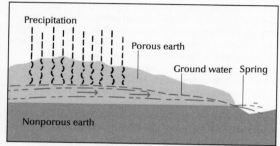

WORLD BOOK illustration

A spring is formed when *ground water*, water from rain or snow that has seeped into the ground, finds a way to the surface. When the water reaches ground level, it bubbles out. Springs are often found at a crack or channel in the surface.

nels. Where such channels reach the surface, great quantities of water may pour from the ground. Famous limestone springs are found in Florida and Missouri.

The temperature of a spring depends on the temperature of the soil or rocks through which its water flows. Ground water that travels close to the surface may produce springs that are warmer in summer than in winter. Springs that come from farther down are always cold. But deep down in Earth, all rocks are hot. In volcanic regions hot rock may lie close to the surface. As a result, spring water that has traveled from deep in Earth, or has originated in volcanic regions, is often hot.

Many springs contain minerals dissolved from the rock by the moving water. They are known as *mineral springs*. The belief that these springs relieve ailments has popularized them as health resorts. Examples of such health springs can be found in Mount Clemens, Michigan; Saratoga Springs, New York; Hot Springs National Park, Arkansas; and in France.   Roy M. Breckenridge

Related articles in *World Book* include:

Arkansas (Springs)	Hot springs
Florida (Rivers, lakes, and springs)	Idaho (Rivers, waterfalls, springs, and lakes)
Geyser	Mineral water
Ground water	Missouri (Springs and caves)

Spring is a device that recovers its shape after an outside force changes that shape and is then removed. Most springs are in the shape of a cylindrical coil or a flat spiral. They are made of metals—commonly steel and bronze.

A coil spring is made by bending a length of wire into the coil shape, then annealing and hardening it. *Annealing,* a process of heating and cooling, removes internal

pressures, called *stresses,* that result from bending.

A coil spring resists forces that tend to elongate or compress the coil. The amount of resistance is proportional to the force applied to the spring.

Adding alloys containing elements such as chromium, cobalt, nickel, and tungsten to steel wire used in springs increases the springs' ability to withstand heat. Stainless-steel springs will perform well at temperatures up to about 500 °F (260 °C). An alloy of nickel and chromium has been used at 900 °F (480 °C).   Stanley T. Rolfe

See also **Automobile** (The support system; diagram).

Spring is the season after winter and before summer. The Northern Hemisphere has spring weather from late March through May. In the Southern Hemisphere, spring weather begins in September and lasts through November. Throughout much of the middle latitudes, spring begins with the melting of winter snow. People living in the tropics rarely consider spring a distinct season because the temperatures there change little from month to month.

The number of daylight hours increases during spring, particularly in the polar regions, and the temperature rises. Nature awakens in spring. Flowers bloom, and hibernating animals leave their winter sleeping places. Many cultures have festivals that celebrate the arrival of spring.

Historically, the year began with spring in many cultures. Evidence of this practice in ancient Rome remains part of the modern calendar. Counting March instead of January as the first month of the year, we find that September, October, November, and December are the seventh, eighth, ninth, and tenth months. The prefixes *sept-, oct-, nov-,* and *dec-* come from the Latin words for 7, 8, 9, and 10.   Jon E. Ahlquist

See also **Equinox; Season.**

Spring-beauty is a type of North American wildflower that blooms in early spring. Spring-beauties are found from Nova Scotia to Georgia and from Saskatchewan to Texas. They also grow in the western United States from Washington to California. The plants are found in woods, thickets, and even lawns.

WORLD BOOK illustration by John F. Eggert

The spring-beauty is a North American wildflower. Its blossoms are white, pink, or rose-colored, with pink to purple veins.

A spring-beauty has white, pink, or rose-colored flowers. The flowers have pink to purple veins. The plant usually has a single pair of leaves about halfway up the stem. Spring-beauties grow 6 to 18 inches (15 to 46 centimeters) tall. The flowers of spring-beauties are *perennials*—that is, they may live for more than two years or growing seasons.   J. Massey

Scientific classification. Spring-beauties belong to the purslane family, Portulacaceae. They are genus *Claytonia.*

Springbok, also called *springbuck,* is an antelope that lives on the grassy open plains of southwestern Africa. It gets its name from its habit of repeatedly springing up to 6 ½ feet (2 meters) into the air when frightened, and then galloping off at high speed. These leaps distract predators, such as lions and cheetahs. The springbok has a fringe of long white hairs in the middle of its back that stand erect when the animal is frightened. Because of this trait, the Portuguese in Angola call this antelope the *goat of the fan.*

The springbok is slender and graceful. It stands about 2 ½ feet (76 centimeters) high and weighs from 73 to 95 pounds (33 to 43 kilograms). The springbok is brownish-red, with a white face and white on its underparts and inner legs. Both the male and the female springbok have curved, lyre-shaped horns. The larger male horns may be from 14 to 19 inches (36 to 48 centimeters) long.

In the past, wandering herds of many thousands of springboks ruined crops while seeking food and water. The Dutch settlers of South Africa called these animals *trekbokken* (traveling bucks). Hunters killed so many springboks that large wild herds today can be found

Charles G. Summers, Jr., Tom Stack & Assoc.

The springbok has long, slender legs and curved horns. This graceful antelope leaps high into the air when frightened.

only in remote regions of Angola and Botswana. Springboks also have been introduced to reserves and private game farms in South Africa.   Anne Innis Dagg

Scientific classification. Springboks are in the cattle family, Bovidae. They are *Antidorcas marsupialis.*

Springer spaniel. See Spaniel.

Springfield, Illinois (pop. 111,454; met. area pop. 201,437), is the state capital and the center of a rich farming region. It lies near a central Illinois coal field. For location, see **Illinois** (political map).

State government is Springfield's largest employer. The city is also a financial, insurance, and medical center for central Illinois. Springfield-area factories make automotive parts and meters, chemical and dairy products, farm equipment, flour and cereal products, house and industrial paints, industrial fans, mattresses. and specialty foods. Trade shows and cultural and sports events are held in the downtown Prairie Capital Convention Center. Lake Springfield, a large artificially created lake, furnishes water for industrial uses and for electric power. It is also used for recreation.

Springfield was founded in 1818 and was chosen as the seat of Sangamon County in 1821. In 1837, it was designated the capital of Illinois, but the state offices were not moved from Vandalia until 1839.

The original statehouse has been restored to its appearance in the mid-1800's. It houses the Illinois State Historical Library. The present Capitol, first occupied in 1876, is west of downtown Springfield.

Abraham Lincoln lived in Springfield from 1837 to 1861. His home still stands at Eighth and Jackson streets, near the city's center. The Lincoln family lived in the two-story frame house from 1844 to 1861. In 1971, the home was designated a national historic site. Lincoln is buried in Springfield's Oak Ridge Cemetery. Larkin G. Mead designed Lincoln's tomb, which was dedicated in 1874.

The pioneer village in which Lincoln lived from 1831 to 1837 has been reconstructed in Lincoln's New Salem State Historic Site, which is 20 miles (32 kilometers) northwest of Springfield. Vachel Lindsay, an American poet of the early 1900's, also lived in Springfield. His home is maintained as a tourist site. The Abraham Lincoln Presidential Library and Museum opened in Springfield in 2005. Springfield has a mayor-council form of government.   Michael E. Kienzler

See also **Illinois** (Climate; pictures); **Lincoln, Abraham** (pictures).

Springfield, Massachusetts (pop. 152,082; met. area pop. 680,014), is a commercial, educational, financial, and industrial center in the southwestern part of the state. The city lies on the Connecticut River, about 90 miles (140 kilometers) southwest of Boston near the Connecticut border. For the location of Springfield, see **Massachusetts** (political map). The Springfield metropolitan area consists of Franklin, Hampden, and Hampshire counties and covers 1,849 square miles (4,789 square kilometers).

Description. Springfield, the county seat of Hampden County, covers 33 square miles (85 square kilometers). Many of the city's cultural attractions are within a block called the Quadrangle. The Quadrangle includes the Connecticut Valley Historical Museum, the Museum of Science, the George Walter Vincent Smith Museum, and the Springfield Museum of Fine Arts.

A weapons museum, operated by the National Park Service, forms part of the Springfield Armory National Historic Site. Many sports fans visit the Naismith Memorial Basketball Hall of Fame in Springfield. It was named for James Naismith, a Springfield teacher who invented basketball in 1891. The city is the home of American International College, Springfield College, and Western New England College.

The city's manufactured products include chemicals, clothing, machinery, and metals. Bradley International Airport lies about 15 miles (24 kilometers) south of the city. Freight and passenger trains also serve Springfield.

Government and history. Springfield has a mayor-council form of government. In 1636, a group of English colonists led by William Pynchon bought the site of what is now Springfield from the Agawam Indians and built a settlement. During King Philip's War (1675-1676), Indians burned most of the buildings in Springfield (see **Philip, King**). But the colonists rebuilt the town, which became a center for farming and trading.

The Continental Army built an armory in Springfield during the Revolutionary War in America (1775-1783). In 1787, a group of farmers led by Daniel Shays tried to capture the armory to protest the imprisonment of debtors. Their revolt failed. See **Shays's Rebellion**.

In 1794, the Springfield armory became the first federal United States armory. Many skilled metalworkers moved to Springfield to work at the armory, and industry began to grow in the town. In 1795, the armory made the first military musket produced in the United States. It also developed the Springfield rifle of World War I (1914-1918) and the M1 rifle of World War II (1939-1945).

The coming of the railroad in 1839 contributed to the steady growth of industry and population in the town. Springfield received a city charter in 1852. During the 1850's, it became a major railroad center. The country's first successful gasoline-powered automobile, the Duryea, made its trial run in Springfield in 1893.

The Springfield armory stopped making weapons in 1968. Springfield Technical Community College and private industry took over most of its buildings.

Several major downtown developments took place in Springfield in the 1970's and 1980's. Baystate West, a hotel-office-retail complex in downtown Springfield, opened in 1971. The Civic Center, which includes facilities for conventions, cultural groups, and sports events, was completed in 1972. Construction in the 1980's included One Financial Plaza, which has office space, and Monarch Place, a downtown office tower and hotel.

In the late 1900's, Springfield's population declined. Many of the city's people moved to the suburbs.

Laurence A. Lewis

Springfield, Missouri (pop. 151,580; met. area pop. 368,374), is the third largest city in the state. Only Kansas City and St. Louis have more people. Springfield lies at the northern edge of the Ozark Mountains in southwestern Missouri (see **Missouri** [political map]).

Products made in Springfield include electronic equipment, machinery, and trailers. The city has one of the largest dairy goods processing plants in the United States. It is also a regional health-care center. The city lies in an area of scenic beauty, and it attracts many tourists. The Burlington Northern and Santa Fe Railway provides jobs and railroad service to Springfield.

The city is the site of the headquarters of the Assemblies of God, a religious denomination. Springfield is the home of the Assemblies of God Theological Seminary, Baptist Bible College, Central Bible College, Drury University, Evangel University, Ozarks Technical Community College, and Missouri State University.

The area was settled in 1830. Springfield became a town in 1838 and a city in 1847. It has a city-council form of government. Springfield is the seat of Greene County.

Paul A. Rollinson

Springhare is a rodent that lives in eastern and southern Africa. It is also called *springhaas.* Springhares live in long burrows with one or many entrances and are active mainly at night. Springhares often bound along like kangaroos, using only their long hind limbs. They may jump as far as 10 feet (3 meters) in one bound.

A springhare has long ears and a long tail. The animal has a tan upper body and whitish underparts. A patch of

© Tom McHugh, Photo Researchers

The springhare is an African rodent.

white fur runs along the inside and front of each thigh and up onto the back. The tail has a black tuft at the end. Adults are 14 to 17 inches (35 to 43 centimeters) long, not including their 15- to 20-inch (37- to 47-centimeter) tail. They weigh up to 9 pounds (4 kilograms).

Springhares feed chiefly on the bulbs and roots of plants. Adults usually live alone, but a pair with young may live together in one or more burrows. Adult female springhares may give birth more than once a year. One offspring is usually born at a time. Charles A. Long

Scientific classification. The springhare belongs to the family Pedetidae. It is *Pedetes capensis.*

Springsteen, Bruce (1949-), is a popular American singer, songwriter, and guitarist. His fans often refer to him as "The Boss." Springsteen is considered to be one of the most dynamic performers in rock music. He composes almost all the songs he performs.

Springsteen's sensitive and emotional lyrics explore the struggles, relationships, and dreams of ordinary people. His songs contain such traditional rock themes as youth's desire for independence and love of cars. His songs also deal with the problems of unemployed workers and veterans of the Vietnam War. Many songs carry a message of hope that life will be better in the future.

Springsteen was born on Sept. 23, 1949, in Freehold, New Jersey. By the mid-1960's, he was singing in small East Coast nightclubs. He signed with Columbia Records in 1972. In the early 1970's, he assembled the E Street Band, which accompanied him through the late 1980's. Springsteen became well known with his third album, *Born to Run* (1975). His most popular album was *Born in the U.S.A.* (1984). It had seven hit songs—"Born in the U.S.A.," "Cover Me," "Dancing in the Dark," "Glory Days," "I'm Goin' Down," "I'm on Fire," and "My Hometown." Other Springsteen hits include "Born to Run" (1975), "Hungry Heart" (1980), "War" (1986), and "Brilliant Disguise" (1987). A collection of his live performances was issued in 1986 as *Bruce Springsteen and the E Street Band Live/1975-1985.*

Springsteen won an Academy Award in 1994 for his song "Streets of Philadelphia" from the movie *Philadelphia.* He reunited with the E Street Band to make the album *The Rising* (2002), inspired by the terrorist attacks in the United States on Sept. 11, 2001. The recording won three Grammy Awards. In 2005, Springsteen released a solo album called *Devils & Dust.*   Don McLeese

See also **Rock music** (picture).

Spruance, Raymond Ames (1886-1969), was a top United States naval commander during World War II (1939-1945). Many experts rate him the best American naval combat commander of the war. Spruance helped devise the circular battle formation that made U.S. carrier groups the most effective fighting fleets in history.

In June 1942, Spruance led the force sent to stop the Japanese at Midway Island. The United States won the Battle of Midway, sinking four Japanese aircraft carriers. Many historians consider the battle the turning point of the Pacific war. After the battle, Spruance was promoted from rear admiral to vice admiral (see **World War II** [The tide turns]). Admiral Chester W. Nimitz, commander of the Pacific Fleet, made Spruance his chief of staff.

In 1943, Spruance led naval forces in the assault on Tarawa in the Gilbert Islands. He was promoted to admiral. In early 1944, he directed attacks on the Marshall Islands and the Japanese naval base at Truk. Later that year, Spruance won a crushing victory in the Battle of the Philippine Sea and led naval forces in the capture of Saipan and Guam. In 1945, he led the first carrier strike on Tokyo and directed the capture of Iwo Jima. After the war, he served as commander in chief of the Pacific Fleet and later as president of the Naval War College.

Spruance was born on July 3, 1886, in Baltimore. He graduated from the U.S. Naval Academy in 1906. Spruance died on Dec. 13, 1969.   Adrian R. Lewis

Spruce is the common name of a group of evergreen *conifers* (cone-bearing trees) in the pine family. About 40 kinds of spruce trees are native to the Northern Hemisphere. Some spruces grow within the Arctic Circle. Others grow as far south as the Pyrenees Mountains in Europe. In North America, they grow as far south as North Carolina and Arizona.

Spruces are more closely related to firs than to any other conifer. But spruces have cones that hang straight downward. Fir trees have cones that stand straight up. The scales on spruce cones remain on the cones. The scales on fir cones fall off when the cones become ripe.

Most spruce tree needles are four-sided, stiff, and less than 1 inch (2.5 centimeters) long. Woody, peglike projections join the needles to the twig. Fir trees do not have these projections. Spruce trees grow tall. Most are shaped like pyramids. In old spruce trees, the drooping

© Ralph Hunt Williams, West Stock

The blue spruce has long, sharp needles. A thick wax coating on the needles gives the spruce a silvery-blue frosted appearance. The blue spruce makes a popular Christmas tree.

lower branches may brush the ground.

Kinds. The *white, black,* and *red* spruces of the North and East and the *Sitka, Engelmann,* and *blue* spruces of the West are the leading commercial spruces in North America. The white and black spruces are named for the general color of the bark and foliage. The white spruce may reach a height of 150 feet (46 meters). The black is a little smaller. These spruces are more widely distributed than any other. They grow between the Bering Strait on the north, and Maine, New York, and Michigan on the south. The red spruce grows between Nova Scotia and North Carolina, and as far west as Tennessee.

The Sitka spruce grows on the Pacific Coast from northern California to Alaska. It sometimes reaches a great height, especially in the swamps or tidewater regions. A number of giant Sitkas are over 300 feet (91 meters) high. The Engelmann spruce grows from British Columbia to New Mexico. The blue spruce grows naturally in valleys in the Rocky Mountains. It is widely planted in yards because of its silver-blue foliage.

The most important spruce in Europe is the *Norway spruce.* This tree is planted in eastern North America as an ornamental. The so-called *Douglas-spruce* (Douglas-fir) of Washington, Oregon, and British Columbia belongs to a different genus but is related to the spruces.

Uses. Spruce wood is widely used for wood pulp in the papermaking industry. The timber is strong, light, and flexible, and is well suited for masts and spars of ships. Spruce is also used to make boxes and sounding boards for musical instruments.

Spruce wood is also used for interior finishing in houses. Resin, tannin, and turpentine are products of spruce bark. Beer is sometimes made from young spruce twigs. The gum of the black spruce, which is hardened resin, is another product. Dyes have been made from turpentine, a by-product of papermaking.

Douglas G. Sprugel

Scientific classification. Spruces belong to the pine family, Pinaceae. They form the genus *Picea.* The scientific name for the white spruce is *P. glauca;* the black, *P. mariana;* and the red, *P. rubens.* The Sitka spruce is *P. sitchensis;* the Engelmann, *P. engelmannii;* the blue, *P. pungens;* and the Norway, *P. abies.*

See also **Conifer; Tree** (Familiar broadleaf and needleleaf trees of North America [picture]).

Spruce budworm is a highly destructive forest insect pest that lives throughout the northern United States and southern Canada. It is a small gray-brown moth with dark markings. During its caterpillar stage, it feeds on the needles of spruce and fir trees.

Female moths lay their eggs on spruce and fir trees in summer. The eggs hatch into caterpillars, which spend winter on the trees. In spring, they begin to eat the new tree buds. The caterpillars spin cocoons in summer and emerge as moths. Spruce budworms can kill a tree by eating its needles for three to six years.

The number of spruce budworms has been controlled naturally by the insect's limited food supply and by birds and other enemies. However, in the eastern United States and eastern Canada, an outbreak of spruce budworms has occurred every 30 to 60 years.

Since the 1940's, more than 20 million acres (8 million hectares) of forests in Maine, New Brunswick, and Quebec have been sprayed at least once with pesticides to kill spruce budworms. However, pesticides kill only part of the spruce budworm population. The survivors thus have a large food supply and can reproduce in great numbers.

In addition, environmentalists argue that widespread use of pesticides harms the environment. During the early 1980's, researchers increased their efforts to control spruce budworms through forest management methods and biological controls. By the late 1980's, outbreaks of spruce budworms in eastern North America had subsided.   Lloyd C. Irland

Canada/United States Spruce Budworms Program

The spruce budworm caterpillar feeds on the needles of spruce and fir trees. This destructive forest insect pest lives throughout the northern United States and southern Canada.

Scientific classification. The spruce budworm belongs to the order Lepidoptera. It is *Choristoneura fumiferana.*

Spurge is the common name for a variety of herbs, shrubs, and other plants, many of which are troublesome weeds. Spurges grow in regions throughout the world. They bear small flowers that often form clusters. Spurges often contain a biting, milky juice that may be poisonous. In dry regions, many spurges resemble cactuses because of their spines and fleshy leaves. Other spurges have small leaves and grow low to the ground.

One damaging species, the *leafy spurge,* ranks as a major weed on the northern plains of the United States and the Canadian prairies. It drives out pasture plants important to livestock. This weed has proved difficult to control because of its deep roots and numerous seeds. In soil, its seeds can remain alive and able to grow for up to eight years. The plant's *secondary roots*—that is, the branching roots that grow from the plant's first root—can provide buds that form new shoots. Farmers normally use chemicals called *herbicides* to control leafy spurge. But scientists are trying to develop biological control agents, such as insects and disease organisms, to combat the weed. Other spurges, including the *spotted spurge* and *prostrate spurge,* can damage gardens, lawns, and open areas.   Michael J. Tanabe

Scientific classification. Spurges are in the spurge family, Euphorbiaceae. The leafy spurge is *Euphorbia esula,* the spotted spurge is *E. maculata,* and the prostrate spurge is *E. humistrata.*

See also **Invasive species.**

Sputnik, *SPUHT nihk,* is the name of a series of unpiloted satellites launched by the Soviet Union. Sputnik 1, launched Oct. 4, 1957, was the first artificial earth satellite. It circled the earth once every 96 minutes at a speed of 18,000 mph (29,000 kph), until it fell to the earth on Jan. 4, 1958. The Soviet Union also launched nine much larger sputniks, from November 1957 to March 1961. The earliest of these carried the first space traveler, the dog Laika.   Cathleen S. Lewis

Spy is a person who tries to get secret information, especially about the enemy in time of war. A spy usually does so by operating in the enemy's territory in disguise. Spies seek valuable military, political, scientific, and economic facts and secrets. They sometimes operate under legal cover as diplomats, commercial representatives, or journalists. Countries use *counterspies* to prevent theft of information. Counterspies called *double agents* pretend to spy for an organization but actually spy against it.

The punishment for wartime spying usually is death. The United States and many other nations have laws making peacetime spying punishable by death as well. In the United States, the first law to establish specific punishments for spying was the Defense Secrets Act of 1911.   Douglas L. Wheeler

Related articles in *World Book* include:

André, John	Edmonds, Sarah	Hale, Nathan
Boyd, Belle	Emma Evelyn	Mata Hari
Chambers, Whittaker	Espionage	Rosenberg, Julius
	Fifth column	and Ethel

Spyri, *SHPEE ree,* **Johanna** (1827-1901), was a Swiss author of books for children. Her best-known book is *Heidi* (1881), the tale of an orphaned Swiss girl who brings joy to her grouchy grandfather and to others in her life.

Spyri was born Johanna Heusser on July 12, 1827, in Hirzel, Switzerland, near Zurich. She spent her whole life in or near Zurich. In 1852, she married Bernhard Spyri. Spyri wrote poetry as a child but did not write professionally until the age of 43. She then wrote several well-received short stories in order to raise money for refugees wounded in the Franco-Prussian War (1870-1871).   Kathryn Pierson Jennings

Squall is a sudden rise in the wind, often with a marked change in wind direction. Rain, hail, or sometimes snow may accompany the wind. A squall may be caused by an advancing mass of cold air that violently lifts the warm air in front of it.   T. Theodore Fujita

Squanto, *SKWAHN toh* (1585?-1622), also called *Tisquantum,* was a Patuxet Indian who befriended the Pilgrims. He helped the Pilgrims survive at Plymouth Colony.

Squanto was born near what is now Plymouth, Massachusetts. In 1614, he was kidnapped by English fishermen and taken to Spain to be sold as a slave. He escaped to England, where he lived for several years and learned to speak English. He also lived in Newfoundland for a time. Squanto returned home in 1619. He found that the Patuxet tribe had been wiped out by disease and the few survivors had joined the Wampanoag tribe. Squanto also joined the Wampanoag.

In 1621, Squanto met the Pilgrims, who were nearly starving after their difficult first winter at Plymouth Colony. The Pilgrims had angered the Wampanoag by stealing the Indians' corn. Squanto served as an interpreter between the colonists and the Wampanoag chief Massasoit and helped arrange a peace treaty (see **Massasoit**). Squanto then stayed with the Pilgrims. He showed them how to plant corn and where to hunt and fish.

Squanto tried to challenge Massasoit's leadership of the Wampanoag. This plot angered the tribe, and Squanto became the enemy of the Wampanoag in 1622. He died from a fever later that year.   Neal Salisbury

See also **Colonial life in America** (picture); **Plymouth Colony** (The first year).

Square, in geometry, is a plane figure that has four equal straight sides and four right (90 °) angles. If each side of a square is 4 inches long, the square can be cut into 4 × 4, or 16, smaller squares that have sides 1 inch long. The *area* of the square equals 16 square inches (see **Square measure**). In arithmetic

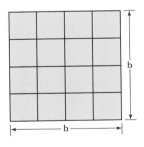

and algebra, the *square* of a quantity is the product of a quantity by itself. For example, 16 is the square of 4, because 4 × 4 = 16. If *b* represents any quantity, the square of *b*, or $b \times b$, is written b^2. The small 2 that appears to the right of and above the *b* is called an *exponent*. The exponent 2 indicates that the quantity *b* is to be taken twice as a factor.   Philip S. Marcus

See also **Power; Square root.**

Square dancing is a type of American folk dancing performed by groups of four couples. The couples may dance in a square formation or in a circle called a *run-*

WORLD BOOK photo by Steven Spicer

Square dancing is a popular type of American folk dancing. The dancers form groups of four couples, who execute various steps and patterns as directed by a caller (not shown).

ning set. They may also dance *longways,* in which two lines of couples face each other.

Square dancers follow the directions of a *caller,* who calls out different movements and patterns. Popular calls include "Promenade," "Swing your partner," and "Form a right-hand (or left-hand) star." The caller may give *singing calls,* in which the directions are sung, or *patter calls,* in which the directions are spoken against a musical background. Most of the music for square dancing is provided by fiddles, banjos, and guitars. It is almost always recorded—usually on records, but also on cassettes or tapes. The music is country or other styles of popular music, and amplified instruments dominate.

Square dancing is popular throughout the United States, especially in rural areas, and different styles have developed in the East and West. Most Eastern square dances are based on simple patterns, with one couple dancing at a time. Western square dances may involve several couples dancing in complex patterns.

Many square dances come from ancient English, Irish, and Scottish folk dances brought to America by early settlers. Different communities adapted the calls and movements in various ways.   Selma Landen Odom

Square measure is the system used in the measurement of surfaces. The unit for the *area* of a surface is the square. Hence *square* is the name of the system used in measuring surfaces. We can describe a tabletop as being 12 inches long and 10 inches wide, or 12 by 10 inches. But these figures represent only lines, which have just one dimension—length.

A plane surface has two dimensions. In the above example, they are length and width. These dimensions can be combined into a single expression using units of square measure. Thus we describe the area of the same tabletop as 120 square inches.

Square measure of any square or rectangular plane surface is obtained by multiplying length by width. The reason for this is easily seen if we draw a picture of the tabletop and mark off its inches. A line should be drawn at every inch along the length and at every inch along the width. The two sets of lines will cross each other. This will give us 120 little squares, each measuring 1 inch in length and 1 inch in width. The measure of each is a square inch. The square measure of other geometrical figures, such as triangles and circles, can be found in a similar way by using special formulas for finding their areas. The units of square measure that describe the area of a figure depend upon the dimensional units that are used. For example, if the above table were 12 meters long and 10 meters wide, its area would be 120 square meters.   Daniel V. De Simone

See also **Weights and measures** (Surface or area).

Square root of a number is a second number whose product with itself gives the original number. For example, a square root of 4 is 2, because $2 \times 2 = 4$. The symbol for a square root, called a *radical sign,* is $\sqrt{\ }$. For example, $\sqrt{25} = 5$ and $\sqrt{4} = 2$. The negative number -2 is also a square root of 4, because $-2 \times -2 = 4$. Each positive number has both a positive and negative square root. These two square roots will always be the positive and negative values of the same numeric figure.

Finding square roots. The easiest and fastest way to find the square root of a number is to use an electronic calculator. Other aids to finding square roots are tables of square roots, tables of logarithms, and slide rules.

It is possible to compute square roots to any desired accuracy using the basic operations of arithmetic. The method described here was discovered by the English mathematician Isaac Newton in the late 1600's.

To find the square root of a number, first make a guess or estimate of the square root of that number. It does not have to be a good guess, and, in fact, the number itself may be used. Next, take the average of the estimate and the number divided by the estimate. This average becomes a new and better estimate for the square root. To tell how good an estimate it is, multiply it by itself and compare the result to the number whose square root is sought. To improve the estimate, repeat the dividing and averaging process.

For example, to find $\sqrt{40}$ using a first estimate of 40, the number divided by the estimate is $40 \div 40$, or 1, and the average of this number and the estimate is $\frac{1}{2} \times (40 + 1)$, or 20.5. Next take the average of this second estimate and its division into 40, $\frac{1}{2} \times [20.5 + (40 \div 20.5)]$, to obtain the third estimate, 11.23. By repeating the procedure, the fourth estimate becomes $\frac{1}{2} \times [11.23 + (40 \div 11.23)] = 7.40$; the fifth, $\frac{1}{2} \times [7.40 + (40 \div 7.40)] = 6.40$; and the sixth, $\frac{1}{2} \times [6.40 + (40 \div 6.40)] = 6.33$. Checking the square, one finds that $6.33 \times 6.33 = 40.07$, which means that 6.33 is a close approximation of $\sqrt{40}$.

The process goes faster if a better guess is used for the first estimate. But, it always eventually gives a good approximation of the square root. Newton gave a logical proof of why this is true using an advanced kind of mathematics called *calculus.* Since the process is completely mechanical if the number itself is used as the first estimate, it can be programmed into a computer. Mathematical processes like these are called *algorithms.*

If a square root of a number that does not fall between 1 and 100 must be found, first multiply or divide the number by 100 to bring it within this range. Consider, for example, finding $\sqrt{4,000}$. Divide 4,000 by 100. This yields 40, a number within the 1 to 100 range. Now multiply the square root of 40, already determined as 6.33, by 10 (the square root of 100) to obtain the square root of 4,000: 63.3. In the same way, $\sqrt{0.4} = 0.633$, which can be found by multiplying by 100, finding the square root of 40, and dividing by 10.

Square roots of negative numbers. What is the square root of -4? Or, what number multiplied by itself gives a product of -4? If there is such a number, it cannot be positive, negative, or zero. None of these multiplied by itself can give a negative number. But, for convenience in solving certain problems, mathematicians have invented a system of *imaginary numbers,* whose squares are negative numbers.   Andy R. Magid

See also **Cube root; Root; Square.**

Squash is any of more than 40 kinds of gourd-shaped vegetables. The word *squash* refers both to the entire plant and to the fruit, which is the part that most people eat. In some regions, squash flowers are fried and eaten. Squashes are closely related to pumpkins. Many plants called pumpkins are actually squashes.

Squashes are highly nutritious. They provide large amounts of vitamins A and C and are low in calories. These vegetables can be cooked in many ways, and one type, zucchini, is often served raw in salads. Some cooks substitute the stringy pulp of the vegetable spaghetti squash for spaghetti in low-calorie dishes.

Squashes are native to the Western Hemisphere. Indians introduced them to the first European explorers who reached the New World. The name comes from *askutasquash,* a Narragansett Indian word meaning *eaten uncooked.* Squashes grow on bushes and vines. The plants have large five-pointed leaves and yellow-orange flowers. Their fruits have many different colors, shapes,

Hubbard

Butternut

Acorn

White scallop

Zucchini and Yellow crookneck

WORLD BOOK illustration by Kate Lloyd-Jones, Linden Artists Ltd.

Squash is a nutritious vegetable that grows on bushes and vines. There are more than 40 kinds of squashes, which differ in color, shape, and taste. Some popular types are shown above.

sizes, tastes, and textures. The two major groups of squashes are *summer squashes* and *winter squashes.*

Summer squashes grow on bushes. The fruit is picked when it is immature and has a soft rind. If a squash grows too large and ripe, it loses some flavor. Summer squashes should be eaten as soon as possible after harvesting. Common types of summer squashes include cocozelle, pattypan, white scallop, yellow crookneck, and zucchini.

Winter squashes grow on vines or bushes. They are frequently not picked until several days before the first freeze. At this time, the fruit is fully ripe and has a hard rind. Winter squashes can be stored for several months in a cool, dry place. Some canned "pumpkin" filling for pumpkin pie actually consists of one or more kinds of winter squashes. Popular winter varieties include acorn, banana, butternut, Hubbard, and vegetable spaghetti.

Growing squashes. Squash plants thrive in any region that has a warm growing season. The seeds should be planted in mounds of rich, well-drained soil. Summer squashes can be harvested in about two months. Winter squashes mature in three or four months.

Squash plants are attacked by several kinds of insects, including cucumber beetles, squash bugs, and squash vine borers. These pests can be controlled with insecticides or by picking them off the plants.

The leading squash-producing states are California, Florida, New Jersey, New York, and Texas. Squash is also popular with home vegetable gardeners.

W. E. Splittstoesser

Scientific classification. Squashes belong to the family Cucurbitaceae. The scientific name for summer squashes is *Cucurbita pepo.* The winter acorn squash is also *C. pepo.* Banana squash is *C. maxima.* Butternut squash is *C. moschata.*

See also **Gourd; Pumpkin; Zucchini.**

Squash, also called *squash rackets* or *squash racquets,* is a fast indoor game similar to handball and racquetball. Squash is played with rackets (or *racquets*) and a hollow rubber ball about the size of a golf ball. The ball is either hard or soft, depending on the version of the game being played. Players use the rackets to hit the ball against the four walls of a court. A variety of shots is possible, and the ball travels at great speed. Two players play *singles.* Two teams of two players each play *doubles.*

There are two forms of squash—*American,* or *hard ball,* and *English,* or *soft ball.* The soft ball form is also called international. Since the early 1990's, most players in North America as well as the rest of the world have adopted the soft ball form. A soft ball court is wider than a hard ball court. Many courts in the United States are hard ball courts, but a majority of people still play soft ball on them. Some matches are played on converted racquetball courts. This article discusses soft ball squash.

A soft ball squash court is 21 feet (6.40 meters) wide and 32 feet (9.75 meters) long. The *out-of-court line,* above which the ball is out-of-bounds, is 15 feet (4.57 meters) high on the front wall. The line slants down the side walls to 7 feet (2.15 meters) on the back wall. Doubles squash is played on a larger court. The surface of most squash courts is plaster, wood, or glass.

A player can only win a point while serving to the opponent, called the *receiver.* The player loses the serve in several ways, such as striking the ball more than once or serving onto or below a metal board called the *telltale board* or *tin.* The telltale board is 19 inches (48 centimeters) high at the bottom of the front wall. Generally, a player must score 9 points to win the game. But if a game is tied 8 to 8, the receiver may choose to continue to 9 points (known as *set one*) or continue to 10 points

© Jeffrey W. Meyers, The Stock Market

Squash is a fast indoor game played on an enclosed court. The players take turns hitting a hard rubber ball with a racket.

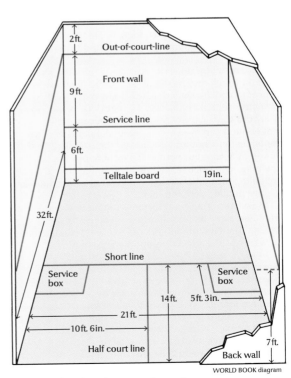

WORLD BOOK diagram

Diagram of an American squash court

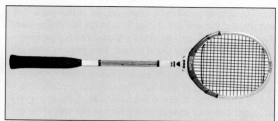

A squash racket, *above,* can be up to 27 inches (68 centimeters) long. The ball, *right,* is about the size of a golf ball. The American form of squash uses a more solid ball than does the English form.

(known as *set two).* The first person to win three games wins the match.

Squash originated at Harrow School in England about 1850. The game was introduced into the United States about 1880.

Critically reviewed by the United States Squash Racquets Association

Squatter is a person who lives on land without having a title or other legal authority and without paying rent. Sometimes a squatter can obtain the title to the land if no one else has a legal claim. During the 1800's, many people moved onto lands in the western United States that had not been surveyed and were not yet for sale. The U.S. Congress passed the Pre-emption Act of 1841, which allowed squatters to gain title to the land they occupied. Today, there are squatter colonies in some developing countries.   Linda Henry Elrod

See also **Homestead Act; Kansas** (The struggle over slavery); **Popular sovereignty; Pre-emption; Squatter's rights.**

Squatter's rights are claims made by settlers to the land on which they have settled. During the westward movement in the United States, many people called *squatters* settled on unsurveyed public land with no title. They did so to avoid buying land or because there was not enough surveyed land to meet the demand. They generally built homes and cleared the land. They believed they had thus earned the right to buy the land at the minimum price when the government sold it. Squatters often formed *claim associations* to protect their land before public sales were held.

Most Westerners supported the squatters, and Western lawmakers backed bills to protect the squatters' interests. The Pre-emption Act of 1841 recognized squatter's rights. See also **Pre-emption; Squatter.**

Robert F. Berkhofer, Jr.

Squeteague. See Weakfish.

Squid is any of a number of soft-bodied marine animals that have 8 or 10 limbs around the mouth. Squids are *invertebrates,* or animals that lack a backbone. They belong to a group of invertebrates called *cephalopods,* which also includes octopuses, nautiluses, and cuttlefish. Squids live in all seas and at all depths.

The body of a squid has two fins, one on each side of the tail. In most squid *species* (kinds), the head is surrounded by eight arms and two often longer limbs

called tentacles. The arms and tentacles possess rows of suckers. Instead of bones, the animal has a *pen* (reduced shell) inside its body. Squids range in length from less than 1 foot (0.3 meters) to about 60 feet (18 meters), including the tentacles.

A squid's head has two well-developed eyes, a pair of powerful beaklike jaws, and a toothed structure called a *radula.* The radula assists the jaws in tearing up food, and it also helps move the food into the digestive system. A muscular, tubelike structure called the *mantle* forms the main part of the body. Attached to the body below the head is a smaller tubelike structure called the *funnel.* A squid propels itself through the water by filling its mantle with water and then forcing the water back out through the funnel. Squids also have three hearts—a main *systemic heart* and two additional *branchial hearts.* The branchial hearts supply blood to the animal's gills.

The life of a squid. Many types of squids live close to the ocean surface or near shores. Coral reefs house some of the most colorful varieties. Other types inhabit the dark, cold waters of the deep sea. Some species have structures called *photophores,* which emit light. Scientists do not completely understand the function of photophores, but a squid may use them for signaling other squids, luring prey, or scaring away predators.

A squid's diet consists of various sea animals, including fish, shellfish, and plankton. Squids often catch their prey by attacking with sudden bursts of speed. They then hold onto the prey using the suckers on their arms and tentacles. Many squids also have glands that emit a poison for stunning prey.

Numerous animals eat squids, including toothed whales, seals, sharks, and bony fishes. Squids avoid these animals in a variety of ways. For example, all squids have an ink sac that spurts out a dark fluid when the squid flees from a predator. This fluid may conceal the squid as it escapes. Many species can also escape danger by rapidly changing color. Skin cells called *chromatophores* contain a colored pigment. When a squid is threatened, these cells contract or expand to produce sudden color changes. Such color changes can either startle the predator or enable the squid to hide by blending into its environment.

Squids have large brains and often exhibit complex behaviors. Many types swim in large groups. To attract females or ward off rivals, male squids sometimes

Parts of a female squid

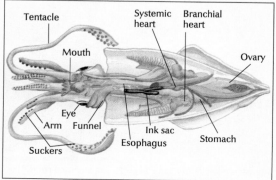

Tentacle

Systemic heart   Branchial heart

Mouth

Ovary

Eye

Arm   Funnel

Ink sac

Suckers   Esophagus   Stomach

A Caribbean reef squid inhabits coral reefs off the Caribbean island of Grand Cayman. This small squid resembles most other squid species. It has a soft, torpedo-shaped body with huge eyes. Two transparent fins grow on either side of the tail.

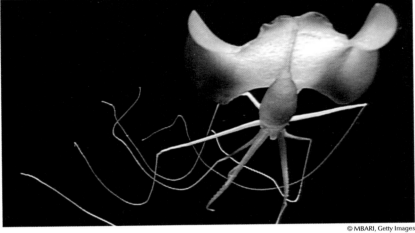

A deep-sea squid inhabits dark waters near the ocean floor. Sometimes called the *longarm squid,* this unusual creature has 10 long, string-like arms. It also possesses huge, flapping fins that resemble elephant's ears. Deep-sea explorers first discovered this squid in the late 1980's.

change color and wave their arms as a form of display.

The number of eggs produced by females varies from a few dozen to many thousands. Newborn squids resemble miniature versions of the adults. Squids generally do not live long. Lifespans typically range from a few months to a few years.

Kinds of squids. Some of the best-known squids live in shallow waters near coasts. The *Caribbean reef squid,* for example, inhabits coral reefs throughout the Caribbean Sea. This small squid grows to about 12 inches (30 centimeters) long. It feeds on crustaceans and small fish.

Two related species, the *longfin inshore squid* and the *veined squid,* rank among the most commercially important types. People around the world eat them and use them as fish bait. Longfin inshore squids inhabit the western Atlantic Ocean from Newfoundland to Venezuela. Veined squids live in eastern Atlantic waters and the Mediterranean Sea. Both species gather in shallow coastal areas to breed and lay eggs. They range from 15 to 36 inches (38 to 91 centimeters) long.

Many squids inhabit deep ocean waters around the world. Scientists know little about most of these animals, which have rarely been seen alive. Deep-sea squids include the huge *giant squids,* which may reach about 60 feet (18 meters) in length. Giant squids probably eat other mollusks, including squids, as well as fish.

In the late 1980's, scientists discovered an unusual deep-sea squid. Sometimes called the *longarm squid,* it has 10 extremely long, threadlike arms of equal size. The arms bend to create elbowlike forms. Nearly all other squids possess eight arms and two tentacles. The long-arm squid also has two huge fins that flap as the animal moves. The total length of this creature probably reaches 10 to 20 feet (3 to 6 meters).

Squids and people. Squids have captured people's imaginations for centuries. Many seafaring cultures, such as those of Japan and Polynesia, created stories of large sea monsters that probably represented squids. Such cultures often prized squids as a source of food. Today, squids play an important role in the fishing industry worldwide, both as food and as bait.

Scientists from a variety of fields study squids. Researchers analyze the nervous systems of squids to learn more about how the human nervous system functions. Biologists and deep-sea explorers continue to discover new squid species.   Robert S. Prezant

Scientific classification. Squids belong to the class Cephalopoda, and they make up different orders and families. The scientific name for the Caribbean reef squid is *Sepioteuthis sepioidea.* The longfin inshore squid is *Loligo pealei,* and the veined squid is *L. forbesi.* Giant squids make up the genus *Architeuthis.*

See also **Giant squid; Mollusk.**

Squill is the name of several plants with bulbous roots. They belong to the hyacinth family. One kind of squill, called sea onion or red squill, grows around the Mediterranean Sea. It produces bulbs that sometimes weigh as much as 4 pounds (1.8 kilograms). The bulbs of this squill have medicinal value. They are also used as a rat poison.

Gardeners collect the bulbs of the sea onion in August. They remove the outer husk, slice the bulb, and dry it in the sun. People make a drug from the bulbs.

Usually they use it in syrup form or in "tincture of squill." The drug stimulates the heart and is rather irritating. It particularly affects the stomach, intestines, and bronchial tracts.

Sometimes doctors use squill as an expectorant and diuretic. They also treat chronic bronchitis with it, but never when the disease is acute.

Squill is also the name given the genus *Scilla* in the hyacinth family. It includes 80 or more species found in the temperate regions of Europe.   August A. De Hertogh

Scientific classification. The sea onion belongs to the hyacinth family, Hyacinthaceae. It is *Urginea maritima.*

Squire. See Knights and knighthood (The squire).

Squirrel is any of a group of small to medium-sized gnawing animals with a long, cylindrical body; a furry tail; and powerful jaws. Squirrels are some of the most popular and easily recognized animals because of their curiosity, liveliness, and wide distribution. They live on every continent except Australia and Antarctica.

Types of squirrels

Squirrels make up one of the largest families of *rodents* (gnawing animals), the order to which beavers, mice, and rats also belong. The squirrel family, Sciuridae, consists of approximately 270 species. They may be divided into three general types: (1) tree squirrels, (2) flying squirrels, and (3) ground squirrels.

Tree squirrels are tree-climbing, bushy-tailed animals that inhabit most of the world's forests. They weigh from ⅓ ounce to 6 ½ pounds (10 grams to 3 kilograms). They are active during the day. Familiar tree squirrels include the eastern gray and eastern fox squirrels of North America, the Eurasian red squirrel, and the giant and tricolor squirrels of Asia.

Flying squirrels are tree climbers that have folds of skin between their front and back legs which enable them to glide long distances. They weigh from ¾ ounce to 5 ½ pounds (22 grams to 2.5 kilograms). Flying squirrels are *nocturnal*—that is, they sleep during the day and become active at night. Most flying squirrel species live in southern Asia. Two small species inhabit North America, but they are rarely seen because they are strictly nocturnal.

Ground squirrels are compact, short-tailed, burrowing rodents that are especially abundant in open country, such as grasslands and tundra. The most common ground squirrels found in North America are the small, striped or spotted rodents that are actually known as *ground squirrels*. These squirrels belong to the genus *Spermophilus.*

Other types of ground squirrels include chipmunks, marmots, and prairie dogs. For more information on these animals, see the *World Book* articles on **Chipmunk; Ground squirrel; Marmot; Prairie dog;** and **Woodchuck.**

The origin and development of squirrels

Scientists believe that squirrels appeared early in the history of rodents. During the Cenozoic Era, beginning about 63 million years ago, forests of seed- and nut-bearing trees began to grow over much of Earth. The growth of such forests was probably a major factor in the evolution of squirrels. It accounts for many of the ways squirrels differ from other rodents. For example, squirrels have sharp *incisor* (front) teeth and powerful jaw muscles, well suited for gnawing through hard-shelled nuts and thick pine cones. Their sharp claws and flexible bodies help them grasp branches and leap from

Gary W. Carter

Common tree squirrels of North America include the American red squirrel, shown eating fruit above, and the eastern gray squirrel, *right.* Their sharp claws and flexible bodies help them climb trees, grasp branches, and leap from limb to limb.

Robert Maier, Animals Animals

© E. Hanumantha Rao, N.H.P.A.

The black giant squirrel lives in forests in Southeast Asia. It weighs up to $6\frac{1}{2}$ pounds (3 kilograms) and has a very long tail.

tree to tree. As a result, they can move easily through the treetops to get food and escape enemies. A squirrel's furry tail acts as a "balancer" when the animal leaps and climbs. The tail also serves as a blanket when wrapped around the body or as a signaling device when waved vigorously from a high perch.

The life of squirrels

Obtaining food. Squirrel behavior has been heavily influenced by the animal's dependence on certain foods. Nuts, seeds, and pine cones are rich sources of energy. But they are hard to eat and may be available only at certain times of the year or in widely scattered areas. Squirrels must spend long periods searching for food and removing the food from its hard covering.

In areas with hot summers and cold winters, many kinds of seeds and nuts are abundant in late summer and fall. In these areas, squirrels often store large supplies of food in the ground, under fallen leaves, or in stockpiles near their nests that can be defended. A good memory and a keen sense of smell help squirrels find and retrieve the hidden food during the winter. Squirrels in most areas supplement their seed-and-nut diet with other foods, including fruit, buds, shoots, bark, sap, insects, eggs, and fungi. In the tropics, these softer foods may replace seeds and nuts completely.

Squirrel feeding habits often benefit the forest. Buried nuts, if not recovered, may grow into trees and help restore the forest. Squirrels also aid tree growth by digging up, eating, and dispersing certain underground fungi, which form beneficial associations, called *mycorrhizae,* with roots. The fungi absorb water and minerals from the soil and pass them on to the plant, receiving energy from the plant in return. Squirrels spread the indigestible spores of these fungi by releasing droppings in areas with young trees.

Obtaining shelter. Second only to food in importance for squirrel survival is the availability of nests. Nests provide protection from heat and cold, a refuge from enemies, a place to raise young, and a storage site for food. A squirrel usually has more than one nest and can move quickly to an alternate nest if threatened.

Many tree and flying squirrels use different kinds of nests for winter and summer. The winter nest consists of a cavity in a tree trunk or branch lined with leaves,

grasses, chewed bark, or other padding. The summer nest is a leaf nest consisting of twigs, leaves, vines, and other plant material woven into a ball in the fork of a tree branch. Some squirrel species use a leaf nest the year around. Such leaf nests are called *dreys.*

Raising young. How far north a squirrel lives affects how often the animal mates and how many young are born in each litter. In the Far North, squirrels usually mate once a year, in late winter or early spring. The resulting litter consists of four to eight young. Farther south, squirrels may have a second litter, but the litter size is smaller. In the tropics, many small litters of one or two have been reported.

A female squirrel carries her offspring inside her body from 36 to 43 days before giving birth. Newborn squirrels are pink, hairless, and helpless. They cannot see because their eyelids are sealed shut. The mother cares for the babies alone. Tree squirrels live with their mother for about 8 weeks before they become independent. Flying squirrels require a longer developmental period, 10 weeks or more, perhaps because they need more time to master the techniques of gliding.

Territories and groups. Most squirrels spend their lives moving about a home area. The size of a squirrel's home area depends on the abundance of resources and the presence of potential mates. Males often have home areas that are much larger than those of females and may even include the ranges of a number of females. Some squirrels fiercely defend their territory. Most species, however, drive away intruders only if they threaten to invade the nest.

Most species of tree and flying squirrels live alone rather than in organized groups. Some species form mated pairs or family groups. Many species share nests, either in family groups or in temporary winter gatherings called *aggregations.* Aggregations help the animals keep warm by sharing their body heat.

Squirrels that do not form groups relate to one another according to a *dominance hierarchy* or "pecking order." In such a hierarchy, larger, stronger, or older individuals dominate other animals and have first choice of food or mates.

Life span. The life span of squirrels is roughly related to their size. Large species of squirrels tend to live longer than small species, are less vulnerable to *predators* (hunting animals), and leave fewer offspring. Small species often suffer a high death rate from predators but have the ability to leave large numbers of offspring.

Squirrels may reach 10 to 12 years of age in the wild. Most squirrels, however, die much younger. Hawks, cats, foxes, weasels, snakes, and other predators kill large numbers of them. Food shortages, diseases, and parasites also take their toll.

Squirrels and people

Many species of tree squirrels may become used to people and seem quite tame. Squirrels should not be kept as pets, however, because of their wild nature.

A few species of squirrels may damage food crops, trees, and pastures, or invade houses or storage areas. Some occasionally carry plague and other diseases that can spread to human beings. Most people, however, enjoy squirrels as neighbors and want to protect them. Nevertheless, the major threat to many squirrel species

Where squirrels live

The yellow areas show where squirrels are found.

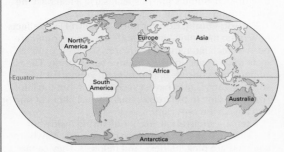

Squirrels inhabit most forests and grasslands. They live on every continent except Australia and Antarctica. A squirrel has sharp *incisor* (front) teeth and powerful jaws that enable it to gnaw through nuts and seeds. The squirrel's tail acts as a "balancer" when the animal climbs or leaps from tree to tree.

The body of a squirrel and squirrel tracks

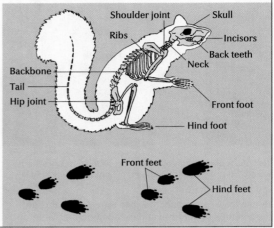

WORLD BOOK illustrations by Tom Dolan

worldwide is the destruction of their forest and grassland homes by human beings.　　Peter D. Weigl

Scientific classification. Squirrels make up the squirrel family, Sciuridae. The scientific name for the American red squirrel is *Tamiasciurus hudsonicus.* The eastern gray squirrel is *Sciurus carolinensis;* the western gray squirrel, *S. griseus;* the eastern fox squirrel, *S. niger;* and the Eurasian red squirrel, *S. vulgaris.* The giant squirrels of southern Asia are genus *Ratufa.* The tricolor squirrels of east Asia are genus *Callosciurus.*

See also **Flying squirrel; Rodent.**

Squirrel monkey is any of several kinds of small monkeys that live in large groups. Most groups have 10 to 50 monkeys, but some have up to 500 animals. Squirrel monkeys live in the forests of Central and South America, from Costa Rica to Bolivia. They move swiftly through trees and on the ground, seeking fruits and insects to eat. They use their long tails for balance when standing or leaping but not for grasping.

Most squirrel monkeys grow about 1 foot (30 centimeters) long, not including the tail, and weigh less than 2 pounds (0.9 kilogram). The monkeys often have an ash-gray or red-brown back, with shades of gold or olive. Their throat, face, and chest are typically white or light

© John Giustina, Bruce Coleman Inc

The common squirrel monkey lives in forests of South America. It has large black eyes, a black nose and mouth, and an ash-gray back with shades of gold.

yellow, and the forearms, hands, and feet are usually yellow or reddish. The black or gray nose and mouth areas contrast with light-colored fur around the eyes.

Squirrel monkeys have become threatened due to the destruction of their forest habitat by people. These monkeys often are captured for use in laboratory research.
Roderic B. Mast and Russell A. Mittermeier

Scientific classification. Squirrel monkeys are in the New World monkey family, Cebidae. The scientific name for the common squirrel monkey, a well-known species, is *Saimiri sciureus.*

Srebrenica massacre, *SREH breh neet sah,* was the worst massacre of the war that raged in Bosnia-Herzegovina from 1992 to 1995. In July 1995, Bosnian Serb forces captured Srebrenica and massacred thousands of Bosnian Muslims who had taken refuge in the town.

Shortly after the war began, the United Nations (UN) sent peacekeeping troops to the area, mainly to protect aid shipments to war refugees. In 1993, the UN declared Srebrenica, four other towns, and the city of Sarajevo to be *safe areas* within Bosnia. Civilians in these areas were supposed to be safe from attack. The UN stationed lightly armed Dutch soldiers in and around Srebrenica to enforce the boundaries of the safe area.

When Serb troops captured Srebrenica on July 11, 1995, the Dutch forces lacked the military strength to stop them. A group of about 15,000 Muslims attempted to flee the safe area, but the Serbs captured most of them. Some escaped or were killed trying to escape. The Serbs claimed that the Muslim civilians who had not fled would be transferred to other safe areas. They separated the men from the women and children, who were sent away on buses and trucks. Over the next few days, the Serbs executed most of the men.

Investigators later found evidence that the Serbs executed over 7,000 Muslim men. The UN convicted several Bosnian Serb military leaders for their roles in the massacre. The UN also charged Ratko Mladić, then head of the Bosnian Serb army, and Radovan Karadžić, then leader of the Bosnian Serbs, with war crimes. But neither man has been captured.　　Sabrina P. Ramet

See also **Bosnia-Herzegovina.**

SRI International is a nonprofit, independent contract research organization. It performs basic and applied research for industry, government, and the public. Its staff provides research services in over 100 subject areas, including economics, electronics, engineering, management, the physical and biological sciences, and urban and social systems. SRI International was founded in 1946 as the Stanford Research Institute. It is based in Menlo Park, California.   Critically reviewed by SRI International

Sri Jayewardenepura Kotte, *sree JY uh wuhr duhn uh PUR uh KOH tay* (pop. 115,826), also called simply Kotte, is the capital of Sri Lanka. It lies about 7 miles (11 kilometers) southeast of Colombo, the country's largest city and former capital. *Sri Jayewardenepura* means *city of victory* in Sinhala, the language of most Sri Lankans.

Kotte was founded in the 1300's. The great kingdom of King Parakramabahu VI, who ruled from 1411 to 1466, was based in Kotte. Sri Lanka's Parliament moved from Colombo to Kotte in 1982.   Robert W. Bradnock

See also **Sri Lanka** (political map).

Sri Lanka, *sree LAHNG kuh,* is an island country in the Indian Ocean that lies about 20 miles (32 kilometers) off the southeast coast of India. Its official name is the Democratic Socialist Republic of Sri Lanka. The country was formerly called Ceylon. Agriculture is Sri Lanka's chief economic activity. Many farmers grow world-famous Sri Lanka tea, also called Ceylon tea. Colombo, a seaport, is the largest city and the commercial center of Sri Lanka. Sri Jayewardenepura Kotte is the country's capital. Sri Lanka became independent in 1948.

Government. A president heads Sri Lanka's government. A 225-member Parliament passes the nation's laws. The voters elect the president and the members of Parliament to six-year terms. The president appoints a Cabinet and a prime minister, who is typically the leader of the ruling party in Parliament.

Sri Lanka has a number of political parties. The most important are the Sri Lanka Freedom Party and the United National Party.

Sri Lanka is divided into nine provinces, which in turn are divided into 25 districts. Provincial councils directly elected by the people govern seven of the provinces. The federal government administers the other two, although Tamil rebels control much of the territory there.

Sri Lanka's highest court is the Supreme Court. The type of law used in private Sri Lankan court cases, such as divorce, depends on the religion of the people involved in the cases. For example, Islamic law applies to Muslims (people of Islamic faith).

People. The people of Sri Lanka belong to several different ethnic groups. The largest groups are the Sinhalese and the Tamils. The Sinhalese make up about 74 percent of the population. They are descended from people from northern India. Their language is called Sinhala, and most of them are Buddhists. Tamils make up about 18 percent of the population. They are descendants of people from southern India. They speak Tamil, and most of them are Hindus. Most Tamils live in

Facts in brief

Capital: Sri Jayewardenepura Kotte.
Official languages: Sinhala and Tamil.
Area: 25,332 mi² (65,610 km²). *Greatest distances*—north-south, 270 mi (435 km); east-west, 140 mi (225 km). *Coastline*—748 mi (1,204 km).
Elevation: *Highest*—Pidurutalagala, 8,281 ft (2,524 m). *Lowest*—sea level.
Population: *Estimated 2008 population*—20,140,000; density, 795 per mi² (307 per km²); distribution, 80 percent rural, 20 percent urban. *2001 census*—16,864,544 (17 of 25 districts only; the government's estimate for the complete 2001 census is 18,732,255).
Chief products: *Agriculture*—rubber, rice, tea, coconuts. *Manufacturing*—food products, rubber products, textiles.
National anthem: "Sri Lanka Matha" ("Sri Lanka, Motherland").
Flag: A yellow lion on a crimson field is a symbol of precolonial Sri Lanka. Ornaments in the corners are bo leaves, which are Buddhist symbols. At the left, a vertical green stripe stands for the Moors and an orange stripe for the Tamils. See **Flag** (picture: Flags of Asia and the Pacific).
Money: *Basic unit*—Sri Lankan rupee. One hundred cents equal one rupee.

Tea is one of Sri Lanka's most important products. Sri Lanka tea, also called Ceylon tea, is famous throughout the world. This woman is harvesting tea leaves by hand.

the northern and eastern parts of the country. Both Sinhala and Tamil are official languages of Sri Lanka.

Moors, who are descendants of Arabs, form Sri Lanka's third largest ethnic group. They make up about 7 percent of the population. Most Moors speak Tamil and are Muslims. Smaller ethnic groups in Sri Lanka include Burghers, Malays, and Veddahs. The Burghers are descendants of European settlers who intermarried with Sri Lankans. The Malays are descended from people who came from what is now Malaysia. The Veddahs are descendants of Sri Lanka's first known residents.

Most of the people of Sri Lanka farm the land and follow the traditions of their ancestors. Colombo is Sri Lanka's largest city by far. Houses that have mud walls and thatched roofs are common among the poorer rural people. The middle class and wealthy have more substantial housing. In both rural and urban areas, many middle- and upper-class houses are surrounded by a

Sri Lanka

▬▬▬	International boundary
────	Road
╪╪╪╪	Railroad
✪	National capital
•	Other city or town
+	Elevation above sea level

WORLD BOOK maps

© Picture Finders/eStock Photo

The Ruwanweliseya in Anuradhapura is an important Buddhist monument. It was built in the 100's B.C. to house Buddhist *relics* (sacred items). Buddhism is Sri Lanka's main religion.

walled compound. Many Sri Lankans, especially rural people, live in *extended families,* in which more than two generations of the same family live together. The *caste* system, which divides people into social classes, is strong among both Sinhalese and Tamils (see **Caste**).

Most rural Sri Lankan men wear a *sarong* (a garment wrapped around the waist to form a long skirt) and a shirt. Many urban men wear Western-style clothing. Sri Lankan women wear a *redde* (skirt similar to a sarong), with a blouse or jacket; or a *sari* (straight piece of cloth draped around the body as a long dress).

Rice is the chief food in Sri Lanka. It is served with *curry* dishes—stewlike dishes of vegetables, meat, fish, or eggs seasoned with spices. Tea is a favorite drink.

Sri Lankans are religious people. The countryside is dotted with Buddhist and Hindu temples and shrines, Islamic mosques, and Christian churches. About 69 percent of the people are Buddhists and about 15 percent are Hindus. Christians and Muslims each account for about 8 percent of the population.

Education in Sri Lanka is free from kindergarten through the university level. Sri Lanka has eight universities. Most Sri Lankans 15 years of age or older can read and write, and the country has one of Asia's highest literacy rates. For Sri Lanka's literacy rates, see **Literacy** (table: Literacy rates for selected countries).

Architecture, painting and sculpture, literature, music, and dance flourished in Sri Lanka before the period of European rule. Much of the island's ancient art focused on religious themes. Remains of this art can still be seen in ruins of some cities and in museums in Colombo and Kandy. Today, dance is an important art form among both Sinhalese and Tamils. Sri Lanka craftworkers make jewelry, pottery, baskets, mats, and wooden masks.

Land and climate. Sri Lanka covers 25,332 square miles (65,610 square kilometers). The south-central part of the country is mountainous. Plains surround the mountains on the east, south, and west, and cover most of the northern half of the island.

A variety of wild animals, including bears, birds, crocodiles, elephants, monkeys, and snakes, live in Sri Lanka. More than 3,000 species of ferns and flowering plants grow there. Common plants include bougainvillea, orchids, poinsettias, and fruit trees. A tropical rain forest covers much of southwestern Sri Lanka.

Temperatures in the low coastal areas average 80 °F (27 °C). Temperatures in the mountains average 60 °F (16 °C). Average annual rainfall ranges from about 50 inches (130 centimeters) in the northeast to about 200 inches (510 centimeters) in parts of the southwest.

Economy. Sri Lanka has a developing economy in which both government control and free enterprise play a part. Agriculture is the main economic activity. It employs about 50 percent of the nation's workers. The chief agricultural products are tea, rubber, rice, and coconuts. Service industries employ about 35 percent of the labor force. Wholesale and retail trade is the country's leading service industry. Other service industries include government activities, and communications and transportation. About 10 percent of the labor force works in manufacturing. Major activities include the processing of agricultural goods, including coconuts, rubber, tea, and tobacco; and the manufacture of textiles. The construction industry employs about 5 percent of the workers.

Sri Lanka has a good transportation system. Most Sri Lankans travel by buses. Less than 1 percent of the people own a car. Sri Lanka's major airport is near Colombo. More than 10 major newspapers are published.

History. The island of Sri Lanka was called Ceylon until 1972. Its first inhabitants were tribal peoples called the *Yaksa* and the *Naga.* The Veddahs are descendants of these peoples. Vijaya, a legendary prince from northern India, is said to have led the Sinhalese culture's founders to Ceylon. The Sinhalese probably began to arrive in the 400's B.C. They settled in the northern part of the island and built advanced irrigation systems to support agriculture. The city of Anuradhapura was the center of Sinhalese civilization from the 200's B.C. until A.D. 993.

Tamils from southern India invaded the island, perhaps as early as the 100's B.C. From the A.D. 400's until the arrival of the Portuguese in the 1500's, the history of Ceylon centered on struggles between Sinhalese kings and Tamil kings. Tamils eventually gained control of the northern half of the island. The Sinhalese moved into the southern half of the island. Arab traders, whose descendants are the Moors, began arriving in the 700's.

European control of Ceylon began in the 1500's. The Portuguese sailed into what is now Colombo Harbor in 1505. They gradually gained control of the island's major coastal areas. The Dutch replaced the Portuguese in the mid-1600's. The British captured the Dutch territories in 1795 and 1796. They made Ceylon a crown colony in 1802. The British took over the Sinhalese mountain kingdom of Kandy in 1815, and became the first Europeans to control the entire island. The British developed coffee, coconut, rubber, and tea plantations.

The colony gradually gained self-government during the 1900's. It became the independent nation of Ceylon on Feb. 4, 1948. The country adopted a parliamentary form of government headed by a prime minister. D. S.

Senanayake became the first prime minister.

S. W. R. D. Bandaranaike became prime minister in 1956. His government passed a law that made Sinhala the country's only official language. The Tamils resented this action, and clashes broke out between Tamils and Sinhalese. Compromises were made to provide for the use of Tamil in many areas. Bandaranaike was assassinated by a Sinhalese extremist in 1959. His widow, Sirimavo Bandaranaike, became prime minister in 1960. She was the world's first woman prime minister. Her party lost control of Parliament in 1965, and Dudley Senanayake then became prime minister. But Sirimavo Bandaranaike regained the office in 1970. In 1972, the country changed its name from Ceylon to Sri Lanka, which means *Resplendent Land.*

In 1977, Bandaranaike's party lost control of Parliament again. Opposition leader J. R. Jayewardene became prime minister. Jayewardene became president in 1978 after a constitutional amendment made the president—not the prime minister—the head of the government. Jayewardene was elected president in 1982. In 1988, Jayewardene announced his retirement. Ranasinghe Premadasa was elected to succeed him as president. Premadasa had been prime minister under Jayewardene.

In the 1970's and 1980's, tension grew between the Sinhalese and the Tamils. Many Tamils felt oppressed by Sinhalese-dominated governments and demanded a separate state called Tamil Eelam in northern and eastern Sri Lanka. Some groups—especially the Liberation Tigers of Tamil Eelam (LTTE)—favored the use of force to achieve a separate state. In 1983, violence broke out in the north between Tamil guerrillas, including the LTTE, and Sinhalese government troops. Thousands of people were killed, and many Tamils fled to India. In 1987, the Sri Lankan government and India worked out a peace plan that called for creating a local government council

Robert Harding Picture Library

Colombo is Sri Lanka's largest city. Many of its buildings were constructed when the country was a British colony.

in the Tamil region. Some Tamil guerrillas agreed to the plan, but others did not. Fighting soon broke out again. A cease-fire was implemented in 1989. Sinhalese nationalists who opposed compromises with the Tamils killed many government officials and government supporters. In 1990, fighting resumed between the LTTE and government troops. In 1994, the LTTE and the government declared a cease-fire. But they could not reach a permanent peace deal. In mid-1995, fighting resumed. Tens of thousands of people have been killed in the violence.

In 1993, Premadasa was assassinated. The prime minister, D. B. Wijetunga, replaced him. In 1994, C. B. Kumaratunga was elected president, and she was reelected in 1999. In February 2002, a cease-fire began between the LTTE and government forces. Later that year, the LTTE abandoned its demand for a separate Tamil state.

In 2004, an undersea earthquake in the Indian Ocean caused a series of large ocean waves called a *tsunami.* The tsunami killed hundreds of thousands of people in coastal areas, including more than 30,000 in Sri Lanka.

In 2005, Prime Minister Mahinda Rajapakse was elected president. Fighting between the LTTE and government forces increased after his election. In 2006, both sides renewed their commitment to the 2002 cease-fire, but heavy fighting continued.   Robert LaPorte, Jr.

See also **Bandaranaike, Sirimavo; Colombo; Sri Jayewardenepura Kotte.**

SSS. See Selective Service System.

St. … See Saint …

Stadium is a large structure for spectators built around a playing field or arena. A stadium has seats arranged in *tiers* (rows) from which spectators view football and baseball games, track meets, boxing matches, and other public events. Universities have built many stadiums for athletic games. Some cities have built municipal stadiums where both civic events and sports events are held. Domed stadiums can be used for baseball, football, circuses, conventions, and other events.

One of the first stadiums was the footrace course in Olympia in ancient Greece. Other famous stadiums were in Delphi, Athens, and Epidaurus in Greece and in Ephesus in Asia Minor. Usually, horseshoe-shaped terraces enclosed the stadiums to give spectators a clear view of the field. Seats were often built on the terraces. The stadium in Athens was rebuilt and used for the Olympic Games in 1896. The word *stadium* comes from the Greek word *stadion,* which referred to the distance between the pillars at each end of the stadium at Olympia (about 630 feet, or 192 meters).   William J. Hennessey

See also **Colosseum; Hippodrome; Olympic Games.**

Staël, *stahl,* **Madame de** (1766-1817), was a prominent French critic and novelist. Her literary work influenced the growth of Romanticism in French literature.

Madame de Staël was one of the first to apply the notion of progress to literature. She felt literature was an extension of society and should reflect social change. In her critical works, such as *On Literature* (1800) and *On Germany* (1810), she emphasized that judgment should be relative, not absolute. *On Germany* introduced the German culture and such great thinkers as Friedrich Schiller to Europe as a model to imitate. Her two novels, *Delphine* (1802) and *Corinne* (1807), reflect her own life. They deal with women who ignore public opinion. Their theme, the conflict between the superior person and society, became popular in the Romantic movement.

Madame de Staël was born Anne Louise Germaine Necker on April 22, 1766, in Paris. She married Baron Staël-Holstein, Swedish ambassador to France, in 1786, but the marriage ended unhappily. She had a famous love affair with novelist Benjamin Constant. In 1811, she married Albert de Rocca, a Swiss military officer. She was exiled from Paris several times by Napoleon I, who opposed her political beliefs. Madame de Staël died on July 14, 1817.   Thomas H. Goetz

Stafford, Jean (1915-1979), was an American novelist and short-story writer famous for her sensitive portrayals of lonely, troubled individuals. Much of her fiction deals with self-conscious children confronted by a difficult, disappointing adult world, or with unhappy women trying to discover satisfaction through marriage and motherhood. Stafford won praise for her rich, realistic prose style. She received the 1970 Pulitzer Prize for fiction for *The Collected Stories of Jean Stafford* (1969).

Stafford's first novel, *Boston Adventure* (1944), explores lower-class life through the eyes of an immigrant girl. *The Mountain Lion* (1947) traces the problems of a teen-aged brother and sister. *The Catherine Wheel* (1952) is a psychological novel about the destructive nature of isolation and ignorance. Stafford's short fiction was collected in *Children Are Bored on Sunday* (1953) and *Bad Characters* (1964). She also wrote for children. Stafford was born on July 1, 1915, in Covina, California, and died on March 26, 1979.   Arthur M. Saltzman

Staffordshire bull terrier, *STAF uhrd shihr,* is a powerful, heavyset dog. It stands from 14 to 16 inches (36 to 41 centimeters) tall and weighs from 28 to 38 pounds (13 to 17 kilograms). The dog has a broad head and a short, muscular neck. Its coat is short and smooth and may be black, blue, red, tan, *brindled* (gray to yellowish-brown, with darker streaks or spots), or white, or a combination of those colors with white.

Missy Yuhl

The Staffordshire bull terrier originated in England.

The breed was developed during the early 1800's by miners of Staffordshire, England. They produced it by mating bulldogs with terriers. Staffordshire bull terriers were once used for dogfighting and for fighting bears and bulls.   Critically reviewed by the American Kennel Club

See also **American Staffordshire terrier.**

Stag. See Deer.

Stag beetle is the name of a family of beetles in which some males have oddly enlarged jaws. These jaws look somewhat like the horns of a male deer and have given the beetle its name. In some cases, these "horns" are nearly as long as the body of the insect. A common American species is the *giant stag beetle* of the Southern States. It has *mandibles* (jaws) 1 inch (2.5 centimeters) long and a body 1 ½ to 2 inches (3.8 to 5 centimeters) long. The *pinchingbug* of the Eastern States is a stag beetle that flies by night. Adult stag beetles eat sap and honeydew. The eggs are laid in cracks in the bark of dead, decaying trees. They hatch into soft white larvae called *grubs.*   David J. Shetlar

Scientific classification. Stag beetles belong to the order Coleoptera and the stag beetle family, Lucanidae. The giant stag beetle is genus *Lucanus elaphus.*

See also **Beetle** (picture).

Stage. See Theater; Motion picture; Drama.

Stagecoach was a horse-drawn coach used to carry passengers and mail on a regular route. Stagecoaches were also sometimes used to carry freight. The first long stage line was established about 1670 between London and Edinburgh, Scotland, a distance of 392 miles (631 kilometers).

Stagecoach lines were established in colonial America in the 1730's. By the mid-1700's, they ran between Boston and Providence, Rhode Island, and linked New York City with Philadelphia. In 1785, Congress began

Granger Collection

Stagecoaches provided the best transportation for passengers and mail between American cities in the 1700's and early 1800's.

mail service by stagecoach. Greater comforts were added to the coaches, such as springs and cushions. Many of the finest coaches were made in Concord, New Hampshire.

Early in the 1800's, travelers from Philadelphia, Baltimore, and Washington traveled to Ohio by the National Road in Concord coaches drawn by six horses. They rode along at 10 miles (16 kilometers) per hour. The trip took 2 ½ days. Horses were changed at relay stations every 15 or 20 miles (24 or 32 kilometers). Later, stagecoach lines operated in the West. But the railroads gradually replaced stagecoaches, except in remote regions.

Robert C. Post

See also **Postal services** (picture: The use of stagecoaches).

Stagg, Amos Alonzo (1862-1965), was one of the most successful and creative coaches in American col-

lege football. Stagg's teams won 314 games. Stagg achieved his greatest success at the University of Chicago, where he coached from 1892 through 1932.

Stagg introduced the basic principles of the T-formation offense, and he invented the tackling dummy. He also devised special plays, including the onside kick, the end-around, the double-reverse, and the flea-flicker.

Stagg was born in West Orange, New Jersey, on Aug. 16, 1862. He played football at Yale University from 1884 through 1889 and was selected to the first all-America team in 1889. Stagg began his coaching career in 1890 at the School for Christian Workers (now Springfield College) and then moved to the University of Chicago in 1892. Stagg coached at the College (now University) of the Pacific from 1933 through 1946. He died on March 17, 1965.   Carlton Stowers

Stain is a liquid similar to paint that is used to color wood and other absorbent materials. Unlike paints, however, most stains are transparent and penetrate wood rather than forming a film on top. The amount of color can be controlled by wiping off excess stain, or by adding more, before it dries. Stains highlight the grain of wood. If used alone, however, they create a dull finish. For this reason, they usually are coated with a clear substance, such as varnish, which provides a gloss.

Stains contain a solvent, a resin, and pigments or dye. They come in many colors.   George J. Danker

Stained glass is colored glass that has been cut into pieces and reassembled to form a picture or decorative design. The pieces are held together by strips of lead. The picture or design shines brightly when the glass is illuminated. However, light must pass through the glass to create this effect. Therefore, stained glass is used chiefly for windows. A well-made stained-glass window glows and sparkles with color in the rays of the sun.

Colorless glass may be painted or chemically treated to look like stained glass. But authentic stained glass is colored during the glassmaking process. The colors are produced by adding certain metal oxides to the other ingredients. For example, cobalt oxide may be added to make blue glass, and copper oxide to make red glass.

Most details of stained-glass pictures, such as shadows and facial features, are painted in. But the art of making stained glass is only distantly related to the art of painting. Stained glass achieves its effects mainly through the colors and shapes of the pieces of glass. The outlines formed by the lead strips also add to the effects of stained glass.

How stained-glass windows are made

Most stained-glass windows are designed by professional artists. In some cases, the artist also makes the window. In others, skilled craftworkers do this work under the artist's supervision.

The artist first makes a sketch of the picture or design to be portrayed by the window. The sketch serves as a model for a full-sized blueprint of the window. On the blueprint, called a *cartoon,* the artist shows the exact shape and color of each piece of glass. The artist also indicates the location of the lead strips and designates the details to be painted in. The cartoon is then traced onto heavy paper. The artist cuts out the patterns of the pieces of glass and marks each one to indicate its color.

Each paper cutout is placed on a sheet of glass of the

designated color, and its outline is traced with a glass-cutter. When the glass is snapped, it breaks neatly along the outlines. After all the pieces have been cut out, they are put in place on the cartoon. The artist then paints the details of the window illustration.

The paint used for the details of stained-glass pictures is an enamel—a mixture of powdered glass, iron oxide, and a liquid, such as oil or water. The liquid makes the enamel flow, and the iron oxide gives it a dark brown color. After the artist has painted in the details of the picture, the pieces are fired in a special furnace called a *kiln*. The heat bonds the powdered glass and the iron oxide to the surface of the colored glass. After the glass has cooled, the pieces are again put in place on the cartoon.

The pieces of the window are now ready to be joined by means of strips of lead. Lead is used because it is soft and can easily be molded to the shapes of the glass pieces. The lead strips used to join segments of stained glass have a groove along each side and are called *cames*. The two grooves of a came are fitted over the edges of adjoining pieces of glass. Thus, each came

Window (1961) created for the synagogue at the Hadassah-Hebrew University Medical Center in Jerusalem, Israel; © Hadassah Medical Relief Association, Inc.

A modern stained-glass window by Marc Chagall is one of a series that honors the 12 tribes of Israel. The window above represents the tribe of Zebulun. The fish and ship symbolize biblical predictions that the tribe would prosper near the sea.

joins several pieces. After all the pieces have been joined, the points where the ends of the cames meet are filled with solder. Putty is forced into the grooves to make them watertight. The finished window is now ready to install.

Large stained-glass windows have a framework of iron bars to hold them in place. The bars divide the window opening into sections. The stained glass for such windows is made in sections that fit the sections of the framework.

History

Early stained-glass windows. The art of making stained-glass windows developed in western Europe during the Middle Ages. From the beginning, the art was closely allied with that of church-building. Stained-glass windows greatly increased the beauty of a church, but they had a more practical purpose as well. Scenes pictured in sparkling light and glowing colors make a strong impression on many people. Stained-glass windows thus became a powerful force in the teaching and encouragement of religion. Most early windows pictured scenes from the Bible or from the lives of saints.

Only fragments of stained glass have survived from the period before the 1000's. Five windows in the cathedral of Augsburg, Germany, are believed to be the oldest stained-glass windows in existence. They date from

The Betrayal of Christ by an unknown German artist; Hessisches Landesmuseum, Darmstadt, Germany

A stained-glass window of the 1200's shows Judas Iscariot giving Jesus Christ the kiss that betrayed Jesus to the Romans. During the Middle Ages, the church used such scenes in stained-glass windows to teach people stories from the Bible.

the last half of the 1000's or the early 1100's. Each of these windows shows a Biblical prophet.

All stained-glass windows made before the mid-1100's were relatively small. At that time, churches had to have extremely thick walls to support their lofty domes and arches. In addition, window openings had to be small to avoid weakening the walls. During the early 1100's, however, architects began to develop a system of roof supports that greatly reduced the stress on the walls. More space could then be devoted to windows. The church of St.-Denis, near Paris, was the first church built in this style of architecture, called Gothic, and the first to have large stained-glass windows. The earliest of these windows were installed in the church in the mid-1100's. During the next 100 years, many Gothic churches were built in Europe, and the art of making stained-glass windows developed rapidly.

Technical improvements. Most large stained-glass windows of the 1100's had a framework of straight iron bars that divided them into rectangular sections. By the early 1200's, blacksmiths had learned to forge iron bars into curved shapes. Window frameworks then began to have round, as well as rectangular, sections. Round sections of stained glass created beautiful medallion-like patterns in a church window. Huge circular stained-glass windows also became common during the 1200's. These windows were divided into sections by delicate stonework called *tracery.* Because of their flowerlike shape, such windows are known as *rose windows.*

As the Gothic system of roof supports was improved, architects designed churches that had more and larger windows. The Ste.-Chapelle, a church built in Paris during the 1240's, has walls made almost entirely of stained glass. The windows are separated only by narrow stone frames and extend from just above the floor to the ceiling, a distance of nearly 50 feet (15 meters). More than 100 large stained-glass windows were installed in the Chartres Cathedral during the 1200's. They include many lovely medallion-style windows and several magnificent rose windows.

The greatest churches of the Middle Ages had many stained-glass windows. But stained glass was expensive, and most churches could afford only a little of it. Then, in the 1300's, craftworkers discovered that colorless glass, if coated with silver nitrate, becomes stained brilliant yellow when fired. The chemical could be applied inexpensively as a solid coating or in patterns. Windows made of this type of stained glass became common in churches during and after the 1300's.

Techniques developed in the 1400's gave artists greater freedom to experiment. One technique involved the use of glass that had only a thin film of color. The film was bonded to the glass during the glassmaking process, but it could be scraped off, exposing the colorless glass underneath. By scraping pictures or designs on the glass, artists produced windows as rich in detail as fine engravings. Also during the 1400's, artists began to use brightly colored enamels to paint elaborate scenes on colorless glass. After the painted glass was fired, it had nearly the same brilliance as stained glass.

Decline and revival. The techniques developed during the 1400's gradually replaced the traditional methods of making stained glass. To make a decorative window, the artist scraped or painted the picture or design on panes of glass. The panes were then installed in the window framework. This method eliminated the need to build a window from many pieces of colored glass and a number of lead strips. However, the windows looked more like paintings than stained glass. By the 1600's, the art of making stained glass was nearly forgotten.

Interest in the art revived during the 1800's. Artists mastered the old techniques of making stained glass, and churches again began to have large stained-glass windows. At first, the windows were designed to look as nearly like those of the Middle Ages as possible. But by the early 1900's, artists had begun to develop new designs and even new uses for stained glass. John La Farge and Louis C. Tiffany were among the leaders of this movement in the United States. Tiffany invented new types of stained glass and used them not only for windows but also for decorative lampshades.

Today, the creation of stained glass ranks as an imaginative, highly developed art. Gifted artists, such as Marc Chagall and Georges Rouault, have designed superb stained-glass windows for modern religious structures. Some artists use techniques similar to those of the Middle Ages. Others have developed new techniques. For example, many stained-glass windows are now made of thick slabs of colored glass. The slabs are cut to shape and then joined with cement rather than with lead.

Jane Hayward

See also **Glass** (picture: Stained-glass windows); **Tracery.**

Stainless steel is the name of a family of alloy steels that resist *corrosion* (rust). As a family, the stainless steels have an easily maintained, attractive appearance. They show remarkable strength and ductility and are unique in their general resistance to weather and to most corrosives. Most stainless steels used in the home are highly polished, with a silvery appearance, but they do not need this finish to resist corrosion. *Stainless-clad steel* is commonly ordinary steel to which a thin layer of stainless steel has been bonded on one or both sides.

The most familiar use of stainless steel in the home is in kitchen knives, flatware, sinks, pots and pans, and other places where cleanliness and easy maintenance are essential. Stainless-steel equipment is used in hospitals, restaurants, chemical industries, dairies, and food-processing plants. Engineers use stainless steel parts for automobiles, aircraft, and railroad passenger cars. Scientists use microporous stainless steel, made with a nickel alloy, to filter gases, liquids, and small particles.

Chromium is the chief metal alloyed with iron, carbon, manganese, and silicon in making stainless steel. Chromium helps steel resist corrosion. However, the carbon in the steel reduces the ability of chromium to provide corrosion resistance. As a result, most stainless steels are improved by reducing the amount of carbon in them to very low levels. Nickel ranks as the second most important alloy in most stainless steels. One or more of the following elements also may be added to iron to make stainless steel: molybdenum, titanium, columbium, aluminum, nitrogen, phosphorus, sulfur, and selenium. Each element modifies stainless steel so it can be used for a specific purpose.   James A. Clum

See also **Haynes, Elwood; Iron and steel** (Stainless steel).

Staked plain. See **Texas** (Land regions).

Michael Habichi, Earth Scenes

Stalactites and stalagmites in Luray Caverns in the Shenandoah Valley of Virginia form beautifully colored columns. The eerie formations are made of deposits of the mineral calcite, or calcium carbonate.

Stalactite, *stuh LAK tyt* or *STAL uhk tyt,* is a beautiful stone formation found in some limestone caves. Stalactites hang from the walls or roofs of the caves. Most look like large icicles, but some resemble draperies or straws with a hole through their center.

Most stalactites form when ground water rich in carbon dioxide dissolves the mineral *calcite* (calcium carbonate) from limestone directly above the cave. As the water drips into the cave, it loses carbon dioxide to the cave atmosphere and leaves behind minute quantities of calcite. The calcite accumulates very slowly, forming stalactites. In many cases, this process occurs over thousands of years.

Formations that build up from the floor of a cave are called *stalagmites* (see **Stalagmite**). In the United States, excellent examples of stalactites and stalagmites exist in Carlsbad Caverns in New Mexico, Luray Caverns in Virginia, Mammoth Cave in Kentucky, Cumberland Caverns in Tennessee, and Blanchard Springs Caverns in Arkansas. Nicholas C. Crawford

See also **Calcite; Cave.**

Stalagmite, *stuh LAG myt* or *STAL uhg myt,* is a stone formation that rises up from the floors of caves, especially in limestone caverns. Stalagmites form when water, dripping on the floor from the walls and roofs of the cave, carries with it deposits of calcium carbonate, or calcite. As the water enters the cave's atmosphere, it loses carbon dioxide and produces calcite. The calcite builds up into colorful stone formations that look like icicles upside down. Similar formations, which hang from the roof of the cave, are called stalactites (see **Stalactite**). Sometimes stalagmites and stalactites join to

form columns or stone curtains against the walls of the cave. Nicholas C. Crawford

See also **Calcite; Cave.**

Stalin, *STAH lihn,* **Joseph** (1879-1953), was dictator of the Union of Soviet Socialist Republics (U.S.S.R.) from 1929 until 1953. He rose from bitter poverty to become ruler of a country that covered about a sixth of the world's land area.

Stalin ruled by terror during most of his years as dictator. He allowed no one to oppose his decisions. Stalin executed or jailed most of those who had helped him rise to power because he feared they might threaten his rule.

Stalin also was responsible for the deaths of millions of Soviet peasants who opposed his program of *collective agriculture* (government control of farms). Under Stalin, the Soviet Union operated a worldwide network of Communist parties. By the time he died, Communism had spread to 11 other countries. His style of government became known as *Stalinism* and continued to influence many governments.

The Soviet people had cause to hate Stalin, and much of the world feared him. But he changed the Soviet Union from an undeveloped country into one of the world's great industrial and military powers. In World War II (1939-1945), the Soviet Union was an ally of the United States and Great Britain against Germany. But Stalin sharply opposed and, on occasion, betrayed his allies even before World War II was over. The last years that Stalin ruled the Soviet Union were marked by the Cold War, in which many non-Communist nations banded together to halt the spread of Communism.

Stalin had little personal charm, and could be brutal to even his closest friends. He seemed unable to feel

Keystone

Joseph Stalin ruled the Union of Soviet Socialist Republics (U.S.S.R.) as dictator from 1929 until 1953.

pity. He could not take criticism, and he never forgave an opponent. Few dictators have demanded such terrible sacrifices from their own people.

After Stalin became dictator, he had Soviet histories rewritten to make his role in past events appear far greater than it really was. In 1938, he helped write an official history of the Communist Party. Stalin had not played a leading part in the revolution of November 1917 (October by the old Russian calendar), which brought Communism to Russia. V.I. Lenin led this revolution, which is known as the October Revolution, and set up the world's first Communist government. But in his history, Stalin pictured himself as Lenin's chief assistant in the revolution.

Stalin died in 1953. He was honored by having his body placed beside that of Lenin in a huge tomb in Red Square in Moscow. In 1956, Nikita S. Khrushchev strongly criticized Stalin for his terrible crimes against loyal Communists. Later, in 1961, the government renamed many cities, towns, and factories that had been named for Stalin. Stalin's body was taken from the tomb and buried in a simple grave nearby.

Early life

Boyhood and education. Stalin was born on Dec. 21, 1879, in Gori, a town near Tbilisi in Georgia, a mountainous area in what was the southwestern part of the Russian empire. His real name was Iosif Vissarionovich Djugashvili. In 1913, he adopted the name *Stalin* from a Russian word that means *man of steel.*

Little is known about Stalin's early life. His father, Vissarion Ivanovich Djugashvili, was an unsuccessful village shoemaker. He is said to have been a drunkard who was cruel to his young son. Stalin's mother, Ekaterina Gheladze Djugashvili, became a washerwoman to help support the family. The Djugashvilis lived in a small shack. The first three children of the family died shortly after birth, and Stalin grew up as an only child. When Stalin was young, his father left the family and went to nearby Tbilisi to work in a shoe factory. The boy had smallpox when he was 6 or 7, and the disease scarred his face for life.

In 1888, at great sacrifice, Stalin's mother sent him to a little church school in Gori. He spent five years there and was a bright student. He then received a scholarship at the religious seminary in Tbilisi. Stalin entered this school in 1894 to study for the priesthood in the Georgian Orthodox Church. At this time, Stalin became interested in the ideas of Karl Marx, a German social philosopher. The people of Tbilisi knew little of Marx and his theories about revolution. But political exiles from Moscow and St. Petersburg were beginning to bring Marxist pamphlets to Tbilisi and other smaller cities.

Czar Alexander III died in 1894, and his son, Nicholas II, became czar. Alexander had ruled Russia with complete power. He closely controlled the press, restricted education, and forbade student organizations. Nicholas continued his father's policies, and Russia made important economic and social progress. However, it was difficult to solve the country's social problems. The peasants were demanding more land. They could not raise enough food for the country on their small farms, and, at times, millions of people faced starvation. The growing class of factory workers was discontented because

Important dates in Stalin's life

1879	(Dec. 21) Born in Gori, Russia.
1901	Joined the Russian Social Democratic Labor Party.
1905	Met Lenin for the first time.
1912	Named by Lenin to Bolshevik Party Central Committee.
1917	Named commissar of nationalities after Bolshevik revolution.
1922	Appointed general secretary of Communist Party.
1928	Began five-year plans to industrialize the U.S.S.R.
1929	Became dictator of the Soviet Union.
1935	Began great purge of Communist Party members.
1939	The U.S.S.R. signed a nonaggression pact with Germany.
1941	Named himself premier of the Soviet Union.
1941	Germany attacked the U.S.S.R. during World War II.
1953	(March 5) Died in Moscow.

of long hours and low wages. For a discussion of conditions in Russia at this time, see **Russia** (History).

In 1898, Stalin joined a secret Marxist revolutionary group. The Tbilisi seminary, like many Russian schools, was a center for the circulation of forbidden revolutionary ideas. In May 1899, Stalin was expelled for not appearing for an examination. His interest in Marxism probably played a part in his dismissal.

Young revolutionist. After Stalin left the seminary, he got a job as a clerk at the Tbilisi Geophysical Observatory. Within a year, he began his career as an active revolutionist. In 1900, Stalin helped organize a small May Day demonstration near Tbilisi. The demonstration was held to protest working conditions.

In March 1901, the czar's secret police arrested a number of socialists in Tbilisi. The police searched Stalin's room, but he was not there and escaped arrest. He left his job and joined the Marxist revolutionary underground movement that was springing up in Russia.

In September 1901, Stalin began to write for a Georgian Marxist journal called *Brdzola* (The Struggle). By this time, he had read revolutionary articles written by Lenin. Stalin's first writings closely imitated the views of Lenin, but lacked Lenin's style or force. In November 1901, Stalin was formally accepted into the Russian Social Democratic Labor (Marxist) Party.

Using various false names, Stalin carried on underground activity in the Caucasus Mountains region. He organized strikes among workers in the Batum oil fields. He helped start a Social Democratic group in Batum and set up a secret press there.

In 1902, Stalin was arrested and jailed for his revolutionary activities. In March 1903, the several Social Democratic groups of the Caucasus united to form an All-Caucasian Federation. Although Stalin was in prison, the federation elected him to serve on its governing body. In November 1903, he was transferred from prison and exiled to Siberia. Also in 1903, the Russian Social Democratic Labor Party, which included many Social Democratic organizations, split into two major groups. Lenin headed the *Bolsheviks,* who demanded that party membership be limited to a small body of devoted revolutionists. The other group, the *Mensheviks,* wanted its membership to represent a wider group of people.

Stalin escaped from Siberia in January 1904. He returned to Tbilisi and joined the Bolsheviks. Stalin met Lenin in Finland in 1905. Between 1906 and 1913, Stalin was arrested and exiled a number of times. He spent 7 of the 10 years between 1907 and 1917 in prison or in exile. In 1912, Stalin was suddenly elevated by Lenin into the small but powerful Central Committee of the Bolshevik party.

In 1913, with Lenin's help, Stalin wrote a long article called "The National Question and Social Democracy." Also in 1913, Stalin was arrested and exiled for the last time. Before his arrest, he served briefly as an editor of *Pravda* (Truth), the Bolshevik party newspaper.

Germany declared war on Russia in 1914 at the beginning of World War I. Stalin was in exile in Siberia, where he remained until 1917.

By the end of 1916, Russia was suffering badly because of the war. Conditions became steadily worse at home. Food shortages in the capital, Petrograd (St.Petersburg), led to riots and strikes. Finally, onMarch 15, 1917, Czar Nicholas II gave up his throne. A *provisional* (temporary) government, run mostly by liberals, was formed the next day. The government released Stalin and other Bolsheviks from exile. They returned to Petrograd on March 25. Stalin took over the editorship of *Pravda* from Vyacheslav Molotov. Lenin became concerned that Stalin did not strongly oppose the provisional government in *Pravda.* Lenin arrived in Petrograd from exile three weeks later and criticized Stalin for not taking a strong Bolshevik stand. Lenin launched a radical program for overthrowing the provisional government. This action led to the Bolshevik seizure of power in November 1917. The month was October in the old Russian calendar, and the Bolshevik take-over is often called the *October Revolution.*

Rise to power

The Bolshevik revolution. Stalin played an important, but not vital, part in the revolution. Lenin worked most closely with Leon Trotsky in the Bolshevik takeover of the government. After Stalin became dictator of the Soviet Union, he had history books rewritten to say that he had led the revolution with Lenin.

Lenin became head of the new government after the revolution and named Stalin commissar of nationalities. Within a few months, opposition to the new government developed in many parts of the country. Armed uprisings broke out and grew into civil war. Stalin was active on the southern military front. In Stalin's version of history, he repeatedly corrected the mistakes of others. Stalin took credit for a victory at Tsaritsyn, the city later named Stalingrad (now Volgograd). Actually, Stalin's military role there was exaggerated.

During the civil war, the Russian Social Democratic Labor Party was renamed the Russian Communist Party (Bolsheviks). Stalin became one of the five members of the newly formed *Politburo* (Political Bureau), the policy-making body of the party's Central Committee. In 1922, the Communist Party's Central Committee elected Stalin as its general secretary.

Stalin takes over. The Bolsheviks won the civil war in 1920. They then began to rebuild the war-torn country. At first, Lenin and the others were unaware of Stalin's quiet plotting. But by the end of 1922, Stalin's growing power began to disturb Lenin. Before a series of strokes prevented Lenin from working, he wrote a secret note warning that Stalin must be removed as general secretary. He wrote that Stalin was too "rude" in personal relations and abused the power of his office. Because of his illness, however, Lenin was unable to remove Stalin.

Lenin died in 1924. The leading Bolsheviks finally learned of the secret note warning against Stalin, but they ignored it. They accepted Stalin's promise that he would improve his behavior. Instead, Stalin continued to build his own power. He cleverly used this power to destroy his rivals. In December 1929, the party praised Stalin on his 50th birthday. He had become a dictator.

Dictator of the Soviet Union

The five-year plan. In 1928, Stalin started the first of the Soviet Union's five-year plans for economic development. The government began to eliminate private businesses. Production of industrial machinery and farm equipment became more important, and production of clothing and household goods was neglected.

In 1929, Stalin began to *collectivize* Soviet agriculture. He ended private farming and transferred the control of farms, farm equipment, and livestock to the government. But the farmers resisted his order and destroyed about half of the U.S.S.R.'s livestock and much of its produce. As punishment, Stalin sent about a million families into exile. The destruction of livestock and grain caused widespread starvation. The economy moved forward, but at the cost of millions of lives.

During the 1930's, Stalin adopted a policy of *Russification.* The minority nationalities in the Soviet Union were subject to increasingly strict control by the government. In 1939, the Soviet Union seized a large part of Poland. In 1940, Soviet troops invaded the Baltic countries—Estonia, Latvia, and Lithuania. Stalin tried to destroy the middle classes in these countries. He set up Communist governments and joined them to the Soviet Union. See **Baltic States.**

Rule by terror. Under the czars, the Russian secret police had often arrested revolutionists and sent them into exile without trial. Stalin set up a police system that was far more terrible. Millions of persons were executed or sent to labor camps. Stalin also turned over many industries to the secret police, who forced prisoners to work in them. Fear spread through the U.S.S.R. as neighbors were ordered to spy on one another. The Soviet government broke up families, and it urged chil-

UPI/Bettmann

Soviet farmworkers had to work on government-controlled farms after Stalin began to end private farming in 1929.

United Press Int.

The U.S.S.R. and Germany divided Poland by a treaty signed in September 1939. Soviet foreign minister Vyacheslav Molotov, *seated,* and German foreign minister Joachim von Ribbentrop, *left,* signed the treaty as Stalin and an aide looked on.

dren to inform on their parents to the police.

In 1935, Stalin started a *purge* (elimination) of most of the old Bolsheviks associated with Lenin. During the next few years, he killed anyone who might have threatened his power. He also executed thousands of other Communist Party members, including the chiefs and countless officers of the Soviet army. Stalin achieved his purpose. When he decided to cooperate with the German dictator Adolf Hitler in 1939, there was no one left to oppose his policies. Even when the Soviet Union later suffered terrible military defeats from Hitler's army, no political opposition to Stalin was possible.

After World War II ended in 1945, Lavrenti P. Beria, chief of the secret police, became a leading figure in Stalin's government. Police control grew tighter. The bloody purges went on, but in secret. No one was safe. Even Politburo members and Communist Party leaders were purged and shot in 1949 and 1950. Anti-Semitism, which had been encouraged by Stalin during the 1930's, was now practiced throughout the country.

World War II. By the late 1930's, Adolf Hitler was ready to conquer Europe. Soviet leaders bargained unsuccessfully with France and the United Kingdom for a defense agreement against Germany. Then, on Aug. 23, 1939, the U.S.S.R. and Germany suddenly signed a treaty agreeing not to go to war against each other. In a secret part of the treaty, Stalin and Hitler also planned to divide Poland between themselves.

On Sept. 1, 1939, German troops marched into Poland. On September 3, France and the United Kingdom declared war on Germany. World War II had begun. Germany quickly conquered western Poland, and the Soviet Union seized the eastern part. On September 28, Germany and the U.S.S.R. signed a treaty which set the boundaries for the division of Poland. The Soviet Union invaded Finland on Nov. 30, 1939, and, after a bitter struggle, took a large portion of that country.

By December 1940, Hitler began planning an attack on the U.S.S.R. Prime Minister Winston Churchill of the United Kingdom and President Franklin D. Roosevelt of the United States told Stalin that their secret agents warned of a coming invasion. But Stalin ignored the warnings, as well as those of his own secret service.

In May 1941, Stalin named himself premier of the Soviet Union. Germany invaded the Soviet Union the next month. In spite of the two extra years that Stalin had to get ready for a war, the country was not prepared. Because of Stalin's purge of the army, the U.S.S.R. lacked experienced officers. The country also lacked up-to-date weapons and equipment. The German army approached Moscow, the capital, in October 1941, and many government officials were moved to Kuybyshev (now Samara). Stalin remained in Moscow to give the Soviet people hope and courage. The army finally beat back German attacks on Moscow in the winter of 1941-1942. Stalin reached the height of his popularity during the war.

In March 1943, Stalin took the military title of Marshal of the Soviet Union. Later in 1943, Churchill, Roosevelt, and Stalin met at Tehran, Iran. The "Big Three" agreed that the United States, the United Kingdom, and the U.S.S.R. would work together until Germany was defeated. The three leaders met again early in 1945 at Yalta in the Crimea to discuss the military occupation of Germany after the war. For the story of the Soviet Union in the war, see **World War II**.

The Cold War. After the Allies defeated Germany in 1945, Stalin gradually cut off almost all contact between the U.S.S.R. and the West. Stalin used the Soviet army's presence in Eastern Europe to set up Communist governments in Bulgaria, Czechoslovakia, East Germany, Hungary, Poland, and Romania. Churchill said that these countries lay behind the *Iron Curtain,* a term he used to refer to Soviet barriers against the West. Stalin also tried unsuccessfully to take over Greece, Iran, and Turkey. Many non-Communist nations joined against the Soviet Union and its *satellites* (countries controlled by the U.S.S.R.) to halt the spread of Communism. This struggle became known as the Cold War (see **Cold War**).

In June 1945, Germany was divided into four zones, each occupied by American, British, French, or Soviet troops. Berlin, which lay deep in the Soviet zone, was also divided among the four powers. Stalin refused to cooperate in administering Germany, and in 1948, France, the United Kingdom, and the United States announced plans to combine their zones into the West German Federal Republic (West Germany). To prevent this action, Stalin tried to drive the Allies out of West Berlin by blockading the city. He hoped the blockade would prevent food and supplies from reaching West Berlin. But the Allies set up the Berlin Airlift and supplied the city entirely by airplanes for 11 months. Stalin was defeated, and he ended the blockade of Berlin in May 1949. The airlift continued until September 1949.

In 1948, Stalin expelled the Yugoslav Communist party from the *Cominform* (Communist Information Bureau), an organization of Communist parties in Europe. Josip Broz Tito, the Communist dictator of Yugoslavia, had refused to allow the Soviet Union to run his country. Under Tito's leadership, Yugoslavia developed its own style of Communism, separate from Stalin's control.

Stalin's aggressive policies led the West in 1949 to form the North Atlantic Treaty Organization (NATO), a mutual defense organization.

During the Korean War (1950-1953), Stalin supported the Communist North Korean forces that invaded South Korea. Korea had been divided into two parts after World War II. At first, Soviet troops occupied the north-

The Battle of Stalingrad ended the Nazis' eastward advance into the Soviet Union during World War II. In a five-month struggle, the Soviets and Germans fought hand-to-hand for single streets, houses, and factories. In this photo, Soviet troops took cover behind mounds of bomb debris as they attacked German soldiers.

AP/Wide World

ern half, and U.S. troops occupied the southern half. Both sides later withdrew their forces. North Korean troops then launched a surprise attack on South Korea to unite the divided country by force. As a result, U.S. troops were sent back to Korea. The war ended a few months after Stalin's death. See **Korean War**.

Death. Early in 1953, Stalin prepared to replace the top men in the Soviet government. Apparently he was planning another great purge. Then, on March 4, 1953, the Central Committee of the Communist Party announced that Stalin had suffered a brain hemorrhage on March 1. Stalin died in Moscow on March 5, 1953.

Stalinism. Even after Stalin's death, many Communist governments continued to use his style of rule, which became known as Stalinism. Stalinist governments eliminate all opposition by employing terrorism—that is, by threatening or using violence to create widespread fear. These governments maintain total control of the media for propaganda and force economic production without considering market conditions or the needs of workers.

Stalinism thrived in countries behind the Iron Curtain until Communism collapsed in Eastern Europe and the Soviet Union in the late 1980's and early 1990's. Outside Europe, Mao Zedong set up a Stalinist government in China in 1949. Ho Chi Minh established a Stalinist dictatorship in North Vietnam in 1954, and Kim Il-sung introduced hard-line Stalinist rule in North Korea in 1948. Under Fidel Castro, a government with many characteristics of Stalinism came to power in Cuba in 1959.

Albert Marrin

Related articles in *World Book* include:

Bolsheviks	Potsdam Conference
Cold War	Russia (History)
Communism	Tehran Conference
(Under Stalin)	Tito, Josip Broz
Khrushchev, Nikita S.	Trotsky, Leon
Lenin, V. I.	Union of Soviet Socialist Re-
Marx, Karl	publics (History)
Molotov, Vyacheslav M.	World War II
Politburo	Yalta Conference

Additional resources

Medvedev, Roy A. and Zhores A. *The Unknown Stalin.* Overlook, 2004.
Montefiore, Simon S. *Stalin.* Knopf, 2004.
Rayfield, Donald. *Stalin and His Hangmen.* Random Hse., 2004.
Service, Robert. *Stalin.* Harvard Univ. Pr., 2005.

Stalinabad. See Dushanbe.
Stalingrad. See Volgograd.

Stalingrad, Battle of, one of the most important battles of history, was a turning point in World War II (1939-1945). It lasted about five months, from August 1942 until early 1943. In the battle, Soviet troops kept German troops from capturing Stalingrad (now Volgograd), an important Soviet industrial city on the Volga River. The German defeat at Stalingrad ended the Nazis' eastward advance into the Soviet Union. The invading German troops had to retreat from the Caucasus oil fields and the lower Don River regions. During the battle, the German army lost about 300,000 soldiers, including about 90,000 prisoners. The prisoners included 24 German generals. Snow and bitter cold took a heavy toll of German troops.

The German Sixth Army launched its drive on Stalingrad on Aug. 21, 1942, from positions about 40 miles (64 kilometers) away on the Don River. By August 23, German tanks had reached the Volga River, north of Stalingrad. Gradually, they forced their way into the city.

By November, German forces had isolated Soviet troops in four "pockets" along the riverbank in the city. German and Soviet units fought hand-to-hand for control of single streets, houses, and factories. When the Volga froze over, Soviet troops pushed supplies across on the ice at night. Soviet armies north and south of Stalingrad counterattacked the German forces on November 19. The Soviet armies met west of Stalingrad on November 23, surrounding the German units in and near the city.

Nazi dictator Adolf Hitler ordered his generals to continue the battle for Stalingrad. He sent other German units to help the troops in the city, but the relief forces could not break through the Soviet lines. The Soviet troops hammered away at the hungry, half-frozen German troops. Finally, German Field Marshal Friedrich von Paulus, Sixth Army commander, surrendered on Jan. 31, 1943. The last German troops in Stalingrad surrendered on February 2.   Daniel Clayton

See also **World War II** (On the Soviet front).
Stallion. See Horse (table: Horse terms).
Stamen. See Flower (The parts of a flower; pictures).
Stamford (pop. 117,083) is an important business center in southwestern Connecticut. The city lies on Long Island Sound, about 35 miles (56 kilometers) northeast of New York City. For location, see **Connecticut** (political map). Stamford, together with Bridgeport and Norwalk, forms a metropolitan area with a population of 882,567.

Stamford ranks among the leading cities as a site for headquarters of large corporations. A number of the nation's biggest companies have home offices in Stamford. The city's leading industries include financial services, information technology, pharmaceuticals, printing and publishing, reinsurance, and the production of office machines and textiles.

Cultural attractions include an art museum, a nature center and museum, an astronomical observatory, and a center for the arts, which features plays and concerts. The city also has an opera company, a chamber music group, and a symphony orchestra. Recreational facilities include golf courses, parks, beaches, and marinas. A branch campus of the University of Connecticut is located in downtown Stamford.

In 1641, European settlers from Wethersfield, Connecticut, moved to the Stamford area after the land was bought from the Paugusset and Siwanog Indians. The establishment of several manufacturing companies in the 1860's changed Stamford from a farming village to a large factory town. In 1893, one part of Stamford was incorporated as a city and the other part as a town. They merged in 1949 under a mayor-council government. Downtown renewal in the middle and late 1900's included the construction of hotels, office buildings, a new city hall, and a large shopping mall.   Joy L. Haenlein

Stammering. See Stuttering.

Stamp is an official mark or seal or a small printed piece of paper with one glued surface. Many documents are not legal until they carry a government stamp. For example, the government may require the payment of a one-dollar tax on a real-estate deed. The collector pastes a revenue stamp of one dollar in value on the deed, as proof that the tax was paid.

The Dutch levied the first stamp taxes in 1624. In 1694, the English used the stamp plan to raise money for carrying on a war with France. The British Stamp Act of 1765 was one of the direct causes of the American colonial revolt against Britain.

In 1814, stamp taxes became a part of the fiscal system of the United States. In 1862, Congress passed an important stamp law. The law required that legal papers and certain kinds of packages carry government stamps. The purpose of the law was to raise funds to pay some of the expenses of the American Civil War. The law was repealed when revenue was no longer needed to pay war expenses. New stamp laws, passed during the Spanish-American War (1898) and World War I (1914-1918), helped raise money to pay the costs of war.

Government stamps for raising money are known as internal revenue stamps. Until 1959, the United States government required that such stamps be placed on luxuries such as tobacco and liquor. Some states also tax these luxuries, and require that they be stamped.

During World War II, the United States government offered war savings stamps for sale to citizens. These stamps raised funds for the war. The ration stamp also came into use during the war. Its purpose was to divide food and clothing equally among civilians. However, people in the United States are probably most familiar with the various forms of postage stamps.   Vito Tanzi

See also **Internal revenue; Postal Service, United States** (Stamps and other mailing materials); **Stamp Act; Stamp collecting.**

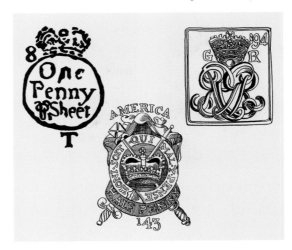

These three stamps were used by the British government under the Stamp Act it imposed upon the American Colonies.

Stamp Act was passed by the British Parliament in March 1765. Its purpose was to raise funds to support the British Army stationed in America after 1763. The act specified that Americans must buy stamps for deeds, mortgages, liquor licenses, law licenses, playing cards, and almanacs. Even newspaper owners and publishers had to buy stamps for their publications.

The Stamp Act was unpopular in the colonies. Societies organized to protest stamp sales. The colonists' slogan became "No Taxation Without Representation."

The Virginia Assembly declared that the Stamp Act was illegal and unjust. The Assembly passed resolutions against taxation by the British Parliament. The Massachusetts House of Representatives invited all colonies to send delegates to a general congress. The colonies that accepted the invitation were New York, New Jersey, Rhode Island, Pennsylvania, Delaware, Connecticut, Maryland, South Carolina, and Massachusetts.

The Stamp Act Congress met in New York in October 1765. It declared that stamp taxes could not be collected without the people's consent. American resistance forced the British Parliament to repeal the Stamp Act in 1766.   John L Bullion

See also **Adams, John** (In New England); **Revolutionary War in America** (The Quartering and Stamp acts).

Stamp collecting is one of the most popular collecting hobbies in the world. Young people, old people, rich people, and poor people in every country collect stamps. Stamp collecting has been called "the hobby of kings and the king of hobbies." King George V of the United Kingdom, Franklin D. Roosevelt, and many other famous people have collected stamps. Students of stamps are called *philatelists.* The name comes from two Greek words, *philos,* meaning *loving,* and *atelos,* meaning *free of tax,* or *paid.* Stamps are signs that the postage, or tax, has been paid.

Origins

The United Kingdom issued the first stamps to prepay postage on letters on May 6, 1840. The stamps were a one-penny stamp (now known as "The Penny Black") and a two-pence stamp. Complete envelopes designed by

Robert A. Siegel, Inc.

The first stamps issued by the U.S. Post Office appeared in 1847. They bore the portraits of George Washington and Benjamin Franklin. Franklin was the first U.S. postmaster general.

William Mulready were also sold in the same values. But these were discontinued. The United States did not issue any stamps until 1847. By that time, several other countries had already tried the newly invented stamp. Among them were Brazil, Mauritius, and the *cantons* (states) of Switzerland. By 1860, almost every country had adopted stamps as a method of paying postage.

No one knows exactly when stamp collecting started. It probably occurred right after the first stamp was issued. We do know that the first stamp catalog was published in 1864 by an Englishman named Mount Brown. Since then, catalogs of stamps have been published in almost every country. A great many books and magazines about stamps have also been published.

People soon discovered that some stamps were harder to find than others, often because smaller quantities were printed. Collectors traded rare stamps and soon began selling them to each other. Prices rose as more people began collecting stamps. A three-shilling 1857 Swedish stamp sold for $2,260,000 in 1996. Sometimes errors are made in printing stamps. Such stamps are usually rare and may become very valuable. For example, 100 24-cent United States airmail stamps were issued in 1918 with the airplane mistakenly appearing upside down.

Ways in which stamps differ

Small differences in stamps mean a great deal to the stamp collector. Stamps which look the same to the beginner might seem entirely different to the expert.

Philatelists study many things, such as the paper and inks used, the way the stamps are separated, the printing process, and postal history.

Paper. The surface of paper may be finished in various ways. Paper with a plain finish is called *wove.* Paper which looks as though it has bars in it when it is held up to the light is known as *laid.* Tiny pieces of colored silk like those in a dollar bill are used in *silk paper.* Pieces of silk so small they can hardly be seen are used in *granite paper,* which is grayish in color. Sometimes paper is made with a design called a *watermark,* which is pressed into the wet paper with wire. The wire can be laid in any shape. Stamps may look the same but have different watermarks. Philatelists consider these as different stamps. The watermark can be seen by holding the stamp up to the light or by placing it face down in a

dark-colored dish and pouring watermark fluid on it.

Ink. Stamps are printed with different colored inks. Variations of the color of the basic ink make the stamps different for the collector. For example, a blue stamp differs from an ultramarine stamp. But sometimes a stamp's color changes with age, making it difficult to determine the original color accurately.

Printing. A stamp may be printed by one of three basic methods—*relief, planographic,* and *intaglio.* Relief printing is made from a raised design. Planographic printing is made from a design level with the surface of the printing plate, and intaglio is printed from a design cut lower than the surface. The most common forms of planographic printing are *offset* and *lithography.* One form of intaglio printing used for stamps is called *engraving.* The ink is slightly raised, just as it is on an engraved calling card. Another intaglio process is *gravure.* See **Printing.**

Separations. The first stamps had to be cut apart with scissors. Such stamps are called *imperforate.* Soon *perforations* (little holes) were punched between the rows of stamps. Stamps that have a different number of holes per two centimeters along any edge are also considered as different stamps. Sometimes the separations are slits cut with a knife, but with no paper punched out. This form is referred to as a *roulette.*

Cancellations. The marks placed on a stamp to show that it has been used are called a *cancellation.* Cancellations show postal history. Used stamps are often left on envelopes, and early stamps may be more valuable that way. Envelopes with a stamp canceled the first day it was issued are called *first day covers.* Collectors are interested in such cancellations, particularly on earlier issues.

Surcharged stamps. Countries often change stamps by overprinting something new on an old stamp, instead of issuing a new one. A new value, called a surcharge, may be printed on an old stamp. When a country is overrun in war, the conquerors often print their names on the stamps of the fallen country.

Special stamps. Many special stamps are issued, in addition to plain postage stamps. A country may honor or commemorate an event or famous person by issuing *commemorative* stamps. The first U.S. commemorative stamps were issued in 1893. They were called the Columbian issue, in honor of the four-hundredth anniversary of the discovery of America. A stamp sold for more than the cost of postage is called a *semipostal.* Such stamps have been issued by many countries, but not by the United States. Extra funds from semipostals have been given to charity, and to help finance fairs, youth clubs, and the rebuilding of a cathedral.

Many types of special stamps are issued by various countries. Among such stamps are airmail, parcel post, official, postage due, provisional stamps for emergencies, pneumatic tube, special delivery, and personal delivery. Other types of special stamps include registration, occupation during war, postal savings, newspaper, special handling, and combinations of special services.

Other reasons for collecting. A large number of people like to collect stamps just for the pictures of odd and out-of-the-way places and things. Some people collect stamps of one country only. Other people collect only stamps showing birds, or railroads, or ships.

WORLD BOOK photos

Commemorative stamps honor important events. The Canadian government issued the two stamps at the left in 1967 to commemorate the centennial of the nation's Confederation. The United States airmail stamp honored the first astronaut to step on the moon. The stamp on the right was issued to celebrate the 150th anniversary of the birth of the American author Henry David Thoreau.

Rare and unusual stamps

Collectors especially value stamps that are rare or have some unusual feature. A number of stamps, called *errors,* have become valuable because of a printing mistake, such as part of the design being upside down. Some collectors have paid thousands of dollars for one error.

Rare stamps are prized by collectors. Only one known copy exists of this one-penny stamp issued in 1856 in British Guiana.

Early stamps, such as this French issue from the 1850's, had no perforations. Collectors call these stamps *imperforates.*

Robert A. Siegel, Inc.

An inverted center makes this 1918 airmail stamp one of the most valuable errors among all United States stamps.

A tête-bêche error occurs when one stamp in a series is accidentally printed upside down. This pair was issued in France in 1870.

Stamp collecting specialties

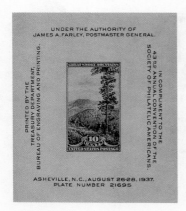

Souvenir sheets have been issued periodically by the U.S. Post Office since 1926. This sheet honored a convention of stamp collectors.

A plate block consists of four or more connected stamps with the serial numbers of the plates from which the stamps were printed.

Stamps showing birds attract collectors who specialize in beautiful stamps or in issues dealing with the same general subject.

WORLD BOOK photos

A first day cover is an envelope bearing a stamp canceled on its first day of issue. On that day, the U.S. Postal Service sells the stamp in only one selected city. The postmark on the example above shows that the first day of issue was Feb. 20, 1987, in Chicago. Private companies sell collectors first day covers decorated with specially designed pictures called *cachets*.

The reason for collecting stamps does not matter as long as the collector has fun.   Richard L. Sine

See also **Stamp.**

Additional resources

Level I
Abeyta, Jennifer. *Stamps.* Children's Pr., 2000.
Briggs, Michael. *Stamps.* Random Hse., 1993.

Level II
Carlton, R. Scott. *The International Encyclopaedic Dictionary of Philately.* Krause, 1996.
Scott Standard Postage Stamp Catalogue. 6 vols. Scott Pub. Co., published annually.
Sine, Richard L. *Stamp Collecting for Dummies.* Hungry Minds, 2001.

Stamp weed. See Velvetleaf.

Standard & Poor's indexes are statistics used to measure the level of American stock market prices. They are compiled and published by Standard & Poor's Corporation, an investment research and advisory firm.

The best-known of the measures is the Standard & Poor's 500 Index. It reflects stock prices for 500 companies whose shares are traded on the New York Stock Exchange. These companies consist of 400 industrial firms, 40 public utilities, 40 financial institutions, and 20 transportation companies. Altogether, the stocks of these companies make up about 80 percent of the market value of all stocks listed on the exchange.

Standard & Poor's computers calculate the 500 Index every five minutes of each business day. The index compares current stock prices with average prices during the period 1941-1943, which is called the *base period.* The average prices during 1941-1943, called *base prices,* are assigned a value of 10.

Current index figures indicate how many times greater than the base prices current average prices are. For example, an index level of 250 means that average share prices are 25 times higher than the base prices. The 500 Index weights each price according to the total market value of the corporation's publicly owned shares, so that larger companies affect the index more than smaller ones do.

The Standard & Poor's Corporation also prepares a 100-industry survey, which appears in its weekly publication *The Outlook.* This survey provides prices and other statistics on 100 industries, giving an overview of the strengths and weaknesses of each industry. In addition, the company publishes separate indexes daily for transportation stocks, for utility stocks, for financial stocks, and for bonds.   Roger G. Ibbotson

See also **Dow Jones averages.**

Standard Model is a theory in physics describing the particles that make up matter and explaining how those particles interact. Since the early 1970's, scientists have subjected the theory to precise experimental tests, and the theory has withstood every test.

According to the Standard Model, the matter we encounter in our daily experiences consists of atoms. A typical atom, in turn, is made up of negatively charged *electrons* and a positively charged *nucleus.* The nucleus contains positively charged *protons* and electrically neutral *neutrons.* And protons and neutrons are made of *quarks,* which can have positive or negative charges.

Particles interact by means of *forces.* The force that attracts electrons to nuclei in atoms is known as the *elec-*tromagnetic force. The *strong force* holds quarks together in protons and neutrons, and it holds protons and neutrons together in a nucleus. The *weak force* is responsible for certain kinds of *radioactive decay.* For example, a *free neutron*—one that is not part of a nucleus—is radioactive. It will decay to a proton, an electron, and a particle known as an *antineutrino.* A fourth force, *gravitation,* is not part of the Standard Model.

The Standard Model explains that forces are transmitted by particles known as *force carriers.* The carrier of the electromagnetic force is the *photon.* In an atom, a proton interacts with an electron by means of a photon. The proton *emits* (sends out) a photon, which the electron then absorbs. The carrier of the strong force is the *gluon.* In a proton, one quark emits a gluon, which another quark then absorbs.

There are three carriers of the weak force: two W *bosons*—one positively charged; the other, negatively charged—and an electrically neutral Z *boson.* A free neutron decays by changing into a proton and a negative W boson. The boson then breaks apart into an electron and an antineutrino.   Michael Dine

See also **Atom** (The parts of an atom); **Force; Gravitation; Quark; Subatomic particle.**

Standard of living usually refers to the economic level achieved by an individual, family, or nation. It may be measured by the value of the goods and services produced or used by the individual, family, or nation in a given period of time. Another interpretation of standard of living is based on the goals that people set for themselves as consumers. That is, when people have enough material things for comfort and happiness, they have achieved their standard of living.

How standard of living is measured. There are several major ways of measuring standard of living. All present problems of interpretation. They do not always provide enough information or the right information.

A nation's living standard may be estimated by determining the proportion of income that "average" citizens spend on certain basic necessities. One basis for comparison is the amount spent for food. According to this measure, the greater the proportion of income spent on food by individuals in a nation, the lower the nation's living standard. But this measure provides only basic information and does not reveal anything about actual levels of consumption. Also, economists cannot easily determine the proportion of individual incomes spent on food and nonfood items.

Another common measure of the standard of living for a nation is obtained by dividing a figure called the *private consumption expenditure* by the population. The private consumption expenditure, also called the *personal consumption expenditure,* represents the value of goods and services bought by individuals over a period of time. But this measure also has drawbacks.

The measure presents a figure for the average citizen of the nation. But such an average does not reveal the distribution of the standard of living in the nation. For example, two nations whose *per capita* (per person) consumption expenditures are $1,000 each year may differ widely. In one nation, all the individuals may spend about $1,000. In the other nation, a few rich individuals may spend much more than $1,000 and many poor individuals may spend much less. The second country has a poorer standard of living for most people, but the measure does not reflect it.

Another drawback to the private consumption measure is that it is not reliable for making international comparisons. There are several reasons for this problem. For one, the official exchange rate with the United States dollar may not accurately reflect the purchasing power of the local currency. Thus, $100 may buy very different amounts of goods in different nations. Secondly, the availability of goods and services differs widely in different nations, a variation that directly affects the ability of the citizens to attain their goals as consumers. Thirdly, nations differ in their ideas concerning consumption. The basic needs of individuals include food, clothing, and shelter. But there are a number of needs that are regarded as basic in some nations and as unimportant in others. Tastes and preferences also differ.

In addition, the private consumption expenditure does not account for some of the social costs associated with citizenship in an industrial society. Certain industrial nations—including Canada, Japan, the United States, and many countries of Western Europe—are said to have the world's highest standard of living. But they also have pollution and overcrowding, which may make life unpleasant in parts of these nations.

Economists also measure standard of living in several other ways. They may divide the amount that a nation produces each year by the number of its population. They also may calculate the average personal income earned by people in a country. This average income, less the amount paid in taxes, shows how much people have to spend or save. It is often adjusted so as to take changing prices into account. However, these measures also have some problems and limitations.

A measure of standard of living

The standard of living for a nation is sometimes measured by dividing its *private consumption expenditure* by its population. This expenditure represents the value of goods and services bought by individuals in a nation during a given period of time. This table lists annual per capita private consumption expenditures in U.S. dollars for 36 selected countries with measurable economies.

Switzerland	$29,870	**South Africa**	$2,850
United States	27,810	**Argentina**	2,510
Norway	24,350	**Malaysia**	2,030
United Kingdom	23,430	**Russia**	1,970
Denmark	21,450	**Brazil**	1,810
Japan	20,630	**Dominican Republic**	1,460
Germany	19,590	**Armenia**	990
France	19,040	**Morocco***	940
Australia	18,460	**Egypt**	780
Canada	17,350	**China***	740
New Zealand	14,500	**Indonesia***	740
Greece	12,190	**Philippines**	730
Singapore*	10,570	**Nicaragua**	690
Israel	10,560	**Pakistan**	440
Czech Republic	5,240	**India***	350
Estonia	4,680	**Tanzania***	230
Mexico	4,380	**Mali***	220
Oman*	3,780	**Nepal**	200

Figures are for 2004, except for *, where figures are for 2003.
Source: *World Book* estimates based on data from the International Monetary Fund.

Area differences. Standards of living vary widely across the world. The world supports about 6 ½ billion people. At the U.S. standard of consumption, the world produces enough grain for only about one-third of the total population. By India's standard, however, there is enough grain for about 11 billion people. China's level of grain consumption falls near the world average. However, people in poor countries actually eat more grain than those in wealthy countries, where much grain is used as feed for animals.

Total food supplies also differ greatly among countries. Some of these differences have been studied by the Food and Agriculture Organization (FAO), a specialized agency of the United Nations. For example, based on FAO estimates of calorie requirements, such countries as the United States and Austria have enough food to provide each of their citizens with about 160 percent of the total calories necessary every day. Russia has 135 percent of the necessary total. China's food supply is 125 percent of its needs, and India has 105 percent. Bangladesh has about 95 percent of the food required for its people, while in Ethiopia there is only about 80 percent of the estimated needed minimum.

More goods per person are consumed in industrial countries than in developing nations. In general, people in industrial nations enjoy better clothing and housing, greater educational opportunities, and more healthful food than people in chiefly agricultural countries.

Louis W. Stern

Related articles in *World Book* include:

Consumption	Income	National income
Cost of living	Industrial Revolu-	Productivity
Gross domestic	tion	Technology
product	Inflation	Wages and hours

Standard Oil Company was one of the richest and most powerful businesses in the world during the late 1800's and early 1900's. The Supreme Court of the United States dissolved the company in 1911, charging it with unfair business practices. Today, several companies stemming from the original Standard Oil Company are among the world's leaders, including ExxonMobil Corporation—the world's largest petroleum company—and Chevron Corporation.

The original Standard Oil Company, also called the Standard Oil Company of Ohio, was established in 1870. The company developed out of a refinery run by American businessman John D. Rockefeller, his younger brother William, and their partners. After 1870, Rockefeller and his business associates bought most of the refineries in Cleveland and many in other cities. They built tank cars, developed a pipeline system, purchased oil-producing lands, and created an organization to market their products.

In 1882, they transferred the stock of all their companies to the newly formed Standard Oil Trust (see **Antitrust laws**). This transfer of control helped unify the management of the organizations and lessened legal difficulties. The Standard Oil Trust immediately became the biggest business in the oil industry. It controlled more than 90 percent of the country's refining capacity, and almost as much of its pipelines.

Since 1870, competitors, journalists, and government agencies had accused Rockefeller and Standard Oil of following illegal practices damaging to other companies. In 1892, the Supreme Court of Ohio ordered Standard Oil Company of Ohio to separate from the trust. The trustees broke up the combination. But many of the same people stayed in control through their positions on the boards of directors of the corporations.

The firms operated independently until 1899, when Standard Oil Company (New Jersey) took control. Standard Oil (New Jersey) exchanged stock in its company for stock in the other corporations of the dissolved Standard trust. It became the holding company for 37 *subsidiaries* (smaller corporations). This reorganization made Standard Oil (New Jersey) one of the richest and most powerful holding companies in the world.

In 1906, the U.S. government brought suit against the combination under the Sherman Antitrust Act. In 1911, under the provisions of the act, the U.S. Supreme Court ordered the company to dissolve. This ruling forced 33 subsidiaries of Standard Oil (New Jersey) to become separate companies. They could have no business connections with one another or with Standard Oil (New Jersey). For years, some of the companies continued to use the well-known Standard name. Only a few still use it in certain areas of the world.   Roger M. Olien

See also **Exxon Mobil Corporation; Rockefeller, John D.**

Standard schnauzer, *SHNOW zuhr,* is a sturdily built dog with a wiry coat, bushy eyebrows, and whiskers and beard. It stands 17 to 20 inches (43 to 51 centimeters) tall at the shoulder. Standard schnauzers have coats that are either pepper-and-salt or black. In the

© Callea Photo

The standard schnauzer makes an excellent watchdog.

pepper-and-salt coats, each hair is banded black, gray, black, blending to a silver-gray on the longer hair on the legs. The ears stand erect if *cropped* (cut). If left natural, the ears fold level with the top of the head.

Standard schnauzers originated during the 1400's in Germany. Farmers used them to catch rats in barns and to guard the farmers' produce carts in the marketplace. The dogs are excellent watchdogs and are loyal to their owners. They also are used in search and rescue efforts and as hearing ear dogs for people who are deaf.

Critically reviewed by the Standard Schnauzer Club of America

See also **Giant schnauzer; Miniature schnauzer.**

Standard time is a worldwide system of uniform time zones. This system divides the world into 24 zones. Each zone is 15° longitude wide (see **Longitude**). The difference in time between neighboring zones is exactly one hour. Within each zone, all clocks keep the same time, except for local variations.

Time zones. The *local,* or *sun,* time for any specific location depends on its longitude. There is a difference of 4 minutes for each degree of longitude, or a difference of an hour for every 15°. Under standard time, the time kept in each zone is that of the central *meridian,* or longitude line. The central meridians are those 15°, 30°, 45°, and so on, east or west of the prime, or Greenwich, meridian (see **Greenwich Meridian**). In theory, the zone boundaries should extend $7\frac{1}{2}$° on either side of the central meridian. In practice, the boundaries are irregular lines. This is to avoid inconvenient changes in time. For example, in the United States, zone boundaries often are located so that a state will lie entirely within one time zone. The Department of Transportation has the authority to establish limits for time zones in the United States. Time zones used in Canada have the same names as the time zones used in the United States.

The standard U.S. and Canadian time zones are—from east to west—Atlantic, Eastern, Central, Mountain, Pacific, Alaska, and Hawaii-Aleutian. Canada also has the Newfoundland Time Zone, but it is not a true standard time zone because it is only a half-hour later than its neighboring zone to the west. For the boundaries of these zones, see **Time** (map).

In summer, residents of most states advance clocks one hour to use daylight saving time. An act of Congress, which took effect in 1967, declared that daylight saving time must be used throughout a state or not at all. However, a 1972 amendment to the act allows states that lie in more than one time zone to use daylight time in one zone without using it in the other. See **Daylight saving time.**

History. Before the adoption of standard time, each U.S. city kept the local time of its own meridian. With the growth of railroads, these differences caused difficulties. Railroads that met in the same city sometimes ran on different times. In 1883, the railroads of the United States and Canada adopted a system for standard time. In 1884, an international conference met in Washington, D.C., to consider a worldwide system of standard time. The meridian passing through the English town of Greenwich (now a borough of London) was chosen as the prime meridian.

In 1918, Congress gave the Interstate Commerce Commission authority to establish limits for time zones in the United States. Congress transferred this authority to the Department of Transportation in 1967.

Today, nearly all nations keep standard time. Only a few small countries and some other regions keep time that differs by a fraction of an hour from standard time.

Donald B. Sullivan

See also **Fleming, Sir Sandford; Time.**

Standish, Miles (1584?-1656), came to America with the Pilgrims on the ship *Mayflower.* He was not a Separatist, and never joined the Pilgrim Church. But he helped the Pilgrims in their plans and in training a militia. See **Pilgrims; Plymouth Colony.**

Standish was short and stout and had a quick temper.

An enemy once called him "Captaine Shrimpe." However, the colonists respected his courage and judgment. He learned American Indian languages and managed the colony's relations with the local Indians. He maintained the peace with his diplomatic skills.

In 1624, Standish became active in the colony as a political leader. For years, he served as the colony's treasurer and advised the governor as a member of the Council of Assistants. In 1625, Standish represented Plymouth in discussions with the English merchants who financed the colony, obtaining loans and important supplies. In 1627, along with other leaders, he assumed the colony's debts. In 1631, Standish helped found Duxbury, Massachusetts, and soon moved there. He lived in Duxbury for the rest of his life and died there on Oct. 3, 1656. His statue now overlooks the town.

Standish was probably born on the Isle of Man. He fought as a young man against the Spanish in the Netherlands. Henry W. Longfellow's account of him in *The Courtship of Miles Standish* is fictitious (see **Longfellow, Henry W.** [Narrative poems]).   Fred W. Anderson

Stanfield, Robert Lorne (1914-2003), was leader of Canada's Progressive Conservative Party from 1967 to 1976. He failed to lead his party to a parliamentary majority in the general elections of 1968, 1972, and 1974. He was premier of Nova Scotia from 1956 to 1967.

Stanfield was born on April 11, 1914, in Truro, Nova Scotia. He graduated from Dalhousie University and Harvard University. In 1948, he became leader of the Nova Scotia Progressive Conservative Party. Stanfield was elected to the Nova Scotia Legislature in 1949. His efforts in encouraging new industry in the province and his administrative skills helped him win reelection in 1953, 1956, 1960, and 1967. He won election to the national House of Commons after the Progressive Conservatives made him their leader. Stanfield succeeded former Canadian Prime Minister John G. Diefenbaker as party leader. Stanfield died on Dec. 16, 2003.   John English

Stanford, Leland (1824-1893), was a railroad builder, governor of California, and United States senator. In 1885, he founded Stanford University with a gift of land and securities. Stanford was born on March 9, 1824, in Watervliet, New York. He moved to California in 1852 and was governor of that state in 1862 and 1863. In 1861, he helped form the Central Pacific Railroad, part of the first transcontinental railway. He was president of the Central Pacific from 1861 until he died on June 21, 1893. Stanford and his partners acquired a near monopoly over California railroads, uniting them under the name *Southern Pacific* in 1884. Stanford was president of the Southern Pacific from 1884 to 1890. From 1885 until his death, he served as a Republican U.S. senator from California. See also **Stanford University.**   Robert W. Cherny

Stanford University is a leading educational and research center in the United States. It has an 8,800-acre (3,600-hectare) campus in Stanford, California, about 30 miles (48 kilometers) south of San Francisco. Stanford is a private, coeducational university. It offers undergraduate and graduate courses of study, and about 25 of its graduate programs rank among the top 10 nationally in their fields. Stanford is also recognized as one of the world's leading centers of research in electronics and physics. Stanford's Web site at http://www.stanford.edu presents information about the university.

Educational program. Stanford has schools of business, earth sciences, education, engineering, humanities and sciences, law, and medicine. These schools are divided into about 70 academic departments. The university also sponsors programs of study in Europe, Asia, and South America.

Undergraduates receive a general education in a wide range of subjects and a specialized education in their chosen field of study. Undergraduates may apply for A.B., B.S., and B.A.S. degrees. Graduate students may apply for A.M., M.S., M.F.A., and Ph.D. degrees and for professional degrees.

Research program. Stanford is a major center of research in the physical, biological, social, and technological sciences. The Stanford Linear Accelerator Center (SLAC) is a world center for the study of high-energy physics. Stanford's medical school is famous for its work on heart transplants, cancer, and *genetic engineering* (altering the genes of a living organism).

The university's Hoover Institution on War, Revolution, and Peace has one of the best collections of books and documents about political, social, and economic movements of the 1900's. This institution was founded in 1919 by Herbert Hoover, a member of Stanford's first graduating class in 1895. Hoover became the 31st president of the United States in 1929.

The Stanford campus is also the home of an industrial park that has about 90 firms. Frederick E. Terman, an electrical engineer who held administrative positions at Stanford University from 1937 to 1965, helped establish the research and manufacturing center in 1951. He supported close ties between the university and industry and persuaded many faculty members and students to form companies in the Stanford area. A number of these firms have manufactured important electronics devices invented by Stanford faculty members. This area, sometimes called Silicon Valley, ranks among the world's leading centers for technological development.

History. Stanford University was founded in 1885 by Leland Stanford and his wife, Jane Lathrop Stanford. Leland Stanford built the Central Pacific Railroad. He was a U.S. senator from California from 1885 until his death in 1893. The Stanfords created the university as a memorial to their son, Leland Stanford, Jr., who died of typhoid fever in 1884. The couple endowed the university with land for a campus and more than $20 million.

Stanford opened for classes in 1891. Its academic departments were organized into seven schools in 1948. Since the late 1950's, Stanford University has been ranked as one of the leading educational institutions in the United States.   Critically reviewed by Stanford University

Stanhope, Philip D. See Chesterfield, Earl of.

Stanislas, *STAN is lus,* **Saint** (1030-1079), is the patron saint of Poland and the city of Kraków, where he served as bishop. He was proclaimed a saint of the Roman Catholic Church in 1253 and is honored as a martyr. His name is also spelled Stanislaus.

Saint Stanislas was born at Szczepanowski, Poland. As a priest, he took charge of a parish near Kraków. He was named bishop of Kraków in 1072 by Pope Alexander II. His outspoken attacks against sin in both low and high places earned him the hatred of King Bolesław II of Poland. Bolesław ordered Stanislas killed. The king accompanied the guards who had been ordered to kill Stanislas. When the guards would not obey, the king killed the bishop himself on April 11, 1079. Saint Stanislas's feast day is celebrated on April 11.   Marvin R. O'Connell

Stanislavski, Konstantin (1863-1938), was the stage name of an influential Russian stage director. While most acting of the 1800's was artificial, Stanislavski taught his actors to seem more natural onstage by recalling their own feelings and behavior in similar situations. They would then transfer those feelings to their characters. The *Stanislavski method* is the basis of most modern acting styles. See **Method acting.**

Stanislavski was born on Jan. 17, 1863, in Moscow. His real family name was Alexeyev. In 1898, he established the Moscow Art Theater with fellow director Vladimir Nemirovich-Danchenko (see **Moscow Art Theater**). The success of the theater and Stanislavski's books on the Method, including *An Actor Prepares* (1926), revolutionized world acting. Stanislavski also wrote an autobiography, *My Life in Art* (1924). He died on Aug. 7, 1938.

Gerald Berkowitz

Stanley, F. A. See **Stanley of Preston, Baron.**

Stanley and Livingstone were two explorers whose travels in Africa excited the Western world and paved the way for Africa's European colonization. David Livingstone (1813-1873) had captured the public's imagination through his writings about his African explorations. But when he disappeared in the late 1860's, rumors about his death began to circulate. In 1869, the *New York Herald* sent Henry Morton Stanley (1841-1904) to find him. In early November 1871, Stanley found Livingstone at the town of Ujiji, on Lake Tanganyika in east-central Africa. Stanley greeted him with the now-famous words: "Dr. Livingstone, I presume?"

Livingstone's discoveries. David Livingstone was born on March 19, 1813, in Blantyre, Scotland, near Glasgow. He received a medical degree from the Uni-

versity of Glasgow. He later joined the London Missionary Society, which sent him to southern Africa in 1841. There he worked to convert Africans to Christianity and to end the business of selling Africans as slaves.

In 1849, Livingstone began to travel into Africa's interior, mapping the land and searching for navigable rivers that British missionaries and traders could use. That year, he arrived at Lake Ngami, in what is now Botswana. In 1851, he traveled to the Zambezi River, on the border between present-day Zambia and Zimbabwe. Livingstone is famous for being the first European to cross Africa. But his trip, taken between 1853 and 1856, was financed and equipped by King Sekeletu of the Lozi Kingdom. On this trip, Livingstone started at the Zambezi and went northwest across Angola to Luanda on the Atlantic Ocean. On the return journey, he followed the Zambezi to its mouth in what is now Mozambique, where Portuguese officials treated him as a representative of Sekeletu. In 1855, he became the first European to sight what are now known as Victoria Falls on the Zambezi. He named the falls for Queen Victoria.

From 1858 to 1864, Livingstone led a large expedition, funded by the British government, across Africa's interior. He became the first European to see Lakes Nyasa and Chilwa, in what is now Malawi. In 1866, Livingstone began to explore the Lake Tanganyika region. Livingstone believed that commerce and Christianity went hand in hand and enthusiastically depicted central Africa as a highly fertile region suitable for the production of sugar and cotton. His discoveries thus helped spark a great competition among European nations for control of Africa. He died on May 1, 1873, in what is now Zambia. His body was brought to London and buried in Westminster Abbey on April 18, 1874.

Stanley's explorations. Henry Morton Stanley was born on Jan. 28, 1841, in Denbigh, Wales, and was bap-

Exploration of Africa by Stanley and Livingstone

David Livingstone explored central Africa to find the source of the Nile River. He was believed lost until Henry M. Stanley found him at Lake Tanganyika in 1871. In 1874, Stanley set out to trace the course of the Congo River. He began in what is now Congo (Kinshasa) and reached the mouth of the river at the Atlantic Ocean in 1877.

------ Livingstone's first
expedition: 1849-1856

—·—·— Livingstone's second
expedition: 1858-1864

———— Livingstone's third
expedition: 1866-1873

·------ Stanley's expedition to
find Livingstone: 1871

———— Stanley's Congo River
expedition: 1874-1877

WORLD BOOK map

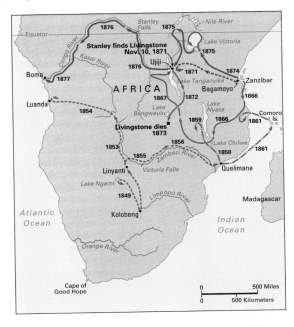

Brown Bros.
Sir Henry M. Stanley

Brown Bros.
David Livingstone

tized John Rowlands. He spent most of his youth in a workhouse for orphans. At the age of 17, he sailed as a cabin boy on a ship to New Orleans. There, Henry Hope Stanley, a cotton dealer, adopted him. Stanley joined the Confederate Army during the American Civil War (1861-1865) and was soon captured. Stanley joined the Union Army to get out of prison but was discharged because of poor health. He joined the Union Navy in 1864.

In 1865, Stanley deserted and became a newspaper reporter. During the late 1860's, he covered Indian wars in the American West and a British military campaign in Ethiopia. But his best-known assignment was to find Livingstone. He wrote about his journey in *How I Found Livingstone* (1872), a best-selling book.

After their meeting, Stanley became interested in Livingstone's hope of finding a source of the Nile River south of the known source in Lake Victoria. Stanley postponed his plans to rush home with news of the great explorer and stayed with him until March 1872.

After Livingstone's death, Stanley became a professional explorer. Although Stanley emphasized his friendship with Livingstone, he was more ruthless in dealing with the African communities he encountered on his journeys. In 1874, he led an expedition of about 350 people into Africa's interior. The group explored Lake Victoria and other lakes, and followed the Congo River west to its mouth at the Atlantic Ocean. By 1877, over two-thirds of the group had died or deserted, and he left for England. Stanley's bold exploration and reputation for ruthlessness earned him the nickname *Bula Matari* (smasher of rocks) from the Africans he exploited.

From 1879 to 1884, Stanley, who had been hired by King Leopold II of Belgium, helped the king claim the Congo Free State, now Congo (Kinshasa). In 1887, Leopold, with financing from English traders and the Royal Geographical Society, sent Stanley to the Sudanese province of Equatoria, prized for its trade routes and ivory stockpiles. Leopold and William Mackinnon, a Scottish businessman, portrayed Stanley's journey as a mission to rescue Equatoria's governor, Emin Pasha. But they secretly hoped to claim Equatoria. The accounts of Stanley's travels made him famous, and he served in the British Parliament from 1895 to 1900. He was knighted in 1899 and died on May 10, 1904.   Timothy H. Parsons

See also **Exploration** (picture); **Lake Edward.**

Stanley brothers were two American inventors and manufacturers who built the Stanley steamer, one of the most famous steam-powered automobiles. The brothers were identical twins.

Francis Edgar Stanley (1849-1918) and Freelan Oscar Stanley (1849-1940) were born in Kingfield, Maine, on June 1, 1849. In 1884, they formed the Stanley Dry Plate Company to manufacture a formula that Francis had developed for use in dry-plate photography. They patented a dry-plate coating machine in 1886. In 1903, they sold their firm to the Eastman Kodak Company.

Meanwhile, the Stanleys were also experimenting with steam engines, and in 1897 they built the first Stanley steamer. They organized a company to produce and market the cars. In 1899, they sold the company and their manufacturing rights. In 1901, the Stanleys bought back their manufacturing rights and formed the Stanley Motor Carriage Company. They then became active in automobile racing. In 1906, one of their cars traveled 128

miles (206 kilometers) per hour, becoming the first car to exceed the speed of 2 miles (3.2 kilometers) per minute.

Sales of steam cars declined as gasoline-powered automobiles, which were easier to start and operate, became increasingly popular. In 1917, the brothers retired and the Stanley Motor Carriage Company was reorganized under new management. The next year, Francis was killed in an automobile accident on July 31, 1918. The Stanley brothers' company went bankrupt in 1924. Freelan died on Oct. 2, 1940.   William L. Bailey

See also **Automobile** (picture).

Stanley Cup is a trophy awarded annually to the team that wins the National Hockey League (NHL) championship. It is the oldest trophy in professional sports competition in North America. In 1893, Baron Stanley of Preston, the governor general of Canada, donated a silver bowl to be awarded annually to the amateur hockey champions of Canada. Professional teams in the National Hockey Association (reorganized into the NHL in 1917) began competing for it in 1910. The Stanley Cup has been under the control of the NHL since 1946. The cup consists of a replica of Baron Stanley's original bowl mounted on a large trophy. It weighs 32 pounds (14.5 kilograms) and stands 35 ¼ inches (89.5 centimeters) high. The original bowl and the Stanley Cup are displayed at the Hockey Hall of Fame in Toronto, Canada, except during the Stanley Cup finals, when the cup is awarded to the winning team. The names of the winning teams and their players are engraved on the cup.   Larry Wigge

Focus on Sports

The Stanley Cup is awarded to the annual champion of the National Hockey League.

See also **Hockey** (table: Stanley Cup finals).

Stanley of Preston, Baron (1841-1908), served as governor general of Canada from 1888 to 1893. Stanley, whose given name was Frederick Arthur Stanley, was an enthusiastic sportsman. In 1893, he donated an ice-hockey trophy called the Stanley Cup (see **Stanley Cup**). Today, the trophy goes to the annual champion of the National Hockey League. Stanley was born on Jan. 15, 1841, in London. He was elected to the British Parliament in 1865 and served in the Cabinet from 1878 to 1880 and in 1885 and 1886. He became Baron of Preston in 1886. After serving as governor general of Canada, Stanley returned to England and succeeded his brother as the Earl of Derby. He was elected lord mayor of Liverpool in 1895. He became the first chancellor of Liverpool University in 1903. He died on June 14, 1908.   Jacques Monet

Stanley steamer. See Automobile (The steam car [picture]); **Stanley brothers.**

Stannous fluoride. See Tin (Uses); **Toothpaste and toothpowder.**

Stanton, Edwin McMasters (1814-1869), an American statesman, served as secretary of war in the Cabinet of President Abraham Lincoln. He later played a major part in the impeachment of President Andrew Johnson.

Stanton was born on Dec. 19, 1814, in Steubenville, Ohio, and was educated at Kenyon College. He studied law and was admitted to the bar in 1836. In 1856, he settled in Washington, D.C., and argued many cases before the Supreme Court. President James Buchanan appointed him attorney general in 1860, and President Lincoln made him secretary of war two years later. Stanton was outspoken, and he made many enemies. As secretary of war, he sometimes quarreled with Lincoln. But despite his many conflicts, Stanton was recognized as an efficient manager of the Department of War.

After Andrew Johnson became president, he and Stanton clashed repeatedly over the treatment of the South. Stanton cooperated with Johnson's enemies in Congress, and after Johnson removed Stanton from the office of secretary of war, the House of Representatives impeached the president. Johnson was acquitted by one vote, and Stanton finally left office in May 1868 (see **Johnson, Andrew** [Increased tension]). Stanton died on Dec. 24, 1869, four days after being appointed to the Supreme Court by President Ulysses S. Grant.

Gabor S. Boritt

Stanton, Elizabeth Cady (1815-1902), was an early leader of the women's rights movement. She and Lucretia Mott, another reformer, organized the first women's rights convention in the United States.

Stanton was born on Nov. 12, 1815, in Johnstown, New York, and graduated from the Troy Female Seminary (now the Emma Willard School). In the 1830's, she became interested in women's rights and in abolition. She and Henry B. Stanton, an abolitionist leader, married in 1840. That same year, they went to London for the World Anti-Slavery Convention. But the delegates voted to exclude women. Elizabeth Stanton discussed the situation with Mott, who also had planned to attend.

Tamiment Institute Library, New York University

Elizabeth Cady Stanton

In 1848, Stanton and Mott called the nation's first women's rights convention. It was held in Seneca Falls, New York, where the Stantons lived. Stanton wrote a Declaration of Sentiments, using the Declaration of Independence as her model. For example, the Declaration of Independence states that "all men are created equal." But Stanton wrote that "all men and women are created equal." She also called for woman suffrage.

During the 1850's and the early 1860's, Stanton worked for women's rights and for abolition. After slavery was abolished in 1865, she broke with abolitionists who favored voting rights for black men but not for any women. In 1869, Stanton and the women's rights leader Susan B. Anthony founded the National Woman Suffrage Association. Stanton was its president until 1890.

In 1878, Stanton persuaded Senator Aaron A. Sargent of California to sponsor a woman suffrage amendment

to the Constitution of the United States. This amendment was reintroduced every year until 1919, when Congress finally approved it. In 1920, it became the 19th Amendment. Stanton died on Oct. 26, 1902.   June Sochen

See also **Mott, Lucretia Coffin.**

Additional resources

Bohannon, Lisa F. *Women's Rights and Nothing Less: The Story of Elizabeth Cady Stanton.* Morgan Reynolds, 2001. Younger readers.
Loos, Pamela. *Elizabeth Cady Stanton.* Chelsea Hse., 2001. Younger readers.
Sigerman, Harriet. *Elizabeth Cady Stanton.* Oxford, 2001.

Staphylococcus, *STAF uh luh KAHK uhs,* is a common organism that belongs to a group of round bacteria. These bacteria are called *cocci* (pronounced *KAHK sy).* Under a microscope, staphylococci are seen in bunches, growing like clusters of grapes.

There are many kinds of staphylococci. They usually can be distinguished by their surface structure or by where they grow. Staphylococci live everywhere in the environment—in the air, in water, on land, and even on the bodies of human beings and animals. Many types are harmless, but some can cause disease. For example, pimples, boils, and

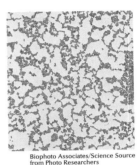

Biophoto Associates/Science Source from Photo Researchers

Staphylococci look like bunches of grapes when seen through a microscope.

a skin infection called *impetigo* are caused by staphylococci that enter the body through a break in the skin. Other staphylococci that penetrate deeper into the body can cause pneumonia or blood poisoning. Such diseases are often treated with antibiotics, but some staphylococci have become resistant to certain drugs.

David Schlessinger

See also **Bacteria; Boil; Carbuncle; Impetigo; Toxic shock syndrome.**

Stapledon, Olaf (1886-1950), was a major British author of science fiction. He wrote imaginary chronicles of the future that he called essays in myth creation. These ambitious stories extend over vast reaches of time and space and often deal with entire civilizations.

Stapledon is best known for the novels *Last and First Men* (1930) and *Star Maker* (1937). *Last and First Men* traces a 2-billion-year progression of humanity to its extinction on Neptune. *Star Maker* records the development of the universe and of all intelligent life. The scope and themes of these novels influenced later science-fiction writers, such as Brian Aldiss and Arthur C. Clarke. Other novels by Stapledon focus on particular characters and situations. In *Odd John* (1935), a man finds himself among the first of a new, superintelligent human species. *Sirius* (1944) concerns the relationship between a girl and a dog with near-human intelligence.

William Olaf Stapledon was born on May 10, 1886, near Liverpool. He wrote several nonfiction books that discuss the ideas in his fiction, including *A Modern Theory of Ethics* (1929) and *Philosophy and Living* (1939). He died on Sept. 6, 1950.   Neil Barron

Star

Star is a huge, shining ball in space that produces a tremendous amount of light and other forms of energy. The sun is a star, and it supplies Earth with light and heat energy. The stars look like twinkling points of light—except for the sun. The sun looks like a ball because it is much closer to Earth than any other star.

The sun and most other stars are made of gas and a hot, gaslike substance known as *plasma*. But some stars, called *white dwarfs* and *neutron stars,* consist of tightly packed atoms or subatomic particles. These stars are much more dense than any substance on Earth.

Stars come in many sizes. The sun's *radius* (distance from its center to its surface) is about 432,000 miles (695,500 kilometers). But astronomers classify the sun as a *dwarf* because other kinds of stars are much bigger. Some of the stars known as *supergiants* have a radius about 1,000 times that of the sun. The smallest stars are the neutron stars, some of which have a radius of only about 6 miles (10 kilometers).

Astronomers think that from about 50 to 75 percent of all stars are members of a *binary system,* a pair of closely spaced stars that orbit each other. The sun is not a member of a binary system. However, its nearest known stellar neighbor, Proxima Centauri, is part of a multiple-star system that also includes Alpha Centauri A and Alpha Centauri B.

The distance from the sun to Proxima Centauri is more than 25 trillion miles (40 trillion kilometers). This distance is so great that light takes 4.2 years to travel between the two stars. Scientists say that Proxima Centauri is 4.2 *light-years* from the sun. One light-year, the distance that light travels in a vacuum in a year, equals about 5.88 trillion miles (9.46 trillion kilometers).

Stars are grouped in huge structures called *galaxies*. Telescopes have revealed galaxies at distances of almost 13 billion light-years. The sun is in a galaxy called the Milky Way that contains hundreds of billions of stars. There are trillions of galaxies in the universe. Each galaxy consists of from hundreds of thousands to trillions of stars. Thus, billions of trillions of stars may exist. But if you look at the night sky far from city lights, you can see only about 3,000 of them without using binoculars or a telescope.

Stars, like people, have life cycles—they are born, they pass through several phases, and eventually they die. The sun was born about 4.6 billion years ago and will remain much as it is for another 5 billion years. Then it will grow to become a *red giant*. Late in the sun's lifetime, it will cast off its outer layers. The remaining core, called a *white dwarf,* will slowly fade, entering its final phase as a *black dwarf*.

Other stars will end their lives in different ways. Some will not go through a red giant stage. Instead, they will merely cool to become white dwarfs, then black dwarfs. A small percentage of stars will die in spectacular explosions called *supernovae*.

The contributor of this article is Paul J. Green, an astrophysicist at Smithsonian Astrophysical Observatory.

Stars at a glance

Number: Perhaps more than 10 billion trillion in the known universe.

Age: Up to about 13 billion years. Most stars are from 1 million to 10 billion years old.

Composition: As determined by mass, at least 71 percent hydrogen and roughly 27 percent helium. Oxygen and carbon account for most of the remaining mass.

Mass: From about $\frac{1}{10}$ of the mass of the sun to more than 100 times the mass of the sun.

Largest known stars: Supergiant stars that have a radius of roughly 650 million miles (1 billion kilometers)—about 1,500 times the radius of the sun.

Smallest known stars: Neutron stars that have a radius of approximately 6 miles (10 kilometers).

Colors: Ranging from reddish for the coolest stars to yellowish for warmer stars, to bluish for the hottest stars.

Temperature: *Surface,* from about 2500 K (2200 °C or 4000 °F) for dark red stars to about 50,000 K (50,000 °C or 90,000 °F) for the hottest blue stars; *core,* about 10 million K (10 million °C or 18 million °F) in stars in which hydrogen is fusing to form helium to nearly 10 billion K (10 billion °C or 18 billion °F) in collapsing stars that are about to produce supernova explosions.

Energy source: Nuclear fusion that changes hydrogen into helium or similar fusion processes that produce heavier and heavier chemical elements up to iron.

The stars at night

If you look at the stars on a clear night, you will notice that they seem to twinkle and that they differ greatly in brightness. A much slower movement also takes place in the night sky: If you map the location of several stars for a few hours, you will observe that all the stars revolve slowly about a single point in the sky.

Twinkling of stars is caused by movements in Earth's atmosphere. Starlight enters the atmosphere as straight rays. Twinkling occurs because air movements constantly change the path of the light as it comes through the air. You can see a similar effect if you stand in a swimming pool and look down. Unless the water is almost perfectly still, your feet will appear to move and change their shape. This "twinkling" occurs because the moving water constantly changes the path of the light rays that travel from your feet to your eyes.

Brightness of stars. How bright a star looks when viewed from Earth depends on two factors: (1) the actual brightness of the star—that is, the amount of light energy the star *emits* (sends out)—and (2) the distance from Earth to the star. A nearby star that is actually dim can appear brighter than a distant star that is really extremely brilliant. For example, Alpha Centauri A seems to be slightly brighter than a star known as Rigel. But Alpha Centauri A emits only $\frac{1}{100,000}$ as much light energy as Rigel. Alpha Centauri A seems brighter because it is

Hubble Heritage Team (STScl/Aura.NASA)

A huge gas cloud surrounds a star that created it—the fainter of the two stars near its center. The faint star was originally the core of a large, bright star, and what is now the cloud made up that star's outer layers. But the core became so hot that it blew away those layers. Such clouds are called *planetary nebulae* because many seem round, like planets, through a small telescope. This cloud is known as NGC 3132 or the Southern Ring Nebula.

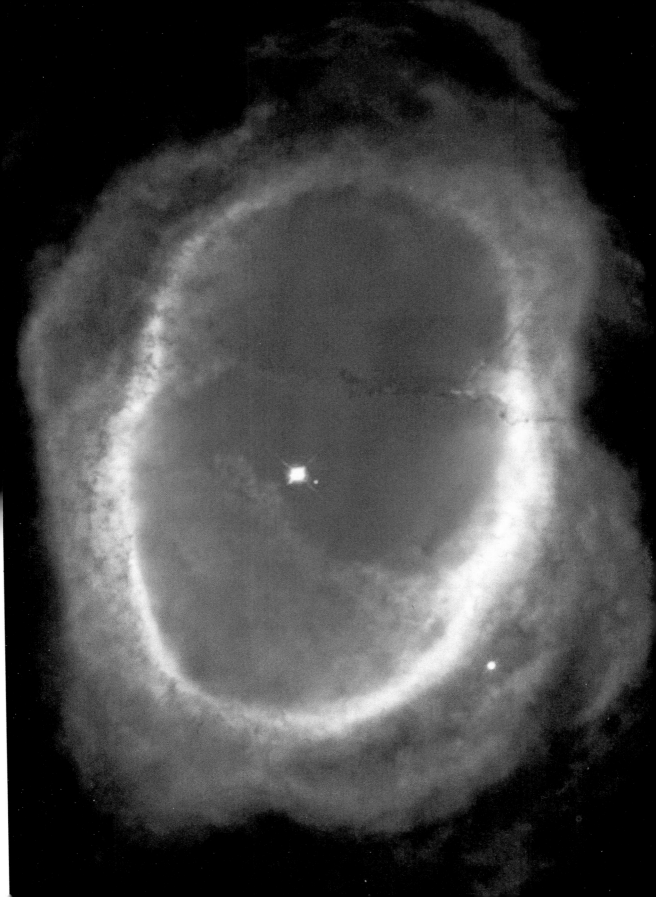

The constellation Orion (the Hunter) contains one of the brightest stars in the sky—Rigel, shown at the figure's right ankle. At Orion's left shoulder is Betelgeuse, one of the largest stars.

© Space.Com

only about ⅟₂₀₀ as far from Earth as Rigel is—4.4 light-years for Alpha Centauri A, compared with 700 to 900 light-years for Rigel.

Rising and setting of stars. When viewed from Earth's Northern Hemisphere, stars rotate counterclockwise around a point called the *celestial north pole.* Viewed from the Southern Hemisphere, stars rotate clockwise about the *celestial south pole.* During the day, the sun moves across the sky in the same direction, and at the same rate, as the stars. These movements do not result from any actual revolution of the sun and stars. Rather, they occur because of the west-to-east rotation of Earth about its own axis. To an observer standing on the ground, Earth seems motionless, while the sun and stars seem to move in circles. But actually, Earth moves.

Names of stars

Ancient people saw that certain stars are arranged in patterns shaped somewhat like human beings, animals, or common objects. Some of these patterns, called *constellations,* came to represent figures of mythological characters. For example, the constellation Orion (the Hunter) is named after a hero in Greek mythology.

Today, astronomers use constellations, some of which were described by the ancients, in the scientific names of stars. The International Astronomical Union

(IAU), the world authority for assigning names to celestial objects, officially recognizes 88 constellations. These constellations cover the entire sky. In most cases, the brightest star in a given constellation has *alpha*—the first letter of the Greek alphabet—as part of its scientific name. For instance, the scientific name for Vega, the brightest star in the constellation Lyra (the Harp), is *Alpha Lyrae. Lyrae* is Latin for *of Lyra.*

The second brightest star in a constellation is usually designated *beta,* the second letter of the Greek alphabet, the third brightest is *gamma,* and so on. The assignment of Greek letters to stars continues until all the Greek letters are used. Numerical designations follow.

But the number of known stars has become so large that the IAU uses a different system for newly discovered stars. Most new names consist of an abbreviation followed by a group of symbols. The abbreviation stands for either the type of star or a catalog that lists information about the star. For example, PSR J1302-6350 is a type of star known as a *pulsar*—hence the *PSR* in its name. The symbols indicate the star's location in the sky. The *1302* and the *6350* are coordinates that are similar to the longitude and latitude designations used to indicate locations on Earth's surface. The *J* indicates that a coordinate system known as J2000 is being used.

Characteristics of stars

A star has five main characteristics: (1) brightness, which astronomers describe in terms of *magnitude* or *luminosity;* (2) color; (3) surface temperature; (4) size; and (5) *mass* (amount of matter). These characteristics are related to one another in a complex way. Color depends on surface temperature, and brightness depends on surface temperature and size. Mass affects the rate at which a star of a given size produces energy and so affects surface temperature. To make these relationships easier to understand, astronomers developed a graph called the *Hertzsprung-Russell* (H-R) *diagram.* This graph, a version of which appears in this article, also helps astronomers understand and describe the life cycles of stars.

Magnitude and luminosity. Magnitude is based on a numbering system invented by the Greek astronomer Hipparchus in about 125 B.C. Hipparchus numbered groups of stars according to their brightness as viewed from Earth. He called the brightest stars *first magnitude* stars, the next brightest *second magnitude* stars, and so on to *sixth magnitude* stars, the faintest visible stars.

Modern astronomers refer to a star's brightness as viewed from Earth as its *apparent magnitude.* But they have extended Hipparchus's system to describe the ac-

The 10 brightest stars as seen from Earth

Common name	Scientific name	Distance (Light-years)	Apparent magnitude	Absolute magnitude	Spectral type
1. Sun		0.00001	−26.72	4.8	G2V
2. Sirius*	Alpha Canis Majoris	8.6	−1.46	1.4	A1V + WD†
3. Canopus	Alpha Carinae	313	−0.72	−2.5	F0Ib
4. Rigel Kentaurus*	Alpha Centauri	4.4	−0.27	4.4	G2V + K1V
5. Arcturus	Alpha Boötis	37	−0.04	0.2	K2III
6. Vega	Alpha Lyrae	25	0.03	0.6	A0V
7. Capella*	Alpha Aurigae	42	0.08	0.4	G6III + G2III
8. Rigel‡	Beta Orionis	700-900§	0.12	−8.1	B8Ia
9. Procyon*	Alpha Canis Minoris	11.5	0.38	2.6	F5IV + WD†
10. Achernar	Alpha Eridani	144	0.46	−1.3	B3V

*Binary star system.   † White dwarf.   ‡ Triple star system.   § Estimate.

tual brightness of stars, for which they use the term *absolute magnitude*. For technical reasons, they define a star's absolute magnitude as what its apparent magnitude would be if it were 32.6 light-years from Earth.

Astronomers have also extended the system of magnitude numbers to include stars brighter than first magnitude and dimmer than sixth magnitude. A star that is brighter than first magnitude has a magnitude less than 1. For example, the apparent magnitude of Rigel is 0.12. Extremely bright stars have magnitudes less than zero— that is, their designations are negative numbers. The brightest star in the night sky is Sirius, with an apparent magnitude of -1.46. Rigel has an absolute magnitude of -8.1. According to astronomers' present understanding of stars, no star can have an absolute magnitude much brighter than -8. At the other end of the scale, the dimmest stars detected with telescopes have apparent magnitudes up to 28. In theory, no star could have an absolute magnitude much fainter than 16.

Luminosity is the rate at which a star emits energy. The scientific term for a rate of energy emission is *power*, and scientists usually measure power in *watts*. For example, the sun's luminosity is 400 trillion trillion watts. But astronomers seldom measure luminosities in watts. Instead, they describe stars in terms of the luminosity of the sun. They say, for instance, that the luminosity of Alpha Centauri A is about 1.3 times that of the sun and that Rigel is about 40,000 times as luminous as the sun.

Luminosity is related to absolute magnitude in a simple way. A difference of 5 on the absolute magnitude scale corresponds to a factor of 100 on the luminosity scale. Thus, a star with an absolute magnitude of 2 is 100 times as luminous as a star with an absolute magnitude of 7. A star with an absolute magnitude of -3 is 100 times as luminous as a star whose absolute magnitude is 2 and 10,000 times as luminous as a star that has an absolute magnitude of 7.

Color and temperature. If you look carefully at the stars, even without binoculars or a telescope, you will see a range of colors from reddish to yellowish to bluish. For example, Betelgeuse looks reddish, Pollux—like the sun—is yellowish, and Rigel looks bluish.

A star's color depends on its surface temperature. Astronomers measure star temperatures in a metric unit known as the *kelvin*. One kelvin equals exactly 1 Celsius degree (1.8 Fahrenheit degree), but the Kelvin and Celsius scales start at different points. The Kelvin scale

Star terms

Absolute magnitude is a measure of a star's actual brightness. Absolute magnitude is what a star's apparent magnitude would be if the star were 32.6 light-years from Earth.

Apparent magnitude is a measure of a star's brightness as viewed from Earth.

Binary system is a pair of closely spaced stars that orbit each other.

Hertzsprung-Russell (H-R) diagram is a graph that displays the main characteristics of stars.

Kelvin, abbreviated K, is the unit in which astronomers measure the temperatures of stars. One kelvin equals 1 Celsius degree (1.8 Fahrenheit degree). A temperature of 0 K equals -273.15 °C (-459.67 °F).

Light-year is the distance that light travels in a vacuum in a year, about 5.88 trillion miles (9.46 trillion kilometers).

Luminosity is the rate at which a star sends light and related forms of energy into space. Thus, luminosity is also a measure of a star's brightness.

Main-sequence star is one that gets all its energy from the fusion of hydrogen nuclei in its core. The sun is a main-sequence star.

Mass is the total amount of matter in an object.

Neutron is a subatomic particle that ordinarily appears only in atomic nuclei. A neutron carries no net electric charge.

Neutron star is a star consisting mostly of neutrons.

Nuclear fusion is a joining of two atomic nuclei to produce a larger nucleus. A star's tremendous energy comes from nuclear fusion in and near its core.

Nucleus is the core of an atom. A nucleus consists of one or more protons and may also have one or more neutrons. The plural of nucleus is *nuclei.*

Proton is a positively charged subatomic particle. All atomic nuclei have at least one proton.

Protostar is a huge, ball-shaped object that has not yet evolved into a star.

Triple-alpha process is the fusion of three nuclei of helium to produce a nucleus of carbon.

Variable star is a star that varies in brightness.

starts at -273.15 °C. Therefore, a temperature of 0 K equals -273.15 °C, or -459.67 °F. A temperature of 0 °C (32 °F) equals 273.15 K.

Dark red stars have surface temperatures of about 2500 K. The surface temperature of a bright red star is approximately 3500 K; that of the sun and other yellow stars, roughly 5500 K. Blue stars range from about 10,000 to 50,000 K in surface temperature.

The 10 known stars nearest Earth

Name	Distance (Light-years)	Apparent magnitude	Absolute magnitude	Spectral type
1. Sun	0.00001	-26.72	4.85	G2V
2. Proxima Centauri	4.2	11.09	15.53	M5V
3. Alpha Centauri A*	4.4	0.01	4.36	G2V
Alpha Centauri B	4.4	1.34	5.69	K0V
4. Barnard's Star	5.9	9.53	13.21	M4V
5. Wolf 359	7.8	13.44	16.55	M6V
6. Lalande 21185	8.1	7.47	10.44	M2V
7. Sirius A*	8.6	-1.43	1.46	A1V
Sirius B	8.6	8.44	11.33	WD†
8. Luyten 726-8 A (UV Ceti)*	8.9	12.43	15.29	M5V
Luyten 726-8 B (BL Ceti)	8.9	13.19	16.05	M6V
9. Ross 154	9.5	10.43	13.06	M3V
10. Ross 248	10.3	12.29	14.79	M5V

*Brighter component of a binary star system.   † White dwarf.

Although a star appears to the unaided eye to have a single color, it actually emits a broad *spectrum* (band) of colors. You can see that starlight consists of many colors by using a prism to separate and spread the colors of the light of the sun, a yellow star. The visible spectrum includes all the colors of the rainbow. These colors range from red, produced by the *photons* (particles of light) with the least energy; to violet, produced by the most energetic photons.

Visible light is one of six bands of *electromagnetic radiation.* Ranging from the least energetic to the most energetic, they are: radio waves, infrared rays, visible light, ultraviolet rays, X rays, and gamma rays. All six bands are emitted by stars, but most individual stars do not emit all of them. The combined range of all six bands is known as the *electromagnetic spectrum.*

Astronomers study a star's spectrum by separating it, spreading it out, and displaying it. The display itself is

also known as a spectrum. The scientists study thin gaps in the spectrum. When the spectrum is spread out from left to right, the gaps appear as vertical lines. The spectra of stars have dark *absorption lines* where radiation of specific energies is weak. In a few special cases in the visible spectrum, stars have bright *emission lines* where radiation of specific energies is especially strong.

An absorption line appears when a chemical element or compound absorbs radiation that has the amount of energy corresponding to the line. For example, the spectrum of the visible light coming from the sun has a group of absorption lines in the green part of the spectrum. Calcium in an outer layer of the sun absorbs light rays that would have produced the corresponding green colors.

Although all stars have absorption lines in the visible band of the electromagnetic spectrum, emission lines are more common in other parts of the spectrum. For in-

The Hertzsprung-Russell diagram

Astronomers use this diagram to classify stars. A star is represented by a dot located according to (1) its surface temperature and (2) its brightness as measured by its *luminosity* or its *absolute magnitude.* Luminosity is a star's energy output relative to that of the sun. The absolute magnitude scale provides a set of numbers that are mathematically related to luminosity and more convenient to use. The diagram also shows how a star's spectral class and color depend on surface temperature.

WORLD BOOK diagram

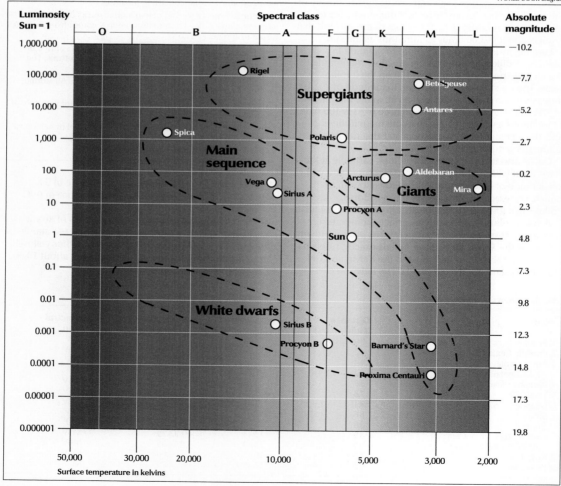

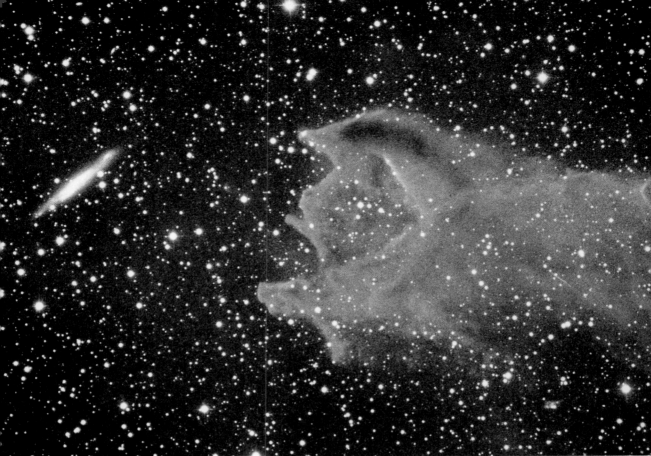

A star-forming cloud called a *cometary globule* consists of gas and dust. This globule, known as CG 4, has enough material to produce several stars the size of the sun. CG 4, like the sun, is in the Milky Way Galaxy. The disk to the left of the globule is a galaxy far beyond the Milky Way.

stance, nitrogen in the sun's atmosphere emits powerful radiation that produces emission lines in the ultraviolet part of the spectrum.

Size. Astronomers measure the size of stars in terms of the sun's radius. Alpha Centauri A, with a radius of 1.05 solar *radii* (the plural of *radius*), is almost exactly the size of the sun. Rigel is much larger at 78 solar radii, and Antares has a huge size of roughly 700 solar radii.

A star's size and surface temperature determine its luminosity. Suppose two stars had the same temperature, but the first star had twice the radius of the second star. In this case, the first star would be four times as bright as the second star. Scientists say that luminosity is proportional to radius *squared*—that is, multiplied by itself. Imagine that you wanted to compare the luminosities of two stars that had the same temperature but different radii. First, you would divide the radius of the larger star by the radius of the smaller star. Then, you would square your answer.

Now, suppose two stars had the same radius but the first star's surface temperature—measured in kelvins—was twice that of the second star. In this example, the luminosity of the first star would be 16 times that of the second star. Luminosity is proportional to temperature *to the fourth power*. Imagine that you wanted to compare the luminosities of stars that had the same radius but different temperatures. First, you would divide the

temperature of the warmer star by the temperature of the cooler star. Next, you would square the result. Then, you would square your answer again.

Mass. Astronomers express the mass of a star in terms of the *solar mass*, the mass of the sun. For example, they give the mass of Alpha Centauri A as 1.08 solar masses; that of Rigel, as about 17 solar masses. The mass of the sun is 2×10^{30} kilograms, which would be written out as 2 followed by 30 zeros.

Stars that have similar masses may not be similar in size—that is, they may have different *densities*. Density is the amount of mass per unit of volume. For instance, the average density of the sun is 88 pounds per cubic foot (1,400 kilograms per cubic meter), about 140 percent that of water. Sirius B has almost exactly the same mass as the sun, but it is 90,000 times as dense. As a result, its radius is only about $\frac{1}{50}$ of a solar radius.

The Hertzsprung-Russell diagram displays the main characteristics of stars. The diagram is named for astronomers Ejnar Hertzsprung of Denmark and Henry Norris Russell of the United States. Working independently of each other, the two scientists developed the diagram around 1910.

Luminosity classes. Points representing the brightest stars appear toward the top of the H-R diagram; points corresponding to the dimmest stars, toward the bottom. These points appear in groups that correspond to different kinds of stars. In the 1930's, American astronomers William W. Morgan and Philip C. Keenan invented what came to be known as the *MK luminosity classification system* for these groups. Astronomers revised and extended this system in 1978. In the MK system, the largest and brightest classes have the lowest classification numbers. The MK classes are: Ia, bright supergiant; Ib, supergiant; II, bright giant; III, giant; IV, subgiant; and V, main sequence or dwarf.

Because temperature also affects the luminosity of a star, stars from different luminosity classes can overlap. For example, Spica, a class V star, has an absolute magnitude of −3.2; but Pollux, a class III star, is dimmer, with an absolute magnitude of 0.7.

Spectral classes. Points representing the stars with the highest surface temperatures appear toward the left edge of the H-R diagram; points representing the coolest stars, toward the right edge. In the MK system, there are eight *spectral classes,* each corresponding to a certain range of surface temperature. From the hottest stars to the coolest, these classes are: O, B, A, F, G, K, M, and L. Each spectral class, in turn, is made up of 10 *spectral types,* which are designated by the letter for the spectral class and a numeral. The hottest stars in a spectral class are assigned the numeral 0; the coolest stars, the numeral 9.

A complete MK designation thus includes symbols for luminosity class and spectral type. For example, the complete designation for the sun is G2V. Alpha Centauri A is also a G2V star, and Rigel's designation is B8Ia.

Fusion in stars

A star's tremendous energy comes from a process known as *nuclear fusion.* This process begins when the temperature of the core of the developing star reaches about 1 million K.

A star develops from a giant, slowly rotating cloud that consists almost entirely of the chemical elements hydrogen and helium. The cloud also contains atoms of other elements as well as microscopic particles of dust.

Due to the force of its own gravity, the cloud begins to collapse inward, thereby becoming smaller. As the cloud shrinks, it rotates more and more rapidly, just as spinning ice skaters turn more rapidly when they pull in their arms. The outermost parts of the cloud form a spinning disk. The inner parts become a roughly spherical clump, which continues to collapse.

The collapsing material becomes warmer, and its pressure increases. But the pressure tends to counteract the gravitational force that is responsible for the collapse. Eventually, therefore, the collapse slows to a gradual contraction. The inner parts of the clump form a *protostar,* a ball-shaped object that is no longer a cloud, but is not yet a star. Surrounding the protostar is an irregular sphere of gas and dust that had been the outer parts of the clump.

Combining nuclei. When the temperature and pressure in the protostar's core become high enough, nuclear fusion begins. Nuclear fusion is a joining of two atomic nuclei to produce a larger nucleus.

Nuclei that fuse are actually the cores of atoms. A complete atom has an outer shell of one or more particles called *electrons,* which carry a negative electric charge. Deep inside the atom is the nucleus, which contains almost all the atom's mass. The simplest nucleus, that of the most common form of hydrogen, consists of a single particle known as a *proton.* A proton carries a positive electric charge. All other nuclei have one or more protons and one or more *neutrons.* A neutron carries no net charge, and so a nucleus is electrically positive. But a complete atom has as many electrons as protons. The net electric charge of a complete atom is therefore zero—the atom is electrically neutral.

However, under the enormous temperatures and pressures near the core of a protostar, atoms lose electrons. The resulting atoms are known as *ions,* and the mixture of the free electrons and ions is called a plasma.

Atoms in the core of the protostar lose all their electrons, and the resulting bare nuclei approach one another at tremendous speeds. Under ordinary circumstances, objects that carry like charges repel each other. However, if the core temperature and pressure become high enough, the repulsion between nuclei can be overcome and the nuclei can fuse. Scientists commonly refer to fusion as "nuclear burning." But fusion has nothing to do with ordinary burning or combustion.

Converting mass to energy. When two relatively light nuclei fuse, a small amount of their mass turns into energy. Thus, the new nucleus has slightly less mass than the sum of the masses of the original nuclei. The German-born American physicist Albert Einstein discovered the relationship $E = mc^2$ that indicates how much energy is released when fusion occurs. The symbol E represents the energy; m, the mass that is converted; and c^2, the speed of light squared.

The speed of light is 186,282 miles (299,792 kilometers) per second. This is such a large number that the conversion of a tiny quantity of mass produces a tremendous amount of energy. For example, complete conversion of 1 gram of mass releases 90 trillion joules of energy. This amount of energy is roughly equal to the quantity released in the explosion of 22,000 tons (20,000 metric tons) of TNT. This is much more energy than was released by the atomic bomb that the United States dropped on Hiroshima, Japan, in 1945 during World War II. The energy of the bomb was equivalent to the explosion of 13,000 tons (12,000 metric tons) of TNT.

Destruction of light nuclei. In the core of a protostar, fusion begins when the temperature reaches about 1 million K. This initial fusion destroys nuclei of certain light elements. These include lithium 7 nuclei, which consist of three protons and four neutrons. In the process involving lithium 7, a hydrogen nucleus combines with a lithium 7 nucleus, which then splits into two parts. Each part consists of a nucleus of helium 4—two protons and two neutrons. A helium 4 nucleus is also known as an *alpha particle.*

Hydrogen fusion. After the light nuclei are destroyed, the protostar continues to contract. Eventually, the core temperature reaches about 10 million K, and hydrogen fusion begins. The protostar is now a star.

In hydrogen fusion, four hydrogen nuclei fuse to form a helium 4 nucleus. There are two general forms of this reaction: (1) the *proton-proton* (p-p) *chain reaction* and (2) the *carbon-nitrogen-oxygen* (CNO) *cycle.*

The p-p chain reaction can occur in several ways, including the following four-step process:

(1) Two protons fuse. In this step, two protons collide,

Spectacularly colored clouds of gas and dust appear in the constellations Scorpio (Scorpion) and Ophiuchus (Serpent Bearer). The clouds receive energy from stars within and near them, then emit the energy, much of it as visible light. At the lower left is Antares, a supergiant in Scorpio.

and then one of the protons loses its positive charge by emitting a *positron*. The proton also emits an electrically neutral particle called a *neutrino*.

A positron is the antimatter equivalent of an electron. It has the same mass as an electron but differs from the electron in having a positive charge. By emitting the positron, the proton becomes a neutron. The new nucleus therefore consists of a proton and a neutron—a combination known as a *deuteron*.

(2) The positron collides with an electron that happens to be nearby. As a result, the two particles annihilate each other, producing two gamma rays.

(3) The deuteron fuses with another proton, producing a helium 3 nucleus, which consists of two protons and one neutron. This step also produces a gamma ray.

(4) The helium 3 nucleus fuses with another helium 3 nucleus. This step produces a helium 4 nucleus, and two protons are released.

The CNO cycle differs from the p-p reaction mainly in that it involves carbon 12 nuclei. These nuclei consist of six protons and six neutrons. During the cycle, they change into nuclei of nitrogen 15 (7 protons and 8 neutrons) and oxygen 15 (8 protons and 7 neutrons). But they change back to carbon 12 nuclei by the end of the cycle.

Fusion of other elements. Helium nuclei can fuse to form carbon 12 nuclei. However, the core temperature must rise to about 100 million K for this process to occur. This high temperature is necessary because the helium nuclei must overcome a much higher repulsive force than the force between two protons. Each helium nucleus has two protons, so the repulsive force is four times as high as the force between two protons.

The fusion of helium is called the *triple-alpha process* because it combines three alpha particles to create a carbon 12 nucleus. Helium fusion also produces nuclei of oxygen 16 (8 protons and 8 neutrons) and neon 20 (10 protons and 10 neutrons).

At core temperatures of about 600 million K, carbon 12 can fuse to form sodium 23 (11 protons, 12 neutrons), magnesium 24 (12 protons, 12 neutrons), and more neon 20. However, not all stars can reach these temperatures.

As fusion processes produce heavier and heavier elements, the temperature necessary for further processes increases. At about 1 billion K, oxygen 16 nuclei can fuse, producing silicon 28 (14 protons, 14 neutrons), phosphorus 31 (15 protons, 16 neutrons), and sulfur 32 (16 protons, 16 neutrons).

Fusion can produce energy only as long as the new nuclei have less mass than the sum of the masses of the original nuclei. Energy production continues until nuclei of iron 56 (26 protons, 30 neutrons) begin to combine with other nuclei. When this happens, the new nuclei have slightly more mass than the original nuclei. This process therefore uses energy, rather than producing it.

Evolution of stars

The life cycles of stars follow three general patterns, each associated with a range of initial mass. There are (1) high-mass stars, which have more than about 8 solar masses; (2) intermediate-mass stars, with about 0.5 to 8 solar masses—the group that includes the sun; and (3) low-mass stars, with about 0.08 to 0.5 solar mass. The exact ranges of mass differ somewhat according to the chemical composition of the star. Objects with less than around 0.1 solar mass do not have enough gravitational force to produce the core temperature necessary for hydrogen fusion.

The life cycles of single stars are simpler than those of binary systems, so this section discusses the evolution of single stars first. And because astronomers know much more about the sun than any other star, the discussion begins with the development of intermediate-mass stars.

Intermediate-mass stars. A cloud that eventually develops into an intermediate-mass star takes about 100,000 years to collapse into a protostar. As a protostar, it has a surface temperature of about 4000 K. It may be anywhere from a few times to a few thousand times as luminous as the sun, depending on its mass.

T-Tauri phase. When hydrogen fusion begins, the protostar is still surrounded by an irregular mass of gas and dust. But the energy produced by hydrogen fusion pushes away this material as a *protostellar wind.* In many cases, the disk that is left over from the collapse channels the wind into two narrow cones or jets. One jet emerges from each side of the disk at a right angle to

the plane of the disk. The protostar has become a *T-Tauri star,* a type of object named after the star T in the constellation Taurus (the Bull). A T-Tauri star is a *variable star,* one that varies in brightness.

Main-sequence phase. The T-Tauri star contracts for about 10 million years. It stops contracting when its tendency to expand due to the energy produced by fusion in its core balances its tendency to contract due to gravity. By this time, hydrogen fusion in the core is supplying all the star's energy. The star has begun the longest part of its life as a producer of energy from hydrogen fusion, the *main-sequence phase.* The name of this phase comes from a part of the H-R diagram.

Any star—whatever its mass—that gets all its energy from hydrogen fusion in its core is said to be "on the main sequence" or "a main-sequence star." The amount of time a star spends there depends on its mass. The greater a star's mass, the more rapidly the hydrogen in its core is used up, and therefore the shorter is its stay on the main sequence. An intermediate-mass star remains on the main sequence for billions of years.

Red giant phase. When all the hydrogen in the core of an intermediate-mass star has fused into helium, the star changes rapidly. Because the core no longer produces fusion energy, gravity immediately crushes matter down upon it. The resulting compression quickly heats the core and the region around it. The temperature becomes so high that hydrogen fusion begins in a thin shell surrounding the core. This fusion produces even more energy than had been produced by hydrogen fusion in the core. The extra energy pushes against the star's outer layers, and so the star expands enormously.

As the star expands, its outer layers become cooler, so the star becomes redder. And because the star's surface area expands greatly, the star also becomes brighter. The star is now a red giant.

Horizontal branch phase. Eventually, the core becomes hot enough to support the triple-alpha process. In red giants that are less than about 2.3 times as massive as the sun, helium fusion begins rapidly in an explosive event called the *helium flash.* The star briefly increases in brightness, then decreases in size and brightness until the energy from the helium fusion stops the core's contraction. At the end of this period, the star is in its *horizontal branch phase,* named for the position of the point representing the star on the H-R diagram. Depending on its composition, a horizontal-branch star may remain red or become hotter and more yellow or blue in appearance.

In red giants that are more than about 2.3 times as massive as the sun, helium fusion begins gradually. The star shrinks slightly and becomes less bright as helium fusion begins. As the helium fusion continues, and the energy from it stops the core's contraction, the star will get somewhat hotter and become more orange in appearance. As the helium gets consumed, the star again becomes cooler and more reddish in appearance.

Asymptotic giant phase. Stars burn helium roughly 10 to 20 percent as long as they burned hydrogen. When all the helium in the core has fused, the core contracts, becoming hotter. The triple-alpha process begins in a shell surrounding the core, and hydrogen fusion continues in a shell surrounding that. Due to the increased energy produced by the burning in the shells, the star's

The life stages of the sun

The stars in this Hertzsprung-Russell diagram represent major phases in the sun's lifetime. The time given beside each star is the number of years to the next phase. The sun is now a main-sequence star, as shown in red. The sun will continue to change its *luminosity* (rate at which it emits energy); its *absolute magnitude* (actual brightness); its surface temperature; and its *spectral class,* a category related to its color. Eventually, it will become so cool that it could not be shown on the diagram.

WORLD BOOK diagram

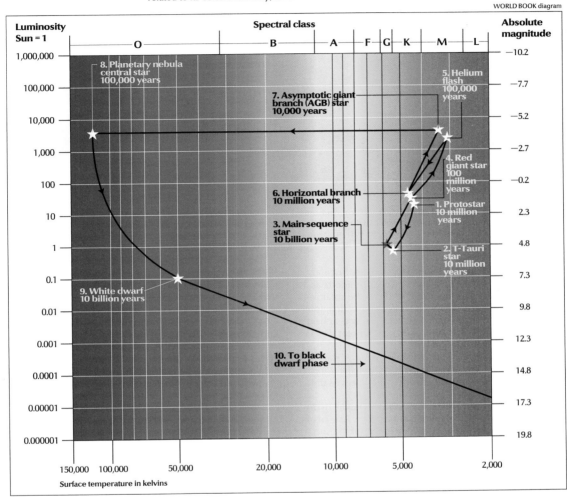

outer layers expand. The star becomes a giant again, but it is brighter than it was the first time.

On the H-R diagram, the point representing the star has moved upward and to the right along a line known as the *asymptotic* (pronounced *as ihm TAHT ihk) giant branch* (AGB). The star is therefore called an *AGB star.*

An AGB star's core is so hot and its gravitational grip on its outermost layers is so weak that those layers blow away from the star in a *stellar wind.* As each layer blows away, a hotter layer is exposed. Thus, the stellar wind becomes even stronger. Out in space, a succession of new, fast stellar winds slam into old, slow stellar winds that are still moving away from the star. The collisions produce dense shells of gas, some of which cool to form dust.

White dwarf phase. In just a few thousand years, all but the hot core of an AGB star blows away, and fusion ceases in the core. The core illuminates the surrounding

shells. Such shells looked like planets through the crude telescopes of astronomers who studied them in the 1800's. As a result, the astronomers called the shells *planetary nebulae*—and today's astronomers still do. The word *nebulae* is Latin for *clouds.*

After a planetary nebula fades from view, the remaining core is known as a *white dwarf star.* This kind of star consists mostly of carbon and oxygen. Its initial temperature is about 100,000 K.

Black dwarf phase. Because a white dwarf star has no fuel remaining for fusion, it becomes cooler and cooler. Over billions of years, it cools more and more slowly. Eventually, it becomes a *black dwarf*—an object too faint to detect. A black dwarf represents the end of the life cycle of an intermediate-mass star.

High-mass stars form quickly and have short lives. A high-mass star forms from a protostar in about 10,000 to 100,000 years.

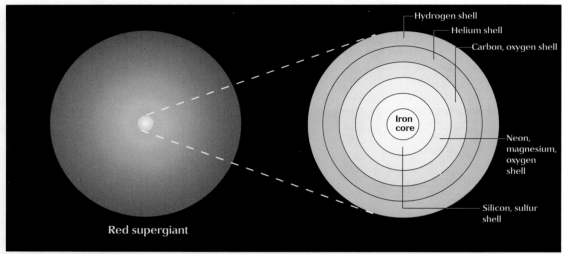

Red supergiant

Hydrogen shell
Helium shell
Carbon, oxygen shell
Iron core
Neon, magnesium, oxygen shell
Silicon, sulfur shell

WORLD BOOK diagram

A huge star creates chemical elements by *nuclear fusion,* the joining of two atomic nuclei to make a larger nucleus. In the outermost shell, hydrogen nuclei fuse, creating helium. In the next shell, helium fuses to make carbon and oxygen. Fusion creates successively heavier elements in shells closer to the core, where iron is produced. The shells in this diagram are not drawn to scale.

High-mass stars on the main sequence are hot and blue. They are 1,000 to 1 million times as luminous as the sun, and their radii are about 10 times the solar radius. High-mass stars are much less common than intermediate- and low-mass stars. Because they are so bright, however, high-mass stars are visible from great distances, and so many are known.

A high-mass star has a strong stellar wind. A star of 30 solar masses can lose 24 solar masses by stellar wind before its core runs out of hydrogen and it leaves the main sequence.

As a high-mass star leaves the main sequence, hydrogen begins to fuse in a shell outside its core. As a result, its radius increases to about 100 times that of the sun. However, its luminosity decreases slightly. Because the star is now emitting almost the same amount of energy from a much larger surface, the temperature of the surface decreases. The star therefore becomes redder.

As the star evolves, its core heats up to 100 million K, enough to start the triple-alpha process. After about 1 million years, helium fusion ends in the core but begins in a shell outside the core. And, as in an intermediate-mass star, hydrogen fuses in a shell outside that. The high-mass star becomes a bright *red supergiant.*

When the contracting core becomes sufficiently hot, carbon fuses, producing a variety of elements, including oxygen, neon, sodium, and magnesium. Red supergiants that are less than roughly 11 times as massive as the sun stop fusing elements when the carbon is exhausted. Such a star then starts cooling and will eventually become a white dwarf. But in most red supergiants, the star goes on to fuse heavier and heavier elements in stages. Each time the fusion of a particular element ceases in the core, it continues in a thin shell surrounding the core. Eventually, the star's central region takes on a layered appearance resembling an onion, with an iron core surrounded by successive shells fusing primarily silicon, oxygen, neon, carbon, helium, and hydrogen.

The fusion of each successive element in the core takes less time. A red supergiant 25 times more massive than the sun and with a similar chemical composition might fuse helium for about 700,000 years, carbon for 1,000 years, neon for 9 months, oxygen for 4 months, and silicon for about 1 day.

Supernovae. At this time, the radius of the iron core is about 1,900 miles (3,000 kilometers). Because further fusion would consume energy, the star is now doomed. It cannot produce any more fusion energy to balance the force of gravity.

When the mass of the iron core reaches 1.4 solar masses, violent events occur. The force of gravity within the core causes the core to collapse. As a result, the core temperature rises to nearly 10 billion K. At this temperature, the iron nuclei break down into lighter nuclei and eventually into individual protons and neutrons. As the collapse continues, protons combine with electrons, producing neutrons and neutrinos. The neutrinos carry away about 99 percent of the energy produced by the crushing of the core.

Now, the core consists of a collapsing ball of neutrons. When the radius of the ball shrinks to about 6 miles (10 kilometers), the ball rebounds like a solid rubber ball that has been squeezed.

All the events from the beginning of the collapse of the core to the rebounding of the neutrons occur in about one second. But more violence is in store. The rebounding of the ball of neutrons sends a spherical shock wave outward through the star. Much of the energy of the wave causes fusion to occur in overlying layers, creating new elements. As the wave reaches the star's surface, it boosts temperatures to 200,000 K. As a result, the star explodes, hurling matter into space at speeds of about 9,000 to 25,000 miles (15,000 to 40,000 kilometers) per second. The brilliant explosion is known as a *Type II supernova.*

Supernovae enrich the clouds of gas and dust from

which new stars eventually form. This enrichment process has been going on since the first supernovae billions of years ago.

Three generations of stars may exist. Astronomers have not found any of what would be the oldest generation, *Population III* stars. But they have found members of the other two generations. *Population II* stars, which would be the second generation, contain relatively small amounts of heavy elements. The more massive ones aged and died quickly, thereby contributing more nuclei of heavy elements to the clouds. For this reason, *Population I* stars, the third generation, contain the largest amounts of heavy elements. Yet these quantities are tiny compared to the amount of hydrogen and helium in Population I stars. For example, elements other than hydrogen and helium make up from 1 to 2 percent of the mass of the sun, a Population I star.

Neutron stars. After a Type II supernova blast occurs, the stellar core remains behind. If the core has less than about 3 solar masses, it becomes a *neutron star.* This object consists almost entirely of neutrons. It packs at least

1.4 solar masses into a sphere with a radius of about 6 to 10 miles (10 to 15 kilometers).

Neutron stars have initial temperatures of 10 million K, but they are so small that their visible light is difficult to detect. However, astronomers have detected pulses of radio energy from neutron stars, sometimes at a rate of almost 1,000 pulses per second.

A neutron star actually emits two continuous beams of radio energy. The beams flow away from the star in opposite directions. As the star rotates, the beams sweep around in space like searchlight beams. If one of the beams periodically sweeps over Earth, a radio telescope can detect it as a series of pulses. The telescope detects one pulse for each revolution of the star. A star that is detected in this way is known as a *pulsar.*

Black holes. If the stellar core remaining after the supernova explosion has about 3 or more solar masses, no known force can support it against its own gravitation. The core collapses to form a *black hole,* a region of space whose gravitational force is so strong that nothing can escape from it. A black hole is invisible because it

A cloud of gas known as the Vela Supernova Remnant has been spreading across the constellation Vela (the Sails) since a gigantic star exploded there about 12,000 years ago. Only part of the cloud is shown here. The explosion also left a neutron star that does not appear in the photo.

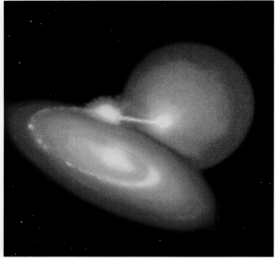

Space Telescope Science Institute

Transfer of mass occurs in a binary star system. Matter flows from a sunlike star, in the background in this illustration, to a disk orbiting a white dwarf star, then to the surface of the dwarf.

traps even light. All its matter is at a single point in its center. This point, known as a *singularity,* is much smaller than an atomic nucleus.

Low-mass stars, from about 0.08 to 0.5 solar mass, have surface temperatures less than about 4,500 K. Their luminosities are less than 2 percent of the sun's. Low-mass stars use hydrogen fuel so slowly that they may shine as main-sequence stars for tens of billions to even several trillions of years. This life span is longer than the present age of the universe, believed to be about 14 billion years. Therefore, no low-mass star has ever died. Nevertheless, astronomers have determined that low-mass stars will never fuse anything but hydrogen. Thus, as these stars die, they will not pass through a red-giant phase. Instead, they will merely cool to become white dwarfs, then black dwarfs.

Binary stars develop from two protostars that form near each other. More than 50 percent of what seem to the unaided eye to be single stars are actually binaries.

One star in a binary system can affect the life cycle of the other if the two stars are sufficiently close together. Between the stars is a location called the *Lagrange point,* named for the French mathematician Joseph-Louis Lagrange, where the star's gravitational forces are exactly equal. If one of the stars expands so much that its outer layers pass the Lagrange point, the other star will begin to strip away those layers and accumulate them on its surface.

This process, called *mass transfer,* can take many forms. Mass transfer from a red giant onto a main-sequence companion can add absorption lines of carbon or other elements to the spectrum of the main-sequence star. But if the stars are close together, the material will flow in the opposite direction when the giant star becomes a white dwarf. The matter will spiral in toward the dwarf, forming a hot disk around it. The disk will flare brilliantly in visible and ultraviolet radiation.

If the giant star leaves behind a neutron star or a black

hole instead of a white dwarf, an *X-ray binary* may form. In this case, the matter transferred from the main-sequence star will become extremely hot. When this matter strikes the surface of the neutron star or is pulled into the black hole, it will emit X rays.

In a third case, the red giant becomes a white dwarf, and the main-sequence star becomes a red giant. When enough gas from the giant accumulates on the dwarf's surface, gas nuclei will fuse violently in a flash called a *nova.* In some cases, so much gas will accumulate that its weight will cause the dwarf to collapse. Almost instantly, the dwarf's carbon will fuse, and the entire dwarf will explode in a *Type I supernova.* This kind of explosion is so bright that it can outshine an entire galaxy for a few months.   Paul J. Green

Related articles in *World Book* include:

Biographies

Outline

Additional resources

Level I
Asimov, Isaac, and Hantula, Richard. *The Life and Death of Stars.* Rev. ed. Gareth Stevens, 2005.
Birch, Robin. *Stars.* Chelsea Clubhouse, 2004.
Driscoll, Michael. *A Child's Introduction to the Night Sky.* Black Dog & Leventhal, 2004.
Miller, Ron. *Stars and Galaxies.* 21st Century Bks., 2006.
Scagell, Robin. *Night Sky Atlas.* DK Pub., 2004.

Level II

Inglis, Mike. *Observer's Guide to Stellar Evolution: The Birth, Life, and Death of Stars*. Springer Pub. Co., 2003.

Kerrod, Robin. *The Star Guide: Learn How to Read the Night Sky Star by Star*. 2nd ed. Wiley, 2005.

Nicolson, Iain. *Stars and Supernovas*. DK Pub., 2001.

Ridpath, Ian, ed. *Norton's Star Atlas and Reference Handbook, Epoch 2000.0*. 20th ed. Pi Pr., 2004.

Tirion, Wil. *The Cambridge Star Atlas*. 3rd ed. Cambridge, 2001.

Star Chamber was a special English court of law during the 1500's and 1600's. It tried people who were too powerful to be brought before the ordinary, common-law courts. The Star Chamber consisted of men from the King's Council, a group of royal advisers. It passed judgment without trial by jury. The court was so named because it held sessions in the Star Chamber of Westminster Palace. Today, the term *star chamber* refers to an unregulated, secret meeting of any court of justice or official organization.

The Star Chamber was popular for a long time because it protected ordinary people from their oppressors. But eventually it abused its powers. Unlike the common-law courts, which protected the accused, it used torture to obtain confessions. King Charles I used the Star Chamber to crush opposition to his policies. In 1641, the Long Parliament abolished the court (see **Long Parliament**). W. M. Southgate

Star cluster is a large grouping of stars held together by their gravitational attraction to one another. The stars in a cluster move as a group. They share the same chemical composition and appear to have formed at the same time. The best-known star cluster, the Pleiades (pronounced *PLEE uh deez)*, appears in the constellation Taurus. The unaided eye can see six stars of the Pleiades. A small telescope reveals hundreds more.

Kinds of clusters. There are three types of star clusters: (1) open clusters, (2) globular clusters, and (3) stellar associations.

Open clusters, such as the Pleiades, are loose collections of stars. An open cluster may include a few hundred to a few thousand stars spread over a roughly spherical region 5 to 10 *light-years* in diameter. A light-year is the distance that light travels in a vacuum in a year—about 5.88 trillion miles (9.46 trillion kilometers).

The open clusters in our own galaxy, the Milky Way, lie in the spiral "arms" of stars that form the galaxy's disk (see **Milky Way** [Shape of the galaxy]). These clusters orbit the galaxy's center, typically at speeds of around 200 kilometers per second (450,000 miles per hour). Even moving at such extremely high rates, they can take 250 million years to complete one trip around the galaxy.

All stars consist primarily of hydrogen and helium, but more than 2 percent of the atoms in open-cluster stars are of heavier elements. These include mainly carbon, oxygen, and nitrogen atoms but also some magnesium, silicon, iron, nickel, and other elements. Most of these heavier atoms originated in exploding stars called *supernovae*. Open clusters thus appear to have formed from clouds of gas and dust produced by supernovae.

Globular clusters contain many more stars than do open clusters. A globular cluster can include tens of thousands to a few million stars in a tight ball a few tens of light-years in diameter. In the Milky Way, globular clusters are not confined to the galaxy's disk. They appear to occur randomly in a sphere stretching 50,000

AURA/STScI/NASA

Globular cluster NGC 6093 ranks among the densest known *star clusters* in our galaxy. A star cluster is a large group of stars held together by their gravitational attraction to one another.

light-years from the center of the galaxy.

The stars in globular clusters contain a much smaller proportion of elements heavier than helium than do those in open clusters. Many globular clusters appear to have formed early in the history of the universe, around 13 billion years ago. Few supernovae had occurred by then, so little of the heavier elements existed.

Stellar associations consist of stars gathered more loosely than those in open clusters. A stellar association features a few tens to a few hundreds of stars spread over tens of light-years. An association has so few stars for its size that their mutual gravitational attraction cannot hold the association together indefinitely. The stars in an association will drift apart within a few million years after their formation.

Like open clusters, stellar associations contain relatively large proportions of heavy elements. In the Milky Way, associations appear only in the galaxy's spiral arms.

Ages of clusters. Astronomers measure the age of a star cluster by the brightness and color of its stars. The more *mass* (amount of matter) a star has, the hotter and bluer it shines. Massive stars also use up their hydrogen fuel and burn out more quickly. Astronomers can thus use a star's brightness to determine its total lifetime. Because the bluest stars will be the first to burn out, the lifetimes of the bluest surviving stars approximate the age of the cluster.

Most open clusters are tens of millions of years to a few billion years old. The Pleiades appear about 100 million years old. Globular clusters are much older, having ages of up to 13 billion years. Michael A. Strauss

See also **Cosmology** (The ages of stars).

Star maps. See Astronomy (illustrations: The stars and constellations).

Star-of-Bethlehem is a small, hardy plant of the hyacinth family. It grew first in Italy, but now has become a common garden plant in the United States. The plant's flowers form the shape of a six-pointed star. The petal-like parts are white, but they have green stripes on the outside. The leaves are green with white stripes. The flower stalk rises from a coated bulb. People grow the star-of-Bethlehem in gardens, in greenhouses, and in window boxes. The plant's flowers bloom in May and June, and tend to close before nightfall. The bulbs of the star-of-Bethlehem are poisonous.

Kenneth A. Nicely

Scientific classification. The star-of-Bethlehem belongs to the hyacinth family, Hyacinthaceae. Its scientific name is *Ornithogalum umbellatum.*

WORLD BOOK illustration by Christabel King

Star-of-Bethlehem

Star of David, also called the *Shield of David,* is the universal symbol of Judaism. The Star of David appears on the flag of the state of Israel, in synagogues, on Jewish ritual objects, and on emblems of various organizations. The star is made up of two triangles that interlace to form a six-pointed star. The figure itself is an ancient one. Scholars do not know when the star became widespread as a Jewish symbol. The figure appeared as early as the 960's B.C. The Hebrew term *Magen David,* which means *Shield of David,* dates from the late A.D. 200's.

The Star of David

Gary G. Porton

Star of India. See Sapphire.

Star-Spangled Banner is the national anthem of the United States. Francis Scott Key, an American lawyer and amateur verse writer, wrote the song during the War of 1812. The melody comes from "To Anacreon in Heaven," a drinking song created by composer John Stafford Smith of Britain in the late 1700's. The U.S. Congress officially approved the song as the national anthem in 1931.

How the song came to be written. In August 1814, British forces near Washington, D.C., arrested an American civilian, William Beanes of Upper Marlborough, Maryland. They held Beanes prisoner aboard a warship in Chesapeake Bay near the mouth of the Potomac River. General John Mason, the United States official in charge of prisoner exchanges, asked two Americans to communicate with the British in an effort to have Beanes released. These Americans were Key, a friend of Beanes's, and John S. Skinner, a government agent.

Key and Skinner went to Baltimore. There, they boarded a United States *flag of truce ship,* a ship used to conduct negotiations with the British. The flag of truce ship took Key and Skinner to the British warship just as the vessel was preparing to bombard Fort McHenry, which stood near Baltimore's harbor. The British agreed to release Beanes. But they did not want the Americans to reveal plans of the attack. They therefore held the Americans on the flag of truce ship at the rear of the British fleet until after the battle ended.

The bombardment started on Tuesday, Sept. 13, 1814,

and continued all day and almost all night. Key and his friends knew that Fort McHenry had little defense. The prisoners paced the deck all night. When dawn came, they saw the American flag still flying over the walls of the fort. Key was deeply moved. He pulled a letter from his pocket and started writing verses. Later that day, the British released the Americans, and Key returned to Baltimore. There, he finished revising the song.

How the song became famous. A few days after the bombardment, Key's poem, titled "Defense of Fort M'Henry," was printed on *handbills* (printed notices) and distributed in Baltimore. A note on the handbills said the poem should be sung to the tune of "To Anacreon in Heaven." Americans knew the melody, which had been used for a popular political song named "Adams and Liberty" and many other patriotic songs. Key himself had used the melody in an earlier song. By November 1814, the song had been published in Baltimore under the name "The Star-Spangled Banner." It was soon published in several other American cities, and it quickly gained popularity. The U.S. Army began to sing it at the daily raising and lowering of the flag in 1895. Today, by government permission, the United States flag flies continuously over Key's grave at Frederick, Maryland, and over Fort McHenry.

Valerie Woodring Goertzen

See also **Baltimore** (picture: Fort McHenry); **Flag** (Saluting the flag); **Key, Francis Scott.**

William S. Weems, Woodfin Camp, Inc.

The Star-Spangled Banner is the flag that inspired Francis Scott Key to write the U.S. national anthem. Key saw the flag flying over Fort McHenry in Baltimore while he was held prisoner by the British during the War of 1812. The flag, which is 50 feet (15 meters) long, covered an entire wall at the Smithsonian Institution's National Museum of American History in Washington, D.C. It has been removed from display, however, so that preservation work can be done on it.

The Star-Spangled Banner

Oh! say, can you see, by the dawn's early light,
What so proudly we hailed at the twilight's last gleaming?
Whose broad stripes and bright stars, through the perilous fight,
O'er the ramparts we watched were so gallantly streaming?
And the rocket's red glare, the bombs bursting in air,
Gave proof through the night that our flag was still there.
Oh! say, does that Star-Spangled Banner yet wave
O'er the land of the free and the home of the brave?

On the shore, dimly seen through the mists of the deep,
Where the foe's haughty host in dread silence reposes,
What is that which the breeze, o'er the towering steep,
As it fitfully blows, half conceals, half discloses?
Now it catches the gleam of the morning's first beam,
In full glory reflected, now shines on the stream.
'Tis the Star-Spangled Banner. Oh! long may it wave
O'er the land of the free and the home of the brave!

And where is that band who so vauntingly swore
That the havoc of war and the battle's confusion
A home and a country should leave us no more?
Their blood has washed out their foul footstep's pollution.
No refuge could save the hireling and slave
From the terror of flight or the gloom of the grave,
And the Star-Spangled Banner in triumph doth wave
O'er the land of the free and the home of the brave.

Oh! thus be it ever when freemen shall stand
Between their lov'd home and the war's desolation,
Blest with vict'ry and peace, may the heav'n-rescued land
Praise the power that hath made and preserved us a nation.
Then conquer we must, when our cause it is just,
And this be our motto—"In God is our trust."
And the Star-Spangled Banner in triumph shall wave
O'er the land of the free and the home of the brave.

Star wars. See Strategic Defense Initiative.

Star Wars is one of the most popular and profitable films in motion-picture history. The science-fiction fantasy, released in 1977, set standards for special effects that revolutionized filmmaking. *Star Wars* was directed and written by George Lucas. It was the first in a trilogy that included *The Empire Strikes Back* (1980) and *Return of the Jedi* (1983). Lucas supervised all three movies and wrote or helped write the screenplays for them, but he did not direct the two later films.

The film's young hero, Luke Skywalker (Mark Hamill), attempts to defeat the evil Galactic Empire with the aid of a mysterious inner power known as "the Force." The film's other famous characters include the robots R2-D2 (Kenny Baker) and C-3PO (Anthony Daniels), the daredevil pilot Han Solo (Harrison Ford), the rebel Princess Leia Organa (Carrie Fisher), the evil Darth Vader (the voice of James Earl Jones), and the mysterious knight Obi-Wan Kenobi (Alec Guinness).

The trilogy formed the last three episodes of a series of six *Star Wars* films. A "prequel" trilogy portrays the early years of key characters in the first trilogy. Lucas directed all three films in the prequel, called *Star Wars: Episode I—The Phantom Menace* (1999), *Star Wars: Episode II—Attack of the Clones* (2002), and *Star Wars: Episode III—Revenge of the Sith* (2005).   Philip Wuntch

Starch is a white, powdery substance found in the living cells of green plants. It can be found in the seeds of corn, wheat, rice, and beans and in the stems, roots, and *tubers* (underground stems) of the potato, arrowroot, or *cassava* (tapioca) plants. Starch is a carbohydrate, one of the most important foods. Starchy foods are an important source of energy for human beings and animals. When starch is digested in the body, energy is directly obtained from it.

During *photosynthesis* (the food-making process in green plants), the energy of sunlight changes water and carbon dioxide into glucose and oxygen. Plant cells can quickly convert glucose into starch. Tiny starch *granules* (grains) are formed in most green leaves during the day. At night, the starch is converted back to sugars, which then move to the root, stem, seeds, fruit, and other parts of the plant. The sugar may be used for growth, or stored again as starch.

Use in foods. Starch or flour that contains starch is often used in cooking to thicken mixtures. The mixtures usually become pasty or jellylike. Uncooked starch does not dissolve in water. But when rice, macaroni, and other starchy foods are cooked, the starch granules swell and absorb water. This property of starch is called *gelatinization*. Cooked, gelatinized starch is easily broken down in the body by digestive *enzymes* (chemicals). However, uncooked starch is too insoluble to be digested easily.

During the cooking of some foods, the starch may change into other substances. For example, slightly scorched starch becomes *dextrin*, a sticky carbohydrate used as glue on envelopes. During breadmaking, a small amount of starch becomes the sugar *maltose*. Maltose is fermented by yeast and changed into carbon dioxide and alcohol. The carbon dioxide forms bubbles in the bread dough and makes it rise.

Chemists use iodine to test for the presence of starch in food. When a small amount of iodine is added to a starch solution, it becomes blue-black. Under the microscope, starch appears as tiny granules. Cornstarch granules are rounded, irregular *polygons* (many-sided figures) about 10 to 20 microns in diameter. Potato starch granules are oval and may be more than 100 microns in diameter. Rice starch has tiny granules about 3 to 5 microns in diameter. With experience, a person can identify a starch by how it looks under a microscope.

Industrial uses. Starch has many uses. It is used to *size* (stiffen) weaving yarn and to finish cloth. Starch gives strength and a smooth, glossy finish to high-quality paper. Starches are also used in making pasteboard, corrugated board, plywood, and wallboard. A starch called *amylopectin* is produced from *waxy maize* (a kind of corn). Amylopectin produces clear and fluid pastes.

To manufacture cornstarch, corn is soaked in warm water and sulfur dioxide for two days. The softened kernels are torn apart and the *germ* (part of the inside) is removed. The kernel fragments are ground and *screened* (sifted) down to starch and *gluten* (proteins). The starch is then filtered, washed, dried, and packaged. Similar processes are used to manufacture starch from waxy maize and sorghum.

To make potato starch, the potatoes are washed and ground, and the starch is separated from potato fibers by screening. After further separation, the starch is

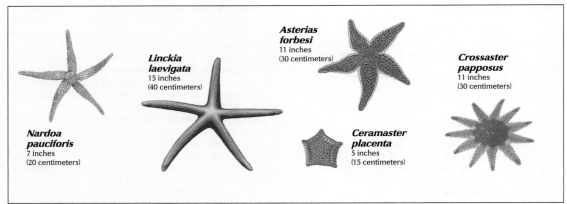

Asterias
forbesi
11 inches
(30 centimeters)

Linckia
laevigata
15 inches
(40 centimeters)

Crossaster
papposus
11 inches
(30 centimeters)

Nardoa
pauciforis
7 inches
(20 centimeters)

Ceramaster
placenta
5 inches
(15 centimeters)

WORLD BOOK illustrations by Alan Male, Linden Artists Ltd.

A great variety of starfish live in the world's oceans. These drawings show the differences in size, shape, and color of several starfish. The sizes given are the diameter.

washed and dried. Arrowroot and tapioca starch may be produced by similar methods.

Wheat starch can be manufactured by *kneading* (mixing) wheat flour into a dough. The starch is washed out of the sticky mass by a stream of water. Rice starch is made by soaking the grain in an alkaline chemical, which dissolves the gluten but not the starch. The starch is then separated and washed.   Kay Franzen Jamieson

Related articles in *World Book* include:

Arrowroot	Cellulose	Dextrin	Tapioca
Carbohydrate	Cornstarch	Sago	

Starfish, also called a *sea star,* is a spiny-skinned sea animal known for its distinctive "star" shape. A starfish has thick, armlike extensions that spread out from its body or *central disk.* Starfish are not fish. They belong to a group of animals called *echinoderms,* which also includes brittle stars, sea cucumbers, sea lilies, sea urchins, and sand dollars. Starfish live in all of the world's oceans, in both shallow and deep waters. They do not live in fresh water.

About 1,500 species of starfish exist. Most have five arms and look somewhat like five-pointed stars. Some species have as many as 40 arms or more. The body of a starfish can measure from less than 1 inch (2.5 centimeters) to more than 3 feet (1 meter).

The body of a starfish. A starfish's mouth lies at the center of its underside and leads directly into a large, baglike stomach. The stomach usually consists of two parts. The *cardiac stomach* extends from the mouth to the *pyloric stomach* above. The pyloric stomach has internal branches called *pyloric caeca* that run the length of each arm and serve as the primary site of digestion.

The surface of the body features *ambulacral grooves* that extend from the mouth to the tip of each arm. Typically, two or four rows of slender *tube feet* line the grooves. The tube feet often have suction disks on their ends. Starfish use tube feet to crawl and obtain food.

Long tube feet at the tips of the arms help starfish to sense their surroundings through touch. Many starfish sense light using a small, colored *eyespot* at the tip of each arm. Starfish do not have a central brain. Nerves run along the length of the ambulacral grooves and surround the mouth.

A complex system of canals carries water through the

body and controls the extension and movement of the tube feet. It also helps to maintain the balance of fluids in the body and distributes gases involved in respiration. The *madreporite,* a small filter on top of the central disc, lets seawater enter the system.

The life of a starfish. Most starfish live for three to five years. In most species, the female releases thousands of eggs into the sea, where sperm from the male fertilizes them. Starfish release eggs and sperm from reproductive organs in their arms. The fertilized eggs develop into tiny, drifting *larvae* (young). After some time, each larva settles on the sea bottom and develops into a juvenile starfish. In some species, the female may hold the eggs on the surface of her body or in her stomach to protect the developing young. Some starfish reproduce through *fission.* In this process, the body of the parent divides to form two or more independent individuals, which then *regenerate* (regrow) missing portions.

Starfish feed on other starfish and on such animals as chitons, coral, sea cucumbers, sea urchins, snails, sponges, and worms. Many starfish feed on *bivalves,* animals with hinged shells, such as clams, mussels, and oysters. The starfish usually attaches its tube feet to the halves of the bivalve's shell, pulling on them until they part slightly. The starfish then pushes its cardiac stomach, turned inside out, through the crack and secretes enzymes to begin digesting the prey. It sucks the partial-

Kenneth R. H. Read, Tom Stack & Assoc.

The underside of a starfish has many slender tubes called *tube feet.* Each tube foot has a tiny suction disk at its tip. The starfish uses its tube feet and suction disks for crawling.

ly digested food into digestive glands in its arms. The *sunflower starfish* consumes its prey whole and digests it internally. Other starfish *ingest* (take in) mud and extract small food particles from it. Still others use their spiny arms to trap small organisms drifting in the water. These *suspension feeders* use their tube feet to pass the food down their arms to the mouth.

Although some crabs, fish, and snails eat them, starfish have few predators. If grabbed, many starfish can drop off arms in a defensive reaction called *autotomy*. They can then regenerate new arms to replace the old ones. If a starfish is cut in two or more pieces, each of the pieces may become a new animal as long as it contains a portion of the central disk. When predators attack, sunflower starfish release fluids that cause nearby sunflower starfish to flee. Some starfish more than triple their speed to escape predators.　　Robert S. Prezant

Scientific classification. Starfish make up the class Asteroidea in the phylum Echinodermata.

See also **Brittle star; Deep sea** (Invertebrates); **Echinoderm.**

Stark, John (1728-1822), was a leading American general in the Revolutionary War in America (1775-1783). His crushing defeat of Colonel Friedrich Baum's raiding party of Germans, Tories, Canadians, and Indians near Bennington, Vermont, on Aug. 16, 1777, was a turning point of the war. It was a severe setback to General John Burgoyne's campaign to cut the American colonies in half.

Stark's New Hampshire regiment defended the American left wing at Breed's Hill in 1775. He helped cover the 1776 retreat from Canada, commanded units at the battles of Trenton and Princeton, and served in the Rhode Island campaign of 1779. Stark was born on Aug. 28, 1728, in Londonderry, New Hampshire. He served with Rogers's Rangers in the French and Indian War from 1754 to 1763. Stark died on May 8, 1822. His statue represents New Hampshire in the U.S. Capitol.　　James H. Hutson

Starling is the name of several songbirds related to mynas. Starlings have pointed wings, a short tail, and a sharp bill. The best-known species is the *common star-*

J. P. Laub, Ardea

The common starling has black feathers with a greenish-purple gloss. It sometimes nests in a hollow tree.

ling, which is native to Europe and Asia. In the early 1890's, about 100 common starlings were set free in Central Park in New York City. Millions now live throughout the United States and southern Canada.

The common starling is about 7 ½ to 8 ½ inches (19 to 22 centimeters) long. Its feathers are black with a greenish-purple gloss. In winter, the feathers are tipped with dull yellow, giving the bird a spotted appearance. The bill is yellow in summer but dark in winter.

The common starling nests in hollow trees, birdhouses, or holes in cliffs. The female lays from four to seven light blue eggs. Starlings compete with North America hole-nesting birds for nest sites, sometimes driving out larger birds. Starlings are helpful to farmers because they eat harmful insects. But in the fruit season, they can be pests because they also eat many berries and cherries, and even apples and pears.　　Martha Hatch Balph

Scientific classification. Starlings belong to the starling family, Sturnidae. The scientific name for the common starling is *Sturnus vulgaris.*

Starr, Belle (1848-1889), has been considered one of the few female outlaws in the United States. According to legends, she became a robber and horse and cattle thief in the Southwest and was known as the Bandit Queen. She married and lived with outlaws. However, most stories about her probably are not true.

Oklahoma Historical Society
Belle Starr

Myra Maybelle Shirley, called Belle, was born on Feb. 5, 1848, near Carthage, Missouri. In 1866, Belle married Jim Reed, who was an outlaw. They had two children, Rosie Lee and Edwin. During the early 1870's, Reed went into hiding because of a reward for his capture. Belle and the children left Reed. In 1874, Reed was killed in a gunfight. Several years later, Belle moved to the Indian Territory (now eastern Oklahoma). She met Sam Starr, a Cherokee Indian, and married him in 1880. They lived in a cabin that became a famous hideout for Jesse James and other bandits. Belle and Sam Starr were convicted of horse stealing in 1883. She served nine months in prison. In 1886, Starr was shot to death in a fight. Belle then lived with Bill July, a part-Cherokee Indian who was a horse thief. A gunman killed Belle on Feb. 3, 1889, in an ambush while July was in court.　　Odie B. Faulk

Starr, Kenneth Winston (1946-　　), is an American lawyer, judge, and law school dean. He served as an independent counsel investigating President Bill Clinton from 1994 to 1999. A judicial panel initially appointed Starr to investigate Clinton's investment in the Whitewater Development Corporation, an Arkansas real estate company accused of illegal and unethical acts.

In 1998, Starr investigated charges of a sexual affair between Clinton and White House intern Monica Lewinsky. Starr delivered a report outlining possible impeachable offenses stemming from the president's attempts to cover up the affair. Starr argued that Clinton lied to a grand jury and encouraged others to lie and to conceal evidence. In December 1998, the House of Representatives impeached Clinton for *perjury* (lying under oath) and obstruction of justice. Two months later, the Senate found Clinton not guilty.

Starr was born in Vernon, Texas, on July 21, 1946. He graduated from Duke Law School in 1973. He worked as a law clerk to Chief Justice Warren E. Burger, counselor to U.S. Attorney General William French Smith, and circuit judge for the U.S. Court of Appeals (District of Columbia Circuit). He served as U.S. solicitor general from 1989 to 1993 under President George H. W. Bush. In 1999, Starr returned to his private law practice. In 2004, he became dean of Pepperdine University School of Law.   Jack M. Kress

See also **Clinton, Bill; Independent counsel.**

Stars and Stripes is a daily newspaper that presents news, editorials, and features of interest to military personnel stationed outside the United States. The United States Department of Defense publishes the paper in Griesheim, Germany, and in Tokyo. People in the U.S. armed forces rely on it for information not available in the general media. This information includes news of military affairs, working benefits, and opportunities for promotion. The paper's staff consists of civilian journalists and military personnel.

Soldier-journalists organized a paper called *The Stars and Stripes* during the American Civil War (1861-1865). They named it after the American flag. In 1918 and 1919, during World War I, American soldiers in France revived *The Stars and Stripes.* Many leading journalists began their careers on the paper, including Grantland Rice, a sports reporter, and Harold W. Ross, founding editor of *The New Yorker* magazine.

The Stars and Stripes appeared again in 1942, after the United States entered World War II. The paper made its greatest impact during this war. Thirty locations in Europe, North Africa, and the Pacific published it. The paper earned respect for its realistic and enterprising coverage of the war. Its reporters often worked under enemy fire and accurately covered discouraging news, such as U.S. naval losses to Japan. In 1945, Bill Mauldin won a Pulitzer Prize for his "Up Front" cartoons in the paper. These cartoons vividly pictured the problems of common soldiers.   Thomas C. Leonard

See also **Mauldin, Bill; Rice, Grantland; Ross, Harold Wallace.**

Starter is a device that sets an engine in motion. Starters are used to start the engines of automobiles, trucks, locomotives, airplanes, and other vehicles.

Automobile starters consist of three main parts: (1) a *motor,* (2) a *pinion* with an *overrunning clutch,* and (3) a *solenoid.* The motor is operated by electric power supplied by the car's battery. The pinion is a small gear that connects the motor to the car's engine and enables it to turn the engine's crankshaft. The solenoid acts as a switch between the battery and the starter motor. It also controls the action of the pinion and overrunning clutch. The overrunning clutch disengages the pinion from the engine when the engine starts and speeds up.

When the driver turns the key in the ignition, electric current flows from the battery to the solenoid. The current produces a magnetic field around the solenoid, pulling in a plunger. When the plunger is in this position, it connects the battery with the starter motor. A wire-wrapped cylindrical conductor in the starter motor, called an *armature,* receives electric current from the battery and begins to rotate. As the plunger connects the battery with the starter motor, it forces a *shift lever* to push the pinion and overrunning clutch onto the drive shaft attached to the armature. The notched teeth of the pinion mesh with those on the *flywheel,* making it spin. The flywheel turns the crankshaft, which moves the pistons and sparks the engine, thus starting the car.

How an automobile starter works

When the driver turns the ignition key, electric current flows from the battery to the solenoid, causing the plunger to be pulled in. This engages the pinion gear with the flywheel and enables current to flow from the battery to the motor, which starts to turn. The pinion gear then spins the flywheel, which turns the crankshaft, moving the pistons and starting the car.

WORLD BOOK diagrams by William Graham

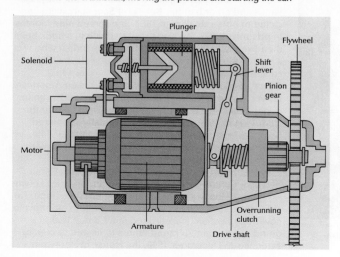

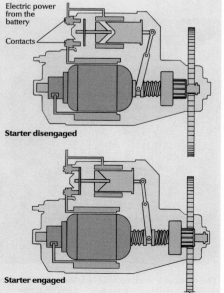

Starter disengaged

Starter engaged

The American engineer and inventor Charles Kettering developed the first successful electric starter for automobiles in 1911. It was first used on the 1912 Cadillac. Prior to Kettering's invention, automobile engines were started manually. Before getting into the car, the driver inserted a crank into the front of the engine. The driver turned the crank, which was connected to the crankshaft, until the engine started. After the engine started, the crank was supposed to disengage from the crankshaft. However, many times the crank did not do so, and the spinning crank would injure the driver.

Diesel starters are used in diesel-powered engines. Such engines are widely used in trucks and locomotives. Diesel engines require more starting power than gasoline engines, since they work at much higher compression. Some diesel engines have powerful electric starters like those in automobile engines. Locomotive diesels use their generators as electric starters. Many diesels are started by pumping compressed air directly to some of the cylinders. The air drives the pistons until the engine can fire on its own. A small *auxiliary* (helper) engine starts other diesels. See **Diesel engine.**

Airplane starters. The first airplanes were started by pulling the propeller by hand, causing the crankshaft to turn. A few small propeller aircraft still start this way. However, most propeller-driven light planes have an electric starter similar to those found in automobiles.

Most large commercial and military airplanes are equipped with an *air turbine starter* or a *jet turbine starter*. These small turbine engines bring the main jet engine up to normal operating speed by supplying it with high-pressure air. A separate *auxiliary power unit* (APU), located on the plane or on the ground, provides power for the starter.   David E. Foster

See also **Gasoline engine; Kettering, Charles F.**

Starvation occurs when a living thing dies from lack of any food substance essential for life. Essential food substances are called *nutrients.* They are classified into six groups: carbohydrates, fats, minerals, proteins, vitamins, and water. Nutrients furnish energy for regulating body processes and for building and maintaining body tissues. Plants derive energy from sunlight by means of photosynthesis. Human beings and other animals derive energy from carbohydrates, fats, and proteins contained in food. Plants, humans, and animals require minerals and water. Human beings and animals also require vitamins. If living organisms do not receive required nutrients, they waste away and finally die of starvation.

In human beings, the most critical nutrient is water. Death occurs when a person loses 20 percent of total body water. Environmental temperature may vary the rate of water loss, but most people will be able to live only about a week without water. How long a person can survive without food depends on the person's supply of body fat. Fat is the body's most efficient form of stored energy. However, most people can survive only 60 to 70 days without food.   Mary Frances Picciano

See also **Fast; Nutrition.**

Stassen, Harold Edward (1907-2001), an American political leader, became famous for repeatedly running for president. He was governor of Minnesota from 1939 to 1943 and served as special assistant for disarmament to United States President Dwight D. Eisenhower from 1955 to 1958. Stassen was a candidate for the Republican nomination for president in the elections of 1948, 1952, 1964, 1968, 1972, 1976, and 1980.

Stassen was born on April 13, 1907, near St. Paul, Minnesota, and graduated from the University of Minnesota. After serving as attorney of Dakota County, Minnesota, he was elected governor in 1938 and was reelected twice. While governor, Stassen revised the civil service laws and lowered the costs of state government. He supported a labor law that provided a "cooling-off" period before strikes. This action brought him national recognition. In his third term as governor, during World War II (1939-1945), Stassen resigned to serve in the U.S. Navy.

In 1945, Stassen became a delegate to the San Francisco Conference, which founded the United Nations. He was appointed president of the University of Pennsylvania in 1948. Stassen resigned from that post in 1953 to serve as U.S. mutual security administrator, and then as foreign operations administrator, directing American aid to many countries. Stassen died on March 4, 2001.
      Stephen E. Ambrose

State. See **Nation; Population** (graph: Ten most densely populated states); **State government; United States.**

State, Department of, is the executive department of the United States government that plans and manages U.S. relations with other governments. It coordinates the actions of other executive departments that affect foreign policy. The department is headed by the secretary of state, a member of the president's Cabinet.

The State Department negotiates treaties and agreements with other governments; handles official business with foreign embassies in Washington, D.C.; speaks for the United States in the United Nations and other international organizations; and arranges for United States participation in international conferences.

Members of the Department of State represent the United States in other countries throughout the world.

Mid Hunt

The Department of State handles United States relations with other countries. Its many responsibilities include negotiating treaties and other international agreements. The department's headquarters, *shown here,* are on C Street in the northwest section of Washington, D.C.

They deal with officials of other governments and report on developments that affect the United States. Their reports provide information on the politics, economics, and social conditions of the other countries. The information is useful to many of the U.S. federal agencies that deal with national security, *intelligence* (confidential information), economic and commercial matters, agriculture, science, and technology. The reports provide a basis for U.S. foreign policy.

Department members also issue passports; grant visas to immigrants or visitors to the United States; help protect and resettle refugees; support human rights worldwide; protect U.S. citizens and their property in other countries; and help businesses promote U.S. trade and investment. The department deals internationally with such matters as aviation, energy, environmental regulations, finance, food and other resources, shipping, tariffs, telecommunications, and trade.

The State Department also develops United States policy on disarmament and the control of military weapons. It also conducts educational and cultural exchanges with other countries and directs information programs to explain U.S. international policy and ways of life. The Department of State guides an independent government agency called the Agency for International Development. This agency manages U.S. economic and humanitarian aid programs in less developed countries. The Agency for International Development also supports programs in democracy, economic growth, the environment, and population planning and health.

The headquarters of the Department of State are in Washington, D.C., on land reclaimed from a swamp near the Potomac River. The area, which was frequently blanketed by fog, became known as *Foggy Bottom*. Today, the name Foggy Bottom is sometimes used to refer to the Department of State. The department has other offices throughout the United States and many overseas posts. The Web site at http://www.state.gov presents information on the department's activities.

Secretary of state

Responsibilities. The secretary of state, head of the State Department, advises the president on international relations. The secretary must identify the major international problems facing the United States and then develop strategies to deal with those problems. The secretary serves on the National Security Council (NSC) and other committees. The NSC, which is a part of the Executive Office of the President, advises the president on international policy, particularly on matters of national security.

The U.S. president appoints the secretary of state with the approval of the Senate. The secretary of state is the highest-ranking member of the Cabinet. In the line of succession to the presidency, the secretary comes after the vice president, the speaker of the House, and the president *pro tempore* of the Senate.

The secretary of state is

The seal of the Department of State

Eric Carle, Shostal

The American Embassy in London houses the State Department delegation that represents the United States government in the United Kingdom.

the custodian of the Great Seal of the United States. Presidential proclamations, treaties, and other official documents carry the seal. For an illustration of the Great Seal, see **United States, Government of the.**

Relationship with the president and Congress. The president consults with the secretary of state on international matters. However, the secretary's role always depends on the president. Some presidents have strong opinions concerning international policy. The secretaries who serve such presidents have less importance and influence than those who serve presidents who are mainly interested in domestic affairs.

The secretary of state's relationship to Congress is also important, because congressional actions often affect international relations. For example, treaties that are arranged by the secretary must be approved by the Senate. The Senate also must approve the appointment of ambassadors. Congress must also authorize the funding needed to carry out the administration's foreign policy.

In the late 1700's and early 1800's, the position of secretary of state frequently served as a gateway to the presidency. Thomas Jefferson, James Madison, James Monroe, John Quincy Adams, Martin Van Buren, and James Buchanan all served in the office before being elected president. Other secretaries of state, such as Henry Clay, Daniel Webster, John C. Calhoun, and William H. Seward, were appointed to the position largely because they were political leaders.

In the 1900's, many secretaries were selected mainly for their ability and international experience. John M. Hay, John Foster Dulles, Henry A. Kissinger, and Warren M. Christopher all had much international experience.

History of the department

Establishment. The Department of State is the oldest executive department of the U.S. government. During the Revolutionary War in America (1775-1783), the Continental Congress dealt with other countries through its

Secretaries of state

Name	Took office	Under president	Name	Took office	Under president
*Thomas Jefferson	1790	Washington	Richard Olney	1895	Cleveland
*Edmund Randolph	1794	Washington	*John Sherman	1897	McKinley
*Timothy Pickering	1795	Washington, J. Adams	William R. Day	1898	McKinley
			*John M. Hay	1898	McKinley, T. Roosevelt
*John Marshall	1800	J. Adams	*Elihu Root	1905	T. Roosevelt
*James Madison	1801	Jefferson	Robert Bacon	1909	T. Roosevelt
Robert Smith	1809	Madison	Philander C. Knox	1909	Taft
*James Monroe	1811	Madison	*William J. Bryan	1913	Wilson
*John Quincy Adams	1817	Monroe	*Robert Lansing	1915	Wilson
*Henry Clay	1825	J. Q. Adams	Bainbridge Colby	1920	Wilson
*Martin Van Buren	1829	Jackson	*Charles E. Hughes	1921	Harding, Coolidge
Edward Livingston	1831	Jackson	*Frank B. Kellogg	1925	Coolidge
Louis McLane	1833	Jackson	Henry L. Stimson	1929	Hoover
John Forsyth	1834	Jackson, Van Buren	*Cordell Hull	1933	F. D. Roosevelt
*Daniel Webster	1841	W. H. Harrison, Tyler	*Edward R. Stettinius, Jr.	1944	F. D. Roosevelt, Truman
Abel P. Upshur	1843	Tyler	*James F. Byrnes	1945	Truman
*John C. Calhoun	1844	Tyler	*George C. Marshall	1947	Truman
*James Buchanan	1845	Polk	*Dean G. Acheson	1949	Truman
*John M. Clayton	1849	Taylor	*John Foster Dulles	1953	Eisenhower
*Daniel Webster	1850	Fillmore	Christian A. Herter	1959	Eisenhower
*Edward Everett	1852	Fillmore	*Dean Rusk	1961	Kennedy, L. B. Johnson
William L. Marcy	1853	Pierce			
*Lewis Cass	1857	Buchanan	William P. Rogers	1969	Nixon
Jeremiah S. Black	1860	Buchanan	*Henry A. Kissinger	1973	Nixon, Ford
*William H. Seward	1861	Lincoln, A. Johnson	*Cyrus R. Vance	1977	Carter
			*Edmund S. Muskie	1980	Carter
Elihu B. Washburne	1869	Grant	*Alexander M. Haig, Jr.	1981	Reagan
*Hamilton Fish	1869	Grant	*George P. Shultz	1982	Reagan
*William M. Evarts	1877	Hayes	*James A. Baker III	1989	G. H. W. Bush
*James G. Blaine	1881	Garfield, Arthur	Lawrence S. Eagleburger	1992	G. H. W. Bush
F. T. Frelinghuysen	1881	Arthur	*Warren M. Christopher	1993	Clinton
Thomas F. Bayard	1885	Cleveland	*Madeleine K. Albright	1997	Clinton
*James G. Blaine	1889	B. Harrison	*Colin L. Powell	2001	G. W. Bush
John W. Foster	1892	B. Harrison	*Condoleezza Rice	2005	G. W. Bush
Walter Q. Gresham	1893	Cleveland			

*Has a separate biography in *World Book*.

Committee of Secret Correspondence. This committee was established in 1775 with Benjamin Franklin as its first chairman. In 1777, it was renamed the Committee for Foreign Affairs.

On Jan. 10, 1781, the Continental Congress created a Department of Foreign Affairs. Robert R. Livingston became the first secretary of foreign affairs, and John Jay succeeded him in 1784. After the adoption of the Constitution, Congress set up a new Department of Foreign Affairs on July 27, 1789, as an executive agency under the president. Congress changed the agency's name to the Department of State on Sept. 15, 1789. The department performed such domestic duties as operating the mint, issuing patents, publishing the census, and regulating immigration. Other departments now handle most United States domestic duties.

President George Washington appointed Thomas Jefferson as the first secretary of state in 1789. However, John Jay served as temporary secretary of state until Jefferson assumed the office in 1790.

Changing responsibilities. During the 1800's and the early 1900's, the interests of the United States centered on domestic matters, and the Department of State grew slowly. The United States avoided alliances with other countries, and the department received little public attention or congressional support. But State Department officials negotiated several important treaties. Some agreements resolved boundary disputes between the United States and the United Kingdom and thus improved relations between the two countries. In the Treaty of Guadalupe Hidalgo of 1848, Mexico surrendered to the United States what is now California, Nevada, and Utah, and parts of Arizona, Colorado, New Mexico, and Wyoming. In 1867, the department accomplished the purchase of Alaska from Russia.

Foreign relations—and the State Department—gained importance during such crises as the American Civil War (1861-1865), the Spanish-American War (1898), and World War I (1914-1918). The work of the department increased greatly during World War I, particularly in providing information and in supporting citizens overseas.

World War II (1939-1945) involved the State Department in many international activities. The department evacuated U.S. citizens from war zones, helped in prisoner-of-war exchanges, and dealt with refugees. It also coordinated wartime agencies and created an effective system of international communications. The war convinced U.S. political leaders that the nation's security depended on U.S. efforts to maintain peace, and influence events, in other parts of the world. As a result, the role of the State Department expanded. After the war, the department took over various agencies that had gathered information and dispensed aid abroad, and it helped in the reconstruction of liberated territories. The department also participated in economic and military aid programs and made security plans with over 40 nations.

Secretary of State William H. Seward, *seated with a map on his lap,* signed a treaty in 1867 that provided for the U.S. purchase of Alaska from Russia. Alaska proved to be rich in natural resources, and it became a U.S. state in 1959.

Copy (about 1934) by Lynn Faucett and Helen Wessells of *Signing of the Alaska Treaty* (1867), an oil painting on canvas by Emanuel Leutze; United States Department of the Interior, Washington, D.C.

Since World War II. In 1961, the Peace Corps and the Agency for International Development were established as agencies under the direction of the Department of State. The Agency for International Development was made part of the International Development Cooperation Agency in 1979. The Peace Corps became an independent agency in 1981.

During the late 1900's, international terrorism became a threat to department members and their families. In 1979, for example, Iranian revolutionaries took over the United States Embassy in Tehran, the capital of Iran. They seized a group of U.S. citizens, most of whom were State Department employees, and held them as hostages until 1981. After several incidents involving kidnappings, killings, or the taking of hostages, the department increased its security precautions, particularly for employees working outside the United States.

Also in the late 1900's, the State Department sometimes played a less central role in foreign affairs than it traditionally had. During the 1980's, for instance, the National Security Council at times operated independently of the department in developing and carrying out certain foreign policies. By the mid-1990's, the State Department's central role in setting much of foreign policy had been reestablished. However, as a result of international developments, many other institutions, especially economic ones, became more important in establishing U.S. policy.   Michael P. Sullivan

Related articles in *World Book* include:

Ambassador	Great Seal of the United
Attaché	States
Consul	International relations
Diplomacy	Minister
Foreign aid	Passport
Foreign policy	Presidential succession
Foreign Service	United States Information
	Agency

State birds. See Bird (table: State and provincial birds); United States (Facts in brief).

State capitals. See United States (Facts in brief).

State flags. See Flag (Flags of the U.S. states and territories).

State flowers. See Flower (table: Flowers of the states); United States (table: Facts in brief about the states); also the picture in each state article.

State government provides many services and regulates many activities for the people of a state. In the United States, a state government maintains law and order, protects property rights, and regulates business. It supervises public education, including schools and state universities. It provides public welfare programs, builds and maintains highways, operates state parks and forests, and regulates the use of state-owned land. It has direct authority over local governments—counties, cities, towns, townships, villages, and school districts.

The government in some countries, such as France and the United Kingdom, operates under the *unitary system.* Under this system, the national government defines and establishes the powers of local governments. The United States has a *federal system,* which divides power between the national and state governments. However, the division of power is subject to dispute. In general, the states reserve the power to take any action that does not conflict with the Constitution of the United States, acts of Congress, or treaties entered into by the national government. See **States' rights.**

The independent powers of state governments arose during the colonial period. After the Declaration of Independence in 1776, each former British colony called itself a state to indicate its *sovereign* (independent) position. The term *state* generally means an area of land whose people are organized under a sovereign government. Each state gave up some of its powers when its citizens approved the federal Constitution.

Since the founding of the United States, the powers and activities of the national government have greatly expanded. The federal government has become involved in many matters, such as education and housing, that once were handled only by state and local govern-

Road construction is one of many services funded by state governments. Every state has a department that is responsible for building and maintaining roads.

ments. Many of these matters required national action or more financial resources than state or local governments could provide. Nevertheless, state and local governments still have numerous responsibilities. In the 1990's, the federal government even began giving authority back to state governments. In 1996, for example, Congress passed welfare reform legislation that gave lump-sum payments to the states to design and carry out their own programs for the poor.

State constitutions

Each state has a constitution that sets forth the principles and framework of its government. Every state constitution has a bill of rights (sometimes called a declaration of rights), which guarantees basic rights, such as freedom of speech. Many state constitutions have provisions on finance, education, and other matters.

The original 13 states had constitutions before the U.S. Constitution was adopted. Those of Massachusetts and New Hampshire are still in use. Constitutional conventions prepared most constitutions now in use.

A state constitution may be amended in several ways. The state legislature may submit a proposed amendment to the people for approval. The Delaware legislature may ratify such an amendment without a popular vote, but only by a two-thirds majority in each of two sessions. In 17 states, the people may suggest an amendment and vote on it in a state election. In some states, constitutional conventions may adopt amendments, subject to ratification by the people. In other states, a constitutional commission may propose an amendment, which must receive legislative approval before being submitted to the people.

Executive branch

The governor, elected by the people, heads the executive branch in each state. The governor has the power to appoint, direct, and remove from office a large number of state officials. The state constitution authorizes this official to see that the laws are faithfully executed. The governor commands the state militia, grants pardons, and may call the state legislature into special session. He or she directs the preparation of the state budget. In all states, the governor may veto bills, and, in some states, may even veto parts of a bill.

Most state governors serve four-year terms and may be removed from office by impeachment and convic-

tion. In most states, a lieutenant governor succeeds a governor who dies in office. For specific information about the length and limits of a governor's term, see the *Government* section of each state article in *World Book.*

The powers of state governors have steadily increased. The first governors had only limited authority because the people had learned to distrust the royal governors appointed by British kings. The office of governor has grown in stature since 1776. Some governors have more authority than other governors to appoint and control subordinate officials. See **Governor.**

Other officers. In most states, the people elect several other executive officials. These officers usually include a lieutenant governor, secretary of state, treasurer, and attorney general. In some states, the governor or legislature appoints one or more of these officials. The secretary of state administers election laws, publishes legislative acts, and directs the state archives. The treasurer collects and maintains state funds. The attorney general advises the governor on legal matters and prosecutes or defends cases that involve the state.

In over half the states, a state board of education or the governor appoints a superintendent of public instruction. In about 20 states, this official is elected. The superintendent administers state schools.

Legislative branch

The legislature of a state passes laws, levies taxes, and appropriates money to be spent by the state government. It takes part in amending the state constitution and has the power to impeach officials.

Organization. Every state except Nebraska has a *bicameral* (two-house) legislature. Nebraska adopted a *unicameral* (one-house) legislature in 1934. Nineteen states call their legislature the General Assembly, North Dakota and Oregon call it the Legislative Assembly, and Massachusetts and New Hampshire call it the General Court. Every upper house is known as the Senate. Most states call the lower house the House of Representatives. But four states use the term Assembly, and three call it the House of Delegates. A speaker presides over the lower house. The lieutenant governor presides over the Senate in about 30 states. In the others, the majority party selects a Senate president.

Senators in most states serve four-year terms. They hold office for two years in the other states. In almost all states, members of the lower house serve two-year terms. In four states, they serve four-year terms. The districts in both houses of a state legislature must be substantially equal in population (see **Apportionment**). For information about the number of members in state legislatures and the limits on their terms, see the *Government* section of each state article.

Salaries of legislators vary widely from state to state. Legislators in some states receive daily payments while the legislature is in session, rather than yearly salaries. Most states give legislators travel allowances, and many give other allowances.

The legislatures of over four-fifths of the states meet annually. The other legislatures meet in regular session *biennially* (every other year). Every legislature may be called into special session by the governor, and more than half may call a special session themselves. Most state constitutions limit the length of regular sessions.

The legislatures do much of their work through *standing committees,* also called *permanent committees.* A typical legislative chamber has about 15 such committees. Some states have joint committees, which include members from both houses and report proposed bills to both houses. Many states set up *ad interim* (temporary) committees to study particular problems while the legislature is not in session. Many states also have legislative councils that meet between sessions to study problems that may arise at the next session. Legislative assistants and other staffers help write laws and assist lawmakers in such areas as budget and technology. Many legislatures have legislative reference services to do research and prepare reports. See **Legislature**.

Initiative and referendum. The people in 24 states have direct power to change the law through procedures called the *initiative* and *referendum.* Through an initiative, a group of voters may propose a bill by petition. Through a referendum, a law or proposed law is submitted to the voters for their approval or rejection.

Since the mid-1990's, for example, voters have used initiatives and referendums to place term limits on legislators. They have also passed measures to put more restraints on the ability of state and local officials to raise and spend revenues.

Some people believe that the power of initiative and referendum gives voters more control of the legislature and increases public interest in government. Others say that it burdens the voters with issues they cannot vote on intelligently and that it tends to weaken the legislature's responsibility.

Judicial branch

State courts settle disputes that come before them under various laws. They handle about nine-tenths of the criminal and civil cases in the United States.

A supreme court heads the judicial system of each state. In a few states, the supreme court is called by another name, such as *court of appeals.* The memberships of state supreme courts range from three to nine judges.

In more than half the states, the voters elect judges to the state supreme court. In several states, the governor or legislature appoints them. In others, the governor appoints the judges, who must later be approved by the voters. Supreme court judges hold office for specified terms in every state except Rhode Island, where they are elected for life. For the specific lengths of these terms,

see the *Government* section of each state article.

Some states have appellate courts to handle some cases that would otherwise go directly to the supreme court. Each state has general trial courts. Most judges in these courts serve four-year, six-year, or eight-year terms. See **Court**.

State services

Education. The states, rather than the federal government, have the main responsibility for public education. State governments support public schools through taxes and administer them through local school districts. Most districts supervise their public elementary and secondary schools under a school board elected by the people or appointed by the mayor. State governments set up general standards for schools and their courses of study. The state funds supplement local property taxes that help pay for education. Every state has at least one state university. The state also maintains such institutions as agricultural colleges, teacher training schools, junior colleges, and vocational schools.

Public safety. The state legislatures enact most criminal laws that protect people and property. State police promote highway safety, preserve the peace, and enforce criminal laws. Each state has prisons, reformatories, or prison camps. Some states have departments of mine safety and sanitation. The governor of each state commands the state's militia, or national guard.

Public works. Each state has a highway, public works, or transportation department that builds and maintains roads. This department may also supervise the construction of bridges, canals, and waterways, and take care of beach protection, flood control, and buildings and grounds. Many toll roads are built and operated by special state authorities appointed by the governor. All states erect and maintain numerous public buildings.

Recreation. Departments or agencies in the various states manage state parks and recreation areas. Many parks and recreation areas have been established in state-owned forests. Other areas have been set up as historical monuments. In addition, state highway departments may operate roadside parks for motorists.

Health. State departments of health, often called boards of health, were first set up in the late 1800's. They supervise and assist local public health agencies. These agencies are responsible for such activities as keeping vital statistics, controlling communicable diseases, and promoting health education, maternal and infant care, sanitation, and hygiene. They have general control over hospitals, nursing, research, and laboratory facilities. State public health work may also include improvement of substandard housing and slum clearance.

Welfare. The federal government pays much of the bill for welfare. But the states have considerable control over the provision of welfare services. Today, state governments emphasize helping welfare recipients enter the job market. Each state operates programs that help the poor, aged, delinquent, and unemployed, and mentally and physically disabled people. States also provide institutional care in hospitals, mental institutions, reformatories, and various types of homes. Welfare agencies administer the welfare programs in most states.

Environment. Environmental agencies exist in every state. Many of the agencies exercise authority from the federal government to issue permits, monitor air and water pollution, and enforce standards for the discharge of waste products. Other environmental activities include soil and forest conservation and protection of water resources through special drainage, irrigation, water supply, and sanitation districts. State governments carry out their responsibilities through education; extension services; and research on water and mineral resources, fish and wildlife, and forests and soils. A director or board heads most environmental agencies. Some states have fish and game commissions and forest services.

Agriculture. The states aid agriculture through county agents, soil conservation districts, agriculture extension services, and agricultural colleges. Most states have a department or board of agriculture. In most of these states, the governor appoints the director or board members. In others, the voters elect these officials.

Business and labor. Each state government grants corporations the charters that allow them to do business. It regulates banks and insurance companies and supervises public utility companies that provide electric power, communication services, and transportation. All states have workers' compensation laws that provide payments to workers who are injured on the job.

State finances

The government of a state must have money to pay for the services the state provides. Most of the money is used for education, highways, public welfare, health and hospitals, insurance trusts for the retirement of employees, and unemployment insurance. In most of the states, the governor receives the financial requests of the state agencies and submits a total budget to the legislature. The legislature must approve all appropriations. Almost all state constitutions impose debt limits on the state.

Grants-in-aid (grants of money) from the federal government are a major source of state income. But reductions in the growth of federal aid have forced state governments to rely more on their own revenue sources. The major tax sources for state governments are sales taxes and income taxes. States also collect revenues through special taxes and fees. Some states impose taxes on the removal of natural resources, such as oil. Many have turned to legalized gambling to secure more revenues. But some people question whether the states should encourage people to gamble.

Traditionally, local authorities have received most of their tax revenues from property taxes. Local governments also rely heavily upon grants-in-aid from the states. They receive these grants upon agreeing to certain conditions imposed by the state. State governments also set debt limits for local governments. See **Taxation.**

In 1995, Congress passed a law to deter *unfunded mandates*—that is, federal programs imposed on state and local governments without grants of federal money to carry them out. The act made it more difficult for the U.S. government to enact programs without providing financial support for them. But the act did not apply to programs that existed when it became law.

Relations with other governments

The federal government has certain constitutional obligations toward the states. It must respect their territorial unity and cannot divide or break up a state without its consent. It must protect the states against invasion and domestic violence. It must guarantee each state a representative form of government.

The U.S. Constitution also puts certain limits on the states. They may not interfere in foreign relations or make compacts among themselves without the consent of Congress. They may not levy import or export taxes. They may not issue currency or pass laws that would weaken the legal obligations of contracts.

The Constitution also places certain obligations on the states in their relations with each other. Each state must give "full faith and credit" to the legal processes and acts of other states. No state may discriminate in favor of its own citizens against people from other states. The Supreme Court of the United States ultimately decides disputes between states that cannot be settled by negotiation and agreement. For a more complete description of the provisions and interpretation of the Constitution, see **Constitution of the United States.**

Issues confronting state governments

Some states have declining populations, and others are experiencing rapid population growth. Most government officials equate population growth with economic development, prosperity, and progress. But some officials in growing states wonder how their states will pay for the increased demands for such government services as education and public safety.

In education, state governments confront other issues as well. Courts have ordered several states to equalize spending on education among rich and poor school districts. States also struggle to improve the overall quality of education. Some states have adopted higher standards for teachers. States also have experimented with coupons called *vouchers,* which families can use to send children to the school of their choice, and with *charter schools,* which operate under special contracts giving them more freedom than other public schools.

State governments also struggle with heavy strains on their judicial and prison systems. Widespread crime and strict law enforcement lead to many arrests and many people going to prison. Under tough sentencing laws, numerous prisoners are locked up for long periods, leading to crowded prisons.

In economics, many states are caught up in the global economy. Their governments try to protect state industries from foreign competition and to prevent industries from moving to nations where wages are lower. Many states encourage tourism, solicit foreign investments in their economies, and try to develop foreign markets for the products of firms in the state.   David R. Berman

Related articles in *World Book.* See the *Government* and *History* sections of each state article, such as **Alabama** (Government; History). See also the following articles:

Additional resources

Book of the States. Council of State Governments, frequently up-
dated.
State and Local Government. CQ Pr., published annually.
Teaford, Jon C. *The Rise of the States: Evolution of American
State Government.* Johns Hopkins, 2002.

State mottoes. See the *table* in each state article. For
example, **Colorado** (table: Colorado in brief).

State parks. See the *Places to visit* section of each
state article.

State popular names. See United States (table: Facts
in brief about the states).

State press is a system of publishing operated by a
government or by a government-controlled political
party. A state press is the opposite of a *free press,* where
individuals are free to publish books, newspapers, and
magazines. Freedom of the press is an important element in political freedom. Dictatorships use state presses to control public opinion, mainly by suppressing un-
favorable facts. See also **Freedom of the press.**

Jethro K. Lieberman

State seals. See the picture in each state article.

State songs. See the *table* in each state article. For example, **Alabama** (table: Alabama in brief). See also **United States** (table: Facts in brief about the states).

State trees. See the picture in each state article; also
United States (table: Facts in brief about the states).

Staten Island forms one of the five *boroughs* (districts) of New York City. It is in New York Bay, about 5
miles (8 kilometers) southwest of Manhattan Island (see
New York [political map]). Staten Island has a population
of approximately 444,000. It is about 14 miles (23 kilometers) long and 7 ½ miles (12 kilometers) across at its
widest point.

The Staten Island Ferry links the island with Manhattan. The Verrazano-Narrows Bridge connects Staten Island with Brooklyn. Three other bridges connect the island with New Jersey.

Like Manhattan Island, Staten Island was purchased
by the Dutch from the Indians in the 1600's. In 1683, the
English changed the name from Staten Island to Richmond, after the Duke of Richmond. The island was officially renamed Staten Island in 1975. In 1993, Staten Islanders voted to secede from New York City. The
measure requires approval by the New York state legislature, and it has been stalled in a legislative committee
since 1995.   Brian J. Laline

See also **New York City** (Staten Island).

States-General. See Estates-General.

States of the Church. See Papal States.

States' rights is a doctrine aimed at protecting the
rights and powers of the states against those of the federal government. The 13 American states gave up many
powers to the federal government when they ratified
the Constitution of the United States. Only those powers
that the Constitution did not grant to the national government were left to the states.

Everyone agrees that the states have rights that the
federal government cannot lawfully touch. But the Constitution says that the federal government can make any
laws that are "necessary and proper" for carrying its specific powers into effect. This provision makes it difficult
to determine exactly what rights the states possess.
Therefore, the major issue is not whether the states have

rights, but rather who is to decide when these rights are
abused.

Early history. Today, most people connect the support of states' rights with the South's position on racial
segregation. But historically, the doctrine has been in-
voked by states in every section of the country whenever they have felt their jurisdiction threatened. One of the
earliest instances was the Kentucky and Virginia Resolutions, passed in opposition to the Alien and Sedition
Acts enacted by the federal government in 1798. This
opposition gave rise to the doctrine of *nullification,*
which asserts that within its own borders, a state can
nullify (declare illegal) those acts of the federal government which it considers an invasion of its own rights.
The doctrine of nullification was developed by John Calhoun and officially adopted by South Carolina in 1832.
See **Nullification.**

In 1860 and 1861, 11 Southern states carried the states'
rights idea to its most extreme point by seceding from
the Union. Their defeat in the American Civil War (1861-
1865) put an end to this particular interpretation of
states' rights. However, it is still generally agreed that
the states have a jurisdiction that the federal government has no right to invade.

The task of drawing the exact line of state jurisdiction
and deciding whether the federal government has over-
stepped it is now left to the federal courts. The decisions
of the courts can be changed only by the courts themselves or by an amendment to the Constitution of the
United States.

Later developments. In the 1950's, supporters of
states' rights claimed that decisions of the federal courts
weakened the powers of the states. The Supreme Court
of the United States declared that state laws ordering
segregation in public schools, in public parks, and on
public transportation systems violated provisions of the
Constitution.

In the controversy over segregation, advocates of
states' rights insisted that each state has the right of *in-
terposition.* This doctrine resembles nullification. It asserts that a state has the right to "interpose the sovereignty of a state against the encroachment upon the
reserved power of the state." Under this doctrine, a state
has the power to overrule a decision of a federal agency
if it conflicts with a state law, and all persons in the state
must obey the state, not the federal, law.

Congress established a Commission on Intergovern-
mental Relations in 1953 to study the extent of federal
aid to the states, and the constitutional limits of federal
and state powers. In 1955, the commission made its recommendations to the president and Congress. The recommendations covered such fields as agriculture, education, and housing. The commission noted that the
Constitution forbids the states to legislate in such fields
as interstate commerce, admiralty laws, and currency. It
also pointed out that the problem of maintaining a federal system arises where both the federal and state
governments have a choice of how to act in a given situation.

States' rights parties have run candidates in most
presidential elections since 1948. The core of these parties came from conservative Democrats and Republicans who opposed the civil rights policies of their own
parties. One of these groups, the States' Rights Demo-

cratic Party (nicknamed the Dixiecrat Party), carried four Southern states in 1948. In 1968, George C. Wallace, who was the presidential candidate of the American Independent Party, also stressed states' rights and carried five of the Southern states.   David R. Berman

See also **Alabama** (Early statehood); **Calhoun, John Caldwell; Dixiecrat Party; Kentucky and Virginia Resolutions; Wallace, George C.**

States' Rights Democratic Party. See Dixiecrat Party.

Statesman is a person with a broad general knowledge of government and politics, who takes a leading part in public affairs. Most people think of statesmen as being concerned with the needs and interests of their country as a whole. In contrast, they think of *politicians* as having only party or political aims. *Elder statesmen,* who are usually retired from active government, continue to give advice on important issues. Japan developed this system in the *genro,* a council of former government leaders who advise the current government.
Kenneth Janda

Static is a term for a disturbance in a radio or television receiver, usually caused by atmospheric electricity. Static may take the form of crackling and grating noises heard over the radio or television. It may also take the form of white or black spots seen on a television picture.

Water droplets and dust particles in the air often carry an electric charge. Any motion of electric charges results in radiation at some frequency. If this radiation has a frequency within the radio or television broadcast bands, it will be heard or seen as static.

Ordinarily, the movement of charged particles in the air produces static in the form of a weak, hissing, background noise. However, severe disturbances to the atmosphere, such as lightning, earthquakes, tornadoes, and volcanoes, make the particles move more rapidly and the air vibrate violently. These disturbances thus cause sudden crashes, pops, and other noises. Certain electric motors and electric sparks from machinery also produce static.   Patrick D. Griffis

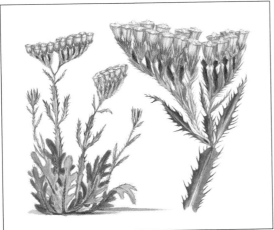

WORLD BOOK illustration by John F. Eggert
Sea lavender, a type of statice, grows wild in salt marshes and deserts worldwide. These illustrations show the entire plant, *left,* and a close-up of flower clusters, *right.*

See also **Frequency modulation.**

Static electricity. See Electricity (Static electricity).

Statice, *STAT uh see* or *STAT ihs,* is a name commonly applied to *sea lavenders,* a group of herbs or shrubs used in rock gardens and flower bed borders. Sea lavenders grow wild throughout the world, especially in salt marshes and desert or semidesert regions. Their purple, rose, white, or yellow flowers are often dried and made into bouquets. A group of evergreen herbs called *thrifts* or *sea pinks* have also been known as statices. Thrifts are found mainly on coasts and in mountainous areas. Their small pink or white flowers grow in dense, globe-shaped clusters.

Both sea lavenders and thrifts grow well in most garden soils. They usually reproduce by seed. The plants should be started in a greenhouse in early spring and then planted outside. Sea lavenders and thrifts have flowers all summer.   Robert A. Kennedy

Scientific classification. Sea lavenders make up the genus *Limonium* in the leadwort family, Plumbaginaceae. Thrifts make up the genus *Armeria* in that family.

Statics is one of the two branches of *mechanics,* the science that studies the effects of forces on bodies at rest or in motion. The other branch of mechanics is *dynamics.*

Statics deals with a body at rest, or in motion at a constant speed and in a constant direction. Such a body is said to be in *equilibrium* because the forces acting on it cancel each other out. Dynamics deals with bodies that change speed, direction, or both, because of forces acting on them.   James D. Chalupnik

Statin, *STAT ihn,* is any one of a class of drugs used to lower cholesterol levels in the blood. Cholesterol is a waxy, fatty substance found in animal tissues and the food that comes from them. The substance is also produced in the liver. High levels of cholesterol in the blood increase a person's risk of *coronary artery disease* (CAD). Statins help prevent CAD by lowering the amount of cholesterol in the blood. This effect helps reduce the risk of heart attack and stroke caused by CAD.

Statins work by *inhibiting* (preventing) the action of an enzyme called *HMG-coA reductase.* This enzyme is necessary for the production of cholesterol in the liver. When statins inhibit the action of the enzyme, the liver takes cholesterol from the blood to make up for the decreased cholesterol production. As a result, the level of cholesterol in the blood falls.

Side effects of statins, such as headache or abdominal pain, are uncommon and usually mild. However, a small number of people develop a severe condition called *rhabdomyolysis* after taking statins. This condition causes muscle cells to break down and cause damage to the kidneys. The side effects cease when people stop taking the drugs.   Michael S. Brown and Joseph L. Goldstein

See also **Cholesterol; Heart** (Coronary artery disease).

Statistics is a set of methods that are used to collect and analyze data. Statistical methods help people identify, study, and solve many problems. They enable people to make informed decisions about uncertain situations.

Statistical methods play an important role in a wide variety of occupations. Doctors and public health officials rely on statistics when determining whether certain drugs and therapies help in the treatment of medical problems. Engineers use statistics to set standards for product safety and quality. Weather forecasters and climate researchers work with statistical models to understand and predict weather patterns and climate trends. Scientists consider statistical ideas when designing and evaluating experiments. Psychologists study statistics to learn about human behavior. Statistical techniques enable economists to discover the impact of government policies and to predict future economic conditions.

People often use the word *statistics* as a plural noun to mean numerical data or numerical summaries of data. Used as a singular noun, *statistics* means the set of methods used to collect and analyze data and report conclusions. This article discusses statistical methods.

Using statistics to study problems

People called *statisticians* specialize in using statistical methods to study problems. They typically study a problem in at least four basic steps: (1) defining the problem, (2) collecting the data, (3) analyzing the data, and (4) reporting the results.

Defining the problem. To obtain accurate data, a statistician must establish an exact definition of the problem. For example, suppose a statistician were asked to count the inhabitants of Lincoln, Nebraska, on a specific date. The statistician would have to define *inhabitant* clearly to know who should be included in the count. The statistician would have to decide whether to include newborn babies in the hospital, students temporarily away from Lincoln at college or attending college in Lincoln, and people visiting Lincoln from other places. If the statistician did not clearly define *inhabitant,* gathering useful data would prove quite difficult.

Collecting the data. Different problems require different kinds of information. The careful study of a single case, such as an airplane crash, can often be useful. But collections of cases, such as the rates of crashes involving various types of airplanes, usually provide more reliable information for reaching general conclusions.

Designing ways to collect data ranks as one of the statistician's most important tasks. Statisticians can collect data from a *population* or from a *sample.* A population is the entire group of objects or people being studied, whereas a sample is only a portion of that group. Statisticians refer to a study in which data are collected on every member of a population as a *census.*

Statisticians often compare populations that differ in some important way, such as where they live or how healthy they are. To make accurate comparisons, statisticians must control the effect of other differences among the members of their samples. For example, imagine a food company asked a statistician to determine if people in two regions react differently to sweetness in food. To ensure that differences in age did not influence the results, the statistician might compare children in one region with children from the other, and adults from one region with adults from the other.

Statisticians gather data using *observational studies* and *controlled experiments.* Observational studies involve collecting data on people or objects in their natural surroundings. A simple type of observational study is the *sample survey,* in which statisticians ask a sample of people about their opinions or situations.

In controlled experiments, statisticians create special conditions and observe how they affect people or ob-

jects. The *randomized controlled experiment* ranks as the most precise and informative method of collecting data for comparisons. In this method, statisticians divide the units to be studied into groups at random to help control the effects of unmeasured differences.

Researchers conducted one of the most famous randomized controlled experiments in the 1950's. They tested a newly developed polio vaccine on 400,000 children. Half the children received the vaccine. The other half received a harmless solution, called a *placebo,* that was known to have no effect on polio. The researchers selected the two groups at random. Because polio affected only a small percentage of children, the groups had to be quite large to reliably reveal whether the vaccine worked. The results showed that the rate of paralysis due to polio was almost three times as great among the children who got the placebo as among those who got the vaccine. Thus, the researchers concluded that the vaccine was effective in helping to prevent polio.

Analyzing the data. Methods for analyzing statistical data fall into two categories: (1) *exploratory methods* and (2) *confirmatory methods.* Statisticians employ exploratory methods to figure out what the collected data reveal about a problem. These methods often involve computing averages or percentages, displaying data on a graph, and estimating levels of association between *variables* (varying quantities) that were measured. Statisticians often use exploratory methods to compare measurements of two or more samples.

Statisticians use confirmatory methods to distinguish between important differences in data and meaningless random variations. Confirmatory methods typically involve using ideas from a branch of mathematics called *probability theory.* In the polio vaccine experiment, confirmatory methods enabled researchers to determine that the difference in polio rates between the two groups was much higher than would be expected due to chance variation.

Statistical analysis often requires extensive calculations. Statisticians rely on computer programs to carry out much of this work. A number of statistical methods use computers to simulate random events for comparison to observed data. Many business people and researchers who do not consider themselves statisticians use statistical computer programs in their work.

Reporting the results. Statisticians analyze data to make *inferences* (logical conclusions) about the populations being studied. They may report their findings in the form of a table, a graph, or a set of percentages.

If a statistician has examined only samples, the reported results must reflect the uncertainty involved in making inferences about the larger population. Statisticians express uncertainty by making statements about the probability of their conclusions and giving ranges of possible values.

Probability

To make accurate inferences, a statistician must understand probability theory. Probability theory enables people to calculate the chance that different possible outcomes of random events will happen.

Suppose you were to toss a penny five times. Each toss would result in one of two possible outcomes: heads or tails. The two outcomes can be thought of as equally likely—that is, the probability that the coin will turn up heads equals ½, as does the probability it will turn up tails. For the collection of five tosses, there are 32 possible sequences of heads and tails, such as heads, heads, heads, tails, tails; or tails, tails, heads, heads, tails. In one possible sequence, the penny never comes up heads, and in another, it comes up heads every time. Each of the 32 sequences is equally likely, so if you counted up how many sequences correspond to zero heads, one head, and so on, you would see that the probabilities for the number of heads are:

Number of heads	0	1	2	3	4	5
Probability	$\frac{1}{32}$	$\frac{5}{32}$	$\frac{10}{32}$	$\frac{10}{32}$	$\frac{5}{32}$	$\frac{1}{32}$

Statisticians call such lists of possible outcomes and their probabilities *probability distributions*. They often display the same information in the form of a graph known as a *probability histogram*. The probability histogram for the distribution given above would be:

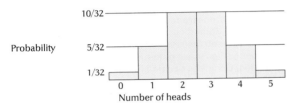

As you toss the penny more times, the probability distribution of the number of heads draws closer and closer to a bell-shaped curve called the *normal distribution:*

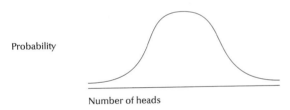

The result of the repeated tosses demonstrates an important mathematical principle called the *central limit theorem*. The theorem holds that for the sum of a large number of independent repeated events, such as coin tosses, the probability distribution will approximate the normal distribution. The theorem enables statisticians to use the normal distribution in making inferences from a sample of observations to the entire population.

All probability distributions have certain properties. For example, each distribution has a *mean* or *average value*. Statisticians calculate the mean of a distribution by multiplying each value by its probability and then adding these products. For five coin tosses, the mean number of heads is found by the following calculation:

$$\text{mean} = (0 \times \tfrac{1}{32}) + (1 \times \tfrac{5}{32}) + (2 \times \tfrac{10}{32})$$
$$+ (3 \times \tfrac{10}{32}) + (4 \times \tfrac{5}{32}) + (5 \times \tfrac{1}{32}) = 2\tfrac{1}{2}$$

If you were to repeatedly toss n times a coin for which the probability of heads is p, the mean number of heads is $n \times p$. In the example above, $n = 5$ and $p = \frac{1}{2}$. The mean is therefore $5 \times \frac{1}{2}$, or $2\frac{1}{2}$. For the normal distribution, the mean occurs at the value directly under the peak of the curve.

Other important properties of probability distributions include the *variance* and the *standard deviation*. Both terms measure how values vary around the mean. The following equation gives the variance:

$$\text{variance} =$$
$$\text{sum of [(value} - \text{mean)}^2 \times \text{(probability of value)]}$$

The standard deviation is the square root of the variance. For the normal distribution, the probability that a value lies within one standard deviation of the mean is about ⅔, and within two standard deviations of the mean is approximately $\frac{95}{100}$.

Sampling

Statisticians must plan carefully to choose samples that will give them useful information. For example, suppose a statistician must estimate the level of unemployment nationwide. The statistician would have to determine how to obtain a sample that would represent the whole nation as accurately as possible. Should many households in each of a few cities be sampled, or should fewer households in each of many cities? How should households in selected cities be chosen?

Statisticians try to avoid choosing samples that do not represent the entire population. Imagine a statistician had to conduct a sample survey to measure the opinions of all the people in a city. The statistician could stand in a public place and survey people walking by, but the location chosen might influence the results. For example, a survey taken in a wealthy neighborhood might strongly reflect the opinions of wealthy people and exclude the opinions of the city's poor. Statisticians use the term *selection bias* to refer to the way that poorly selected samples can lead to inaccurate conclusions.

To reduce selection bias, statisticians often choose the units that make up a sample randomly. A *simple random sample* is selected in such a way that all possible samples of the same size have an equal probability of being selected. The larger a random sample is, the more reliably a statistician can infer such quantities as means or proportions for the population. Larger samples also usually justify drawing more precise conclusions. Statisticians can measure the reliability of a sample using the standard deviation of the sample average. The standard deviation decreases in proportion to the square root of the sample size. Thus to double the reliability, the statistician must take a sample four times as large.

Sample sizes vary greatly depending on the purposes of the statistical study. Most well-known public opinion polls survey samples consisting of from 500 to 2,000 people. The sample survey used to measure the official national unemployment rate in the United States involves interviews with over 50,000 individuals. Such a survey produces averages and proportions over five times as reliable as a survey of 1,500 people. Although statisticians use fairly complex methods to choose the samples in these surveys, they still rely in part on the idea of simple random samples.

History

People gathered numerical data as far back as ancient times, and the Bible describes the details of several censuses. Political and religious leaders collected information about people and property throughout the Middle Ages and the Renaissance. In the 1700's, the word *statis-*

tik was commonly used in German universities to describe a systematic comparison of data about nations.

In the late 1800's, British scientists and mathematicians, including Francis Ysidro Edgeworth, Francis Galton, Karl Pearson, and George Udny Yulesuch, developed many of the statistical ideas and methods of analysis used today. However, many of these ideas remained unrefined until the 1920's. At that time, statistics emerged as a branch of science through the work of a small group of statisticians, also working in England. Statistical inference grew out of the work of Ronald A. Fisher, Jerzy Neyman, and Egon Pearson. Fisher also developed a theory of experimental design based on random assignment of treatments. Neyman proposed a theory of sample surveys with ideas similar to those in the theory of experimental design.

During World War II (1939-1945), statisticians developed many ideas and methods as part of the war effort in the United Kingdom and the United States. After the war, the field of statistics grew, and statistical ideas came into use in a wide variety of areas.

Careers in statistics

Statisticians find career opportunities in a wide variety of fields, including *actuarial science* (the estimation of risk), agriculture, biology, business, education, engineering, environmental science, health and medicine, quality control, and the social sciences. In all of these fields—and in many others—statisticians work closely with other scientists and researchers to develop new statistical techniques, adapt existing methods to new problems, design experiments, and direct the analysis of surveys and observational studies. As the ability to collect and process data improves, statisticians frequently take up key roles in new and expanding fields. In the early 2000's, areas of rapid development included astronomy and astrophysics, environmental and climate

studies, statistical genetics, and *data mining* (extracting useful information from large stores of data) in business.

Many national governments employ professional statisticians at various levels of responsibility and policymaking. Statistical experts at local levels help solve problems concerning the environment, the economy, transportation, public health, and other matters of public concern. Lawyers and judges have increasingly turned to statisticians to help weigh evidence and determine reasonable doubt. Universities employ statisticians for teaching and research. Many statisticians engage in private consulting practice.   Michael D. Larsen

Related articles in *World Book* include:

Average	Median	Public opinion
Census	Mode	poll
Galton, Sir Francis	Pearson, Karl	Vital statistics
Mean	Probability	

Statistics, Vital. See Vital statistics.

Statuary Hall is a room in the United States Capitol in Washington, D.C., that houses statues of outstanding American citizens from many states. The hall itself is a semicircular domed chamber. It lies near the magnificent Rotunda on the side of the Capitol leading to the chamber of the House of Representatives.

In 1864, Congress decided that each state should be invited to send two statues to be displayed in the Capitol. The states were asked to contribute statues of distinguished citizens who were "worthy of this national commemoration." Congress set aside the former House of Representatives chamber to display the statues.

The first statue arrived in 1870. The collection grew over the years. In 1933, architects discovered that the hall was overloaded. As a result, Congress then authorized that some of the statues be moved to other sites.

By 1971, all 50 states had sent at least one statue. By 2005, each state had sent two. The statues honor pioneers, political and religious leaders, and other out-

Kurt Scholz, Shostal

Statuary Hall displays statues of outstanding Americans. The hall itself is a semicircular domed chamber in the United States Capitol in Washington, D.C. The House of Representatives met in this chamber until 1857.

standing citizens. Thirty-eight stand in Statuary Hall. The others are in the Rotunda or elsewhere in the building.

In 2005, Congress unanimously approved legislation to add a statue of civil rights activist Rosa Parks to the hall. When the statue is dedicated, it will be the first in the hall to honor an African American woman.

Many important events in American history took place in what is now Statuary Hall. The House of Representatives met there from 1807 to 1857, except for a period of repair work from 1815 to 1819. The chamber needed the repairs after the British burned the Capitol during the War of 1812. The House met in the hall to choose the president in the contested election of 1824 and elected John Quincy Adams. Millard Fillmore took the oath as president in Statuary Hall in 1850.

In honor of the bicentennial celebration of 1976—the 200th anniversary of the founding of the United States—workers redecorated Statuary Hall. They partially restored the room to look much as it did when the House of Representatives met there. They reopened the original fireplaces, put in reproductions of the old mantels, and installed replicas of the red draperies and oil-burning chandelier that hung there.

The floor of Statuary Hall has nine bronze markers. They honor the nine presidents who served in the chamber as representatives when the House met there.

Critically reviewed by the Office of the Architect of the Capitol

Statue. See Sculpture.

National Statuary Hall Collection

This table lists the statues of outstanding Americans that each state has placed in the U.S. Capitol and the date each statue was presented. Many of the figures stand in Statuary Hall. Others are in the east front lobby, in the Rotunda, or elsewhere in the building.

State	Statue	Date presented	State	Statue	Date presented
Alabama	J. L. M. Curry	1908	**Montana**	Charles M. Russell*	1959
	Joseph Wheeler*	1925		Jeannette Rankin	1985
Alaska	Edward Lewis (Bob) Bartlett	1971	**Nebraska**	William Jennings Bryan*	1937
	Ernest Gruening	1977		J. Sterling Morton	1937
Arizona	John C. Greenway*	1930	**Nevada**	Patrick A. McCarran*	1960
	Eusebio Francisco Kino	1965		Sarah Winnemucca	2005
Arkansas	Uriah M. Rose*	1917	**New Hampshire**	John Stark	1894
	James P. Clarke	1921		Daniel Webster*	1894
California	Thomas S. King	1931	**New Jersey**	Philip Kearny	1888
	Junipero Serra*	1931		Richard Stockton	1888
Colorado	Florence Rena Sabin*	1959	**New Mexico**	Dennis Chavez	1966
	John L. (Jack) Swigert	1997		Po'Pay (Popé)	2005
Connecticut	Roger Sherman	1872	**New York**	George Clinton	1873
	Jonathan Trumbull	1872		Robert R. Livingston	1875
Delaware	John M. Clayton	1934	**North Carolina**	Zebulon Baird Vance*	1916
	Caesar Rodney	1934		Charles B. Aycock	1932
Florida	John Gorrie*	1914	**North Dakota**	John Burke*	1963
	Edmund Kirby Smith	1922		Sakakawea (Sacagawea)	2003
Georgia	Crawford W. Long	1926	**Ohio**	James A. Garfield	1886
	Alexander H. Stephens*	1927		William Allen*	1887
Hawaii	Joseph Damien de Veuster	1969	**Oklahoma**	Sequoyah*	1917
	Kamehameha I*	1969		Will Rogers	1939
Idaho	George L. Shoup*	1910	**Oregon**	Jason Lee*	1953
	William E. Borah	1947		John McLoughlin	1953
Illinois	James Shields	1893	**Pennsylvania**	Robert Fulton*	1889
	Frances E. Willard*	1905		John Peter G. Muhlenberg	1889
Indiana	Oliver P. Morton	1900	**Rhode Island**	Nathanael Greene	1870
	Lew Wallace*	1910		Roger Williams	1872
Iowa	James Harlan	1910	**South Carolina**	John C. Calhoun	1910
	Samuel J. Kirkwood*	1913		Wade Hampton	1929
Kansas	John J. Ingalls*	1905	**South Dakota**	William H. H. Beadle*	1938
	Dwight D. Eisenhower	2003		Joseph Ward	1963
Kentucky	Henry Clay*	1929	**Tennessee**	Andrew Jackson	1928
	Ephraim McDowell	1929		John Sevier*	1931
Louisiana	Huey P. Long*	1941	**Texas**	Stephen F. Austin	1905
	Edward Douglass White	1955		Sam Houston*	1905
Maine	William King	1878	**Utah**	Brigham Young*	1950
	Hannibal Hamlin*	1935		Philo T. Farnsworth	1990
Maryland	Charles Carroll of Carrollton	1903	**Vermont**	Ethan Allen*	1876
	John Hanson	1903		Jacob Collamer	1881
Massachusetts	Samuel Adams	1876	**Virginia**	Robert E. Lee*	1934
	John Winthrop	1876		George Washington	1934
Michigan	Lewis Cass*	1889	**Washington**	Marcus Whitman*	1953
	Zachariah Chandler	1913		Mother Joseph	1980
Minnesota	Henry Mower Rice*	1916	**West Virginia**	John E. Kenna	1901
	Maria L. Sanford	1958		Francis H. Pierpont*	1910
Mississippi	Jefferson Davis*	1931	**Wisconsin**	Jacques Marquette	1896
	James Z. George	1931		Robert M. La Follette, Sr.*	1929
Missouri	Thomas H. Benton*	1899	**Wyoming**	Esther Hobart Morris	1960
	Francis P. Blair, Jr.	1899		Washakie	2000

*In Statuary Hall.

The Statue of Liberty, a symbol of the United States and a beacon of freedom for immigrants, stands on Liberty Island in New York Harbor. France gave the Statue of Liberty to the United States in 1884 as an expression of friendship. The monument rises above star-shaped Fort Wood, built during the early 1800's.

© George Goodwin, Monkmeyer

Statue of Liberty is a majestic copper sculpture that towers above Liberty Island at the entrance to New York Harbor in Upper New York Bay. This famous figure of a robed woman holding a torch is one of the largest statues ever built. The statue's complete name is *Liberty Enlightening the World.*

The people of France gave the Statue of Liberty to the people of the United States in 1884. This gift was an expression of friendship and of the ideal of liberty shared by both peoples. French citizens donated the money to build the statue, and people in the United States raised the funds to construct the foundation and the *pedestal* (base). The French sculptor Frédéric Auguste Bartholdi designed the statue and chose its site.

The Statue of Liberty is a monumental feat of sculpture, engineering, and architecture. It attracts visitors from all over the world. The Statue of Liberty and a former immigration station at Ellis Island make up the Statue of Liberty National Monument, which is administered by the National Park Service.

The statue as a symbol

The Statue of Liberty has become a symbol of the United States and an expression of freedom to people throughout the world. The statue shows Liberty as a goddess draped in the graceful folds of a loose robe. In her uplifted right hand, she holds a glowing torch. She wears a crown with seven spikes that stand for the light of liberty shining on the seven seas and seven continents. With her left arm, she cradles a tablet bearing the date of the Declaration of Independence. A chain that represents *tyranny* (unjust rule) lies broken at her feet.

From the 1890's to the 1920's, many millions of immigrants passed the Statue of Liberty as they entered the United States. For them, the statue was a strong, welcoming figure holding out the promise of freedom and opportunity. The American poet Emma Lazarus expressed this idea of the statue as "Mother of Exiles" in a famous poem written in 1883. This poem, entitled "The New Colossus," was inscribed on a bronze plaque placed on the interior wall of the pedestal of the monument in 1903. The poem reads:

> Not like the brazen giant of Greek fame,
> With conquering limbs astride from land to land;
> Here at our sea-washed, sunset gates shall stand
> A mighty woman with a torch, whose flame
> Is the imprisoned lightning, and her name
> Mother of Exiles. From her beacon-hand
> Glows world-wide welcome; her mild eyes command
> The air-bridged harbor that twin cities frame.
> "Keep, ancient lands, your storied pomp!" cries she
> With silent lips. "Give me your tired, your poor,
> Your huddled masses yearning to breathe free,
> The wretched refuse of your teeming shore.
> Send these, the homeless, tempest-tost to me.
> I lift my lamp beside the golden door!"

Description

The Statue of Liberty stands on Liberty Island, a 12-acre (5-hectare) island in Upper New York Bay. The island lies about $1\frac{1}{2}$ miles (2.4 kilometers) southwest of the tip of Manhattan Island. The island was originally called Bedloe's Island after Isaac Bedloe, a Dutch merchant who owned it in the late 1600's. It came under federal jurisdiction after the Revolutionary War in America (1775-1783). The United States government completed construction of a star-shaped fort on the island in 1811 to defend New York against naval attack. The government later named the installation Fort Wood after Eleazar Wood, a hero of the Battle of Fort Erie during the War of 1812 (1812-1815). The statue's pedestal rises from within the old fort's walls. In 1956, the U.S. Congress changed the island's name to Liberty Island.

The pedestal is an enormous mass of concrete reinforced with steel beams and covered with Connecticut granite. It was designed by Richard Morris Hunt, an American architect famous for designing magnificent mansions. The pedestal is 89 feet (27 meters) tall. It rests on a huge concrete foundation 65 feet (20 meters) tall. When the pedestal was completed in 1886, its foundation was the largest single concrete structure in the world. Stairs and a passenger elevator run up through the interior of the pedestal. Partway up the pedestal stands a row of pillars called a colonnade. A balcony extends around the top of the pedestal.

The statue stands 151 feet 1 inch (46.05 meters) high from its feet to the top of the torch. It weighs 225 tons (204 metric tons). The figure consists of 300 sheets of Norwegian copper fastened together with *rivets* (threadless bolts). This copper skin is only $\frac{3}{32}$ inch (2.4 millimeters) thick. Sculptor Auguste Bartholdi chose pure copper instead of an *alloy* (mixture) because it was lighter and it could be hammered thin. The statue is one of the most celebrated examples of *repoussé* work, a process of shaping metal by hammering it into a mold.

Gustave Eiffel, the French engineer who later built the famous Eiffel Tower in Paris, designed the structural

Facts about the statue

Height, overall (foundation to torch)	305 ft 1 in (92.99 m)
Height of figure (feet to torch)	151 ft 1 in (46.05 m)
Weight, overall	225 tons (204 metric tons)
Weight of copper skin	100 tons (91 metric tons)
Weight of framework	125 tons (113 metric tons)
Number of steps in the statue	162
Date presented to the United States	July 4, 1884
Date dedicated	Oct. 28, 1886

framework that supports the copper covering. The framework for the Statue of Liberty resembles what he later devised for the Eiffel Tower. It consists of a central tower of four vertical iron columns connected by horizontal and diagonal crossbeams. Iron girders leading up and out from the tower support the raised right arm.

Eiffel's strong but flexible design enables the copper skin to react to wind and temperature changes without placing great stress on the statue's framework. Iron bars extend from the central tower to stainless steel "ribs" that follow the shape of the statue's inner surface. These ribs are not rigidly attached to the copper skin. Instead, they fit into special copper brackets connected to the inside of the skin. This indirect method of attaching the copper skin to the ribs enables the statue to absorb the force of the strong winds that often blow across the bay. The attachment method also allows the copper skin to expand and contract as the temperature rises and falls.

Two parallel, spiral stairways wind up through the interior of the statue to the crown on the statue's head. A small elevator runs from the ground level in the base to the shoulder level of the statue. The elevator is used only in emergencies or for maintenance of the statue.

The torch towers 305 feet 1 inch (92.99 meters) above the base of the monument. At night, its gold-covered flame glows with reflected light from 16 powerful lamps

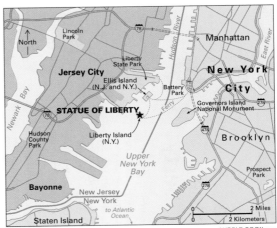

WORLD BOOK map

The Statue of Liberty National Monument includes the statue on Liberty Island and the Ellis Island immigration station. Although the two islands are closer to New Jersey, Liberty Island is officially under the jurisdiction of New York. Most of Ellis Island is under New Jersey's jurisdiction. But the National Park Service actually operates both sites.

The Statue of Liberty

The enormous copper statue stands on Liberty Island in Upper New York Bay. Its official name is *Liberty Enlightening the World.* France gave the statue to the United States in 1884 as a symbol of the ideal of liberty shared by the people of both countries. The statue also became a symbol of the freedom and opportunity for millions of immigrants entering the United States through the immigration station on nearby Ellis Island.

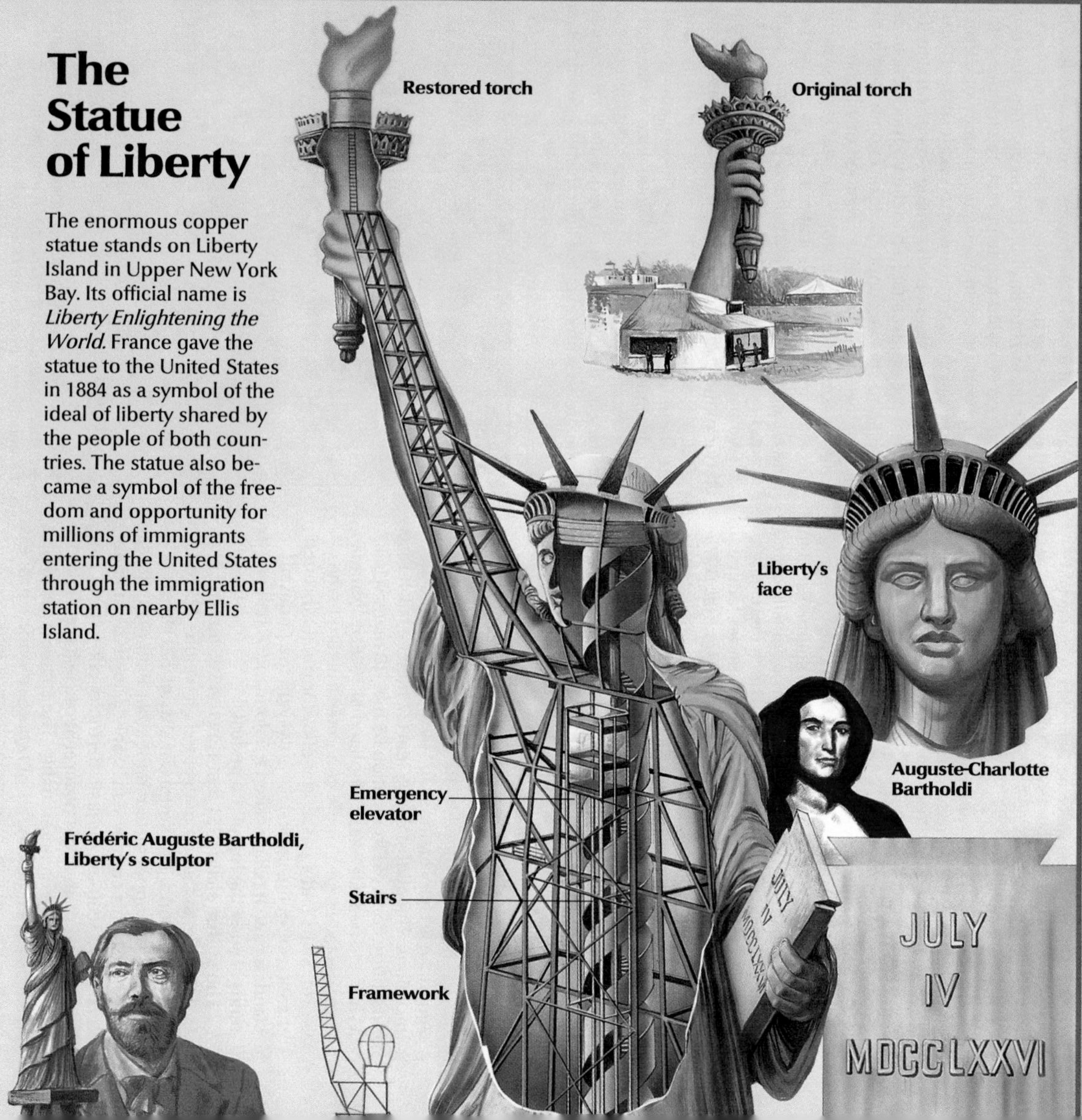

Restored torch

Original torch

Liberty's face

Auguste-Charlotte Bartholdi

JULY
IV
MDCCLXXVI

JULY
IV
MDCCLXXVI

Emergency elevator

Stairs

Framework

Frédéric Auguste Bartholdi, Liberty's sculptor

The restored torch, which follows more faithfully the original design, measures 21 feet (6.4 meters) from bottom to top. At night, the shiny surface of its gilded flame reflects light from 16 powerful electric lamps located around the torch's rim.

The original torch was displayed at the Centennial Exposition in Philadelphia in 1876. For a fee of 50 cents, visitors could climb a ladder inside the arm to the balcony. The money raised in this way was used to help fund the construction of the rest of the statue in Paris.

Liberty's face was modeled after the features of Auguste-Charlotte Bartholdi, the sculptor's mother. The nose is $4\frac{1}{2}$ feet (1.4 meters) long, and each eye is $2\frac{1}{2}$ feet (0.8 meter) across.

Frédéric Auguste Bartholdi, Liberty's sculptor, designed the statue, chose its site, and supervised its construction in Paris. Bartholdi also spent a great deal of time and energy promoting the project in France and the United States. His other works include statues of the French soldier and statesman the Marquis de Lafayette and of George Washington, both in New York City.

Gustave Eiffel, the brilliant French engineer who later created the Eiffel Tower in Paris, designed the framework that supports Liberty's copper skin. The unique iron and steel tower enables the statue to withstand fierce winds.

The pedestal was designed by American architect Richard Morris Hunt. Made of granite and concrete, the pedestal stands 89 feet (27 meters) high on a foundation that is 65 feet (20 meters) tall.

The inspiration for the Statue of Liberty came from Édouard Laboulaye, a French legal scholar. He envisioned the statue as a monument to U.S. independence. The figure of Liberty holds a tablet inscribed with the date of the Declaration of Independence in Roman numerals.

Mother of Exiles is the name given to the statue in "The New Colossus," a poem by the American poet Emma Lazarus. Lazarus wrote the poem in 1883 for a literary auction to raise money for the construction of the pedestal. In the poem, the statue welcomes immigrants seeking freedom and opportunity in the United States. A bronze plaque inscribed with the poem is exhibited in the Statue of Liberty Museum in the pedestal.

A model of the statue stands on a small island in the Seine River, just downstream from the Eiffel Tower in Paris. This model, about one-fourth the size of the original Statue of Liberty, was given to France in 1885 by U.S. citizens living in Paris.

Édouard Laboulaye

Gustave Eiffel designer of Liberty's framework

The pedestal

Pedestal balcony

Elevator to top of pedestal

Emma Lazarus

"Give me your tired, your poor, / Your huddled masses yearning to breathe free...."

Model of Liberty in Paris

Colonnade

WORLD BOOK illustration by Tony Gibbons, Linden Artists Ltd.; critically reviewed by Swanke Hayden Connell Architects arranged around the rim of the torch. Lamps shining up from below illuminate the rest of the statue.

History

Inspiration and preparations. The idea for the statue came from Édouard Laboulaye, a prominent French politician and historian. Laboulaye greatly admired the United States. At a dinner party in 1865, after the end of the American Civil War, he proposed the construction of a joint French and American monument celebrating the ideal of liberty.

In 1871, Frédéric Auguste Bartholdi, Laboulaye's friend and a noted French sculptor, sailed to the United States to seek support for the project. During his trip, Bartholdi selected Bedloe's Island, in Upper New York Bay, as the site for the monument.

Upon returning to France, Bartholdi began designing the statue. In the late 1860's, he had proposed a lighthouse for the newly constructed Suez Canal in Egypt. He had suggested a colossal sculpture of a woman bearing a torch, to be called *Egypt (or Progress) Bringing the Light to Asia*. That project was never built. For the monument to liberty, Bartholdi planned a similar sculpture that would be the largest built since ancient times. He modeled the figure's face after the face of his mother.

In 1875, the French-American Union was established to raise funds and oversee the project. Laboulaye became chairman of the organization in France. The French people donated about $400,000 for the construction of the statue. In 1877, the American Committee was organized in the United States to raise funds needed to build the pedestal. In 1881, the American architect Richard Morris Hunt was selected to design the pedestal. Hunt had studied architecture in Paris at the École des Beaux-Arts, a famous school of fine arts. He had designed many mansions for rich families in New York City and Newport, Rhode Island. He planned a massive pedestal of concrete, granite, and steel that would not detract attention from the statue.

Construction and dedication. Construction of the statue began in 1875 at a workshop in Paris. First, Bartholdi built a small clay model of the figure. Then the sculptor and his assistants built three plaster models, each larger than the previous one. For the final version, workers made a strong wooden framework for each major section of the statue. A layer of plaster was then applied over this wooden framework, forming a full-scale model for each major part of the figure.

Next, carpenters built large wooden forms that followed the shape of the plaster model of the statue. Metalworkers then placed thin sheets of copper in the wooden forms. They bent the copper sheets and hammered them into the shape of the forms. When the hammered copper sheets were removed from the forms, they matched the shape of the plaster model from which the wooden forms had been made.

Designing a framework to support the statue presented a difficult engineering challenge. French engineer Gustave Eiffel devised a support system with a central iron tower. A strong but flexible framework of iron bars would connect the copper skin to the tower. Eiffel's support system was erected outside the Paris workshop where the statue was being made. Then workers attached the sections of copper skin to the framework.

Bartholdi had hoped to present the statue to the United States on July 4, 1876—the centennial of the Declaration of Independence. But a late start and subsequent delays made this impossible. He had completed the

The New York Public Library

Building the enormous statue required several steps. First, full-scale wooden models of sections of the statue were built in a Paris workshop, *above.* Each section was then covered with plaster. Next, carpenters made wooden forms that followed the shape of the plaster. Copper sheets were placed in the forms and hammered into the desired shape. Finally, the copper sheets were attached to the iron support system outside the workshop, *right.*

The Unveiling of the Statue of Liberty (1886), an oil painting on canvas by Edward Moran; Museum of the City of New York

Dedication of the Statue of Liberty on Oct. 28, 1886, was celebrated on land and sea. President Grover Cleveland and representatives of France took part in the ceremonies.

right hand and torch by 1876, however, and sent this section of the statue to the United States. It was displayed at the Centennial Exposition in Philadelphia and later shown in New York City before it was returned to Paris. In 1878, an international exposition in Paris displayed Liberty's head. The people of France officially presented the entire statue to the U.S. minister to France in Paris on July 4, 1884.

Construction of the pedestal began in 1884 but soon came to a halt because of a lack of funds. In March 1885, Joseph Pulitzer, the new publisher of a New York newspaper called *The World,* launched a front-page campaign to raise funds for the completion of the pedestal. By mid-August, about 121,000 people had contributed a total of more than $100,000—enough to finish building the pedestal. Pulitzer listed every contributor's name in his paper, which greatly boosted sales of *The World.* The pedestal was completed in April 1886, at a final cost of about $300,000.

Meanwhile, the statue had been disassembled in Paris and packed in 214 wooden crates for shipment to the United States. The French ship *Isère* carried the statue across the Atlantic Ocean and arrived at New York City on June 17, 1885. Assembly of the statue began soon after the pedestal was completed.

On Oct. 28, 1886, *Liberty Enlightening the World* was dedicated in Upper New York Bay. New York City celebrated with a grand parade, and boats filled the harbor. United States President Grover Cleveland and members of his Cabinet attended the ceremonies. Bartholdi and

representatives of the French government and the French-American Union also participated.

Growth as a symbol. The Statue of Liberty was dedicated in 1886 as a memorial to the alliance between France and the American colonists who fought for independence in the Revolutionary War in America. It also served as a symbol of the friendship between France and the United States. Over the years, however, it has taken on additional meanings. Bartholdi, aware of his statue's commercial potential as an image, had copyrighted it in both France and the United States. But even by 1886, he found himself powerless to enforce his rights. The statue's image came to be used in countless advertisements, campaigns, and trademarks.

During World War I (1914-1918), the Statue of Liberty became a powerful symbol of the United States. The statue's image appeared on posters for war bonds sold by the U.S. Treasury. Sales of these bonds, called *Liberty*

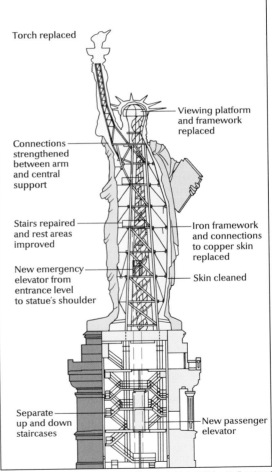

Torch replaced

Viewing platform and framework replaced

Connections strengthened between arm and central support

Stairs repaired and rest areas improved

New emergency elevator from entrance level to statue's shoulder

Iron framework and connections to copper skin replaced

Skin cleaned

Separate up and down staircases

New passenger elevator

WORLD BOOK illustration by Zorica Dabich; critically reviewed by Swanke Hayden Connell Architects

Major repairs and renovation were carried out for the 1986 centennial of the statue. A new flame was built that more faithfully matches the design of Liberty's original flame. The surface of the statue was cleaned, its framework repaired, and new elevators added. The ventilation system was also improved.

Bonds, raised about $15 billion and helped pay for the cost of the war. As the statue gained in popularity, its formal title, *Liberty Enlightening the World,* was replaced in common usage by the name *Statue of Liberty.*

From the 1890's to the 1920's, many millions of immigrants passed the Statue of Liberty as they entered the United States at Ellis Island. Increasingly, newcomers looked upon the statue as a welcoming presence. In 1903, a plaque with Emma Lazarus's poem, "The New Colossus," had been placed on an interior wall of the pedestal of the statue. But it was not until a second wave of immigrants arrived after World War II (1939-1945) that the statue became popularly linked with the poem's image of the "Mother of Exiles."

Repairs and changes. Bartholdi had intended the Statue of Liberty to serve as a lighthouse, with kerosene lamps burning in the crown. Before the statue was dedicated, however, officials decided to light the torch instead. They had electric lights installed that shone through two rows of windows cut in the flame. The federal lighthouse board administered the Statue of Liberty from 1886 to 1902. But the light from the torch was too dim to serve as an effective beacon. In 1902, the U.S. War Department, which administered Fort Wood, took over responsibility for the statue.

In 1916, the War Department installed floodlights at the base of the statue and changed the torch lighting system. Visitors were no longer allowed in the torch or on the torch's observation deck. Hundreds of windows were cut in the copper flame of the torch, and powerful lamps inside lit the torch.

In 1924, the Statue of Liberty became a national monument. The National Park Service took over responsibility for maintaining the statue in 1933.

By the early 1980's, the Statue of Liberty required major repairs. A group of engineers and friends of the monument formed the French-American Committee for Restoration of the Statue of Liberty. In cooperation with the National Park Service, the committee inspected the statue and planned a $30-million restoration project. However, the final cost of the restoration totaled more than twice that amount. Private donations to the Statue of Liberty—Ellis Island Foundation raised the funds. The foundation also set out to raise $160 million to restore the immigration station at Ellis Island.

For two and a half years, while the restoration work went on, aluminum scaffolding hid the statue. During the original assembly process, the workers had used no scaffolding, only ropes. A major part of the restoration was the replacement of the torch. Restorers removed the old torch and fashioned a new one, duplicating Bartholdi's original design and construction methods. The new torch has no windows. Its flame is covered with gold leaf and glows with reflected light. The old torch now stands on display in the lobby of the pedestal.

When the statue was erected in 1886, workers did not attach the statue's head and right arm to the framework in the right place. Instead, they attached the head and arm about 2 feet (60 centimeters) to the right of where Eiffel had planned their attachment. This caused a weak connection at the right shoulder. The restoration strengthened this connection.

The restoration also included replacing the statue's many ribs that link the skin to the frame. The original

© 1984 Peter B. Kaplan

Replacing Liberty's flame required removing the torch from the statue and dismantling the original flame. The windows had been cut in the flame in 1886 and again in 1916.

ribs were made of iron, and many had rusted badly. Restoration workers shaped new stainless steel ribs to replace those made of iron. Workers also replaced many rivets that had pulled loose from the copper skin.

Cleaning crews carefully removed stains from the exterior of the statue but preserved the familiar greenish color of the exposed copper. In fact, the restorers coated any copper they added to match the existing copper. The cleaning also stripped layers of dirt, paint, and tar from the inside.

The Park Service installed a new passenger elevator in the pedestal and added an emergency elevator that reaches to the shoulder level. The restoration also improved the ventilation system and installed a new lighting system. Landscapers redesigned the plantings around the monument to provide a new approach from the ferry landing. New doors were installed at the entrance in the statue's base.

Official celebrations marked the opening of the newly restored Statue of Liberty on July 4, 1986, with President Ronald Reagan and an audience of 2 million people in attendance. Another grand ceremony took place on Oct. 28, 1986—100 years after the original dedication.

The early 2000's. On Sept. 11, 2001, the United States experienced the worst terrorist attacks in the nation's history. About 3,000 people were killed, and the World Trade Center towers in New York City and part of the Pentagon Building, near Washington, D.C., were destroyed (see **September 11 terrorist attacks**). After these attacks, the Statue of Liberty and other important symbols of the United States were closed to the public until increased security measures could be put in place.

© 1984 Peter B. Kaplan

© Dan Cornish, ESTO

Restoring the torch. A plaster model of the torch was used to fashion the new flame, *left.* The restored torch, *right,* measures 21 feet (6.4 meters) from bottom to top. The new flame has no windows and is covered with gold. It is lit at night by 16 powerful lamps around the rim of the torch.

Until September 11, visitors had been free to climb the staircase inside the Statue of Liberty and look out a window from an observation deck in the crown. For three months after the events of September 11, visitors were not allowed on Liberty Island. On Dec. 20, 2001, ferry rides to the island began again. However, the statue itself remained closed while new fire-alarm systems were installed and other changes were made for the protection of visitors and the monument.

Officials reopened the Statue of Liberty in the summer of 2004. Visitors can go inside the pedestal and up to an observation area at the top of the pedestal. There, they can view the harbor, and they can also look up through a glass ceiling to see the statue's interior. Visitors can also view exhibits in the pedestal. The exhibits include full-sized replicas of the statue's head and feet.

Margaret Heilbrun

Related articles in *World Book* include:

Bartholdi, Frédéric A.
Eiffel, Gustave
Ellis Island
Hunt, Richard M.
Lazarus, Emma
Liberty Island

Statue of Liberty National Monument is on Ellis and Liberty islands in New York Harbor. The colossal statue by Frédéric Auguste Bartholdi stands on Liberty Island. The people of France presented it to the United States minister to France in Paris on July 4, 1884. The statue was dedicated in 1886. The site was designated a national monument in 1924. Ellis Island was an immigration station until 1954. It became part of the monument in 1965. See also **Ellis Island; Statue of Liberty**.

Critically reviewed by the National Park Service

Statute. See Law (Civil law systems).

Statute of limitations is a law that sets a time limit for the filing of lawsuits. Statutes of limitations are designed to prevent suits in which the facts of the case have become unclear because of a long lapse of time. Suits filed after the time limit are barred, no matter how just they may be and even if the facts are still clear.

The governments of most independent countries and many states and provinces, including the United States government and each U.S. state, have their own statute of limitations. A single statute may establish many different limitation periods, each for a different kind of claim. Typical statutes set limits of 1 year for cases involving such offenses as libel, slander, and assault and battery; 2 or 3 years for personal injury resulting from negligence; 3, 5, or 10 years for cases involving written contracts; and 20 years for actions to recover land. A few crimes, such as murder, are not subject to statutes of limitations. In most cases, the limitation period begins at the completion of the supposed act or acts upon which the lawsuit is based.   Sherman L. Cohn

Statutory law. See Code.

STD. See Sexually transmitted disease.

Ste. … See Sainte …

Stealth aircraft. See Aircraft, Military (Recent developments); Bomber (History).

Steam is water that has been changed into gas and is at least as hot as 212 °F (100 °C), the boiling point of water. It is colorless and transparent. The white vapor often visible over the spout of a teakettle, in geysers, and in the white gases coming from smokestacks is not actually steam. Instead, this *wet steam* consists of tiny droplets of liquid water. It forms as invisible steam cools. Steam at a temperature much higher than the boiling point is called *superheated steam.*

Steam is produced by boiling water. Although water remains at 100° C until it all turns to steam, it absorbs a large amount of heat in undergoing this change. For example, 100 calories of heat must be absorbed to raise 1 gram (0.04 ounce) of water from the freezing point (0 °C or 32 °F) to the boiling point. But to change the same gram of boiling water into steam takes 540 calories of heat (see **Calorie**). The amount of heat absorbed to change boiling water to steam is called the *heat of vaporization.* This heat is released when the steam cools and changes back to liquid water.

Steam is used as a means of transferring heat from a source, such as the burning of coal, wood, or natural gas, to a place where this energy is needed. For example, steam is used to drive turbines that extract heat from the steam and use some of this energy to turn generators for the production of electricity. Steam is also commonly used in heating homes, in chemical processing, and in sterilizing food.   John P. Chesick

Related articles in *World Book* include:

Boiling point	Steam engine
Electric power (Sources of electric power)	Steamboat
Evaporation	Turbine (Steam turbines)

Steam engine is any engine that is operated by the energy of expanding steam. The steam may be used to power an engine by spinning a turbine or by pushing pistons. Huge turbines drive electric generators and giant ships. Piston steam engines power large pile drivers. In some countries, locomotives with piston steam engines are still used to pull railroad trains. In the United States, diesel locomotives pull most trains.

The development of the steam engine in the 1700's made modern industry possible. Until then, people had to depend on the power of their own muscles or on animal, wind, and water power. One steam engine could do the work of many horses. It could supply the power needed to run all the machines in a factory. A steam locomotive could haul heavy loads of freight great distances in a single day. Steamships provided safe, fast, dependable water transportation.

How steam engines work

A steam engine uses steam to change heat energy into rotary or *reciprocating* (back-and-forth) motion. Most steam engines have a *furnace* in which coal, oil, or some other fuel is burned to produce heat energy. In atomic power plants, a nuclear reactor supplies the heat energy (see **Nuclear energy** [Steam production]).

Every steam engine has a *boiler.* The heat energy produced inside the furnace or reactor changes water into steam inside the boiler. The steam expands, taking up many times the space of the original water. This energy of expansion can be used in two ways: (1) to spin a turbine, or (2) to push a piston back and forth.

Steam turbines produce a rotary motion. A steam turbine has many sets of bladed wheels mounted on a long shaft. The steam enters at one end and spins the bladed wheels as it rushes past them. Steam turbines, which are more efficient than reciprocating steam engines, are used to turn electric generators and ship propellers. See **Turbine** (Steam turbines).

Reciprocating steam engines have pistons that slide back and forth in cylinders. Various valves allow the steam to enter a cylinder and drive a piston first in one direction and then the other before they exhaust the used steam. Steam hammers that drive piles and forge metal require reciprocating motion (see **Forging; Steam hammer**). A locomotive, however, requires rotary motion to turn its wheels. This motion is achieved by attaching a crankshaft to the pistons. In some reciprocating steam engines, called *compound engines,* the steam may flow through two, three, or four cylinders and operate the same number of pistons.

History

Hero, a scientist who lived in Alexandria, Egypt, described the first known steam engine about A.D. 60. The

How a steam engine works

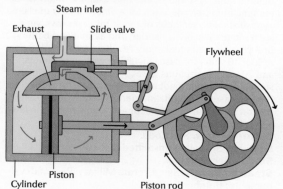

Steam operates the engine by pushing first on one side of the piston and then on the other. A slide valve directs the steam from side to side. In the diagram above, steam enters from the left side of the cylinder and forces the piston to the right. As the piston moves, the piston rod turns the flywheel half a turn.

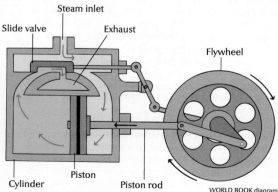

When the piston reaches the right side of the cylinder, *above,* the slide valve moves and directs the steam behind the piston again. The steam forces the piston to the left. The piston rod then pulls the flywheel around to complete one turn. Steam in the left side of the cylinder escapes through the exhaust.

device consisted of a small, hollow globe mounted on a pipe running to a steam kettle. Two L-shaped pipes were fastened to opposite sides of the globe. When steam rushed out of the two L-shaped pipes, it caused the globe to whirl. However, this device performed no useful work. Hundreds of years passed before the first successful steam engines were developed during the 1600's.

The first steam engines operated on the ability of steam to *condense* back into a liquid rather than on its ability to expand. When steam condenses, the liquid takes less space than the steam. If this condensation takes place in a sealed *vessel* (container), it creates within this vessel a *partial vacuum* (a pressure much lower than that of the surrounding atmosphere). Liquids and gases tend to flow from regions of higher pressure to regions of lower pressure, so when a vessel containing a partial vacuum is opened, the vacuum exerts a sucking action on whatever is on the other side of the opening. Thus, the partial vacuum and the surrounding atmosphere act together to perform work.

In 1698, Thomas Savery (1650-1715), an Englishman, patented the first practical steam engine, a pump to drain water from mines. Savery's pump had no moving parts other than valves operated by hand. These were turned to let steam enter a sealed vessel. Cold water was poured on the vessel to chill it and condense the steam. Then a valve was opened so the vacuum in the vessel could suck water up a pipe.

In 1712, Thomas Newcomen (1663-1729), an English tool seller, invented anther steam-engine pump for mines. Newcomen's engine had a large horizontal beam balanced in the middle like a seesaw. A piston that fitted into a cylinder hung from one end of the beam. When steam was let into the cylinder, it forced the piston up, lowering the other end of the beam. Cold water was then sprayed into the cylinder, the steam condensed, and the vacuum sucked the piston down again. This raised the other end of the horizontal beam, which was attached to the piston of a pump in a mine.

Watt's engine. When James Watt began his experiments in 1763, the Newcomen engine was the best known. It set Watt to thinking because it used an enormous quantity of steam and therefore a large amount of fuel. Watt saw that the alternate heating and cooling of the cylinder wasted much heat. He invented an engine in which the condenser and the cylinder were separate. The cylinder remained hot. This arrangement saved three-fourths of the fuel cost because little steam was lost through condensation by entering a cold cylinder.

Watt took out his first patent on a steam engine in 1769 and continued to improve his engines. Perhaps his most important improvement was the use of the *double-action* principle. In engines based on this principle, the steam is used first on one side of the piston, then on the other. Watt also learned to shut off the steam when the cylinder was only partly filled. The steam already in the cylinder completed the piston's stroke. Many people believe Watt invented the steam engine. But he only improved previous designs. He made it practical to use *condensing* engines for work other than pumping.

Modern steam engines. The main improvement in the years after Newcomen and Watt was the development of engines that could use high-pressure steam. Watt never experimented in the use of high-pressure steam because he feared an explosion. The pressures in his engines were not much greater than normal atmospheric pressure, or about 15 pounds per square inch (p.s.i.), or 103 kilopascals. Then, in the late 1700's and early 1800's, Richard Trevithick of England designed and built the first high-pressure steam engines. One of his first engines operated under 30 p.s.i. (207 kilopascals) of pressure. By 1815, Oliver Evans, an American, had built an engine that used 200 p.s.i. (1,379 kilopascals) of pressure. Today, many engines use steam under a pressure of more than 1,000 p.s.i. (6,895 kilopascals).

Other improvements made in steam engines included the development of the compound engine, and the use of *superheated* steam. In superheating, the temperature of the steam is raised above the boiling point at the engine's pressure. This process helps keep the incoming steam from condensing because superheated steam does not cool as quickly as ordinary steam. In the late 1800's, the invention of steam turbines marked another big improvement in steam engines. During the early 1900's, steam turbines replaced piston steam engines in electrical generating stations.　J. P. Hartman

Related articles in *World Book* include:

Bettmann Archive

Thomas Newcomen's steam engine drove a pump that removed water from mines. This bulky engine of the early 1700's turned only a fraction of the energy it received into useful work.

Steam hammer is a power-driven hammer that is used to make heavy forgings. The hammer head is raised by the pressure of steam that is admitted into the lower part of a cylinder connected to the head. When the hammer reaches the desired height, the steam is released and the hammer falls. Steam admitted into the upper part of the cylinder increases the speed of the fall. The speed of the hammer's fall also determines its force. Steam hammers vary in weight from 100 pounds (45 kilograms) to 100 short tons (91 metric tons).

Steam drop hammers are raised like ordinary steam hammers. But they differ from other steam hammers in that they fall by their own weight. The steam hammer was invented by the Scottish engineer and manufacturer James Nasmyth in 1839.   M. O. M. Osman

See also **Forging; Nasmyth, James.**

Steam turbine. See Turbine.

Steamboat is a term used for steam-driven vessels that sail on rivers. The term also refers to the smaller vessels on lakes or in coastal waters of the sea. *Steamship* is used for large vessels such as those on the open sea. In 1787, John Fitch demonstrated the first workable steamboat in the United States. The first financially successful steamboat was Robert Fulton's *Clermont.* In 1807, it steamed the 150 miles (241 kilometers) up the Hudson from New York City to Albany in about 30 hours. Steamboats carried passengers on the great rivers before the development of railroads and other faster or more efficient means of transportation. Steamships are still used in many parts of the world.   Joseph A. Gutierrez, Jr.

Related articles in *World Book* include:
Clermont
Fitch, John
Fulton, Robert (with picture)
Louisiana (picture)
Roosevelt, Nicholas J.
Ship

Steamship. See Ship; Steamboat.

Stearic acid, *stee AR ihk,* is a valuable organic fatty acid that comes from many animal and vegetable fats and oils. It gets its name from a Greek word meaning *tallow.* It is also called *octadecanoic acid.*

Stearic acid is prepared commercially by treating animal fats with water at high temperature and at high pressure. It can also be obtained from the hydrogenation of vegetable oils, including cottonseed oil. Stearic acid is used for softening rubber and in manufacturing wax candles, cosmetics, and soaps.

Stearic acid is a waxy solid that melts at about 70° C. It is a saturated fatty acid and it is found in many saturated fats. Its chemical formula is $CH_3(CH_2)_{16}COOH$.

Roger D. Barry

Steatite. See Soapstone.

Steel. See Iron and steel.

Steele, Sir Richard (1672-1729), an Irish-born writer, created the popular journalistic essays that were published as *The Tatler.* In addition, Steele worked with Joseph Addison in writing the essays published as *The Spectator.*

The Tatler (1709-1711) dealt in a humorous, good-natured way with family life, the theater, and literature. Steele tried to inform and entertain his readers, especially women, and to develop their taste. Steele did most of the writing in *The Tatler,* though Addison helped him. Addison contributed more essays to *The Spectator* (1711-1712) than his friend did. Steele was a frank, warm person, and his essays are livelier than Addison's (see **Addison, Joseph**).

Steele later published several less successful series of essays. He also wrote poems and four comic plays. The first play, *The Funeral* (1701), was very popular. His last play, *The Conscious Lovers* (1722), was the best example of sentimental comedy, which flourished in English drama during the 1700's.

Steamboats were an important method of transportation on waterways throughout the United States during the 1800's and early 1900's. This photograph shows steamboats on the Ohio River in 1911.

Steele was born in Dublin. In 1684, he entered the Charterhouse School in London, where he began his long friendship with Addison, a fellow student. Steele went to Oxford University in 1689, but left without a degree to join the army. He served several terms in Parliament beginning in 1713. He was knighted in 1715.

Gary A. Stringer

Steelworkers of America, United (USWA). See United Steelworkers.

Steen, *stayn,* **Jan,** *yahn* (1626?-1679), was a Dutch painter. He became known for his many lively and often humorous portrayals of everyday life, such as schoolroom activities, festive customs, and holiday celebrations. Many of Steen's colorful compositions are crowded with people of all ages. Some of the figures represent well-known characters from the Dutch popular theater. The artist sometimes included a self-portrait in his paintings. In his many cheerful scenes, people laugh, drink,

Oil painting on canvas (1667); Rijksmuseum, Amsterdam

A Jan Steen painting called *The Feast of St. Nicholas* illustrates the artist's skill at painting lively scenes of everyday life and holiday celebrations in the Netherlands of his day.

eat, play games, and dance. The floor and tables are often littered with discarded objects, such as eggshells. Today, a lively, untidy Dutch home is traditionally called a "Jan Steen household."

Steen also painted works based on proverbs, such as "Easy come, easy go." He often inscribed the proverbs clearly in the paintings. Many of his works try to teach a moral lesson. Steen also painted numerous religious subjects, treating some of the scenes humorously. Steen was born in Leiden. Linda Stone-Ferrier

Steenbok, *STEEN bahk,* also spelled *steinbok,* is a small antelope that lives in southern and east-central Africa. Its name means *brick buck* in Afrikaans and refers to the steenbok's reddish color. Adult steenboks stand about 21 inches (53 centimeters) high at the shoul-

ders and weigh about 24 pounds (11 kilograms). Males have short, straight horns and females are hornless. Steenboks usually live alone in woodlands and remain within a specific area called a *territory.* They can survive without drinking water. Steenboks get the moisture that they need from the grasses and leaves they eat.

Anne Innis Dagg

Scientific classification. The steenbok is a member of the family Bovidae. Its scientific name is *Raphicerus campestris.*

Steeplechasing is a sport in which horses ridden by jockeys race over a series of obstacles on a course 2 to 4 ½ miles (3 to 7.2 kilometers) long. These obstacles include fences and ditches. The steeplechase is also a running event in track and field (see **Track and field** [The steeplechase]).

Steeplechasing is popular in the United Kingdom and several other European countries, as well as in Australia, New Zealand, Japan, and the United States. The most famous steeplechase race is the Grand National, held each March or April at the Aintree race course near Liverpool, England. As many as 40 horses compete (see **Grand National**).

Steeplechasing originated in Ireland in the mid-1700's. According to legend, two men decided to test their horses' speed after a fox hunt. A church steeple was the most visible landmark in the area, so they agreed to "race to yon steeple." Charles T. Colgan

Steer. See Cattle.

Steffens, Lincoln (1866-1936), was an American author, editor, lecturer, and reformer. He was one of a group of writers known as *muckrakers* because their magazine articles during the early 1900's exposed corruption in government, business, and labor. Starting in 1902 with an exposé of crooked political practices in St. Louis, Steffens went on to write about conditions in many U.S. cities and states.

Joseph Lincoln Steffens was born in San Francisco and studied at the University of California and in Europe. He began his career with the *New York Commercial Advertiser.* He soon joined *McClure's Magazine,* and there wrote the articles that made him famous. Later, he wrote for the *American Magazine* and *Everybody's Magazine.* His *Autobiography* (1931) is considered one of the great American autobiographies. Michael Emery

Stegner, Wallace (1909-1993), was an American author best known for his fiction set in the Great Plains and mountains of the American and Canadian West. Stegner won the 1972 Pulitzer Prize for fiction for his novel *Angle of Repose* (1971), a family chronicle partly based on the life of Western novelist Mary Hallock Foote. Another acclaimed Stegner novel is *The Big Rock Candy Mountain* (1943). In it, the restless hero, who resembles Stegner's father, moves his family from place to place in an unsuccessful quest for prosperity.

In addition to his many novels, Stegner wrote short stories, essays, and biographical and historical works. *Beyond the Hundredth Meridian* (1954) is a powerful biography of the geologist, explorer, and naturalist John Wesley Powell. *Wolf Willow* (1962) combines Western history, autobiography, and fiction. Stegner's historical writings include *Mormon Country* (1942) and *The Gathering of Zion: The Story of the Mormon Trail* (1964). Many of his essays were collected in *One Way to Spell Man* (1982). The *Collected Stories of Wallace Stegner* was published in 1990. Stegner was born in Lake Mills, Iowa, on Feb. 18, 1909. He taught at Stanford University. Stegner died on April 13, 1993.   Alan Gribben

Stegosaurus, STEHG uh SAWR uhs, was a large, plant-eating dinosaur that lived about 150 million years ago in what is now the western United States. *Stegosaurus* had two rows of bony plates shaped like huge arrowheads sticking out of its back and tail.

Stegosaurus grew up to 30 feet (9 meters) long and had a heavy, bulky body. The dinosaur's small, narrow head had a beak at the front and teeth farther back. The front legs were less than half as long as the back legs, and so the body sloped down from the hips. At the end of the tail, the animal had pairs of bony spikes, each about 3 feet (0.9 meter) long. *Stegosaurus* could have defended itself by swinging its heavy tail and hitting an attacker with its sharp spikes.

No one really knows why *Stegosaurus* had its bony plates. They may have discouraged attackers or attracted mates. The plates may also have helped *Stegosaurus* warm up and cool down. It could warm up by turning the broad, flat sides of the plates toward the sun to soak up heat. If the dinosaur became too warm, air moving along its back could have cooled blood flowing through the thin plates.   Peter Dodson

See also **Dinosaur** (pictures).

Steichen, STY kuhn, **Edward** (1879-1973), was an American photographer who helped develop photography as a creative art. Early in his career, Steichen was a painter as well as a photographer. He became known for his soft, hazy photographs of landscapes and people.

Greta Garbo, 1928, by Edward Steichen, is a dramatic black-and-white photograph of the famous actress. Steichen produced many sharply defined fashion photographs and portraits.

Reprinted with the permission of Joanna T. Steichen (Museum of Modern Art, New York City)

Steichen was a member of the Photo-Secession, a group formed in 1902 by Alfred Stieglitz, another American photographer. The group promoted photography as a fine art. Steichen helped Stieglitz publish the magazine *Camera Work.* They also worked together in organizing art exhibits in New York City.

During World War I (1914-1918), Steichen organized an aerial photography unit for the United States Army. After the war, he began to take sharp, detailed photographs. From 1923 to 1938, he was chief photographer for two fashion magazines, *Vanity Fair* and *Vogue.* From 1947 to 1962, Steichen directed the photography department of the Museum of Modern Art in New York City. He assembled a famous exhibit there in 1955 called "The Family of Man," which consisted of 503 photographs of people throughout the world.

Edward Steichen was born Eduard Jean Steichen on March 21, 1879, in Luxembourg. His family settled in the United States in 1882. He died on March 25, 1973.
        Charles Hagen

Stein, Gertrude (1874-1946), was an American author who introduced a unique style of writing. She influenced many writers—among them Sherwood Anderson and Ernest Hemingway—who were trying to develop new ways to express themselves.

In her writing style, Stein repeated basic words. Her style is exemplified by her statement, "Rose is a rose is a rose is a rose." Stein felt that such repetition of words helped communicate the feelings that they expressed, as well as depict the natural behavior of a mind in motion. Stein believed that punctuation and difficult words distracted the reader from these feelings, and so she used little punctuation and simple words. In her fiction, she placed more importance on revealing the feelings of the characters than on telling a story.

Stein was born on Feb. 3, 1874, in Allegheny, Pennsylvania, and graduated from Radcliffe College. She studied under the American philosopher William James, and his teaching strongly influenced her writing style.

In 1903, Stein settled in Paris. Her apartment became a gathering place for many writers, musicians, and painters. Stein was one of the first people to realize the importance of various experimental movements in painting. She encouraged such artists as Henri Matisse and Pablo Picasso in their work. She also became an art critic and collector.

Stein's best-known book is *The Autobiography of Alice B. Toklas* (1933). She wrote it about herself from the viewpoint of Alice B. Toklas, who was her friend and secretary. Stein's other works include *Three Lives* (1909), a book of stories; and *Lectures in America* (1935), a collection of lectures on literature, painting, and music. She wrote the text for two operas composed by Virgil Thomson, *Four Saints in Three Acts* (1934) and *The Mother of Us All* (1947). Stein died on July 27, 1946. Stein's *Operas & Plays* was published in 1987.   Arthur M. Saltzman

See also **Lost Generation.**

Additional resources

Curnutt, Kirk, ed. *The Critical Response to Gertrude Stein.* Greenwood, 2000.
Meyer, Steven. *Irresistible Dictation: Gertrude Stein and the Correlations of Writing and Science.* Stanford, 2001.

Steinbeck, John (1902-1968), an American author, won the 1962 Nobel Prize in literature. Steinbeck's best-known fiction sympathetically explores the struggles of poor people. His most famous novel, *The Grapes of Wrath* (1939), won the 1940 Pulitzer Prize. The novel tells the story of the Joads, a poor Oklahoma farming family, who migrate to California in search of a better life during the Great Depression of the 1930's. Steinbeck effectively demonstrated how the struggles of one family mirrored the hardship of the entire nation. Through the inspiration of the labor organizer Jim Casy, the Joads learn that the poor must work together to survive.

Steinbeck set much of his fiction in and around his birthplace of Salinas, California, where he was born on Feb. 27, 1902. His first novel, *Cup of Gold* (1929), is based on the life of Sir Henry Morgan, a famous English pirate of the 1600's. Steinbeck's next work, *The Pastures of Heaven* (1932), is a collection of stories about the people of a farm community near Salinas. In this work, Steinbeck focused on the struggle between human beings and nature. *Tortilla Flat* (1935) deals with migrant workers and poor farmers. *In Dubious Battle* (1936) realistically portrays labor strife in California during the 1930's. *Of Mice and Men* (1937) is a short novel that Steinbeck adapted into a popular play in 1937. It is a tragic story about a physically powerful farmworker with mental retardation and his best friend and protector.

Steinbeck's most ambitious novel is *East of Eden* (1952). It follows three generations of a California family from the 1860's to World War I (1914-1918). The title refers to the family's strife, which parallels the conflict between the Biblical figures of Cain and Abel. Steinbeck's last novel was *The Winter of Our Discontent* (1961). It is a modern story of moral failure.

Steinbeck wrote the humorous novels *Cannery Row* (1945), *The Wayward Bus* (1947), *Sweet Thursday* (1954), and *The Short Reign of Pippin IV* (1957). *Travels with Charley* (1962) describes a cross-country trip with his pet poodle. Other nonfiction was published in *America and Americans* in 2002, after his death. He also wrote screenplays for several films, notably *Viva Zapata!* (1952). Steinbeck died on Dec. 20, 1968.   Barbara M. Perkins

Additional resources

Florence, Donnë. *John Steinbeck.* Enslow, 2000.
Parini, Jay. *John Steinbeck: A Biography.* 1995. Reprint. Henry Holt, 1996.
Simmonds, Roy S. *A Biographical and Critical Introduction of John Steinbeck.* Edwin Mellen Pr., 2000.
Tessitore, John. *John Steinbeck.* Watts, 2001.

Steinberg, Saul (1914-1999), was an artist noted for his humorous and thought-provoking pen-and-ink drawings. His works often involve puns on the meanings of images and words. The majority of Steinberg's drawings have no captions or explanations. In many of Steinberg's drawings, however, figures utter "words" indicated by fantastic forms coming from their mouths.

Two important themes appear in Steinberg's works, identity and transformation. Some of his drawings reproduce such documents as passports. Steinberg also created drawings featuring fingerprints.

Steinberg was born on June 15, 1914, in Rîmnicu Sărat, Romania, and settled in the United States at the age of 28. Much of his work appeared in *The New Yorker* magazine. Steinberg died on May 12, 1999.

Pamela A. Ivinski

Steinbok. See Steenbok.

Steinem, *STYN uhm,* **Gloria** (1934-   ), is a writer and a leading supporter of the women's liberation movement in the United States. She has campaigned for women's rights in employment, politics, and social life. Steinem cofounded *Ms.,* a magazine published and edited by women. The magazine, which first appeared in 1972, features articles that tell women about career opportunities and meaningful ways of life.

From the WORLD BOOK Collection

Saul Steinberg's *Sam's Art* shows how the artist used sharp line and an unusual combination of images to make witty comments about modern life. Much of his work appeared in *The New Yorker* magazine.

In 1971, Steinem helped found the National Women's Political Caucus, which encourages women to seek political office and to work for women's rights laws. That same year, she helped establish the Women's Action Alliance, which fights discrimination against women.

Gloria Steinem was born on March 25, 1934, in Toledo, Ohio. She graduated from Smith College in 1956. She worked as a magazine and television writer before becoming active in the women's liberation movement in 1968. She is the author of *Outrageous Acts and Everyday Rebellions* (1983), a collection of articles; *Marilyn* (1986), a biography of film star Marilyn Monroe; and *Revolution from Within* (1992).   Cynthia Fuchs Epstein

Steiner, Rudolf (1861-1925), was an Austrian-born philosopher who founded a spiritual movement called Anthroposophy. Anthroposophy claims that divine wisdom is naturally accessible and can be used to develop the potential of the individual. Steiner believed that through the pure soul's understanding of divine wisdom, people had the capacity for self-healing. Anthroposophy developed from a system of philosophic and religious thought called Theosophy (see **Theosophy**).

Steiner was born on Feb. 27, 1861, in Kraljevica, near Rijeka, in what is now Croatia. He studied natural science at the University of Vienna and edited the scientific writings of the German Romantic poet Johann von Goethe from 1889 through 1896. Steiner included many ideas of Romanticism, such as its emphasis on imagination and intuition, in Anthroposophy.

In 1902, Steiner became the head of the German section of the Theosophical Society. In 1912, he established the Anthroposophical Society. The next year, he established the society's international headquarters in Dornach, near Basel, Switzerland. Steiner wrote on a wide range of topics, including special education, mental illness, agriculture, religion, and architecture. He died on March 30, 1925.   Susan M. Setta

Steinmetz, Charles Proteus, *STYN mehts, charlz PROH tee uhs* (1865-1923), was a German-born mathematician and engineer. He is best known for his development of a method for solving problems in alternating-current circuits, and for his experiments with artificially created lightning. Despite poverty, political misfortune, and a crippling spinal deformity, Steinmetz became an engineering genius.

Steinmetz established his reputation in the American engineering community in 1892. He established a formula for calculating *hysteresis loss,* a magnetic effect peculiar to alternating current. He was soon invited to join the newly founded General Electric Company, where he spent his career in research on electricity. Out of his home laboratory, which the company funded, came many experimental discoveries and inventions.

Steinmetz was born on April 9, 1865, in Breslau, Germany (now Wrocław, Poland). Fearing arrest for socialist activity, he fled the country in 1888, just before receiving a Ph.D. degree from Breslau University. He came to the United States in 1889. He taught electrical engineering at Union College in Schenectady, New York, and wrote several books on electrical engineering theory. Steinmetz also held political office in Schenectady as a socialist. He died on Oct. 26, 1923.   Ronald R. Kline

Steinway, *STYN way,* **Henry Engelhard** (1797-1871), was a German-born piano maker who founded the

Steinway & Sons piano company. Steinway established his firm in New York City in 1853, about three years after he immigrated to the United States. The pianos are famous for their high quality.

In 1855, Steinway introduced the first successful piano with an interior cast-iron frame and a string arrangement known as the *overstrung scale*. This arrangement had bass strings that stretched diagonally across the other strings. The frame and the diagonal strings greatly improved the sound of a piano. These features have been used in nearly all pianos built since the 1850's.

Steinway was born on Feb. 25, 1797, near Seesen, Germany. His real name was Heinrich Engelhard Steinweg. Although Steinway received training as a cabinetmaker, he started to make pianos in the 1830's. He died on Feb. 7, 1871.   Barry W. Poulson

See also **Piano** (History).

Stella, Frank (1936-   ), is an American artist famous for his abstract paintings. Stella was one of the first painters and theorists of the Minimalist art movement during the 1960's. See **Minimalism.**

Stella first gained recognition with a series of pictures called the *Black Paintings* (1959-1960). The pictures were square or rectangular in shape, and they were composed of rows of stripes that made designs on the canvas. Each stripe or band was the same width as all the others. Stella wanted to dispense with the pictorial drama and complex compositions of the Abstract Expressionist movement that had been popular since the mid-1940's. Stella stated, "What you see is what you see," meaning that there was nothing more to be understood from a painting than its obvious pattern and color.

During the 1960's, Stella experimented with bands of stripes on increasingly complex, geometrically shaped canvases, such as L shapes, pentagons, semicircles, and parallelograms. The *Black Paintings* and the geometrically shaped canvases were painted with commercial house paint. Later in the 1960's, Stella used fluorescent Day-Glo paint. He again was reacting against the complexity of previous abstract painting by creating work that was simpler, more direct, and more logical as the eye moved from one stripe to the next.

Lac Laronge III (1969); Albright-Knox Art Gallery, Buffalo, New York, gift of Seymour H. Knox, 1970

A Frank Stella painting shows the geometric forms and vivid colors that were typical of his style during the middle and late 1960's. Stella made color the primary element of these large works, emphasizing the bright shades through the use of fluorescent paint.

During the 1970's, Stella's paintings changed radically. His work shifted from the carefully painted stripes and geometric shapes of Minimalism. He created three-dimensional sculptures in space, with large planes of industrial metals and fiberglass jutting away from the wall. Stella continued these metallic reliefs into the 2000's.

Frank Philip Stella was born on May 12, 1936, in Malden, Massachusetts. He received a B.A. degree from Princeton University in 1958. A series of his lectures on abstract art was published as *Working Space* (1986).

Michael Plante

Stem is the part of a plant that produces and supports the buds, leaves, flowers, and fruit. Most stems hold the leaves in a position to receive sunlight needed to manufacture food. The stem also carries water and minerals from the roots to the leaves for use in food production. In addition, the sugar made in the leaves is conducted through the stem to other parts of the plant.

All plants have stems except liverworts, hornworts, and mosses. However, the stems of various kinds of plants differ considerably in size and appearance. For example, lettuce plants have extremely short stems that are barely visible under the large leaves. California redwood trees have huge stems—their trunks—that may grow 12 feet (3.7 meters) wide and more than 350 feet (107 meters) high.

Most stems grow erect above the ground. A few kinds grow underground or horizontally along the ground. Buds develop on the stem at points called *nodes* and produce branches, leaves, or flowers. The space between each node is called an *internode.*

Kinds of stems

There are two chief kinds of stems, *herbaceous stems* and *woody stems.* Herbaceous stems have soft tissues, produce small plants, and grow little in diameter. Most herbaceous stems live only one growing season. Such plants as roses, water lilies, alfalfa, and garden peas have herbaceous stems.

Woody stems are hard and thick. They have tough, woody tissues and may live for hundreds of years. Each growing season, woody stems grow in diameter. Trees and shrubs have woody stems.

Herbaceous stems. Herbaceous stems consist only of *primary tissues.* Such tissues develop as a result of cell division at the tip of the stem. Primary tissues include the *epidermis,* the *phloem,* the *xylem,* and the *parenchyma.*

The epidermis tissue forms the outer protective layer of the stem. On many stems, the epidermis has a thin waxy covering that keeps the stem from drying out. Phloem tissue includes living cells that form *sieve tubes,* which carry sugar down from the leaves. Xylem tissue consists mainly of dead tubes that carry water up from the roots to other parts of the plant. Parenchyma is tissue that stores food and other substances for a plant.

Herbaceous stems differ in internal structure among various groups of plants. For example, the stems of the two kinds of flowering plants, *monocotyledons* and *dicotyledons,* have different structures.

Monocotyledonous stems have bundles containing both xylem and phloem scattered throughout the stem. These bundles are surrounded by *ground tissue,* which consists of parenchyma cells.

Dicotyledonous stems have a circular layer of cells, called the *cortex,* that lies directly under the epidermis. The cortex consists mainly of parenchyma cells. Bundles of xylem and phloem are arranged in a ring beneath the cortex, with the xylem toward the inside of each bundle and the phloem toward the outside. A band of cells called the *cambium* runs through the bundles between the xylem and the phloem. The cambium cells make woody stems grow wider. The cambium is not active in most herbaceous stems. The core of a dicotyledonous stem is called the *pith* and consists of parenchyma cells.

Woody stems have primary tissues that resemble those of herbaceous dicotyledonous stems. During their first year of growth, woody stems begin to develop *secondary tissues* through cell division in the cambium and in tissue called the *cork cambium.* The secondary tissues support or replace primary tissues by producing wood and bark. Woody stems increase greatly in diameter over time because they develop new layers of secondary tissues each year. As the stem grows in width, the epidermis and cortex are pushed outward. These tissues break up and fall away.

A cross section of a mature woody stem shows circular layers of the primary and secondary tissues. These layers, from the innermost layer to the outermost layer, are the (1) primary xylem, (2) secondary xylem, (3) cambium, (4) secondary phloem, (5) phelloderm, (6) cork cambium, and (7) cork. Secondary xylem and secondary phloem result from cell division in the cambium. Immature woody stems contain a layer of primary phloem that is destroyed as the plant grows. Phelloderm and cork are produced by cell division in the cork cambium.

Primary xylem and secondary xylem form a core of wood, which makes up the greatest part of a woody stem. During each growing season, the cambium produces a new layer of secondary xylem that can be distinguished from previous layers. The new layers are called *growth rings,* or *annual rings.* The approximate age of a stem can be determined by counting these rings.

Secondary phloem and phelloderm make up the stem's inner bark. As new layers of secondary phloem develop, they press outward and crush the older phloem into the outer bark. The phelloderm is a layer of parenchyma cells that replaces the cortex.

Outer bark consists of cork, a hard dead tissue that replaces the epidermis as a protective covering. Stems develop new layers of cork yearly. However, the older outer bark wears away or splits apart and falls off as the stem grows wider. Therefore, the thickness of the outer bark of most woody stems does not increase greatly through the years. In the outer bark of older stems, bands of cork are alternated with bands of dead phloem that have been pushed outward by the growth of secondary phloem.

Specialized stems

Some stems perform special functions, such as food storage, reproduction, or protection or support of the plant. Such stems do not look like herbaceous or woody stems. However, specialized stems are true stems because they have nodes on their surface.

Certain specialized stems, including *bulbs, corms, rhizomes,* and *tubers,* are underground stems that can store large amounts of food. Bulbs consist of a short

E. R. Degginger   E. R. Degginger   © G. I. Bernard, NHPA

Plant stems can be divided into two kinds, *herbaceous* and *woody.* Herbaceous stems, like those of the orchid, *left,* and the rose, *center,* have soft tissue and produce small plants. A woody stem, like that of the atlas cedar, *right,* has hard, tough tissue. Trees and shrubs have woody stems.

stem surrounded by fleshy leaves. Corms resemble bulbs but have a thicker stem and thinner leaves. Onions and tulips grow from bulbs, and gladiolus plants have corms. Rhizomes are thick stems that grow horizontally. Irises and violets have rhizomes. Tubers are short and swollen. They grow underground at the tip of the stems of such plants as potatoes.

Strawberry plants have *runners,* a kind of specialized stem that is active in reproduction. Runners grow horizontally along the ground and produce new plants at places where their nodes touch the surface. Boston ivy and grape plants have modified stems called *tendrils,* which coil around or stick to objects, providing support for these climbing plants. The *thorns* of the honey locust are modified stems that protect the plant from animals.

How people use stems

Stems provide many important foods. Asparagus, bamboo shoots, onions, and potatoes are stems. Sugar is obtained from stems of sugar cane and sorghum. Sap from stems of maple trees is used to make maple sugar.

Stems are also used to make many products. For example, wood produced by woody stems is used for furniture, paper, and building materials. Such fabrics as burlap and linen are made from fibers in the phloem of some stems. Stems of certain trees provide substances used in rubber and turpentine.   Richard C. Keating

Related articles in *World Book* include:

Bark	Grafting	Rhizome	Tuber
Bulb	Leaf	Root	Wood
Corm	Plant (Stems)	Sap	

The structure of stems   The various kinds of stems differ in structure. Herbaceous stems have only *primary tissues,* which develop from cell division at the tip of the stem. Woody stems have both primary and *secondary tissues.* Secondary tissues cause woody stems to develop wood and bark and to grow thicker. The diagrams below show the internal structures of the herbaceous stems and of a woody stem.

WORLD BOOK diagrams by Marion Pahl

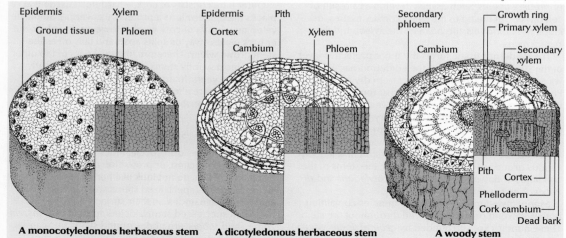

A monocotyledonous herbaceous stem   A dicotyledonous herbaceous stem   A woody stem

Stem cell is a cell with the ability to develop into any of the cell types that make up the tissues and organs of the body. The original cells from which an entire organism develops are stem cells. These cells are also found in adult organs. Stem cells have the ability to divide endlessly, producing more stem cells or other types of cells.

In 1998, scientists succeeded in isolating and growing stem cells from a human embryo in a laboratory. Such stem cells are called *embryonic stem cells.* Scientists think that stem cells can be used to replace damaged tissues and treat diseases, such as Parkinson disease and diabetes, in people.

Early in development, a human embryo consists of a hollow ball of cells called a *blastocyst.* Blastocyst cells divide and eventually develop into all the tissues and organs of a human being, a process called *differentiation.*

Embryonic stem cells can be grown in the laboratory from blastocysts and made to differentiate into nerve, liver, muscle, blood, and other cells. Scientists hope to control the differentiation of the cells to replace cells in diseased or damaged organs in human beings. Learning how to control the differentiation of stem cells will help scientists understand how human tissues and organs develop. It may also lead to new treatments for many diseases, such as cancer. Embryonic stem cells can also be used to test the effects of new drugs without harming animals or people.

In adults, stem cells are found in many places in the body, including the skin, liver, bone marrow, and muscles. In these organs, stem cells remain inactive until they are needed. The stem cells supply each organ with the cells needed to replace damaged or dead cells. Some stem cells in the bone marrow may produce new bone and cartilage cells when needed.

Other bone marrow stem cells divide to produce more stem cells, additional cells called *precursor cells,* and all of the different cells that make up the blood and immune system. Precursor cells have the ability to form many different types of cells, but not more stem cells. Scientists can isolate bone marrow stem cells to use as donor cells in transplants. Adult stem cells, however, are rare and more difficult to detect and isolate. Scientists have also found that damaged stem cells may play a role in the development of certain cancers.

The discovery and isolation of embryonic stem cells has led to debate over whether it is right to use cells taken from human embryos for research. People have expressed concern about using human embryos and collecting some of their cells. Some people who oppose stem cell research consider embryos already to be human beings. The embryos are destroyed in the process of isolating the stem cells. Many people consider it wrong to destroy human embryos, but other people believe that the potential medical benefits of stem cells justify their use.

By 2004, scientists in the United Kingdom and South Korea began producing cloned human embryos to produce stem cells. This process first involves destroying the nucleus of a human egg cell. A nucleus is then removed from another human cell and injected into the egg cell. The egg, with its new nucleus, develops into an embryo with the same genetic makeup as the donor. Some scientists are working to clone human embryos to produce a collection of stem cells that are genetically identical to sick and injured patients. This kind of cloning is known as *therapeutic cloning* because doctors might be able to use the stem cells to replace damaged human tissues and treat diseases.

In the United States, the National Institutes of Health (NIH) sets the standards for medical research that can receive federal funding. The NIH forbids laboratories that receive federal funding from isolating human embryonic stem cells. In 2001, President George W. Bush allowed federal funds to support research on existing supplies of stem cells that had been isolated previously in privately funded laboratories. But in 2006 and 2007, Bush vetoed legislation that would have further eased restrictions on using federal funds for embryonic stem cell research.

A law passed by the California Legislature in 2002 allows laboratories that receive funding from that state to isolate human embryonic stem cells. In 2004, California voters approved a plan to provide state funds for stem cell research. Other states, including Massachusetts and New Jersey, have passed similar laws. Studies of new embryonic stem cells remain ineligible for federal funds.

In 2007, Japanese scientists announced that they had developed a technique to transform skin cells into stem cells in mice. Scientists hope to develop this technique for use with human cells. If they are successful, scientists would no longer need to use embryonic stem cells for research. Meri T. Firpo

See also **Reproduction, Human** (Development of the embryo).

Stendhal, *stehn DAHL* (1783-1842), is the pen name of Marie Henri Beyle, one of the chief figures in the history of the French psychological novel. Stendhal was born on Jan. 23, 1783, in Grenoble. He served in the Napoleonic Wars, and Napoleon I became his hero. Julien Sorel, the hero of Stendhal's masterpiece *The Red and the Black* (1830), lives a life of action and has great ambition, as Napoleon did. Stendhal's other great novel, *The Charterhouse of Parma* (1839), begins with Napoleon's defeat at the Battle of Waterloo and tells of intrigue in Italy. Stendhal died on March 23, 1842.

In his writings, Stendhal was concerned basically with the search for happiness, which he believed could be achieved by the exercise of physical energy and will. Elements of Realism and Romanticism can be found in his work. He usually neglected other aspects of his novels in favor of analyses of the minute, changing emotional states of his characters. Thomas H. Goetz

Stengel, Casey (1890-1975), was one of the most successful managers in baseball history. Stengel's colorful use of language and outgoing personality made him one of the best-known sports celebrities of his time. He managed the New York Yankees from 1949 through 1960. During those 12 seasons, the Yankees won 10 American League pennants and 7 World Series titles.

Stengel had previously managed the Brooklyn Dodgers from 1934 to 1936 and the Boston Braves from 1938 through 1943. He also served as the first manager of the New York Mets from 1962 through 1965.

Charles Dillon Stengel was born on April 30, 1890, in Kansas City, Missouri. He was an outfielder from 1912 to 1925 with Brooklyn, Pittsburgh, Philadelphia, New York, and Boston of the National League. Stengel was elected to the Baseball Hall of Fame in 1966. He died on Sept. 29, 1975. Dave Nightingale

Stepashin, *styeh PAH shihn,* **Sergei Vadimovich,** *sehr GAY vahd DEEM uh vihch* (1952-   ), is a Russian politician who was prime minister briefly in 1999. Stepashin was born on March 2, 1952, on a Soviet military base in Port Arthur (Lüshun), China. He joined the Soviet Union's internal security agency after graduating in 1973 from a political and military school run by the Ministry of Internal Affairs. In 1981, he graduated from the V. I. Lenin Higher Military Political Academy. He earned a doctor of law degree in 1986.

In 1994, Stepashin became head of Russia's Federal Counterintelligence Service (now the Federal Security Service) and helped increase its powers. Also in 1994, he helped direct an invasion of Chechnya, a Russian republic fighting for independence. President Boris N. Yeltsin fired Stepashin in 1995 for his poor handling of a Chechen hostage crisis, which ended in more than 100 deaths. But in 1997, Yeltsin appointed Stepashin justice minister and, a year later, minister of internal affairs. In 1999, Yeltsin elevated Stepashin to prime minister in May, then removed him in August.   Donald J. Raleigh

Stephen (1097?-1154) was a king of England whose reign was so full of strife that it came to be known as *The Anarchy.* Stephen was a son of Adela, daughter of William the Conqueror. He claimed the throne after William's son King Henry I died in 1135. But Henry's daughter Matilda challenged Stephen's claim. Stephen fought Matilda and her supporters for most of his reign. Finally, in 1153, Stephen recognized as his successor Matilda's son Henry. After Stephen died on Oct. 25, 1154, Henry became the first Plantagenet king as Henry II (see **Plantagenet**).   Emily Zack Tabuteau

Stephen, George (1829-1921), was a Canadian financier. He was a founder, and the first president, of the Canadian Pacific Railway. Born in Dufftown, Scotland, on June 5, 1829, he went to Canada in 1850 and became a cloth manufacturer in Montreal. In 1876, Stephen became president of the Bank of Montreal. In 1880, he became a member of the company that built the Canadian Pacific, Canada's first transcontinental railway. He moved to England in 1888 and was made Baron Mount Stephen in 1891. He died on Nov. 29, 1921.   George H. Drury

Stephen, Saint, was the first Christian martyr. He was stoned to death outside Jerusalem after the Crucifixion. His story is told in the Acts of the Apostles 6:1 to 8:2.

Stephen was one of the seven deacons chosen by the apostles to take over certain practical duties in the church in Jerusalem. Stephen was the spokesman for this group. The New Testament portrays him as an inspired figure who speaks on behalf of God. His speech before the Jewish authorities, reported in Acts 7, criticized Israel for being slow to accept any dramatic, unexpected action by God. The speech angered a mob, which stoned him to death. Stephen's feast day is December 26.   Richard A. Edwards

Stephens, Alexander Hamilton (1812-1883), was vice president of the Confederate States during the American Civil War (1861-1865). He was opposed to secession but remained loyal to Georgia when it left the Union in 1861. He was a delegate to the Montgomery Convention, which formed the Confederacy, and he was chosen vice president of the new government. During the war, he often disagreed with Jefferson Davis, the Confederacy's president, on questions of states' rights.

In February 1865, Stephens led an unsuccessful peace commission that met with United States President Abraham Lincoln at Hampton Roads (see **Hampton Roads Conference**). After the war, Stephens was arrested and imprisoned for six months at Fort Warren in Boston Harbor. Georgia elected him to the U.S. Senate in 1866, but Congress refused him his seat. He then wrote *A Constitutional View of the Late War Between the States* (1867-1870). Later, he wrote other books, and he became editor of the Atlanta *Southern Sun* in 1871. Stephens was again elected to Congress in 1872 and served 10 years. He was elected governor of Georgia in 1882 but died on March 4, 1883, a few months after taking office.

Stephens was born near Crawfordville, Georgia, on Feb. 11, 1812. He was educated at the University of Georgia. He had intended to become a minister but changed his mind and studied law instead. In 1834, he was admitted to the bar, and two years later, he became a member of the Georgia state legislature. He opposed vigilance committees, and the "slicking clubs," which were the parent of the Ku Klux Klan. From 1843 to 1859, he served as a congressman from Georgia. He represents Georgia in Statuary Hall in Washington, D.C.   Thomas L. Connelly

Stephens, James (1882?-1950), was an Irish author. He was regarded chiefly as a poet, but his best-known work is the novel *The Crock of Gold* (1912), which gained him his first literary recognition. This story of a leprechaun is an original blend of fantasy, humor, and realism. Like much of Stephens's other writing, *The Crock of Gold* draws on Irish legend and folklore. His fiction and poetry have been described as sentimental, playful, and filled with whimsy. However, modern critics have also praised their subtle irony and satire. Stephens was born into a poor family in Dublin and was educated in an orphanage. He later studied Irish culture, including Gaelic literature and art and Irish mythology. He strongly supported Irish independence from the United Kingdom. His major writings include *Collected Poems* (1926) and the novels *Deirdre* (1923) and *In the Land of Youth* (1924). Stephens died on Dec. 26, 1950.   Janet Egleson Dunleavy

Stephens, John Lloyd (1805-1852), was an American explorer and writer who aroused wide interest in the ancient Maya civilization of Central America. He visited the Maya ruins twice between 1839 and 1841 and wrote two books about his adventures and observations. These books featured beautifully written descriptions of the ruins and became best sellers. Until Stephens's explorations, the Maya civilization had been almost unknown.

Stephens was not trained in archaeology and did little digging at the ruins. But his explorations established the Maya civilization as a subject of archaeological study. His books included excellent illustrations by Frederick Catherwood, an English artist who traveled with him.

Stephens was born in Shrewsbury, New Jersey, on Nov. 28, 1805. He practiced law in New York City. He eventually became involved in politics. President Martin Van Buren assigned him to make a diplomatic trip to Central America. There Stephens saw the Maya ruins for the first time. He died on Oct. 12, 1852.   Richard G. Klein

Stephenson, George (1781-1848), was a British engineer whose inventions helped create the British railroad system. In 1814, while working as chief mechanic at a coal mine in Killingworth, near Newcastle, he completed his first locomotive. This locomotive, *Blucher,* could pull eight coal cars at 4 miles (6 kilometers) per hour. Stephenson helped his son, Robert, build the *Rocket,* a locomotive that became the model for almost all later steam locomotives. He also created such useful inventions as a miner's lamp and an alarm clock. In addition, Stephenson sponsored schools and libraries for miners and their children.

Stephenson built the world's first public railroad, the Stockton and Darlington, which opened in 1825. He then began the complicated task of building the Liverpool and Manchester Railway, using his ideas for tunnels, grading, and bridges to make a level roadbed.

Stephenson was born on June 9, 1781, in Wylam, near Newcastle. He died on Aug. 12, 1848.   John H. White, Jr.

See also **Railroad** (Invention of the locomotive); **Stephenson, Robert.**

Stephenson, Robert (1803-1859), was a British engineer best known for designing and building the *Rocket,* a locomotive that served as the model for almost all later steam locomotives. He is also noted for building bridges, railroads, and viaducts. Stephenson introduced the use of tubular girders in the construction of iron bridges. His best-known bridges are the Britannia Bridge over the Menai Strait in Wales and the Victoria Bridge over the St. Lawrence River in Montreal, Canada.

Stephenson was born on Oct. 16, 1803, at Willington Quay, near Newcastle. In 1823, he joined his father, George, a well-known engineer and inventor, and Edward Pease, a businessman, to form Robert Stephenson & Company, a locomotive manufacturing firm. In 1824, Robert went to Colombia as a mining engineer. He returned to the United Kingdom in 1827 and devoted himself to building railroads and managing the locomotive factory. In 1829, the *Rocket* gained fame for winning the Rainhill Trials, a competition among locomotives held by the Liverpool and Manchester Railway. From 1833 to 1838, Stephenson was chief engineer for the construction of the London and Birmingham Railway, the first

main rail line to enter London. In 1856, he completed Africa's first railroad, in Egypt. Stephenson served in the House of Commons from 1847 until 1859. He died on Oct. 12, 1859.   John H. White, Jr.

See also **Locomotive** (picture); **Rocket** (locomotive); **Stephenson, George.**

Steppe, *stehp,* is an area covered chiefly by short grasses. Steppes are found in dry areas that have hot summers and cold winters. Most steppes receive an average of from 10 to 20 inches (25 to 51 centimeters) of rain a year—less rain than on a prairie, but more than on a desert. In North America, steppes cover most of the Great Plains from northern New Mexico to southern Alberta. In Eurasia, they extend from southwestern Russia into central Asia.

Most steppe plants grow less than 1 foot (30 centimeters) high. They do not grow as dense as the tall grasses of prairies grow. Plants of the North American steppes include blue grama, buffalo grass, cactuses, sagebrush, and spear grass. Before people farmed the steppes, many bison, deer, jack rabbits, prairie dogs, pronghorns, hawks, and owls lived there.

Today, people use steppes to graze livestock and to grow wheat and other crops. Overgrazing, plowing, and excess salts left behind by irrigation waters have harmed some steppes. Strong winds may blow away loose soil after plowing, especially during a drought. A combination of plowing, winds, and drought has caused severe dust storms in the Great Plains region of the United States (see **Dust Bowl**).   René W. Barendregt

Stereophonic sound system is electronic equipment that reproduces lifelike sound, especially music, that seems to have depth and to come from many directions. Such a system is often called a *stereo system* or simply a *stereo.* Stereophonic sound requires the distribution of sound signals through at least two separate channels. The resulting sound provides the illusion of the sound effects of musicians spread out on a stage.

Pioneer

A rack system consists of a compact disc player, phonograph, radio receiver, speakers, and other parts that a manufacturer has wired together and assembled into a frame or cabinet. Rack systems cost less to produce than component systems, which are made up of individual parts purchased separately.

Most stereo systems maintain the greatest possible *fidelity,* or faithfulness, to a sound source while producing little distortion or background noise. Such systems are sometimes called *high-fidelity systems.*

Types of systems

There are several types of stereo systems, including (1) component systems, (2) rack systems, (3) portable systems, and (4) home theater systems.

Component systems are made up of individual *components* (parts) that are purchased separately and connected by the consumer. People can combine different models and types of components to suit their individual needs, budgets, and tastes. In general, component systems provide the best sound quality.

Rack systems consist of units that a manufacturer has wired together and assembled into a frame or cabinet. In the past, such systems were called *consoles.* Rack systems have the same kinds of audio parts as component systems, but the parts cannot be separated. Some preassembled systems are small enough to fit on a table or desk. These are known as *tabletop,* or *desktop, systems.* Rack systems, as well as smaller preassembled systems, cost less to produce than component systems but generally have poorer sound quality.

Portable systems are lightweight preassembled systems that can be carried easily while in use. They are powered by batteries. Some portable systems, popularly called *boom boxes,* have small speakers. Others are small enough to fit into a pocket. Such units are used with headphones.

Home theater systems combine high-quality sound with picture playback. In such systems, components are connected to a large-screen television set. The sound and picture come from a video component, such as a videocassette recorder (VCR) or a DVD player (see **DVD**).

Parts of a stereo system

Every stereo system has three basic types of parts: (1) a program source, (2) an amplifier, and (3) speakers or headphones. Program sources produce electric signals that represent sound waves. Amplifiers strengthen the signals. Speakers and headphones use the amplified signals to duplicate the original sound.

Program sources include tuners, compact disc players, tape decks, and phonographs.

A tuner receives signals broadcast from radio stations and converts them into electric signals. The user adjusts the tuner to receive a radio signal of only a certain *frequency* (vibrations per second). Each radio station broadcasts its program signals at a specific frequency. In many stereo systems, the tuner is combined with the amplifier into a single unit called a *receiver.*

A compact disc (CD) player produces sound that has been recorded on a small, round disc in *digital* (numerical) code. The disc is made of hard plastic with a reflective metal coating. As the player spins the disc, a laser beam shines on the disc. The beam reflects off the disc as pulses of light. The CD player uses the pulses, which correspond to the code on the disc, to create a signal.

CD players are an excellent program source because they produce virtually no background noise. In addition, playback does not damage the disc. As a result, CD's last longer than tapes and records. With a CD player, the user can quickly access any part of the recording. Most models can be programmed so that *tracks* (recordings) can be played in a certain order. A device called a *CD changer* accepts multiple discs for extended playback.

A tape deck, also called a *cassette deck,* records and reproduces sounds on magnetic tape. During recording, electromagnetic heads convert electric signals into varying magnetic patterns on the tape. During playback, heads translate the magnetic patterns into electric signals. Decks typically have electronic noise reduction systems that reduce the faint hissing noise made by the tape during playback.

A phonograph, also called a *record player,* reproduces sound from a plastic disc called a *record.* An *analog* (likeness) of the original sound waves is stored as jagged waves within a spiral groove on the record. The record is placed on a circular *turntable.* As the turntable spins the record, a needle called a *stylus* rides along the groove. The waves in the groove cause the stylus to vibrate. The phonograph converts the vibrations into electric signals.

An amplifier strengthens the electric signals that it receives from the program source. Most home stereo systems use amplifiers with at least 50 watts of power per channel. Stereo systems require at least two amplifier channels. Amplifiers used in portable systems produce only a few watts because of the limitations of battery power and size. In general, amplifiers with greater power provide better sound because distortion is lessened. However, speakers are designed to use only a certain range of power, so the amplifier in a system must be coordinated with the speakers. Too much power from an amplifier can damage speakers.

Amplifiers or receivers serve as the control center of stereo systems. These components may have switches to adjust loudness, *tone,* and the balance of stereophonic sound between the channels. Tone controls alter the strength of sound signals within limited ranges of frequencies. There are three basic types of tone controls— *bass, treble,* and *midrange.* Bass controls cut or boost low-frequency signals, which produce low-pitched sounds. Treble controls control high-frequency signals, which produce high-pitched sounds.

An amplifier may include an *equalizer* to improve sound quality. An equalizer operates similarly to tone controls but can cut or boost more specific ranges of frequencies, thus enabling more precise tone control. An equalizer can correct acoustic problems caused by the speakers or by the shape of the room in which the speakers are kept.

A speaker receives electric signals from the amplifier and converts them into vibrations, which create sound waves. Stereophonic systems require at least two speakers for reproducing sound—one for each channel of recorded sound. Because it is difficult for one speaker element to reproduce the entire range of frequencies, high-quality units contain three speakers, one each for bass, midrange, and treble.

Speakers in component systems are mounted in wooden or plastic cabinets. The size and shape of the cabinet affects the tone quality of the sound made by the speakers. The location of speakers in a room also affects the quality of the sound they produce.

Headphones, like speakers, change electric signals

into sound waves. Headphones, also called *earphones,* typically have two cushioned earpieces connected by a band. The device fits over the head and ears for private listening. Each earpiece carries one sound channel.

History

Stereophonic phonographs and discs first appeared on the market in 1958. Previously, records and phonographs were *monaural,* or *monophonic*—that is, they reproduced sound from only one channel. Radio stations began broadcasting programs in stereo on a large scale in 1961. By the late 1960's, almost all new recorded music was stereophonic. Until the mid-1980's, phonographs were the most common program source. Since that time, however, many people have replaced their records with tapes or compact discs.   Ken C. Pohlmann

Related articles in *World Book* include:

Compact disc	Headphones	Radio	Tape recorder
DVD	Phonograph	Speaker	

Stereoscope, *STEHR ee uh SKOHP,* is an optical viewing device that makes photographs seem to have three dimensions. An ordinary camera sees things only in a flat plane, and not in the round, the way our eyes usually see things. But a camera with two lenses set a small distance apart can work like our eyes. It can be used to take two photographs of an object at the same time. These photographs are then mounted side by side and viewed through a combination of lenses and prisms inside the stereoscope. To the user, the two photographs seem to blend into a single three-dimensional image.

If two stereo photographs are mounted side by side, a person can view them without prisms or lenses and still see an image that appears to have depth. However, viewing images in this way may cause eyestrain.

During the late 1800's and early 1900's, many families enjoyed looking at pictures with a stereoscope, sometimes called a *stereopticon.* The old-style stereoscope consisted of a rack and handle, special slides, and a set of lenses or prisms. The present-day stereoscope is a plastic box with two viewing holes. One popular type, a toy called the View-Master, has picture slides mounted in a cardboard or plastic disk.

Today, mapmakers and geographers use stereoscopes in aerial surveys to map out land elevations. The images are produced from photographs of the ground taken at two slightly different times from a camera mounted in the belly of an airplane. Botanists and forest rangers also use stereo images and viewers to help them identify plants and trees. Astronomers use a special type of stereoscope for finding comets, asteroids, and other heavenly bodies.   Jack Feinberg

See also **Eye** (Depth perception); **Camera** (Stereo cameras); **Polarized light.**

Stereotyping, *STEHR ee uh typ ihng,* is the method of making metal plates for use in printing. In the process, workers set the type and lock it into a steel *chase* (frame). Others brush the face of the type with a thin coating of oil. A sheet of thick, composite paper, called *flong,* is laid on the type and beaten or pressed tightly against it. This sheet takes an impression of the face of the type or *cut* (picture) in the frame. The paper mold thus formed then goes into an oven and bakes until it becomes hard and dry. This mold, known as a *matrix* or *mat,* is placed in a box faceup. A worker pours melted

stereotype metal, made up of tin, antimony, and lead, over the mold. The metal hardens at once, forming a solid plate, and the page is printed from this plate.

Introduction of the stereotype process helped speed up newspaper printing. The stereotype plates used on small presses were flat. Those used on rotary presses for newspapers were in the form of half cylinders. It took only about 15 minutes to make stereotype plates, and they were inexpensive compared to other printing plates. One matrix could produce a number of plates. Today, stereotyping has been replaced by offset lithography for most general printing in the United States (see **Printing** [Offset lithography]). But it is still used in less developed countries.   J. C. McCracken

See also **Type.**

Stereotyping is the act of holding or promoting generalized and oversimplified beliefs about members of a group. These beliefs—which commonly involve personality traits, physical appearance, and types of behavior—are called *stereotypes.* In many cases, the use of stereotypes is unfair and harmful. Some people hold negative stereotypes about others based on such characteristics as ethnicity, lifestyle, race, sex, and sexual orientation. Common negative stereotypes include the mistaken beliefs that women are overly emotional and that African Americans are lazy.

Whenever individuals are organized into groups, people expect group members to share some common qualities. For example, an observer might classify basketball players as tall or children as lively. Such general observations become stereotypes when they are exaggerated and applied to all members of a group without regard to individual characteristics. Stereotypes can provide a basis for *prejudice*—that is, unfair negative attitudes or feelings directed at members of a group.

Numerous cultural, sociological, and psychological factors affect the creation and maintenance of stereotypes. Television programs, motion pictures, and other mass media presentations can influence popular beliefs about certain groups. Families and peer groups are probably the most important sources of children's attitudes toward other groups.   Kenneth B. Nunn

See also **Prejudice; Racism.**

Sterility, *stuh RIHL uh tee,* refers to the inability to reproduce. It applies to all forms of life, from microorganisms to higher plants, animals, and human beings.

Some antibiotics, such as penicillin, interfere with the reproductive powers of disease-producing bacteria. As a result, the number of bacteria remain low, and the body is able to overcome disease.

A plant may be sterile because of imperfectly developed reproductive organs. If the stamens and pistils are imperfect or absent, the plant cannot reproduce. Sterility in animals results if the reproductive organs do not develop properly. Certain hybrid animals, such as the mule, cannot reproduce.

Sterility in human beings may have several causes. It may result from defects in the structure of the reproductive organs. Certain diseases affect the reproductive organs and may cause sterility. Improper balance of the hormones produced by the pituitary gland, the thyroid gland, the adrenal glands, and the *gonads* (sex glands) may result in failure to produce eggs or sperm. Human beings may intentionally become sterile by undergoing surgical sterilization (see **Birth control** [Methods of birth control]). P. Landis Keyes

See also **Infertility**.

Sterilization, STEHR *uh luh ZAY shuhn,* in medicine and bacteriology, means the killing of germs. Germ killing helps to prevent infection and the spread of disease. Doctors and dentists sterilize their tools before they touch the human body. The bandages and many of the medicines we buy are sterilized before they are packed. Sterilization has been practiced only since the late 1800's. The English surgeon Joseph Lister introduced antiseptic, germ-killing methods into surgery.

A sterile object has no living germs on it. Proper sterilization is done by fire, steam, heated air, radiation, or certain chemicals. Steam and heated air are the best, for they leave no foreign matter on the sterilized object. Fire is commonly used in the home to sterilize a needle with which to prick a blister or remove a splinter. Steam cabinets are often used to sterilize medical instruments. Heated dry air is used to sterilize oily medicines.

The method of sterilization chosen depends upon the type of germ to be killed. For example, passing a solution through a fine filter will eliminate bacteria from the solution. However, many viruses are small enough to pass through such filters. Bacterial spores, unlike bacteria, usually can withstand boiling in water. But such spores can be killed by high-pressure steam. Some viruses, including the virus that causes AIDS, can be killed by heating at 113 °F (45 °C). However, certain *slow viruses* and viruslike germs called *viroids* can be killed only by much more extensive treatments.

The word *sterilization* is also used to refer to surgical procedures that prevent a female from becoming pregnant or a male from fathering a child. For information on such surgical sterilizations, see **Birth control** (Methods of birth control). David Schlessinger

See also **Disinfectant; Food preservation** (Canning); **Pasteurization.**

Sterling. See **Pound.**

Stern, Isaac (1920-2001), was an outstanding American violinist. He performed and recorded violin concertos from nearly all musical periods with virtually every major orchestra in the world. Stern also gained praise for his performances in chamber music, especially with pianist Eugene Istomin and cellist Leonard Rose. Stern helped in the career development of numerous violinists, including Itzhak Perlman, Pinchas Zukerman, and Schlomo Mintz. In 1960, Stern led a successful movement to save Carnegie Hall in New York City from demolition. He became president of the Carnegie Hall Corporation, which is responsible for cultural programs at Carnegie Hall. Stern's influence helped create the National Endowment for the Arts in 1964.

Stern was born on Oct. 21, 1920, in Kremenets, near Ternopol, in Ukraine and was brought to the United States when he was about 1 year old. He made his performing debut with the San Francisco Symphony Orchestra at the age of 15 and earned his first major recognition with a recital at Carnegie Hall in 1943. He wrote an autobiography, *My First 79 Years* (1999). Stephen Clapp

Sterne, Laurence (1713-1768), was an English clergyman who suddenly became famous as the author of *The Life and Opinions of Tristram Shandy, Gentleman* (1760-1767). *Tristram Shandy* is an unconventional novel of conversations and reminiscences rather than action. Tristram is only about 5 years old when the story ends. This is partly because the work was never finished, but mainly because Sterne was more interested in other characters—Tristram's family, their friends and servants. The book is lively and extremely witty. Its popularity reflects the growing regard for humor and laughter and for feeling and sentiment during that period. Tristram's Uncle Toby, the simple and good-hearted soldier, climaxed a long line of lovable but comic eccentrics in the literature of the 1700's.

The novel's conversations and incidents do not follow a straightforward time sequence. Sterne was influenced by the philosopher John Locke. Locke thought that at birth the mind is a blank tablet upon which ideas take form only through the association of experiences gained through our senses. Locke observed that we may sometimes associate ideas that are logically unrelated. Such illogical chains of ideas form the basis of the narrative development in *Tristram Shandy.* Although readers may at first be confused by the way Sterne jumps from one idea to another, the book eventually may seem closer to our own experience of life than more conventional novels. Sterne's method in *Tristram Shandy* anticipates the stream-of-consciousness novels of James Joyce and Virginia Woolf.

Sterne was born on Nov. 24, 1713, in Clonmel, Ireland. He suffered from tuberculosis and made trips to the milder climate of southern France for his health. These trips inspired *A Sentimental Journey Through France and Italy* (1768). Gary A. Stringer

Steroid, *STEHR oyd,* is any of a class of chemical compounds important in chemistry, biology, and medicine. Steroids play a key role in the body processes of living things. They are produced naturally by plants and animals. They are also made commercially. Steroids include sterols, such as cholesterol; bile acids from the liver; adrenal hormones; sex hormones; and poisons in certain toads (see **Cholesterol; Liver**).

All steroids are alike in basic chemical structure. But each steroid has a slightly different arrangement of atoms. Because of this difference, steroids have different effects on living things. Also, individual organisms may react differently to the same steroid.

Steroids influence body *metabolism,* the process by which the body changes food into energy and living tissue. In plants, they help form certain vitamins and other important substances. Some steroids are used in medicine to treat diseases. *Digitalis,* a plant steroid, is often used to treat heart failure (see **Digitalis**).

The sex steroids *progesterone* and *estrogens* are primarily secreted by the *ovaries* (female sex organs). Progesterone helps regulate menstruation and maintain pregnancy. Estrogens are essential for female sexual development, including the development of breasts. Birth control pills contain powerful synthetic forms of progesterone. Some birth control pills also contain estrogens (see **Birth control**).

Androgens are sex steroids chiefly produced by the *testes* (male sex glands). Androgens are responsible for maturation of the male's sex organs and his beard, large muscles, and deep voice. Small amounts of androgens are also secreted by the sex glands in females. Similarly, male sex glands produce small amounts of estrogens.

Anabolic steroids are produced by chemical methods from the male hormone *testosterone.* Some athletes use anabolic steroids because the drugs increase strength and body weight. But this use is considered unethical. The use of these drugs can also cause many undesirable effects. These effects include liver damage, high blood pressure, aggressive behavior, and the appearance of male physical characteristics in females. The use of anabolic steroids in most sports competition is prohibited.

The adrenal steroids. The *cortex* (outer layer) of the adrenal gland produces *cortisol, corticosterone*, and small amounts of *cortisone.* These steroids help regulate protein and carbohydrate metabolism. *Aldosterone,* another steroid from the adrenal cortex, influences mineral and water balance of the body.

Doctors use adrenal steroids to reduce *inflammation* (redness and swelling) and to provide treatment for arthritis, allergies, and other diseases. If the adrenal glands are surgically removed, a person will die unless treated with steroids.

A part of the brain called the *hypothalamus* regulates the steroid secretion of the ovaries, testes, and adrenal glands. The hypothalamus controls the release of the protein hormones *gonadotropins* and *adrenocorticotropic hormone* (ACTH) from the pituitary gland. The hormones cause the ovaries, testes, and adrenal glands to release their steroids. The steroids then affect other body parts and characteristics.   Eugene M. Johnson, Jr.

See also **Hormone; Progesterone; Testosterone.**

Stethoscope, *STEHTH uh skohp,* is a device physicians use to hear the sounds produced by certain organs of the body, such as the heart, lungs, intestines, veins, and arteries. The stethoscope picks up the sounds made by these organs and excludes other sounds.

The stethoscope consists of a body contact piece, which is placed against the body of the patient, and earpieces, which are placed in the ears of the physician. Hollow rubber tubing connects the body contact piece to the earpieces. Physicians use either a bell, diaphragm, or combination bell-diaphragm body contact piece. The

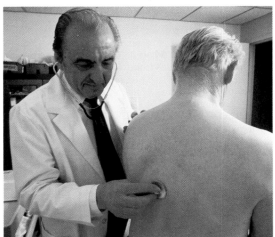

© Michael Geissinger, Comstock

A stethoscope enables a physician to hear sounds made by the heart, the lungs, and certain other organs. In this photograph, a doctor uses a stethoscope to examine a patient.

bell type of contact piece picks up low-pitched sounds. The diaphragm type picks up high-pitched sounds.

Before the invention of the stethoscope, the physician placed an ear next to the patient's body to hear the sounds made by the organs. René Laënnec, a French physician, made the first stethoscope from a hollow wooden tube in 1816.   Edward J. Shahady

See also **Laënnec, René T. H.**

Stetson, John Batterson (1830-1906), was an American hat manufacturer and philanthropist. He went West in the early 1860's to regain his health, and used his knowledge of Western tastes and hatmaking to design his famous ten-gallon hat. He established a factory in Philadelphia in 1865, and became the leading hat manufacturer in America. Although he had little formal education, Stetson endowed a small academy in De Land, Florida, which later became Stetson University. He was born on May 5, 1830, in Orange, New Jersey.

John N. Ingham

Stettin. See Szczecin.

Stettinius, *stuh TIHN ee uhs,* **Edward Riley, Jr.** (1900-1949), was secretary of state under Presidents Franklin D. Roosevelt and Harry S. Truman. When the national defense program was set up in 1940, Stettinius held key posts. From 1941 to 1943, he was the Lend-Lease administrator (see **Lend-Lease**). He became secretary of state in 1944 and participated in the Dumbarton Oaks Conference in 1944 and the Yalta Conference in 1945. He led the United States delegation to the 1945 San Francisco Conference, which organized the United Nations (UN). After the conference, Stettinius resigned as secretary of state so that Truman could appoint him head of the U.S. delegation to the UN. He became rector of the University of Virginia in 1946.

Stettinius was born on Oct. 22, 1900, in Chicago and attended the University of Virginia. In 1938, he took the post of chairman of the board of United States Steel Corporation. He died on Oct. 31, 1949.   Alonzo L. Hamby

Steuben, *STOO buhn* or *SHTOY buhn,* **Baron von** (1730-1794), was a Prussian soldier who served in the American army during the Revolutionary War in America (1775-1783). He became responsible for military training and made the army an effective fighting force.

Steuben was born on Sept. 17, 1730, in Magdeburg, Prussia. His given name was Friedrich Wilhelm Ludolf Gerhard Augustin. He served as a captain in the Prussian Army during the Seven Years' War (1756-1763). He came to the American Colonies in 1777 and offered to help the Americans defeat Britain. George Washington, commander of the American army, made Steuben a major general and asked him to direct the army's training.

Steuben quickly turned the undisciplined troops into a superb army. He personally drilled the soldiers in the basic principles of marching and of fighting with muskets and bayonets. He also commanded some American forces and fought the British at Monmouth and Yorktown. After the war, he enjoyed a comfortable retirement in New York state.   Charles W. Ingrao

Stevens, John (1749-1838), was an American engineer who urged the use of railroads rather than canals for transportation in the United States. In 1815, he received a charter to build a railroad from Trenton to New Brunswick in New Jersey. He designed and built the first U.S. steam locomotive in 1825. With his sons, Stevens set up the Camden and Amboy Railroad and Transportation Company in 1830. He also helped develop a railroad from Philadelphia to Columbia, Pennsylvania, that later became part of the Pennsylvania Railroad.

Stevens was born in New York City. He graduated from King's College (now Columbia University). At first, he was more interested in steamboats than in railroads. His ship, the *Phoenix,* which traveled from New York City to Philadelphia in 1809, was the first steamship to make an ocean voyage.   George H. Drury

Stevens, John Paul (1920-   ), became an associate justice of the Supreme Court of the United States in 1975. President Gerald R. Ford chose him to replace Justice William O. Douglas, who retired.

On the Supreme Court, Stevens has increasingly taken liberal positions on a variety of issues. At first, he opposed *affirmative-action programs,* which are designed to remedy the effects of past discrimination against such groups as women and minorities. But later, he voted to uphold such programs. He has also supported the 1973 Supreme Court decision in the case of *Roe v. Wade.* In this case, the court ruled that, except under certain conditions, the states could not prohibit a woman's right to have an abortion during the first six months of pregnancy (see *Roe v. Wade*).

Stevens was born on April 20, 1920, in Chicago. He graduated from the University of Chicago in 1941 and from Northwestern University School of Law in 1947. In 1947 and 1948, he served as a law clerk to U.S. Supreme Court Justice Wiley B. Rutledge. Stevens began practicing law in Chicago in 1948. In 1970, President Richard M. Nixon appointed him to the U.S. Court of Appeals for the Seventh Circuit.   Dennis J. Hutchinson

See also **Supreme Court of the U.S.** (picture).

Stevens, Robert Livingston (1787-1856), an American engineer, designed and built more than 20 steam-powered ships. He aimed always for faster, safer, and more efficient vessels.

Stevens was born on Oct. 18, 1787, in Hoboken, New Jersey. His father, John Stevens, pioneered in developing steam transportation in the United States. Stevens helped his father build the *Phoenix,* the first steamship to make an ocean voyage in 1809. In 1830, Stevens went to England to study steam locomotives and purchase iron rails. He bought the English locomotive *John Bull* for use on the Camden and Amboy Railroad in New Jersey. He also developed a safer type of railroad track, the T-rail, and invented a hook-headed spike to attach the rail to the wooden ties. In 1844, Stevens designed the *Maria,* the fastest sailing ship of its time.   J. P. Hartman

Stevens, Thaddeus (1792-1868), of Pennsylvania was a leader of the Radical Republicans, a powerful group of Northern congressmen in the United States House of Representatives. The Radicals wanted strict government protection for the rights of blacks and firm treatment of the South after the Civil War (1861-1865).

Stevens served in the House from 1849 to 1853 and from 1859 to 1868. He was first elected as a Whig, but he joined the Republican Party in the mid-1850's.

During the Civil War, Stevens pressed for freeing the slaves. He also served as chairman of the House Ways and Means Committee, which played a key role in financing the North's war effort. After the war, he urged federal control of the South until a new leadership

could emerge there and until the freed slaves were protected by law and gained land ownership. Stevens believed the government should seize land from former slaveowners and give it to the former slaves. He helped form, and served on, the Joint Committee on Reconstruction, which formulated a plan for dealing with the defeated South.

Stevens strongly opposed President Andrew Johnson because of Johnson's mild policies toward the South. He served on the House committee that recommended impeachment and voted in 1868 to send the president to trial in the Senate, where he was acquitted by one vote.

Stevens was born April 4, 1792, in Danville, Vermont. He began to practice law in Gettysburg, Pennsylvania, in 1816. He often defended fugitive slaves without charging a fee. Stevens served in Pennsylvania's legislature several times in the 1830's and 1840's.   Michael Perman

See also **Johnson, Andrew** (Plans for Reconstruction); **Reconstruction** (The Radicals and the Moderates).

Stevens, Wallace (1879-1955), was an American poet. Stevens had a unique writing style. Although his language is often difficult and abstract, his poems also have an extraordinary richness of imagery and sound. They are playful, colorful, and philosophical.

Stevens's major theme is the relationship between the mind and physical reality. In his view, people constantly face the disorder of the world and the certainty of their own death. They are rescued from this potentially tragic situation by the use of imagination. Imagination can give meaning to the confusion of reality and can also discover beauty in nature and joy in the face of death. Because Stevens believed that only the imagination can make sense of the universe, he thought that "God and the imagination are one." Stevens explored the virtues of the imaginative life in such brief poems as "Sunday Morning" (1915), "The Emperor of Ice-Cream" (1922), and "The Idea of Order at Key West" (1934). He dealt with the same theme in such longer works as "Notes toward a Supreme Fiction" (1942) and "Esthétique du Mal" (1944).

Stevens was born on Oct. 2, 1879, in Reading, Pennsylvania. He wrote his poetry while also succeeding as a lawyer and later an insurance executive. Stevens's *Collected Poems* (1954) won the 1955 Pulitzer Prize. His *Collected Poetry and Prose* was published in 1997, after his death. See also **Poetry** (Imagery).   Steven Gould Axelrod

Stevenson, Adlai Ewing (1835-1914), was vice president of the United States from 1893 to 1897 under President Grover Cleveland. He was the grandfather of Adlai E. Stevenson, the Democratic presidential nominee in 1952 and 1956.

Most members of the Cleveland administration stood for a national currency backed by gold. But Stevenson supported a policy known as *free silver,* which called for coining unlimited amounts of silver. Largely for this reason, the public was never informed when Cleveland had emergency surgery during the business panic

Chicago Historical Society
**Adlai E. Stevenson
(1835-1914)**

of 1893. His advisers feared the panic might increase if there seemed to be any possibility of Stevenson succeeding to the presidency. Stevenson was nominated for the vice presidency again in 1900 as the running mate of William Jennings Bryan. But the Democrats lost to William McKinley and Theodore Roosevelt.

Stevenson served in the House of Representatives for two terms. He became the first U.S. assistant postmaster general in 1885. Stevenson was born on Oct. 12, 1835, in Christian County, Kentucky, and attended Illinois Wesleyan University.   Edward A. Lukes-Lukaszewski

Stevenson, Adlai Ewing (1900-1965), was the Democratic nominee for president of the United States in 1952 and 1956. Dwight D. Eisenhower defeated him both times. Stevenson's running mates were John J. Sparkman in 1952 and Estes Kefauver in 1956. Stevenson served as U.S. ambassador to the United Nations from 1961 until his death.

Stevenson was a grandson of Vice President Adlai E. Stevenson. He was born in Los Angeles on Feb. 5, 1900. After graduating from Princeton University, he studied law at Harvard and Northwestern universities. He worked on his family newspaper, the *Bloomington* (Illinois) *Daily Pantagraph,* and practiced law in Chicago. In 1933 and 1934, Stevenson held

**Adlai E. Stevenson
(1900-1965)**

his first public office, serving as special counsel to the Agricultural Adjustment Administration. During World War II (1939-1945), Stevenson served as a special assistant to Secretary of the Navy Frank Knox and led a U.S. mission on occupation policies in Italy. After the war, he became an alternate delegate to the United Nations.

In 1948, Stevenson was elected governor of Illinois by the largest plurality in the state's history. He was considered by many for his party's 1952 presidential nomination, but he refused to campaign. Nevertheless, the party nominated him after a dramatic convention struggle. During his campaigns, he became noted for his wit, speaking ability, and the high literary quality of his speeches. In 1952, his book *Major Campaign Speeches* was published. He also wrote and published *Call to Greatness* (1954), *What I Think* (1956), *Friends and Enemies* (1959), *Putting First Things First* (1960), and *Looking Outward: Years of Crisis at the United Nations* (1963). His son Adlai III represented Illinois in the U.S. Senate from 1970 to 1981.   James I. Lengle

Stevenson, Robert (1772-1850), was a Scottish civil engineer noted as a builder of lighthouses. He built 23 lighthouses along the coast of Britain and invented a flashing light with which they guided ships. His most noted work is the Bell Rock Lighthouse, which he designed and built with John Rennie. The lighthouse stands in the North Sea near Dundee, Scotland. Stevenson was born June 8, 1772, in Glasgow. The author Robert Louis Stevenson was his grandson.   Robert L. Scheina

Stevenson, Robert Louis (1850-1894), was a Scottish novelist, essayist, and poet who became one of the

world's most popular writers. His exciting adventure stories *Treasure Island* and *Kidnapped* have long appealed to both children and adults. His essays and travel books are considered models of sophisticated English prose style, while the tender, simple poems collected in *A Child's Garden of Verses* are masterpieces of children's literature.

Stevenson's life was as varied and fascinating as his work. He fought illness constantly, writing many of his best books from a sickbed. He traveled widely for his health and to learn about people. He spent his last years on the South Sea island of Samoa, and the Samoans honored him with the title *Tusitala* (Teller of Tales).

Stevenson's life

Early life. Stevenson was born on Nov. 13, 1850, in Edinburgh, Scotland. His full name was Robert Lewis Balfour Stevenson. He later adopted the name Robert Louis Stevenson. He was a sickly boy who suffered from a lung disease that later developed into tuberculosis. Young Stevenson loved the open air, the sea, and adventure, but he also loved to read. He preferred literature and history, especially Scottish history, which supplied the background for many of his novels.

When he was 17, Stevenson entered Edinburgh University to study engineering, his father's profession. Stevenson's father, Thomas Stevenson (1818-1887), designed the Stevenson Screen in 1864. This device was used to house meteorological thermometers. Stevenson himself gave up engineering for law. He passed his bar examination in 1875, but he did not enjoy law and never practiced it. His real love was writing.

Stevenson began publishing short stories and essays in the mid-1870's. His first book, *An Inland Voyage,* appeared in 1878. It relates his experiences during a canoeing trip through France and Belgium. In *Travels with a Donkey in the Cévennes* (1879), Stevenson describes a walking tour through part of France. Although both books reveal Stevenson's inexperience as a writer, they gave signs of the graceful, charming essay style for which he was to become famous.

Marriage. In 1876, Stevenson met Fanny Osbourne, a married American woman who was studying art in Paris. Although she was 11 years older than Stevenson and had a son and daughter, Stevenson fell in love with her. In 1879, he followed her to San Francisco in spite of the opposition of his parents. They were married in Oakland in 1880, after her divorce. The long journey from Europe to California severely affected Stevenson's frail health. To speed his recovery, he moved his family to a rough mining camp in the mountains near Calistoga, California. Stevenson described his experiences there in *The Silverado Squatters* (1883).

The Stevensons returned to Scotland in 1880. For the next seven years, they moved through Europe from one resort to another, hoping that a change of air would improve Stevenson's health. In 1887, Stevenson returned with his family to the United States, where he entered a sanitarium at Saranac Lake, New York.

The South Seas. For Stevenson, the sea had always been bracing. When his health improved, he boldly decided to sail a yacht to the South Seas. He left San Francisco with his wife, widowed mother, and stepson in June 1888, and for the next six years traveled through the

Brown Bros.

Robert Louis Stevenson settled with his family near Apia on Upolu, one of the Samoan islands in the South Seas. There he built a large house which he called *Vailima*. This picture shows Stevenson seated next to his wife, Fanny. His mother and stepson Lloyd Osbourne (standing) are shown on the author's right.

South Sea islands. He came to know the life of the islanders better than any writer of his time.

Eventually, Stevenson decided to settle in the South Seas, the one place that seemed to promise some lasting improvement in his health. He bought some forestland near Apia, Samoa, and built a large house, which he called *Vailima* (Five Rivers). He became a planter and took an active part in island affairs. Stevenson's kindness, understanding, and tolerance gained the affection of the Samoans, who built a road to his house which they called *The Road of the Loving Heart*.

Tragedy clouded Stevenson's last years when his wife became mentally ill. This misfortune moved him deeply, affecting his ability to complete his last books. Stevenson's life was beginning to brighten when his wife partially recovered, but he died suddenly of a stroke on Dec. 3, 1894. Local chiefs buried him on top of Mount Vaea, where his gravestone is inscribed with his own poem "Requiem." Its concluding lines make a fitting epitaph for a gallant adventurer:

> Here he lies where he longed to be;
> Home is the sailor, home from the sea,
> And the hunter, home from the hill.

Stevenson's writings

Novels. In 1881, Stevenson amused his stepson, Lloyd Osbourne, with a little tale about pirates and the buried treasure of Captain Kidd. It grew into *Treasure Island,* Stevenson's first and most famous novel. The story, first published in a boy's magazine, was revised for book publication in 1883. The boy hero Jim Hawkins, the two villains Long John Silver and blind Pew, and the hair-raising search for the buried treasure have become familiar to millions of readers.

With the publication of Stevenson's second major novel, *The Strange Case of Dr. Jekyll and Mr. Hyde* (1886), his reputation was assured. The story tells of a doctor who takes a drug that changes him into a new person,

physically ugly and spiritually evil. As a psychological inquiry into the nature of the evil that exists in all people, the novel brilliantly anticipates much modern psychological fiction and is one of the most fascinating horror stories ever written.

Stevenson also published *Kidnapped,* his best long novel, in 1886. Based on considerable historical research, it weaves an exciting fictional story around an actual Scottish murder committed in 1745. The novel displays Stevenson's matchless ability to create adult entertainment out of the materials of children's adventure stories. Because of its length, Stevenson ended *Kidnapped* before the plot was completed. He finally finished the story in 1893 with a sequel, *David Balfour* (published in England as *Catriona*).

The Master of Ballantrae (1889) is set against the background of Scotland's revolt against England in the 1740's. The novel tells a story of bitter hatred between two brothers. *The Master of Ballantrae* begins as a promising psychological study, but suffers from its melodramatic ending.

Stevenson's later novels, far different from his early light-hearted romances, are often bitter in tone. Less popular, they still have merit. The short novel *The Beach of Falesá* (1892), which Stevenson described as "the first realistic South Sea story," was called "art brought to a perfection" by novelist Henry James.

Stevenson wrote three other novels, in collaboration with Lloyd Osbourne—*The Wrong Box* (1889), *The Wrecker* (1892), and *The Ebb Tide* (1894). Stevenson also left two novels unfinished at his death. *St. Ives,* which was completed by Sir Arthur Quiller-Couch, describes the adventures of a French prisoner in Britain in 1813. *Weir of Hermiston,* a story of Scotland in the 1700's, promised to be Stevenson's finest novel.

Other writings. Stevenson wrote many short stories, some of which were collected into *New Arabian Nights* (1882) and *More New Arabian Nights* (1885). Many of the short stories are rich in imagination and fantasy, though the early ones are often written in an artificial style.

Stevenson's concern with prose style is most apparent in his essays, which are among the finest in the English language. His observations on people and manners are marked by a delicate fancy. For charm and perceptiveness, they can be compared only to the essays of Charles Lamb and William Hazlitt. Stevenson's most memorable essays were collected in *Virginibus Puerisque and Other Papers* (1881), *Familiar Studies of Men and Books* (1882), and *Memories and Portraits* (1887).

Stevenson wrote several travel books later in his career. The *Amateur Emigrant* (1880, 1895) describes his voyages to the United States. *Across the Plains* (1892) tells of his trip from New York to San Francisco. *In the South Seas* (1890) contains his reflections on his Pacific voyages. All demonstrate Stevenson's extraordinary stylistic quality—the sudden word or phrase that lights a page with meaning.

In addition to the works mentioned above, Stevenson composed some delightful letters, wrote several volumes of poetry, and collaborated with William Ernest Henley on some unsuccessful dramas. *A Child's Garden of Verses* (1885) reveals the world of a child's imagination with a deceptive simplicity that still holds appeal for readers young and old. Stevenson's adult poetry, however, is almost totally ignored today, in spite of occasional pieces of considerable merit.

Stevenson's place in literature

Stevenson was both the most popular and the most successful among writers of the late 1800's who developed romance as a reaction to the literary movements of Realism and Naturalism. If his influence has declined today, it is not necessarily because modern writers are more skillful, but rather that Stevenson's optimistic view of life has become unfashionable.

Stevenson insisted that novels are to adults what play is to children, and that one of the legitimate and necessary functions of literature is to supply adventure for people who lead unexciting lives. A theory of fiction seemingly so limited and naive might well have produced literary trifles. In fact, it resulted in art of such high quality that the disciplined Henry James once praised Stevenson as "the only man in England who can write a decent English sentence."

Stevenson's faults are obvious. His plots are a bit melodramatic, his pirates rather stagy, and, as he readily admitted, his heroines entirely unreal. However, his sure handling of narrative pace, his strong sense of atmosphere, and above all his masterly command of style give his novels and stories enduring vitality.

The reading public has never lost its admiration for Stevenson, and it appears likely that as long as there is a taste for romance written with artistry, he will continue to have an audience. Furthermore, there are signs that critics are reevaluating his works, finding more fine shades of meaning in his writings than they had suspected.   Sharon Bassett

See also **Apia.**

Additional resources

Callow, Philip. *Louis: A Life of Robert Louis Stevenson.* Ivan R. Dee, 2001.
Colley, Ann C. *Robert Louis Stevenson and the Colonial Imagination.* Ashgate Pub. Ltd., 2004.
Gray, William. *Robert Louis Stevenson: A Literary Life.* Palgrave, 2004.
Menikoff, Barry. *Narrating Scotland: The Imagination of Robert Louis Stevenson.* Univ. of S.C. Pr., 2005.

Stewart, James (1908-1997), was a lanky American motion-picture actor who spoke with a distinctive drawl. Stewart appeared in over 70 motion pictures. He was best known for his roles portraying an honest, middle-class American who courageously faces some crisis.

Stewart won the 1940 Academy Award as best actor for his performance in the comedy *The Philadelphia Story.* He starred in three popular films directed by Frank Capra—*You Can't Take It With You* (1938), *Mr. Smith Goes to Washington* (1939), and *It's a Wonderful Life* (1946). His roles have achieved almost mythic stature as portraits of all-American decency. Stewart played in the Westerns *Destry Rides Again* (1939), *Winchester '73* (1950), and *The Man Who Shot Liberty Valance* (1962). In addition, he starred in four suspense movies directed by Alfred Hitchcock—*Rope* (1948), *Rear Window* (1954), *The Man Who Knew Too Much* (1956), and *Vertigo* (1958). Stewart's other films include *Harvey* (1950), *The Glenn Miller Story* (1953), and *Anatomy of a Murder* (1959).

Warner Bros.

James Stewart

James Maitland Stewart was born on May 20, 1908, in Indiana, Pennsylvania. His first movie was *Murder Man* (1935). He died on July 2, 1997.   Louis Giannetti

Stewart, Potter (1915-1985), was an associate justice of the Supreme Court of the United States from 1958 to 1981. On the court, Stewart could not be labeled as a conservative or a liberal. He voted with the conservative justices on some cases and with the liberals on others.

Stewart was born on Jan. 23, 1915, in Jackson, Michigan. His father, James Garfield Stewart, became an Ohio Supreme Court judge. Potter Stewart attended Yale University, Yale Law School, and Cambridge University. He practiced law in Cincinnati, and he was elected to the Cincinnati city council in 1949. Stewart served as a judge of the federal court of appeals from 1954 to 1958. He died on Dec. 7, 1985.   Bruce Allen Murphy

Stewart, Robert. See Castlereagh, Viscount.

Stibnite. See Antimony; Mineral (picture).

Stickleback is a name given to a family of small fishes of the Northern Hemisphere. These fish are called sticklebacks because some of their fins are made of strong, sharp, separated spines. Instead of having scales, the sides of the fish's body may have a series of hard plates. There are both freshwater and ocean sticklebacks. The freshwater ones reach a length of 1 to 4 inches (2.5 to 10.2 centimeters). The ocean ones grow as much as 7 inches (18 centimeters) long. The *brook stickleback* is common in the interior parts of Canada and in the Great

Lakes states. These fish, like other sticklebacks, build muff-shaped nests of sticks and roots for receiving the *spawn* (fish eggs). The male carefully guards the spawn. He also watches over the young for several days after the eggs hatch. Sticklebacks usually eat insect larvae, worms, and other small animals. They also feed on the eggs and young of other fish.   David W. Greenfield

Scientific classification. Sticklebacks make up the stickleback family, Gasterosteidae. The brook stickleback is *Eucalia inconstans.*

See also **Instinct.**

Stiegel, *STEE guhl,* **Henry William** (1729-1785), was an important early American manufacturer of fine glass. His factories were the first in the American Colonies to make glassware as good as that being imported from Europe. Stiegel typically adapted European designs for his wares, which included clear and colored vases, bottles, glass tableware, and decanters. Many pieces had enameled or engraved decorations. He was among the first glass manufacturers to insist on production in which every piece of glassware matched a set model.

Stiegel was born on May 13, 1729, near Cologne, Germany. He came to Philadelphia in 1750. He began making glass at Elizabeth Furnace in 1763. He opened two more glass factories in Manheim, Pennsylvania, in 1765 and 1769. At the height of his success, he lived in a large house, wore fine clothes, and was called baron. But his extravagance and risky investments led to financial ruin. In 1774, the Stiegel company closed. Stiegel died on Jan. 10, 1785.   John W. Keefe

See also **Antique** (picture: A glass bottle).

Stieglitz, *STEEG lihts,* **Alfred** (1864-1946), was an American photographer who pioneered in photography

The Art Institute of Chicago, the Alfred Stieglitz Collection

The Steerage is one of Alfred Stieglitz's best-known photographs. He took this picture of travelers on a ship to Europe in 1907 and considered it one of his best works.

as an art form. He also helped introduce and promote Modern art in the United States.

During the 1880's and 1890's, Stieglitz became famous for *pictorial photographs,* which featured hazy, romantic scenes. He later produced sharply focused, realistic photographs of everyday subjects.

In 1902, Stieglitz formed the Photo-Secession, a group of photographers who worked to develop photography as an expressive art. He began publishing the magazine *Camera Work* in 1903. It included work by leading photographers, artists, and critics. In 1905, he opened a gallery, known as "291," in New York City. It exhibited paintings, sculpture, and other works by Modern artists of Europe and the United States. Stieglitz later opened other galleries. Stieglitz was born in Hoboken, New Jersey, on Jan. 1, 1864. In 1924, he married the painter Georgia O'Keeffe, whom he often photographed. Stieglitz died on July 13, 1946.   Charles Hagen

See also **O'Keeffe, Georgia; Photography** (Artistic advances).

Still, Clyfford (1904-1980), an American painter, was a leading member of the Abstract Expressionist movement. He was known chiefly for his imaginative use of large expanses of color. His paintings contain large, vertical, jagged-edged, flamelike shapes. He combined thickly applied paint with bright, aggressive, sharply contrasting colors to create works that are dramatic and disturbing. The rough surfaces formed by the paint suggest natural formations, such as canyons and crevices.

Still was born in Grandin, North Dakota, on Nov. 30, 1904. He used large areas of color in nearly all his works. During the 1930's and early 1940's, he painted the landscape of the western United States, especially the vast western plateaus. In the late 1940's, he ceased to use recognizable subjects and developed the style associated with his work. He taught in San Francisco from 1946 to 1950, inspiring many young artists to experiment freely. Still died on June 23, 1980.   Dore Ashton

See also **Abstract Expressionism.**

Still, William Grant (1895-1978), was an American composer whose numerous works include five symphonies and nine operas. *Afro-American Symphony* (1931), his first symphony, was the first work by an African American composer to be performed by a major orchestra, the Rochester Philharmonic. It remains his best-known composition.

Still's characteristic style is conservative and richly melodic, drawing heavily upon African and African American themes. These themes appear in his first symphony, as well as in his second symphony, *Symphony in G Minor: Song of a New Race* (1937).

Still was born on May 11, 1895, in Woodville, Mississippi. In the 1920's, he began writing concert music. In the 1920's and 1930's, Still also played violin and oboe in orchestras and dance bands. In 1934, he settled in Los Angeles. He wrote his operas there, including *Troubled Island* (completed 1941, first performed 1949), *A Bayou Legend* (completed 1941, first performed 1974), and *Highway 1, U.S.A.* (1962). Still died on Dec. 3, 1978.
Stewart L. Ross

Stillwater, Minnesota (pop. 15,143), is one of the state's earliest settlements. It lies in southeast Minnesota, on the boundary with Wisconsin. It stands near the mouth of the St. Croix River, at a point where the river widens into a lake (see **Minnesota** [political map]).

Stillwater was established in 1843. For many years, it served as an important logging center for lumbering in the nearby pine forests. It is called the *Birthplace of Minnesota*. The convention that petitioned Congress to form the territory of Minnesota met there in 1848. Congress created the Minnesota Territory the following year.

Stillwater's historical importance and its beautiful river setting attract many tourists. The city has a mayor-council form of government. Mark Brouwer

Stilt is a wading bird with long, slender legs. These slender legs make it look as if it walks on stilts. The stilts are related to the avocets and live in both the Eastern and Western hemispheres.

The *black-necked stilt* is about 15 inches (38 centimeters) long. The upper part of the bird's body is black, and the underpart is white. Its long legs are bright red. The stilt builds its nest by lining a low place in the ground with grasses. The female lays three or four eggs of an

Keith H. Murakami, Tom Stack & Assoc.

The black-necked stilt is the only American variety of this wading bird. The stilt is named for its long, slender legs.

olive or buff color, thickly spotted with chocolate tones. Stilts live along shallow ponds in freshwater and saltwater marshes. See also **Avocet**. Fritz L. Knopf

Scientific classification. The stilt belongs to the stilt and avocet family, Recurvirostridae. The black-necked stilt is *Himantopus mexicanus.*

Stilwell, Joseph Warren (1883-1946), commanded all the United States forces in the China-Burma-India theater of war during World War II (1939-1945). He also served as chief of staff to Generalissimo Chiang Kai-shek, supreme commander of the Chinese theater, and was the first American general to command a Chinese army. Stilwell won the nickname of *Vinegar Joe* because of his forthright manner.

Stilwell was sent to Burma (now Myanmar) in 1942 to assist the Chinese and British troops defending Burma against Japan. When the Allied forces were defeated in Burma, Stilwell retreated to India. In India, he trained several Chinese divisions to recapture Burma and open a line of communication to China. With these forces and a small American force called "Merrill's Marauders," Stilwell opened a route to China late in 1944 (see **Merrill's**

Marauders). In June 1945, Stilwell took command of the U.S. Tenth Army on Okinawa. After the war ended, he held an Army command in the United States.

Stilwell was born on March 19, 1883, in Palatka, Florida. He graduated from the U.S. Military Academy in 1904 and later served in World War I (1914-1918). He studied Chinese and served as a military attaché in China from 1935 to 1939. He died on Oct. 12, 1946. Adrian R. Lewis

Stimulant is a substance that causes an increase in the activity of an organ of the body. The term usually refers to chemicals that excite or increase certain activities of the central nervous system (see **Nervous system** [The central nervous system]). Such compounds as strychnine and picrotoxin are toxic stimulants of the central nervous system. They are classified as *analeptics* or *convulsants.* An overdose of these types of stimulants may cause severe disturbance, convulsions, and death. Caffeine, nicotine, and amphetamines also stimulate the central nervous system, but only extremely high doses cause convulsions. Caffeine is found in coffee, tea, and a number of nonprescription analgesic preparations. Tobacco products contain nicotine. Barbara M. Bayer

Related articles in *World Book* include:

Amphetamine	Drug abuse
Caffeine	Epinephrine
Drug (Drugs that affect the nervous system)	Nicotine
	Ritalin

Stimulus. See Learning (How we learn); **Reflex action.**

Stine, R. L. (1943-   ), became one of the best-selling children's authors in history with his novels of suspense and horror. Stine, an American, wrote most of the children's paperbacks that became best sellers during the middle and late 1990's.

Stine writes the "Goosebumps" novels for younger readers and the "Fear Street" series for older children. His books tell stories of ordinary young people who unexpectedly encounter the supernatural, the terrifying, and the unusual. In many novels, the young characters must find a way to defeat evil forces, which can range from ghosts or monsters to insane killers. Many of Stine's supernatural stories occur during such commonplace activities as a trip to a store, a family's move to a new house, or a high school homecoming weekend.

Robert Lawrence Stine was born on Oct. 8, 1943, in Bexley, Ohio. His first book of horror fiction was *Blind Date* (1986). Its success led Stine to begin his "Fear Street" series, which started with *The New Girl* (1989). In 1992, he began his "Goosebumps" series with *Welcome to Dead House.* In 2000, Stine started a series called "The Nightmare Room" with *Don't Forget Me!* and *Locker 13.* Stine created another series called "Mostly Ghostly" with *Who Let the Ghosts Out?* (2004). John Cech

Stingray, also called *stingaree,* is a ray, or flattish fish. Its long, whiplike tail has one or two sharp spines near the base. These spines have poisonous glands at the base and barbs along the edges. When a bather or a predatory fish disturbs the stingray, it swings its tail upward, inflicting a painful wound that can be as dangerous as a poisonous snakebite.

More than 150 species of stingrays exist. Most live on sandy to muddy bottoms in shallow parts of the ocean and in bays. Some species live in fresh water. In South America, small, freshwater stingrays live in rivers that flow into the Atlantic Ocean. Some of these stingrays

WORLD BOOK illustration by John F. Eggert

The roughtail stingray can inflict a serious wound with the strong, sharp spine on its whiplike tail.

live as far as 2,000 miles (3,200 kilometers) above the mouth of the Amazon River. A stingray that lives in the waters off Australia reaches a length of 14 feet (4 meters). John E. McCosker

Scientific classification. Most marine stingrays belong to the family Dasyatidae. River stingrays belong to the family Potamotrygonidae. The roughtail stingray is *Dasyatis centroura.*

Stink bug is a kind of insect that gives off a foul odor when it is disturbed. The stink bug's body is shaped like a shield. Each of the bug's two antennae is made up of five sections. Some species of stink bugs eat only plants, some eat only other insects, and some eat both plants and insects. Many species of stink bugs attack plants that are not economically important, but the brightly colored *harlequin bug* damages cabbage. James E. Lloyd

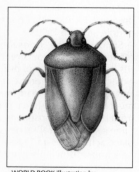

WORLD BOOK illustration by
Shirley Hooper, Oxford Illustrators Limited

Stink bug

Scientific classification. Stink bugs are members of the stink bug family, Pentatomidae. The harlequin bug is *Murgantia histrionica.*

Stirling, Robert. See Stirling engine.

Stirling engine is an experimental source of power that someday may be used in cars, boats, and other vehicles. It runs more efficiently and produces less air pollution than do most other engines.

A typical Stirling engine has a sealed cylinder that contains a gas—either helium or hydrogen. The gas goes through a cycle of pressure changes by means of a process of alternate heating and cooling. A device called the *regenerator* partially heats the gas at the beginning of the cycle. A heater outside the cylinder provides additional heat by burning a fuel, such as diesel oil, kerosene, or alcohol. At the end of the cycle, the regenerator cools the gas by absorbing its heat.

How a Stirling engine works

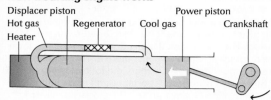

A cycle of a Stirling engine begins when the power piston moves toward the displacer piston. This action causes the cool gas between the pistons to start flowing up to the regenerator.

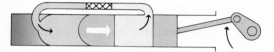

The displacer piston moves toward the power piston, forcing the cool gas through the regenerator to be heated. The heated gas then flows into the space behind the displacer piston.

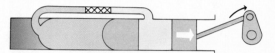

The heater outside the cylinder supplies additional heat to make the gas expand. The expanding gas causes both the displacer piston and the power piston to move in a *power stroke.*

WORLD BOOK diagrams by Arthur Grebetz

The displacer piston returns to its original position, forcing the gas to flow back through the regenerator, which absorbs its heat. The cooled gas reenters the space between the pistons.

The gas expands and contracts as it goes through the cycle of pressure changes. In doing so, it causes a *power piston* to move back and forth inside the cylinder. A rod connects the power piston to a crankshaft that converts the piston's *reciprocating* (back-and-forth) motion to the rotary motion of the drive shaft. This action, in turn, causes a *displacer piston* to move back and forth and force the gas through the regenerator.

Robert Stirling, a Scottish minister, invented the Stirling engine in 1816. Stirling engines have never come into general use because they cost more to build than other types. The chief difficulties of Stirling engines involve their complexity, their heat exchange requirements, the sealing of their cylinders, and containing hydrogen at high temperatures. David E. Cole

Stitch. See Sewing (Kinds of stitches).

Stoat. See Ermine.

Stock is a name given to about 50 species of garden flowers. A species called the *Grecian stock* bears fragrant lilac or purple flowers that open at evening. This small, branching annual plant comes from southern Europe. Its pods have two noticeable horns on the end. The *Virginian stock* is another annual with small white, red, or lilac-colored flowers. It has a short stalk and pods with no horns. The *Brampton,* or *common, stock* is about 2 feet (60 centimeters) high. It bears fragrant white, pink, red, purple, or yellow blossoms.   W. Dennis Clark

Scientific classification. Stocks are in the mustard family, Brassicaceae or Cruciferae. Grecian stock is *Matthiola bicornis.* Brampton stock is *M. incana.* Virginian stock is *Malcolmia maritima.*

Derek Fell
Stock blossoms

Stock is a right of ownership in a corporation. The stock is divided into a certain number of *shares,* and the corporation issues stockholders one or more *stock certificates* to show how many shares they hold. The stockholders own the company and elect a board of directors to manage it for them.

Stockholders may sell their stock whenever they want to, unless the corporation has some special rule to prevent it. Prices of stock change according to general business conditions and the earnings and future prospects of the company. If the business is doing well, stockholders may be able to sell their stock for a profit. If it is not, they may have to take a loss.

Large corporations may have many thousands of stockholders. Their stock is bought and sold in marketplaces called *stock exchanges.* When a sale is made, the seller signs the certificate. The buyer turns this over to the corporation and gets a new certificate.

When the corporation has made a profit, the directors may divide the profit among the stockholders as *dividends,* or they may decide to use it to expand the business. Dividends may be paid only out of the corporation's profits. When profits are used to expand the business, the directors and stockholders may decide to issue more stock to show that there is more money invested in the business. This new stock will be divided among the stockholders as a *stock dividend.*

Kinds of stock. The Articles of Incorporation—papers signed when the corporation is formed—may specify the different kinds of stock. *Par stock* must be issued for not less than a set price, called the *par value,* for each share. If the articles provide for *no-par* stock, the directors determine the issuing price of the stock and may change it whenever they wish.

All shares of stock have equal dividend and voting rights unless the articles provide differently. There may be different classes of stock, such as *voting* and *nonvoting.* Many articles provide for *common* and *preferred* stock. Preferred stock is entitled to a preference on dividends. That is, the directors must pay a certain amount —usually a percentage of par value—to the holders of preferred stock before they pay anything to the holders of common stock. If preferred-stock holders share with common-stock holders in dividends beyond the percentage, the stock is called *participating preferred.*

Preferred stock may also be *cumulative.* That is, if there are no dividends given in a year, the preferred-stock holders must be given double their dividend the next year. This dividend is paid before anything is paid to the common-stock holders. It will continue to multiply for as many years as dividends are not paid.

When a corporation goes out of business, it divides its property among the stockholders. This process is called *liquidation.* When a company liquidates, the preferred-stock holders may be given the par value of their stock before the common-stock holders are given anything. This preferred stock is said to be *preferred up to par on liquidation.*   Robert Sobel

See also **Employee Stock Ownership Plan; Investment; Stock exchange.**

Stock car. See Automobile racing.

Stock exchange is a marketplace where brokers act as agents for the public in buying and selling stocks and bonds. Stock exchanges play an important role in business and society. People invest money in *securities* (stocks and bonds) in hopes of gaining more money in the future. These investments make money available to companies and governments, thus enabling them to provide goods and services.

Investors trade billions of shares of stock worth hundreds of billions of dollars each year. In the United States, major stock exchanges operate in Chicago, Los Angeles, New York City, and San Francisco. Major exchanges in other countries include those in London, Paris, and Tokyo, and those in Amsterdam, the Netherlands; Frankfurt, Germany; Hong Kong, China; Johannesburg, South Africa; Sydney, Australia; Toronto, Canada; and Zurich, Switzerland.

How a stock exchange operates

At a stock exchange, only brokers who are members of the exchange can buy and sell securities. At most exchanges, brokers must pay a fee and meet certain membership requirements before they can obtain a *seat* (membership). Only a limited number of seats are available at each exchange.

Stocks traded on exchanges are known as *listed stocks.* A company that wants its shares listed must qualify under the rules of the exchange. For many exchanges, a company must show that it possesses a certain amount of capital, is a lawful enterprise, and is in good financial condition. *Listed bonds* may also be traded on stock exchanges. Unlisted stocks and most bonds are bought and sold in *over-the-counter* trading, which takes place outside of stock exchanges.

Stock prices and indexes. All stocks *fluctuate* (change) in value. Unforeseen circumstances may diminish the earning power of a company and thus lower the price investors are willing to pay for its stock. Other circumstances—such as improved management or the introduction of new products—may increase the value of a stock. Stock prices often reflect the state of a country's economy. If business conditions are good, stock prices have a tendency to rise, creating what is called a *bull market.* If business conditions are poor, stock prices drop, causing a *bear market.*

All stock exchanges have at least one *stock index.* Stock indexes are numbers that measure the overall rise and fall of stock prices on an exchange. Dow Jones averages are indexes for stocks traded in the United States. Other major indexes include the Financial Times Stock Exchange Index, which tracks prices on the London

Stock Exchange, and the Nikkei Index, which tracks prices on the Tokyo Stock Exchange.

Trading. An investor who wishes to buy or sell shares of stock can place an order with a *brokerage company,* or *brokerage house.* Once an order is placed, the company relays the instructions to a broker at the exchange, who makes the transaction. Brokers receive *commissions* (transaction fees) for their services. Many investors use online brokerage services to conduct transactions over the Internet.

Stock is often traded under a contract called an *option.* An option allows the stockholder to buy or sell a certain amount of stock at a specific price within a designated period. For example, an investor may believe that a stock will increase in value. The investor can buy an option that will allow the purchase of shares of that stock at a specific price before a certain date. If the value of the stock rises above the price set by the option, the holder can profit by buying the stock and immediately reselling it.

Information about stock transactions appears on electronic displays called *stock tickers.* Brokers and investors throughout the world use stock tickers to keep informed of stock market developments.

Regulation. Countries around the world have laws that regulate the issuance, listing, and trading of securities. In the United States, the Securities and Exchange Commission (SEC) administers federal laws concerning stock exchanges. Additional laws exist at the state level. In Canada, stock exchanges are regulated primarily at the provincial and territorial levels. The Financial Services Authority is an independent, nongovernment body that regulates financial markets in the United Kingdom.

History

The first European stock exchange was established in Antwerp, Belgium, in 1531. The first stock exchange in England was formed in 1773 by the brokers of London. Before that time, people who wished to buy or sell stock had to find a broker to conduct the transactions. In London, brokers traditionally gathered at coffee houses.

In New York City, brokers met under an old buttonwood tree on Wall Street. In 1792, they established the New York Stock Exchange, the oldest and largest stock exchange in the United States. Another major stock exchange, the American Stock Exchange, was formerly called the Curb Exchange because of its origins on the streets of New York City.   Roberto Serrano

Related articles in *World Book* include:

American Stock Exchange	Investment banking
Bears and bulls	Margin
Blue-sky laws	Mutual fund
Bond	Nasdaq
Commodity exchange	New York Stock Exchange
Cornering the market	Securities and Exchange
Dow Jones averages	Commission
Europe (picture: Major stock	Securities Exchange Act
exchanges)	Standard & Poor's Indexes
Initial public offering	Stock
Insider trading	Stock ticker
Investment (How to read a	Wall Street
newspaper stock report)	

Stock market crash of 1929. See **Great Depression.**

Stock ticker is an electronic display that shows purchases and sales of stock. It usually appears on a video

screen. The display of each stock transaction begins with a *stock symbol.* This symbol consists of one or more letters that represent the name of the corporation issuing the stock. The transaction display also includes the number of shares involved and the price at which they were bought or sold.

Stockbrokers throughout the United States relay orders to a stock exchange by telephone, facsimile, or some other type of electronic device. At the exchange, another broker buys or sells the stock. An exchange reporter puts the details of the transaction into one of the many computers on the trading floor. A vast telecommunications network then carries the information to video screens and other devices across the country.

The New York Stock Exchange introduced an early form of stock ticker in 1867. These tickers were teletype machines that recorded stock transactions on a 1-inch (2.5-centimeter) wide paper called *ticker tape.* Since the early 1900's, these machines have been replaced by electronic display devices. One of the most common of the electronic devices is a video screen called a *quote machine.* This device may also display such information as historical trading summaries, graphs, and related news items.   Roger G. Ibbotson

See also **Edison, Thomas A.** (Telegraph innovator).

Stockhausen, *SHTOHK how zehn,* **Karlheinz** (1928-), a German composer, has been a leading force in the development of modern music since the early 1950's. Stockhausen creates music from unusual sounds. His music uses synthetic electronic sounds and such everyday noises as radio static, speech, and street sounds. He sometimes distorts these sounds electronically.

Stockhausen has experimented with *chance music,* in which the performer determines the order in which the sections of a composition are played. In such works as *Gruppen (Groups,* 1955-1957) for three orchestras, Stockhausen scattered performers throughout the concert hall to produce a live stereo effect called *music in space.* He composed *Kontakte* (1960), for electronic sounds, piano, and percussion; and the electronic work *Hymnen* (1967), which weaves together the national anthems of more than 40 countries. Stockhausen was born on Aug. 22, 1928, in Mödrath, near Cologne.

Stephen Jaffe

See also **Electronic music.**

Stockholm is the capital and largest city of Sweden. The municipality of Stockholm has a population of 765,044. A municipality may include rural areas as well as the urban center. Stockholm is the heart of Swedish commercial and cultural life and a major center for international trade and communications. The city lies on the east coast of Sweden, between Lake Mälaren and the Baltic Sea. For the location of Stockholm, see **Sweden** (political map).

The city is built on 14 islands and a part of the mainland. About 50 bridges connect these parts of Stockholm. Careful city planning and a magnificent natural setting among heavily wooded hills have made Stockholm one of the world's most beautiful cities. The contrasts of land and water and of old and new architecture add to its charm.

The heart of Stockholm is Gamla Stan (Old Town). This old section is the site of the huge Royal Palace, which dates from the 1700's. Sweden's Parliament build-

Stockholm covers 14 islands and a part of the mainland. About 50 bridges connect the parts of the city. The small island of Riddarholmen, *foreground,* is one of the oldest parts of the city. The Riddarholm Church, *right,* dates from the late 1200's and houses the tombs of many Swedish monarchs.

ing stands near the palace, on its own island. The modern main business and shopping district lies north of Gamla Stan. Most Stockholmers live in large, modern apartment buildings.

Stockholm is the home of Stockholm University and of Sweden's Royal Ballet, Library, Opera, and Theater. It also has many art galleries and museums. Skansen, a popular park, features an amusement park, a zoo, and an open-air museum.

Thousands of islands of various sizes in the sea east of Stockholm form an archipelago. The islands have many cabins and tiny settlements. People visit the islands the year around for recreation and relaxation.

Economy. Stockholm is Sweden's economic and administrative center. Most workers have service jobs, and more than a third are employed by the national or local government. Trade, manufacturing, banking, insurance, and commerce also employ many people. The chief industries include publishing and the manufacture of chemicals, machinery, and metal products. The city is Sweden's second largest port, after Göteborg, and the hub of the nation's air, highway, and railroad travel. Buses and a subway system serve the city and its suburbs.

History. Stockholm probably was founded in the early 1250's by a Swedish leader named Birger Jarl. He built a castle in the area that is now Gamla Stan. Stockholm grew as a trade center, and the city became the capital of Sweden in 1523. Through the years, Stockholm expanded and prospered. Like other cities, it developed such problems as congestion and urban decay. But a long tradition of sensible city planning has helped Stockholm deal with many of its problems. For example, the city's population grew rapidly after World War II ended in 1945. During the 1950's and 1960's, residential suburbs were built on land purchased by the city as long ago as 1904. Since the mid-1900's, entire sections of Stockholm have been rebuilt to provide new housing and to replace run-down buildings with new ones. A major project of the 1980's was the complete renovation of the Parliament building.   M. Donald Hancock

See also **Sweden** (Climate; pictures).

Stockings are articles of clothing that fit snugly over the feet and part or all of the legs. Two forms of stock-

ings, pantyhose and tights, cover the feet and legs and reach to the waist. People wear stockings chiefly for comfort, warmth, and decoration and to protect their shoes from perspiration and foot odor.

How stockings are made. Most pantyhose and women's stockings are *sheer* (transparent). Most tights, men's hose, and children's stockings and some women's stockings are *opaque* (nontransparent). Nearly all sheer stockings are made of some kind of nylon yarn. Almost all opaque stockings are made from cotton, wool, or manufactured fibers, such as nylon, olefin, and acrylic and polyester fibers. Support and surgical hosiery contain some spandex or rubber for stretch and elasticity.

Stockings are made from knitted fabric, using one of two basic methods. Most seamless stockings are made on a *circular machine* that knits each stocking into a tubelike shape. The toe is then closed by hand or machine. Stockings with a seam, called *full-fashioned* hose, are made on a *flat-bed machine.* This machine knits a flat piece of fabric, varying the stitches to shape the leg and foot. Another machine sews the edges together to form a seam.

History. As early as the 400's B.C., people in ancient Greece and some other lands occasionally wore socklike foot coverings for warmth. The stockings were made of fabric and worn inside shoes. During the A.D. 400's, clergymen in western Europe began to wear long, tight stockings as a symbol of purity. By the 1000's, noblemen had also adopted this style of stocking.

Although a group of ancient Egyptians called *Copts* knew how to knit hosiery, stockings were made of woven cloth until the 1500's, when rich people began to wear hosiery produced by professional hand-knitters. In 1589, William Lee, an English minister, invented a machine that could knit stockings. By the late 1600's, many people wore machine-knitted hose. Most stockings were made of cotton, silk, or wool until nylon was introduced in 1939.   Lois M. Gurel

See also **Clothing** (Clothing through the ages).

Stocks. See Stock; Investment.

Stocks are an old device used for punishment. Stocks are a wooden framework with holes for the legs of the victim, and sometimes also for the arms. People were placed in the stocks for minor offenses, such as drunkenness, for periods of a few hours to several days. Stocks were commonly used for punishment in American colonial days. In the North, women charged with being "common scolds" were sometimes punished in the stocks. In the South, disobedient slaves were placed in the stocks. Stocks were used until the early 1800's. See also **Pillory**.   Marvin E. Wolfgang

Stockton, Frank Richard (1834-1902), was an American author who wrote humorous short stories and novels. His best-known work is the short story "The Lady or the Tiger?" (1882), famous for its unusual ending. Most of Stockton's fiction is based on actual events and concerns polite, well-mannered people. He retold the stories with comic invention and genial good humor.

Critics consider Stockton's best work to be *The Casting Away of Mrs. Lecks and Mrs. Aleshine* (1886). This comic novel tells about two middle-aged women who are shipwrecked and set up housekeeping on a deserted island. Stockton's first popular work was the comic fantasy *Rudder Grange* (1879).

Stockton was born on April 5, 1834, in Philadelphia. In his first major job, he worked as a wood engraver. He died on April 20, 1902.   Ronald T. Curran

Stockton, Richard (1730-1781), was a New Jersey signer of the Declaration of Independence. He served in the Continental Congress in 1776. The British captured him that same year, during the Revolutionary War in America. Stockton was imprisoned in New York, where he suffered harsh treatment from which he never fully recovered. He remained an invalid for the rest of his life.

A statue of Stockton represents New Jersey in the United States Capitol in Washington, D.C. Stockton was born on Oct. 1, 1730, in Princeton, New Jersey. He died on Feb. 28, 1781.   Robert A. Becker

Stoddert, Benjamin (1751-1813), was the first secretary of the Navy of the United States. He directed naval operations from 1798 to 1801, while the nation fought an undeclared war against France. Stoddert built the Navy up to some 50 vessels and 6,000 sailors. He purchased navy yard sites and began construction of shore facilities at Portsmouth, New Hampshire; Charlestown, Massachusetts; Brooklyn (now part of New York City); Philadelphia; Washington, D.C.; and Gosport, Virginia. Stoddert, born in Charles County, Maryland, was a merchant shipper. He died on Dec. 17, 1813.   Michael J. Crawford

Stoic philosophy flourished from about 300 B.C. to A.D. 300. It began in Greece and then spread to Rome. The Stoics believed that the world was a unique, finite, intelligent creature whose life was identical to the life of God. This world, they believed, came about not by chance but by divine providence and is the best of all possible worlds despite apparent evil. At periodic intervals, the world becomes a wholly creative fire from which an identical world is regenerated.

The Stoics emphasized the role of fate. The goal of each human being is to understand the divine plan and to act according to it. This means acting in accord with virtue, which, for the Stoics, is the only good. The Stoics believed that happiness was achieved by following reason, by freeing themselves from passions, and by concentrating only on things they could control.

The Stoic philosophers had their greatest influence on law, ethics, and political theory, but they also formulated important views on logic, the theory of knowledge, and natural philosophy. Zeno is considered the founder of Stoic philosophy. The early Stoics, particularly Chrysippus, were interested in logic and natural philosophy as well as ethics. The later Stoics, especially Seneca, Marcus Aurelius, and Epictetus, emphasized ethics.   Carl A. Huffman

See also **Epictetus; Marcus Aurelius; Seneca, Lucius Annaeus; Zeno of Citium.**

Stoke-on-Trent (pop. 240,643), a city in west-central England, is the pottery center of the United Kingdom. It lies on the River Trent. For the location of Stoke-on-Trent, see **England** (political map). Stoke-on-Trent was formed in 1910 by combining six pottery-manufacturing towns. The English writer Arnold Bennett used five of these communities as the setting for his "Five Towns" series of stories.

As early as the 1300's, crude pots were made from clays found near what is now Stoke-on-Trent. By the mid-1700's, the manufacture of fine pottery had become a small, specialized industry. Josiah Wedgwood, a leading English potter, opened a factory in the area in 1759. Today, Stoke-on-Trent's chief products include pottery, bricks, and tiles. Tourism is also a significant industry.

G. Malcolm Lewis

Stoker, Bram (1847-1912), an Irish author, wrote *Dracula* (1897), one of the most famous horror stories of all time. Count Dracula, the book's main character, is a nobleman who is really a vampire. He lives in Transylvania (now part of Romania) and is several hundred years old. At night, he changes into a huge bat and flies about the countryside drawing blood from the necks of sleeping victims. Dracula moves to England and terrorizes the people there. He is finally caught during the day and killed. Stoker wrote other novels and some nonfiction, but none of his other books approached the success of *Dracula*. See **Dracula.**

Abraham Stoker was born in Dublin, Ireland. He was theater manager for actor Sir Henry Irving and wrote *Personal Reminiscences of Henry Irving* (1906). Stoker died on April 20, 1912.   David Geherin

Stokes, Carl Burton (1927-1996), served as mayor of Cleveland from 1967 to 1971. Stokes was the first black person to be elected to head a major United States city.

Stokes was born on June 21, 1927, in Cleveland. His family was poor, and Stokes left high school at age 17 to go to work. He served in the Army from 1944 to 1946. Then he finished high school and worked his way through college. He graduated from the University of Minnesota and from Cleveland-Marshall Law School. He began practicing law in Cleveland in 1957.

Stokes served as an assistant city prosecutor in Cleveland from 1958 to 1962. In 1962, he was elected to the Ohio House of Representatives. He was reelected twice. In 1965, he ran for mayor of Cleveland as an independent but lost. In 1967, he ran as a Democrat and won. He was reelected in 1969.

From 1972 to 1980, Stokes worked as a TV newscaster in New York City. From 1983 to 1994, Stokes served as a judge on the Cleveland Municipal Court. He served as the United States ambassador to Seychelles from 1994 to 1996. He died on April 3, 1996. Stokes's brother, Louis, served in the U.S. House of Representatives from 1969 to 1999.   Nancy J. Weiss

Stokowski, *stuh KOW skee,* **Leopold** (1882-1977), was a flamboyant and somewhat controversial conductor. During his long and influential career, he extended the range of music played by symphony orchestras. He worked to improve the quality of recorded sound and to bring music to more people. He conducted the Philadelphia Orchestra in the Walt Disney animated film *Fantasia* (1940), which spread his fame beyond the music world.

Stokowski was born on April 18, 1882, in London. He moved to the United States in 1905. In 1909, he became conductor of the Cincinnati Symphony Orchestra. From 1912 to 1938, he was chief conductor of the Philadelphia Orchestra, sharing the last two seasons with Eugene Ormandy. In 1962, he founded the American Symphony Orchestra of New York City. Some criticized him for tampering with musical scores to suit his own ideas, but few questioned his technical skill. Stokowski died on Sept. 13, 1977.   Martin Bernheimer

STOL. See V/STOL.

Stolen Generation is a term that refers to Australian children, mainly of mixed Aboriginal and European descent, who were taken from their homes by Australian governments. The removals started in about 1870 and lasted until about 1970. Thousands of children were separated from their families and placed in institutions, missions, and foster homes. In many cases, all ties between parents and children ended once they were separated.

The removals took place as part of colonial policies, and later state and territorial policies, to control Aborigines and make them adopt Western culture. Mixed-race Aboriginal children were targeted for removal for several reasons. The governments thought that such children would benefit from an education like that received by white children. Many people believed the Aboriginal children would eventually marry whites and the Aboriginal culture would die out. The governments said they were taking the children to protect them from neglect. But many of them had been in happy, stable families.

In 1997, the Australian federal government issued a report on the Stolen Generation called *Bringing Them Home.* Since then, the Stolen Generation has been a subject of much debate in Australia. Some Australians say the governments should issue public apologies and make payments to people who were wrongly separated from their families. But others argue that past governments only did what they thought was best for Aboriginal children. Some members of the Stolen Generation have filed lawsuits in an effort to receive *compensation* (payment). The federal government has made efforts to help displaced Aborigines gain information about themselves and be reunited with families.   Richard Broome

Stomach is an enlarged part of the alimentary canal. It lies between the *esophagus* and the small *intestine.* In people and most animals, it is a simple baglike organ. In cows, sheep, and other *ruminants* (animals that chew their cud), it has four compartments and is more complicated than a human stomach.

A human being's stomach is shaped much like a *J.* In most people, it is in the upper left side of the abdomen. The upper end of the stomach connects with the esophagus. The lower end opens into the *duodenum,* the beginning of the small intestine. The stomach is a muscular organ. The muscles in the stomach's wall enable it to churn and mix its contents and fit its shape to the amount of food it holds. The average adult stomach can hold a little over 1 quart (0.95 liter).

The stomach's work. The stomach serves as a storage place for food, so that a large meal may be eaten at one time. Food in the stomach is discharged slowly into the intestines. The stomach also helps digest food.

Glands in the stomach wall secrete mucus to lubricate the food. Other glands give off hydrochloric acid and the enzyme pepsin to help digest the food, and a substance called *intrinsic factor* to aid the absorption of vitamin B_{12}. The hydrochloric acid kills many *microorganisms* (tiny living organisms, such as bacteria) in the food.

The stomach muscles churn food and digestive juices into a mass called *chyme* (pronounced *kym*). The muscles then contract and squeeze the chyme toward the *pyloric* (intestinal) end of the stomach. These contractions, called *peristaltic waves,* occur about 20 seconds apart. They start at the top of the stomach and move downward. The *pyloric sphincter,* a ringlike muscle around the duodenal opening, keeps the chyme in the stomach until it is almost a liquid. The pyloric sphincter then relaxes and lets some chyme enter the duodenum.

The churning action of the stomach tends to begin at usual mealtimes. When people say their stomach is "growling," they are referring to these peristaltic waves. Sometimes, these movements grow so strong that they squeeze acid gastric juice up into the lower part of the esophagus. Fluids from the stomach can irritate or damage the lining of the esophagus and produce heartburn.

The pyloric sphincter allows water to pass through almost as soon as it enters the stomach. The time that the stomach retains food varies. On the mixed diet most people eat, the stomach empties in three to five hours.

The enzymes secreted in the stomach are *pepsin,* which partially digests proteins and clots milk; and *rennin,* which also clots milk. Rennin is probably important only in infants. Infants also have significant amounts of *gastric lipase,* an enzyme that helps digest fat in the

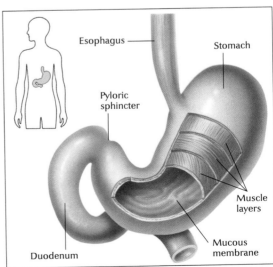

WORLD BOOK illustration by Charles Wellek

The human stomach is shaped somewhat like the letter *J.* The cutaway view shows the mucous membrane that lines the organ, and the three muscle layers of the stomach wall.

stomach. Although the stomach performs several useful functions, it is not absolutely essential for life. Many people lead long lives after their stomachs are either partially or wholly removed because of cancer or ulcers.

Peptic ulcers. Hydrochloric acid and other digestive juices can eat through the tissues that form the lining of the stomach and adjacent organs. Normally, the body replaces these tissues at about the same rate that they wear away. However, in some cases, the tissues erode faster than the body can replace them and open sores develop in the affected organ. Such sores, called *peptic ulcers,* can cause chronic stomach pain.

The two most common kinds of peptic ulcers are *gastric ulcers* and *duodenal ulcers.* Gastric ulcers develop in the stomach, typically from a weakening in the stomach's defense against tissue erosion. They sometimes result from the overuse of aspirin, which can irritate the stomach lining. The consumption of alcoholic beverages also can damage the stomach lining and cause gastric ulcers. Duodenal ulcers form in the duodenum. They usually result from excessive secretion of stomach acid.

Medications to relieve peptic ulcers include histamine H2-receptor antagonists, which reduce secretion of stomach acid. Antacids also help by neutralizing the acid. Doctors may prescribe antibiotics. Most people with peptic ulcers are infected with *Helicobacter pylori,* a bacterium. Scientists believe that this bacterium, which can live in the stomach, is associated with the development of ulcers and some stomach cancers. Controlling emotional stress can lessen the chance of developing a duodenal ulcer. Stress stimulates the production of acid, which contributes to ulcer formation.   Charles Liebow

Related articles in *World Book.* See the Trans-Vision three-dimensional picture with **Human body.** See also:

Alimentary canal	Gastritis	Nausea
Antacid	Gastroscope	Ruminant
Digestive system	Heartburn	Ulcer
Esophagus	Indigestion	Vomiting
Food	Intestine	

Stone. See Building stone; Rock.

Stone, Edward Durell (1902-1978), was an American architect best known for his decorative use of concrete. Stone's most famous buildings are almost completely enclosed in elaborate concrete screens that provide protection from the sun.

Stone was born on March 9, 1902, in Fayetteville, Arkansas. His early designs were influenced by the German architect Walter Gropius in their clear geometric shapes, smooth surfaces, and extensive use of glass. This influence appears in the Museum of Modern Art (1939) in New York City and the Mandel House (1935) in Mount Kisco, New York. Stone began designing his best-known buildings in the 1950's. The buildings include the American Embassy (1958) in New Delhi, India; the Huntington Hartford Museum (1964) in New York City; the Kennedy Center for the Performing Arts (1971) in Washington, D.C.; and the Standard Oil Building (now the Aon Center, 1973) in Chicago. Stone died on Aug. 6, 1978.   Nicholas Adams

Stone, Harlan Fiske (1872-1946), served as chief justice of the United States from 1941 until his death. His years as chief justice were marked by changing constitutional views and by division within the Supreme Court. He became an associate justice in 1925. Although a con-

servative, Stone often joined Louis D. Brandeis and Oliver Wendell Holmes in upholding liberal measures.

Stone was born on Oct. 11, 1872, in Chesterfield, New Hampshire. He graduated from Amherst College and studied at the Columbia University Law School. From 1899 to 1905, he taught law at Columbia. Stone was dean of the Columbia University Law School from 1910 to 1923. He became attorney general of the United States in 1924 and cleaned up scandals in the Department of Justice. Stone died on April 22, 1946.   Bruce Allen Murphy

Stone, Lucy (1818-1893), helped organize the women's rights movement in the United States. She was one of the first American women to lecture on women's rights and probably the nation's first married woman to keep her maiden name.

Brown Bros.
Lucy Stone

Stone was born on Aug. 13, 1818, near West Brookfield, Massachusetts. Few women of her day went to college, but Stone began to teach school at the age of 16 to earn money so she could go. She entered Oberlin College in 1843 and joined the abolitionist movement there. In 1847, she became one of the first Massachusetts women to earn a degree. After graduating from college, Stone lectured in the United States and Canada on abolitionism and, later, on women's rights. She viewed slavery and discrimination against women as linked evils of society. Stone helped organize the first national convention on equal rights for women, held in Worcester, Massachusetts, in 1850.

In 1855, Stone married Henry Blackwell, a merchant and abolitionist. They omitted the word *obey* from their marriage vows and promised to treat each other equally. Stone continued to use her maiden name and even refused to open mail addressed to Mrs. Henry Blackwell. The phrase *Lucy Stoners* came to refer to women who kept their maiden names after marriage.

In 1869, Stone helped establish the American Woman Suffrage Association, which worked for women's right to vote. She also founded the group's newspaper, *Woman's Journal.* She died on Oct. 18, 1893.   June Sochen

See also **Woman suffrage** (Growth of the movement).

Stone, Oliver (1946-   ), is an American film director, screenwriter, and producer. Stone is best known for his often controversial films about American society.

Stone served as a combat soldier in the Vietnam War in 1967 and 1968. He wrote and directed three films about the Vietnam War era. He won an Academy Award as best director for *Platoon* (1986), a realistic portrayal of a young soldier's experiences during the war. Stone also won an Academy Award for his direction of *Born on the Fourth of July* (1989), a true story about a soldier who was paralyzed during the war. *Heaven and Earth* (1993) depicts the war's devastation of the Vietnamese people.

Stone first became well known for writing the film *Midnight Express* (1978), a grim tale of an American's experiences in a Turkish prison. He won an Academy Award for the film's screenplay. Stone co-wrote and directed *Wall Street* (1987), a story about corrupt values in the world of finance; *The Doors* (1991), a portrayal of the 1960's rock group of the same name; *JFK* (1991), a controversial interpretation of the assassination of President John F. Kennedy; *Natural Born Killers* (1994), a satire about American fascination with violence; *Nixon* (1995), a biography of President Richard M. Nixon; *Any Given Sunday* (1999), an exploration of professional football in the United States; and *Alexander* (2004), a historical epic about the Macedonian general Alexander the Great. Stone directed *World Trade Center* (2006), a realistic account of the terrorist attacks on Sept. 11, 2001. He was born on Sept. 15, 1946, in New York City.   Louis Giannetti

Stone, Thomas (1743-1787), was a Maryland signer of the Declaration of Independence. Although he favored independence for the American colonists, he urged negotiation with Britain instead of war. Stone served in the Second Continental Congress and helped frame the Articles of Confederation. He was elected to the Maryland Senate three times. He died on Oct. 5, 1787, during his third term. Stone was born in Charles County, Maryland, and studied law at Annapolis.   Gary D. Hermalyn

Stone Age is a term used to designate the period in all human cultures when people used stone, rather than metal, tools. The Stone Age began about 2 ½ million years ago, when small stones were first made into crude chopping tools. It ended in the Near East about 3000 B.C., when bronze replaced stone as the chief material from which tools were made (see **Bronze Age**).

Scientists have divided the Stone Age on the basis of toolmaking techniques into *Paleolithic, Mesolithic,* and *Neolithic* phases. But only the term *paleolithic* (Old Stone Age) is still commonly used. This phase includes the prehistory of all human beings until about 8000 B.C. Paleolithic people were hunters and gatherers. After 8000 B.C., hunting and gathering became more specialized. Some people mainly gathered wild vegetables, while others fished or hunted large game. Many early farmers in the Near East, Asia, and the Americas had no metals and lived in the Stone Age. They used polished stone axes and flint sickles to harvest crops.

Many peoples were still using Stone Age technology when Europeans began their voyages of exploration and discovery in the A.D. 1400's. The Aborigines of Tasmania and Australia were making Stone Age tools when white explorers discovered them in the 1700's. Europeans found groups in southern Africa living like their Stone Age ancestors. Islanders of the South Pacific Ocean and most American Indians lacked metal farming tools when they first met Europeans. A few groups in New Guinea and Australia are still in the Stone Age.   Brian M. Fagan

See also **City** (How cities began and developed; picture: Neolithic villages); **Lake dwelling; Paleo-Indians; Prehistoric people; Tool** (History of tools).

Stone Mountain is a huge, rounded mass of light-gray granite, about 16 miles (26 kilometers) east of Atlanta, Georgia (see **Georgia** [physical map]). It is the largest stone mountain, or smooth-sided rock dome, in North America. At its highest point, it rises more than 700 feet (210 meters) above the surrounding terrain. It measures about 2 miles (3.2 kilometers) long and 1 mile (1.6 kilometers) wide. A kind of cactus grows on thin pockets of soil that lie on top of the granite.

In 1923, an ambitious sculpture project began on

Stone Mountain. It was designed as a memorial to the struggle of the South in the American Civil War (1861-1865). The American sculptor Gutzon Borglum was the first to work on the monument, but he left Stone Mountain and later worked on the Mount Rushmore carvings (see **Borglum, Gutzon**). Henry Augustus Lukeman, another American sculptor, also worked on the project. The work was discontinued in 1929 due to lack of funds.

In 1958, Georgia purchased 1,613 acres (653 hectares), including Stone Mountain, to establish a state park there. DeKalb County donated another 400 acres (160 hectares). Since then, the state has bought more land, and the area of the park now totals 3,200 acres (1,290 hectares). It features a lake at the base of Stone Mountain and a skylift. Other attractions include a beach, a golf course, museums, trails, and a restored plantation.

In 1964, carving resumed under the direction of a new sculptor, Walker Kirtland Hancock. The figures were completed in 1969. The sculpture includes Jefferson Davis, Robert E. Lee, and Stonewall Jackson, on horseback. The sculpture is about 90 feet (27 meters) high and 190 feet (58 meters) wide.   James O. Wheeler

See also **Georgia** (picture: Sculpture of Confederate leaders on Stone Mountain).

Stonechat is the name of a small bird that lives in Europe, Asia, and Africa. Its name comes from its peculiar note, a sound like that of two stones struck together.

H. D. Brandl, Okapia from NAS/PR
The stonechat

The male has a black head and throat and chestnut underparts. The female is duller in coloring. The stonechat is restless and active, and it usually lives in open, grassy locations. It builds its nest on the ground, under a tuft of grass, and feeds on insect larvae, worms, beetles, and seeds. It lays from three to six greenish-blue, faintly spotted eggs. European and Asian stonechats migrate south for the winter.

David M. Niles

Scientific classification. The stonechat belongs to the thrush family, Turdidae. Some scientists place it in the Old World flycatcher family, Muscicapidae. It is *Saxicola torquata.*

Stonefish is an extremely poisonous type of fish that lives along the bottom of tropical, shallow waters

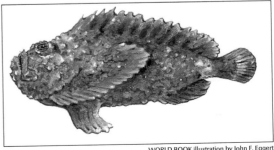

WORLD BOOK illustration by John F. Eggert
A stonefish has a stout body with wartlike skin.

around coral reefs. Stonefishes are found from French Polynesia in the South Pacific Ocean to the coast of Africa in the Indian Ocean. They can grow to a length of about 15 inches (38 centimeters). A stonefish has a large, spiny head, a stout body, and large *pectoral fins* (fins behind the gill openings). Its skin is grayish-brown with blotches of orange and looks wartlike. The fish resembles a stone when it hides between rocks and when it waits half-buried in sand and mud to ambush small fish.

A stonefish has sharp, grooved spines in the fins on its back and underside. Each spine has a pair of poison glands at the base that produce the deadliest of all fish poisons. When a spine penetrates an object, the pressure on the spine causes the glands to burst and forces the poison out the tip of the spine. In human beings, this poison causes instantaneous and intense pain. It also may cause difficult breathing, convulsions, and even death. Gary T. Sakagawa

Scientific classification. Stonefishes make up the subfamily Synanceiinae in the order Scorpaeniformes.

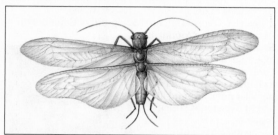

WORLD BOOK illustration by Shirley Hooper, Oxford Illustrators Limited
The stonefly usually lives near brooks or streams.

Stonefly is a weak-flying insect. It is not a true fly because it has four wings. True flies have only two wings. Stoneflies are sometimes found in great numbers along the shores of moving water, where they mate.

The name *stonefly* refers to the *nymphs* (young), which live under the stones in streams or along the shores of lakes or ponds. Trout and other fish eat the nymphs. Adult stoneflies are drab in color. They measure up to 2 ½ inches (6.4 centimeters) long. Adult stone-

flies feed on small aquatic plants and animals and on *cyanobacteria* (blue-green algae). Sandra J. Glover

Scientific classification. Stoneflies make up the order Plecoptera.

Stonehenge, STOHN hehnj, an ancient ruin in southwestern England, consists of huge, rough-cut stones set in a circle. Stonehenge lies on the Salisbury Plain in Wiltshire. Archaeologists think that the ancient inhabitants of the region constructed the site, using it as a gathering place and religious center. Stonehenge ranks as the most famous and elaborate of many similar ruins or *henges* found in the United Kingdom and Ireland.

Archaeologists have determined that Stonehenge was built in three phases over about 1,500 years. Beginning around 3100 B.C., *Neolithic* (late Stone Age) people dug a circular ditch about 360 feet (110 meters) in diameter at the site. They piled material removed from the ditch along its outside to construct a low earthen wall. A series of pits about 3 feet (1 meter) in diameter run along the inner edge of the ditch. These pits likely held wooden posts erected in a giant circle.

Around 2600 B.C., ancient people replaced the wooden circle with stone. They used dark volcanic rocks called *bluestones* quarried at a site in Wales. Scholars think workers dragged the bluestones—some of which weigh up to 4 tons (3.6 metric tons)—to the sea. There, they loaded the stones onto barges and sent them up Hampshire's Avon River, unloading them near the site of Stonehenge—a journey of about 245 miles (395 kilometers). Workers dragged the stones on sledges or rolled them into place on logs. However, the builders abandoned the site before completing the stone circle.

Workers rearranged the bluestones in the next phase of construction around 2300 B.C. At this time, they brought in huge gray sandstones called *sarsens* from quarries about 20 miles (32 kilometers) away. These stones weigh up to 25 tons (23 metric tons) and stand up to 13 ½ feet (4.1 meters) tall. Builders used them to construct an outer circle surrounding the bluestones. They laid other sarsens atop the upright stones to form horizontal beams called *lintels*. This outer circle measured 108 feet (33 meters) in diameter. Its center contained five archlike stone settings, called *trilithons,* and a large altar stone. By 1500 B.C., this construction phase had ended.

Aerofilms

Stonehenge, *shown in the photograph,* was probably used as a gathering place and religious center by ancient inhabitants of what is now England. It was built between about 3100 and 1500 B.C. The drawing shows what scholars believe was the original arrangement of the monument's huge stones.

Over the years, many of the stones fell, and people took some stones to make bridges and dams. But scholars have learned what the site looked like from the positions of the remaining stones. Scientists think that ancient people used Stonehenge for religious ceremonies linked to the rising and setting of the sun at the summer *solstice* and to the rising of the moon at the summer and winter solstices. The solstices mark the start of summer and winter. Archaeologists know that Stonehenge was part of a larger ceremonial center. Today, Stonehenge is a popular tourist attraction. Christine Hamlin

See also **Megalithic monuments.**

Stoneware is a hard, nonporous kind of pottery. Stoneware containers are used in restaurants to store food and in factories to store chemicals. Stoneware also makes durable dishes and pipes. Potters also use it to create statues and other art objects. Stoneware is made by baking a mixture of special clays at extremely high temperatures. Heat causes stoneware to become nonporous, and so the material need not be glazed.

Stoneware was first produced in China during the A.D. 400's. Production was based in the Rhine River region of Germany until about 1671, when the potter John Dwight began manufacturing stoneware in England (see **Dwight, John**). Stoneware was popular among artistic potters in France during the 1800's and was called *grès.* Early settlers in America made stoneware pitchers, crocks, and other useful items. The manufacture of

The Metropolitan Museum of Art, gift of Robert M. Jackson, 1920

A stoneware pitcher

stoneware eventually centered in western Pennsylvania and eastern Ohio, where the pottery is still made today.

William C. Gates, Jr.

See also **Pottery** (Types of pottery).

Stoppard, Tom (1937-   ), is a British dramatist. His works are noted for their imaginative blend of philosophical themes, witty dialogue, and broad comic technique. Stoppard's plays often dramatize actual historical figures and events.

Stoppard first gained fame for *Rosencrantz and Guildenstern Are Dead* (1967). In this play, he used two minor characters from William Shakespeare's *Hamlet* to probe the meaninglessness he saw in human existence. In *Jumpers* (1972), Stoppard mixed acrobatics, murder, and philosophy. *Travesties* (1974) uses famous literary and political figures to explore questions of art and politics. *Every Good Boy Deserves Favor* (1977) includes a symphony orchestra and deals with Soviet dissidents. *Night and Day* (1978) is a realistic play that discusses the role of journalism in the modern world. In *Hapgood* (1988), Stoppard blends espionage and the quantum theory of physics. *Arcadia* (1993) investigates the mysteries of love, time, and thermodynamics.

Stoppard wrote a trilogy called *The Coast of Utopia* (2002), focusing on Russian intellectuals during the 1800's. The individual plays are *Voyage, Shipwreck,* and

Salvage. Stoppard divides the action in *Rock 'n' Roll* (2006) between Prague in the Czech Republic and Cambridge University in England from 1968 to 1989.

Stoppard's other plays include *The Real Inspector Hound* (1968), *After Magritte* (1970), *Dirty Linen* (1976), and *The Real Thing* (1982). He shared the 1998 Academy Award for best original screenplay with Marc Norman for *Shakespeare in Love,* one of his several screenplays.

Stoppard was born on July 3, 1937, in Zlín, in what is now the Czech Republic. He moved with his family to England in 1946. Stoppard worked as a reporter until the early 1960's, when he began writing plays. Stoppard was knighted by Queen Elizabeth II in 1997. Thomas P. Adler

Store. See Chain store; Cooperative; Department store; Food (Marketing).

Stork is the name of a group of birds with long legs, strong wings, and a long, pointed beak. Many more *species* (kinds) of storks live in the Eastern Hemisphere than in the Western Hemisphere. Storks feed on insects, fish, frogs, reptiles, young birds, and small mammals. Most storks feed in swamps and marshes, but some hunt in grassy plains and farm fields.

The best-known stork, the *white stork,* lives in parts of Europe, Asia, and northern Africa in the summer and in Africa, northern India, and southern China in the winter. This stork is white with black markings on its wings. It has a red beak, and its legs and feet are a reddish-pink. White storks frequently nest on roofs and chimneys. A pair of storks will return to the same nest year after year. The white stork is a respected and protected bird in many places. The familiar legend that the stork brings the new baby into the home arises from the fact that the bird takes loving care of its own young.

Other storks of the Eastern Hemisphere are the *marabou,* the *black stork,* and the *woolly-necked stork.* The *maguari stork* and the *jabiru,* which measures 5 feet (1.5 meters) in height, live in Central and South America.

The *wood stork,* formerly called the *wood ibis,* is the

© Manfred Danegger, N.H.P.A.

The white stork often nests on roofs and chimneys in cities and towns in Asia, Africa, and Europe. The bird is white with black wing markings, a red beak, and reddish-pink feet and legs.

only true stork native to the United States. It lives in the cypress swamps of Florida, as well as coastal regions of Central and South America. This large, white bird stands about $3\frac{1}{2}$ feet (1.1 meters) tall. The undersides of the wings are mostly black, as are the tail feathers. The number of wood storks in Florida declined dramatically during the mid-1900's, mainly because of loss of swamp lands where the birds fed.   James J. Dinsmore

Scientific classification. Storks make up the stork family, Ciconiidae. The white stork is *Ciconia ciconia*. The wood stork is *Mycteria americana*.

See also **Bird** (picture: Birds of Europe); **Jabiru; Marabou.**

Storm usually refers to unpleasant or destructive weather, consisting of rain, snow, freezing precipitation, hail, strong winds, or a combination of these. Storms are atmospheric *cyclones*—that is, low-pressure areas circled by winds that spiral inward. In the middle latitudes, cyclones travel from west to east and produce widespread rain, thunderstorms, tornadoes, and blizzards. Tropical cyclones produce hurricanes and typhoons.

If there is little or no moisture in the air, a cyclone may travel a great distance without bringing precipitation. But if a cyclone meets a mass of warm, humid air, the swirling winds draw it in. The moist air rises in the low-pressure center, then cools and *condenses* (changes from vapor to liquid) or *sublimes* (changes from vapor to ice). Drops, flakes, and ice crystals form. When they grow heavy enough, they fall to the ground.

Storms vary widely in size and in how long they last. The smallest storms—tornadoes and thunderstorms—usually affect areas of about 10 square miles (25 square kilometers) and last a few hours. The largest storms—tropical storms and cyclones—may affect whole continents and last for weeks.   Wayne M. Wendland

Related articles in *World Book* include:

Air   Blizzard   Cloud (Storms)   Cyclone

NASA

The clouds of a storm front, *shown here,* move across the central plains of India. They were photographed by special cameras from an orbiting spacecraft.

Dust devil	Lightning	Snow	Typhoon
Dust storm	Rain	Sunspot	Waterspout
Hail	Sandstorm	Thunder	Weather
Hurricane	Sleet	Tornado	Wind

Stormalong, Alfred Bulltop, was a gigantic sea captain in New England folklore. He commanded a huge wooden ship that was so big that the crew rode horseback on deck. Its masts had hinges so they could bend to let the sun and moon pass. Sailors who climbed its rigging as young men came down with gray beards.

Folk tales and a sea song tell about Stormalong's amazing seamanship. For example, he suggested soaping the sides of his ship so it could squeeze through the English Channel. The soap scraped off on the cliffs of Dover, leaving them white.   Ellen J. Stekert

Story, Joseph (1779-1845), served as an associate justice of the Supreme Court of the United States from 1812 to 1845. As an outstanding member of the Supreme Court, he followed closely in the footsteps of John Marshall (see **Marshall, John**). His *Commentaries,* a series of important legal essays, helped shape American concepts of the common law.

Story was born on Sept. 18, 1779, at Marblehead, Massachusetts. He graduated from Harvard University in 1798. He began to practice law in 1801 and later served in Congress. He was also a professor of law at Harvard University from 1829 until his death on Sept. 10, 1845.
                Jerre S. Williams

Storytelling is the art and craft of telling stories orally. Storytelling is an ancient tradition, developed long before written language, which connects generations, cultures, and societies. In storytelling, a person prepares a story to present to an audience. Although some storytellers tell stories from their own imagination, most storytellers learn a story that appears in a book.

Storytelling provides great benefits for listeners. Hearing a story can expand creativity, and create a sense of community and a feeling of connection with history. In libraries and classrooms, storytelling is used to motivate children to read, to improve listening and writing skills, and to introduce young people to good literature. Storytelling sources include folklore, primarily folk tales, myths, epics, legends, and fables. Literary tales also provide material for stories.

Kinds of stories for telling

Folk tales are stories that have been handed down from generation to generation either in writing or by word of mouth. Folk tales are simple stories that concentrate almost entirely on plot. Because they are short and simple, these tales are perfect for storytelling. Many collections of folk tales from around the world have been rewritten and edited especially for the storyteller.

Myths, epics, and legends are closely related to folk tales. Myths are stories that attempt to describe the nature of the world and human existence. Greek, Roman, and Norse myths are the most familiar to Western audiences, and are the kind most often told by storytellers. An epic is a body of stories that concern a hero, such as Robin Hood or King Arthur. Legends usually relate some aspect of the history of a culture. Stories describing the building of railroads in the United States or the adventures of *bushrangers* (outlaws) in Australia often take the form of legends.

Fables are short tales that attempt to teach a lesson or convey a moral. Many of the characters are animals who act like human beings. The Greek stories of Aesop and the French tales of Jean de la Fontaine are probably the best-known fables, but African, Asian, Russian, and other fable collections include colorful tales as well.

Literary tales are stories created by an author but written in the style of a folk tale. Most literary tales contain more descriptive passages than folk tales, and the characters are more fully developed. Because the literary tale is more complex, it is usually told by an advanced storyteller.

Urban legends are modern fictional stories passed from one person to another as truth, even though few actually happened. Most of these tales are funny or shocking and have unexpected endings that are highly improbable. In place of evidence, the storyteller relies upon the word of a supposedly trustworthy friend. These stories are often referred to as "friend of a friend" stories. The term *urban legend* entered the popular vocabulary with the publication of *The Vanishing Hitchhiker: American Urban Legends and Their Meanings* (1981) by Jan Harold Brunvand.

How to tell a story

Selecting a story is the first step in the storyteller's preparation. The best place to find a good story is in books on the art of storytelling. These books contain discussions of sources, hints for learning and telling stories, and story collections ready to tell.

The type of audience determines what kind of story the storyteller will choose. It is important to adjust the story's length and complexity to the age of the audience. The storyteller can tell short folk tales to young children. School-age children are ready for longer stories. However, for first-, second-, and third-graders, the plots should be simple with few characters. Older children and adults enjoy longer folk tales, myths, epics, historical legends, and urban legends.

Learning the story is the next step for the storyteller. First, read the story over several times and try to organize the order of events and the characters in your mind. Then, tell the story to yourself or to a willing listener.

You will find that you have memorized a key phrase or two and possibly some sentences at the beginning and end of the story. After you have learned the story well enough that you no longer have to look at the book, you can begin to refine your technique.

Most professional tellers agree that it is not necessary to memorize every word in a story. However, you should memorize a literary tale if the style of writing is important.

Telling the story should be easy for anyone who prepares properly. The words should tell the story. You do not need to mime or act. If you are "seeing" the characters and scenes in your mind, the audience will see them as well. As the storyteller, you will have to decide when to expand your description so that your audience will better appreciate your story.

History

The earliest storytelling probably consisted of simple chants that praised the dawn or the stars, or expressed the joy of being alive. People sang other chants to accompany some task, such as grinding corn or sharpening tools or weapons.

As people began to wonder about the world around them, they created myths to explain natural occurrences. They assigned superhuman qualities to ordinary people, thus originating the hero tale.

Early storytelling combined stories, poetry, music, and dance. Many people told stories, but the best storytellers became entertainers for the community. These people also became historians for the group, marking the beginning of professional storytelling.

The Middle Ages, from about the A.D. 400's through the 1400's, saw the flowering of the storyteller's art. Storytellers were welcome in royal courts as well as in marketplaces. Traveling storytellers journeyed from land to land, gathering news and learning the favorite stories of various regions. Storytellers exchanged stories so often that it became difficult to trace the origin of many of their tales.

The storytellers of the Middle Ages had thorough training. Ruth Sawyer, a noted American storyteller and author of children's books, described the training of a

Lawrence Migdale

A storytelling session entertains a group of young listeners. This teacher dramatizes the action of the story with her expressive gestures and facial expressions.

troubadour, who was a medieval poet-musician. She wrote that a good troubadour was expected "to know perfectly all the current tales, to repeat all the noteworthy theses from the universities, to be well informed on court scandal, to know the healing power of herbs and *simples* (medicines), to be able to compose verses to a lord or lady at a moment's notice, and to play on at least two of the instruments then in favor at court."

No one knows how many storytellers entertained during the Middle Ages. Some writings say 426 minstrels were employed at the wedding of Princess Margaret of England in 1290. The many minstrels in the court of King Edward I included two women who performed under the names of Matill Makejoye and Pearl in the Egg.

After the invention of movable type in Europe about 1440, reading replaced listening, and the influence of the professional storyteller faded. Inexpensive pamphlets of popular tales known as *chapbooks* provided entertainment and also preserved some of the earliest stories. Oral storytelling survived mainly in rural areas.

The 1800's were a time of growing scholarly interest in folk literature. In 1812 and 1815, the brothers Jakob and Wilhelm Grimm published collections of German tales that became probably the best-known works of their kind. The brothers gathered their stories from the common people and faithfully preserved the unique structure and language pattern of the tales. See **Grimm.**

Peter Asbjørnsen and Jørgen Moe followed the example of the Grimms and collected Norwegian folk tales (see **Asbjørnsen, Peter Christen**). The *Fairy Tales* of Hans Christian Andersen of Denmark appeared in England in 1846. Many of his stories were his own adaptations of folk tales he had heard from storytellers. However, Andersen also added his own literary tales. In England, Joseph Jacobs searched folklore journals for tales of England, Scotland, Wales, and Ireland and rewrote them for children. The Folklore Society, founded in London in 1878, was devoted to the study of traditional culture, including stories.

The 1900's were a period when storytelling continued to flourish. During the early 1900's, Marie Shedlock, a retired English schoolteacher and gifted storyteller, made several tours throughout the United States to lecture on the art of storytelling. She emphasized the importance of storytelling as a natural way to introduce literature to children. Her work encouraged organized storytelling that had already begun in Sunday schools, kindergartens, and libraries throughout the United States. In 1903, a group of schoolteachers formed what is now the National Story League, a volunteer organization to promote the art of storytelling.

In 1973, the first National Storytelling Festival was held in Jonesborough, Tennessee. The success of the festival led to the founding of the National Association for the Preservation and Perpetuation of Storytelling, later the National Storytelling Association (NSA). In 1998, the NSA divided into two organizations, the National Storytelling Network and the International Storytelling Center. These groups and such organizations as the Australian Storytelling Guild in Australia and the Society for Storytelling in the United Kingdom provide resources and training for storytellers throughout the world. Regional, national, and international storytelling festivals inspire new types of stories.

The 2000's. The Internet has connected storytellers in the 2000's. There are numerous Web sites devoted to storytelling and folklore research. There are also online discussion groups and home pages for individual storytellers and storytelling organizations.

Today's storytellers are no longer limited primarily to traditional folklore. They also tell personal stories, autobiographical material, and original pieces.

Ann D. Carlson

Related articles in *World Book.* See Folklore and its list of *Related articles* for some famous stories and characters. See also:

Storytellers

Andersen, Hans C.	Grimm (family)	Perrault, Charles
Asbjørnsen,	Meistersinger	Sawyer, Ruth
Peter Christen	Minnesinger	Skald
Bard	Minstrel	Troubadour

Other related articles

Ballad	Mythology
Library (picture: Music helps	Nursery rhyme
tell a story)	Tennessee (picture: The Na-
Literature for children	tional Storytelling Festival)
Mother Goose	

See the *Books to read* section of the **Literature for children** article. See also the following books:

Additional resources

Stories for telling

Andersen, Hans Christian. *The Complete Fairy Tales and Stories.* Trans. by Erik Haugaard. 1974. Reprint. Anchor, 1983.

Asbjørnsen, P. C., and Moe, Jørgen. *East of the Sun and West of the Moon.* Various editions.

Babbitt, Natalie. *The Devil's Storybook.* Farrar, 1974. *The Devil's Other Storybook.* Farrar, 1987.

Baker, Augusta. *The Golden Lynx.* Lippincott, 1960.

Baltuck, Naomi. *Apples from Heaven.* Linnet, 1995. *Crazy Gibberish.* 1996.

Bruchac, Joseph, and Ross, Gayle. *The Girl Who Married the Moon: Tales from Native North America.* Bridgewater, 1994.

Bryan, Ashley. *Beat the Story-Drum, Pum-Pum.* Atheneum, 1980.

Chase, Richard. *The Jack Tales.* Houghton, 1943. *Grandfather Tales.* 1948.

Cole, Joanna. *Best Loved Folktales of the World.* Doubleday, 1983.

Colwell, Eileen. *A Storyteller's Choice.* Walck, 1964. *A Second Storyteller's Choice.* 1965. *The Magic Umbrella and Other Stories for Telling: With Notes on How to Tell Them.* Bodley Head, 1976.

Courlander, Harold, and Herzog, George. *The Cow-Tail Switch and Other West African Stories.* Holt, 1947. *The Fire on the Mountain.* Holt, 1950. *The Hat-Shaking Dance and Other Tales from the Gold Coast.* Harcourt, 1957. *The Piece of Fire and Other Haitian Tales.* Harcourt, 1964. *People of the Short Blue Corn: Tales and Legends of the Hopi Indians.* Harcourt, 1970.

DeSpain, Pleasant. *Eleven Nature Tales: A Multicultural Journey.* August Hse., 1996. *The Emerald Lizard: Fifteen Latin American Tales to Tell in English and Spanish.* 1999. *Sweet Land of Story: Thirty-Six American Tales to Tell.* 2000.

Fang, Linda. *The Ch'i-lin Purse: A Collection of Ancient Chinese Stories.* Farrar, 1995.

Forest, Heather. *Wisdom Tales from Around the World.* August Hse., 1996. *Wonder Tales from Around the World.* 1997.

Grimm, Jakob and Wilhelm. *Grimms' Tales for Young and Old: The Complete Stories.* Trans. by Ralph Manheim. Doubleday, 1983.

Hamilton, Edith. *Mythology.* Little, Brown, 1942.

Hamilton, Martha, and Weiss, Mitch. *Through the Grapevine: World Tales Kids Can Read and Tell.* August Hse., 2001.

Hamilton, Virginia. *Her Stories: African American Folktales, Fairy Tales, and True Tales.* Blue Sky, 1995. *The People Could Fly: The Book of Black Folktales.* Knopf, 1985.

Haskins, James. *The Headless Haunt and Other African-American Ghost Stories.* HarperCollins, 1994.

Holt, David, ed. *Ready-to-Tell Tales.* August Hse., 1994. *More Ready-to-Tell Tales from Around the World.* 2000.

Holt, David, and Mooney, Bill. *Spiders in the Hairdo: Modern Urban Legends.* August Hse., 1999. *The Exploding Toilet: Modern Urban Legends.* 2004.

Hutchinson, Veronica. *Chimney Corner Fairy Tales.* Minton, Balch, 1926.

Jacobs, Joseph. *English Folk and Fairy Tales.* Putnam, 1898. *More English Fairy Tales.* Putnam, 1904.

Kennedy, Richard. *Collected Stories.* Harper, 1987.

Kipling, Rudyard. *Just So Stories.* Country Life, 1912.

Lang, Andrew. *Blue Fairy Book, Green Fairy Book,* etc. 1891-1910. Reprints. Dover, 1965-1968. Twelve books, each title featuring a different color.

Leach, Maria. *Whistle in the Graveyard: Folktales to Chill Your Bones.* Viking, 1974.

Lester, Julius. *Tales of Uncle Remus: The Adventures of Brer Rabbit.* Dial, 1987. *More Tales of Uncle Remus.* 1988. *Further Tales of Uncle Remus.* 1989. *The Last Tales of Uncle Remus.* 1994.

Liyi, He. *The Spring of Butterflies and Other Folktales of China's Minority Peoples.* Lothrop, 1986.

Mabie, Hamilton Wright. *Folk Tales Every Child Should Know.* Grosset, 1912.

MacDonald, Margaret R. *Celebrate the World: Twenty Tellable Folktales for Multicultural Festivals.* Wilson. 1994. *Twenty Tellable Tales: Audience Participation Folktales for the Beginning Storyteller.* 1986. *When the Lights Go Out: Twenty Scary Tales to Tell.* 1988. *Shake-It-Up Tales!: Stories to Sing, Dance, Drum, and Act Out.* August Hse., 2000. *Tuck-Me-in Tales: Bedtime Stories from Around the World.* August Hse., 1996.

Martin, Rafe. *The Hungry Tigress: Buddhist Legends and Jataka Tales.* Parallax, 1990. *Mysterious Tales of Japan.* Putnam, 1996.

National Association for the Preservation and Perpetuation of Storytelling. *Best-Loved Stories at the National Storytelling Festival.* National Storytelling Pr., 1991. *Best-Loved Stories Told at the National Storytelling Festival.* 1992.

Miller, Teresa. *Joining In: An Anthology of Audience Participation Stories & How to Tell Them.* Yellow Moon Pr., 1988.

Nic Leodhas, Sorche. *Heather and Broom: Tales of the Scottish Highlands.* Holt, 1960. *Thistle and Thyme: Tales and Legends from Scotland.* 1962.

Oodgeroo. *Dreamtime: Aboriginal Stories.* Lothrop, 1994.

Phelps, Ethel J., ed. *The Maid of the North: Feminist Folk Tales from Around the World.* Holt, 1981.

Power, Effie. *Bag O' Tales: A Source Book for Story-Tellers.* Dutton, 1934. *Blue Caravan Tales.* 1935.

Quayle, Eric. *The Shining Princess and Other Japanese Legends.* Arcade, 1989.

Ransome, Arthur. *Old Peter's Russian Tales.* Nelson, 1916.

Ritchie, Alice. *Treasure of Li-Po.* Harcourt, 1949.

Ross, Eulalie Steinmetz. *The Lost Half-Hour.* Harcourt, 1963.

San Souci. *Cut from the Same Cloth: American Women of Myth, Legend, and Tall Tale.* Philomel, 1993.

Sandburg, Carl. *More Rootabagas: Stories by Carl Sandburg.* Random Hse., 1993.

Schwartz, Alvin. *Scary Stories to Tell in the Dark.* Lippincott, 1981. *More Scary Stories to Tell in the Dark.* 1987.

Seeger, Pete, and Jacobs, P. D. *Pete Seeger's Storytelling Book.* Harvest Bks., 2001.

Sherlock, Philip M. *Anansi, the Spider Man: Jamaican Folk Tales.* Crowell, 1954.

Singer, Isaac Bashevis. *Stories for Children.* Farrar, 1962. *When Schlemiel Went to Warsaw and Other Stories.* 1968.

Uchida, Yoshiko. T*he Dancing Kettle and Other Japanese Folk Tales.* Harcourt, 1949. *The Sea of Gold and Other Tales from Japan.* Scribner, 1965.

Vuong, Lynette D. *The Brocaded Slipper and Other Vietnamese Tales.* Harper, 1992.

Walker, Barbara. *The Dancing Palm Tree and Other Nigerian Folktales.* Tex. Tech Univ. Pr., 1990. *A Treasury of Turkish Folktales for Children.* Shoe String Pr., 1988.

Wolkstein, Diane. *The Magic Orange Tree and Other Haitian Folktales.* Knopf, 1978.

Young, Richard and Judy. *African-American Folktales for Young Readers: Including Favorite Stories from African and African-American Storytellers.* August Hse., 1993.

Yee, Paul. *Tales from Gold Mountain: Stories of the Chinese in the New World.* Macmillan, 1989.

Yep, Laurence. *The Rainbow People.* Harper, 1989.

Yolen, Jane. *Favorite Folktales from Around the World.* Random Hse., 1986. *Gray Heroes: Elder Tales from Around the World.* Penguin, 1999.

Yolen, Jane, and Stemple, H. E. L. *Mirror, Mirror: Forty Folk Tales for Mothers and Daughters to Share.* Viking, 2000.

Storytelling guides

Baker, Augusta, and Greene, Ellin. *Storytelling: Art and Technique.* 2nd ed. Bowker, 1987.

Bauer, Caroline Feller. *Caroline Feller Bauer's New Handbook for Storytellers: With Stories, Poems, Magic, and More.* Am. Lib. Assn., 1992.

Bryant, Sara Cone. *How to Tell Stories to Children.* 1924. Reprint. Gale, 1973.

Clarkson, Atelia, and Cross, G. B., eds. *World Folktales: A Scribner Resource Collection.* Scribner, 1980.

Colum, Padraic. *Story Telling, New and Old.* 1927. Reprint. Macmillan, 1968.

Colwell, Eileen. *Storytelling.* Bodley Head, 1980.

Cook, Elizabeth. *The Ordinary and the Fabulous: An Introduction to Myths, Legends and Fairy Tales for Teachers and Storytellers.* 2nd ed. Cambridge, 1975.

De Vos, Gail. *Storytelling for Young Adults: A Guide to Tales for Teens.* 2nd ed. Lib. Unlimited, 2003. *Tales, Rumors, and Gossip: Exploring Contemporary Folk Literature in Grades 7-12.* Lib. Unlimited, 1996.

De Wit, Dorothy. *Children's Faces Looking Up: Program Building for the Storyteller.* Am. Lib. Assn., 1979.

Leeming, David A., ed. *Storytelling Encyclopedia: Historical, Cultural, and Multiethnic Approaches to Oral Traditions Around the World.* Oryx, 1997.

Lipman, Doug. *Improving Your Storytelling: Beyond the Basics for All Who Tell Stories in Work or Play.* August Hse., 1999. *The Storytelling Coach.* 1995.

Livo, Norma J., and Rietz, S. A. *Storytelling: Folklore Sourcebook.* Lib. Unlimited, 1991. S*torytelling: Process and Practice.* 1986.

MacDonald, Margaret R. *The Parent's Guide to Storytelling.* 2nd ed. August Hse., 2001. *The Storyteller's Start-Up Book: Finding, Learning, Performing, and Using Folktales Including Twelve Tellable Tales.* 1993.

Maguire, Jack. *Creative Storytelling: Choosing, Inventing, and Sharing Tales for Children.* Yellow Moon Pr., 1992.

Mooney, Bill, and Holt, David. *The Storyteller's Guide: Storytellers Share Advice for the Classroom, Boardroom, Showroom, Podium, Pulpit and Center Stage.* August Hse., 1996.

Pellowski, Anne.*The Storytelling Handbook: A Young People's Collection of Unusual Tales and Helpful Hints on How to Tell Them.* The World of Storytelling. Bowker, 1977. Simon & Schuster, 1995.

Sawyer, Ruth. *The Way of the Storyteller.* 1942. Reprint. Penguin, 1977.

Schimmel, Nancy. *Just Enough to Make a Story: A Sourcebook for Storytelling.* 3rd ed. Sisters' Choice, 1992. (Visit her Web site at www.sisterschoice.com for more information.)

Shedlock, Marie L. *The Art of the Storyteller.* 3rd ed. Dover, 1951.

Ziskind, Sylvia. *Telling Stories to Children.* Wilson, 1976.

Zipes, Jack. *Creative Storytelling: Building Community, Changing Lives.* Routledge, 1995.

Scholarly studies

Bettelheim, Bruno. *The Uses of Enchantment: The Meaning and Importance of Fairy Tales.* Knopf, 1976.

Birch, Carol, and Heckler, Melissa, eds. *Who Says? Essays on Pivotal Issues in Contemporary Storytelling.* August Hse., 1996.

Campbell, Joseph. *The Hero with a Thousand Faces.* 1949. Reprint. Princeton, 2004.

MacDonald, Margaret Read, ed. *Traditional Storytelling Today: An International Sourcebook.* Fitzroy Dearborn, 1999.

Opie, Iona and Peter. *The Classic Fairy Tales.* 1974. Reprint. Oxford, 1992.

Stone, Kay. *Burning Brightly: New Light on Old Tales Told Today.* Broadview, 1998.
Tatar, Maria. *Annotated Classic Fairy Tales.* Norton, 2003. *The Hard Facts of the Grimms' Fairy Tales.* 2nd ed. Princeton, 2003.
Zipes, Jack. *Don't Bet on the Prince.* Methuen, 1986. *Happily Ever After: Fairy Tales, Children, and the Culture Industry.* Routledge, 1997.

Web sites related to storytelling

August House, Inc. at: http://www.augusthouse.com
Library of Congress American Folklife Center at: http://www.loc.gov/folklife/
National Storytelling Network at: http://www.storynet.org

Stoss, *shtohs,* **Veit,** *fyt* (1440?-1533), was a German sculptor. His works have a rich, complex appearance. Stoss and the German sculptor Tilman Riemenschneider used a late Gothic style. Both represented Christian themes almost entirely, but Stoss's sculpture is more dramatic and expressive than Riemenschneider's quiet, lyrical sculpture.

Stoss was born in Germany. He went to Kraków, Poland, in 1477. There, he worked for 12 years on what is probably his masterpiece, the huge altar for the Church of St. Mary. The stagelike altarpiece is filled with larger than life-sized figures representing episodes from the life of the Virgin Mary. Stoss later settled in Nuremberg, Germany. He died in September 1533.

Germanisches Nationalmuseum, Nuremberg, Germany

A Veit Stoss statue in wood called *Madonna and Child* was carved about 1510 in the late Gothic style of sculpture.

Alison McNeil Kettering

Stout, Rex (1886-1975), was an American detective-story writer. He created the fat, beer-drinking, orchid-loving detective Nero Wolfe. Wolfe stays in his New York City brownstone residence and sends his able assistant Archie Goodwin out for clues. Later, while sitting with a glass of beer, Wolfe solves the mystery. Wolfe first appeared in *Fer-de-Lance* (1934). Other Nero Wolfe mysteries include *Too Many Cooks* (1938), *Some Buried Caesar* (1939), *And Be a Villain* (1948), and *A Family Affair* (1975).

Rex Todhunter Stout was born on Dec. 1, 1886, in Noblesville, Indiana. He devised a school banking system, which he set up in about 400 cities and towns between 1917 and 1927. Profits from the system made him wealthy and enabled him to devote his time to writing. Stout died on Oct. 27, 1975.   David Geherin

Stove. See Heating (Local heating devices); **Range.**

Stowe, Harriet Beecher (1811-1896), is remembered chiefly for her antislavery novel, *Uncle Tom's Cabin*

Brown Bros.

Harriet Beecher Stowe

(1851-1852). But when most people think of the book's famous characters, Uncle Tom, Little Eva, Topsy, and Simon Legree, they are not remembering the book. They are thinking instead of George L. Aiken's play of 1852, or of crude and violent spectacles called "Tom Shows," which played in small towns in the North. Aiken's play and the Tom Shows only faintly suggest Stowe's book.

Uncle Tom's Cabin is melodramatic and sentimental, but it is more than a melodrama. It re-creates characters, scenes, and incidents with humor and realism. It analyzes the issue of slavery in the Midwest, New England, and the South during the days of the Fugitive Slave Law. The book intensified the disagreement between the North and the South that led to the American Civil War (1861-1865). Stowe's name became hated in the South.

Other works. Stowe's works, dealing with New England in the late 1700's and early 1800's, are important for anyone who wants to understand the American past. These include *The Minister's Wooing* (1859), *The Pearl of Orr's Island* (1862), and *Oldtown Folks* (1869), all novels; and *Sam Lawson's Oldtown Fireside Stories* (1872), a collection of stories. They present everyday life of the New England village, and make clear the good and bad aspects of Puritanism. Another novel, *Dred, A Tale of the Great Dismal Swamp* (1856), deals with slavery in the South. Of her later books, the most shocking to her contemporaries was *Lady Byron Vindicated* (1870). It told of Lady Byron's separation from her husband, the famous poet Lord Byron. Stowe's account was based on Lady Byron's talk with her in 1856.

Her life. Stowe was born on June 14, 1811, in Litchfield, Connecticut. Her father, Lyman Beecher, was a Presbyterian minister. Stowe was educated at the academy in Litchfield and at Hartford Female Seminary. From 1832 to 1850, she lived in Cincinnati, Ohio, where her father served as president of Lane Theological Seminary. In 1836, she married Calvin Stowe, a member of the Lane faculty. Her years in Cincinnati furnished her with many of the characters and incidents for *Uncle Tom's Cabin,* which she wrote in Brunswick, Maine. After the publication of the book, Stowe became famous overnight. On a visit to England, she was welcomed by the English abolitionists. She died on July 1, 1896.

Stowe was the sister of the clergyman Henry Ward Beecher and the reformer and educator Catharine Beecher. See **Beecher, Catharine Esther; Beecher, Henry Ward.**   John Clendenning

See also **Abolition movement; Uncle Tom's Cabin.**

Additional resources

Gelletly, LeeAnne. *Harriet Beecher Stowe.* Chelsea Hse., 2000. Younger readers.
Hedrick, Joan D. *Harriet Beecher Stowe.* Oxford, 1994.
Thulesius, Olav. *Harriet Beecher Stowe in Florida, 1867 to 1884.* McFarland, 2001.

Strabismus, *struh BIHZ muhs,* is an abnormal condition of the eyes in which one eye is fixed on one object and the other eye is fixed on another object. This condition is also known as *heterotropia, cross-eye,* and *squint.* Normally, the position of the eyes enables both eyes to see the same object at the same time and in the same place. In strabismus, one eye turns away from its normal position. If this eye turns inward toward the nose, the condition is known as *convergent strabismus.* In *divergent strabismus,* the eye turns outward. In *supravergent strabismus,* the eye turns upward or downward. Strabismus may be constant or periodic and may involve only one eye or alternating eyes.

Convergent strabismus is the most common form of strabismus. Most cases of convergent strabismus occur in far-sighted children under 4 years of age. To see clearly, far-sighted children often force their eyes together, resulting in strabismus. Strabismus is sometimes caused by weakened, overactive, or restricted eye muscles. Damaged nerve connections can also cause the condition. The tendency to have strabismus is inherited.

Strabismus can be corrected in children, especially if treatment starts early. Treatment of strabismus usually involves wearing glasses, forced development of the weaker eye, and training the eyes to function together. However, many cases of strabismus eventually require surgery or the use of drugs to weaken an overactive muscle. If strabismus is not corrected, vision in the affected eye may never develop properly or may be lost entirely.   Ramesh C. Tripathi and Brenda Tripathi

See also **Eye** (Strabismus).

Strabo, *STRAY boh* (63 B.C.?-A.D. 24?), was a Greek geographer and historian. He became famous for his 17-volume *Geography,* which described all parts of the known world. These volumes are the best source of geographical information about the Mediterranean countries at the beginning of the Christian Era. Strabo also wrote a lengthy history that is now lost. He was born in Amasia, Pontus. He studied in Rome and Alexandria, and traveled in Arabia, southern Europe, and northern Africa.   Howard B. Wolman

Strachey, *STRAY chee,* **Lytton,** *LIHT uhn* (1880-1932), was an English biographer, essayist, and literary critic. His best-known works are biographies—*Eminent Victorians* (1918) and *Queen Victoria* (1921). *Eminent Victorians* is a group of sketches about four famous figures of Victorian England—the educator Thomas Arnold, General Charles Gordon, Cardinal Henry Manning, and the nurse Florence Nightingale. He later published *Elizabeth and Essex* (1928) and *Portraits in Miniature* (1931). Stressing personality over political context, Strachey's sketches are written in an unorthodox, ironic style that advanced the craft of biography as aesthetic portraiture.

Giles Lytton Strachey was born in London. He formed most of his ideas and lifelong friendships while studying at Cambridge University from 1899 to 1903. Strachey gained a place in the center of London literary life through the wit, elegance, and skeptical nature of his personality and writings. Strachey and his Cambridge friends formed the nucleus of what became known as the Bloomsbury Group (see **Bloomsbury Group**). This group included some of the leading English intellectuals of the day.   Garrett Stewart

Stradivari, *STRAD uh VAIR ee,* **Antonio** (1644?-1737), was one of the leading instrument makers in music history. He used Stradivarius, the Latin form of his name, on the labels of his instruments. Stradivari was probably born in Cremona, Italy. He studied there with Nicolo Amati, a noted instrument maker, and served for a time as Amati's assistant. During his long career, Stradivari made about 1,100 instruments. Of these, about 635 violins, 17 violas, and 60 cellos still exist.

Stradivari's instruments combine excellent wood, outstanding craftsmanship, beautiful shape and proportion, and superb varnish. His masterpieces provide an incomparable blend of strength and sweetness of sound. Stradivari's instruments, like others of his time, were later modified. These changes gave the instruments in-

Ashmolean Museum, Oxford, England
Stradivari made a violin called *the Messiah* **in 1716.**

creased string tension and the structural strength to resist that tension. The modified instruments gained the volume needed to perform in the large concert halls and with the large orchestras of the 1800's and 1900's.
Abram Loft

Strafford, Earl of (1593-1641), was an English statesman. His given and family name was Thomas Wentworth. From 1614 to 1628, he was a leader of Parliament in its struggle with Kings James I and Charles I. But he drew away from his parliamentary friends as their criticism of Charles I grew more vigorous. In 1628, he joined the king's side and in 1633 became lord deputy of Ireland. His administration was harsh.

Wentworth returned to England in 1639 and became Earl of Strafford in 1640. He served as one of Charles's chief advisers in his struggle against Parliament. Parliamentary leaders saw Strafford as a threat and in 1640 decided to try him for treason. Instead, Parliament passed a bill of attainder, an act to punish him without trial. Charles had promised protection but, fearing mob violence, signed the bill. Two days later, Strafford was executed. Wentworth was born in London.   Charles Carlton

Strait is a narrow waterway connecting two larger bodies of water. Many wars have been fought and many treaties negotiated for control and use of important straits. These include the Strait of Gibraltar between the Atlantic Ocean and the Mediterranean Sea, and the straits of Bosporus and Dardanelles between the Mediterranean and Black seas. The Strait of Magellan at the tip of South America is the only strait between the Atlantic and Pacific oceans. The terms *strait, passage,* and *channel* are often used in place of one another. See the separate articles in *World Book* on the various straits, such as **Gibraltar, Strait of.**   James C. Walters

Straits Settlements, in Southeast Asia, were part of colonial British Malaya. The British East India Company formed the settlements in 1826. They became a colony in 1867. The Straits Settlements included Singapore, Melaka, Penang-Wellesley, and the islands of the Dindings district. The mainland of the Dindings district was added to the settlements in 1874. Christmas Island joined the settlements in 1900. The Cocos Islands joined in 1903, and Labuan Island joined in 1907.

During World War II (1939-1945), the Japanese occupied the settlements and Malaya. The Straits Settlements colony was dissolved in 1946. Singapore, with Cocos and Christmas islands, became a colony, and Labuan Island was added to North Borneo. In 1957, the United Kingdom ceded Penang and Melaka to the Federation of Malaya. In 1963, the former Straits Settlements, Malaya, Singapore, Sarawak, and Sabah (formerly North Borneo) merged to form Malaysia. Singapore became an independent country in 1965.   Markus P. M. Vink

Strand, Paul (1890-1976), an American photographer, helped develop photography as an art. Strand took detailed, focused photos that presented subjects simply and directly. He rejected the hazy, out-of-focus style that had become popular during the late 1800's.

Some of Strand's photographs show the influence of the cubist painters, who emphasized the basic geometric shapes of their subjects. To create a similar effect, Strand took photos of everyday objects, such as bowls and fences, from close and unusual angles. He later took detailed photographs of machines and landscapes.

In 1915, Strand began to take unposed portraits of

Photograph from the *Mexican Portfolio;* © 1967 Estate of Paul Strand (Art Institute of Chicago)
Plaza—State of Puebla, a photograph taken by Paul Strand in 1933, portrays the beauty of a simple scene in Mexico.

people he saw on the streets of New York City. He later visited many countries, including Egypt, Ghana, Italy, and Mexico, and photographed the people for a book of pictures on each nation. He was born on Oct. 16, 1890, in New York City.   Charles Hagen

Strasbourg, *STRAS burg* or *strahz BOOR* (pop. 267,051; met. area pop. 427,245), is a trading center in France. Its location on the Ill River and its canal link with the Rhine make it an important port. It stands 250 miles (402 kilometers) east of Paris (see **France** [political map]). Strasbourg's plants produce chemicals, leather, metals, paper, plastics, and textiles.

Strasbourg is an old city with many medieval buildings. The city's Gothic cathedral, with its famous clock and magnificent rose window, is one of the most beautiful in Europe. Its spire is 466 feet (142 meters) high.

G. Marche, FPG
Strasbourg is famous for its magnificent Gothic cathedral, *shown here.* This beautiful church was completed in 1439.

Strasbourg University was founded in 1538.

The location of Strasbourg near the German-French border has made the city important commercially, but it has also made it a prize of war for many years. It was a German free town until 1681, when it was united with France. During the French Revolution in 1792, "The Marseillaise," the French national anthem, was written in Strasbourg. After the Franco-Prussian War in 1870, France ceded Strasbourg to Germany. The city became French again after the Treaty of Versailles in 1919. German troops occupied Strasbourg during World War II (1939-1945). Strasbourg has been the headquarters of the Council of Europe since 1949.   William M. Reddy

See also **Alsace-Lorraine.**

Strassmann, *STRAHS manh,* **Fritz** (1902-1980), was a German chemist. His work with Otto Hahn, a German chemist, and Lise Meitner, an Austrian nuclear physicist, led to the discovery of *nuclear fission* (the splitting of atomic nuclei). In 1938, Strassmann and Hahn found that the bombardment of uranium atoms with neutrons produces the element barium. Meitner and Austrian physicist Otto R. Frisch explained in 1939 that the neutrons had split uranium nuclei, producing nuclei of barium and other elements.

Strassmann was born in Boppard, Germany, on Feb. 22, 1902. He studied at the Technological Institute in Hanover. In 1929, he joined the Kaiser Wilhelm Institute for Chemistry in Berlin (now the Max Planck Institute for Chemistry in Mainz). He became director of the institute in 1946. In 1985, Yad Vashem, Israel's memorial to victims of the Holocaust, honored Strassmann for risking his life to save a Jew from the Nazis in 1943. Strassmann died on April 22, 1980.   Matthew Stanley

See also **Hahn, Otto; Meitner, Lise.**

Strategic Air Command (SAC) was the largest organization of the United States Air Force until June 1992, when an Air Force reorganization eliminated the command. SAC bombers were put under the authority of a new Air Combat Command. See **Air Force, United States** (Combat commands). SAC missiles became part of the Air Force Space Command in 1993.

SAC's main purpose was to deter nuclear war. It could launch its forces within minutes of a warning and strike anywhere in the world. It had more than 120,000 military and civilian personnel, about 300 bombers, and approximately 1,000 nuclear-armed intercontinental ballistic missiles (ICBM's). The bombers could deliver either nuclear or conventional weapons.

The Army Air Forces set up SAC in 1946, with headquarters in Washington, D.C. In 1948, the headquarters were moved to Offutt Air Force Base, near Omaha, Nebraska. Also in 1948, SAC introduced in-flight refueling, which gave its bombers intercontinental range. SAC added ICBM's to its forces in 1958.   Wayne Thompson

See also **Offutt Air Force Base.**

Strategic Arms Limitation Talks (SALT), a series of meetings between the Soviet Union and the United States, took place between 1969 and 1979. The two nations met in an attempt to limit the production and distribution of nuclear weapons. United States President Lyndon B. Johnson proposed the talks in January 1967 to try to end the costly U.S.-Soviet arms race. At that time, the Soviets were trying to overtake the United States in the production of offensive intercontinental ballistic missiles (ICBM's) and submarine-launched missiles. Later, the Soviets began building an antiballistic missile (ABM) system to defend Moscow.

The first round of SALT meetings lasted from 1969 to 1972. The meetings took place in Helsinki, Finland; Vienna, Austria; and Geneva, Switzerland. A second round, held in Geneva, lasted from 1973 to 1979.

The first round of meetings led to two major U.S.-Soviet agreements which were signed in 1972. The two agreements together became known as SALT I. One agreement was a treaty limiting each country's defensive missile system to two ABM sites with no more than 100 missiles at each site. The treaty was later changed to allow each nation only one site. The other SALT I pact limited distribution of certain offensive nuclear weapons for five years. Both of the agreements went into effect in 1972.

In 1979, another round of SALT talks led to the signing of a U.S.-Soviet treaty limiting long-range bombers and missiles. But the pact, known as SALT II, did not officially go into effect because the United States Senate never ratified it. The Senate stopped considering the treaty in 1980, partly to protest a Soviet invasion of Afghanistan. However, the limits under SALT II were observed until 1986.

In 1991, the Soviet Union was dissolved. Most of the former Soviet republics formed a loose confederation of independent states. Key members agreed to abide by the ABM Treaty of SALT I.

In 2002, however, the United States withdrew from the ABM Treaty. United States President George W. Bush claimed that the development of an extensive missile defense system was central to the security of the United States.   Robert J. Pranger

Strategic Arms Reduction Treaty (START) refers to certain arms control agreements designed to reduce the numbers of long-range nuclear weapons. The United States and the Soviet Union signed the first, START I, in July 1991. START I called for a reduction in the number of long-range nuclear warheads and bombs held by each country by about one-third over a period of seven years.

In late 1991, however, the Soviet Union broke apart. Afterward, the former Soviet weapons were in the newly independent countries of Belarus, Kazakhstan, Russia, and Ukraine. The United States ratified START I in 1992, and the four former Soviet republics with nuclear weapons did so by 1994. The treaty took effect in 1994. By the end of 1996, Belarus, Kazakhstan, and Ukraine turned over all their nuclear weapons to Russia.

The second START agreement, START II, was signed in 1993 by the United States and Russia. START II aimed to cut the total number of United States and former Soviet long-range nuclear warheads and bombs to less than half that proposed by START I. Russia and the United States would then each be left with between 3,000 and 3,500 of these weapons. To take effect, START II required ratification by the United States and Russia and the beginning of the implementation of START I. The United States ratified START II in 1996. In 2000, Russian leaders approved START II, but only after making changes in it. The United States did not ratify the changes, and the treaty never went into effect.

Dan Caldwell

Strategic Defense Initiative was a United States effort lasting from 1983 to 1993 to develop a high-technology system of defense against nuclear missiles. The research centered on the use of both ground-based systems and weapons mounted aboard artificial satellites in outer space. Such weapons were to have included *lasers* (instruments that produce intense light beams) and other devices capable of destroying missiles and warheads in flight.

The Strategic Defense Initiative, also called SDI or "Star Wars," was announced in 1983 by United States President Ronald Reagan. Reagan planned a large-scale system of defense that would shield the nation from a massive *first strike* (initial nuclear attack) by the Soviet Union.

In 1991, the Soviet Union broke apart. As a result, fears of a major nuclear war decreased significantly. In 1993, the administration of President Bill Clinton formally ended SDI as a program.

The SDI program was controversial for a number of

reasons. Many critics argued that several technologies needed to complete a full SDI system might not work. But supporters believed these challenges could be met.

In 2002, the United States began developing a land- and sea-based missile defense system along its west coast. However, the planned system is more limited than an SDI system would have been. The new system will be designed to intercept a single missile launched by a "rogue nation"—that is, a nation that ignores international law and supports terrorism—rather than to protect against a massive missile strike.   George W. S. Kuhn

Strategic Petroleum Reserve is a system of United States government storage facilities that hold supplies of crude oil. The government created the reserve to protect the nation from disruptions in the flow of petroleum supplies. The reserve is maintained by the U.S. Department of Energy. It has the capacity to store more than 700 million barrels of oil in underground salt caverns along the Gulf Coast.

The U.S. Congress created the Strategic Petroleum Reserve in 1975 as a response to nationwide fuel shortages. In 1973 and 1974, oil-producing nations in the Middle East had halted their exports of oil to the United States to punish it for supporting Israel in the 1973 Arab-Israeli war. In 1977, the U.S. government acquired existing salt caverns to store the reserve's first stockpile of oil. The Department of Energy then began to create additional caverns within salt deposits along the Gulf Coast. Today, four storage facilities—two in Louisiana and two in Texas—contain a total of 62 caverns. A typical cavern measures about 2,000 feet (610 meters) from top to bottom and lies at a depth of about 2,000 to 4,000 feet (610 to 1,220 meters) below ground.

The president of the United States has the authority to order the sale and transfer of oil from the reserve to commercial distributors if the nation faces an oil supply disruption that threatens its economy. Such transfers occurred in 1991 at the start of the Persian Gulf War and in 2005 after Hurricane Katrina hit the Gulf Coast.

In 2005, Congress authorized the Department of Energy to expand the reserve's capacity to 1 billion barrels. To reach the desired capacity, the department chose in 2007 to develop a new storage site in southeastern Mississippi and to expand the capacities of existing sites in Louisiana and Texas.

Critically reviewed by the U.S. Department of Energy

Strategic Services, Office of (OSS), was a secret United States government agency responsible for foreign intelligence during World War II (1939-1945). William J. Donovan headed the office under the direction of the Joint Chiefs of Staff. The OSS was set up in 1942 to gather and analyze information and to conduct psychological and guerrilla warfare. Its functions were divided between the Department of State and the War Department after the war. In 1947, the Central Intelligence Agency was formed to coordinate the activities of all intelligence agencies (see **Central Intelligence Agency**).   Donald P. Steury

Stratemeyer, Edward (1862-1930), was an American author who created some of the most popular characters in children's literature. About 1903, he founded the Stratemeyer Syndicate, which employed a staff of authors who wrote many of the books. Stratemeyer wrote —or outlined for others to write—more than 800 chil-

dren's books published under more than 60 pen names.

Stratemeyer's best-known books are adventure stories that feature teen-aged characters. As Franklin Dixon, he wrote about the Hardy Boys. His other pen names included Victor Appleton for books about Tom Swift, Laura Lee Hope for stories about the Bobbsey Twins, and Arthur Winfield for tales about the Rover Boys. Just before his death on May 10, 1930, he created the character of Nancy Drew under the name of Carolyn Keene (see **Keene, Carolyn**). Stratemeyer was born in Elizabeth, New Jersey, on Oct. 4, 1862.   Nancy Lyman Huse

Stratford-upon-Avon is a quiet English market town famous as William Shakespeare's birthplace. It is one of the oldest towns in England. It lies in the green valley of the River Avon (see **England** [political map]). High-peaked Old English-style houses line its narrow streets. It is the largest town in the district of Stratford-on-Avon.

The house where Shakespeare probably was born has been kept as a memorial. It is always open to visitors. At Shottery, 1 mile (1.6 kilometers) west of Stratford, is the thatch-roofed cottage that was the home of Anne Hathaway, Shakespeare's wife. The Guild Hall and grammar school are kept as they were in Shakespeare's day. Visitors also go to Wilmcote, 2 ½ miles (4 kilometers) northwest of Stratford, to see the cottage of Mary Arden, Shakespeare's mother. Shakespeare and his wife are buried in Stratford's Holy Trinity Church. See **Shakespeare, William** (Shakespeare's life: pictures).

In 1879, a Shakespeare Memorial was completed on the riverbank above the church. It includes a theater, a museum, and a library. The theater burned in 1926, but people donated funds to rebuild it. The new theater, designed by Elisabeth Scott, opened in 1932. It is called the Royal Shakespeare Theatre. The Royal Shakespeare Company performs Shakespeare's plays there. This permanent company includes many of the finest British actors and directors. A Shakespeare Center opened in 1964 to house the Shakespeare collections and provide a meeting place for scholars.   Peter R. Mounfield

Strathcona and Mount Royal, Baron of (1820-1914), Donald Alexander Smith, was a Canadian fur trader, railroad builder, financier, and statesman. He was closely associated with the Hudson's Bay Company from 1838 until his death on Jan. 21, 1914, and became a governor of the company in 1889. He went to Labrador when he was 18 and became a fur trader. Afterward, he moved to Canada and helped the Canadians acquire the territories of the Hudson's Bay Company.

When Manitoba became a province of Canada, Smith was elected to the Manitoba Assembly. The next year, he was appointed commissioner for the North West Territories and was elected to the Dominion House of Commons, serving from 1871 to 1880 and from 1887 to 1896. Smith was the chief promoter of the Canadian Pacific Railway. He served as president of the Bank of Montreal and as chancellor of McGill University. From 1896 to 1906, he acted as Canadian high commissioner in London. Smith was born in Forres, Scotland, on Aug. 6, 1820.   John Elgin Foster

Stratosphere is a layer of Earth's atmosphere. It lies above the *troposphere,* the atmospheric layer nearest Earth. The stratosphere begins about 6 miles (10 kilometers) above Earth's surface in the polar regions and about 12 miles (19 kilometers) near the equator. The upper boundary, called the *stratopause,* lies at an altitude of about 30 miles (48 kilometers).

The stratosphere generally has a lower layer of nearly steady temperature and an upper layer in which the temperature increases with altitude. The lower layer has a temperature of about –67 °F (–55 °C). Near the top, the stratosphere reaches a maximum temperature of about 28 °F (–2 °C). The increase in temperature with height is due mainly to the absorption of sunlight by *ozone* (a form of oxygen) in the stratosphere. Stratospheric ozone also shields human beings from ultraviolet radiation of the sun. About 80 to 90 percent of the total ozone in the atmosphere is found in the stratosphere. See **Ozone.**

The stratosphere has complex wind systems, but violent storms do not occur there. It is nearly cloudless and extremely dry, except for the polar regions, where ice clouds form during winter.   Veerabhadran Ramanathan

See also **Air; Balloon** (Balloon explorations of the upper atmosphere); **Ionosphere; Mesosphere; Thermosphere; Troposphere.**

Stratton, Charles Sherwood (1838-1883), was an American midget who became best known by his circus name, General Tom Thumb. As a youth, Stratton was only 25 inches (64 centimeters) tall and weighed 15 pounds (6.8 kilograms). He was so bright that at the age of 6 he was exhibited by P. T. Barnum as though he were a full-grown man. Later, Stratton grew to be 40 inches (100 centimeters) tall and weighed 70 pounds (32 kilograms).

Stratton was born on Jan. 4, 1838, in Bridgeport, Connecticut, to parents of normal height. Barnum persuaded Stratton's parents to allow the boy to join his museum in New York City in 1842.

Barnum took him to Europe in 1844, where he entertained royalty and caused a sensation. In 1863, Stratton married Lavinia Warren (1841-1919), another one of Barnum's midgets. Stratton toured with Barnum's circus in 1881. He died on July 15, 1883.

Robert L. Parkinson

See also **Barnum, P. T.**

Stratus. See Cloud (Kinds of clouds; picture).

Straus, Oscar (1870-1954), an Austrian composer, was the last of the successful Viennese operetta composers. Straus composed more than 40 operettas. The most popular were *A Waltz Dream* (1907) and *The Chocolate Soldier* (1908). His last successful operetta, *Three Waltzes* (1935), used the waltz music of Johann Strauss, Sr., and Johann Strauss, Jr., in the first two acts and his own music for the third act.

Straus was born on March 6, 1870, in Vienna. Beginning in 1900, he worked for several years composing music for a Berlin cabaret, writing about 500 cabaret songs. He lived in New York City and Hollywood from 1940 until 1948, when he returned to Austria. He composed several motion-picture scores as well as a serenade for string orchestra, a piano trio, and many solo piano pieces. He died on Jan. 11, 1954.   Charles H. Webb

Brown Bros.
Charles S. Stratton

Strauss, *strows* or *shtrows,* **Johann,** *YOH hahn,* **Sr.** (1804-1849), was an Austrian composer who became known as the "Father of the Waltz." He was also a violinist and the leader of a popular orchestra that played light, entertaining music. Several of Strauss's sons became famous for composing and conducting waltzes, notably Johann Strauss, Jr.

Strauss's compositions include all the favorite types of dance music in Austria in the early 1800's. He composed about 250 works, including more than 150 waltzes. His waltzes embody the popular, tuneful qualities of Austrian folk music. As his waltz style matured, he began to insert rhythmic surprises to add interest and variety to these graceful, lilting pieces for string orchestra. His most famous composition is the "Radetzky March" (1848).

Strauss was born on March 14, 1804, in Vienna. After studying violin and harmony for a time, he joined the popular orchestra of Michael Pamer at age 15. Strauss organized his own orchestra in about 1825 to play in Viennese taverns and inns, becoming well known for his waltzes. As his reputation grew, his orchestra increased in size and played in many Austrian cities and towns. Later, the Strauss orchestra performed throughout Europe, enjoying great success wherever it played. Strauss died of scarlet fever on Sept. 25, 1849.   Daniel T. Politoske

See also **Strauss, Johann, Jr.; Waltz.**

Strauss, *strows* or *shtrows,* **Johann,** *YOH hahn,* **Jr.** (1825-1899), was an Austrian composer who became known as the "Waltz King." Strauss composed nearly 400 waltzes that represent the peak of their style. He also composed other popular orchestral dance works and 16 operettas. In addition, he was a violinist and the leader of a successful orchestra that played light music.

Strauss's music includes all the popular dance types of the mid-1800's in Austria, notably the waltz, polka, and quadrille. He also wrote many marches. The long, lyrical melodies of Strauss's waltzes dominate the music, while unusual rhythmic patterns disguise or cover the ¾ waltz meter. Strauss's most popular operettas include *Die Fledermaus (The Bat,* 1874) and *Die Zigeunerbaron (The Gypsy Baron,* 1885).

Strauss was born on Oct. 25, 1825, in Vienna, the oldest son of composer Johann Strauss, Sr. The father wanted his three sons—Josef, Johann, and Eduard—to enter business when they were old enough. However, his wife wanted them to have some musical training. With her encouragement, Johann received violin lessons secretly from a member of his father's orchestra. Johann, Jr., received more thorough musical training after Johann, Sr., left his family in 1842 to live with his mistress.

When he was almost 19, Strauss formed a small orchestra that performed with great success. The orchestra soon was a rival to his father's orchestra. After Johann, Sr., died in 1849, Johann, Jr., merged the two orchestras. The group performed throughout Austria, Germany, Poland, and Russia. From 1863 to 1871, Strauss served as music director of the court balls in Vienna. During this time, he wrote such famous waltzes as "On the Beautiful, Blue Danube" (1867), "Tales from the Vienna Woods" (1868), and "Wine, Women, and Song" (1869).

In 1871, Strauss gave up his music director position and began to compose operettas. He also composed many other popular waltzes, including "Vienna Blood" (1873) and "The Emperor Waltz" (1888). Among his popular polkas are "Thunder and Lightning" (1868) and "Pizzicato Polka" (1870), which he composed with his brother Josef. Strauss died on June 3, 1899.   Daniel T. Politoske

See also **Waltz; Strauss, Johann, Sr.**

Additional resources

Kemp, Peter. *The Strauss Family.* 1985. Reprint. Omnibus, 1996.
Strauss, Johann, Jr. *The Great Piano Works of Johann Strauss.* Ed. by Dale Tucker. Warner Bros. Pubns., 1997.

Strauss, Levi (1829-1902), was an American clothing manufacturer. He founded Levi Strauss & Co., the world's first and largest manufacturer of denim jeans, which are sold under the brand name Levi's.

Strauss was born on Feb. 26, 1829, in Buttenheim, a town near Forchheim in what is now Germany. He came to the United States in 1847 to join the dry goods business of his two brothers in New York City. In 1853, he opened a San Francisco wholesale business and began making sturdy work pants for miners. The business later became Levi Strauss & Co. A Nevada tailor, Jacob Davis, wrote to the firm in 1872 suggesting the company make work pants with rivets to reinforce the seams. Strauss hired Davis, and in 1873 the company began producing riveted blue denim jeans and jackets. Gradually, the firm expanded to make other clothing in many fabrics. Today, the company is one of the world's leading clothing manufacturers. Strauss died on Sept. 26, 1902.   Ed Cray

See also **Jeans.**

Strauss, *strows* or *shtrows,* **Richard,** *RIHK ahrt* (1864-1949), was a German composer. He is best known for a series of operas he composed to *librettos* (texts) by the Austrian poet Hugo von Hofmannsthal. Strauss also became famous as a composer of songs and instrumental works and as a conductor.

Strauss was born on June 11, 1864, in Munich. His first important works for orchestra were symphonic poems based on literary narratives. They include, with dates of composition, *Don Juan* (1889), *Death and Transfiguration* (1889), *Till Eulenspiegel's Merry Pranks* (1895), *Thus Spake Zarathustra* (1896), *Don Quixote* (1897), and *A Hero's Life* (1898). Strauss also composed most of his almost 150 songs during this period. His best songs rank among the finest ever composed.

Strauss's first operas, *Guntram* (1894, revised 1940) and *Feuersnot* (1901), were unsuccessful. But they reflected the influence of the operas of Richard Wagner and had many of the qualities of Strauss's later operas. Like Wagner, Strauss used a stream of expressive and often complex music throughout each act. *Salomé* (1905), Strauss's third opera, was his first success. It outraged many listeners with its *dissonant* (not in a key) passages. Many listeners believe that the passages trace the unbalanced mind of the main character.

Strauss met Hofmannsthal soon after the premiere of *Salomé.* Their first collaboration, *Elektra* (1909), was an adaptation of the tragedy by the Greek playwright Sophocles. Strauss carried the dissonant style of *Salomé* even further in *Elektra*—and created greater controversy. In *Der Rosenkavalier* (1911), Strauss and Hofmannsthal tried to re-create, in a more conservative work, the vanished aristocratic world of Vienna in the 1700's. This work is still Strauss's most popular opera.

Strauss wrote his most elaborate score in *The Woman Without a Shadow* (1919), a later collaboration with Hof-

mannsthal. This work echoes *The Magic Flute,* an opera by Wolfgang Amadeus Mozart. It is highly symbolic and features both mortal and supernatural elements.

Other works produced by Strauss and Hofmannsthal include *Ariadne auf Naxos* (1912, final version, 1916), *The Egyptian Helen* (1928, revised 1933), and *Arabella* (first performed in 1933, after Hofmannsthal's death). Strauss's score for *Arabella* contains some of his most delicate and beautiful orchestral writing.

Strauss was one of the finest conductors of his day. He particularly excelled in interpreting the works of Wagner and Mozart. Strauss was conductor of the Berlin Royal Opera from 1898 to 1918 and codirector of the Vienna State Opera from 1919 to 1924.

Strauss wrote five operas after Hofmannsthal's death in 1929. They include *The Silent Woman* (1935) and *Capriccio* (1942). During his last years, Strauss concentrated on a series of small-scale instrumental and vocal pieces. The best-known of these are *Metamorphoses* (1945) and *Four Last Songs* (1948). Strauss died on Sept. 8, 1949.
    Carolyn Abbate

See also **Hofmannsthal, Hugo von; Opera** (The opera repertoire).

Additional resources

Boyden, Matthew. *Richard Strauss.* Northeastern Univ. Pr., 1999.
Kennedy, Michael. *Richard Strauss.* Cambridge, 1999.

Stravinsky, *struh VIHN skee,* **Igor,** *EE gawr* (1882-1971), was a Russian-born composer. Stravinsky and Arnold Schoenberg are generally considered the two most influential composers of the 1900's.

Early works. Stravinsky first gained world fame for three major ballets—*The Firebird* (1910), *Petrouchka* (1911, revised 1947), and *The Rite of Spring (Le Sacre du Printemps)* (1913). All were produced in Paris in collaboration with the famous Russian ballet manager Sergei Diaghilev and remain Stravinsky's best-known works. *The Rite of Spring,* with its huge orchestration, savage rhythms, and innovative harmonies, caused a riot at its first performance. All three ballets were based on Russian folklore, as were Stravinsky's ballet *Les Noces (The Wedding,* 1923) and his stage work *L'Histoire du soldat (The Soldier's Tale,* 1918).

Neoclassical works. From 1919 through 1951, Stravinsky wrote in a neoclassical style, using scales, chords, and tone color in a generally clear and traditional way. During this period, Stravinsky modeled his works on music from the past. His ballet *Pulcinella* (1920) is based on themes by the Italian baroque composer Giovanni Pergolesi. *The Rake's Progress* (1951), Stravinsky's only full-length opera, is stylistically similar to the operas of Wolfgang Amadeus Mozart.

Stravinsky's other major neoclassical works include the Octet for winds (1923, revised 1952), Symphony in C (1940), and *Symphony in Three Movements* (1946). *Symphony of Psalms* (1930, revised 1948) is a choral work whose orchestration

Schaal, Pix

Igor Stravinsky

excludes clarinets, violins, and violas while including two pianos. Here, as in most of his later choral works, Stravinsky used Latin texts.

The 12-tone works. Though long opposed to Schoenberg's 12-tone system, Stravinsky eventually came to adopt it in his own way (see **Music** [Tone]). From 1952 to 1954, Stravinsky used rows of fewer than 12 notes in his compositions. This use is consistent throughout *In Memoriam Dylan Thomas* (1954), for tenor and instruments. The abstract ballet *Agon* (1957) has a 12-tone row in some movements but not in others. The same is true of the choral composition *Canticum Sacrum* (1956). The choral work *Threni* (1958) marks Stravinsky's first consistent use of a single 12-tone row in an extended composition.

Stravinsky's last major works, from *Movements* for piano and orchestra (1960) through *Requiem Canticles* (1966), display a use of 12-tone technique that was increasingly unconventional and personal. In these works, Stravinsky composed as if the orchestra were a collection of chamber ensembles.

Life. Igor Fyodorovich Stravinsky was born on June 17, 1882, near St. Petersburg. He began piano lessons at the age of 9 and studied composition and orchestration with Russian composer Nikolai Rimsky-Korsakov from 1903 to 1908. Stravinsky left Russia in 1914, settling first in Switzerland, and then in France in 1920 and in the United States in 1939. Stravinsky became a French citizen in 1934 and a U.S. citizen in 1945. He died on April 6, 1971.   Stewart L. Ross

See also **Classical music** (The 1900's).

Additional resources

Cross, Jonathan, ed. *The Cambridge Companion to Stravinsky.* Cambridge, 2003.
Whiting, Jim. *The Life and Times of Igor Stravinsky.* Mitchell Lane, 2005. Younger readers.

Straw consists of the dried stems of such grains as wheat, rye, oats, and barley. Straw has many different uses. Farmers use it as bedding for animals, and for soil improvement. Manufacturers use straw to make hats, baskets, and paper. In the chemical laboratory, straw is used to produce carbon and acetic acid. Straw may someday serve as an energy source.

Wheat straw makes the best hats. The stalks are pulled out of the ground, cut into short lengths, and laid in the sun. The sun bleaches the straw almost white. The leaves are then pulled off, leaving only the stem, which is bleached again with sulfur. The straw is sorted according to color and is ready for weaving into hats. In some countries, mechanical looms do the weaving. However, in many parts of Europe, Japan, and China, the work is done by hand. Some of the best hand-braided straw comes from Tuscany, Italy. Panama hats are not made from a straw, but from the leaf fiber of a tropical plant. Straw differs from hay, which is dried grasses or other plants used as feed for animals.   David S. Seigler

Strawberry, a small plant of the rose family, is grown for its tasty heart-shaped fruit. Strawberry plants grow close to the ground and produce small, white flowers that have a pleasant odor. The fruit is greenish white at first and then ripens to a bright red. It is a good source of vitamin C and is often eaten fresh. Strawberries are also canned or frozen or used in making jam, jelly, and wine.

WORLD BOOK illustration by James Teason
Strawberry plants produce heart-shaped red fruit and tiny white flowers. The delicious fruit can be eaten fresh or made into jam, jelly, and other food products.

Botanists do not classify the strawberry as a true berry. True berries, such as blueberries and cranberries, have seeds within their fleshy tissue. The fleshy part of the strawberry is covered with dry, yellow "seeds," each of which is actually a separate fruit.

Strawberry plants have short roots and long, slender stems called *runners* that grow along the surface of the soil. Leaves grow from the stem, and each leaf has three sections, or leaflets. The fruit seems to be *strewn* (scattered) among the leaves, and this may be why the plant was first called *strewberry.* It later came to be called *strawberry.*

Strawberries grow wild or are raised commercially in almost every country. Plant breeders have developed hundreds of varieties of strawberries that are suited for different growing conditions. Varieties that are raised in the United States include the *Tribute, Tristar, Earliglow, Honeoye, Kent,* and *Chandler.* California produces about three-fourths of the strawberries grown in the United States. Other leading strawberry states include, in order of production, Florida, Oregon, Michigan, and Washington.

Strawberries grow best in a cool, moist climate and in many kinds of soil. They are usually planted in fall or spring and may produce fruit the first year. The plants reproduce by means of their runners. Roots extend from the runners into the soil and produce new plants. The harvesting season varies, depending on the climate and the type of strawberry. Some types, called *everbearing,* produce fruit through the summer and fall. In most states, strawberries are produced from May or June to September or November. In California and Florida, strawberries also are produced in the winter months. Most strawberry plants bear fruit for five or six years, but the best crops grow during the first year or two.

Many gardeners raise strawberries because the fruit grows so easily. Several scientific advances have led to increased commercial strawberry production. For example, plant breeders have developed varieties suited to specific climates. Researchers also have found various methods to control the major diseases and insects that attack strawberries. Also, many commercial growers use mechanical equipment to plant and harvest strawberries more efficiently. Large greenhouses are also used to control the environment and improve production.

Wild strawberries were grown in ancient Rome. During the 1700's, a hybrid variety was developed in France by breeding wild strawberries brought from North America with others from Chile. The first important American variety, the *Hovey,* was grown in 1834 in Massachusetts.   John L. Maas

Scientific classification. The strawberry belongs to the genus *Fragaria* in the rose family, Rosaceae. Some common American species are *F. chiloensis, F. vesca,* and *F. virginiana.*

Strawflower is a tall herb grown for its yellow, orange, red, or white flowers. The strawflower is cultivated as an *annual*—that is, for one growing season. But the plant is actually a *perennial* and thus can live for more than one year. The flowers are dried and used in winter bouquets. The strawflower belongs to a group of plants called *everlastings.* All everlastings have flowers that last a long time when dried. The strawflower originated in Australia and now grows in Europe and America. It grows 3 feet (91 centimeters) tall.

James E. Simon

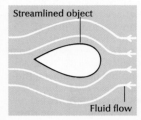

WORLD BOOK illustration
by Christabel King

Strawflowers

Scientific classification. The strawflower belongs to the composite family, Asteraceae or Compositae. It is *Helichrysum bracteatum.*

Stream. See River.

Streamlining is the shaping of a body so that it meets the smallest amount of resistance as it moves through a *fluid* (liquid or gas). The best streamlined shape for a body depends on whether it is to travel slower or faster than sound through the fluid. For *subsonic* (slower than sound) travel, a body should be somewhat blunt and rounded in front, and then taper to a point at the tail. Submarines and subsonic airplanes have this shape. In nature, fish have this type of streamlining. For *supersonic* (faster than sound) travel, a body should have a pointed front to reduce the effects of shock waves. Engineers design supersonic airplanes and rockets in this shape.

The resisting force acting on a body as it travels through a fluid is called *drag.* The amount of drag acting on a body depends on how smoothly the fluid flows around the body. The path that any bit of fluid follows around the body in a steady flow is called a *streamline.* If a body is streamlined, the streamlines divide smoothly at the front, pass smoothly around the body, and meet again at the tail. If the body is not streamlined, however, the fluid may swirl and twist violently as it passes around the body. These motions are called *eddy flows,* or *eddies.* The fluid may separate from the surface of the body and cause a partial vacuum behind it. The amount of drag increases because of the lack of pressure behind the body to balance pressure in front.

The effects of streamlining

A streamlined object, *below left,* offers the least resistance to a fluid flowing past it. A round object, *below right,* causes eddy flows that increase its resistance to the flowing fluid.

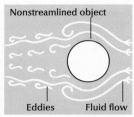

WORLD BOOK diagrams

Researchers can measure the effects of streamlining by using a *wind tunnel.* In the tunnel, air is blown past a body so the drag can be measured. Researchers can make streamlines visible by adding smoke to the air at several points. When a flat plate set upright against the flow of air is tested in the tunnel, streamlines curve around the edges of the plate. The air behind it is disturbed, forming eddies and a partial vacuum. The drag on the plate is relatively large. When a properly streamlined body is tested in a wind tunnel, the streamlines follow the surface more smoothly. No rotating eddy flows are produced behind the body, and there is less drag.

Besides a body's shape, three other factors affect the drag: (1) the density of the fluid, (2) the amount of the body's area that meets the fluid, and (3) the speed of the body through the fluid. The drag doubles if the density of the fluid is doubled. The drag also doubles if the area of the body meeting the fluid is doubled. If the speed of the body is doubled, the drag is multiplied by four.

The term *streamlining* is also used in business and manufacturing. In these fields, it refers to the simplification of management and production processes.

Leonard Scott Miller

See also **Aerodynamics; Wind tunnel.**

Streep, Meryl, *MAIR uhl* (1949-   ), is an American actress. Streep became known for her sensitive portrayals of a wide variety of characters and her great technical skill, especially in imitating regional and foreign accents. Streep has been nominated for a record 14 Academy Awards. She won the 1979 award as best supporting actress for her role in the motion picture *Kramer vs. Kramer.* She won the 1982 award as best actress in *Sophie's Choice.* Streep won Emmy Awards in 1978 and 2004 for her performances in the television dramas *Holocaust* and *Angels in America,* respectively.

Streep was born June 22, 1949, in Summit, New Jersey. Her given and family name is Mary Louise Streep. She studied acting at Vassar College and at the Yale School of Drama. Streep won immediate recognition after her stage debut in New York City in 1975. She made her movie

AP/Wide World

Meryl Streep

debut in *Julia* (1977) and had her first major success in *The Deer Hunter* (1978). Her other important films include *Manhattan* (1979), *The Seduction of Joe Tynan* (1979), *The French Lieutenant's Woman* (1981), *Silkwood* (1983), *Out of Africa* (1985), *Ironweed* (1987), *A Cry in the Dark* (1988), *Postcards from the Edge* (1990), *Death Becomes Her* (1992), *The River Wild* (1994), *The Bridges of Madison County* (1995), *One True Thing* (1998), *Music of the Heart* (1999), *Adaptation* (2002), *The Hours* (2002), *Lemony Snicket's A Series of Unfortunate Events* (2004), and *The Manchurian Candidate* (2004). Louis Giannetti

Streetcar is a passenger vehicle that runs on rails laid in city streets. Streetcars were originally pulled by horses and were called *horsecars.* Today, most streetcars are powered by electric current from an overhead power line or an electrified third rail. Some, such as those in San Francisco, are pulled by a cable.

The first horsecar lines in the United States were established in New York City in 1852. Horsecars were soon in use in most large U.S. cities, despite various problems associated with them. For example, some people objected to horsecars because of the sanitary problems caused by the horses. Many also thought the animals were overworked and mistreated. In addition, horses could not climb the steep hills in many cities.

During the 1870's and 1880's, inventors tried to find a suitable kind of mechanical power for streetcars. In 1888, Frank J. Sprague, an American engineer, demonstrated a streetcar in Richmond, Virginia, that was economical, durable, and powerful enough to ascend hills. His streetcars had motors powered by an electric current from an overhead power line. The current traveled from the line to the car's motor by a long pole. The pole had a small wheel called a *shoe* that slid or rolled along the line. This overhead mechanism was called a *trolley,* a term that was later applied to the entire vehicle.

In the late 1890's and early 1900's, electric streetcar systems based on Sprague's design were built in many U.S. cities and some small towns. But competition with the automobile and high repair and replacement costs led to the abandonment of most streetcar lines in the United States during the mid-1900's. However, such lines were maintained in other countries.

Since the 1970's, there has been renewed interest in streetcars in the United States because they use less energy per person and create less pollution than automobiles or buses do. Streetcar lines built today are often called *light rail transit systems.* They differ from earlier streetcar lines mainly in the location of the tracks. Most light rail tracks lie alongside the roadway. As a result, light rail vehicles interfere less with automobile traffic than do streetcars that run down the middle of the street. Many of the new systems also have automated braking and speed controls. For example, Vancouver, Canada, has a light rail system controlled by computer.

Today, streetcar lines operate in a number of U.S. cities, including Boston; Cleveland; Dallas; New Orleans; Philadelphia; Pittsburgh, Pennsylvania; San Diego; San Francisco; and Seattle. Canadian cities with streetcar lines include Calgary and Edmonton, Alberta; and Toronto. Darwin H. Stapleton

See also **Cable car; Electric railroad; Transportation** (Urban public transportation; pictures: Transportation in the 1800's; Vehicles of the early 1900's).

Streisand, Barbra (1942-   ), is an American singer and actress who became famous for her dramatic interpretation of popular songs. She also gained praise as a comedienne both on the stage and in motion pictures.

Streisand was born in New York City. Her career began in 1961 when she entered a talent contest in a New York City nightclub, winning $50 and a nightclub engagement. She made her Broadway debut in the musical *I Can Get It for You Wholesale* (1962) and became a star in the musical *Funny Girl* (1964). Her first motion-picture appearance came in the adaptation of *Funny Girl* (1968). She won an Academy Award as best actress for her performance.

Wide World
Barbra Streisand

Streisand starred in the film musicals *Hello, Dolly!* (1969), *Funny Lady* (1975), and *A Star Is Born* (1976). She shared an Academy Award as best songwriter with Paul Williams for the song "Evergreen" from *A Star Is Born.* She directed and starred in the musical *Yentl* (1983), the drama *The Prince of Tides* (1991), and the romantic comedy *The Mirror Has Two Faces* (1996). Streisand's nonmusical films include *The Way We Were* (1973) and *Nuts* (1987). Rachel Gallagher

Strength of materials. See Materials (Properties of materials).

Strep throat is an infectious disease that affects the membranes of the throat and tonsils. It develops mainly in children from 5 to 12 years of age. The disease is also called *septic sore throat, acute streptococcal pharyngitis,* and *acute streptococcal tonsillitis.*

Strep throat is caused by bacteria of a type called *group A beta-hemolytic streptococci* (see **Streptococcus**). The bacteria generally spread from person to person through droplets of moisture sprayed from the nose and mouth. People called *carriers,* who harbor the streptococci but do not have symptoms of disease, can spread strep bacteria. Laboratory tests can confirm the presence of strep bacteria in material from the patient's throat. See **Disease** (Spread of infectious diseases).

Symptoms of strep throat include sore throat, fever, headache, and, in some cases, chills, nausea, and vomiting. The patient usually experiences swelling of the tonsils and of the lymph nodes in the neck. The disease disappears rapidly following treatment with penicillin. Untreated cases generally last four or five days, though some may last as long as two weeks.

Complications can follow strep throat. The infection may spread to the ears, sinuses, lungs, bones, or bloodstream. In other cases, patients later develop *rheumatic fever* or a kidney disease called *acute glomerulonephritis* (see **Rheumatic fever; Nephritis**). Prompt treatment with penicillin can prevent the infection from spreading to other parts of the body. Penicillin also ends the risk of rheumatic fever but does not always prevent acute glomerulonephritis. Russell W. Steele

Streptococcus, *STREHP tuh KAHK uhs* (plural, streptococci, *STREHP tuh KAHK sy),* is any of a group of round bacteria that look, under a microscope, like strings of beads. Some forms of streptococci are harmless. But *pathogenic* (disease-causing) streptococci can cause many illnesses.

Bacteriologists classify some groups of streptococci as *hemolytic (hee muh LIHT ihk)* bacteria. When these bacteria are grown in laboratories, they harm or destroy red blood cells in their culture medium (source of food). There are two chief types of hemolytic streptococci, *alpha-hemolytic* and *beta-hemolytic*. Alpha-hemolytic streptococci damage red blood cells. Some of these bacteria are found in the mouth and are linked to tooth decay. A related species, *Streptococcus pneumoniae,* is a major cause of bacterial pneumonia, ear infections, and sinus infections.

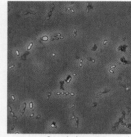

© Manfred Kage, Peter Arnold

Streptococcus bacteria often form beadlike chains.

Beta-hemolytic streptococci completely destroy red blood cells. Biologists recognize many groups of beta-hemolytic streptococci. One of the groups—*group A*—causes most streptococcal diseases in human beings. Group A streptococcal infections include strep throat, a skin infection called *impetigo (IHM puh TY goh),* scarlet fever, and *septicemia* (blood poisoning, pronounced *SEHP tuh SEE mee uh).* Group A infections also can lead to rheumatic fever. Some doctors think the number of severe group A infections began to increase in the 1980's. These illnesses include *necrotizing fasciitis (NEHK ruh tyz ihng fash ee EYE tihs),* sometimes called the "flesh-eating" infection because it can destroy infected tissue.

Doctors prescribe disease-fighting drugs called antibiotics to treat streptococcal infections. But due to the use and overuse of these drugs, several types of streptococci have developed resistance to antibiotics. Some kinds of *Streptococcus pneumoniae,* for example, became resistant to penicillin.   James K. Todd

See also **Disease** (picture: Bacteria).

Streptomycin, *STREHP tuh MY sihn,* is an antibiotic that fights certain disease-causing bacteria. It is produced by *Streptomyces griseus,* a microbe that grows in soil. Streptomycin was one of the first antibiotics discovered. The American microbiologist Selman A. Waksman and a student of his discovered it in 1943. Their discovery resulted from tests on about 10,000 soil microbes for antibiotic activity. Streptomycin is one of the *aminoglycosides,* a group of chemically similar antibiotics that also includes gentamicin and neomycin.

After its discovery, streptomycin was used to treat tuberculosis and many other bacterial infections. Its use greatly decreased as scientists developed safer and more effective antibiotics. The popularity of streptomycin also declined because certain bacteria acquired resistance to its effects. Today, it is seldom used. However, physicians use other aminoglycosides in the treatment of a wide variety of serious disorders, including peritonitis, pneumonia, and infections of the urinary tract.

Streptomycin weakens or kills bacteria by interfering with the process by which they make proteins. Too large a dose of streptomycin can cause a person to suffer dizziness, nausea, and deafness due to damage to the nerves of the ear. An overdose of streptomycin also can cause kidney damage.   Eugene M. Johnson, Jr.

See also **Antibiotic; Waksman, Selman Abraham.**

Stress. See Elasticity.

Stress is the body's emergency response to real or imagined danger. A stress reaction prepares the body for a burst of action to fight or flee a threat. The heart races, the hands get cold and sweaty, the muscles tense, and the stomach feels jittery. Stress that lasts a long time can exhaust the body and frazzle the mind with worry. Any event, thought, or situation that causes stress is called a *stressor.*

Stress aids survival, especially in cases when extraordinary effort can overcome real physical dangers. Stress prepares the body to fight against or escape from danger. This so-called *fight-or-flight response* was particularly useful for prehistoric people who faced life-threatening predators. As civilization developed, life for most people became less physically dangerous. But as society became more complex, mental and emotional challenges increased and became common stressors.

Stress is not always useful as a response to mental or emotional stressors. Mild stress can provide a sense of excitement and help people perform at their peak. But severe stress can fill people with worry, disrupt sleep, and interfere with efficiency. Stress that lasts a long time can weaken health and undermine happiness.

Causes of stress. Many experts consider modern life particularly stressful because it exposes people to many stressors. Some physical stressors remain, including natural disasters, illnesses, and noise. Certain life experiences, such as the death of a loved one, are major stressors. Day-to-day problems, such as taking tests or driving in traffic jams, may also be stressful. In addition, the increasing demands of jobs, school, and other activities are stressors for children and for their overworked parents.

People need not experience events directly to feel stress. Television, radio, newspapers, and the Internet flood people with information about crime, disasters, terrorism, and other upsetting occurrences throughout the world. People can also imagine future misfortunes and regret past failures, causing stress.

How stress affects the body. The Canadian scientist Hans Selye pioneered studies of stress in the 1930's. He used the term *general adaptation syndrome* to describe the body's reaction to stressors. The first part of the general adaptation response, called an *alarm reaction,* occurs when a person or other animal first senses danger.

An alarm reaction begins in the brain when a frightening experience activates an area called the *hypothalamus.* The hypothalamus then sends nerve signals to the *adrenal glands,* which sit above the kidneys. These nerve signals stimulate the *medulla* (inner core) of the adrenals to release chemical messengers called *hormones.* One important hormone is *epinephrine,* which is also called *adrenalin.* Epinephrine raises heart rate, breathing rate, blood pressure, and the amount of sugar in the blood. These effects increase alertness and deliver more blood, oxygen, and food to active muscles.

If danger persists, a stage called *resistance* follows the alarm reaction. During resistance, the body attempts to return to a state of balance. Breathing and heart rate decrease to normal levels. But the hypothalamus sends a hormone signal to a nearby gland in the brain called the *pituitary.* The pituitary gland then releases *adrenocorticotropic hormone,* also called ACTH. ACTH travels to the *cortex* (outer layer) of the adrenal glands. The adrenal cortex responds by releasing hormones called *glucocorticoids.* These hormones keep blood sugar high to provide extra energy.

If stress continues at high levels, the body enters the final stage of the general adaptation syndrome, called *exhaustion.* In exhaustion, energy reserves are used up, leading to extreme fatigue and inability to resist new stressors.

Scientists have found that women respond to stress differently than men do. In addition to the fight-or-flight response, women may react to a stressor with a *nurturing and protecting* response, where they tend to seek support of others. This response may be due in part to the release of *oxytocin,* a hormone that also prompts childbirth and milk production in females.

Stress-related illnesses. Many physicians recognize that stress is involved in a large number of illnesses. Hormones released during a stress reaction affect organs throughout the body. Heredity, learning, and injuries all play a role in determining where or when a stress-related illness may occur in a particular individual.

Stress hormones that act on the heart, blood vessels, and lungs may contribute to heart disease, high blood pressure, and asthma. Prolonged elevation of blood sugar can influence development of diabetes. Diseases of the stomach and intestines are often linked to stress because blood leaves these organs and moves to muscles during stress. Extended exposure to mental and emotional stressors can lead to difficulties in eating, sleeping, and making decisions. People may also feel angry, depressed, and overwhelmed.

Glucocorticoid hormones can suppress the body's *immune* (disease-fighting) system. During prolonged or repeated stress, people are more likely to get colds, flu, and many other diseases.

Managing stress. Stress is an individual reaction to something that a particular person finds alarming. Understanding how they react to stress can enable people to control or reduce some of their stress reactions. One important way people can manage stress is to learn to question whether experiences that they fear are truly dangerous. By asking questions and sharing information about the world, people can avoid jumping to conclusions and exaggerating the importance of events. For example, someone who finds taking tests extremely stressful might ask such questions as (1) Is there a friend who could help me study? (2) How much does the test really count? (3) Can I talk with the teacher if I feel that my performance does not reflect my knowledge of the subject? Relaxation techniques are another useful means of managing stress. These techniques include breathing deeply and slowly, tensing and then relaxing each muscle in the body, and imagining a calm, peaceful place. More formal relaxation techniques include meditation, yoga, hypnosis, recorded relaxation programs, and biofeedback training.

Healthy lifestyle choices increase the body's ability to cope with stress. People can manage stress by exercising regularly, eating nutritious foods, avoiding nicotine, and reducing use of caffeine and alcohol. Friendships, pets, and other social connections aid greatly in managing stress. Talking with others helps people sort through problems and explore possible solutions. Many people find that spiritual activities reduce stress. Religions can offer forms of meditation, traditional wisdom, and the fellowship of other members.   Ronald G. Nathan

See also **Gland; Hormone; Post-traumatic stress disorder; Selye, Hans.**

Additional resources

Charlesworth, Edward A., and Nathan, R. G. *Stress Management.* Rev. ed. Ballantine, 2004.
Fink, George, ed. *Encyclopedia of Stress.* 3 vols. Academic Pr., 2000.
Lenson, Barry. *Good Stress, Bad Stress.* Marlowe, 2002.
McEwen, Bruce S., and Lasley, E. N. *The End of Stress as We Know It.* Joseph Henry, 2002.

Stress test, also called *exercise stress test* or *stress ECG,* is a test that measures the functioning of the heart during physical exercise. Physicians use stress tests to detect heart problems, particularly coronary artery disease (CAD). CAD involves narrowing of the coronary arteries, the blood vessels that supply oxygen to the heart. It is the most common form of heart disease. Early detection of CAD can lead to treatment that prevents heart attacks and saves lives.

In a stress test, the patient exercises at increasing speed and incline on a treadmill or on a stationary bicycle while hooked up to an *electrocardiograph.* This device produces a record called an electrocardiogram (ECG), which displays the electrical activity of the heart. During exercise, the heart demands more blood and oxygen. When the heart's demand for blood and oxygen exceeds its supply, an ECG shows changes from the normal pattern of activity. Such changes may indicate a narrowed coronary artery.

Because stress tests are not completely reliable, an abnormal test result requires further procedures to diagnose CAD. After the stress test, doctors sometimes inject a radioactive substance into a patient's vein. A spe-

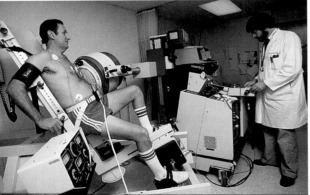

Ken Sherman, Phototake

A stress test shows the pattern of the heart's activity during exercise. An abnormal pattern may be due to lack of oxygen caused by narrowed coronary arteries.

cial camera then shows areas of the heart not getting enough blood. In some cases, the patient must undergo *coronary angiography,* a technique that makes the coronary arteries visible on an X-ray image (see **Angiography**).   James J. Foody

See **Electrocardiograph; Heart** (picture: Rehabilitation).

Strike, in business and industry, is a stopping of work by a group of employees. All or some of a company's employees may be involved. A strike is designed to interrupt the normal flow of goods or services that a company produces or handles. The workers use the strike as a bargaining weapon. They hope that a strike or the threat of a strike will persuade the company to agree to their demands for higher wages, improved working conditions, or other benefits.

The term *strike* also refers to any stoppage of normal operations or activities to protest an action or condition. During the 1950's and 1960's, some civil rights workers in the United States staged *sit-down strikes.* They sat down in public places and refused to move to protest racial injustice. Some prison inmates have gone on *hunger strikes* and refused to eat until officials considered their grievances. College students have struck for various kinds of changes. But strikes are most closely associated with work stoppages in business and industry. This article chiefly discusses such labor strikes.

Functions of strikes. A strike is a sign of dissatisfaction among workers in a plant or industry. By striking, workers take action to express a grievance or to enforce a demand. In the 1800's and early 1900's, many strikes in the United States resulted from workers' efforts to get employers to recognize unions as their bargaining agents. However, most strikes today involve disputes over wages, hours, and other conditions of employment.

Strikes are an important part of the *collective bargaining* process between workers and employers. In this process, representatives of both parties meet to establish conditions of employment that will be jointly acceptable. There are more than 150,000 collective bargaining contracts in the United States. Most collective bargaining agreements are reached—and renegotiated periodically—without strikes.

Strikes occur occasionally in any society that encourages free collective bargaining. No matter how reasonable the two sides may be, disagreements will arise between labor and management. During bargaining, a strike or the threat of a strike increases the cost of being unreasonable. It encourages each side to seriously consider the other's arguments and demands.

Kinds of strikes. There are various kinds of strikes. An *authorized strike* is one agreed upon by union officials or a majority of the union members. A *wildcat strike* is a strike called by a group of workers without official union support. Most strikes are *walkouts,* in which the workers leave their jobs. A *sit-down strike* is a strike in which people stop working but do not leave their place of employment. A *sympathy strike* is called by one union to support another union that is on strike. A *jurisdictional strike* may result when two or more rival unions claim the exclusive right to do certain work. A *secondary strike* occurs when people stop working to try to force their employer to stop doing business with

Bettmann Archive
Clothing workers in New York City went on strike for higher wages and better working conditions in 1910.

another employer who is involved in a labor dispute.

Generally, nonpublic employees have the right to strike. Similarly, private employers may close their plants in order to keep employees from working. Such action is called a *lockout.* Almost all collective bargaining agreements prohibit strikes and lockouts during the term of a contract. In the United States, federal laws also prohibit or limit certain kinds of strikes. For example, the Taft-Hartley Act bans jurisdictional strikes, secondary strikes, and sympathy strikes. The Taft-Hartley Act and the Railway Labor Act include provisions to delay strikes that might create a national emergency.

Many states have laws forbidding strikes by employees of the state or local government. But strikes by such public employees as police and teachers became common in the 1960's and 1970's. Several states passed laws giving government workers the right to strike.

Strike tactics in the United States and other industrial countries have been relatively peaceful for many years. But fights, loss of life, and destruction of property were common in the 1800's and early 1900's.

Union members usually follow authorized strike-vote procedures, though occasionally a wildcat strike may occur. Many unions have special strike funds to help support the strikers.

When a strike begins, union members usually set up *picket lines* at entrances to the employer's place of business. The pickets carry signs telling why they are striking. The purpose of the picket line is to turn away other workers, to discourage customers, and to keep goods from being taken into or out of the plant. Union members often refuse to cross another union's picket line.

Strike settlements. Most strikes are settled through negotiations between representatives of labor and management. A neutral third party may help the parties reach a settlement. Third parties participate in both *mediation* and *arbitration.* In mediation, the third party tries to promote discussion, to work out compromises, and to find areas of agreement. A mediator has no power to force a settlement. In arbitration, the third party has the power to settle a strike. An arbitrator is given the power of *binding arbitration* through voluntary agreement of the parties involved or by law. Binding arbitration requires both sides to accept the recommendations of the arbitrator.   Daniel Quinn Mills

Related articles in *World Book* include:

Arbitration
Boycott
Federal Mediation and Conciliation Service
Haymarket Riot
Homestead Strike
Industrial relations
Labor movement

Lockout
National Labor Relations Board
National Mediation Board
Pullman Strike
Railway Labor Act
Taft-Hartley Act

Additional resources

Norwood, Stephen H. *Strikebreaking & Intimidation.* Univ. of N.C. Pr., 2002.
Stein, R. Conrad. *The Pullman Strike and the Labor Movement in American History.* Enslow, 2001. Younger readers.
Watson, Bruce. *Bread and Roses: Mills, Migrants, and the Struggle for the American Dream.* Viking, 2005.

Strindberg, August (1849-1912), was a Swedish author who became one of the most influential dramatists of his time. His experiments in two major literary movements—Naturalism and Expressionism—made him second in importance only to Norwegian playwright Henrik Ibsen in the development of modern drama. Strindberg's Naturalism provided a philosophic foundation for subsequent Realist writers. In addition, numerous modern writers have been influenced by the emphasis in Strindberg's later works on anxiety, the irrational, alienation, and the fragmentation of personality. Strindberg wrote more than 65 plays. He also wrote novels, poetry, short stories, autobiography, and history.

Johan August Strindberg was born on Jan. 22, 1849, in Stockholm. He was hypersensitive from childhood on, displaying throughout his life the sudden and violent changes in mood that mark many of his plays. Strindberg wrote his first play in 1869. His first major drama was *Master Olof* (written in 1872), the finest historical play in Swedish drama. In 1877, Strindberg began the first of his three marriages, all of which ended in bitterness and divorce. His *The Red Room* (1879) was the first Naturalistic novel in Swedish (see **Naturalism**).

Strindberg lived most of the time from 1883 to 1898 in southern Europe. His collection of satirical short stories, *Married* (1884), aroused charges of blasphemy against him. The "battle of the sexes," especially love-hate relationships between husbands and wives, dominated several plays, notably *The Dance of Death* (written in 1900), *The Father* (1887), *Comrades* (written in 1887), *Creditors* (1889), and *Miss Julie* (1889). His life in Europe ended in an emotional disturbance after his first marriage collapsed. Strindberg had a mental breakdown, which he recorded in the autobiographical novel *Inferno* (1897).

After Strindberg returned to Sweden in 1898, he wrote a number of Expressionistic plays that convey the fleeting unreality of existence (see **Expressionism**). The best of these dramas was *A Dream Play* (written in 1901), which influenced the Surrealism movement of the 1920's and 1930's. He also wrote five shorter, mysterious "chamber plays," notably *The Ghost Sonata* (1908). Four were written for the Intimate Theatre in Stockholm, which Strindberg cofounded in 1907. His last play was *The Great Highway* (1910), a spiritual autobiography presented as a symbolic fantasy. Strindberg died on May 14, 1912.   Frederick C. Wilkins

Additional resources

Adler, Stella. *Stella Adler on Ibsen, Strindberg, and Chekhov.* Knopf, 1999.
Meyer, Michael L. *Strindberg.* Random Hse., 1985. A standard biography.

String theory is a theory of the fundamental forces of nature. Since the mid-1980's, physicists have developed many forms of the theory, including a group of *superstring theories.* However, the theory is still incomplete.

The key to string theory is its description of *elementary particles,* objects that are not made up of other objects. According to conventional theories of physics, these objects—which include electrons and quarks—are pointlike. But in string theory, they are tiny strings that can vibrate in various ways. Different patterns of vibration would appear to us as different particles.

A successful string theory would be the first single theory to describe all four of the known fundamental forces: (1) the *electromagnetic force* that underlies electricity and magnetism; (2) the *strong nuclear force* that binds together quarks in protons, neutrons, and other objects; (3) the *weak nuclear force,* responsible for the radioactive decay of atomic nuclei; and (4) *gravitation,* the attraction between material objects. Physicists have developed successful conventional theories of the four forces, but they have not combined those theories.

The conventional theories of the electromagnetic, strong, and weak forces are *quantum theories*—that is, they use the principles of the theory of quantum mechanics. According to that theory, particles transmit forces to one another by means of *quanta,* or "chunks" of energy. *(Quanta* is the plural of *quantum.)* For example, a quantum called the *photon* transmits electric and magnetic forces.

The gravitational theory is the theory of general relativity, developed by the German-born physicist Albert Einstein. The theory of relativity is not a quantum theory. Rather, the theory says, gravitation is an effect of a distortion of space and time by the presence of matter. A successful string theory would combine aspects of general relativity and quantum mechanics.   Michael Dine

See also **Gravitation; Quantum mechanics; Relativity.**

Stringed instrument. See **Music; Orchestra.**

Stroke is the sudden loss of brain function. It is a medical emergency that may result in paralysis, severe brain damage, or death. Most strokes occur when a blood clot blocks the flow of blood to the brain, interrupting the brain's supply of oxygen and nutrients. If the blockage lasts for more than a few minutes, permanent damage occurs. Strokes also may result when a blood vessel ruptures and bleeds into the brain or the fluid around the brain. The bleeding produces pressure that damages brain tissue.

Stroke is a major health problem throughout the world. It is the third leading cause of death in the United States, behind heart disease and cancer. Each year, about 300,000 Americans suffer strokes. About a third of these strokes are fatal. Most people who survive their first stroke soon regain some lost brain function and may regain more over several years. People who suffer two or more strokes are more often permanently disabled. Most stroke victims are age 65 or older.

Symptoms of stroke depend on the areas of the brain affected. The most common symptoms include sudden weakness, loss of sensation on one side of the body, partial loss of vision, dizziness, slurred speech, mental confusion, and personality changes. Symptoms commonly worsen over the next several hours or days. In some patients, the progression of symptoms leads to coma and death. In some minor strokes, symptoms disappear in less than a day. Such *transient ischemic attacks* (TIA's) often precede more serious strokes.

Causes. The majority of strokes are caused by blockage of blood circulation to the brain. Such blockage may result from either *cerebral thrombosis* or *cerebral embolism.* Cerebral thrombosis occurs when a blood clot forms in one of the major blood vessels supplying the brain. It is most often associated with *atherosclerosis* (hardening of the arteries) in the brain or the neck. Factors that increase the risk of cerebral thrombosis from atherosclerosis include *hypertension* (high blood pressure), diabetes, high blood levels of cholesterol, and cigarette smoking (see **Arteriosclerosis**). Cerebral embolism involves a clot that forms in another part of the body, usually the heart or a major artery. The clot is then carried in the bloodstream until it lodges in a blood vessel that supplies the brain. Cerebral embolism is common in patients with heart disease and atherosclerosis of the large arteries.

Another major cause of strokes is *cerebral hemorrhage*—that is, bleeding into the brain from a ruptured blood vessel. Cerebral hemorrhage can be caused by hypertension, malformations of the brain's arteries and veins, or especially in elderly people, disease of brain arteries (see **Cerebral hemorrhage**).

Strokes also may result from bleeding into the cerebrospinal fluid. This bleeding is called *subarachnoid hemorrhage.* It often results from a *cerebral aneurysm,* a defect in the wall of a blood vessel in the brain.

Prevention. To avoid strokes, people should have their blood pressure checked frequently. Those with elevated blood pressure should take measures to bring down their blood pressure by changing their diet or by taking medication, as directed by their doctor. In many people with atherosclerosis or irregular heartbeats, doctors prescribe taking aspirin daily to help prevent stroke. Doctors also prescribe a drug called *ticlopidine.*

Drugs called *anticoagulants* thin the blood and can help prevent strokes in patients with certain types of heart disease. Patients with severe atherosclerosis and narrowing of the large arteries, especially the carotid arteries in the neck, may benefit from a surgical procedure called *carotid endarterectomy.* This procedure removes the hardened inner lining of the carotid arteries, allowing blood to flow freely and preventing the formation of clots in the arteries.

Treatment. For many years, no direct treatment for stroke existed. Medical care was aimed at preventing complications and reducing the risk of a second stroke. Complications from stroke include pneumonia and other infections and bed sores. In 1995, a major study showed that the clot-dissolving drug *tissue plasminogen activator* could improve eventual recovery of strokes due to blood clots. Doctors may also use a device called the *Merci Retriever,* a corkscrew-shaped device that is threaded through an artery to remove the clot and restore blood flow. Because stroke treatments must be given within three hours of a stroke's onset, patients with symptoms of stroke should seek immediate care.

Rehabilitation helps many of those who are able to work with therapists regain lost function. Stroke patients work chiefly with physical therapists, speech therapists, and occupational therapists. Physical therapists help paralyzed stroke patients move to prevent muscle stiffening. Physical therapists also use exercises and treatment with heat, water, and massage to help patients perform daily tasks. Speech therapists help those with language disabilities. Occupational therapists help patients coordinate hand and eye movements to perform such basic tasks as writing and preparing food. See **Physical therapy; Speech therapy; Occupational therapy.**

Scientists have conducted much research on how the brain recovers its ability to function following stroke. A new rehabilitation technique called *constraint-induced movement therapy* helps stroke patients regain use of paralyzed limbs. In this type of therapy, patients perform up to six hours of exercise with the paralyzed limb while the opposite, unaffected limb is restrained. Scientists believe the intensive therapy causes the brain to grow new nerve connections to restore lost function. Such research offers hope that someday all stroke patients will be able to regain full use of their brain.   James N. Davis

See also **Aphasia; Hypertension.**

Additional resources

Hachinski, Vladimir and Larissa. *Stroke.* Firefly Bks., 2003.
Hutton, Cleo, and Caplan, L. R. *Striking Back at Stroke.* Dana Pr., 2003.
Shannon, Joyce B., ed. *Stroke Sourcebook.* Omnigraphics, 2003.

Stromboli, *STRAHM buh lee,* is an Italian island in the Tyrrhenian Sea off the northeastern coast of Sicily (see **Italy** [terrain map]). The island covers 4.6 square miles (12.1 square kilometers) and has a few hundred inhabitants. It is famous for its volcano, which rises 3,031 feet (924 meters). The volcano is one of the few in Europe that are constantly active. Ancient writers reported this activity centuries ago. Disastrous eruptions rarely occur because the lava flows freely instead of building up internal pressure for violent eruptions.   David I. Kertzer

See also **Volcano** (Describing eruptions).

Strontium, *STRAHN shee uhm,* a chemical element, is a soft, silvery metal. It exists as a number of *isotopes,* forms of the element with the same number of protons but different numbers of neutrons. Strontium 90 is a dangerous radioactive isotope found in the fallout from some nuclear explosions. The isotope's radioactivity kills the tissues that produce blood in people and animals.

Strontium is found in the minerals celestite and strontianite. It combines readily with oxygen, nitrogen, and hydrogen. Strontium nitrate ($Sr(NO_3)_2$) burns with a crimson flame and is used in flares and fireworks.

Strontium has the chemical symbol Sr. Its *atomic number* (number of protons) is 38. Its *relative atomic mass* is 87.62. An element's relative atomic mass equals its *mass* (amount of matter) divided by $\frac{1}{12}$ of the mass of carbon 12, the most abundant isotope of carbon. Strontium melts at 769 °C and boils at 1384 °C. It was discovered in 1790 by Adair Crawford of Ireland.

Duward F. Shriver

Stuart, Gilbert Charles (1755-1828), was an American artist. He became famous for his unfinished portrait of George Washington, probably the best-known portrait in the United States.

Stuart was born on Dec. 3, 1755, near Newport, Rhode Island, and began painting at the age of 13. His early works were simple, thinly painted portraits. In 1775, he went to London, and in 1777, he began four years of study under artist Benjamin West. In 1782, Stuart exhibited *The Skater* at the Royal Academy. This graceful, luminous picture received so much praise that Stuart opened a portrait studio in London. For the next five years, the wealthy of England and Scotland sat for portraits by him. But Stuart lived so extravagantly that in 1787 he moved to Dublin to escape his debts.

In early 1793, Stuart returned to the United States, again heavily in debt. He planned to make money by painting Washington's portrait. Washington sat for three different portraits in 1795 and 1796. The "Vaughan" type, a bust portrait, shows Washington's head and upper body. "Lansdowne" is a full-length portrait of Washington as statesman. "Atheneum" is the familiar unfinished oval of Washington's head. Stuart sold many copies of the portraits that he, his daughter Jane, and others made.

Stuart moved to Boston in 1805. He became noted for his charm, his ability to complete portraits quickly, and his advice to young artists. He died on July 9, 1828.

Elizabeth Garrity Ellis

For reproductions of Stuart's works, see **Adams, John Quincy; Madison, James; Monroe, James; Washington, George.**

Stuart, House of, was a royal family of England and Scotland. The Stuarts were kings and queens of Scotland from 1371 to 1603, and of England and Scotland from 1603 to 1649 and 1660 to 1714. Much of their rule in the 1600's was characterized by disputes over foreign policy, religion, and the power of the monarchy. The family's name is sometimes spelled *Stewart.*

James VI of Scotland, the son of Mary, Queen of Scots, became king of England and Ireland at the death of his third cousin, Queen Elizabeth I, in 1603. He took the title of James I. His son Charles I succeeded him in 1625. Charles's attempt to rule without Parliament, as well as his religious, economic, and foreign policies, turned many English leaders against him. As a result, civil war broke out in Scotland in 1639, in Ireland in 1641, and in England in 1642. Charles was beheaded in 1649. After his execution, England became a republic.

In 1660, a new Parliament restored the monarchy under Charles II, son of Charles I. When Charles II died in 1685, his brother, James II, became king. In Scotland, James reigned as James VII. He wished to provide some religious freedom for Roman Catholics. Without Parliament's consent, he suspended laws against Catholics and against Protestants who did not belong to the Church of England. Alarmed by the king's actions, key political leaders united against him. They forced him to give up the throne in 1688. Parliament gave the crown to James's daughter Mary and her husband, William of Orange, in 1689. Anne Stuart, Mary's sister, became queen in 1702. She was the last Stuart ruler. During her reign, England and Wales joined Scotland to form a united kingdom of Great Britain.

After Anne died in 1714, her distant cousin George I of the House of Hanover in Germany became king of Britain. But James Francis Edward Stuart, the son of James II, also claimed the throne. In 1715, thousands of his supporters, mostly Scots, rebelled against George. In 1745, James Francis Edward Stuart's son, Charles Edward Stuart, led a more threatening uprising against George II. Both rebellions failed.

Richard L. Greaves

Related articles in *World Book* include:

Stuart, Jeb (1833-1864), was a Confederate cavalry general. He distinguished himself in the First Battle of Bull Run (Manassas). He served with Stonewall Jackson at Chancellorsville and commanded Jackson's corps after Jackson was wounded. As commander of all General Robert E. Lee's cavalry, Stuart fought successful actions in the Wilderness Campaign in 1864. But he had gained his widest fame for his two daring rides "around McClellan." In these rides, Stuart took his cavalry all the way around the Union Army.

Stuart became the center of a controversy following the Battle of Gettysburg. He had taken his command off on an independent operation while Lee invaded the North, and Stuart's absence deprived Lee of the "eyes" of his army. On May 11, 1864, Stuart was wounded at Yellow Tavern, Virginia, in the battle for Richmond. He died the following day.

James Ewell Brown Stuart was born on Feb. 6, 1833, in Patrick County, Virginia, and graduated from the United States Military Academy. Stuart served in Kansas and on the frontier from 1855 to 1861. He left the U.S. Army in 1861 and joined the Confederacy. James M. McPherson

See also **Civil War, American** (The peninsular campaign).

Stuart, Jesse Hilton (1906-1984), was an American author known for his writings about the mountain region of Kentucky. Stuart wrote more than 30 works, including novels, collections of poetry and short stories, and autobiographies. His major works show his simple, realistic writing style and his affection for the people of the Kentucky mountains, where he was born and raised.

Stuart's novels include *Taps for Private Tussie* (1943) and *Daughter of the Legend* (1965). Among the collections of his short stories are *Head o' W-Hollow* (1936) and *My Land Has a Voice* (1966). Collections of his poems include *Man with a Bull-Tongue Plow* (1934) and *Hold April* (1962). Stuart described his childhood and family in *God's Oddling* (1960). He based *To Teach, To Love* (1970) on his experiences as a teacher and writer. Stuart was born on Aug. 8, 1906, near Riverton, Kentucky. He died on Feb. 17, 1984. Noel Polk

Stuart, Mary. See Mary, Queen of Scots.

Studebaker, Clement (1831-1901), an American manufacturer, founded a wagon-building business that later developed into the Studebaker Corporation. With $68 in cash, Clement and his brother Henry opened a blacksmith and wagon shop in South Bend, Indiana, in 1852. Henry left the business in 1858, and another brother, John, joined it. Clement and John, along with their brother Peter, organized the Studebaker Brothers Manufacturing Company in 1868, and Clement became its first president. Over the years, Clement traveled widely, opening branches of the company around the United States and in Europe. By 1895, the company had become the world's largest producer of horse-drawn vehicles.

Clement Studebaker was born on March 12, 1831, near Gettysburg, Pennsylvania. He was trained as a blacksmith and wagon-builder by his father. He died on Nov. 27, 1901.   William L. Bailey

Studebaker, John Mohler (1833-1917), was an American automobile manufacturer. In 1901, he became president of the Studebaker Brothers Manufacturing Company, later called the Studebaker Corporation.

Studebaker was born on Oct. 10, 1833, near Gettysburg, Pennsylvania. In 1853, he went to California to seek a fortune in mining during the gold rush. However, Studebaker earned money instead by building wheelbarrows for the miners at $10 each. In 1858, Studebaker moved to South Bend, Indiana, where he became a partner with his brother Clement in a wagon-building business. John used the $8,000 he had earned in California to expand the company. The Studebakers' firm made its first electric-powered automobile in 1902 and began making gasoline-powered cars in 1904. John Studebaker died on March 16, 1917.   William L. Bailey

Student government is the process by which students take part in the management of their school, college, or university. Student government usually involves an organization, sometimes called a *student council,* that represents the interests of students. The organization may also be called a *student cabinet, student congress, student legislature, student union,* or *G.O.* (general organization). Most high schools, colleges, and universities have some form of student government.

In most student governments, students elect representatives to a council, governing board, or other group. The group then meets regularly to discuss curriculum, student benefits, alumni relations, and other matters of interest to the students. In many cases, a faculty member serves as a sponsor or adviser to the group. The group also meets with the faculty and administration to discuss student issues.

Student government activities may include sponsoring scholarship and award programs; coordinating student activities; and organizing assembly programs, community projects, fund-raising efforts, conferences, lectures, and other events. In addition, student organizations may campaign for students' rights. During the mid-1900's, for instance, many student groups fought to end racial and sexual discrimination in college admissions. Student governments may sponsor student courts, conduct faculty evaluations, and help manage cafeterias, health centers, and other student services. In some cases, a student government may organize travel programs for students.

Most high schools in the United States belong to the National Association of Student Councils (NASC). Many collegiate student organizations belong to the United States Student Association (USSA). Other national student groups include the Student Leadership Network, the National Conference on Student Leadership, and the Student Empowerment Training Project.

In the United Kingdom and in Australia, the National Union of Students represents the interests of student organizations throughout each country. The Canadian Federation of Students performs a similar role in Canada. Student organizations from numerous countries belong to the International Union of Students, based in Prague, in the Czech Republic.   Lawrence O. Picus

Student National Education Association. See National Education Association.

Student Nonviolent Coordinating Committee (SNCC), also called "Snick," was a civil rights organization in the United States during the 1960's. It was founded in 1960 in Raleigh, North Carolina, and originally consisted of black and white college students. In the early 1960's, SNCC organized peaceful protests and demonstrations to speed desegregation in the South. In 1964, SNCC sponsored the Mississippi Project, in which about 800 volunteers helped thousands of African Americans register to vote.

In 1966, SNCC's new leader, Stokely Carmichael, expressed the frustration and impatience of many young blacks with the slow progress being made through nonviolent protests. He called for a campaign to achieve Black Power and to fight the "white power" that had oppressed blacks. Carmichael urged blacks to gain political and economic control of their own communities. He rejected much of SNCC's white support.

In 1966, SNCC was the first civil rights organization to oppose U.S. involvement in the Vietnam War (1957-1975). Carmichael and other SNCC leaders said the United States was interfering in the struggle of nonwhite people to become independent.

Carmichael resigned in 1967, and H. Rap Brown succeeded him. SNCC changed its name to Student National Coordinating Committee in 1969, but the organization disbanded soon after that.   Alton Hornsby, Jr.

See also **Carmichael, Stokely.**

Students for a Democratic Society (SDS) was a radical political organization in the United States during the 1960's. Most members were college students or other young people. They opposed what they believed to be the hypocrisy that existed in American society.

SDS members believed that American society theoretically supported liberal democratic principles but had failed to correct such injustices as poverty, racial discrimination, and international aggression. SDS strongly opposed U.S. participation in the Vietnam War (1957-1975) and tried to arouse public opinion against the war. The organization also demanded more student influence in the administration of colleges and universities.

SDS tactics included propaganda and such direct action as student strikes and mass demonstrations. The organization was often accused of using or provoking violence to advance its demands.

SDS was organized in 1962 at Port Huron, Michigan. SDS was not united on its ideas and tactics, and internal disputes reduced its effectiveness. In the late 1960's, SDS split into several factions and soon ceased to be a significant organization.   Murray Clark Havens

Study is an effort to learn about any subject. Studying is an important part of learning because your achievement in school greatly depends on how much you study. You cannot expect to learn everything you need to know about a subject during class. It is the combination of classroom learning and regular study outside of class that determines how well you do in school. Study becomes more important as you move from elementary school to high school and on to college.

This article offers suggestions on how to develop good study habits. You can use these suggestions to improve your grades in school. Good study habits can also help you learn new job skills or simply investigate a subject that interests you. For more information about study, see *A Student Guide to Better Writing, Speaking, and Research Skills* in the Research Guide/Index, Volume 22. It discusses how to use such important study tools as reference books and other resource materials.

Where to study. Every student needs a special place to study with a desk or table and a chair. There should also be enough daylight or artificial light so that you can read for long periods of time without straining your eyes. In addition, a study area should have enough space for your textbooks; such reference books as a dictionary, an encyclopedia, and an atlas; and, perhaps, a computer. You should also have a place to store paper, pencils, pens, notebooks, and other study materials.

Most people can study almost anywhere—if the subject fascinates them. But they have difficulty concentrating on something they consider uninteresting. Therefore, your study area should be as free as possible of noise and visual distractions. Find out what distracts you and remove it from your study area.

Many students have a problem finding a quiet place to study. You must adapt your study habits to your own situation. For example, if you have your own room, you could make one corner into a good study area. If you share a room with a brother or a sister, both of you could agree to study at the same time in opposite corners. Or you could get up early and study when your brother or sister is asleep. If your home is crowded or noisy, you could ask permission to study at the home of a friend or relative who has more space.

When to study. Students should study regularly throughout the school year. You will remember more about a subject if you study it soon after it has been presented in class. Never wait until just before an exam to start reviewing the work for the entire period to be covered by the test. Anything you learn by such *cramming* is usually soon forgotten.

You may find it helpful to plan a weekly study schedule. A large number of students fill out a chart showing the times they are in school or are involved with other activities. They then set aside a certain time each day for study. It is easier to keep up with your schoolwork if you have the habit of studying at the same time daily. Two points to consider in developing a study schedule are (1) the best time of the day for studying and (2) the length of each session.

The best time of day for study depends on you and your situation. Many students prefer to study immediately after arriving home from school. Others have a job or participate in after-school activities, and so they study in the early evening. Some students study later at night, or in the morning before school, because their home is too noisy early in the evening.

The length of your study sessions depends on your age, your ability as a student, and whether you already have good study habits. If you are still in elementary school or have just begun to develop good study habits, you should probably allow about an hour a day for study. As your schoolwork becomes more difficult, you should plan longer study sessions to keep your homework assignments up to date.

How to study. Ask yourself two questions before you start to study: "Why am I studying this topic?" "What do I want to learn about it?" You cannot study effectively unless you understand what you are supposed to accomplish. Simply memorizing dates, mathematical formulas, or passages in literature is not enough to make you a good student.

Many good students sometimes have trouble concentrating. There are several study methods that can help keep your mind from wandering. For example, you should study the most difficult subjects first, when you are the most mentally alert. Also, take breaks between subjects. A short walk or some simple exercises can help freshen your mind. If you still have trouble concentrating, work on such tasks as writing out next week's study schedule or reviewing the previous day's work.

There are a number of ways to study more effectively. Some students try to link a fact they want to remember with something they already know. Others use rhymes, mental pictures, and other memory aids called *mnemonic devices* to help recall certain information (see **Memory** [Improving memory]). You may find it useful to repeat out loud something you have just learned. Some students like to study in pairs so that they can test each other orally on a subject.

At the end of each study session, test yourself to make sure you understand the major points of the topic. If you are still confused by the topic, study it again later. Do not hesitate to ask your teacher or school counselor for help with a study problem or for general advice about improving your study habits.   Samuel Ball

See also **Learning** (Efficient learning); **Outline; Reading** (Study-type reading).

Additional resources

Fry, Ronald W. *How to Study.* 5th ed. Career Pr., 2000.
Gold, Mimi. *Help for the Struggling Student.* Jossey-Bass, 2003.
    A guide for parents and teachers.
Robinson, Adam. *What Smart Students Know.* Crown, 1993.
Schumm, Jeanne S. *School Power.* Rev. ed. Free Spirit, 2001.

Sturgeon, *STUR juhn,* is a large fish whose long, slender body is covered in tough skin and bony plates, instead of scales like most other fish. Sturgeons live in both fresh and salt water in the North Temperate Zone, the region between the Tropic of Cancer and the Arctic Circle. Fishing crews catch sturgeon for their flesh, which processors usually *smoke* (preserve and flavor by exposure to smoke and heat). Manufacturers salt the eggs of sturgeon to make the delicacy called *caviar.*

Rows of bony plates protect the body of the sturgeon, and additional plates protect the head. Beneath an adult sturgeon's long snout lies a small, toothless mouth with thick, sucking lips. The fish uses these lips to suck up crustaceans, fish, worms, and other animals that live on the water's bottom. Four long, thin, fleshy growths called *barbels* project from in front of the mouth. A single *dorsal* fin rises from the the sturgeon's back. A sturgeon's body extends into the long upper part of its tail fin.

Most sturgeon live in salt water, migrating into streams during the *spawning* (egg-releasing) season. However, some species of sturgeon live only in fresh waters.

Sturgeon belong to an ancient group of fish whose bodies have changed relatively little since the time of the dinosaurs. Early ancestors of the sturgeon appeared more than 150 million years ago, during the Jurassic Pe-

WORLD BOOK illustration by Colin Newman, Linden Artists Ltd.

The sturgeon is a large, primitive-looking fish. Rows of bony plates protect its head and most of its long, slender body. People eat the fish's meat, often smoked, and use its eggs in caviar.

riod. The sucking mouth and plated body of the sturgeon developed later.

The sturgeon family includes about two dozen species. The *common sturgeon,* one of the best-known species, lives in European waters. A related species, the *Atlantic sturgeon,* lives along the North American coast from Labrador to the Gulf of Mexico. The *white sturgeon* of the American Pacific Coast ranks as the largest American freshwater fish. It grows to 20 feet (6 meters) long and may weigh more than 1,500 pounds (680 kilograms). The *lake sturgeon* lives in the Great Lakes and the waters of the Mississippi Valley.

Scientists consider the *beluga* or *Russian sturgeon* to be the largest freshwater fish. It lives in the Black and Caspian seas. The longest known beluga measured 28 feet (8.5 meters). The heaviest known beluga weighed 4,568 pounds (2,072 kilograms). Beluga eggs produce the most valuable caviar. Along with giant white sturgeons, belugas can live more than 100 years.

Worldwide, sturgeon were once abundant. However, overfishing, pollution, and the construction of dams have greatly reduced their numbers and caused several species to become endangered.   John E. McCosker

Scientific classification. Sturgeon make up the family Acipenseridae. The common sturgeon is *Acipenser sturio;* the Atlantic sturgeon, *A. oxyrhynchus;* the white sturgeon, *A. transmontanus;* the lake sturgeon, *A. fulvescens;* and the beluga or Russian sturgeon, *Huso huso.*

See also **Caviar; Fish** (picture: Fish of temperate fresh waters).

Sturgeon, *STUR juhn,* **Theodore** (1918-1985), was an American author of fantasy and science fiction. Most of his stories deal with the meaning of love in various human relationships. Many of his characters are abnormal human beings or beings from other worlds. But these characters seem real to the reader because Sturgeon described them with sympathetic understanding.

Sturgeon's finest and best-known work is *More Than Human* (1953). This novel tells about several young outcasts who blend their odd talents to form a superior organism. *Venus Plus X* (1960) is one of several Sturgeon novels that intelligently explore alien and human sexuality. *Godbody* (published in 1986, after his death) deals with the redeeming power of love. Sturgeon's short fiction has been collected in such books as *E Pluribus Unicorn* (1953); *Aliens 4* (1959), which includes the well-known story "Killdozer" (1944); and *Sturgeon Is Alive and Well* (1971).

Sturgeon was born on Feb. 26, 1918, in Staten Island,

New York. His given and family name was Edward Hamilton Waldo. He died on May 8, 1985.   Neil Barron

Sturges, Preston (1898-1959), was an American motion-picture writer and director. He became famous for films that brilliantly satirize aspects of American life. *The Great McGinty* (1940) satirizes crooked politicians. *Sullivan's Travels* (1941) attacks the false values Sturges saw mirrored in Hollywood. *The Miracle of Morgan's Creek* (1944) and *Hail the Conquering Hero* (1944) deal with small-town politics and the idealization of military heroes. Sturges also wrote and directed *Christmas in July* (1940), *The Lady Eve* (1941), and *Unfaithfully Yours* (1948). All show Sturges's skill at writing witty dialogue and creating slapstick comedy.

Sturges was born on Aug. 29, 1898, in Chicago. He wrote several Broadway plays before going to Hollywood in 1932. They include the Broadway comedy hit *Strictly Dishonorable* (1929). Sturges died on Aug. 6, 1959. His autobiography, *Preston Sturges,* was published in 1990.   Robert Sklar

Sturluson. See Snorri Sturluson.

Stuttering, also called *stammering,* is a form of speech characterized by involuntary disruptions in a person's utterances, including repetitions of sounds or syllables, prolonging of sounds, hesitations and interjections, or complete verbal blocks when no sound is produced. These speech interruptions may be accompanied by distracting bodily movements, such as eye blinks, facial contortions, or head jerks.

Stuttering is a *variable disorder.* A person who stutters may be more fluent at some times or in some situations than others. People who stutter may avoid words and situations where they are at risk to stutter, and therefore they may show few or no symptoms.

Most people lose some *fluency* (smoothness of speech) if they have trouble thinking of the word they want to say, when they try to speak too rapidly, or when they are upset or excited. These fluency breakdowns are normal and should not be confused with stuttering.

Stuttering usually begins between the ages of 2 and 5, when language skills develop. It is about 3 to 4 times more common among males than females. Speech experts do not know the exact cause of stuttering, but they believe that it results from the interaction of several factors in the nervous system. They do know that stuttering is not caused by nervousness, by psychological factors, or by a parent drawing attention to a child's speech.

Stuttering can become so serious that it interferes with a person's social life, education, or career. Most young children who show symptoms of stuttering will outgrow the problem. However, if fluency problems cause concern to the child or parents, a speech professional should be consulted as soon as possible.

Speech therapists use various methods to reduce or eliminate stuttering. Treatments are determined by the individual needs of the person who stutters. Early treatment, as close to the onset of stuttering as possible, increases the chances of success. Some people never recover completely from stuttering, but they can instead learn techniques to manage it so that the stuttering is less severe.   Robert W. Quesal

Stuttgart, *STUHT gahrt* (pop. 579,988), is the capital of the German state of Baden-Württemberg (see **Germany** [political map]). It was formerly the capital of the duchy

Shostal

Stuttgart is the capital of Baden-Württemberg, a German state. The Neues Schloss (New Palace), *center,* is a former royal residence that today houses ministries of the state government.

and kingdom of Württemberg. Stuttgart lies along the Neckar River. It is a center of German cultural, economic, and political life. Many buildings in Stuttgart are noted for their fine architecture. They include the Altes Schloss (Old Palace) in Renaissance architectural style and the Neues Schloss (New Palace) in Baroque and rococo styles. Both palaces served as residences for the dukes and kings of Württemberg. Stuttgart has dedicated a square and a monument to the German playwright and poet Friedrich Schiller, who was born in the Duchy of Württemberg.

Allied air raids hit Stuttgart heavily in World War II (1939-1945) because the city had automobile and machine tool factories. These industries, as well as the manufacture of precision instruments and such electronic products as computers, still dominate the city's economy. Stuttgart is also a publishing center. In addition, the city lies in a rich farming area that is famous for its wine.   Uwe Altrock

Stuyvesant, *STY vih suhnt,* **Peter** (1610?-1672), was the last Dutch governor of New Netherland. This area included land in present-day New York and several nearby states (see **New Netherland**).

Stuyvesant was born at Scherpenzeel, near Heerenveen, the Netherlands. Around 1632, he entered the service of the Dutch West India Company. By 1643, its directors had appointed him governor of the Caribbean islands of Curaçao, Aruba, and Bonaire. The next year, he lost a leg while taking part in an unsuccessful attempt to capture the Spanish island of St. Martin.

In 1646, Stuyvesant became director-general of all Dutch territory in the Caribbean and North America. In 1647, he arrived in New Amsterdam (now New York City) to take charge of New Netherland. In New Netherland, Stuyvesant had to deal with disorder in the colony's government, boundary disputes with other European colonies, and conflicts with a number of local Indian tribes.

He soon negotiated peace treaties with several Indian groups. In 1650, he established the colony's eastern border by agreeing to give New England colonists much disputed land. But Stuyvesant protected all land under actual Dutch control from further English expansion. In 1655, he captured New Sweden, including lands in what are now New Jersey, Delaware, and Pennsylvania. He named the region New Amstel and made it a part of New Netherland.

New York Historical Society
Peter Stuyvesant

Stuyvesant governed with absolute power. His methods were often effective, but they caused tension between him and the colonists. In 1664, an English fleet ordered the surrender of New Amsterdam. The colonists refused to support Stuyvesant, and he was forced to give in. He sailed to Holland in disgrace, but he later returned to New York and settled on his *bouwerij* (farm), part of which later became the Bowery of New York City. Stuyvesant died there in February 1672. He lies buried on the site of St. Mark's Church.   T. H. Breen

See also **Fire department** (History); **New Sweden; New York City** (History).

Sty is an infection of a *follicle* (sac) from which an eyelash grows or of a gland in the eyelid. A sty resembles a pimple. It is usually caused by *staphylococcus bacteria* that enter the root of the eyelash, grow there, and form pus. Sties often occur one after another because the germs spread from one hair follicle to another. Rubbing the eye may spread the bacteria more quickly.

White blood cells in the body usually kill the germs that cause a sty. Then the sty softens, breaks, lets out the pus, and heals. In some cases, the pus may have to be drained by minor surgery. When sties continue for a long time, doctors may treat them with antibiotics. Doctors can prevent sties from occurring with a vaccine made from staphylococcus bacteria.

Ramesh C. Tripathi and Brenda Tripathi

See also **Boil; Eye** (picture: Disorders).

Style. See Art and the arts; Fashion; Interior design.

Styracosaurus, *sty RAK uh sawr uhs,* was a horned dinosaur known for the giant spikes at the back of its skull. Its name means *spiked lizard.*

Styracosaurus had a bulky body with a short, pointed tail. It measured about 18 feet (5.5 meters) long and weighed 2 to 3 tons (1.8 to 2.7 metric tons). The dinosaur traveled on four short legs, and it probably could not run faster than about 14 miles (22 kilometers) per hour.

Styracosaurus had a remarkable head. At the back of its skull, a bony frill resembling a thin, oval shelf extended backward and upward. A number of long, tapering spikes spread out like a fan from the edge of the frill. Some of these spikes grew up to 2 feet (0.6 meter) long. *Styracosaurus* also had a nose horn about 2 feet (0.6 meter) long and two smaller horns above its eyes. It probably used its spikes and horns in self-defense or to attract mates. The animal ate fibrous plants using its parrotlike beak and the many *cheek teeth* in the sides of its jaws.

Styracosaurus lived about 77 million to 70 million years ago, during the Cretaceous Period. It inhabited what is now western North America. Fossils indicate that the animal may have gathered in herds. It also may have cared for its young, unlike other dinosaurs that left their young to fend for themselves. David B. Weishampel

See also **Dinosaur** (picture: The huge head of *Styracosaurus*).

Styrofoam. See Polystyrene.

Styron, *STY ruhn,* **William** (1925-2006), was an American novelist. Although the settings in his fiction are diverse, Styron has usually been called a Southern writer. His often powerful, elaborate prose reveals the influence of the noted Southern writer William Faulkner.

Styron was born on June 11, 1925, in Newport News, Virginia. His themes reflect a concern for the loss or corruption of such traditional values as family stability, religion, and regional culture. In his first novel, *Lie Down in Darkness* (1951), a young woman from Virginia becomes involved in a violent conflict between her parents and runs away from home. She commits suicide, partly as a result of the loss of moral authority represented by the failure of family order.

AP/Wide World

William Styron

Styron received the Pulitzer Prize for fiction in 1968 for *The Confessions of Nat Turner* (1967). In the book, Styron tried to imagine the psychological motivations that drove Turner, a black minister, to lead a bloody slave revolt in Virginia in 1831 (see **Turner, Nat**). *Sophie's Choice* (1979) deals with a Polish woman who survives the Nazi concentration camps during World War II (1939-1945). She settles in New York City and has a tragic love affair with an emotionally unstable Jewish man. A young Southern writer narrates the story. *A Tidewater Morning* (1993) is a collection of three interrelated tales. While not strictly autobiographical, they reflect the author's experiences as a young man growing up in Virginia. Styron also wrote the novelette *The Long March* (1953) and the novel *Set This House on Fire* (1960).

A collection of Styron's essays and other nonfiction pieces was published as *This Quiet Dust* (1982). Styron suffered from mental illness. He wrote an account of this struggle in *Darkness Visible* (1990). Styron died on Nov. 1, 2006. Marcus Klein

Styx, *stihks,* was a gloomy river of the underworld in Greek and Roman mythology. *Styx* is a Greek word meaning *hateful.* The boatman Charon was often described as ferrying the souls of the dead across the Styx. The gods took their most sacred oaths by the name of the Styx. If they broke such an oath, they were punished by spending nine years in Tartarus, a deep pit in the underworld. The Styx supposedly began as an actual waterfall in the region of ancient Greece called Arcadia. Its waters, which were said to be poisonous, plunged down a steep gorge to the underworld. See also **Elysium; Hades; Tartarus.** Justin M. Glenn

Su-chou. See Suzhou.

Suárez, *SWAHR ehz* or *SWAH rayth,* **Francisco** (1548-1617), was a Spanish theologian and a founder of the philosophy of international law. In his famous treatise *On Laws,* he attacked the theory of the divine right of kings and insisted on the need for the consent of the people in a just political order. Suárez saw that the medieval idea of a Christian empire was no longer possible with the rise of self-governing national monarchies. Suárez was born on Jan. 5, 1548, in Granada. He became a Jesuit in 1564. Suárez died on Sept. 25, 1617.

Carla Rahn Phillips and William D. Phillips, Jr.

Subatomic particle is a unit of matter smaller than an atom. Subatomic particles include the three major particles found in atoms: (1) *protons,* which carry a positive electric charge; (2) negatively charged *electrons;* and (3) electrically neutral *neutrons.* Protons and neutrons form an atom's nucleus. Electrons surround the nucleus.

Electrons and several other subatomic particles are *elementary particles*—that is, they are not made up of smaller units of matter. Protons and neutrons are *composite particles.* They are made up of elementary particles called *quarks.*

Some subatomic particles do not occur naturally in atoms. Rather, they are produced as a result of collisions involving at least one particle that is moving with an extremely large amount of energy—either a cosmic ray or a particle whose energy has been greatly boosted in a device called a *particle accelerator.*

For every type of ordinary subatomic particle, there also exists an *antiparticle.* An antiparticle has the same *mass* (amount of matter) as its corresponding particle, but it carries an opposite charge. For example, the antiparticle of the electron is the *positron,* which carries a positive electric charge. The antiparticle of the proton is the *antiproton,* which is negatively charged. If a particle and its antiparticle collide, they destroy each other, releasing energy. When an extremely large amount of energy is released, much of it is quickly converted into particles and antiparticles. See **Antimatter.**

All particles also have properties of waves, including *frequency* (rate of vibration) and *wavelength* (distance between successive wave crests). For information on the wave properties of particles, see **Quantum mechanics.**

Fundamental forces

Subatomic particles interact with one another mainly through three fundamental forces. These forces, from the strongest to the weakest, are (1) the strong nuclear force, also called the *strong interaction;* (2) electromagnetism; and (3) the weak nuclear force, also called the *weak interaction.* A fourth fundamental force, gravity, is relatively unimportant for subatomic particles because it is much weaker than the other three forces.

The strong nuclear force binds protons and neutrons in an atomic nucleus. It also holds together the quarks that make up protons and neutrons. Electromagnetism includes electric and magnetic forces. It holds molecules together and keeps electrons in orbit around an atomic nucleus. The weak nuclear force causes one form of *radioactive decay,* in which, for example, a neutron changes into a proton in the atomic nucleus and *emits* (gives off) an electron and an electrically neutral particle called an *antineutrino.*

The strong and weak forces act over only extremely

short distances—one trillionth of a millimeter or less. Electromagnetism can act over any distance.

Kinds of subatomic particles

Physicists distinguish between elementary particles and composite particles. They also classify subatomic particles according to such properties as electric charge, mass, and *spin*. Spin is a measure of the internal rotation of a particle.

Elementary particles. Scientists divide elementary particles into three classes: (1) leptons, (2) quarks, and (3) fundamental bosons.

Leptons. There are six known leptons. These particles are *electrons, muons, taus,* and three kinds of *neutrinos.* All leptons have a $\frac{1}{2}$ unit of spin. Particles with half-integer spins ($\frac{1}{2}, \frac{3}{2}, \frac{5}{2}$, and so forth) are called *fermions.* Each electron, muon, and tau has one unit of negative electric charge.

An electron is an extremely light particle. The mass of an electron is 0.0000000000000000000000000009 gram. That numeral is a decimal point followed by 27 zeros and a 9, or, in scientific notation, 9×10^{-28} (see **Scientific notation**).

However, scientists usually measure the mass of subatomic particles in terms of equivalent energy. They do so by applying Einstein's equation $E=mc^2$, where E is energy, m is mass, and c^2 is the speed of light multiplied by itself. For the unit of energy, they commonly use 1 million electronvolts, abbreviated *MeV,* or 1 billion electronvolts *(GeV).* One electronvolt is the amount of energy gained by an electron as it moves freely through a potential difference of 1 volt (see **Volt**). In terms of energy, the mass of an electron is 0.51 MeV. A muon is 207 times as massive as an electron; a tau, 3,477 times as massive as an electron.

Neutrinos have no electric charge, but they do have a tiny amount of mass. Their mass has so far proved too small to measure. Leptons have no measurable size; physicists describe them as "pointlike." See **Lepton**.

Quarks. There are six known quarks. They are known as *up, down, charm, strange, bottom,* and *top.* Physicists are almost certain there are no more to be found.

Scientists often refer to quarks by the first letter of the names of these particles. For example, a down quark is called a *d quark,* or simply a *d.*

The *u, c,* and *t* quarks have $\frac{2}{3}$ unit of positive electric charge. The *d, s,* and *b* quarks have $\frac{1}{3}$ unit of negative electric charge. Like leptons, quarks have a $\frac{1}{2}$ unit of spin. However, quarks interact by means of the strong force, but leptons do not. The strong force binds quarks together with such strength that they are never found as free particles. They are found only in composite particles known as *hadrons.*

The lightest quark is the *u,* whose mass is about 5 MeV. The heaviest is the *t.* Physicists believe that this particle's mass is about 175 GeV. Quarks, like electrons, are described as "pointlike."

Fundamental bosons, also called *gauge bosons,* make up the third class of elementary particles. Fundamental bosons transmit the fundamental forces, and they have no known smaller parts. All bosons have a whole number value of spin (0, 1, or 2).

A fundamental boson called a *photon* transmits the electromagnetic force. Thus, all forms of electromagnetic radiation—including visible light—consist of photons. According to the theory of electromagnetism, electrically charged particles interact with one another by *exchanging* (giving off and absorbing) photons. A photon has no mass, and is pointlike.

The *Z boson,* which is electrically neutral, and two *W bosons,* one with a positive charge and one with a negative charge, carry the weak force. Each *W* boson has a mass of 80 GeV. The mass of the *Z* boson is 91 GeV.

Eight bosons called *gluons* transmit the strong force. These bosons "glue" the quarks together to form hadrons. The quarks interact with one another by exchanging gluons. Gluons are always bound in hadrons. Gluons have no mass.

Physicists believe the gravitational force is transmitted by a particle called the *graviton.* However, the gravitational force is so weak that this particle has never been observed. See **Boson; Higgs boson; Gluon; Photon**.

Composite particles. Quarks make up composite particles called hadrons. There are two types of hadrons—*baryons* and *mesons.*

Baryons are composed of three quarks. The most familiar baryons are the proton, composed of two *u* quarks and a *d* quark, and the neutron, composed of two *d* quarks and a *u* quark.

All atoms of the same chemical element have the same number of protons. Each proton carries one unit of positive electric charge. The mass of a proton is approximately 938 MeV, or about 1,836 times the mass of an electron.

A neutron has no net electric charge because the charges of its quarks cancel one another out. A neutron's mass is 940 MeV. Protons and neutrons are about 10^{-12} millimeter across. See **Neutron; Proton**.

Experimenters have observed more than 100 kinds of baryons besides protons and neutrons. These other baryons have more mass than protons and neutrons, and they decay quickly. A subatomic particle decays by releasing energy and turning into one or more other particles.

Mesons are composed of a quark and an antiquark. For example, the positively charged *pi meson* is composed of a *u* quark and a *d* antiquark. All mesons decay quickly and are produced only in particle collisions. Mesons are also classified as bosons because they have a whole number value of spin. Experimenters have observed about 150 kinds of mesons. See **Baryon; Hadron; Meson; Quark**.

Theories of forces

Scientists have developed several theories of forces to explain natural phenomena and to predict the outcome of experiments. Researchers are now trying to develop a single theory for all the forces.

Early theories. The earliest successful theories have become known as *classical theories.* These theories apply only to objects larger than atoms and molecules. The first such theory was a theory of gravity formulated by the English scientist Isaac Newton in the 1600's. It was refined by the German-born physicist Albert Einstein in 1915 in his general theory of relativity. In the 1860's, James Clerk Maxwell, a Scottish physicist and mathematician, developed another classical theory, the theory of electromagnetism.

During the early 1900's, scientists found that classical theories could not explain the inner workings of atoms. By the 1920's, they had developed the theory of quantum mechanics to help them understand the physics of such minute objects as atoms. Since then, theories of forces have had to be consistent with the theory of quantum mechanics and with Einstein's special theory of relativity—published in 1905—to be acceptable to the scientific community. As a result, such theories are often called *relativistic quantum theories.* See **Relativity.**

The Standard Model. Physicists developed three successful relativistic quantum theories beginning in the 1940's. These theories explain electromagnetism, the weak force, and the strong force. All three have the same basic mathematical structure, and are known as *gauge theories.* Together, these theories are known as the *Standard Model.* Gravity is the only fundamental force that does not have a satisfactory quantum theory.

The relativistic quantum theory of electromagnetism is called *quantum electrodynamics,* or *QED.* This theory was developed during the 1940's by physicists Richard P. Feynman and Julian S. Schwinger of the United States and Sin-Itiro Tomonaga of Japan.

The electromagnetic and weak forces are closely related. The *electroweak theory* describes their relationship. It was completed in the early 1970's by physicists Sheldon L. Glashow and Steven Weinberg of the United States and Abdus Salam of Pakistan.

The theory of the strong interaction, called *quantum chromodynamics,* or *QCD,* was proposed by the American physicists David J. Gross and Frank A. Wilczek in 1973, and independently by the American physicist H. David Politzer in 1974. This theory predicted the existence of gluons.

One of the main differences among the three theories concerns the number and types of charges involved in the three forces. Electromagnetism has only one charge, the familiar electric charge. The weak and strong forces have associated with them certain properties that are believed to be similar to, but not exactly the same as, electric charges. The weak force has two such "charges," called *weak isospin,* and the strong force has three, fancifully called *color.* These color "charges" have no relationship to actual colors.

Most gauge theories require that the gauge bosons be massless particles, and photons and gluons meet this requirement. However, the weak gauge bosons, the W and Z particles, are extremely massive. As a result, scientists have concluded that the gauge theory of electroweak interactions can be correct only if there exists another particle, called a *Higgs boson,* to contribute mass to the W's and Z. There is no experimental evidence for this particle.

Theoretical research on particles and forces is aimed at the development of a single theory that explains all four fundamental forces. This theory will also have to explain why the leptons and quarks have their particular masses.

The theory must also explain why there are three "families" of subatomic particles. Each family has a neutral lepton, a negatively charged lepton, a quark with an electric charge of $+\frac{2}{3}$, and a quark whose charge is $-\frac{1}{3}$.

The first family consists of the electron neutrino, the electron, and the u and d quarks, respectively. All the material around us is made up of only members of the first family.

In the second family are the muon neutrino, the muon, and the c and s quarks. The third family consists of the tau neutrino, the tau, and the t and b quarks.

The members of the second and third families seem to be identical to those of the first family, except for mass. Each member of the second family has more mass than the corresponding member of the first family. Each member of the third family has more mass than the corresponding member of the second family.

One group of theories, called *grand unified theories,* or GUTs, describe electroweak and strong forces as aspects of a single force. However, these theories do not deal with gravity.

Another group of theories, *superstring theories,* attempt to unify all four fundamental forces, including gravity, into a single force. According to these theories, objects called *strings* underlie all matter and forces. String length is only about 10^{-32} millimeter.

Gary J. Feldman

See also **Atom; Particle accelerator; String theory.**

Subconscious. See Unconscious.

Sublette, *SUHB leht,* **William Lewis** (1799?-1845), was an American fur trader and merchant. He was born in Lincoln County, Kentucky, but grew up in St. Charles, Mo. He left Missouri in 1822 to become a trapper. He became wealthy through his business relationships with other fur traders. Sublette operated trading posts on the Platte and upper Missouri rivers. He helped open the Oregon Trail by using wagons in the Rocky Mountains, and by finding a shortcut, *Sublette's Cutoff.*

William E. Foley

Sublimation, *SUHB luh MAY shuhn,* is the process by which a solid substance changes into a gas, or vapor, without first becoming a liquid. There are a few substances, such as iodine, arsenic, camphor, and dry ice, that change into a gas without first melting. These substances are said to *sublime.* The most familiar example of sublimation can occur when wet clothes are hung out on the line on a winter day when the temperature is below freezing. The water on the clothes freezes and then evaporates into vapor without melting. Solid iodine will change into a vapor when it is warmed without becoming a liquid. Then, when the vapor is cooled, the iodine will change back into crystals. The change of a vapor back into a solid is part of sublimation.

Sublimation is used in industry to purify substances. When a solid changes directly into a vapor, only the pure substance evaporates, while the impurities remain. Pure sulfur, benzoin, and sal ammoniac are made by this process.

Albert G. Anderson

See also **Melting point.**

Subliminal, *suhb LIHM uh nuhl,* refers to stimuli that are so weak or last so short a time that a person is not aware of them. Such stimuli are said to be *subliminal* (below the threshold of consciousness). The consciousness threshold varies from person to person and from time to time, even in the same person. Psychologists have been trying to determine whether subliminal stimuli can influence people, perhaps through the unconscious. Some use has been made of such subliminal stimuli in advertising and in attempts by retail stores to reduce shoplifting.

Phillip L. Rice

U.S. Navy

An attack submarine is designed to search out and destroy enemy ships during wartime. Many attack submarines have nuclear-powered engines and carry torpedoes and missiles. Crew members use such devices as periscopes and radar to locate enemy ships on the water's surface.

Submarine is a ship that can travel underwater. Most submarines are designed for use in war—to attack enemy ships or to fire missiles at enemy countries. These submarines range in length from about 200 feet (61 meters) to more than 550 feet (168 meters). Their rounded hulls are about 30 feet (9 meters) in diameter. More than 150 crew members can live and work in a large submarine. Some submarines are used for scientific research. These underwater craft explore the ocean depths and gather scientific information. They are smaller than military submarines and carry only a few crew members. See **Ocean** (Exploring the ocean).

In war, a submarine usually attacks from beneath the surface of the water. A submarine must remain underwater to be effective. Early submarines could not stay submerged for long periods. They had to surface every few hours for air for their engines and crews. Enemy planes and ships could then attack them. Today, nuclear submarines can stay underwater for months at a time. Nuclear engines do not need oxygen to operate, and modern submarines can produce air.

A submarine's long, cigar-shaped body enables it to move swiftly underwater. Its working and living spaces, weapons, and machinery are encased in a *pressure hull* made of high-strength steel or *titanium* (a strong, lightweight metal). At operating depths, a pressure hull cannot be crushed by the pressure of the water around it.

Norman Polmar, the contributor of this article, is a former editor of the U.S. sections of Jane's Fighting Ships *and the author of* Atomic Submarines *and* Death of the Thresher.

Built into the bow and stern of the pressure hull are tanks that, when filled with water, give the submarine *ballast* (weight) for diving. Submarines that are not built in the United States usually have a second, outer hull. The space between the hulls is used to store ballast tanks and equipment that does not need protection from water pressure.

A tall, thin structure called the *sail* rises from the middle of a submarine's deck. The sail stands about 20 feet (6.1 meters) high. It holds the periscopes and the radar and radio antennas. The top of the sail also serves as the *bridge,* from which the captain directs the craft when on the surface. Steel fins called *diving planes* stick out from both sides of the sail or bow and from the stern. They guide the ship to different depths. One or two propellers in the stern drive the submarine. Rudders mounted above and below the propellers steer the craft.

Kinds of submarines

There are two main kinds of submarines, *attack submarines* and *ballistic missile submarines.*

Attack submarines are designed to search out and destroy enemy submarines and surface ships. They also are used to attack targets on land and to gather information about enemy vessels.

Most attack submarines in the United States Navy range in length from about 290 to 360 feet (88 to 110 meters). They have about 130 crew members. Most of these submarines have nuclear-powered engines and carry torpedoes and guided missiles. Attack submarines track and locate their underwater targets with *sonar* (*so*und *n*avigation *a*nd *r*anging) equipment, which detects

Basic parts of an attack submarine

The illustration below shows the basic parts of an attack submarine. A nuclear reactor furnishes the power for the vessel. Small wings called *diving planes* stick out from both sides of the sail or bow and from the stern, and help guide the ship underwater. The rudders, which are mounted on the stern, help steer the submarine. Torpedoes are fired from tubes located along each side of the vessel.

WORLD BOOK illustration by George Suyeoka

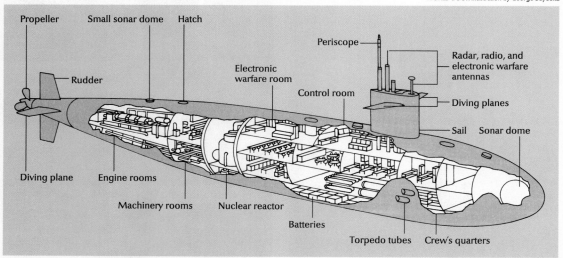

Propeller   Small sonar dome   Hatch   Periscope   Radar, radio, and electronic warfare antennas   Electronic warfare room   Control room   Diving planes   Sail   Sonar dome   Rudder   Diving plane   Engine rooms   Machinery rooms   Nuclear reactor   Batteries   Torpedo tubes   Crew's quarters

sounds underwater. They use periscopes and radar equipment to identify enemy ships on the surface.

Modern U.S. attack submarines fire their torpedoes from four tubes located along the sides of the hull. Torpedoes have *homing devices* that follow the target and guide the torpedo to it (see **Torpedo**). Older submarines had their torpedo tubes in the bow. But in modern submarines, the sonar is located in the bow—far away from the noise of the ship's propeller.

Some submarines can also fire antisubmarine missiles from the torpedo tubes. These short-range weapons have a torpedo or a nuclear warhead that can destroy submerged submarines from as far away as 30 miles (48 kilometers). Other submarines can attack surface ships and onshore targets with *cruise missiles,* which have short wings that open after launching.

Basic parts of a ballistic missile submarine

The illustration below shows the basic parts of a ballistic missile submarine. The exterior of this vessel is similar to that of an attack submarine. But ballistic missile submarines are larger than attack submarines, and they carry long-range missiles for bombing enemy cities and military bases on shore. The missiles are launched from tubes through openings at the top of the vessel.

WORLD BOOK illustration by George Suyeoka; adapted from a *Newsweek* illustration by Oliver Williams

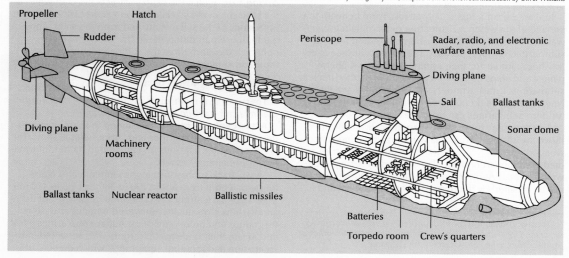

Propeller   Hatch   Periscope   Radar, radio, and electronic warfare antennas   Rudder   Diving plane   Sail   Ballast tanks   Sonar dome   Diving plane   Machinery rooms   Ballast tanks   Nuclear reactor   Ballistic missiles   Batteries   Torpedo room   Crew's quarters

Ballistic missile submarines are designed to attack enemy cities and military bases ashore. They carry long-range missiles that can strike targets from about 1,500 to 4,000 miles (2,400 to 6,400 kilometers) away.

Ballistic missile submarines are larger than attack submarines, measuring from about 380 to 560 feet (115 to 170 meters) long. Their crews number about 150 members. Missiles are fired from *silos* (launching tubes) in the submarine's hull. The missiles can carry multiple *warheads* (explosive sections). Each warhead can be aimed at a separate target. Ballistic missile submarines also carry torpedoes for defense.

Special equipment aboard the submarine plots the craft's exact location and determines the path of the ballistic missile to its destination. This equipment, called the *inertial navigation system,* consists of accurate measuring devices linked to computers. The system helps navigate the submarine by recording its starting position on a voyage and its movement in all directions. This information is fed into a guidance system in the missile to provide the precise distance and direction to the target. After launching, the missile's own inertial navigation system guides the weapon. See **Inertial guidance.**

The power plant

The engine of a nuclear submarine consists of a nuclear reactor and a steam generator. The reactor uses uranium for fuel and splits uranium atoms in a controlled process called *fission.* This process produces intense heat. See **Nuclear energy.**

Pipes carry water from the steam generator to the reactor, where the water is heated to about 600 °F (315 °C). This water is kept under pressure so it will not boil. Instead, it returns to the steam generator and boils a supply of unpressurized water that turns to steam. The steam spins large *turbines* (wheels), producing power to rotate the propeller shaft and run the ship.

Nuclear engines operate without air and consume much less fuel than do other engines. About 4 pounds (1.8 kilograms) of uranium fuel produce more energy than 10 million gallons (38 million liters) of fuel oil.

Some submarines run on diesel engines. However, the U.S. Navy has not built a diesel-powered submarine for combat since 1959. Diesel engines burn fuel oil and need air for combustion. A submarine can use these engines only when on or near the surface. Electric batteries supply power underwater. Late in World War II (1939-1945), the German Navy equipped submarines with an air tube called a *snorkel.* The snorkel drew air into the submarine when the craft was near the surface. This air replaced oxygen used up by the diesel engines and crew. But the snorkel left a trail through the water and could reveal the submarine's location.

Submarines did not become true underwater ships until the development of nuclear-powered engines. In the early 1990's, however, some countries began building submarines with *air-independent systems,* which allow diesel engines to operate underwater for several weeks at low speeds without taking in air.

How a submarine operates

Surface operation. On the surface of the water, a submarine performs much like any other ship. A submarine can cruise at about 20 *knots* (nautical miles per hour) on the surface. However, modern submarines spend little time on the surface.

Diving. A submarine dives by flooding its ballast tanks with water. The added weight causes the ship to lose its *positive buoyancy* (ability to stay afloat), and it becomes *neutrally buoyant.* Then the submarine's diving planes are tilted down and the craft glides smoothly down into the water.

A submarine can dive to a depth of over 100 feet (30 meters) in less than a minute. Most modern U.S. combat submarines operate at a depth of about 1,300 feet (400 meters) or less. If they were to dive significantly deeper, they would be destroyed by water pressure.

Underwater operation. A submarine travels underwater somewhat as an airplane moves through the air. The diving planes angle up and down to raise or lower the ship. Two crew members sit at aircraftlike controls. They push the control wheel forward to make the submarine descend or pull the wheel toward them to make the craft rise. Turning the wheel to the right or left moves the rudder and steers the ship.

A nuclear submarine can travel faster than 30 knots underwater. Its sonar warns of any obstacles in its path, and the inertial guidance system keeps a constant check on the position of the submarine. However, submarines normally travel at about 10 knots or less to avoid detection by sonar.

Resurfacing. A submarine is brought to the surface in one of two ways. Water is blown out of the ballast tanks by compressed air, or the diving planes are tilted so the submarine angles up.

Life aboard a submarine

Attack submarines of the United States Navy go on patrol for two or three months. They frequently stop in ports during the voyage. Ballistic missile submarines stay on patrol for about 60 days and spend almost the entire period underwater.

The sailors on attack submarines and ballistic missile submarines have many comforts during their cruise. For example, large air-conditioning units keep the temperature and humidity at comfortable levels. Libraries, motion pictures, and game rooms help ease the monotony of life beneath the sea.

On most submarines, every member of the crew works a daily four-hour shift called a *watch.* At the end of their watch, the crew members are relieved and go off duty for eight hours. They may have to do some maintenance work on the ship but are mostly free to relax or study until they return to their stations. The work assignments vary so that all the crew members have days off.

Nuclear submarines produce their own air and drinking water. A process called *electrolysis* extracts oxygen from seawater and provides all the air needed for the crew. Chemical filters remove any harmful elements from the air in a submarine. Thick lead plates around the nuclear reactor shield the crew from radiation. Machines distill ocean water into pure drinking water.

A submarine returns to port at the end of its cruise. It receives any needed repairs and takes on additional supplies. A ballistic missile submarine also changes crews. Each ballistic missile submarine in the U.S. Navy has two crews, the *blue crew* and the *gold crew.* After

U.S. Navy

An early submarine called the *Turtle* was powered by a hand-cranked propeller and operated by one person. In 1776, the *Turtle* made the first known submarine attack on a warship.

U.S. Navy

The United States Navy's first submarine, the U.S.S. *Holland,* was powered by a gasoline engine and electric batteries. An Irish-born inventor, John P. Holland, launched it in 1898.

one crew completes a patrol, it is replaced by the other. The oncoming crew takes the submarine on another mission. The men returning to shore go on leave and then receive additional training. After the crew of an attack submarine completes a patrol, it spends six months in port and in local operations.

History

Early submarines. The first workable submarine was a wooden rowboat covered with waterproof hides. The builder, a Dutch scientist named Cornelius van Drebbel, demonstrated his invention in England about 1620. Designers constructed many undersea craft during the next century. But little use was made of such ships until the Revolutionary War in America (1775-1783). During that war, David Bushnell, a student at Yale College, designed the *Turtle,* a one-man submarine powered by a hand-cranked propeller. In 1776, the *Turtle* failed in an attempt

to sink a British warship in New York Harbor. This mission was the first known attack by a submarine.

In 1800, the American inventor Robert Fulton built the *Nautilus,* a copper-covered submarine 21 feet (6.4 meters) long. Fulton tried to sell the *Nautilus* to France and Britain. But neither nation showed much interest in it, even though it sank several ships in demonstrations.

During the Civil War (1861-1865), the Confederate submarine *Hunley* became the first underwater vessel to sink a ship in wartime. The *Hunley* carried an explosive attached to a long pole on its bow. In 1864, it rammed the Union ship *Housatonic* in Charleston Harbor off the coast of South Carolina. The explosion sank the *Housatonic,* but the *Hunley* went to the bottom with its victim. In 1995, a search team led by amateur marine archaeologist Clive Cussler of the United States found the wreckage of the *Hunley.*

In 1898, the American inventor John P. Holland

U.S. Navy

German submarines called *U-boats* sank thousands of merchant ships during World War II (1939-1945). The U-boat shown at the left was captured by the United States during the war.

launched a 53-foot (16-meter) submarine powered by a gasoline engine and electric batteries. It could reach a speed of 6 knots submerged. The U.S. Navy bought this ship—its first submarine—in 1900 and named it the U.S.S. *Holland.*

Simon Lake, another American, invented the submarine periscope in 1902. His periscope used magnifying lenses that enabled a submerged submarine to sight distant targets. Lake also built submarines with wheels so they could roll along the bottom of the sea. In 1908, the United Kingdom launched the first diesel-powered submarine. Its engines were more powerful, cost less to operate, and produced fewer dangerous fumes than did gasoline engines. Most submarines used diesel engines until the development of nuclear power in the 1950's.

World Wars I and II. During World War I (1914-1918), Germany proved the submarine's effectiveness as a deadly warship. In 1914, the German submarine *U-9* sank three British cruisers within an hour. German submarines, called *Unterseeboote* or *U-boats,* blockaded the United Kingdom and took a heavy toll of merchant and passenger ships. U-boats became the terror of the seas by waging unrestricted war on Allied ships.

In May 1915, a German submarine torpedoed the British liner *Lusitania.* The attack killed 1,201 passengers, including 128 Americans. Public anger increased in the United States as U-boats sank one American merchant ship after another during the next year. These submarine attacks helped lead to the entry of the United States into the war in April 1917.

During World War II (1939-1945), U-boats sank thousands of merchant ships. The U-boats hunted in groups of up to 40. These groups were called *wolf packs.*

The Allies fought to protect their ships from the German submarines. Merchant ships formed large *convoys* (fleets) that were protected by destroyers and other ships. The development of radar and sonar helped locate the U-boats and reduced the danger of attack.

The U.S. submarines operated chiefly in the Pacific Ocean. They sank more than half of Japan's merchant ships and many of its warships. The Navy's submarines also carried troops to raid enemy islands, laid mines in enemy harbors, and performed rescue missions.

Nuclear submarines. In 1954, the U.S. Navy commissioned the first nuclear-powered submarine, the *Nautilus.* On its first voyage, the *Nautilus* broke all previous submarine records for underwater speed and endurance. In 1958, the *Nautilus* became the first submarine to sail under the ice at the North Pole. In 1960, the *Triton* traveled underwater around the world. That same year, the *Seadragon* navigated the Northwest Passage, the northern route from the Atlantic to the Pacific Ocean.

In the late 1950's, the U.S. Navy developed the first modern ballistic missile submarines. Each of these submarines had 16 missiles in the hull behind the sail. The early missiles carried nuclear weapons and could strike targets up to 1,200 miles (1,930 kilometers) away.

In 1981, the United States commissioned the first *Ohio*-class submarine. The last ship of this class was commissioned in 1997. *Ohio*-class ships are the largest and most powerful U.S. submarines ever built. They are sometimes known as Trident submarines. *Ohio*-class submarines measure 560 feet (171 meters) long and carry 24 Trident missiles. Each missile has a range of about 4,000 miles (6,400 kilometers) and can hold several individual warheads. Each warhead can be aimed at a separate target. The only longer submarines to ever be built were those of the Soviet *Typhoon* class of the 1980's. In 1982, during the conflict between the United Kingdom and Argentina in the Falkland Islands, the British Royal Navy became the first navy to use nuclear-powered submarines in combat.

At the time of its breakup in 1991, the Soviet Union had the world's largest submarine fleet—about 310 ships. Today's submarine fleets are much smaller. The United States operates the largest fleet. The U.S. fleet consists of about 55 attack submarines and about 18 ballistic missile submarines. Major classes of U.S. attack and ballistic missile submarines include the *Ohio, Los Angeles, Seawolf,* and *Virginia.*   Norman Polmar

Related articles in *World Book* include:

Depth charge	Periscope
Diving, Underwater (Diving in	Rickover, Hyman G.
vehicles)	World War I
Guided missile	World War II
Holland, John P.	

Additional resources

Cross, Wilbur, and Feise, G. W., Jr. *Encyclopedia of American Submarines.* Facts on File, 2003.
Parrish, Thomas. *The Submarine: A History.* Viking, 2004.
Payan, Gregory, and Guelke, Alexander. *Life on a Submarine.* Children's Pr., 2000. Younger readers.

Subpoena, *suh PEE nuh,* also spelled *subpena,* is a written legal order to appear as a witness and give testimony in court. The name comes from two Latin words, *sub,* which means *under,* and *poena,* which means *penalty.* A person who receives a subpoena must obey it *under penalty* of being held in contempt of court (see **Contempt**). The *subpoena duces tecum* (Latin for *bring with you under penalty)* requires a person to bring into court specified things, such as papers, books, financial records, or other documents. See also **Witness.**

James O. Finckenauer

Subsidy, *SUHB suh dee,* is a money payment or other form of aid that the government gives to a person or organization. Its purpose is to encourage some needed activity by furnishing funds, free land, tax relief, or legal rights that might otherwise be lacking.

In the 1800's, the United States government gave large tracts of land to the railroads on the condition that they would build lines across the continent. Altogether, the railroads received about 160,000,000 acres (64,700,000 hectares) of land in this way. The government also granted subsidies to telegraph and cable companies. In the 1920's, it granted subsidies to ship companies. It gave them generous mail-carrying contracts and allowed them to buy government-owned ships at a fraction of their actual cost. Government airmail contracts have also aided the airlines since the 1920's.

Federal, state, and local governments award subsidies for a variety of activities. Taxes on goods imported into the United States are indirect subsidies to U.S. manufacturers who make the same kind of goods. Subsidies also help finance many schools. Subsidies are sometimes improperly awarded to gain the political support of those receiving the aid.   Daniel Quinn Mills

See also **Education; Tariff** (Why tariffs are levied).
Substance abuse. See **Alcoholism; Drug abuse.**

WORLD BOOK photo by Steven Spicer

Subtraction is a way of taking away a number of things from a larger number. You take them away to find how many things are left. Only *like things* can be subtracted. That is, you cannot subtract apples from pencils.

Suppose you have a set of 8 oranges.

Suppose you want to take away a set of 5 oranges.

You find that you have 3 oranges left.

Learning to subtract

A question such as "3 from 6 is how many?" is a subtraction problem. To find out how many things are left in a subtraction problem, you can *count* or find the answer by *thinking*.

Subtraction by counting. Here are two groups of chocolate cupcakes.

How many cupcakes are there in the first group? Count them. There are 6 cupcakes in the first group. Mary took 3 cupcakes from the second group. How many cupcakes are left in the second group? Count them. There are 3 cupcakes left. You counted to find how many cupcakes are left if you take 3 from 6. You discovered that 3 taken from 6 leaves 3.

Subtraction by thinking. Tommy has 5 pennies.

He wants to spend 2 pennies for a pencil. How many pennies will Tommy have left? Cover 2 pennies in the picture. You should be able to tell how many pennies are left by just looking at the picture, without counting. You should learn to *think* "2 from 5 leaves 3." This article will show you the facts you need to know to subtract by thinking. Thinking the answer is a quicker way of subtracting than counting.

You can learn to think the answer to a subtraction problem from what you know about addition. For example, you know that 3 and 2 are 5. This means that if you take 2 from 5, you have 3. You can practice this method of subtraction by writing the addition and subtraction facts in groups of four.

3 and 4 are 7	4 from 7 leaves 3
4 and 3 are 7	3 from 7 leaves 4

Subtraction questions. Subtraction tells you how many things are left when you take away one set of things from another. It also lets you *compare* two sets of things. Suppose Mary has 5 balloons and Sue has 3 balloons.

To compare the two sets of balloons, you must find the *difference* between the two sets. You can find the difference by subtracting. When you subtract 3 from 5, you discover that the difference between the two sets is 2 balloons, or 2.

Subtraction terms

Borrow in subtraction means to change a 10 in the minuend into 1's, to change a 100 into 10's, or to change a 1,000 into 100's, and so on.

Difference. In 12−7=5, the number 5 is the difference. It means that 12 and 7 are being compared.

Minuend. In 12−7=5, the number 12 is the minuend.

Minus in subtraction means *less* or *take away*. For example, 12 *minus* 7 is 5.

Remainder. In 12−7=5, the number 5 is the remainder. It is the answer to the subtraction problem.

Subtraction fact is a basic statement in subtraction. For example, 16−9=7 and 4−3=1 are two subtraction facts.

Subtrahend. In 12−7=5, the number taken away (7) is the subtrahend.

You can also use subtraction to find out how many more things are needed. Suppose John needs 12 pennies. He has 5 pennies. How many more pennies does he need?

When you subtract 5 from 12, you discover that John needs 7 more pennies to make 12.

Subtraction can tell you (1) how many things are left, (2) what the difference is, and (3) how many more things are needed.

Writing subtraction. It is best to write your subtraction problems and their answers. This gives you a record of your thinking.

You can make a record with pictures.

The picture shows that 3 taken from 5 leaves 2.

You can write this in numbers and words.

3 from 5 leaves 2

But you must learn to write with numbers and signs.

$$5-3=2$$

The − sign means to subtract or take away. So 5−3 means "3 taken from 5." We call the − sign the *minus sign,* and read 5−3 as "5 *minus* 3." The = sign means that the sets on one side of the = sign are *equal* to the sets on the other side. Here is how it works:

$$5-3 \qquad = \qquad 2$$

There is another way to use numerals and signs.

$$\begin{array}{r} 5 \\ -3 \\ \hline 2 \end{array}$$

Each part of a subtraction problem has a name. When we are subtracting to find out how many things are left, we call the answer the *remainder.* When we are subtracting to compare two groups or to find how many more things are needed, we call the answer the *difference.* We call the number being taken away or subtracted the *subtrahend.* The number from which the subtrahend is taken is called the *minuend.*

$$\begin{array}{r} 5 \\ -3 \\ \hline 2 \end{array}$$

5 ◄——— Minuend
−3 ◄——— Subtrahend
2 ◄——— Remainder or difference

Subtraction facts. By subtracting one group from another, you discover that 8−5=3, 6−3=3, and 12−5=7. We call these *subtraction facts.*

Each subtraction fact consists of a minuend, a subtrahend, and a remainder, or difference. You can discover each subtraction fact for yourself by counting and taking away one set of things from another. For example, you can practice by crossing off squares as you have seen crossing off done in an earlier example.

Some subtraction facts

2	3	4	5	6	7	8	9	10
−1	−1	−1	−1	−1	−1	−1	−1	−1
1	2	3	4	5	6	7	8	9
3	4	5	6	7	8	9	10	11
−2	−2	−2	−2	−2	−2	−2	−2	−2
1	2	3	4	5	6	7	8	9
4	5	6	7	8	9	10	11	12
−3	−3	−3	−3	−3	−3	−3	−3	−3
1	2	3	4	5	6	7	8	9
5	6	7	8	9	10	11	12	13
−4	−4	−4	−4	−4	−4	−4	−4	−4
1	2	3	4	5	6	7	8	9
6	7	8	9	10	11	12	13	14
−5	−5	−5	−5	−5	−5	−5	−5	−5
1	2	3	4	5	6	7	8	9
7	8	9	10	11	12	13	14	15
−6	−6	−6	−6	−6	−6	−6	−6	−6
1	2	3	4	5	6	7	8	9
8	9	10	11	12	13	14	15	16
−7	−7	−7	−7	−7	−7	−7	−7	−7
1	2	3	4	5	6	7	8	9
9	10	11	12	13	14	15	16	17
−8	−8	−8	−8	−8	−8	−8	−8	−8
1	2	3	4	5	6	7	8	9
10	11	12	13	14	15	16	17	18
−9	−9	−9	−9	−9	−9	−9	−9	−9
1	2	3	4	5	6	7	8	9

There are other subtraction facts. For example, any number minus itself is zero. Thus, 5−5=0 and 9−9=0. Also, any number minus zero is the number itself. Thus, 6−0=6 and 3−0=3. It is best to learn the subtraction facts so that you can recall them without stopping to work them out. You can use them to solve problems right away.

To learn the harder facts, it is sometimes useful to *regroup.* For example, many people find it easier to subtract numbers from 10. Suppose you wanted to solve the problem 14−7. You know that 14 is the same as one 10 and four 1's. So you could regroup it like this.

1	2	3	4	5	6	7	8	9	10

First, you can take away 4. You know that 7−4=3, so you must still take away 3. Subtracting 3 from 10 is simple.

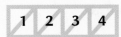

You can see that 10−3=7. So 14−7=7.

You can probably invent other ways to help you learn the subtraction facts.

Subtracting larger numbers

Subtracting larger numbers is not difficult, if you know the subtraction facts and understand the number system.

Subtracting 10's and 100's. Suppose you have 5 dimes. This is the same as 50¢. Suppose you want to spend 3 dimes on a book. This is the same as 30¢. How much money will you have left? The problem is 5 dimes −3 dimes or 50¢−30¢. You can find the answer by counting.

You can also find the answer by using the subtraction facts and thinking.

$$\begin{array}{r} 5\text{ dimes} \\ -3\text{ dimes} \\ \hline 2\text{ dimes} \end{array} \qquad \begin{array}{r} 50¢ \\ -30¢ \\ \hline 20¢ \end{array}$$

If you know that 5−3=2, you can see that 3 dimes taken from 5 dimes leaves 2 dimes. A dime is 10¢, so you can see that 50−30=20. The subtraction fact 5−3=2 helps you find the answer. *You subtract 10's the same way that you subtract 1's. But you must write the remainder in the 10's place.* And you must remember to write in a zero to show that the remainder is 10's, not 1's.

Subtracting 100's is done in the same way. Suppose you had to subtract 3 dollars from 5 dollars.

$$\begin{array}{r} 5\text{ dollars} \\ -3\text{ dollars} \\ \hline 2\text{ dollars} \end{array} \qquad \begin{array}{r} 500¢ \\ -300¢ \\ \hline 200¢ \end{array} \qquad \begin{array}{r} 500 \\ -300 \\ \hline 200 \end{array}$$

You subtract 100's (and 1,000's and so on) the same way that you subtract 1's and 10's. Once again, you can see how the subtraction fact helps you find the answer to the subtraction example.

Subtracting 10's and 1's. Tom had 45 tickets to sell. He sold 23 of them. How many tickets should he have left? That is, what is 45−23? We call numbers such as 45 and 23 *two-place* numbers, because 45 has two places, four 10's and five 1's; and 23 has two places, two 10's and three 1's.

$$\begin{array}{r} 4\text{ tens and 5 ones} \\ -2\text{ tens and 3 ones} \\ \hline 2\text{ tens and 2 ones} \end{array} \qquad \begin{array}{r} 45 \\ -23 \\ \hline 22 \end{array}$$

To subtract one two-place number from another, you

begin by subtracting the 1's: 5−3=2. Write the 2 in the 1's place in the remainder.

$$\begin{array}{r} 45 \\ -23 \\ \hline 22 \end{array}$$

Next, subtract the 10's: 4−2=2. Remember that the 4−2 stands for 10's, not 1's. Write the 2 in the 10's place in the remainder.

$$\begin{array}{r} 45 \\ -23 \\ \hline 22 \end{array}$$

So Tom should have 22 tickets left.

Here is an example of subtracting *three-place numbers.*

$$\begin{array}{r} 647 \\ -123 \\ \hline 524 \end{array}$$

First, subtract the 1's: 7−3=4. Write the 4 in the 1's place of the remainder. Next, subtract the 10's: 4−2=2. Write the 2 in the 10's place in the remainder. Next, subtract the 100's: 6−1=5. Write the 5 in the 100's place. Subtracting two- and three-place numbers is easy, but you must remember two things. You must subtract the 1's, 10's, 100's, 1,000's, and so on, *in that order.* Always begin at the right—in the 1's place—and work to the left. Second, you must write your work carefully, so that the numbers of the remainders are in the proper places.

How to borrow. When you subtract larger numbers, you often cannot solve a problem unless you know how to *borrow.* For instance, look at the example 62−27. How can you subtract seven 1's from two 1's? Borrowing helps solve this kind of example.

To understand borrowing, you must follow an example step by step. In the example 62−27, the first step is to write the numbers as 10's and 1's.

$$\begin{array}{r} 62 \\ -27 \end{array} \qquad \Rightarrow \qquad \begin{array}{r} 6\text{ tens 2 ones} \\ -2\text{ tens 7 ones} \end{array}$$

You cannot subtract seven 1's from two 1's. *But you can take one of the 10's in the minuend and change it into 1's.* Now you can solve the problem.

$$\begin{array}{r} 6\text{ tens 2 ones} \\ -2\text{ tens 7 ones} \end{array} \Rightarrow \begin{array}{r} 5\text{ tens }10+2\text{ ones} \\ -2\text{ tens 7 ones} \end{array} \Rightarrow \begin{array}{r} 5\text{ tens 12 ones} \\ -2\text{ tens 7 ones} \\ \hline 3\text{ tens 5 ones} \end{array}$$

So 62−27=35. There were too many 1's in the subtrahend to subtract. You "borrowed," or changed a 10 from the 10's part of the minuend into the 1's. This is what borrowing means. You can also borrow 100's, 1,000's, and so on, in solving problems.

You do not have to write out a problem every time you borrow. You can *think* the steps and write in little numbers as a guide. Here is the same example:

$$\begin{array}{r} 62 \\ -27 \end{array}$$

First, you study the example. "I cannot take 7 from 2,"

you think, "so I must change a 10 to 1's." You draw a line through the 6 in the minuend and write a 5 above it. This means that there are now five 10's in the 10's place instead of six. Next, you write a little 1 just above and to the left of the 2. This means that there are now twelve 1's, instead of two.

$$\begin{array}{r} \overset{5}{\cancel{6}}\overset{1}{2} \\ -27 \end{array}$$

Now you can do the subtraction. "Seven 1's from twelve 1's leave 5," you think, and write a 5 in the 1's place of the remainder. "Two 10's from five 10's leave 3," you think, and write a 3 in the 10's place of the remainder. This completes the example.

$$\begin{array}{r} \overset{5}{\cancel{6}}\overset{1}{2} \\ -27 \\ \hline 35 \end{array}$$

The same method of "borrowing" a 10 can be used for 100's and 1,000's.

$$\begin{array}{r} 628 \\ -361 \\ \hline 7 \end{array}$$

First, you subtract one 1 from eight 1's, and write a 7 in the 1's place of the remainder. But you see that you cannot subtract six 10's from two 10's. You must borrow a 100, or ten 10's, from the six 100's in the minuend.

$$\begin{array}{r} \overset{5}{\cancel{6}}28 \\ -361 \\ \hline 7 \end{array}$$

You draw a line through the 6 in the minuend and write a 5 above it. This means that there are now five 100's in the 100's place, instead of six. Next, you write in a little 1 just above and to the left of the 2. This means that there are now twelve 10's, instead of two. Now you can finish the subtraction. Six 10's from twelve 10's leaves six. You write a 6 in the 10's place of the remainder. Three 100's from five 100's leaves two. You write a 2 in the 100's place of the remainder.

$$\begin{array}{r} \overset{5}{\cancel{6}}\overset{1}{2}8 \\ -361 \\ \hline 267 \end{array}$$

You use the same method for 1,000's. You borrow a 1,000 just as you borrowed a 10 or a 100.

Checking subtraction

You should always check your work in subtraction to make sure that you have done it correctly.

Checking by subtraction. One way to check a subtraction problem is to subtract the remainder from the minuend.

Problem		Check	
628	Minuend	628	Minuend
−361	Subtrahend	−267	Remainder
267	Remainder	361	

The new remainder should be the same as the old subtrahend. This checks your work.

Checking by addition. A good way to check subtraction problems is by addition, because addition is the opposite of subtraction. You add the subtrahend and the remainder.

Problem		Check	
628	Minuend	361	Subtrahend
−361	Subtrahend	+267	Remainder
267	Remainder	628	

The sum of the addition should be the same as the old minuend in the subtraction problem.

Estimating helps you know if your answer is reasonable. Try to estimate the answer *before* you work the problem. Here is an example:

$$\begin{array}{r} 476 \\ -254 \\ \hline 222 \end{array}$$

Estimating
(Think)
476 is about 475.
254 is about 250.
475 is 400 and 75.
250 is 200 and 50.
75 − 50 is 25.
400 − 200 is 200.
The answer should be about 225

This is almost the exact answer. You can estimate in larger numbers. For example, 476 is about 500, and 254 is about 250. Subtracting 500−250 gives you 250. This gives you a good idea of what the answer should be. Estimating the answer before you work a problem will save you time if you make a mistake, because you know about what the answer should be.

Subtraction rules to remember

Here are six rules that will help you solve subtraction problems.

1. Remember what subtraction means. You can find the answers to subtraction problems by counting. But it is quicker and easier to *think* the answers.

2. Learning the subtraction facts will help you think the answers to subtraction problems quickly.

3. Subtraction is the opposite of addition. Because of this, addition will help you learn the subtraction facts and check problems.

4. The subtraction facts help you subtract larger numbers to solve problems.

5. You can only subtract quantities of the same kind. That is, you must subtract 1's from 1's and 10's from 10's.

6. Subtraction answers three kinds of questions: how many are left, what is the difference, and how many more are needed.

Other ways to subtract

There are several ways of thinking out a subtraction problem. The method we have used is called the "*take-away-borrow*" *method*. Here is another example:

$$\begin{array}{r} 72 \\ -28 \end{array} \qquad \begin{array}{r} \overset{6}{\cancel{7}}\overset{1}{2} \\ -28 \\ \hline 4 \end{array} \qquad \begin{array}{r} \overset{6}{\cancel{7}}\overset{1}{2} \\ -28 \\ \hline 44 \end{array}$$

First, you see that you cannot take eight 1's from two 1's. You borrow a 10, making the minuend six 10's and twelve 1's. Then you subtract eight 1's from twelve 1's: $12-8=4$. You write the 4 in the 1's place in the answer. Next you subtract two 10's from six 10's: $6-2=4$. You write the 4 in the 10's place in the answer.

Another method is called the *"addition-borrow" method.*

$$
\begin{array}{r} 72 \\ -28 \\ \hline \end{array}
\Rightarrow
\begin{array}{r} 72 \\ -28 \\ \hline 4 \end{array}
\Rightarrow
\begin{array}{r} 72 \\ -28 \\ \hline 44 \end{array}
$$

The numbers are the same as in the "take-away-borrow" method, but the *thinking* is different. You see that you cannot take eight 1's from two 1's, and borrow a 10. Instead of subtracting eight 1's from twelve 1's, you think "what *added* to 8 makes 12?" You know that $8+4=12$, so you write the 4 in the 1's place in the answer. Instead of subtracting two 10's from six 10's, you think "what *added* to 2 makes 6?" You know that $2+4=6$, so you write the 4 in the 10's place in the answer.

A third method is called the *"addition-carry" method* or the *"Austrian" method.*

$$
\begin{array}{r} 72 \\ -28 \\ \hline \end{array}
\Rightarrow
\begin{array}{r} 7\overset{1}{2} \\ -28 \\ \hline 4 \end{array}
\Rightarrow
\begin{array}{r} 7\overset{1}{2} \\ -\ {}^{3}8 \\ \hline 44 \end{array}
$$

First, you see that you cannot take eight 1's from two 1's. Instead of borrowing, you add ten 1's to the two 1's: $2+10=12$. Next, you think "what *added* to 8 makes 12?" You already know that $8+4=12$, so you write the 4 in the 1's place in the answer. Now you think "I added a 10 to the 1's, so I must subtract a 10 from the 10's." To do this, you change the two 10's in the subtrahend to three 10's. You think "what *added* to 3 makes 7?" You know that $3+4=7$, so you write the 4 in the 10's place in the answer.

Fun with subtraction

Many games that can be played with the addition, multiplication, and division facts can be changed a little for the subtraction facts.

To play a game called *More or Less,* make a pack of 36 cards. Write the numbers from 1 to 18 separately on two sets of cards. There will be two cards for each number. Shuffle the cards and place the pile facedown. The leader of the game takes the first card and holds it up for the players to see. Suppose it is 14. The first player takes a card from the pile and shows it. Suppose it is 6. The player compares it with the 14 card and says "It is less." Then he must tell how much less. In this case, the player would say "It is 8 less than 14." He must find the answer by thinking the subtraction. Suppose the next player turns up 17. She compares it with the first card. She must say "It is more. It is 3 more than 14." A player who gives the wrong answer is out of the game. When you have gone through the cards once, you can mix them up and play again with new numbers.

John M. Smith

Related articles in *World Book* include:

Addition	Decimal system	Multiplication
Algebra (Subtraction)	Division	Numeration systems (Working with numeration systems)
Arithmetic	Fraction	
	Mathematics	

Outline

I. Learning to subtract
  A. Subtraction by counting
  B. Subtraction by thinking
  C. Subtraction questions
  D. Writing subtraction
  E. Subtraction facts
II. Subtracting larger numbers
  A. Subtracting 10's and 100's
  B. Subtracting 10's and 1's
  C. How to borrow
III. Checking subtraction
  A. Checking by subtraction

Practice subtraction examples

1. $8-5=$	4. $18-5=$	7. $15-9=$	10. $7-5=$	13. $9-3=$
2. $7-4=$	5. $17-4=$	8. $15-7=$	11. $7-2=$	14. $14-8=$
3. $8-6=$	6. $18-6=$	9. $15-6=$	12. $9-6=$	15. $14-6=$

16. $\begin{array}{r}5\\-2\\\hline\end{array}$	21. $\begin{array}{r}120\\-30\\\hline\end{array}$	26. $\begin{array}{r}90\\-30\\\hline\end{array}$	31. $\begin{array}{r}67\\-23\\\hline\end{array}$	36. $\begin{array}{r}83\\-48\\\hline\end{array}$	41. $\begin{array}{r}923\\-465\\\hline\end{array}$
17. $\begin{array}{r}50\\-20\\\hline\end{array}$	22. $\begin{array}{r}8\\-4\\\hline\end{array}$	27. $\begin{array}{r}7\\-4\\\hline\end{array}$	32. $\begin{array}{r}628\\-115\\\hline\end{array}$	37. $\begin{array}{r}65\\-39\\\hline\end{array}$	42. $\begin{array}{r}307\\-186\\\hline\end{array}$
18. $\begin{array}{r}8\\-3\\\hline\end{array}$	23. $\begin{array}{r}80\\-40\\\hline\end{array}$	28. $\begin{array}{r}70\\-40\\\hline\end{array}$	33. $\begin{array}{r}843\\-531\\\hline\end{array}$	38. $\begin{array}{r}625\\-241\\\hline\end{array}$	43. $\begin{array}{r}503\\-280\\\hline\end{array}$
19. $\begin{array}{r}80\\-30\\\hline\end{array}$	24. $\begin{array}{r}6\\-4\\\hline\end{array}$	29. $\begin{array}{r}84\\-22\\\hline\end{array}$	34. $\begin{array}{r}6725\\-3513\\\hline\end{array}$	39. $\begin{array}{r}729\\-381\\\hline\end{array}$	44. $\begin{array}{r}700\\-265\\\hline\end{array}$
20. $\begin{array}{r}12\\-3\\\hline\end{array}$	25. $\begin{array}{r}9\\-3\\\hline\end{array}$	30. $\begin{array}{r}95\\-34\\\hline\end{array}$	35. $\begin{array}{r}52\\-26\\\hline\end{array}$	40. $\begin{array}{r}90\\-36\\\hline\end{array}$	45. $\begin{array}{r}900\\-189\\\hline\end{array}$

Answers to the practice examples

1. 3	6. 12	11. 5	16. 3	21. 90	26. 60	31. 44	36. 35	41. 458
2. 3	7. 6	12. 3	17. 30	22. 4	27. 3	32. 513	37. 26	42. 121
3. 2	8. 8	13. 6	18. 5	23. 40	28. 30	33. 312	38. 384	43. 223
4. 13	9. 9	14. 6	19. 50	24. 2	29. 62	34. 3,212	39. 348	44. 435
5. 13	10. 2	15. 8	20. 9	25. 6	30. 61	35. 26	40. 54	45. 711

Suburb is a community next to or near a central city. Each central city and its suburbs form a continuous *metropolitan area.* In the early 2000's, about half of all Americans lived in suburbs.

People dwell in suburbs for various reasons. Many families seek a house and a yard and freedom from overcrowded, declining city neighborhoods. Others believe their children will get a better education in the suburbs. Still others move to escape the crime, pollution, and other problems of the central city.

Characteristics of suburbs. Most suburbanites live in single-family houses, though the number of town houses and apartment dwellings has increased rapidly since 1980. Many suburbs each consist of people with similar social characteristics, incomes, and lifestyles. Some suburbs serve as retirement communities.

In the suburbs, homes, workplaces, and shopping centers are spread over greater distances than in central cities. For this reason, most suburbanites consider automobiles essential to daily life. In the past, a majority of suburban residents traveled regularly to the central city to work or for recreational or cultural activities. But today, most suburbanites work and seek entertainment in the suburbs.

Most suburbs in the United States have their own governments, with a mayor or city manager, a council, and such municipal services as police and fire protection. County officials directly govern other suburbs.

Growth of the suburbs. Extensive suburban growth in the United States began in the late 1800's with the development of streetcar lines and railroads. People could live in the "country" and ride the trolley or train to their jobs in the city. During the 1950's and 1960's, general prosperity increased the move to the suburbs, as more families became able to buy one or two automobiles.

Since 1960, U.S. suburbs have experienced massive growth in nonresidential activities. By the 1990's, so many shopping malls, office complexes, and industrial parks had been built in suburban areas that the suburbs passed the central cities in total number of jobs. The most notable growth has been concentrated near expressways, especially where these highways intersect. At such locations, suburban downtowns, or *edge cities,* have developed. Today, the suburban ring can itself be regarded as an *outer city,* which increasingly dominates the social and economic life of the metropolitan area.

The rapid growth of suburbs has created many problems. Numerous suburbs have had difficulty raising enough money for such basic services as police and fire protection. Residents often engage in disputes over the quality of the community's schools and the amount of taxes needed to support them. Especially in older suburbs, population change may produce friction between ethnic groups. Many suburbs now face the crime, congestion, and other problems that some residents sought to escape by leaving the central cities.   Peter O. Muller

See also **City; City government; Levitt, William Jaird; Local government; Metropolitan area** (The development of suburbs).

Subway is an underground railway that usually serves as part of a rapid transit system in an urban area. Although parts of such a railway system may be at ground level or elevated, the system as a whole is generally referred to as a "subway" if any part of it is underground. Subways are most useful in crowded urban areas, where heavy traffic often slows travel by bus or car. Subway passenger capacities in such cities as Chicago, New York City, and Washington, D.C., can be up to 10 times higher than those of other modes of transportation.

There are three types of subway tunnel construction. *Cut and cover* construction involves digging up streets, building the tunnel, and then covering it. In *cover and cut* construction, a crew lays a concrete slab cover and then digs the tunnel underneath it. In a third method of construction, the tunnel is drilled and lined at the same time using a special tunnel-boring device commonly known as a *tunneler.* The tunneler uses a cutting head to drill the tunnel and then immediately assembles the lining behind the head using precast concrete pieces.

London's subway system, the longest in the world, provides quick, cheap transportation to all parts of the city and suburbs. It handles more passengers than any other system in the world. London's system is often called the *tube* or the *underground.* Some of its lines are so far underground that passengers take elevators down to board trains. New York City's subway system is the longest in the United States.

Many of the world's other major cities also have extensive subway systems, including Baltimore; Beijing; Buenos Aires, Argentina; Cairo, Egypt; Chicago; Edmonton, Canada; Istanbul, Turkey; Kolkata, India; Los Angeles; Mexico City; Montreal; Moscow; Paris; Philadelphia; San Francisco; São Paulo, Brazil; Seoul, South Korea; Shanghai; Tokyo; Toronto; and Washington, D.C.

London was the first city to have a subway. Its first underground passenger line opened in 1863. It used steam locomotives. The first deep-level line opened in London in 1890 and had electric locomotives. All subways since then have used electric power. Boston was the first U.S.

David R. Frazier

Washington, D.C.'s, modern subway extends throughout the city and into the suburbs. Thousands of tourists and government workers travel on the subway system each day.

city to have a subway. It opened a line of $1\frac{1}{2}$ miles (2.4 kilometers) in 1897. The first sections of New York City's subway opened in 1904.   Alypios Chatziioanou

See also **Electric railroad; New York City** (Transportation); **Tunnel.**

Succession, Presidential. See Presidential succession.

Succession wars, *suhk SEHSH uhn.* Wars growing out of disputes over who should *succeed to* (inherit) a throne are called *succession wars.* Four important conflicts in European history are known by this name. They are the War of the Spanish Succession, the War of the Polish Succession, the War of the Austrian Succession, and the War of the Bavarian Succession.

The War of the Spanish Succession began in 1701 and lasted until 1714. Its American phase was known as Queen Anne's War (1702-1713).

Charles II, king of Spain, had no children, and all Europe was interested in the question of who would be his successor. The laws governing succession were so involved, and the claims of the different heirs were so conflicting, that it is almost impossible to say who rightfully should have worn the Spanish crown.

When King Charles II died in Spain on Nov. 1, 1700, he left a will that gave the crown to the French prince, Philip of Anjou. Philip's grandfather, King Louis XIV of France, then proclaimed him King Philip V of Spain, and the Spanish ambassador said that the Pyrenees no longer separated the two kingdoms. Since French power was already feared in Europe, other countries were alarmed that France might annex the Spanish Empire.

During 1701, the Grand Alliance was formed by England, the Netherlands, Prussia, Austria, and most of the other states of the Holy Roman Empire. This alliance sought to prevent Philip of Anjou from becoming king of Spain, and to put the Archduke Charles of Austria on the throne instead. Fighting had begun in 1701, but the Grand Alliance did not declare war on France and Spain until 1702. The French were defeated decisively in the battles of Blenheim, Ramillies, Turin, and Oudenaarde. The English general, the Duke of Marlborough, and the imperial general, Prince Eugene of Savoy, commanded the forces of the Grand Alliance.

In spite of the allies' victories, England grew tired of war, especially after the bloody battle of Malplaquet in 1709. In 1710, England began secret talks with France. In 1711, Joseph I, the Holy Roman emperor and ruler of Austria, died. He was succeeded by his brother, the Archduke Charles, who was the allies' candidate for the Spanish throne. Austria's allies feared the possibility that Charles might rule both Spain and Austria, and so they agreed to negotiate peace with France.

In 1713, most of the participating powers in Europe agreed to the Treaty of Utrecht. Under this treaty, King Louis XIV of France obtained fairly favorable terms. His grandson, Philip, was recognized as king of Spain on the condition that Spain and France would never be united. Charles refused to sign the Treaty of Utrecht. But in March 1714, he was forced to sign the Treaty of Rastatt, which was almost the same. The Treaty of Baden, signed six months later, concluded the peace settlement between France and the states of the Holy Roman Empire.

The War of the Polish Succession (1733-1738) was caused when Polish noblemen elected Stanislas

Leszczyński, father-in-law of King Louis XV of France, as king of Poland. Russia and Austria forced the Poles to accept the Elector Augustus of Saxony as king. War followed with France, Spain, and Sardinia opposing Austria, Russia, and several German states. France won most of the battles. But treaties signed in Vienna in 1735 and 1738 allowed Augustus of Saxony to remain king of Poland. However, France and its allies won considerable territory from Austria in Germany and Italy.

The War of the Austrian Succession (1740-1748) was known in America as King George's War. It was caused by the death of Charles VI, ruler of Austria and Holy Roman emperor. Charles had no sons and left his vast lands to his daughter Maria Theresa. The great powers of Europe had recognized her right to succeed by the terms of the Pragmatic Sanction (see **Pragmatic Sanction**). But after Charles died, several of the powers broke their word and tried to take her lands.

The first to attack was Frederick the Great, king of Prussia, who conquered the Austrian province of Silesia. Early in the war, France, Spain, Bavaria, Saxony, and Sardinia joined Prussia, threatening Maria Theresa with the loss of her other territories. But she saved her crown and most of her lands through her own great courage and leadership. Britain and the Netherlands became her allies, and eventually Sardinia and Saxony also switched to her side. Britain gave her money to build up her army. Maria Theresa separated Frederick the Great from his allies by giving him most of Silesia. The Treaty of Aix-la-Chapelle, signed in 1748, ended the war. It allowed her to keep Austria, Bohemia, and Hungary.

The War of the Bavarian Succession (1778-1779) was a short quarrel between Prussia and Austria over the succession to the throne of Bavaria and claims to Bavarian territory. In 1777, the Elector of Bavaria, Maximilian Joseph, died and left no direct heirs. Austria then persuaded the new elector to give a large part of Bavaria to Austria. This move aroused the jealousy of Frederick the Great. Austrian forces occupied Bavaria, and war seemed inevitable. But neither Austria nor Prussia was anxious for war. No battles were fought, and the war is often called the "Potato War." Hungry soldiers spent their time searching for food in the fields. Catherine II of Russia mediated peace. In the Treaty of Teschen, which was signed in 1779, Austria accepted only minor territorial gains.   Charles W. Ingrao

Related articles in *World Book* include:

Blenheim, Battle of	Louis XIV
Charles VII (Holy Roman emperor)	Louis XV
	Maria Theresa
Frederick II (of Prussia)	Marlborough, Duke of
French and Indian wars	Philip V (of Spain)
(Queen Anne's War; King George's War)	Seven Years' War
	Utrecht, Peace of

Succulent, *SUHK yuh luhnt,* is the name for a fleshy plant, such as a cactus, that has large stems or leaves in which water is stored. Succulent plants grow in deserts and other places where there is little water. By using the water stored in their leaves and stems, succulents can survive long droughts.   James D. Mauseth

See also **Cactus; Sedum; Spurge.**

Sucker is the name given to several kinds of fishes closely related to the minnow family. Most of them have mouths with thick, fleshy lips that help them suck up animal and plant life on the bottom of lakes and streams.

WORLD BOOK illustration by Colin Newman, Linden Artists Ltd.

The white sucker has thick lips on the underside of its snout. Its mouth has no teeth, but its throat is lined with thin, comblike teeth. Suckers live in lakes and streams.

Suckers are dull-colored except in the spring, when the males of some species have yellow to red fins and a rose or orange stripe.

Except for two species in China and one in eastern Siberia, all suckers are native to North America. The *white sucker* is one of the most common North American suckers. It lives in streams in much of Canada and the northern United States east of the Rocky Mountains. The larger species of suckers are food fishes. Large, carplike suckers known as *buffalo* are caught in the Mississippi Valley (see **Buffalo**).   David W.

Scientific classification. Suckers belong to the sucker family, Catostomidae. The white sucker is *Catostomus commersoni.*

Suckling, Sir John (1609-1642), was the most famous member of the *Cavalier poets,* a group associated with the court of King Charles I of England. In his comedy *The Way of the World* (1700), William Congreve called the poet "natural, easy Suckling." His best verse has a witty and knowing quality.

Suckling's plays include *Aglaura* (1637). His short poems were published four years after his death in a collection titled *Fragmenta Aurea.* Suckling's ability as a literary critic can be seen in "A Session of Poets" (1637), a verse review of poetry in his day.

Suckling was born in Middlesex (now part of London) in February 1609 and served in the army. In 1641, he was accused of plotting to gain control of the army for the king. Suckling was notorious for his wild living. He fled to Paris and died there in May or June 1642, perhaps having poisoned himself.   Gary A. Stringer

WORLD BOOK illustration by Lorraine Epstein

Sempervivum is an example of a succulent plant.

Sucre, *SOO kray* , is the official capital of Bolivia. But all government offices except those of the Supreme Court are in La Paz, the actual capital. The municipality of Sucre has a population of 215,778. A municipality may include rural areas as well as the urban center. Sucre lies in south-central Bolivia in the *Cordillera Real* (Royal Range) of the Andes Mountains. Its altitude is about 8,900 feet (2,700 meters). For location, see **Bolivia** (map).

Sucre is one of the oldest cities in South America, and it preserves much of its charming historic character. Most of the city's buildings are painted white, as they were in the days of the Spanish empire. Sucre's main square has a cathedral that was begun in the 1500's and the Legislative Palace, in which Bolivia's Declaration of Independence was signed in 1825. The University of St. Francis Xavier is in Sucre. Founded in 1624, it is one of the oldest universities in the Western Hemisphere.

Many of Sucre's people work on nearby farms or in factories that process farm products. Others are employed by the government or in such industries as oil refining and cement manufacturing.

Sucre was founded as an administrative center by Spanish settlers in 1538 on the site of an Indian settlement. During the Spanish colonial period, the town was known at different times as Charcas, La Plata, and Chuquisaca. It grew rapidly after the discovery in 1545 of silver mines at nearby Potosí. In 1839, it was renamed Sucre after Bolivia's first constitutional president, General Antonio José de Sucre. Most of the government moved from Sucre to La Paz in 1899, largely because La Paz had become Bolivia's major economic and transportation center.   Nathan A. Haverstock

Sucre, *SOO kray,* **Antonio José de** (1795-1830), was commander of the armies that liberated Ecuador, Peru, and Bolivia from Spain. He served as president of Bolivia and was one of the ablest generals of his time.

Sucre was born in Cumaná, Venezuela, on Feb. 3, 1795. When he was 15, he joined the army that opposed Spanish rule in South America. Sucre became a friend and the chief lieutenant of Venezuelan general Simón Bolívar, the army's chief commander (see **Bolívar, Simón**). In 1822, Sucre freed Ecuador by winning the Battle of Pichincha near Quito, Ecuador. In 1824, he led the troops that defeated a large Spanish force at Ayacucho in south-central Peru. In 1825, Sucre's forces defeated the Spanish in Bolivia.

Sucre became Bolivia's first constitutional president in 1826. He was an able administrator. He resigned the presidency in 1828 to prevent war with the Peruvians, who objected to Sucre's loyalty to Bolívar. The Peruvians thought Bolívar wanted to control Peru. Sucre was killed by an assassin on June 4, 1830.   Michael L. Conniff

Sucrose, *SOO krohs,* is the chemical name for common table sugar. Sucrose belongs to a class of foods called *carbohydrates.* It is a product of *photosynthesis,* the food-making process in plants. Sucrose is extracted from sugar beets and sugar cane and is widely used as a sweetener. Its chemical formula is $C_{12}H_{22}O_{11}$.

Sucrose destroys organisms that cause spoilage and is used as a preservative for some foods, especially fruits, jams, and jellies. It is also used to prepare substances used in industry and medicine, including ethyl alcohol, glycerin, and citric acid.   Dorothy M. Feigl

See also **Sugar.**

© Mike Yamashita, Woodfin Camp, Inc.

Sudan, Africa's largest country in area, is a land of widely differing geography. Northern Sudan is largely a desert, as in the scene shown here. The central part of the country consists chiefly of a grass-covered plain. Southern Sudan features dense, junglelike vegetation.

Sudan, *soo DAN,* is Africa's largest country in area. It lies in the northeastern part of the continent. Sudan is a land of widely differing geography. It sprawls across vast deserts in the north, grassy plains in its center, and steamy jungles and swamps in the south. The Nile River is the most important geographic feature. Khartoum, the capital, and Omdurman, the largest city, lie on the Nile. Most Sudanese live near the Nile or one of its branches.

Most northern Sudanese consider themselves Arabs, speak Arabic, and practice the religion of Islam. In the southern third of Sudan, most people belong to groups that are *indigenous* (native) to Africa. They speak a number of languages, and most follow traditional African religions or are Christians. Most Sudanese are farmers.

People have lived in what is now Sudan for thousands of years. Ancient kingdoms flourished in the area, and Egypt controlled parts of Sudan at various times. Sudan became independent in 1956.

Government

In 2005, as part of a peace deal between Sudan's government and rebels in the south, the country's National Assembly approved an interim constitution for Sudan. It provides for power to be shared between northerners and southerners. It also establishes a regional government in southern Sudan with a large degree of self-rule.

Sudan's president is the head of state, head of government, and commander in chief of the armed forces. The interim National Assembly has 450 appointed members.

People

Ethnic groups. About 40 percent of Sudan's people consider themselves Arabs. They make up the country's

Jok Madut Jok, the contributor of this article, is Associate Professor of History at Loyola Marymount University.

largest ethnic group. Some are descended from Arab immigrants. Others belong to Sudanese groups that gradually adopted the Arabic language and culture. Most Arabs live in the northern two-thirds of the country. Other ethnic groups in this area include Nubians, Beja, Fur, and descendants of West African immigrants.

The Dinka make up the largest ethnic group in the southern third of Sudan. Other ethnic groups in the south include the Nuer, the Shilluk, and the Azande.

Languages. The people of Sudan use more than 100 different languages. More than half the people speak Arabic, which is one of Sudan's official languages and the dominant language in the north. In the south, most people speak Dinka or another African language. English, which is Sudan's other official language, serves as the language of trade and government in the south.

Religion. About 70 percent of Sudan's people are Sunni Muslims. Most Muslims live in northern and cen-

Facts in brief

Capital: Khartoum.
Official languages: Arabic and English.
Area: 967,500 mi² (2,505,813 km²). *Greatest distances*—north-south, 1,275 mi (2,050 km); east-west, 1,150 mi (1,850 km). *Coastline*—400 mi (644 km).
Elevation: *Highest*—Mount Kinyeti, 10,456 ft (3,187 m) above sea level. *Lowest*—sea level.
Population: *Estimated 2008 population*—39,076,000; density, 40 per mi² (16 per km²); distribution, 59 percent rural, 41 percent urban.
Chief products: *Agriculture*—cotton, livestock, millet, peanuts, sesame, sorghum, sugar cane, wheat. *Forestry*—gum arabic, timber. *Manufacturing*—food products, petroleum products, shoes, textiles. *Mining*—chromium, gold, gypsum, petroleum.
Flag: Three equal horizontal stripes of red, white, and black, with a green triangle symbolizing Islam. Adopted in 1970. See Flag (picture: Flags of Africa).
Money: *Basic unit*—Sudanese pound.

tral Sudan. In the south, most people practice traditional African religions. About 5 percent of Sudanese are Christians. Nearly all the Christians live in the south.

Way of life. About 60 percent of Sudan's people live in rural areas. Most of them farm the land or herd animals along the Nile River and its two major branches—the White Nile and the Blue Nile. Most farmers own small plots of land. They use old-fashioned tools and methods, and many must struggle to grow enough food for their families. Some Sudanese work as tenant farmers on irrigated land owned by the government or by private corporations. A few rural people are nomads who travel the desert region with their herds.

About 40 percent of Sudanese live in cities and towns. The largest urban center consists of three cities where the White and Blue Nile come together. These cities—Khartoum, Khartoum North, and Omdurman—have a combined population of more than 4 million. In addition, nearly 2 million people who have been displaced from their villages by war and drought live in camps around Khartoum. Other urban centers include Port Sudan, on the Red Sea; Wad Madani; El Obeid (Al Ubaid); and Juba, the capital of the southern region. Many of Sudan's city dwellers work in offices, shops, and factories. Many others are unemployed.

Housing. The most common rural dwellings in northern Sudan are flat-roofed, rectangular houses made of sun-dried mud-brick. In the south, the people build thatch-roofed shelters. Most city dwellers live in apartment buildings or small houses similar to those in Western cities. In poor urban neighborhoods, houses resemble those in rural areas. Tents and other temporary shelters house many people on the outskirts of cities.

Clothing. Throughout Sudan, people wear both traditional garments and clothing similar to that worn by North Americans and Europeans. In southern Sudan, many rural people wear little clothing because of the heat. In northern Sudan, most women wear a traditional outer garment called a *taub,* which covers the head and reaches to the feet. Many men in northern Sudan wear a long robe called a *jallabiyah.* On their heads, they wear a small skullcap called a *taqiyah* or a white turban called an *immah.* Sandals are the most common footwear.

Food and drink. The main dish in the Sudanese diet is *ful* (also spelled *fool).* Ful consists of broad beans cooked in oil. Goat, lamb, beef, and chicken are served occasionally, but most people eat little meat. *Karkadai,* a beverage made from the hibiscus plant, is a national drink. The people of Sudan also drink tea and coffee.

Recreation. Soccer is the country's most popular sport. Visiting with family members and neighbors is the most common Sudanese recreational activity.

Education. The school system in Sudan calls for two years of preschool and eight years of elementary education provided free by the government. But only about half of the country's children attend elementary school.

Sudan

National park

International boundary

Road

Railroad

Cataract (waterfall)

River

Seasonal stream

Swamp

National capital

Other city or town

Elevation above sea level

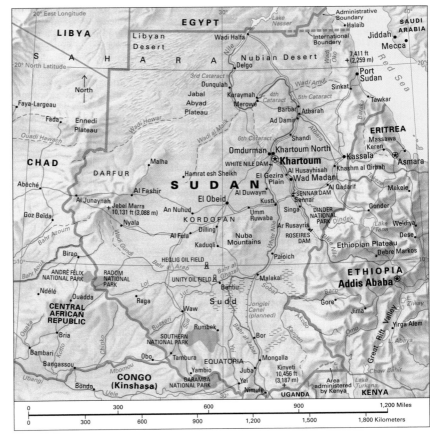

WORLD BOOK maps

© H. Rogers, Trip

An ornate tower of the Grand Mosque of Khartoum rises above a bustling street in the city. Khartoum is Sudan's capital and its second largest city, after Omdurman.

Secondary school lasts three years, but only about a third of Sudan's children attend secondary school.

Sudan has about 25 universities. Many of them were founded in the 1990's and are still being developed. About 60 percent of Sudan's adults can read and write. For the literacy rate, see **Literacy** (table: Literacy rates).

The arts. Traditional handicrafts are the most common form of art in Sudan. Some Sudanese writers have achieved recognition in other countries. Al-Tayyib Salih (also spelled Tayeb Salih) is probably Sudan's best-known writer. Several of his books, including the novel *Season of Migration to the North* (1966) and the short story collection *The Wedding of Zein* (1966), have been translated into English.

Land and climate

Sudan's vast area includes plains, swamps, and desert. Northeastern Sudan borders the Red Sea. The country's most important geographic feature is the Nile River. The river is called the Bahr al Jabal in southern Sudan. It floods the flatland of the south to form a vast swamp called the Sudd. North of the Sudd, the Bahr al Jabal is called the White Nile. It meets the Blue Nile, which flows from the mountains of Ethiopia, at Khartoum. Together, the two rivers form the main Nile River.

Northern Sudan. North of Khartoum, Sudan is primarily desert. Rainfall rarely exceeds 4 inches (10 centimeters) a year. Average summer high temperatures reach about 110 °F (43 °C). Average winter lows drop to about 60 °F (16 °C). People live along the banks of the Nile and the Red Sea, but much of the north is uninhabited. A few nomads travel with herds of camels near the southern edge of the region and in the Red Sea Hills in the east.

Central Sudan consists largely of a grass-covered plain. Annual rainfall varies from about 4 to 30 inches (10 to 75 centimeters). Most of this area has enough water for farming. Average winter temperatures are slightly warmer, and average summer temperatures a little cooler, than those in northern Sudan. Between the Blue and White Nile rivers lies El Gezira (Al Jazirah), the most fertile area in Sudan. Farmers also grow crops in an upland area in the west, in the Nuba Mountains along the White

Nile, and in an irrigated clay plain in the east.

Southern Sudan. Most of southern Sudan consists of a flood plain formed by the branches of the Nile River. Dense, junglelike vegetation covers much of the region. Mountain ranges rise along Sudan's borders with Uganda, Kenya, and Ethiopia. Rainfall averages from about 30 to 60 inches (75 to 150 centimeters) annually. Average temperatures are lower in the south than in the rest of Sudan. Wild animals, including gazelles, giraffes, lions, leopards, and elephants, roam the south. Hippopotamuses and crocodiles live along the Nile's branches.

Economy

Sudan has an economy based on agriculture. The government controls the main industries, most irrigated farmland, and the transportation and communications networks. But in 1992, the government began selling some government-owned companies to private firms.

Agriculture employs more than 50 percent of Sudan's workers and accounts for more than 30 percent of the value of the nation's total economic production. Sudan's main crops are cotton, gum arabic, millet, peanuts, sesame, sorghum, sugar cane, and wheat. Cotton is the main export crop. Cattle, sheep, goats, and camels provide food and a source of income for Sudan's herders and nomadic groups.

Manufacturing and mining employ about 5 percent of all workers and account for about 10 percent of the value of Sudan's economic production. Factories produce food products, petroleum products, shoes, and textiles. Most factories are in the Nile Valley, especially around Khartoum and in El Gezira. Chromium, gold, gypsum, and petroleum rank as leading mineral products. Other mineral deposits include copper, iron ore, lead, nickel, silver, tungsten, and zinc.

Energy sources. Before the late 1990's, Sudan relied on imported petroleum for its energy needs. In the mid-1990's, Sudan began to cooperate with international companies to develop oil fields in the south and southwest. Sudan now produces much of its own petroleum. The country's forests supply fuel for rural households. Dams along the Nile provide hydroelectric power.

© Mike Yamashita, Woodfin Camp, Inc.

Two nomad women watch over a herd of goats near their desert camp. Nomads make up a small portion of Sudan's population. They live in the desert region of northern Sudan.

© Nedra Westwater, Black Star

A village in southern Sudan fills a clearing in a lush, tropical forest. The village has mud-walled huts. It is near Juba.

© Marc & Evelyne Bernheim, Woodfin Camp, Inc.

Workers pick cotton in the Gezira area of central Sudan, which lies between the Blue and White Nile rivers. Cotton is Sudan's most important export crop.

Trade. Since Sudan began petroleum production in 1999, it has become the leading export. Other exports include cotton, gold, gum arabic, live animals, peanuts, and sesame. Imports include food products and heavy machinery. Trade partners include China, Egypt, France, Germany, Saudi Arabia, and the United Kingdom.

Transportation and communication. The government-operated Sudan Railway is the only railroad system. Most roads are unpaved. The major paved roads are in the north. A national airline provides local flights and flights to European, Asian, and other African countries. Few of Sudan's people own a car. Buses, taxis, and pickup trucks carry passengers in the cities, and long-distance buses and trucks link cities and towns. River transportation is important in the south. Port Sudan, on the Red Sea, is the only important port. About 10 daily general-interest newspapers are published in Sudan.

History

Early days. As early as the 7000's B.C., people lived along the Nile River in what is now Sudan. By about 4000 B.C., they had built villages and developed methods of farming and raising animals. Most settlements were in Nubia, in the northern part of Sudan. After about 2600 B.C., Egypt brought Nubia under its control. A new civilization, influenced by Egyptian culture, developed there after 1000 B.C. The Egyptians called the civilization Kush. Kush existed as an independent kingdom at various times until its collapse around A.D. 350.

In the 500's, missionaries from Egypt converted the rulers of southern Egypt and northern Sudan to Christianity. But by the mid-600's, Arab Muslims had conquered Egypt and had begun to raid Nubia. The Arabs made agreements with the Nubians to conduct trade in Sudan. Arab tribesmen then migrated to Nubia and married local women. Arab merchants and religious leaders also moved there. By the early 1500's, the last Christian kingdoms in the north had come under Muslim control.

The Funj, a Muslim group, conquered much of Sudan

during the 1500's. Meanwhile, the Dinka, the Shilluk, the Nuer, the Azande, and other indigenous African groups had been settling in central and southern Sudan.

Egyptian and British control. In 1821, Egypt conquered the Funj. The Egyptians eventually gained control over all of Sudan. In 1881, a Sudanese Muslim religious teacher named Muhammad Ahmed proclaimed himself the *Mahdi* (divinely appointed guide). Over the next four years, he led a successful revolt against the Egyptians. Charles Gordon, a famous British soldier and adventurer, was killed while defending Khartoum against Muhammad Ahmed (see **Gordon, Charles G.**).

In 1898, the United Kingdom and Egypt joined forces to defeat the Sudanese at the Battle of Omdurman. The United Kingdom and Egypt agreed to rule the country together, but the British provided most high officials.

In the early 1900's, many Sudanese began to demand an end to British rule. Some favored Egyptian control, and others wanted complete independence. In 1924, Sudanese troops under Egyptian leadership rose up against the British. The mutiny failed, and the British expelled most Egyptian officials from Sudan. The Egyptian officials did not return to Sudan until 1936, when Egypt signed a new agreement with the United Kingdom.

Independence. During the 1940's and early 1950's, the Sudanese *nationalist* (self-government) movement grew. In 1953, the United Kingdom and Egypt agreed on steps leading to self-government for Sudan. In 1955, the Sudanese parliament voted for self-government. Sudan officially became an independent nation on Jan. 1, 1956.

After independence, southern leaders feared that northern leaders would not share power equally. They objected to the use of Arabic as the national language. They also feared that northern administrators in the south would force southerners to become more like Arab Muslims. Differences in ethnicity, language, and religion resulted in years of suspicion and fighting between the north and south. Sudan's first independent government failed to improve north-south relations.

In 1958, General Ibrahim Abboud overthrew the government. He banned political parties and jailed many politicians. His attempts to force southern leaders to cooperate with his government only increased tensions in the south. In 1964, teachers, students, lawyers, and union organizers held a strike against Abboud. They forced him to return the government to civilian control.

In 1969, Colonel Gaafar Nimeiri seized control of the government. He outlawed political parties and arrested most leading politicians. In 1971, Nimeiri became president of Sudan. In 1972, he brought an end to the rebellion in the south and signed agreements that gave the southern provinces a single regional government.

Sudan adopted a new constitution in 1973. The Constitution established a strong presidency and a weak legislature. It provided for one official political party, the Sudanese Socialist Union. Nimeiri served as party head.

Civil war. In 1983, Nimeiri established Islamic law throughout Sudan. He also ended the regional government in the south. Southerners protested against these actions. Fighting broke out between government forces and southerners. In addition, severe nationwide economic problems led to general strikes and rioting.

In 1985, a group of military officers forced Nimeiri out of power, disbanded the Sudanese Socialist Union, and established a military government. But they soon helped set up a transitional government that included civilians. Political parties were organized again. In 1986, elections were held for a new legislature, and Sadiq al Mahdi, head of the Umma Party, became prime minister.

In 1989, Brigadier General Umar Hassan Ahmad al-Bashir led a group of military officers that overthrew Mahdi. Bashir was backed by a political group called the National Islamic Front. The NIF (now called the National Congress) has sought to shape Sudan's government according to traditional Islamic law. Bashir dissolved the legislature and replaced it with a military council. He suspended the Constitution and banned all political parties. In 1993, the military council appointed Bashir president. The council then dissolved itself.

In 1996, Sudan held presidential and parliamentary elections. Bashir was elected president. The new parliament elected Hassan al-Turabi, the leader of the NIF, as speaker. The NIF came to be known as the National Congress in the late 1990's. In 1998, Sudan adopted a new constitution that allowed the formation of political parties. Several parties were organized in 1999.

In the late 1990's, tension grew between Bashir and Turabi. In 1999, Bashir removed Turabi as speaker, dissolved the National Assembly, and suspended parts of the Constitution. In June 2000, after being expelled from the National Congress, Turabi formed a party called the Popular National Congress (PNC). Bashir was reelected in December 2000, and the National Congress won a majority in the Assembly. Opposition parties, including the PNC, boycotted the vote. In 2001, police arrested and detained Turabi and other PNC members. He was released in 2003, but detained again in 2004 and 2005.

In the late 1990's, Sudan began cooperating with international companies to develop the oil reserves in the southern part of the country. Sudan began to export oil in 1999. Oil soon became the country's leading export.

From 1983 to 2004, the fighting between Sudan's government and rebels in the south killed about 2 million people. The fighting interfered with the production and distribution of food and caused widespread hunger. Many civilians in the south fled to the north or to neighboring countries. Droughts in the late 1900's and the early 2000's contributed to the spread of hunger and disease, especially in the south and west.

In July 2002, the government and the rebels signed an agreement providing that Islamic law would apply in northern Sudan but not in southern Sudan. The government also agreed to eventually allow southerners to hold a referendum on independence. In 2003 and 2004, the government and the rebels signed further agreements on the sharing of power, the distribution of oil wealth, and other issues. In January 2005, the two sides signed a full peace agreement that ended their conflict. In July 2005, the National Assembly approved a new constitution that was to remain in effect until 2011. It established a temporary power-sharing government, as well as a regional government in the south.

Violence in Darfur. In early 2003, a separate conflict erupted in the western region of Darfur. Indigenous African rebels claimed that the Sudanese government was ignoring Darfur and began attacking government targets in the region. In response, government forces and government-backed Arab militias known as the Janjaweed began attacking rebels and civilians in Darfur. There have long been tensions over land and grazing rights in Darfur between herders, who are mostly Arabs, and farmers, who are mostly indigenous Africans.

Violence in Darfur rose in late 2003 and in 2004. Hundreds of thousands of people have died, and about 2 ½ million people have been forced from their homes.

Many international groups accused the government and the Janjaweed of human rights abuses, including murder and rape. The United States described the atrocities as *genocide* (extermination of an entire people). In 2006, the government signed a peace deal with one rebel group. But other rebel groups rejected the deal, and violence in Darfur continued.   Jok Madut Jok

Related articles in *World Book* include:

Arabs	Funj Sultanate	Nubia
Baker, Sir Samuel White	Khartoum	Nuer
Dinka	Kush	Omdurman
Emin Pasha	Nile River	Port Sudan

Sudan grass is a tall grass plant primarily used as feed for livestock. It is closely related to grain sorghum. Sudan grass grows from 6 ½ to 10 feet (2 to 3 meters) high. It is an *annual,* and therefore new seeds must be planted each growing season. This grass is native to dry regions of northwestern Africa. It was introduced into the United States in 1909 from Khartoum, Sudan, by the U.S. Department of Agriculture.

Since the 1950's, Sudan grass has been crossed with grain sorghum to make hybrids that are more productive and more resistant to disease. These hybrids are more widely used than Sudan grass.   Douglas A. Johnson

Scientific classification. Sudan grass is in the grass family, Poaceae or Gramineae. It is *Sorghum x drummondii.*

See also **Grain sorghum; Grass** (picture); **Sorghum** (Grassy sorghums).

Sudbury. See Greater Sudbury.

Sudden infant death syndrome, also called *SIDS, crib death,* or *cot death,* is a term used to describe the unexpected death of an apparently healthy baby. In most cases, the baby is found dead a few hours after being put to bed. Most SIDS deaths occur among infants between 1 and 6 months of age. In many countries, SIDS is the leading cause of death during the first year of life.

To be considered SIDS, an infant's death must remain unexplained after an investigation, including an autopsy and review of the child's medical history. Scientists call SIDS a "diagnosis of exclusion" because it is based on finding no cause of death after a thorough search.

Scientists have identified several risk factors for SIDS, including the infant's sleeping position, hazardous sleeping conditions, and exposure to cigarette smoke before and after birth. Babies sleeping on their stomach have a higher risk for SIDS, while babies sleeping on their back have the lowest risk. Doctors recommend that healthy babies be placed on their back for sleep during the first six months of life. Crib bedding material can also partially block an infant's ability to get enough fresh air, which is thought to play a role in some SIDS deaths. Toys and pillows that can block the flow of air should be removed from a child's bed. But researchers have found that using a pacifier may actually reduce the risk of SIDS.

Some medical studies suggest that victims of SIDS may have been born with a defect that interferes with the nervous system's ability to control breathing, heart rate, or blood pressure. Many scientists believe that research may eventually lead to tests that can detect infants who are at risk for SIDS. John L. Carroll

Sudermann, *ZOO duhr MAHN,* **Hermann** (1857-1928), was a German dramatist and novelist associated with the Naturalism movement. *Dame Care* (1887), his best-known novel, concerns a young man burdened with his father's failure in life. Through sacrifice, the son must master fate's repeated challenges. *Regina* (1890) is a historical novel showing a man's struggle against the prejudices of his community.

Sudermann gained fame in Europe with his plays *Honor* (1889) and *Magda* (1893). In these dramas, he stripped away the pretenses of the middle-class society of the late 1800's. Sudermann's *Lithuanian Tales* (1917) skillfully portray working-class characters and carry a genuine sense of tragedy. Sudermann was born on Sept. 30, 1857, in Matzicken in East Prussia. He died on Nov. 21, 1928. Walther L. Hahn

Sudetenland, *SOO DAYT uhn LAND,* is a mountainous and forested region in what is now the Czech Republic. It stretches from the southern part of the Moravia region; around the southern, western, and northern edges of Bohemia; and back to northern Moravia. For location, see **Czechoslovakia** (map). The Sudetenland was named after the Sudeten Mountains, which line much of the northern part of the region.

During the A.D. 800's, Bohemia—a Czech-speaking kingdom that included most of the Sudetenland—came under control of the Premyslid dynasty, which ruled for nearly 500 years. In the mid-1200's, German speakers began migrating into Bohemia. In 1526, Austria's Habsburg family began ruling the region and made German the official language. In 1867, the Austrian Empire became Austria-Hungary. After Austria-Hungary's defeat in World War I (1914-1918), the Sudetenland became part of Czechoslovakia, a new country that was formed from Austria-Hungary's territory. Because nearly 3 million Germans lived in the Sudetenland, tension developed between Czechoslovakia and Germany.

In 1938, the German dictator Adolf Hitler demanded that the Sudetenland become part of Germany. That year, in an attempt to avoid war, British and French leaders signed the Munich Agreement, which forced Czechoslovakia to surrender the region to Germany (see **Munich Agreement**). Nevertheless, Germany invaded Czechoslovakia in March 1939. Several months later, World War II (1939-1945) began. Following Germany's defeat in the war, Czechoslovakia was restored, and most Germans were expelled from the Sudetenland. In 1993, Czechoslovakia broke apart into the independent nations of the Czech Republic—which includes the Sudetenland—and Slovakia. Norman J. W. Goda

Suede. See **Leather** (Kinds of leather).

Suess, *zyoos,* **Eduard** (1831-1914), an Austrian geologist, became famous for his work on changes of Earth's surface. His most important book was the four-volume *Face of the Earth* (1885-1901). He served as an assistant at the Hofmuseum in Vienna from 1852 to 1862 and taught at the University of Vienna from 1857 to 1901. From 1869 to 1896, he served as leader of the Liberal Party in the Austrian Parliament. Suess was born on Aug. 20, 1831, in London and died on April 26, 1914. Rachel Laudan

Suet, *SOO iht,* is the hard, white fat around the kidneys and loins of cattle and mature sheep. Suet can be melted to form tallow. Tallow is used as shortening for cooking and to prevent baked goods from hardening. Tallow also is used in making candles and soap. Suet can serve as bird feed in winter. Donald H. Beermann

Suetonius, *swih TOH nee uhs* (A.D. 69?-140?), was a Roman biographer and historian. As secretary for the Roman emperor Hadrian until 121 or 122, Suetonius had access to the Roman archives. He used official documents and hearsay evidence in his writings. His most notable work is *Lives of the Caesars,* the biographies of 12 Roman emperors, from Julius Caesar to Domitian. Suetonius wrote an earlier collection of biographies known as *Lives of Famous Men.* The work originally included sketches of Roman grammarians, historians, orators, and poets. Only fragments exist today.

Suetonius was less critical of his sources than modern historians would be. His biographies combine historical fact with anecdotes about his subjects' private and public lives. He often gave information that historians and other biographers had omitted. Suetonius's full name was Gaius Suetonius Tranquillus. Joseph R. Tebben

Suez, *soo EHZ* (pop. 417,527), is an Egyptian city at the southern entrance to the Suez Canal. The city lies on the Gulf of Suez. For location, see **Suez Canal** (map).

Suez has been an Egyptian seaport since ancient times. The city became an especially important port and one of Egypt's chief industrial centers after the Suez Canal opened in 1869. Major industries of Suez included oil refining and fertilizer production.

Suez was heavily damaged during the Arab-Israeli wars of 1967 and 1973. The wars hit the city's industries particularly hard. The 1967 war also forced the closing of the Suez Canal, which sharply reduced the importance of Suez as a port. The canal was reopened in 1975. Since then, increased revenue from canal tolls and the construction of new factories and oil refineries have helped Suez regain its former importance. Robert L. Tignor

Suez Canal, *soo EHZ,* is a narrow, artificial waterway in Egypt that joins the Mediterranean and Red seas. The main canal is just under 100 miles (160 kilometers) long. Including entrance canals at both ends, the Suez Canal is about 118 miles (190 kilometers) long. When it was opened in 1869, it made the route between England and India about half as long. The canal had been the world's busiest interocean waterway until it closed during the 1967 Arab-Israeli war. Egypt reopened the canal in 1975.

Description. The canal stretches north and south across the Isthmus of Suez, between the cities of Port Said and Suez. It has no locks because there is no great difference between the levels of the Red and Mediterranean seas. Most of the canal can handle only single-lane traffic. When the canal was built, it measured 26 feet (8 meters) deep, 72 feet (22 meters) wide at the bottom, and about 230 feet (70 meters) wide at the surface. It has been enlarged several times. Today, it is 64 feet (19.5 meters) deep, 302 feet (92 meters) wide at the bottom, and 741 feet (226 meters) wide at the surface.

History. Canals were built to connect the Nile River and the Red Sea hundreds of years before the time of Christ. For a time in the A.D. 600's, the Red and Mediterranean seas were joined by a canal. Napoleon I of France saw advantages of a waterway across the Isthmus of Suez when he invaded Egypt in 1798. But Ferdinand de Lesseps, a French diplomat and canal builder, carried out the plan. He got permission for the project from Said Pasha, Egypt's ruler, in 1854. An International Technical Commission met in 1855 to plan the canal route. By 1858, the Suez Canal Company had been organized with a capital stock of about $40 million. Frenchmen and the Ottoman Empire owned most of the stock. Construction began on April 25, 1859, and the canal was opened on Nov. 17, 1869. The Suez Canal Company was given a concession to operate the canal until 1968.

Although the United Kingdom gained more from the construction of the canal than any other country, it had no part in building the canal and bought none of the original shares of stock. But in 1875, the British bought the shares of the ruler of Egypt, Ismail Pasha, who had succeeded Said Pasha in 1863. After that, a commission composed mostly of British and French directed management of the canal.

In 1888, an international convention agreed that the canal should be open to all nations in peace and in war. However, the United Kingdom stationed troops near the canal in World War I (1914-1918) and kept ships of nations at war with it from using the waterway. Axis ships

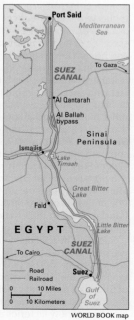

Suez Canal

WORLD BOOK map

were denied use of the canal in World War II (1939-1945). In 1950, as a result of the Arab-Israeli war of 1948-1949, Egypt banned Israeli ships from the canal.

Under the terms of a 1954 agreement with Egypt, British troops left the canal zone in June 1956. In July, the United States and the United Kingdom withdrew their offers to help finance the Aswan High Dam across the Nile River. This and other factors, including a strong Egyptian nationalist movement, led to the take-over of the canal by Egyptian President Gamal A. Nasser on July 26. He said Egypt would use the canal tolls to build the dam. The United Kingdom, France, and other Western nations protested the take-over.

On Oct. 29, 1956, Israel invaded Egypt. The United Kingdom and France attacked Egypt on October 31 in an effort to restore international control of the canal. United Nations (UN) action ended the fighting on November 6. A UN police force restored peace in the area. The canal was reopened in March 1957 under Egyptian management. It was blocked by sunken ships during an Arab-Israeli war in June 1967. The Suez Canal was not reopened until June 1975. In 1979, Egypt ended its ban against Israeli use of the canal. In 1980, a tunnel for motor vehicles was completed under the canal 10 miles (16 kilometers) north of the city of Suez.   Hartmut S. Walter

See also **De Lesseps, Ferdinand Marie; Suez crisis.**

Suez crisis, *soo EHZ,* began on July 26, 1956, when Egypt took control of the Suez Canal from its French and British owners. Israel, the United Kingdom, and France used the canal take-over to justify an attack on Egypt in October 1956. But international pressure forced the attackers to end military operations the next month.

In the 1950's, Western countries, led by the United States, and Communist countries, led by the Soviet Union, both tried to gain influence in Egypt. The two *blocs* (groups of countries) were engaged in an intense rivalry known as the Cold War. Egyptian President Gamal Abdel Nasser wanted Egypt to remain neutral in the Cold War. He sought funding from both sides for economic development projects in Egypt. The United Kingdom and the United States offered to help pay for the construction of the important Aswan High Dam (see **Aswan High Dam**). But they were troubled by Egypt's refusal to join an anti-Communist alliance and by its purchase of military supplies from the Soviets.

In July 1956, the United States and the United Kingdom abruptly decided to withdraw their offers of funding for the dam. Nasser, angered by this action, quickly responded by *nationalizing* (taking control of) the Suez Canal Company, the international company that owned the Suez Canal. He planned to use revenue from the canal to pay for the dam.

The United Kingdom and France, which had controlled the Suez Canal Company, plotted with Israel to overthrow Nasser and regain control of the canal. On Oct. 29, 1956, Israeli forces invaded Egypt and advanced across the Sinai Peninsula toward the canal. The United Kingdom and France demanded that both Israel and Egypt withdraw from the canal zone and allow a joint British-French force to occupy the area. On October 31, the British and French began air strikes against Egypt. In November, French and British troops captured Port Said and Port Fuad, two ports in the canal zone. Thousands of Egyptians were killed or wounded in the fighting.

The United States, the Soviet Union, and many other countries condemned the invasion. The Soviet Union threatened armed intervention. Faced with this pressure, the United Kingdom and France agreed to a cease-fire on November 6. A United Nations (UN) peacekeeping force was sent to Egypt. In December, the UN force finished evacuating the French and British troops. Israeli forces, which had occupied the Sinai Peninsula, withdrew from that area in March 1957 under U.S. pressure.

Despite his military losses, Nasser was regarded in Egypt as a victor, and he became an Arab hero for standing up to the West. The United Kingdom and France were compensated for the shares they had held in the canal. But the two countries lost influence in the Middle East. The Suez crisis proved that the United States and the Soviet Union had become the leading powers in world politics. Michael J. Reimer

See also **Nasser, Gamal Abdel; Suez Canal.**

Suffrage. See Voting; Woman suffrage.

Sugar is a food widely used as a sweetener. People sprinkle sugar on such foods as grapefruit and cereal to improve their taste. Some people add it to coffee, tea, and other beverages. In addition, manufacturers include sugar in such foods as ice cream and soft drinks.

All green plants produce sugar. But most sugar that people use comes from sugar cane or sugar beets, which produce a sugar called *sucrose*. This sugar is the one that people keep in a sugar bowl. Other sources of sugar include cornstarch, milk, maple syrup, and honey. Cornstarch is an especially important source of sugar-rich syrups in the United States. The consumption of corn sweeteners in the United States is about equal to the consumption of sucrose.

Sugar belongs to the class of foods called *carbohydrates.* Carbohydrates provide energy for plants and animals. Sugar is *refined* (purified) before it is used for food. The refining process also removes vitamins and other *nutrients* that are necessary for growth and health. Thus, refined sugar serves only as a source of energy.

Eating large amounts of sugar may increase the risk of tooth decay and help cause a person to become overweight. To avoid these problems, many people use artificial sweeteners, such as aspartame and saccharin, instead of sugar (see **Artificial sweetener**).

Uses of sugar

In the food industry. Most of the world's sugar crop is used in food. Much of the sugar eaten by people in the United States is contained in *processed* (specially prepared) foods. For example, candy, canned fruit, jams, jellies, and soft drinks all include large amounts of sugar. Sugar is also added to many bakery products.

Manufacturers sell sugar in several forms. Most is sold in the form of white *granules* (small grains). Some sugar is ground into powdered sugar and used in cake frostings. Brown sugar, which is often used in baking, is a mixture of molasses-flavored syrup and sugar.

In other industries. A small amount of the world's sugar crop is used by nonfood industries to make various products. For example, sugar is used for mixing cement, tanning leather, and making plastics. Some medicines contain sugar to disguise their unpleasant taste.

Certain products obtained from the sugar-refining process are also made into nonfood items. For example, after sugar has been removed from sugar cane, a material called *bagasse* remains. Bagasse is burned as a source of energy or is made into paper or wallboard.

Kinds of sugar

There are two kinds of sugar, *monosaccharides* and *disaccharides.* In pure form, both are white crystals. Monosaccharides are the simplest carbohydrates. Common monosaccharides include *glucose* and *fructose.* Glucose is the most important carbohydrate in the blood. Fructose, also called *levulose,* is found in fruits and vegetables. Disaccharides are made up of two monosaccharides. For example, the disaccharide sucrose can be broken down by enzymes into glucose and fructose. Other common disaccharides include *lactose* and *maltose.* Lactose is found in milk and is used in making some medicines. Maltose, formed from starch, is used in the production of bread and baby food.

The sources of sugar

Sugar beets and sugar cane are the world's main sources of sugar. Sugar beets grow in temperate climates. Sucrose is stored in the plant's fleshy root. Sugar cane is a tall grass plant that thrives in tropical and semi-

Hans & Judy Beste, Tom Stack & Assoc.

Sugar cane, one of the leading sources of sugar, thrives in tropical and semitropical climates. Most sugar cane is cut and gathered by hand, but some is harvested by machine, as *shown here.*

© John Messineo

Sugar beets, a major source of sugar, grow in temperate climates. They store sugar in their large, fleshy roots, which are harvested after the leaves have been removed, as *shown here.*

How raw sugar is obtained from sugar cane

To obtain raw sugar from sugar cane, processors first wash and shred the cane. The cane is then placed in a crushing machine, which forces a sugary juice called *cane juice* from the stalks. After the juice is heated and filtered, an evaporator and vacuum pan remove much of the water from it, forming a syrup. A centrifuge separates sugar crystals from the syrup, producing raw sugar.

WORLD BOOK diagram by Steven Liska

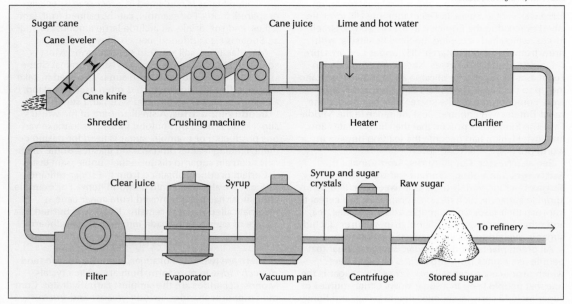

Sugar cane · Cane leveler · Cane knife · Shredder · Crushing machine · Cane juice · Lime and hot water · Heater · Clarifier

Clear juice · Filter · Syrup · Evaporator · Vacuum pan · Syrup and sugar crystals · Centrifuge · Raw sugar · Stored sugar · To refinery →

tropical climates. It stores sucrose in its stalks. For more detailed information, see **Sugar beet; Sugar cane.**

Cornstarch and other starches are made up of sugars. Starches can be broken down to form individual sugars by mixing them with acid or *enzymes* (molecules that speed up chemical reactions). For example, the partial breakdown of cornstarch produces *corn syrup,* which consists primarily of glucose and maltose. Corn syrup is used to flavor such foods as candy and salad dressing. Solid *corn sugar,* also formed from cornstarch, is made up chiefly of glucose. A liquid called *high-fructose corn syrup* is produced by converting some of the glucose in cornstarch to fructose. High-fructose corn syrup is used in place of sucrose in many baked goods and soft drinks. See **Corn syrup; Cornstarch.**

Honey is the sweet liquid that bees make from the nectar they drink from flowers. Bees collect sucrose from the nectar and convert it into *invert sugar,* an equal mixture of fructose and glucose. Invert sugar is the primary ingredient of honey, which also contains small amounts of vitamins and other nutrients. See **Honey.**

Maple syrup is the concentrated sap of certain maple trees. It consists chiefly of sucrose. But the syrup gets its maple taste from nonsucrose compounds that form during processing. People pour the syrup on pancakes, waffles, and other foods, and manufacturers use it to flavor certain candies. See **Maple syrup.**

Milk. Lactose, also called milk sugar, is found in the milk of all *mammals* (milk-producing animals). It is obtained commercially from skimmed milk and *whey,* a liquid by-product of the cheese-making process.

Molasses is a by-product of sugar-beet and sugar-cane refining processes. It contains 40 to 50 percent sugar. It is used chiefly in making alcoholic beverages,

candy, and livestock feed. The word *molasses* also refers to the extracts of many sugar-bearing plants. For example, the syrup produced by the sweet sorghum plant is called molasses. See **Sorghum** (Sweet sorghums).

Sugar production

Making cane sugar. Sugar cane stalks grow 7 to 15 feet (2 to 5 meters) high. When the cane is ready to harvest, the field is set on fire for a few minutes to burn off the plants' dry leaves. The stalks do not burn because of their high moisture content and tough outer shell. The cane is then harvested and taken to a factory. There, the stalks are washed, shredded, and placed in a crushing machine or into vats of hot water that dissolve the sugar. Crushing machines burst the stalks, squeezing out the sugary liquid. Sprays of water dissolve more sugar from the stalks. The mixture of sugar and water, called *cane juice,* is then taken away for purifying.

Obtaining raw sugar. The cane juice, still diluted with water, is heated. Lime (calcium hydroxide) is added to the juice to settle out impurities, and carbon dioxide is used to remove the excess lime. Workers then put the clarified juice in huge evaporator tanks, where most of the water is evaporated and the juice becomes thick and syrupy. However, still more water must be removed from the syrup so that sugar crystals will form. To remove the excess water, the syrup is heated in large, dome-shaped vacuum pans. Sugar and sugar syrup scorch easily. But the vacuum lowers the boiling point of the syrup so that it will heat without scorching.

After large sugar crystals form in the thick syrup, workers put the mixture in a *centrifuge.* This machine separates most of the syrup from the crystals. The remaining *raw sugar* contains 97 to 99 percent sucrose.

Refining cane sugar. To obtain pure white sugar for table use, the yellowish-brown raw sugar must go through several more steps. The film that gives raw sugar its yellow-brown color is rinsed off. Next, the sugar crystals are dissolved in water, and the solution is poured through filters until it becomes a clear, colorless liquid. The liquid is then evaporated until crystals form again. The crystals are again spun in the centrifuge, and sugar flows from the machine into drying drums. Heated air in the drums absorbs any remaining moisture.

Some of the syrup does not form crystals during evaporation and spinning. The process is repeated several times to form more of the white crystals. The remaining syrup is then used to make brown sugar.

Making beet sugar. After sugar beets are dug out of the ground, they are shipped to a factory. There, they are washed and cut into thin slices called *cossettes*. The cossettes are placed in machines called *diffusers* to soak. The soaking removes the sugar from the slices. The cossettes are then dried and mixed with molasses to make cattle feed.

The solution obtained by soaking the cossettes is heated and treated with lime to settle out impurities. Carbon dioxide is added to remove the excess lime in the solution. The juice is then filtered to remove the impurities. The purified solution is called *thin juice*. The juice is evaporated to remove water and crystallize the sugar. From this point, the process for making sugar from sugar beets is the same as for sugar cane. However, in the United States and some other countries, beet-sugar processing is carried out in a single operation.

The sugar industry

About 150 million tons (136 million metric tons) of sugar are produced worldwide every year. Brazil and India lead the world in sugar production.

World consumption of sweeteners

This graph shows the average amounts of sweeteners consumed per capita in major regions of the world since 1961.

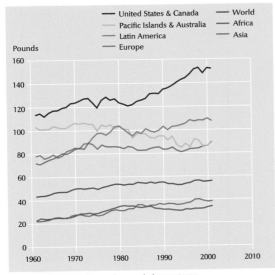

Figures include sugar, maple syrup, honey, and other sweeteners.
Source: Food and Agriculture Organization of the United Nations.

Leading sugar-producing countries

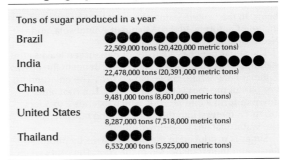

Tons of sugar produced in a year

Brazil — 22,509,000 tons (20,420,000 metric tons)
India — 22,478,000 tons (20,391,000 metric tons)
China — 9,481,000 tons (8,601,000 metric tons)
United States — 8,287,000 tons (7,518,000 metric tons)
Thailand — 6,532,000 tons (5,925,000 metric tons)

Figures are for a three-year average, 2000-2002.
Source: Food and Agriculture Organization of the United Nations.

The United States produces more than 8 million tons (7.25 million metric tons) of sugar a year. Florida, Hawaii, and Louisiana are major producers of cane sugar. The Red River Valley in Minnesota and North Dakota is the largest sugar-beet growing region in the United States.

History

Sugar from sugar cane. Inhabitants of South Pacific islands grew sugar cane more than 8,000 years ago. The plants were also widely grown in ancient India. Sugar cane is specifically mentioned in records of an expedition by the Macedonian king Alexander the Great to what is now Pakistan in 326 B.C.

The cultivation and refining of sugar cane spread east from India to China about 100 B.C. but did not reach Europe until about A.D. 636. In the early 1400's, Europeans planted sugar cane in northern Africa and on islands in the Atlantic Ocean. Portuguese settlers later planted sugar cane on the west coast of Africa and in Brazil. The Italian navigator Christopher Columbus brought sugar-cane cuttings to islands in the Caribbean Sea in 1493.

The first sugar mill in the Western Hemisphere was built in 1515 in what is now the Dominican Republic. Jesuit missionaries brought sugar cane to Louisiana in 1751. In 1791, the first sugar mill on the North American mainland was built in New Orleans by Antonio Mendez, a Louisiana planter.

Sugar from sugar beets. The people of ancient Babylonia, Egypt, and Greece grew sugar beets. In 1744, Andreas Sigismund Marggraf, a German chemist, found that sugar from the sugar beet was the same as that removed from sugar cane. In 1799, Franz Achard, a student of Marggraf's, developed a practical method of removing sugar from sugar beets. Sugar mills then sprang up quickiy in Europe and Russia. Beet sugar was first produced in the United States in 1838. E. H. Dyer, an American businessman, established the country's first successful sugar-beet processing factory in Alvarado, California, near Oakland.   Roger E. Wyse

Related articles in *World Book* include:

Candy	Corn syrup	Fructose	Rillieux,
Carbohydrate	Dextrose	Glucose	Norbert
		Molasses	Sucrose

Sugar beet is a plant grown for the sugar contained in its large, fleshy root. Sugar beets supply about 40 percent of the world's commercial sugar. Only sugar cane provides more. France leads the countries of the world in growing sugar beets. Germany, Turkey, Ukraine, and the United States are also important producers of sugar beets. In the United States, the chief beet-growing states include California, Idaho, Michigan, Minnesota, and North Dakota.

The sugar beet has a cluster of dark-green leaves atop a short stocky stem called the *crown.* Beneath the crown is the creamy-white, cone-shaped root. The enlarged upper part of the root is called the *beet.* The root tapers down to form a thin *taproot,* which extends 2 to 5 feet (0.6 to 1.5 meters) into the soil. The long taproot can obtain water that lies far belowground.

Sugar is produced in the plant's leaves by photosynthesis and then transported to the root. The roots weigh from 1 ½ to 3 pounds (0.7 to 1.4 kilograms). About 15 to 20 percent of this weight is a sugar called *sucrose.*

Raising sugar beets. Sugar beets grow best in regions that have sunny days and cool nights. Farmers plant the seeds in early spring and apply fertilizer early in the growing season. Sugar beets require a large amount of water to prevent them from wilting, and in most growing areas, the plants are irrigated.

Plants grown for sugar are harvested at the end of the first growing season, after the roots have developed. When grown for seed, the plants require a second year of growth. In areas that have mild winters, roots are simply left in the ground after the first growing season. In areas with cold winters, farmers dig up the roots in the autumn, store them over the winter, and then replant them in the spring. During the second year, the plants develop tall, branched stalks with tiny flowers that produce the seeds. In the United States, Oregon is the leading producer of sugar-beet seeds.

A number of diseases, insect pests, and nematodes (roundworms) attack sugar beets. *Leaf spot* and other fungal diseases are troublesome in regions with hot, humid summers. In areas with mild winters, sugar beets

WORLD BOOK illustration by James Teason
Sugar beets consist of a creamy-white storage root, *right,* with a crown of large, dark-green leaves, *left.* Sugar makes up 15 to 20 percent of the weight of the root.

Leading sugar-beet growing countries

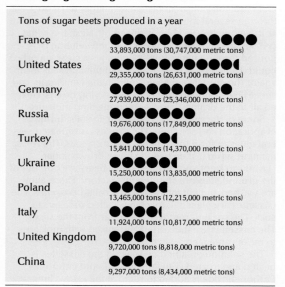

Tons of sugar beets produced in a year

France	33,893,000 tons (30,747,000 metric tons)
United States	29,355,000 tons (26,631,000 metric tons)
Germany	27,939,000 tons (25,346,000 metric tons)
Russia	19,676,000 tons (17,849,000 metric tons)
Turkey	15,841,000 tons (14,370,000 metric tons)
Ukraine	15,250,000 tons (13,835,000 metric tons)
Poland	13,465,000 tons (12,215,000 metric tons)
Italy	11,924,000 tons (10,817,000 metric tons)
United Kingdom	9,720,000 tons (8,818,000 metric tons)
China	9,297,000 tons (8,434,000 metric tons)

Figures are for a three-year average, 2002-2004.
Source: Food and Agriculture Organization of the United Nations.

may be damaged by such viral diseases as *curly top* and *beet yellows.* During winter, viruses that cause these diseases are found in insects and weeds. In spring, they are transmitted to sugar beets by such insects as aphids and leaf hoppers. Farmers control these diseases and pests by planting disease-resistant varieties of sugar-beet plants, by applying pesticides, and by crop rotation.

Harvesting. Sugar beets that are grown for sugar are harvested in late September or early October in most states, though California has a longer growing season. First, a plant is *topped*—that is, its leaves and crown are removed—and then its root is dug up. Both operations are done mechanically. The tops are fed to livestock or are used as fertilizer. The beets are shipped to a factory, where sugar is extracted. For a detailed description of how sugar is obtained from sugar beets, and for the history of such production, see **Sugar.**   Myrna P. Steinkamp

Scientific classification. The sugar beet belongs to the goosefoot family, Chenopodiaceae. It is *Beta vulgaris.*

Sugar cane is a tall grass plant that grows in tropical and semitropical countries. Sugar-cane plants consist of sturdy stalks 7 to 30 feet (2 to 9 meters) high and about 2 inches (5 centimeters) in diameter. These stalks contain a large amount of sugary juice from which sugar and molasses are made. The plant fiber that remains after the juice is extracted is frequently burned as fuel to generate electricity. The fiber may also be used to make fiberboard and paper.

Sugar cane grows as *tillers* (shoots) from underground branches called *rhizomes.* The numerous stalks aboveground have no branches, but they have long, narrow leaves that are arranged in two rows. The sugar-cane stalk is divided into several sections, like a bamboo cane. These sections, called *internodes,* are connected by joints known as *nodes.* Each node bears a bud, much like a potato eye. The buds can be used to plant a new crop. The stem's color varies from yellow to reddish.

Leading sugar-cane growing countries

Tons of sugar cane produced in a year

Brazil	●●●●●●●●●●●●
	427,910,000 tons (388,193,000 metric tons)
India	●●●●●●●●◖
	302,624,000 tons (274,536,000 metric tons)
China	●●◖
	101,942,000 tons (92,481,000 metric tons)
Thailand	●●◖
	79,416,000 tons (72,045,000 metric tons)
Pakistan	●◖
	55,901,000 tons (50,712,000 metric tons)
Mexico	●◖
	49,930,000 tons (45,296,000 metric tons)
Colombia	●◖
	40,381,000 tons (36,633,000 metric tons)
Australia	●
	39,360,000 tons (35,707,000 metric tons)

Figures are for a three-year average, 2002-2004.
Source: Food and Agriculture Organization of the United Nations.

South Pacific islanders grew sugar cane more than 8,000 years ago. The plant was also widely grown in ancient India. Its cultivation and refining spread from India to China about 100 B.C. but did not reach Europe until about A.D. 636. Colonizers brought sugar cane to America and the West Indies during the 1500's. Today, the leading sugar-cane growing nations include Brazil, China, India, Pakistan, and Thailand. Florida, Hawaii, and Louisiana are the leading U.S. cane-producing states.

Growth and cultivation. Most sugar cane is grown in regions where temperatures generally range be-

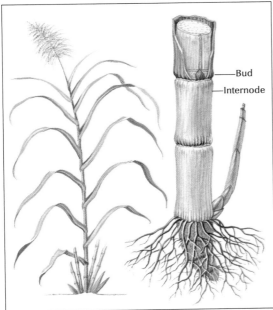

WORLD BOOK illustration by James Teason

Sugar cane grows in the form of stalks, *left,* which contain sugary juice. The stalks are divided into *internodes, right.* Buds and roots occur at the *nodes* (joints) between the internodes.

tween 75 and 86 °F (24 and 30 °C) and where rainfall is high. Sugar cane needs about 60 to 120 inches (150 to 300 centimeters) of water a year. In regions with little rainfall, growers irrigate the plants.

Sugar cane is grown chiefly from stem cuttings placed in *furrows* (narrow grooves) in the field and covered with soil. The buds on the nodes germinate into leafy shoots that emerge from the soil. In a few weeks, the shoots produce stalks with nodes and internodes. The underground nodal buds then germinate to produce the tillers that make up the multistalked plant.

Harvesting. Most sugar cane is harvested from 8 to 24 months after planting. In some countries, particularly Australia and the United States, machines are used to cut off the cane stalks. But in most other sugar-cane growing areas, workers cut the cane by hand using a large steel knife called a *machete.* The cut stalks are gathered into heaps called *windrows* and then placed into carts, trucks, or railway cars that take them to the sugar mill. The stubble left in the field produces from 2 to 10 additional crops, depending on the location.

For a detailed discussion of how sugar is obtained from sugar cane, see **Sugar** (Sugar production).

Paul H. Moore

Scientific classification. Sugar cane belongs to the grass family, Poaceae or Gramineae. It is *Saccharum officinarum.*

See also **Cuba** (picture); **Hawaii** (Agriculture); **Sugar.**

Suggestion, in psychology, is the acceptance of an idea by the mind without critical thought. For example, if someone merely makes a throwing motion, many observers will be sure that something actually was thrown. They get this impression because the mind tends to complete a partial picture. Similarly, if a parent touches the forehead of a child who feels ill, the parent may believe that the child has a fever, even though a thermometer would show a normal temperature.

Professional magicians rely on suggestion for most of their effects. If a magician goes through the motion of tossing a coin into a cup, and if people in the audience hear the expected jingling sound, they assume the coin is in the cup. Advertisers use suggestion in many ways. No advertiser would dare guarantee that a person will become popular by using a certain product. But the advertisements may strongly suggest this result.

Children accept suggestions more easily than adults do, because they are less critical and less experienced. Most uneducated or prejudiced people also accept suggestion easily. People are more suggestible when they are worried, tired, or ill. Leonard M. Horowitz

See also **Hypnotism; Magic; Magician.**

Suharto, *soo HAHR toh* (1921-   ), also spelled *Soeharto,* was president of Indonesia from 1968 to 1998. Under Suharto, Indonesia experienced strong economic growth. But Suharto suppressed human rights and used his power to make his family and allies wealthy.

Suharto was born on Java when Indonesia was a colony of the Netherlands called the Dutch East Indies. He joined the Dutch colonial army in 1940, beginning a military career. Later, he fought the Dutch for Indonesian independence. Suharto seized power in 1966, after putting down a violent feud within the military. Suharto became acting president in 1967. The national legislature elected him president in 1968 and reelected him, unopposed, every five years through 1998.

In 1997 and 1998, Indonesia suffered one of the worst financial slumps in its history. Suharto's management of the economic crisis led to calls for his resignation. Violent protests in key cities forced Suharto to resign in May 1998. In 2000, the government brought corruption charges against him. In 2006, it dropped the charges, saying he was too ill to stand trial.   David T. Hill

Sui dynasty, *sway,* was a Chinese *dynasty* (family of rulers) that governed from A.D. 581 to 618. The dynasty's first ruler, Yang Jian (also spelled Yang Chien), united most of northern and southern China after almost 400 years of civil war. He issued a new law code, built a new capital near Xi'an, and promoted Buddhism. Yang Jian died in 604, possibly murdered by his son, Sui Yangdi (Sui Yang-ti), who then ruled.

Yangdi built the first Grand Canal, a waterway for shipping grain and other products. It extended almost 1,200 miles (1,930 kilometers), from Hangzhou to Luoyang to near Beijing. Yangdi tried but failed to conquer Korea and Manchuria. After the Koreans defeated the Sui army in 612, the Chinese people became dissatisfied with the emperor and revolted. In 615, the Sui army suffered another defeat, by the Eastern Turks, and Yangdi retreated to the south. He was assassinated in 618, and the Sui dynasty ended. The Tang dynasty was founded that same year.   Grant Hardy

Suicide is the act of deliberately killing oneself. According to the World Health Organization, hundreds of thousands of people throughout the world commit suicide every year. The worldwide rate of suicide among teen-agers and young adults is rising faster than in any other age group. Rates of suicide are generally higher among men than among women. The individuals most likely to commit suicide are those who have thought about it, threatened to commit it, or attempted it.

Causes. Most people who commit suicide do so for personal reasons, such as despair or loss of a loved one. Fears of the future, of failure, or of not being loved contribute to some suicides, especially among adolescents. A mental illness—especially depression—or hopeless physical illness may also increase risk of suicide.

Society plays a part in some suicides. As a society becomes more complex, for example, loneliness and stress can lead some people to kill themselves. People who believe that they have betrayed the ideals of their country may also kill themselves. Such suicides were common among defeated Japanese warriors, who committed a ritual form of suicide called *hara-kiri* (see **Hara-kiri**). Some people commit suicide as a dramatic form of protest against a government.

Prevention. People considering suicide may exhibit certain warning signs. They may express feelings of hopelessness, a loss of interest in living, or a wish to die. Other signs include listless behavior, sleep disturbances, weight gain or loss, loss of appetite, and headaches. The role of suggestion in bringing on suicides is well documented. Suicides often increase after a famous person commits suicide. Mental health professionals often work to prevent a series of teen-age suicides in a community after one takes place there.

Counseling and support can help people overcome a wish to die. Many communities have set up suicide prevention centers where people considering suicide can call in and discuss their problems. Doctors prescribe drugs, such as antidepressants, to treat many mental illnesses that increase risk of suicide. Limiting access to firearms and other means of killing oneself may help prevent some suicides.

Physician-assisted suicide. Some people believe that hopelessly ill people are entitled to *physician-assisted suicide,* in which a doctor helps a patient die. Other people think physician-assisted suicide is morally wrong. Many nations and most states of the United States have laws against the practice.

Supporters of physician-assisted suicide think that life-extending medical techniques have created a need for new approaches to care at the end of life. They believe such care should include help with dying if patients can think clearly and freely request help. A few doctors have said publicly—and more have admitted privately—that they would help patients die in some situations. Other doctors strongly oppose the idea of helping someone die. Throughout the world, citizens, lawmakers, and physicians are struggling to create policies that protect people and prevent suffering.   David Lester

See also **Adolescent** (Suicide); **Death** (The right to die); **Euthanasia** (Physician-assisted suicide); **Mental illness** (Mood disorders).

Additional resources

Jamison, Kay R. *Night Falls Fast: Understanding Suicide.* 1999. Reprint. Vintage Bks., 2000.
Murphy, James M. *Coping with Teen Suicide.* Rosen Pub. Group, 1999.

Suit. People who seek the help of a court of law to enforce their rights are said to "bring suit." Someone who has suffered injury at the hands of another may bring suit for damages. A person may also bring suit to recover property, to collect money, to enforce the terms of a contract, or to accomplish one of many other purposes. A governmental unit may bring suit in the same way as a private person or a corporation. In general, a suit is any civil action brought before a court of law. Criminal cases are not called suits. See also **Class action; Court** (How courts work); **Malpractice suit; Statute of limitations.**

          Sherman L. Cohn

Suite, *sweet,* is a type of musical composition. Most suites are made up of a number of short works, usually in the same key. These suites generally consist of dance pieces that have contrasting tempos and moods. The suite developed during the 1500's and declined in popularity after about 1750.

After the 1800's, the term *suite* also was used to describe several other types of musical compositions. A group of instrumental selections from a ballet or opera is called a suite. For example, music from *The Nutcracker* (1892), a ballet by the Russian composer Peter Ilich Tchaikovsky, was arranged into the *Nutcracker Suite.* A suite can also be a series of descriptive musical pieces. *The Grand Canyon Suite* (1931) by the American composer Ferde Grofé is an example.   R. M. Longyear

Sukarno, *soo KAHR no* (1901-1970), also spelled *Soekarno,* was Indonesia's first president, serving from 1945 to 1967. He founded the Indonesian National Party (PNI) in 1927 to end Dutch colonial rule.

In 1945, Sukarno created national principles called Pancasila to unify the diverse country and to block demands for an Islamic state. In 1955, Sukarno helped found the Non-Aligned Movement, a political group of developing nations. In 1957, with the help of the United States Central Intelligence Agency, rebel movements began. In response, Sukarno closed parliament in 1959 and imposed a system called "guided democracy."

In 1964, Sukarno sent forces into newly independent Malaysia to challenge the United Kingdom's influence there. In 1965, he withdrew Indonesia from the United Nations after Malaysia's election to the Security Council. In 1966, Lieutenant General Suharto overthrew Sukarno after a failed coup blamed on Indonesian Communists. Sukarno kept the title of president until 1967.

Sukarno was born on June 6, 1901, in Surabaya, on the island of Java. Sukarno died on June 21, 1970. His oldest daughter, Megawati Sukarnoputri, served as president of Indonesia from 2001 to 2004. Jeffrey Winters

See also **Indonesia** (History).

Sukkot, *su KOHTH* or *su KOHT,* is a Jewish festival that begins on the 15th day of the Hebrew month of Tishri (approximately September and October). It lasts seven days. The festival is also called the *Feast of Tabernacles.*

The ancient Hebrews celebrated Sukkot as a festival of thanksgiving and brought sacrifices to the Temple in Jerusalem. Jews still observe the holiday by making joyous parades in synagogues and carrying *lulabs* (palm branches), *etrogs* (citrons), and myrtle and willow branches. During Sukkot, traditional Jews live in a hut called a *sukkah* as a reminder of the temporary dwellings in which their ancestors lived during their wanderings in the wilderness in Biblical times. Following Suk-

A *sukkah* is a temporary hut used during the Jewish festival of *Sukkot.* Branches or straw are laid across the top of the sukkah to form a roof. Sukkahs remind Jews of the temporary dwellings in which their ancestors lived during their wanderings in the desert in Biblical times. Many Jews eat and sleep in a sukkah during the festival, in accordance with Jewish law.

kot is a supplementary two-day celebration called Shemini Atzeret, the second day of which is called Simhat Torah (see **Simhat Torah**). B. Barry Levy

Süleyman I, *SOO luh MAHN* or *soo lay MAHN* (1494-1566), became known in the Western world as The Magnificent. However, his own people called Süleyman I The Lawgiver. He was the 10th ruler of the Ottoman Empire. His name is sometimes spelled Suleiman I. During Süleyman's rule, the empire was the richest and most powerful in Europe and the Middle East. Süleyman led armies into Hungary, and stormed the walls of Vienna. In Asia, his armies invaded Persia (Iran) and captured Tabriz and Baghdad. Süleyman's fleets dominated the Mediterranean Sea, the Red Sea, and the Persian Gulf. His sailors held North Africa, and raided the coasts of Spain, France, and Italy. Süleyman took Rhodes from the Knights Hospitallers. He revised the legal system of the Ottoman Empire. See also **Ottoman Empire** (History); **Knights Hospitallers.** Justin McCarthy

Sulfa drug is any of a group of chemically related antibacterial compounds. Sulfa drugs, also called *sulfonamides* (pronounced *suhl FAHN uh mydz),* were the first drugs to be proved safe and effective against many common bacterial infections. Sulfa drugs played a major role in antibacterial treatment from the late 1930's until the mid-1940's, when penicillin became widely available. The development of sulfa drugs resulted in a sharp decline in the number of deaths caused by many infectious diseases. These drugs helped save many lives during World War II (1939-1945). Today, physicians prescribe sulfa drugs chiefly to treat urinary tract infections.

How sulfa drugs work. Normally, sulfa drugs do not kill bacteria. Instead, they prevent the bacteria from multiplying. The bacteria are then killed by the body's normal defense mechanisms. Bacteria sensitive to sulfa drugs require a chemical called para-aminobenzoic acid (PABA) in order to multiply. Sulfa drugs have a chemical structure similar to PABA and are readily absorbed by bacteria that require this compound. The sulfonamides then block the chemical reactions that involve PABA, so that the bacteria can no longer divide and multiply.

Uses in treating diseases. Sulfonamides are not effective against all bacteria. Therefore, physicians need to identify the type of bacteria causing an infection before they know whether to use a sulfa drug. Sulfa drugs are most commonly taken by mouth, but they may be given by injection or applied directly to the skin.

In the past, sulfa drugs were used in the treatment of such diseases as pneumonia and blood poisoning. The use of sulfa drugs has decreased because more powerful drugs—such as penicillin and other antibiotics—are now used to treat many bacterial diseases. In addition, many bacteria have become resistant to sulfa drugs.

In the late 1960's, researchers developed a combination drug consisting of sulfamethoxazole (a sulfonamide) and a compound called trimethoprim. This drug is effective in treating certain bacterial infections not sensitive to sulfonamides alone. Recurrent urinary tract infections, middle-ear infections, and shigellosis are among the diseases that may be treated with this drug.

Development of sulfa drugs. In 1908, Paul Gelmo, a German chemist who was looking for better dyes for woolen goods, discovered chemicals that eventually led to sulfa drugs. However, it was not until the early 1930's that sulfonamides were used in medicine.

In 1935, a German pathologist named Gerhard Domagk reported that the dye Prontosil killed streptococcal bacteria in mice. Further research revealed that Prontosil was broken down to sulfanilamide in the body. Scientists determined that sulfanilamide was the chemical responsible for blocking the bacteria's growth. Researchers tested thousands of related chemicals before they found the few that were most useful.

A major problem with sulfanilamide and other early sulfa drugs was that they sometimes *crystallized* (solidified) in the urine of the patient, causing kidney damage. Scientists later developed sulfa drugs that are much more water soluble and, therefore, much less likely to crystallize in the urine.   Eugene M. Johnson, Jr.

Sulfate is a chemical compound that contains a certain group of associated atoms of sulfur and oxygen. This group is known as the *sulfate radical.* The chemical formula of the radical is SO_4. The radical has an electrical charge of -2. Most sulfates are stable compounds, formed in crystals. Common sulfates are celestite, a sulfate of strontium; Epsom salt, a sulfate of magnesium; and gypsum, a sulfate of calcium. Many sulfates are soluble in water, but some, such as barium, strontium, and lead sulfates, do not dissolve in water.

Sulfates have a number of important industrial uses. Copper sulfate, also known as blue vitriol, is used in many industries, including dyeing and *calico printing,* a process of imprinting color designs on cloth. Iron sulfate is used in making ink and as a medicine. Zinc sulfate is used in surgery as an antiseptic, in calico printing, and in making drying oils for varnishes. Some baking powders contain *alum,* a double sulfate of potassium and aluminum. See also **Alum; Gypsum.**   C. Frank Shaw III

Sulfide is a chemical compound that contains sulfur and another element, usually a metal. All sulfides contain the *sulfide ion,* a single sulfur atom with an electrical charge of -2. All living beings have sulfide ions in proteins that play a role in the use of food energy.

Sulfides are also important in chemistry and industry. Chemists can use hydrogen sulfide (H_2S), a poisonous gas, to test for various metals. Carbon disulfide (CS_2) is a solvent of rubber and sulfur, and a local anesthetic. Industries use it to make cellophane, pesticides, and other products. Several sulfides give paints their color. They are also important sources of metals. Sulfides commonly found in rocks include chalcocite, a sulfide of copper; and cinnabar, a sulfide of mercury. See also **Hydrogen sulfide.**   C. Frank Shaw III

Sulfonamide. See Sulfa drug.

Sulfur is a yellow, nonmetallic chemical element that is found in many parts of the world. It has been used for hundreds of years. The ancient Greeks and Romans used sulfur as a cleanser, bleach, and medicine. The element was later important as one of the main ingredients in gunpowder. Today, sulfur is used in a wide variety of products and industrial processes.

Sulfur occurs alone in nature, and it is also found in coal, crude oil, natural gas, oil shales, and many minerals. The most abundant of all sulfur minerals is a compound of sulfur and iron called *pyrite.* The atmosphere of Venus contains sulfur, and some scientists believe the core of Mars consists of pure *iron sulfide,* another compound of sulfur and iron. Astronomers have found sul-

fur compounds in interstellar clouds and in meteorites.

All plants and animals need small amounts of sulfur to live. Plants obtain sulfur from the soil. Many foods from plants, including cabbage, garlic, onions, and soybean flour, are rich in sulfur compounds. *Methionine,* a sulfur-containing substance required in the human diet, is found in such foods as eggs, dairy products, and meats.

Uses. Almost all sulfur produced today is used to prepare *sulfuric acid,* a sulfur compound. This substance is the world's most important commercial chemical. Manufacturers use sulfuric acid to make such products as dyes, paints, paper, textiles, and a number of industrial chemicals. The compound is also used in the production of metals and in petroleum refining.

Products that contain sulfur—but not sulfuric acid— include fertilizers and some types of explosives, fungicides, insecticides, rubber, shampoos, storage batteries, and chemicals used to develop photographic film. Sulfur is also an ingredient in many medicines, and it may be used in highway construction instead of asphalt.

Properties. Sulfur has no taste or odor. Its *atomic number* (number of protons in its nucleus) is 16. Its *relative atomic mass* is 32.065. An element's relative atomic mass equals its *mass* (amount of matter) divided by $\frac{1}{12}$ of the mass of carbon 12, the most abundant form of carbon. The chemical symbol for sulfur is S. Sulfur melts at 120 °C if it is heated slowly, and 113 °C if it is heated rapidly. It boils at 444.6 °C. Between 150 °C and 444.6 °C, sulfur goes through many changes in density and color as it takes on different forms called *allotropes.*

Sulfur is a very reactive element. At 250 °C, it ignites with air. As it burns, it combines with oxygen to form *sulfur dioxide,* a colorless gas. Large amounts of sulfur dioxide are found in the air of many densely populated areas. This gas has been associated with respiratory disorders, damage to buildings, and a type of precipitation called *acid rain* (see **Acid rain**). Much of the sulfur dioxide in the air is formed when coal that contains sulfur is burned. In the United States and certain other countries, environmental protection laws limit the amount of sulfur that coal-burning power plants can emit.

Forms. Sulfur exists in several allotropes. The most common allotrope is *orthorhombic sulfur,* also called *rhombic sulfur,* a lemon-yellow, crystalline material that is stable at room temperature. *Monoclinic sulfur,* or *pris-*

Field Museum of Natural History (WORLD BOOK photo)
Sulfur is a yellow, nonmetallic element. It is used mainly to make sulfuric acid, an important industrial chemical.

How sulfur is obtained

Most of the sulfur used today is recovered from sulfur compounds in oil and natural gas through *Claus conversion*. This diagram shows the basic steps involved in the process.

WORLD BOOK diagram by Zorica Dabich

Separating raw natural gas from crude oil obtained from a well is the first step in recovering sulfur. After the gas has been separated, it is transferred to a cleaning plant. There, a complex purification process removes hydrogen sulfide from the gas.

Conversion of the hydrogen sulfide to sulfur occurs in a *Claus kiln*. Air and water are added to this combustion chamber, and the hydrogen sulfide is heated to form a mixture of sulfurous gases and water vapor. Much of the sulfur condenses to liquid form. The remaining waste gas is removed and incinerated.

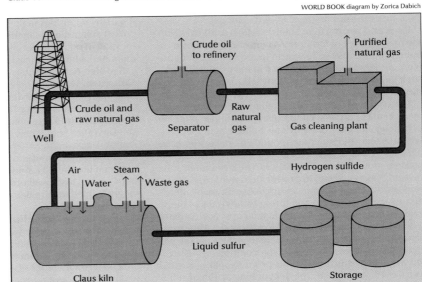

matic sulfur, is stable only between 94 and 120 °C. It occurs in long, almost colorless, needlelike crystals. *Amorphous sulfur,* also called *plastic sulfur,* is soft and sticky and stretches like rubber. Both monoclinic sulfur and amorphous sulfur change to the orthorhombic form at room temperature.

Orthorhombic sulfur is prepared in several ways for commercial use. For example, fine grains of sulfur are produced when sulfur vapor condenses. These grains are called *flowers of sulfur* because they occur in flowerlike patterns. *Roll sulfur* is made by hardening liquid sulfur in cylinder-shaped molds. *Sulfur nuggets* are prepared by spraying molten sulfur into a water bath.

How sulfur is obtained. Before 1900, many industries obtained sulfur from volcanic deposits, sulfur mines in Sicily, and roasted pyrites. The United States led the world in sulfur production during the 1900's. In the early 2000's, the United States and Canada ranked as the leading producers of sulfur. Other sulfur-producing countries included China, Japan, and Russia.

From 1900 until the mid-1950's, the chief process used to produce sulfur was the *Frasch method.* In 1891, Herman Frasch, an American chemical engineer, discovered that sulfur could be melted underground with superheated steam. In the Frasch process, water is heated under pressure to a temperature above sulfur's melting point. Pumps force the water into the ground, where it melts sulfur into a frothy liquid. Compressed air then forces the liquid sulfur to the surface. Most sulfur produced by the Frasch method is about 99.5 to 99.9 percent pure. See **Mining** (diagram: The Frasch method).

Today, most sulfur comes from sulfur compounds found in oil and natural gas. In natural gas, sulfur takes the form of *hydrogen sulfide,* a compound of hydrogen and sulfur. Petroleum companies extract hydrogen sulfide to prevent the release of sulfur dioxide when the natural gas is burned. After removal from natural gas,

the hydrogen sulfide is heated and converted to sulfur that is 99.9 percent pure. This process, called *Claus conversion,* was invented in 1883 by C. F. Claus, an English chemical engineer. Sulfur is also obtained by roasting pyrites and other minerals containing sulfur to form sulfur dioxide. This gas is then used to manufacture sulfuric acid.   Adrian L. Schwan

See also **Sulfa drug; Sulfate; Sulfide; Sulfur dioxide; Sulfuric acid.**

Sulfur dioxide is a colorless, poisonous gas with a sharp odor. Sulfur dioxide forms naturally from volcanic activity and from the decay of organic matter. It can be made by burning sulfur or heating metallic sulfur compounds. It is also released into the atmosphere by oil refineries, by some metal smelters, and by factories and electric power plants that burn coal or oil. In the air people breathe, the substance can irritate the eyes and respiratory system. It may also dissolve in water droplets to form *acid rain,* which can harm or even kill wildlife and damage buildings. Acid rain also may form when sulfur dioxide in the air is converted into sulfur trioxide. United States government regulations limit the amount of sulfur dioxide that industries can discharge into the air.

Manufacturers combine sulfur dioxide with water to make sulfurous acid, which serves as a bleach and as a food preservative. Sulfur dioxide is also used to prepare such chemicals as sulfites and sulfuric acid. The gas becomes liquid under pressure or at a temperature of −10 °C (+14 °F). The liquid is a refrigerant. Sulfur dioxide has the chemical formula SO_2.   C. Frank Shaw III

See also **Acid rain.**

Sulfuric acid is a colorless, dense, oily liquid that is extremely corrosive. It is one of the most important commercial chemicals, with many uses in production and manufacturing. Chemists classify sulfuric acid as a strong mineral acid. Its chemical formula is H_2SO_4.

Sulfuric acid is one of the strongest acids. It can burn

the skin and irritate the lining of the nose, *trachea* (windpipe), and lungs. Safety standards established by the United States government protect industrial workers from overexposure to the acid or its fumes.

Uses and properties. Sulfuric acid is used chiefly in the manufacture of fertilizer. Manufacturers of petroleum products use sulfuric acid in the refining of petroleum. Other manufacturers use it in the production of such items as automobile batteries, explosives, pigments, iron and other metals, and paper pulp.

The chemical industry uses sulfuric acid in producing many kinds of organic chemicals. For example, it is used in making alcohol from ethylene. Sulfuric acid reacts with benzene and other compounds to make *sulfonates,* which are used in powerful detergents. It is also used in making some dyes and medicines. The strength of sulfuric acid makes it useful in producing other acids and in removing soluble materials from minerals. Many metals dissolve in sulfuric acid and form *sulfates* (salts of the acid), which have important industrial uses (see **Sulfate**).

Sulfuric acid combines quickly with water. The strong chemical attraction of sulfuric acid to water enables it to remove hydrogen and oxygen, the components of water, from many substances. This property makes it useful as a dehydrating agent. The dehydrating action of sulfuric acid can be shown with sugar, which contains carbon, hydrogen, and oxygen. When the acid is poured on sugar, the mixture decomposes and turns into black, foamy carbon "charcoal."

Water and concentrated sulfuric acid react violently when they are combined, and the mixture becomes boiling hot. Small amounts of acid should be added slowly and carefully to water. Water should never be added to sulfuric acid. This action causes dangerous spattering.

Some sulfuric acid contains excess *sulfur trioxide,* a chemical that gives off gas when combined with moisture in the air. Chemists call this type of sulfuric acid *oleum* or *fuming sulfuric acid.* It is used in one of the methods of manufacturing sulfuric acid.

How sulfuric acid is made. Commercial preparation of sulfuric acid was first described in the 1600's. In the past, manufacturers mainly used the *lead-chamber method* to produce sulfuric acid. Today, the acid is primarily manufactured from sulfur by the *contact method.*

The lead-chamber method starts with the burning of sulfur to form sulfur dioxide. The sulfur dioxide then reacts with nitrogen compounds called *nitric oxides* in a lead-lined chamber, producing sulfuric acid. This process is inexpensive, but it produces relatively weak acid.

The contact method produces purer, more highly concentrated sulfuric acid than does the lead-chamber process. In the contact method, sulfur trioxide is made by passing *sulfur dioxide,* a colorless gas, through a heated reaction tube that contains either vanadium or platinum, each of which acts as a *catalyst* (see **Catalysis**). Next, the sulfur trioxide is dissolved in concentrated sulfuric acid, forming oleum. The oleum is added to water to produce sulfuric acid of any desired concentration.

Sulfuric acid can also be produced from sulfur dioxide obtained as a by-product of *roasting* copper and iron pyrites and other sulfide ores. Roasting is a process used in separating and refining metal ores by heating the ores in air.

In the future, electric power plants that burn coal for fuel may provide a practical source of sulfuric acid. The acid could be produced from sulfur dioxide obtained by purifying gases released during coal combustion. But the many impurities in these gases make it difficult to collect sulfur dioxide in this manner. Also, the remote location of many power plants complicates the shipment of the highly corrosive sulfuric acid.   B. Meyer

See also **Acid; Sulfur.**

Sulgrave Manor is an estate in Northamptonshire, England, which is regarded as the home of George Washington's ancestors. The Washington family owned it from 1539 to 1610, when Robert Washington and his son Lawrence sold it. Lawrence Washington built the manor house in the 1500's. In 1914, the British government bought the house to celebrate 100 years of peace between the United Kingdom and the United States. The house is still fairly well preserved. American patriotic societies helped furnish and restore the building's interior.
Kathryn Kish Sklar

Sulla, Lucius Cornelius (138-78 B.C.), reformed the Roman government. He was the first Roman general to use his army against political foes. Later politicians, including Julius Caesar, followed this example.

Sulla was a member of a *patrician* (aristocratic) family. In 88 B.C., he was a *consul* (chief government official) and commander of a Roman army. When Mithridates VI, king of Pontus (in Asia Minor), attacked Roman lands in Asia, the Roman Senate put Sulla in command of an army to fight him. But the Roman Assembly overruled the Senate and voted the command to Gaius Marius. Sulla was driven out of Rome. He returned with his army, drove out Marius, and then went to fight Mithridates. In 87 and 86 B.C., Sulla attacked Athens, an ally of Pontus, and defeated two of Mithridates' armies. When Sulla entered Asia, Mithridates asked for and got peace.

Sulla hurried back to Rome because Marius and other leaders had returned and killed many of his supporters. Marius was dead when Sulla returned in 83 B.C., but Sulla fought and won a civil war against Marius' followers. As dictator from 82 to 79 B.C., Sulla reorganized the state. He destroyed the power of the *tribunes* (representatives of the people), and gave the Senate control of Rome. After Sulla retired in 79 B.C., most of his reforms were discarded.   Arther Ferrill

Sullivan, Anne Mansfield (1866-1936), became known as the teacher of Helen Keller, a deaf and blind woman who won international fame. Sullivan was born on April 14, 1866, in Feeding Hills, near Springfield, Massachusetts. She had visual problems as a child and in 1880 became a student at the Perkins Institution for the Blind in Boston (now Perkins School for the Blind in Watertown, Massachusetts). At Perkins, she roomed with Laura Bridgman, the first deaf-blind person to be educated in the United States (see **Bridgman, Laura D.**). In 1881 and 1887, Sullivan underwent surgery that restored most of her vision.

In 1887, Sullivan went to Tuscumbia, Alabama, to become the private teacher of Helen Keller, who was nearly 7 years old. Sullivan first communicated with the girl through a manual alphabet by which she spelled out words on Helen's hands. She also taught Helen to read and write braille. In 1900, she accompanied Keller to Radcliffe College and spent four years there translating lectures for Helen by manual communication.

In 1904, Sullivan married John A. Macy, then an editor and a Harvard University instructor. But she and Keller remained together. The two women traveled widely and made lecture tours. The film *The Miracle Worker* (1962) deals with Sullivan's difficulties in communicating with the young Keller before finally breaking through. Sullivan died on Oct. 20, 1936.   Kenneth A. Stuckey

See also **Keller, Helen.**

Sullivan, Sir Arthur Seymour (1842-1900), was an English composer and conductor best known for a series of comic operettas he wrote with the English playwright Sir William Gilbert. Sullivan also won recognition for several hymns, notably the familiar "Onward, Christian Soldiers" (1871).

Sullivan was born on May 13, 1842, in London. He studied at the Royal Academy of Music in London and at the Leipzig Conservatory in Germany. In 1860 and 1861, while still a student, Sullivan wrote incidental music for William Shakespeare's play *The Tempest,* his first successful composition. Sullivan's first successful operetta was *Cox and Box* (1867). He began working with Gilbert in 1871. During his lifetime, Sullivan was considered the leading English composer. However, other than his operettas and hymns, none of his works have remained popular. Sullivan died on Nov. 22, 1900. For information about his collaboration with Gilbert, see **Gilbert and Sullivan.**   Katherine K. Preston

Sullivan, Harry Stack (1892-1949), was an American psychiatrist who believed that personality is formed by an individual's relationships with others. Sullivan called this the *interpersonal theory* of personality.

Sullivan's theory describes several stages of personality formation. In each stage, different interpersonal relationships determine how the individual's personality develops. For example, in infancy, the relationship with the mother counts the most. From ages 5 to 8, relationships with *peers* (friends and acquaintances) are the most important. In adolescence, relationships with members of the opposite sex have the greatest significance. During each stage, the individual learns to behave in a way that will enable him or her to deal successfully with the anxieties that arise from the relationships.

Sullivan was born in Norwich, New York, on Feb. 21, 1892. He graduated from the Chicago College of Medicine and Surgery in 1917 and served as head of the William Alanson White Psychiatric Foundation in Washington, D.C., from 1933 to 1943. In 1948, he helped to found the World Federation for Mental Health. Sullivan died on Jan. 14, 1949.   Hannah S. Decker

Sullivan, John L. (1858-1918), was a famous American heavyweight boxing champion. He was the last boxer to win the heavyweight championship fighting with bare knuckles. Sullivan won the heavyweight title by knocking out Paddy Ryan in 1882. He successfully defended his crown against Charley Mitchell in 1888 and Jake Kilrain in 1889. The Sullivan-Kilrain fight lasted 75 rounds and

Culver Pictures
John L. Sullivan

was the last bare-knuckle championship bout. Thereafter, all championship bouts were fought under the *Queensberry Rules,* which require the use of boxing gloves. Sullivan popularized the use of gloves during exhibition tours of the United States. He lost the heavyweight title to James J. Corbett in 1892, his only defeat.

John Lawrence Sullivan was born on Oct. 12, 1858, in Roxbury, Massachusetts. He began his boxing career in 1878. He died on Feb. 2, 1918.   Bert Randolph Sugar

See also **Boxing** (From bare knuckles to gloves).

Sullivan, Leon Howard (1922-2001), was a Baptist minister and civil rights leader who organized economic self-help programs for African Americans. In 1971, Sullivan became the first black member of the board of directors of General Motors Corporation. He worked to hire and train black men and women for jobs at all levels throughout the company and to improve its economic ties to blacks and black-owned businesses.

Sullivan was born on Oct. 16, 1922, in Charleston, West Virginia. He began his programs in the 1950's. He regarded unemployment as the basic cause of black juvenile delinquency. In 1959, he led 400 black ministers and their congregations in starting what turned out to be a three-year boycott of about 30 Philadelphia companies. These firms had refused to hire blacks but opened many jobs to them as a result of the boycott.

In 1964, Sullivan founded the Opportunities Industrialization Center (OIC) in Philadelphia to provide training and job placement for minority groups. OIC has trained thousands of workers and has opened centers in more than 100 United States cities and eight African countries. In 1965, Sullivan founded Zion Investment Associates. He persuaded members of his Zion Baptist Church—and later other blacks—to give this corporation $10 a month for three years to establish black businesses. The corporation built and managed an apartment complex, a shopping center, a garment manufacturing company, and other businesses—all in Philadelphia. In 1981, Sullivan helped establish the International Foundation for Education and Self-Help. This organization works to reduce hunger and illiteracy, and to promote health care and economic development, in developing nations.

In 1977, Sullivan began a campaign to help end *apartheid,* the South African government's policy of rigid racial segregation. He asked United States companies operating in South Africa to follow a code that became known as the *Sullivan Principles.* This code, in part, required employers to ban segregation in workplaces and use more nonwhite managers. About 130 U.S. firms agreed to follow the principles. But the code did little to end apartheid. As a result, in 1987, Sullivan urged U.S. firms to leave South Africa. The firms that had followed the principles then left the country. In 1991, the South African government repealed the last of the laws that had formed the legal basis of apartheid. In 1993, it set a date for South Africa's first national elections in which blacks could vote. Sullivan then began to urge U.S. companies to invest in South Africa.   Edgar Allan Toppin

Sullivan, Louis Henri (1856-1924), was one of the greatest American architects. Sullivan's influence comes from the quality and originality of his designs and his perceptive writings on architectural theory. He was a leader in the Chicago School of architecture. The architect Frank Lloyd Wright worked briefly for Sullivan and

Guaranty Building (1894-1895); Patricia Layman Bazelon

Sullivan's Guaranty Building in Buffalo, New York, is an early example of a skyscraper. The horizontal rows of windows and thin vertical columns create patterns of harmonious simplicity.

credited him with enormous influence.

More than any other American architect of the 1800's, Sullivan united the major threads of architecture and engineering with broad theories of nature and social change. Sullivan considered the creation of a building more than a problem of design, a solution of practical needs, or the development of a structural scheme. To him, a building was the expression of a view of humanity, nature, and society. He used ornament, design, utility, and structure to express his philosophy. Sullivan popularized the phrase "form follows function." He argued that function meant more than satisfying practical needs or arriving at a logical structure. Sullivan declared that a building should be organic—that is, it should express a

© Louis Bunde, Unicorn Stock Photos

Late Sullivan works include small Midwestern banks and office buildings. One of his finest designs of the early 1900's is the National Farmers' Bank, *shown here,* in Owatonna, Minnesota.

person's view of nature and society in the broadest sense. He intended his architecture as a fulfillment of the American spirit of progress and democracy.

Sullivan was born on Sept. 3, 1856, in Boston. From 1873 to 1875, he studied architecture in Philadelphia, Chicago, and Paris. He finally settled in Chicago and joined the firm of Dankmar Adler in 1879. He became a full partner in 1881. Sullivan and Adler seem to have had an ideal relationship. Sullivan was responsible for designing buildings, and Adler concentrated on solving engineering problems and obtaining clients. Their Chicago Auditorium Building (1889) is considered Sullivan's first original design. Sullivan also designed the Wainwright Building (1891) in St. Louis, Missouri. It was one of the first buildings to clearly express the vertical thrust of a skyscraper. In a later skyscraper, the Guaranty Building (1895) in Buffalo, New York, the vertical forces were expressed in ornamental details as a giant vine that climbs over the top cornice.

Sullivan and Adler separated in 1895, and Sullivan's business success as an architect declined rapidly. After about 1900, he got only a few commissions for small Midwestern banks and office buildings. These buildings rank among Sullivan's finest creations. During his later years, Sullivan concentrated much of his effort on writing. His most notable works include *Kindergarten Chats* (1901-1902, revised in 1918) and *The Autobiography of an Idea* (1924). He died on April 14, 1924.   Nicholas Adams

See also **Adler, Dankmar; Architecture** (Early modern architecture in America).

Additional resources

Morrison, Hugh. *Louis Sullivan.* 1935. Reprint. Norton, 1998. A classic biography with updates.
Twombly, Robert C. *Louis Sullivan.* Viking, 1986. A standard biography.

Sullivan, Louis Wade (1933-   ), was United States secretary of health and human services from 1989 to 1993 under President George H. W. Bush. He was the second African American to hold that office. The first was Patricia R. Harris, who served from 1979 to 1981. Before becoming secretary of health and human services, he was president of the Morehouse School of Medicine.

Sullivan was born on Nov. 3, 1933, in Atlanta, Georgia. He graduated with a B.S. degree from Morehouse College in 1954. In 1958, he earned an M.D. degree from Boston University. From 1963 to 1975, Sullivan taught at the Harvard Medical School, the New Jersey College of Medicine, and the Boston University School of Medicine. From 1972 to 1975, he also conducted research on sickle cell anemia. In 1975, Sullivan returned to Morehouse College as a professor of biology and medicine. That year, he founded the Morehouse School of Medicine and became its president.   Lee Thornton

Sully, *SUHL ee,* **Thomas** (1783-1872), an American painter, was noted for his elegant portraits. Sully portrayed women in refined poses and fashionable costumes and with beautiful complexions. He painted elegant but sturdier portraits of men. A portrait painted by Sully is reproduced in the **Adams, John Quincy,** article.

Sully was born on June 19, 1783, in Horncastle, England, and moved to America when he was 9. He began studying painting when he was about 12. In 1808, Sully settled in Philadelphia, where he soon became the leading portrait painter. He visited London in 1809 and 1810,

Oil painting on canvas (1820); Museum of Fine Arts, Boston

The Torn Hat by Thomas Sully is a study of this American artist's son. The winsome face, torn hat, and simple charm of the boy have made this a favorite among paintings of children.

and met the painters Benjamin West and Sir Thomas Lawrence, who greatly influenced his style. Sully died on Nov. 5, 1872.   Elizabeth Garrity Ellis

Sully Prudhomme, *soo LEE proo DAWM* (1839-1907), a French poet, won the first Nobel Prize in literature in 1901. He wrote several collections of poetry from 1865 to 1888, to considerable acclaim. His poetry can be divided into two periods. His earlier verse is lyrical and melancholy. Poems from this period include "The Broken Vase," his best-known poem, from *Stances et poèmes* (1865), and "The Swan" from *Les Solitudes* (1869). His second period reflects philosophical and scientific concerns. Many critics consider these poems less successful. His later works include *La Justice* (1878) and *Le Bonheur* (1888). Sully Prudhomme died on Sept. 7, 1907.

Sully Prudhomme was born on March 16, 1839, in Paris. His real name was René François Armand Prudhomme. He studied law, philosophy, and science, but decided to become a poet.   Jean-Pierre Cauvin

Sulphur. See Sulfur.

Sultan is a title given to some Muslim rulers. The title of sultan has been used since about A.D. 1000. In the past, it described Muslim rulers with complete political and military power. The Turkish rulers of the Seljuk and Ottoman empires were called sultans. Today, sultan is used as a title of honor for some Muslim rulers, though many of them have little real power. See also **Ottoman Empire** (Government).   Justin McCarthy

Sulu Sea, *SOO loo,* lies between the Philippine Islands and Borneo. The sea is also called the Sea of Mindoro. The Sulu Sea is surrounded by the Visayan Islands on the northeast, the island of Palawan on the northwest, Borneo on the southwest, and the Sulu Archipelago and the island of Mindanao on the southeast (see **Philippines** [map]). The sea has an average depth of 14,600 feet (4,450 meters).   David A. Ross

Sulzberger, *SUHLZ bur guhr,* **Arthur Hays** (1891-1968), was the publisher of *The New York Times* from 1935 to 1961. He succeeded his father-in-law, Adolph S. Ochs (see **Ochs, Adolph S.**).

Under Sulzberger's leadership, the *Times* printed more editorials and technological articles than ever before and expanded its news coverage and analysis. The daily circulation of the *Times* increased by about 40 percent, and the Sunday circulation nearly doubled.

Sulzberger was born on Sept. 12, 1891, in New York City. He joined the *Times* in 1918 as an assistant to the general manager. He was a vice president before becoming publisher. He also became chairman of the board in 1957 and held that post until his death on Dec. 11, 1968.   Daniel W. Pfaff

Sulzberger, *SUHLZ bur guhr,* **Arthur Ochs** (1926-), was the publisher of *The New York Times* from 1963 until his retirement in 1992. Under his leadership, the *Times* modernized its layout and type style and added several regular feature sections to increase its appeal to both advertisers and readers. In 1980, the *Times* began a national edition. In 1973, Sulzberger was elected chairman of the newspaper's parent firm, the New York Times Company. He remained chairman after retiring as publisher. Sulzberger was succeeded as publisher by his son, Arthur Ochs Sulzberger, Jr.

Arthur Ochs Sulzberger was born on Feb. 5, 1926, in New York City. He served as an assistant treasurer of the *Times* before becoming its publisher. His grandfather Adolph S. Ochs was publisher of the *Times* from 1896 to 1935. Sulzberger's father, Arthur Hays Sulzberger, served as publisher from 1935 to 1961.   Daniel W. Pfaff

Sumac, *SOO mak* or *SHOO mak,* is the name of a group of small trees and shrubs in the cashew family. Some kinds of sumacs are poisonous, but many kinds are nonpoisonous and have commercial uses. Some species found in eastern Asia are important sources of natural lacquers and waxes. Other species provide tannin, a substance used in tanning and dyeing.

There are about 120 species of nonpoisonous sumacs. They grow in regions with mild or subtropical climates. About 15 species are found in North America. These sumacs have long leaves that consist of numerous leaflets. The flowers grow in dense clusters at the ends of twigs. The small, berrylike fruits are mostly red in color. Most North American sumacs are shrubs and grow rapidly. They form dense thickets that provide important cover for wildlife. The fruits, twigs, and leaves also provide food for animals. Sumac tea is made from the berries of some species. The leaves of species in eastern North America turn bright red or orange in autumn.

One of the best-known North American sumacs is the *staghorn sumac.* This shrub or small tree is common in the Great Lakes region and the Northeast. It grows up to 30 feet (9 meters) high. It takes its name from the young branches, which resemble deer antlers in the velvet stage. Other common North American sumacs include the *smooth sumac* and the *shining sumac,* both found in the eastern part of the United States. The smooth sumac

© Joy Spurr, Bruce Coleman Inc.

The sumac has dark green leaves that turn brilliant colors in fall. The leaves and bark of some sumacs have commercial uses.

also grows in parts of the West.

Twenty-two species of poisonous sumacs grow in Asia and North America. Oils in their sap cause rashes and *dermatitis* (skin inflammation). Some people are sensitive to the poisons and suffer pain. The entire plant is poisonous. Even indirect contact can cause poisoning.

The *poison sumac,* also known as *poison elder* or *swamp sumac,* is found in bogs and swamps, especially in the Atlantic Coast and Great Lakes regions. It grows up to 25 feet (8 meters) tall. Its berries are white or yellowish and grow in drooping clusters.   Michael J. Baranski

See also **Poison ivy.**

Scientific classification. Sumacs belong to the cashew family, Anacardiaceae. Nonpoisonous sumacs are in the genus *Rhus.* Poisonous sumacs belong to the genus *Toxicodendron* or *Rhus.* The staghorn sumac is *R. typhina;* the shining sumac, *R. copallina;* and the smooth sumac, *R. glabra.* The poison sumac is *T. vernix* or *R. vernix.*

Sumatra, *soo MAH truh,* is an island in western Indonesia and the sixth largest island in the world. It covers an area of 186,253 square miles (482,393 square kilometers). Sumatra lies on the eastern edge of the Indian Ocean. For location, see **Indonesia** (map).

Sumatra has many ethnic groups, but the four largest are the Acehnese, Batak, Malay, and Minangkabau. The Acehnese live in Aceh, on the northern tip of the island. They are mostly Muslim, as are the Malay and Minangkabau. The Malay inhabit the eastern coastal areas, and the Minangkabau are in west-central Sumatra. The Batak live in northern Sumatra and are mostly Christian.

The Barisan Mountains stand along Sumatra's western coast. Monsoons control the climate. Rainfall is heaviest from December to February, and lightest from May to September. Animals on Sumatra include elephants, orangutans, tapirs, and tigers. Two of the world's largest flowers, the rafflesia and the titan arum, grow there. Natural gas and oil are important to the economy. Sumatra also produces coffee, palm oil, rubber, and tobacco.

Sumatra has been a trading center since at least the 600's, when Asian and Middle Eastern merchants traded there. European traders began arriving in the 1500's. The Dutch began to expand their empire into Sumatra in the early 1800's but did not defeat the Acehnese until 1903. During World War II (1939-1945), the Japanese occupied what is now Indonesia. After the war, Sumatrans fought against Dutch recolonization. In 1949, the Dutch recognized Indonesia's independence.

In the 1970's, the Free Aceh Movement began. Its supporters fought against central government forces for an independent Acehnese state. By 2004, over 15,000 people had died in the conflict. In December 2004, a powerful earthquake in the Indian Ocean near Sumatra generated a series of large waves called a *tsunami.* It killed more than 216,000 people, including more than 156,000 on Sumatra and nearby islands. The Indonesian government and Acehnese rebels declared an informal truce to allow aid to reach Aceh. They signed a peace agreement in 2005. As part of the agreement, the rebels gave up their weapons, and the government withdrew over 24,000 troops from Aceh.   Jeffrey Hadler

See also **Indonesia.**

Sumer, *SOO muhr,* an ancient region in southern Mesopotamia (now southeastern Iraq), was the birthplace of the world's first civilization. This civilization began about 3500 B.C. and flourished until about 2000 B.C. It was later absorbed by the great empires of Babylonia and Assyria. The Sumerians invented the world's first writing system, chiefly a set of word pictures. This system developed into a script called *cuneiform,* which used symbols composed of triangular marks. Cuneiform was used to write various languages throughout southwestern Asia during ancient times.

Way of life. The Sumerian civilization developed in the fertile plain formed by the Tigris and Euphrates rivers. The Sumerians built cities that had magnificent palaces and temples. The Sumerians built walls around their cities for protection against invaders.

Most Sumerians grew crops or raised livestock for a living. Sumer's dry climate prompted them to construct canals to irrigate their fields. The major crops were barley, wheat, dates, and vegetables. Sumerians also raised cattle, donkeys, sheep, and goats. Wool from the sheep was used to make textiles, the main export of the area.

Sumerians were accomplished craftworkers and traders. Many were skilled in metalwork or stonework even though nearly all stone and metal had to be imported. Textile workers wove fine cloth. Other craftworkers made jewelry, pottery, armor, and weapons. Traders carried their goods to nearby regions by land and by boat. Sumerian ships sailed to lands bordering the Persian Gulf to obtain ivory and other luxury items.

The Sumerians invented cuneiform about 3000 B.C. They made the cuneiform symbols by pressing a tool with a wedge-shaped tip into wet clay tablets. The tablets were then dried in the sun. Hundreds of thousands of these tablets have survived. They provide information about Sumerian politics, literature, economy, law, and religion. They also indicate that the Sumerians had knowledge of mathematics, astronomy, and medicine.

The Sumerians founded some of the earliest schools, mainly to train scribes. Scribes kept records for government offices, temples, and other institutions.

History. People had inhabited the Sumer region since the 5000's B.C. Scholars do not know where these people originally came from. Cities first developed in Sumer about 3500 B.C. Several Sumerian cities grew into independent city-states. The more powerful city-states conquered their neighbors and became small kingdoms, including Kish, Lagash, Umma, Ur, and

The University Museum, University of Pennsylvania

Giraudon/Art Resource

Sumerian cuneiform writing was invented about 3000 B.C. The Sumerians did most of their writing on clay tablets and stone slabs, many of which have been preserved. A detail of a clay tablet, *far left*, shows medical prescriptions. Cuneiform on a detail of a stone slab, *near left*, describes a military victory.

Uruk. During the 2300's B.C., Uruk controlled Sumer for a brief time until Sargon of Akkad conquered it. Shortly before 2100 B.C., Ur won control first of Sumer and then of nearby Assyria and Elam. But Semites, who may have come from the Arabian Peninsula, ruled Sumer for most of the period from 2300 until 539 B.C., when the Persians conquered the region. The Semites spoke languages related to Arabic and Hebrew, but they absorbed most of the traditions of Sumerian civilization.   John A. Brinkman

Related articles in *World Book* include:

Assyria
Babylonia
Clothing (Ancient times; picture: The kaunakes)
Cuneiform
Gilgamesh, Epic of
Sargon of Akkad
Ur
World, History of the (The Tigris-Euphrates Valley)

Summer is the warmest season of the year. The Northern Hemisphere has summer weather from late June through August. In the Southern Hemisphere, summer weather lasts from late December through February. People living in the tropics rarely consider summer a distinct season because the temperatures there change little from month to month. Summer's highest temperatures usually occur in the middle of each continent. Days of summerlike weather may also occur in mid-autumn, an event sometimes called *Indian summer.*

During summer in North America, warm winds carry moisture north from the Gulf of Mexico. These winds can bring warm, humid weather to much of the region east of the Rocky Mountains and as far north as Canada. In the southeastern United States, afternoon thunderstorms are common during summer.   Jon E. Ahlquist

See also **Indian summer; Season.**

Summons is an order *served* (delivered) by a sheriff or other officer of a court. It notifies a person that a complaint has been made and that the person must come to court to answer it. A summons may be used instead of an arrest for traffic violations or other minor offenses. If a person does not come to court, the court can have that person arrested. A summons also may be issued by other governmental bodies, such as congressional committees. See also **Subpoena; Writ.**   James O. Finckenauer

Sumner, Charles (1811-1874), was a famous statesman and antislavery leader in the United States. He helped found the Republican Party in 1854. He favored freeing the slaves and giving them the right to vote.

Sumner was born on Jan. 6, 1811, in Boston. He graduated from Harvard Law School in 1833. He joined the antislavery Free Soil Party in 1848 and was elected to the U.S. Senate from Massachusetts in 1851. Before the start of the American Civil War (1861-1865), Sumner opposed any compromise with the South on slavery. His Senate speeches were often directed at Southern senators. One speech in 1856 included sneering remarks about Senator Andrew P. Butler of South Carolina. Two days later, Representative Preston S. Brooks, a relative of Butler's, attacked Sumner in the Senate, beating him severely.

Sumner supported President Abraham Lincoln's policies during the Civil War. But he believed that Lincoln's reconstruction plans for the South did not protect the civil rights of blacks or guarantee against further rebellion by the South. For these same reasons, Sumner also opposed the postwar plans of President Andrew Johnson. Sumner died on March 11, 1874.   James E. Sefton

See also **Grant, Ulysses S.** (Foreign relations).

Sumner, William Graham (1840-1910), was an American sociologist known for his study of popular traditions and customs. Social groups unconsciously develop ways of doing things that are handed down from generation to generation. Such customs, which Sumner called *folkways,* include rules of etiquette and standards of personal grooming. Sumner used the Latin word *mores* (pronounced *MAWR ayz*) for folkways that reflect ideas of morality and that a society considers vital to its welfare. Mores include remaining loyal to one's country and preventing close relatives from intermarrying.

Sumner pointed out that folkways vary from society to society. Each society believes its own are the best and most natural. He called this attitude *ethnocentrism.*

Sumner was born on Oct. 30, 1840, in Paterson, New Jersey. He taught at Yale University. He introduced the ideas of folkways, mores, and ethnocentrism in his book *Folkways* (1906). He died April 12, 1910.   Irving M. Zeitlin

See also **Ethnocentrism; Mores; Social Darwinism.**

Sumptuary law, *SUHMP chu EHR ee.* The word *sumptuary* comes from a Latin word that means *expenditure.* In ancient Greece and Rome, laws limited the amount of money that anyone could spend on private luxuries. Laws of this kind were called *sumptuary laws.*

Similar laws have been common at various times in England, France, Scotland, Spain, and Italy. From the days of Edward III (1327-1377) until the Reformation in the early 1500's, the English Parliament restricted the number of courses of a meal to two, except on holidays. It also regulated the amount that members of each class of society could spend on clothes.   Douglas Greenberg

See also **Blue laws; Prohibition.**

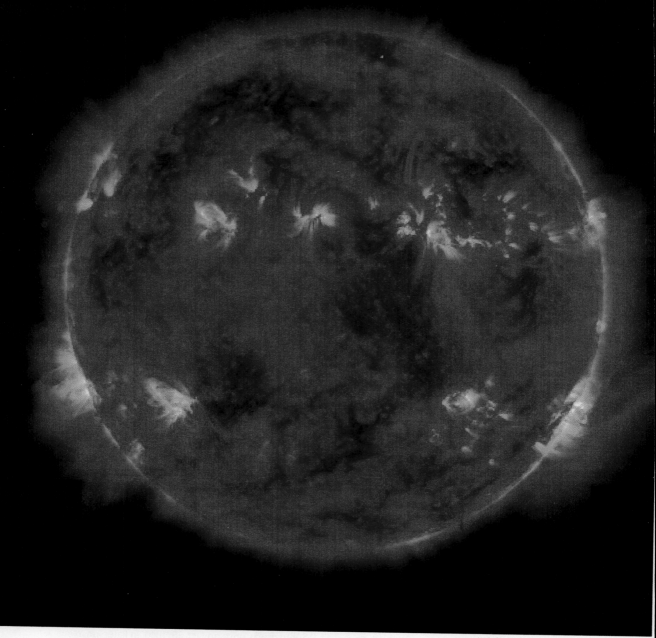

NASA/Transition Region & Coronal Explorer

The sun blazes with energy. On its surface, magnetic forces create loops and streams of gas that extend tens of thousands of miles or kilometers into space. This image was made by photographing ultraviolet radiation given off by atoms of iron gas that are hotter than 9 million °F (5 million °C).

Sun

Sun is a huge, glowing ball at the center of our solar system. The sun provides light, heat, and other energy to Earth. The sun is made up entirely of gas. Most of it is a type of gas that is sensitive to magnetism. This sensitiv-

The contributors of this article are Jay M. Pasachoff and Leon Golub. Pasachoff is Field Memorial Professor of Astronomy and Director of the Hopkins Observatory at Williams College. Golub is an astrophysicist at the Harvard-Smithsonian Center for Astrophysics.

ity makes this type of gas so unique that scientists sometimes give it a special name: *plasma.* The solar system's planets and their moons, tens of thousands of asteroids, and trillions of comets revolve around the sun. The sun and all these objects are in the solar system. Earth travels around the sun at an average distance of about 92,960,000 miles (149,600,000 kilometers) from it.

The sun is one of hundreds of billions of stars in the Milky Way Galaxy. It is about 25,000 *light-years* from the center of the galaxy, and it revolves around the galactic center once about every 240 million years. One light-year, the distance that light travels in a vacuum in a year, equals about 5.88 trillion miles (9.46 trillion kilometers).

The sun's *radius* (distance from its center to its surface) is about 432,000 miles (695,500 kilometers), approximately 109 times Earth's radius. The following example may help you picture the relative sizes of the sun and Earth and the distance between them: Suppose Earth were the size of a man. The sun would be roughly the size of a 60-story building, and the sun would be about 13 miles (21 kilometers) from Earth.

The part of the sun that we see has a temperature of about 5500 °C (10,000 °F). Astronomers measure star temperatures in a metric unit called the *kelvin* (abbreviated K). One kelvin equals exactly 1 Celsius degree (1.8 Fahrenheit degrees), but the Kelvin and Celsius scales begin at different points. The Kelvin scale starts at absolute zero, which is −273.15 °C (−459.67 °F). Thus, the temperature of the solar surface is about 5800 K. Temperatures in the sun's core reach over 15 million K.

The energy of the sun comes from *nuclear fusion reactions* that occur deep inside the sun's core. In a fusion reaction, two atomic nuclei join together, creating a new nucleus. Fusion produces energy by converting nuclear matter into energy.

The sun, like Earth, is magnetic. Scientists describe the magnetism of an object in terms of a *magnetic field*. This field is a region that includes all the space occupied by the object and much of the surrounding space. Physicists define a magnetic field as the region in which a magnetic force can be detected—as with a compass. Physicists describe how magnetic an object is in terms of *field strength*. Field strength is a measure of the force that the field would exert on a magnetic object, such as a compass needle. The typical strength of the sun's field is only about twice that of Earth's field.

But the sun's magnetic field becomes highly concentrated in small regions, with strengths up to 3,000 times as great as the typical strength. These regions shape solar matter to create a variety of features on the sun's surface and in its *atmosphere*, the part that we can see. These features range from relatively cool, dark structures known as *sunspots* to spectacular eruptions called *flares* and *coronal mass ejections*.

Flares are the most violent eruptions in the solar system. Coronal mass ejections, though less violent than flares, involve a tremendous *mass* (amount of matter). A single ejection can spew approximately 20 billion tons (18 billion metric tons) of matter into space. A cube of lead $\frac{3}{4}$ mile (1.2 kilometers) on a side would have about the same mass.

The sun was born about 4.6 billion years ago. It has enough nuclear fuel to remain much as it is for another 5 billion years. Then it will grow to become a type of star called a *red giant*. Later in the sun's life, it will cast off its outer layers. The remaining core will collapse to become an object called a *white dwarf* and will slowly fade. The sun will enter its final phase as a faint, cool object sometimes called a *black dwarf*.

Characteristics of the sun

Mass and density. The sun has 99.8 percent of the mass in the solar system. The sun's mass is roughly 2×10^{27} tons. This number would be written out as a 2 followed by 27 zeros. The sun is 333,000 times as massive as Earth. The sun's average density is about 90 pounds per cubic foot (1.4 grams per cubic centimeter).

The sun at a glance

Distance from Earth: *Shortest,* about 91,400,000 miles (147,100,000 kilometers); *longest,* about 94,500,000 miles (152,100,000 kilometers); *average,* about 92,960,000 miles (149,600,000 kilometers). Sunlight takes about 8 minutes to reach Earth, traveling at 186,282 miles (299,792 kilometers) per second.

Radius, distance from the sun's center to its surface: About 432,000 miles (695,500 kilometers), approximately 109 times the radius of Earth.

Volume: About 33×10^{16} cubic miles. This number would be written out as 33 followed by 16 zeroes. It is equivalent to 14×10^{17} cubic kilometers and is 1,300,000 times the volume of Earth.

Mass, amount of matter: About 2×10^{27} tons or metric tons. The sun's mass makes up 99.8 percent of the mass of the solar system and is about 333,000 times as great as the mass of Earth.

Density: *Average,* about 90 pounds per cubic foot (1.4 grams per cubic centimeter), roughly 1.4 times the density of water; *core,* about 100 times the density of water; *radiative zone,* about equal to the density of water; *convection zone,* about $\frac{1}{10}$ the density of water.

Temperature: *Surface,* about 5800 kelvins (5500 °C or 10,000 °F); *core,* more than 15 million kelvins (15 million °C, or 27 million °F).

Age: About 4,600,000,000 years.

Chemical makeup: By mass, hydrogen, about 72 percent; helium, approximately 26 percent; other elements, roughly 2 percent. By number of atoms, hydrogen, about 94 percent; helium, about 6 percent; other elements, about 0.1 percent.

Luminosity, the rate at which the sun sends out energy: About 4×10^{26} watts.

Solar constant, the amount of energy from the sun that arrives at the top of Earth's atmosphere: About 1,370 watts per square meter.

Rotation period: About 25 days at the equator; about 28 days at higher latitudes.

Revolution period (in the Milky Way Galaxy): About 250 million years.

This density is about 1.4 times that of water and less than one-third of Earth's average density.

Composition. The sun, like most other stars, is made up mostly of atoms of the chemical element hydrogen. The second most plentiful element in the sun is helium, and almost all the remaining matter consists of atoms of seven other elements. For every 1 million atoms of hydrogen in the entire sun, there are 98,000 atoms of helium, 850 of oxygen, 360 of carbon, 120 of neon, 110 of nitrogen, 40 of magnesium, 35 of iron, and 35 of silicon. So about 94 percent of the atoms are hydrogen, and 0.1 percent are elements other than hydrogen and helium.

But hydrogen is the lightest of all elements, and so it accounts for only about 72 percent of the mass. Helium makes up around 26 percent.

The inside of the sun and most of its atmosphere consist of plasma. Plasma is basically a gas whose temperature has been raised to such a high level that it becomes sensitive to magnetism. Scientists sometimes emphasize the difference in behavior between plasma and other gas. They say that plasma is a fourth state of matter, alongside solid, liquid, and gas. But in general, scientists make the distinction between plasma and gas only when technically necessary.

The essential difference between plasma and other gas is an effect of the temperature increase: This in-

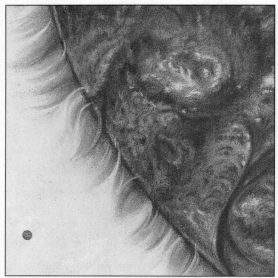

WORLD BOOK illustration by Roberta Polfus

The sun is much larger than Earth. From the sun's center to its surface, it is about 109 times the radius of Earth. Some of the streams of gas rising from the solar surface are larger than Earth.

crease has made the gas atoms come apart. What is left—the plasma—consists of electrically charged atoms called *ions* and electrically charged particles called *electrons* that move about independently.

An electrically neutral atom contains one or more electrons that act as though they form a shell or shells around the atom's central region, its nucleus. Each electron carries a single unit of negative electric charge. Deep inside the atom is the nucleus, which has almost all the atom's mass. The simplest nucleus, that of the most common form of hydrogen, consists of a single particle known as a *proton*. A proton carries a single unit of positive electric charge. All other nuclei have one or more protons and one or more *neutrons*. A neutron carries no net charge, and so every nucleus is electrically positive. But a neutral atom has as many electrons as protons. The net electric charge of a neutral atom is therefore zero.

An atom or molecule that comes apart by losing one or more electrons has a positive charge and is called an ion or, sometimes, a *positive ion*. Most of the atoms inside the sun are positive ions of the most common form of hydrogen. Thus, most of the sun consists of single protons and independent electrons.

The relative amounts of plasma and other gas in a given part of the solar atmosphere depends on the temperature. As the temperature increases, more and more atoms become ionized, and the atoms that are ionized lose more and more electrons. The highest part of the solar atmosphere, called the *corona*, is strongly ionized. The corona's temperature is usually about 3 million to 5 million K, more than enough to strip away over half the 26 electrons in its iron atoms.

How much of a gas is made up of single atoms and how much of molecules also depends upon its temperature. If the gas is relatively hot, the atoms will move about independently. But if the gas is relatively cool, its

atoms may *bond* (combine chemically), creating molecules. Much of the sun's surface consists of a gas of single atoms. But sunspots are so cool that some of their atoms can bond to form molecules.

The remainder of this article follows the general practice of scientists by referring to both plasma and other gas simply as *gas.*

Energy output. Most of the energy *emitted* (sent out) by the sun is visible light and a related form of radiation known as *infrared rays,* which we feel as heat. Visible light and infrared rays are two forms of *electromagnetic radiation.* The sun also emits *particle radiation,* made up mostly of protons and electrons.

Electromagnetic radiation consists of electrical and magnetic energy. The radiation can be thought of as waves of energy or as particlelike "packets" of energy called *photons.*

Visible light, infrared rays, and other forms of electromagnetic radiation differ in their energy. Six bands of energy span the entire *spectrum* (range) of electromagnetic energy. From the least energetic to the most energetic, they are: radio waves, infrared rays, visible light, ultraviolet rays, X rays, and gamma rays. Microwaves, which are high-energy radio waves, are sometimes con-

Sun terms

Core is the center of the sun, where nuclear fusion reactions produce the sun's energy.
Corona is the highest part of the solar atmosphere.
Coronal mass ejection is a large-scale eruption of material from the corona into interplanetary space.
Electromagnetic radiation is a flow of electric and magnetic energy. Visible light is a form of electromagnetic radiation.
Electromagnetic spectrum is the entire band of electromagnetic radiation, including radio waves, infrared rays, visible light, ultraviolet rays, X rays, and gamma rays.
Flare is a sudden brightening of a part of the sun's atmosphere.
Helioseismology is the study of the vibrations inside the sun.
Kelvin, abbreviated K, is the unit in which astronomers measure the temperature of the sun and other stars. One kelvin equals 1 Celsius degree (1.8 Fahrenheit degrees). A temperature of 0 K equals −273.15 °C (−459.67 °F).
Magnetic field is a region in which magnetic force can be detected, as with a compass.
Magnetic field lines are imaginary lines that define the strength, shape, and direction of a magnetic field.
Mass is the amount of matter in an object.
Nuclear fusion reaction is a process that produces energy in the sun's core. In a nuclear fusion reaction, two atomic nuclei join to create a new, larger nucleus.
Photon is a "packet" of electromagnetic radiation.
Photosphere is the lowest layer of the solar atmosphere. The photosphere sends out the light that we see.
Plasma is a substance similar to a gas. A plasma consists of positive ions and of electrons that move about independently.
Positive ion is an atom that has lost one or more of its electrons, giving it a positive electric charge.
Solar activity includes such phenomena as sunspots, flares, and coronal mass ejections.
Solar atmosphere consists of the visible layers of the sun.
Solar wind is the continual flow of protons and electrons from the corona.
Spectrum is a band or range of energy of a particular kind. For example, the visible spectrum is the band of the energy of the electromagnetic radiation that we can see. *Spectrum* also means the display of the colors in visible light when they are separated and spread out, as by a prism.
Sunspot is a dark, often roughly circular feature on the sun's surface.

sidered to be a separate band. The sun emits radiation of each type in the spectrum.

The amount of energy in electromagnetic waves is directly related to their *wavelength,* the distance between successive wave crests. The more energetic the radiation, the shorter the wavelength. For example, gamma rays have shorter wavelengths than radio waves. The energy in an individual photon is related to the position of the photon in the spectrum. For instance, a gamma ray photon has more energy than a photon of radio energy.

All forms of electromagnetic radiation travel through space at the same speed, commonly known as the *speed of light:* 186,282 miles (299,792 kilometers) per second. At this rate, a photon emitted by the sun takes only about 8 minutes to reach Earth.

The amount of electromagnetic radiation from the sun that reaches the top of Earth's atmosphere is known as the *solar constant.* This amount is about 1,370 watts per square meter. But only about 40 percent of the energy in this radiation reaches Earth's surface. The atmosphere blocks some of the visible and infrared radiation, almost all the ultraviolet rays, and all the X rays and gamma rays. But nearly all the radio energy reaches Earth's surface.

Particle radiation. Protons and electrons flow continually outward from the sun in all directions as the *solar wind.* These particles come close to Earth, but Earth's magnetic field prevents them from reaching the surface.

However, more intense concentrations of particles from flares and coronal mass ejections on the sun reach Earth's atmosphere. These particles are known as *solar cosmic rays.* Most of them are protons, but they also include heavier nuclei as well as electrons. They are extremely energetic. As a result, they can be hazardous to astronauts in orbit or to orbiting satellites.

The cosmic rays cannot reach Earth's surface. When they collide with atoms at the top of the atmosphere, they change into a shower of less energetic particles. But, because the solar events are so energetic, they can create *geomagnetic storms,* major disturbances in Earth's magnetic field. The storms, in turn, can disrupt electrical equipment on Earth's surface. For example, they can overload power lines, leading to blackouts.

Color. In the visible-light band of the electromagnetic spectrum are all the colors of the rainbow. Sunlight consists of all these colors. Most solar radiation comes to us in the yellow-green part of the visible spectrum, but sunlight is white. When the atmosphere acts as a filter for the setting sun, the sun may look yellow or orange.

You can view the colors in sunlight by using a prism to separate and spread them out. Red light, which is produced by the radiation with the least energy per photon—and the longest waves—will be at one end of the spectrum. The red light will gradually shade into orange light, which, in turn, will shade into yellow light. Next to yellow will be green, and then will come blue. In some lists of the colors of the rainbow, indigo comes after blue. The last color will be violet, produced by the radiation with the most energy per photon—and the shortest waves. Such color listings are not meant to indicate that sunlight has only six or seven colors. Each shading is itself a color. Nature produces many more colors than people have ever named.

Rotation. The sun makes a complete rotation in about a month. But because the sun is a gaseous body rather than a solid one, different parts of the sun rotate at different rates. Gas near the sun's equator takes about 25 days to rotate once, while gas at higher latitudes may take slightly more than 28 days. The sun's axis of rotation is tilted by a few degrees from the axis of Earth's orbit. Thus, either the sun's north geographic pole or its south geographic pole is usually visible from Earth.

Vibration. The sun vibrates like a bell that is continually struck. But the sun produces more than 10 million individual "tones" at the same time. The vibrations of the solar gas are mechanically similar to the vibrations of air—also a gas—that we know as sound waves. Astronomers therefore refer to the solar waves as sound waves, though the vibrations are much too slow for us to hear. The fastest solar vibrations have a *period* of about 2 minutes. A vibration's period is the amount of time taken for a complete *cycle* of vibration—one back-and-forth movement of the vibrating object. The slowest vibration that a human being can hear has a period of about $\frac{1}{20}$ of a second.

Most of the sun's sound waves originate in *convection cells*—large concentrations, or clumps, of gas beneath the surface. These cells carry energy to the surface by rising, just as water boiling in a pan rises to the surface. The word *convection* refers to the boiling motions of the cells. As the cells rise, they cool. They then fall back down to the level at which the upward motion started. As the cells fall, they vibrate violently. The vibrations cause sound waves to move out from the cells.

Because the sun's atmosphere has so little mass, sound waves cannot travel through it. Therefore, when a wave reaches the surface, it turns back inward. As a result, a bit of the surface bobs up and down. As the wave travels inward, it begins to curve back toward the surface. The amount by which it curves depends on the density of the gas through which it travels and other factors. Eventually, the wave reaches the surface and turns inward again. It continues to travel until it loses all its energy to the surrounding gas.

The waves that travel downward the greatest distance have the longest periods. Some of these waves approach the sun's core and have periods of several hours.

Magnetic field. Some of the time, the sun's magnetic field has a simple overall shape. At other times, the field is extremely complex. The simple field resembles the field that would be present if the sun's axis of rotation were a huge bar magnet. You can see the shape of a bar magnet's field by conducting an experiment with iron filings. Place a sheet of paper on a bar magnet and then sprinkle iron filings on the paper. The filings will form a pattern that reveals the shape of the magnetic field. Many of the filings will gather in D-shaped loops that connect the ends of the magnet. For an illustration of these loops, see **Magnetism** (picture: A magnetic field).

Physicists define the field in terms of imaginary lines that give rise to the loops of filings. These lines are called *field lines, flux lines,* or *lines of force.* Scientists assign these lines a direction, and the bar magnet is said to have a *magnetic north pole* at one end and a *magnetic south pole* at the other end. The field lines go out of the magnet from the north pole, loop around, and return to the magnet at the south pole.

The cause of the sun's magnetic field is, in part, the movement of the convection cells. Any electrically charged object can create a magnetic field simply by moving. The convection cells, which are composed of positive ions and electrons, circulate in a way that helps create the solar field.

When the sun's magnetic field becomes complex, field lines resemble a kinked, twisted garden hose. The field kinks and twists for two reasons: (1) The sun rotates more rapidly at the equator than at higher latitudes, and (2) the inner parts of the sun rotate more rapidly than the surface. The differences in rotational speed stretch field lines in an easterly direction. Eventually, the lines become so distorted that the kinks and twists develop.

In some areas, the field is thousands of times stronger than the overall magnetic field. In these places, clusters of field lines break through the surface, creating loops in the solar atmosphere. At one end of the loop, the breakthrough point is a magnetic north pole. At this point, the direction of the field lines is upward—that is, away from the interior. At the other end of the loop, the breakthrough point is a magnetic south pole, and the lines point downward. A sunspot forms at each point. The field lines guide ions and electrons into the space above the sunspots, producing gigantic loops of gas.

The number of sunspots on the sun depends on the amount of distortion in the field. The change in this number, from a minimum to a maximum and back to a minimum, is known as the *sunspot cycle*. The average period of the sunspot cycle is about 11 years.

At the end of a sunspot cycle, the magnetic field quickly reverses its polarity and loses most of its distortion. Suppose the sun's magnetic north pole and its geographic north pole were at the same place at the start of a given cycle. At the beginning of the next cycle, the magnetic north pole would be at the same place as the geographic south pole. A change of polarity from one orientation to the other and back again equals the periods of two successive sunspot cycles and is therefore about 22 years.

Nuclear fusion can occur in the core of the sun because the core is tremendously hot and dense. Because nuclei have a positive charge, they tend to repel one another. But the core's temperature and density are high enough to force nuclei together.

The most common fusion process in the sun is called the *proton-proton chain*. This process begins when nuclei of the simplest form of hydrogen—single protons—are forced together one at a time. First, a nucleus with two particles forms, then a nucleus with three particles, and finally a nucleus with four particles. The process also produces an electrically neutral particle called a *neutrino*.

The final nucleus consists of two protons and two neutrons, a nucleus of the most common form of helium. The mass of this nucleus is slightly less than the mass of the four protons from which it forms. The lost mass is converted into energy. The amount of energy can be calculated from an equation discovered by the German-born physicist Albert Einstein: $E = mc^2$. In this equation, the symbol E represents the energy; m, the mass that is converted; and c^2, the speed of light *squared* (multiplied by itself).

Comparison with other stars. Fewer than 5 percent of the stars in the Milky Way are brighter or more massive than the sun. But some stars are more than 100,000

© National Optical Astronomy Observatories

The main mirror at the McMath-Pierce Telescope Facility is a *heliostat mirror* 82 inches (208 centimeters) in diameter. The mirror is mounted on a frame that weighs 27 tons (24 metric tons).

© National Optical Astronomy Observatories

The McMath-Pierce Telescope Facility has the largest telescope structure on Earth. A mirror mounted on a tower reflects sunlight down a diagonal shaft to underground laboratories. The shaft is about 500 feet (170 meters) long, and most of it is underground. The facility is at Kitt Peak, Arizona, near Tucson.

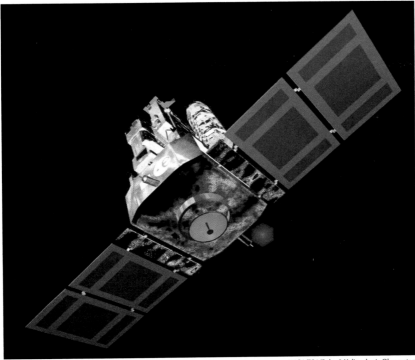

NASA/ESA/Solar & Heliospheric Observatory

An orbiting solar telescope known as the Solar and Heliospheric Observatory (SOHO) studies the sun's interior, its atmosphere, and the *solar wind,* a stream of electrically charged particles that flow from the sun's surface. The European Space Agency launched the telescope in 1995. NASA provided some of SOHO's scientific equipment.

times as bright as the sun, and some have as much as 100 times the sun's mass. At the other extreme, some stars are less than $\frac{1}{10,000}$ as bright as the sun, and a small star can have as little as $\frac{7}{100}$ of the sun's mass. There are hotter stars, which are much bluer than the sun; and cooler stars, which are much redder.

The sun is a relatively young star, a member of a generation of stars known as *Population I* stars. An older generation of stars is called *Population II.* There may have existed an earlier generation, called *Population III.* However, no members of this generation are known. The remainder of this section refers to three generations of stars.

The three generations differ in their content of chemical elements heavier than helium. First-generation stars have the lowest percentage of these elements, and second-generation stars have a higher percentage. The sun and other third-generation stars have the highest percentage of elements heavier than helium.

The percentages differ in this way because first- and second-generation stars that "died" passed along their heavier elements. Many of these stars produced successively heavier elements by means of fusion in and near their cores. The heaviest elements were created when the most massive stars exploded as *supernovae.* Supernovae enrich the clouds of gas and dust from which other stars form. Other sources of enrichment are *planetary nebulae,* the cast-off outer layers of less massive stars.

Zones of the sun

The sun and its atmosphere consist of several zones or layers. From the inside out, the solar interior consists of the core, the *radiative zone,* and the *convection zone.*

The solar atmosphere is made up of the *photosphere,* the *chromosphere,* a *transition region,* and the corona. Beyond the corona is the solar wind, which is actually an outward flow of coronal gas.

Because astronomers cannot see inside the sun, they have learned about the solar interior indirectly. Part of their knowledge is based on the observed properties of the sun as a whole. Some of it is based on calculations that account for phenomena in the observable zones.

Core. The core extends from the center of the sun about one-fourth of the way to the surface. The core has about 2 percent of the sun's volume, but it contains almost half the sun's mass. Its maximum temperature is over 15 million kelvins. Its density reaches 150 grams per cubic centimeter, nearly 15 times the density of lead.

The high temperature and density of the core result in a pressure of about 200 billion times Earth's atmospheric pressure at sea level. The core's pressure supports all the overlying gas, preventing the sun from collapsing.

Almost all the fusion in the sun takes place in the core. Like the rest of the sun, the core's initial composition, by mass, was 72 percent hydrogen, 26 percent helium, and 2 percent heavier elements. Nuclear fusion has gradually changed the core's contents. Hydrogen now makes up about 35 percent of the mass in the center of the core and 65 percent at its outer boundary.

Radiative zone. Surrounding the core is a huge spherical shell known as the *radiative zone.* The outer boundary of this zone is 70 percent of the way to the solar surface. The radiative zone makes up 32 percent of the sun's volume and 48 percent of its mass.

The radiative zone gets its name from the fact that energy travels through it mainly by radiation. Photons emerging from the core pass through stable layers of gas. But they scatter from the dense particles of gas so often that an individual photon may take 10,000 years to pass through the zone.

At the bottom of the radiative zone, the density is 22 grams per cubic centimeter—about twice that of lead—and the temperature is 8 million K. At the top of the zone, the density is 0.2 gram per cubic centimeter, and the temperature is 2 million K.

The composition of the radiative zone has remained much the same since the sun's birth. The percentages of the elements are nearly the same from the top of the radiative zone to the solar surface.

Convection zone. The highest level of the solar interior, the *convection zone,* extends from the radiative zone to the sun's surface. This zone consists of the "boiling" convection cells. It makes up about 66 percent of the sun's volume but only slightly more than 2 percent of its mass. At the top of the zone, the density is near zero, and the temperature is about 5800 K. The convection cells "boil" to the surface because photons that spread outward from the radiative zone heat them.

Astronomers have observed two main kinds of convection cells—(1) *granulation* and (2) *supergranulation.* Granulation cells are about 600 miles (1,000 kilometers) across. Supergranulation cells reach a diameter of about 20,000 miles (30,000 kilometers).

Photosphere. The lowest layer of the atmosphere is called the *photosphere.* This zone emits the light that we see. The photosphere is about 300 miles (500 kilometers) thick. But most of the light that we see comes from its lowest part, which is only about 100 miles (150 kilometers) thick. Astronomers often refer to this part as the sun's surface. At the bottom of the photosphere, the temperature is 6400 K, while it is 4400 K at the top.

The photosphere consists of numerous *granules,* which are the tops of granulation cells. A typical granule exists for 15 to 20 minutes. The average density of the photosphere is less than one-millionth of a gram per cubic centimeter. This may seem to be an extremely low density, but there are tens of trillions to hundreds of trillions of individual particles in each cubic centimeter.

Chromosphere. The next zone up is the *chromosphere.* The main characteristic of this zone is a rise in temperature, which reaches about 10,000 K in some places and 20,000 K in others.

Astronomers first detected the chromosphere's spectrum during total eclipses of the sun. The spectrum is visible after the moon covers the photosphere, but before it covers the chromosphere. This period lasts only a few seconds. The emission lines in the spectrum seem to flash suddenly into visibility, so the spectrum is known as the *flash spectrum.*

The chromosphere is apparently made up entirely of spike-shaped structures called *spicules* (pronounced *SPIHK yoolz).* A typical spicule is about 600 miles (1,000 kilometers) across and up to 6,000 miles (10,000 kilometers) high. The density of the chromosphere is about 10 billion to 100 billion particles per cubic centimeter.

Transition region. The temperature of the chromosphere ranges to about 20,000 K, and the corona is hotter than 500,000 K. Between the two zones is a region of intermediate temperatures known as the *chromosphere-corona transition region,* or simply the *transition region.*

The transition region receives much of its energy from the overlying corona. The region emits most of its light in the ultraviolet spectrum.

The thickness of the transition region is a few hundred to a few thousand miles or kilometers. In some places, relatively cool spicules extend from the chromosphere high into the solar atmosphere. Nearby may be areas where thin, hot coronal structures reach down close to the photosphere.

Corona is the part of the sun's atmosphere whose temperature is greater than 500,000 K. The corona consists of such structures as loops and streams of ionized gas. The structures connect vertically to the solar surface, and magnetic fields that emerge from inside the sun shape them. The temperature of a given structure varies along each field line. Near the surface, the temperature is typical of the photosphere. At higher levels, the temperature has chromospheric values, then values of the transition region, then coronal values.

In the part of the corona nearest the solar surface, the temperature is about 1 million to 6 million K, and the density is about 100 million to 1 billion particles per cubic centimeter. The temperature reaches tens of millions of kelvins when a flare occurs.

Solar wind. The corona is so hot that it extends far into space and continually expands. The flow of coronal gas into space is known as the solar wind. At the distance of Earth from the sun, the density of the solar wind is about 10 to 100 particles per cubic centimeter.

The solar wind extends far into interplanetary space as a large, teardrop-shaped cavity called the *heliosphere.* The sun and all the planets are inside the heliosphere. Far beyond the orbit of Pluto, the farthest planet, the heliosphere joins the *interstellar medium,* the dust and gas that occupy the space between the stars.

Solar activity

The sun's magnetic fields rise through the convection zone and erupt through the photosphere into the chromosphere and corona. The eruptions lead to *solar activity,* which includes such phenomena as sunspots, flares, and coronal mass ejections. Areas where sunspots or eruptions occur are known as *active regions.* The amount of activity varies from a *solar minimum* at the beginning of a sunspot cycle to a *solar maximum* about 5 years later. The number of sunspots at a given time varies. On the side of the solar disk that we see, this number ranges from none to approximately 250 individual sunspots and clusters of sunspots.

Sunspots are dark, often roughly circular features on the solar surface. They form where denser bundles of magnetic field lines from the solar interior break through the surface.

Sunspots form in pairs that have opposite magnetic polarity. The orientation of the pairs is generally in the east-west direction. Consider, for example, the western spot of a pair in the Northern Hemisphere and the western spot of a pair in the Southern Hemisphere. If the spot in the Northern Hemisphere has a polarity of south, the spot in the Southern Hemisphere will have a polarity of north. In the next sunspot cycle, the polarities of the sunspots will be reversed.

The reversal of magnetic polarity actually begins before the end of a sunspot cycle. At the start of a cycle, spots form in two belts about 30° north and south of the equator. As the cycle progresses, new spots form closer to the equator. Toward the end of the cycle, spots that "belong" to the next cycle—and which therefore have a reversed magnetic polarity—often form at high latitudes. At the same time, spots that are part of the existing cycle are still forming near the equator.

Prominences. Projecting into the corona are denser threads of gas that have chromospheric temperatures. The threads can be over 100 times as dense as the surrounding corona. When viewed with the disk of the sun in the background, a thread appears dark and is called a *filament.* When a thread is seen projecting above the *limb* (edge of the sun), it can appear bright against the dark background of the sky. In this case, it is called a *prominence.*

There are two kinds of prominences: (1) *active prominences,* which form in and near active regions, and (2)

quiescent (kwy EHS uhnt) prominences, which form where the magnetic fields are relatively old, large, and weak. Active prominences are closely associated in time and location with the eruption of flares and coronal mass ejections. A typical active prominence is a few thousand miles or kilometers wide and long. This kind of prominence changes greatly in size and shape from day to day.

Many quiescent prominences are 5 to 10 times the size of active prominences. A quiescent prominence may last several weeks or longer. Large quiescent prominences often erupt to form coronal mass ejections.

Flares. A flare is a sudden brightening of a part of the solar atmosphere. The main feature of a flare is an increase in the temperature of the corona to about 10 million K, and sometimes higher. Flares are strong sources of radio waves. A flare's *rise phase*—the stage in which its temperature increases—may last from tens of sec-

Zones of the sun

The sun and its atmosphere consist of several zones. Energy flows from the *core* through *radiative* and *convection* zones. The thin *photosphere,* the lowest part of the atmosphere, produces the light we see. Then come the *chromosphere,* the *transition region,* and the *corona,* with its fiery loops.

WORLD BOOK illustration by Roberta Polfus

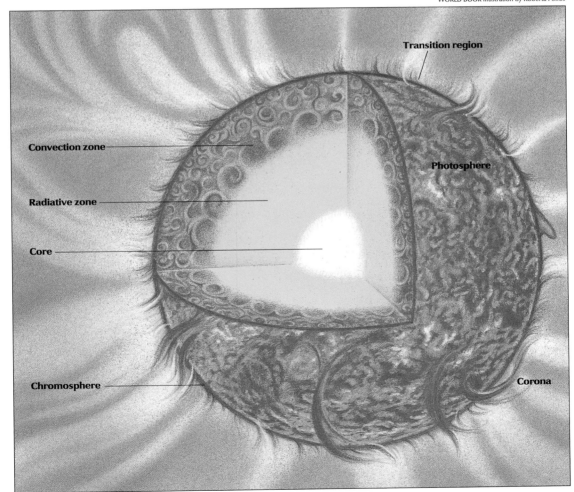

Transition region

Convection zone

Photosphere

Radiative zone

Core

Chromosphere

Corona

onds to tens of minutes. The *decay phase,* in which the temperature declines to normal, may last from minutes to hours. Flares are almost certainly a result of the release of energy from magnetic fields that extend into the corona. The fields release the energy by reconnecting field lines in a way that eliminates twists and kinks.

Spicules, which apparently make up the entire chromosphere, consist of spikes of gas just large enough for telescopes to detect. At any given moment, there are hundreds of thousands of them on the sun. They contain enough gas to replace the corona in a few minutes. After they rise, some of them fall, while others seem to fade. Spicules have lifetimes of about 15 minutes.

Coronal mass ejections are large eruptions of coronal material into interplanetary space. One of these eruptions occurs when a large bubble or tube of magnetic field lines erupts from the sun. This structure sweeps a large volume of the corona outward, creating a cloud of gas. A typical ejection leaves the sun at a speed of about 500 miles (800 kilometers) per second.

A coronal mass ejection releases about 5 trillion trillion joules of energy, enough to supply Earth's commercial energy needs for more than 12,000 years. These eruptions also increase the sun's X-ray emissions and create bursts of radio energy.

Evolution of the sun

The sun formed when part of an immense, slowly spinning cloud of dust and gas became denser than the surrounding parts. This region may have become denser because a kind of pressure wave called a *shock wave,* created by a supernova, passed through it. On the other hand, the increase in density may have been due merely to random motion within the cloud. Whatever the cause, the dense region began to shrink, pulled together by its own gravity.

As the region shrank, its spin increased, just as spinning ice skaters turn more rapidly when they pull in their arms. The region eventually became a rapidly spinning disk. Because of compression, the gas in the center of the disk became hotter. Clumps of matter in the surrounding, relatively cool part of the disk grew into objects known as *planetesimals.* Groups of planetesimals then came together to form the planets.

Eventually, the central mass became hot and dense enough for nuclear fusion to begin. At that time, about 4.6 billion years ago, the sun was born as a star.

About 5 billion years from now, all the hydrogen in the sun's core will have fused into helium. The sun's interior will then contract, heating the core and the region around it. As a result, hydrogen fusion will begin in a thin shell outside the core. This fusion will produce so much energy that the sun will expand enormously. The sun will become a type of star known as a *red giant.* Its outer layers will probably expand nearly to the current orbit of Mercury.

Eventually, the core will become so hot that the helium there will begin to fuse. As this process continues, the core will expand, and its temperature will drop. This decrease in temperature will cause the temperature of the hydrogen-burning shell to drop. Consequently, the energy output of the shell will decrease, the outer layers of the sun will contract, and the sun will shrink.

When all the helium in the core has fused, the core will contract and therefore become hotter. Helium fusion will therefore begin in a shell surrounding the core, and hydrogen fusion will continue in a shell surrounding that. The increased energy output will cause the sun to become a giant again.

In time, the core's gravitational grip on the outer layers will become so weak that the outer layers will drift away. These layers will form a huge, shell-like planetary nebula. The hot core of the sun will then be exposed. The core will cool and shrink, becoming a *white dwarf.*

All the changes from the sun's red giant stage to its white dwarf stage will take more than 100 million years. The white dwarf will continue to cool. After a few billion years, it will become a faint, cool object sometimes called a *black dwarf.*

Studying the sun

Scientists study the sun by producing solar images and by analyzing electromagnetic and particle radiation from the sun. They also use powerful computers to *simulate* (represent) how solar processes occur. This kind of simulation is similar to the manner in which an electronic game simulates a real situation.

Producing images. Astronomers use cameras mounted on telescopes to photograph objects in the sky. The cameras record images on photographic film or with electronic detectors, such as *charge-coupled devices* (CCD's). A CCD in a large telescope is similar to the device that takes pictures in an ordinary digital still or video camera. However, the telescope device is more sensitive and more carefully made.

Astronomers have produced images of the sun in all parts of the electromagnetic spectrum. To obtain images in the parts of the spectrum that are blocked by Earth's atmosphere, they have sent rockets and satellites into outer space.

The sun's corona requires special attention because it is faint compared with the everyday blue sky. Scientists must use special techniques or special instruments to observe the corona with ground-based telescopes. One technique is simply to wait for a total eclipse of the sun.

© Williams College & EIT Consortium

The sun's corona appears as a whitish glow in this composite photo. Scientists on Earth photographed the corona during a total eclipse. A satellite imaged the solar surface at the same time.

During an eclipse, the moon blocks out the light from the lower parts of the sun's atmosphere.

A device for studying the corona is a *coronagraph,* a telescope with a disk in the middle. The disk blocks out the light from the lower, brighter layers of the sun. A coronagraph's artificial eclipse does not block this light as well as a real one, however.

Astronomers also use space-based telescopes to observe the corona. The telescopes that observe visible light are equipped with coronagraphs. Telescopes that observe X rays or ultraviolet light do not need them.

Analyzing electromagnetic radiation. Astronomers use instruments called *spectrographs* to produce images of the sun's spectrum. The scientists study two kinds of *spectral lines:* (1) thin, dark gaps in the spectrum of the photosphere; and (2) places where the spectrum of the chromosphere and corona is unusually bright. They also study *Doppler shifts* in the spectrum. The lines and shifts reveal information about the motions, the chemical makeup, and the temperature of the sun.

Spectral lines. The dark gaps in the spectrum are *absorption lines.* When the spectrum is spread out from side to side, they appear as vertical lines. A line appears when a chemical element or compound in the sun's atmosphere absorbs radiation. Absorption occurs in the visible spectrum when the white light emitted by low, relatively hot parts of the atmosphere passes through cooler areas. Every element or compound absorbs radiation that corresponds to certain specific lines. The locations of the lines in the spectrum depend on the temperature of the element or compound. Thus, the pattern of absorption lines in the solar spectrum reveals the composition and the temperature of the cooler areas.

The absorption lines in the sun's spectrum have a special name: *Fraunhofer lines.* They are named for German optician Joseph von Fraunhofer, who discovered them and mapped them accurately in 1814. The spectrum of the photosphere contains a large number of Fraunhofer lines.

In the sun's chromosphere, the dark Fraunhofer lines give way to *emission lines,* which appear as bright lines in the spectrum. Emission lines appear in the spectrum where radiation of specific wavelengths is especially

The development of sunspots

Sunspots develop as a result of a distortion of the sun's magnetic field. These diagrams show a simplified version of that field. The actual field develops kinks and twists as distortion progresses.

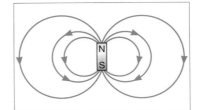

A bar magnet has a magnetic field like that of the sun. Field lines, which represent the field, exit the north pole and enter the south pole.

The sun's magnetic field lines exit the northern hemisphere of the sun, loop around through space at distances too vast to show in this diagram, and re-enter the sun in its southern hemisphere.

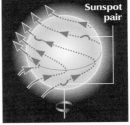

WORLD BOOK diagrams by Precision Graphics

The sun's rotation distorts the field because the sun rotates more rapidly at its equator than at higher latitudes.

Field lines break the surface when the field is greatly distorted. Pairs of sunspots form at the breakthrough points.

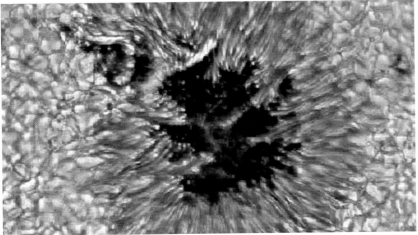

A sunspot is a dark feature that is slightly cooler than the remainder of the solar surface. This sunspot is larger than Earth. The yellowish clumps outside the sunspot are *granulation cells,* which are about 600 miles (1,000 kilometers) across.

strong. This radiation comes from extremely hot elements in the solar atmosphere. Each element emits a
characteristic pattern of lines in the same pattern as its
absorption lines.

Doppler shift occurs in a spectrum when the source
of the spectral image is moving toward or away from
the spectrograph. This phenomenon is known as the
Doppler effect. Movement toward the observing instrument shifts the wavelengths toward the blue end of the
spectrum. Movement away from the instrument shifts
the wavelengths toward the red end.

Astronomers use the Doppler effect to study the vibrations of the solar surface. Sound vibrations make the
sun's surface move in and out. They therefore cause the
light emitted from the sun's surface to be slightly shifted
to higher and lower wavelengths. Special instruments
analyze the vibrations and produce much information
about the inside of the sun.

One kind of analysis has determined the temperature
at various depths. This analysis works because vibration
rates depend in part upon how rapidly sound waves
move through solar gas, and because the speed of
sound in a gas depends on temperature. The study of

the sun's interior using solar vibrations is known as *helioseismology.*

Analyzing charged particles. The space above
Earth's atmosphere is filled with charged particles from
the sun and from objects beyond the solar system.
Earth's magnetic field deflects most of these particles.
But instruments on satellites orbiting between the sun
and the field detect the particles before they reach the
field. Astronomers use data gathered by these instruments to determine the composition, amount of ioniza-
tion, speed, and direction of flow of the particles.

Analyzing neutrinos. The study of solar neutrinos is
advancing scientists' understanding of how the sun
shines. Physicists have calculated the rate at which neutrinos form during fusion in the sun's core. They base
their calculation on the *Standard Model,* the currently
accepted group of theories of subatomic interactions.
But experiments have detected only one-half to one-
third the number of neutrinos predicted by the model.

The fact that the predictions and the experimental
data differ is known as the *solar neutrino problem.* Scientists are not sure how to solve this problem. They may
have to change the Standard Model slightly.

How coronal loops form

Huge loops of gas, such as the those shown in the photo, form in the sun's corona when magnetic
field lines break through the solar surface. The field lines resemble those of a bar magnet, shown
in the diagram at the left. Particles of hot, electrically charged gas travel along the sun's field lines,
center. The looping structures that result have the same shape as many of the field lines, *right.*

WORLD BOOK diagrams by Precision Graphics

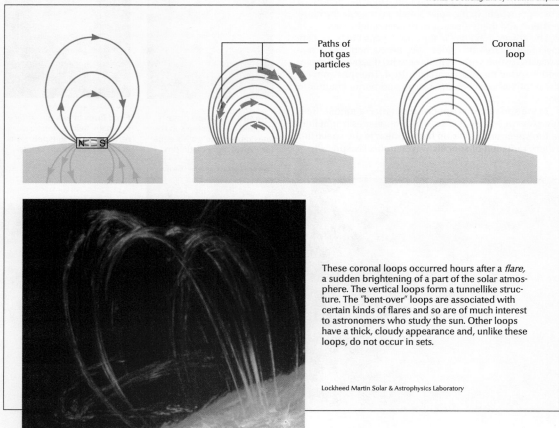

Paths of
hot gas
particles

Coronal
loop

These coronal loops occurred hours after a *flare,*
a sudden brightening of a part of the solar atmosphere. The vertical loops form a tunnellike structure. The "bent-over" loops are associated with
certain kinds of flares and so are of much interest
to astronomers who study the sun. Other loops
have a thick, cloudy appearance and, unlike these
loops, do not occur in sets.

Lockheed Martin Solar & Astrophysics Laboratory

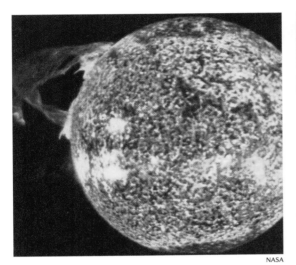

NASA

A flare, a brightening of the sun's atmosphere, releases tremendous energy. The gas loop associated with the flare shown here spanned about 365,000 miles (588,000 kilometers) of the surface.

Scientists must take extraordinary measures to detect neutrinos. Neutrinos rarely interact with other particles. So, to detect enough neutrino interactions for study, researchers must build enormous detectors that weigh many tons. In addition, the neutrino detectors must lie deep underground because sensors that can detect neutrinos also detect other particles. The other particles are plentiful at and near Earth's surface, but most of them cannot penetrate far into the ground.

The most sensitive detector is the Sudbury Neutrino Observatory, 6,800 feet (2,075 meters) underground in a mine near Greater Sudbury, Ontario. The facility uses 1,000 tons of *heavy water.* In heavy water, the nucleus of each hydrogen atom consists of a proton and a neutron, rather than a single proton. A reaction of a neutrino

National Solar Observatory

Sharp-pointed spicules make up the *chromosphere,* the zone above the part of the atmosphere that sends out the light we see. Typical spicules are up to 6,000 miles (10,000 kilometers) high.

NASA/ESA/Solar & Heliospheric Observatory

A prominence erupts from the sun's atmosphere, creating a handle-shaped loop that extends into space a distance equal to one-fourth of the solar diameter. Prominences are normally suspended in the sun's outer layer, the corona. A wedge-shaped prominence is visible beneath the "handle." The dense, cloudlike structures that appear elsewhere on the edge of the sun in this photo are also prominences.

A coronal mass ejection is the most massive kind of eruption in the solar system. A satellite telescope took this photo with the aid of a *coronagraph,* a device that creates an "artificial eclipse."

with the heavy water creates a flash of light that is detected by devices called *photomultiplier tubes.* The Sudbury facility began taking measurements in 1999.

Computer modeling. Astronomers use *scientific models* to investigate solar phenomena that they cannot directly observe. A scientific model consists of a set of equations that represent certain natural phenomena, such as the "boiling" motion of convection cells. Most of what astronomers know about the solar interior is based on helioseismology and computer modeling.

In using the computer modeling technique, an astronomer first assumes that a set of physical conditions existed at a certain time in the past. Next, the astronomer feeds the numbers corresponding to those conditions into the computer and runs the model. He or she then compares the computer's results with actual observations. If the comparison does not match the observations closely enough, the astronomer modifies the assumed conditions and runs the model again. This process continues until the model produces an acceptable comparison with the observations. Some models can create animated images of solar processes.

History of modern solar study

Beginnings. Modern study of the sun began around 1610 with observations by a number of European astronomers, including Galileo in Italy, Christoph Scheiner in Germany, and Thomas Harriot in England. Many scientists, working separately, used the newly developed telescope to project images of the sun onto surfaces where the images could be viewed safely. The scientists observed sunspots in the images.

Before that time, people had occasionally seen sunspots by looking directly at the sun with the unaided eye. This practice was extremely dangerous, though sun watchers usually had looked when the sun was dimmed by haze near sunset. But they could not determine whether the sunspots were actually on the sun or were an effect of Earth's atmosphere.

The 1800's. By the 1850's, scientists determined that the number of sunspots increases and decreases over a

period of about 11 years. Observers photographed sunspots as early as 1858—as soon as photography became sensitive enough to do so.

By viewing eclipses in the late 1800's, astronomers determined that prominences and the corona appeared the same from widely separated locations on Earth. This discovery showed that these structures were also solar features rather than effects of Earth's atmosphere.

In 1868, the French astronomer Jules Janssen and the British astronomer Norman Lockyer independently developed a method to view certain bright emission lines in the spectrum of the sun. Previously, these lines could only be seen during a solar eclipse. Both scientists made their observations with the newly invented spectroscope. Lockyer later concluded that the lines were created by a previously unknown element, which came to be called helium. Scientists named it *helium,* from the Greek word for *sun,* because they had not yet found it on Earth and thought it existed only on the sun.

The following year's eclipse brought the discovery of what seemed to be an element that existed only in the corona. Scientists called this element *coronium.* But in the 1930's, scientists showed that "coronium" is actually extremely hot gas composed of iron and other previously known elements. All these elements were in previously unknown states. This discovery showed that the temperature of the corona is millions of kelvins.

In the late 1800's, the American astronomer George Ellery Hale developed an instrument called the *spectroheliograph* to photograph the sun in different colors of the spectrum. His photos revealed that the inner atmosphere of the sun had a layered structure. Beginning in 1908, Hale mapped the sun's magnetic field. His work showed that the field is extremely strong in sunspots.

Space-based studies. Starting in the late 1940's, researchers sent rockets above Earth's atmosphere to measure X rays and ultraviolet radiation emitted by the sun. In the 1960's, researchers first used satellites to detect particles from the sun.

In 1973, the National Aeronautics and Space Administration (NASA) launched the Skylab space station, which carried a set of solar telescopes. The telescopes produced ultraviolet and X-ray images and spectra of the sun. Observations from space continued with NASA's Solar Maximum Mission Satellite, launched in 1980. This craft studied solar flares in much detail and carried a coronagraph to map the corona continually.

In 1991, the Japanese satellite Yohkoh began to produce X-ray images of the sun. In 1994, the space probe Ulysses became the first craft to observe the sun from an orbit that carried it over the sun's polar regions. NASA and the European Space Agency (ESA) had launched Ulysses from the space shuttle Discovery in 1990. In 1995, the ESA launched the Solar and Heliospheric Observatory (SOHO). This satellite carries a dozen instruments for studying the solar interior, the solar atmosphere, and the solar wind. NASA provided some of this equipment. NASA's Transition Region and Coronal Explorer (TRACE), launched in 1998, makes high-resolution observations of the chromosphere and corona in the ultraviolet part of the spectrum.

In 2001, NASA launched the Genesis spacecraft to gather samples of the solar wind. Genesis returned to Earth in September 2004, but the craft's parachutes failed to open, and it crashed to the ground. A recovery team located the craft and salvaged some of the damaged samples.

In the 2000's, NASA began its Solar Terrestrial Probes program, a series of missions to study solar variations and their influence on the solar system. In 2001, the agency launched the Thermosphere Ionosphere Mesosphere Energetics and Dynamics (TIMED) mission to study the effects of the sun on Earth's middle atmosphere. In 2006, the Japan Aerospace Exploration Agency launched the Hinode spacecraft. The craft, developed by Japan, the United States, and the United Kingdom, was designed to study the sun's magnetic field and its interactions with the sun's atmosphere and solar flares. Also in 2006, NASA launched the Solar Terrestrial Relations Observatory (STEREO), a set of two satellites designed to help scientists predict coronal mass ejections.

Earth-based studies. In 1962, the McMath-Pierce Telescope Facility, the largest solar telescope on Earth, went into operation at Kitt Peak, Arizona. The telescope's main mirror is mounted on a 100-foot (30-meter) tower. A diagonal shaft slants 200 feet to the ground, where a tunnel continues another 300 feet underground. Laboratories underground analyze the solar spectrum, photograph the sun, and project a 30-inch (75-centimeter) image of the sun onto a screen for direct viewing.

In the 1960's, scientists discovered that the surface of the sun vibrates with a period of five minutes. This discovery ushered in the science of helioseismology. In the late 1960's, scientists began experiments to detect neutrinos emitted by the sun.

Studies of the solar interior through helioseismology led to the formation of the Global Oscillation Network Group (GONG). This organization studies the sun by means of a network of six special telescopes around the globe. The network arrangement enables the telescopes to collect data continuously—sunset cannot disrupt their work. The telescopes began to collect data in 1995.

Jay M. Pasachoff and Leon Golub

Related articles in *World Book* include:

Astronomy	Neutrino
Aurora	Radiation (Sources of
Bode's law	radiation)
Charge-coupled device	Rainbow
Corona	Solar energy
Cosmic rays	Solar system
Earth	Solar wind
Eclipse	Space exploration (Solar
Heat (Sources of heat)	probes)
Heliosphere	Star
Light	Subatomic particle
Magnetic storm	Sun worship
Magnetism (The magnetism	Sundial
of the sun)	Sunspot
Midnight sun	Tide
Milky Way	

Outline

I. Characteristics of the sun
 A. Mass and density
 B. Composition
 C. Energy output
 D. Color
 E. Rotation
 F. Vibration
 G. Magnetic field
 H. Nuclear fusion
 I. Comparison with other stars

II. Zones of the sun
 A. Core
 B. Radiative zone
 C. Convection zone
 D. Photosphere
 E. Chromosphere
 F. Transition region
 G. Corona
 H. Solar wind

III. Solar activity
 A. Sunspots
 B. Prominences
 C. Flares
 D. Spicules
 E. Coronal mass ejections

IV. Evolution of the sun

V. Studying the sun
 A. Producing images
 B. Analyzing electromagnetic radiation
 C. Analyzing charged particles
 D. Analyzing neutrinos
 E. Computer modeling

VI. History of modern solar study

Additional resources

Level I
Barnes-Svarney, Patricia L. *Secrets of the Sun.* Raintree Steck-Vaughn, 2001.
Bourgeois, Paulette. *The Sun.* Kids Can Pr., 1997.
Cole, Michael D. *The Sun.* Enslow, 2001.

Level II
Golub, Leon, and Pasachoff, Jay M. *Nearest Star: The Surprising Science of Our Sun.* Harvard Univ. Pr., 2001.
Kippenhahn, Rudolf. *Discovering the Secrets of the Sun.* Wiley, 1994.
Lang, Kenneth R. *The Cambridge Encyclopedia of the Sun.* Cambridge, 2001. *The Sun from Space.* Springer-Verlag, 2000.

Sun Belt. See **United States** (Urban life).

Sun dance ranks as one of the most important religious ceremonies of almost all the Indian tribes of the Great Plains of the United States. It was originally performed to give thanks to the Supreme Being, represented by the sun. The Indians also used the dance to ask the Supreme Being to provide for their needs during the coming year. Today, the ceremony has different meanings for each tribe. Tribes that have long performed the sun dance include the Arapaho, Cheyenne, Cree, Crow, Pawnee, Sioux, and Ute.

The Oglala band of the Teton Sioux hold the ceremony for four days during the summer. The dance symbolizes both their unity and their separateness from all other peoples. During the first three days, the ceremony includes selecting, cutting, trimming, and erecting a tall, straight tree to serve as the sun dance pole. On the fourth day, several young men dance around the pole. In some cases, a long pin is inserted through cuts in the dancers' chest or back muscles. Leather ropes connected to the pins are attached to the pole or to buffalo skulls dragged behind the dancers. The dance continues until the pin rips through the muscle. The Oglala believe that the dancers, while they are dancing, have visions or communicate in other ways with the Supreme Being and thus gain sacred power. Michael D. Green

See also **Buffalo ceremonials; Crow Indians; Indian, American** (picture: Sun dance).

Sun lamp is an electrical device that produces artificial ultraviolet radiation. The energy given off by a sun lamp is similar to the ultraviolet radiation found in natural sunlight. Sun lamps are used primarily to produce a suntan, but they also have therapeutic uses.

Most sun lamps operate with an electric current that passes between two electrodes and is surrounded by a gas vapor, often mercury. The electric current and the gas vapor react to produce ultraviolet radiation—that is, ultraviolet light. Wavelengths of ultraviolet light are shorter than wavelengths in the visible spectrum and thus cannot be seen by the human eye. However, most sun lamps also produce some visible light.

The majority of sun lamps are designed for home use. They are small and lightweight, and they can be plugged into a standard household electric outlet. Many health clubs and tanning parlors feature large booths equipped with ultraviolet lights and reflectors to provide an even, allover tan. People should exercise great care when using these devices, however, because the intensity of light they produce is much more powerful than sunlight.

Most sun lamp users can achieve a tan with repeated moderate exposures over a period of several weeks. But individuals with fair skin may suffer severe sunburns after only a few seconds of exposure to sun lamps and thus should not use these devices. Repeated exposure to sun lamps leads to premature aging of the skin and skin cancer. In addition, concentrated amounts of ultraviolet radiation can cause a variety of eye disorders, ranging from mild irritation to temporary blindness. To help prevent injuries caused by overexposure, laws require sun lamp manufacturers to provide protective eye goggles, timing switches that limit the length of exposure, and other safety features.

Some dermatologists use sun lamps to treat certain skin diseases. A type of sun lamp known as a *germicidal lamp* emits short ultraviolet wavelengths that kill bacteria and viruses. These lamps are used to disinfect the air in hospital operating rooms and to sterilize surgical equipment.   Charles J. McDonald

See also **Ultraviolet rays**.

Sun Valley, Idaho (pop. 1,427), a famous resort, lies in the Sawtooth Mountains of south-central Idaho, next to the town of Ketchum. For location, see **Idaho** (political map). In 1936, Averell Harriman, chairman of the board of directors of the Union Pacific Railroad, picked the site for development as a center for skiing and other winter sports because of its brilliant sunshine and frequent snowfalls.

The resort now serves tourists the year around. Summer activities include golf, tennis, and trout fishing. Chair lifts serve over 2,000 acres (810 hectares) and about 60 ski runs in Sun Valley. The resort also has numerous cross-country ski trails.   Harley Johansen

See also **Idaho** (Visitor's guide).

Sun worship was a religious practice that developed in some lands as people came to associate the sun with the growing season and with warmth. It developed especially among agricultural peoples, who needed sunshine for their crops. Sun worship was important in the cultures of ancient Egypt, Babylonia, Persia, and northern India. The peoples of Scandinavia also worshiped the sun. Teutonic peoples named the first day of the week for the sun. Sun worship was important to American Indians in the agricultural lands that are now the southeastern and southwestern United States. It also grew up among the Aztec, Inca, and Maya peoples who lived in Central and South America.

Kings and queens in some lands believed themselves to be brothers, sisters, or children of the sun, and they came to be worshiped as gods. For hundreds of years, the Japanese worshiped their emperor as a descendant of the sun goddess, Amaterasu-O-Mi-Kami. The Bible warns against the worship of the sun, which it says was created by God.   J. H. Charlesworth

See also **Apollo; Helios; Re**.

Sun Yat-sen, *soon yaht sen* (1866-1925), a Chinese statesman and revolutionary leader, fought to establish a republic of China. He is generally called the *Father of the Revolution.* Sun was too idealistic to become an effective political leader. However, his *Three People's Principles* (nationalism, democracy, and socialism) became the guiding principles of the Chinese republic, which was established in 1912.

Sun was born in the Zhongshan district of Guangdong Province on Nov. 12, 1866. He attended mission schools in Hong Kong and Honolulu, and became a doctor. From 1895 to 1911, he traveled widely in the United States, Japan, and Europe to organize sympathy for republican principles and to seek financial aid for his revolutionary movement against the Manchu (Qing) dynasty. He was aided by Chinese overseas communities and English, American, and Japanese sympathizers.

The Kuomintang Party. From 1911 to 1922, Sun tried to unite China and establish a stable government. The Kuomintang Party, headed by Sun, became a leading political force after the 1911 Wuhan uprising to overthrow the Manchu regime. In 1912, Sun's party adopted a constitution, and Sun became the temporary president of

Akhenaton worshiping the sun god, Aton (about 1360 B.C.), a limestone relief sculpture (© Erich Lessing, Magnum)

Many ancient peoples thought the sun was a god. They worshiped the sun and made offerings to it. This carving from ancient Egypt shows the pharaoh Akhenaton praying to the sun.

the first Chinese republic. The political situation was turbulent. To further ensure the unity of China, Sun resigned as president in favor of Yuan Shikai after only six and one-half weeks in office.

His later efforts. In 1913, Sun disagreed with Yuan's policies and organized a revolt. Sun fled to Japan, and the Kuomintang members of parliament were thrown out of office. Once again, the revolutionists assembled to set up a separate government under the 1912 Constitution. In 1921, Sun became president of this government in Guangzhou. He was driven out of his capital in 1922 but returned in 1923.

Sun continued to work for the unification of China. After failing to get assistance from the West, he turned to the Soviet Union. With funds and help from the Soviet Union, he reorganized the Kuomintang Party and Army in 1923 and formed a united front with the Chinese Communist Party. He set up the Whampoa Military Academy, with Chiang Kai-shek as superintendent. Sun died of cancer on March 12, 1925, in Beijing.

In 1929, Sun's body was transferred to a national mausoleum erected in his honor in Nanjing. Politically, he was more effective after his death. His principles became slogans of both the Communists and the Nationalists. In 1928, Chiang Kai-shek achieved Sun's goal of a China united under a central government.   Lanxin Xiang

See also **Chiang Kai-shek; China** (History).

Sunbird is the common name of about 115 species of small songbirds. Sunbirds live in Africa and Asia, and one species is found in northern Australia. Sunbirds are similar in appearance and in feeding habits to the hummingbirds of North and South America. However, these two groups of birds are not related.

In most species of sunbirds, males are brightly colored during the breeding season. They may be various combinations of yellow, blue, purple, green, and red. Females and nonbreeding males are dull yellow, yellowish-green, or gray. Sunbirds have thin, curved bills and long, tube-shaped tongues.

Sunbirds feed on the nectar of flowers and on spiders and small insects that live in the blossoms. Like hummingbirds, sunbirds can probe into a flower while hovering in front of it. But they mostly feed by perching on the flower or on a nearby twig. Sunbirds build small, purse-shaped nests. Females lay two or three dull gray eggs, usually with black or brown markings.

David M. Niles

Scientific classification. Sunbirds belong to the sunbird family, Nectariniidae.

Sunburn is a painful inflammation of the skin that is caused by overexposure to the invisible ultraviolet rays of the sun. Sunburn ranges from mild redness that disappears in a few hours to blistering, swollen, scarlet skin that peels before it heals. A severe sunburn can cause chills, dizziness, fever, and weakness. Repeated, prolonged exposure to the sun also can lead to premature aging of the skin and to skin cancer.

The seriousness of a sunburn depends on the intensity of the light and the length of time spent in the sun. The sun's burning rays shine most intensely during the summer and from late morning to early afternoon. They travel through clouds and water, and so a person can be burned on a cloudy day or while swimming. Sand and snow reflect the rays and increase the chances of being burned on a beach or ski slope.

The skin contains a brown-black pigment called *melanin,* which partially provides natural protection from sunburn. Blue-eyed blonds, redheads with freckles, and other fair-skinned people have little melanin and burn easily. However, dark-skinned people rarely burn because their skin has much more melanin. Most fair-skinned people can tan without burning if they stay in the sun for only 15 minutes the first day and then increase the time by 10 to 15 minutes daily.

Sunburn can also be avoided by covering the skin or by using a lotion containing chemicals that act as a *sun block* or a *sunscreen.* A sun block filters out all the sun's burning rays, and a sunscreen filters most of them. Commercial sunscreens are available in various strengths indicated by a number called a *sun protection factor* (SPF). An SPF of 2 means that, once applied, twice the normal time passes before the skin becomes sunburned. Skin experts recommend that fair-skinned people use a sunscreen with an SPF of 15 or higher. Darker-skinned people may use one with a lower SPF. Sunscreens should be applied 15 to 20 minutes before prolonged exposure to the sun and should be reapplied frequently.

The best treatment for sunburn is aspirin, which relieves the pain and reduces the inflammation. Cool baths, wet compresses, and medicated creams also provide relief.   Critically reviewed by the American Red Cross

See also **Skin** (Burns); **Sun lamp.**

Sunday is the first day of the week. For Christians, it is the day set aside for rest and for worship of God. Sunday was the day sacred to the sun among the old Teutonic peoples. Its name means the "day of the sun." The French call Sunday *dimanche,* the Spanish call it *domingo,* and the Italians call it *domenica.* These names come from the Latin *dies dominica,* which means Lord's Day.

The early Christians lived hard lives and had to work on Sunday as well as the other days in the week. But they made Sunday a day for special worship, because they believed that the resurrection of Jesus occurred on that day. By the A.D. 300's, both the church and the state officially recognized it as a day of rest in Europe.

In the United States, all government agencies and banks are closed on Sunday. Some states and communities have laws that restrict the hours during which stores may open on Sunday, prohibit certain types of businesses from opening, or restrict the sale of certain products, such as alcoholic beverages. Such laws are called *blue laws* (see **Blue laws**).   Jack Santino

See also **Colonial life in America** (A colonial Sunday).

Sunday, Billy (1862-1935), was a baseball player who became a famous evangelist. He used his baseball background, slangy language, flamboyant manners, and highly developed promotional methods to become the most popular evangelist of the time. He was supposed to have preached to over 100 million people, and to have converted over a million people.

William Ashley Sunday was born on Nov. 19, 1862, in Ames, Iowa. His early years were spent with his grandparents and at an orphans home. Sunday played baseball for major league teams in Chicago, Pittsburgh, and Philadelphia from 1883 to 1890. During these years, he was converted and began working with the YMCA. Billy Sunday became a Presbyterian minister in 1903. He died on Nov. 6, 1935.   Charles H. Lippy

Sunday school. See Religious education (Private education).

Sundew is an unusual plant that traps and digests insects. It gets its name because drops of sticky fluid produced by glands appear on its leaves. In the sunlight, these drops glitter like dewdrops. Sundews live in bogs and marshes worldwide. The *round-leaved sundew,* the most common kind, thrives in moist, acid soil in all but the southwestern part of the United States. The plant also grows in some parts of Canada, Europe, and Asia.

The sundew's slender stem is topped by small white flowers. A cluster of flat, rounded leaves grows at the base of the stem, near the ground. These leaves are the size of a small coin and are covered with small, red hairs that bear glands. An insect may easily become stuck to the drops of sticky fluid on the leaves. Then the hairs fold in around the insect and hold it. Fluid covers the insect and suffocates it. The glands produce juices that digest the victim.   David A. Francko

Scientific classification. The sundews are in the sundew family, Droseraceae. They form the genus *Drosera.* The scientific name for the round-leaved sundew is *Drosera rotundifolia.*

See also **Carnivorous plant; Plant** (picture: Plants that eat insects).

Sundial is one of the oldest known devices for the measurement of time. It is based on the fact that the shadow of an object will move from one side of the object to the other as the sun moves from east to west during the day. The sundial is believed to have been used in Babylon at least as early as 2000 B.C.

The earliest description of a sundial comes from Berossus, a Babylonian priest and author of the 200's B.C. His sundial was a hollow half-sphere, or dome, set with its edge flat and with a small bead fixed at the center. During the day the shadow of the bead moved in a circular arc, divided into 12 equal parts. These were called *temporary hours* because they changed with the seasons. *Equal hours* were decided upon about A.D. 1400, when clocks were invented.

Artstreet

A sundial tells time by measuring the angle of a shadow cast by the sun. Many sundials have faces numbered in Roman numerals from 5 a.m. to 7 p.m. When the sun hits the *gnomon,* a flat piece of metal in the center, it casts a shadow that tells the time. The time on the sundial shown here is 3:30 p.m.

A sundial consists of two parts: the *plane* (dial face) and the *gnomon* (style). The dial face is divided into hours and sometimes half and quarter hours. The gnomon is a flat piece of metal set in the center of the dial. It points toward the North Pole in the Northern Hemisphere and toward the South Pole in the Southern Hemisphere. The upper edge of the gnomon must slant upward from the dial face at an angle equal to the latitude of the location of the sundial.   James Jespersen

Sundiata Keita, *sun JAHT ah KAY tah* (1210?-1260?), also known as Mari-Diata, founded the Mali Empire in West Africa in 1235 and ruled it until about 1260. Sundiata transformed Kangaba—a small kingdom of the Malinke people—into the core of the Mali Empire. It grew to be one of the largest and wealthiest of Africa's ancient empires.

In the early 1200's, Kangaba's independence was threatened by Soso, one of several kingdoms that succeeded the Ghana Empire. Sundiata, who had become king of Kangaba, rallied his people and sought battle with the Soso army. In 1235, he destroyed the army of Sumanguru, the ruler of Soso, at the Battle of Kirina, near present-day Koulikoro, Mali. Further military successes led to the expansion of the Mali Empire. The empire prospered because it controlled major gold fields and was an important center of trans-Saharan trade.

Sundiata successfully combined Islamic and traditional African beliefs. His followers believed he had magical powers. Today, the Malinke people of West Africa still regard Sundiata as a hero.   Kevin C. MacDonald

See also **Mali Empire.**

Sunfish is a name for several kinds of fishes. The two chief kinds of sunfish are (1) *true sunfishes,* also called *panfishes,* and (2) *pygmy sunfishes.* These fishes belong to the sunfish family, which also includes *crappies* and *black bass* (see **Crappie; Bass**).

Panfish are common, brightly colored game fish that rarely measure more than 10 inches (25 centimeters) in length. They are found in bodies of water of all types and are native to all regions of North America east of the Rocky Mountains. The males become brightly colored in the breeding seasons. They clear out a nest on the bottom of a lake or stream and guard the eggs against intruders. The most widely favored game fish among the panfishes is the *bluegill.*

The *pumpkinseed,* another kind of true sunfish, is found abundantly in brooks and ponds from Maine to Florida, and in the northern Mississippi Valley. It has a roundish body and considerable orange in its color. There is a bright red spot on the ear flap. This fish grows up to 8 inches (20 centimeters) long and weighs as much as 8 ounces (230 grams). People enjoy fishing for it because it bites with so much vigor. Panfish are popular with many fishing enthusiasts because the fish are widespread and easily caught with worms as a bait. Other species of the fish also are common. Some smaller, more brilliant sunfish are kept in home aquariums.

Pygmy sunfish are small, less common sunfish found in marshy areas in the southeastern United States. They grow up to 2 inches (5 centimeters) in length.

The name *sunfish* also refers to a group of grotesque-appearing ocean fish. Their bodies are scaleless, silvery, and clumsy, and seem to consist of one great head with small fins. They often rest on the surface in sunny weather, with one fin above water. These fish may weigh 1,000 pounds (450 kilograms). They are never eaten. They are not closely related to freshwater sunfish.   Robert D. Hoyt

Scientific classification. Freshwater sunfish belong to the family Centrarchidae. The bluegill is *Lepomis macrochirus.* The pumpkinseed is *L. gibbosus.* Ocean sunfish belong to the mola family, Molidae. The most common kind is *Mola mola.*

See also **Crappie; Fish** (pictures: Fish of temperate fresh waters [Bluegill; Pumpkinseed]).

Sunflower is a tall plant known for its showy yellow flowers. There are more than 60 species of sunflowers. The most common type grows from 3 to 10 feet (1 to 3 meters) tall and has one or more heads of flowers. Each head consists of a disk of small, tubular flowers surrounded by a fringe of large yellow petals. A sunflower head may measure more than 1 foot (30 centimeters) in diameter and produce up to 1,000 seeds. The head turns and faces toward the sun throughout the day.

Sunflower seeds are rich in protein. They yield a high-quality vegetable oil used in making margarine and cooking oil. Some types of sunflowers have large striped seeds, which are roasted for snack food or blended with other grains to make birdseed. Special *oil-seed* varieties produce small black seeds that contain up to 50 percent oil. Sunflower seed oil accounts for about one-eighth of all vegetable oils produced throughout the world. Sunflower seed oil is sometimes used as a replacement for diesel fuel.

Argentina and Russia lead the world in the production of sunflower seeds. In the United States, production increased rapidly during the mid-1970's as a result of improved varieties and in response to a growing demand for sunflower oil. The chief sunflower-producing states are Kansas, Minnesota, North Dakota, and South Dakota.

Sunflowers originated in North America and were introduced into Europe during the 1500's. Some species come up every year, but the most common ones must be grown annually from seeds.   David E. Zimmer

Scientific classification. Sunflowers make up the genus *Helianthus* of the composite family, Asteraceae or Compositae. The scientific name for the common annual sunflower is *H. annuus.*

See also **Flower** (picture: Common annuals).

Sunflower State. See **Kansas**.

Sung dynasty. See **Song dynasty**.

Sunni Ali, *SUN ee AHL ee* (? -1492), ruled the Songhai Empire in West Africa from 1464 to 1492. He began to absorb the Mali Empire about 1464 and developed Songhai into the most powerful state in the western Sudan. Sunni Ali conquered many neighboring countries. He captured Timbuktu in 1468 and threw out the Tuareg who had held the city since 1433. About 1475, he conquered Djénné, another center of trade.

Sunni Ali established law and order in the Songhai Empire and encouraged trade. He died while returning from a military expedition in 1492. Historians believe he may have been assassinated.   Kevin C. MacDonald

See also **Songhai Empire**.

Sunnis, *SOON eez,* are the followers of the Sunni division of the Islamic religion. Sunnis belong to the larger of the two major divisions of Islam. The other major division is called Shi'ah, and its followers are called Shiites. Sunnis make up more than 80 percent of the *Muslims* (followers of Islam) in the world, and they live everywhere Islam has spread. This name comes from the Sun-

nis' claim that they follow the *Sunnah* (example) of Muhammad, the prophet of Islam.

In all matters of religion, conduct, and law, Muslims recognize two primary sources of guidance. One is the Qur'an, the sacred book of Islam. The other source is the Sunnah of Muhammad. Sunnis call themselves "the people of the established way and the community." They claim to follow faithfully the Islamic community's beliefs and practices and thus to represent true Islam. For this reason and because they make up a majority of Muslims, Sunnis are sometimes called *orthodox Muslims.*

The Sunnis and Shiites differ little in their basic beliefs about God, prophecy, revelation, and the Last Judgment. But throughout Islamic history, there has been hostility between the two groups that has often led to persecution and repression of one by the other.

The issue that most sharply divides the Sunnis from the Shiites is the leadership of the religious community. When Muhammad died in A.D. 632, he named no one to succeed him and did not establish any method for choosing a new leader. The majority, which became the Sunnis, united behind Abū Bakr, one of Muhammad's prominent disciples, and acclaimed him as *caliph* (leader or successor). A smaller group, which became the Shiites, rejected Abū Bakr and the two caliphs who succeeded him. They argued that Muhammad had designated his son-in-law, Alī ibn Abi Talib, as leader, and that leadership should have remained in the family of Muhammad.   Charles J. Adams

See also **Black Muslims; Islam; Muhammad; Muslims; Shiites**.

Sunset laws are laws that require certain state government agencies and programs to be reviewed regularly by the state legislature. An agency or program is automatically abolished—that is, its sun will set—if it cannot be proven essential. Even if the agency or program is essential, it may be restructured.

Sunset laws were passed in an effort to eliminate unnecessary agencies and force other agencies to become more efficient. Agencies authorized to continue are reviewed on a regular basis, such as every four or six years. A related budgeting technique, also aimed at controlling public spending, is called *zero-base budgeting.*

In 1976, Colorado, Florida, Louisiana, and Alabama, in that order, became the first states to adopt sunset laws. By the mid-1980's, most states had passed some form of sunset legislation.   Robert T. Golembiewski

Sunshine laws are laws that require federal, state, and local government agencies to conduct their meetings as openly as possible. These laws permit the public to attend various government meetings. By opening meetings to "let the sunshine in," the laws help discourage secrecy in government.

Sunshine laws originated in 1905, when the Florida Supreme Court ruled that the public could attend city and town government meetings in that state. In 1953, California and New Mexico passed the first state sunshine laws. The problem of secrecy in government reached a height during the Watergate scandal of the 1970's (see **Watergate**). By 1977, all the states had passed sunshine laws. The federal government, through the "Government in the Sunshine Act" of 1976, opened meetings of many agencies to the public.

Sunshine laws vary widely. Some require government

agencies to admit the public to almost all their meetings. Others allow preliminary meetings to be closed if the final vote on an issue is held in open session. Many sunshine laws also permit closed meetings on certain topics, such as personnel matters and real estate purchases.

Robert T. Golembiewski

See also **Freedom of Information Act.**

Sunshine State. See Florida.

Sunspot is a relatively dark area on the surface of the sun. Sunspots appear dark because they are cooler than the rest of the sun's visible surface. They may have a temperature of only about 7000 °F (4000 °C), compared with 11,000 °F (6000 °C) for their surroundings.

A typical large sunspot may have a diameter of about 20,000 miles (32,000 kilometers)—several times larger than Earth's diameter—and last for months. Such a large spot consists of a dark central region called the *umbra* and a lighter surrounding region known as the *penumbra.* A small sunspot, known as a *pore,* has no penumbra. Pores may be several hundred miles in diameter, and they may last only for hours.

The number of sunspots and solar latitudes at which they appear vary over a period of about 11 years. This period is called the *sunspot cycle.* At the beginning of a cycle, sunspots appear chiefly between 20° and 40° north and south of the sun's equator. Later, the spots increase in number and occur closer to the solar equator. By the time the sunspots are greatest in number, they lie primarily between 5° and 40° north and south latitude. At the end of the cycle, the number of spots drops to a minimum and the spots occur chiefly between about 5° and 15° north and south latitude.

How sunspots form. Sunspots have magnetic fields of a strength up to 3,000 times as great as the average magnetic field of either the sun or Earth. Astronomers believe the cause of sunspots is closely related to this fact. According to a standard explanation, the strong magnetic fields of the sun have the shape of tubes just below the solar surface at the beginning of a sunspot cycle. These tubes lie perpendicular to the sun's equator. The sun rotates faster at its equator than at its poles, and so the tubes are stretched out in the east-west direction. Kinks then develop in the magnetic tubes and push through the solar surface. A pair of sunspots appears wherever a kink penetrates, because the kink both leaves and reenters the surface.

Another model for solar activity suggests that giant, doughnut-shaped rolls of turbulent gas rotate beneath the sun's surface. These rolls encircle the sun and lie parallel to its equator. The gas in each carries a magnetic field and rotates perpendicularly to the ring of the rolls. Where gas in adjacent rolls pushes together, the magnetic field increases and sunspots arise.

The two members of a pair of sunspots have opposite magnetic polarities, much like the poles of a magnet. The two spots are called the *preceding spot* and the *following spot* because one "leads" the other in the direction of the sun's rotation. During any given 11-year sunspot cycle, the magnetic polarity of sunspot pairs north of the solar equator is opposite to the polarity of the pairs south of the equator. For example, if the preceding spots in the Northern Hemisphere behave like the north-seeking end of a magnet, the preceding spots in the Southern Hemisphere behave like the south-seeking

end. However, during the next sunspot cycle the behavior of the preceding spots is reversed. Thus, a complete sunspot cycle lasts about 22 years.

Other findings. Astronomers have discovered that the sunspot cycle is only part of a more basic solar activity cycle, which includes *solar flares, plages,* and *prominences* (see Sun [Solar activity]). Such phenomena are closely associated with sunspots and occur in the region around the spots.

In the late 1890's, E. Walter Maunder, a British astronomer, concluded that no sunspots occurred from 1645 to 1715. Research during the 1970's showed that only a small number of sunspots occurred in those 70 years. The existence of that period, called the *Maunder minimum,* indicates that the sunspot cycle may not be as basic a property of the sun as astronomers had thought. Some research has shown that certain aspects of Earth's weather might be linked to solar activity. But these studies remain inconclusive.

From 1980 to 1989, a United States satellite called *Solar Maximum Mission* studied solar activity. Its data showed that changes in the amount of solar energy reaching Earth's atmosphere correspond to changes in the amount of the sun's surface covered by sunspots. For example, when a large sunspot appears, the amount of energy reaching the atmosphere decreases. But on a longer time scale, the sun is overall slightly brighter at the time of a sunspot maximum—which corresponds to the maximum of the solar activity cycle.

The most recent maximums occurred in 1989-1991 and 2000-2001. The next will likely occur in 2011-2012.

Jay M. Pasachoff

See also **Aurora; Climate** (Activity on the sun's surface); **Magnetic storm; Sun** (picture: A sunspot).

Sunstroke. See Hyperthermia.

Super Bowl. See Football (Professional competition).

Superconductivity is the ability of some materials to conduct electric current without resistance at extremely low temperatures. These materials, called *superconductors,* have many useful properties. Electric current can flow through a superconductor without loss of energy. Superconductors can also produce powerful *magnetic fields,* some more than 400,000 times stronger than Earth's magnetic field. A magnetic field is the region around a magnetic object or electric current in which its magnetic force can be detected. The Dutch physicist Heike Kamerlingh Onnes discovered superconductivity in 1911.

Superconductors include many metallic elements, compounds, and *alloys* (combinations of two or more metals). In addition, some *copper oxides* (compounds that contain copper and oxygen) and *organic* (carbon-based) materials can superconduct. A superconductor loses its resistance below a certain temperature, called the *critical temperature.* Many metallic superconductors have critical temperatures near *absolute zero* (0 K or −273.15 °C). Mercury, for example, has a critical temperature of about 4 K (−269 °C). Scientists achieve such low temperatures using expensive cooling equipment with liquid helium as a refrigerant.

Researchers have developed superconductors that work at higher temperatures. One metallic superconductor used in industry, an alloy of niobium and tin, has a critical temperature near 18 K (−255 °C). Magnesium diboride, which superconducts below approximately 39 K (−234 °C), has the highest critical temperature of any known metallic compound. Some copper oxide ceramics have higher critical temperatures. Yttrium-barium-copper oxide superconducts below about 93 K (−180 °C), and mercury-barium-calcium-copper oxide below 133 K (−140 °C). Liquid nitrogen, which is cheaper and easier to handle than liquid helium, can cool these materials to their critical temperature.

A theory explaining one type of superconductivity was proposed in the mid-1950's by three American physicists—John Bardeen, Leon N. Cooper, and John Robert Schrieffer. Their theory is called the *BCS theory,* from the initials of their last names. Normal conductors consist of positive *ions* (charged atoms) surrounded by free-moving electrons that can carry electric current. These electrons scatter off the positive ions, creating resistance. In the BCS theory, superconductivity occurs when the electrons stop behaving as individual particles and begin to move in a more organized way.

The organized state consists of electron pairs called *Cooper pairs,* named for Leon Cooper. Normally, negatively charged electrons repel each other. In superconductivity, a passing electron gently tugs nearby positive ions closer together, leaving behind a trail of slight positive charge. This short-lived charge attracts a second electron toward the first, forming a Cooper pair. When the electrons in a metal are linked as Cooper pairs, they no longer scatter off the positive ions. As a result, they move through the material without resistance.

The BCS theory describes superconductivity in metallic elements and alloys and most compounds. Scientists have not yet developed a model that explains superconductivity in copper oxides and some other compounds.

The need for expensive, bulky cooling equipment limits the use of superconductors. However, they are used in *magnetic resonance imaging* (MRI) machines, which employ magnetic fields to produce images of tissue inside the body. Physics laboratories use superconducting magnets in devices called *particle accelerators* that enable scientists to study tiny bits of matter. Scientists and engineers are working to develop cheaper high-temperature superconductors for use in efficient power lines, high-speed electronic devices, and extremely sensitive magnetic field detectors.   Paul C. Canfield

See also **Cable** (Recent developments); **Cryogenics; Magnetism** (Modern research in magnetism); **Matter** (Superconductors).

Superfluid is a liquid that flows absolutely freely. An ordinary liquid flows with an internal mechanical resistance called *viscosity.* A familiar example of a liquid with high viscosity—that is, a large amount of internal resistance—is molasses. Water has low viscosity, but a superfluid has none. Scientists have found only two substances that can become superfluids. Both are *isotopes* (forms) of helium, and both must be chilled to extremely low temperatures to become superfluids.

Besides zero viscosity, a superfluid has other unusual properties. For example, spinning a container of superfluid produces microscopic whirlpools called *vortexes* (singular *vortex)* in the superfluid. A vortex will continue to spin as long as the liquid remains a superfluid. In addition, a superfluid can flow through a finely packed powder. It can also *conduct* heat—that is, allow heat to pass through itself—at a tremendous rate.

The two isotopes that can become superfluids are known as helium 3 and helium 4. They differ in the composition of their nuclei. A helium 3 nucleus consists of two protons and one neutron, while a helium 4 nucleus has two protons and two neutrons. At atmospheric pressure, helium 3 becomes a superfluid when chilled to less than 0.0016 Fahrenheit degree (0.0009 Celsius degree) above absolute zero (−459.67 °F or −273.15 °C). Helium 4 becomes a superfluid at atmospheric pressure when chilled to less than 3.91 Fahrenheit degrees (2.17 Celsius degrees) above absolute zero.

The Soviet physicist Pyotr Kapitsa discovered superfluidity in 1937. Kapitsa received the Nobel Prize in 1978 for his research in low-temperature physics.

Kieran Mullen

See also **Matter.**

Superior, Lake. See Lake Superior.

Supernova is an exploding star that can become billions of times as bright as the sun before gradually fading from view. At its brightest, a supernova may outshine an entire galaxy. The explosion throws a large cloud of gas into space at speeds of up to 10 percent of the speed of light, which is 186,282 miles (299,792 kilometers) per second. The mass of the expelled material may exceed 10 times the sun's mass (see **Sun** [Mass and density]). Most supernovae reach their peak brightness in one to three weeks and shine intensely for several months. Astronomers often classify a supernova according to the type of explosion involved. The two main types are: (1) *thermonuclear supernovae* and (2) *core-collapse supernovae.*

WORLD BOOK illustrations by Bensen Studios

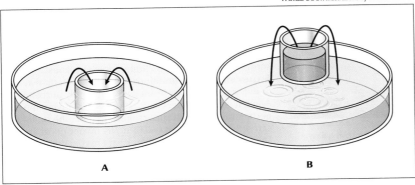

Two experiments show how a superfluid's lack of viscosity enables it to "crawl" up the side of a beaker. In figure A, an empty beaker sitting in a bowl of superfluid helium gradually fills. In B, the beaker is above the liquid, and the helium "crawls" back out.

A   B

Thermonuclear supernovae are thought to occur in certain *binary stars.* A binary star is actually a pair of stars that lie close together and orbit each other. Some such pairs include a *white dwarf*—a small, dense star made up of mostly carbon and oxygen. If the two stars lie close enough to each other, the gravitational pull of the white dwarf draws mass from the larger companion. When the white dwarf reaches a mass about 1.4 times that of the sun, atomic nuclei begin to *fuse* (join) in its interior. This reaction, a type of *thermonuclear fusion,* releases a tremendous amount of energy. The rapid release of energy produces a thermonuclear explosion that destroys the white dwarf.

Thermonuclear supernovae serve an important role in *cosmology,* the study of the universe's structure and development. Because all thermonuclear supernovae explode at about the same mass, they reach almost exactly the same peak brightness. Astronomers can therefore determine such a supernova's distance by measuring how bright it appears from Earth. Studies of the distances of supernovae have revealed information about the universe's size, shape, and development. Astronomers sometimes refer to thermonuclear supernovae as *Type Ia* supernovae, using a classification system based on the *spectrum* (range of light) a supernova emits.

Core-collapse supernovae occur when single stars that are at least roughly 11 times as massive as the sun run out of fuel to sustain fusion. When this happens, the core of iron built up by the fusion process suddenly collapses. The collapse releases a huge amount of energy in the form of *neutrinos* (electrically neutral subatomic particles) and *electromagnetic radiation* (electric and magnetic energy). This energy causes the star to explode as a supernova.

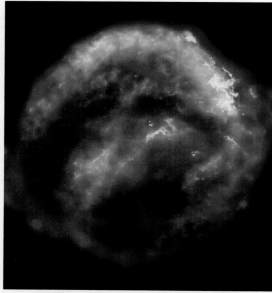

Supernova 1604 was a star that exploded in our own galaxy. The supernova blasted off the shell of gas and dust seen in this false-color composite image. The shell continues to expand at around 2,000 kilometers (1,200 miles) per second. The German astronomer Johannes Kepler observed the explosion in 1604.

Results of supernovae. Supernovae leave behind various types of objects. Some leave a small, extremely dense object called a *neutron star* (see **Neutron star**). After other supernovae, an invisible object called a *black hole* may remain. A black hole has such a powerful gravitational pull that not even light can escape it (see **Black hole**). Some supernovae leave behind no object at all.

In 1054, Chinese astronomers recorded a supernova so bright that it was visible during the day. The explosion left behind a *pulsar* (rapidly spinning neutron star) and a huge cloud of gas and dust now known as the Crab Nebula. In 1987, an exploding star in the Large Magellanic Cloud, the galaxy closest to our own Milky Way, became the first supernova to be visible to the unaided eye in almost 400 years.

Scientists think that supernovae created all the heavier elements, such as iron, gold, and uranium, that are found on Earth and throughout the universe. Many *cosmic rays* appear to originate in supernovae. Cosmic rays are electrically charged, high-energy particles that travel through space (see **Cosmic rays**). Observations suggest that some core-collapse supernovae may produce *gamma-ray bursts.* A gamma-ray burst is a brief, extremely powerful flash of *gamma rays*—the most energetic form of electromagnetic radiation.   Peter E. Nugent

See also **Cosmology** (Faint supernovae); **Star** (Supernovae).

Supersaurus, *SOO pur sawr uhs,* was one of the largest dinosaurs that ever lived. It measured from 100 to 130 feet (30 to 40 meters) long, stood about 27 feet (8.2 meters) tall at the hips, and may have weighed more than 40 tons (36 metric tons). This enormous reptile lived about 150 million years ago, during the late Jurassic Period. It inhabited what is now the western United States.

Supersaurus belonged to a group of gigantic, long-necked dinosaurs called *sauropods.* The animal's slender neck may have stretched as long as 40 feet (12 meters). Its huge, whiplike tail probably extended about 50 feet (15 meters). Because of its large size, *Supersaurus* moved slowly on its four short, thick legs.

Supersaurus ate plants. Its mouth probably had peg-shaped teeth for stripping bark and leaves from trees. Such a huge animal would have eaten tons of plant material every day.

The American paleontologist James A. Jensen discovered *Supersaurus* in 1972. Jensen found a fossilized shoulder blade in Colorado that measured about 8 feet (2.4 meters) long. Few fossils of *Supersaurus* exist, and no complete skeleton has been assembled. Most of what scientists know about the dinosaur comes from comparing its fossils to those of better-known sauropods, such as *Apatosaurus.*   David B. Weishampel

See also **Dinosaur** (Saurischians).

Supersonic flight. See **Aerodynamics** (Supersonic aerodynamics); **Airplane** (Supersonic airplanes).

Superstition is a traditional belief that a certain action or event can cause or foretell an apparently unrelated event. It is often viewed as irrational or involving the supernatural. Common superstitions include the belief that carrying a rabbit's foot will bring its owner good luck. Many people say that if a black cat crosses their path, they will have bad luck. In each case, the action and the event it foretells are traditionally thought to be connected. For instance, the rabbit's foot is likely associated with growth and prosperity because the animal is perceived as especially fertile, energetic, and independent.

Most people, including highly educated individuals, act superstitiously from time to time. Even if people do not express a superstition, they may nonetheless knock on wood or avoid walking under a ladder to prevent bad luck. Many people view superstitions as things of the past. But people create superstitions in everyday life, and new superstitions circulate in modern times. Superstition is common in sports. Many baseball players believe, for example, that a pitcher will give up a hit if anyone mentions that a no-hit game is being pitched. Other athletes have items of clothing that they consider lucky and believe they cannot win without.

Kinds of superstitions. Many superstitions deal with important events in a person's life, such as birth, entering adulthood, marriage, pregnancy, and death. Such superstitions supposedly ensure that a person will pass safely from one stage of life to the next. For example, a person born on Sunday will always have good luck. A bride and groom will have bad luck if they see each other on their wedding day before the ceremony. A pregnant woman must eat the right food, or she will give her child an unwanted birthmark. After a person dies, the doors and windows of the room should be opened so the spirit can leave.

Some superstitions involve a type of magic. One form of such magic comes from the belief that similar actions produce similar results. Many people believe a newborn baby must be carried upstairs before being carried downstairs. In this way, the child will be assured of rising in the world and having success. The same principle appears in the custom of putting money in a purse or wallet being given as a gift. The giver wants to make sure the purse or wallet will always have money in it.

A number of superstitions involve someone taking a deliberate action to cause something to happen or to prevent something from occurring. Most of these *causal* superstitions involve ensuring good luck, avoiding bad luck, or making something good happen. For example, in the United States, carrying a silver dollar is supposed to bring good luck. Some people will not start a trip on a Friday, especially if it is the 13th day of the month. Friday and the number 13 are both associated with bad luck in Western cultures. According to a Japanese belief, the number 4 is unlucky. This is because *shi,* the Japanese word for 4, sounds like the Japanese word for *death.* Thus, many buildings in Japan have no fourth floor.

Other superstitions foretell an event without any conscious action by the person involved. Some of these *sign* superstitions foretell good or bad luck. For example, finding a horseshoe or a four-leaf clover means good luck. Breaking a mirror or spilling salt brings bad luck. Other sign superstitions foretell a certain event or condition. A ring around the moon means rain will soon fall. A person with red hair has a quick temper.

Some sign superstitions may be changed into causal superstitions. If a person hangs a horseshoe over a door, witches cannot enter. In some cases, a person may avoid the bad luck involved in a sign superstition by taking immediate action. For example, someone who has spilled salt may cancel the bad luck by throwing a pinch of salt over the left shoulder.

The role of superstitions. Many people scoff at superstitions because they consider such beliefs to be unscientific. But many scholars believe some superstitions have a scientific basis. For example, people in England once used tea made from foxglove plants to treat some forms of heart disease. Today, physicians often prescribe digitalis, a drug made from dried leaves of the purple foxglove, for patients with weak hearts.

Most people have fears that make them insecure. Superstitions help overcome such fears by providing security. They reassure people that they will get what they want and avoid trouble. For example, millions of people believe in astrology and base important decisions on the position of the sun, moon, planets, and stars (see **Astrology**). Superstitions will probably have a part in life as long as people wonder about the world and their society, seek control in their lives, and have uncertainties about the future.   Simon J. Bronner

Related articles in *World Book* include:

Amulet	Exorcism	Halloween	Occultism
Augur	Fetish	(Halloween	Omen
Birthstone	Fortunetelling	symbols)	Palmistry
Blarney Stone	Friday	Magic	Vampire
Divination	Ghost	Mental illness	Voodoo
Evil eye		(History)	Witchcraft

Additional resources

Shermer, Michael. *Why People Believe Weird Things.* 2nd ed. Owl Bks., 2002.
Vyse, Stuart A. *Believing in Magic: The Psychology of Superstition.* 1997. Reprint. Oxford, 2000.
Waring, Philippa. *A Dictionary of Omens and Superstitions.* 1978. Reprint. Souvenir Pr., 1997.

Supersymmetry is a theory about the relation between the two major groups of *elementary particles.* Elementary particles are subatomic particles, such as electrons, quarks, and neutrinos, that have no known smaller parts. Physicists divide all such particles into two groups: *bosons* and *fermions.* Bosons and fermions differ primarily in *spin,* a measure of internal rotation.

According to supersymmetry theory, each type of boson shares a special relationship with a type of fermion called its *superpartner.* Similarly, each fermion has a boson superpartner. Under certain conditions, a boson or fermion could transform into its superpartner simply by changing its spin. The existence of boson and fermion superpartners would establish an orderly mathematical relation between the two groups of particles. In physics, such a relation is known as a *symmetry.* Physicists call supersymmetry a *hidden symmetry* because the relationship between superpartners would not be apparent under most conditions.

No known boson and fermion share a superpartner relationship. Therefore, if supersymmetry exists, the superpartners of the known particles must be bosons and fermions that are yet to be discovered. Scientists search for subatomic particles using devices called *particle accelerators.* The undiscovered superpartners may be too massive to be produced in current particle accelerators.

Physicists have developed supersymmetry for many reasons. Similar symmetries underlie many laws of physics, and earlier symmetry theories have led to the discovery of new particles. Supersymmetry could also solve many important questions in physics and mathematics. For example, calculations indicate that the universe contains much more matter than we observe. Undiscovered superpartners of known particles might account for the missing mass. Michael Dine

See also **Boson; Fermion.**

Suppé, ZOO pay, **Franz von,** frahnts fuhn (1819-1895), was an Austrian composer and conductor. He primarily wrote theater music, including overtures, incidental music for plays, and operas. His most important works were Viennese-style operettas. His operettas are noted for their rhythmic drive; strong emphasis on waltz rhythms; and light, elegant, and appealing melodies. His first operetta was The Boarding School (1860). Others include The Jolly Pirates (1863), Light Cavalry (1866), and Fatinitza (1876). His masterpiece is the opera Boccaccio (1879). Suppé's most famous composition is the Poet and Peasant overture (1846).

Suppé was born in Spalato, Dalmatia (now Split, Croatia). From 1845 until his retirement in 1883, he served as orchestra director at several major theaters in Vienna, where he conducted his own works as well as performances of many important operas. Katherine K. Preston

Supply and demand are economic forces that determine the amount of a product that is produced and its price. The supply of a product is the amount of it that businesses are willing and able to offer for sale at alternative prices. Generally, the higher the price is, the greater the amount supplied will be. Similarly, the demand for a product is the amount of it that users can and would like to buy at alternative prices. Demand also depends on the price, but in the opposite way. Usually, the quantity demanded is lower at high prices than at low ones. Because the amount that producers actually sell must be the same as the amount that users actually buy, the only price at which everyone can be satisfied is the one for which supply equals demand. This is called the equilibrium price.

The supply and demand diagram with this article shows how these economic forces operate. Using the market for onions as an example, the supply curve SS shows the number of pounds produced each month at every possible market price. Higher prices encourage farmers to produce more onions, and low prices discourage production. Consumers' reactions are shown by the demand curve DD, which shows how many pounds of onions customers want to buy each month at every possible price. At low prices, they want many onions. At high prices, they use other vegetables.

Supply and demand curves cross at a certain price (20 cents a pound in the example). When this is the market price, suppliers will offer just the quantity that users wish to buy. At any higher price, farmers will produce more onions than consumers are willing to buy, and competition among farmers will force the price down. At prices lower than equilibrium, purchasers will demand more onions than are available, and the scarcity of onions will drive the price up. Henry J. Aaron

See also **Price.**

Supreme Court of Canada is Canada's highest court. It is the final court of appeal in all areas of Canadian law. The court hears cases involving provincial or federal laws or Canada's constitution. The Supreme Court also advises the federal government on constitutional questions. The court meets in Ottawa.

Organization. The Supreme Court has nine members—a chief justice and eight associate judges called puisne (pronounced PYOO nee) judges. The term puisne means junior, or associate. Traditionally, three of the nine judges come from Ontario, two from the Prairie Provinces and British Columbia, and one from the Atlantic Provinces. In addition, by law, at least three of the judges must come from Quebec. This rule ensures that at least three members of the court have a background in Quebec's distinctive civil law system. All the other provinces have common law systems. In civil law systems, judges base their decisions on written codes. In common law systems, judges base their rulings on previous court decisions in similar cases.

The prime minister of Canada chooses the Supreme Court judges. The judges are then appointed by the governor general in council. The governor general in council is the governor general of Canada acting with the advice and consent of the Cabinet. The judges are usually selected from the judges of provincial courts of appeal. Lawyers who have belonged to a provincial bar (body of lawyers) for at least 10 years also are eligible to serve on the Supreme Court. Judges of the Supreme Court must retire at the age of 75.

Authority. The Supreme Court deals primarily with cases of broad public significance. Most cases brought before the court involve Canada's Criminal Code, other federal or provincial laws, or administrative acts of the federal government. But the court also decides constitutional cases. Most of the constitutional cases deal with the Canadian bill of rights, called the Charter of Rights and Freedoms, or with the division of powers between the federal and provincial governments.

Lawsuits involving private law can be appealed to the Supreme Court only if the court grants a person or group leave (permission) to make the appeal. Private law deals with the rights and obligations people have in their relations with each other (see **Law** [Branches of law]). The court grants leave to appeal if a panel of three of its judges decides the case is of sufficient public importance. The Supreme Court also must decide whether to grant leave in most cases involving criminal, administrative, or constitutional law. Certain criminal cases may be brought before the court without leave. For example, any conviction of first-degree murder carries with it an automatic right of appeal to the Supreme Court.

Before it can hear any case, the court must form a quorum. A quorum consists of five judges. All nine

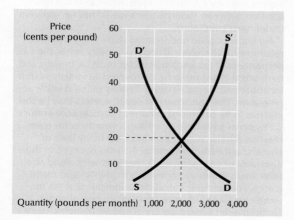

Price
(cents per pound)

Quantity (pounds per month) 1,000 2,000 3,000 4,000

The Supreme Court of Canada is the highest court of appeal in all areas of Canadian law. The Supreme Court has nine members—a chief justice and eight *puisne* (associate) judges. All nine judges may serve until they reach the age of 75. The court meets in Ottawa.

Rosalie Silberman Abella

Michel Bastarache

Ian Binnie

Louise V. Charron

Chief Justice Beverley McLachlin

Marie Deschamps

Morris J. Fish

Louis LeBel

Marshall Rothstein

Photos of Michel Bastarache, Ian Binnie, and Beverley McLachlin © Larry Munns, Supreme Court of Canada; photos of Rosalie Silberman Abella, Louise V. Charron, Marie Deschamps, Morris J. Fish, Louis LeBel, and Marshall Rothstein © Philippe Landreville Inc., Supreme Court of Canada

Judges of the Supreme Court of Canada

Name	Year appointed	Province	Appointing government	Judicial position prior to Supreme Court service	Year retirement due*
Beverley McLachlin (chief justice)	1989	British Columbia	Mulroney	Supreme Court of British Columbia	2018
Michel Bastarache	1997	New Brunswick	Chrétien	New Brunswick Court of Appeal	2022
Ian Binnie	1998	Ontario	Chrétien	None	2014
Louis LeBel	2000	Quebec	Chrétien	Quebec Court of Appeal	2015
Marie Deschamps	2002	Quebec	Chrétien	Quebec Court of Appeal	2027
Morris J. Fish	2003	Quebec	Chrétien	Quebec Court of Appeal	2013
Louise V. Charron	2004	Ontario	Martin	Ontario Court of Appeal	2026
Rosalie Silberman Abella	2004	Ontario	Martin	Ontario Court of Appeal	2022
Marshall Rothstein	2006	Ontario	Harper	Federal Court of Appeal	2015

*Judges must retire at age 75.

judges usually do not participate in a single case, but the full court assembles for important constitutional cases. Most Supreme Court cases are heard by a panel of seven judges or by the full court. In most of its cases, the court explains the reasoning behind its decision.

History. Canada's Parliament created the Supreme Court in 1875 as a general court of appeal. At that time, the court had six judges. A seventh judge was added in 1927. The court was expanded to nine members in 1949.

From 1875 to 1949, the Supreme Court was supreme in name only. In reality, it was merely an intermediate appellate court. Its legal decisions could be appealed to the Judicial Committee of the Privy Council in London, England. Canadians could even choose to bypass the Supreme Court by appealing their case directly to the Judicial Committee from the highest court of appeal in their province. The committee, which consisted chiefly of judges from the United Kingdom's highest courts, served as Canada's highest court of appeal. Distinguished members of the Supreme Court of Canada occasionally served on the committee.

In 1933, all appeals of Canadian criminal cases to the Judicial Committee were abolished. In 1949, all other

Canadian appeals to the committee were eliminated, and the Supreme Court became Canada's highest court of appeal in all areas of law.

Until 1975, parties to any private lawsuit that involved $10,000 or more were granted an automatic right of appeal to the Supreme Court from the federal court of appeal or from any of the provincial courts of appeal. As a result, many of the cases heard by the Supreme Court involved no significant issue of public law. In 1975, the court was granted the authority to decide which cases involving private lawsuits were important enough for it to hear. Afterward, the court significantly reduced the number of private lawsuits it handled annually.

The Supreme Court gained a more prominent role in Canadian life after the government adopted the Charter of Rights and Freedoms in 1982. Since then, in cases involving the charter, the court has declared a number of federal and provincial laws unconstitutional. In 1988, for example, the court overturned a federal law that made abortions illegal unless they were authorized by special hospital committees.   Peter H. Russell

See also **Dickson, Brian; Lamer, Antonio; McLachlin, Beverley Marian.**

Supreme Court of the United States is the highest court in the United States. The court meets regularly in the Supreme Court Building in Washington, D.C. Its main duty is to determine the legality of conduct at all levels of government—federal, state, and local—as measured either by the Constitution of the United States or by other laws passed by Congress. Much of the court's work involves the interpretation of general legal rules and the application of these rules to specific cases.

The Supreme Court accepts only a small percentage of the cases brought before it. Because the court is the nation's highest judicial authority, its decisions have great importance. Once it decides a constitutional question, all other courts in the United States are expected to follow the decision in similar cases.

The Supreme Court is the only court specifically created by the Constitution. Congress later created federal district and circuit courts (now known as courts of appeals), above which stands the Supreme Court. State judicial systems also have high courts that are supreme in interpreting state statutes and state constitutions. However, the Supreme Court of the United States can review the decisions of the highest state courts when the Constitution of the United States or acts of Congress are involved. This article deals only with the Supreme Court of the United States. For information on the federal court system and on state courts, see the article **Court.**

The role of the Supreme Court and its interpretation of the law have shifted throughout history. These changes depend largely on the beliefs of its members, and on the national conditions of the time. In the early days of the nation, for example, the court concerned itself chiefly with the proper division of authority between the state and federal governments. Since the mid-1900's, the protection of the rights and liberties of individuals has been a major concern.

How the Supreme Court is organized

Article III of the Constitution provides for the creation of the Supreme Court and states the limits of its jurisdiction. But the Constitution leaves most details of the court's organization and of the work it can do to Congress, which set up the initial federal court system with the Judiciary Act of 1789.

Membership. The Supreme Court has nine members—a chief justice and eight associate justices. Congress sets the number and has changed it through the years. The first Supreme Court had six members. During Abraham Lincoln's presidency, it had 10 members. Since 1869, the court has had nine members.

The Constitution sets no qualifications for justices but states that they shall be appointed by the president, with the advice and consent of the Senate. All justices, however, have been lawyers. Most have been judges, and some have been government officials or law school professors. In the late 1900's, most justices appointed to the court served on the U.S. courts of appeals before their nomination. The Senate has rejected outright only 12 Supreme Court nominees.

Salary and terms. Once appointed, justices may remain in office for life, and Congress cannot reduce their salaries. These provisions protect the justices from political control and help ensure their independence. In 2005, the salaries were $212,100 for the chief justice and $203,000 for the associate justices. Congress can remove a justice through impeachment for corrupt behavior or other abuses of office, but the lawmakers have never done so. A justice 70 years of age, who has served as a justice or judge of the United States for 10 or more years, may retire and continue to receive a full salary. A justice who has served at least 15 years as a justice or judge may retire at 65 and receive the salary.

Authority of the Supreme Court

The Supreme Court declares what the law is only when an actual case comes before it. The case must involve a real dispute between opposing parties. The Supreme Court of the United States, unlike some state supreme courts, does not give legal advice or advisory opinions on pending legislation, even if requested to do so by the president or by Congress.

The Constitution permits the court to decide cases arising under the Constitution, federal laws, and treaties. The Supreme Court also decides disputes involving the United States or two or more states. The most important of these cases are those that require the court to interpret the Constitution or the laws enacted by Congress.

The Supreme Court has the power to decide whether a federal or state law or executive action is constitutional. The Constitution does not expressly grant the court this power, known as *judicial review.* However, the Constitution, by its own terms, is the "supreme law of the land." The court has ruled that it must review conflicts between the Constitution and federal or state law to preserve the supremacy of the Constitution.

Original and appellate jurisdiction. The Constitution gives the Supreme Court two types of authority: (1) *original jurisdiction* and (2) *appellate jurisdiction.* The court has original jurisdiction in cases affecting ambassadors or other representatives of foreign countries and in cases in which a state is one of the parties. These cases go directly to the Supreme Court, though they make up only a small part of the court's workload.

Most of the work of the court comes from its appellate jurisdiction, which is its authority to confirm or reverse lower court decisions. Most Supreme Court cases come from the federal courts of appeals and the highest

Photri

The courtroom of the Supreme Court Building in Washington, D.C., is shown here from the back of the room, where spectators can sit and watch court proceedings. At the front of the room is the bench, where the nine justices sit.

© Mark Wilson, Getty Images

John G. Roberts, Jr.

© Mark Wilson, Getty Images

Samuel A. Alito, Jr.

Stephen G. Breyer

Ruth Bader Ginsburg

Anthony M. Kennedy

Antonin Scalia

David H. Souter

John Paul Stevens

All other photos from the Collection, Supreme Court Historical Society

Clarence Thomas

state courts. The courts of appeals normally review federal district court decisions before the Supreme Court does. In a few cases, the Supreme Court may review the decisions of federal district courts or of lower state courts. The Supreme Court also reviews the decisions of the Court of Appeals for the Federal Circuit, a specialized court, and of the Supreme Court of Puerto Rico.

The Supreme Court decides which of the cases under its appellate jurisdiction it will review. Because it cannot possibly review all of the cases brought before it, it selects the ones it considers most important or the ones where earlier rulings have left confusion about the law.

Writ of certiorari. The court agrees to hear a case by granting a *writ of certiorari* (pronounced *SUR shee uh RAIR ee*), a written order calling the case up from a lower court for review. The attorney for the side requesting a review submits a written *petition for certiorari.* It explains why the lower court judge is in error and why the case is of sufficient significance to merit review by the Supreme Court. The opposing attorney can file a written statement opposing the petition. If four justices vote to grant the petition, the court agrees to hear the case.

The court in action

Attorneys who have been admitted to the bar of the Supreme Court plead most cases before the court. However, other attorneys who meet specific qualifications may be allowed to present certain cases. Most litigants hire and pay their own attorneys. If a litigant has no money, the court may provide free legal service. When the U.S. government has an interest in a case before the Supreme Court, the solicitor general or members of the solicitor general's staff usually represent the government. The attorney general of the United States may sometimes argue an important case.

Deciding cases. The justices decide a case after they have considered written and oral arguments from each side. The written argument is called a *brief.* During oral arguments, the justices often interrupt and ask questions. After the attorneys' oral arguments, the justices discuss the case *in conference* (in private). The chief justice begins the discussion. Then, in order of *seniority* (time served on the court), the associate justices give their opinions. After discussion ends, the justices vote in reverse order of seniority. Cases are decided by majority vote. If a tie occurs, the lower court decision stands and the parties have no further appeal.

Written opinions. If the chief justice has voted with the majority, he or she selects a justice to write the *opinion of the court,* also called the *majority opinion.* If the chief justice has not voted with the majority, the senior justice of the majority assigns the opinion. A justice who disagrees with this opinion may write a *dissenting opinion.* Justices may also write *concurring opinions* if they agree with the conclusion of the majority but not with the reasons for reaching it, or if they wish to express similar reasons in their own words. If a majority of participating justices disagree, there is no majority opinion. In this case, there may be a *plurality opinion* signed by several, but not a majority, of the justices. A plurality opinion does not establish a precedent for later cases.

A government publication called the *United States Reports* publishes all Supreme Court opinions. The publishing of opinions allows lawyers, legal officials, and the general public to study the decisions of the court. This publishing is an important tradition in a free society and a safeguard against unreasonable use of power.

Effects of decisions. Supreme Court decisions have far-ranging effects because lower courts are expected to follow the decisions in similar cases. The Supreme Court itself usually follows its earlier decisions. The policy of following previous decisions is known as *stare decisis.* It lends stability and predictability to the law. But the court may not consider itself bound by an earlier de-

U.S. Supreme Court justices

Name	Term	Appointed by	Name	Term	Appointed by
Chief justices			Stanley Matthews	1881-1889	Garfield
*John Jay	1789-1795	Washington	Horace Gray	1882-1902	Arthur
*†John Rutledge	1795	Washington	Samuel Blatchford	1882-1893	Arthur
*Oliver Ellsworth	1796-1800	Washington	*Lucius Q. C. Lamar	1888-1893	Cleveland
*John Marshall	1801-1835	J. Adams	David J. Brewer	1890-1910	Harrison
*Roger B. Taney	1836-1864	Jackson	Henry B. Brown	1891-1906	Harrison
*Salmon P. Chase	1864-1873	Lincoln	George Shiras, Jr.	1892-1903	Harrison
*Morrison R. Waite	1874-1888	Grant	Howell E. Jackson	1893-1895	Harrison
*Melville W. Fuller	1888-1910	Cleveland	*Edward D. White	1894-1910	Cleveland
*Edward D. White	1910-1921	Taft	*Rufus W. Peckham	1896-1909	Cleveland
*William H. Taft	1921-1930	Harding	Joseph McKenna	1898-1925	McKinley
*Charles E. Hughes	1930-1941	Hoover	*Oliver W. Holmes, Jr.	1902-1932	T. Roosevelt
*Harlan F. Stone	1941-1946	F. D. Roosevelt	William R. Day	1903-1922	T. Roosevelt
*Frederick M. Vinson	1946-1953	Truman	William H. Moody	1906-1910	T. Roosevelt
*Earl Warren	1953-1969	Eisenhower	Horace H. Lurton	1910-1914	Taft
*Warren E. Burger	1969-1986	Nixon	*Charles E. Hughes	1910-1916	Taft
*William H. Rehnquist	1986-2005	Reagan	Willis Van Devanter	1911-1937	Taft
*John G. Roberts, Jr.	2005-	G. W. Bush	Joseph R. Lamar	1911-1916	Taft
			Mahlon Pitney	1912-1922	Taft
Associate justices			James C. McReynolds	1914-1941	Wilson
*James Wilson	1789-1798	Washington	*Louis D. Brandeis	1916-1939	Wilson
*John Rutledge	1789-1791	Washington	John H. Clarke	1916-1922	Wilson
William Cushing	1790-1810	Washington	George Sutherland	1922-1938	Harding
*John Blair	1790-1796	Washington	Pierce Butler	1923-1939	Harding
James Iredell	1790-1799	Washington	Edward T. Sanford	1923-1930	Harding
Thomas Johnson	1792-1793	Washington	*Harlan F. Stone	1925-1941	Coolidge
*William Paterson	1793-1806	Washington	*Owen J. Roberts	1930-1945	Hoover
*Samuel Chase	1796-1811	Washington	*Benjamin N. Cardozo	1932-1938	Hoover
Bushrod Washington	1799-1829	J. Adams	*Hugo L. Black	1937-1971	F. D. Roosevelt
Alfred Moore	1800-1804	J. Adams	Stanley F. Reed	1938-1957	F. D. Roosevelt
William Johnson	1804-1834	Jefferson	*Felix Frankfurter	1939-1962	F. D. Roosevelt
H. Brockholst Livingston	1807-1823	Jefferson	*William O. Douglas	1939-1975	F. D. Roosevelt
Thomas Todd	1807-1826	Jefferson	Frank Murphy	1940-1949	F. D. Roosevelt
Gabriel Duvall	1811-1835	Madison	*James F. Byrnes	1941-1942	F. D. Roosevelt
*Joseph Story	1812-1845	Madison	*Robert H. Jackson	1941-1954	F. D. Roosevelt
Smith Thompson	1823-1843	Monroe	Wiley B. Rutledge	1943-1949	F. D. Roosevelt
Robert Trimble	1826-1828	J. Q. Adams	Harold H. Burton	1945-1958	Truman
John McLean	1830-1861	Jackson	*Tom C. Clark	1949-1967	Truman
Henry Baldwin	1830-1844	Jackson	Sherman Minton	1949-1956	Truman
James M. Wayne	1835-1867	Jackson	John M. Harlan	1955-1971	Eisenhower
Philip P. Barbour	1836-1841	Jackson	*William J. Brennan, Jr.	1956-1990	Eisenhower
John Catron	1837-1865	Van Buren	Charles E. Whittaker	1957-1962	Eisenhower
John McKinley	1838-1852	Van Buren	*Potter Stewart	1958-1981	Eisenhower
Peter V. Daniel	1842-1860	Van Buren	*Byron R. White	1962-1993	Kennedy
Samuel Nelson	1845-1872	Tyler	*Arthur J. Goldberg	1962-1965	Kennedy
Levi Woodbury	1845-1851	Polk	*Abe Fortas	1965-1969	Johnson
Robert C. Grier	1846-1870	Polk	*Thurgood Marshall	1967-1991	Johnson
Benjamin R. Curtis	1851-1857	Fillmore	*Harry A. Blackmun	1970-1994	Nixon
John A. Campbell	1853-1861	Pierce	*Lewis F. Powell, Jr.	1972-1987	Nixon
Nathan Clifford	1858-1881	Buchanan	*William H. Rehnquist	1972-1986	Nixon
Noah H. Swayne	1862-1881	Lincoln	*John P. Stevens	1975-	Ford
*Samuel F. Miller	1862-1890	Lincoln	*Sandra Day O'Connor	1981-2006	Reagan
*David Davis	1862-1877	Lincoln	*Antonin Scalia	1986-	Reagan
*Stephen J. Field	1863-1897	Lincoln	*Anthony M. Kennedy	1988-	Reagan
William Strong	1870-1880	Grant	*David H. Souter	1990-	G. H. W. Bush
Joseph P. Bradley	1870-1892	Grant	*Clarence Thomas	1991-	G. H. W. Bush
Ward Hunt	1873-1882	Grant	*Ruth Bader Ginsburg	1993-	Clinton
*John M. Harlan	1877-1911	Hayes	*Stephen G. Breyer	1994-	Clinton
William B. Woods	1881-1887	Hayes	*Samuel A. Alito, Jr.	2006-	G. W. Bush

*Has a separate biography in *World Book*.
†Served during U.S. Senate recess and later rejected by the Senate.

cision if it is convinced an error has been made, or if new circumstances require a different approach. This policy enables the court to recognize a previous error or to reflect social, political, and economic change.

Landmark decisions

The Supreme Court has decided cases that touch almost every aspect of American life. One of the most important early Supreme Court cases was *Marbury v. Mad-* *ison* in 1803. In the decision, Chief Justice John Marshall stated that the court may rule an act of Congress unenforceable if it violates the Constitution. This ruling was the first instance of judicial invalidation of a federal law.

Federalism. The court has interpreted the Constitution as granting broad powers to the federal government. These powers bar certain exercises of state power when they conflict with national interests. For example, in the 1819 case of *McCulloch v. Maryland*, the court determined that Congress had the power to charter a national bank. The court then struck down a Maryland law that would have taxed the bank.

The power of the federal government increased during the mid-1800's, aided by the adoption of the 14th Amendment in 1868. This amendment forbids the states from denying any person due process, equal protection, or the rights and privileges of citizens of the United States. Since the amendment's passing, the court has varied in the extent to which it prevents states from trespassing on these protected rights.

Civil rights. In 1857, in *Dred Scott v. Sandford,* the court held that blacks, even those freed from slavery, were not and could not become U.S. citizens. Then in 1868, the 14th Amendment made blacks citizens and guaranteed to all people "equal protection of the laws." In 1896, in *Plessy v. Ferguson,* the court interpreted that provision to allow "separate but equal" facilities for whites and blacks. But in 1954, in *Brown v. Board of Education of Topeka,* the court ruled that a state could not separate students by race. Later, the court decided that it is sometimes permissible to give preference to racial minorities in jobs and other matters as a way to correct the effects of past discrimination.

In 1873, in *Bradwell v. State,* the Supreme Court decided that Illinois could exclude women from the practice of law. The 19th Amendment, adopted in 1920, gave women the right to vote, but many laws continued to treat men and women differently. Women's rights generally remained restricted until the 1960's, when Congress began to pass laws expanding the employment and educational opportunities of women and the court actively enforced those laws.

A landmark decision in the area of women's rights occurred in the 1973 case of *Roe v. Wade.* In this case, the court declared that a state may not prohibit abortion during the first three months of pregnancy, and may do so only under limited conditions in the second three months. Later decisions modified *Roe* somewhat, but its basic principle remained intact.

Election issues. For most of its history, the Supreme Court was reluctant to hear challenges to election districting. But in 1962, in *Baker v. Carr,* the court changed its position and said that unfair distribution of seats in state legislatures could be challenged in federal courts. Then in 1964, in *Reynolds v. Sims,* it ruled that states must redraw election districts to guarantee that all districts are roughly equal in population.

In 2000, the Supreme Court played a major role in deciding the presidential race between Texas Governor George W. Bush and Vice President Al Gore. Five weeks after the election, the court ruled in *Bush v. Gore* that the state of Florida should not continue vote recounts, because a consistent statewide standard did not exist. The court also ruled that there was not enough time to develop a statewide standard and to perform a manual recount. Gore then conceded the election to Bush.

Freedom of speech. Starting around World War I (1914-1918), the Supreme Court heard many cases involving the guarantee of free speech in the First Amendment. Early decisions upheld lower courts that found dissenters guilty of a crime for protesting United States entry into the war. The legal protection of free speech grew steadily from the 1930's to the 1960's. In 1964, in

New York Times v. Sullivan, the court ruled that a newspaper could not be punished for publishing false statements about a public official unless it knew or should have known that the statements were false. In 1969, in *Brandenburg v. Ohio,* the court held that a person could not be punished for urging a violation of the law unless it was clear that the violation would likely occur.

Criminal law. In the 1960's, the Supreme Court strengthened the protections given a person accused of a crime. In the 1961 case of *Mapp v. Ohio,* the court ruled that prosecutors could not introduce into a trial evidence obtained without a search warrant, though later court rulings provided for certain exceptions. In 1963, in *Gideon v. Wainwright,* the court held that states must provide free legal counsel to any person charged with a felony who could not afford to hire a lawyer. In 1966, *Miranda v. Arizona* ruled that the police must inform an accused person of his or her right to remain silent and to consult with a lawyer before questioning the person. The court reaffirmed *Miranda* in a 2000 decision.

The Supreme Court has also placed limits on the power of the state to impose the death penalty. In 1972, in *Furman v. Georgia,* the court held that some state laws authorizing the penalty were unconstitutional. The court claimed that the death penalty, as administered under the laws, qualified as cruel and unusual punishment. In response to this decision, more than 35 states enacted new laws authorizing the death penalty. The Supreme Court basically approved these laws in *Gregg v. Georgia* in 1976. Still, the court's members remained sharply divided about actual administration of the death penalty.

Church and state. The Bill of Rights prohibits laws establishing religion or interfering with the free exercise of religion. The Supreme Court has spent many years trying to interpret these clauses, which may appear to contradict each other. In the 1962 case of *Engel v. Vitale,* the court banned prayer in public schools. The justices upheld this ruling in a 2000 case involving prayers at school football games. But in the 1995 case of *Rosenberger v. University of Virginia,* the court held that a state could not deny funding to a religion-oriented student publication if it funded other, nonreligious ones.

Controversy on the court

The Supreme Court has divided sharply on many cases. Divisions on the court often mirror divisions within the wider American public, regarding such matters as the scope of minority rights or the relationship between church and state. Legal experts believe that the court's lack of complete agreement in such cases should be expected and is even desirable. It reflects the seriousness of the cases and the presence of different points of view.

The court's members also divide sharply on matters of *judicial methodology*—that is, the approach that courts should take when interpreting the Constitution. Some justices insist that the court should interpret and apply the Constitution to agree with its authors' original intentions. Others argue for a more creative role for the court in building "a living Constitution" that responds to the nation's new and changing problems.   Sanford Levinson

Related articles in *World Book.* See the separate articles for the justices and the landmark decisions listed in the *tables* in this article. See also the following articles:
Chief justice

Landmark decisions of the Supreme Court

Powers of the court, federal government, and states

1803 *Marbury v. Madison.* If a law passed by Congress conflicts with the Constitution, the Supreme Court must base its decision on the Constitution. This ruling established the court's power of *judicial review*—that is, its authority to declare laws unconstitutional.

1810 *Fletcher v. Peck.* Georgia could not revoke a land grant after the land had been sold to a third party. The Constitution protects contracts against interference by the states, and a sales agreement is a type of contract.

1819 *McCulloch v. Maryland.* The Constitution gives *implied powers* to Congress in addition to the *express powers* that are specifically granted. Implied powers are those necessary to carry out express powers.

1819 *Dartmouth College v. Woodward.* New Hampshire could not alter a royal charter and make Dartmouth a state college. A charter is a contract, and the Constitution protects contracts against state interference.

1995 *U.S. Term Limits v. Thornton.* The states cannot limit the number of terms their senators and representatives may serve in Congress.

Powers of the president

1974 *United States v. Nixon.* The president cannot withhold evidence needed in a criminal trial. This ruling established that the president's executive privilege—the right to keep records confidential—is not unlimited.

1982 *Fitzgerald v. Nixon.* No president may be sued for damages for any official action taken while in office. This immunity applies to civil suits, not to criminal prosecution or other types of judicial action.

Powers of business and industry

1824 *Gibbons v. Ogden.* The powers of the federal government are superior to those of the states in all matters of *interstate* commerce (trade between states).

1905 *Lochner v. New York.* A law limiting bakers to a 60-hour work week was unconstitutional because it violated "freedom of contract" between employer and employee.

1935 *Schechter v. United States.* The National Industrial Recovery Act of 1933, which provided for fair-competition codes for businesses, was unconstitutional.

Election issues

1962 *Baker v. Carr.* Citizens can challenge unfair distribution of seats in state legislatures before a federal court.

1964 *Reynolds v. Sims.* The U.S. House of Representatives and both houses of a state legislature must follow the rule of "one person, one vote" and create election districts roughly equal in population.

2000 *Bush v. Gore.* Vote recounts conducted without a consistent statewide standard are unconstitutional. This ruling played a major role in the victory of Texas Governor George W. Bush over Vice President Al Gore in the 2000 presidential election.

Freedom of speech and of the press

1919 *Schenck v. United States.* The government can restrict freedom of speech if the speech creates a "clear and present danger" of violence or some other evil that the government has a right to prevent.

1957 *Roth v. United States.* Freedom of the press, guaranteed by the First Amendment to the Constitution, protects publication of material thought to be obscene if such material meets certain standards.

1964 *New York Times Co. v. Sullivan.* A newspaper cannot be punished for untrue statements about a public official unless it deliberately published a falsehood.

1969 *Brandenburg v. Ohio.* The government cannot punish a person for advocating (supporting) ideas.

1973 *Miller v. California.* Material can be considered obscene if it fulfills certain requirements established by the court (see **Obscenity and pornography**).

1989 *Texas v. Johnson.* The government cannot punish a person for burning the flag of the United States as part of a peaceful protest.

Church and state

1962 *Engel v. Vitale.* Public schools cannot require the recitation of prayers.

1984 *Lynch v. Donnelly.* A city or town can include a *crèche*, or Nativity scene, in its Christmas display.

Rights of people accused of crime

1866 *Ex Parte Milligan.* Military courts cannot try civilians outside military areas if civilian courts are available.

1961 *Mapp v. Ohio.* Evidence obtained by illegal means cannot be used in a criminal trial.

1963 *Gideon v. Wainwright.* The states must provide free legal counsel to any person accused of a felony who cannot afford a lawyer.

1966 *Miranda v. Arizona.* An accused person must be informed of his or her constitutional rights, including rights to remain silent and to have the assistance of a lawyer, before being questioned.

1972 *Argersinger v. Hamlin.* The states must provide free legal counsel to any person accused of a misdemeanor that involves a jail term if the person cannot afford a lawyer.

1972 *Furman v. Georgia.* The death penalty, as it was then administered, was cruel and unusual punishment in violation of the 8th and 14th amendments to the Constitution.

1976 *Gregg v. Georgia.* The death penalty is constitutional when statutes adequately guide its use.

Rights of women and minority groups

1857 *Dred Scott v. Sandford.* Blacks could not be U.S. citizens, and Congress could not prohibit slavery in the U.S. territories. The first part of this ruling was overturned in 1868 by the 14th Amendment. The second part was changed in 1865 by the 13th Amendment.

1896 *Plessy v. Ferguson.* "Separate but equal" public facilities for whites and blacks did not violate the Constitution. The court reversed this decision in 1954.

1948 *Shelley v. Kraemer.* State or federal courts cannot enforce *restrictive covenants,* which are agreements to prevent real-estate owners from selling their property to members of minority groups.

1954 *Brown v. Board of Education of Topeka* (Kansas). Separate but equal facilities for blacks in public schools do not meet the constitutional requirement for equal protection under the law.

1973 *Roe v. Wade.* The states may not prohibit a woman's right to have an abortion during the first three months of pregnancy and may do so only under certain conditions in the second three months. But under certain circumstances, the states may prohibit the abortion of a fetus that is capable of living outside the mother's body.

1978 *Regents of the University of California v. Bakke,* also called the *Bakke* case. University and college admissions programs may not use specific quotas to achieve racial balance. But they may give special consideration to members of minority groups.

1986 *Meritor Savings Bank v. Vinson.* Sexual harassment is a form of discrimination prohibited under the Civil Rights Act of 1964. Sexual harassment includes unwelcome sexual requests or comments from an employer, teacher, or other person in a position of power.

2003 *Lawrence v. Texas.* States may not ban private homosexual conduct.

*Has a separate article in *World Book.*

Constitution of the United States
Court
Roosevelt, Franklin D. (The Supreme Court)
Scottsboro case
Washington, D.C. (picture: The Supreme Court Building)

Additional resources

Hall, Kermit L., and others, eds. *The Oxford Companion to the Supreme Court of the United States.* 2nd ed. Oxford, 2005.
Horn, Geoffrey M. *The Supreme Court.* World Almanac Lib., 2003. Younger readers.
Jost, Kenneth, ed. *The Supreme Court A to Z.* 3rd ed. CQ Pr., 2003.
Justices of the United States Supreme Court. Macmillan Reference, 2001.
Patrick, John J. *The Supreme Court of the United States: A Student Companion.* 2nd ed. Oxford, 2001.

Surabaya, SUR *uh BAH yuh* (pop. 2,610,477), sometimes spelled Surabaja, is the second largest city in Indonesia. Only Jakarta has more people. Surabaya is the capital of the province of East Java and is Indonesia's second busiest port after Jakarta. Indonesia's navy has a major naval base in Surabaya. Surabaya lies on the northeast coast of the island of Java (see **Indonesia** [political map]).

Surabaya is a major industrial center. Its industries include shipbuilding, motor assembly, textile production, and rubber processing. The city is the home of a large university and a major technical school.

Surabaya's founding date is uncertain. But the city has been the chief trading and shipping center of eastern Java since the 1300's.   Harold Crouch

Surface measure. See Area; Square measure.

Surface tension is an effect produced at the boundary of a liquid that can cause the boundary to act like a thin, elastic film. For example, surface tension enables the surface of a pool of water to support some objects that would normally sink—including needles, razor blades, and certain insects—if they are placed carefully on the water. Surface tension can also draw liquid into a thin tube, an effect known as *capillarity* (see **Capillarity**).

Surface tension occurs because molecules near the boundary of a liquid experience different forces than do molecules in the liquid's interior. Deep inside the liquid, each molecule is attracted to other liquid molecules all around it. Such forces typically balance in all directions. However, molecules near the boundary also interact with molecules in the neighboring material. Such forces may not balance the attractive forces of the liquid molecules, producing surface tension. At the surface of a pool of water, for example, air molecules only weakly attract water molecules. The molecules inside the pool attract the surface water molecules more strongly, resulting in an overall inward force that causes the surface to act like a thin, elastic skin.   Michael Schatz

Surfactant. See Detergent and soap.

Surfing is an exciting water sport in which a person rides waves, usually in the ocean. People in what is now Hawaii were surfing before explorer Christopher Columbus sailed to the New World in 1492. Today, surfing is popular in many countries, including Australia, Brazil, Indonesia, South Africa, and the United States.

All forms of surfing require exact timing and sharp reflexes to stay balanced. Surfers should also be able to anticipate what a breaking wave will do. There are nine aquatic activities that can be classified as surfing. In surfing, the surfer lies, kneels, sits, or stands on a board or sits in a kayak or canoe. In the three wintersurf events, the surfer maneuvers a surfboard or sailboard on snow.

This article discusses *standup surfing,* the most popular form of this sport. It is often simply called *surfing.*

Ancient Hawaiians surfed on wooden boards that were up to 18 feet (5.5 meters) long. Today, surfers use boards made of a strong, lightweight plastic called polyurethane foam wrapped in fiberglass sealed with resins.

Generally, boards less than 7 feet (2 meters) in length are called *shortboards,* and those 7 feet or more are called *longboards.* Shortboards are more popular today. A typical shortboard is about 6 feet (1.8 meters) long, about 20 inches (51 centimeters) wide, and about 2 ½ inches (6.4 centimeters) thick. It weighs from 6 to 8 pounds (2.7 to 3.6 kilograms).

To prepare for a shortboard ride, the standup surfer lies facedown on the board. On a longboard, the surfer usually kneels on the board. Then the surfer paddles out beyond where the waves begin to break, called the *outside.* When a wave, ideally at least 3 feet (0.9 meter) high, starts to move toward the shore, the surfer paddles the

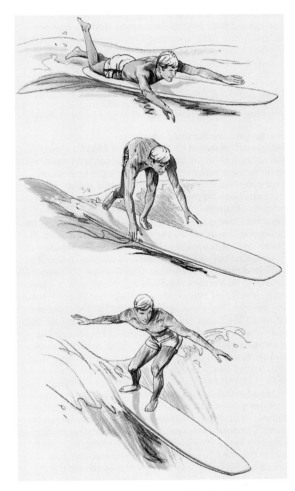

Catching a wave, the surfer paddles with his hands to gain speed. When the wave lifts the board, he stands up and puts his weight on his front foot, aiming the board toward the shore.

board just ahead of it. The surfer stands just as the wave begins to lift the board and carry it toward shore. The surfer shifts weight to steer the board across the wave's *face*—that is, the smooth wall of water just below the crest. The surfer may also skim along the wave's crest.

Expert surfers tend to stand at the front of the board. Less experienced surfers tend to stand in the center to maintain better control. Skilled surfers may perform such difficult maneuvers as *360's* (complete circular turns on the face of the wave), *aerials* (flying out of the water above the wave), and *roller coasters* (riding up and down the face of the wave).

Many surfers train for surfing by running on the beach, bodybuilding, and bodysurfing. To bodysurf, they enter the water and wait until a high wave starts moving toward the shore. Then the bodysurfers do a *scissors kick,* spreading their legs apart and bringing them together forcefully in the direction of the shore. After swimming a few strokes at the crest, bodysurfers put their head down, arch their back, place their arms along their sides, and keep their body rigid. The wave sweeps them toward the shore in this position. As the wave dies out, bodysurfers push their hands forward and spread their legs to slow down. Bodysurfing provides a sense of balance and a knowledge of waves that is good training for all other aquatic surfing events.

Gary Fairmont R. Filosa II

Additional resources

Cralle, Trevor, ed. *The Surfin'ary: A Dictionary of Surfing Terms and Surfspeak.* 2nd ed. Ten Speed, 2000.
Warshaw, Matt. *The Encyclopedia of Surfing.* Harcourt, 2003.

Surgeon. See Surgery; Medicine.

Surgeon general of the United States serves as the nation's chief health adviser. The surgeon general commissions research concerning major health concerns and issues warnings to the public about health dangers. Such warnings include the statement about the hazards of smoking that appears on every package of cigarettes that is sold in the United States. The surgeon general is appointed by the president of the United States with the consent of the United States Senate.

Congress created the position of surgeon general in 1870 to direct the Marine Hospital Service. This service provided health care mainly to American sailors. However, it developed into a national public health service during the late 1800's and early 1900's. In 1912, Congress renamed it the Public Health Service (PHS). Today, the PHS is a division of the U.S. Department of Health and Human Services and is directed by the department's assistant secretary for health. The surgeon general is a top PHS official with a rank equivalent to that of vice admiral in the U.S. Navy. Critically reviewed by the Public Health Service

See also **Public Health Service.**

Surgery is the branch of medicine that deals with the treatment of disease, deformities, or injuries by operations. The doctor who performs the operation is called a *surgeon.* Every physician has some training in surgery and is qualified to perform simple operations. But surgeons are specially trained so that they have the judgment and skill to perform complicated operations.

Modern surgery stresses accurate diagnosis of the disease and proper care of the patient before and after the operation. Thus, the surgeon not only needs to

know how to perform an operation, but also must have a wide knowledge of anatomy, physiology, chemistry, and pathology. Five to eight years of training after medical school are necessary for physicians to qualify as surgeons.

The surgeon's tools

A surgical operation is complicated. Many people, medicines, equipment, and techniques help assure the greatest possible safety and comfort for the patient. The elimination of pain, the prevention of infection, and advanced means of diagnosis are all part of modern surgery. A qualified *surgical team* is essential to the success of both the operation and the patient's recovery. This team usually consists of a surgeon, at least one assistant, an anesthesiologist, and one or more nurses.

Anesthesia refers to methods that cause a loss of sensation, particularly the loss of pain. Before the use of modern anesthetics, surgeons tried to deaden the pain by giving large quantities of alcoholic beverages or by using compounds containing opium. But the relief from pain was not complete and lasted only a short time. As a result, surgeons could perform only short operations.

In the mid-1840's, diethyl ether and chloroform were first used as anesthetics. Since then, researchers have developed many safer anesthetics. *General anesthetics,* such as the gases nitrous oxide and halothane, are used to put the patient to sleep. General anesthesia also may be induced by injecting such intravenous drugs as thiopental (see **Thiopental**). *Local anesthetics,* such as procaine or lidocaine, affect only the area near the place of injection. They are used to block nerve impulses on a specific part of the body (see **Lidocaine**). They also may be injected into the spinal canal to produce spinal anesthesia. This type of nerve block is useful for surgery of the lower abdomen or legs.

Anesthesiologists use many other drugs to keep the patient safe during surgery and to help the surgeon. For example, the drug *curare* relaxes the stomach muscles during abdominal operations (see **Curare**). Doctors learned about curare centuries ago from the South American Indians who used it during hunting to immobilize birds and other small animals. See **Anesthesia**.

Antiseptics and asepsis. Infection once was a great danger in surgery. Even when the surgery was successful, patients often died if infection occurred. But in 1865, Joseph Lister of the United Kingdom introduced methods for preventing infection. He used various antiseptics to kill bacteria in the operating room during the course of an operation. He often sprayed carbolic acid around the room to kill germs. Later, the method of *aseptic* (completely sterile) surgery was developed. With this method, all germs that cause infection are kept out by cleaning and sterilizing all equipment and linens used in the operating room. Thus, while antiseptics kill germs that are present, asepsis keeps them out altogether. See **Antiseptic; Lister, Sir Joseph.**

Instruments. A surgeon uses many instruments in the course of an operation. These instruments include holders for needles and sponges, *clamps* to close off blood vessels, and *retractors* to hold back folds of skin. Sharp instruments include scissors and *scalpels* (knives). Since the 1970's, lasers have been used to make delicate cuts in body tissues. Doctors use the high-energy light

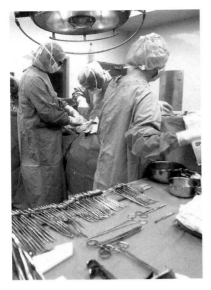
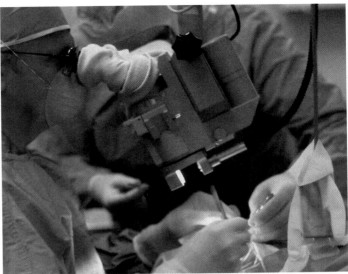

© Terry Wild

Modern surgery is a team effort. Surgeons perform an operation, *left,* while nurses supply them with instruments. Two physicians are using a microscope to perform delicate eye surgery, *right.*

of the laser to cut tissue by burning fine lines in the skin or other organs.

Many instruments aid the surgeon in making an accurate diagnosis. One of the most useful of these, the X-ray machine, permits the surgeon to detect broken bones and diagnose many diseases of the internal organs. A special kind of X-ray machine called a *computerized tomographic scanner (CT scanner)* enables the surgeon to view a cross section of the patient's body.

Other instruments are used to examine body cavities. For example, the *bronchoscope* is used to look into the lungs and to remove small pieces of tissue for examination. The *laparoscope* allows the doctor to view the abdominal and pelvic cavities and identify diseases of various internal organs, such as the uterus, ovary, and liver. These instruments also may be used during surgery. For example, a laser can be directed through a bronchoscope or a laparoscope to cut tissue in places beyond the reach of a surgeon's knife.

In 2000, the first *robotic surgical device* was approved by the United States Food and Drug Administration (FDA). This mechanical device is used to assist a surgeon in delicate procedures, such as nerve operations. The robot's ability to perform precise movements in very small spaces allows surgeons to perform operations with much smaller incisions and fewer risks.

Sutures are threads used to tie severed blood vessels and to close surgical wounds so that the tissues heal properly. Modern surgery would be impossible without sutures. Some kinds of sutures, such as catgut, are absorbed by the body. Others, such as nylon or silk, must be removed after several days. Sutures made from fine steel wire are nonirritating and do not need to be removed. Sometimes a surgeon uses metal staples to hold the edges of the skin together until healing occurs.

Technique. Modern techniques enable the surgeon to operate successfully upon all parts of the human body. For example, a surgeon can remove a long section of diseased intestine and sew the remaining intestinal sections together. The body will function normally after the operation. A kidney, or even a major part of the stomach, can be removed by an operation. In heart surgery, a doctor may replace one of the heart valves with an artificial one. A neurosurgeon can remove brain tumors, repair head injuries, and cut nerves to correct painful conditions.

Transplanting organs involves taking a healthy organ from one person and using it to replace the diseased organ in another person. The kidney is a commonly transplanted organ. The transplanted tissue must closely match that of the patient, or the patient's body will reject the new organ. See **Transplant.**

A technique called *cryosurgery* makes use of extreme cold in surgery. It usually involves freezing tissues. Surgeons sometimes use cold probes to treat detached retinas, or freeze diseased tissue in order to remove it. See **Cryobiology.**

In *microsurgery,* the surgeon operates while viewing the procedure through a microscope or magnifying glass. This technique enables physicians to perform operations on some of the tiniest body structures. For example, surgeons can rejoin extremely small blood vessels and nerves by microsurgery. It has led to the successful reattachment of severed fingers, hands, and even arms and legs. Doctors also use microsurgery to operate on the delicate structures in the eye, the kidney, the brain, and many other parts of the body.

A typical operation

Perhaps the best way to understand what is involved in a surgical operation is to consider a typical one. After a thorough examination, including laboratory tests, the doctor diagnoses the disease as an infected appendix. The patient is brought to the hospital and prepared for an appendectomy. Sedative drugs are given to relax the patient before the operation.

The operating room has been prepared for the patient's arrival by a thorough cleaning and scrubbing. All equipment not to be used for the operation has been removed. A large table is set up near the operating table. This will hold all the sterilized instruments and sponges that the surgeon might need. A nurse or an operating room technician has charge of this equipment.

The patient is anesthetized either in a room next to the operating room designed for this purpose or in the operating room itself. The anesthesiologist may inject an anesthetic intravenously or place a mask over the face and allow the patient to breathe anesthetic gases mixed with oxygen. After a few minutes, the patient is asleep and feels no pain. The anesthesiologist delivers precise amounts of oxygen and anesthetic gases to the patient, and monitors the patient's breathing, heart activity, blood pressure, and other vital information.

Meantime the doctors and nurses on the surgical team prepare for the operation. They spend 8 to 10 minutes scrubbing their hands and forearms to remove germs. They also wear sterilized rubber gloves because the skin cannot be made completely sterile even with strong antiseptics. The members of the surgical team put on sterilized gowns to cover their clothing and caps to cover their hair. In addition, they wear masks of gauze or other material to cover their mouths and noses so they will not breathe germs onto the patient.

After the patient has been anesthetized and is ready for surgery, sterile sheets are placed over the patient in such a manner that the area in which the *incision* (opening) is to be made is left open. This area is thoroughly cleansed and antiseptics are applied. Nurses place the sterile instruments on the tables, and put the small table over the operating table, within easy reach of the surgeon. The surgeon starts the operation by making an incision in the skin of the abdomen. The muscle tissue is pulled back, and retractors are placed in position to hold the tissue out of the way. This exposes the appen-

dix and that part of the intestine to which it is attached.

While working, the surgeon closes the severed ends of small blood vessels with clamps called *hemostats*. Thus, little bleeding occurs in the operation. *Sponges*, which are pieces of gauze folded into small pads, are used to remove surplus blood. The surgeon quickly removes the appendix, ties the stump that remains with a suture, and *inverts* (turns) the stump into the large intestine. Then the "closing-up" procedure begins.

The sponges are removed. The surgeon unclamps the blood vessels and ties them so that there is no bleeding. The retractors are then removed, and the muscles move back into their normal position. Finally, the edges of the cut skin are sewed together.

The anesthesiologist, nurses, and surgeon function like members of any well-drilled team. During the course of the operation, the anesthesiologist has been careful to give exactly the right amounts of drugs so the patient is safe and will awake quickly after surgery. At the end of the operation, the surgeon applies a gauze bandage to the incision area, and nurses remove the sheets used for draping. The patient is taken to the recovery room to awaken completely. Afterward, the patient is taken to a hospital bed. Recovery is usually uneventful. Yet such a routine operation would have been impossible a hundred years ago.

A person having an appendectomy may need to spend a day or two in the hospital. Certain major operations may require a longer hospital stay. However, for many operations, patients enter the hospital, undergo surgery, recover, and return home the same day. This procedure, called *ambulatory surgery* or *same-day surgery*, accounts for about three-fifths of all operations.

Surgical specialties

As in other branches of medicine, special branches of surgery have developed. These specialties came about because of the need for specialized types of surgery for

---

Some common surgical operations

Amputation is the removal of a limb (or part of a limb) or another appendage. Usually performed if a limb is damaged beyond repair, or if a seriously diseased appendage resists treatment and threatens to infect other parts of the body. See **Amputation**.

Appendectomy is the removal of the vermiform appendix. Commonly performed in cases of appendicitis. See **Appendicitis**.

Arthroscopy is the insertion of a straight, tubelike instrument through a small incision to examine and repair or remove damaged tissue, most often in the joints. See **Arthroscopy**.

Colostomy is the creation of an artificial opening in the *colon*, a part of the large intestine. Usually performed if the rectum is diseased or has been removed. Solid body waste passes through an opening made in the wall of the abdomen.

D and C is the *dilation* (stretching) of the opening of the uterus and the *curettage* (scraping) of the inside of the uterus. Commonly performed to diagnose such problems as excessive uterine bleeding or cancer of the uterus. May also be performed to remove placental tissues following childbirth, miscarriage, or induced abortion.

Gastrectomy is the removal of part or all of the stomach. Commonly performed to remove cancerous tissue or peptic ulcers.

Hysterectomy is the removal of the uterus. Usually performed to treat uterine diseases, including cancer. Hysterectomy does not affect sexual desire or function, but it does cause sterility. See **Hysterectomy**.

Mastectomy is the removal of part or all of a breast. Commonly performed to remove diseased tissue, especially cancerous tissue. *Radical mastectomy* includes the removal of additional muscle and *axillary* (armpit) tissue. See **Mastectomy**.

Nephrectomy is the removal of a kidney. Generally performed to remove cancerous tissue or a kidney that no longer functions properly. Removal of one kidney causes no disability. But removal of both kidneys results in death, unless the patient receives a kidney transplant or undergoes *dialysis* (regular treatments with an artificial kidney machine).

Oöphorectomy is the removal of an ovary. Usually performed to remove diseased tissue, such as a cancerous tumor. Removal of both ovaries causes *menopause* (the end of menstruation) and prevents the patient from having children.

Pneumonectomy is the removal of lung tissue. Commonly performed to remove cancerous tissue; occasionally to remove a long-term abscess or infection. *Total pneumonectomy* is the removal of an entire lung.

Tracheotomy is the creation of an artificial opening leading from the *trachea* (windpipe) to the outside of the body. Commonly performed to enable a patient with a blocked larynx to breathe.

Vasectomy is the cutting and tying of the *vasa deferentia*, the tubes that carry sperm from the testicles. Usually performed to cause sterility. Vasectomy does not affect sexual desire or function.

Robotic surgery allows a surgeon to perform precise movements within a tiny incision. Patients benefit from the technique with faster healing. Robotic surgery may even be performed at a great distance. This photo shows a surgeon in New York City operating by remote control on a patient in Strasbourg, France, over 4,000 miles (6,400 kilometers) away.

Reprinted with permission of *Nature* © Macmillan Magazines Ltd. (photo by Jacques Marescaux)

specific areas of the body. Surgeons in these fields require additional training to be certified as specialists.

Ophthalmology is a specialty concerned with treating diseases of the eyes. Ophthalmologists cure blindness that results from *cataracts* (a clouding of the eye lens) by removing the lens. Ophthalmologists also operate on the eye muscles to correct a condition called *strabismus* or *cross-eyes*. See **Ophthalmology**.

Plastic surgery helps people whose appearance has been harmed by injury, illness, or aging. Plastic surgeons can remove scars and blemishes. They also can replace damaged skin with grafts from healthy tissue. Many operations are performed to remove wrinkles from the face, to straighten a crooked nose, or to change the size of breasts. New noses and ears have been created, even though the original ones were completely destroyed. In addition, surgeons can fashion new jaws from living bone, cartilage, and flesh. See **Plastic surgery**.

Obstetrics and gynecology is a specialty that deals with childbirth and the female reproductive system. In the 1800's, Caesarean section for childbirth resulted in the death of about 86 of every 100 women on whom it was performed. Today, developments in surgical technique, blood transfusions, and drugs that fight infection have helped reduce the number of women who die during childbirth to less than 1 in 10,000.

Cardiac surgery is a specialty that treats heart diseases. Surgeons commonly treat *angina pectoris* (heart pain) by replacing obstructed segments of the heart's arteries with pieces of veins taken from the patient's leg. This procedure, called *coronary artery bypass*, increases the amount of blood that goes to the heart. Surgeons also have successfully transplanted human hearts and implanted artificial hearts. See **Heart** (Coronary artery disease [Treatment]; Heart failure; pictures).

Other specialty fields. There are a large number of other fields in which special types of surgery have developed. The *thoracic surgeon* operates on the lungs and chest. The *urologist* operates on the kidneys and urinary bladder. The *otolaryngologist* specializes in diseases of the ears, nose, and throat. The *orthopedist* operates on bones. The *proctologist* treats diseases of the lower bowel and anus.

History

Surgery has been known since ancient times. The word *surgery* comes from a Greek word meaning *working by hand*. The first surgeon's tool was probably a piece of flint stone. Some skeletons of Stone Age people show evidence of *trephining*. In this operation, a hole was cut in the skull of the patient, probably as an attempt to release spirits that were thought to cause headaches and other ailments. Primitive tribes fixed broken legs with splints. Even in the earliest times, *cautery* (searing the flesh) was used to stop bleeding. Circumcision, performed during certain religious rites, was one of the earliest operations.

Some operations were known to the ancient Babylonians, Greeks, and Romans. Military surgery has been important for two or three thousand years. The early Hindus used at least 125 surgical instruments. They also developed plastic surgery techniques to replace noses and ears that had been cut off. In the Middle Ages, surgeons and barbers both performed operations. But only barbers did bloodletting. Surgeons thought it too demeaning. It is from this bloodletting that the red-and-white striped barber pole developed—the red standing for blood and the white for the bandage.

Among the many famous surgeons of the past was a Frenchman, Ambroise Paré, who lived in the 1500's. He has been called the father of military medicine. He abolished the harmful practice of pouring boiling oil on wounds to sterilize them. John Hunter, a British surgeon of the 1700's, was the founder of experimental surgery.

Many of the great modern surgeons have been Americans. Ephraim McDowell of Kentucky performed the first successful operation to remove a tumor of the ovary in 1809, the beginning of successful abdominal surgery. Crawford W. Long of Georgia is credited with having first used diethyl ether as a surgical anesthetic in 1842. William Halsted, a surgeon of the late 1800's and early 1900's, introduced many of the surgical procedures and techniques that are used today, including the use of sterile gloves in aseptic surgery. Fred H. Albee, an orthopedist, introduced bone grafting in 1915. In 1933, Evarts Graham became the first surgeon to successfully remove a cancerous lung.

An American surgical team in Boston performed the first successful human organ transplant, a kidney transplant from one identical twin to another, in 1954. A South African surgeon, Christiaan Barnard, performed the first human heart transplant in 1967. By 2001, surgeons had gained the ability to use remote-controlled surgical instruments to perform surgery on patients who were thousands of miles or kilometers away.

Modern surgery has advanced in five main ways. These are (1) the development of aseptic surgery; (2) the technical improvements in surgical instruments; (3) the increased knowledge of body processes; (4) the development of anesthesia; and (5) the use of chemicals to prevent and treat infections.   Edwin S. Munson

Related articles in *World Book* include:

Biographies

Barnard, Christiaan	Drew, Charles R.	Mayo, William J.
Crile, George W.	Lister, Sir Joseph	Mayo, William W.
Cushing, Harvey	Long, Crawford W.	Paré, Ambroise
DeBakey, Michael	Mayo, Charles H.	Penfield, Wilder G.

Other related articles

Acupuncture	Bronchoscope	Hysterectomy	Plastic surgery
Amputation	Circumcision	Laparoscopy	Sterilization
Anatomy	Colostomy	Laser	Transplant
Anesthesia	Endoscope	LASIK surgery	Trephining
Angioplasty	Gastroscope	Mastectomy	Vasectomy
Arthroscopy	Hypothermia	Medicine	X rays
Bloodletting			

Surinam. See Suriname.

Surinam toad, *SUR uh nam,* is an odd-shaped toad known for the unusual way it raises its young. The toad is named for Suriname (also spelled Surinam), a country in northeastern South America, where it was first discovered. The animal is flat with a head shaped like a triangle. The Surinam toad has small eyes and no tongue or teeth. The fingers of its front legs are not webbed, but its hind feet have webbed toes.

The Surinam toad lives in the water and has rough, brown skin. At breeding time, the skin of the female Surinam toad grows thick and spongy. The female lays her eggs while she and her mate turn over in the water. The male fertilizes the eggs and places them in the skin of the female's back. There, the eggs develop into tiny toads. The Surinam toad does not have a tadpole stage as in most other toads and frogs. The toads come out of the skin when they are about $2\frac{1}{2}$ months old or older.

Laurie J. Vitt

Scientific classification. The Surinam toad is in the family Pipidae. Its scientific name is *Pipa pipa.*

Suriname, *SUR ree NAHM uh* or *SOOR uh NAHM,* is a country on the northeast coast of South America. The country's name is also spelled *Surinam.* Mountainous rain forests cover about 80 percent of Suriname, and most of the people live in the flat coastal area. Suriname is the smallest independent country in South America, both in area and population. Nearly half of the people live in Paramaribo, the capital, largest city, and chief port. The Netherlands ruled the country during most of the period from 1667 until 1975, when Suriname gained independence.

Government. The people elect 51 members to a National Assembly for five-year terms. The National Assembly passes the country's laws and elects a president and vice president for five-year terms. The president heads the government. The president appoints a Council of Ministers, who help carry out the operations of the gov-

The female Surinam toad carries eggs in the thick skin of her back until they are fully developed into tiny toads.

© Heather Angel

Suriname

— International boundary
— Road
⊛ National capital
• Other city or town
+ Elevation above sea level

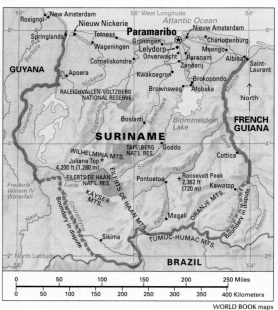

WORLD BOOK maps

© Frank Fournier, Contact from Woodfin Camp, Inc.

Paramaribo is Suriname's capital, largest city, and chief port. Wooden buildings line the streets of the city, the country's center of business, cultural, and government activity.

ernment. The vice president presides over the Council of Ministers and also serves as prime minister. A Council of State composed of civilian and military members has an advisory role in the government. In addition, the council can veto laws passed by the National Assembly. The president chairs the Council of State.

People of many ethnic backgrounds live in Suriname. Hindustanis, who are descendants of people from India, make up more than a third of the country's population. Creoles—people with mixed European and African ancestry—make up about a third. The rest of Suriname's people are, in order of number, Indonesians, Maroons, American Indians, Chinese, and Europeans. Maroons are the descendants of Africans who escaped from slavery in the 1600's and 1700's.

Each ethnic group in Suriname has preserved its own culture, religion, and language. Dutch is the nation's official language. But the most commonly used language is Sranan Tongo, also called Suriname Creole. Sranan Tongo combines elements of English, Dutch, and several

Facts in brief

Capital: Paramaribo.
Official language: Dutch.
Area: 63,251 mi² (163,820 km²). *Coastline*—226 mi (364 km). *Greatest distances*—north-south, 285 mi (459 km); east-west, 280 mi (451 km).
Elevation: *Highest*—Mount Juliana Top, 4,200 ft (1,280 m). *Lowest*—sea level.
Population: *Estimated 2008 population*—458,000; density, 7 per mi² (3 per km²); distribution, 74 percent urban, 26 percent rural. *2004 census*—492,829.
Chief products: Aluminum, bananas, bauxite, rice.
National anthem: "Opo Kondre Man Oen Opo" ("Arise People, Arise").
Flag: The flag has five horizontal stripes of green, white, red, white, and green. A yellow star lies in the center. See **Flag** (picture: Flags of the Americas).
Money: *Basic unit*—Suriname dollar. One hundred cents equal one dollar.

African languages. Many Surinamese also speak English.

Some Hindustanis own small farms. Others are skilled industrial workers. Most Creoles work in government or for businesses. Many Indonesians are tenant farmers, who rent their land from large landowners. Most Maroons live in the rain forests and follow African customs.

About 65 percent of Suriname's people from 15 to 59 years of age can read and write. The law requires children from 7 to 12 years old to attend elementary school, and some students continue on to high school. Suriname has one university, just outside of Paramaribo.

Land and climate. Suriname has a narrow coastal area of flat swampland that has been drained for farming. This area extends inland 10 to 50 miles (16 to 80 kilometers) to a sandy plain that rises about 150 feet (46 meters) high. Mountainous rain forests with about 2,000 kinds of trees lie farther inland, and a high *savanna* (grassy, thinly wooded plain) runs along the country's southwest border. Rivers flow north to the Atlantic Ocean. Suriname is warm and moist, with an average annual temperature of 81 °F (27 °C). The annual rainfall averages 76 inches (193 centimeters) in western Suriname and 95 inches (241 centimeters) in Paramaribo.

Economy is based on mining and metal processing. Suriname produces large amounts of bauxite, an ore from which aluminum is made. Raw bauxite and aluminum account for about 75 percent of the exports.

Agriculture also has an important part in Suriname's economy. Rice, a major export crop, is grown on about three-fourths of the farmland. Other crops include bananas, coconuts, and sugar. The forests yield a large supply of hardwoods from which Suriname's lumber industry produces logs and plywood.

The country's chief means of transportation is an extensive system of rivers. Suriname has only about 800 miles (1,300 kilometers) of main roads, and railroad service is limited. An international airport operates near Zanderij. Suriname has two major newspapers, a television station, and four radio stations.

History. Christopher Columbus sighted what is now Suriname in 1498, and Spaniards and Portuguese explored the area during the 1500's. In 1651, British explorers built the first permanent settlement there. They established cotton and sugar cane plantations and brought Africans to work as slaves on the land. In 1667, the Dutch took control of it and in exchange gave the British what became the state of New York.

Suriname's economy declined in the 1700's because of slave uprisings and Dutch neglect. In the early 1800's, ownership shifted several times between the United Kingdom and the Netherlands. In 1815, the United Kingdom gave up its claim to Suriname, and the Dutch regained control. The Dutch abolished slavery in 1863 and brought laborers from India and Indonesia to work on the plantations. However, plantation farming declined in the early 1900's, and many people moved to urban areas.

Suriname became a self-governing Dutch territory in 1954. During the 1970's, the Creoles led a movement for full independence, which was supported by the Dutch government. But the Hindustanis opposed independence, leading to conflicts between the two groups. Suriname gained independence on Nov. 25, 1975. It adopted a democratic form of government, in which the people elected a Parliament. Shortly before independence, thousands of Suriname's people emigrated to the Netherlands. This caused a shortage of skilled labor and greatly restricted economic development in Suriname.

Early in 1980, a group of noncommissioned officers in Suriname's armed forces seized control of the country's government and abolished the Parliament. Later in 1980, Suriname established a new government in which both civilians and the military held power. However, the Parliament was not reestablished.

In 1987, the military leaders permitted elections. Voters approved a new constitution that provided for an elected parliament called the National Assembly. However, a Council of State, composed of military and civilian leaders, has the power to veto the Assembly's legislation. In 1988, the National Assembly elected a president and vice president. In 1990, military leaders staged a coup and forced the resignation of the civilian government. In 1991, Suriname returned to civilian government when a new Assembly and president were elected.　　　Gary Brana-Shute

See also **Aluminum** (graph); **Maroons; Paramaribo.**

Surrealism is a movement in art and literature. It was founded in Paris in 1924 by the French poet André Breton. Like Dadaism, from which it arose, Surrealism uses art as a weapon against the evils and restrictions that Surrealists see in society. Unlike Dadaism, however, Surrealism tries to reveal a new and higher reality than that of daily life. *Surrealism,* an invented word meaning *super realism,* derived much of its theory from the psychology of the Austrian physician Sigmund Freud.

The Surrealists claim to create forms and images not primarily by reason, but by unthinking impulse and blind feeling—or even by accident. Using these methods, the Surrealists declare that alternative realities can be created in art and literature. These realities are as valid as conventional realities and more beautiful because of their unexpectedness.

Much of the beauty sought by Surrealism is violent and cruel. In this way, the Surrealist artists and writers try to shock the viewer or reader into a realization that "normal" realities are arbitrary. In the process, the Surrealists reveal what they consider the deeper, truer part of human nature.

Although the movement is not so strong as it once was, it still influences artists and writers. Leading Surrealist painters include André Masson, René Magritte, Salvador Dali, Joan Miró, and Max Ernst. The leading Surrealistic writer was André Breton.　　　Stephen C. Foster

Related articles in *World Book* include:

Breton, André	French literature	Miró, Joan
Dadaism	(Surrealism)	Painting (Surrealism)
Dali, Salvador	Magritte, René	ism)
Ernst, Max	Masson, André	Ray, Man

Additional resources

Bolton, Linda. *Surrealism.* Peter Bedrick, 2000. Younger readers.
Caws, Mary A., ed. *Surrealist Painters and Poets.* MIT Pr., 2001.
Durozoi, Gérard. *History of the Surrealist Movement.* Univ. of Chicago Pr., 2002.

Surrey, Earl of (1517?-1547), is usually linked in literary history with Sir Thomas Wyatt. They are considered the two greatest English poets at the dawn of the English Renaissance. Surrey, a courtier during the reign of Henry VIII, introduced blank verse into English literature. He and Wyatt also imported the Italian sonnet form into English poetry. The poems of Surrey and Wyatt were first published in *The Book of Songs and Sonnets* (1557), a text usually called *Tottel's Miscellany.* Surrey was beheaded on a charge of high treason. His full name was Henry Howard.　　　John N. King

Surrogate birth is the result of a legal arrangement in which a woman agrees to give birth to a child to be raised by others. The woman who bears the child is called the *surrogate mother.* In *traditional surrogacy,* the surrogate mother's egg is fertilized through artificial insemination by the intended father. In *gestational surrogacy,* the intended mother's egg is fertilized by sperm from the intended father in a laboratory in a process called *in vitro fertilization* (IVF). The resulting embryo is then implanted in the surrogate's womb. Either before or at birth, the surrogate mother signs a document stating that the individual or couple with whom she made the arrangement will raise the baby. Surrogate births are usually sought by couples who are infertile or cannot carry a pregnancy to term.

Many legal and ethical complications can develop from surrogate births and threaten the child's welfare. The surrogate mother may refuse to give up the newborn child even if she has made a legal agreement to

Europe After the Rain (1942), an oil painting on canvas; Wadsworth Atheneum, Hartford, Conn., Ella Gallup Sumner and Mary Catlin Sumner Collection

Surrealistic painting combines recognizable forms in unusual ways, creating a feeling of mystery. Max Ernst painted this scene and others that resemble fantastic rocky landscapes.

do so. Other complications involve questions about whether the surrogate should be paid for carrying a child and whether the surrogate should have any parental rights. Some people worry that surrogate birth is essentially a commercial enterprise in which children and women are reduced to commodities that can be bought, sold, or rented.

In the United States, some states have banned surrogate agreements or do not recognize them as legal. But in other states and many countries, surrogate birth agreements are largely unregulated.

Margaret R. McLean

See also **Adoption.**

Survey. See Public opinion poll.

Surveying is the technique of measuring to determine the position of points, or of marking out points and boundaries. The points may be on, beneath, or above Earth's surface. Surveying is as old as civilization. The technique began in Egypt. Every year, after the Nile River overflowed its banks and washed out farm boundaries, the Egyptians fixed new boundaries by surveying.

Types of surveys

Surveys can either be *plane surveys* or *geodetic surveys*. Plane surveys do not take into consideration the curved shape of Earth's surface. They are used for all but the largest areas. Geodetic surveys make adjustments for Earth's curvature. In the United States, the National Geodetic Survey, a unit of the federal government, establishes the location of *geodetic control points.* Plane surveys use these points as reference points.

The land survey is the most familiar type of survey. It is used to find the areas of plots of ground and to fix boundaries. For example, a landowner who plans to build a fence might have a land survey done to determine the property lines.

The topographic survey includes the measurement of elevations and depressions as well as horizontal distances for the making of maps. The U.S. Geological Survey produces topographic maps of the United States.

The aerial survey determines distances and sizes on the ground by means of photographs usually taken from airplanes. These photographs include an enormous amount of detail that a ground observer cannot easily obtain. Aerial surveying is frequently used for topographic mapping of large areas.

Other surveys meet special needs. For example, *construction,* or *engineering, surveys* are made where buildings, bridges, roads, canals, and other structures are to be built. *Underground surveys* help engineers determine where to lay pipes or dig tunnels. *Nautical,* or *hydrographic, surveys* map out the bed of a river, lake, or ocean. By studying riverbeds, people can learn to control the flow of water and prevent water erosion.

Surveying tools

Modern tools. The most important surveying tool is the *total station.* This is a small telescope equipped with an electronic distance-measuring device and set up on a *tripod* (three-legged stand). The telescope pivots horizontally above a horizontal plate on which angles are marked. The telescope also pivots vertically beside a plate that has angle markings. Electronic devices measure the angles and display the results on a liquid crystal panel. Total stations also calculate the horizontal and vertical angles between points. In some total stations, the measurements are accurate to *1 second of arc.* One second equals ⅟₃,₆₀₀ of 1 degree.

The total station uses a laser to measure distance. The measuring device with the laser is mounted on top of or inside the telescope. A laser beam sent out from this device reflects from a prism mounted on a pole held over the target point, then returns to the device. The device measures the time it takes for the signal to travel to and from the reflector, then uses the measurement to calculate the distance. The total station measures distances to the nearest millimeter (0.04 inch). The liquid crystal panel displays the distance in feet or meters. Some total stations also calculate differences in elevation.

Surveyors sometimes use a long *steel tape* to measure or set out distances. Most steel tapes are 100, 200, or 300 feet (30, 60, or 90 meters) long. Surveyors use an *invar tape* when making extremely precise measurements. Invar is a mixture of nickel, iron, and other metals. Temperature variations change the length of an invar tape much less than the length of a steel tape.

Surveyors also measure lines with the *Global Positioning System,* which consists of artificial satellites, radio receivers, computers, and other equipment. Satellites transmit signals that indicate their positions relative to the receivers. Computers use these signals to determine the lengths of lines. The Global Positioning System has 24 satellites. A receiver must obtain signals from at least three of them to compute latitude and longitude. A receiver must obtain signals from at least four satellites to compute elevation as well.

Early tools. Early surveyors in the United States measured distance with a *Gunter's chain,* and direction with a *surveyor's compass.* Today's surveyors rarely use these instruments.

A Gunter's chain is 66 feet (20 meters) long and has 100 links that each measure 7.92 inches (20.12 centimeters). The English mathematician Edmund Gunter invented this tool in the early 1600's. The Gunter's chain gave rise to a unit of distance for surveys, the *chain,* equal to 66 feet (20 meters). Surveyors no longer use this unit. However, the acre, which is based on the chain, is still in common use. Ten square chains, or 100,000 square links, make 1 acre (0.4 hectare).

A surveyor's compass determines directions with a magnetic needle. The needle generally pivots on a jeweled bearing to keep friction at a minimum. The ends of the needle, sharpened to knifelike points, pass near ruled degree markings. Some compasses have a hinged lid with a mirror on the inside. Surveyors can read the reflection of the compass face while sighting a target.

Sighting instruments called *transits* and *theodolites* began to replace the surveyor's compass in the early 1800's. These instruments measure angles and determine directions. A theodolite provides more precise readings than does a transit and is sometimes used today. The theodolite and the transit, like the total station, have a telescope that pivots horizontally and vertically.

Surveyors and engineers formerly set a theodolite over a specific point using a string or line called a *plumb line.* A plumb line has a weight called a *plumb bob* attached to one end to keep the line hanging straight. Modern theodolites—and total stations—have a special telescope device called an *optical plummet* that provides more precise placement over a point.

Surveyors once made topographic surveys with a *plane table* and an *alidade*. These instruments are rarely used today. A plane table consists of a drawing board mounted on a tripod. The surveyor levels the drawing board and places a map on it. An alidade, which consists of a telescope fastened to a straightedge, is then set up on the map. The telescope and straightedge move parallel with one another. The surveyor sights an object through the telescope and uses the straightedge to draw a line on the map parallel to the line of sight. A mapmaker uses vertical angles measured with the alidade and distances read off the map to calculate elevations and depressions.

Careers in surveying

Modern surveying is closely connected with the various branches of engineering, especially civil engineering. Surveyors find work to do whenever there are roads, dams, bridges, and residential areas to be built. They determine the boundaries of private property and the boundaries of various political divisions. They also provide input for *geographic information systems,* computer databases that contain data on land features and boundaries.

Surveyors must have a thorough knowledge of algebra, basic calculus, geometry, and trigonometry. They must also know the laws that deal with surveys, property, and contracts. In addition, they must be able to use delicate instruments with precision and accuracy.

Howard Turner

Related articles in *World Book* include:

Bench mark	Level	Photogrammetry
Geodesy	Map	Public lands
Global Positioning System	Parallax	Sextant

Survival of the fittest. See Natural selection.

Susa, *SOO sah,* called *Shush* in the Farsi language, was once a capital of the ancient Kingdom of Elam and of the Persian Empire. Its partly uncovered ruins lie in the province of Khuzistan, in southwestern Iran.

Susa was founded around 4000 B.C. It is mentioned many times in Mesopotamian texts and in the Bible, where it is called *Shushan.* The Old Testament story of Esther took place in Susa. The tomb of the Biblical figure Daniel is said to be there. French archaeologists unearthed a famous group of Babylonian laws, called the Code of Hammurabi, in Susa's ruins in 1901 and 1902.

The Assyrians plundered Susa in 640 B.C. Around 520 B.C., Darius I built a palace in Susa and made it a capital of the Persian Empire. Alexander the Great conquered Susa in the late 300's B.C. One of his successors, Seleucus I, refounded Susa as Seleucia-on-the-Elaios. The city declined after the A.D. 300's. Daniel Potts

Sushi is a traditional Japanese food made with seasoned rice and other ingredients, often including fish. Some people mistakenly believe that the word *sushi* refers to raw fish. However, the term refers to *vinegared rice* (rice sprinkled with vinegar, salt, and sugar). The Japanese term for raw fish is *sashimi.*

Sushi originated in China by at least the A.D. 100's as a method of preserving fish meat by packing it in rice and salt and then allowing it to ferment for several months.

The Chinese generally threw away the rice and ate only the fish. The process spread to Japan about the 600's. The Japanese came to prefer eating the rice and fish together. In the 1600's, they began using vinegar in making sushi, and this shortened the fermentation time. In 1824, Hanaya Yohei, a Japanese chef, first prepared modern sushi. He served sashimi with vinegared rice. This meal could be prepared in minutes rather than days.

There are several types of sushi. Common types include *nigiri sushi,* shaped rice topped by raw fish, and *maki sushi,* seaweed layered with rice and strips of vegetables and seafood, then rolled tightly and sliced to form short cylinders. Sushi is traditionally served with *wasabi,* a rare condiment made from the ground root of a mustardlike plant. However, imitation wasabi made with horseradish is commonly used. Frank Toshi Sugiura

Suspension is a mixture in which the particles of a substance separate from a liquid or gas slowly. Each of the particles consists of many atoms or molecules, and so a suspension can be visually recognized as a mixture of two different substances.

There are several types of suspensions. They include (1) a solid in a gas, such as dust and smoke; (2) a liquid in a gas, such as fog and aerosols; (3) a solid in a liquid, such as muddy or soapy water; (4) a gas in a liquid, such as foam; and (5) a liquid in a liquid, such as latex or water-based paints. A suspension that contains extremely small particles is called a *colloid.* The particles in many colloids can be seen only with the aid of a microscope. Homogenized milk with its tiny particles of suspended fat is a common colloid. See **Colloid.**

The molecules of a liquid or gas in a suspension move rapidly and collide with the suspended particles. The buffeting effect of these collisions is important in resisting the natural tendency of the particles to settle because of gravity. The rapid, random motion of the suspended particles that results from the collisions is called *Brownian motion.*

A suspension has certain other basic properties that distinguish it from another type of mixture called a solution. When a beam of light is shone through a colloidal suspension, such as smoke or dust-filled air, its path becomes clearly visible. This phenomenon, called the *Tyndall effect,* occurs because the suspended particles reflect and scatter light. A solution shows no such effect because its particles are too small to scatter light.

A suspension can also be separated into its component parts by filtration. However, a solution cannot. Particle size is again the determining factor. J. D. Corbett

See also **Solution.**

Susquehanna River, *SUHS kwuh HAN uh,* is a swift but shallow waterway that flows through industrial and farm areas in the eastern United States. The river rises at Otsego Lake in central New York state. It flows southward across Pennsylvania into Maryland, where it empties into Chesapeake Bay (see **Pennsylvania** [physical map]).

The river is 444 miles (715 kilometers) long. Its swift current, rock obstructions, and shallow bed discourage shipping. But the Susquehanna has the greatest water-power potential of the rivers in the northeastern United States. Several hydroelectric generation stations, coal-fired power plants, and nuclear power plants are along the river. William C. Rense

Sussex spaniel, *SUHS ihks,* is a breed of dog that originated in England. It was named for the county of Sussex in southern England. The dog is strong and stocky with short legs. It weighs from 35 to 45 pounds (16 to 20 kilograms). Its coat is a golden liver color. The Sussex spaniel makes an excellent hunting dog and pet.

Critically reviewed by the Sussex Spaniel Club of America

Sutherland, Joan (1926-   ), an Australian operatic soprano, won acclaim for her brilliant vocal technique. Her voice had a depth and richness not usually associated with the ornate style of her roles. Her voice had magnificent range, flexibility, and resonance. She sang usually with her husband, Richard Bonynge, as conductor.

Sutherland was born on Nov. 7, 1926, in Sydney and received her training there. She moved to London in 1951 and the following year made her debut at the Covent Garden Opera in *The Magic Flute.* She first performed in the United States with the Dallas Opera in 1960. Sutherland made her debut at the Metropolitan Opera in New York City in 1961 in *Lucia di Lammermoor.* Queen Elizabeth II made Sutherland a dame commander in the Order of the British Empire in 1978, and she became known as Dame Joan Sutherland. She retired as a performer in 1990.   Charles H. Webb

See also **Opera** (picture: An opera ensemble).

Sutherland Falls is the fifth highest mountain waterfall in the world. It lies 16 miles (26 kilometers) from the head of Milford Sound, in the Southern Alps of New Zealand's South Island. Its waters plunge down a mountainside in three leaps for a total of 1,904 feet (580 meters). Water from melting glaciers forms the falls. The waters eventually flow into Milford Sound. The falls are named after the Scottish explorer Donald Sutherland, who is thought to have discovered the falls in the 1880's. See also **Waterfall** (table; picture).   Giselle M. Byrnes

Suttee, *suh TEE* or *SUHT ee,* is a Hindu custom once widely practiced in India. It is sometimes spelled *sati.* The name comes from the Sanskrit word *sati,* which means *faithful wife.* By the custom, a widow allows herself or is forced to be put to death. She is usually burned with her husband's body or an article of his clothing.

The origin of suttee is unknown. But a few ancient writings stated that a good wife should follow her husband in death. In 1829, the British rulers of India made suttee illegal. But the practice continued to a lesser degree throughout the 1800's. Today it is reported only rarely.   Charles S. J. White

SUV. See **Sport utility vehicle.**

Suva, *SOO vah* (pop. 71,608), is the capital and largest city of Fiji, an island country in the South Pacific Ocean. The city lies on the southeastern coast of Viti Levu, Fiji's largest island. For location, see **Fiji** (map). Suva is Fiji's chief seaport and commercial center. Ships stop there to load *copra* (dried coconut meat), sugar, tropical fruit, and other goods. Tourist ships also visit. Factories in Suva produce processed sugar, coconut oil, clothing, and other goods. In 1874, Fiji became a British colony. Suva became the capital of Fiji in 1882. Fiji gained independence from the United Kingdom in 1970. Suva is the headquarters of the University of the South Pacific. The city's Fiji Museum stands inside the Thurston Gardens. See also **Fiji** (picture).   Robert C. Kiste

Suwannee River, *suh WAHN ee,* winds for about 190 miles (306 kilometers) through southern Georgia and northern Florida and empties into the Gulf of Mexico. Stephen Foster, who called the river *Swanee,* made it famous with his song, "Old Folks at Home." The river rises south of Waycross, Georgia. It helps drain the Okefenokee Swamp. Only small boats can navigate the river. The Suwannee reaches the Gulf of Mexico at Suwannee Sound, where Hog Island divides the river into two distributaries (see **Florida** [terrain map]).   James O. Wheeler

Suzhou, *soo joh* (pop. 3,273,010), is an ancient Chinese city known for its canals, gardens, and *pagodas* (temples). Its name is also spelled *Su-chou* or *Soochow.* Suzhou is in a rich agricultural region in Jiangsu Province, between Nanjing and Shanghai. For the location, see **China** (political map). Suzhou's factories produce chemicals and machinery. Skilled craftworkers in the city carve jade and weave silks.   Mingzheng Shi

Suzuki, *suh zoo kee,* **Ichiro,** *ee chee roh* (1973-   ), a Japanese baseball player, became a star playing for the Seattle Mariners of the American League. In 2001, he became the first Japanese player other than a pitcher to play major league baseball in the United States. Ichiro, as he is widely called, became the first player in major league history with at least 200 hits in each of his first six seasons. In 2004, he set a new single-season record for hits with 262, breaking the record of 257 set by George Sisler of the St. Louis Browns in 1920. Suzuki also led the American League in hits in 2001 with 242 and in 2006 with 224.

Suzuki was named the American League Rookie of the Year and Most Valuable Player in 2001. Only Fred Lynn of the Boston Red Sox had won both honors in the same season (1975). In 2001, Suzuki led the league in batting with a .350 average. He led the major leagues in stolen bases with 56 and set a record for hits by a rookie with 242. He led the American League in batting again in 2004 with a .372 average.

Suzuki, a right fielder, won praise for his speed in the outfield and his strong throwing arm. He won an American League Gold Glove award for outfielders each season from 2001 through 2006.

Suzuki was born in Kasugai, Japan, on Oct. 22, 1973. Before playing in the United States, he was a star in Japanese baseball. As a member of the Orix Blue Wave, Suzuki led Japan's Pacific League in batting for a record seven consecutive seasons. He won seven Gold Glove awards and was named the league's Most Valuable Player three times. After joining the Mariners, he became a national hero in Japan.   Neil Milbert

Suzuki method, *suh ZOO kee,* is a way of teaching children how to play certain musical instruments at an early age. It is most widely used with the violin but is also applied to such instruments as the cello, flute, and piano. Shinichi Suzuki, a Japanese violinist, developed the method in the 1940's.

The Suzuki method is based on an educational philosophy known as Talent Education. According to this philosophy, most children have the potential to play a musical instrument. Youngsters learn to speak by imitating the speech of their parents and others, and they acquire a large vocabulary before they begin to learn to read. Similarly, Suzuki students listen to recorded music while learning to play the music on their instruments.

The Suzuki teacher instructs the students individually and in groups. Parents play an important role by attending lessons with their child and supervising practice sessions at home. They work with the teacher to create an atmosphere that encourages the child to enjoy music.

Critically reviewed by the Suzuki Association of the Americas

Svalbard, *SVAHL bahr,* is a group of islands in the Arctic Ocean, about midway between Norway and the North Pole. The islands belong to Norway, and Svalbard is their Norwegian name. They are sometimes called by their German name, Spitsbergen.

Svalbard has five large islands and many smaller ones. The main islands, in order of size, are Spitsbergen, North East Land, Edge Island, Barents Island, and Prince Charles Foreland. Svalbard covers 23,958 square miles (62,050 square kilometers). It is about 700 miles (1,100 kilometers) from the North Pole (see **Arctic Ocean** [map]; **Norway** [map]).

Svalbard has a population of about 3,500. Mining companies, radio and weather stations, and a scientific research station provide jobs on the islands. More than half of the people are Russians who work in Russian-owned coal mines. Tourists visit Svalbard to see Arctic animal and plant life. Svalbard has served as the base for many Arctic explorations.

Norse Vikings probably visited the islands. Early Norwegian stories mention Svalbard. In the Middle Ages, the Norwegian kings claimed Svalbard. A Dutch expedition under Willem Barents rediscovered the islands in 1596 (see **Barents, Willem**). The English explorer Henry

Hudson sighted them in 1607. No one settled on the islands until after the Norwegians began mining coal there in the 1890's. In 1920, other nations formally recognized Norway's claim to the islands.   Ian W. D. Dalziel

Sverdlovsk. See Yekaterinburg.

Swahili, *swah HEE lee,* are an African people of mixed Bantu and Arab ancestry. The Swahili live along the east coast of Africa, from Somalia to Mozambique. The word *Swahili* means *coast people.* The Swahili language, known by the Swahili as Kiswahili, is used in East Africa for business and communication among various ethnic groups. It serves as the official language of Kenya and Tanzania. All the Swahili are Muslims.

Historians believe that Arab traders began to settle in East African coastal villages about the time of Jesus Christ. The native and Arab cultures gradually mixed and developed into the Swahili civilization. From about 1200 to 1500, many Swahili city-states became thriving commercial centers. They included Kilwa, Lamu, Malindi, Mombasa, and Zanzibar. The Swahili traded gold, ivory, and slaves from the African interior for goods from China, India, and Persia.

In the 1500's and 1600's, the Portuguese looted many Swahili cities and seriously damaged the Swahili trade. In the early 1700's, Omani Arabs replaced the Portuguese as rulers of the Swahili people.   T. O. Beidelman

Swallow is a type of small, graceful bird. A swallow has long, powerful, pointed wings and small feet suited only

Tree swallow
Tachycineta bicolor
Found throughout North and Central America
Body length: 5 to 6 $\frac{1}{4}$ inches (13 to 16 centimeters)

Barn swallow
Hirundo rustica
Found throughout North and South America, Africa, Asia, and Europe
Body length: 5 $\frac{3}{4}$ to 7 $\frac{3}{4}$ inches (15 to 20 centimeters)

Bank swallow
Riparia riparia
Found in North and South America, Africa, Asia, and Europe
Body length: 4 $\frac{1}{2}$ to 5 $\frac{1}{2}$ inches (11 to 14 centimeters)

Cliff swallow
Hirundo pyrrhonota
Found throughout most of North and South America
Body length: 5 to 6 inches (13 to 15 centimeters)

WORLD BOOK illustrations by Albert Earl Gilbert

for perching. It has a wide mouth that it uses to catch flying insects, which make up nearly all its food. Swallows eat many mosquitoes.

Swallows are found in almost all parts of the world. They usually live in open or partly open country, often near water. Most swallows migrate over long distances between their summer and winter homes. Some, such as the *cliff swallow* and the *barn swallow,* travel thousands of miles. These movements help swallows avoid cold weather and find food. During their migrations, swallows fly by day and spend the nights in woods or marshes.

Swallows generally are sociable birds. Some nest in pairs, but most live in colonies. Some species make their nests in holes in riverbanks or trees. Others build nests of clay or mud on beams of bridges, on rafters in barns, or under eaves. Female swallows lay three to eight eggs that are solid white or white with brown spots.

Several species of swallows live in North America. The barn swallow has a steel-blue back, chestnut breast, and a deeply forked tail. The cliff swallow has a rectangular tail and a light brown patch on its rump. The *tree swallow* is dark bluish-green and white and often nests in birdhouses. The *bank swallow* is brown and white with a narrow dark band across its chest. The *purple martin* is the largest swallow in North America. It may grow to $8\frac{1}{2}$ inches (21 centimeters) long. The adult male is black all over.   Martha Hatch Balph

Scientific classification. Swallows belong to the swallow family, Hirundinidae. The scientific name for the purple martin is *Progne subis.*

See also **Bird** (picture: Kinds of bird nests); **Martin; San Juan Capistrano.**

Swammerdam, *SVAHM uhr DAHM,* **Jan,** *yahn* (1637-1680), a Dutch anatomist and zoologist, helped pioneer the use of the microscope. He studied tiny structures in animals and was the first to observe red blood cells.

Swammerdam's observations on the life history, anatomy, and development of insects led to a system of insect classification that is still considered useful. This system is based on the different patterns of *metamorphosis* in various insects. Metamorphosis is the change in form that many insects undergo to become adults (see **Metamorphosis**). Swammerdam also made important observations on how nerves and muscles function.

Swammerdam was born on Feb. 12, 1637, in Amsterdam, the Netherlands. He studied medicine before beginning his anatomical research.   G. J. Kenagy

Swamp is a wet area of land where trees and shrubs grow and where surface water is present for at least part of the year. Swamps occur worldwide in lowland and coastal areas, and near slowly flowing rivers. They have more woody plants than do marshes (see **Marsh**).

A wide variety of plants and animals live in swamps. The moist soil supports trees, shrubs, vines, and other plant life. Ponds and streams in swamps provide a home for fish, frogs, and such reptiles as alligators, crocodiles, snakes, and turtles. Birds and insects live in swamps, as do such mammals as bears, deer, and rabbits.

Swamps may have either fresh water or salt water. Freshwater swamps have constantly changing water levels that reflect changes in rainfall. Most freshwater swamps flood during only part of each year. The water

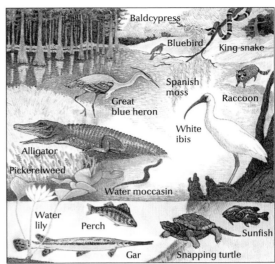

WORLD BOOK illustration by Jean Helmer

Life in a swamp includes a variety of plants and animals. Trees, shrubs, and other plants thrive in the muddy soil. Many kinds of birds, reptiles, fish, and other animals also inhabit swamps.

level of saltwater swamps depends on the water level of the body of salt water that supplies the swamp.

The length of time a swamp is flooded and the depth of flooding determine the plants that grow there. In permanently flooded areas, such water plants as water lilies are common. Somewhat drier areas that flood regularly or in certain seasons have baldcypresses, water tupelos, and red maples. Oaks and elms grow at slightly higher ground levels, where less flooding occurs. Where flooding occurs for longer periods, few plants other than trees grow at ground level. Poison ivy and other woody vines climb the tree trunks, and Spanish moss hangs from the branches. Higher areas of ground, called *hummocks* or *ridges,* remain damp but not flooded. Trees, ferns, shrubs, vines, and wild flowers grow there. Algae, lichens, and mosses cover many of the tree trunks.

A *mangrove swamp* is a kind of a saltwater swamp. Mangrove swamps lie along tropical seacoasts. They are named for the mangrove trees that grow there. Pelicans, snails, and various sea animals live in such swamps.

The best-known swamps in the United States are the Dismal Swamp in North Carolina and Virginia, the Everglades in Florida, the Okefenokee Swamp in Georgia and Florida, and swamps near the White River in Arkansas and the Atchafalaya River in Louisiana. Conservationists work to keep many swamps from being drained for use as farmland or as commercial or residential areas.

Leigh H. Fredrickson

Related articles in *World Book* include:

Bog	Marsh
Dismal Swamp	Okefenokee Swamp
Everglades	Wetland

Swan is a water bird closely related to ducks and geese. Like ducks and geese, swans have a flattened bill; a long neck; water-repellent feathers; long, pointed wings; a short tail; short legs; and webbed feet. But most swans are larger and have a much longer neck than ducks or geese.

Swans nest on all continents except Africa and Antarctica. They live chiefly in regions with a mild or cold climate. Their webbed feet make them good swimmers, but they also walk well on land. Swans make several vocal sounds, from whistles to trumpetlike calls. Male swans are called *cobs,* females are called *pens,* and their offspring are called *cygnets.*

Kinds. There are seven species of swans. Four species live in the Northern Hemisphere, and the others are found in the Southern Hemisphere. Northern swans have white feathers over their entire body. Southern swans have at least some black coloration.

The *mute swan* is the most common northern species. It is native to northern Europe and Asia, but people can also see it in parks and zoos throughout the world. In some places outside of Europe and Asia, mute swans have escaped parks and now live in the wild. The mute swan has a curved neck and holds its wings high over its back. This swan is more quiet than other swans. But it hisses loudly when angry. The bill of the mute swan is orange with a black knob at the base.

The other three northern swans have straight necks and black bills. The *tundra swan* nests on the cold, treeless tundra of northern Asia, Europe, and North America. The *whooper swan* of Europe and Asia and the *trumpeter swan* of North America live in slightly warmer regions. The trumpeter swan is also the largest swan. The adult male weighs about 26 pounds (12 kilograms).

The three southern swans are the *black swan* of Australia, and the *black-necked swan* and the *Coscoroba swan* of South America. The black swan has black feathers with white wing tips, and a red bill. The black-necked swan has white feathers except for its neck and head. The Coscoroba swan has white feathers with black wing tips and is the smallest swan. The female weighs about 8 pounds (3.6 kilograms).

Habits. Most swans nest along the shores of marshes and ponds in the summer. They move to large lakes and bays in the winter. Swans are strong, graceful flyers. But many swans in public parks have their wings clipped and cannot fly. Swans feed mostly on underwater plants. Because of their long necks, they can graze in deeper water than can many ducks. Swans also eat grass along the shore. Occasionally, they eat grain in upland fields.

The swan swims and flies gracefully, though it is one of the largest birds. Its beauty has inspired composers, painters, and writers. Four of the seven species of swans are shown below.

Black-necked swan
Cygnus melanocoryphus
Found in South America
Body length: 45 inches
(114 centimeters)

Black swan
Cygnus atratus
Found in Australia
Body length: 40 inches
(100 centimeters)

Mute swan
Cygnus olor
Found in temperate Eurasia
Body length: 60 inches
(150 centimeters)

Tundra swan
Cygnus columbianus
Found in North American
and Eurasian tundras
Body length: 52 inches
(132 centimeters)

WORLD BOOK illustrations by Walter Linsenmaier

When they are 2 or 3 years old, swans choose mates during highly vocal courtship displays. In one such display, called the *triumph ceremony,* the male and female swans face each other, raise their wings, and call loudly. Mated swans usually stay together for life. Some swans in captivity have lived more than 50 years.

Swans use grasses and other plant material to build large nests. The female usually lays four to six whitish eggs. Among most swans, only the female sits on the eggs to keep them warm. But the female and male black swans share this duty. The eggs must be warmed 30 to 35 days before they hatch. During this period, swans will attack foxes, dogs, people, and any other possible threats to their eggs. When cygnets hatch, they are covered with grayish-white down. They soon grow their flight feathers and can fly at 7 to 14 weeks of age. Small cygnets may ride on their parents' backs. Swans have strong family ties. The young may remain with their parents until it is time to choose a mate.   Fritz L. Knopf

Scientific classification. Swans are in the family Anatidae.

Swansea, *SWAHN see* (pop. 223,293), is a local government area in Wales. It became a unitary authority in 1996. Swansea is located about 45 miles (72 kilometers) west of Cardiff. It lies on Swansea Bay, on the northern side of the Bristol Channel. For location, see **United Kingdom** (political map).

Swansea is a center of trade, manufacturing, and shipping. The manufacture of electronics products is an important industry in the city. Other products include automobile parts and tin plate. Swansea's port handles general cargo and exports of coal from local mines.

Swansea was founded in the 1000's. It became important in the 1800's, after the development of the smelting industry and the hard-coal trade. Swansea became the chief British center for the shipping of tin plate. Since the early 1930's, the city has declined as a manufacturing center and port. To help offset this decline, Swansea became the site of Britain's first *enterprise zone* in 1981. This zone provides space for new commercial and industrial activities.   D. Q. Bowen

Swastika, *SWAHS tuh kuh,* is an ancient symbol often used as an ornament or a religious sign. The swastika is in the form of a cross with the ends of the arms bent at right angles in a given direction, usually clockwise. The swastika has been found on Byzantine buildings, Buddhist inscriptions, Celtic monuments, and Greek coins.

Swastikas were widely used among the Indians of North America and South America. The clockwise swastika was adopted in 1920 as the symbol of the National Socialist Party of Germany. As such, it came to be one of the most hated symbols in human history. It came to

stand for all the evil associated with the Nazis as they took control of Europe before and during World War II. After the Allies defeated Germany in 1945, they banned the display of the swastika emblem.   Whitney Smith

Swaziland, *SWAH zee LAND,* is a small, beautiful country in southern Africa. It is surrounded by the Republic of South Africa on three sides and by Mozambique on the east. Swaziland has rich mineral deposits, large forests, and good farm and ranch land. But most mines, processing plants, and profitable farms are owned by people of European origin. Most people of African origin in Swaziland are peasant farmers.

Swaziland was formerly a British protectorate. It became independent in 1968 as the Kingdom of Swaziland. Mbabane is Swaziland's administrative capital (see **Mbabane**). Lobamba, a village, is the traditional, or royal, capital, and the legislative capital. Manzini is the country's main commercial center.

Government. Swaziland is a monarchy. The *Ngwenyama* (king), a hereditary leader, rules with the help of a council of ministers and a national legislature. The *Ndlovukazi* (queen mother, or mother of the king) is in charge of national rituals. If the king's mother is no longer living, one of his wives may act as Ndlovukazi.

People. The vast majority of Swaziland's people belong to the Swazi ethnic group. They speak siSwati, a Bantu language. Small numbers of people belong to other African ethnic groups or are Europeans. Most of Swaziland's people farm and raise livestock. Some live in towns and work in factories, offices, and shops.

Swazi farmers prize their cattle and respect people with large herds. Traditionally, Swazi do not kill cattle for food, but some are sold for cash or sacrificed at reli-

Swaziland

▬▬▬	International boundary
———	Road
——	Railroad
⊛	National capital
•	Other city or town
+	Elevation above sea level

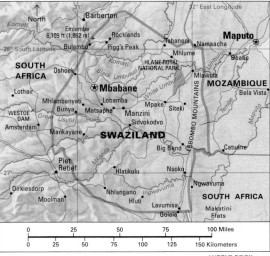

WORLD BOOK maps

Swastika

Oriental and American Indian

Nazi

gious ceremonies. When a man marries, his family gives his wife's family cattle to legalize her status as his wife.

Swazi men may have more than one wife. The traditional family includes a man, his wives, his unmarried children, and his married sons and their families. Each family lives in a separate homestead. For hundreds of years, the homesteads consisted of circular houses built around a cattle pen. Today, many wealthy Swazi live in houses like those of North Americans or Europeans. In traditional, rural homesteads with more than one wife, each wife has her own living quarters and a garden plot where she grows beans, corn, gourds, and other crops. The Swazi men and boys tend the family's cattle.

Traditional Swazi clothing is made of animal skins, leather, or brightly colored cloth. Swazi also wear beaded ornaments. Today, most Swazi wear clothing similar to that worn by North Americans or Europeans.

Each Swazi man belongs to an *age group* organized by the Ngwenyama. All the men in a particular group are about the same age. Different age groups have spe-

Facts in brief

Capitals: Mbabane (administrative) and Lobamba (traditional).
Official languages: siSwati and English.
Area: 6,704 mi² (17,364 km²). *Greatest distances*—north-south, 120 mi (193 km); east-west, 90 mi (140 km).
Elevation: *Highest*—Mount Emlembe, 6,109 ft (1,862 m) above sea level. *Lowest*—70 ft (21 m) above sea level.
Population: *Estimated 2008 population*—1,102,000; density, 164 per mi² (63 per km²); distribution, 76 percent rural, 24 percent urban. *1997 census*—929,718.
Chief products: *Agriculture*—citrus fruits, corn, cotton, hides and skins, pineapples, rice, sugar cane, tobacco. *Manufacturing*—food products, soft drink concentrates, wood products. *Mining*—asbestos, barite, coal, gold, kaolin, tin.
Flag: The flag has five horizontal stripes. The top and bottom stripes are blue (for peace). The wide center stripe is red (for past battles) with a black and white shield, spears, and staff. Between the blue and red stripes are yellow stripes (for natural resources). See **Flag** (picture: Flags of Africa).
Money: *Basic unit*—lilangeni (plural spelled emalangeni). One hundred cents equal one lilangeni.

cial parts in Swazi ceremonies. Many of Swaziland's adults cannot read and write. For the country's literacy rate, see **Literacy** (table: Literacy rates). About 90 percent of Swazi belong to Christian churches. Most of the rest practice traditional African religions or are Muslims.

The Europeans in Swaziland own farms, mines, and forests. Many *Eurafricans* (people of mixed descent) work for Europeans, and others are farmers, craftworkers, or business people. There are some Asian immigrants who work in small businesses.

Land. Mountains up to 6,000 feet (1,800 meters) above sea level rise along Swaziland's western border. Vast pine forests cover much of the land there. Temperatures average 60 °F (16 °C), and from 45 to 75 inches (114 to 191 centimeters) of rain falls each year. Rolling, grassy midlands lie east of the mountains. More people live in this region than in any other. Temperatures average 66 °F (19 °C), and from 30 to 45 inches (76 to 114 centimeters) of rain falls there each year. Farther east, the land levels off into a low plain covered by bushes and grass. Temperatures average 72 °F (22 °C), and only about 20 inches (51 centimeters) of rain falls per year. The high, narrow Lebombo Mountains rise along the eastern border.

Swaziland is one of the best-watered areas in southern Africa. Four main rivers flow eastward across the country. They are the Ingwavuma, Komati, Umbuluzi, and Great Usutu. The rivers supply the water needed to irrigate crops and to run hydroelectric power plants.

Economy. More than half the country's land is owned by the Ngwenyama and is called Swazi Nation Land (SNL). Most Swazi graze cattle and grow food for their families on SNL. Since the 1960's, an increasing number of Swazi have been raising cash crops, especially cotton and corn, on SNL. Europeans own about half of all the privately owned land in Swaziland. They raise many of the cash crops, including citrus fruits, cotton, pineapples, rice, sugar cane, and tobacco. They also raise cattle for meat, skins, and hides.

Since the 1940's, European companies have planted mountainous land in Swaziland with pine and eucalyptus trees. Today, the area has one of the largest artificial-

Shostal

Mbabane, the administrative capital of Swaziland, lies in the country's western highlands. Most of the people of Swaziland live in rural areas.

ly created forests in Africa. European-owned mills process wood pulp and other forest products.

Rich mineral deposits lie in the mountains, and much of the nation's income comes from the European-owned mining industry. Swaziland has deposits of asbestos, coal, gold, tin, *barite* (ore used in making barium), and *kaolin* (clay used in making pottery).

Since the 1960's, a number of small manufacturing firms have developed in Swaziland. During the 1980's, a number of South African companies transferred part of their operations to Swaziland to avoid economic sanctions imposed against their country. After sanctions were lifted in the early 1990's, most of these operations stayed in Swaziland. Industries in Swaziland include sugar milling, fruit processing, and the production of soft drink concentrates and wood products.

Swaziland has about 1,000 miles (1,600 kilometers) of tar or gravel roads and about 2,000 miles (3,200 kilometers) of unpaved roads. Winding footpaths run between most homesteads. A railroad connects Sidvokodvo with the port at Maputo, Mozambique. Airplane service links Manzini with South Africa and Mozambique.

History. According to the legends of the Swazi, their ancestors once lived near what is now Maputo, Mozambique. In the late 1700's, the Swazi chief Ngwane II led a small band of people over the mountains to what is now southeastern Swaziland. There, the Swazi found other African peoples. Ngwane II and the chiefs who ruled after him united several of these peoples with the Swazi.

British traders and *Boers* (chiefly Dutch farmers from South Africa) first came to Swaziland in the 1830's. In the 1880's, the settlers discovered gold. Hundreds of prospectors rushed into the region. They asked the Swazi chief and his advisers to sign documents granting them rights to mine minerals and to use land for farming and grazing. The Swazi leaders could not read and did not realize that they were giving up control of the land.

In 1894, the British and Boers agreed that the Boers would govern Swaziland. But in 1902, the Boers lost a war with the British, and the United Kingdom took control of Swaziland. It ruled Swaziland until the mid-1960's. In 1967, Swaziland gained control over its internal matters. It received full independence on Sept. 6, 1968.

In 1968, the United Kingdom introduced a constitution to Swaziland. It established Swaziland as a constitutional monarchy, headed by King Sobhuza II. Many Swazi opposed it because they felt it disregarded Swazi interests and traditions. In 1973, Sobhuza—at the urging of other conservative Swazi leaders—abolished the Constitution and suspended the country's legislature. The king began to rule the country with the assistance of a council of ministers. A new legislature was established in 1979.

King Sobhuza died in 1982 after a reign of 61 years. In 1983, one of his sons, 15-year-old Prince Makhosetive, was named heir to the throne. In 1986, the prince was installed as king. He took the name King Mswati III. In the 1990's, popular unrest forced the government to consider political reforms. In 2005, King Mswati approved a new constitution for Swaziland but maintained his hold on power.   Donald L. Sparks

Sweat gland. See Gland; Perspiration.

Sweatshop is a factory in which poverty-stricken people—mostly women and children—work long hours for low wages. Working conditions are often bad enough to

endanger the health and safety of the workers.

The sweatshop, often called the *sweating system,* began when the factory system developed in the early 1800's. Many factories were too small to house all the workers. So factory owners assigned part of the work to subcontractors. The subcontractors set up makeshift factories in dimly lighted and poorly ventilated buildings. They hired workers on a *piecework* basis—that is, each worker's pay was based on the number of product units he or she completed. Nearly all industrialized countries had sweatshops.

In the United States, people began to object to sweatshops as early as 1830. The problem became serious after 1880, when the rate of immigration to the United States increased. Sweatshop owners took advantage of immigrants' ignorance and poverty to get them to work for low wages. The cigar and needlework industries in particular, as well as some mechanical industries, relied heavily on the sweating system.

In the 1900's, some northern European nations began to pass laws banning sweatshop conditions. Many states of the United States passed such laws after a fire in 1911 killed 146 workers at the Triangle Shirtwaist Company in New York City. States also passed minimum-wage laws that made it impractical for factories to assign work to subcontractors. Laws that abolished child labor and limited the hours women could work also hurt the sweatshop system. Another factor hastening the sweatshops' decline was that more women took jobs in metalworking and other trades. In these trades, laborers could not work outside the regular factories.

By the 1990's, some sweatshops reappeared in the United States, especially in Saipan and other U.S. territories overseas, and in northern Europe. The shops employed mainly immigrants, some of whom lacked work permits or other necessary documents. Sweatshops also sprang up in some Asian and Latin American nations, even where they were illegal. A number of these shops supplied clothing, shoes, toys, and other products to American companies for sale in the United States. Student protesters, human rights groups, and labor leaders campaigned to end sweatshops.   Daniel Quinn Mills

See also **Child labor; Wages and hours.**

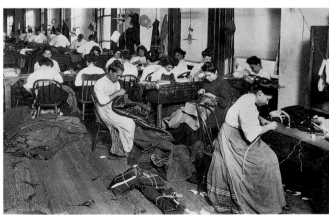

Brown Bros.

Sweatshops employed people for very low pay. Workers put in long hours in makeshift factories under miserable conditions.

The landscape of Sweden includes many swift rivers, thick forests, and snow-capped mountains. Camping, hiking, and other outdoor activities are popular among the Swedish people. In this photo, great spruce and pine forests blanket the hills of scenic Jämtland, a region of central Sweden.

Sweden

Sweden is a country in northern Europe. It is one of Europe's largest countries in area. However, it is also one of Europe's most thinly populated countries. Forests cover more than half of Sweden's land. Only about one-tenth of the country is farmland. The northernmost part of Sweden lies inside the Arctic Circle in a region of continuous cold called the *Land of the Midnight Sun.* The region has that name because for periods during the summer, the sun shines 24 hours a day.

Sweden is also a land of beautiful lakes, snow-capped mountains, swift rivers, and rocky offshore islands. Part of its long coastline has sandy beaches, and other parts have rocky cliffs. Stockholm is Sweden's capital and largest city. It lies on the east coast of Sweden, on the Baltic Sea, and it includes small offshore islands. Wooded hills add to the beauty of Stockholm's setting.

Sweden and its neighbor Norway occupy the Scandinavian peninsula. Sweden, Norway, and Denmark are called the Scandinavian countries. The three nations have close cultural and economic ties. Their languages are similar, and Swedes, Norwegians, and Danes can usually understand each other.

The Swedish standard of living is one of the highest in the world. Sweden ranks among the leading European nations in the number of automobiles, telephones, and television sets it has in relation to its population. Many Swedish families have country homes where they enjoy

spending their weekends and vacations.

Sweden's way of life has often been called the "middle way," because it combines private enterprise with some government ownership of industry. Also, the Swedish government offers extensive social security benefits. It provides free education and largely free medical service. It pays pensions to old people, widows, and orphans. After most Swedes retire, they receive annual pensions that amount to a large percentage of their av-

Facts in brief

Capital: Stockholm.
Official language: Swedish.
Official name: Konungariket Sverige (Kingdom of Sweden).
Area: 173,732 mi² (449,964 km²). *Greatest distances*—north-south, 977 mi (1,572 km); east-west, 310 mi (499 km). *Coastline*—4,700 mi (7,564 km).
Elevation: *Highest*—Mount Kebnekaise, 6,926 ft (2,111 m) above sea level. *Lowest*—sea level along the coast.
Population: *Estimated 2008 population*—9,179,000; density, 53 per mi² (20 per km²); distribution, 84 percent urban, 16 percent rural. *2005 official government estimate*—9,028,944.
Chief products: *Agriculture*—barley, beef cattle, dairy products, hogs, oats, potatoes, sugar beets, wheat. *Forestry*—beech, oak, pine, spruce. *Manufacturing*—agricultural machinery, aircraft, automobiles, ball bearings, diesel motors, electrical equipment, explosives, pharmaceuticals, plastics, precision tools, safety matches, ships, stainless steel goods, steel, telephones. *Mining*—copper, gold, iron ore, lead, silver.
National anthem: "Du gamla, du fria, du fjällhöga nord" ("Thou Ancient, Thou Free, Thou Mountain-Crowned North").
National holiday: Flag Day, June 6.
Money: *Basic unit*—Swedish krona. One hundred öre equal one krona.

M. Donald Hancock, the contributor of this article, is Professor of Political Science and Director, Center for European Studies at Vanderbilt University.

Damm, ZEFA

Gripsholm Castle houses the Swedish National Portrait Gallery, which contains about 3,000 paintings. The castle lies on Lake Mälaren, near Stockholm, and was built in the 1500's.

Damm, ZEFA

Stockholm, Sweden's capital and largest city, is the center of the country's commercial and cultural life. It also serves as a major center for international trade and communications.

erage earnings. The government also provides health insurance and financial aid for housing.

Government

National government. Sweden is a constitutional monarchy with a king or queen, a prime minister and Cabinet, and a parliament. It had the same constitution from 1809 to 1975, when a new constitution went into effect. The 1809 constitution gave the king executive power, but divided legislative power between the king and parliament. The power of parliament gradually increased, and parliamentary rule was established in 1917. Under the 1975 constitution, the king lost his remaining executive powers and became a ceremonial figure, though he remained head of state. In 1980, a constitutional change made the royal couple's eldest child—male or female—heir to the throne. Today, the monarch formally opens the sessions of parliament and must be present at the meeting at which the prime minister turns over the government to the new prime minister.

Executive power lies in the hands of the prime minister and other members of the Cabinet. The prime minister is nominated by the speaker of parliament and must be confirmed by the members of parliament.

Sweden's prime minister is usually the leader of the largest political party in parliament or the designated leader of a *coalition* (combination of political parties) that includes a majority of the members of parliament. On rare occasions, the leader of a smaller party or a minority coalition has served as prime minister. The prime minister appoints the remaining Cabinet members. Ministries and central administrative agencies, which are made up partly of civil servants, carry out the work of the government.

Sweden's parliament, called the *Riksdag,* is a one-

The Swedish flag, first used in the mid-1400's, was made official in 1663. The colors come from the coat of arms.

Sweden's coat of arms features three gold crowns, symbols of Sweden since the early 1300's.

WORLD BOOK map

Sweden lies in northern Europe on the eastern part of the Scandinavian peninsula. It is bordered by Norway and Finland.

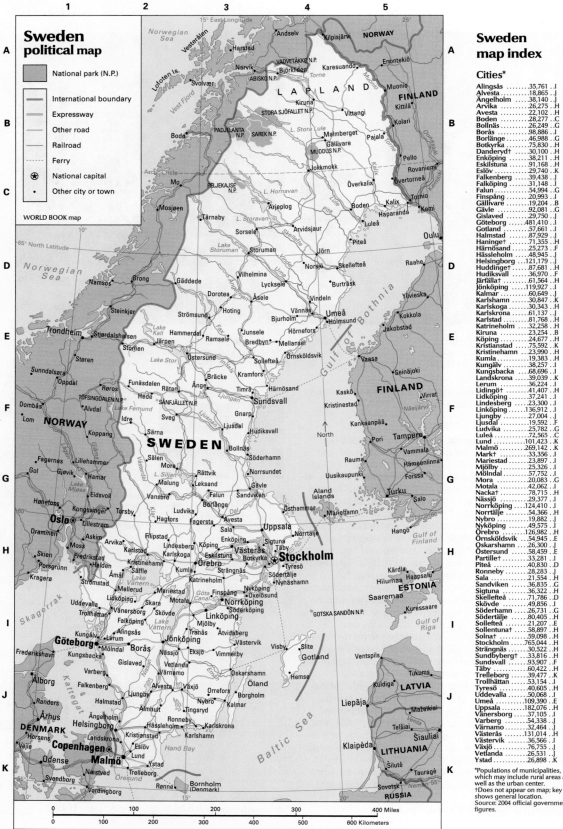

Sweden political map

National park (N.P.)

International boundary
Expressway
Other road
Railroad
Ferry
National capital
Other city or town

WORLD BOOK map

house legislature. It has 349 members, who are elected for four-year terms.

Voters choose 310 of the members of parliament by voting for political parties in their local districts, called *constituencies*. The remaining 39 seats are distributed among the parties according to each party's proportion of the nationwide vote. A party must win at least 4 percent of the nationwide vote, or 12 percent in any constituency, in order to receive any seats in the parliament. All Swedish citizens 18 years and older may vote in national elections.

The Riksdag meets in full session from October through May. During this time, the Riksdag hears and debates the Cabinet's legislative proposals. The Riksdag has the power to remove the entire Cabinet or an individual Cabinet member from office through a vote of no confidence.

Ombudsmen. The Riksdag appoints officials called *ombudsmen* to protect citizens from the illegal or incompetent use of power by government officials or agencies. Specialized ombudsmen offices exist for issues involving antitrust and competition, consumer affairs, equal opportunity in work, and allegations of ethnic discrimination. An ombudsman for the press is appointed by a special committee.

The ombudsmen, who are assisted by expert staffs, may either initiate their own investigations or respond to the complaints of citizens. Sweden created the office of ombudsman in 1809 to help ensure that judges, civil servants, and military officers observed the laws. It was the first country to have an ombudsman.

Politics. The Social Democratic Party ranks as Sweden's largest political party. This socialist party helped establish the country's welfare system.

The Moderate Party, a nonsocialist party, ranks as Sweden's second largest political party. The country's other political parties include the Center Party, the Christian Democrats, the Green Party, the Left Party, and the Liberal Party.

Local government. Sweden is divided into 21 counties. Each county is administered by a governor appointed by the national government and a council elected by the people.

Courts. District courts serve the towns and counties of Sweden. Regional courts of appeal hear appeals from the district courts.

The Supreme Court is the highest court in the country. This court hears final appeals in important civil and criminal cases.

Armed forces. Swedish men between the ages of 18 and 47 are required to serve from 7 to 15 months in the country's armed forces. The nation's regular army, navy, and air force have a total of about 55,000 members.

People

Sweden is one of the most thinly populated countries of Europe. Most of Sweden's people live in urban areas, mainly in the central and southern parts of the country. Sweden's three largest cities are Stockholm, Göteborg, and Malmö.

Ancestry. Most Swedes are descendants of ancient Germanic tribes who settled in the Scandinavian region beginning in 8000 to 5000 B.C. They are thus closely related to the Danes and Norwegians.

People of Finnish origin make up the country's largest ethnic minority. Most of them live in the northern part of the country or along the eastern coast.

The Sami are another large ethnic group in Sweden. They live in the northernmost part of the country, known as Sapmi or Lapland. The Sami are also known as Lapps. They differ in appearance, language, and way of life from most other Swedes. For thousands of years, they earned a living by hunting, fishing, and tending herds of reindeer. Many Sami continue to migrate with their reindeer herds from summer pastures to winter pastures, though most of the Sami now have permanent residences. Their other economic activities include the production of artwork, handicrafts, and textiles (see **Sami**).

A large number of people from other countries have settled in Sweden. During the 1960's, people from Denmark, Finland, Greece, Norway, Turkey, and Yugoslavia moved to Sweden to find jobs. In the late 1900's, many people immigrated to Sweden from the Balkan region in southeastern Europe and other areas of conflict around the world.

Language. Swedish is a Germanic language that closely resembles Danish and Norwegian. People from Sweden, Denmark, and Norway can usually understand one another.

Spoken and written Swedish are similar throughout the country, but some regional dialects exist. Many Swedes of Finnish origin speak Finnish as their first language but learn Swedish beginning at an early age in school. The Sami speak a language that is related to Finnish. The majority of adult Swedes speak some Eng-

Population density

This map shows the population density of Sweden. About a third of the people live in or near the country's three largest cities—Stockholm, Göteborg, and Malmö.

WORLD BOOK map

Persons per sq. mi.	Persons per km²
More than 60	More than 25
25 to 60	10 to 25
2 to 25	1 to 10
Less than 2	Less than 1

lish, and in many cases, they speak a second foreign language as well.

Way of life

Sweden is a land of striking physical and visual contrasts. While it is a highly urbanized nation, it also has countless lakes and vast stretches of forests scattered with villages and towns.

City life. Sweden's cities are modern and efficient. They feature blends of traditional and functional modern architecture. Many Swedish cities, especially Stockholm and Kalmar on the southeastern coast, have imposing castles and churches dating from the Middle Ages. Suburbs of the larger cities have high-rise apartment buildings. Many of these buildings were built during the 1950's and 1960's in response to rapid urbanization.

Highways and public transportation facilities, such as railways and buses, link Sweden's city centers and suburbs. In addition, Stockholm has a sprawling subway system. As in other industrialized nations, highway congestion presents a daily challenge for people who work and live in Sweden's cities. However, because Sweden relies heavily on electrical energy for heating and industry, pollution is less of a problem there than in many other countries.

Rural life. Economic and social development in Sweden have caused a diminishing of economic differences between urban and rural residents. As a result, people in rural areas maintain a standard of living similar to that of urban dwellers, because the government provides special payments and other supports to farmers and because many rural citizens work in industry or services in nearby towns. In addition, many people who live in rural areas work part-time on farms and part-time in factories.

Food and drink. Sweden is famous for *smörgåsbord,* an assortment of cold and hot foods placed on a large table for self-service. Smörgåsbord is served on holidays, in fine restaurants, and on board many Swedish cruise ships. Swedes often eat the foods in a particular order. First they eat cold fish dishes, including anchovies, eels, herring, salmon, sardines, and shrimp. Next, they eat such cold meats as liver pâté, smoked reindeer, sliced beef, and ham with vegetable salad. Next come small hot dishes, such as meatballs, omelets, sausages, anchovies, or herring cooked in breadcrumbs. Favorite desserts include cheese, fresh fruit, fruit salad, and pastry.

On a daily basis, Swedes usually eat more simple fare. Breakfast often consists of cold cereal or a pastry and strong coffee or milk. Lunch may consist of open-faced sandwiches on thin, hard bread. Dinner is often a meat or fish dish with boiled potatoes.

Swedes, like their Scandinavian neighbors, drink vast quantities of coffee at mealtime and during breaks from work. Many Swedes also enjoy beer, which is sometimes accompanied by a strong, colorless liquor known as *aquavit.* They also drink vodka, wine, and other alcoholic beverages.

Religion. Most Swedes are members of the Lutheran Church. In fact, Lutheranism was Sweden's official religion from about 1540 until 2000. Other religious groups include Baptists, Jews, the Mission Covenant Church, Pentecostals, and Roman Catholics. Many immigrants are Eastern Orthodox or Muslim.

The churches pioneered much welfare work in the country, but the government has taken over most of this work. Swedish churches have a long tradition of missionary activities, particularly the Lutheran Church in India and South Africa.

Education. The Swedish government requires children from 7 to 16 years of age to attend school. Elementary and high school education are free for Swedish children. The government also operates all the universities and most of the technical and other specialized colleges in the country.

Many children under the age of 7 attend kindergar-

© Eric A. Wessman

Sidewalk cafes in Swedish cities and towns provide a pleasant place for people to eat, drink, and visit with friends.

Many small villages lie along the southwestern coast of Sweden, just south of the border with Norway. Fishing is an important economic activity in this area.

Mohn, ZEFA

tens run by private individuals or organizations. The government assists the kindergartens, but attendance is not required.

The Swedish primary school, called the *grundskola,* has three three-year divisions. The *junior stage* consists of first grade through third grade, and the *intermediate stage* covers fourth grade through sixth grade. The *senior stage* consists of seventh through ninth grade. In the seventh and eighth grades, students begin to choose their own subjects. In the ninth grade, they select one of nine courses of study. Most pupils continue their general education. Others also learn such practical skills as home economics or workshop methods. Some select special courses in languages, technology, or commerce. Every child in the fourth through seventh grade is required to study English, and about 90 percent continue English after that.

After completing the grundskola, some children go to a secondary school. There are three kinds of secondary schools. The three-year *upper secondary schools* prepare students to attend a university. The two-year *continuation schools* give courses in social, economic, and technical subjects. The *vocational schools* offer day and evening courses for one to three years in such subjects as industry, handicrafts, and home economics.

Sweden has six universities—in Göteborg, Linköping, Lund, Stockholm, Umeå, and Uppsala. The oldest, the University of Uppsala, was founded in 1477.

Libraries and museums. Sweden has four general research libraries—the Royal Library in Stockholm and the university libraries in Göteborg, Lund, and Uppsala. The Royal Library, established in the 1600's, has a large collection of early Swedish manuscripts. Sweden also has about 400 public libraries.

The country's leading museums include the Skansen open-air museum, which exhibits old Swedish houses, and the Nationalmuseum, which has a collection of Swedish sculpture and paintings. Both museums are located in Stockholm.

Recreation. Outdoor activities are popular in Sweden. Skiing and hockey are the chief winter sports. Every March, thousands of Swedes take part in a cross-country ski race called the Vasa Race, held in the county of Dalarna in central Sweden. The race covers about 55 miles (89 kilometers). Hunting and fishing are also popular activities. Hunters shoot deer, fox, moose, and various wild fowl. Game fish include pike, salmon, and trout. When the rivers are frozen, people cut holes in the ice and drop their fishing lines through them.

The people of Sweden also like hiking and camping,

© Klingwalls

Swedes celebrate St. Lucia Day, also called the Festival of Light, on December 13. Young girls dress in white, serve their families hot coffee and buns, and sing a traditional song.

Leif R. Jansson, Svenskt Pressfoto

Seaside beaches dot the long southern coastline of Sweden. Many Swedes, along with tourists from other countries, spend their vacations at these beaches.

Swedish Tourist Board

The Vasa Race, a cross-country ski event, is held every March. The race from Sälen to Mora, in the county of Dalarna in central Sweden, covers 55 miles (89 kilometers).

soccer, swimming, sailing, and tennis. A number of Swedes, including Bjorn Borg and Stefan Edberg, have become international tennis stars. Graceful exercises called *gymnastics* are popular in Sweden and are a feature of school training.

Many Swedes spend their vacations by the sea or on the country's offshore islands, such as Gotland or Öland. Others relax near one of Sweden's many lakes or in the vast wilderness that covers the northern part of the country. Tourists enjoy three-day trips along the Göta Canal, which flows across southern Sweden. This canal

links lakes and rivers, making a trip of about 350 miles (560 kilometers) from Göteborg to Stockholm. In cities, people enjoy Sweden's many urban parks, or sip coffee and watch passers-by at sidewalk cafes.

Holidays. The major winter festivals in Sweden take place in December. On December 13, the Swedes celebrate St. Lucia Day, the Festival of Light. Before dawn, young girls dress in white with a crown of evergreen leaves. They awaken their families with a traditional song and serve them hot coffee and buns. Swedes have their Christmas celebration on Christmas Eve. Families gather for dinner, which usually includes ham and a fish course. After dinner, everyone receives presents.

Midsummer's Eve festivities are held on the Friday between June 19 and 26. The people celebrate the return of summer to Sweden. They stay up most of the night and dance around gaily decorated Maypoles. Flag Day, the national holiday, is June 6. The monarch presents the national flag to Swedish organizations and societies at a special ceremony.

Social welfare. The Swedes pay high taxes, but the government provides extensive welfare benefits. Every family receives an allowance for each child under 16. The government also provides housing allowances for families with children. The allowance is based on family income, the number of children, and the cost of housing. Every employed person is guaranteed a five-week annual vacation with pay.

Swedes who lose their jobs receive unemployment benefits representing about 80 percent of their former earnings. The people have largely free medical service. After retirement, most Swedes receive annual pensions of about 65 percent of their average earnings during their 15 highest paid years. The government also provides pensions for widows, orphans, and children who have lost one parent.

Arts

Literature. The roots of Swedish literature can be traced back to the Middle Ages, but the first internationally recognized Swedish authors did not appear until the 1800's. August Strindberg became the most influen-

© Eric A. Wessman

Hiking is a popular sport among Swedes, and Sweden's northern wilderness poses an exciting challenge for hikers. In this photo, a lone hiker treks north of the Arctic Circle.

tial writer in Swedish literary history with his novels and plays of the late 1800's and early 1900's. Strindberg's plays, because of their surrealistic quality and bold themes, helped revolutionize modern drama.

A number of Swedish authors have been honored with Nobel Prizes for literature. In 1909, Selma Lagerlöf became the first Swede to receive the prize. She still ranks as the country's best-known novelist for her stories about life in her native Värmland. Other Nobel Prize winners were Verner von Heidenstam in 1916 for his poetry, Eric Axel Karlfeldt in 1931 for his lyric poems, and Pär Fabian Lagerkvist in 1951 for his novels. In 1974, Eyvind Johnson and Harry Edmund Martinson shared the prize. Johnson received recognition for his novels and short stories and Martinson for his dramas, essays, novels, and poems.

In the middle and late 1900's, the husband-and-wife team of Per Wahlöö and Maj Sjöwall gained international popularity for their series of novels about Stockholm policeman Martin Beck. Astrid Lindgren became known for her popular children's books. Lars Gustafsson won attention as a novelist and social critic.

Fine arts. Few Swedish artists have gained international recognition. Most Swedish painters, sculptors, and architects have followed styles developed elsewhere in Europe. During the early 1900's, Carl Milles became the best-known Swedish sculptor, primarily for his monuments and sculpture fountains. Painter Anders Zorn won a reputation in the late 1800's and early 1900's for his landscapes and portraits. In architecture, Ragnar Östberg designed the Stockholm City Hall, which was completed in 1923. The hall's modern style influenced architects throughout Scandinavia.

Industrial design. Sweden, along with other Scandinavian countries, made its greatest contribution to the arts in the field of industrial design. Scandinavia became influential in industrial design in the 1920's and 1930's with the creation of simple, harmonious textiles, furniture, glassware, and ceramics. Swedish furniture designers emphasized light-colored wood and bright upholstery and drapery.

Music. Classical music in Sweden generally has followed the models of the major composers and movements of other European countries. Sweden has an important folk music tradition that extends back to the Middle Ages. The Swedish soprano Jenny Lind became one of the most famous opera and concert singers of the 1800's. Tenor Jussi Bjoerling and dramatic soprano Birgit Nilsson ranked among the greatest opera singers of the 1900's.

Motion pictures. Sweden developed an important motion-picture industry in the early 1900's. Victor Sjöström and Mauritz Stiller were two influential directors of the era. Many of their films were based on Scandinavian literature. The famous movie actress Greta Garbo began her career in Swedish silent films before moving to the United States in 1925. Ingrid Bergman was another movie actress who started her career in

Royal Dramatic Theater, Stockholm

The plays of August Strindberg have won international fame. A scene from his play *Miss Julie* is shown here as directed by famous Swedish stage and film director Ingmar Bergman.

Midsummer Dance (1897), an oil painting on canvas;
Nationalmuseum, Stockholm

Swedish painter Anders Zorn became famous for his portraits and scenes of rural Swedish customs. The painting here depicts the traditional Midsummer Dance.

Sweden and then achieved fame in the United States. The most important figure in modern Swedish motion pictures is director Ingmar Bergman. He achieved worldwide recognition for his symbolic, brilliantly photographed films.

The land

Sweden occupies the eastern part of the Scandinavian peninsula. From Sweden's hilly and, in parts, mountainous border with Norway, the land slopes gently eastward to the Gulf of Bothnia and the Baltic Sea. The country's scenery varies from the unpopulated, treeless Kölen Mountains in the northwest to the fertile plains in the south. Thousands of lakes cover about a twelfth of the country's area.

The long coastline of Sweden has sandy beaches in the south and rocky cliffs in parts of the west and north. Many groups of small islands lie off the coast. The largest islands are Gotland, a fertile island covering about 1,160 square miles (3,004 square kilometers), and Öland, which covers about 520 square miles (1,350 square kilometers). Both of these islands are located in the Baltic Sea.

Sweden has four main land regions: (1) the Mountain Range, (2) the Inner Northland, (3) the Swedish Lowland, and (4) the South Swedish Highland.

The Mountain Range is part of the Kölen Mountains. Sweden's northern boundary with Norway runs through these mountains, which Norwegians call the Kjølen Mountains. Hundreds of small glaciers cover the higher slopes of the snow-capped range. Sweden's highest mountain, 6,926-foot (2,111-meter) Mount Kebnekaise, is in this rugged region.

The land is completely treeless above about 1,600 feet (488 meters) in the northernmost part of the mountains. There, the climate is too cold for trees. Some birch trees grow on the warmer, lower slopes.

The Inner Northland is a vast, thinly populated, hilly region. Great forests of pine and spruce trees cover most of the land, and lumbering is an important industry. Many swift rivers flow southeast across the Inner Northland and provide much hydroelectric power. The rivers have formed deep, narrow valleys, some of which have long lakes. The valleys broaden toward the coast of the Gulf of Bothnia. Most of the region's people live in these valleys or on the coast.

The Torne River forms part of the boundary between the Inner Northland and Finland. Other rivers in the region include the Lule, the Ume, the Ångerman, and the Dal rivers. Bergslagen, a hilly area rich in minerals, lies south of the Dal River in the southernmost part of the Inner Northland.

The Swedish Lowland has more people than any other part of the country. This region includes the central and southern plains of Sweden. The broad central plains are broken by lakes, tree-covered ridges, and small hills. Farmland covers more than 40 percent of these plains.

Sweden's largest lakes, Vänern and Vättern, are in the Swedish Lowland. Lake Vänern covers 2,156 square miles (5,584 square kilometers) and is one of the largest lakes in Europe. Lake Vättern has an area of 738 square miles (1,911 square kilometers).

The southern plains include some of Sweden's most

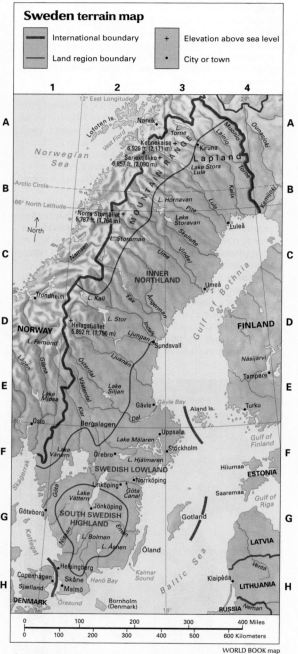

Sweden terrain map

| | International boundary | + | Elevation above sea level |
| | Land region boundary | • | City or town |

WORLD BOOK map

Physical features

Ångerman River	.D	3	Lake Kall	.D	1
Baltic Sea	.H	3	Lake Mälaren	.F	3
Bergslagen (region)	.F	2	Lake Siljan	.E	2
Dal River	.E	2	Lake Stor	.D	2
Gävle Bay	.E	3	Lake Torne	.A	3
Göta Canal	.F	2	Lake Vänern	.F	1
Gotland (island)	.G	3	Lake Vättern	.G	2
Gulf of Bothnia	.C	4	Lule River	.B	3
Hanö Bay	.H	2	Öland (island)	.G	2
Helagsfjället			Sarjektjåkko		
(mountain)	.D	1	(mountain)	.B	3
Kalmar Sound	.H	2	Skåne (region)	.H	1
Kattegat (channel)	.G	1	Torne River	.B	4
Kebnekaise			Ume River	.C	3
(mountain)	.A	3	Västerdal River	.E	1
Lake Hjälmaren	.F	2	Vindel River	.C	3

The Swedish Lowland includes some of the country's most fertile land. Farmland covers more than 40 percent of this land region. The farm shown here is in the Östergotland region, near Norrköping.

J. Pfaff, ZEFA

fertile land. Farmland and forests of beechwood cover most of Skåne, which is the southernmost region of the country. Skåne is the most thickly populated and richest farming area of Sweden.

The South Swedish Highland, also called the Götaland Plateau, is a rocky upland that rises to about 1,200 feet (366 meters) above sea level. This thinly populated area has poor, stony soils and is covered mostly by forests. The southern part of the region is flat, with small lakes and swamps.

Climate

The climate of Sweden varies greatly between the southern and northern parts of the country. Southwesterly winds from the Atlantic Ocean give southern Sweden pleasant summers and mostly mild winters. In contrast, the northern part of the country has pleasant summers but cold winters. The Atlantic winds are blocked by the Kölen Mountains and therefore have less effect on northern Sweden.

In Sweden's extreme south, temperatures in January and February, the coldest months, average 32 °F (0 °C). In Kiruna, in the far north of the country, temperatures average about 10 °F (−12 °C) during these months. In July, which is Sweden's warmest month, temperatures average from 59 to 63 °F (15 to 17 °C) in the south, and 54 to 57 °F (12 to 14 °C) in the north. In winter, eastern air masses may lower the temperature to −10 °F (−23 °C) in Stockholm in the south, and to −45 °F (−43 °C) in the northern part of Sweden.

Rainfall is generally greater in the Kölen Mountains and the southern highlands than on the plains that border the Gulf of Bothnia. In the south, snow covers the ground in January and February. The north has snow from mid-October through mid-April.

Economy

Sweden is a highly industrialized nation. Its economy is based on a combination of advanced engineering and service industries. It also relies heavily on exports. Most of Sweden's industry is privately owned. Government ownership is concentrated in mines, public transportation, energy, and telecommunications.

Abundant natural resources, such as vast forests and

Average January temperatures
The northern regions of Sweden have cold winters. The southern part of the country has milder winters.

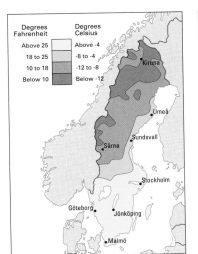

Degrees Fahrenheit	Degrees Celsius
Above 25	Above -4
18 to 25	-8 to -4
10 to 18	-12 to -8
Below 10	Below -12

Average July temperatures
Summers are cool in northern Sweden and in most inland regions. The southern region of Sweden has warm summers.

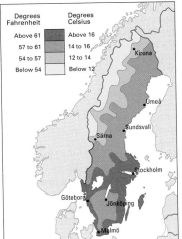

Degrees Fahrenheit	Degrees Celsius
Above 61	Above 16
57 to 61	14 to 16
54 to 57	12 to 14
Below 54	Below 12

Average yearly precipitation
The mountainous areas receive the most precipitation. The Inner Northland and Swedish Lowland receive the least.

WORLD BOOK maps

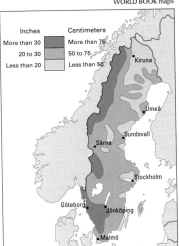

Inches	Centimeters
More than 30	More than 75
20 to 30	50 to 75
Less than 20	Less than 50

Average monthly weather

	Stockholm								Särna					
	Temperatures °F		Temperatures °C		Days of rain or snow				Temperatures °F		Temperatures °C		Days of rain or snow
	High	Low	High	Low					High	Low	High	Low	
Jan.	31	23	-1	-5	8		Jan.		19	4	-7	-16	8
Feb.	31	22	-1	-6	7		Feb.		24	5	-4	-15	5
Mar.	37	26	3	-3	7		Mar.		33	11	1	-12	5
Apr.	45	32	7	0	6		Apr.		42	23	6	-5	7
May	57	41	14	5	8		May		56	32	13	0	6
June	65	49	18	9	7		June		63	41	17	5	11
July	70	55	21	13	9		July		69	46	21	8	13
Aug.	66	53	19	12	10		Aug.		65	44	18	7	12
Sept.	58	46	14	8	8		Sept.		54	36	12	2	10
Oct.	48	39	9	4	9		Oct.		42	28	6	-2	9
Nov.	38	31	3	-1	9		Nov.		30	19	-1	-7	9
Dec.	33	26	1	-3	9		Dec.		24	11	-4	-12	9

rich deposits of iron ore, helped change Sweden from a poor agricultural nation to an advanced industrial society. Nuclear power plants, along with hydroelectric power, provide much of the nation's energy needs. Rich farmland in the southern and central regions of Sweden provides most of the country's food.

Close cooperation among government, employer groups, and labor unions have helped in bringing about Sweden's economic development. These groups have sought to promote full employment through a labor policy based on the retraining and relocation of displaced workers. In addition, Sweden's government has assisted the country's economic development indirectly through its industrial and tax policies. The government has invested public funds in research and development to encourage innovation in technology and other fields. In addition, the Cabinet has devalued the krona periodically in an effort to reduce the cost of Swedish exports and thus make them more competitive abroad.

Service industries provide about three-fourths of Sweden's jobs and produce more than two-thirds of the total value of Sweden's economic production. Service industries provide services rather than produce goods.

Community, government, and personal services are by far the leading employer among service industries in Sweden. Community services include such economic activities as education and health care. Personal services consist of such activities as advertising and data processing and the operation of cleaning establishments, repair shops, and beauty salons. Government includes both public administration and defense. Other important service industry groups include finance, insurance, real estate, and business services, and trade, restaurants, and hotels.

Manufacturing industries are scattered along the coast and throughout central Sweden and the western part of the region called Skåne, which is the southernmost part of Sweden. The iron and steel industry produces high-quality steel, which is used for such products as ball bearings, stainless steel goods for the home, and precision tools. Steel is widely used in the engineering industry, which accounts for about half of Sweden's industrial production and also for about half of the country's exports.

Sweden's important engineering products include

agricultural machinery, aircraft, automobiles, and ships. Linköping is the chief center of the country's aircraft industry, and Trollhättan has aircraft engine and diesel motor plants. Göteborg, Linköping, and Stockholm have major automobile plants. About a third of the automobiles made in Sweden are exported to the United States. Volvo and Saab are leading Swedish carmakers. The main shipbuilding centers are Göteborg and Malmö. The electrical engineering industry makes equipment for power supplies and communications, and telephones are an important export.

The Swedish chemical industry imports most of its raw materials. The industry's chief products include explosives, pharmaceuticals, plastics, and safety matches. Safety matches were invented in Sweden in 1844, and the country is still one of the world's leading producers.

Agriculture. Farmland covers less than 10 percent of Sweden. The region of Skåne, in the extreme south, has a good climate and is the most fertile area. Other agri-

Sweden's gross domestic product

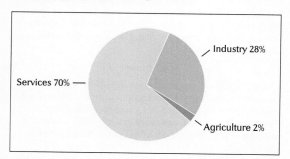

Services 70% — Industry 28% — Agriculture 2%

Sweden's gross domestic product (GDP) was $346,410,000,000 in 2004. The GDP is the total value of goods and services produced within a country in a year. *Services* include community, government, and personal services; finance, insurance, real estate, and business services; trade, restaurants, and hotels; and transportation and communication. *Industry* includes construction, manufacturing, mining, and utilities. *Agriculture* includes agriculture, forestry, and fishing.

Production and workers by economic activities

Economic activities	Percent of GDP produced	Employed workers Number of people	Employed workers Percent of total
Community, government, & personal services	27	1,615,000	38
Finance, insurance, real estate, & business services	24	632,000	15
Manufacturing	20	679,000	16
Trade, restaurants, & hotels	12	653,000	16
Transportation & communication	7	265,000	6
Construction	4	242,000	6
Utilities	3	27,000	1
Agriculture, forestry, & fishing	2	90,000	2
Mining	*	6,000	*
Total†	100	4,209,000	100

*Less than one-half of 1 percent.
†Figures may not add up to 100 percent due to rounding.
Figures are for 2004.
Sources: International Labour Organization; International Monetary Fund; Statistics Sweden.

Gunnar Lundmark, Svenskt Pressfoto

A lumberjack cuts logs for transport to a sawmill. Forests cover more than half of Sweden, and forestry is an important economic activity. Lumber and wood products are among Sweden's chief exports.

cultural areas lie in the south and around the lakes in central Sweden. However, much of northern Sweden is too cold and infertile for farming. Less than 1 percent of the Inner Northland region is cultivated. About three-fourths of the farms in Sweden are less than 50 acres (20 hectares) in size. Most Swedish farmers own their own land.

Dairy farming and livestock raising are important sources of income for Swedish farmers. Beef, milk, and pork are the leading livestock products. The chief crops include barley, oats, potatoes, sugar beets, and wheat. Almost all farmers belong to Sweden's agricultural cooperative movement. Cooperatives collect, process, and market farm products (see **Cooperative**).

Mining. Sweden has some of the richest iron ore deposits in the world. Most of Sweden's iron ore is found near Kiruna in Lapland. The Lapland mines have some of the world's best high-grade ores. Most of the Lapland ore is exported.

In summer, the Lapland ore is shipped from the port of Luleå, on the Gulf of Bothnia. In winter, Luleå's harbor is icebound, and the ore must be carried across the mountains to the ice-free port of Narvik in Norway.

The Swedish iron and steel industry gets most of its ore from the Lapland mines. The Skellefteå region in northern Sweden has copper, gold, lead, and silver.

Forestry. Forests cover more than half of Sweden, and about a tenth of the nation's exports are lumber or products made from wood. The main lumber regions are in the north and north-central sections, where the most important trees include birch, pine, and spruce. Almost all lumber is carried to sawmills by truck and railroad. Then, it is processed into many products for domestic use and export. Forestry is less important in southern Sweden, even though beech, oak, pine, spruce, and other trees cover large areas.

Fishing. Cod and herring are the most important fish caught in Swedish waters. Other fish caught in Sweden include mackerel and salmon. Leading fishing ports lie along the western coast, from the Bohuslän region in the north to the Halland region in the south.

International trade. The value of Sweden's exports is greater than the value of its imports. Sweden exports large amounts of paper products and imports almost

Economy of Sweden

This map shows the economic uses of land in Sweden. It also indicates the country's main farm products, its chief mineral deposits, and its most important fishing products. Major manufacturing centers are shown in red.

WORLD BOOK map

© Douglas Mesney, The Stock Market
Automobiles are one of Sweden's most important manufactured products. Swedish automobiles, such as those being built in this photo, are shipped worldwide.

none. However, the country imports much larger amounts of petroleum and farm products than it exports. Sweden both exports and imports various types of transportation equipment, electrical machinery, chemicals, and other goods. Its major trading partners include Denmark, Finland, France, Germany, the Netherlands, Norway, the United Kingdom, and the United States.

Transportation. Sweden has a good railroad network, most of which is owned by the government. Ferries connect Swedish railroads with those in Denmark and Germany. Sweden has a network of good roads and highways, and trucks carry more freight than the railroads do.

The Öresund Link is a bridge and tunnel connection between Malmö, at the southern tip of Sweden, and Copenhagen, Denmark. The link serves railroad trains as well as automobiles.

Stockholm has an international airport at nearby Arlanda. Other important airports serve Göteborg and Malmö. Ships carry goods between coastal towns. Sweden's most important port is Göteborg. Other port cities include Helsingborg, Malmö, and Stockholm.

Communication. Sweden has more than 150 daily newspapers. The largest newspapers are *Aftonbladet, Dagens Nyheter,* and *Expressen,* all published in Stockholm. Most of Sweden's newspapers are privately owned. Freedom of the press is guaranteed by law, and government censorship is forbidden even in wartime.

The Swedish Broadcasting Corporation, run partly by the government, operates two television networks and several radio networks. Sweden also has some private radio stations. Sweden's telephone services are operated by the government.

History

Early times. Sweden was one of the last regions to lose the ice that covered most of Europe thousands of years ago. The ice had melted from the southern tip of Sweden by about 8000 B.C., and groups of people that hunted and fished began to move from south of the Baltic Sea into this region. People settled farther north as the climate improved.

Beginning about 50 B.C., the people traded with the Roman Empire. They exchanged furs and amber for glass and bronze objects and silver coins. The Romans were the first people to make written records about the Swedes. About A.D. 100, the Roman historian Tacitus wrote about the Svear, a Scandinavian people. *Sverige* (Sweden) means *land of the Svear.*

The Swedish Vikings. Beginning about A.D. 800, Scandinavian adventurers called Vikings sailed to many parts of the world. They acquired wealth by trade and conquest. Most of the Norwegian and Danish Vikings sailed westward. The Swedish Vikings went eastward across Russia, as far as the Black and Caspian seas. The Swedes traded slaves and furs for gold, silver, and luxury goods. The Viking expeditions lasted until the 1000's. Much of Sweden's trade with the east then fell to German merchants, who settled in the town of Visby on the island of Gotland.

The early kingdom. Christianity was first preached in Sweden in A.D. 829 by Saint Anskar, a Frankish monk. His missionary work began a struggle between Christianity and paganism that lasted about 200 years. The first Christian king of Sweden was Olof Skötkonung, who ruled from the late 900's until the early 1000's. Christianity brought about great changes in Sweden. The clergy founded schools, encouraged the arts, and set down Sweden's laws in writing.

By the 1000's, Sweden, Denmark, and Norway had become separate kingdoms. Sweden began to develop along partly feudal lines (see **Feudalism**). There were three social classes—the clergy, the nobles, and the peasants. Above them was the king, who was elected by the provincial lawmaking assemblies. In 1249, Sweden conquered much of Finland.

Union with Norway and Denmark. During the 1200's and 1300's, constant struggles took place between

Important dates in Sweden

c. 6000 B.C. The first settlers came to Sweden.
c. A.D. 800's to 1000's Swedish Vikings attacked other countries, traded, and colonized.
829 Christianity was introduced into Sweden.
1397 Sweden, Denmark, and Norway were united in the Union of Kalmar.
1523 Gustavus Vasa was elected king, and Sweden became independent.
c. 1540 Lutheranism became Sweden's official religion.
1630-1632 Gustavus Adolphus won victories for Sweden in the Thirty Years' War (1618-1648).
1709 Swedish power declined after the Battle of Poltava.
1809 Sweden lost Finland to Russia. A new constitution was adopted.
1814 Sweden gained Norway from Denmark.
1867 Alfred Nobel, a Swedish chemist, patented dynamite.
1867-1886 Many Swedes immigrated to the United States because of harsh economic conditions in Sweden.
1905 Norway dissolved its union with Sweden.
1914-1918 Sweden was neutral in World War I.
1939-1945 Sweden remained neutral in World War II.
1960 Sweden helped form the European Free Trade Association (EFTA).
1975 Sweden adopted a new constitution that greatly reduced the power of the king.
1986 Prime Minister Olof Palme was killed by an assassin.
1995 Sweden left EFTA and joined the European Union (EU).
2000 Sweden separated church and state, ending the status of Lutheranism as the country's official religion.

Ronald Sheridan

Picture stones were carved by Swedish Vikings, usually as monuments for heroes. This stone dates from about A.D. 700.

the rulers of Sweden and the nobles. In 1388, to oppose the growing German influence in Sweden's affairs, the nobles turned for help to Queen Margaret of Denmark and Norway. The Germans were defeated in 1389, and the three Scandinavian countries were united under Margaret in 1397. A treaty called the *Union of Kalmar* laid down the conditions of the union between the three countries. This treaty provided for a common foreign policy, but separate national councils and the continuation of existing laws in each country. Except for a few short periods of separation, the union lasted more than 100 years.

Under the influence of German merchants, Sweden's economy developed considerably during the 1200's and early 1300's. These merchants developed Sweden's mineral resources and controlled Swedish trade. Plague wiped out a large part of Sweden's population in 1350 and caused an economic decline. The German mer-

chants, with their powerful association called the Hanseatic League, increased their control of Swedish trade (see **Hanseatic League**).

During the late 1400's, the *Riksdag* (parliament) developed into a lawmaking and tax-raising body. Members of a new social class, the merchants, joined the other three classes as members of the Riksdag.

The beginnings of modern Sweden. The union with Norway and Denmark continued throughout most of the 1400's. But many struggles took place between supporters and opponents of the union. Gustavus Vasa, a Swedish noble, finally broke away from the union in 1523 after defeating the Danes. He became King Gustav I Vasa of independent Sweden that year. Norway remained under Danish rule.

Gustav encouraged the followers of Martin Luther, the German religious reformer, to spread their ideas. About 1540, the Lutheran religion became the state religion of Sweden. Gustav also increased the power of the throne and laid the foundations of the modern Swedish state. He centralized the administration, dealt harshly with revolts, built an efficient army, and encouraged trade and industry.

The age of expansion. Beginning in the late 1500's, the Swedes fought a series of wars to gain control of the lands surrounding the Baltic Sea. King Gustavus Adolphus, also known as Gustav II Adolf, won many victories for Sweden and the Protestant cause in the Thirty Years' War. Sweden gained new possessions in Europe, and these gains led to continual wars against Denmark, Poland, and Russia. Between 1617 and 1648, war victories over Russia, Poland, and Denmark gave Sweden territories on both sides of the Baltic Sea, as well as some areas in what are now Germany and Poland. In 1658, under the Treaty of Roskilde, the Swedes forced the Danes to give up their provinces on the Swedish mainland.

Charles XII, who ruled from 1697 to 1718, won many victories during the first half of his reign, making Sweden one of the greatest powers in Europe for a time. In 1709, however, the Swedes were defeated by Czar Peter the Great of Russia in the battle of Poltava. During the next few years, Sweden was forced to give up most of

Oil painting on canvas (1633) by Jan Marsende Jonge; Palace of Stockholm (The Royal Collections)

King Gustavus Adolphus, shown here leading a cavalry charge, won many victories for Sweden and the Protestant cause in the Thirty Years' War. He died in battle in 1632.

its European possessions, including its Baltic provinces and Bremen and Verden in Germany.

The Age of Liberty. Charles XII died in 1718. Before agreeing to elect a new king, the Riksdag insisted that any monarch chosen should accept a new constitution. This constitution, which was passed in 1720, transferred many of the crown's powers to the Riksdag. The period of parliamentary government that followed was called the Age of Liberty and lasted until 1772. That year, an unsuccessful war in Germany and serious economic and political troubles at home resulted in a peaceful revolution that reestablished the power of the king.

The Napoleonic Wars. Because of its growing trade with the United Kingdom, Sweden became involved in wars against the French Emperor Napoleon in the early 1800's. As a result of these wars, Sweden lost Finland to Russia, but gained Norway from Denmark. In 1809, Sweden adopted a new constitution.

In 1810, the Swedish Riksdag elected Jean Baptiste Jules Bernadotte, a French general, to be the heir of the childless King Charles XIII. In 1818, Bernadotte succeeded to the Swedish throne as Charles XIV John. Sweden's present royal family is descended from him.

Emigration. During the 1800's, more land was available for farming. However, food was often in short supply because of a great increase in the population. There were not enough jobs, and nearly 450,000 people left Sweden between 1867 and 1886. Most of them moved to the United States and settled mainly in the Midwest.

Growth of industry. Emigration decreased after Sweden developed manufacturing, mining, and forest industries. Engineers built many railroads in the 1860's and 1870's, and Sweden's lumber resources were put

☐	Sweden in 1560
☐	Areas gained 1561-1660
—	Boundary of present-day Sweden

Lapland

Norwegian Sea

1617

Russia

Trondheim 1658-60

Finland

Jämtland 1645

Karelia 1617

SWEDEN

Norway (part of Denmark)

Ingria 1617

Stockholm

Dagö 1582

Estonia 1561

North Sea

Bohuslän 1658

Ösel 1645

Livonia 1629

Halland 1645

Gotland 1645

Russia

Skåne 1658

Baltic Sea

Memel 1629-35

Denmark

Bornholm 1658-60

Pillau 1629-35

Lithuania

Bremen 1648

Wismar 1648

West Pomerania 1648

Elbing 1629-35

0   200 Miles

Germany

Poland

0   200 Kilometers

WORLD BOOK map

Sweden fought a series of wars from the late 1500's to the late 1600's to gain control of lands surrounding the Baltic Sea. For a time, it was one of the greatest powers of Europe.

into use. In 1867, Alfred Nobel, a Swedish chemist, patented dynamite. The availability of dynamite speeded the growth of mining. Engineering industries based on iron and steel were developed. By 1900, Sweden had become an important industrial nation.

Period of reform. The 1800's and early 1900's was a period of sweeping political and social reform in Sweden. Workers formed labor unions and demanded higher wages, shorter workdays, and workers' compensation for industrial accidents. Many strikes broke out as workers demanded improved work conditions. Workers also sought the right to vote—a privilege previously granted only to those with a certain level of income. The Social Democratic Party was founded in 1889 on the strength of the Swedish labor movement.

The Swedish government responded to these movements by passing a series of laws. An 1881 law limited the employment of children in factories, a 1901 law created workers' compensation insurance, and a 1913 law authorized a fund for workers' old-age pensions. In 1909, Sweden provided for proportional representation in parliament and granted all adult males the right to vote for members of one chamber of the Riksdag. Women with property had been able to vote in local elections since the mid-1800's. Women received voting rights equal with men in 1921.

In 1905, Norway broke away from Sweden. The Norwegians elected a king, and Sweden recognized Norway's independence.

Neutrality. Sweden was neutral during World War I (1914-1918) and World War II (1939-1945). After Germany conquered Norway in 1940, Sweden let German troops pass through on their way to Norway. Many Swedes opposed this policy, and Sweden stopped it in 1943.

Economic growth. From the end of World War II through the 1960's, Sweden experienced strong growth and rapid change in its economy. The economy expanded and diversified as more workers took jobs in the commerce, transportation, and service industries. The number of employees in agriculture, mining, manufacturing, and construction declined proportionately.

Close cooperation among government, employer groups, and labor unions helped to make Sweden's economic growth possible. Sweden's high standard of living spread to all income groups by means of the government welfare system that developed fully after World War II. Critics of the system say it makes people so secure that they become bored. Critics also say the system has helped cause high taxation and inflation. But most Swedes support the system.

Political changes. A new constitution took effect in Sweden in 1975. It reduced the king's power and placed power in the hands of Sweden's parliament and Cabinet.

In 1976 elections, the party that had long held power in Sweden, the Social Democratic Party, was defeated, largely because voters were dissatisfied with the country's high taxes. Except for a few months in 1936, the Social Democrats had controlled Sweden's government continuously from 1932 to 1976. Various nonsocialist coalitions governed the country from 1976 to 1982, when the Social Democratic Party regained control. A tragedy struck Sweden in 1986, when Prime Minister Olof Palme was shot and killed by an assassin. In 1991, a nonsocialist coalition won control of the government, but the Social Democrats returned to power in 1994.

In the early 1990's, Sweden's economic performance faltered and unemployment increased. The government trimmed its budget deficits and enacted measures to help Swedish businesses. By the late 1990's, these efforts resulted in increased prosperity without sacrificing Sweden's social programs.

Recent developments. In 1995, Sweden left the European Free Trade Association (EFTA), a European economic organization that it had helped to form in 1960. It joined the European Union (EU), a larger organization that works for political as well as economic cooperation among its member nations.

Also in 1995, the Lutheran Church of Sweden agreed to a government move to separate church and state. The church agreed to phase out by 2000 from its position as Sweden's official church. Lutheranism had been the country's official religion since the 1500's. But the government recognized that the Swedish population had come to include many people from other countries who practiced other faiths.

In 1998 elections, the Social Democratic Party won the most seats in parliament. But it did not win a majority and needed the support of other parties to govern. Elections in 2002 returned the Social Democrats and their political allies to power. In 2003, Sweden's voters rejected a proposal to replace their nation's currency, the krona, with the euro, a currency used by most of the other countries of the European Union. In 2006 elections, a center-right union of political parties led by the Moderate Party won control of parliament.   M. Donald Hancock

Related articles in *World Book* include:

Monarchs of Sweden

Bernadotte, Jean B. J.
Carl XVI Gustaf
Charles X
Charles XI
Charles XII
Gustav I Vasa
Gustavus Adolphus

Other biographies

Alfvén, Hannes O. G.
Bergman, Ingmar
Bergman, Ingrid
Berzelius, Jöns J.
Bjoerling, Jussi
Ericsson, John
Garbo, Greta
Hammarskjöld, Dag
Lagerkvist, Pär F.
Lagerlöf, Selma
Lind, Jenny
Linnaeus, Carolus
Milles, Carl
Myrdal, Alva R.
Myrdal, Gunnar
Nilsson, Birgit
Nobel, Alfred B.
Nordenskjöld, Nils A.
Oldenburg, Claes
Oxenstierna, Axel G.
Siegbahn, Karl M. G.
Strindberg, August
Wallenberg, Raoul

Cities

Göteborg
Malmö
Stockholm

History

Denmark (History)
Finland (History)
Goths
Norway (History)
Thirty Years' War
Vikings

Physical features

Baltic Sea
Torne River

Other related articles

Christmas (In Denmark, Norway, and Sweden; picture: On St. Lucia Day)
Clothing (picture: Traditional costumes)
Lapland
Ombudsman
Sami
Scandinavia
Theater (Scandinavia)

Outline

Questions

Why are Sweden's forests important to its economy?
What social reforms took place in Sweden during the late 1800's and early 1900's?
What languages does Swedish closely resemble?
Who was the most important writer in Swedish literary history?
How long did the Union of Kalmar last?
Why did Sweden create the office of ombudsman?
Who founded Sweden's present royal family?
What is the Vasa Race?
Where are Sweden's two largest lakes located?

Additional resources

Fast, April, and Thomas, Keltie. *Sweden: The Culture.* Crabtree Pub. Co., 2004. *Sweden: The Land.* 2004. *Sweden: The People.* 2004. All for younger readers.
Gan, Delice, and Jermyn, Leslie. *Sweden.* 2nd ed. Benchmark Bks., 2003. Younger readers.
Hutchings, Jane, and others, eds. *Insight Guide: Sweden.* Rev. ed. APA Productions, 2003.
Nordstrom, Byron J. *The History of Sweden.* Greenwood, 2002.

Swedenborgians, SWEE duhn BAWR jee uhns, follo[w] the formulation of Christian doctrine as set forth by Emanuel Swedenborg, a Swedish theologian. A chur[ch] based on this doctrine was organized in London in 1[ ] and in the United States in 1792. Churches in the Un[ited] States and Canada set up the General Convention [of] New Jerusalem in 1817. A separate body, the Gen[eral] Church of the New Jerusalem, formed in 1890. Sw[eden]borgians have societies and missions in many p[arts of] the world. These societies and missions are us[u]ated with the American bodies or with the Co[uncil] of the New Church in the United Kingdom.

Swedenborg's teachings emphasize one G[od a]Lord and Savior Jesus Christ, in whom is the [Fa]ther, Son, and Holy Spirit. Swedenborgian[s] [re]al hu[mans?] the Holy City, New Jerusalem, is symbolic [al, or] man society. They regard Jesus as truly [I]n[enborg] *God with us.* They believe that God calle[d] to reveal deeper spiritual meanings in scripture. As humanity accepts and practices a truer Christianity, Jesus makes his Second Coming in spirit, rather than in physical form. *Critically reviewed by the Swedenborgian Church*

Sweeney, John Joseph (1934-   ), became president of the American Federation of Labor and Congress of Industrial Organizations (AFL-CIO) in 1995. The AFL-CIO is a federation of labor unions in the United States. From 1980 to 1995, Sweeney had been president of the Service Employees International Union (SEIU). That union was, until 2005, an AFL-CIO member. The SEIU represents many nurses' aides, janitors, and other workers in health care and building services.

As president of the AFL-CIO, Sweeney launched an effort to expand union membership. He also urged unions to negotiate more aggressively with employers. He was reelected in 1997, 2001, and 2005. In 2005, major unions, including the Teamsters Union and the SEIU, left the AFL-CIO because of disagreements over strategy.

Sweeney was born in the Bronx, in New York City, on May 5, 1934. He graduated from Iona College. From 1957 to 1960, he was a researcher with the International Ladies' Garment Workers' Union. Beginning in 1960, he held a series of positions with the SEIU. He was an SEIU vice president from 1973 to 1980 and an AFL-CIO vice president while he was SEIU president. *James G. Scoville*

Sweet alyssum, *uh LIHS uhm,* is a low, spreading plant with clusters of tiny lavender or white flowers. It is an *annual*—that is, it lives for only one growing season. It can be planted in early spring and usually blooms within six weeks. Some varieties are cultivated as dwarfs, and others grow about 12 inches (30 centimeters) high.

Theodore R. Dudley

Scientific classification. Sweet alyssum is in the mustard family, Brassicaceae or Cruciferae. Its scientific name is *Lobularia maritima.*

© Giuseppe Mazza

Sweet alyssum

Sweet cicely, *SIHS uh lee,* is a European herb with fragrant leaves that taste like anise. It grows about 3 feet (91 centimeters) high and has downy gray leaves and clusters of small white flowers. The seeds of the plant are used for flavoring in candies, syrups, and liqueurs. Europeans use the leaves in soups and salads. The roots may be cooked and eaten as a vegetable. The term *sweet cicely* also refers to a group of related plants that grow in ~~As~~ia, North America, and South America. *Lyle E. Craker*

~~S~~cientific classification. Sweet cicely belongs to the parsley ~~fami~~ly, Apiaceae or Umbelliferae. It is *Myrrhis odorata.*

~~Se~~e also **Herb** (picture).

~~Swee~~t corn. See **Corn.**

~~Sweet~~ flag is a tall, reedlike plant of the arum family. It ~~grows a~~long brooks and in marshy places in almost all ~~parts of t~~he Northern Hemisphere. Its leaves are flat and ~~sword~~like ~~and 2 to 6 feet~~ (61 to 180 centimeters) long. They are shaped ~~like pointe~~d but ~~ed~~ged swords. The stems resemble the leaves ~~in shape~~ blosser ~~and~~ bear spiky clusters of small green ~~flowers ne~~ar the top. The leaves and stems rise

© Giuseppe Mazza

The sweet flag's tiny flowers cluster on a stem.

directly from a thick, fleshy underground *rhizome* (horizontal stem). The rhizome has been used medicinally since ancient times. Today, it is also used in the manufacture of perfume and cosmetic preparations. In Europe, the rhizome is valued as a food. *David A. Francko*

Scientific classification. The sweet flag is in the arum family, Araceae. Its scientific name is *Acorus calamus.*

Sweet gum, also called *red gum,* is a tall, stately tree. It grows naturally from Connecticut and southern New York to Florida and westward to southern Illinois, Oklahoma, and eastern Texas. It is also native to mountainous regions of Mexico and Guatemala and has been planted widely in the western United States. Normally, the sweet gum reaches a height of 80 to 100 feet (24 to 30 meters). When mature, the tree's straight trunk is 3 to 4 feet

© Irvin L. Oakes, Photo Researchers

The sweet gum has a long, straight trunk and star-shaped leaves that turn beautiful colors in autumn.

(91 to 120 centimeters) thick at the base. Sweet gum leaves are deeply lobed and star-shaped. They turn gold, red, or a deep crimson in autumn. The fruit is a brownish, spiny ball that remains on the tree through the winter. The sweet gum is so named because it produces a gummy compound, called *storax,* that is used in making perfumes, adhesives, and salves. Sweet gum wood is fairly hard and heavy. People use it to make veneer, cabinets, and other products. Kenneth R. Robertson

Scientific classification. Sweet gum trees belong to the witch hazel family, Hamamelidaceae. They are *Liquidambar styraciflua.*

Sweet pea is a favorite garden flower that belongs to the same family as the kind of pea that we eat. People grow the sweet pea for the beauty and fragrance of its flowers. The sweet pea is one of the special flowers for the month of April. Sweet pea flowers are blue, red, pink, purple, and white. Some look like butterflies. There are more than 1,000 varieties of sweet pea. In some, the flower petals are smooth and velvety. In others, they are crinkled and wavy. The plants may be *dwarf,* which grow close to the ground, or *climbing,* which grow along strings or trellises.

Rich, well-drained soil, plenty of sunshine, and free circulation of air are needed to raise sweet peas. Gardeners should sow the seed in April. They use 1 ounce (28 grams) of seed to 30 feet (9 meters) of row. The plants should be at least 2 inches (5 centimeters) apart in the

Richard Kolar, Earth Scenes

The sweet pea is a popular garden plant because of its lovely, fragrant blossoms. The petals vary in color and shape.

row, and the rows should be 4 feet (1.2 meters) apart. The gardener should cultivate the ground as soon as the plants appear. The soil should be stirred lightly every week and should be kept free of weeds. Once a week the plants should be given a liquid fertilizer.

The vines should be trained on strings. The flowers should be picked as they open, before seeds develop. The sweet pea stops blooming soon after seeds form.

Daniel F. Austin

Scientific classification. Sweet peas belong to the pea family, Fabaceae or Leguminosae. Common garden sweet peas are *Lathyrus odoratus.*

Sweet potato is a vegetable with large, fleshy, edible roots. Sweet potatoes are believed to have been first grown in South America. Today, they are grown throughout the world, and they are an important food in many countries. About 85 percent of the world's sweet potato crop is produced in China.

Sweet potatoes contain high amounts of carbohydrates and vitamins A and C. People buy them fresh, canned, frozen, or *dehydrated* (dried by removing the water). Sweet potatoes are also used for animal feed, alcohol, and starch. The American scientist George Washington Carver created 118 products and numerous recipes from the sweet potato. The flesh and skin of sweet potatoes vary in color from purple to white. The most common flesh colors are orange, yellow, and white. Some sweet potatoes, such as the *Porto Rico* and *Jewel* varieties, have moist flesh. Others, including the *Jersey* and *Triumph* varieties, have dry flesh.

Sweet potato plants are commonly grown from roots placed in moist, warm, sandy soil or sawdust in greenhouses or hotbeds about four to six weeks before planting time. The roots produce sprouts called *slips.* The slips are cut from the roots and transplanted to fields. There, they are generally placed 12 to 15 inches (30 to 38 centimeters) from one another in rows 3 to 4 feet (90 to 120 centimeters) apart. In tropical regions, the plants are grown from vine cuttings rather than from slips.

In tropical areas where frost is not a problem, sweet potatoes may remain in the soil for as long as 7 to 12 months. In colder regions, however, sweet potato crops are harvested in the early fall, before the first killing frost. Immediately after harvesting, the potatoes are *cured* (partially dried) and stored at temperatures from

Leading sweet potato growing countries

Tons of sweet potatoes grown in a year	
China	●●●●●●●●●●●●●●●● 117,810,000 tons (106,870,000 metric tons)
Uganda	❨ 2,890,000 tons (2,620,000 metric tons)
Nigeria	❨ 2,770,000 tons (2,520,000 metric tons)
Indonesia	❨ 2,110,000 tons (1,910,000 metric tons)

Figures are for a three-year average, 2003-2005.
Source: Food and Agriculture Organization of the United Nations.

Leading sweet potato growing states

Tons of sweet potatoes grown in a year	
North Carolina	●●●●●●●●●●● 292,800 tons (265,700 metric tons)
California	●●●●●●❨ 158,600 tons (143,900 metric tons)
Louisiana	●●●●●❨ 122,500 tons (111,100 metric tons)
Mississippi	●●●●●❨ 115,800 tons (105,100 metric tons)

Figures are for a three-year average, 2002-2004.
Source: U.S. Department of Agriculture.

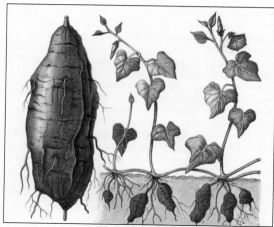

WORLD BOOK illustration by Jill Coombs

Sweet potatoes are vegetables that grow underground.

55 to 60 °F (13 to 16 °C). Curing and storing the storage roots help keep them in good condition for marketing during the winter and spring.

Conrad K. Bonsi and Bobby R. Phills

Scientific classification. The sweet potato belongs to the morning-glory family, Convolvulaceae. It is *Ipomoea batatas.*

Sweet William is a popular garden plant that is native to northern Europe and Asia. The plant usually grows about 2 feet (61 centimeters) high and bears dense, round clusters of velvety flowers. The flowers may be white, pink, rose, or purple, and they often are ringed or dotted with contrasting colors. Cultivated plants may bear double flowers. Gardeners usually cultivate sweet William as a *biennial* (a plant that requires two years to mature).

A kind of phlox native to eastern North America is known as the *wild sweet William.* This plant may grow 5 feet (1.5 meters) high. It has pink or purple flower clusters. See **Phlox.**   W. Dennis Clark

Scientific classification. Sweet William belongs to the pink family, Caryophyllaceae. Its scientific name is *Dianthus barbatus.* Wild sweet William is in the phlox family, Polemoniaceae. Its scientific name is *Phlox maculata.*

See also **Flower** (picture: Garden biennials).

Sw... © Giuseppe Mazza
cluste...m is a popular garden plant. It forms large, velvety ...end of the stem.

Sweetbread is a mild-flavored meat that comes from the *thymus* of a young calf or lamb, or the *pancreas* of a hog. The thymus is a glandlike organ located inside the animal's chest cavity. The pancreas is a gland situated near the stomach. The largest and most tender sweetbreads come from young calves because the thymus shrinks as the animal ages. Fine restaurants serve sweetbread as a main dish. Some supermarkets sell calf sweetbreads, but lamb sweetbreads are too small to be sold in markets. Few markets sell hog sweetbreads because demand is low. Most sweetbreads in the United States are exported to Europe, where they are more popular.   Donald H. Beermann

Sweetbrier. See Eglantine.

Swift is a small bird that can fly for many hours with its long, strong wings. Swifts capture their insect food while flying. They almost always return at dusk to the cave, chimney, cliff, or hollow tree where they live in flocks. A chimney swift may fly 135,000 miles (217,000 kilometers) a year. Swifts build nests made of sticks that they cement together with their saliva. Some of these nests are almost entirely made up of saliva. In Asia, some people eat the nests of certain species of swifts.

More than 75 different kinds of swifts live in various parts of the world. They are sooty-brown or greenish-black. Some swifts have white throats or rumps. Their song, continually repeated, is little more than short, indistinct sounds. The chimney swift of eastern North America almost always builds its nest in chimneys. Vaux's swifts of western North America and chimney swifts may roost by the thousands in large chimneys

Stephen Dalton, Photo Researchers

Swifts are strong, fast fliers. Some can travel over 100 miles (160 kilometers) per hour for short distances. They feed on insects while in the air. Some swifts spend the night in flight.

Steve Maslowski, Photo Researchers

Swifts usually roost on vertical surfaces, clinging with sharp toenails and using the tail as a prop, *above*. They rarely perch on branches because their feet and legs are small and weak.

while migrating. They perform spectacular maneuvers in the air as they fly into the chimneys for the night.

Donald F. Bruning

Scientific classification. Swifts make up the swift family, Apodidae. The chimney swift is *Chaetura pelagica.* Vaux's swift is *C. vauxi.*

See also **Animal** (picture: Animals of the mountains ([House swift]); **Bird** (picture: How birds feed); **Bird's-nest soup.**

Swift is the name of certain small, quick-moving lizards. Swifts live in dry, warm areas of the United States, Mexico, and Central America. These lizards have scales with sharp ridges and points. Many swifts have brilliant blue colors on their bellies and are often called *blue bellies.*

© Terry L. Hibbitts

A swift called the *blue spiny lizard, above,* has bright blue markings on its upper body. Swifts live in dry, warm areas of the United States, Mexico, and Central America.

Swifts eat insects. Most types of swifts lay eggs. But, some species give birth to live young. Raymond B. Huey

Scientific classification. Swifts belong to the New World lizard family, Iguanidae. They are genus *Sceloporus.*

Swift, Gustavus Franklin (1839-1903), was an American businessman who founded one of the world's leading meat-packing companies, Swift & Company. Swift pioneered in the development of modern meat-packing techniques. He was also one of the first business leaders to promote the idea that the employees of a company should own stock in the firm.

Swift was born in West Sandwich (now called Sagamore), Mass. He quit school at the age of 14 to work in his brother's butcher shop and opened his own shop about six years later. He soon had several of his own shops. To keep them supplied with fresh meat, Swift bought cattle from nearby farms and ran a small slaughtering operation and packing plant.

In 1875, Swift moved to Chicago, the major center of the cattle market. He soon developed the idea of shipping fresh meat rather than live cattle from Chicago to the East Coast. To do so, Swift hired an engineer to design a refrigerated railroad car. Swift formed Swift & Company in 1885, combining into one firm all of the various operations involved in selling meat. The company ran feed lots for the cattle and used an early form of the assembly line to butcher large quantities of meat. It also operated refrigerated transportation, regional warehouses that distributed the meat, and retail stores.

William R. Childs

Swift, Jonathan (1667-1745), an English author, wrote *Gulliver's Travels* (1726), a masterpiece of comic literature. Swift is called a great *satirist* because of his ability to ridicule customs, ideas, and actions he considered silly or harmful. His satire is often bitter, but it is also delightfully humorous. Swift was deeply concerned about the welfare and behavior of the people of his time, especially the welfare of the Irish and the behavior of the English toward Ireland. Swift was a Protestant churchman who became a hero in Roman Catholic Ireland.

His life. Swift was born in Dublin on Nov. 30, 1667. His parents were of English birth. Swift graduated from Trinity College in Dublin, and moved to England in 1688 or 1689. He was secretary to the distinguished statesman Sir William Temple from 1689 until 1699, with some interruptions. In 1695, Swift became a minister in the Anglican Church of Ireland.

While working for Temple, Swift met a young girl named Esther Johnson, whom he called Stella. He and Stella became lifelong friends, and Swift wrote long letters to her during his busiest days. The letters were published after Swift's death as the *Journal to Stella.*

Temple died in 1699, and in 1700 Swift became of a small parish in Laracor, Ireland. He visited Eng often between 1701 and 1710, conducting church ness and winning influential friends at the highe of government. His skill as a writer became wid known.

In 1710, Swift became a powerful supporter new Tory government of Great Britain. Throu many articles and pamphlets that were writt effense of Tory policies, Swift became one of itish fective behind-the-scenes spokespersons administration.

Queen Anne recognized Swift's political work in 1713 when she made him *dean* (head clergyman) of St. Patrick's Cathedral in Dublin. Swift would have preferred a church position in England. The queen died in 1714, and George I became king. The Whig Party won control of the government that year. These changes ended the political power of Swift and his friends in England.

Jonathan Swift by Charles Jervas.
National Portrait Gallery, London

Jonathan Swift

Swift spent the rest of his life—more than 30 years—as dean of St. Patrick's. In many ways, these years were disappointing. Swift was disheartened because his political efforts had amounted to so little. He also missed his friends in England, especially the poets Alexander Pope and John Gay. However, he served in Ireland energetically by taking up the cause of the Irish against abuses he saw in British rule. It was as dean that Swift wrote *Gulliver's Travels* and the satiric pamphlets that increased his fame, *The Drapier's Letters* and *A Modest Proposal.* Swift's health declined in his last years and finally his mind failed. He died on Oct. 19, 1745. He left his money to start a hospital for the mentally ill.

Gulliver's Travels is often described as a book that children read with delight, but which adults find serious and disturbing. However, even young readers usually recognize that Swift's "make-believe" world sometimes resembles their own world. Adults recognize that, in spite of the book's serious themes, it is highly comic.

Gulliver's Travels describes four voyages that Lemuel Gulliver, who was trained as a ship's doctor, makes to strange lands. Gulliver first visits the *Lilliputians* (pronounced LIHL *uh PYOO shuhnz*)—tiny people whose bodies and surroundings are only $\frac{1}{12}$ the size of normal people and things. The Lilliputians treat Gulliver well at first. Gulliver helps them, but after a time they turn against him and he is happy to escape their land. The story's events resemble those of Swift's own political life.

Gulliver's second voyage takes him to the country of *Brobdingnag (BRAHB dihng nag),* where the people are 12 times larger than Gulliver and greatly amused by his puny size.

Gulliver's third voyage takes him to several strange kingdoms. The conduct of the odd people of these countries represents the kinds of foolishness Swift saw in his world. For example, in the academy of Lagado, scholars spend all their time on useless projects such as extracting sunbeams from cucumbers. Here Swift was satirizing impractical scientists and philosophers.

In his last voyage, Gulliver discovers a land ruled by wise and gentle horses called *Houyhnhnms (hoo IHN* [...] *or HWIHN uhmz).* Savage, stupid animals called [...] also live there. The Yahoos look like human beings. The Houyhnhnms distrust Gulliver because they [...] he is a Yahoo. Gulliver wishes to stay in the [...] company of the Houyhnhnms, but they force [...] ve. After Gulliver returns to England, he con[...]st only with the horses in his stable.

Some people believe Swift was a *misanthrope* (hater of humanity), and that the ugliness and stupidity in his book reflect his view of the world. Other people argue that Swift was a devoted and courageous Christian who could not have denied the existence of goodness and hope. Still others claim that in *Gulliver's Travels,* Swift is really urging us to avoid the extremes of the boringly perfect Houyhnhnms and the wild Yahoos, and to lead moderate, sensible lives.

Scholars are still trying to discover all the ways in which real people, institutions, and events are represented in *Gulliver's Travels.* But readers need not be scholars to find pleasure in the book and to find themselves set to thinking about its distinctive picture of human life.

Swift's other works. *A Modest Proposal* (1729) is probably Swift's second best-known work. In this essay, Swift pretends to urge that Irish babies be killed, sold, and eaten. They would be as well off, says Swift bitterly,

Engraving by Bernard Lens the elder for the 1710 edition of *The Battle of the Books.* Newberry Library, Chicago

The Battle of the Books ridicules scholars who argued the relative merits of ancient and modern writers. This picture shows a battle between ancient and modern books in a library.

Culver

Gulliver's Travels is Swift's most famous book. In its best-known episode, Gulliver is shipwrecked in the country of Lilliput, where the people are only ½ his size. He awakes to find that the Lilliputians have tied him down with hundreds of tiny ropes.

as those Irish who grow up in poverty under British rule. Swift hoped this outrageous suggestion would shock the Irish people into taking sensible steps to improve their condition. He had in mind such steps as the earlier refusal of the Irish to allow the British to arrange for Irish copper coins. The Irish rejected these coins because it was widely believed that the coins would be debased. Swift's series of *Drapier's Letters* (1724) actually forced a change in British policy on this matter.

A Tale of a Tub (1704), on the surface, is a story of three brothers arguing over their father's last will. But it is actually a clever attack on certain religious beliefs and on humanity's false pride in its knowledge.

In *The Battle of the Books* (1704), a lighter work, Swift imagines old and new library books warring with each other. This work reflected a real quarrel between scholars who boasted of being modern and scholars who believed the ancient thinkers could not be bettered.

Swift could be very playful. He loved riddles, jokes, and hoaxes. One of his best literary pranks was the *Bickerstaff Papers* (1708-1709). In this work, he invented an astrologer named Isaac Bickerstaff to ridicule John Partridge, a popular astrologer and almanac writer of the time. Swift satirized Partridge by publishing his own improbable predictions, including a prediction of Partridge's own death. Swift then published a notice that Partridge had died, which many people believed.

Swift wrote a great deal of poetry and light verse. Much of his poetry is humorous, and it is often sharply satirical as well. But many of his poems, both comic and serious, show his deep affection for his friends.

Swift's personality. Whether Swift hated humanity or whether he mocked people to reform them is still disputed. But there are some things Swift clearly either hated or valued. He hated those who attacked religion, particularly when they pretended to be religious them-

selves. He also hated the tyranny of one nation over another. Above all, he hated false pride—the tendency of people to exaggerate their accomplishments and overlook their weaknesses. Swift valued liberty, common sense, honesty, and humility. His writings—whether bitter, shocking, or humorous—ask the reader to share these values.   Michael Seidel

See also **Gulliver's Travels.**

Additional resources

Connery, Brian A., ed. *Representations of Swift.* Univ. of Del. Pr., 2002.
Crook, Keith. *A Preface to Swift.* Longman Pub. Group, 1998.
Glendinning, Victoria. *Jonathan Swift.* Henry Holt, 1999.
Kelly, Ann C. *Jonathan Swift and Popular Culture.* Palgrave, 2002.

Swigert, John Leonard, Jr. (1931-1982), a United States astronaut, served as command module pilot of the Apollo 13 lunar flight in April 1970. Swigert made the flight with astronauts Fred W. Haise, Jr., and James A Lovell, Jr.

About 56 hours after the flight began, an explosion caused by a short circuit severely damaged the command module's life-support and electrical systems. T crew switched to the lunar module's systems and u them to return to Earth. The tense return trip ende ly nearly four days later.

Swigert was born in Denver, Colorado, on Aug 1931. He was in the Air Force from 1953 to 1956. then worked as a civilian test pilot until 1966, wl became an astronaut. Swigert resigned from th naut program in 1977. In 1982, Swigert won el the United States House of Representatives fr orado. But he died before taking office, on Din of that year. A statue of Swigert represents 6h the Statuary Hall collection in the U.S. Capi ington, D.C.   James R. Hansen

Paul J. Sutton, Duomo

Swimming is an exciting sport and a popular form of recreation. The swimmers shown above are competing in a world championship race. Most people enjoy swimming as a pastime and as a healthful form of exercise in community and backyard pools.

Swimming

Swimming is the act of moving through water by using the arms and legs. Swimming is a popular form of recreation, an important international sport, and a healthful exercise.

People of all ages—from the very young to the elderly—swim for fun. Throughout the world, millions of people enjoy swimming in lakes, oceans, and rivers. Others swim in indoor or outdoor pools. Many schools, recreation centers, motels, apartment buildings, and private clubs have an indoor or outdoor pool. Thousands of communities provide pools for residents. Many families even have a pool in their backyard.

During the 1900's, swimming became a major competitive sport. Today, thousands of swimmers compete in meets held by schools, colleges, and swimming clubs. The best international swimmers take part in annual meets in many parts of the world. Swimming races have always been a highlight of the Summer Olympic Games. Many long-distance swimmers attempt such as swimming across the English Channel or from southern California coast to Santa Catalina Island. swimmers can also enjoy various other water

sports. Such sports include springboard and platform diving, surfing, water skiing, board sailing, water polo, scuba diving, and synchronized swimming. The ability to swim well makes such sports as fishing and boating safer and more fun. Above all, the ability to swim may save a person's life in an emergency in the water.

Swimming is one of the best exercises for keeping physically fit. Swimming improves heart action, aids blood circulation, and helps develop firm muscles.

Water safety

Swimming, boating, fishing, and other water sports are among the most popular forms of recreation. Yet many people lack knowledge of water safety rules or take dangerous chances. Every year, about 4,000 people drown in the United States and about 400 people in Canada. Most of these drownings would not occur if everyone knew how to swim and observed basic water safety rules. The following discussion deals with basic rules and techniques that could save your life or help you save another person's life.

First of all, know how to swim. Many schools and community recreation departments provide swimming lessons. Lessons are also frequently offered by organizations such as the YMCA and the American Red Cross.

Never swim alone. Always swim with a companion and know where that person is at all times. Swim only in areas protected by lifeguards. A swimming area should be free of obstacles and the water should be clean and

James Freas, the contributor of this article, is President national Swimming Hall of Fame.

Robert E. Daemmrich, Tony Stone Images

Children take swimming lessons to learn the correct and safe way to enjoy the activity. Many schools and community recreation centers offer lessons conducted by qualified instructors.

clear. It is dangerous to swim in an unprotected ocean, river, or lake.

Water used for diving must be deep and be clear enough to see the bottom. Look for swimmers before you dive. Plan your dive and, following your entry into the water, avoid hitting the bottom by steering up with your hands out in front.

Whether you are a beginning or experienced swimmer, a knowledge of *survival bobbing* can help you survive an accident or other difficulty in the water. Survival bobbing, also known as *drown proofing,* enables you to float a long time on your front while using very little energy. You fill your lungs with air and relax your body. Your arms and legs hang down limply, and your chin flops down to the chest. The air in your lungs holds your back above the water's surface. When you need a breath, you quickly exhale through the nose, lift your face out of the water, and inhale through your mouth. You then return to the restful floating position. You can raise your mouth higher out of the water for a breath by pressing your hands down or squeezing your legs gently together.

Only a trained lifeguard should attempt a swimming rescue. But even if you are a nonswimmer, you can help a swimmer who is in trouble. If the person is nearby, you can extend a board, pole, shirt, towel, or similar object and pull the swimmer to safety. But be sure to lie down or keep your body low to avoid being pulled into the water. If the swimmer is too far away to reach an ob-

ject, you can throw a life preserver, a board, or any other object that will float and support the swimmer.

Swimming kicks and strokes

Swimmers move their legs, feet, arms, and hands in certain ways to propel themselves through the water easily and quickly. The movements of the legs and feet are called *kicks.* These movements combined with movements of the arms and hands are called *strokes.*

The basic kicks. Swimmers use four types of kicks: (1) the flutter kick, (2) the breaststroke kick, (3) the dolphin kick, and (4) the scissors kick. Each of these kicks is used in doing one or more of the strokes described later in this section.

The flutter kick is the most popular kick and the easiest for swimmers to learn. The power to do the kick should come from the upper leg. The legs are alternately moved up and down with a slightly relaxed bend at the knees. The propulsion comes from the feet as if kicking mud off the toes.

The breaststroke kick begins with your legs fully extended and the toes pointed to the rear. By bending your knees, you bring your heels toward your hips just under the surface of the water. As your feet near the hips, turn your ankles so the toes point outward. Then, without pause, push your feet outward and backward, squeezing your legs together until the toes again point to the rear.

The dolphin kick resembles the flutter kick. But in the dolphin kick, you move both of your legs up and down at the same time and keep more bend in your knees.

The scissors kick begins with your body turned to either side. Your legs are together and the toes pointed back. Draw your knees up and then spread your legs wide apart like the open blades of a scissors, moving your top leg forward from the hip. Then snap both legs together to their original position.

The basic strokes are (1) the front crawl, (2) the backstroke, (3) the breaststroke, (4) the butterfly, and (5) the sidestroke.

The front crawl is the fastest and most popular stroke. You move your arms in a steady, circular motion in combination with the flutter kick. One hand reaches forward above the water while the other pulls beneath the water. You breathe by turning your head to one side just as the hand on that side passes your leg. You inhale through the mouth. You exhale through the mouth or nose while keeping your face in the water.

The backstroke, or *back crawl,* is performed as you lie on your back. It is a restful stroke because your face is always out of the water and breathing is easy. As in the front crawl, each arm alternately moves in a steady circular motion in and out of the water while your le do the flutter kick.

The breaststroke is another restful stroke. It is d in combination with the breaststroke kick. You be with your face in the water, arms and legs fully e ed, and the palms facing outward. You then swe your arms as your hands push downward and The hands continue to circle and come togeth the chin. As the hands begin to push down, y head for a breath. Finally, you again extend y and legs and glide forward. You then repea quence. You make a breaststroke kick at th

Competitive swimming strokes

The front crawl

The backstroke

The breaststroke

The butterfly

the stroke as your arms extend for the glide.

The butterfly is a difficult stroke to learn, but it is smooth and graceful if performed correctly. In this stroke, you swing both arms forward above the water and then pull them down and back to your legs. As your arms start to move toward your legs, you lift your head forward and take a breath. Then you dip your head into the water and exhale as your arms move forward again. You make two dolphin kicks during each complete stroke, one as your hands enter the water and the other as your arms pass under your body.

The sidestroke is done on your side, whichever side is more comfortable. Your head rests on your lower arm, which is extended ahead with the palm turned downward. The top arm is at your side. The palm of the lower hand presses down in the water until it is beneath the shoulder. At the same time, the top hand slides up to meet the lower hand. The legs do a scissors kick while the lower arm returns to an extended position and the palm of the upper hand pushes toward the feet. You then glide forward before repeating the sequence.

Other strokes. Swimmers use a number of other strokes besides the basic five. The most important include the *dog paddle* and the *elementary backstroke*. To perform the dog paddle, cup your hands and rotate them in a circular motion underwater, with one hand forward when the other one is back. You do a flutter kick with the dog paddle. Your head remains out of the water throughout the stroke. The elementary back-stroke, like the regular backstroke, is performed on your back. You bring your hands up along the sides of your body to your shoulders. Next you turn out the hands and point the fingers outward. Then you push your hands out and glide. Swimmers do the breaststroke kick with this stroke.

Swimming as a sport

The Fédération Internationale de Natation (FINA) governs international swimming and other water sports at the amateur level. FINA consists of national associations from about 190 countries. These associations include United States Aquatic Sports, Inc.; the Aquatic Federation of Canada; Australian Swimming; and the Amateur Swimming Federation of Great Britain.

The pool. Swim meets are held in both *long-course* pools, which measure 50 meters (164 feet) long, and *short-course* pools, most of which measure 25 meters (82 feet) long. A 25-yard (22.9-meter) short-course pool is used almost exclusively in the United States but is not recognized in international competition. Long-course pools are divided into 6, 8, or 10 lanes, each of which is 2.5 meters (8.2 feet) wide. Short-course pools have 6 or 8 lanes. Each lane measures 2.1 or 2.4 meters (7 or 8 feet) wide. In U.S. championship meets, 8 lanes must be used in both long- and short-course pools. FINA recognizes world records set only in long-course pools or 25-meter short-course pools.

Water in a regulation pool must be at least 4 feet (1.2 meters) deep and have a temperature of about 74 °F (24 °C). Floats called *lane lines* run the length of the pool. They mark lane boundaries and help keep the surface of the water calm.

Kinds of races. Swimmers participate in five kinds of races—freestyle, breaststroke, backstroke, butterfly, and individual medley. In a freestyle race, a swimmer may choose any stroke. But swimmers always use the front crawl because it is the fastest stroke. In the individual medley, athletes swim an equal distance of each of four strokes. In order, the strokes are the (1) butterfly, (2) backstroke, (3) breaststroke, and (4) front crawl.

WORLD BOOK illustrations by Robert Keys

A regulation swimming pool

Swimming pools are divided into lanes for races, one lane for each swimmer. Wall targets, lane lines, and lane markers guide each swimmer. Near each end of the pool, a flag line is hung over the water to warn swimmers in backstroke races that they are approaching the end of the lane.

WORLD BOOK diagram by Arthur Grebetz

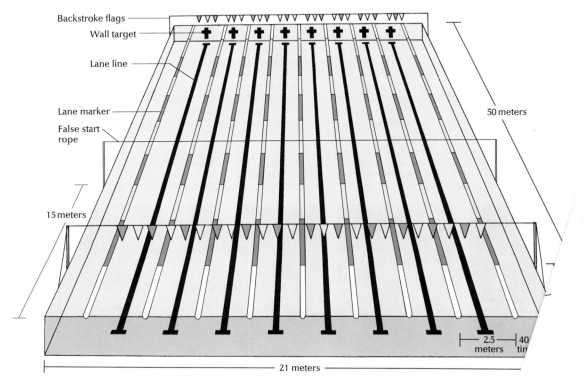

Backstroke flags

Wall target

Lane line

Lane marker

False start rope

15 meters

50 meters

2.5 meters

40 tin

21 meters

Team stunt performed by the Santa Clara (Calif.) Aquamaids;
Lee Pillsbury, *Swimming World*

Synchronized swimming is a water sport in which swimmers *synchronize* (match) graceful, acrobatic movements to music. Competition is divided into solo, duet, trio, and team events.

In national and international meets, individual freestyle races are held at distances of 100, 200, 400, 800, and 1,500 meters. Breaststroke, backstroke, and butterfly events are 100 and 200 meters long. The individual medley covers 200 and 400 meters. Open water races—held in rivers, lakes, or oceans—cover 25 kilometers (15.5 miles) in international competition and 5, 10, or 15 kilometers (3.1, 6.2, or 9.3 miles) in national races.

Team *relays* are among the most exciting swimming races. A team consists of four swimmers, each of whom swims an equal distance. Men's and women's teams participate in a 400-meter freestyle relay, a 400-meter medley relay, and an 800-meter freestyle relay. In the medley relay, each member of the team swims a different stroke for 100 meters in the following order: (1) backstroke, (2) breaststroke, (3) butterfly, and (4) front crawl.

Swim meets are held at various levels of competition, from local to international. So many swimmers participate in competitive swimming that qualifying times are established for large meets. To qualify for an event, a swimmer must at least equal the qualifying time for that race.

Large meets have several officials. The chief official is the referee. The referee supervises the other officials and makes sure that the swimmers follow regulations.

Each swimmer in a race is assigned a lane. The swimmers with the fastest qualifying times get the center lanes, and the slowest swimmers receive the outside lanes. The race begins at the sound of the starter's gun or horn. During the race, lane judges watch each swimmer's strokes and the turns at the end of the pool. An illegal stroke or turn disqualifies a swimmer.

In many meets, an electronic timing and judging system determines the order of finish and each swimmer's time to $\frac{1}{100}$ of a second. The system begins automatically at the starter's signal. It records the time for each swimmer as the swimmer's hand touches a plate attached to the end of the pool.

Starts and turns. A swimmer's performance in a race partly depends on the skill used in starting the race and in turning at the end of each lap. At the start of a freestyle, breaststroke, or butterfly race, a swimmer gains time by diving as far as possible through the air before hitting the water. In these races, swimmers dive off a raised starting platform. In backstroke events, they begin in the water with their back to the lane. They hold onto a starting block attached to the end of the pool. At the starting signal, with their back slightly arched, the swimmers use both feet to push off from the pool's end as forcibly as possible.

Fast turns also save a swimmer time. Freestyle and backstroke swimmers use the *flip,* or *somersault,* turn. In this turn, they make an underwater somersault to reverse their direction after touching the end of the pool. Breaststroke and butterfly swimmers use an *open* turn, in which they keep their head above the water while reversing their direction.

Training. Most young people interested in competitive swimming begin by racing against swimmers in their own age group. In the United States, United States Swimming has established an age-group program for young swimmers. This program divides swimmers into four groups: (1) age 10 and under; (2) ages 11 and 12; (3) ages 13 and 14; and (4) ages 15 to 18.

Starting a swimming race

A proper start is important in a race. In the grab start position, the swimmer bends down, grabs the front of the starting block, and curls her toes over the edge, *left.* She then rolls her body forward, lifts her head, swings her arms out, and pushes off the block with her legs, *center.* Over the water, *right,* she stretches forward and tries to enter the water cleanly to minimize resistance.

WORLD BOOK photos by Steven Spicer

Most swimmers in age-group programs work out once or twice a day for five or six days each week. Their training includes land and water exercises to increase endurance, speed, and strength. They also practice kicks and strokes.

Synchronized swimming is a water sport that combines grace, rhythm, and acrobatic skills. In this sport, swimmers perform certain movements to music that they have selected. They *synchronize* (match) these movements with the rhythm and the mood of the music.

Synchronized swimming was once called *water ballet*. It began as a form of exhibition swimming at water shows and remains popular. In 1952, the first international rules were established for synchronized swimming as a sport. It became an Olympic sport in 1984.

International competition is divided into solo, duet, and team events. A team may have four to eight members. Each solo, duet, or team event has three sections:

World swimming records*

Event	Time	Holder	Country	Made at	Date
Men's events					
50-meter freestyle	21.64 s	Alexander Popov	Russia	Moscow	June 16, 2000
100-meter freestyle	47.84 s	Pieter van den Hoogenband	Netherlands	Sydney, Australia	Sept. 19, 2000
200-meter freestyle	1 min 43.86 s	Michael Phelps	United States	Melbourne, Australia	March 27, 2007
400-meter freestyle	3 min 40.08 s	Ian Thorpe	Australia	Manchester, England	July 30, 2002
800-meter freestyle	7 min 38.65 s	Grant Hackett	Australia	Montreal, Canada	July 27, 2005
1,500-meter freestyle	14 min 34.56 s	Grant Hackett	Australia	Fukuoka, Japan	July 29, 2001
50-meter backstroke	24.80 s	Thomas Rupprath	Germany	Barcelona, Spain	July 27, 2003
100-meter backstroke	52.98 s	Aaron Peirsol	United States	Melbourne, Australia	March 27, 2007
200-meter backstroke	1 min 54.32 s	Ryan Lochte	United States	Melbourne, Australia	March 30, 2007
50-meter breaststroke	27.18 s	Oleg Lisogor	Ukraine	Berlin, Germany	Aug. 2, 2002
100-meter breaststroke	59.13 s	Brendan Hansen	United States	Irvine, CA, U.S.	Aug. 1, 2006
200-meter breaststroke	2 min 08.50 s	Brendan Hansen	United States	Victoria, Canada	Aug. 20, 2006
50-meter butterfly	22.96 s	Roland Schoeman	South Africa	Montreal, Canada	July 25, 2005
100-meter butterfly	50.40 s	Ian Crocker	United States	Montreal, Canada	July 30, 2005
200-meter butterfly	1 min 52.09 s	Michael Phelps	United States	Melbourne, Australia	March 28, 2007
200-meter individual medley	1 min 54.98 s	Michael Phelps	United States	Melbourne, Australia	March 29, 2007
400-meter individual medley	4 min 06.22 s	Michael Phelps	United States	Melbourne, Australia	April 1, 2007
400-meter freestyle relay	3 min 12.46 s	National team (M. Phelps, C. Jones, N. Walker, J. Lezak)	United States	Victoria, Canada	Aug. 18, 2006
800-meter freestyle relay	7 min 03.24 s	National team (M. Phelps, R. Lochte, K. Keller, P. Vanderkaay)	United States	Melbourne, Australia	March 30, 2007
400-meter medley relay	3 min 30.68 s	National team (A. Peirsol, B. Hansen, I. Crocker, J. Lezak)	United States	Athens, Greece	Aug. 21, 2004
Women's events					
50-meter freestyle	24.13 s	Inge de Bruijn	Netherlands	Sydney, Australia	Sept. 22, 2000
100-meter freestyle	53.30 s	Britta Steffen	Germany	Budapest, Hungary	Aug. 2, 2006
200-meter freestyle	1 min 55.52 s	Laure Manaudou	France	Melbourne, Australia	March 28, 2007
400-meter freestyle	4 min 02.13 s	Laure Manaudou	France	Budapest, Hungary	Aug. 6, 2006
800-meter freestyle	8 min 16.22 s	Janet Evans	United States	Tokyo	Aug. 20, 1989
1,500-meter freestyle	15 min 42.54 s	Kate Ziegler	United States	Mission Viejo, CA, U.S.	June 17, 2007
50-meter backstroke	28.16 s	Leila Vaziri	United States	Melbourne, Australia	March 28 and 29, 2007
100-meter backstroke	59.44 s	Natalie Coughlin	United States	Melbourne, Australia	March 27, 2007
200-meter backstroke	2 min 06.62 s	Krisztina Egerszegi	Hungary	Athens, Greece	Aug. 25, 1991
50-meter breaststroke	30.31 s	Jade Edmistone	Australia	Melbourne, Australia	Jan. 30, 2006
100-meter breaststroke	1 min 05.09 s	Leisel Jones	Australia	Melbourne, Australia	March 20, 20
200-meter breaststroke	2 min 20.54 s	Leisel Jones	Australia	Melbourne, Australia	Feb. 1, 2
50-meter butterfly	25.57 s	Anna-Karin Kammerling	Sweden	Berlin, Germany	July 30, 7
100-meter butterfly	56.61 s	Inge de Bruijn	Netherlands	Sydney, Australia	Sept. 17,
200-meter butterfly	2 min 05.40 s	Jessicah Schipper	Australia	Victoria, Canada	Aug. 17
200-meter individual medley	2 min 09.72 s	Yanyan Wu	China	Shanghai, China	Oct. 1
400-meter individual medley	4 min 32.89 s	Katie Hoff	United States	Melbourne, Australia	April
400-meter freestyle relay	3 min 35.22 s	National team (P. Dallmann, D. Götz, B. Steffen, A. Liebs)	Germany	Budapest, Hungary	July
800-meter freestyle relay	7 min 50.09 s	National team (N. Coughlin, D. Vollmer, L. Nymeyer, K. Hoff)	United States	Melbourne, Australia	Marc
400-meter medley relay	3 min 56.30 s	National team (S. Edington, L. Jones, J. Schipper, L. Lenton)	Australia	Melbourne, Australia	M

*Includes only records set in 50-meter pools.   Source: USA Swimming.

(1) *figures,* (2) *technical routines,* and (3) *free routines.* Figures are acrobatic movements. Technical routines must include required figures as directed by FINA. Free routines may consist of any listed figures, strokes, or parts of figures or strokes.

Almost 200 figures may be used in international competition. They are divided into four categories. The meet organizers draw lots to select one figure from each category that swimmers must perform.

The *dolphin* is an example of a commonly performed figure. It is also used in many routines. Swimmers begin the dolphin by floating on their back. They then pull themselves under the water head first, make a complete circle, and return to the floating position. In the *dolphin bent knee* figure, swimmers bend one knee while they perform the circular movement underwater.

A panel of judges awards points for each figure and routine. After each figure, the judges grade swimmers according to the difficulty of the figure and how well they performed it. The judges give each routine two scores, one for technical merit and one for artistic impression. Technical merit scores rate the difficulty and execution of strokes and patterns and the synchronization of swimmers with the music and with each other. Artistic impression scores include choreography, musical interpretation, and total presentation.

In water shows and swimming exhibitions, swimmers often base their synchronized routines on a story. For example, a team might act out a tale, such as *Alice in Wonderland,* with the aid of a narrator. The Cirque du Soleil water show called "O" has become internationally popular. It features synchronized swimming as well as high diving, acrobatics, and circus acts.

History

Ancient peoples may have learned to swim by imitating the way dogs and other animals moved through water. Swimming became a popular form of exercise and recreation in many ancient lands, including Assyria, Egypt, Greece, and Rome. Its popularity fell in the Middle Ages, from about the A.D. 400's through the 1400's. Many people feared swimming because they thought plague and certain other diseases were spread by water. Swimming regained popularity in the early 1800's.

Organized swim meets became common during the mid-1800's. At that time, many swimmers used the breaststroke. A faster stroke, the *Australian crawl,* was developed in the late 1800's. Johnny Weissmuller, an American swimmer who later played Tarzan in motion pictures, changed this stroke slightly in the early 1900's. His version, now called the front crawl, is the fastest, most widely used stroke.

Men's international swim meets began in 1896 in the first modern Olympic Games. Women's meets were added in the 1912 Olympics. That year, Fanny Durack, an Australian, became the first woman to win an Olympic gold medal in swimming. Weissmuller won a total of [fi]ve gold medals in the 1924 and 1928 Olympic Games. [Du]ring his career, he set 67 world records. Dawn Fraser [and] Murray Rose, two Australian swimmers, starred in [O]lympics of the 1950's and 1960's. In 1972, Mark [Spitz o]f the United States won seven gold medals, more [than an]y other athlete had ever won in a single Olym[pics. Jane]t Evans of the United States was the dominant

woman freestyle swimmer of the 1980's and early 1990's.

Swimming stars at the 2000 Summer Olympic Games included Ian Thorpe of Australia, Pieter van den Hoogenband and Inge de Bruijn of the Netherlands, and Lenny Krayzelburg of the United States. Stars at the 2004 Summer Olympics included Michael Phelps, Natalie Coughlin, and Aaron Peirsol of the United States; Thorpe, Petria Thomas, and Jodie Henry of Australia; Kosuke Kitajima of Japan; and de Bruijn. Phelps won eight medals, tying a record for most individual medals won during a Summer Olympics.   Samuel James Freas

Related articles in *World Book* include:

Diving	Skin diving
Diving, Underwater	Spearfishing
Drowning	Surfing
Ederle, Gertrude Caroline	Swimming pool
Life jacket	Triathlon
Olympic Games	Water polo
Safety (In water sports)	Water-skiing

Outline

I. Water safety

II. Swimming kicks and strokes
   A. The basic kicks   B. The basic strokes

III. Swimming as a sport
   A. The pool   D. Starts and turns
   B. Kinds of races   E. Training
   C. Swim meets   F. Synchronized swimming

IV. History

Questions

How did Johnny Weissmuller contribute to swimming?
How can a nonswimmer help a swimmer in trouble?
What are the five basic swimming strokes?
What is FINA?
How do swimmers start in a backstroke race?
What part does music play in synchronized swimming?
What are some basic water safety rules?
Why is swimming a good exercise for keeping fit?
What is a freestyle race?
What is survival bobbing?

Additional resources

Bean, Dawn P. *Synchronized Swimming: An American History.* McFarland, 2005.
Crossingham, John, and Walker, Niki. *Swimming in Action.* Crabtree Pub. Co., 2003. Younger readers.
Manley, Claudia B. *Ultra Swimming.* Rosen Central, 2002.
Mason, Paul. *A World-Class Swimmer.* Heinemann Lib., 2004. Describes the creation of a top swimmer. Younger readers.

Swimming pool is a large tank used for swimming and diving. Many people throughout the world enjoy the fun and recreation provided by swimming pools. Some pools are used for swimming races. This article discusses backyard pools. For information on pools used in swim meets, see the article on **Swimming.**

Manufacturers produce a wide variety of backyard pools. Both the expense and the type of swimming activities planned should be considered when selecting a pool. There are two main kinds of backyard swimming pools, *in-ground pools* and *above-ground pools.*

In-ground pools are pools in which the water is below the ground's surface. Most cost as much as a new car, but they last almost indefinitely. Some in-ground pools are made of concrete or fiberglass. Others consist of a vinyl liner in a shell of steel, aluminum, or special wood. Many in-ground pools have diving boards.

Above-ground pools are pools in which the water is in a metal or plastic frame above the surface of the ground. Such pools are less expensive than in-ground pools. However, they do not last as long.

Any backyard pool should have basic equipment. Ladders are necessary for getting into and out of the pool. A filtration system for removing impurities from the water is essential. The pool should also have an automatic *skimmer,* a device that clears the surface of trash.

Critically reviewed by the National Swimming Pool Institute

Swinburne, Algernon Charles (1837-1909), was a major English poet. He shocked Victorian England with his devotion to pleasure and his unorthodox religious and political beliefs. The sensuality of his verse scandalized many readers. Today, Swinburne's life and poetry do not seem so unconventional and shocking as they once did. However, the unusual technical skill of his poetry still retains its power to surprise.

Swinburne was born on April 5, 1837, in London. He attended Oxford University but left in 1860 to lead a bohemian life in London. For several years, Swinburne wrote much passionate but carefully composed poetry. His style emphasized long melodic lines with varied meters and complex rhyme schemes. Even more than most poets, Swinburne achieved beautiful and strange effects through the sound of words.

Drawing and water color (1861) by Dante Gabriel Rossetti; Fitzwilliam Museum, Cambridge, England

Algernon Swinburne

For example, the knight of "Laus Veneris" wishes to die "where tides of grass break into foam of flowers,/or where the wind's feet shine along the sea." Many of Swinburne's poems were inspired by Elizabethan writers, French poets, and ancient Greek and Roman writers. Swinburne first gained fame with his verse play *Atalanta in Calydon* (1865) and his collection *Poems and Ballads* (1866).

Swinburne's pleasure-seeking way of life led to his collapse in 1879. For the rest of his life, he lived in the home of a friend, Theodore Watts-Dunton. Swinburne continued to write poetry as well as drama and literary criticism.   K. K. Collins

Swine. See Hog (table: Hog terms).

Swing, in music. See Jazz (The swing era).

Swiss is a fine, sheer, plain weave cloth. It is used in making aprons, dresses, and curtains and other household textiles. It is also used as a foundation for embroidery. Swiss is usually woven from cotton or a blend of cotton and synthetic fibers. The cloth may be plain or figured, or may have woven, flocked, or paste dots. It may be processed to stay crisp and stiff after washing. Swiss was originally made in Switzerland.   Phyllis Tortora

Swiss chard is a garden vegetable plant. Its leaves are eaten as greens. Swiss chard is related to the common beet plant. It resembles the beet, except that it does not have a large fleshy root. Swiss chard has a small woody root which cannot be eaten. The vegetable has fleshy leafstems, large leaves, and a dark green color. Some varieties of Swiss chard have pale yellow leaves and others have bright red leaves and leafstems. The plant has

attractive, brilliant colors.

Swiss chard is one of the few garden greens that grow throughout the summer. The seeds are sown in the spring. The large outer leaves are harvested as soon as they develop. Later the inner leaves are taken, and the harvest continues until frost kills the plant.

People grew Swiss chard as long ago as 350 B.C. It is a favorite crop in

©Runk/Schoenberger, Grant Heilman

Swiss chard

Switzerland and was introduced in the United States in 1806. Massachusetts is one of the leading states in growing Swiss chard. Swiss chard is an excellent source of vitamin A and contains a fair amount of vitamins of the B complex and C. Like most leafy vegetables, Swiss chard is also rich in minerals.   Hugh C. Price

Scientific classification. Swiss chard belongs to the goosefoot family, Chenopodiaceae. It is *Beta vulgaris,* variety *cicla.*

Swiss Family Robinson. See Wyss family.

Swiss Guard. This famous body of Swiss soldiers grew out of a group of 250 Swiss who were picked to guard the pope in the late 1400's. In 1506, Pope Julius II secured the position of the Swiss Guard by a treaty with the Swiss cantons of Zurich and Lucerne. According to the agreement, the cantons supplied 250 men to serve as a bodyguard for the pope from that time on.

As a result of the agreement, the pope has always had a body of the Swiss Guard around him at the Vatican. But through the years, the number of guards has been reduced and the type of service they provide has changed. Today, they are called the Pontifical Swiss Guard. Their uniform style is still essentially medieval.

Another body of Swiss soldiers, called Swiss Guards, or Switzers, was organized in 1616 to protect King Louis XIII of France. These soldiers served France for 175 years. On Aug. 10, 1792, during the French Revolution, most of the Swiss Guards were killed while defending the royal palace in Paris from attack by an angry mob. The memory of these Swiss Guards is preserved in the famous *Lion of Lucerne,* which is carved in the face of a rock in Lucerne, Switzerland. It bears the words, "To the Fidelity and Courage of the Helvetians."

King Louis XVIII formed a second corps of Swiss Guards in 1815. They were defeated in the Revolution of 1830, and the corps disbanded.   Richard A. Sauers

Switch, Electric. See Electric switch.

Swithin, Saint, also spelled *Swithun,* was appointed bishop of Winchester, England, in 852. Swithin was born in Wessex in southwestern England and raised at the abbey of Winchester. After his ordination as a priest, h served as chaplain and chief adviser to Egbert and Etwulf, kings of the West Saxons. Swithin died in 862 was *canonized* (declared a saint) in the 900's. St. Sw Day is July 15. According to an old rhyme, the we that day will last for 40 days:

St. Swithin's Day, if thou dost rain/for forty days it sha'
St. Swithin's Day, if thou art fair/for forty days 'twill r

Neil J. Roy

© J. Messerschmidt, The Stock Market

Switzerland is famous for its magnificent mountain scenery. Picturesque towns in the Swiss Alps, such as Arosa, *shown here,* are popular tourist centers that feature winter sports.

Switzerland

Switzerland is a small European country known for its beautiful, snow-capped mountains and freedom-loving people. The Alps and the Jura Mountains cover more than half of Switzerland. But most of the Swiss people live on a plateau that extends across the middle of the country between the two mountain ranges. In this region are most of Switzerland's industries and its richest farmlands. Switzerland's capital, Bern, and largest city, Zurich, are also there.

The Swiss have a long tradition of freedom. About 700 years ago, people in what is now central Switzerland agreed to help each other stay free from foreign rule. Gradually, people in nearby areas joined them in what came to be known as the Swiss Confederation. Various Swiss groups speak different languages. Switzerland has three official languages—German, French, and Italian. The Latin name for Switzerland, *Helvetia,* appears on Swiss coins and postage stamps.

The Swiss show great pride in their long independence. Switzerland has no regular army, but almost all

Facts in brief

Capital: Bern.
Official languages: German, French, and Italian.
Official names: Schweizerische Eidgenossenschaft (in German), Confédération Suisse (in French), Confederazione Svizzera (in Italian).
Area: 15,940 mi^2 (41,284 km^2), including 523 mi^2 (1,355 km^2) of inland water. *Greatest distances*—east-west, 213 mi (343 km); north-south, 138 mi (222 km).
Elevation: *Highest*—Dufourspitze of Monte Rosa, 15,203 ft (4,634 m) above sea level. *Lowest*—shore of Lake Maggiore, 633 ft (193 m) above sea level.
Population: *Estimated 2008 population*—7,542,000; density, 473 per mi^2 (183 per km^2); distribution, 68 percent urban, 32 percent rural. *2000 census*—7,288,010.
Chief products: *Agriculture*—dairy products, fruits, potatoes, sugar beets, wheat. *Manufacturing*—chemicals, drugs, electrical equipment, machine tools, precision instruments, processed foods, textiles, watches, wine.
National holiday: Swiss National Day, August 1.
Money: *Basic unit*—Swiss franc. One hundred centimes equal one Swiss franc.

young men receive military training yearly. They keep their weapons and uniforms at home, and can be called up quickly in an emergency. Local marksmanship contests are held frequently.

In the early 1500's, Switzerland established a policy of not taking sides in the many wars that raged in Europe. During World Wars I and II, Switzerland remained an island of peace. Almost all the nations around it took part in the bloody struggles. Switzerland provided safety for thousands who fled from the fighting, or from political persecution. The nation's neutrality policy helped the Swiss develop valuable banking services to people of countries throughout the world, where banks are less safe. The League of Nations, the major world organization of the 1920's and 1930's, had its headquarters in the Swiss city of Geneva. Today, many international organizations, including various United Nations agencies, have headquarters in Geneva.

Switzerland has limited natural resources, but it is a thriving industrial nation. Using imported raw materials, the Swiss manufacture high-quality goods including electrical equipment, machine tools, and watches. They also produce chemicals, drugs, chocolate, and cheese and other dairy products.

Government

The government is based on the Swiss Constitution, which was created in 1848 and revised in 1874 and 1999. The Constitution establishes a *federal republic* in which political powers are divided between the central government and *cantonal* (state) governments.

In some ways, the Swiss government is one of the most democratic in the world. Swiss citizens enjoy close control over their laws through the rights of the *referendum* and the *initiative*.

The referendum allows the people to demand a popular vote on laws passed by the legislature. A vote must be held if 50,000 people request it. The people can accept or veto the law.

The initiative gives Swiss citizens the right to bring specific issues before the people for a vote. Such a vote may force a change in government policy or may amend the Constitution. An initiative requires a petition by at least 100,000 citizens. All voters must be at least 18 years old.

National government. The executive branch of Switzerland's government is a seven-member cabinet called the Federal Council. The Council serves in place of a single chief executive. Its members are elected by the Swiss legislature to four-year terms. The legislature elects one member of the Federal Council as president, but the president's duties are largely ceremonial. The president serves a one-year term and may not serve two terms in a row.

Switzerland's legislature, the Federal Assembly, is made up of the Council of States and the National Council. The Council of States has 46 members. Each canton elects two of its members, and each half-canton elects one. The terms of members of the Council of States range from one to four years. The National Council has 200 members, elected to four-year terms from election districts based on population.

Cantonal and local government. Swiss voters elect executive councils and legislatures in the 20 cantons, 6 half-cantons, and cities. The country's six half-cantons were originally three undivided cantons. They split into separate political units with as much power of self-government as the full cantons. But each half-canton sends only one representative to the national legislature's Council of States, instead of two.

In one canton and in four of the half-cantons, the people vote by a show of hands at an open-air meeting called a *Landsgemeinde*. Similar meetings of voters are held in the small towns and villages.

Politics. Switzerland has a wide range of political parties. Since 1959, however, a *coalition* (alliance) of the four largest political parties has held a great majority in the Federal Assembly. The four parties have divided most government posts between themselves. The four are the Christian Democratic, Radical Democratic, and Social Democratic parties and the Swiss People's Party.

Courts. Switzerland's highest court is the Federal Tribunal. It has 26 judges and 12 alternate judges, elected to six-year terms by the Federal Assembly. Various lower courts are in the cantons.

Defense. Switzerland has a *militia* (citizens' army) instead of regular armed forces. Swiss men are required to begin a series of military-training periods at the age of 20. They can be called into service until the age of 30. Women are not required to serve in the militia, but they

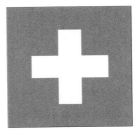 

The Swiss flag was used in an earlier form in 1240 by the region of Schwyz. The cross represents Christianity.

The coat of arms of Switzerland, like the Swiss flag, was established with its present dimensions in 1889.

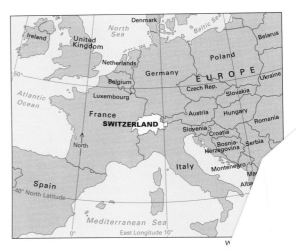

Switzerland lies in western Europe and is bordere[d] many, Austria, Liechtenstein, Italy, and France.

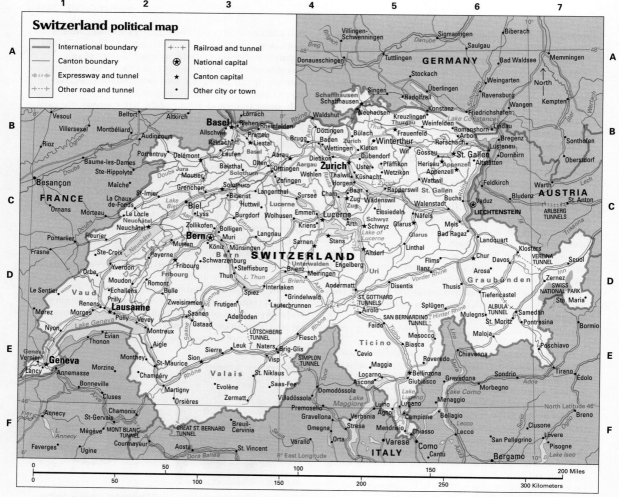

Switzerland political map

———	International boundary	+‑+‑+	Railroad and tunnel
———	Canton boundary	✪	National capital
‑‑‑‑	Expressway and tunnel	★	Canton capital
+‑‑+	Other road and tunnel	•	Other city or town

WORLD BOOK map

Switzerland map index

.... in German, French, or Italian, alternative name in parentheses.
.... antons.
.... ion of metropolitan area, including suburbs.

§Does not appear on map; key shows general location.
Sources: 2000 census for cantons, larger cities, and metropolitan areas; 2002 official estimates
for other cities and towns.

may volunteer for service. About 220,000 people serve in Switzerland's armed forces.

People

Even after the Swiss began to join forces about 700 years ago to defend themselves, people from different areas kept their own ways of life. They defended these ways of life in the same spirit of independence that has made Switzerland famous. As a result, the Swiss still differ greatly among themselves in language, customs, and traditions. These differences are apparent from region to region, and even among some small communities.

In the past, the local patriotism of the Swiss was so strong that most of them thought of themselves as part of their own local area more than of their country. They considered the Swiss of other areas almost as foreign rivals, and feuds among various areas lasted for hundreds of years. But at most times when their country faced danger, the Swiss stood together as one people. Today, local patriotism has largely been replaced by national patriotism.

Population. About one-fifth of the people of Switzerland are foreign-born. The country has one of the highest percentages of foreign-born residents of any country in Europe. More than one-fourth of Switzerland's foreign-born population came from Italy. Large groups of people from Germany, Portugal, Spain, and the former Yugoslavia also reside in Switzerland. Foreign workers have been recruited to fill newly created jobs because Switzerland's economy has grown faster than its domestic population.

The majority of Switzerland's people live in cities and towns. Bern is the country's capital. Zurich is Switzerland's largest city. Other large Swiss cities include Basel, Geneva, and Lausanne.

Language. The Swiss Constitution provides for three *official* languages and four *national* languages. The official languages are German, French, and Italian. As a result, Switzerland has three official names—Schweizerische Eidgenossenschaft (in German), Confédération Suisse (in French), and Confederazione Svizzera (in Italian). All national laws are published in each of these three languages. The Federal Tribunal, Switzerland's highest court, must include judges who represent each language group.

The four national languages are the three official ones plus *Romansh* (also spelled *Romansch)*, which is closely related to Latin. Romansh is spoken only in the mountain valleys of the canton of Graubünden, by about 50,000 people.

About two-thirds of the people speak a form of German that is called *Schwyzerdütsch* (Swiss German). They live in the northern, eastern, and central parts of Switzerland. Schwyzerdütsch is almost a separate language, and even people who speak German find it hard to understand. The language and its name vary from place to place. For example, it is called *Baseldütsch* in Basel and *Züridütsch* in Zurich. However, wherever Schwyzerdütsch is spoken, standard German is used in newspapers, books, television and radio programs, plays, and church sermons.

French, spoken in western Switzerland, is the language of almost 20 percent of the people. Italian is used by nearly 10 percent of the people, in the south. Both these languages, as spoken by the Swiss, are much like their standard forms in France or Italy.

One difficulty, especially for visitors, is that many place names in Switzerland vary by language. The most complicated example—the city known as *Geneva* to English-speaking people—is called *Genf* in German, *Genève* in French, and *Ginevra* in Italian. English-speaking people know almost all other Swiss cities and towns by their French or German name.

Religion. Switzerland has complete freedom of religion. About 45 percent of the people are Roman Catholics, and about 40 percent are Protestants. Of the 26 cantons and half-cantons in Switzerland, 15 have a Roman Catholic majority, and 11 are chiefly Protestant.

The Protestant Reformation took a special form in Switzerland. Calvinism developed there and spread to France and many other countries during the 1500's. As a result, the Protestant movement split into two major camps, Calvinists and Lutherans. See **Calvin, John; Reformation** (Zwingli and the Anabaptists); **Zwingli, Huldreich.**

Education. Swiss children are required by canton law to go to school, but the age limits vary. In most cantons, children must attend school from 6 through 14. Instruction is held in the local national language, and each child also has the opportunity to learn one of the other national languages.

Students who plan to attend a university may go to one of three kinds of high schools. These schools specialize in (1) Greek and Latin, (2) modern languages, or (3) mathematics and science. Other students go to trade or technical schools while serving an apprenticeship. An increasing number of people take adult education courses in order to achieve their career goals.

Switzerland has seven universities and various other schools of higher learning. The oldest, the University

Population and language

This map shows Switzerland's largest population centers. It also shows where the national languages are spoken. Most Swiss speak a form of German called *Schwyzerdütsch.*

WORLD BOOK map

A cafe in Zurich includes outdoor tables where people can eat and drink in a charming urban setting. Zurich is Switzerland's largest city.

Swiss National Tourist Office

of Basel, was founded in 1460. The University of Zurich, with about 16,000 students, is the largest. All universities are public institutions. Their students pay no tuition.

Arts. Most Swiss literature has been written in German. Famous books include two children's classics, *Heidi* by Johanna Spyri and *The Swiss Family Robinson* by the Wyss family. Major Swiss authors of the 1800's were Jeremias Gotthelf, Gottfried Keller, and Conrad Ferdinand Meyer. Carl Spitteler won the Nobel Prize in literature in 1919 for his epic poetry and other writings. Later writers of the 1900's included Max Frisch and Friedrich Dürrenmatt, whose plays have been performed in many countries. Charles Ferdinand Ramuz wrote novels in French.

The art movement called *Dadaism* was founded in Zurich in 1916 (see **Dadaism**). Outstanding Swiss artists of the 1900's included the painter Paul Klee and the sculptors Alberto Giacometti and Jean Tinguely. Le Corbusier won fame in modern architecture.

Several Swiss cities have symphony orchestras. The Orchestre de la Suisse Romande of Geneva became world famous under conductor Ernest Ansermet. An annual music festival in Lucerne attracts thousands of music lovers. Almost every town and village has a singing group that practices weekly for local festivals, and for regional and national competitions. Band music and folk dancing in colorful costumes are also popular. Some mountaineers enjoy yodeling or playing a musical instrument known as the alphorn (see **Alphorn**).

Sports. The mountains of Switzerland provide grand opportunities for a variety of sports. About a third of the nation's people ski. Many also enjoy bobsledding, camping, climbing, and hiking in the mountains. Target shooting, stressed by the Swiss military system, is extremely popular. Shooting matches are held frequently. Other favorite sports of the Swiss include bicycling, [ska]ting, gymnastics, soccer, swimming, and wrestling.

Hornussen, a game somewhat like baseball, is played by two teams. The batter hits a wooden disk with a wooden club 8 feet (2.4 meters) long. Fielders catch the disk with wooden rackets.

The land

Switzerland has three main land regions: (1) the Jura Mountains, (2) the Swiss Plateau, and (3) the Swiss Alps. The two mountain regions make up about 65 percent of Switzerland's area. But the plateau between them has about four-fifths of the country's population.

The Jura Mountains consist of a series of parallel ridges that are separated by narrow valleys. These ridges extend along Switzerland's western border and

Paolo Koch, Photo Researchers

In the game of hornussen, a batter uses a long, flexible pole to hit a disk. The game is hundreds of years old.

into France. Within Switzerland, the highest mountain of the range is 5,518-foot (1,682-meter) Mont Tendre. The Jura Mountains are the home of Switzerland's important watchmaking industry. Other industries in the region include dairy farming, lumbering, and the manufacture of electronics.

The Swiss Plateau is a hilly region with rolling plains. It lies from 1,200 to 2,200 feet (366 to 671 meters) above sea level. The movement of ancient glaciers formed many lakes, including Lake Constance and Lake

Geneva. Switzerland's richest farmland is in this region, as are most of the large cities and manufacturing industries. See **Lake Constance; Lake Geneva.**

The Swiss Alps are part of the mighty Alps, the largest mountain system in Europe. This region covers about 60 percent of Switzerland, but less than a fifth of the people live there. There are glaciers as low as 3,500 feet (1,070 meters) above sea level, and snow blankets most of the region from three to five months a year. Much of the region is forested. The forests help prevent

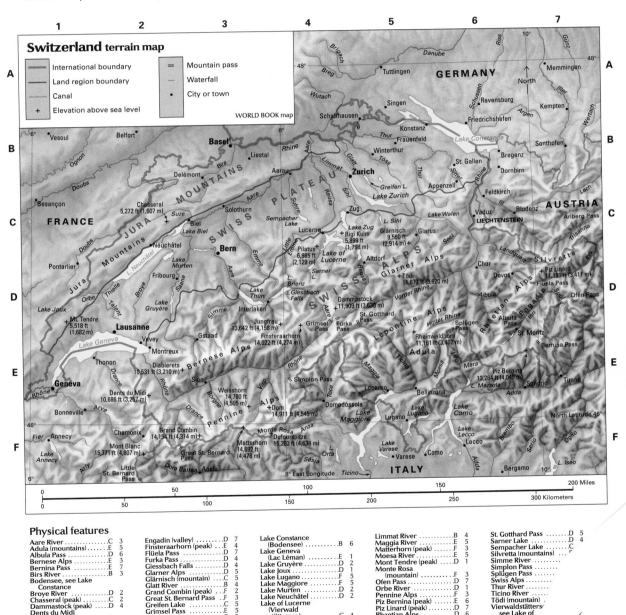

Physical features

Aare River . . . . .C 3	Engadin (valley) . . . . .D 7	Lake Constance
Adula (mountains) . . . . . .E 5	Finsteraarhorn (peak) . . .E 4	(Bodensee) . . . . .B 6
Albula Pass . . . . .D 6	Flüela Pass . . . . .D 7	Lake Geneva
Bernese Alps . . . . .E 3	Furka Pass . . . . .D 4	(Lac Léman) . . . . .E 1
Bernina Pass . . . . .E 7	Giessbach Falls . . . . .D 4	Lake Gruyère . . . . .D 2
Birs River . . . . .B 3	Glarner Alps . . . . .D 5	Lake Joux . . . . .D 1
Bodensee, see Lake	Glärnisch (mountain) . . . .D 5	Lake Lugano . . . . .F 5
Constance	Glatt River . . . . .B 4	Lake Maggiore . . . . .F 5
Broye River . . . . .D 2	Grand Combin (peak) . . . .F 2	Lake Murten . . . . .D 2
Chasseral (peak) . . . . .C 2	Great St. Bernard Pass . . .F 2	Lake Neuchâtel . . . . .D 2
Dammastock (peak) . . . . .D 4	Greifen Lake . . . . .C 5	Lake of Lucerne
Dents du Midi	Grimsel Pass . . . . .E 5	(Vierwald
(mountain) . . . . .E 2	Inn River . . . . .D 7	stättersee) . . . . .C 4
Diablerets	Jungfrau (peak) . . . . .D 3	Lake Sihl . . . . .C 5
(mountains) . . . . .E 2	Jura Mountains . . . . .C 2	Lake Thun . . . . .D 3
Dom (peak) . . . . .F 2	Lac Léman, see	Lake Walen . . . . .C 6
Doubs River . . . . .C 1	Lake Geneva	Lake Zug . . . . .C 4
Dufourspitze (peak) . . . .F 4	Lake Biel . . . . .C 3	Lake Zurich . . . . .C 5
Emme River . . . . .D 3	Lake Brienz . . . . .D 4	Lepontine Alps . . . . .D 5

Limmat River . . . . .B 4	St. Gotthard Pass . . . . .D 5
Maggia River . . . . .E 5	Sarner Lake . . . . .D 4
Matterhorn (peak) . . . . . .F 2	Sempacher Lake C
Moesa River . . . . .E 5	Silvretta (mountains) . . . .
Mont Tendre (peak) . . . .D 1	Simme River . . . .
Monte Rosa	Simplon Pass . . . .
(mountain) . . . . .F 3	Splügen Pass . . . .
Ofen Pass . . . . .D 7	Swiss Alps . . . .
Orbe River . . . . .D 1	Thur River . . . .
Pennine Alps . . . . .F 3	Tödi (mountain) . .
Piz Bernina (peak) . . . . . .E 6	Ticino River . . . .
Piz Linard (peak) . . . . . . .D 7	Vierwaldstätters
Rhaetian Alps . . . . .D 6	see Lake of
Rheinwaldhorn	Lucerne
(peak) . . . . .E 5	Visp River . . .
Rhine River . . . . .B 6	Weisshorn (p
Rhône River . . . . .E 4	
Ruess River . . . . .C 4	
Saane River . . . . .D 2	

snow from sliding, but avalanches sometimes occur.

The upper valleys of the Rhine and Rhône rivers divide the Swiss Alps into a northern and a southern series of ranges. These ranges include the Bernese, Lepontine, Pennine, and Rhaetian Alps. Their sharp peaks, jagged ridges, and steep gorges create many scenic areas. Many mountain streams form plunging waterfalls. The highest waterfall is the 1,982-foot (604-meter) Giessbach Falls in the Bernese Alps. The Pennine Alps include Switzerland's highest peak, the 15,203-foot (4,634-meter) Dufourspitze of Monte Rosa. The beauty of the Swiss Alps attracts tourists from around the world. See **Alps.**

Rivers. The Swiss Alps form part of Europe's main drainage divide. They are the source of rivers that flow in all directions. The Rhine and the Rhône rivers rise within 15 miles (24 kilometers) of each other in the Alps. The Rhine flows into the North Sea, and the Rhône into the Mediterranean Sea. The Inn River winds into the Danube River, which goes into the Black Sea. The Ticino River is a tributary of the Po River, which flows into the Adriatic Sea. See **Rhine River; Rhône River.**

Climate

The climate of Switzerland varies greatly from area to area because of the wide variety in altitude. In general, temperatures decrease about 3 °F (2 °C) with each 1,000-foot (300-meter) increase in elevation, and higher areas of the country receive more rain and snow. Atlantic air held up by the mountains often settles over lower areas, producing dampness and fog. Fog sometimes covers the entire Swiss Plateau like a sea of clouds. Some areas may be covered by fog for as many as 120 days a year.

January temperatures average from 29 to 33 °F (−2 to 1 °C) on the central plateau and in the Swiss mountain valleys. During the winter, there is colder though drier and sunnier weather above the layer of fog than below it.

In summer, the Swiss Plateau is warm and sunny. However, severe storms may occur there. July temperatures on the plateau average from 65 to 70 °F (18 to 21 °C). Sheltered valleys sometimes become uncomfortably hot. In summer, the higher slopes of the mountains are cool or even cold. The canton of Ticino, which extends southward to the Italian plains, has hot summers and mild winters.

EPA from Pictorial Parade

Ticino, the southernmost Swiss canton, is the warmest part of the country. It has hot summers and mild winters.

The central plateau receives from 40 to 45 inches (100 to 114 centimeters) of *precipitation* (rain, snow, and other forms of moisture) a year. Sheltered valleys usually have less. In some high areas, the yearly precipitation totals more than 100 inches (250 centimeters). Above 6,000 feet (1,800 meters), snow covers the ground at least six months a year.

A dry, warm southerly wind called the *foehn* sometimes blows down the valleys of the Swiss Alps. It causes rapid changes in temperature and air pressure, which makes many people uncomfortable. The foehn melts mountain snows earlier than such snows would otherwise melt. The foehn can also cause avalanches.

Economy

Switzerland is a prosperous country with one of the world's highest standards of living. The nation's highly specialized industries are extremely profitable. These industries include banking, insurance, and watchmaking. Tourism also contributes significantly to the country's economy. Switzerland has more jobs than its own people can fill. Foreign workers make up about a fifth of the country's labor force.

Switzerland trades with nations throughout the world, but chiefly with Western European countries and the United States. Leading exports include drugs and medicines, industrial equipment, and watches.

Natural resources. Switzerland lacks important deposits of coal, iron ore, petroleum, and other minerals on which heavy industry is based. Most of the land is too high or too rugged to be good farmland. In addition, the climate is generally better for producing hay and

Average monthly weather

Bern						Lugano					
	Temperatures				Days of rain or snow		Temperatures				Days of rain or snow
	°F		°C				°F		°C		
	High	Low	High	Low			High	Low	High	Low	
Jan.	35	26	2	−3	11	Jan.	43	29	6	−2	7
Feb.	40	27	4	−3	10	Feb.	48	30	8	−1	6
Mar.	48	33	9	1	12	Mar.	56	36	13	2	9
Apr.	56	39	13	4	14	Apr.	63	43	17	6	11
May	64	46	18	8	15	May	70	50	21	10	14
June	70	52	21	11	14	June	78	56	26	13	12
July	74	56	23	13	13	July	83	60	28	16	11
Aug.	73	55	23	13	12	Aug.	82	59	28	15	10
Sept.	66	50	19	10	11	Sept.	75	54	24	12	9
Oct.	55	42	13	6	12	Oct.	63	46	17	8	11
Nov.	44	34	7	1	12	Nov.	52	38	11	3	10
Dec.	36	27	2	−3	12	Dec.	45	31	7	−1	8

Meteorological Office, London

other livestock feeds rather than such crops as wheat and fruit. Crops are raised on only about a tenth of Switzerland's total area, chiefly on the plateau. About a fourth of the country consists of meadows or grazing land, much of which can be used only in summer. Forests cover about a fourth of Switzerland. But air pollution has damaged many trees in the forests. The government has established strict pollution controls for automobiles in an effort to combat forest damage.

Switzerland's rushing mountain rivers are its greatest natural resource. About 60 percent of the electric power produced in Switzerland is generated at hydroelectric power stations on the rivers. Nuclear power plants supply most of the rest of the country's electric power.

Manufacturing. Switzerland is one of the most industrialized countries in the world. Its manufacturing industries are based on the processing of imported raw materials into high-quality products for export. To keep the cost of materials and transportation as low as possible, these industries specialize in skilled, precision work on small, valuable items. In Switzerland's watchmaking industry, for example, the cost of materials is only about one-twentieth the cost of labor. More than 95 percent of the watches made in Switzerland are exported.

The Swiss make chemical products, generators and other electrical equipment, industrial machinery, machine tools, precision instruments, and motor vehicles. Other major products are paper, processed foods including cheese and chocolate, and textiles.

Most Swiss factories are small- or medium-sized because of the stress on quality goods rather than mass production. There are factories in small towns and even in villages. The use of hydroelectric power to run the factories and railroads helps keep the busiest industrial centers almost free of smoke.

Agriculture in Switzerland supplies only about three-fifths of the people's needs. The rest of the nation's food must be imported. Livestock raising is the most important agricultural activity because of the limited cropland resources and the climate. It provides about 70 percent of Switzerland's farm income, largely through dairy farming. Most of the dairy cattle graze on the high mountain pastures in summer and are brought down to the valleys in winter. Much of the milk is used to make

Switzerland's gross domestic product

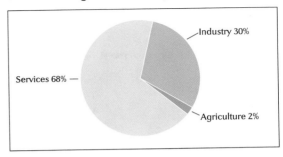

The gross domestic product (GDP) of Switzerland totaled $258,620,000,000 in 1999. The GDP is the total value of goods and services produced within a country in a year. *Services* include community, social, and personal services; finance, insurance, real estate, and business services; government; and trade, restaurants, and hotels; and transportation and communication. *Industry* includes construction, manufacturing, mining, and utilities. *Agriculture* includes agriculture, forestry, and fishing.

Production and workers by economic activities

Economic activities	Percent of GDP produced	Employed workers	
		Number of people	Percent of total
Finance, insurance, real estate, & business services	26	580,000	15
Manufacturing & mining	21	689,000	18
Trade, restaurants, & hotels	15	886,000	23
Government	13	153,000	4
Community, social, & personal services	7	813,000	21
Transportation & communication	7	253,000	6
Construction	6	289,000	7
Utilities	3	25,000	1
Agriculture, forestry, & fishing	2	187,000	5
Total	100	3,875,000	100

Figures are for 1999.
Sources: Swiss Federal Statistical Office; International Monetary Fund.

cheeses for export. These cheeses include Emmentaler, also known as *Swiss cheese,* and Gruyère. Farmers also raise hogs, goats, sheep, and chickens.

Swiss farms are small, averaging only 35 acres (14 hectares). Farmers work the land carefully to make it as productive as possible. Crops include fruits, wheat and other grains, and potatoes. Grapes are grown near Lakes Geneva, Lugano, and Neuchâtel, and in other sunny areas. Olive trees grow in the canton of Ticino.

Tourism. Since the early 1800's, large numbers of tourists have come to Switzerland. Today, more than 7 million tourists visit yearly. Switzerland has thousand⌐ hotels and inns for tourists. Sports centers in the A' including Davos and St. Moritz, attract many vaca Skiing is especially popular. Most of the ski run⌐ of trees because they are higher than the eleva' which trees stop growing. In summer, guides tourists mountain climbing. Many visitors co' healthful clear, dry, mountain air, as well as

Alan Band Associates
Switzerland's watchmaking industry is world famous. Almost all Swiss watches are exported to other countries.

Cattle graze in high Swiss mountain pastures during the summer. They are brought down to the valleys for the winter. Livestock raising is the most important agricultural activity in Switzerland. Crop production is limited by the climate and a shortage of good farmland.

© Michael Yamashita, Woodfin Camp, Inc.

beauty of the Alps. Water sports on Lake Geneva and other lakes are also popular vacation attractions.

Banking also ranks as one of Switzerland's major industries. Swiss banks attract deposits from people in many countries. The banks are probably the safest in the world, partly because of the nation's neutrality. Depositors can choose to be identified by a number known only to themselves and a few bank officials. In this way, a private fortune can be kept secret. Under Swiss law, a bank employee who violates this secrecy may be fined and imprisoned. But the secrecy may be broken in the investigation of criminal cases.

© Marche, FPG

Tourists who enjoy skiing flock to the snowy Swiss Alps. Switzerland's economy depends heavily on tourism. Outstanding facilities contribute greatly to the tourist trade.

Transportation. Switzerland has fine transportation systems in spite of the mountains, which make travel difficult. The government owns and operates almost the entire railroad network. Railroad tunnels—including the Furka Base, Lötschberg, St. Gotthard, and Simplon tunnels—cut through the Alps. The 21.5-mile (34.6-kilometer) Lötschberg Base Tunnel is one of the world's longest railroad tunnels.

Switzerland's paved roads and highways provide travel even to mountain areas. But roads that wind through the higher mountain passes are open only a few months of the year. Heavy snow makes them unusable except in summer. The 3 ½ mile (5.6-kilometer) Great St. Bernard Tunnel, opened in 1964, was the first automobile tunnel through the Alps. It links Switzerland and Italy. The 10.5-mile (16.9-kilometer) St. Gotthard Road Tunnel is one of the longest highway tunnels in the world.

The Rhine River connects Basel, Switzerland's only port, with the North Sea. Large barges can reach Basel, which handles about 9 million tons (8.2 million metric tons) of cargo a year. Geneva and Zurich have the country's busiest international airports.

Communication. Switzerland has about 80 daily newspapers. The largest newspapers include *Der Blick, Tages Anzeiger Zürich,* and *Neue Zürcher Zeitung,* all published in Zurich. Most of the country's newspapers are published in German, and some are published in French or Italian. A few of the nondaily newspapers are published in Romansh.

Government-controlled corporations operate a radio network and a television network in each of the three official languages. A few programs are broadcast in Romansh. In addition, several privately owned radio stations broadcast in Switzerland. Almost all Swiss families own at least one radio and one television set. The government operates the postal, telegraph, and telephone services.

History

Early days. Before the time of Christ, a Celtic people called the Helvetians lived in what is now Switzerland.

They were conquered in 58 B.C. by Roman armies led by Julius Caesar. The region, known as *Helvetia,* became a Roman province. By the A.D. 400's, two Germanic tribes, the Alemannians and the Burgundians, settled there. Another Germanic people, the Franks, defeated these tribes by the early 500's. The Frankish kingdom later expanded and became powerful under Charlemagne, but it broke apart during the 800's. See **Franks**.

Most of present-day Switzerland became part of the Holy Roman Empire in 962, when the empire began, and the rest was part of the kingdom of Burgundy. That part came into the empire in 1033. Switzerland consisted of many territories, towns, and villages ruled by local lords, and some communities directly under the emperor. See **Holy Roman Empire**.

The struggle for freedom. By the 1200's, the Habsburg family had gained control over much of Switzerland. The free men of what are now the *cantons* (states) of Schwyz and Uri feared the growth of the Habsburgs' power. In 1273, Rudolf I became the first Habsburg to rule the Holy Roman Empire. He began to take control of the two regions. In 1291, Schwyz and Uri decided to defend their freedom. They invited the nearby region of Unterwalden to join them.

Leaders of the three regions met in August 1291, and signed the Perpetual Covenant, a defense agreement. They declared their freedom and promised to aid each other against any foreign ruler. The Perpetual Covenant was the start of the Swiss Confederation. The confederation came to be known as Switzerland. It took its name from the canton of Schwyz.

The Habsburgs ruled Austria, and the Swiss fought several wars of independence against Austrian forces. In 1315, at Morgarten, Swiss peasants trapped and defeated an Austrian army 10 times their strength. Between 1332 and 1353, five more cantons joined the Swiss Confederation. The Swiss again defeated the Austrians at Sempach in 1386 and at Näfels in 1388. See **Habsburg, House of**.

The wars with Austria were full of dramatic incidents, and many famous stories have been told about Swiss heroes. For two exciting tales, see the articles on **Tell, William** and **Winkelried, Arnold von**.

Independence and expansion. Switzerland became a strong military power during the 1400's. The Swiss entered several wars to gain land, and won many territories. In three battles in 1476 and 1477, the Swiss defeated Charles the Bold, Duke of Burgundy. In 1499, they crushed the forces of Maximilian I, the Habsburg ruler of the Holy Roman Empire. Switzerland won complete independence, though the empire did not officially recognize it until 1648. In 1512 and 1513, the Swiss drove French armies out of northern Italy. Almost all the lands won in these wars of expansion remained under Swiss control for nearly 300 years, and then were admitted into the confederation as cantons.

In 1515, the French defeated the Swiss at Marignano in Italy. The Swiss suffered great losses, and began to question their policy of expansion. Switzerland soon adopted a policy of neutrality, and has stayed out of foreign wars ever since.

Five more cantons joined the Swiss Confederation between 1481 and 1513, making a total of 13. Each canton governed itself as it chose, almost like a separate country. Some cantons were peasant democracies, and others were governed by powerful families or by craftsmen's groups called *Zünfte* (guilds). Many cantons owned nearby territories either by themselves or with other cantons. The confederation had no central government. Delegates from each canton occasionally met in

By an unknown artist from the *Stumpf Chronicle.* Zentralbibliothek, Zurich, Switzerland

The Battle of Sempach was fought in 1386 against the Austrians during the Swiss wars of independence. That battle, won by the Swiss, is shown in a woodcut dating from 1548.

Important dates in Switzerland

58 B.C. Roman armies under Julius Caesar conquered Helvetia (now Switzerland).

A.D. 400's Germanic tribes occupied Helvetia.

962 Most of what is now Switzerland became part of the Holy Roman Empire.

1291 Three Swiss *cantons* (states) signed the Perpetual Covenant, a defense agreement that marked the start of the Swiss Confederation.

1315-1388 Switzerland defeated Austria in three wars of independence.

1470's Victories over Charles the Bold, Duke of Burgundy, established Switzerland as a European power.

1515 The Swiss were defeated by the French in Italy and began their policy of permanent neutrality.

1648 The Holy Roman Empire recognized Switzerland's independence.

1798 French forces occupied Switzerland and established the Helvetic Republic under their control.

1815 The Congress of Vienna expanded Switzerland to 22 cantons and restored the old confederation.

1848 Switzerland adopted a constitution that established federal power over the confederation.

1863 The Red Cross was founded in Switzerland. Geneva became the seat of the International Committee of the Red Cross.

1874 Constitutional changes increased federal power.

1920 The League of Nations met at its headquarters in Geneva, Switzerland, for its first session.

1958 Basel became the first Swiss city to let women vote in local elections.

1960 Switzerland helped form the European Free Trade Association.

1963 Switzerland joined the Council of Europe.

1971 Women won voting rights in Swiss national elections.

1979 Jura was created as the 23rd canton of Switzerland.

1984 Elisabeth Kopp became the first woman to be elected to the Federal Council.

2002 Switzerland joined the United Nations.

---

an assembly called *Tagsatzung* to discuss various matters. But this assembly had no real power.

Religious civil wars. The Reformation spread quickly in Switzerland during the early 1500's. Huldreich Zwingli, one of the great leaders of the Protestant movement, preached in Zurich. John Calvin, another great Protestant leader, made Geneva an international center of Protestantism (see **Reformation**). The Reformation split Switzerland into two armed camps, Protestant and Roman Catholic. The two groups fought in 1529, 1531, 1656, and 1712, without either side gaining control.

French control. In 1798, during the French Revolution, French armies swept into Switzerland and quickly occupied the country. The French set up the *Helvetic Republic* and gave the new Swiss government strong central power. The Swiss cantons became merely administrative districts of the government.

The great political change caused much confusion and dissatisfaction among the Swiss. As a result, Napoleon of France reestablished the 13 Swiss cantons in 1803 and created 6 new ones from their territories. He reduced the power of the central government and restored much of the cantons' self-government.

After Napoleon's final defeat in 1815, the Congress of Vienna gave Switzerland three more cantons that had been under French control (see **Vienna, Congress of**). The old confederation system was largely restored, with the central government having little power. The Con-

gress of Vienna also guaranteed Swiss neutrality. The European powers at the congress recognized Swiss neutrality as being for the good of all Europe. The neutrality of Switzerland has never since been broken.

The Constitution of 1848. By 1830, many Swiss had begun to demand political reforms—including individual rights and freedom of the press—and greater national unity. Governments were overthrown peaceably in some cantons, but rioting occurred in others. The reform movement grew in strength. Seven cantons banded together to oppose the changes, but were defeated in a three-week civil war in 1847.

Switzerland adopted a new Constitution in 1848. This Constitution set up a federal democracy with a two-house legislature. It established federal power over the confederation and guaranteed religious freedom and other individual rights. The Constitution was changed in 1874 to increase the government's powers, especially in military and court matters.

In 1863, Jean Henri Dunant, a Swiss businessman and writer, founded the Red Cross in Geneva. The Red Cross flag was copied from that of Switzerland, with the two colors reversed. See **Red Cross**.

Neutrality in the world wars. World War I began in 1914, and Switzerland immediately declared its neutrality. The fighting nations respected this policy because Switzerland acted in a strictly neutral manner throughout the war. Food imports decreased during the four years of fighting, but farmers in Switzerland increased their grain production to feed the people. In 1920, Geneva became the headquarters of the newly created League of Nations, an association of countries organized to prevent war. Switzerland was one of the original members of the League. See **League of Nations**.

After World War II began in 1939, Switzerland again declared its neutrality. German forces did not invade

Expansion of Switzerland—1291 to 1815

In 1291, three Swiss *cantons* (states) allied to form the Swiss Confederation, shown at the center of this map. Other cantons joined in the 1300's, and still others from 1481 to 1513. Territory added in the 1800's brought the nation to its present size.

WORLD BOOK map

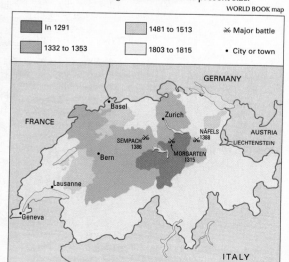

Switzerland. They feared the Swiss would blow up transportation tunnels in the Alps if they did. Switzerland became a major supply link between Germany and its ally Italy. It also represented the United States and other Allied nations in enemy countries. During the war, Switzerland cared for more than 100,000 refugees from a number of countries.

Switzerland did not join the United Nations (UN), which was founded after World War II ended in 1945. The Swiss felt that UN membership, which requires possible military action by member nations, would violate their neutrality policy. But the UN made Geneva its European headquarters, and Switzerland joined most of the UN's specialized agencies.

After the wars, Switzerland continued to avoid membership in international organizations that might endanger its neutrality. But it participated when there was no danger of losing its independence. In 1960, the Swiss helped form the European Free Trade Association, an economic organization of European nations. In 1963, Switzerland joined the Council of Europe, an organization of European countries that seeks closer unity among its members for economic and social progress.

In 1979, Switzerland increased its number of cantons from 22 to 23. It created a new canton called Jura from territory that was part of the canton of Bern. In most of Bern, most people are German-speaking Protestants. But in the part of Bern that became Jura, most people are French-speaking Roman Catholics. Jura was created to give the French-speaking Catholics their own canton.

Switzerland was the last major European country to grant women political equality. In 1958, Basel became the first Swiss city to allow women to vote in local elections. In 1971, women in Switzerland were given the right to vote in national elections. The Swiss voters approved an equal rights amendment for women in 1981.

In 1984, Elisabeth Kopp became the first woman to be elected to Switzerland's Federal Council. Kopp resigned from the council in 1988, after admitting that she had advised her husband to resign from a firm she knew the government was going to investigate.

Recent developments. In 1992, voters approved Switzerland's membership in the International Monetary Fund and the World Bank. In 1993, many of Europe's leading nations joined together to form the European Union, an organization that promotes economic and political cooperation. The Swiss declined to join, preferring to preserve their traditional independence. In 2002, however, the Swiss voted to join the United Nations. Switzerland became a UN member in September 2002.

In 1999, Ruth Dreifuss, the second woman elected to the Federal Council, became Switzerland's first female president. The largely ceremonial post is for one year and rotates among council members.   Patrick Ireland

Related articles in *World Book* include:

Biographies

Agassiz, Louis	Gallatin, Albert	Piaget, Jean
Barth, Karl	Hesse, Hermann	Piccard, Auguste
Calvin, John	Hingis, Martina	Piccard, Jacques
Dunant, Jean H.	Jung, Carl G.	Piccard, Jean
Dürrenmatt,	Klee, Paul	Rousseau, Jean-
Friedrich	Le Corbusier	Jacques
Euler, Leonhard	Paracelsus, Philippus A.	Spyri, Johanna
Frisch, Max	Pestalozzi, Johann H.	Tussaud, Marie G.

Winkelried, Arnold von
Wyss family
Zwingli, Huldreich

Cities

Basel	Geneva	Lucerne	Zurich
Bern	Lausanne	Saint Moritz	

Physical features

Alps	Saint Bernard Passes
Lake Constance	Saint Gotthard Pass
Lake Geneva	Saint Gotthard tunnels
Lake of Lucerne	Simplon Pass and Tunnel
Matterhorn	

Other related articles

Clothing (picture: Traditional costumes)	Helvetians
	Lake dwelling
Europe, Council of	League of Nations
European Free Trade Association	Tell, William

Outline

I. Government
  A. National government
  B. Cantonal and local government
  C. Politics
  D. Courts
  E. Defense
II. People
  A. Population
  B. Language
  C. Religion
  D. Education
  E. Arts
  F. Sports
III. The land
  A. The Jura Mountains
  B. The Swiss Plateau
  C. The Swiss Alps
  D. Rivers
IV. Climate
V. Economy
  A. Natural resources
  B. Manufacturing
  C. Agriculture
  D. Tourism
  E. Banking
  F. Transportation
  G. Communication
VI. History

Questions

When did women in Switzerland gain the right to vote in national elections?
What are the three official languages of Switzerland?
Where does the name *Switzerland* come from?
How much of Switzerland do the Alps cover?
What was the first automobile tunnel through the Alps?
How did the Swiss Confederation start?
Why do Swiss banks attract deposits from people around the world?
In what region do about two-thirds of the Swiss live?
How does Switzerland keep itself prepared for military defense?
Why are Swiss industrial areas almost free of smoke?

Additional resources

Birmingham, David. *Switzerland: A Village History.* St. Martin's, 2000.
Dame, Frederick W. *History of Switzerland.* 3 vols. Edwin Mellen Pr., 2001.
Harvey, Miles. *Look What Came from Switzerland.* Watts, 2002. Younger readers.
Levy, Patricia, and Lord, Richard. *Switzerland.* 2nd ed. Benchmark Bks., 2005. Younger readers.

Sword is a sharp-edged metal weapon. It is used in hand-to-hand fighting to stab or cut.

Swords consist chiefly of a blade and a handle called a *hilt.* Sword blades have either one cutting edge or two, and they are made in a variety of sizes and shape Some are broad like that of the Scottish *claymore,* others are narrow like that of the *rapier.* The Pe shamshir, sometimes called a *scimitar,* has a curved blade. But the *saber* has one that is o

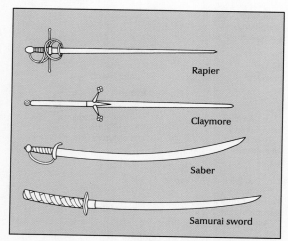

Rapier

Claymore

Saber

Samurai sword

WORLD BOOK illustrations by Zorica Dabich

Various types of swords have played a role in the warfare of many civilizations. Swords differ chiefly in size, the shape of the blade, and the number of cutting edges the blade has.

curved. Hilts also vary. For example, the hilts on some of the swords of European Vikings and Japanese samurai warriors are highly ornamental works of art. But the hilt on the Roman *gladius* is purely practical.

About 3500 B.C., people discovered how to make bronze, and early swords were made of this metal. By about 1000 B.C., swords were commonly made of iron, a metal harder than bronze and so better suited for sword making. Most early iron swords were only 18 to 24 inches (46 to 61 centimeters) long. Few armies used them as their principal weapon.

During the Middle Ages, sword makers in Europe and Japan perfected the long sword. Long swords ranged from 3 to 6 feet (0.9 to 1.8 meters) in length, and could be swung with either one or two hands. They were extremely deadly, and they were among the most important weapons in warfare of the time.

By the 1600's, firearms had been developed and the use of swords declined as a result. However, cavalry soldiers continued to use such swords as sabers and broadswords into the 1900's. At that time, tanks and other advanced weapons made cavalry itself useless. Today, some military officers still wear swords as a sign of authority. In addition, blunt-edged swords are used in the sport of fencing (see **Fencing**).   Joseph Goering

See also **Dagger**; **Vikings** (picture: The sword).

Swordfish is one of the fastest of all fish. Its scaleless, muscular body is designed for high-speed swimming. This fish can swim at speeds up to 60 miles (97 kilometers) per hour.

The swordfish is known for its long, flattened upper jaw, which looks like a sword. Most swordfish have a brownish-black body with a light brown underside. They also have large eyes and dark, crescent-shaped fins.

Most swordfish measure 5 to 8 feet (1.5 to 2.4 meters) long and weigh about 150 to 300 pounds (70 to 135 kilograms). The largest swordfish ever caught was nearly 15 feet (4.6 meters) long and weighed 1,182 pounds (536 kilograms).

The "sword" or bill of a swordfish is strong and may measure about one-third as long as its body. The bill is probably used to break up schools of fish and leave individual fish open to attack. A swordfish swallows its prey whole because it has no teeth. The bill may also aid the swordfish in swimming. Its coarse surface breaks the flow of water around the fish. Rough water allows the swordfish to swim more easily. Swordfish sometimes use their bills to attack small boats.

This fish lives in temperate to tropical ocean waters. On calm days, its back and tail fins can be seen above the water, and it occasionally leaps completely out of the water. But swordfish are able to swim more than 2,000 feet (610 meters) below the surface, and they often feed on deep-sea fishes. Swordfish also eat squid.

Swordfish, which was once considered unsafe to eat, is a popular food fish. Because it is difficult and dangerous to catch, the swordfish is also prized as a sport fish.

John D. McEachran

Scientific classification. The swordfish belongs to the billfish family Xiphiidae. It is *Xiphias gladius.*

See also **Marlin**; **Sailfish**; **Fish** (picture: Fish of coastal waters and the open ocean).

Sycamore, *SIHK uh mawr,* is a shade tree with reddish-brown wood. It grows in fertile lowlands and along streams. The *American sycamore* is found in great numbers in the United States from southern Maine to Nebraska and as far south as Texas and Florida. This tree may reach a height of 175 feet (53 meters) and be 14 feet (4 meters) through the trunk. The bark on the lower trunk is reddish-brown, and the bark on the branches is olive-green. The bark on the branches breaks off in tiny scales. When these scales break off, they show an inner bark that is light cream in color. This light bark gives rise to the phrase "hoary-antlered sycamore." Some sycamores are known as *buttonwoods,* others as *plane trees.*

A sycamore tree can be recognized by its leaves, which are broad and have large teeth. The stem of each leaf is hollow at the base where it encloses the next year's bud. The flowers of a sycamore are of two types, those that bear *stamens* and those that bear *pistils.* Each type of flower grows in separate flower heads on different parts of the same tree. The fruits of a sycamore are borne in small balls which hang from drooping stems. Each ball is made up of many tiny dry fruits tightly packed together. The fruits are known as *achenes.*

Norman L. Christensen, Jr.

Scientific classification. Sycamores belong to the plane tree family, Platanaceae. They make up the genus *Platanus.* The scientific name for the American sycamore is *P. occidentalis.*

See also **Tree** (Familiar broadleaf and needleleaf trees of North America [picture]).

Sydenham, *SIHD uhn uhm,* **Baron** (1799-1841), was a British statesman and governor general of Canada from 1839 to 1841. He succeeded the Earl of Durham, who had served briefly as governor general. Sydenham carried out the Act of Union that united Upper Canada (now Ontario) and Lower Canada (now Quebec) in 1841.

Sydenham was born Charles Edward Poulett Thomson at Waverly Abbey, near Farnham, England. He became a merchant and an early supporter of free trade. In 1826, he was elected to Parliament and, in 1834, became president of Britain's Board of Trade. Queen Victoria gave him the title Baron Sydenham in 1840. Sydenham resigned as governor general in 1841. He died of tetanus on Sept. 19, 1841, after a riding accident. J. M. Bumsted

Sydenham, *SIHD uhn uhm,* **Thomas** (1624-1689), an English physician, was one of the most widely admired doctors of his time. He believed that medicine must be learned through experience at the patient's bedside and that the practice of medicine should be based on observation rather than book learning or theory. He was a keen observer and gave excellent descriptions of gout, scarlet fever, measles, and influenza.

Sydenham was born in early September 1624 at Wynford Eagle, Dorset. He served as a captain in the army led by Oliver Cromwell during the English Civil War in the 1640's. Later, Sydenham finished his medical studies at Oxford University and opened a practice. He came to believe that medical treatment was justified by results, not by physiological theory. Experience led him to use the plant cinchona, from which quinine is extracted, as a remedy for certain fevers. Many physicians at that time opposed using specific medicines for specific ailments.

Sydenham worked to improve understanding of the origins and nature of disease. He suggested that diseases could be classified as plants had been. Sydenham also believed that changes in the atmosphere led to epidemics. He died on Dec. 29, 1689. Matthew Ramsey

Sydney (pop. 3,997,321) is Australia's oldest and largest city and the capital of the state of New South Wales. The city is also Australia's leading industrial city and a major port. Sydney lies on a huge, deep harbor on the nation's southeastern coast (see **Australia** [political map]). This harbor, officially called Port Jackson, is also known as Sydney Harbour. It is considered one of the most beautiful harbors in the world. The Sydney Harbour Bridge links the southern and northern shores, and the Sydney Opera House stands on the harbor's southern side.

Britain (now also called the United Kingdom) founded Sydney as a prison colony in 1788. At that time, many nations sent criminals to distant prison colonies. The colony's first governor, Captain Arthur Phillip, chose the site for its harbor and supply of fresh water. He named it for Thomas Townshend, Baron (later Viscount) Sydney, a British nobleman.

The city and its suburbs cover about 4,690 square miles (12,100 square kilometers). Downtown Sydney lies on the south side of Sydney Harbour. An area called the Rocks, part of the oldest section of Sydney, is built on sandstone cliffs that rise along part of the waterfront. Many of the historic buildings in the area have been restored, and it is now a major tourist attraction with shops, hotels, and restaurants. Southeast of the Rocks is the Darling Harbour area, which includes a casino, a large entertainment center, an exhibition hall, an aquarium, and many restaurants and hotels.

The city's main street, George Street, runs through downtown Sydney. The downtown area includes many high-rise office buildings. A series of parks, including Hyde Park, the Domain, and the Royal Botanic Gardens, lie east of the downtown area. Nearby Macquarie Street is the site of the Parliament House of New South Wales. The street also has many historic buildings, including some constructed by convicts in the early 1800's. One of the most famous of these buildings, the Hyde Park Barracks, originally housed convicts but is now a museum.

Sydney Harbour Bridge and the Sydney Harbour Tunnel, which runs under the harbor, link the downtown area with suburbs on the north shore. Other suburbs spread south beyond Botany Bay, west to the Blue Mountains, and east to the Pacific coastline. Royal National Park, one of the oldest national parks in the world, is south of the city. Ku-ring-gai Chase National Park, north of the city, has rock paintings and carvings made by Aborigines, the original inhabitants of Australia.

The people of Sydney are called *Sydneysiders.* About two-thirds of them were born in Australia. British descent is the most common ancestry among Sydneysiders. But other Europeans, especially people from Italy and Greece, and many Asians have settled in Sydney. The city also has a significant Aboriginal population.

Most Sydney-area families live in houses in the suburbs. But an increasing number of people live in apartments in central Sydney to be close to jobs and services.

The city's mild climate enables Sydneysiders to spend much time outdoors. Sydney's beaches, such as Bondi and Manly, attract thousands of swimmers, surfers, and sunbathers. Sailing is also popular. Sydneysiders enjoy watching and playing a variety of sports, including Australian Rules football, cricket, Rugby Union and Rugby

© Bill Bachman, Photo Researchers

Sydney's landmarks include the Sydney Opera House, with its white, shell-like structure, and Sydney Harbour Bridge. The opera house has facilities for symphony concerts, ballets, and theater productions. The bridge spans Sydney Harbour and links the downtown area with the suburbs to the north.

Sydney

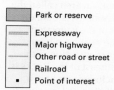

Park or reserve

Expressway
Major highway
Other road or street
Railroad
■ Point of interest

Location of Sydney

Sydney Metro Area

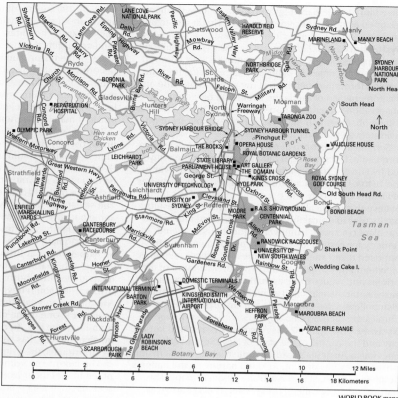

WORLD BOOK maps

League football, soccer, and tennis. Local and international sporting events are held at Sydney Cricket Ground and Aussie Stadium. Homebush Bay, a suburb west of the city, is the site of Olympic Stadium, which was built for the 2000 Summer Olympics.

The Sydney Festival takes place every January. Sydneysiders flock to art shows, open-air concerts, and other festival activities. The Royal Easter Show, held every April in Homebush Bay, features livestock judging, commercial exhibits, performances, and other events.

Cultural life. The Sydney Symphony Orchestra, Opera Australia, the Sydney Dance Company, and the Australian Ballet Company perform in the Sydney Opera House. Completed in 1973, the opera house has towering white shells that resemble billowing sails. Architects consider the opera house, designed by Danish architect Jørn Utzon, one of the finest buildings of the 1900's.

The University of Sydney, founded in 1850, is the oldest and largest institution of higher learning in Australia. The Art Gallery of New South Wales displays artworks from many cultures. The Museum of Contemporary Art exhibits works by modern artists. Motion pictures for the Australian and overseas markets are produced at studios in Moore Park.

Economy. Goods manufactured in Sydney account for about a fifth of the value of all goods made in Australia. The city's chief factory products include chemical and paper goods, food products, machinery equipment, and metal products. Rich cattle- and sheep-raising areas in New South Wales make Sydney a major livestock and wool market. It is also a business and finance center.

The city is sometimes called *the gateway to Australia.* Many visitors enter Australia through Sydney's Kingsford Smith International Airport. Sydney Ports Corporation controls both Sydney Harbour and Port Botany, which is about 8 miles (12 kilometers) south of Sydney Harbour. Port Botany handles about two-thirds of Sydney's cargo, and Sydney Harbour handles the rest. The city's chief exports include aluminum, chemicals, coal, machinery, meat, wheat, and wool.

History. Aborigines lived in the area of what is now Sydney as early as 40,000 or 50,000 years ago. The first shiploads of convicts from Great Britain (now the United Kingdom) arrived in Sydney on Jan. 26, 1788. The newcomers included about 750 convicts plus their guards and officials. The prison colony grew slowly at first because the convicts knew little about building or farming.

In the early 1800's, a farmer named John Macarthur helped found Australia's wool industry. He successfully bred Merino sheep and introduced the wool from this breed to the London market. The new industry attracted free settlers to the colony. In 1842, Sydney was incorporated as a city with a population of about 30,000.

In 1849, Sydney received its last convicts from the United Kingdom. In 1851, gold was discovered in New South Wales, and Sydney grew rapidly during the gold rush that followed. By the 1890's, the population had risen to nearly 400,000.

Since the mid-1900's, Sydney has become a sprawling urban region. Many European immigrants arrived in the 1950's, and the city's population grew to 2 million. The city's rapid growth led to a number of problems, including water and air pollution and traffic jams. In the 1980's, the city built new sewers and tunnels to take sewage out to sea. The city also constructed tollways and traffic tunnels, including one completed in 1992 under Sydney Harbour, to reduce road congestion.

Parts of downtown Sydney have also undergone redevelopment. In 1988, for example, the Darling Harbour complex opened. In 2000, Sydney hosted the Summer Olympic Games.

In 2005, mobs of white Australians attacked people who appeared to be Middle Eastern at North Cronulla beach, south of Sydney. The attacks seemed to be motivated by racial tensions. Dozens of people were injured and arrested.   Brian Kennedy

See also **Australia** (pictures); **Botany Bay; New South Wales.**

Sylvester I, Saint (? -335), was elected pope in 314. Little is known about his life, but many legends sprang up about his reign. He was pope during the rule of the Roman emperor Constantine the Great. Constantine was converted to Christianity on his deathbed by an Arian bishop. But according to one legend, Sylvester converted Constantine after curing him of leprosy. Such tales were widely known during the Middle Ages and contributed to the hoax called the *Donation of Constantine.* The Donation was a forged document probably composed in the 760's. The document falsely stated that Constantine gave most of his property, rights, and honors as emperor to Sylvester and the pope's successors.

Sylvester was the first pope to acquire important buildings in Rome for the church. The best known were the Lateran Palace and basilica, which served as the papacy's headquarters until the 1300's.   Thomas F. X. Noble

Sylvester II (940-1003), elected pope in 999, became the first French pope. He was born in the Auvergne region of southern France. His given name was Gerbert. He showed extraordinary intelligence throughout his life and became the most accomplished mathematician and philosopher of his time.

Sylvester had a remarkable career before becoming pope. He traveled widely in Europe, attracting patrons and supporters such as popes and German emperors. He was abbot of the great Italian monastery of Bobbio, master of the famous French cathedral school at Reims, archbishop of Reims, and patriarch of Ravenna, Italy.

As an intellectual, Sylvester promoted the close study of original manuscripts and raised interest in many classical authors. As a churchman, he was a sincere and strong reformer, working for a clergy that was more highly educated and also more pious and moral. Sylvester died on May 12, 1003.   Thomas F. X. Noble

Symbiosis, SIHM *by OH* sihs or SIHM *bee OH sihs,* means *living together.* Any two different species of organisms that live together in a close relationship are symbiotic. In a symbiotic relationship, one member always benefits from the relationship. The other member may also benefit, or it may be harmed or unaffected by the relationship. There are three forms of symbiosis: parasitism, commensalism, and mutualism.

In *parasitism,* one organism lives on or in another organism—called the *host*—at the host's expense. Parasites may harm the host. An example of parasitism is the hookworm. Hookworms may live in the intestines of human beings and other animals. See **Parasite.**

In *commensalism,* one organism benefits from the host, which is unaffected. For example, a type of marine worm lives in the shells occupied by hermit crabs. When the crab feeds, the worm comes out to share the host's meals.

In *mutualism,* both parties benefit. For example, certain kinds of ants live in thorny plants. The plants provide food and nesting sites for ants. In return, the ants provide protection from insect pests. Mutualism also occurs when an alga and a fungus grow together to form a lichen, which differs from either organism. The fungus, which cannot produce its own food, gets its food from the alga. The fungus helps the alga get water. See **Lichen.**   Alan R. Templeton

Symbol, also called *emblem,* communicates a fact or an idea or stands for an object. Some symbols, such as flags and stop signs, are visual. Others, including music and spoken words, involve sounds. Symbols rank among humanity's oldest and most basic inventions.

Almost anything can be a symbol. For example, the letters of the alphabet are among the most important symbols because they form the basis for almost all written and spoken communication. Gestures and sounds made by human beings also symbolize ideas or feelings. A symbol can be used alone or with other symbols.

Uses of symbols. Individuals, nations, and organizations use symbols every day. Symbols also play an important part in religious life. People throughout the world have agreed on certain symbols that serve as a shorthand for recording and recalling information. Every branch of science, for example, has its own system of symbols. Astronomy uses a set of ancient symbols to identify the sun, the moon, the planets, and the stars. In mathematics, Greek letters and other symbols make up an abbreviated language.

Other symbols appear in such fields as commerce, engineering, medicine, packaging, and transportation. Since the 1930's, many nations have been working together to create a system of road and traffic signs that could be universally understood.

All countries have official or unofficial national symbols. A flag or an anthem may symbolize a nation. Familiar symbols of the United States include Uncle Sam, the Statue of Liberty, and the eagle. Symbols for other coun-

Canada	France	United States
Christianity	Islam	Judaism

WORLD BOOK illustrations by Mas Nakagawa

Symbols are signs that stand for an idea or an object. Nations and religions use pictorial symbols to identify themselves and to express their ideals.

tries include the maple leaf for Canada, John Bull for England, and the fleur-de-lis for France. Many political parties use symbols for identification. In the United States, a donkey symbolizes the Democratic Party, and an elephant represents the Republican Party.

Most religions use symbols to represent their beliefs. The cross symbolizes Christ's death and all Christian beliefs. The Star of David represents Jewish teachings.

Many rituals have a symbolic nature. Such symbolic acts include coronations, inaugurations, military salutes, and religious sacraments.

Symbols with different meanings. Several societies may use the same symbols, but these symbols may stand for different things. In many societies, for example, the color red symbolizes war and violence. But this color also has other meanings. In China, red represents marriage. Among American Indians, it stands for the East. Red symbolizes life in the Shinto religion of Japan, but in France it represents law schools.

A symbol only has the meaning people give it. Even a powerful symbol can lose its meaning if the society dishonors or ignores it for a time period. Throughout early history, many people considered the swastika a good luck charm. But the Nazi Party of Germany adopted it as its symbol in 1920. The swastika came to represent the Nazi attempt to conquer Europe. Today, it ranks as one of the most hated symbols in history. 		Whitney Smith

Related articles in *World Book* include:

Algebra (Symbols in algebra)	Element, Chemical (tables)	John Bull
Alphabet	Flag	Map (Map legends)
Cartouche	Heraldry	Mythology (Mythical symbols)
Crescent	Indian, American (Language; pictures)	Ranching (picture)
Easter (Easter symbols)		Seal
	Insignia	Swastika

Symbolism was a literary movement that developed in France between 1885 and 1895. It involved the quest for a reality beyond the physical world. Symbolist poets developed the musical suggestiveness of words, experimenting with existing verse forms. Symbolism inspired innovative works in music, painting, and the theater.

The symbolist movement was inspired by the French poets Charles Baudelaire, Stéphane Mallarmé, Arthur Rimbaud, and Paul Verlaine. Baudelaire's famous sonnet "Correspondences" evokes the world as "a forest of symbols" that speak mysterious words to the poet. Leading symbolist theorists included René Ghil, Jules Laforgue, Gustave Kahn, and Jean Moréas. The most prominent symbolist poet was Paul Valéry. Other symbolist poets included Henri de Régnier, Émile Verhaeren, Maurice Maeterlinck, Francis Viélé-Griffin, and Stuart Merrill.

Some symbolists were called *decadents* due to their preoccupation with death and decay—tendencies typified by Joris-Karl Huysmans's novel *À Rebours (Against Nature,* 1884) and the play *Axël* (about 1885) by a French nobleman, the Comte de Villiers de l'Isle-Adam. Symbolism's pessimistic tone was influenced by the German philosopher Arthur Schopenhauer. 		Edward K. Kaplan

Related articles in *World Book* include:

Baudelaire, Charles	Rimbaud, Arthur
Drama (Symbolism)	Russian literature (Symbolism)
French literature (Symbolism)	Valéry, Paul
Maeterlinck, Maurice	Verlaine, Paul
Mallarmé, Stéphane	

Symington, Stuart (1901-1988), a Missouri Democrat, served as a United States senator from 1953 until he retired from office in 1976. He campaigned for the 1960 Democratic presidential nomination but failed to win it.

In the Senate, Symington sat on the Armed Services and Foreign Relations committees and specialized in military matters. In 1954, he charged that the Department of Defense had wasted millions of dollars on outdated weapons. He became a leading critic of U.S. involvement in the Vietnam War (1957-1975).

William Stuart Symington was born on June 26, 1901, in Amherst, Massachusetts. He served in the Army in 1918, during World War I. He studied at Yale University from 1919 to 1923. He then held executive positions in several companies. He was president of the Emerson Electric Manufacturing Company from 1938 to 1945. Symington became assistant secretary of war in 1946 and served as the first secretary of the U.S. Air Force from 1947 to 1950. He died on Dec. 14, 1988.

		Mark J. Rozell

Symmetry, in geometry, is a correspondence, or matching, of parts of an object. These parts correspond in size, shape, and position after certain geometric operations are carried out. One major use of the concept of symmetry is to classify crystals (see **Crystal**). In this application, three kinds of symmetry are especially useful. The operations that produce these symmetries occur relative to (1) a plane of symmetry, (2) an axis of symmetry, and (3) a center of symmetry.

A plane of symmetry divides an object into two symmetrical parts. These parts are *mirror images* of each other—that is, the reflection of one of the parts matches the other part. This kind of symmetry is therefore called *reflectional symmetry*. In chemistry, molecules that display reflectional symmetry are known as *chiral* (pronounced *KY ruhl*) forms.

An axis of symmetry is an imaginary line through the center of an object. Rotating the object about this line produces a number of identical appearances of the object. For example, a square-based pyramid displays

WORLD BOOK illustration by Linda Kinnaman

| 0° | 90° | 180° | 270° | 360° |

Symmetry is a balanced arrangement of a figure's features. The figure pictured at left has *fourfold rotational symmetry*—it can be rotated 360° to show four identical faces. The imaginary line through the center of the figure, around which the figure can be rotated, is the *axis of symmetry*.

four identical appearances when rotated 360° about its axis of symmetry. The number of identical appearances displayed in a 360° rotation is known as the *fold of the axis.* Thus, the pyramid has a *fourfold axis of symmetry.*

A center of symmetry is a midpoint of an object. Located at equal distances from this point are equal and opposite pairs of parts. In crystals, such parts include faces, edges, and corners. William B. Simmons, Jr.

Symphonic poem is an orchestral composition that tries to portray a nonmusical idea in music. Composers have based symphonic poems on poems, plays, stories, episodes from history, scenes from nature, paintings, and philosophical statements. The symphonic poem developed from the *concert overture* (see **Overture**). Like the concert overture, most symphonic poems consist of one *movement* (section). However, symphonic poems are written more freely, and they are longer.

Composer Franz Liszt of Hungary created the first symphonic poems about 1850. The German composer Richard Strauss expanded the form with his works *Thus Spake Zarathustra* (1896) and *A Hero's Life* (1898). Jean Sibelius of Finland and Claude Debussy of France were the last major composers of symphonic poems.
  R. M. Longyear

Symphony is a large-scale musical composition for an orchestra. Symphonies are divided into sections called *movements.* Most symphonies consist of four movements, but some have only one and others have as many as six. The first movement of most symphonies is moderately fast. The second movement is the slowest, and the third has a dancelike quality. The fourth movement is a lively or triumphant conclusion.

Symphonies developed from the overtures of Italian operas of the early 1700's. The Austrian composer Joseph Haydn wrote more than 100 symphonies in the late 1700's, and they reflect the development of the symphony into a major musical form. The last four symphonies of the Austrian composer Wolfgang Amadeus Mozart, written in 1786 and 1788, are examples of especially elegant works called *classical symphonies.*

Many composers of the 1800's and early 1900's modeled their works after one or more symphonies by Ludwig van Beethoven of Germany. For example, Beethoven's symphonies influenced such composers as Hector Berlioz of France; Franz Liszt of Hungary; Anton Bruckner, Gustav Mahler, and Franz Schubert of Austria; Felix Mendelssohn and Robert Schumann of Germany; and Jean Sibelius of Finland. The symphonies of Schumann influenced Johannes Brahms of Germany, Antonín Dvořák of what is now the Czech Republic, and Peter Ilich Tchaikovsky of Russia.

Leading symphony composers of the 1900's include Sergei Prokofiev, Dimitri Shostakovich, and Igor Stravinsky of Russia; Aaron Copland and Charles Ives of the United States; Ralph Vaughan Williams of the United Kingdom; and Anton Webern of Austria. R. M. Longyear

Each composer discussed in this article has a biography in *World Book.* See also **Minuet; Orchestra; Sonata.**

Synagogue is the Jewish house of worship and the center of Jewish education and social life. The word *synagogue* usually refers to the place where worship and other activities take place. The synagogue has become one of the most important centers for the transmission and preservation of Judaism.

A synagogue has many functions. People gather there for worship services every morning and evening, as well as on the Sabbath and on holy days. Synagogues have schools where children and adults study the scriptures, the Hebrew language, and Jewish history. Such important events as a wedding or a *bar mitzvah* are celebrated in the synagogue (see **Bar mitzvah**). In the United States, many synagogues also serve as meeting places for Jewish organizations in the community.

Jews began to gather for formal prayer in Biblical times at the Temple in Jerusalem when it was the center of Jewish life. The Temple was destroyed in 587 or 586 B.C. Later, buildings called synagogues were built. They served as places of prayer and study, and as centers of Jewish life worldwide. Lawrence H. Schiffman

See also **Judaism** (The synagogue).

Synchrotron, *SIHNG kruh trahn,* is a device that accelerates electrons and protons to high energies. It is a type of *particle accelerator* that makes particles travel in circular orbits. Physicists use the synchrotron to study the structure and forces of the atomic nucleus. For a diagram of a synchrotron, see **Particle accelerator.** See also **X rays** (Synchrotron radiation).

Syndicalism, *SIHN duh kuh LIHZ uhm,* was a revolutionary labor movement that was most popular in France in the late 1800's and early 1900's. Its goal was to create a society in which associations of workers owned and operated all means of production and controlled the government. Such associations would develop from existing labor unions. The word *syndicalism* came from the French word *syndicat,* which means *union.*

Syndicalists called for the abolition of *capitalism,* the economic system of the United States and most European nations, and for the abolition of national governments (see **Capitalism**). They believed capitalism and these governments benefited private owners at the expense of workers. Syndicalists wanted to replace capitalism and national governments with small associations of workers. These associations would control all resources and industries, handle all political affairs, and form the basis of a free and just society.

Syndicalism rejected political activity as a method of working for its goals. Instead, it proposed a general strike of all workers, organized by the associations.

Syndicalism influenced the labor movements in Italy, Spain, France, and other countries. In the United States, the Industrial Workers of the World (IWW) had many aims and methods in common with syndicalism, especially after 1908 (see **Industrial Workers of the World**). By the 1920's, however, syndicalism had lost much of its influence on the world's labor movements.
  James G. Scoville

Synfuel. See Synthetic fuel.

Synge, *sihng,* **John Millington** (1871-1909), was an Irish dramatist who portrayed the rugged life of Irish peasants of the 1800's. Most of his plays are written in a vigorous poetic language based on folk speech.

Synge had a particular genius for plays having both tragic and comic elements. Like other Irish writers of his time, Synge dealt imaginatively with heroism and the apparent gap between the real and the ideal. This gap forms the theme of *In the Shadow of the Glen* (1903), *The Well of the Saints* (1905), and *The Playboy of the Western World* (1907), his masterpiece. The dramatist wrote two tragedies, *Riders to the Sea* (1904), and *Deirdre of the Sorrows* (first performed in 1910, after his death). In both plays, heroism is tied to the central character's confrontation with mortality.

Synge was born on April 16, 1871, near Rathfarnham, a suburb of Dublin. From 1898 to 1902, he spent periods of time on the Aran Islands off the western coast of Ireland, which provided the material for his plays.

Edward Hirsch

Synonym, *SIHN uh nihm,* is a word that has the same, or nearly the same, meaning as another word. There are many cases when one word will serve the same purpose as another word, such as *small* boy and *little* boy and *smart* idea and *clever* idea. However, although two words may be *synonymous* (used in the same way) in one sense, they may not be synonymous in another sense. For example, *dull* and *stupid* may both be used to describe a person. However, one does not use the word *stupid* to describe the *dull* blade of a knife. Synonyms enrich the language by helping the speaker or writer to use words with precise meanings and associations as well as to avoid the monotony of repetition.

Marianne Cooley

Syntax. See **Linguistics** (The components of a grammar).

Synthesizer, *SIHN thuh SY zuhr,* is a musical instrument that produces sounds electronically. Most synthesizers are played by means of a keyboard. A person can create and combine many kinds of sounds by operating various controls that determine such characteristics as pitch, tone color, tuning, and loudness.

Synthesizers are used in all styles of music and frequently replace live musicians. They have become especially popular in recordings, because a single synthesizer can duplicate the sound of many traditional instruments.

American physicist Robert A. Moog and American inventor Donald Buchla independently developed the first commercially successful synthesizers in the 1960's. They used controlled levels of voltage to produce different sounds on the instrument. The *digital synthesizer,* which uses a computer to create and control sounds, was developed in the 1970's.　　Jon H. Appleton

See also **Electronic music.**

Synthetic fuel is a fuel that can be substituted for crude oil and natural gas. The chief sources of synthetic fuels, also called *synfuels,* include coal, oil shale, bituminous sands, and biomass.

Coal can be turned into gas and liquid fuels through processes called *gasification* and *liquefaction.* In one method of gasification, mined coal is combined with steam and oxygen to produce a mixture of carbon monoxide, hydrogen, and methane. This gaseous mixture can be used in place of natural gas or can be further processed to make synthetic natural gas.

Liquefaction of coal can be carried out by any of several processes. In one process, called *pyrolysis,* coal is heated rapidly, causing its liquids to evaporate. The vaporized coal tars are then combined with hydrogen to produce liquid fuels. The charcoallike solid that remains can also be burned as fuel.

Oil shale is a soft, fine-grained, sedimentary rock that consists partly of an organic substance called *kerogen.* Kerogen breaks down and releases vapors when heat-

ed. These vapors condense into liquid oil.

Bituminous sands, also called *oil sands* or *tar sands,* are saturated with *bitumen.* Bitumen is a gluelike black substance used to produce liquid fuel. The method used to recover bitumen depends on the location of the sands. Sands mined from deposits near the surface of the ground are heated with water or an organic liquid that will separate the bitumen from the sand. Further processing turns the bitumen into oil. Sands deep underground are heated where they lie to melt the bitumen, which is then pumped through heated pipes to the surface. There, it is heated further to convert it to oil and other fuels.

Biomass is any type of organic matter. All plant and animal matter has energy that can be recovered by heating or through gasification. Some biomass can be fermented to make *ethanol,* also called ethyl alcohol, which is used in some gasolines in order to improve performance.

Some types of synthetic fuels are expensive to develop. When gas or petroleum prices are low, it may not be cost effective to produce synfuels. For example, operations to develop synfuels from oil shale deposits in Colorado's Rocky Mountains began in the 1980's. But a sharp decline in oil prices, and other factors, led to a shutdown of the last of those operations in 1991.

Geoffrey E. Dolbear

See also **Biomass; Bituminous sands; Coal** (Coal research); **Energy supply; Oil shale.**

Synthetics are artificially created substances in which two or more elements are chemically combined to make a new compound. Synthetics include all plastics and such manufactured fibers as acrylic, acetate, and nylon. Most synthetic substances have been developed when natural products became scarce or inadequate to meet specific industrial needs.

Manufacturers use synthetics in making countless products for the home and industry. For example, they use tough plastics in furniture, machinery parts, and packaging. Synthetic fibers form part of such products as rubber tires, brushes, electric insulating material, and clothing. Other items that can be made *synthetically* (chemically) include gems as well as various types of foods.

Chemists can give synthetics various properties. Some synthetics are brittle and strong, for example, and others are elastic. Many resist chemicals, insects, mildew, and sunlight. In many ways, synthetics are superior to natural products.

Manufacturers produce most synthetics by combining such raw materials as carbon, hydrogen, nitrogen, and oxygen. The manufacturers change these raw materials into chemical compounds through one of several chemical processes. The most common of these chemical processes is *polymerization,* which involves the transformation of small molecules into much larger ones. After the chemical process has been completed, the synthetic may be formed into fibers, a film, or a liquid that can be molded into various shapes.

Richard F. Blewitt

Related articles in *World Book* include:
Acrylic
Artificial sweetener
Artificial turf

Diamond (Synthetic diamonds)	Hormone (Synthetic hormones)	Polyester
		Polyvinyl chloride
Fiber (Synthetic fibers)	Materials	Resin, Synthetic
	Microfiber	Rubber
Fiberglass	Nylon	Silicone
Gem (Imitation and synthetic gems)	Olefin	Spandex
	Paint	Teflon
	Plastics	

Syphilis, *SIHF uh lihs,* is a sexually transmitted disease that can lead to a variety of severe symptoms if left untreated. Syphilis is caused by a *spirochete* (corkscrew-shaped bacterium) named *Treponema pallidum.* This organism is usually spread during intimate sexual activity.

Syphilis typically progresses through three stages if left untreated: (1) primary, (2) secondary, and (3) tertiary, or late. A *latent* period, characterized by the total absence of symptoms, may occur between the second and third stages.

Primary syphilis develops 10 days to three months after infection. It begins as a small, red pimple at the site of infection. This pimple develops into a sore called a *chancre.* The chancre is usually painless and may go unnoticed. It disappears within six weeks.

Secondary syphilis usually begins about 2 to 8 weeks after the chancre disappears. This stage is recognized chiefly by a rash. The rash may appear on many parts of the body, especially the soles of the feet and the palms. The patient may also experience such symptoms as fever, headache, and hair loss. The symptoms may be mild and may again go unnoticed. These symptoms usually disappear within several weeks.

In the latent period, infection can only be detected by a blood test. If the disease still goes untreated, late syphilis may result in severe, irreversible complications later in the patient's life. In this final stage, the spirochete may attack the brain, heart, skin, bones, and spinal cord, causing blindness, deafness, mental illness, dementia, heart problems, paralysis, and bone deformities. A pregnant woman who has syphilis can pass it to her unborn child. Many such babies die before birth. Those born alive may suffer from such disorders as blindness, deafness, abnormal bone growth, or mental retardation.

Doctors diagnose syphilis through a blood test. It can also be diagnosed by identifying *Treponema pallidum* in scrapings from chancres or other sores. Syphilis is treated with penicillin or other antibiotics. Penicillin cures syphilis if given early in the course of the disease. Given later, antibiotics can prevent development of further complications of late syphilis.

In 1998, researchers identified the complete sequence of genes in syphilis bacteria. Scientists hope that knowledge of these genes will reveal new ways to prevent and treat the disease. Janet N. Arno

See also **Sexually transmitted disease; Tabes.**

Syracuse, *SIHR uh KYOOS,* on the southeastern coast of Sicily, was one of the most powerful cities of the ancient Greek world. Greeks from Corinth founded the city about 734 B.C. It grew rapidly and became a cultural center under Hiero I, who built an empire in southern Italy. A democracy was established at Syracuse after Hiero's death. It defeated a strong Athenian force that besieged the city from 415 to 413 B.C. But internal troubles and threats from Carthage brought to power a harsh military ruler—Dionysius the Elder. After Dionysius's death in 367 B.C., Syracuse declined.

After 345 B.C., the Corinthian general Timoleon defeated the Carthaginians and rebuilt the city. During the rule of Hiero II, in the 200's B.C., Syracuse was allied with Rome. But the city later sided with Carthage, and Romans captured it in 212 B.C., after a three-year siege. The mathematician Archimedes aided the defenders during the siege with several defensive devices he invented (see **Archimedes**). Syracuse then became the capital of the Roman province of Sicily. In A.D. 878, the Muslims destroyed Syracuse. The town of Siracusa now stands on its site. Peter Krentz

Syracuse, *SIHR uh KYOOS* (pop. 163,860; met. area pop. 650,154), is an industrial center of New York. It lies along Onondaga Lake in the central part of the state. For the location of Syracuse, see **New York** (political map).

The city's factories manufacture such products as chemicals, chinaware, drugs, electrical machinery, paper, and transportation equipment. Syracuse is a market center for nearby farming areas. Passenger trains and freight railroads serve the city. Hancock International Airport lies just outside Syracuse.

Syracuse's central location has made it one of New York's chief convention centers. The city is at the intersection of interstates 81 and 90. The annual New York State Fair is held in the city in August and September.

Syracuse is an important educational center. It is the home of Syracuse University, Le Moyne College, State University of New York Upstate Medical Center, and State University of New York College of Environmental Science and Forestry. Cultural attractions include the Canal Museum, the Everson Museum of Art, and the Syracuse Symphony Orchestra. A replica of Fort Sainte Marie de Gannentaha, a French fort built in 1658, stands near Onondaga Lake. The nearby Salt Museum features exhibits of the area's earliest industry, the drying of salt.

Iroquois Indians lived in what is now the Syracuse area when Ephraim Webster became the first permanent white settler there in 1786. Webster opened a trading post near the salt springs that surrounded Onondaga Lake. Veterans of the Revolutionary War in America (1775-1783) built a small settlement in the area in 1788. They established several saltworks in 1788 or 1789.

In 1825, the settlement was named after the ancient Greek city of Syracuse, which also lay near salt springs. Also in 1825, the Erie Canal was completed. The canal, which linked the Atlantic Ocean and the Great Lakes, ran through the settlement and stimulated economic and population growth. The community soon became a center of the salt industry. It was chartered as a city in 1848. The coming of railroads in the mid-1800's brought new industries. The salt industry declined in the early 1900's.

In the 1960's and early 1970's, urban renewal projects cleared land in Syracuse for banks, department stores, and office buildings. The Onondaga County Civic Center, which opened in 1976, combines a 16-story government office building and a cultural center. The Oncenter Complex, completed in the early 1990's, includes a convention center, an arena, and three theaters.

In 2002, a real estate developer announced plans to expand the Carousel Center mall into a gigantic shopping and entertainment complex that would become a tourist destination.

Syracuse is the seat of Onondaga County. It has a mayor-council government. John Rennie Short

Damascus is Syria's capital and one of the country's main population and trade centers. It is also one of the world's oldest cities. Historians believe Damascus may have been founded about 3000 B.C. The large Umayyad, or Great Mosque, *shown here,* is a fine work of Islamic architecture.

Syria

Syria, *SEER ee uh,* is an Arab country in southwestern Asia at the eastern end of the Mediterranean Sea. It is a land of rolling plains, fertile river valleys, and barren deserts. Damascus is Syria's capital. Damascus and Aleppo are the largest cities.

Syria is an extremely ancient land with a rich cultural heritage. Some of the oldest known civilizations existed in this region, and one of the world's first alphabets was developed there. Syrian artists and scholars greatly influenced the cultures of ancient Greece and Rome and the later culture of the Muslim empire (see **Muslims**).

Syria lies along major trade routes linking Africa, Asia, and Europe. Camel caravans followed these routes more than 4,000 years ago carrying goods between Asia and Mediterranean ports. Such Syrian cities as Damascus and Aleppo grew up along the caravan routes and became centers of world trade as early as 2000 B.C.

Syrians have also profited from agriculture. The country is at the western end of a rich farmland that is called the Fertile Crescent (see **Fertile Crescent**). Farmers raise chiefly cotton and wheat on the rich Syrian plains.

Most Syrians are Muslim Arabs, but the population also includes several ethnic and religious minorities. Most of Syria's people live in the western part of the country. About a fourth of all workers are farmers. Syrian industries are expanding, and rural people have increasingly moved to the cities to seek industrial and service jobs.

Government

Syria is a republic. Its Constitution, adopted in 1973, calls the country a *socialist popular democracy.* Syrians 18 years of age or older may vote.

As`ad AbuKhalil, the contributor of this article, is Associate Professor of Politics at California State University, Stanislaus.

National government. A president is Syria's head of state and most powerful government official. The people elect the president to a seven-year term. A 250-member parliament called the People's Council makes Syria's laws. Voters elect council members to four-year terms.

The president heads the Arab Socialist Baath (Renaissance) Party, which controls Syrian politics. The party's power rests on its control of the country's armed forces. The Baath Party and Syria's other legal political parties form a broad nationalist organization known as the National Progressive Front.

Local government. Syria is divided into 13 provinces and the city of Damascus, which is considered a separate unit. The national government appoints all provincial governors. Each province also has a people's council made up of elected and appointed members.

Courts. The Court of Cassation is Syria's highest court of appeals for civil, commercial, and criminal cases.

Facts in brief

Capital: Damascus.
Official language: Arabic.
Official name: Al-Jumhuriyah al-Arabiyah as-Suriyah (Syrian Arab Republic).
Area: 71,498 mi² (185,180 km²). *Greatest distances*—east-west, 515 mi (829 km); north-south, 465 mi (748 km). *Coastline*—94 mi (151 km).
Elevation: *Highest*—Mount Hermon, 9,232 ft (2,814 m) above sea level. *Lowest*—sea level along the coast.
Population: *Estimated 2008 population*—20,423,000; density, 286 per mi² (110 per km²); distribution, 50 percent urban, 50 percent rural. *2002 official government estimate*—16,924,000.
Chief products: *Agriculture*—barley, cotton, grapes, milk, sugar beets, wheat. *Manufacturing*—cement, fertilizer, glass, petroleum products, processed foods, textiles. *Mining*—petroleum, phosphates.
National anthem: "Humata al-Diyari" ("Guardians of the Homeland").
Money: *Basic unit*—Syrian pound (also called lira). One hundred piasters equal one pound.

Björn Klingwall

Cotton is one of Syria's main crops. These men are handling a cotton harvest in northern Syria. About half of all the Syrian people live in rural areas, mostly in small villages.

Each of Syria's religious communities has its own courts for such matters as marriage, divorce, and inheritance.

Armed forces. About 420,000 people serve in Syria's armed forces. All eligible males serve 30 months of military service. Women may volunteer for service. Syria also has about 650,000 people in its military reserves.

People

Ancestry. More than 90 percent of Syrians speak Arabic, Syria's official language. About 90 percent consider themselves to be Arabs. Most of them are descended from people called Semites who settled in ancient Syria. Non-Arab Syrians include Armenians and Kurds. Their ancestors came from the north. Most of these Syrians still speak Armenian or Kurdish in everyday life.

Way of life. Syria has some of the world's oldest cities. They have narrow, winding streets and ancient marketplaces. But the cities also have newer sections where life resembles that in most modern cities. The people live in modern houses or apartments and work in government, services, industry, and other fields.

Most people in rural areas live in small villages. Some villagers live much as their ancestors did. They farm small plots and build houses of stone or of sun-dried mud bricks. Nomadic herders called Bedouins make up a tiny percentage of Syria's rural people. These people live in tents and move about the countryside grazing their livestock. However, increasing numbers of Bedouins have abandoned their traditional nomadic lives and settled on farms or in cities.

Some Syrians, especially in rural areas, wear traditional clothing, such as billowy trousers and a large cloth head covering. In the cities and towns, most people wear clothing similar to that worn by North Americans and Europeans. *Pita bread,* which is a flat bread made of wheat, is widely eaten in Syria. Most Syrians also eat cheese, fresh fruits and vegetables, and rich stews. Lamb dishes are commonly served, and they are often prepared for special occasions. Syrians, like other

Arabs, enjoy strong coffee. They also drink milk, tea, beer, and *arak* (a strong liquor flavored with the seeds of the anise plant).

Family ties are close among most Syrians. Many parents share their home with their sons and the sons' families. However, the *nuclear family* is becoming more and more standard. The nuclear family consists of a father, a mother, and their children, typically living by themselves away from grandparents, aunts, and uncles.

As in most traditional societies, women in Syria face tremendous challenges in gaining social privileges and freedoms. However, increasing educational opportunities and exposure to modern ideas are improving the position of women. Several Syrian women now occupy prominent roles in government, Baath party leadership, and society in general.

Religion. Muslims make up about 90 percent of Syria's population. Most of them belong to the Sunni branch of Islam. Syria also has smaller groups of Muslims, including Alawites and Shi`ites. Christians account for most of the rest of the people. Some Syrians are Druses. They practice a secret religion related to Islam. Syria also has a small number of Jews.

Religion, especially Islam, is a powerful political and social force in Syria. However, the ruling Baath party is not officially tied to any religion, and some Christians serve in leading government positions. Many Syrians

Syria's flag, which was adopted in 1980, bears traditional Arab colors. Two green stars appear on the flag.

Syria's coat of arms shows a hawk. This bird was the emblem of the tribe of Muhammad, the prophet of Islam.

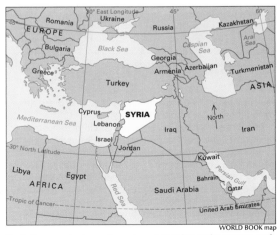

WORLD BOOK map

Syria is a country in southwestern Asia. It lies at the eastern end of the Mediterranean Sea and borders on five other countries.

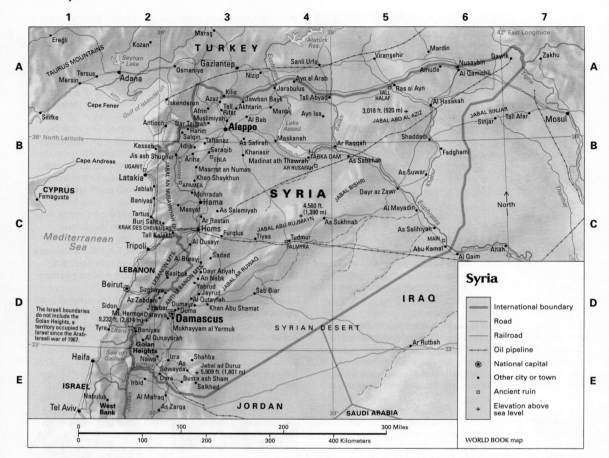

Syria map. Grid columns 1–7, rows A–E.

Syria

―――	International boundary
―――	Road
―――	Railroad
∙∙∙∙∙	Oil pipeline
⊛	National capital
•	Other city or town
▫	Ancient ruin
+	Elevation above sea level

WORLD BOOK map

0   100   200   300 Miles
0 100   200   300   400 Kilometers

Cities and towns

Abu Kamal	20,000	.C	6
Afrin	16,000	.B	3
Al Bab	27,000	.B	3
Aleppo	1,583,000	.B	3
Al Hasakah	60,000	.B	6
Al Mayadin	13,000	.C	5
Al Qamishli	144,000	.A	6
Al Qusayr	13,000	.C	3
Al Qutayfah	17,000	.D	3
An Nabk	22,000	.D	3
Ariha	18,000	.B	3
Ar Raqqah	165,000	.B	4
Ar Rastan	8,000	.C	3
As Safirah	15,000	.B	3
As Salamiyah	31,000	.C	3
As Saqlabiyah*	10,000	.C	3
As Suwayda	48,000	.E	2

At Tall*	18,000	.D	2
Ayn al Arab	12,000	.A	4
Azaz	15,000	.A	3
Az Zabdani	16,000	.D	2
Baniyas	22,000	.C	2
Burj Safita	12,000	.C	2
Damascus	1,394,000	.D	2
Dara	44,000	.E	2
Darayya	33,000	.D	2
Dayr az Zawr	140,000	.C	5
Dayrik	11,000	.A	7
Duma	42,000	.D	2
Hama	264,000	.C	2
Harim	7,000	.B	2
Homs	540,000	.C	2
Idlib	50,000	.B	3
Izra	8,000	.E	2
Jablah	26,000	.C	2

Jisr ash Shughur	22,000	.B	2
Latakia	312,000	.B	2
Maarrat an Numan	24,000	.B	3
Madinat ath Thawrah	35,000	.B	4
Manbij	25,000	.B	4
Masyaf	13,000	.C	2
Muhradah	13,000	.C	3
Mukhayyam al Yarmuk	90,000	.D	2
Qatana	20,000	.D	2
Ras al Ayn	12,000	.A	5
Salkhad	7,000	.E	3
Tall Kalakh	9,000	.C	2
Tartus	58,000	.C	2
Tudmur	17,000	.C	4

Physical features

Anti-Lebanon Mountains	.D	2
Apamea (Ancient ruin)	.C	2
Ar Rusafah (Ancient ruin)	.B	4
Assad Reservoir	.B	4
Balikh River	.B	4
Ebla (Ancient ruin)	.B	3
Euphrates River	.C	6
Galilee, Sea of	.E	2
Golan Heights	.E	2
Jabal Abu Rujmayn (Mountains)	.C	4
Jabal ad Duruz (Mountain)	.E	3
Jabal an Nusayriyah (Mountains)	.C	2

Jabal ar Ruwaq (Mountains)	.D	3
Jabal Bishri (Ridge)	.C	4
Khabur River	.B	6
Krak des Chevaliers (Ancient ruin)	.C	2
Mari (Ancient ruin)	.C	6
Mount Hermon	.D	2
Orontes River	.B	2
Palmyra (Ancient ruin)	.C	4
Syrian Desert	.D	4
Tabka Dam	.B	4
Tall Halaf (Ancient ruin)	.A	5
Tigris River	.A	7
Ugarit (Ancient ruin)	.B	2
Yarmuk River	.E	2

*Does not appear on the map; key shows general location.
Sources: 1994 census for cities over 100,000; 1980 official estimates for all other places.

feel strong ties to their religious group, and these ties have often hindered national unity.

Education. Syrian law requires all children from 6 through 11 years old to go to school. However, many children do not attend school because of a shortage of classrooms and teachers. About three-fourths of all Syrians 15 years of age or older can read and write. Universities operate in Aleppo, Damascus, Homs, and Latakia.

The arts. Syria's cultural heritage goes back thousands of years. Since ancient times, Syrian craftworkers have been famous for their beautiful glassware, metalwork, and textiles. Semites who lived in Syria and Palestine developed one of the earliest alphabets there about

1500 B.C. Some basic ideas in architecture, shipbuilding, and ironwork also originated in Syria.

Syria's greatest contribution to the arts has been in literature, the Arabs' supreme art. Two of Syria's finest poets were al-Mutanabbi, who lived in the 900's, and Abu al-Ala al-Maarri, who lived in the 1000's. During the 900's, the Syrian al-Farabi became one of Islam's leading philosophers. Important Syrian writers of the 1900's included Umar Abu Rishah, Nizar Qabbani, and Syrian-born Ali Ahmad Said (known as Adunis or Adonis).

The land and climate

Syria can be divided into three main land regions.

They are, from west to east: (1) the coast, (2) the mountains, and (3) the valleys and plains.

The coast is a narrow strip of land that extends along the Mediterranean Sea from Turkey to Lebanon. Moist sea winds give the region a mild, humid climate. Temperatures average about 48 °F (9 °C) in January and about 81 °F (27 °C) in July. About 40 inches (100 centimeters) of rain falls yearly. The coast is one of the few areas in Syria where crops do not have to be irrigated, and most of the land is cultivated.

The mountains run mostly from north to south. The region includes the Jabal an Nusayriyah range east of the coast; the Anti-Lebanon Mountains along the border with Lebanon; and the Jabal ad Duruz, a mountain southeast of the Anti-Lebanon range. The western slopes of the Jabal an Nusayriyah and Jabal ad Duruz are well populated, and most land is cultivated. The Anti-Lebanon Mountains have a dry, stony surface and are thinly populated. The mountains catch sea winds blowing inland and force them to drop their moisture on the western side of the mountains. Thus, the western slopes have up to 40 inches (100 centimeters) of rain yearly, but the land to the east remains dry. Temperatures average about 41 °F (5 °C) in January and about 72 °F (22 °C) in July.

The valleys and plains include fertile river valleys, grassy plains, and sandy deserts. The Orontes River and mountain streams water the plains along the eastern edge of the mountains. These plains have rich, productive farmlands and are the home of most of Syria's people. The Euphrates River and its tributaries provide water for a developing agricultural area in the northeastern part of Syria. Most of the rest of Syria is covered by deserts and by dry grasslands where Bedouins graze their livestock. Little rain falls in the valleys and plains region. Temperatures average about 41 °F (5 °C) in January and about 88 °F (31 °C) in July.

Economy

Syria is a developing country with good potential for economic growth. The government controls most of the economy, but the majority of farms, small businesses, and small industries are privately owned. In the 1990's, the government adopted a policy of reducing economic restrictions and allowing more privatization, including private banking.

Natural resources. Syria's most valuable natural resources are agricultural land and petroleum. The Euphrates and Orontes rivers provide irrigation water for farmlands. In addition, hydroelectric power is produced at Syria's huge Tabka Dam on the Euphrates River.

Service industries account for 60 percent of the value of Syria's economic production. They employ about 40 percent of the country's workers. The leading service industries are wholesale and retail trade, tourism, and government services. Aleppo, Damascus, and Latakia are the leading trade centers. Much of the money spent on government services in Syria goes to military and *intelligence* (information-gathering) activities. Other service industries include education, finance, health care, and utilities.

Agriculture accounts for 20 percent of the value of Syria's production. Cotton and wheat are Syria's main crops. Farmers also grow barley; sugar beets; tobacco; and such fruits and vegetables as grapes, olives, and tomatoes. Bedouins raise cattle, goats, and sheep.

Most Syrian farmers work small plots of land. Some use old-fashioned methods. However, government funds have helped provide modern machinery for many small farms. Syria also has a few large, state-owned farms. On about 90 percent of Syria's land, the rainfall is too light and irregular for raising many kinds of crops. Irrigation thus plays a vital role in farming.

Mining makes up 7 percent of Syria's production value. Petroleum is Syria's chief mineral product. Most of the petroleum comes from fields in the northeastern part of the country. Phosphate rock is another important source of mining income. Phosphate, which is used to make fertilizer, is mined in the Palmyra area of central Syria. The country's other mineral products include gypsum, limestone, and natural gas.

Manufacturing accounts for 6 percent of the value of Syria's production. The manufacture of cotton fabrics

© Age Fotostock/SuperStock

Agriculture is an important part of Syria's economy. The farmer shown here is using a traditional plow, but many Syrian farmers use modern machinery.

© Tibor Bognar, Corbis Stock Market

People shop for vegetables at an outdoor market in Aleppo, one of Syria's largest cities. Aleppo, which lies in northwestern Syria, is an important agricultural, industrial, and education center.

and other textiles is one of Syria's most important industries. Other chief products include Arabic candy and sweets, beverages, cement, fertilizer, glass, processed foods, and sugar. Syria also has a growing oil-refining industry. The main industrial centers are Damascus, Aleppo, Homs, and Latakia.

International trade. Syria's chief exports are petroleum, raw cotton, and woolens and other textiles. Other exports include food products, phosphates, and tobacco. Major imports include fuels, grain, machinery, metals and metal products, and motor vehicles. Syria's main trading partners include China, France, Germany, Italy, Lebanon, Saudi Arabia, South Korea, Turkey, and Ukraine.

Transportation and communication. Many Syrians own automobiles, and many others travel by bus. Damascus has an international airport. The port of Latakia handles most of Syria's foreign trade. About 30 percent

of all Syrians own a radio, and about 7 percent own a television set. Syria has 10 major daily newspapers. The use of computers is spreading among educated urban Syrians.

History

Until 1918, Syria included much of what are now Israel, Jordan, Lebanon, and parts of Turkey. This region, often called *Greater Syria,* has a long, colorful past. Throughout history, Syria's rich soil and location on major trade routes have made the country a valuable prize. As a result, many battles were fought for Syria, and it became part of many empires.

Semitic settlement. Unidentified peoples lived in northern Syria before 4500 B.C. The first known settlers in Syria were Semites who probably arrived about 3500 B.C. They established city-states throughout the region. One city-state, Ebla, flourished sometime between 2700

© Styve Reineck, Shutterstock

Ruins of Palmyra stand in central Syria. This ancient city thrived more than 2,000 years ago as a major stop for caravans.

Important dates in Syria

2300's B.C. The Akkadians conquered northern and eastern Syria.

c. 1500 B.C. The Arameans arrived in Syria.

732 B.C. The Assyrians conquered most of Syria.

539 B.C. Syria became part of the Persian Empire.

331 B.C. Alexander the Great gained control of Syria.

64 B.C. Syria fell to the Romans.

A.D. 636 Muslim Arabs defeated Byzantine forces and gained control of Syria.

1516 The Ottomans added Syria to their empire.

1914-1918 Syrians and other Arabs revolted against Ottoman rule during World War I.

1920 France occupied Syria under a League of Nations mandate.

1946 Syria gained complete independence from France.

1948 Syrian and other Arab troops went to war with Israel. The United Nations eventually arranged a cease-fire.

1967 Israel defeated Syria, Egypt, and Jordan in a brief war, and Israel occupied Syria's Golan Heights.

1973 Syria and Egypt led an Arab war with Israel. Cease-fires ended the fighting.

1976 Syria sent troops into Lebanon in an effort to stop a civil war there.

1981 Israel claimed legal and political authority in the Golan Heights. Syria and many other countries denounced this action.

1991 Syrian troops helped end the Iraqi occupation of Kuwait.

and 2200 B.C. Ebla was a powerful kingdom with a highly advanced civilization. See **Ebla.**

Various Semitic groups ruled parts of Syria until 539 B.C. For example, the Akkadians conquered much of northern and eastern Syria during the 2300's B.C. The Canaanites may have moved into the southwest and along the Mediterranean coast about 2000 B.C. The Greeks later called the people living along the coast Phoenicians. Phoenician sailors carried Syrian culture throughout the Mediterranean world.

By 1700 B.C., the Amorites ruled much of eastern Syria. The Arameans arrived in Syria about 1500 B.C. Their culture gradually spread through most of Syria. By 1200 B.C., Damascus was a prosperous Aramean city. During the late 1200's B.C., the Hebrews entered southern Syria. In 732 B.C., the Assyrians conquered most of Syria. They ruled until 612 B.C., when the Babylonians took control.

The age of non-Semitic rule. Persian forces defeated the Babylonians in 539 B.C. and made Syria part of the Persian Empire. Greek and Macedonian armies under Alexander the Great conquered the Persians in 331 B.C. Under Alexander and his successors, the Seleucids, Greek culture spread throughout most of the Middle East. The Seleucids ruled from 312 to 64 B.C. During their reign, trade flourished, and many agricultural advances were made.

Syria fell to the Romans in 64 B.C. Syrians then lived under the Roman system of law for nearly 700 years, first as part of the Roman Empire, then of the East Roman Empire, and finally of the Byzantine Empire. During this period, Christianity was born and developed in a part of Greater Syria called Palestine. It became the state religion of Syria in the A.D. 300's.

The Muslim Arabs. Muslims from the Arabian Peninsula invaded Syria in 633 and defeated the Byzantine forces in 636. Islam gradually took the place of Christianity, and Arabic became the common language of the

area. Beginning in 661, a vast Islamic empire was governed from Damascus by the Umayyad dynasty. In 750, the Umayyads were overthrown. The Abbāsid dynasty gained control of the empire and ruled it from Baghdad, in what is now Iraq.

Christian crusaders from Europe invaded Syria during the late 1000's. The crusaders hoped to capture the Holy Land (Palestine) from the Muslims. Saladin, the Muslim ruler of Egypt, swept into Syria to fight off the crusaders. By the late 1100's, Saladin had become the ruler of most of Syria.

The Mamluks and Ottomans. From 1260 to 1516, Syria was governed by the Mamluk dynasty of Egypt. In 1516, the Ottoman Empire conquered Syria. Ottoman rule lasted about 400 years. During the late 1500's, European explorers discovered sea routes to India. Syria's position as a trade center then declined. By the 1700's, the power of the Ottoman Empire was growing weak. By 1900, many Syrians were demanding independence.

World War I to independence. During World War I (1914-1918), Syrians and other Arabs revolted against the Ottomans and helped the United Kingdom fight the Ottoman Empire. The Arabs had agreed to aid the United Kingdom in return for its support of Arab independence. But after the war, the League of Nations divided Greater Syria into Syria and Palestine. Palestine was later divided into Palestine and Transjordan, and Syria was later divided into Syria and Lebanon. The League gave France a *mandate* to manage Syrian and Lebanese affairs (see **Mandated territory**). France used force to gain control of Syria. Most Syrians resented French control, the presence of French troops, and the division of their land, and they demanded independence.

Independence. France finally withdrew all its troops from Syria in 1946, and Syria gained complete independence. Many Syrians wanted to reunite Greater Syria. But in 1947, the United Nations (UN) divided Palestine into a Jewish state (Israel) and an Arab state. Israel declared its independence in 1948. Syrian and other Arab forces then went to war with Israel but were unable to defeat Israeli forces, which were larger and better equipped. The UN eventually arranged a cease-fire. More than 700,000 Palestinian Arabs fled or were driven out of their homes in the new Jewish state. They became refugees in neighboring Arab countries.

Many Syrians blamed their government for failing to prevent the division of Palestine. In 1949, army officers overthrew the government. During the next 20 years, control of the government changed hands many times through military revolts.

In a move toward Arab unity, Syria joined Egypt in 1958 in a political union called the United Arab Republic (U.A.R.). But Egypt soon threatened to take complete control, and Syria withdrew from the U.A.R. in 1961.

During the early 1960's, Syria's Baath Party rose to power. The government took over most industry and all international trade in Syria. In 1970, Hafez al-Assad (also spelled Hafiz al-Asad), a Baathist leader and commander of the air force, seized power in Syria. He was elected president the next year.

The continuing Arab-Israeli conflict. During the early 1960's, border clashes between Syrian and Israeli troops occurred frequently. On June 5, 1967, Israel went to war with the Arab states of Syria, Jordan, and Egypt.

© Courtney Kealy, Liaison

A Syrian woman casts her vote during a presidential election. All Syrians 18 years of age or older are allowed to vote. The photograph on the wall is of President Bashar al-Assad.

After six days of fighting, Israel had won the war and occupied much Arab land. This included an area called the Golan Heights, in the southwestern corner of Syria. Thousands of Arabs then fled from territory occupied by Israel to seek refuge in neighboring Arab countries.

Fighting between Syria and Israel continued occasionally around the Golan Heights. The presence in Syria of Arab refugees from Palestine and the Golan Heights increased tension between Syria and Israel.

In October 1973, Syria and Egypt went to war with Israel. Cease-fires ended most of the fighting by November. But Syrian and Israeli forces continued fighting each other off and on until May 1974.

In 1981, Israel claimed legal and political authority in the Golan Heights. Syria and many other nations denounced Israel for this action.

Tension between Syria and Israel has continued. Syria calls for the return of the Golan Heights and the creation of a Palestinian state.

Other conflicts. In 1976, Syria sent troops into Lebanon, with the approval of the Lebanese government then in power, in an effort to stop a civil war there. Syrian troops remained in Lebanon as part of an Arab peacekeeping force. Starting in 1979, this force consisted entirely of Syrian troops. This force periodically fought against participants in the Lebanese conflict. Most fighting in Lebanon ended in 1991. But the Syrian forces remained in Lebanon.

In August 1990, Iraq invaded and occupied Kuwait. After the invasion, Syria, the United States, and many other countries formed an alliance to oppose Iraq's occupation of Kuwait. War broke out in January 1991, and the allies defeated Iraq in February. Approximately 20,000 Syrian troops took part in the war effort. See **Persian Gulf War of 1991.**

The early 2000's. In June 2000, President Hafez al-Assad died. The Baath Party chose his son, Bashar al-Assad (also spelled Bashar al-Asad), to take over as president. Bashar was also appointed commander of the armed forces. In July, voters confirmed Bashar as president.

In the early 2000's, many Lebanese citizens and for-

eign governments urged Syria to withdraw its forces from Lebanon. In February 2005, Rafik Hariri, a former Lebanese prime minister who had called for an end to the Syrian troop presence, was killed in Beirut, Lebanon. Many people accused Syria of playing a role in his death, but Syria denied the charge. The assassination sparked large anti-Syrian protests in Lebanon and led to increased demands for Syrian withdrawal. There were also large pro-Syrian protests. In response to international pressure, Syria withdrew its troops from Lebanon by the end of April 2005.   As`ad AbuKhalil

Related articles in *World Book* include:

Aleppo	Bedouins	Middle East
Arab-Israeli conflict	Damascus	Palestine
	Druses	Palmyra
Arabs	Euphrates River	Phoenicia
Assad, Bashar al-	Golan Heights	Sèvres, Treaty of
Assad, Hafez al-	Latakia	

Outline

I. Government
   A. National government   C. Courts
   B. Local government   D. Armed forces
II. People
   A. Population and   C. Religion
      ancestry   D. Education
   B. Way of life   E. The arts
III. The land and climate
   A. The coast   C. The valleys and plains
   B. The mountains
IV. Economy
   A. Natural resources   E. Manufacturing
   B. Service industries   F. International trade
   C. Agriculture   G. Transportation and
   D. Mining   communication
V. History

Questions

What are Syria's main agricultural products?
When did Syria gain full independence from France?
What is the chief religion in Syria?
Who were the first known settlers in Syria?
For what products have Syrian craftworkers been famous since ancient times?
Who is Syria's most powerful government official?
Why was ancient Syria a major trade center?
What is Syria's chief mineral product?
How do Syria's mountains affect the distribution of rainfall in the country?

Additional resources

George, Alan. *Syria.* Zed Bks., 2003.
Ginat, Rami. *Syria and the Doctrine of Arab Neutralism.* Sussex Academic, 2005.

Syrian Desert, *SEER ee uhn,* is a desert located in southwestern Asia that covers portions of Jordan, Syria, Iraq, and Saudi Arabia. The Syrian Desert is the northwestern part of the Arabian Desert. For the location of the Syrian Desert, see **Iraq** (map).

The Syrian Desert is mostly a plateau that slopes downward to the Euphrates River, its eastern boundary. The southern two-thirds of the plateau is rocky. A mountainous area about 3,000 feet (910 meters) high stands above the central part of the plateau, near the point where Jordan, Iraq, and Saudi Arabia meet. Deeply cut *wadis* (dry valleys) wind down from these mountains to the Euphrates. The northern third of the plateau is a flat, sandy plain that forms the natural bridge between Syria and Iraq.

The Syrian Desert contains historic ruins and several towns that have grown up around oases. The area includes the famous ruins of Palmyra in central Syria. Palmyra thrived more than 2,000 years ago as a major stop for caravans. Wayne Lambert

Syringe, *suh RIHNJ,* is a pumplike device. It is a tube, tapered at one end, with a plunger or a soft, hollow bulb at the other. The plunger or bulb either creates suction or forces fluid from the syringe. Syringes are used to spray or inject liquids, or to remove them by suction. Edward J. Shahady

See also **Hypodermic injection; Intravenous injection.**

Syringa. See **Mock orange.**

Syrinx. See **Pan.**

Syrup. See **Corn syrup; Maple syrup; Molasses; Sorghum.**

System. See **Human body; Life** (Tissues, organs, and organ systems).

Systems analysis is the study of how the parts of a system work together. A system is any group of people, machines, or processes that combine to do a certain job.

The goal of systems analysis is to find the best way for a system to accomplish its task. For example, a high school is a system that includes students, teachers, teaching materials, and classrooms. Systems analysis can develop student schedules that make the most efficient use of the teachers, materials, and classrooms. Systems analysis is used in many fields, including the armed forces, business, economics, education, government, industry, the sciences, and transportation.

Systems analysis usually uses advanced mathematics. A systems analyst uses mathematical equations to describe the relationships between the different parts of a system. These equations make up a *mathematical model* of the system. Then the model is analyzed mathematically. This stage requires the solution of long, difficult mathematical problems. Systems analysts frequently use computers to help find the answers to these problems.

The techniques of systems analysis were developed starting in the late 1930's. The later development of electronic computers resulted in the widespread use of systems analysis. Ronald G. Askin

See also **Computer** (Careers); **Management information systems.**

Systolic pressure. See **Blood pressure.**

Szczecin, *SHCHEH cheen,* or in German, Stettin (pop. 413,294), is the leading port of Poland. The city lies on the Baltic Sea at the mouth of the Oder River (see **Poland** [political map]). Szczecin serves as a port for the Czech Republic, Hungary, and Slovakia, as well as for Poland. The city produces machines, metals, paper, and ships.

Szczecin became part of Poland at the end of World War II in 1945. The city had previously formed part of Germany. Leslie Dienes

Szell, *sehl,* **George** (1897-1970), was a Hungarian-born symphony orchestra conductor. Earlier in his career, Szell was equally noted as a pianist. From 1946 until his death, Szell conducted the Cleveland Orchestra, which he built into one of the world's great orchestras. Szell's insistence on precision and clarity made some observers think his interpretations lacked sufficient emotion. Actually, Szell used his brilliant technique to produce music of unique emotional force.

Szell was born on June 7, 1897, in Budapest. During the 1920's and 1930's, he established himself as a conductor of operas, particularly those composed by Wolfgang Amadeus Mozart of Austria and Richard Wagner of Germany. Szell later concentrated on conducting orchestral music. Szell became a United States citizen in 1946. He died on July 29, 1970. Martin Bernheimer

Szent-Györgyi, *sehnt JAWRJ ee,* **Albert** (1893-1986), a Hungarian-born American biochemist, discovered *actin,* a muscle protein. Through his research, he explained the catalytic action in cellular *oxidation* (combustion), the role of vitamins in metabolism, and the chemistry and structure of muscle tissue. He received the 1937 Nobel Prize in physiology or medicine for his discoveries in connection with oxidation in tissues, Vitamin C, and *fumaric acid,* a substance in the cells. He was born on Sept. 16, 1893, in Budapest as Albert Szent-Györgyi von Nagyrapolt. He died on Oct. 22, 1986.

Szilard, *SIHL ahrd* or *zih LAHRD,* **Leo** (1898-1964), an American physicist, pioneered in the development of nuclear energy. With Enrico Fermi, he originated the method of arranging graphite and uranium which made possible the first self-sustaining nuclear reactor in 1942. In 1939, Szilard and Eugene Wigner visited Albert Einstein. Einstein then wrote to President Franklin D. Roosevelt and initiated federal support of nuclear energy.

Szilard was born in Budapest, Hungary, on Feb. 11, 1898. He became a U.S. citizen in 1943. He and Wigner shared the 1959 Atoms for Peace Award. Szilard died on May 30, 1964. Richard L. Hilt

CORBIS/Bettmann

Leo Szilard, *second from the left,* chats with fellow scientists in 1945. Szilard, an American physicist, pioneered in the development of nuclear energy.

Szoka, *SHAHK ah,* **Edmund Casimir** (1927-   ), was appointed a cardinal of the Roman Catholic Church by Pope John Paul II in 1988. He served as archbishop of Detroit from 1981 to 1990, when he became president of prefecture for economic affairs of the Holy See.

Szoka was born in Grand Rapids, Michigan, on Sept. 14, 1927. He was ordained a priest in 1954. He served as bishop of the diocese of Gaylord, Michigan, from 1971 to 1981. Szoka became a trustee of the National Shrine of the Immaculate Conception in Washington, D.C., in 1981 and became chairman of the board of directors of the Catholic Telecommunications Network of America in 1984.   Kenneth Guentert

CORBIS/Bettmann

Henrietta Szold, the founder of Hadassah, directed *Youth Aliyah,* which rescued Jewish children from Nazi persecution. Szold, *left,* welcomed these Polish refugees to Palestine in 1943.

Szold, *zohld,* **Henrietta** (1860-1945), an American social worker, founded Hadassah, the largest Jewish women's organization in the world. She established Hadassah in 1912 and dedicated its activities to improving the living conditions of Jews in Palestine. Szold served as president of Hadassah until 1926. Under her leadership, the organization built many hospitals and schools in Palestine. In 1933, she became director of *Youth Aliyah,* a program sponsored by Hadassah to rescue Jewish children from Nazi Germany and resettle them in Palestine. See **Hadassah.**

Szold was born in Baltimore. During the 1880's, she organized Americanization classes for Jews who had emigrated there from eastern Europe. From 1892 to 1916, she served as an editor and translator for the Jewish Publication Society of America. During part of that period, from 1904 to 1910, she also was coeditor of the *American Jewish Year Book.* In 1902, Szold became the first woman to study at the Jewish Theological Seminary of America.   Critically reviewed by Hadassah

Szymborska, *shihm BAWR skuh,* **Wisława,** *vees WAH wah* (1923-   ), a Polish poet, won the 1996 Nobel Prize for literature. Her spare, witty verse emphasizes interpersonal relationships and the oddities and unexpected turns of everyday life. She also explores Communist totalitarianism and the threat to individualism in modern mass society.

Szymborska was born near Poznań. She graduated from Jagiellonian University and earned a living for several years editing a literary journal. She describes her later poetry as personal rather than political, but her first volume, *That's What We Live For* (1952), was heavily influenced by Communism. *Calling Out to Yeti* (1957) compares Soviet dictator Joseph Stalin to the Abominable Snowman. Her other volumes include *A Hundred Joys* (1967), *People on a Bridge* (1986), and *View with a Grain of Sand* (1995). Szymborska is highly popular in Poland, where her verse has even been set to rock music.

Paul B. Diehl